Encyclopedia of the Confederacy

Editorial Advisers

Encyclopedia of the Confederacy

RICHARD N. CURRENT, Editor in Chief
Emeritus, University of North Carolina, Greensboro

Volume 3

SIMON & SCHUSTER
A Paramount Communications Company

New York London Toronto Sydney Tokyo Singapore

Simon & Schuster
Academic Reference Division
15 Columbus Circle
New York, New York 10023

Printed in the United States of America

printing number
1 2 3 4 5 6 7 8 9 10

Library of Congress Cataloging-in-Publication Data

Encyclopedia of the Confederacy

Richard N. Current, Editor in Chief; editorial board, Paul D.
Escott . . . [et al.].
p. cm..

Includes bibliographical reference and index (p.).
ISBN 0-13-275991-8 (set: alk. paper)
1. Confederate States of America—Encyclopedia.
I. Current, Richard Nelson.

E487.55 1993 973.7′13—dc20 93-4133 CIP

ISBN 0-13-275991-8 (set)
ISBN 0-13-276031-2 (v. 3)

*Acknowledgments of sources, copyrights, and
permissions to use previously printed materials
are made throughout the work.*

*The paper used in this publication meets the minimum requirements of
American National Standard for Information Sciences—Permanence
of Paper for Printed Library Materials ANSI Z39.48-1984.*

ABBREVIATIONS AND SYMBOLS USED IN THIS WORK

A.D. *anno Domini*, in the year of the (our) Lord
Adj. Gen. adjutant general
Adm. admiral
Ala. Alabama
A.M. *ante meridiem*, before noon
Ariz. Arizona
Ark. Arkansas
b. born; beam (interior measurement of width of a ship)
B.C. before Christ
brig. brigade
Brig. Gen. brigadier general
c. *circa*, about, approximately
Calif. California
Capt. captain
cf. *confer*, compare
chap. chapter (pl., chaps.)
cm centimeters
Col. colonel
Colo. Colorado
Comdr. commander
Como. commodore
Conn. Connecticut
Cpl. corporal
C.S. Confederate States
C.S.A. Confederate States of America, Confederate States Army
CSS Confederate States ship
cwt. hundredweight (equals 772 lbs.)
d. died
D.C. District of Columbia
Del. Delaware
diss. dissertation
div. division
dph. depth of hold
ed. editor (pl., eds.); edition; edited by
e.g. *exempli gratia*, for example
Eng. England
enl. enlarged
Ens. ensign
esp. especially
et al. *et alii*, and others
etc. *et cetera*, and so forth
exp. expanded
f. and following (pl., ff.)
1st Lt. first lieutenant
fl. *floruit*, flourished
Fla. Florida
frag. fragment
ft. feet
Ga. Georgia
Gen. general
Gov. governor
HMS Her Majesty's ship
ibid. *ibidem*, in the same place (as the one immediately preceding)
i.e. *id est*, that is
Ill. Illinois
Ind. Indiana
Kans. Kansas
km kilometers
Ky. Kentucky
l. length
La. Louisiana
lb. pound (pl., lbs.)
Lt. lieutenant
Lt. Col. lieutenant colonel
Lt. Comdr. lieutenant commander
Lt. Gen. lieutenant general
m meters
M.A. Master of Arts
Maj. Major
Maj. Gen. major general
Mass. Massachusetts
mi. miles
Mich. Michigan
Minn. Minnesota
Miss. Mississippi
Mo. Missouri
Mont. Montana
n. note
N.C. North Carolina
n.d. no date
N.Dak. North Dakota
Neb. Nebraska
Nev. Nevada
N.H. New Hampshire
N.J. New Jersey
N.Mex. New Mexico
no. number (pl., nos.)
n.p. no place
n.s. new series
N.Y. New York
Okla. Oklahoma
Oreg. Oregon
p. page (pl., pp.)
Pa. Pennsylvania
pdr. pounder (weight of pro-
jec tile in pounds; pl., pdrs.)
pl. plural, plate (pl., pls.)
P.M. *post meridiem*, after noon
Pres. president
pt. part (pl., pts.)
Pvt. private
r. reigned; ruled; river
Rear Adm. rear admiral
regt. regiment
Rep. representative
rev. revised
R.I. Rhode Island
S.C. South Carolina
S.Dak. South Dakota
sec. section (pl., secs.)
2d Lt. second lieutenant
Sen. senator
ser. series
Sgt. sergeant
sing. singular
sq. square
supp. supplement; supplementary
Tenn. Tennessee
Tex. Texas
trans. translator, translators; translated by; translation
U.S. United States
USS United States ship
Va. Virginia
var. variant; variation
vol. volume (pl., vols.)
Vt. Vermont
Wash. Washington
Wis. Wisconsin
W.Va. West Virginia
Wyo. Wyoming
° degress
′ feet; minutes
″ inches; seconds
£ pounds
? uncertain; possibly; perhaps

Key to Map Symbols

Troops, Confederate
Troops, Union
Cavalry, Confederate
Cavalry, Union
Tactical Movement, Confederate
Tactical Movement, Union
Strategic Movement, Confedederate
Strategic Movement, Union
Retreat
Engagement
Artillery
Encampment
Headquarters
Fortifications
Entrenchments

Casemate Ironclad
Gunboat
Monitor
Warship

Trees
Marsh
Elevation
River
Railroad
Unfinished Railroad
Road
State Boundary

Building
Church
Village
Town, Strategic
Town, Tactical
Pontoon Bridge
Bridge

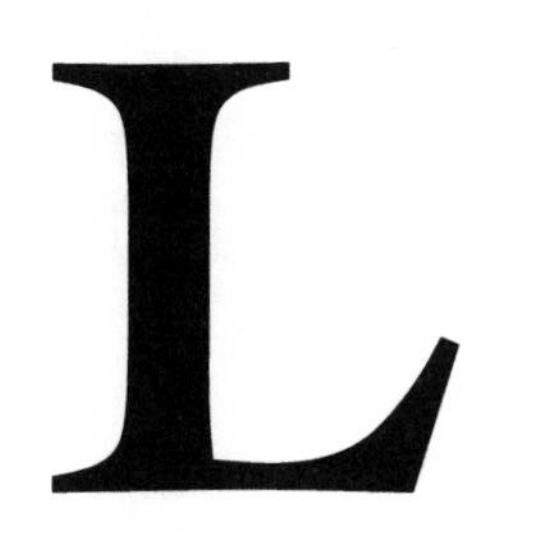

(CONTINUED)

LONG, ARMISTEAD LINDSAY (1827–1891), brigadier general. Born in central Virginia's Campbell County on September 13, 1827, Long was a member of the class of 1850 at West Point. He joined the Second Artillery and for ten years performed the usual duty at frontier posts. In June 1861, Long was serving on the staff of his father-in-law, Gen. Edwin V. Sumner, when he left the army for the Confederate cause.

Appointed major and chief of artillery for Gen. W. W. Loring, Long participated in the autumn campaign in western Virginia. He then went to South Carolina and joined the staff of Gen. Robert E. Lee. Late in May 1862, Long became Lee's military secretary. The association between Long and Lee, fellow officer Jedediah Hotchkiss observed, continued "with intimate friendship and confidence" thereafter.

Long displayed astute judgment in artillery emplacement at Fredericksburg, Chancellorsville, and Gettysburg. On September 21, 1863, at Lee's urging, Long was promoted to brigadier general and given command of the batteries of the Second Corps. He commanded Confederate artillery throughout the second Shenandoah Valley campaign and then surrendered with his troops at Appomattox.

After the war Long served a short time as chief engineer for the James River and Kanawha Canal Company. In 1870 he became totally blind because of "exposure during his campaigns." Even though he spent the last twenty years of his life in darkness, Long mastered the art of writing on a slate and produced a number of works. These included a half-dozen articles for the *Southern Historical Society Papers* and an 1886 life of Lee which was praised as "a model of biographical history." Long died April 29, 1891, in Charlottesville, Virginia, where he was buried.

ARMISTEAD LINDSAY LONG. LIBRARY OF CONGRESS

BIBLIOGRAPHY

Hotchkiss, Jed. *Virginia.* Vol. 3 of *Confederate Military History.* Edited by Clement A. Evans. Atlanta, 1899. Vol. 4 of extended ed. Wilmington, N.C., 1987.

Long, Armistead L. *Memoirs of Robert E. Lee.* New York, 1886.

JAMES I. ROBERTSON, JR.

LONGSTREET, JAMES (1821–1904), lieutenant general. Born January 8, 1821, on his grandparents' plantation in the Edgefield District, South Carolina, Longstreet spent most of his youth outside Gainesville, Georgia. After his father died in 1833, his mother sent him to live with his uncle, Augustus Baldwin Longstreet, humorist, minister, and an ardent secessionist in 1860, while she relocated in Alabama. James received an appointment to West Point from Alabama (Georgia's slots were filled) and entered the academy in 1838. His academic record was hardly impressive; he graduated fifty-fourth of sixty-two in the class of 1842.

With a brevet second lieutenant's commission in hand, Longstreet served with the Fourth U.S. Infantry at Jefferson Barracks in Missouri and in Louisiana. Transferring to the Eighth Infantry in 1845, he was stationed in Florida until the outbreak of the Mexican War. From 1847 to 1849, Longstreet served as regimental adjutant and fought under Gens. Zachary Taylor and Winfield Scott. Always brave and alert, Longstreet was wounded while charging the Mexican bastion at Chapultepec. His gallant behavior earned him brevets as captain on August 20 and major on September 8, 1847. After the war, Longstreet saw duty in Texas where he received a captain's commission on December 7, 1852. On July 19, 1858, he was promoted to major in the Paymaster Department in Albuquerque, New Mexico Territory. Longstreet tendered his resignation from the U.S. Army on June 1, 1861.

Longstreet (called "Old Pete" by his men) was made a brigadier general, dated June 17, and led a Virginia brigade near Manassas Junction. He did not see action at First Manassas on July 21, but he had been engaged three days earlier at Blackburn's Ford where he repelled an advancing Federal brigade. The fight at Blackburn's Ford demonstrated the superiority of the defense and probably influenced Longstreet's tactical thinking for the rest of the war. He almost always preferred receiving the enemy's assault and then striking back with a well-directed counterattack.

Longstreet often lacked finesse when dealing with his fellow officers and civilian officials. Though he received a

JAMES LONGSTREET. *HARPER'S PICTORIAL HISTORY OF THE GREAT REBELLION*

promotion to major general, dated October 7, 1861, he risked his career by supporting Gen. Joseph E. Johnston in his dispute with Jefferson Davis over strategy and by blaming the president for the army's failure to capture Washington after Manassas. His arrogant manner and strong opinions rankled subordinates and superiors alike. Longstreet became moody and withdrawn after he lost three of his four children to scarlet fever in January 1862.

When Johnston shifted his forces to the peninsula in the spring of 1862, Longstreet directed many of the complex movements and handled responsibilities beyond his rank. During a rearguard action at Williamsburg on May 5, Longstreet tenaciously held his ground, allowing the bulk of Johnston's force to continue its retreat. He did not, however, enjoy success at Seven Pines on May 31. Johnston's confusing orders resulted in an argument between Longstreet and Maj. Gen. Benjamin Huger, which delayed the Confederate advance. Longstreet made matters worse by swinging his troops farther south than Johnston had intended, but he redeemed himself by aggressively fulfilling his orders during the Seven Days' campaign (June 25–July 1). Longstreet especially impressed his new commander, Gen. Robert E. Lee, who told Davis that "Longstreet is a Capital soldier."

When Lee reorganized the Army of Northern Virginia after the Seven Days' Battles, he gave Longstreet the right wing, which included five divisions, while giving Maj. Gen. Thomas J. ("Stonewall") Jackson only three. At Second Manassas Longstreet arrived on the field on August 29, just to the right of Jackson. Although urged by Lee to launch an attack immediately, Longstreet warned that a premature assault would not allow him to concentrate his forces. Lee acquiesced, permitting Longstreet to bring his entire command to bear on the enemy the next day, when he drove the Federals off in confusion.

Longstreet further enhanced his reputation at Sharpsburg, Maryland, on September 17. Conspicuously wearing a pair of carpet slippers because of a foot injury, Longstreet was omnipresent, encouraging his men and even holding his staff officers' horses so they could operate the cannon of a depleted battery. One of his subordinates remembered that Longstreet was "like a rock in steadiness when sometimes in battle the world seemed flying to pieces." Throughout the day he brilliantly shifted his troops to meet each Union threat. When Longstreet returned to headquarters that night, Lee embraced him and exclaimed, "Ah! here is Longstreet; here is my old *war-horse*" (which led to Longstreet's being called "Lee's War Horse" on occasion). Lee pushed for Longstreet's promotion to lieutenant general, which was approved, dated October 9. With the boost in rank, he also received command of the First Corps.

The Battle of Fredericksburg on December 13, 1862, must have confirmed Longstreet's faith in superiority of the defense. In repulsing over 25,000 Federals at Marye's Heights, he not only took advantage of the natural terrain but improved it with entrenchments. Longstreet, in fact, deserves credit as one of the first officers to demonstrate the decisive advantage in constructing fieldworks. During the winter, he ordered the use of traverses—earthen walls that cut across a trench and protected the flanks of the men inside.

Unable to feed his army adequately at the beginning of 1863, Lee dispatched Longstreet with two divisions of the First Corps to the area south of the James River. Although he furnished his troops with sufficient supplies, Longstreet cautiously besieged Suffolk and decided against a major assault. Controversy surrounded Longstreet's decision, since he himself had admitted that the place could be captured. Some detractors point to this failure as proof that he was not aggressive. A British observer, however, wrote that Longstreet "was never far from General Lee, who relies very much upon his judgement. By the soldiers he is invariably spoken of as 'the best fighter in the whole army.' " Because Longstreet was on detached service, he missed the Battle of Chancellorsville but marched with the army into Pennsylvania.

Longstreet and Lee collided over strategy during the Gettysburg campaign. Longstreet had favored a concentration of forces in the West, but Lee insisted on a raid into the

North. Longstreet felt comfortable with his superior's plan as long as Lee would retire to a strong defensive position and force the Federals to assault the Army of Northern Virginia. When Lee decided to attack the Northern position south of Gettysburg on July 2, Longstreet felt betrayed. Lee, in fact, rejected Longstreet's suggestion to flank the Union left that day, instructing his subordinate to press straight ahead. Unusually apathetic and sluggish in his movements, Longstreet nevertheless launched a fierce assault through the Peach Orchard and Wheat Field which nearly captured Little Round Top.

Lee continued his frontal assaults the next day against Cemetery Hill. Longstreet adamantly opposed such a move, desiring a flanking maneuver instead. Lee held firm, however, and ordered Maj. Gen. George E. Pickett's division and elements of the Third Corps to strike the Union center. Before the attack, Longstreet told artillerist Col. Edward Porter Alexander that "I do not want to make this charge. I do not see how it can succeed." Alexander thought Longstreet "obeyed *reluctantly* at Gettysburg, on the 2nd and 3rd. But it must be admitted that his judgment in both matters was sound and he owed it to Lee to be reluctant, for failure was *inevitable.*" After the battle, Longstreet privately expressed the hope that all of Lee's subordinates would share responsibility for the army's defeat and that Lee would still enjoy the South's full support.

Longstreet and two of his divisions were detached to the Army of Tennessee after Gettysburg, a plan consistent with Longstreet's strategic view that emphasized a concentration of Confederate forces in the western theater. At Chickamauga on September 20, 1863, Longstreet exploited a gap in the enemy's line, routing the entire Union army, an accomplishment that earned him a new nickname—"Bull of the Woods." He followed this triumph with a poor showing during the siege of Chattanooga when he allowed the Federals to gain a foothold at the base of Lookout Mountain at the end of October.

Longstreet also became embroiled in the feud surrounding Gen. Braxton Bragg that fall. Longstreet fueled divisiveness among the officers in the Army of Tennessee by openly criticizing Bragg. Rumors surfaced that Longstreet would replace Bragg as the army's new commander, but Jefferson Davis suggested that Longstreet receive an independent command and move toward Knoxville, which he did on November 5. A few weeks later the mission ended in failure, marking the nadir of Longstreet's career as he feuded with his subordinates, notably Maj. Gen. Lafayette McLaws, while his men suffered from a lack of rations and clothing.

Longstreet and his two divisions returned to Virginia in April 1864, a welcome addition to the Army of Northern Virginia. One of Lee's staff officers wrote to Longstreet: "I really am beside myself, General, with joy of having you back. It is like the reunion of a family."

Longstreet recaptured his former glory at the Battle of the Wilderness on May 6 by completing a forced march and then directing a counterattack that saved the Confederate right flank. In circumstances remarkably similar to the wounding of Stonewall Jackson the previous year, Longstreet's own men fired at the general and his staff, hitting the First Corps commander in the throat and right arm—a serious injury that required an extended period of absence. Because his officer corps had been thinned, Lee desperately needed the services of his lieutenant for the rest of the Overland campaign and beginning of the siege of Petersburg. One Confederate staff officer felt "very anxious that Genl. Longstreet should get back to the army. . . . Genl. Lee needs him not only to advise with, but Genl. Longstreet has a very suggestive mind and none of the other Lt. Genls. have this."

With a husky voice and a paralyzed arm, Longstreet returned to the First Corps in October. The general's condition presented Lee with a perfect opportunity to reassign his subordinate to a less critical post, but Lee immediately gave Longstreet command of the army's left flank, a line that stretched north of the James River. After the Federals broke through the Petersburg defenses on April 2, 1865, Longstreet guided his own troops as well as remnants of the Third Corps during the retreat to Appomattox. When a fellow officer suggested that Longstreet impress upon Lee the need to surrender, Longstreet sharply rebuked him, saying that only Lee could make that decision and that he would follow the general to the end.

Longstreet's reputation declined precipitously after the war, largely owing to the efforts of a cadre of Southern officers headed by Jubal Early. Through the *Southern Historical Society Papers,* these men blamed Longstreet for the loss at Gettysburg and characterized him as a sulky, insubordinate officer who consistently undermined Lee's operations. Longstreet's published criticism of Lee's actions at Gettysburg in the *Philadelphia Weekly Times* of November 3, 1877, and February 28, 1878, and his affiliation with the Republican party after the war made him a convenient scapegoat for the South's defeat. Edward Porter Alexander, who had been at Gettysburg, noted that "Longstreet's *great* mistake was not in the *war,* but in some of his awkward and apparently bitter criticisms of Gen Lee." The negative sentiments held against Longstreet are reflected in an 1876 letter written by Early: "He [Longstreet] is sincerely purporting to lay claim to the chief glory for the seven days around Richmond, but the rebut I gave him on that head has taken the wind out of his sails."

Nevertheless, although Longstreet did not always agree with Lee's decisions, they maintained a warm relationship and respected each other professionally. Lee frequently camped next to Longstreet, and a British observer noted in 1863 that the friendship between the two officers was "quite touching—they are almost always together." Longstreet exhibited shortcomings as an independent commander and lacked delicacy in dealing with subordinates. In combat, however, he had few equals. Unlike Stonewall Jackson who frequently attacked in a piecemeal fashion, Longstreet delivered well-coordinated assaults by concentrating his forces against a specific point.

Pardoned on June 19, 1867, Longstreet, through connections with the Republican party, obtained a number of governmental appointments, including surveyor of the port of New Orleans in 1869; postmaster at Gainesville, Georgia, in 1879; U.S. minister to Turkey in 1880; and Federal marshal for northern Georgia in 1881. President William McKinley appointed him U.S. commissioner of railroads in 1897. Longstreet spent the remaining years of his life near Gainesville where he died on January 2, 1904.

BIBLIOGRAPHY

Alexander, Edward Porter. *Fighting for the Confederacy: The Personal Recollections of General Edward Porter Alexander.* Edited by Gary W. Gallagher. Chapel Hill, N.C., 1989.

Eckenrode, H. J., and Bryan Conrad. *James Longstreet: Lee's War Horse.* Chapel Hill, N.C., 1933. Reprint, Chapel Hill, N.C., 1986.

Longstreet, James. *From Manassas to Appomattox.* Philadelphia, 1896.

Piston, William Garrett. *Lee's Tarnished Lieutenant: James Longstreet and His Place in Southern History.* Athens, Ga., 1987.

Sorrel, G. Moxley. *Recollections of a Confederate Staff Officer.* New York, 1905. Reprint, Dayton, Ohio, 1978.

Peter S. Carmichael

LORING, W. W. (1818–1886), Confederate major general and Egyptian Army officer (1869–1879). William Wing Loring was born December 4, 1818, in Wilmington, North Carolina. His long military career probably included more of interest before and after the Civil War than during his four Confederate years. He was fighting Seminoles at the age of fourteen and held a commission when he was eighteen. Loring won a seat in the Florida legislature while in his early twenties and was commissioned as captain in the U.S. Army during the Mexican War. He came out of that war a brevet colonel and missing an arm. Loring remained in the army until 1861, at which time he was by far its youngest colonel.

After a brief stint as a Confederate colonel, Loring received brigadier general's rank on May 20, 1861. He participated in the complex and disappointing campaigns in northwestern Virginia in 1861 before receiving orders to collaborate with Thomas J. ("Stonewall") Jackson early in 1862. The two generals soon found themselves in violent disagreement over the location of winter quarters assigned to Loring's men. Richmond sided with Loring, who was promoted in the midst of the controversy. After commanding near Charleston, Virginia, in 1862, Loring went west to join John C. Pemberton's army. He evaded the Vicksburg entrapment and commanded a division in the army led by Joseph E. Johnston and then by John Bell Hood, participating in the late-1864 disasters in Tennessee. Loring surrendered with Johnston in North Carolina.

General Loring went to Egypt in 1869 to accept a commission as brigadier from the khedive. During a decade in that service Loring earned decorations and promotion. For the last seven years of his life the veteran officer lived in New York and Florida. He died December 30, 1886, and was buried in St. Augustine, Florida.

[*See also* Loring-Jackson Incident.]

BIBLIOGRAPHY

Loring, William W. *A Confederate Soldier in Egypt.* New York, 1884.

Wessels, William L. *Born to Be a Soldier.* Fort Worth, Tex., 1971.

Robert K. Krick

LORING-JACKSON INCIDENT. In the winter of 1861–1862 Maj. Gen. Thomas J. ("Stonewall") Jackson conducted a controversial winter campaign in the mountains and the Shenandoah Valley of northwestern Virginia. After receiving reluctant approval for his plans, Jackson was reinforced by troops under Brig. Gen. William W. Loring.

The small Army of the Valley left Winchester on New Years' Day, 1862, and occupied the town of Romney two weeks later, after difficult marching and countermarching in snow and sleet. Jackson's troops fought the bitter weather, widespread illness, and each other more than they did the Federals and were in no condition to continue the campaign. Loring and his men, to make matters worse, were near mutiny over Jackson's supposed incompetence and favoritism toward his own brigades. Jackson, however, ordered Loring to occupy Romney for the winter while the rest of the army returned to Winchester and operated from there.

When Loring complained to Secretary of War Judah P. Benjamin, Benjamin ordered Jackson to send Loring back to Winchester immediately. Though Jackson complied with Benjamin's order, he tendered his resignation on January 31, 1862, protesting, "with such interference in my command I cannot expect to be of much service in the field."

A host of allies, including Governor John Letcher of Virginia, pressured Jackson to stay and persuaded him to withdraw his resignation in mid-February. The Romney campaign was overshadowed by the bitter Loring-Jackson dispute, with the result that Confederate civil authorities would not overlook Jackson's insistence on military authority again.

BIBLIOGRAPHY

Chambers, Lenoir. *"Stonewall" Jackson.* Vol. 2. New York, 1959.

Tanner, Robert G. *Stonewall in the Valley: Thomas J. "Stonewall" Jackson's Shenandoah Valley Campaign, Spring 1862.* Garden City, N.Y., 1976.

Vandiver, Frank E. *Mighty Stonewall.* New York, 1957. Reprint, Texas A & M University Military History Series, no. 9. College Station, Tex., 1988.

J. Tracy Power

LOSSES AND NUMBERS. *For discussion of the number of combatants and casualties in the Civil War, see* Civil War, *article on* Losses and Numbers, *and entries on particular battles.*

LOST CAUSE. [*This entry is composed of two articles,* An Overview, *which discusses changing Southern interpretations of the Civil War and Confederate defeat, and* Iconography, *which discusses graphic and sculptural depictions of Confederate heroes and military incidents. See also* Burial of Latané; Civil War, *articles on* Causes of War *and* Causes of Defeat; Confederate Veteran; Film and Video; Julio, E. D. B.; Juneteenth; Literature, *article on* The Confederacy in Literature; Memorial Day; Memorial Organizations; Monuments and Memorials; Printmaking; Southern Historical Society; Volck, Adalbert.]

An Overview

The Lost Cause, the title of Edward A. Pollard's 1866 history of the Confederacy, first referred to the South's defeat in the Civil War, but in time it came to designate the region's memory of the war as well.

Appomattox brought defeat, desolation, and despair to the white South. Almost at once, Southerners began to memorialize their failed cause, establishing Confederate Memorial Day and dedicating funeral monuments to the Confederate dead. These activities, usually held in cemeteries, evoked mourning and melancholy even as they honored the soldiers. They formed part of a larger process through which white Southerners assimilated defeat. Former Confederates reexamined their defense of slavery and decision to secede from the Union and judged both legal and moral. To explain their defeat, some Southerners pointed to the Confederates' personal sins, such as drinking or swearing. But most Southerners proclaimed the South blameless, sought solace in biblical promises that God tested those whom he loved best, and concluded that God had chosen the South for some great destiny. Having decided God had not abandoned them, white Southerners sought other explanations for their defeat. A few leaders blamed each other; others questioned the unity, discipline, or commitment of the Southern people. Almost no one criticized the fighting mettle of Confederate soldiers; rather, their heroism was praised.

In the 1870s the process of coming to terms with defeat entered a new phase. Jubal A. Early and a few other former Confederate leaders organized the Southern Historical Society (SHS), which, through its publications and the other Southern writings it endorsed, established certain "truths" about the Confederate cause: the South had not fought to preserve slavery; secession was a constitutional and justifiable response to Northern violations of the national compact; and Robert E. Lee and Thomas J. ("Stonewall") Jackson were perfect heroes whose very existence testified to Confederate nobility. When explaining Confederate defeat, Early and the SHS offered two not

"The Conquered Banner." Sheet music cover for a postwar song mourning the defeat of the Confederacy. Lithograph printed in black, red, blue, and buff on wove paper. Published by A. E. Blackmar, New Orleans, Louisiana, 1866. Library of Congress

altogether consistent explanations: James Longstreet's tardiness at Gettysburg led to the loss of the war, and the Confederate armies succumbed only to overwhelming numbers and resources.

Beginning in the late 1880s, the mourning and self-examination of the early postwar years gave way by the turn of the century to a popular celebration of the war. Communities throughout the South dedicated Confederate monuments. A few of these statues memorialized generals or other leaders, but most honored the common soldiers and took the form of a lone soldier, often at rest, atop a tall shaft on the courthouse square or a central street. In 1889 the United Confederate Veterans formed and chose as its leader John B. Gordon, a Confederate general committed to a New South and reconciliation with the North. Within a decade, the United Daughters of the Confederacy and the Sons of Confederate Veterans organized. All three groups participated in annual reunions of Confederate veterans, which became regional festivals that drew huge crowds. Some scholars argue that this turn-of-the-century Confederate celebration expressed a civil religion that preserved a distinctive regional identity and Lost Cause mentality. It did indirectly foster white supremacy, state rights, and Democratic party solidarity, as well as incorporate most of the positions held by the SHS. But its rituals primarily celebrated the sacrifice and heroism of the soldiers and vindicated the honor of the South. The celebration thereby rendered the Lost Cause a glorious memory with much of the war's pain, passions, and such issues as slavery or independence expunged. In fact, it did little to revive wartime ideology or forge a distinctively regional identity, but instead reinforced Southerners' deference to leaders and loyalty to country, now the reunited nation.

In 1898 the Spanish-American War allowed the South to demonstrate its loyalty and honor under fire. In the war's wake, and amid a national resurgence of racism that rendered reconciliation among whites easier, most Northerners joined in the celebration of the Confederate soldiers. Robert E. Lee became a national hero, and Blue-Gray reunions demonstrated the North's respect for its former foes. With Northern acknowledgment of Southern honor and with regional confidence restored, the Confederate celebration lost much of its intensity. As the twentieth century progressed, fewer Confederate monuments were erected. As the veteran generation died off, Confederate reunions became less spectacular, and in 1932 the old soldiers held their last major review. Sons' and daughters' organizations persisted, but neither assumed the central role in Southern society the veterans had held. With this decline of the organizations and ceremonies of the Lost Cause, no one interpretation of the war dominated Southern culture as it once had.

Southern academics and other intellectuals developed independent, conflicting interpretations of the war. In their 1930 manifesto, *I'll Take My Stand,* the Nashville agrarians sought to counter both New South commercialism and the ills of modern industrial society by promoting an image of an agrarian South, although one that all but ignored the existence of slavery. Thereafter a few conservative Southern intellectuals similarly evoked the memory of the Old South and the Confederacy in opposition to modern developments they disdained. A larger number of Southern intellectuals, however, rethought their society's celebration of the Confederacy. Novelist William Faulkner, journalist W. J. Cash, historian C. Vann Woodward, and others saw slavery as central to the sectional confrontation, stressed the Civil War's devastating effects on the South, and claimed that defeat helped create a distinctive regional mentality characterized by guilt and an appreciation for human limitations. By the 1960s, a few historians influenced by this tradition even attributed Confederate defeat to guilt over slavery which had led to a failure of Confederate nationalism. Not all historians embraced such explanations; over the course of the century scholars attributed the war to a conflict of civilizations, a blundering generation, the collapse of the political party system, and a host of other factors. They offered myriad explanations of Confederate defeat, although perhaps the overwhelming-numbers-and-resources argument remained preeminent. Most Southern historians and intellectuals, though, emphasized the importance of slavery to the conflict and viewed the war as more tragic than did the Confederate celebration or twentieth-century popular culture.

A few scholars find popular acceptance of failure, guilt, and human limits, which they label the Lost Cause mentality, in twentieth-century country music. Such sentiments appeared in many country songs, but that probably reflected the hard realities of Southern rural and lower-class life rather than any influence of the Lost Cause. The popular memory of the Civil War more often took heroic form. Novels and films—especially the silent classic *Birth of a Nation* and one of the most popular movies of all time, *Gone with the Wind*—portrayed the Old South as a conservative but romantic place that suffered a terrible defeat. Yet in most, as in *Gone with the Wind,* Confederates appeared as heroic figures who survived, if not triumphed, in the end, and slavery seemed a benign if not beneficial institution. Once again, an absence of concern about the plight of African Americans made it easier for both Northern and Southern whites to honor the heroes of the Southern cause. With twentieth-century popular culture's glorification of the Confederacy, following its celebration at the turn of the century, many white Southerners even joked that the South had not actually lost the war, which suggested that the heritage of defeat had ceased to be very important to or even very real for them. Rather than displaying some special caution or wisdom rooted in defeat, white Southerners became among the most patriotic of Americans; the Lost Cause had primarily fostered respect for the military and unquestioning patriotism.

The Civil War Centennial, more a Northern than a Southern celebration, did little to reverse the decline of interest in the Lost Cause or to reshape its definition. Rather, the centennial further demonstrated the increasing commercialization and trivialization of the memory of the war. During the civil rights revolt of the 1950s and 1960s, many white Southerners did revive the use of Confederate symbols, especially the Confederate flag and "Dixie," in behalf of segregation and white supremacy. They thereby did much to reverse what the turn-of-the-century Confederate celebration had done to render them symbols of honor and loyalty to country. In the 1980s continued display of the Confederate flag exacerbated tensions between white and black Southerners. By then blacks who objected to Confederate symbols as an assertion of white supremacy probably reacted more to the battles of the 1960s than to those of the 1860s. But with few exceptions, black Southerners had never participated in or embraced the Lost Cause. For them the Civil War brought not defeat but deliverance from slavery. They gloried not in Confederate legions but in their ancestors' participation in a Union army that brought emancipation, which many black communities after the war, and into the present, celebrated on January 1, June 19, or various other dates.

These conflicts over Confederate symbols exposed, more than anything else, the nation's failure to establish a biracial society after it emancipated the slaves, but they also revealed that the Civil War remained important for some Southerners. Even in the 1970s and 1980s, many people, not just Southerners, reenacted Civil War battles. The Daughters of the Confederacy and Sons of Confederate Veterans persisted; many of their members continued to interpret the war much as the SHS had. But only a small minority of Southerners participated in reenactments or descendants' organizations; for the majority, Confederate symbols and evocations of the Lost Cause had little fixed meaning and little clear relationship to the issues that motivated Confederates from 1861 through 1865. When a neoconservative Harvard student flew the Confederate flag out her window to challenge liberal calls for cultural diversity on campus; when a country-music singer bragged that if the South had won the war, murderers would be hanged and the day Elvis Presley died would be a national holiday; and when an advertisement for an Atlanta hotel featured William Tecumseh Sherman's picture and told patrons "Say Sherman sent you" to receive a discount, then defining any specific ideological or cultural content to the Lost Cause became difficult, if not futile. Moreover, in the 1980s most white Southerners displayed limited knowledge of or interest in the history of the Civil War. One survey found that just 39 percent of white Southerners claimed to have had an ancestor in the Confederate army; another 37 percent did not know if their ancestors had fought or not. Only 30 percent of the same respondents admitted they had a great deal of interest in Southern history, though another 51 percent claimed to have some interest.

By the 1990s the memory of the Civil War had not totally disappeared from Southern culture, but certainly the specificity and power of the Lost Cause had dramatically declined.

BIBLIOGRAPHY

Connelly, Thomas L., and Barbara L. Bellows. *God and General Longstreet: The Lost Cause and the Southern Mind.* Baton Rouge, La., 1982.

Foster, Gaines M. *Ghosts of the Confederacy: Defeat, the Lost Cause, and the Emergence of the New South, 1865–1913.* New York, 1987.

Kirby, Jack Temple. *Media-Made Dixie: The South in the American Imagination.* Athens, Ga., 1986.

Neely, Mark E., Jr., Harold Holzer, and Gabor S. Boritt. *The Confederate Image: Prints of the Lost Cause.* Chapel Hill, N.C., 1987.

Pressly, Thomas J. *Americans Interpret Their Civil War.* New York, 1962.

Weaver, Richard M. *The Southern Tradition at Bay: A History of Postbellum Thought.* Edited by George Core and M. E. Bradford. New Rochelle, N.Y., 1968.

Wilson, Charles Reagan. *Baptized in Blood: The Religion of the Lost Cause, 1865–1920.* Athens, Ga., 1980.

Wilson, Charles Reagan. " 'God's Project': The Southern Civil Religion, 1920–1980." In *Religion and the Life of the Nation: American Recoveries.* Edited by Rowland A. Sherrill. Urbana, Ill., 1990.

GAINES M. FOSTER

Iconography

One of the great ironies of Confederate iconography is that while the cause lived, it was rarely depicted in the popular arts, but after it was lost, it was widely celebrated in postwar graphics. In yet a further irony, much of this retrospective Lost Cause parlor art was created not by Southern publishers but by Northern ones eager to profit from the reopening of the Southern marketplace, where the native print industry had all but died during the war.

Lost Cause icons—engravings and lithographs of the Confederacy's great heroes and most famous military incidents—came pouring off the presses in New York, Philadelphia, Boston, and Chicago after 1866. So did sentimental genre scenes illuminating Southern defeat and suffering, typified by Currier & Ives's lithograph of a Confederate veteran returning to a war-ravaged home, a print aptly titled *The Lost Cause.* A landmark example of the Lost Cause icon was the print of William D. Washington's painting, *The Burial of Latané,* published in 1868 and popular for generations. As late as 1863 the Virginian who owned the original canvas noted that throughout his life he had seen "many of the steel engravings hanging on the walls of this county and neighboring counties," adding, "I really believe that these engravings helped to hold the Southern People together as one after the war."

Another important Lost Cause icon celebrating two wartime generals, *The Last Meeting of Lee and Jackson,* first appeared in a print adaptation in New Yorker Frederick Halpin's 1872 engraving. It won far greater acclaim and acceptance than the original E. B. D. Julio painting on which it was based.

Robert E. Lee and Thomas J. ("Stonewall") Jackson, together with Jefferson Davis, constituted a Lost Cause "trinity" of icons portrayed more often in prints than any other Confederate heroes. Jackson, surprisingly, proved an object of fascination for Northerners, perhaps because this "Cromwell in Gray" seemed more comprehensible to the Puritan Union culture than cavaliers like Lee. Currier & Ives even celebrated Jackson's martyrdom in a reverential deathbed print granting him a wholly military setting for his final moments, when in fact Jackson had died in a house, not a tent.

Davis had a checkered career in Lost Cause art. At first he was mercilessly lampooned in caricatures that vivified the story that he had donned hoopskirts to evade capture by Union troops. But Davis recovered from this symbolic emasculation when he was shackled at Fortress Monroe. Overnight he became a living martyr of the Lost Cause, and his reemergence was celebrated in engraved and lithographed tributes from then until his death in 1889.

No Confederate hero inspired as many prints—or as consistently reverential ones—as did Robert E. Lee. Although the enfeebled Confederate print industry had been unable to produce a single Lee portrait while the war raged, Northern publishers filled the void once the war ended, first portraying him nobly in defeat in an array of Appomattox prints in 1865. Lee's death in 1870 ignited demand for his image, and when competing memorial associations organized fund-raising appeals to erect statues in Lexington and Richmond, both offered Lee prints as premiums. "A grateful people," one observer reported, "gave of their poverty gladly" to purchase the prints—one of which showed Lee in beatific close-up, the other astride his beloved horse, Traveller.

Lost Cause prints proliferated as long as the fashion for home art itself endured. A journalist visiting a Mobile home in 1871 noted what had become true of innumerable Southern dwellings after the war: "Upon the walls were portraits of Gen. R. E. Lee, and Stonewall Jackson, and

Last Meeting of Lee and Jackson. Painting by E. B. D. Julio, 1869. Photography by Katherine Wetzel.

The Museum of the Confederacy, Richmond, Virginia

Jefferson Davis." Added the eyewitness: "Indeed, the first two mentioned I see everywhere in the South, in private as well as in public houses."

Financed in part by the sale of popular prints, Edward Virginius Valentine's recumbent statue of Robert E. Lee was installed in 1883 atop the general's tomb in the chapel of Washington College in Lexington, Virginia. In 1890, the Lee Monument Association's heroic equestrian statue of Lee by sculptor Marius Jean Antonin Mercie was unveiled before a throng of 100,000 in Richmond. An orator for the occasion declared it a blessing that "future generations may see the counterfeit presentment of this . . . bright consummate flower of our civilization."

Completion of these two Lee monuments ushered in a golden age of Confederate statuary. The city of Richmond, in particular, was soon crowded with dazzling sculpture, including a series of large equestrian statues of Jackson, J. E. B. Stuart, and others, crowning the same broad avenue where the Mercie Lee had been installed.

Atlanta, too, became an important outdoor gallery of public icons. The installation of one such tribute, Solon Borglum's sculpture of Gen. John B. Gordon, may best be remembered because it ushered in the saga of the most ambitious of all Confederate sculpture memorials—and also the most disastrous.

Around 1915, a journalist named John Graves and the president of the national United Daughters of the Confederacy, Mrs. Helen Plane, conceived of the idea of a Confederate Memorial for one of the South's grandest vistas: the face of Stone Mountain, Georgia. Appropriately, they turned to Solon Borglum's brother, Gutzon Borglum, who would later sculpt Mount Rushmore.

Borglum's plans proved even more ambitious than Grant's and Mrs. Plane's. Dismissing their proposal for a mere Lee portrait as nothing more than a "stamp on a barn door," Borglum conceived of a far grander monumental frieze that would portray artillery and infantry, and colossal sculptures of Lee, Jackson, and Davis. He began work in 1915, but was interrupted by World War I. Work resumed in 1922, and on January 19, 1924—Lee's 117th birthday—the Stone Mountain Monumental Association unveiled the massive head of Lee.

This proved the apex of the movement to create Confederate memorial statuary. Soon after, Borglum began feuding with the Monumental Association over artistic details and money. When the Association fired him, he destroyed all his models, leaving Stone Mountain permanently unfinished—a monument not only to Lee but to the passionate, three-generation-long effort to create permanent sculpted tributes to Confederate heroes.

BIBLIOGRAPHY

Buttre, J. C. *Catalogue of Engravings for Sale by J. C. Buttre & Co.* New York, 1884.

Connelly, Thomas L. *The Marble Man: Robert E. Lee and His Image in American Society.* Baton Rouge, La., 1977.

Neely, Mark E., Jr., Harold Holzer, and Gabor S. Boritt. *The Confederate Image: Prints of the Lost Cause.* Chapel Hill, N.C., 1987.

Smith, Rex Alan. *The Carving of Mount Rushmore.* New York, 1985.

HAROLD HOLZER

LOUISIANA. As part of the Confederacy's Trans-Mississippi Department, Louisiana was on the military periphery during much of the Civil War. The capture of New Orleans by Federal forces on May 1, 1862, was a pivotal event, but the state's major battles seem like skirmishes compared to Virginia's titanic struggles. For the conflict's last three years, two governments vied for control of the Pelican State: a military-dominated Unionist regime centered in New Orleans and a Confederate administration that was repeatedly forced to shift its state capital farther north. Exercising tenuous authority over southern Louisiana (designated the Department of the Gulf by occupying authorities), the Unionist state government played an important role in molding federal race and Reconstruction policy.

If the state was confined to the military sidelines, white Louisianians were often in the thick of things. Masses of them mobilized for war. Approximately 56,000 whites enlisted in Confederate armies, while another 10,000 served in the state militia. Together they represented 64 percent of Louisiana's white military manhood as of 1860 (men between the ages of thirteen and forty-five). Louisianians in gray mostly saw action beyond state borders, in places like Shiloh, Manassas, and Malvern Hill. New Orleans's famed Washington Artillery served more or less continuously with Robert E. Lee's Army of Northern Virginia, although a battery fought in Tennessee. Roberdeau Wheat's Louisiana Tigers, comprising roustabouts from the New Orleans waterfront, participated in every major campaign in Virginia, Maryland, and Pennsylvania. Moreover, Louisiana made important contributions to the Confederacy's top brass. Creole Gen. P. G. T. Beauregard, who commanded Confederate forces in Charleston during the bombardment of Fort Sumter, led Southern armies to victory at First Manassas. Braxton Bragg, one of eight full generals commissioned by the Confederacy (Beauregard was another), went from being a colonel on Louisiana Governor Thomas O. Moore's staff to overall commander of the Army of Tennessee. Richard Taylor, Zachary's son, served with distinction under Thomas J. ("Stonewall") Jackson before assuming charge of the newly formed District of Western Louisiana (as Confederate-controlled northern Louisiana was called) in August 1862.

Several civilians left their mark on the Confederacy. Without question the smartest man in Jefferson Davis's cabinet was former U.S. Senator Judah P. Benjamin, whose portfolio variously included Justice, War, and State. John Slidell, Benjamin's Senate colleague, became Confederate Commissioner to France, and Judge Pierre A. Rost joined in the Confederacy's first diplomatic mission to Europe. Confederate Congressman Duncan F. Kenner, chairman of the Ways and Means Committee, spearheaded the eleventh-hour effort by the expiring Richmond government to barter emancipation for European intervention.

Secession

As a general rule, support for the cause of Southern rights was strongest in states with large slave populations. But Louisiana, one-half of whose 1860 population of 708,000 was black, is a case apart. John C. Breckinridge, for example, the Southern Democratic presidential candidate during the 1860 presidential election, polled less than 45 percent of the vote—his lowest proportion in the Gulf South and second lowest among the eleven states that

Map of Louisiana.

Harper's Pictorial History of the Great Rebellion

eventually formed the Confederacy. The south Louisianian sugar industry's dependence on tariff protection accounts for some of this residual Unionism. Another explanation was yeoman dissent in places like Winn Parish, historically a seedbed of radical protest. But most of the state's surprisingly buoyant Unionism can be traced to the influence of New Orleans, the South's largest and oldest city, and home to a quarter of the state's population. Linked to national markets by the Mississippi River, the city's largely Northern-born commercial community was reluctant to cut its lifeline to the free states. Pro-Union feeling was even stronger at the bottom of the white social structure, where recent immigrants predominated. (Nearly 40 percent of New Orleans's 1860 population was foreign-born.) Angry that Stephen A. Douglas had outpolled Breckinridge in every New Orleans district, Senator Slidell complained that "here in the city seven-eighths of the vote for Douglas were cast by the Irish and Germans." Had it not been for strict registration laws that reduced the number of immigrant voters, Breckinridge's statewide percentage would likely have been even smaller. Later in the war thousands of New Orleans's foreign-born residents joined the Union army.

Because of the strength and breadth of pro-Union sentiment, Louisiana's secessionists pulled out all stops to sever the state's ties with Washington. Calling the legislature into special session shortly following Abraham Lincoln's election, Governor Moore declared: "I do not think it comports with the honor and self-respect of Louisiana as a slaveholding state, to live under the government of a Black Republican president." Moore was an immediate secessionist; he favored separate state action, as opposed to the strategy of having Louisiana leave the Union in concert with other slave states. Before the secession convention met, he ordered state militiamen to seize federal military installations in Baton Rouge, New Orleans, and along the river. The election for convention delegates took place in a climate of intimidation. The immediate secessionists, organized into various home guards, vigilance committees, and Southern rights associations, placed those favoring compromise on the defensive. In New Orleans, South Carolina native Benjamin A. Palmer, the city's foremost Presbyterian minister, delivered a two-hour fire-breathing sermon that effectively silenced the wavering Unionists within his up-scale congregation.

Immediate secessionists scored a narrow 52-to-48-percent victory on January 7, 1861, because many demoralized Unionist voters stayed home on election day. Compared to the presidential election two months earlier, turnout among rural voters had dropped by nearly a quarter. Owing to the fact that seats in the secession convention were apportioned on the basis of total population, this slim electoral majority for disunion ballooned into an 80-to-44 margin in the delegate count. On January 26 the ordinance of secession passed by a vote of 113 to 17, despite the lonely prediction by the Unionist judge James Taliaferro of war and anarchy. As was the case in most states that joined the Confederacy, Louisiana never submitted its secession ordinance to a popular vote. Abetted by the cross-pressures of regional loyalty and racial hysteria, a resolute secessionist minority had brilliantly undermined the conditional Unionism of Louisiana's white majority.

Military Action

Trainloads of embalmed corpses and wounded soldiers from Shiloh were still arriving in New Orleans in early April 1862 when a Federal flotilla under Adm. David Farragut steamed up the Mississippi toward the Confederacy's largest port. Seventy-five miles downriver, near Forts Jackson and St. Phillip, Confederate defenders had strung a makeshift defensive chain of vessels and a fire raft across the Mississippi, but Farragut's fleet successfully ran the gauntlet on April 24. Five days later the Union navy dropped anchor outside the New Orleans levee; two days after that, following Union Gen. Benjamin F. Butler's capture of Fort Jackson, Farragut raised the Stars and Stripes over the U.S. Custom House on Canal Street in downtown New Orleans. Meanwhile, Mayor John Monroe's obstructionism had given Confederate Gen. Mansfield Lovell enough time to evacuate the four thousand troops still in the city and torch the cotton stacked near the riverfront.

The fall of New Orleans opened up southern Louisiana for Union army forays, and they were not long in coming. Farragut's fleet forced the surrender of Baton Rouge on May 12 and then continued upstream to threaten Vicksburg. Three months later, on August 5, 1862, Confederate troops under Gen. John C. Breckinridge drove the Union garrison back to New Orleans, but had to abandon the state capital for the second and final time in December 1862. Even before retaking Baton Rouge, blue-clad soldiers began punching their way up and down the state's major north-south bayous, disrupting plantation routine and forcing wide-scale planter refugeeing to Texas. In October 1862, for example, the Bayou LaFourche expedition resulted in the loss of southeastern Louisiana to a Federal force under the command of Gen. Godfrey Weitzel.

The next spring another Union expedition, this one up Bayou Teche, farther to the west, tried to squeeze Confed-

Burning of Baton Rouge, Louisiana, December 30, 1862.
Frank Leslie's Illustrated Famous Leaders and Battle Scenes of the Civil War

erate troops out of southern Louisiana altogether. By this time, Louisiana had been reassigned to Gen. E. Kirby Smith's Trans-Mississippi Department and placed under the command of Richard Taylor in the District of Western Louisiana. To clear an invasion path to Texas, in early April 1863 the Department of the Gulf's new commander, Nathaniel P. Banks, moved against Taylor's scattered Confederate forces west and north of Brashear City. Banks's army was three times larger than Taylor's, and his gunboats threatened to outflank every defensive position Confederates managed to erect on the narrow neck of land between the bayou and the swamps. There was some sharp fighting at Irish Bend on April 14, but most of the campaign consisted of rearguard skirmishing. Burning bridges as they went, Confederates retreated from New Iberia through Vermilionville and Opelousas. By May 7 Banks had reached Alexandria, the traditional dividing point between Franco southern and Anglo northern Louisiana, obliging Taylor to relocate his headquarters to Natchitoches. The Confederate state government meanwhile had fallen all the way back to Shreveport.

The expulsion of Southern forces from southwestern Louisiana was only temporary. Less than a week after arriving in Alexandria, Banks redeployed the bulk of his army against Maj. Gen. Franklin Gardner's Confederate garrison at Port Hudson, twenty-five miles north of Baton Rouge. Port Hudson was the southern hinge on the Confederacy's remaining door to the Trans-Mississippi West. Throughout the winter and spring of 1863 Ulysses S. Grant had been hammering away at the northern hinge at Vicksburg. After reaching Vicksburg's rear in May, Grant expected his Louisiana counterpart to join him for the final blow. But Banks, reluctant to become Grant's second fiddle, moved on Port Hudson instead.

Situated, like Vicksburg, on a hairpin curve of the Mississippi River, Port Hudson was fortified along a several-mile front approachable only through thick forests and deep ravines, some of them blocked by felled trees. Enjoying a huge manpower advantage (40,000 to 5,700), Banks twice tried to take the Confederate works by frontal assault, only to suffer stunning casualties. Thereafter he settled in for a protracted siege, which included tunneling mine shafts under Confederate lines. Union forces were ready to detonate explosive charges beneath Gardner's fortifications, when the Confederate commander surrendered Port Hudson on July 9, 1863. Gardner realized Vicksburg's fall five days earlier ruled out Confederate forces coming to the relief of his beleaguered garrison. The Confederacy was now cut in two, and Taylor's troops were forced to regroup in northern Louisiana.

Conceived to unify Louisiana under Unionist rule, liberate Texas, and capture stores of cotton, Banks's Red River campaign in the spring of 1864 was the last major military action on Louisiana soil. Having cleared Confederate forces from Alexandria, Bank's 27,000-man army waited until the Red River rose high enough to permit Como. David Porter's gunboats to float past the double rapids above the city. Because Banks enjoyed the supporting fire of Union gunboats, Taylor was leery of giving battle near the river. But the Union commander threw away his naval advantage by leaving the river road for a shorter inland route to Shreveport. Taylor furiously attacked Banks's advancing columns at Mansfield on April 8, 1864, throwing them back in confusion. The next day he followed up with another assault on Federal forces dug in at Pleasant Hill. Banks thereupon fell back to the Mississippi River, where naval transports carried his army to the safety of New Orleans.

Banks's abortive Red River campaign effectively concluded full-scale military operations in the Confederate District of Western Louisiana. Guerrilla bands composed of deserters and camp followers from both sides desolated the no-man's land between Union and Confederate lines, especially in north central Louisiana, where arson and rustling were rampant. They were active in the contraband trade in cotton, which boomed after Confederate and Federal officials concluded the illicit commerce was mutually beneficial. The guerrilla bands became more wanton as defeat swelled the ranks of Confederate desertion.

The Civil War inflicted wholesale destruction on Louisiana. During the Teche campaign, for example, footsore soldiers from both armies plundered mules and horses, carts and carriages, as they marched up the bayou. The following year Alexandria was badly burned, and each side blamed the other. The most devastating Southern loss may have been the destruction of the saltworks at Avery Island, which, since its founding in May 1862, had produced more than 22 million pounds of salt for the Confederacy.

Government and Politics

Avery Island is one of the better-known examples of Confederate involvement in the economy. But there were others, especially under Governor Henry W. Allen, a Confederate brigadier general who had been wounded in the Battle of Baton Rouge. Assuming office in January 1864, Allen built state laboratories to provide medicine, erected an iron foundry in Shreveport, opened trade with Mexico to secure arms and scarce civilian goods, and distributed free cotton cards to enable hard-pressed families to spin their own cloth. He was keenly concerned with the welfare of soldiers' families. Under his administration state stores were established to provide affordable necessities to the common folk and soak up surplus state treasury certificates. Allen was also one of the first prominent Confederates to advocate arming the slaves. Historian Douglas S. Freeman described him as "the single great administrator produced by the Confederacy."

In part because of Allen's governing style, relations between Richmond and Confederate state authorities never deteriorated to the degree they did in Georgia and North Carolina. To be sure, there was ongoing friction over Louisiana's defenses. Governor Moore wrangled with the Davis administration about keeping munitions and soldiers within the state. Sharp words were exchanged over Richmond's choice of military commanders for Louisiana. But comparatively speaking, these difference never festered into open sores. Allen and Moore both cooperated with Davis's efforts to strengthen the value of Confederate currency, which was worth more in Louisiana than almost anywhere else. The Confederate legislature also helped dampen class conflict by postponing debt and tax collections. As for partisanship, according to historian Jefferson Davis Bragg, "Politics of the ordinary sort took a vacation in Louisiana during the war."

Politics, ironically, did not take a holiday in the Federal Department of the Gulf. New Orleans was a hotbed of political controversy. From almost the moment the city fell into Union hands, President Lincoln looked on Louisiana as a laboratory for field-testing Federal race and Reconstruction policy, and his two political generals were eager assistants. Of the two, Butler was more controversial because of his brusque treatment of recalcitrant Confederate sympathizers. His relief and public works program offered employment to thousands of destitute whites, especially from immigrant households, and laid the groundwork for the Free State party, which eventually metamorphosed into the postwar Republican party. Banks, on the other hand, tilted to the wealthy sugar planters and New Orleans merchants who controlled the conservative Union movement.

Butler's and Banks's clashing Reconstruction priorities were shaped by their different approaches to black free labor. The Department of the Gulf had been exempted from the Emancipation Proclamation, but that technicality did not prevent thousands of slaves from fleeing to Union lines. To give only one illustration, almost eight thousand bondsmen flocked to the five-mile-long caravan that trailed Banks's Teche expedition back to New Orleans. As contraband camps swelled with black refugees, Butler induced the slaves to return to plantations by ordering planters to pay wages and prohibiting the use of the whip. In contrast, Banks, who was cultivating political support among old slave owners, cut wages and used Federal provost marshals to bolster planter authority. Both generals, however, sought to enlist African Americans in the Union military, once arming the slaves became official policy. Over twenty-four thousand black Louisianians served in blue, the most from any state. Two of their regiments—one composed of prewar free blacks, the other of slaves—fought with valor in the bloody May 27 assault on Port Hudson.

Just as Federal race policy was framed with reference to Louisiana developments, so was early Reconstruction policy. In December 1862, a year before Lincoln unveiled his own plan of Reconstruction, two south Louisiana Unionists were elected to Congress, though they served only temporarily and as delegates. Lincoln's mild program—which authorized a return to civilian rule whenever 10 percent of the 1860 white population swore allegiance to the United States—resulted in the 1864 election of a Unionist state government under Michael Hahn and a new constitution that abolished slavery but stopped short of enfranchising blacks. Andrew Johnson applied Lincoln's Louisiana model to the rest of the former Confederacy when he succeeded the slain president, only to have Congress overthrow the wartime plan in favor of a Reconstruction program based on black suffrage.

That turn toward radicalism vindicated New Orleans's self-confident free black community. Since 1862 its leaders had been arguing that justice and the future safety of the country dictated giving blacks citizenship. Creole blacks had also been in the forefront of the effort to arm African Americans. Both policies were eventually adopted, but their most persistent advocates were seldom elevated to positions of leadership in the new political order. Whites from outside the state had captured control of the Republican party.

The Civil War ended in Louisiana when Kirby Smith surrendered the Trans-Mississippi Department on May 26, 1865. By this time most of his command had decamped for home fires. The final accounting of Louisiana's failed bid to switch national loyalties was a 73 percent decline in farm value, a 70 percent decline in livestock value, unenumerated machinery losses, broken levees, destroyed railroads, and a terrible loss of young life—a demographic calamity by any definition.

[*For further discussion of battles and cities in Louisiana, see* Baton Rouge, Louisiana; Mansfield, Louisiana; New Orleans, Louisiana; Port Hudson, Louisiana; Red River Campaigns. *See also* Butler's Woman Order; Creoles; Louisiana State Seminary and Military Academy; Louisiana Tigers; *and biographies of numerous figures mentioned herein.*]

BIBLIOGRAPHY

Bragg, Jefferson Davis. *Louisiana in the Confederacy.* Baton Rouge, La., 1941.

Dew, Charles B. "The Long Lost Returns: The Candidates and Their Totals in Louisiana's Secession Election." *Louisiana History* 10 (Fall 1969): 353–369.

McCrary, Peyton. *Abraham Lincoln and Reconstruction: The Louisiana Experiment.* Princeton, 1978.

Moneyhon, Carl, and Bobby Roberts. *Portraits of Conflict: A Photographic History of Louisiana in the Civil War.* Fayetteville, Ark., 1990.

Ripley, C. Peter. *Slaves and Freedmen in Civil War Louisiana.* Baton Rouge, La., 1976.

Winters, John D. *The Civil War in Louisiana.* Baton Rouge, La., 1963.

LAWRENCE N. POWELL

LOUISIANA STATE SEMINARY AND MILITARY ACADEMY. There was no viable public institution of higher learning in antebellum Louisiana until January 2, 1860, when the Louisiana State Seminary of Learning and Military Academy opened for its first session in Pineville, on the north bank of the Red River opposite Alexandria in the center of the state. (The so-called University of Louisiana, established some years earlier in New Orleans, never received legislative support and therefore existed largely on paper. In 1884 its few remaining assets were merged with those of Tulane University, a private institution.) Determined to avoid the mistakes of other states, which had divided public funding among several schools only to see all of them fail, Louisiana officials decided to establish and support only one public institution.

Although languages, science, and mathematics formed the core curriculum, the seminary was operated as a military academy in which both faculty and students wore uniforms and military discipline prevailed. Virginia Military Institute was the explicit model for the Louisiana institution. Five professors, headed by Superintendent William Tecumseh Sherman of Ohio, and 62 cadets comprised the academy community by May 1860. During the second session of 1860–1861, 115 cadets were enrolled, virtually all of whom subsequently served in the Confederate army.

Sherman resigned immediately after state forces seized the Federal arsenal in Baton Rouge and left the seminary on February 20, 1861. Two of the remaining four professors, one of them the future superintendent David F. Boyd, later obtained leaves of absence to serve the Confederacy in the field. With both its faculty and corps of cadets depleted by wartime military service, the seminary closed in the fall of 1861 but reopened on November 2, 1862, with 112 enrolled cadets, mostly young boys in their midteens. As Federal troops approached the school, Superintendent William A. Seay dismissed the cadets for the second time, urging them on April 23, 1863, to either return home or "go fight the enemy." The institution remained closed for the duration of the war. During the 1864 Red River campaign, Federal forces looted and burned the central building.

Little is known of individual cadets who attended the seminary prior to 1863. (Only one of them, however, is known to have supported the Union—Cadet H. B. Taliaferro.) The leading authority on the subject concluded that no similar American institution furnished a higher proportion of its former students to military service during the Civil War. Throughout the Confederate army, Louisiana Seminary cadets were apparently in great demand as drill instructors, small unit leaders, and company grade officers.

Whenever Federal troops under Major General Sherman captured anyone formerly associated with the seminary, Sherman treated the individual with compassion and respect, as he did his former colleague, Lt. Col. David F. Boyd, C.S.A. Sherman retained his affection for the seminary after the war. When the institution was relocated in Baton Rouge in 1869 and renamed Louisiana State University the following year, Sherman, as commanding general of the army, made possible the transfer of the old Pentagon Barracks in Baton Rouge to LSU for use as cadet dormitories.

BIBLIOGRAPHY

Fleming, Walter L. *Louisiana State University: 1860–1896.* Baton Rouge, La., 1936.

Reed, G. M. *David French Boyd.* Baton Rouge, La., 1977.

MARK T. CARLETON

LOUISIANA TIGERS. The name "Louisiana Tigers" derived in 1861 from the Tiger Rifles, a Zouave company in Roberdeau Wheat's Battalion. Wheat's men became so notorious for thievery, brawling, and drunkenness that the battalion soon became known as the Louisiana Tiger Battalion. When other Louisiana commands showed similar behavior, the name was applied to all the Louisiana troops in the Army of Northern Virginia. Almost without exception the units that became notorious for bad behavior were New Orleans commands. The fact that hundreds, if not thousands, of Tigers could not speak English made them even more conspicuous. In fact, many units drilled completely in French for the first year of the war.

There were the approximately thirteen thousand infantry from the Pelican State who served in the Army of Northern Virginia. Originally comprising nine regiments and five battalions, the Tigers were eventually consolidated into two brigades in the Second Corps. The First Louisiana Brigade was composed of the Fifth, Sixth, Seventh, Eighth, and Ninth Louisiana Volunteers; the Second contained the First, Second, Tenth, Fourteenth, and Fifteenth Louisiana Volunteers.

The Tigers fought in every major battle of the eastern theater and at times played a crucial role in them. At First Manassas, Wheat's Battalion first engaged the enemy and delayed them for a crucial time. Under Richard Taylor the First Louisiana Brigade marched through the Shenandoah Valley in 1862 with Thomas ("Stonewall") Jackson, who gave it much of the credit for winning the battles of Front Royal, Winchester, and Port Republic. At Second Manassas, William Edwin Starke's Second Louisiana Brigade earned fame by holding the famous railroad cut with rocks after running out of ammunition. Starke was later killed at Sharpsburg, where the First Louisiana Brigade, now under Harry Thompson Hays, lost 60 percent of its men in thirty minutes. Francis Nicholls led the Second Louisiana Brigade at Chancellorsville and lost his foot during Jackson's celebrated flank attack. Hays's brigade aided Jubal Early in holding the enemy at Fredericksburg and gained acclaim for winning some temporary success at Salem Church.

A LOUISIANA TIGER. NATIONAL ARCHIVES

During the Gettysburg campaign, Hays's brigade made the critical charge that captured Winchester, and the Second Louisiana Brigade captured six hundred Federals at Stephenson's Depot, Virginia. At Gettysburg, Hays's men helped rout the Northerners on the first day and briefly broke the Union line and captured two batteries on Cemetery Hill on July 2. The year ended in disaster when over six hundred of Hays's men were captured during a surprise attack on their position at Rappahannock Station on November 7. Both brigades suffered heavily in the Wilderness, where Leroy A. Stafford, commanding the Second Louisiana Brigade, was mortally wounded.

Because of the heavy losses, the two brigades were consolidated under Hays but kept their separate organizations. Hays was wounded at Spotsylvania on May 9. The Second Louisiana Brigade was mostly overrun and captured at the Mule Shoe, but Hays's brigade played a crucial role in containing the Union breakthrough on the Confederate left. The consolidated brigade, under Zebulon York, accompanied Early to the Monocacy and Washington and fought well throughout the Shenandoah Valley campaign of Sheridan. When York was wounded at Third Winchester, William Raine Peck took command until early 1865. In the last days of the war, the Louisiana Brigade, under Col. Eugene Waggaman, led the attempted breakout of Petersburg at Fort Stedman and was among the last troops to leave the city. At Appomattox only 376 Tigers remained. During the war about 3,300 Tigers had died and at least 10 percent deserted.

[*See also* Foreigners *and biographies of numerous figures mentioned herein.*]

BIBLIOGRAPHY

Jones, Terry L. *The Civil War Memoirs of Capt. William J. Seymour: Reminiscences of a Louisiana Tiger.* Baton Rouge, La., 1991.

Jones, Terry L. *Lee's Tigers: The Louisiana Infantry in the Army of Northern Virginia.* Baton Rouge, La., 1987.

TERRY L. JONES

LOVELL, MANSFIELD (1822–1884), major general. Born on October 20, 1822, in Washington, D.C., Lovell finished ninth of fifty-six at West Point in 1842. Promoted to first lieutenant early in the Mexican War, Lovell survived a severe wound at Belen Gate and earned a brevet captaincy at Chapultepec. He resigned his commission on December 18, 1854, and became deputy street commissioner of New York City, a position he resigned on September 19, 1861, to join the Confederacy.

Appointed major general October 7, 1861, Lovell commanded at New Orleans. Hampered by inferior cannon and a shortage of troops, Lovell abandoned the city in April 1862 after a Federal fleet passed the forts downriver. Although Lovell was vilified by many, Robert E. Lee and others commended his defense and a court of inquiry eventually cleared him. After commanding a division at Vicksburg, he led the right wing at Corinth in October, where, on the second day, he withheld his troops from a hopeless assault. His unappreciative men continued singing the "New Ballad

MANSFIELD LOVELL. NATIONAL ARCHIVES

of Lord Lovell," which memorialized his loss of New Orleans and his drinker's red nose. Despite his skillful rearguard action, he was relieved. In 1864 both Joseph E. Johnston and John Bell Hood futilely requested him as a corps commander. In March 1865, however, Johnston successfully sought Lovell's services, and Lovell was presumably en route when Johnston surrendered.

Lovell returned to New York City after the war. After serving as assistant engineer in the removal of obstructions in the East River, he worked as a civil engineer. He died in New York City June 1, 1884, and was buried in Woodlawn Cemetery.

BIBLIOGRAPHY

Dufour, Charles L. *The Night the War Was Lost.* Garden City, N.Y., 1960.

Heleniak, Roman J., and Lawrence L. Hewitt, eds. *The 1989 Deep Delta Civil War Symposium: Leadership during the Civil War.* Shippensburg, Pa., 1992.

Sutherland, Daniel L. "Mansfield Lovell's Quest for Justice: Another Look at the Fall of New Orleans." *Louisiana History* 24 (1987): 233–259.

LAWRENCE L. HEWITT

LOWREY, MARK PERRIN (1828–1885), brigadier general. Born in McNairy County, Tennessee, December 30, 1828, Lowrey moved with his widowed mother to Mississippi in 1845. After Mexican War service, he worked as a brickmason. Much of his education came from a schoolteacher who boarded in his home. In 1853 he became a Baptist minister.

MARK PERRIN LOWREY. LIBRARY OF CONGRESS

Early in the Civil War Lowrey commanded some troops raised for sixty days' service. In February 1862—"when gloom was upon every Southern home" because of recent defeats (as he later put it)—he conceived it his duty to help organize what became the Thirty-second Mississippi Infantry Regiment. Lowrey became the regiment's commander. Intending to serve but a short time, he found that circumstances required his continued presence.

Remaining in service, Lowrey participated in the battles of the Army of Tennessee from mid-1862 to March 1865. "One of the best officers of his grade in the Army of Tenn," as Lt. Gen. Alexander P. Stewart wrote, he was promoted to brigadier general in October 1863. In early 1865 he acted as division commander.

On March 5 of that year, noting that the army was so reduced in strength that it had twice as many generals as it needed, Lowrey submitted his resignation so he could return to the ministry. It was accepted on March 14.

Lowrey continued in Baptist religious work until his death February 27, 1885. He founded the Blue Mountain

Female Institute at Blue Mountain, Mississippi. He died in Middleton, Tennessee, and is buried in the Blue Mountain Cemetery.

BIBLIOGRAPHY

Bergeron, Arthur W., Jr. "Mark Perrin Lowrey." In *The Confederate General.* Edited by William C. Davis. Vol. 5. Harrisburg, Pa., 1991.

Warner, Ezra J. *Generals in Gray: Lives of the Confederate Commanders.* Baton Rouge, La., 1959.

RICHARD M. MCMURRY

LOWRY, ROBERT (1830–1910), brigadier general and postwar governor of Mississippi. Born March 10, 1830, in Chesterfield District, South Carolina, Lowry moved with his family to Tennessee and then on to Tishomingo County, Mississippi. Raised by an uncle who was a judge in Raleigh, Mississippi, he became a lawyer and served in the Mississippi State Senate.

In 1861 he joined and was quickly elected major of the Sixth Mississippi Infantry Regiment. On May 23, 1862, he became the regiment's colonel. In 1863 he was with the Confederate forces that tried to prevent the capture of Vicksburg, and he won much praise for his performance in the Battle of Port Gibson on May 1. In the following year he was with the Army of Tennessee in the Atlanta and Franklin and Nashville campaigns. At the Battle of Franklin (November 30, 1864), he took command of the brigade when Brig. Gen. John Adams was killed. Seizing a flag, he bravely led the men on in the assault.

Maj. Gen. W. W. Loring called him "an officer of the first order," and in February 1865 he was promoted to brigadier general. He served in the Carolinas campaign of 1865 and surrendered with the Southern forces there. He was paroled at Greensboro, North Carolina (probably on May 1).

Lowry was active in state politics after the war. He served in the legislature, helped overthrow the Republican Reconstruction government, and was twice elected governor (1881, 1885). He died in Jackson on January 19, 1910 and is buried in the city cemetery in Brandon, Mississippi.

BIBLIOGRAPHY

Jones, Terry L. "Robert Lowry." In *The Confederate General.* Edited by William C. Davis. Vol. 4. Harrisburg, Pa., 1991.

Warner, Ezra J. *Generals in Gray: Lives of the Confederate Commanders.* Baton Rouge, La., 1959.

RICHARD M. MCMURRY

LOYALL, BENJAMIN, P. (fl. 1861), naval officer. Born in Virginia, Loyall was a lieutenant in the U.S. Navy when the Civil War began. He soon resigned to offer his services to the Confederacy and was briefly imprisoned at Fort Warren, Massachusetts, by Union naval authorities. After his release, he became a first lieutenant in the Confederate navy, effective November 26, 1861. Loyall commanded the shore defenses of Roanoke Island, carrying an army commission as captain in addition to his naval rank. On February 7 and 8, Federal naval forces landed troops on the island and defeated a Confederate flotilla led by Capt. William F. Lynch. Loyall was forced to abandon the batteries and was captured.

After his parole at Elizabeth City, North Carolina, on February 21, Loyall served aboard the ironclad CSS *Richmond,* part of the James River Squadron. He also participated in the Confederate raid on Johnson's Island Prison in 1863. Later that year, Loyall was among the twenty-one officers sent to Halifax and Wilmington, North Carolina, to help oversee the construction of ironclad vessels.

In January 1864, Loyall joined Captain Lynch in a boat attack on the Federal flotilla at New Bern, North Carolina. As Lynch's second-in-command, Loyall was among the first boarders of the Federal gunboat USS *Underwriter.* Although the Confederates were forced to destroy the vessel instead of escaping aboard it, Loyall won promotion to commander and was given command of the CSS *Neuse,* an armored ram under construction at Whitehall, North Carolina.

Chronic shortages of material, a yellow fever outbreak, and a Federal raid that damaged the hull of the vessel all delayed completion. By the time *Neuse* finally started downstream on April 27, 1864, the river level was dropping steadily, and the vessel traveled only some four miles before running firmly aground. In April 1865 the Confederates destroyed the stranded ironclad upon the approach of Sherman's Federal army.

By this point, Loyall was serving aboard *Patrick Henry,* the school ship for the Confederate Naval Academy. He was paroled at Greensboro, North Carolina, on April 28, 1865.

BIBLIOGRAPHY

Civil War Naval Chronology, 1861–1865. Washington, D.C., 1971.

Gibbons, Tony. *Warships and Naval Battles of the Civil War.* New York, 1989.

Scharf, J. Thomas. *History of the Confederate States Navy.* New York, 1887. Reprint, New York, 1977.

Still, William N., Jr. *Iron Afloat: The Story of the Confederate Armorclads.* Nashville, Tenn., 1971.

ROBERT S. BROWNING III

LUBBOCK, FRANCIS R. (1815–1905), governor of Texas and lieutenant colonel. A native South Carolinian born October 16, 1815, Francis Richard Lubbock was a prominent rancher and politician in Texas prior to the Civil War and a resident of Velasco, near Houston, Harris County. He was elected lieutenant governor of the state in 1857 but was not reelected two years later. In 1860 he was a delegate to the Democratic National Convention at Charleston and supported the Southern rights faction that walked out of the convention. Following the election of Abraham Lincoln, Lubbock became a strong advocate of secession.

In 1861 Lubbock was elected governor over Edward Clark, and upon taking office he began to organize the state for defense. At his suggestion a board was created to direct military preparations, a frontier cavalry regiment was organized, and funds were raised to support these measures. As a member of the military board, Lubbock actively encouraged the development of war industries in the state. Private firms received contracts for the construction of a foundry, a percussion-cap factory, and other munitions works. Machinery was acquired to make cloth and shoes at the state penitentiary.

In the summer of 1862, Lubbock joined with the governors of Arkansas and Louisiana to ask the Confederate government to establish a branch of the Treasury in the Trans-Mississippi, to send more supplies to the district, and to provide additional troops. Lubbock was concerned particularly with the problems on the frontier and feared that the removal of able-bodied men from the state increased the threat of Indian attacks in the West. President Jefferson Davis responded by increasing the autonomy of the Trans-Mississippi region and sending General Theophilus H. Holmes to take command of it.

Lubbock decided not to run for reelection in 1863. He served on the staff of Gen. John B. Magruder who commanded Confederate forces in Texas. He then joined the staff of Gen. John Austin Wharton, who was named commander of Gen. Richard Taylor's cavalry division following the death of Gen. Thomas Green on April 12, 1864. Lubbock was with Wharton in the cavalry action against the Federal rear guard as Gen. Nathaniel Banks retreated from his Red River campaign that spring. In 1864 Lubbock went to Richmond where he received a lieutenant colonel's commission and served on the staff of President Davis as an adviser on Trans-Mississippi affairs.

At the war's end Lubbock accompanied Davis in his effort to escape Union capture, but he was taken with him at Irwinville, Georgia. Lubbock was sent to Fort Delaware where he remained for several months. After being paroled, he returned to Texas, living in Houston, Galveston, and Austin and actively participating in Democratic party politics and holding public office. Lubbock died at Austin on June 22, 1905.

BIBLIOGRAPHY

Lubbock, Francis R. *Six Decades in Texas: The Memoirs of Francis R. Lubbock.* Austin, Tex., 1900.

Yearns, W. Buck, ed. *The Confederate Governors.* Athens, Ga., 1985.

CARL H. MONEYHON

LUTHERAN CHURCH. The Lutheran Church was a muted voice in the Confederacy, both because of its relatively small constituency and because it was divided into separate synods, chiefly along state lines. The several Southern synods were, moreover, markedly ethnic (especially German and Scandinavian) in their origin and had never been significantly increased by immigration to a South to which only a small stream of immigrants was attracted. Lutherans were more numerous in the upper South, especially in Virginia and the Carolinas, than elsewhere. Those in rural areas were more likely to live in the backcountry than in the plantation areas.

The church as an organized entity was committed to a conservative theology and to a tradition of quietism in private life; it was disinclined to enter publicly into secular controversy. Most leaders tended to deplore the secession movement, and after the firing on Fort Sumter they continued to urge conciliation and compromise.

Official relations between the synods were occasionally embarrassed by sharp differences over questions of doctrine and polity, the use of the English language, and the morality of slavery. By 1856 the General Synod, formed of Southern and Northern synods in 1820, was weakened by both inter- and intrasynodical disputes, and in 1862 five of the Southern synods (of North Carolina, South Carolina, Virginia, West Virginia, and Georgia) withdrew, eliciting from the diminished General Synod a resolution of rebuke: "the rebellion against the constitutional Government of this land is most wicked . . . unjustified . . . unnatural . . . inhuman, oppressive, and destructive in its result to the highest interest of morality and religion."

In the main, Lutherans in the Confederacy were as loyal to their national government as were Northern Lutherans to theirs. Curiously, differences among leaders as well as lay members concerning the morality and biblical standing of slavery continued to be vigorously argued as late as 1868.

BIBLIOGRAPHY

Jacobs, Henry Eyster. *A History of the Evangelical Lutheran Church in the United States.* 2d ed. New York, 1899.

Nelson, E. Clifford, ed. *The Lutherans in North America.* Philadelphia, 1975.

RICHARD BARDOLPH

LYNCH, JOHN ROY (1847–1939), African American Reconstruction leader and Republican politician. Lynch was born the son of a slave mother and a white father in Louisiana. After the Civil War and emancipation, he attached himself to the Republican party in Mississippi, and despite some disappointment with its racial policies, he maintained party allegiance until his death.

Before his twentieth birthday, Lynch had become a party activist, leading a fight in Mississippi, for example, to ratify a new state constitution in 1867. He went to the Mississippi House of Representatives from his Natchez district in 1869 and later became Speaker of that body. As a member of the state legislature, he played an important role in reorganizing the judicial system, establishing stronger public schools, and improving the prison system.

In the fall of 1872, Lynch won a seat in the U.S. House of Representatives. During his time in Congress, he played an important role in the debate over the successful 1875 Civil Rights Act, a measure invalidated by the U.S. Supreme Court eight years later. Defeated for reelection in 1876, Lynch made another bid in 1880 and won a contested election that required congressional action to seat him. Although he lost his seat in 1882, he remained active in Republican politics in the following decades, serving as chairman of the Republican state executive committee in Mississippi and as a delegate to the Republican National Conventions of 1884, 1888, 1892 and 1900.

After he left Congress in 1883, Lynch wrote *The Facts of Reconstruction,* a work designed to stress the favorable aspects of that era and to correct what he considered mistaken notions about it. Before his death in Chicago in 1939, he completed his autobiographical work *Reminiscences of an Active Life.* He was buried in Arlington National Cemetery.

BIBLIOGRAPHY

Christopher, Marvin. *Black Americans in Congress.* Rev. ed. New York, 1976.

Lynch, John Roy. *The Facts of Reconstruction.* New York, 1913.

Lynch, John Roy. *Reminiscences of an Active Life: The Autobiography of John Roy Lynch.* Edited by John Hope Franklin. Chicago, 1970.

Rabinowitz, Howard N., ed. *Southern Black Leaders of the Reconstruction Era.* Urbana, Ill., 1982.

Smith, Samuel Denny. *The Negro in Congress, 1870–1901.* Chapel Hill, N.C., 1940.

JIMMIE LEWIS FRANKLIN

LYNCH, WILLIAM F. (1801–1865), naval captain. Lynch ended a forty-two-year career in the U.S. Navy in April 1861 when he resigned a captaincy to become a captain in the Confederate navy. Born on April 1, 1801, in Norfolk, Virginia, he became a midshipman in 1819 and a lieutenant in 1829. By 1849, he was noted for a survey he had made of the Dead Sea.

Confederate service engaged Lynch in action as commander of the Aquia Creek Batteries in May and June 1861; in the defense of New Orleans and the Mississippi in 1862; and especially as flag officer in command of North Carolina naval defenses from 1862 to 1865. His command came under attack in February 1862 when a combined U.S. navy and army expedition captured Roanoke Island. Lynch's small complement of ships was inadequate to defend the North Carolina sounds where blockade runners found passage or to prevent the U.S. navy from closing off supply lines to Norfolk, which fell three months later.

A devout Episcopalian and cultivated gentleman, Lynch was brave and daring in combat. Blockade running near Wilmington created relatively more action in his squadron than in Savannah and Mobile. He was more successful in command than in managing construction of ironclads at Wilmington, New Bern, Whitehall, Edward's Ferry, and Tarboro. Conflicts over transportation and materials which plagued many naval construction projects were especially severe. In the disorganized command system of a new army and navy, he was jealous of his authority and fiercely protective of naval interests. Because of his conflicts with Confederate and state political officials, army and navy officers, and transportation and industry representatives, coordinating his command with the army was difficult and at times impossible.

In 1865, Secretary of the Navy Mallory assigned Lynch the task of writing a history of the Confederate navy. Lynch survived the war's end by only a few months, however, dying in Baltimore on October 18, 1865.

BIBLIOGRAPHY

Lynch, William F. *Narrative of the United States Expedition to the River Jordan and the Dead Sea.* Philadelphia, 1849.

Lynch, William F. *Naval Life; or, Observations Afloat and On Shore.* New York, 1851.

Still, William N., Jr. *Iron Afloat: The Story of the Confederate Armorclads.* Rev. ed. Columbia, S.C., 1985.

MAXINE TURNER

LYNCHBURG, VIRGINIA. A tobacco manufacturing center before the Civil War, the city of Lynchburg in the course of the conflict became one of the principal supply depots for the Confederate forces operating in Virginia. The primary reason for this was the city's strategic location far behind the front lines. The Confederate War Department could stockpile vast quantities of supplies—munitions, foodstuffs, clothing—secure in the knowledge that they were safe from the enemy. In addition, the city had direct railroad connections with Richmond and Petersburg to the east, Charlottesville and Gordonsville to the north, and Knoxville, Tennessee, to the west, which enabled the Confederacy to transport men and materials quickly and efficiently. Over time Lynchburg increased in importance, becoming by 1864 an indispensable source of supply for the Army of Northern Virginia.

The Federals were aware of how valuable Lynchburg was to the Confederate war effort, and on June 6, 1864, Lt. Gen. Ulysses S. Grant directed Maj. Gen. David Hunter, commander of the Federal forces in the Shenandoah Valley, to occupy the city. To accomplish his mission Grant wanted Hunter to move east of the Blue Ridge Mountains at Staunton, join forces with Maj. Gen. Philip H. Sheridan's cavalry nearby, and advance on Lynchburg from the north, destroying the southern branch of the Orange and Alexandria Railroad as he went. But when Hunter reached Staunton he did not move east of the mountains and unite with Sheridan; instead, he elected to continue up the valley on his own and approach Lynchburg from the west. He occupied Lexington on June 11, and after destroying everything of value, he passed through the Blue Ridge Mountains via Buford's Gap and began his advance on Lynchburg, reaching the outskirts of the city on June 17.

When the Federals occupied Lexington, Gen. Robert E. Lee foresaw that Lynchburg would be their next objective, and he moved quickly to protect his supply base. On June 12 he sent Lt. Gen. Jubal Early and the entire Second Corps of the Army of Northern Virginia, approximately eight thousand men, west to defend the city and defeat Hunter. A lack of rolling stock delayed the Confederates' arrival, but by midday of June 17 Early and half of his command had reached the city. Prior to Early's arrival, the city had been protected by nine thousand troops commanded by Maj. Gen. John C. Breckinridge, half of which were reserve forces made up of several disorganized infantry units, the cadets of the Virginia Military Institute, and invalids from the hospitals.

Confined to bed because of an injury, Breckinridge called upon Lt. Gen. D. H. Hill to take charge of the city's defense. Hill established a defensive line just outside the city limits, but after surveying the field Early created a second line of breastworks covering both sides of the Salem Turnpike about two miles from the city. That night half of the Second Corps, Breckinridge's division, and about fifteen pieces of artillery took up positions along the advance line of defense while the reserve forces occupied the interior line of works.

When Hunter descended on Lynchburg he commanded an army composed of two divisions of infantry, two divisions of cavalry, and several batteries of artillery, a total of about eighteen thousand men. If he had acted boldly and decisively, he could have captured the city with few difficulties; but because he was under the impression that he was greatly outnumbered, he failed to do so. On the afternoon of the seventeenth, his artillery opened fire on the Confederate positions, but no infantry assault was attempted. The next day Hunter ordered several small-scale attacks, but they were easily repulsed and he made no further attempts to seize the city. When he discovered that Early had arrived, Hunter immediately issued orders for the army to retreat. That night under the cover of darkness he led his command back toward the Shenandoah Valley.

Compared to other engagements, the Battle of Lynchburg, in terms of troops involved, was not very large, but it did have a significant impact on the course of the war in Virginia in 1864. When Hunter withdrew, Early pressed his rear guard hard and sent his cavalry over the Blue Ridge to prevent Hunter from retreating down the valley. Unable to use the valley as an avenue of escape, Hunter had no choice but to retreat into the mountains of West Virginia, taking his army out of the war for several weeks and leaving the valley unprotected. With no one to oppose him, Early marched down the valley, crossed over the Potomac River, and threatened Washington, D.C.

Early's raid and his continued presence in the lower valley, in turn, compelled Grant to alter his plans to defeat the Confederate forces in Virginia. To protect the Union's capital and drive the Confederates from the valley, he had to transfer two full corps from the Army of the Potomac to northern Virginia. The departure of nearly forty thousand men severely limited Grant's offensive capabilities; unable to penetrate or outflank his opponents' defenses, he had to place Richmond and Petersburg under siege. Hunter's failure also caused Grant to abandon his idea of attacking Richmond from the west, and Lynchburg remained a vital supply base for the Confederates until the end of the war.

BIBLIOGRAPHY

Blackford, Charles M. "The Campaign and Battle of Lynchburg." *Southern Historical Society Papers* 30 (1902): 279–331. Reprint, Wilmington, N.C., 1991.

Catton, Bruce. *Grant Takes Command.* New York, 1968.

Freeman, Douglas S. *Lee's Lieutenants: A Study in Command.* 3 vols. New York, 1942–1944. Reprint, New York, 1986.

Johnson, Robert U., and C. C. Buel, eds. *Battles and Leaders of the Civil War.* Vol. 4. New York, 1888. Reprint, Secaucus, N.J., 1982.

MICHAEL G. MAHON

LYON, FRANCIS STROTHER (1800–1882), congressman from Alabama. Born on February 25, 1800, in Danbury, North Carolina, he attended school in North Carolina before moving to St. Stephens near Mobile. He studied law there, was admitted to the bar in 1821, and opened a law practice in Demopolis. He served as secretary of the Alabama Senate from 1822 to 1830. In 1833 he was elected to the state senate and in 1834 was chosen senate president. He served in the U.S. House of Representatives as a Whig from 1835 to 1839.

A secessionist, he was chairman of the 1860 state

Democratic convention and was a delegate to the 1860 Democratic National Convention, where he walked out with William Lowndes Yancey. In 1861 he served in the Alabama legislature, and although elected to the Provisional Confederate Congress, he declined to serve. Elected to the First and Second Confederate House of Representatives, he served until the end of the war. He supported President Jefferson Davis and was a member of the Ways and Means, Currency, War Tax, and other committees. Lyon invested heavily in the Confederacy, and the war destroyed him financially.

During Reconstruction he joined Josiah Gorgas in the unsuccessful Brierfield Ironworks near Montevallo. A delegate to the 1875 Alabama Constitutional Convention, he was elected to the Alabama Senate in 1876. He died in retirement on December 31, 1882, in Demopolis.

BIBLIOGRAPHY

Owen, Thomas McAdory. *History of Alabama and Dictionary of Alabama Biography.* 4 vols. Chicago, 1921.

Thornton, J. Mills, III. *Politics and Power in a Slave Society: Alabama, 1800–1860.* Baton Rouge, La., 1978.

Vandiver, Frank E. *Ploughshares into Swords: Josiah Gorgas and Confederate Ordnance.* Austin, Tex., 1952.

Wakelyn, Jon L. *Biographical Directory of the Confederacy.* Edited by Frank E. Vandiver. Westport, Conn., 1977.

SARAH WOOLFOLK WIGGINS

LYON, HYLAN BENTON (1836–1907), brigadier general. Lyon was born in Caldwell County, Kentucky, on February 22, 1836. Orphaned as a child and educated in local schools, he attended the U.S. Military Academy, graduating nineteenth in his class in 1856. Prior to the Civil War, he served in Florida and Washington Territory.

Lyon resigned his commission in the U.S. Army on April 30, 1861, and entered the Confederate army as a captain of artillery. In February 1862, he became lieutenant colonel of the Eighth Kentucky Infantry. He was captured at Fort Donelson and remained a prisoner at Johnson's Island until the fall of 1862. Lyon emerged from prison a colonel and fought in Mississippi, escaping from Vicksburg during the 1863 siege, and later at Chattanooga, where he temporarily took command and saved much of the Army of Tennessee's artillery.

Lyon received his commission as brigadier general on June 14, 1864. He commanded a brigade of four Kentucky regiments under Brig. Gen. Abraham Buford in Nathan Bedford Forrest's cavalry corps almost until the end of the war. During that time he served well at Brice's Cross Roads and Johnsonville and took part in Gen. John Bell Hood's Tennessee campaign. Lyon finished the war as commander of the District of Western Kentucky, ostensibly sent there to raise additional recruits and harass the Federals.

HYLAN BENTON LYON. NATIONAL ARCHIVES

Lyon fled to Mexico at the end of the war, but returned to Kentucky in 1866 and farmed near Eddyville. Later, he became involved with the state penitentiary system, serving as a commissioner to build a branch prison at Eddyville. He died on his farm April 25, 1907.

BIBLIOGRAPHY

Bearss, Edwin C. *Forrest at Brice's Cross Roads.* Dayton, Ohio, 1979.

Henry, Robert Selph. *"First with the Most" Forrest.* Indianapolis, 1944.

Wills, Brian Steel. *A Battle from the Start: The Life of Nathan Bedford Forrest.* New York, 1992.

Wyeth, John Allan. *Life of General Nathan Bedford Forrest.* New York, 1899. Reprint, Baton Rouge, La., 1989.

BRIAN S. WILLS

LYONS, JAMES (1801–1882), congressman from Virginia and judge. Born in Hanover County, Virginia, Lyons graduated from the College of William and Mary and began to practice law in 1818. He married Henningham Watkins and, after her death, Imogen Bradfute Penn. A state rights Whig and later Democrat, Lyons served in the Virginia House of Delegates (1845–1846) and Senate (1839–1843) and in the Virginia convention of 1850 to 1851. He became an ardent and early secessionist.

In November 1861 he came in third after John Tyler and William H. MacFarland in a race for the Provisional Congress but won the special election to fill the seat in the First Congress that fell vacant when Tyler died. In Congress he served on the Buildings and Commerce committees. Like other state righters confronted with the practicalities of winning a war, he opposed the centrifugal forces of localism and approved the strictest measures demanded by the Davis administration for the central government. The Confederacy happily declined Lyons's proposed response to the Emancipation Proclamation: take no prisoners and pay African Americans bounties for killing Federal soldiers. The *Richmond Enquirer* supported Lyons's reelection because he "was its advocate when to avow secession principles found more frowns than smiles." When he nevertheless lost the race, the defeat was seen as a rebuke to the president.

Later in the war, Lyons was appointed a judge to hear cases involving political prisoners and, ironically, after the war became defense counsel for the most prominent prisoner of conscience, Jefferson Davis. Lyons continued practicing law in Richmond until his death there in his home on December 18, 1882.

BIBLIOGRAPHY

Wakelyn, Jon L. *Biographical Dictionary of the Confederacy.* Edited by Frank E. Vandiver. Westport, Conn., 1977.

Warner, Ezra J., and W. Buck Yearns. *Biographical Register of the Confederate Congress.* Baton Rouge, La., 1975.

Yearns, Wilfred B. *The Confederate Congress.* Athens, Ga., 1960.

NELSON D. LANKFORD

MCCALLUM, JAMES (1806–1889), congressman from Tennessee. Little is known about the early life of this native North Carolinian, whose parents moved from Sumner County, Tennessee, in 1809, to make their home in or near Pulaski. There McCallum eventually worked as a planter, attorney, and clerk and master of the chancery court (1842–1861). A former Whig turned Democrat, he owned as many as twenty-five slaves on the eve of the war and an estate worth $65,000.

McCallum, who later claimed to have been not an original secessionist but a Unionist, served a term in the Tennessee (Confederate) House (1861–1863) before he was elected to represent Tennessee's Seventh District in the Second Confederate Congress. Admitted on May 3, 1864, he served continually until Congress adjourned in March 1865, except for a week in November 1864, when he was on official leave.

Appointed to the Accounts, Medical Department, and Post Office and Post Roads committees, McCallum proved to be a strong supporter of the Davis government and the war effort. Among the sixteen bills and resolutions he introduced, one provided for salary increases to soldiers in the field and another supported the impressment of property for the army. During the last months of the war, McCallum sponsored or approved more drastic measures, such as the government's seizure of the rail system, the impressment of all gold and silver plate, taxes on cotton and tobacco to be paid in kind, the repeal of all military exemptions, and the drafting into military service of all white males between the ages of sixteen and fifty. He opposed the conscription of slaves, however, and was one of only two Tennessee congressmen who refused on March 15, 1865, to authorize Jefferson Davis to suspend the writ of habeas corpus.

Following the surrender of Gen. Joseph E. Johnston's forces in North Carolina, McCallum returned to Pulaski, where on July 12, 1865, he appealed to President Andrew Johnson for executive amnesty. He was pardoned on September 30 and resumed his law practice. The extent of his involvement (if any) in the activities of the first Ku Klux Klan, which was founded in Pulaski in 1866, is not known. But some evidence has been located to support McCallum's January 1865 assertion that, despite his advanced age, he had once served in the Confederate army, probably as a private in Company A, Third (Clack's) Tennessee Infantry.

BIBLIOGRAPHY

Amnesty File. James McCallum. Microcopy M1003, Roll 50. Record Group 94. National Archives, Washington, D.C.

Journal of the Congress of the Confederate States of America, 1861–1865. 7 vols. Washington, D.C., 1904–1905.

McCallum, James. *A Brief Sketch of the Settlement and Early History of Giles County, Tennessee, 1876.* Pulaski, Tenn., 1928.

Warner, Ezra J., and W. Buck Yearns. *Biographical Register of the Confederate Congress.* Baton Rouge, La., 1975.

R. B. Rosenburg

MCCAUSLAND, JOHN (1836–1927), brigadier general. Born in St. Louis, Missouri, September 13, 1836, the son of Irish immigrants, McCausland graduated from the Virginia Military Institute in 1857. While a professor at VMI, he went with a number of cadets to witness the hanging of John Brown in Charlestown.

Upon Virginia's secession he formed the Rockbridge Artillery but declined its command. Later, however, he organized troops in the Kanawha Valley and assumed command of the Thirty-sixth Virginia Infantry with the rank of colonel. He was present at the surrender of Fort Donelson, Tennessee, in 1862 but escaped with his troops to safety. After serving with the infantry in southwestern

JOHN MCCAUSLAND. LIBRARY OF CONGRESS

Virginia until May of 1864, he was promoted to brigadier general and given command of a cavalry brigade.

McCausland saved Lynchburg, Virginia, by delaying David Hunter's advance until reinforcements could arrive. He then led a gallant charge at Monocacy, Maryland, and took his cavalry to the suburbs of Washington, D.C., at the head of Jubal Early's army.

In July of 1864 he was ordered by General Early to Chambersburg, Pennsylvania. He demanded $500,000 as retribution for damage caused by Hunter in the Shenandoah Valley. When the townspeople refused to pay, McCausland ordered the town burned. On the retreat from Chambersburg, his cavalry was surprised at Moorefield and many of his men were captured.

McCausland served throughout the Shenandoah Valley campaign and was present at Appomattox. Once again he refused to surrender; instead he cut his way through the Union lines and returned home.

Threats arising from the episode at Chambersburg caused him to flee to Europe and Mexico for two years. After his return, McCausland spent the rest of his life farming in Mason County, West Virginia. At his death on January 22, 1927, he was survived only by Felix Robertson as the last Confederate general.

BIBLIOGRAPHY

Brown, James Earl. "The Life of Brigadier General John McCausland." *West Virginia History* 5 (1942): 1094.

Lewis, Thomas A. *The Shenandoah in Flames.* Alexandria, Va., 1987.

Scott, J. L. *Thirty-Sixth Virginia Infantry.* Lynchburg, Va., 1987.

J. L. SCOTT

MCCOMB, WILLIAM (1828–1918), brigadier general. Born in Mercer County, Pennsylvania, November 21, 1828, McComb moved to Tennessee in 1854 to superintend the construction of a flour mill at Price's Landing on the Cumberland River.

At the outbreak of the war McComb enlisted as a private in Company L of the Fourteenth Tennessee Infantry. He was promoted to lieutenant shortly thereafter and was adjutant of the regiment during the Cheat Mountain campaign. McComb was with W. W. Loring's division during Thomas J. ("Stonewall") Jackson's Romney expedition and, upon the reorganization of the army in the spring of 1862, was elected major of the Fourteenth Tennessee. In that role he participated in the engagements around Richmond. Because of deaths among officers of higher rank, McComb rose rapidly and became colonel of the regiment, September 2, 1862, shortly after Second Manassas.

For several months in 1864 fellow officers sought promotion for McComb. A petition containing the signatures of many officers stated that he had earned promotion "by his gallantry on many a hard contested field—by his uniformly strict discipline—his close and earnest attention to his duties." Henry Heth also recommended promotion, calling McComb "a gallant and deserving officer." Robert E. Lee declared that McComb was the "best officer to command the brigade" formed by the consolidation of James Jay Archer's old brigade with that of Bushrod Rust Johnson even though he was not the senior colonel. McComb was commissioned a brigadier, February 27, 1865.

After his parole at Appomattox, McComb resided in Mississippi and Alabama for several years. He moved to Louisa County, Virginia, in 1869 and engaged in farming for nearly fifty years.

McComb was one of the last six surviving general officers of the Confederacy when he died at his plantation, July 21, 1918. He was buried in Louisa County.

BIBLIOGRAPHY

Compiled Military Service Records. William McComb. Microcopy M331, Roll 170. Record Group 109. National Archives, Washington, D.C.

"The Last Roll." *Confederate Veteran* 26 (1918): 404. Reprint, Wilmington, N.C., 1985.

Porter, James D. *Tennessee.* Vol. 8 of *Confederate Military History.* Edited by Clement A. Evans. Atlanta, 1899. Vol. 10 of extended ed. Wilmington, N.C., 1987.

Warner, Ezra J. *Generals in Gray: Lives of the Confederate Commanders.* Baton Rouge, La., 1959.

LOWELL REIDENBAUGH

MCCORD, LOUISA CHEVES (1810–1879), writer and volunteer worker. One of the antebellum South's most remarkable women, Louisa Susanna Cheves McCord defies stereotypical description. Possessed of both rare intellect and the opportunity to use it, she was a powerful, independent, and greatly respected figure in South Carolina in the mid-nineteenth century. A perceptive political economist, an astute and passionate social commentator, an efficient manager of a plantation, she was also a creative writer and poet, while never abandoning the principle that her foremost duties were as wife and mother. Her contributions to the Confederate cause during the war years were perhaps unmatched by any other Southern woman. Mary Boykin Chesnut, a friend of McCord's, described her as "the clearest-headed, strongest-minded woman I ever knew—and the best and the truest."

Daughter of South Carolina statesman Langdon Cheves, in her youth Cheves was encouraged to pursue, along with traditional feminine academic studies, those subjects usually reserved for a male's education. She traveled extensively with her family, and when her father's career took him to Philadelphia as president of the Bank of the United States, she accompanied him to pursue her studies there. In 1840 she married David James McCord, lawyer and man of letters, and together they continued their commitment to political, social, and literary matters, often publishing articles together in learned journals. They had three children and settled at Lang Syne Plantation, near Fort Motte, South Carolina.

During the Civil War, McCord gave unstintingly to the cause in which she believed so fervently. In devotion, time, energy, and resources expended, her dedication was unparalleled. Spending the war years in Columbia, the state capital, in 1861 she became president of both the Soldier's Relief Association and the Lady's Clothing Association. After her only son's death at the Second Battle of Manassas in 1862, she devoted herself primarily to working with the military hospital in Columbia.

Believing from the beginning that her country should be self-supporting, she immediately planted large provision crops and set up workshops of all kinds on the plantation. Workers turned out cloth and shoes, cut up carpets into blankets, and opened mattresses so their contents could be spun into yarn for soldiers' socks. McCord herself, while supervising this activity, knitted twenty-one pairs of socks every week. Even the hair of rabbits killed on the plantation was saved, and, combined with scraps of wool and old black silk, made into a fine gray yarn for officers' gloves. All lead on the plantation, including the pipes of her newly installed water system, was sent off to be melted into bullets. The horses were sent to the army.

Her Columbia house was so close to the hospital that it became a food depot for the wounded who were able to walk across the street. Every day fifty to a hundred men were fed from her kitchen. Friends and neighbors donated whatever food scraps they could to McCord's huge pot of stew, and she helped the plates herself.

She tended the sick and dying with the devotion of a mother. After seeing the stew or soup distributed, she would go to the hospital, carrying a basket of whatever delicacies she could find for bedridden soldiers. She would sit with a boy about to go under chloroform and promise him that she wouldn't let them take too much of a limb. She would be beside him when he woke from the anesthetic and cried for his wife or mother. She would ride miles in search of a priest of a particular denomination when the hospital chaplain could not comfort a dying soldier. At night she would return home, change her dress after inspecting it for the dreaded "greybacks" (lice), and resume her knitting, oftentimes late into the night.

When St. Julien Ravenel was asked why he let McCord manage his hospital, he replied, "The more she manages the better; every bit of her that isn't enthusiasm is common sense." McCord's service ranks among the best testimonies to the heroism and fidelity on the home front of the women of the Confederacy.

At the war's end, embittered, McCord moved first to Virginia and then to Canada. Returning at last to South Carolina, she lived her final years in Charleston and was buried there in Magnolia Cemetery.

BIBLIOGRAPHY

Forrest, Mary. *Women of the South Distinguished in Literature.* New York, 1961.

Thorp, Margaret Farrand. *Female Persuasion: Six Strong-Minded Women.* Hamden, Conn., 1971.

ANNE BLYTHE MERIWETHER

MCCOWN, JOHN P. (1815–1879), major general. Born near Sevierville, Tennessee, McCown graduated from West Point in 1840. After receiving assignment with the Fourth U.S. Artillery, he served in Florida during the Seminole War and then was transferred to the frontier, where he participated in Indian fighting and scouting. Seeing action in the Mexican War, McCown won a brevet at the Battle of Cerro Gordo for bravery. Transferred again to the frontier, he participated in the Utah expedition against the Mormons, attaining the rank of captain of artillery.

Resigning his commission on May 17, 1861, McCown entered Confederate service as colonel of the Tennessee Artillery Corps. After receiving promotion to brigadier general in October 1861, he participated in battles at

Belmont, Island Number 10, and Fort Pillow and served temporarily as commander of the Army of the West while Earl Van Dorn led the department. McCown received promotion to major general in March 1862 and was given divisional command under E. Kirby Smith in eastern Tennessee. McCown's division was attached to William J. Hardee's corps and participated in the initial attack by Braxton Bragg's army at the Battle of Murfreesboro in December 1862. The following February, Bragg preferred charges against him for disobeying orders during that battle, reporting that McCown was unfit for responsible command. Court-martialed the following month at Shelbyville, Tennessee, he was found guilty and served the remainder of the war in relative obscurity. He participated in actions in April 1865 along the Catawba River in western North Carolina.

At war's end, McCown returned to Tennessee, where he taught school before moving to Magnolia, Arkansas, to operate a farm. He died at Little Rock while attending a meeting of the Masonic Lodge and was buried at Magnolia.

BIBLIOGRAPHY

Faust, Patricia, ed. *Historical Times Illustrated's Encyclopedia of the Civil War.* New York, 1986.

Johnson, Robert U., and C. C. Buel, eds. *Battles and Leaders of the Civil War.* 4 vols. New York, 1887–1888. Reprint, Secaucus, N.J., 1982.

Warner, Ezra J. *Generals in Gray: Lives of the Confederate Commanders.* Baton Rouge, La., 1959.

CHRISTOPHER PHILLIPS

MCCULLOCH, BEN (1811–1862), brigadier general. Born November 11, 1811, in Rutherford County, Tennessee, the elder brother of Gen. Henry Eustace McCulloch, Ben moved to Texas in 1835 at the urging of his friend Davy Crockett and fought in the Texas Revolution. He served a term in the Republic of Texas legislature and was a well-known Indian fighter. He led Texas Rangers in the Mexican War and in the late 1840s joined the California gold rush. He served as sheriff of Sacramento County from 1850 until 1852 and then returned to Texas to become a U.S. marshal.

When Texas seceded, McCulloch became a colonel of state troops and took the surrender of Federal forces under David Emanuel Twiggs at San Antonio. Commissioned a brigadier general on May 11, 1861, he was assigned to command in Arkansas. His troops fought with the Missourians under Sterling Price at Oak Hills. Because of a personality clash between McCulloch and Price, the Confederate government created the Trans-Mississippi District in January 1862 and sent Maj. Gen. Earl Van Dorn to take command. In Van Dorn's attack at Elkhorn Tavern, Arkansas, McCulloch directed the right wing and was fatally wounded by a Union sharpshooter on March 7, 1862. McCulloch refused to wear the Confederate uniform and was dressed in his customary black velvet when shot through the heart. He is buried in Austin in the Texas State Cemetery beside his father, a brigadier general in the War of 1812.

BEN MCCULLOCH.

HARPER'S PICTORIAL HISTORY OF THE GREAT REBELLION

BIBLIOGRAPHY

Hughes, Michael A. "A Forgotten Battle in a Region Ignored . . . Pea Ridge, or Elkhorn Tavern, Arkansas—March 7–8, 1862: The Campaign, the Battle, and the Men Who Fought for the Fate of Missouri." *Blue & Gray Magazine* 5 (1988): 8–36.

Nunn, W. C., ed. *Ten More Texans in Gray.* Hillsboro, Tex., 1980.

Pea Ridge National Park. "The Battle of Pea Ridge, 1862." Pamphlet. Rogers, Ark., n.d.

Wright, Marcus, J., comp., and Harold B. Simpson, ed. *Texas in the War, 1861–1865.* Hillsboro, Tex., 1965.

ANNE J. BAILEY

MCCULLOCH, HENRY EUSTACE (1816–1895), brigadier general. McCulloch was born December 6, 1816, in Rutherford County, Tennessee, the younger brother of Ben McCulloch. After moving to Texas in 1837 Henry served as sheriff of Gonzales County, fought in several Indian campaigns, and commanded a company of

Texas Rangers in the Mexican War. He was elected to the state legislature in 1853 and the Texas senate in 1855.

McCulloch, when the Civil War began, was a U.S. marshal. The secession convention appointed him a colonel and authorized him to demand the surrender of the U.S. forts on the northwestern frontier. McCulloch briefly headed the Department of Texas and was made commander of the Submilitary District of the Rio Grande early in 1862. He was promoted to brigadier general in March 1862. McCulloch took command in the eastern district of Texas and forwarded over twenty-thousand Texans toward Little Rock. In September he joined them and took command of a division of Texas infantry. In December he was replaced by Maj. Gen. John G. Walker and was assigned a brigade. McCulloch fought at Milliken's Bend on June 7, 1863, but his performance was so poor that he was transferred to an administrative post. In September 1863 he took over the Northern Subdistrict of Texas and remained there until the war's end.

Although he apparently had little talent for leading troops, McCulloch was an excellent administrator. Following the war he engaged in shipping cattle to Cuba, and worked for the railroad, and was appointed superintendent of the Asylum for the Deaf and Dumb in Austin, a position he held until he retired in 1879. He died in Rockport, Texas, on March 12, 1895, and is buried in Seguin.

BIBLIOGRAPHY

Bailey, Anne J. *Between the Enemy and Texas.* Fort Worth, Tex., 1989.

Wright, Marcus J., comp., and Harold B. Simpson, ed. *Texas in the War, 1861–1865.* Hillsboro, Tex., 1965.

ANNE J. BAILEY

MCDOWELL, THOMAS D. (1823–1898), congressman from North Carolina.

Born on January 4, 1823, in Bladen County, North Carolina, McDowell graduated from the University of North Carolina in 1843 and commenced planting in his native county. He served three terms as a Democrat in the house of commons (1846–1851) and another three in the state senate (1852–1855, 1858–1859). Like most North Carolina Democrats, he espoused the constitutional right of secession; nonetheless, he opposed disunion until after Abraham Lincoln's call for troops. Although he owned fifty-seven slaves in 1860 and ran a plantation valued at $65,000, McDowell later claimed that he would have readily "consented to a just and equitable plan of gradual emancipation . . . at any time before the war."

Elected to the secession convention in May 1861, McDowell resigned that position to take a seat in the Provisional Congress. There he generally supported the measures of the Davis administration, his principal concern being the defense of the North Carolina coast. He was subsequently elected without opposition to the First Congress and served on the Commerce Committee. A staunch adherent to the state rights school of politics, he became increasingly disenchanted with the centralizing tendencies of the Davis administration, voted against the suspension of habeas corpus, and opposed most of the administration's economic and military measures. He was not a candidate for reelection in 1863.

McDowell quickly reconciled himself to the outcome of the war, claiming that the abolition of slavery had "relieved [me] of the greatest trouble of my life." Avoiding politics, he concentrated instead on the management of his agricultural interests. He died at his plantation on May 1, 1898.

BIBLIOGRAPHY

Alexander, Thomas B., and Richard E. Beringer. *The Anatomy of the Confederate Congress: A Study of the Influences of Member Characteristics on Legislative Voting Behavior, 1861–1865.* Nashville, Tenn., 1972.

Powell, William S. *Dictionary of North Carolina Biography.* 4 vols. to date. Chapel Hill, N.C., 1979–.

Wakelyn, Jon L. *Biographical Dictionary of the Confederacy.* Edited by Frank E. Vandiver. Westport, Conn., 1977.

Warner, Ezra J., and W. Buck Yearns. *Biographical Register of the Confederate Congress.* Baton Rouge, La., 1975.

THOMAS E. JEFFREY

MACFARLAND, WILLIAM H. (1799–1872), congressman from Virginia.

A native of Lunenburg County, Virginia, MacFarland attended college at Hampden-Sydney and William and Mary. He entered law practice after study in Connecticut, and in the Virginia House of Delegates he represented Lunenburg (1822–1824) and later Petersburg (1830–1831). By 1836 MacFarland had moved on to Richmond where he prospered in banking, coal mining, railroads, and civic affairs. An Episcopalian Whig prominent and successful in the community, he nevertheless struck some as pompous, overbearing, and "nearly overcome with dignity and fat."

Elected to the 1861 Virginia convention as a Unionist, he cast his vote with the majority both times: against secession on the first ballot and for it on the second. He became an anti-administration member of the Provisional Congress, where he championed local interests against the demands of the central government in matters of taxation, sequestration, and confiscation. On the other hand, he did not oppose centralized control of transportation and commerce. He served on the Commercial Affairs and Inauguration committees and on the special committee for wounded soldiers. In the election for the First Congress he lost his race against former president John Tyler, who accused him of threatening to foreclose on his debtors unless they voted for him. He provided business advice to the government and in 1864 helped supply wounded soldiers with artificial limbs.

After his defeat by Tyler, MacFarland returned to banking until the end of the war and retired from public life during Reconstruction. He died at his summer home in Greenbrier County, West Virginia, on January 10, 1872.

BIBLIOGRAPHY

Gaines, William H., Jr. *Biographical Register of Members, Virginia State Convention of 1861, First Session.* Richmond, Va., 1969.

Wakelyn, Jon L. *Biographical Dictionary of the Confederacy.* Edited by Frank E. Vandiver. Westport, Conn., 1977.

Warner, Ezra J., and W. Buck Yearns. *Biographical Register of the Confederate Congress.* Baton Rouge, La., 1975.

NELSON D. LANKFORD

MCGOWAN, SAMUEL (1819–1897), brigadier general. The son of Scotch-Irish immigrants, McGowan was born October 9, 1819, in Laurens District, South Carolina. After graduating from South Carolina College in 1841, he studied law in Abbeville and was admitted to the bar in 1842. McGowan served twelve years in the state house of representatives. His legal career was interrupted by military service in the Mexican War. Enlisting as a private in the Palmetto Regiment, McGowan rose to the rank of captain and was cited for gallantry in the storming of Chapultepec. He resumed the practice of law upon the end of hostilities and also retained his interest in military matters, becoming a major general in the state militia.

Following the secession of South Carolina, McGowan was commissioned a brigadier general of state troops and aided P. G. T. Beauregard in the reduction of Fort Sumter. Later he was a volunteer aide to Gen. Milledge L. Bonham at Blackburn's Ford and First Manassas. Subsequently, he returned to his native state and was elected lieutenant colonel of the Fourteenth South Carolina Infantry on September 1, 1861. He was promoted to colonel on May 10, 1862.

Thereafter, McGowan joined Maxcy Gregg's brigade in the Army of Northern Virginia. Following the death of Gregg at Fredericksburg, McGowan's fellow South Carolinian Christopher G. Memminger conducted an ardent campaign for McGowan's promotion to command of the brigade. The secretary of the treasury, writing to Secretary of War James A. Seddon, praised McGowan highly and added that A. P. Hill also desired McGowan's promotion. McGowan received his brigadier's commission on April 23, 1863, to date from January 17.

McGowan was wounded four times during the war, at Gaines Mill, Second Manassas, Chancellorsville, and Spotsylvania. The gunshot wound to his left leg suffered at Chancellorsville idled him until February 1864.

After his parole at Appomattox, McGowan returned to Abbeville where he resumed his law practice. He was a member of the state constitutional convention in 1865 and was elected to the U.S. House of Representatives the same year. He was denied his seat, however. In 1879 he was elected an associate justice of the state supreme court but was defeated for reelection in 1893.

McGowan died at his home in Abbeville on August 9, 1897, and was buried in Long Cane Cemetery.

BIBLIOGRAPHY

Caldwell, J. F. J. *The History of a Brigade of South Carolinians, Known First as "Gregg's" and Subsequently as "McGowan's Brigade."* Philadelphia, 1866. Reprint, Dayton, Ohio, 1987.

Capers, Ellison. *South Carolina.* Vol. 5 of *Confederate Military History.* Edited by Clement A. Evans. Atlanta, 1899. Vol. 6 of extended ed. Wilmington, N.C., 1987.

Compiled Military Service Records. Samuel McGowan. Microcopy M331, Roll 171. Record Group 109. National Archives, Washington, D.C.

Warner, Ezra J. *Generals in Gray: Lives of the Confederate Commanders.* Baton Rouge, La., 1959.

LOWELL REIDENBAUGH

MACHEN, WILLIS BENSON (1810–1893), congressman from Kentucky. Machen typified the "strong nationalists" in the Confederate Congress. Like other legislators from states occupied by Union troops and represented in the Federal Congress, Machen was a war hawk, wholeheartedly supporting the Confederate war effort. In 1862, for example, he urged the Confederate army to go on the offensive and invade Ohio.

Born in Caldwell County, Kentucky, Machen attended Cumberland College and settled in Eddyville, Kentucky. As a farmer, merchant, and manufacturer, he amassed a modest fortune, including twenty-six slaves and an estate valued at more than $90,000 in 1860. He was a member of Kentucky's 1849 constitutional convention and, in the 1850s, served one term in the Kentucky Senate and two terms in the Kentucky House of Representatives.

A Democrat, Machen adamantly favored secession and was elected from Lyon County to Kentucky's November 1861 sovereignty convention. He served as president of the Executive Council of the Provisional Government of Kentucky. In 1862 Machen was elected to the First Congress from the First District and was reelected in 1864. He served on the Accounts, Ways and Means, and Quartermaster's and Commissary Departments committees. Machen supported the Davis administration's impressment measures and its policy of exempting skilled laborers from military service. But he nonetheless upheld the right of private property and opposed nationalization of the South's railroads and specie. According to historians Thomas B. Alexander and Richard E. Beringer, Machen exemplified "the lawmaker who did not have to be concerned about whether or not his constituents could carry the burdens he proposed to place on other backs." Given the peculiar circumstances of a Confederate congressman from a state overrun by Union troops, Machen "did not labor under the remotest possibility of any assertion of Confederate control at home."

Following Appomattox, Machen returned to Lyon County, Kentucky, where he farmed and operated iron furnaces. After the death of Garrett Davis, he completed Davis's term in the U.S. Senate, serving in 1872 and 1873. In 1880 Machen was appointed Kentucky railroad commissioner.

BIBLIOGRAPHY

Alexander, Thomas B., and Richard E. Beringer. *The Anatomy of the Confederate Congress: A Study of the Influences of Member Characteristics on Legislative Voting Behavior, 1861–1865.* Nashville, Tenn., 1972.

Quisenberry, A. C. "The Alleged Secession of Kentucky." *Register of the Kentucky State Historical Society* 15 (1917): 15–32.

Warner, Ezra J., and W. Buck Yearns. *Biographical Register of the Confederate Congress.* Baton Rouge, La., 1975.

John David Smith

MCINTOSH, JAMES MCQUEEN (1828–1862),

brigadier general. Born in the Florida Territory while his father, Col. James S. McIntosh, was stationed there, McIntosh graduated from West Point in 1849, last in his class of forty-three. He served in the infantry until 1855 when he was transferred to the First U.S. Cavalry on the frontier.

McIntosh resigned from the regular army on May 7, 1861, and after offering his services to the Confederacy, reported to Ben McCulloch in Arkansas. He took part in the Battle of Oak Hills, Missouri, where he was commended for bravery under fire. In December 1861 he fought at Chustenahlah in the Indian Territory and was promoted to brigadier general on January 24, 1862. During the Battle of Elkhorn Tavern, Arkansas, McIntosh headed a cavalry brigade and was killed while leading a charge on March 7, 1862. His death occurred soon after McCulloch's. McIntosh was interred in the National Cemetery in Fort Smith, Arkansas.

James's younger brother, John Baillie McIntosh, fought in the Union army and always considered it "a blot on his family honor" that his brother had joined the Confederacy.

BIBLIOGRAPHY

Pea Ridge National Park. "The Battle of Pea Ridge, 1862." Pamphlet. Rogers, Ark., n.d.

Hughes, Michael A. "A Forgotten Battle in a Region Ignored . . . Pea Ridge, or Elkhorn Tavern, Arkansas—March 7–8, 1862: The Campaign, the Battle, and the Men Who Fought for the Fate of Missouri." *Blue & Gray Magazine* 5 (1988): 8–36.

Anne J. Bailey

MACKALL, WILLIAM W. (1817–1891),

brigadier general. Mackall was born in Cecil City, Maryland, January 18, 1817, and graduated in 1837 from West Point eighth in a class of fifty. A career soldier, he was wounded in the Seminole War and wounded and brevetted in the Mexican War. He resigned from the U.S. Army on July 3, 1861, to join the Confederate army.

In March 1862 Brigadier General Mackall took command of New Madrid and Island Number 10, where on April 7 he surrendered with 3,500 men to the Federals. Exchanged in August 1862, Mackall held minor posts until he became Gen. Braxton Bragg's chief of staff on April 17, 1863. Mackall served Bragg and the Army of Tennessee well, particularly during Bragg's frequent illnesses. Although he supported Bragg and attempted to ease the general's burdens, Mackall became dissatisfied with his position, believing Bragg did not clearly define his duties and too often interfered in what Mackall considered his own administrative domain. On October 16, 1863, Mackall left Bragg. He returned to his old position, however, in January 1864 when Gen. Joseph E. Johnston replaced Bragg as commander of the Army of Tennessee. When Gen. John Bell Hood, in turn, took the command in July 1864, Mackall again asked to be relieved of duty. He held no further military assignments.

Mackall always believed he failed to receive deserved promotions because as a Marylander he had no one in the South to promote his interests out of either familial or political motives. He retired to farm in Virginia until his death in Fairfax County on August 12, 1891.

BIBLIOGRAPHY

Gow, June I. "Chiefs of Staff in the Army of Tennessee under Braxton Bragg." *Tennessee Historical Quarterly* 27 (1968): 341–360.

Gow, June I. "Military Administration in the Confederate Army of Tennessee." *Journal of Southern History* 40 (1974): 183–198.

Hallock, Judith Lee. *Braxton Bragg and Confederate Defeat.* Vol. 2. Tuscaloosa, Ala., 1991.

Mackall, William W. *A Son's Recollections of His Father.* New York, 1930.

Judith Lee Hallock

MCLAWS, LAFAYETTE (1821–1897), major general. McLaws, who was born January 15, 1821, in Augusta, Georgia, attended the U.S. Military Academy at West Point, where he graduated in the class of 1842, ranking forty-eighth among fifty-six graduates. For nearly two decades after graduation McLaws performed routine duty in seven states, the Indian Territory, and Mexico. When the Civil War broke out, he had been stuck at the rank of captain for almost ten years.

McLaws served briefly as a quartermaster in Georgia early in 1861 before receiving appointment as colonel of the Tenth Georgia Infantry on June 17. He took his new command to Virginia, where he made a strong enough impression on the Confederacy's military hierarchy to win promotion to brigadier general on September 7, 1861, and to major general on May 23, 1862. McLaws's commission as major general was dated earlier than that of most of the other division commanders in the Army of Northern Virginia. As a result, he outranked most of that army's more familiar division commanders.

For two years McLaws led a sturdy division in Robert E. Lee's army that included Joseph B. Kershaw's South Carolina brigade, William Barksdale's (later Benjamin Grubb Humphreys's) Mississippi brigade, and the two Georgia brigades commanded by Thomas R. R. Cobb (later William Tatum Wofford) and Paul J. Semmes (later Goode Bryan). McLaws managed to weld his brigades into a solid fighting force noted for its defensive prowess. In the words of a staff officer, McLaws "was an officer of much experience and most careful. Fond of detail, his command was in excellent condition, and his ground and position well examined and reconnoitered."

McLaws saw action on Virginia's peninsula early in 1862 under John B. Magruder, whose judgment he soon came to distrust. In Maryland during September 1862, McLaws commanded with marked success on Maryland Heights and then led his division to a great, if lucky, triumph in the West Woods near Sharpsburg. At Fredericksburg, McLaws executed an assignment that played to his strength when he guarded the riverfront. He was, wrote an observant artillerist, "about the best general in the army for that sort of job."

Perhaps because he irritated Lee by his lack of initiative around Salem Church in May 1863, McLaws did not receive either of the promotions to corps command issued later that month. At Gettysburg, McLaws was so disgusted with James Longstreet, who had been his mentor, that he called him "a humbug, a man of small capacity, very obstinate, not at all chivalrous, exceedingly conceited, and totally selfish." The deadly impact of the rift on McLaws's career became apparent in the aftermath of Longstreet's botched Knoxville campaign that fall when Longstreet brought six formal charges against him. Five of them were patently absurd, as attested by dozens of witnesses, and the sixth was misrepresented. Although the War Department overturned the one negative finding and censured Longstreet for his behavior, the corps commander remained far more important to Lee's army than did McLaws.

McLaws spent the rest of the war in defense of Savannah, vainly attempting to stem William Tecumseh Sherman's onslaught and then following the Southern retreat northward. After the war the general lived in straitened circumstances. In 1886 he declared, "I am without means, having lost all." He died July 22, 1897, at Savannah, Georgia.

BIBLIOGRAPHY

Freeman, Douglas S. *Lee's Lieutenants: A Study in Command.* 3 vols. New York, 1942–1944. Reprint, New York, 1986.

McLaws, Lafayette. Papers. Southern Historical Collection, University of North Carolina, Chapel Hill; Duke University, Durham, North Carolina.

ROBERT K. KRICK

MACLAY, ROBERT P. (1820–1903), major and acting brigadier general. Maclay, who was born in Pennsylvania, was appointed to the U.S. Military Academy from that state. After his graduation in 1840, he served on the frontier and fought in the Mexican and Seminole wars, rising to the rank of captain. He resigned December 31, 1860, to become a planter in Louisiana. When the state seceded, Maclay joined the Confederate army as a major of artillery and became chief of staff in Maj. Gen. John G. Walker's division.

After the death of Brig. Gen. Horace Randal, Gen. E. Kirby Smith assigned Maclay as a brigadier general on May 13, 1864, to command Randal's First Brigade, Walker's division. He apparently was accepted by his new colleagues, for surgeon Edward W. Cade wrote in a letter on May 14 that he "has so far given great satisfaction to the officers and men in his brigade." But the appointment by Kirby Smith of a Louisianian to command a Texas brigade after he had appointed a North Carolinian (Maj. Gen. John Horace Forney) to command a Texas division aggravated Smith's difficulties with Governor Pendleton Murrah of Texas. The two men were already embroiled in disputes over the Cotton Bureau and Texas conscription laws. To alleviate tensions, Smith granted Maclay a leave of absence until his appointment as brigadier general was confirmed by the Richmond government. Because the confirmation never materialized, Maclay remained on leave until the end of the war. Afterward, he returned to his plantation at Cook's Landing, Louisiana.

BIBLIOGRAPHY

Anderson, John Q. *A Texas Surgeon in the C.S.A.* Tuscaloosa, Ala., 1957.

Blessington, James P. *Campaigns of Walker's Texas Division*. New York, 1875.

Confederate States Army, Trans-Mississippi Department. *General Orders, Headquarters, Trans-Mississippi Department, from March 6, 1863 to January 1865*. Houston, Tex., 1865.

ROY R. STEPHENSON

MCLEAN, JAMES ROBERT (1823–1870), congressman from North Carolina. McLean was born in Enfield, North Carolina, September 21, 1823. He lost his parents while still a child, and relatives accepted responsibility for his education at subscription schools in Mebane and Greensboro. After studying law, he was licensed to practice in 1844. Beginning his career in Greensboro, he moved to Surry County, which in 1850 sent him as a Democrat to the North Carolina House of Commons. Soon thereafter he returned to Greensboro where he was master of a small plantation and twenty-five slaves.

By 1860 he had become one of the state's "original secessionists" and was elected in 1861 as a delegate to the Confederate House of Representatives, defeating two candidates who had been slower to call for withdrawal from the Union. He served as a diligent but inconspicuous legislator, loyal to the Davis administration, and then declined to run for another term because of physical infirmity. Late in 1864, however, McLean was elected major of the Seventy-seventh North Carolina Regiment, a unit of senior reserves from Alamance County, which participated in some minor military operations near Savannah before its fall to Gen. William Tecumseh Sherman.

The end of the war saw McLean in greatly reduced circumstances and increasingly enfeebled in health. His efforts to overcome his hardships met with some success, but he died in Greensboro April 15, 1870. McLean was described by contemporaries as a highly gifted lawyer and a man of wit and of brilliant mind.

BIBLIOGRAPHY

Connor, Robert D. W., ed. *History of North Carolina*. Vol. 6. Chicago and New York, 1919.

Powell, William S., ed. *Dictionary of North Carolina Biography*. Vol. 4. Chapel Hill, N.C., 1990.

RICHARD BARDOLPH

MCLEAN, WILMER (1814–?), army volunteer. In 1861 McLean was a forty-seven-year-old Virginian who owned a farm near Manassas Junction. Too old to fight but an ardent Confederate, he did what he could to support the Southern cause. In June 1861 he assisted Gen. P. G. T. Beauregard in a reconnaissance of the local countryside and soon after permitted the Confederates to place a signal station on his property. Beauregard used his house as army headquarters during the affair at Blackburn's Ford on July 18—the first engagement between the two opposing armies in Virginia. After the First Battle of Manassas, he worked as a volunteer for the Confederate Quartermaster Department.

By the spring of 1862, however, his dedication to the cause had waned considerably. He saw nothing but waste and mismanagement in the Quartermaster Department, and he grew tired of donating his time for free while others were reaping tremendous profits through speculation. In March 1862, he sold his home and began speculating in the sugar market, traveling widely throughout the South.

Toward the end of 1863, he returned to Virginia and settled down in a house at Appomattox Court House—a small peaceful village some two hundred miles from Manassas—with the hope of never seeing another soldier. He lived there in quiet seclusion until April 9, 1865, when Gen. Robert E. Lee used his residence to surrender the Army of Northern Virginia.

BIBLIOGRAPHY

Foote, Shelby. *The Civil War: A Narrative*. Vol. 3. New York, 1974.

Gallagher, Gary W., ed. *Fighting for the Confederacy: The Personal Recollections of General Edward Porter Alexander*. Chapel Hill, N.C., 1989.

McPherson, James M., ed. *Battle Chronicles of the Civil War*. Vol. 5. New York, 1989.

MICHAEL G. MAHON

MCMULLEN, FAYETTE (1805–1880), congressman from Virginia. Born in Bedford County, Fayette (as he was commonly known; his real name was LaFayette) McMullen had perhaps the most humble background of any Virginian who sat in the Confederate Congress. He never went to college and worked as a young man in his father's business as a wagon driver and teamster before turning to farming. Despite this inauspicious beginning, McMullen won repeated election as a Democrat to the Virginia legislature (1832–1848) and the U.S. House of Representatives (1849–1857). President James Buchanan appointed him governor of Washington Territory in 1857, but he returned to Virginia after a year and resumed farming in Marion.

An early secessionist, McMullen lost in his first bid for election to the Confederate Congress but defeated the incumbent, his old opponent Walter Preston, in the race for the Second Congress. He chaired the Public Buildings committee and championed the rights of the small farmer. To this end, he tried to have taxes based on financial assets rather than land and proposed exempting farmers and artisans from the draft. He saw by the end of 1864 that the war was lost—he called it "unholy and uncivilized"—and proposed a peace commission. His Confederate credentials were intact, however, for on the last day Congress was in session he called for the arrest of all absent congressmen as deserters.

After the war he returned to his farm and was soundly defeated in his run for governor in 1878 as a Conservative-Independent-Greenback candidate. McMullen died on November 8, 1880, after being struck by a train.

BIBLIOGRAPHY

Biographical Directory of the United States Congress, 1774–1989. Washington, D.C., 1989.

Wakelyn, Jon L. *Biographical Dictionary of the Confederacy.* Edited by Frank E. Vandiver. Westport, Conn., 1977.

Warner, Ezra J., and W. Buck Yearns. *Biographical Register of the Confederate Congress.* Baton Rouge, La., 1975.

NELSON D. LANKFORD

MCNAIR, EVANDER (1820–1902), brigadier general. McNair was born April 15, 1820, in Richmond County, North Carolina. The next year his family moved to Mississippi and settled in Simpson County. McNair became a merchant in Jackson and served in the Mexican War as sergeant in Jefferson Davis's First Mississippi Rifles.

In the 1850s McNair moved to Arkansas and, when the Civil War began, raised what became the Fourth Arkansas Infantry. He fought at Oak Hills, Missouri, and at Elkhorn Tavern, Arkansas. In March 1862 he participated in E. Kirby Smith's Kentucky campaign where he earned distinction in the Battle of Richmond. He was promoted to brigadier general on November 4, 1862, and his brigade took part in the Battle of Murfreesboro and the Vicksburg campaign. Following Vicksburg's surrender, McNair remained in Mississippi until ordered to Atlanta in September 1863. He fought at Chickamauga where he was seriously wounded on September 20. After he recovered, he returned briefly with his brigade to Mississippi and then went back to Atlanta in January 1864. McNair fought in the Atlanta campaign and at its end was transferred to the Trans-Mississippi Department. After September 1864, he commanded an Arkansas infantry brigade until the war's end.

After the war, McNair moved to Louisiana and then Mississippi, where he died at Hattiesburg on November 13, 1902. He is buried at the home of his son-in-law at Magnolia, Mississippi.

BIBLIOGRAPHY

Bunn, H. G. "Gen. Evander McNair." *Confederate Veteran* 11 (1903): 265–266.

Tucker, Glenn. *Chickamauga: Bloody Battle in the West.* Indianapolis, 1961.

ANNE J. BAILEY

MACON, GEORGIA. Proclaimed "Queen Inland City of the South," Macon dominated the economy of central Georgia. Situated on the fall line of the Ocmulgee River and at the intersection of the Central of Georgia Railroad and the Macon and Western Railroad, the city served the heart of the state's cotton belt. This rail center linked Atlanta, Columbus, Americus, Milledgeville, Augusta, and Savannah.

Macon's population was 8,034 in 1860, making it the fifth largest Georgia city. Famed poet and resident Sidney Lanier boldly declared its future as the "cultural capital of the young South" and the "next American Athens." Residents numbered 5,337 whites, 2,664 slaves, and 33 free blacks. Ironically, the free black population was 55 less than in 1850. Bibb County, with Macon as its county seat, was the only one in the area to have a white population majority. One-fifth of the city's residents were foreign-born and 60 percent of the white households owned slaves. Planters headed 9 percent of resident families; 37 percent described themselves as "professionals, merchants, manufacturers, or proprietors." Master craftsmen and journeymen also headed 37 percent of families; semiskilled and day laborers composed 14 percent. Overseers headed 2 percent of households, and the remaining 1 percent included widows and the retired or unemployed.

Almost all slaves worked as domestics, building tradesmen, proprietors of small shops (typically the city's barbers were blacks), or laborers on the railroad. Many negotiated with their masters to permit them to operate their own small businesses, free from daily contact with their owners. Urban slaves experienced only limited opposition in engaging in such commercial ventures.

The minuscule free black population worked primarily in the construction trades, domestic service, or other service occupations. A notable exception was Solomon Humphries who purchased his family's freedom from his plantation master, became a successful merchant, made a fortune, and was widely respected.

Macon's economy rested primarily on King Cotton. One-seventh of Georgia's total production was baled in the city on the eve of the Civil War and transported via rail or river to Northern or European mills. The railroad and its supporting iron industry also were major elements of the economy. The Macon and Western Railroad boasted a cash surplus of $131,000 in 1860 and paid a 9 percent dividend. The Central of Georgia Railroad connected the city with Savannah, the state's busiest deepwater port, enabling Maconites to enjoy seafood as "common luxuries" in winter and cheap ice in summer. Several roundhouses attested to the importance of rail transportation to the city's economic vitality.

In the presidential election of 1860, Maconites voted for either John Bell of the Constitutional Union party or John

FORT MACON. Surrender of Fort Macon. *FRANK LESLIE'S ILLUSTRATED FAMOUS LEADERS AND BATTLE SCENES OF THE CIVIL WAR*

C. Breckinridge, the proslavery nominee of the fragmented Democrats. Bell carried the city by a small margin, while Breckinridge won the state. The announcement of Abraham Lincoln's victory forced the city's moderates to join the secession camp or cease public political discussion.

Lincoln's election caused the city to begin preparing for armed conflict with the Federal government. On November 8 the Minutemen announced their unit's uniform style and color. The following week a Committee of Safety prepared to take "protective measures" within the city. The Macon volunteers unfurled their unit's colors with fifteen stars in anticipation of the formation of the Southern nation. Sidney Lanier soon joined this unit, which was one of Georgia's first to fight at the Virginia front. During the war, twenty-six companies of infantry, artillery, and cavalry went into battle. The city's Camp Oglethorpe was a major staging location for soldiers ordered to the front. No county in the Confederacy sent more troops in proportion to its population than Bibb, and roughly one-tenth of the county's white males died in the war.

While the recently established *Macon Telegraph* urged the electorate to guard against hasty action on the part of their representatives in the legislature, Mayor M. S. Thomson, the first of Macon's three Civil War mayors, also urged careful thought and tried to maintain public order. In mid-December the city chose three delegates to the state secession convention. One of these, Eugenius A. Nisbet, drafted the Georgia Ordinance of Secession, which declared the state an independent republic on January 19, 1861. Troops from Macon had already been ordered by Governor Joseph E. Brown to seize Fort Pulaski near Savannah.

Numerous aid societies, most patterned after the Macon Ladies Soldiers' Relief Society, contributed to war preparations even before the fall of Fort Sumter. These groups sewed, solicited contributions, and tended the sick and wounded. They were instrumental in converting the Macon Hotel, the vacant Georgia Academy for the Blind, and other buildings into treatment facilities as casualties mounted. Arrival of wounded from Chickamauga transformed City Hall into a hospital.

The city enjoyed unique security from enemy assault during the first years of war. Its location in the heart of the Piedmont and upstream from the shoals at the confluence of the Ocmulgee and Altamaha rivers ensured its relative safety from either land or water assault until late in the war.

The Confederate government established three ordnance installations in the city in 1861. An armory for manufacturing and repairing small arms, an arsenal for molding cannons and other heavy arms, and a laboratory for producing ammunition became major employers. These factories ranked in size only behind the Tredegar Iron Works in Richmond and the Selma, Alabama, Ordnance Works. Other government offices quickly located in the city. A Quartermaster Depot, the Medical Purveyor's Office, and a steam bakery produced necessities. By war's end, the Confederate government controlled a great portion of the city's land and labor, both free and slave. Over a thousand slaves and several hundred white civilians worked in these factories. The Confederate Treasury Department used Macon as a depository for $1.5 million in gold.

Private businesses, though plagued by chronic labor and material shortages, similarly prospered. Articles for military and civilian use—from steam engines, cotton presses, and sawmills to spurs, swords, pistols, and uniforms—poured from the city. The twin problems of rampant inflation and shortages of food and cloth precipitated a riot by some Macon women in 1864.

Though the Georgia Academy for the Blind moved to Fort Valley, Wesleyan College managed to remain open throughout the war. Public entertainment provided welcome diversion from the hardships. Residents supported and regularly attended various stock companies whose productions ranged from *Macbeth* to *Pizzaro*.

By 1864, Macon was exhibiting the overcrowding, lawlessness, disease, and disorder of a refugee city. Dislocated civilians, wounded and ill soldiers, and prostitutes poured in following Confederate defeats in northern Georgia and Alabama.

In the spring of 1864, the Army of Georgia Reserves and Georgia Militia, commanded by Howell Cobb, headquartered in Macon. Union forces under the command of George Stoneman raided the city on July 30, but they were repulsed and failed in their attempt to free Union officers held as prisoners of war. Earthworks now guarded the city's perimeter.

Following the fall of Atlanta, Macon anticipated a direct Union attack. Because Cobb's militia numbered only 1,500, the armory was dismantled and removed to keep it from falling into enemy hands. The city did escape Sherman's March to the Sea as he swept across the state from the ashes of Atlanta to Savannah. With the Union capture of the state capital, Milledgeville, Macon's City Hall served as the capitol building until war's end.

Cobb surrendered the city to Union commander James H. Wilson on April 20, 1865, eleven days after Appomattox. Though some looting and pillaging occurred, Macon fared better than many occupied cities, for Wilson and Cobb cooperated in maintaining order. Nor had the city sustained substantial war-related damage.

James Johnson, the presidentially appointed provisional governor of Georgia, inspected Macon in mid-July and found the city rebuilding. Businesses reopened and banking revived, though barter was still widely used. Tracks and rolling stock of the Central of Georgia Railroad were repaired and the company refinanced. Most of the residents who had fled during the war's final months returned quickly; by decade's end the population had grown to over seven thousand and Macon continued its dominance of central Georgia.

BIBLIOGRAPHY

Anderson, Nancy B. *Macon: A Pictorial History.* Virginia Beach, Va., 1979.

Reidy, Joseph P. "Masters and Slaves, Planters and Freedmen: The Transition from Slavery to Freedom in Central Georgia, 1820–1880." Ph.D. diss., Northern Illinois University, 1982.

Simms, Kristina. *Macon: Georgia's Central City.* Chatsworth, Calif., 1989.

Young, Ida, Julius Gholsow, and Clara Nell Hargrove. *History of Macon, Georgia.* Macon, Ga., 1959.

RALPH B. SINGER, JR.

MCQUEEN, JOHN (1804–1867), congressman from South Carolina. Born at Queensdale in Robeson County, North Carolina, on February 9, 1804, McQueen attended the University of North Carolina. He was admitted to the South Carolina bar in 1828 and began to practice in Bennettsville. After 1850 he considered himself a planter, not an attorney. In 1844 McQueen was defeated in a race for the U.S. Congress, but he was appointed to the House of Representatives in 1849 to fill an unexpired term and served until 1860. He was an early state rights advocate, and in 1856 he predicted dire results if Kansas became a free state. On December 21, 1860, McQueen resigned his seat with the entire South Carolina delegation.

In 1861 he was elected unopposed to the Confederate Congress and became chairman of the Accounts Committee. He also served on the Foreign Affairs and Inauguration

JOHN MCQUEEN. *HARPER'S PICTORIAL HISTORY OF THE GREAT REBELLION*

committees. He supported the central government except in the areas of taxation and conscription. He backed suspension of the writ of habeas corpus and the right of the president to make appointments and conduct diplomacy. He consistently opposed all peace negotiations. McQueen defended Secretary of War Judah P. Benjamin after the loss of Forts Henry and Donelson. In 1863, McQueen, in a fierce campaign, was defeated for reelection by James Hervey Witherspoon, a critic of Jefferson Davis.

After the war McQueen moved to Society Hill, where he farmed and practiced law until his death on August 30, 1867.

BIBLIOGRAPHY

Biographical Directory of the American Congress, 1774–1989. Washington, D.C., 1989.

Warner, Ezra J., and W. Buck Yearns, eds. *Biographical Register of the Confederate Congress.* Baton Rouge, La., 1975.

A. V. HUFF, JR.

MCRAE, COLIN J. (1812–1877), Mississippi governor and congressman, and chief financial agent for the Confederacy in Europe. McRae was born in Sneedsboro (present-day McFarlan), North Carolina, on October 22, 1812. In 1817 his family moved to Mississippi where his father became a well-established merchant and trader. Eventually the family settled in Pascagoula, Mississippi, on the Gulf coast; however, as his father's business expanded, the family maintained another home in Mobile, Alabama. McRae, although he was a Presbyterian, attended the Catholic College of Biloxi, Mississippi, for one year.

McRae's father died in 1835, and he took over the operation of the family's extensive mercantile business and assumed responsibility for his ten brothers and sisters. McRae quickly became a respected cotton commissioner and was one of the most successful businessmen along the Gulf coast, where he operated a fleet of coastal trading vessels. He also invested heavily in railroad development and real estate. He was one of the founders of Mississippi City, located about eighteen miles west of Biloxi. In addition he owned thousands of acres of land and many slaves.

Active in Mississippi politics, McRae was appointed a general of militia, and in 1838 he was elected to the Mississippi legislature. In 1840, he moved his base of operations to Mobile and entered into a partnership with Burwell Boykin as commission merchants. He also became involved in Democratic politics during this period. During the 1840s, McRae formed a business arrangement with his brother John J. McRae to promote the Mobile and Ohio Railroad and later the Mobile and New Orleans Railroad. The brothers also became slave dealers, real estate brokers, and land speculators. John McRae went on to become a U.S. senator from 1851 to 1852, governor of Mississippi from 1854 to 1858, a member of the U.S. House of Representatives from 1858 until secession, and a member of the Confederate House of Representatives from 1861 to 1863.

Colin McRae was a staunch secessionist, and in January 1861 he was elected to represent Mobile County in the Provisional Congress of the Confederacy. He was named to the Finance Committee as well as the Engrossment and Enrollment, Buildings, and Naval Affairs committees. He was also appointed to the Special Committee for the Inauguration of the President and Vice-President.

Because of his vast mercantile interests, McRae was concerned with keeping the port of Mobile open and argued strongly for its defense, pointing out its value as a major shipping point in correspondence with Confederate officials. He suggested that the Confederate navy construct four patrol boats to protect Mobile's harbor area. In addition he opposed transferring large numbers of Alabama troops to the regular army, insisting that they remain under state control and be used to protect Alabama. Because he understood the importance of commerce to the Federal government and realized that one way to weaken the North's war effort was to cripple its overseas trade, McRae also pushed for the issuance of letters of marque to Southern privateers who would scour the oceans in search of Northern shipping.

McRae did not stand for reelection. Instead he became involved in equipping the Southern military and entered the arms and munitions business. In 1861, he became an agent of the Confederate Ordnance Bureau, working in an unofficial capacity until July 16, 1862, when he was appointed an Ordnance Bureau agent for the Confederacy and the state of Alabama.

In 1861 he became interested in the construction of a major arms foundry at Selma, Alabama. Selma offered an ideal location: it was inland and therefore safe from a seaborne assault, it had excellent river and rail connections, and it was close to the coal and iron deposits of central Alabama. In addition, there existed in the city a small foundry and machine shop, the Selma Manufacturing Company, which the Confederacy could purchase for $35,000. In March 1865, President Jefferson Davis approved McRae's plan and authorized the purchase of the Selma company and the construction of an arms and munitions center. In addition to his official connection with the Selma ordnance works through his Confederate and Alabama commissions, McRae had a personal financial interest in the operation.

McRae spent much time putting the plan into effect, traveling to New Orleans to purchase equipment. The Selma operation developed into one of the largest iron manufacturing centers in the South, second only to the Tredegar Iron Works in Richmond, Virginia. Eventually the entire operation was taken over by the Confederate War and Navy departments. At the peak of its production, the Naval Arms Foundry at Selma employed three thousand workers and specialized in casting heavy cannons as well as operating an arsenal, powdermill, ironworks, and navy yard. It was at Selma that the Confederacy built the machinery and hulls for its naval vessels.

During the fall of 1862, McRae purchased cotton throughout the South and arranged for its shipment through the blockade to European markets, where it would be sold or exchanged for arms and munitions. The operation was so successful that during the first two years of the conflict European arms dealers were the principal source of Confederate weapons and military equipment.

In January of 1863 McRae served as the European manager of the Erlanger loan, negotiated with Emile Erlanger and Company of Paris, France. In return for Confederate bonds backed by cotton, Erlanger agreed to market a loan of 5 million pounds sterling in Europe for a fee equal to 5 percent of the bond issue. At the time cotton was considered an excellent financial investment for Europeans, and bond purchasers were offered two options for redeeming their investment: they could take possession of the cotton that backed the loan in New Orleans at the close of the war for a price of six pence a pound, or if they wanted their cotton before the war ended, they could demand that it be delivered to points within the Confederacy not more than ten miles from a railway or navigable stream for shipment at the bondholders' risk and expense.

The bonds were discounted 40 percent, and Erlanger was secretly allowed to take over the bonds at 77 percent and sell them in foreign financial markets at 90 percent of face value. Although the rates were exorbitant, they were not out of line with the interest charged on other loans of the period. The arrangement also allowed Erlanger and Company to repurchase the bonds, with Confederate capital, as a means of supporting the market and preventing their value from plunging. Because the bonds were backed by cotton, their successful distribution depended on the willingness of purchasers to speculate on the price of cotton.

The agreement allowed Erlanger and Company to make an enormous profit of about 13.5 million francs. The arrangement was criticized by many; however, the loan and subsequent bond issue provided the South with $15 million with which to continue the war effort, and it proved to be the mainstay of Confederate purchasing power in Europe. In spite of its drawbacks, the loan underwrote most of the arms purchases made by the Confederacy abroad until 1864, and at the time its terms were about the best that McRae could have negotiated. The value of the bonds fluctuated greatly during the war years, and the price of cotton rose and fell as the Federal blockade restricted trade and new cotton-producing areas were opened in Egypt. When the war ended the bonds became worthless, but their holders continued to scheme for their redemption for several years.

McRae returned home briefly in 1863 to complete the transfer of the Selma operation to the Confederate government. That same year he was named the chief Confederate overseas financial agent and devoted most of his time and energy to maintaining the South's credit, an increasingly difficult task as the North began to assert its supremacy on the battlefield and the Union's navy tightened its blockade of Southern ports.

At first the blockade was enforced by only one warship responsible for approximately three hundred miles of coastline. It had little effect on Southern trade with Europe and caused McRae little trouble. By 1864, however, the Federal navy had grown from 42 warships to 671 vessels, and their stranglehold on the South threatened to cut communications with other countries. Although McRae did everything possible to maintain trade, his efforts failed, and with the fall of Wilmington, North Carolina, which was evacuated by Southern forces on February 11, 1865, his task became impossible.

In October 1863, McRae suggested a plan to Confederate officials to reestablish Southern credit. First, he proposed the revoking of all contracts in which profits or commissions were allowed. Second, he demanded that a single contracting or purchasing officer be appointed for the War Department and another for the Navy Department. Third, he wanted to appoint a general agent in Europe with broad discretionary powers who would control all Southern credit, raise money, and take charge of all contracting and purchasing agents abroad. Fourth, McRae wanted the Confederate government to take control of all exports and imports, allowing nothing into or out of the South unless it was on a government account or an account of a bondholder demanding cotton. Finally, he urged that Confederate officials seize all cotton and tobacco in the South at a price fixed by Congress. This, he pointed out, would allow the government, rather than speculators, to make a profit. The plan was approved by President Davis and his cabinet and enacted into legislation in January 1864. McRae hoped that through these measures the Confederacy could restructure its credit by maintaining a monopoly on the shipping of cotton. It came too late in the war effort, however, to have much effect.

In the fall of 1864, at the urging of Secretary of State Judah P. Benjamin, McRae embarked on a secret mission to recruit Poles, who had unsuccessfully rebelled against Russia earlier that year, into Confederate service. In August 1864, four Polish officers had run the Federal blockade and offered their services to President Davis in return for the Confederacy setting aside an area in which the exiles could settle. Davis agreed and authorized the Poles to organize their own military units. On September 1, Benjamin ordered McRae to oversee the arrangements to ship the exiles to Mexico and from there into the Confederacy. He was not to induce any Poles to volunteer; they had to offer their services on their own. McRae was given 50,000 British pounds from the Secret Service fund to carry out the plan. The project failed to generate support among exiles, and in February 1865, McRae admitted to Benjamin that the recruitment effort had not succeeded.

With the downturn in Confederate military fortunes, several holders of Southern bonds in Europe sued McRae in an effort to force payment of their notes. In every instance the courts ruled in McRae's favor and acquitted him of any legal obligation. At the end of the war McRae returned to Mississippi and reestablished many of his former businesses.

When Davis was indicted for treason in 1867, McRae was among those supplying funds for the defense. Although Davis was charged under a statute enacted in 1790, Federal prosecutors never brought the matter to trial, as the defense maintained that the Fourteenth Amendment precluded any further punishment of ex-Confederates. After numerous delays the charges were dropped, and Davis was released under the provisions of a presidential proclamation of general amnesty in December 1868.

In the fall of 1867, McRae joined a group of Confederate expatriates to form a colony of exiles in Central America. He purchased a plantation and mercantile establishment at Puerto Cortés in Honduras. Applying his business talents to the new endeavor, McRae quickly became involved in the cattle and mahogany trade and expanded his mercantile business. He was joined in Honduras by his brother John and one of their sisters. John died in British Honduras (present-day Belize) while visiting Colón in May 1868 and was buried there. Colin McRae also died in British Honduras in February 1877 and was buried beside his brother.

BIBLIOGRAPHY

Brewer, W. *Alabama: Her History, Resources, War Record, and Public Men from 1540 to 1872.* Montgomery, Ala., 1872.

Davis, Charles S. *Colin J. McRae: Confederate Financial Agent.* Tuscaloosa, Ala., 1961.

Eaton, Clement. *A History of the Southern Confederacy.* New York, 1954.

Fleming, Walter L. *Civil War and Reconstruction in Alabama.* New York, 1905.

Huse, Caleb. *The Supplies for the Confederate Army: How They Were Obtained in Europe and How Paid For.* Boston, 1904.

McRae, John Colin. Letters. Alabama State Department of Archives and History. Montgomery, Ala.

Thompson, Samuel B. *Confederate Purchasing Operations Abroad.* Chapel Hill, N.C., 1935.

KENNY A. FRANKS

MCRAE, DANDRIDGE (1829–1899), brigadier general. A practicing attorney and clerk of the courts, McRae was named inspector general of the state of Arkansas when the war began. He mustered hundreds of Arkansas troops into service and as a lieutenant colonel, he led the Third Arkansas Battalion at the Battle of Oak Hills, Missouri, August 10, 1861, winning a citation for "coolness and bravery." Promoted to colonel, he commanded the Twenty-first Arkansas Infantry and won fresh plaudits at the Battle of Elkhorn Tavern, Arkansas, March 10, 1862.

In the spring of 1862, McRae was transferred east of the Mississippi River with Maj. Gen. Earl Van Dorn's Army of the West but returned to the Trans-Mississippi Department that summer to raise another regiment, the Twenty-eighth Arkansas Infantry.

Commissioned brigadier general on November 5, 1862, McRae served creditably at the Battle of Prairie Grove, Arkansas, December 9. During the Confederate assault on Fort Hindman, Arkansas, July 4, 1863, his troops captured their initial objective but were unable to respond when Lt. Gen. Theophilus H. Holmes ordered them to renew the attack. Holmes made McRae a scapegoat for the resulting Confederate defeat, but a court of inquiry dismissed charges of "misbehavior before the enemy."

When the Federal capture of Little Rock divided Arkansas in half, McRae was reassigned to command Confederate forces in the northern part of the state in October 1863. He served on Maj. Gen. Sterling Price's staff as a volunteer aide during the Battle of Jenkins's Ferry, Arkansas, April 30, 1864, and then spent the rest of the war leading Confederate guerrillas in northern Arkansas.

With the close of hostilities in 1865, McRae resumed his law practice. Appointed deputy secretary of state in 1881, he represented Arkansas at various trade expositions and served as vice president of the State Bureau of Information.

BIBLIOGRAPHY

"Gen. Dandridge McRae." *Confederate Veteran* 7 (August 1899): 368.

Hanks, C. J. "Steele's Escape at Jenkins's Ferry." *Confederate Veteran* 25 (February 1917): 79.

Harrell, John M. *Arkansas.* Vol. 10 of *Confederate Military History.* Edited by Clement A. Evans. Atlanta, 1899. Vol. 14 of extended ed. Wilmington, N.C., 1988.

DAVID EVANS

MCRAE, JOHN JONES (1815–1868), Mississippi governor and congressman. With his family, McRae moved when he was two years old from North Carolina to Mississippi. After graduating from Miami University of Ohio in 1834, he studied law in Mississippi and was

JOHN JONES MCRAE.

HARPER'S PICTORIAL HISTORY OF THE GREAT REBELLION

admitted to the bar. In 1837 he founded the *Eastern Clarion* at Paulding and became its editor and a politician. Reuben Davis remembered him as "a bright speaker, gay, humorous, and fascinating." He was elected to the state legislature in 1848 and 1850. After Jefferson Davis resigned from the U.S. Senate to run for governor in 1851, McRae was appointed to fill the post but was defeated in the next election.

From 1854 to 1858 McRae served two terms as governor. He said he owed his election to his support of the "great doctrine" of state rights, "based upon the individuality and sovereignty of the several States, as co-equals in the Confederacy." Despite the revival of secession as an emotional issue during McRae's terms, his primary interest was in state affairs—finances, railroad development, levee building, and especially education. He said that to appreciate life's two most important ideas—God and liberty—a man "must be educated; to be educated, the means must be provided, and this is the duty of the State."

In 1858 McRae became a U.S. congressman. He vowed that he would never accept a Republican president and warned that the election of Abraham Lincoln would precipitate secession. He served until 1861, when he, along with the other members of the Mississippi delegation, withdrew from the U.S. Congress.

McRae ran for a seat in the First Congress and won. The temper of the times favored his extreme Southern nationalism. McRae attended all four sessions and served on the Ways and Means, the Commissary and Quartermaster's Departments, and the Military Transportation committees. During his tenure, he consistently supported the policies of Jefferson Davis. He rarely contributed legislation but in 1862 introduced an unsuccessful bill to place a war tax on cotton. On February 12, 1863, McRae introduced a bill on exemptions that never got out of committee, and on March 31, 1863, after a bill defining who could be exempted from military service was reported from the Senate, McRae had his chance to present his version as an amendment. Like previous versions, McRae agreed to exempt people unfit for service; government officials; people needed to run ships, railroads, and telegraphs; newspaper personnel; ministers; hospital workers; educators; and indispensable workers in manufacture and construction. In McRae's amendment, the Secretary of War had the authority to set policies not specified in the law.

Later in 1863 when McRae sought a seat in the Second Congress, the public had become weary of the war, and he lost to the more moderate John T. Lamkin, whom he had defeated for the First Congress.

After the war McRae practiced law. Then, in 1868, despondent over the fall of the Confederacy, his wife's death, financial losses, and the failure of his own health, he went to Belize, British Honduras, to be with his brother, who had served in Europe as the Confederacy's chief financial officer. McRae died there a few days after his arrival.

BIBLIOGRAPHY

Alexander, Thomas B., and Richard E. Beringer. *The Anatomy of the Confederate Congress: A Study of the Influences of Member Characteristics on Legislative Voting Behavior, 1861–1865.* Nashville, Tenn., 1972.

Warner, Ezra J., and W. Buck Yearns. *Biographical Register of the Confederate Congress.* Baton Rouge, La., 1975.

RAY SKATES

MACRAE, WILLIAM (1834–1882), brigadier general. MacRae was the seventh son of Gen. Alexander MacRae and a descendant of Scottish warriors who fought with distinction from the Crusades to Waterloo. Born at Wilmington, North Carolina, September 9, 1834, he trained as a civil engineer and followed that profession until the start of the Civil War.

MacRae enlisted as a private in the Monroe Light Infantry in 1861 and was elected captain when the company was incorporated in the Fifteenth North Carolina. MacRae was promoted to lieutenant colonel in April 1862; to colonel in February 1863; to temporary rank of brigadier general, June 23, 1864; and to permanent rank of brigadier, November 5, 1864.

Small of stature but an iron disciplinarian, MacRae was

said to have the ability of instilling more fight in his troops than any other Confederate officer with the exception of John B. Gordon. He took part in the battles on the peninsula and the Seven Days' campaign. At Malvern Hill, MacRae took 300 men into action, only 35 of whom survived. At Sharpsburg, commanding a brigade that numbered only 250 effectives, MacRae repelled three assaults and fell back only when his ammunition was exhausted and his force was reduced to 50 men.

At Fredericksburg, MacRae fought stubbornly before Marye's Heights and held his ground despite the loss of nearly half his strength. Early in 1863 the Fifteenth was transferred to North Carolina and did not take part in the invasion of Pennsylvania. It rejoined the Army of Northern Virginia in time for the Bristoe Station engagement. Following the wounding of William Whedbee Kirkland at Cold Harbor, MacRae was given command of the brigade. According to a fellow Confederate, under MacRae's leadership "the highest degree of discipline and proficiency was attained, for no position was considered too strong to be assaulted if MacRae ordered it." At Reams' Station, MacRae's men captured a battery while driving Winfield Scott Hancock's troops from their entrenchments. For this feat, MacRae received the compliments of Robert E. Lee.

His many battles notwithstanding, MacRae was wounded only once, when a bullet struck his jaw. Twice his sword was shot in two. When he surrendered at Appomattox, his personal property consisted of two horses and a sword.

Returning to North Carolina, MacRae served as superintendent of the Wilmington and Manchester Railroad, later the Macon and Brunswick line, and finally of the State Road of Georgia, which became the Western and Atlantic. He died at Augusta, Georgia, February 11, 1882, and was buried in Oakdale Cemetery, Wilmington.

BIBLIOGRAPHY

Compiled Military Service Records. William MacRae. Microcopy M331, Roll 161. Record Group 109. National Archives, Washington, D.C.

Hill, D. H., Jr. *North Carolina.* Vol. 4 of *Confederate Military History.* Edited by Clement A. Evans. Atlanta, 1899. Vol. 5 of extended ed. Wilmington, N.C., 1987.

Kenan, William R. "Letter." *Confederate Veteran* 7 (1899): 397–398. Reprint, Wilmington, N.C., 1985.

MacRae, David. *The Americans at Home.* New York, 1952.

LOWELL REIDENBAUGH

MACWILLIE, MARCUS H. (fl. 1860), congressman from Arizona Territory. Nothing is known of Marcus Macwillie's early life. He does not appear on any census record, and there is disagreement even over his first name, which sometimes is given as Malcolm. At the height of the secession movement in 1860, Macwillie was an attorney practicing at La Mesilla in Dona Ana County, New Mexico Territory, and a prominent citizen of the surrounding Mesilla valley. He was deeply involved in the secession movement in Arizona and New Mexico.

The two regions played an important part in the South's initial plans. President Jefferson Davis had served as the U.S. secretary of war under President Franklin Pierce. As such he oversaw the survey of possible railway routes between the East and the West Coast and thus realized the potential of controlling the communication route between the two. To Davis the two most feasible routes were both southern: one ran from Preston, Texas, on the Red River across Texas through the Gadsden Purchase area of New Mexico and Arizona to San Diego, California; the other ran from Fort Smith, Arkansas, across Indian Territory, New Mexico, and Arizona to Los Angeles. In addition, the Butterfield overland stage route, which ran from Fort Smith, across Indian Territory, Texas, New Mexico, and Arizona, was the principal east-west route to California. Moreover, New Mexico and Arizona bordered Mexico—controlling them would give the Confederacy an overland connection with a neutral country and allow the South to bypass the Federal naval blockade.

President Davis and other Southern leaders hoped to extend Confederate power westward into the two regions, cut off Federal contact with the West Coast, deprive the North of the area's mineral wealth, and possibly encourage the territory to secede from the Union and support the South. Macwillie played a major role in their plans.

Macwillie became one of the leading spokesmen for secession in the mining camps of present-day southern Arizona. The movement for secession in the region was tied as much to the so called Indian problem as to Southern rights. The territory of New Mexico—present-day New Mexico, Arizona, and the southern tip of Nevada—had been created in 1850, but the inhabitants of present-day Arizona and New Mexico south of the Jornado del Muerto desert were so disgruntled over the Federal government's inability to control the Apaches that they organized the unofficial territory of Arizona in 1860.

La Mesilla, a depot on the Butterfield overland stage route, was the center of pro-Southern sympathy in the region. As early as late summer of 1860 Macwillie was urging local residents to support the extralegal Arizona territorial government, and on September 30, 1860, he appeared before a large meeting of miners in Pinto Alto urging them to abandon their ties to New Mexico Territory.

On March 16, 1861, a pro-Southern convention was held at La Mesilla, and it declared that portion of New Mexico Territory south of 34° north latitude to have seceded from the Union and asked to be annexed to the Confederacy. Their action was supported by Texas troops commanded by

Lt. Col. John R. Baylor and the withdrawal of Northern forces from the region. At a mass meeting in Tucson on August 5, Granville H. Oury was selected as an unofficial representative of the region to the Confederate Congress in Richmond, Virginia. On August 8, 1861, Baylor reported to Brig. Gen. Earl Van Dorn, the commander of the Department of Texas, that a pro-Southern provisional government of Arizona had been established.

La Mesilla was named the capital of Confederate Arizona Territory, and Macwillie was appointed territorial attorney general. Baylor, however, who was serving as territorial governor, called for a second territorial election to select a representative to the Confederate Congress. For some reason he was determined to replace Oury with Macwillie and sent letters to justices of the peace of the various voting precincts, instructing them to vote for the attorney general. In the correspondence Baylor stressed the need to select a congressional delegate who would protect the interests of the territory; Macwillie, he believed, was the person best suited to fill the position. Oury's supporters were outraged by Baylor's action and boycotted the voting, claiming that it was illegal because sufficient notice had not been given of the election. When the votes were counted on December 30, 1861, Macwillie was chosen to replace Oury.

On January 13, 1862, Congress passed an act creating Arizona Territory, which was signed into law by President Davis on January 18. The act, which went into effect on February 14, allowed the territory one nonvoting delegate in the Confederate House of Representatives. Oury, who was already in Richmond as the territory's unofficial delegate, took Arizona's seat on January 18, but he was replaced by Macwillie on March 11.

Although Macwillie was not allowed to serve on committees, he did become a steadfast supporter of the Davis administration. He also introduced legislation to control Indian depredations in Arizona Territory and to aid Baylor in preventing Federal forces from retaking the region. He was a staunch defender of Baylor's policy of exterminating the Apaches. He also worked with Elias C. Boudinot, the Cherokee Nation's representative to the Confederate Congress, to provide payment for material seized by Southern officials in Indian Territory.

Macwillie introduced House Resolution 124, on January 8, 1864, which amended the Organic Act for Arizona Territory to allow the present Arizona Territory delegate to remain in office until a new one was elected. By this time Confederate Arizona Territory had ceased to exist, for Federal troops had reoccupied the region early in 1862. Macwillie's act, however, which was approved by Congress and signed by Davis, allowed him to remain in office until the end of the Civil War. When the fighting ceased, Macwillie disappeared from history.

BIBLIOGRAPHY

Colton, Ray C. *The Civil War in the Western Territories: Arizona, Colorado, New Mexico, and Utah.* Norman, Okla., 1959.

Faulk, Odie B. *Arizona: A Short History.* Norman, Okla., 1970.

Kerby, Robert L. *The Confederate Invasion of New Mexico and Arizona, 1861–1862.* Los Angeles, 1958.

Sacks, B. "The Creation of the Territory of Arizona." *Arizona and the West* 5 (1963): 109–148.

Waldrup, William I. "New Mexico during the Civil War." *New Mexico Historical Review* 27 (1953): 163–182.

PAUL F. LAMBERT

MAFFITT, JOHN N. (1819–1886), naval officer and commander of blockade runners. Maffitt enlisted in the U.S. Navy in 1832 and resigned his commission in 1861 after twenty-nine years of service, including fourteen in the coastal survey. This latter service was probably responsible for the success of his blockade running.

Maffitt was commissioned a lieutenant in the Confederate navy in May 1861. His first command was *Savannah,* flagship of Josiah Tattnall's squadron, which tried to prevent the capture of Port Royal. His next assignment was as captain of a blockade runner. At Nassau on May 6, 1862, Maffitt took command of *Oreto,* which soon became *Florida.* Unable to begin his cruise immediately because of an inadequate crew, incomplete armament, and yellow fever among his men, he began an odyssey in Cuba that eventually took the ship on a spectacular run through the Union blockade in full daylight at Mobile, a feat he accomplished by disguising *Florida* as an English warship. He finally began his first cruise on January 17, 1863. Although he constantly encountered difficulty in supplying his ship, Maffitt captured twenty-five merchant ships. His auxiliaries seized another twenty-two, making the captures attributed to *Florida's* first cruise a total of forty-seven.

After leaving *Florida* Maffitt returned to duty as a blockade runner and briefly commanded the ram *Albermarle* in 1864. His superiors, fearing that the aggressive Maffitt would lose *Albermarle,* had him removed. He climaxed his career by running the blockades at Wilmington, Charleston, and Galveston with *Owl.* Maffitt served for a time in the British merchant service before returning to his home in North Carolina, where he spent his remaining years on a small farm near Wilmington.

BIBLIOGRAPHY

Boykin, Edward. *Sea Devil of the Confederacy: The Story of the Florida and Her Captain John Newland Maffitt.* New York, 1959.

Dalzell, George W. *Flight from the Flag.* Chapel Hill, N.C., 1940.

Owsley, Frank L. *The C.S.S. Florida: Her Building and Operations.* Tuscaloosa, Ala., 1987.

FRANK LAWRENCE OWSLEY

MAGAZINES. [*This entry contains four articles:*

De Bow's Review
Southern Illustrated News
Southern Literary Messenger
Northern Magazines in the South.

See also Literature, *article on* Literature in the Confederacy; War Correspondents.]

De Bow's Review

Although *De Bow's Review* was one of the most persistent advocates of the Southern cause, it did not appear often during the years of the Confederacy. Between the middle of 1862 and January 1866, it was published only once: the July-August issue of 1864.

Yet the scheduled monthly had been the semiofficial voice for the Southern cause since the latter part of the 1850s. Originally meant to be an economic organ when started by James Dunwoody Brownson De Bow in January 1846, the *Review* gradually abandoned its avoidance of politics as the issues of slavery and civil conflict heated up. De Bow himself became one of the South's key promoters of the slavery system, being elected president of both the 1857 Southern Convention and the African Labor Supply Association in 1859.

By the 1850s, *De Bow's Review* was devoting considerable space to the fundamental economic questions involved in the slavery dispute; between 1849 and 1851, the magazine ran four serials defending slavery and an article by De Bow asserting that slavery was a personal matter. On occasion, *De Bow's* collected inflammatory Northern statements under the title "The War Against the South." *De Bow's* appealed to white racial pride and Southern economic independence with its proslavery stance. The magazine promoted the growth of Southern nationalism and called upon its readers "as Southerners, as Americans, and as MEN" to make "no explanation . . . no apology" for slavery. At another point, the magazine asserted, "It is sufficient that we, the people of a state, we the people of half the states of this Union, in our sovereign independence . . . have decreed our institutions as they are, *and so will dare maintain them.*" The 1850s represented *De Bow's* most secure period. After a shaky start and interruptions in publication, the magazine was able to appear monthly because of financial help from a wealthy sugar planter.

After the Harpers Ferry episode, *De Bow's* was full of discussions on secession and the approaching conflict; in April 1860, the magazine appealed to the South to secede and form an empire composed of the Southern states, Texas, Mexico, Central America, and the West Indies. When the firing commenced, De Bow wrote: "The glorious action at Fort Sumter excited to enthusiasm the entire South." The shortages and dislocations brought on by the war, however, caused distress for *De Bow's*—double numbers, poor quality printing and paper, and a move from New Orleans to Charleston, South Carolina, in 1861. These problems culminated in a quadruple number in August 1862 and the complete suspension of publication for two years thereafter. The magazine published its final issue during the war in 1864 at Columbia.

De Bow's role in the postbellum South was once again central. Publishing out of Nashville, the magazine was "Devoted to the Restoration of the Southern States, and the Development of the Wealth and Resources of the Country," as it proclaimed in its logotype. De Bow urged diversification of the South's economy and investments from the North. He died in 1867; his magazine lived on until 1880.

BIBLIOGRAPHY

McCardell, John. *The Idea of a Southern Nation.* Vol. 2. New York, 1979.

Mott, Frank L. *A History of American Magazines.* Vol. 1. Cambridge, Mass., 1938.

Riley, Sam. *Magazines of the American South.* Westport, Conn., 1986.

JOHN A. LENT and KOHAVA SIMHI

Southern Illustrated News

Founded in September 1862 to fill a void left when *Harper's Weekly* and other Northern illustrated periodicals could no longer circulate in the South, the *Southern Illustrated News* attracted some of the most distinguished writers of the Confederacy. Among them were John R. Thompson, a Virginia lawyer who was editor for a time; James R. Randall, author of "Maryland, My Maryland"; Paul Hamilton Hayne, the poet; George W. Bagby, a Virginia physician and writer of dialect stories; William Gilmore Simms; Henry Flash; and Henry Timrod.

Some of these writers had close connections to the *Southern Literary Messenger* as well; both Thompson and Bagby served as editor and Simms had merged his *Southern and Western Monthly Magazine and Review* with the *Messenger* in 1845.

The weekly's major war correspondent was the novelist John Esten Cooke, who at various times served as staff officer for both J. E. B. Stuart and Thomas J. ("Stonewall") Jackson. Like many correspondents, he also filed stories for other publications, especially the Richmond dailies. Other *Southern Illustrated News* writers, including Bagby and Timrod, had also been war correspondents.

The *Southern Illustrated News,* the second magazine of that name (the first published in Atlanta in 1860), was patterned after a London pictorial. Its early success was rather remarkable; within a few weeks of its launching, there were at least 20,000 subscribers. The magazine had to raise its subscription rate to twenty dollars at the end of 1863 as the economic situation worsened, and it ceased publication in the waning weeks of the war.

BIBLIOGRAPHY

Mott, Frank L. *A History of American Magazines.* Vol. 1. Cambridge, Mass., 1938.

Riley, Sam. *Magazines of the American South.* Westport, Conn., 1986.

JOHN A. LENT and KOHAVA SIMHI

Southern Literary Messenger

The *Southern Literary Messenger,* published in Richmond, Virginia, had been around for more than two decades and was already considered the cultural voice of the South when the Confederacy was established. But its stance was inconsistent, its tone and causes changing with its numerous proprietors and editors.

In the beginning, editor James Ewell Heath gave the monthly a moralistic flavor; his successor, Edgar Allan Poe, was more prone to outspokenness. They and proprietor and third editor Thomas W. White emphasized literary fare, although not necessarily about the South. Benjamin B. Minor, who bought the magazine and edited it from 1843 to 1847, used it as a recorder of Southern history. John Reuben Thompson's thirteen-year tenure as *Messenger* editor restored its literary stature, at least temporarily.

In its earliest years, the *Messenger* strove for political neutrality, but by 1841, White had put his magazine in the camp of those defending Southern interests and rights, including slavery. Benjamin Minor, his successor, used the arousal of sectionalism as a stratagem to keep the struggling magazine alive. Minor took a strong stance, declaring, "We will vindicate Southern interests from assault, Southern manners from aspersion, and Southern literature from disparagement."

During Thompson's initial period as editor, the *Messenger* appealed less to sectionalism than at any time in its past. His policy of emphasizing literature over politics changed, however, as disputes over slavery intensified and the magazine edged closer to bankruptcy. Eventually, Thompson followed the same expedient route traveled by Minor, taking up a sectional, but Unionist position and publishing proslavery articles in the hope of capturing a larger Southern readership. When he could no longer stand to watch his *Messenger* decline as an outlet for belles lettres, Thompson resigned as editor in May 1860.

The magazine's Unionist position was abandoned after Thompson's departure. The new editor, George W. Bagby, a Virginia physician and writer of dialect stories, strongly favored secession. The great difference between Thompson's and Bagby's editorial stands has been summarized by historian Frank Luther Mott: "the chief interest of the Bagby editorship was political. . . . Thompson had been forced by currents of opinion to the publishing of many articles with a political bearing; Bagby soon came to writing politics with gusto for his 'Editor's Table.' "

Bagby declared for a Southern Confederacy in December 1860 and called upon Virginia to initiate such action in succeeding issues of the *Messenger.* As early as January 1861, he proposed Jefferson Davis as president of such a confederacy. When Virginia did secede in April 1861, Bagby immediately enlisted in the military, even though he was not physically fit. He edited the *Messenger* from the field until August, when he returned to Richmond, having been discharged because of poor health.

During the next two and a half years, Bagby vigorously attacked the North, while simultaneously criticizing the South's conduct of the war. He was especially incensed with the incompetence of the Southern leadership in 1862 and 1863, declaring on one occasion, "From the Chief Magistrate down none of us have got any common sense, any real energy, and certainly not any forecast."

Bagby's outspoken criticism cost the *Messenger* almost all of its Northern readers and many from the South. As a result, he was forced to raise the price of the magazine three times in 1863 alone. The magazine was sold late that year to Wedderburn and Alfriend; its last number appeared the following June.

BIBLIOGRAPHY

Chielens, Edward E., ed. *American Literary Magazines: The Eighteenth and Nineteenth Centuries.* Westport, Conn., 1986.

Jacobs, Robert D. "Campaign for a Southern Literature: *The Southern Literary Messenger.*" *Southern Literary Journal* 2 (Fall 1969): 66–98.

Mott, Frank L. *A History of American Magazines.* Vols. 1, 2. Cambridge, Mass., 1938.

Riley, Sam. *Magazines of the American South.* Westport, Conn., 1986.

JOHN A. LENT and KOHAVA SIMHI

Northern Magazines in the South

Although most American periodicals between 1850 and 1865 were local or regional, a few, such as *Harper's Monthly, Godey's Lady's Book, New York Ledger,* and *Frank Leslie's Illustrated,* had national circulations, and some were very popular in the South.

The latter fact caused Southern magazine editors much consternation, especially in the decade before the Civil War, when the South spawned a number of its own periodicals. The lack of support for these magazines embittered their editors, some of whom savagely blasted Northern periodicals that had large circulations in the South.

The *Southern Quarterly* typified such a reaction. Claiming *Harper's* in 1854 received $150,000 from subscriptions, its editor bluntly declared "that one-third of that sum, centered annually upon almost any southern monthly or quarterly, would insure a better work than Harper's and Putnam's together." In a similar vein, *De Bow's* countered arguments that said Northern periodicals gave more for the dollar: "More what? More trash, more abuse, more reports of anti-slavery conventions, of anti-Sabbath, anti-matrimony, and anti-everything-in-general mass meetings."

When the *Southern Literary Messenger* faced suspension for financial reasons in early 1855, editor John R. Thompson could not resist a comparison with the lucrative Northern periodicals: "*Harper's Magazine* has probably five times as many subscribers south of the Potomac . . . and even *Putnam's Monthly,* which has recently outraged the entire slave holding portion of the Union by lending itself to the extremist views of the abolitionists, has a larger circulation among slave-holders."

Another aspect of the problem was that some of the best writers of the South sent their choice work to Northern magazines of greater repute and circulation. An early editor of the *Southern Literary Messenger* lamented this situation.

Over the years, some Northern periodicals gained a strong foothold in the South because of the paucity of important publishing centers there and because Northern periodicals often published laudatory articles about the South.

Especially prominent in the South were *Harper's Monthly* and *Putnam's Monthly.* Eschewing all partisan and controversial questions, especially that of slavery, *Harper's* ventured opinions only when they were universally acceptable. Such a policy helped the magazine build a large Southern circulation, which it sustained until the fighting actually began in the Civil War. Despite its political bias, *Putnam's* gained a following in the South because it paid attention to the region, using Southern fiction and writers. The magazine was chastised often by Southern editors, especially for its role as the organ for the "Black Republican Party."

Still other Northern periodicals popular in the South were *Harper's Weekly, Godey's Lady's Book, Frank Leslie's Illustrated, New York Mercury,* and *New York Ledger,* as well as religious quarterlies and medical, legal, and technical journals. *Leslie's,* which was in direct competition with *Harper's Weekly,* aimed at nonpartisanship, but found itself criticized by both North and South. By the middle of 1861, the paper became a Northern sympathizer; the switch was out of character, as *Leslie's* had been anti-abolitionist for years. The breakoff of communication between the North and South once hostilities commenced abruptly reduced the circulation of these Northern magazines.

BIBLIOGRAPHY

Mott, Frank L. *A History of American Magazines.* Vol. 2. Cambridge, Mass., 1938.

Stanchak, John E., ed. *Leslie's Illustrated Civil War.* Jackson, Miss., 1992.

JOHN A. LENT and KOHAVA SIMHI

MAGOFFIN, BERIAH (1815–1885), governor of Kentucky. Magoffin was born in Harrodsburg, Kentucky, on April 18, 1815. He graduated from Centre College in 1835 and completed the law course at Transylvania University in 1838.

A Democratic stalwart, Magoffin was a delegate to several national conventions and a frequent candidate for presidential elector. Elected to the state senate in 1850, he was defeated for lieutenant governor in 1855. Magoffin won the governorship in 1859 over Joshua F. Bell, 76,187 to 67,283. His troubled administration was dominated by the sectional crisis and the Civil War.

Magoffin never concealed his Southern sympathies. He accepted slavery, and he charged that the Republicans ("obstinate in spirit, and sullen in temper") had violated Southern rights in regard to the territories and fugitive slaves. Although he believed in the right of secession, Magoffin hoped that collective demands from the slave states would force the North to make concessions. If compromise failed, he predicted that Kentucky would go with the other slave states.

When his efforts to secure a compromise failed, Magoffin advocated calling a convention to determine the state's policy, but Unionist legislators refused it for fear that it might be a plot to take Kentucky out of the Union. After the fall of Fort Sumter, Magoffin rejected the Union call for troops; Kentucky would supply "no troops for the wicked purpose of subduing her Sister Southern States." But he also refused to supply troops to the Confederacy, and he helped formulate Kentucky's neutrality policy, which he proclaimed on May 20, 1861.

After summer elections the Unionist majorities in the legislature easily overrode his vetoes. When opposing forces entered the state in early September, the legislature ordered him to demand the withdrawal of only the Confederates. When his veto failed, Magoffin obeyed the directive; he explained that his oath of office required him to obey the will of the majority, regardless of his own views. He puzzled his opponents by retaining his office and denouncing the Confederate government of Kentucky that was established in November. But his efforts to halt what he saw as Federal violations of constitutional rights convinced his opponents of his pro-Confederate stance, and the legislature stripped him of many of his powers. His position became increasingly untenable. But the lieutenant governor had died in 1859, and Magoffin would not accept Speaker of the Senate John F. Fisk as his successor. After secret negotiations, Fisk resigned as Speaker on August 16, 1862, and was replaced immediately by James F. Robinson. Two days later Magoffin resigned as governor, Robinson replaced him, and Fisk was reelected Speaker.

Magoffin retired to his Harrodsburg farm and law practice. Chicago real estate investments made him wealthy. When the war ended, he urged Kentuckians to ratify the Thirteenth Amendment and extend civil rights to blacks. Magoffin served a term (1867–1869) in the statehouse. He died on February 28, 1885, and was buried at Harrodsburg.

BIBLIOGRAPHY

Commonwealth of Kentucky. House of Representatives. *Journal*. 1859–1862.

Commonwealth of Kentucky. Senate. *Journal*. 1859–1862.

Coulter, E. Merton. *The Civil War and Readjustment in Kentucky*. Chapel Hill, N.C., 1926.

Dues, Michael T. "The Pro-Secessionist Governor of Kentucky: Beriah Magoffin's Credibility Gap." *Register of the Kentucky Historical Society* 67 (July 1969): 221–231.

Harrison, Lowell H. "Beriah Magoffin, 1859–1862." In *Kentucky's Governors, 1792–1885*. Edited by Lowell H. Harrison. Lexington, Ky., 1985.

Harrison, Lowell H. "Governor Magoffin and the Secession Crisis." *Register of the Kentucky Historical Society* 72 (April 1974): 91–110.

LOWELL H. HARRISON

MAGRATH, ANDREW G. (1813–1893), district judge and governor of South Carolina. Born in Charleston February 8, 1813, Magrath attended Catholic Bishop John England's school and graduated from South Carolina College in 1831. After attending Harvard Law School and reading law, he was admitted to the bar in 1835. He served in the state legislature in 1840 and 1842. Magrath married Emma C. Mikell in 1843. He was a cooperationist in the secession crisis of 1852 and joined James L. Orr's National Democratic faction in 1856. He was elected to the Democratic National Convention but resigned to become federal district judge.

After Abraham Lincoln's election in 1860, Magrath resigned from the judiciary, declaring that "the Temple of Justice, raised under the Constitution of the United States, is now closed." He was elected to the secession convention and on December 30, 1860, became secretary of state. He served on the Executive Council until 1862. Then he was appointed Confederate district judge. Although he held the Conscription and Sequestering acts constitutional, his opinions increasingly reflected a state rights position. He declared the war tax on securities unconstitutional. His later decisions made him popular with the anti–Jefferson Davis faction.

On November 16, 1864, Magrath urged Senator James Chesnut, Jr., a leader of the pro-Davis faction, to run for governor. Mrs. Chesnut noted: "I take it for granted he wants to be governor himself, and to use Mr. Chesnut in the canvass as a sort of lightning rod." Chesnut refused, and four names emerged: John Smith Preston and Samuel McGowan, who were pro-Davis, and Magrath and A. C. Garlington, anti-Davis. On December 14 Magrath won on the sixth ballot. He declared his efforts would be directed toward defending the state equally from the Union and from the Confederate government.

The legislature gave Magrath power to exempt from Confederate service whomever he deemed necessary for the defense of the state and restricted the power of the Confederacy to impress slaves in South Carolina. With William Tecumseh Sherman's invasion imminent, Magrath urged Davis to save Charleston.

In January 1865 Magrath received word that P. G. T. Beauregard had ordered the evacuation of the garrison there. The governor appealed to Davis and Robert E. Lee, and Davis sent a brigade of Charlestonians. Meanwhile, Magrath appealed unsuccessfully to the governors of Georgia and North Carolina. By February the state was invaded, and the governor urged citizens to defend their homes and to destroy or remove what was of value to the enemy. With Sherman before Columbia on February 16, Magrath moved to Winnsboro, Union, and then Spartanburg. He called the legislature to meet in Greenville on April 25, but no quorum appeared. Magrath returned to Columbia and ordered other state officials to do the same. After Joseph E. Johnston's surrender on April 26, Magrath demanded that Confederate supplies be turned over to the state.

On May 15, 1865, Union Gen. Quincy A. Gillmore charged Magrath with treason. The governor suspended the functions of his office, and on May 25 he was arrested and imprisoned at Fort Pulaski. On November 23, 1865, President Andrew Johnson ordered Magrath released. Shortly afterward he married Mary McCord (his first wife having died) and moved to Charleston. He resumed the practice of law until his death on April 9, 1893.

BIBLIOGRAPHY

Cauthen, Charles E. *South Carolina Goes to War, 1860–1865*. Chapel Hill, N.C., 1950.

Edmunds, John B., Jr. "South Carolina." In *The Confederate Governors*. Edited by W. Buck Yearns. Athens, Ga., 1985.

A. V. HUFF, JR.

MAGRUDER, JOHN B. (1807–1871), major general. Born in Port Royal, Virginia, Magruder graduated from West Point in 1830. Serving in the First United States Artillery, he earned distinction in the Mexican War. Magruder, who became known as "Prince John," was fond of finery, drink, and revelry, which made him a conspicuous figure but raised questions about his competency among his superiors. On April 20, 1861, shortly after Virginia seceded from the Union, Magruder resigned his brevet lieutenant colonel commission in the U.S. Army. He received a Confederate commission as colonel on May 21, 1861, to date from March 16, 1861. Promotion came rapidly: he became a brigadier general on June 17 and a major general on October 7, 1861.

Command of the Confederate troops on the peninsula in May 1861 offered Magruder a critical assignment. He defeated the Federals at Big Bethel, a minor skirmish on June 10, which won him acclaim throughout the South. A more serious threat materialized in the spring of 1862, when Gen. George B. McClellan's Union army plodded up the peninsula. To slow the Federal advance, Magruder brilliantly disguised the numerical weakness of his force. His subterfuges stalled McClellan at Yorktown for an entire month. This allowed Gen. Joseph E. Johnston to shift his forces to the peninsula and assume overall command there. Magruder's performance, however, did not impress Johnston. His criticisms reached Jefferson Davis whose estimation of Magruder fell considerably.

Magruder's part in the Seven Days' Battles remains the most controversial aspect of his career in Confederate service. While Gen. Robert E. Lee concentrated the bulk of his forces on the Confederate left, Magruder and Gen. Benjamin Huger were left with 25,000 men to stave off more than 65,000 Federals south of the Chickahominy River. Repeating his tactics on the peninsula, Magruder deluded McClellan into believing that he faced a superior force. As Lee chased the retreating Federal army, Magruder joined the pursuit on June 28. The dapper Virginian suddenly became lethargic, punctuated by occasional outbursts of anger. Physical exhaustion, an allergic reaction to some medicine, and the mental strain of holding Lee's thin right flank had taken a toll on Magruder. He did not handle his troops energetically at Savage's Station on June 29 or the next day at Frayser's Farm. At Malvern Hill on July 1, Magruder fell apart. One Confederate officer observed that there was a "wild expression" in Magruder's eyes and "his excited manner impressed me at once with the belief that he was under the influence of some powerful stimulant."

The press singled out Magruder for the failure to destroy McClellan's command while Lee and Jackson largely escaped criticism. Persistent rumors of his drunkenness largely explains why Magruder became a scapegoat of the Seven Days' Battles. Shortly thereafter, he was transferred to the Trans-Mississippi and assigned to Texas in October 1862. Magruder protected the state's coast and launched a successful raid against Galveston on the first day of 1863. In 1864, Magruder detached most of his troops to Gen. Richard Taylor in Louisiana. He stayed in Texas with his small force until the end of the war.

After the war, Magruder emigrated to Mexico, where he served in the army of Maximilian. Magruder returned to the United States after Maximilian's regime fell. He died in Houston, Texas, on February 18, 1871.

BIBLIOGRAPHY

Capers, Ellison. *South Carolina.* Vol. 5 of *Confederate Military History*. Edited by Clement A. Evans. Atlanta, 1899. Vol. 6 of extended ed. Wilmington, N.C., 1987.

Gallagher, Gary W. "The Fall of 'Prince John' Magruder." *Civil War Times Illustrated* 19 (August 1989): 8–15.

PETER S. CARMICHAEL

MAHONE, WILLIAM (1826–1895), major general and U.S. senator. Mahone was born December 1, 1826, in Southampton County, Virginia. He was the grandson of veterans of the War of 1812 and son of a tavernkeeper who commanded a militia regiment during the Nat Turner insurrection.

WILLIAM MAHONE. NATIONAL ARCHIVES

As a youth, Billy Mahone carried mail from Jerusalem (Courtland) to Hill's Ford (Emporia) and was described as a congenial chap and a whiz at the gaming table. With financial aid from friends, he attended the Virginia Military Institute, graduating in 1847. During his two years as a teacher at the Rappahannock Military Academy, Mahone continued his studies and was appointed engineer of the Orange and Alexandria Railroad and later of the Norfolk and Petersburg line.

Offering his services to the state upon its adoption of the ordinance of secession, Mahone was appointed quartermaster general of Virginia and then colonel of the Sixth Virginia Infantry. He took part in the capture of the Norfolk Navy Yard, commanded the Norfolk district until it was abandoned, and then joined the Army of Northern Virginia for the remainder of the war.

As commander of a brigade at Seven Pines, Mahone was criticized by D. H. Hill for creating a gap in the Confederate line. But at Malvern Hill he was lauded by John B. Magruder who said he "could not speak too highly" of Mahone and his men. James Longstreet also praised Mahone for his performance at Second Manassas where a severe wound incapacitated Mahone for the Maryland campaign.

Longstreet was in the forefront of those urging that Mahone, who was commissioned a brigadier on November 16, 1861, be promoted to major general. In February 1863, he called his subordinate "one of our best brigadiers and . . . worthy of promotion." Richard Anderson, Robert E. Lee, and members of Congress also endorsed him. But when the promotion came on June 1, 1864, Mahone immediately declined it, apparently because it was only a temporary advancement. He was promoted to the permanent rank of major general on August 3 to date from July 30, when Mahone and his division performed heroically at the Battle of the Crater. Commenting on Mahone's feat of first containing the Federals and then routing them, W. H. Stuart of the Sixty-first Virginia wrote: "The whole movement was under his immediate and personal direction, and to him, above all, save the brave men who bore the muskets, belongs the honor and credit of recapturing the Confederate lines."

Billy Mahone, "short, spare and long-bearded, always in gray slouch hat and peg-top trousers, eyes blue and restless, voice thin and piping," surrendered at Appomattox and returned to his railroad interests in Virginia. He took an active part in politics as an organizer of the Readjuster party. He lost a bid for the gubernatorial nomination in 1877, but won a seat in the U.S. Senate in 1880 when he became identified with the Republican party. He made his home in Washington during his later years and died there October 8, 1895. He was buried in Blandford Cemetery, Petersburg, his adopted city.

BIBLIOGRAPHY

Blake, Nelson Morehouse. *William Mahone of Virginia.* Richmond, Va., 1935.

Bridges, Hal. *Lee's Maverick General: Daniel Harvey Hill.* New York, 1961.

Compiled Military Service Records. William Mahone. Microcopy M331, Roll 162. Record Group 109. National Archives, Washington, D.C.

Hotchkiss, Jed. *Virginia.* Vol. 3 of *Confederate Military History.* Edited by Clement A. Evans. Atlanta, 1899. Vol. 4 of extended ed. Wilmington, N.C., 1987.

LOWELL REIDENBAUGH

MAJOR, JAMES PATRICK (1836–1877), brigadier general. Born May 14, 1836, in Fayette, Missouri, Major graduated from West Point in 1856, twenty-third out of forty-nine. In 1857 he joined the Second U.S. Cavalry and was on the Texas frontier when the Civil War began.

He resigned from the regular army on March 21, 1861, and returned to Missouri where he participated in the Battle of Oak Hills. Soon after, Major left for Texas to recruit troops for the Confederate army. Although he did not return to Arkansas until after Elkhorn Tavern, Major accompanied his friend Earl Van Dorn across the Mississippi River in March 1862. Van Dorn recommended Major for promotion to brigadier general in September 1862, but nothing came of this. Major served on Van Dorn's staff as acting chief of artillery and remained with him until his death. In May 1863 he returned to the Trans-Mississippi Department and reported to Richard Taylor, where he was assigned to command a Texas cavalry brigade. He saw action with Brig. Gen. Thomas Green (a relative by marriage) in Louisiana and was promoted to brigadier general July 21, 1863. Major fought at Mansfield and Pleasant Hill in the Red River campaign and was with Green when he was killed. Major was paroled at New Iberia, Louisiana, on June 11, 1865.

After the war Major lived in France before returning to farm in Louisiana and Texas. He died in Austin on May 7, 1877. Because his second marriage was to a sister of Brig. Gen. Paul O. Hébert of Louisiana, he was buried in his in-laws' tomb at Donaldsonville, Louisiana.

BIBLIOGRAPHY

Johnson, Ludwell H. *Red River Campaign: Politics and Cotton in the Civil War.* Baltimore, 1958.

Parks, Joseph H. *General Kirby Smith, C.S.A.* Baton Rouge, La., 1954.

Taylor, Richard. *Destruction and Reconstruction.* New York, 1955.

ANNE J. BAILEY

MALLORY, STEPHEN R. (1811–1873), U.S. senator and Confederate secretary of the navy. Mallory was born at Port of Spain on the island of Trinidad, British West Indies. His father was a construction engineer from Connecticut, and his mother was Irish. The Mallorys left Trinidad when Stephen was about a year old and lived at several places before settling in Key West in 1820. Stephen's formal education was rudimentary, consisting of six to twelve months in a country school near Blakely, Alabama, at age nine and about three years at a Moravian academy at Nazareth, Pennsylvania. He helped his mother run her boardinghouse at Key West after his father's death. In 1833 he became inspector of customs at Key West and read voraciously to improve himself. Having decided to become a lawyer, he studied law under Judge William Marvin from 1830 to 1834 and was soon admitted to the Florida bar. He commanded a small vessel in campaigns against the Seminoles in the Everglades (1836–1838). In July 1838, he married Angela Moreno, a Spanish woman from Pensacola. From 1837 to 1845, he was county judge of Monroe County and was named collector of the port at Key West in 1845.

In 1850, the Florida legislature elected Mallory (a Democrat) as a U.S. senator, and he was reelected in 1856. Appointed chairman of the Naval Affairs Committee in 1853, he unsuccessfully supported appropriations for the development of an ironclad floating battery that was something of a forerunner of Confederate armorclads. His Naval Retiring Board removed Matthew Fontaine Maury from active duty in 1855, prompting much criticism. This board and other reforms designed to streamline the navy's personnel became the model for the Union Navy Department's reorganization during the Civil War. In 1858, President James Buchanan offered to appoint Mallory minister to Spain, but he declined the appointment.

STEPHEN R. MALLORY.

NAVAL HISTORICAL CENTER, WASHINGTON, D.C.

Although he had been a strong supporter of the South while in the Senate, Mallory opposed secession. Nevertheless, he resigned on January 21, 1861, after Florida left the Union. Offered the post of chief justice of the state's Admiralty Court, he turned it down. Mallory's political enemies accused him of preventing the Florida authorities from seizing Fort Pickens in January 1861, but he had conferred with and received support from senators from other Southern states in advising against bloodshed at that time. Mallory did use his influence with Buchanan to keep warships from entering Pensacola Harbor and to prevent reinforcements from being landed at the fort.

Jefferson Davis named Mallory head of the Navy Department on February 25, 1861. He had not sought the office and was unaware of his nomination. One reason for his appointment was that he came from Florida, which was allotted a prominent cabinet position because of the date of its secession. Mallory had also had experience in naval affairs during his long career, and he had shown great interest in innovations and improvements in both ship design and naval ordnance. The Florida delegation to Congress opposed his nomination because of their misunderstanding of his actions involving Fort Pickens. Mallory's was the only appointment delayed in the Congress, though he was ultimately confirmed on March 4. He and Postmaster General John H. Reagan were the only two men who remained in their cabinet positions throughout the conflict.

Mallory's department at the beginning of the war consisted of approximately twelve small ships and some three hundred officers who had left the U.S. Navy. Although he allowed these officers to retain their Union ranks, he based promotions entirely on gallant or meritorious conduct. In May 1863, Mallory persuaded Congress to create the Provisional Navy. Through it, he could promote young and energetic officers, which was a significant reform. One of Mallory's major accomplishments as secretary was recruiting and training sailors for the navy. Many of these men transferred to their vessels from the army, despite some opposition by several secretaries of war.

To create a navy, Mallory had to purchase ships built abroad or have them built there. The department also issued thirty-two contracts from June 1861 to December 1862 for construction of gunboats and other vessels within the Confederacy. He emphasized the building of several powerful ironclads. Mallory wrote in May, "I regard the possession of an iron-armored ship as a matter of the first necessity." He hoped to use ironclads to break the Union blockade of the Southern coast. After Mallory called for acquisition of an ironclad, Congress appropriated $2 million to purchase or construct such ships in Europe.

Capt. James D. Bulloch was sent to England to purchase ironclads that could sink the wooden blockaders, and fast commerce raiders that would clear the oceans of Northern merchant ships. Mallory hoped the activities of the commerce raiders would draw blockaders away from the Southern ports. Bulloch succeeded in having *Florida* and *Alabama* constructed by the Laird shipyards and turned over to Confederate commanders. Lt. James H. North also went to Europe to purchase one or more existing ironclads. Although he failed to buy such a vessel, he did have construction of an ironclad ram *(Stonewall)* started in Scotland. It was eventually sold to Denmark before its completion and was acquired by the Confederacy from that country, though too late to participate in the conflict. Bulloch's efforts to obtain two additional ironclad rams from the Laird shipyards in Liverpool failed when the British government gave in to Union diplomatic pressure and seized them in October 1863 before they were completed.

To help pay for these activities, Mallory sent other agents to Europe with the authority to promise cotton for ship construction. This use of cotton bonds set a precedent, and the government authorities in Richmond tried to make better use of their large cotton reserves. In 1863, after the Navy Department's funds began dwindling, Mallory became involved in blockade running and ordered Bulloch and Comdr. Matthew Fontaine Maury to buy a speedy runner to take cotton to Europe. Eventually Bulloch acquired three vessels, which brought him sufficient amounts of cotton to finance his work. Mallory kept these operations small so that they would not interfere with those of the War Department, which conducted most of the blockade running.

Mallory put some of his best officers, men like Raphael Semmes and John N. Maffitt, aboard the commerce raiders because of the importance he attached to their activities. The efforts of his raiders failed to secure one of the objectives for which he had obtained them. Though these vessels destroyed millions of dollars of Northern shipping, the Union government chose to accept the loss of its merchant ships rather than weaken or abandon the blockade. The warships that did go in search of the raiders were mostly older and heavier vessels that would have been of little use in patrolling the coastline.

To create a navy in the South, Mallory acquired gunboats through purchase, construction, and capture. He set up workshops for producing naval supplies and machinery and foundries for casting cannons and projectiles. As with his overseas program, the naval secretary stressed construction of ironclads. The design he preferred was that of a casemated, armor-plated wooden vessel similar to the floating battery he had supported in the 1850s. Mallory intended for the first of his ironclads to attack the Union blockading ships and open Southern ports. He also hoped that his gunboats would be seagoing vessels that would take the war to the North. None of them, however, was seaworthy, nor did any possess adequate engines for such ambitious projects.

Confederate work crews at Norfolk raised the frigate *Merrimack* from where it had been scuttled. It was converted into an ironclad ram and renamed *Virginia.* Mallory contracted for construction of four armored vessels on the Mississippi River, two at New Orleans and two at Memphis. Various delays prevented completion of all of these gunboats. At New Orleans, *Louisiana* had to be used as a floating battery because its machinery could not propel it against the flow of the river. Memphis fell before the two vessels there were finished, but one, *Arkansas,* was taken up the Yazoo River in Mississippi and completed there. That ship, too, had problems with faulty engines, which led ultimately to its being blown up by its crew to avoid capture.

After the summer of 1862, however, Mallory changed both the mission and the size of his new ironclads. Their primary duty became the defense of the Confederacy's rivers and harbors by supporting the masonry and earthen fortifications that guarded those areas. Instead of the large, deep-draft vessels designed by Lt. John M. Brooke, Mallory switched over to smaller and lighter ironclads based upon the plans of John L. Porter, chief naval constructor. The loss of Norfolk and New Orleans forced Mallory to establish new shipyards at various places in the interior. In addition to facilities at Richmond and Charleston, ironclad construction was started or completed at Selma, Mobile, Oven Bluff, and Montgomery, Alabama; Columbus, Georgia; Shreveport, Louisiana; Yazoo City, Mississippi; and Whitehall and Edward's Ferry, North Carolina. Despite their weaknesses, the presence of vessels such as *Tennessee* at Mobile Bay caused Union naval authorities to delay or even cancel attacks on Southern ports.

At first, the Confederate navy could obtain new cannons only from the Tredegar Iron Works in Richmond. Mallory sent Lt. Catesby Jones to Selma, Alabama, in the spring of 1863 to assume control of a foundry there that had been converted to produce heavy ordnance, armor plate, and projectiles. From January 1864 to March 1865, the Selma works turned out fifteen rifled and banded cannons designed by John Brooke. With the rifled pieces produced in Richmond, the Selma guns meant that the navy never had a shortage of modern armament for its vessels. Naval ordnance works at Atlanta, Richmond, Charleston, and Charlotte manufactured gun carriages and other equipment. A powder mill established originally at Petersburg, Virginia, was moved to Columbia, South Carolina, and after 1864 it was producing all the navy's needs.

Mallory played an active and early role in the development and use of torpedoes, or mines. The use of these devices became one of the most successful aspects of the navy's activities during the war. Confederate minefields helped keep the Union navy from entering Charleston Harbor and delayed the attack on Mobile Bay. By the end of the war, torpedoes had sunk or damaged forty-three enemy vessels, including four monitors. These devices destroyed more Federal warships than did all the Confederate gunboats. Mallory also supported the development and employment of torpedo boats and submarines. One of the first submarines was *Pioneer,* which was built at New Orleans. It was scuttled upon the fall of the city, having never had an opportunity to attack the enemy. *H. L. Hunley* became the first submarine in history to attack and sink an enemy vessel, the steam sloop *Housatonic.* A number of semisubmersible torpedo boats called Davids were constructed at Charleston, and the Confederates were planning to build a model that could venture into the open sea. Because of this latter development, one historian has stated that the Davids might have become a more prominent offensive weapon if the war had lasted longer.

The construction of the Eads ironclads at St. Louis for the Union navy concerned Mallory greatly. Because of them, he decided that it was more important to defend New Orleans from the north than from the Gulf of Mexico. In early April 1862, Flag Officer George N. Hollins at Memphis received a message from Como. William C. Whittle at New Orleans that Flag Officer David G. Farragut's Union squadron had entered the Mississippi River. Whittle asked Hollins to come to his assistance. Hollins did so and telegraphed Mallory asking permission to order his vessels southward. He felt that his wooden gunboats would be more effective against Farragut's wooden ships than against the ironclads. Mallory declared that it was more important to oppose the latter, and he even proposed sending the ironclad *Louisiana* northward. He thought that the forts on the lower river would be able to stop Farragut.

When the Federal squadron steamed past the forts, forced the destruction of the ironclads *Mississippi* and *Louisiana,* and captured New Orleans, Mallory was virtually incapacitated by the distress he suffered as a result of these disasters. He came under severe criticism not only for the fall of the Crescent City but also for the loss of Norfolk, Memphis, and *Virginia,* which all occurred about the same time. In August 1862, the Confederate House of Representatives called for an investigation into the Navy Department's role in these events, and a joint committee conducted hearings for about a year and a half. In its report, however, the committee exonerated Mallory from any guilt and praised him for the achievements his department had accomplished so far.

Occasionally, Mallory directed his subordinates to attempt unusual or unrealistic schemes. His message to Capt. Franklin Buchanan in March 1862 suggesting that *Virginia* sail into the Atlantic Ocean and attack New York City was one such order. In February 1863, he proposed an expedition whereby sailors would use small boats to carry them at night to Union monitors stationed off the coast. Once aboard, the men would douse the ironclads with inflammable substances and set them afire. A lieutenant went to Charleston to set up such a force, but the project was stopped by the naval commander there in favor of using spar torpedoes. This small unit was called the Special Service Detachment, and ten boats were acquired for it. By September, the force had been broken up and the project abandoned without any attacks on the blockaders.

Mallory and his wife were well liked by Richmond society, even though they were not well known there when the war started. One historian has written of the Floridian that "his wit, his powers as a raconteur, his genial manners and frank courtesy soon won general esteem." The Mallory home accommodated a number of distinguished visitors to the capital during the course of the war. Mallory was not only adept at spinning tales and flattering the ladies, but he cooked well and mixed excellent mint juleps. Despite the long hours he devoted to his job, he found time to relax with his family.

In mid-January 1865, Mallory urged his naval commander at Richmond, Flag Officer John K. Mitchell, to sortie down the James River with his squadron and attack the giant Federal base at City Point. He hoped that, if they were successful in destroying the base, the Confederates would force Ulysses S. Grant to break off his siege of Richmond and Petersburg. Mitchell delayed sending his vessels downstream, and when they finally moved, their attempt failed. This plan of Mallory's had a fair chance of succeeding. If it had, it might have delayed Grant's operations for some months. Disappointed with Mitchell's handling of this affair, Mallory soon replaced him with Adm. Raphael Semmes.

Mallory accompanied Jefferson Davis and the cabinet in the retreat from Richmond to Danville in early April. They then spent a week at Greensboro, North Carolina. At Charlotte, Davis asked his cabinet about accepting the agreement signed by Gen. Joseph E. Johnston and Maj. Gen. William Tecumseh Sherman. With four other cabinet members, Mallory advised Davis to accept the convention's terms, rejecting a proposal that the Confederacy turn to guerrilla warfare. He did not believe that it would succeed and recognized that the Southern people no longer supported the war effort. Mallory went with Davis as far as Washington, Georgia, where, on May 3, 1865, he resigned and left the party to join his family at LaGrange. Mallory did not intend to try to escape from the South.

Most historians have treated Mallory's performance as secretary of the navy better than did many of his contemporaries. The press, public, and politicians criticized him frequently for inefficiency, lack of aggressiveness, and, in some cases, doing too much himself. Given the gigantic difficulties under which he worked, Mallory accomplished a great deal and can be ranked as one of the best Confederate cabinet members. He was intelligent and not reluctant to heed the advice of his staff and his naval officers. Mallory worked well with Davis and most of his fellow cabinet members. His imagination, hard work, and enthusiasm for his job all contributed to his success. Joseph T. Durkin, Mallory's chief biographer, concluded, "He was by no means a great administrator, but he was a conscientious, methodical, and generally reliable one."

After leaving Davis's entourage, Mallory went briefly to Atlanta and then traveled on to LaGrange. On the night of May 20, he was arrested with Senator Benjamin H. Hill in the latter's home and was imprisoned at Fort LaFayette in New York Harbor. Mallory was released on parole on March 10, 1866, and joined his family at Bridgeport, Connecticut. His health had deteriorated because of the pressures of the war years and the months he had spent in prison. Mallory returned to Pensacola in July 1866 and resumed his law practice. He opposed black suffrage and Radical Reconstruction, expressing his views in numerous editorials in the *West Florida Commercial*. Mallory died at his home early on November 12, 1873, and was buried in St. Michael's Cemetery.

[*See also* Navy, *article on* Navy Department.]

BIBLIOGRAPHY

Clubbs, Occie. "Stephen Russell Mallory, the Elder." Master's thesis, University of Florida, 1936.

Durkin, Joseph T. *Stephen R. Mallory: Confederate Navy Chief.* Chapel Hill, N.C., 1954. Reprint, Columbia, S.C., 1987.

Hendrick, Burton J. *Statesmen of the Lost Cause: Jefferson Davis and His Cabinet.* New York, 1939.

Mallory, Stephen R. Papers. Southern Historical Collection, University of North Carolina, Chapel Hill.

Melvin, Philip. "Stephen Russell Mallory, Naval Statesman." *Journal of Southern History* 10 (1944): 137–160.

Patrick, Rembert W. *Jefferson Davis and His Cabinet.* Baton Rouge, La., 1944.

Still, William N., Jr. *Iron Afloat: The Story of the Confederate Armorclads.* Nashville, Tenn., 1971.

Wells, Tom H. *The Confederate Navy: A Study in Organization.* University, Ala., 1971.

ARTHUR W. BERGERON, JR.

MALVERN HILL, VIRGINIA. On July 1, 1862, the last major confrontation of the Seven Days' Battles between Maj. Gen. George B. McClellan's Army of the Potomac and Gen. Robert E. Lee's Army of Northern Virginia took place at Malvern Hill. The site was located on high ground five miles from the Union base at Harrison's Landing on the James River. McClellan had chosen this naturally strong position to make his last stand before reaching Harrison's Landing and the safety of the gunboats waiting there.

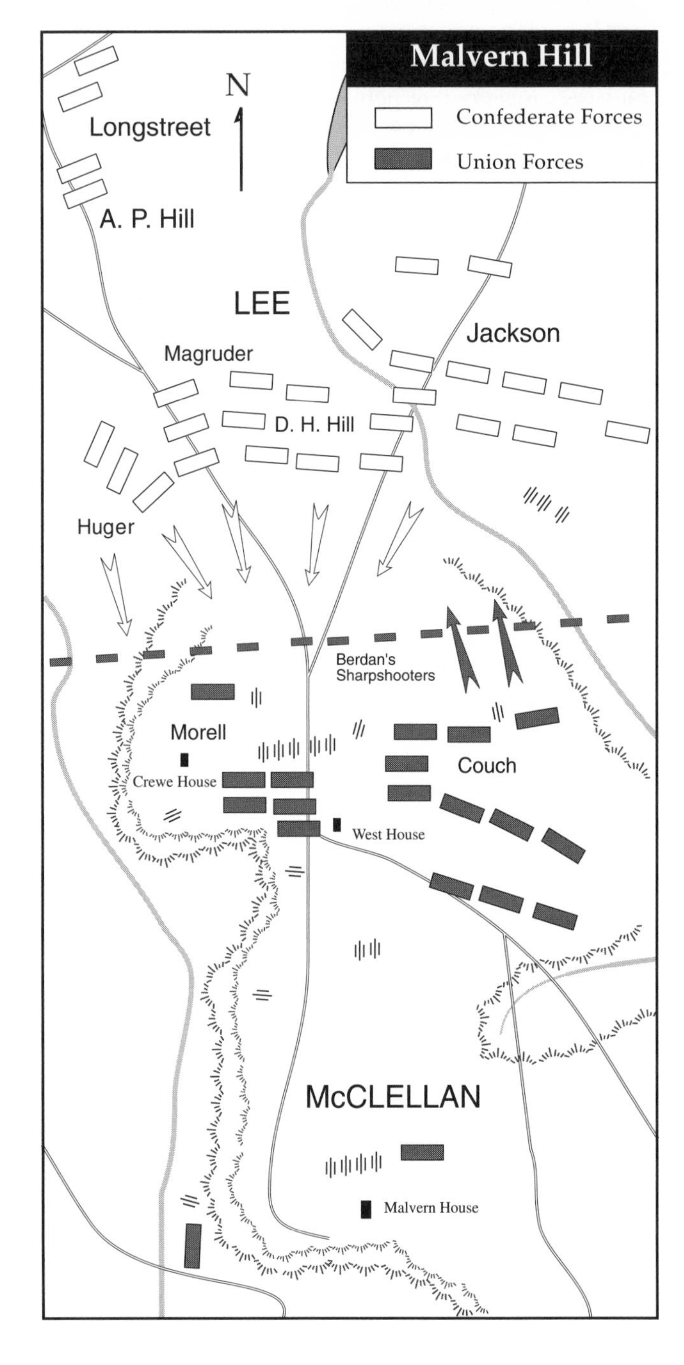

For the sixth time in seven days, the opposing armies massed to confront each other in battle. Lee had achieved his goal of relieving pressure on Richmond by driving McClellan away from the city, but had failed to accomplish his overriding aim of annihilating the Army of the Potomac. He had devised several masterful plans to destroy the Federals, but on every occasion the failure of one or more of his subordinates and the consequently uncoordinated attacks left the Southerners short of their objective and badly bloodied. At one point during the battle of Malvern Hill, Lee answered an officer's concern that McClellan might escape: "Yes, he will get away because I cannot have my orders carried out."

Calculating that McClellan's men were demoralized by the steady repetition of fighting and retreat and believing that one final push might accomplish his elusive goal of destroying the enemy army, Lee determined to attack. The decision would prove costly. The Union position was a formidable one. Maj. Gen. Fitz John Porter's men had been preparing it since the day before, and its creeks and ravines ensured that any attacking columns would be funneled into a frontal assault. With as many as 100 Union artillery pieces dotting the high ground and another 150 in reserve, the Confederates would be heavily pounded.

Despite warnings from Maj. Gen. D. H. Hill, Lee gave his approval for the advance. To prepare for the attack, Maj. Gen. James Longstreet suggested that the Confederates mass their artillery so as to create a powerful cross fire. But the Southerners failed to bring more than a fraction of their artillery into play, and when batteries came forward, the Federals quickly pounded them into silence or retreat.

Lee assigned the task of assaulting McClellan's right flank to Maj. Gen. Thomas J. ("Stonewall") Jackson's troops. He directed Maj. Gen. John B. Magruder to form his men on Jackson's right. Next to Magruder would come Maj. Gen. Benjamin Huger's division. The exhausted soldiers

FIELD BATTERIES, MALVERN HILL. Union field guns engaged during the Peninsular campaign, July 1, 1862. Watercolor-tinted engraving by A. Castaigne, 1892. NAVAL HISTORICAL CENTER, WASHINGTON, D.C.

under Longstreet and Maj. Gen. A. P. Hill would remain in reserve.

True to form in this series of battles, Lee's plan for the attack miscarried. Because of faulty communication, the Confederates thought McClellan might be retreating, when in fact he was not.

About 3:30 P.M. Brig. Gen. Lewis A. Armistead of Huger's division advanced. This was to have been the signal for a general offensive along the line, made with artillery support. That support was missing, however, and the Federal guns hammered the exposed Confederates. Huger's men had little choice but to seek cover. But as D. H. Hill's men moved past them, the Union cannons had no shortage of targets, and Hill's men suffered badly from the fire. Magruder's men had marched away and then countermarched, and as they reached the battlefield, they too began to feel the brunt of the Federal artillery fire. The Union projectiles tore wide gaps in the Confederate lines. As daylight faded, the Southern brigades continued to feed themselves into a bloody maelstrom. Darkness finally brought the fighting to an end, and the Federals moved away to their base at Harrison's Landing.

On the slopes of Malvern Hill, Lee had lost a staggering 5,355 casualties; McClellan, 3,214. Mercifully for the combatants, the bitter fighting at Malvern Hill ended the Seven Days' Battles. In assessing what he had seen that day, D. H. Hill observed, "It was not war—it was murder."

BIBLIOGRAPHY

Cullen, Joseph P. *The Peninsula Campaign, 1862: McClellan and Lee Struggle for Richmond.* Harrisburg, Pa., 1973.

Freeman, Douglas S. *Lee's Lieutenants: A Study in Command.* 3 vols. New York, 1942–1944. Reprint, New York, 1986.

Johnson, Robert U., and C. C. Buel, eds. *Battles and Leaders of the Civil War.* 4 vols. New York, 1887–1888. Reprint, Secaucus, N.J., 1982.

Sears, Stephen W. *To the Gates of Richmond: The Peninsula Campaign.* New York, 1992.

U.S. War Department. *War of the Rebellion: A Compilation of the Official Records of the Union and Confederate Armies.* Washington, D.C. Ser. 1, vol. 11, pt. 1, pp. 67–70; ser. 1, pt. 2, pp. 495–497.

BRIAN S. WILLS

MANASSAS, FIRST. Ten hours of combat near Manassas, Virginia, on July 21, 1861, changed the way a nation viewed war. Both Federals and Confederates came to these fields confident of swift, relatively bloodless victories. They left behind more than 800 dead and 2,700 wounded. They also left behind any illusions that the war could be won or lost on a single Sunday afternoon. Wrote Confederate Samuel Melton: "I have no idea that they intend to give up the fight. On the contrary, five men will rise up where one has been killed, and in my opinion, the war will have to be continued to the bloody end."

As the confluence of the Orange and Alexandria and the Manassas Gap railroads, Manassas Junction assumed preeminent importance for the Confederates in the summer of 1861. Defending at Manassas were 22,000 Confederates under the command of P. G. T. Beauregard. Beauregard knew his force to be insufficient to stop a Union overland advance on Richmond. Instead, Confederate success depended on the ability of a second Confederate army (10,000 men) in the Shenandoah Valley under Joseph E. Johnston to move swiftly to Beauregard's support when the Federals advanced. Johnston's army would move to Manassas Junction via the Manassas Gap Railroad.

On July 16, 1861, Union Gen. Irvin McDowell led 33,000 slightly trained soldiers out of Washington and Alexandria toward Manassas. Beauregard quickly sent word to Johnston and then assumed a defensive position along Bull Run. His line extended for nearly eight miles, from the Stone Bridge on the north to Union Mills on the south.

On July 18 the Federals tested the Confederate center at Blackburn's Ford. In a sharp skirmish that left 83 Union troops killed or wounded, Confederates under James Longstreet repulsed the Federals. Convinced that he could not force his way across Bull Run, McDowell, at Centreville, spent the next two days searching for an undefended ford. The Confederates made good use of the Union delay. Johnston's army slipped away from a Union force under Robert Patterson in the Shenandoah Valley and took the trains to join Beauregard at Manassas Junction. By July 21, Beauregard's and Johnston's combined forces totaled 32,000, only 1,000 less than the Federals.

McDowell's search along Bull Run uncovered an undefended crossing at Sudley Ford, about two miles north of the Confederate left at the Stone Bridge. On Sunday morning, July 21, McDowell's army moved forward in three columns. Two of them were diversionary—one toward Blackburn's and Mitchell's Ford in the Confederate center and the other toward the Stone Bridge. At 6:00 A.M. a Union 30-pounder Parrott rifle, drawn to its position near the Stone Bridge by a team of ten horses, fired the first shot of the first major land battle of the Civil War.

Meanwhile the main Union column (13,000 men with five batteries) marched northwestward toward Sudley Ford, bent on crossing the stream and sweeping southward behind the Confederates. The march proceeded slowly but without incident until about 8:30 A.M. At that time Confederate signal officer E. P. Alexander, on the Wilcoxen farm about eight miles south of the Stone Bridge, by chance spotted the Union column. Alexander immediately sent warning to Col. Nathan Evans, whose two regiments had charge of defending the Confederate left: "Look out for your left, you are turned." At the same time, Evans received

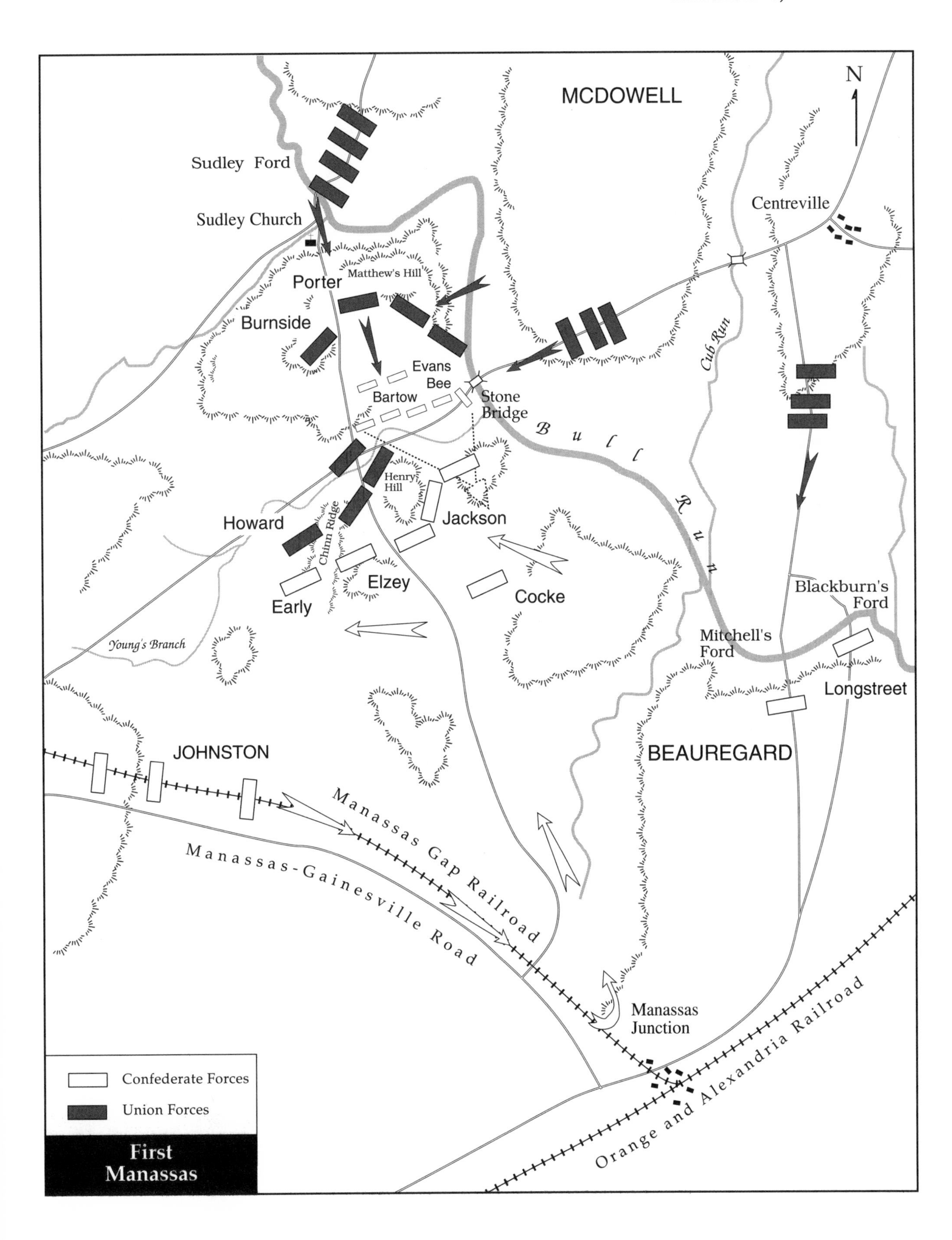
N
MCDOWELL
Sudley Ford
Sudley Church
Centreville
Matthew's Hill
Porter
Burnside
Evans
Bee
Bartow
Stone
Bridge
Bull Run
Cub Run
Henry
Hill
Jackson
Howard
Chinn Ridge
Elzey
Early
Cocke
Blackburn's
Ford
Mitchell's
Ford
Young's Branch
Longstreet
JOHNSTON
BEAUREGARD
Manassas Gap Railroad
Manassas-Gainesville Road
Manassas
Junction
Orange and Alexandria Railroad
Confederate Forces
Union Forces
First
Manassas

warning of the Union flanking movement from his pickets near Sudley. Leaving 200 men to defend the Stone Bridge, Evans moved with his remaining 900 to block the Union flanking column. His job: delay the Federals long enough for Confederate reinforcements from the center and right to arrive.

Evans met the head of the Federal column on the slopes of Matthew's Hill. For perhaps thirty minutes his two regiments fought alone, while the Federals piled troops from Ambrose Burnside's and Andrew Porter's brigades into the fight. At about 11:00 A.M. Confederate reinforcements arrived. Four regiments under Barnard E. Bee and Francis S. Bartow moved up on Evans's right. Along fence lines and in pine thickets the battle raged. But the Federals, outnumbering the Confederates by nearly 10,000 men, soon lapped around both Confederate flanks. The Southern lines gave way. Soon nearly 3,000 Confederates were streaming rearward to the heights of Henry Hill.

Had McDowell continued his assault at this moment, the battle might have ended as a crushing Confederate defeat. But the Federal advance stopped on Matthew's Hill. The delay gave Beauregard and Johnston the time they needed to rush reinforcements to Henry Hill to stabilize the shattered Confederate line. Thomas J. Jackson's Virginia brigade arrived first and formed behind a thirteen-gun line of artillery on the southeastern edge of Henry Hill. Behind these Virginians the fugitives from Matthew's Hill rallied. By 2:00 P.M. the Confederates on Henry Hill were presenting a strong front. It was a rejuvenation made possible only by Union delay.

At about 2:30 the Federals moved against Jackson's line on Henry Hill, first with Charles Griffin's and James B. Ricketts's batteries of artillery and then with infantry. Jackson's regiments met the Federals with a fire that routed the infantry and devastated Ricketts's battery. Later Griffin moved two of his Union cannons to within two hundred yards of the Confederate line. The Thirty-third Virginia lunged forward and captured them—the first tangible Confederate success of the day. Then the Second and Fourth Virginia of Jackson's brigade charged and captured Ricketts's battery, too. The tide of the battle turned.

For the next ninety minutes the fighting surged across Widow Henry's farm. The Confederates captured and recaptured the Union cannons three times. In this fighting General Bee and Colonel Bartow became the two highest-ranking Confederates to die in the battle. Beauregard and Johnston haphazardly threw regiments into the battle as they arrived; a frantic procession of crises allowed for little coordination. McDowell, too, fed regiments into the fight singly, or at best in pairs, until by 4:00 he had few regiments left to send forward (about half the Union army remained east of Bull Run and never joined the battle). A final advance by the Eighth and Eighteenth Virginia of Philip St. George Cocke's brigade drove the last Federals off Henry Hill into the valley of Young's Branch.

Foiled in his efforts to dislodge the Confederates from Henry Hill by direct attack, McDowell tried finally to flank the Confederates by sending a brigade under O. O. Howard over Chinn Ridge, around the Confederate left. But before Howard could manage the movement, Johnston had directed two fresh brigades under Jubal Early and Arnold Elzey to Chinn Ridge. When Howard's four regiments crested the ridge, they found themselves caught in a pocket of Confederate fire. Elzey attacked. Howard's regiments broke after a brief fight. With that, from right to left, McDowell's lines began to crumble.

Harassed by Confederate artillery fire, disorganized Union regiments retreated the way they had come—some northward across Sudley Ford, a few eastward across Stone Bridge. The Confederates followed and opened fire on the Federals as they struggled across the bridge over Cub Run, about a mile east of Bull Run. A shell overturned a wagon on the bridge. The Federals panicked. "Before the third shell struck near us, every man as far as the eye could see seemed to be running for very life," recorded one Federal. For hours, frightened Union soldiers and a few hundred civilians who had come out from Washington to catch a glimpse of the battle jammed the roads leading to the Union capital. The Confederates, nearly as disorganized in victory as were the Federals in retreat, did not pursue beyond Cub Run and later returned to their bivouacs along Bull Run.

The battle produced several heroes for the Confederates. Johnston and Beauregard were foremost. Evans received just praise for his delaying action in the morning, and Elzey garnered much notice for his decisive attack on Chinn Ridge in the afternoon. But the most famous would be Jackson. His brigade had provided a focal point for rallying the fugitives from the morning fight on Matthew's Hill. And in the afternoon, his regiments had engineered the initial capture of Ricketts's and Griffin's guns. On these fields Jackson won his sobriquet "Stonewall."

The 387 Confederate dead and 1,582 wounded initially did little to dim Southern euphoria over the victory. One Southern soldier told his wife, "Sunday last . . . was the happiest day of my life, our wedding-day not excepted. I think the fight is over forever." But Confederate glee soon yielded to the realization that the Federals had no intention of giving up. Strategically, the battle changed little in the Virginia theater; each side simply returned to its starting point to prepare for the next campaign. And people North and South soon realized that the next campaign would be infinitely larger and bloodier. It would be shown that First Manassas elevated the war to a higher, more awful and costly level. The next campaign would involve not 30,000 Federals but almost 130,000. And by 1864 the hundreds lost

STONE BRIDGE. Ruins of the bridge after the Battle of First Manassas. Photograph by George N. Bernard and James F. Gibson, 1861.
NATIONAL ARCHIVES

at Manassas would pale in comparison to the thousands lost at Gettysburg, the Wilderness, and a dozen other fields. But no battle of the war—perhaps no battle in American history—would have so dramatic an emotional impact as First Manassas.

BIBLIOGRAPHY

Beattie, Russell H., Jr. *Road to Manassas.* New York, 1961.

Davis, William C. *Battle at Bull Run.* Garden City, N.Y., 1977.

Freeman, Douglas S. *Lee's Lieutenants: A Study in Command.* 3 vols. New York, 1942–1944. Reprint, New York, 1986.

Gallagher, Gary W., ed. *Fighting for the Confederacy: The Personal Recollections of General Edward Porter Alexander.* Chapel Hill, N.C., 1989.

Hennessy, John. *The First Battle of Manassas: An End to Innocence.* Lynchburg, Va., 1989.

Johnston, Robert M. *Bull Run, Its Strategy and Tactics.* Boston, 1913.

U.S. Committee on the Conduct of the War. *Report of the Joint Committee on the Conduct of the War.* Washington, D.C., 1863.

JOHN J. HENNESSY

MANASSAS, SECOND. War came a second time to the plains of Manassas in August 1862—this time in a form bigger, bloodier, and strategically more significant than in 1861. More than 100,000 troops participated in the battle, leaving behind more than 23,000 casualties (9,000 Confederate). Robert E. Lee's decisive victory over Federal Maj. Gen. John Pope and the Army of Virginia here laid the groundwork for his first raid into the North. Conversely, it brought the Union war effort to a dangerously low ebb. The aftermath of Second Manassas represented perhaps the South's best opportunity to win the war.

After his successful repulse of Union Gen. George B.

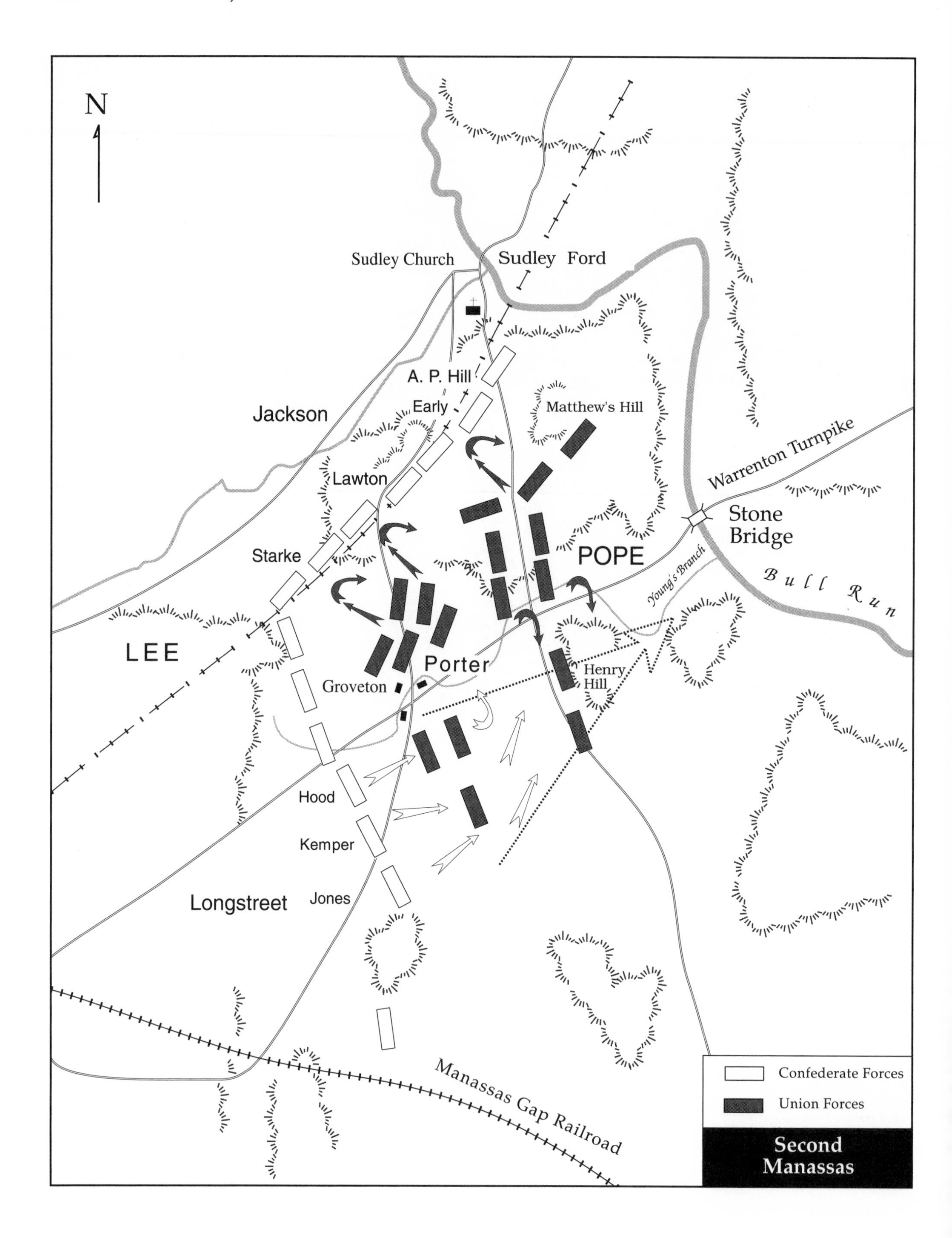
N
Sudley Church
Sudley Ford
A. P. Hill
Early
Jackson
Matthew's Hill
Lawton
Warrenton Turnpike
Stone
Bridge
Starke
POPE
Young's Branch
Bull Run
LEE
Porter
Henry
Hill
Groveton
Hood
Kemper
Longstreet
Jones
Manassas Gap Railroad
Confederate Forces
Union Forces
Second
Manassas

McClellan's Army of the Potomac in the Seven Days' Battles around Richmond, Lee turned his attention northward to a second Union threat: the newly formed Army of Virginia, commanded by Pope. Fearful that Pope would menace the Virginia Central Railroad—Richmond's communications with the Shenandoah Valley—or, worse, move on Richmond from the northwest, Lee on July 15 dispatched a force under Thomas J. ("Stonewall") Jackson to confront Pope. Jackson and Pope eyed each other across the Rapidan River until August 9, when Jackson attacked an exposed part of Pope's army near Cedar Mountain, just south of Culpeper. Though a Confederate victory, after the battle Jackson had to retire across the Rapidan in the face of increasing Union numbers.

On August 15, confident that McClellan intended no further trouble in front of Richmond, Lee and James Longstreet joined Jackson near Gordonsville. Anxious to force Pope out of central Virginia before McClellan's army, now retiring from the Virginia Peninsula, could join him, Lee hunted for a chance to strike Pope or at least drive him back. From August 17 until August 25 the armies sparred, first along the Rapidan and then, after a short retreat by Pope, along the Rappahannock.

On August 25, 1862, Lee found an opening. Holding Longstreet with 30,000 men in front of Pope, Lee sent 24,000 men under Jackson (about half the army) on a wide flanking march around Pope's right flank. They first marched northward to Salem and then turned to the southeast, through Thoroughfare Gap and Gainesville. On the evening of August 26 Jackson's troops cut the Orange and Alexandria Railroad—the Federal supply line—at Bristoe Station and Manassas Junction. In thirty-six hours Jackson's men had marched fifty-four miles to the rear of the Union army. Few strategic maneuvers of the war would surpass this one in nerve and effectiveness.

Surprised and outmaneuvered, Pope turned away from the Rappahannock and fanned out in search of Jackson's command. Jackson spent August 27 pillaging the stores at Manassas and beating back two mild Union advances. That night he set fire to the remaining plunder and marched northward to elude Pope. On August 28 he assumed a position in woods and behind ridges north of the Warrenton Turnpike near Groveton. There, Jackson knew, he could monitor the Federal march and perhaps lure Pope into battle. At the same time he would be in position to await the arrival of Lee and Longstreet, then marching to join him with almost 30,000 men.

Jackson and his troops passed a quiet day on August 28 until about 5:30 P.M. Then Jackson received word of a Union column (Rufus King's division) marching eastward on the Warrenton Turnpike, only a few hundred yards in front of his position. After watching the Union troops march unwarily by for several minutes, Jackson ordered an attack. Soon shells burst above the Federal column. Union brigade commander John Gibbon ordered his regiments to turn off the road and move against the Confederates. For the next ninety minutes the fighting raged on the Brawner and Dogan farms. Though Jackson outnumbered the Union division in front nearly three to one, he was unable to launch a coordinated assault sufficient to overwhelm the Federals. Instead the battle amounted to a brutal, largely static musketry fight waged from behind fence lines. Darkness brought an end to the indecisive fighting. Among the Confederate casualties was Richard S. Ewell, who would lose his leg and be absent from the army for nine months.

Though Jackson had failed to destroy King's division, he had revealed his position to Pope, who responded by ordering his entire army to converge on Jackson's position. The next morning, August 29, Jackson discovered that King had retreated but that additional Union troops had arrived on Henry Hill to the east. He deployed his troops along the cuts and fills of an old unfinished railroad and prepared for battle.

Meanwhile, the rest of the Confederate army, led by Lee and Longstreet, moved to join Jackson. Following Jackson's earlier route, Longstreet on August 28 pushed aside a Union force at Thoroughfare Gap. Resuming the march the next morning, the head of Longstreet's column reached the battlefield at about 10:00 A.M. Longstreet formed on Jackson's right, extending his line southward across the Warrenton Turnpike for more than a mile. Once formed, the Confederate line resembled a huge pair of jaws, ready to snap shut.

John Pope knew nothing of Longstreet's presence south of the turnpike on August 29. Instead he focused all his attention on Jackson. During the morning Franz Sigel's corps and John F. Reynolds's division moved against Jackson along a two-mile front. In what amounted to a protracted heavy skirmish, the Federals managed no progress against Jackson's lines. During the afternoon Pope intensified his efforts. At 3:00 Cuvier Grover's brigade launched a violent bayonet attack that threatened to dislocate part of A. P. Hill's division on the left of Jackson's line. Only hard fighting by Maxcy Gregg's brigade of South Carolinians and Edward L. Thomas's Georgia brigade drove the Federals back.

An hour later another Union charge, this by Col. James Nagle's brigade, plunged into Alexander Lawton's (formerly Ewell's) division, in Jackson's center. The Federals maintained their position for minutes only, until an advance by two brigades of Starke's division to Lawton's right relieved the pressure against Jackson's center and forced the Federals back.

The largest Union attack of August 29 came at 5:00 P.M., and it came against the most beleaguered part of Jackson's line: A. P. Hill's division on the left. Parts of three Union brigades surged against Gregg's brigade on a knoll southeast of Sudley Church. In an episode that would become part of Confederate lore, General Gregg unsheathed his grandfather's Revolutionary War sword and paced his line: "Let us die here, my men, let us die here," he said. Despite Gregg's urgings, his men yielded. The left of Hill's line bent back more than three hundred yards. Only the timely arrival of Jubal Early's brigade restored the Confederate front and forced the Federals to retreat.

Lee had little to do with the fighting on Jackson's front this day. Instead, he focused on launching an attack against Pope's dangling left flank. But in this he was frustrated. First Longstreet prudently requested time to examine the ground to his front. Then Lee received word of a threatening Union force hovering opposite Longstreet's right flank (this was Fitz John Porter's corps along the Manassas-Gainesville road). Not until almost 5:00 would Lee decide this force meant no trouble. But by then it was too late to launch an attack. Instead, Longstreet mounted a reconnaissance in force that ran into strong Union resistance near Groveton. Based on this, Lee canceled all plans for an attack against Pope's left.

The repulses of August 29 did nothing to dissuade Pope from continuing the battle. Indeed, on the morning of August 30 he concluded that the Confederates were retreating. At noon he launched a pursuit—one of the shortest of the war. Lee, Longstreet, and Jackson had, of course, gone nowhere. Pope decided to renew his attacks against Jackson's line. He remained unaware of Longstreet's presence opposite his left.

At 3:00 P.M. Pope launched his largest attack of the battle: more than 5,000 men under the command of Fitz John Porter surged against Starke's division on Jackson's right. In the battle's most intense burst of fighting, Jackson's men clung tenaciously to their position on the unfinished railroad, though in places the Federals closed to within ten yards. After thirty minutes of fighting many Confederates ran out of ammunition. Some met the Union attack with stones. This was, wrote one Federal, "an unlooked for variation in the proceedings." The rock-throwing episode would become the most famous incident of the battle. It lasted only moments, however, until Confederate reinforcements from Hill's division arrived. The Federals retreated, pelted all the while by the cannon of S. D. Lee's battalion, a few hundred yards to the west.

Porter's retreat threw the Union line into a spasm of disorganization. Lee and Longstreet simultaneously sensed the opportunity. Lee ordered Longstreet to attack—to seize Henry Hill and cut off the Union retreat. At the same time, he ordered Jackson to "look out for and protect Longstreet's left." Less than thirty minutes after receiving orders to advance, Longstreet had more than 20,000 soldiers moving forward toward the Union left. Less than 3,000 Federals stood in their path.

John Bell Hood's division, along the Warrenton Turnpike, led Longstreet's assault. Near Groveton the Texas Brigade struck and demolished a brigade of New York troops commanded by Gouverneur K. Warren. One Union regiment, the Fifth New York, had more men killed here than any other infantry regiment in any other battle of the war.

Next, Hood's men routed a Union brigade just west of Chinn Ridge, capturing a battery in the process. Then, joined by Nathan Evans's brigade, Hood ascended the west slope of Chinn Ridge into the face of Col. Nathaniel McLean's brigade of Ohioans. Soon the division of James Lawson Kemper arrived on Hood's right. Col. Montgomery Corse's Virginia brigade wheeled left down the crest of the ridge and crashed into the flank of the Union line. The Federals resisted stoutly, buying time for reinforcements to arrive. For the next hour both sides piled troops into the most intense sustained fighting of the battle. The fighting here would be decisive; it would determine the magnitude of the Union defeat.

While the combat raged on Chinn Ridge, Jackson stood still on the north flank. This in turn allowed Pope to pull troops from the right of his line and put them into position on Henry Hill. By the time the Federals yielded on Chinn Ridge—which they did only after buying precious time and extracting heavy Confederate casualties—four brigades of Union troops were waiting on Henry Hill. David Rumph Jones's division led the Confederate advance against Henry Hill, joined soon by Richard Heron Anderson's division and Cadmus Wilcox's brigade. But an hour of assaults left the Federals unmoved. Darkness brought an end to the fighting. The beaten but intact Union army retreated from the field that night.

The next day Lee moved again to cut off Pope's retreat to Washington by again sending Jackson on a flank march. This time, however, Pope responded promptly. He blocked Jackson's march near Germantown and then attacked him with two divisions. The resultant Battle of Ox Hill on September 1 ended in stalemate after two hours of combat in a driving rainstorm. The battle, which claimed the lives of Union Gens. Isaac Stevens and Philip Kearny, marked the end of the campaign.

The Second Manassas campaign helped chisel the identity of the Army of Northern Virginia. The army's three dominant figures assumed the roles they would henceforth play. Lee showed himself to be the master strategist—patient, trusting of subordinates, and incredibly bold. It would be his most successful campaign. By swift marching and unmatched daring, Jackson showed himself to be the master creator of opportunities. His strategic brilliance during the last week of August 1862 was second only to his Shenandoah Valley campaign. And Longstreet showed himself to be cautious—prudently so, it would prove—but swift, strong, and decisive once moved. On no other battlefield would he contribute more to Confederate victory.

Bringing a Union army to the brink of destruction—and indeed the Union cause to the edge of collapse—cost Lee some 9,000 casualties. More than 16,000 Federals fell or were captured during the campaign. The victory at Second Manassas bared the strategic table for Lee. From here he moved unfettered into Maryland, where what was perhaps the Confederacy's greatest hope for victory perished on the banks of Antietam Creek.

BIBLIOGRAPHY

Allan, William. *The Army of Northern Virginia in 1862.* Boston, 1892. Reprint, Dayton, Ohio, 1984.

Freeman, Douglas S. *Lee's Lieutenants: A Study in Command.* Vol. 2. New York, 1943. Reprint, New York, 1986.

Gordon, George H. *History of the Campaign of the Army of Virginia, under John Pope: From Cedar Mountain to Antietam.* Boston, 1880.

Hennessy, John J. *Return to Bull Run: The Campaign and Battle of Second Manassas.* New York, 1992.

Hennessy, John J. *Second Manassas Battlefield Map Study.* Lynchburg, Va., 1991.

Johnson, Robert U., and C. C. Buel., eds. *Battles and Leaders of the Civil War.* Vol. 2. New York, 1888. Reprint, Secaucus, N.J., 1982.

Ropes, John C. *The Army under Pope.* New York, 1881. Reprint, Wilmington, N.C., 1989.

Stackpole, Edward J. *From Cedar Mountain to Antietam, August-September, 1862.* Harrisburg, Pa., 1959.

JOHN J. HENNESSY

MANEY, GEORGE EARL (1826–1901), brigadier general and U.S. diplomat. Maney was born August 24, 1826, in Franklin, Tennessee. He studied at the Nashville Seminary and the University of Nashville, served as a lieutenant in the Mexican War, and practiced law in Nashville in the 1840s and 1850s.

In April 1861 he entered Confederate service as captain of what became Company D, Eleventh Tennessee Infantry Regiment. He was soon elected colonel of the First Tennessee Regiment. He and his unit served with Confederate forces in western Virginia for several months before being returned to the West early in 1862 to help try to restore Southern fortunes in Tennessee. Maney became part of the Army of Tennessee and was assigned as a brigade commander.

Distinguished at Shiloh (April 6–7, 1862), Maney was promoted to brigadier general in April 1862. From that time until the Battle of Jonesboro, Georgia (August 31–September 1, 1864), he commanded either his brigade or, by seniority, a division in the Army of Tennessee. At Jonesboro he was wounded, and the records show him absent on a surgeon's certificate as late as January 1865. He was paroled at Greensboro, North Carolina, that spring (probably on May 1).

After the war Maney was president of the Tennessee and Pacific Railroad Company. From 1881 until 1894, he held diplomatic posts in Latin America. He died in Washington, D.C., February 9, 1901, and is buried in Mount Olivet Cemetery in Nashville.

BIBLIOGRAPHY

Hewitt, Lawrence L. "George Earl Maney." In *The Confederate General.* Edited by William C. Davis. Vol. 4. Harrisburg, Pa., 1991.

Warner, Ezra J. *Generals in Gray: Lives of the Confederate Commanders.* Baton Rouge, La., 1959.

RICHARD M. MCMURRY

MANIGAULT, ARTHUR MIDDLETON (1824–1886), brigadier general. Born in Charleston and into the South Carolina aristocracy, October 26, 1824, Manigault was a commission merchant and rice planter in the 1840s and 1850s. During the Mexican War he served as a lieutenant in the Palmetto (South Carolina) Regiment.

In the winter of 1860–1861 Manigault was captain of a local militia company and helped prepare the defenses of Charleston Harbor. That April he was appointed special aide-de-camp on the staff of the governor, who assigned him to serve with Brig. Gen. P. G. T. Beauregard, commander of Confederate forces at Charleston. In May 1861 Manigault was promoted to lieutenant colonel and named Beauregard's assistant adjutant and inspector general.

ARTHUR MIDDLETON MANIGAULT. LIBRARY OF CONGRESS

Elected colonel of the Tenth South Carolina Infantry Regiment, Manigault served with that unit on the South Atlantic coast. In the spring of 1862 he and his unit went west to reinforce the Army of Tennessee. For two and a half years Manigault served with that army, first as a regimental and then as a brigade commander. He was promoted to brigadier general in April 1863. Manigault was so badly wounded at the Battle of Franklin, November 30, 1864, that he was disabled from further service.

Manigault resumed rice planting after the war. Elected South Carolina's adjutant and inspector general in 1880, he held that office until his death August 17, 1886. He is buried in Magnolia Cemetery, Charleston. His memoirs constitute an invaluable source on the Army of Tennessee.

BIBLIOGRAPHY

Manigault, Arthur Middleton. *A Carolinian Goes to War: The Civil War Narrative of Arthur Middleton Manigault.* Edited by R. Lockwood Tower. Columbia, S.C., 1983.

Warner, Ezra J. *Generals in Gray: Lives of the Confederate Commanders.* New York, 1959.

RICHARD M. MCMURRY

MANN, A. DUDLEY

MANN, A. DUDLEY (1801–1889), diplomat. Ambrose Dudley Mann had experienced a long career in diplomacy before President Jefferson Davis appointed him, with William Lowndes Yancey and Pierre A. Rost, a Confederate commissioner to Europe. Born at Hanover Court House, Virginia, Mann attended West Point but did not graduate, preferring a diplomatic to a military career. By 1842 he was U.S. consul in Bremen, Germany, where he negotiated a series of commercial treaties with German states. In 1849 Secretary of State John Clayton sent him as a special agent to the revolutionary government of Louis Kossuth in Hungary. From 1853 to 1856 he served as assistant secretary of state.

As commissioner for the Confederacy, Mann reached London in April 1861 and remained there until autumn promoting the Confederate cause. In September 1861 the Confederate government assigned him to Belgium. For three years he cultivated King Leopold, reporting forcefully, yet often naively, on Europe's mistreatment of the Confederacy. Mann's unique venture as commissioner came in November 1863 when he interviewed the pope in Rome. "How strikingly majestic," he informed Secretary of State Judah P. Benjamin, "the conduct of the Pontifical State in its bearing toward me when contrasted with the sneaking subterfuges to which some of the Governments of western Europe have had recourse in order to evade intercourse with our Commissioners!" In December he forwarded a papal letter addressed to President Davis, asserting that it represented "a positive recognition of our government." For Benjamin the pope's letter demonstrated only politeness, not meaningful recognition. With the Confederate defeat Mann retired to Paris where he resided until his death.

BIBLIOGRAPHY

Henry, Robert Selph. *The Story of the Confederacy.* Indianapolis, 1931.

Owsley, Frank Lawrence. *King Cotton Diplomacy: Foreign Relations of the Confederate States of America.* Revised by Harriet Chappell Owsley. Chicago, 1959.

NORMAN A. GRAEBNER

MANPOWER

MANPOWER. *See* Army *and* Navy, *articles on* Manpower. *See also* Civil War, *article on* Losses and Numbers.

MANSFIELD, LOUISIANA

MANSFIELD, LOUISIANA. On April 8, 1864, three miles southeast of Mansfield, Louisiana, Maj. Gen. Nathaniel P. Banks's Red River campaign was halted in battle by a small Confederate army under Lt. Gen. Richard Taylor. Also known as the Battle of Sabine Cross Roads, Mansfield was the largest Civil War battle west of the Mississippi River and was one of the Confederacy's last major victories. Banks lost almost 2,200 men in the disastrous defeat, while Taylor suffered about 1,000 casualties.

Banks began his Red River campaign from Baton Rouge in March 1864 with almost 30,000 troops. He hoped to destroy the Confederate forces in Louisiana, seize vital cotton in the Red River valley and open Texas to invasion by capturing the capital at Shreveport. Accompanying Banks was Rear Adm. David Dixon Porter's fleet of river gunboats and transports. Confederate departmental commander Gen. E. Kirby Smith had only Taylor's small 8,800-man army to oppose this formidable force.

Banks and Porter moved up the Red River and reached Natchitoches on March 30. Here Banks made a critical error. Having faced little opposition from the outnumbered Taylor, Banks was convinced the Southerners would not fight outside Shreveport. Thus he decided to leave the protective gunboats and move on Shreveport by way of an inland road that passed through Mansfield.

Not expecting a fight, Banks had his men poorly prepared for battle as he marched along the narrow woods road. Only a few thousand infantry led the advance, separated from the main force by a long wagon train. On the afternoon of April 8 the head of the column emerged into a broad field near the Sabine Cross Roads and found Taylor's men in line of battle on the other side.

After watching the enemy deploy behind a rail fence, Taylor chose to attack before Banks could bring up his entire force. At approximately 4:00 P.M. Brig. Gen. Alfred Mouton's division, on Taylor's left, charged across the open field. The Louisianians and Texans were cut down by a murderous fire from the Federals behind the fence. Mouton fell dead, along with three of his regimental commanders. One-third of the division was lost, but Brig. Gen. Camille J. Polignac assumed command and pressed on the attack. Taylor then sent in Maj. Gen. John G. Walker's Texas division on the right. The Northerners put up a fierce fight but were forced to fall back to a new position after being overrun and losing several cannon.

Breaking this second line, the Confederates surged through the thick woods and overran Banks's wagon train. Panic seized the Federals and their orderly withdrawal soon turned into a rout. Fortunately for Banks, the Confederates slowed their pursuit to loot the wagons, thus giving Brig. Gen. William Emory time to form a line on a ridge overlooking a small creek three miles from their original position. A last vicious fight erupted in the woods at dark, but Emory held on and gave Banks time to withdraw fifteen miles to Pleasant Hill.

The day had been a disaster for the Federals. Not only had their advance on Shreveport been stopped, but they also had suffered more than 2,000 casualties (over 1,000 of whom were prisoners) and lost twenty cannon and over two hundred wagons. Despite winning a second battle at Pleasant Hill on April 9, Banks accepted defeat and retreated to Baton Rouge.

BIBLIOGRAPHY

Johnson, Ludwell H. *Red River Campaign: Politics and Cotton in the Civil War.* Baltimore, 1958.

Taylor, Richard. *Destruction and Reconstruction: Personal Experiences of the Late War.* New York, 1879. Reprint, New York, 1955.

Winters, John D. *The Civil War in Louisiana.* Baton Rouge, La., 1963.

TERRY L. JONES

MARCH TO THE SEA, SHERMAN'S. Union Gen. William Tecumseh Sherman completed the Atlanta campaign with the capture of that Georgia city on September 2, 1864. He allowed the Confederate Army of Tennessee under Gen. John Bell Hood to escape destruction, however, and on October 3 found himself chasing Hood back toward

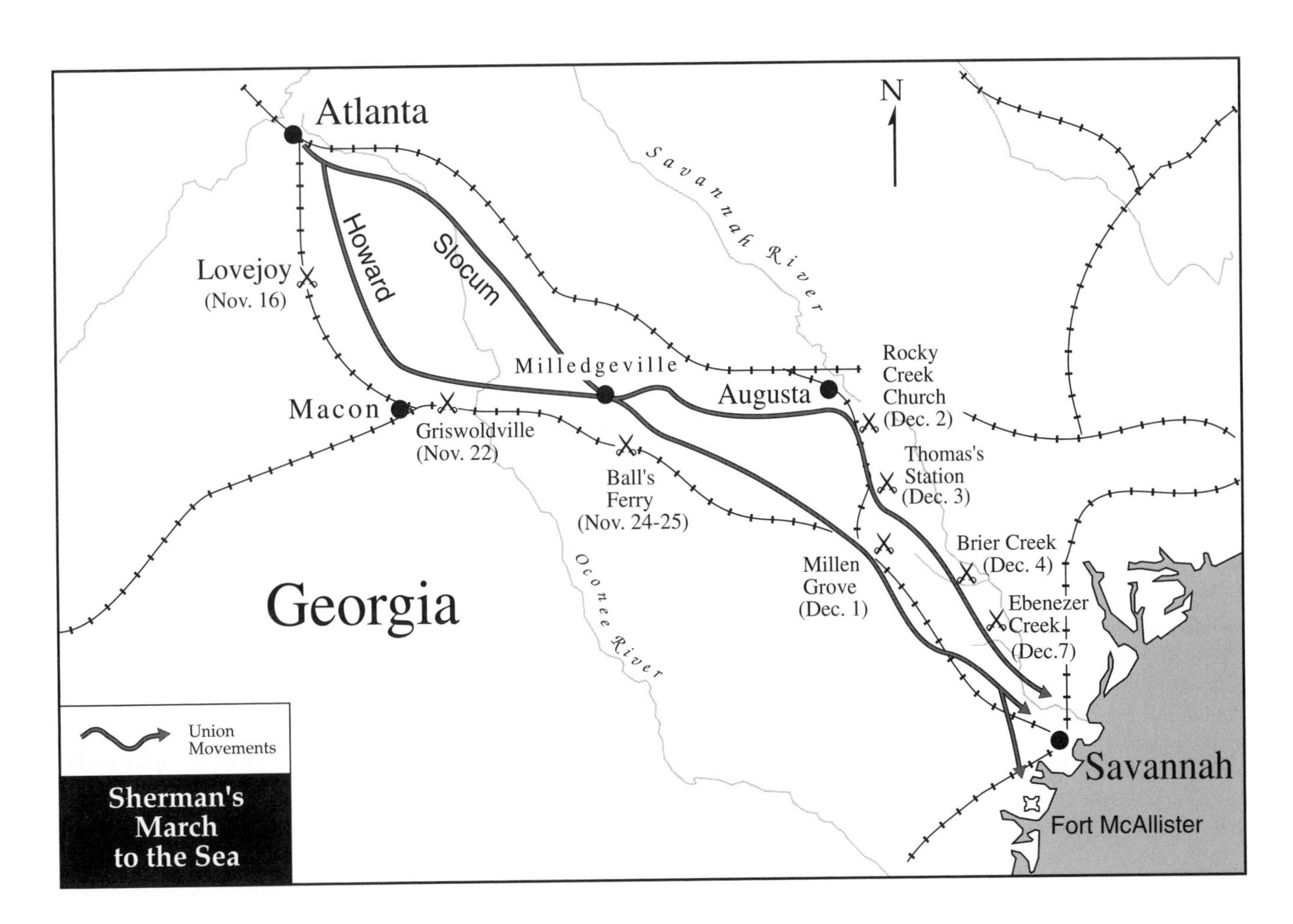

Chattanooga over the same ground he and Gen. Joseph E. Johnston had contested during the recently completed campaign. Frustrated, Sherman reached back to a lifetime of civilian and military experiences and decided to undertake something different. Instead of continuing to try to protect his railroad supply line by chasing Hood all over Georgia, he would send Gens. George H. Thomas and John M. Schofield with some 60,000 troops to Tennessee to handle Hood, while he cut loose from his supply line with approximately 62,000 of his best troops and marched across Georgia to the Atlantic Ocean.

In later years, Sherman called his action nothing more than a change of military base from Atlanta to Savannah, but actually he implemented psychological warfare, demonstrating to Confederate soldiers and the civilian population that the Confederacy could not defend its home front and therefore was doomed. He saw his raid as the only way to end the war quickly. It was much more effective and humane, he believed, than slaughtering troops in conventional warfare.

As he had done in his raid on Meridian, Mississippi, in early 1864, Sherman divided his invading force into two approximately equal wings (under O. O. Howard and Henry W. Slocum) with Hugh J. Kilpatrick's cavalry protecting the flanks. Since he had no supply line, the army was to consume the twenty-day rations it carried with it and the three thousand beef cattle driven along behind. For the rest, it would live off the countryside. The army left Atlanta on November 15, destroying the city's war-making capacity but leaving many of its structures standing. Opposing it was a varied collection of Confederate troops numbering perhaps 8,000: mainly Joseph Wheeler's cavalry corps and Gustavus W. Smith's Georgia militia. On November 17, William J. Hardee became overall Confederate commander in Georgia, but he could do little to stop Sherman and concentrated his small military force on fortifying Savannah. Hood and his Army of Tennessee were far away to the rear, still hoping to draw Sherman into Tennessee.

The March to the Sea covered about fifteen miles a day. The two columns traveled along separate paths, sometimes as far as fifty miles apart, throwing out foragers (bummers) in all directions to supply the troops. Sherman tried to make it appear that he was moving against Macon, Augusta, or Savannah and then brought his wings together to capture Milledgeville, the wartime state capital, on November 23. This indirect approach confused the outmanned Confederates and made their task even more impossible.

There were a number of skirmishes during the march, including those at Lovejoy on November 16; Griswoldville on November 22; Ball's Ferry, November 24 through 25; Millen Grove, December 1; Rocky Creek Church, December 2; Thomas's Station, December 3; Brier Creek, December 4; and Ebenezer Creek, December 7. The most memorable encounter of the march occurred on November 22 at Griswoldville, ten miles outside of Macon. Union troops brushed aside the attacking Georgia militia and to their horror found that the dead were young boys and old men. Wheeler and Smith could never offer any significant opposition to the advancing Union force. Sherman's casualties for the entire campaign were only around 2,200 men.

William Tecumseh Sherman.

Harper's Pictorial History of the Great Rebellion

As the troops marched, they terrorized the countryside. Physical assault against civilians was rare, but destruction and confiscation of property was widespread. Food was regularly taken, though at times Southerners in need were helped. Clothes and household furnishings were often carried away or destroyed. It was not a scorched earth policy, however, because everything in the path of the invaders was not routinely burned. Only property connected with slavery and Union prisoners of war was systematically destroyed. For example, dogs were killed because of their use in chasing fugitive slaves and escaping Union prisoners.

There was a great deal of destruction in Georgia during the March to the Sea, but Sherman's troops were not the sole perpetrators. Ironically, Confederates helped him create the terror of war on civilians. The plundering by Confederate deserters and elements of Wheeler's cavalry, as well as runaway slaves and Union deserters, intensified the havoc. Sherman regularly wished there was some other way to end the conflict, but he was convinced there was none.

Slaves played an important role in the march. Many ran

away from their masters and acted as spies for the army, and even those who simply stood by the roadside and cheered the advancing troops buoyed the soldiers with their exuberance. Sherman, whom the slaves viewed as a conquering messiah, found them an encumbrance to his army, though he treated them with respect on the personal level.

Union officers and men as a rule agreed with their commander's position that the thousands of fugitives following the army were a nuisance. There were some soldiers who were kind to the slaves, but military attitudes were usually racist at worst and condescending at best. On December 9, Gen. Jeff C. Davis, commander of the Fourteenth Corps, demonstrated army attitudes with his actions at Ebenezer Creek. Davis's unit, with black fugitives to the rear and Joe Wheeler's Confederate cavalry not far behind, was crossing the creek on pontoon bridges. As soon as the troops had crossed, the bridges were removed, and the blacks were left stranded. Fearing for their lives at the hands of Wheeler's approaching cavalry, the fugitives made desperate attempts to cross the creek. Many tragically drowned in the effort. Davis and Sherman never admitted any blame.

By December 10, only Savannah and nearby Fort McAllister stood in the way of Sherman's reaching the sea. He chose his old division from Shiloh, now under William B. Hazen, to assault the fort, and this force easily overran the garrison on December 13. William J. Hardee still held Savannah, and on December 17 Sherman demanded its surrender. He clamped a siege on the city, but, as he had in Atlanta, he allowed the Confederate force to escape when he took Savannah on December 21. Meanwhile, John M. Schofield defeated John Bell Hood at Franklin, Tennessee, on November 30, and George H. Thomas finished the job at Nashville on December 15 and 16. It was a happy Sherman who telegraphed Abraham Lincoln on December 22 offering Savannah as a Christmas gift.

Upon entering the city, Sherman continued his psychological warfare, but now he put his troops on their best behavior to show the populace the benefits of returning to the Union. He wanted Confederates to know that he believed in a hard war but a soft peace. He wanted them to quit fighting so that more death and destruction would be unnecessary.

The March to the Sea confused, frustrated, frightened, and angered the people of the Confederacy. At its start, Georgians were encouraged to rise up in opposition and burn what they could not carry away from the invaders. In the midst of the campaign, rumors were rife about the size, location, and activities of the invaders. Their arrival in an area created panic and helplessness. Throughout, Confederate newspapers predicted imminent disaster for the Federals and criticized Sherman for raiding rather than fighting, but desertions increased in Robert E. Lee's army in Virginia and the optimism of the Confederate populace plummeted. From Savannah, Sherman marched through the Carolinas during the early months of 1865, moving toward a juncture with Ulysses S. Grant against Lee in Virginia. The March to the Sea was a harbinger of modern total war, and it created the fodder for later Lost Cause arguments that Sherman was a villian and the Confederate leaders were corresponding exemplars of virtue.

[*See also* Bummers; Savannah, Georgia, *article on* Savannah Campaign.]

BIBLIOGRAPHY

Cox, Jacob D. *The March to the Sea—Franklin and Nashville.* Introduction by Nat C. Hughes. New York, 1882. Reprint, Wilmington, N.C., 1989.

DeLaubenfels, David J., ed. "With Sherman through Georgia: A Journal [John Rzeha]." *Georgia Historical Quarterly* 41 (September 1957): 288–300.

Glatthaar, Joseph T. *The March to the Sea and Beyond: Sherman's Troops in the Savannah and Carolinas Campaign.* New York, 1985.

Hitchcock, Henry M. *Marching with Sherman.* Edited by M. A. deWolfe Howe. New Haven, 1927.

Jones, James P. "General Jeff C. Davis, U.S.A., and Sherman's Georgia Campaign." *Georgia Historical Quarterly* 47 (March 1962): 231–242.

Marszalek, John F. *Sherman: A Soldier's Passion for Order.* New York, 1992.

Marszalek, John F. "W. T. Sherman, Was He Really a Brute?" *Blue and Gray* 7 (December 1989): 46–51.

JOHN F. MARSZALEK

MARINE CORPS. Section 5 of "An Act to provide for the organization of the Navy," passed by the Provisional Congress of the Confederate States on March 16, 1861, established a Corps of Marines, commanded by a major and consisting of six companies. An amendatory act, passed May 20, 1861, expanded the corps to ten companies and elevated the grade of the commanding officer to that of colonel. All laws and regulations of the U.S. Marine Corps not inconsistent with these acts were applied to the government of its Confederate counterpart.

Lloyd J. Beall, former paymaster in the U.S. Army, was appointed colonel of the Confederate States Marines on May 23, 1861. Colonel Beall served throughout the war as the first and only commanding officer of the corps. Fifty-six officers were appointed to the corps during the war period. Nineteen were formerly officers of the U.S. Marine Corps, four had served in the U.S. Navy or Coast Survey, three were appointed directly from civilian pursuits, one, the commandant, with service in the U.S. Army, and the rest came from the ranks of the Provisional Army of the Confederate States.

The Confederate States Marines served in many of the coastal operations of the war: Pensacola, 1861–1862; Port Royal, November 5–7, 1861; Hampton Roads, March 8–9, 1862; New Orleans, April 24, 1862; Drewry's Bluff, May 15, 1862; Charleston Harbor, 1863–1865; Mobile Bay, August 5, 1864; and Fort Fisher, December 24–25, 1864, and January 13–15, 1865. Marines also served ashore at Second Drewry's Bluff, May 13–16, 1864; Fort Gaines, August 5–8, 1864; Savannah, December 11–20, 1864; Sayler's Creek, April 6, 1865; and Spanish Fort (Fort Blakely), April 9, 1865.

Marine Guards served aboard many of the warships of the Confederate States Navy including the commerce raiders CSS *Sumter, Georgia, Tallahassee (Olustee), Chickamauga, Stonewall,* and *Shenandoah.* One solitary Marine, Capt. Becket K. Howell, cruised aboard CSS *Alabama.*

The headquarters of the marines was located at Richmond, Virginia. Three companies garrisoned the post at Drewry's Bluff from May 1862 until the evacuation of Richmond in April 1865. Companies were regularly assigned to the naval stations at Mobile, Alabama, and Savannah, Georgia, with detachments on duty at various times at the navy yards at Richmond, Charleston, South Carolina, and Wilmington and Charlotte, North Carolina.

The marines were utilized on numerous occasions as a rapid deployment force, being called upon for missions to Charleston Harbor in February 1862 and the proposed attack upon the Federal prisoner of war compound at Point Lookout, Maryland, in July 1864. Marines also assisted in the capture of USS *Underwriter* at New Berne, North Carolina, February 2, 1864, and USS *Waterwitch* off Ossabaw Island, Georgia, June 3, 1864.

The irresistible tide of Federal ground and naval forces eliminated the Confederate naval bases at Savannah, Charleston, and Wilmington during late 1864 and early 1865. Contingents of Marines from those stations made their way to the post at Drewry's Bluff, where they were organized with sailors into a naval battalion under the command of Capt. John R. Tucker. The majority of marines were killed or captured at the Battle of Sayler's Creek on April 6, 1865. A few managed to escape, only to surrender at Appomattox on April 9, 1865. Others, components of a naval brigade made up of shipless crew from the James River Squadron, surrendered at Greensboro, North Carolina, on April 28, 1865. The last organized force of Confederate Marines, the remnant of the Mobile Company, surrendered north of that city on May 10, 1865.

BIBLIOGRAPHY

Donnelly, Ralph W. *The Confederate States Marine Corps: The Rebel Leathernecks.* Shippensburg, Pa., 1989.

Gardner, Donald R. "The Confederate Corps of Marines." Master's thesis, Memphis State University, 1973.

Sullivan, David M. "Leathernecks in Gray: A Perspective of the War through the Letters of Confederate States Marine Officers." *Journal of Confederate History* 1, no. 2 (1988): 351–386.

DAVID M. SULLIVAN

MARMADUKE, JOHN SAPPINGTON (1833–1887), major general and postwar governor of Missouri. Both Marmaduke's father and his uncle served as Missouri's governor, the first in 1844 and the latter in 1860. The younger Marmaduke attended Yale and Harvard before accepting a cadetship at West Point, graduating in 1857, and then serving in Utah during the Mormon War.

Though his father favored the Union, Marmaduke in 1861 resigned his commission in the Federal army and was made colonel of cavalry in the Missouri State Guard. He

JOHN SAPPINGTON MARMADUKE. LIBRARY OF CONGRESS

BIBLIOGRAPHY

Eliot, Ellsworth, Jr. *West Point in the Confederacy.* New York, 1941.

Faust, Patricia L., ed. *Historical Times Illustrated Encyclopedia of the Civil War.* New York, 1986.

Warner, Ezra J. *Generals in Gray: Lives of the Confederate Commanders.* Baton Rouge, La., 1959.

KENNETH L. STILES

MARTIN, JOHN MARSHALL (1832–1921), congressman from Florida and colonel. Born in Edgefield District, South Carolina, Martin graduated from the Citadel in 1852 and moved to Ocala, Florida in 1856, where he became a prominent cotton planter. He was active in the Democratic party and strongly supported secession.

In 1861, he organized the Marion Light Infantry and was elected captain but was also elected to the First Confederate House of Representatives from the First District of Florida at the same time. He served in Congress for only one term and was on a special committee for the relief of sick soldiers and the Naval Affairs Committee. Martin refused a second term and returned to his regiment. At the Battle of Richmond, Kentucky, in August 1862, he was severely wounded and had to leave the field for several months. In 1864, he became colonel of the Ninth Florida Regiment of the Army of Tennessee and served in the Nashville campaign late that year.

After the surrender, Martin returned to his Ocala plantation and remained there, an honored and admired resident, until his death on August 10, 1921.

BIBLIOGRAPHY

Ott, Eloise R., and Louis H. Chazal. *Ocali Country, Kingdom of the Sun: A History of Marion County, Florida, 1559–1965.* Ocala, Fla., 1966.

Wakelyn, Jon L. *Biographical Dictionary of the Confederacy.* Edited by Frank E. Vandiver. Westport, Conn., 1977.

ARCH FREDRIC BLAKEY

MARTIN, WILLIAM THOMPSON (1823–1910), major general. Before the war Martin, a district attorney in Mississippi, opposed secession. But when his state seceded, he organized the Adams County Cavalry Company, and after the bombardment of Fort Sumter, he volunteered his company to the Confederacy.

Promoted to major in November 1861, Martin commanded the Second Mississippi Cavalry during the Peninsular campaign. He fought at Yorktown and Williamsburg, and participated in J. E. B. Stuart's ride around George B. McClellan in June 1862. At Sharpsburg in September 1862, he served as a personal aide to Gen. Robert E. Lee.

WILLIAM THOMPSON MARTIN. LIBRARY OF CONGRESS

Appointed brigadier general in December 1862, Martin was transferred to the Army of Tennessee to command a division of cavalry under Joseph Wheeler. His division participated in the fighting at Spring Hill in March 1863 and later took part in the Tullahoma and Chickamauga campaigns. Promoted to major general in November 1863, Martin commanded all the cavalry that accompanied James Longstreet in the operations against Knoxville. During the Atlanta campaign his division participated in numerous skirmishes and was constantly involved in reconnaissance activities. From February 1865 until the end of the war, he commanded the district of Mississippi and East Louisiana. There is no record of where he surrendered.

After the war, Martin resumed his law practice and was active in Mississippi politics, serving in the Mississippi Senate from 1882 to 1894. He died in Natchez, Mississippi, on March 16, 1910.

BIBLIOGRAPHY

Hooker, Charles E. *Mississippi.* Vol. 7 of *Confederate Military History.* Edited by Clement A. Evans. Atlanta, 1899. Vol. 9 of extended ed. Wilmington, N.C., 1987.

U.S. War Department. *War of the Rebellion: A Compilation of the Official Records of the Union and Confederate Armies.* Washington, D.C., 1880–1901. Ser. 1, vol. 11, pt. 2, p. 513; ser. 1, vol. 23, pt. 2, p. 695; ser. 1, vol. 31, pt. 3, p. 740; ser. 1, vol. 49, pt. 1, p. 985.

Wakelyn, Jon L. *Biographical Dictionary of the Confederacy.* Edited by Frank E. Vandiver. Westport, Conn., 1977.

MICHAEL G. MAHON

MARYLAND. *See* Border States.

MASON, JAMES M. (1798–1871), congressman from Virginia and diplomat. Though by middle age James Murray Mason had attained the high office his prominent Virginia family had raised him to expect, he could not have anticipated that he would be remembered most because of the actions of others rather than his own. As the grandson of Revolutionary giant George Mason, he grew up with the arrogant confidence of a member of the Virginia gentry. He was born in the northern corner of the state that was then part of the District of Columbia, and he graduated from the University of Pennsylvania. After studying law at William and Mary, he settled in Winchester, Virginia, on a modest estate called Selma.

JAMES M. MASON. NATIONAL ARCHIVES

Mason served in the Virginia legislature in the 1820s and sat in the state's constitutional convention of 1829 and 1830, where he upheld backcountry interests against those of the Tidewater. After a single term in the U.S. House of Representatives (1838–1839), he won election in 1847 to the U.S. Senate and remained there until the secession crisis.

A state rights Democrat, Mason moved in the congenial company of his fellow Virginia senator Robert M. T. Hunter and South Carolinian John C. Calhoun. He served as chairman of the Senate Foreign Relations Committee and drafted the Fugitive Slave Law that was part of the Compromise of 1850. Like Calhoun, whose constitutional views he admired, Mason viewed sectional antagonism as something too deep to be assuaged by palliative measures. For him, Abraham Lincoln's election spelled the end of the Union. He left the Senate on March 28, 1861—nearly a month before Virginia seceded—and served briefly in the Provisional Congress in his old role as Foreign Relations chairman.

Mason's greatest challenge came when Jefferson Davis appointed him the fledgling Confederacy's diplomatic commissioner to Great Britain. Mason's letter of instruction came from his fellow Virginian Hunter, whose own Confederate reincarnation in 1861 was as secretary of state. Hunter told Mason to go to London immediately and present the South's request for diplomatic recognition not as "revolted provinces or rebellious subjects" but as a "new Confederacy and a new Government." In words hardly suited to such a proud nation, he suggested that Mason remind the English—erroneously thought to be in great need of cotton—that the supply of that staple to Britain from an independent South "would be as abundant, as cheap and as certain as if these States were themselves her colonies."

On his way to Charleston in search of a ship to run the blockade, Mason traveled in the company of another former U.S. senator, John Slidell, a Louisianan sent by the Confederacy as emissary to France. Slidell took his family with him and, like Mason, was also accompanied by a secretary of legation. At first they planned to take the steamship *Nashville,* but an unexpected increase in activity by the blockading Northern ships made them consider going to Mexico before embarking. When they concluded that the overland route would unduly delay their mission, they found another ship, a privateer with a shallower draft than the *Nashville* and a better chance of eluding the blockading vessels. On the evening of October 11, 1861, *Gordon* slipped out of Charleston in a driving rain and through the blockade without incident. "Here we are," Mason wrote his wife, "on the deep blue sea; clear of all the Yankees."

The ship arrived in the Bahamas three days later. On learning that the only regularly scheduled British vessel leaving from Nassau stopped, inconveniently, at New York, the commissioners decided to continue on to Cuba where they expected to find passage to the West Indies and then to London. When they reached Havana they were feted by sympathetic Spanish citizens and introduced by the obliging British consul general to Cuban authorities as diplomats of the Confederacy. They made no attempt to keep their mission a secret. Capt. Charles D. Wilkes of the warship USS *San Jacinto* learned of their presence when he put in at a port down the coast. He quickly cast off for Havana in hopes of capturing them when their ship put out to sea. The common knowledge in the Cuban capital that the Southerners had booked passage on the British mail packet *Trent* eliminated guesswork for Wilkes. On November 8 *San Jacinto* intercepted *Trent* on the high seas, and Wilkes, ignoring the cautions of his executive officer not to spark an international incident, did just that.

After firing shots across the mail packet's bow, Wilkes sent across a boarding party to take prisoner the two Confederate diplomats whose names would ever after be linked in history. For Mason and Slidell, their diplomatic role was beginning much sooner than expected. After much glowering, brandishing of bayonets, and hurling of insults between members of the boarding party and the largely Southern company of passengers, *Trent* gave up its soon-to-be-famous passengers. Though the Northern sailors did not search the British ship for papers or take it as a prize, seizing the two commissioners and their assistants was enough. While Slidell was gathering his bags to leave the mail packet, his wife asked who commanded *San Jacinto.* When told it was someone she knew, she blurted out the bald truth before Mason could stop her: "Captain Wilkes is playing into our hands!"

The incident lasted less than three hours but reverberated across the ocean for weeks to come. As *San Jacinto* sailed up the coast, often within sight of Confederate territory, Mason while pacing the decks lectured his secretary on how this act of "piracy" would force the British to join hands with the South. On November 24 *San Jacinto* dropped anchor in Boston Harbor and turned over its captives to the prison at Fort Warren. Mason and Slidell were ushered into their spartan but clean and warm quarters—an eighteen-by-eighteen-foot room that the two men shared. It was not an uncomfortable arrangement. Far from eating prison gruel in a damp cell, the Southerners enjoyed professionally cooked meals replete, as one disgusted Bostonian reported, with "champagne, fruit, cigars, English papers and letters of sympathy." "Indeed," Mason admitted, "we have a better daily table than any hotel affords."

While Mason and Slidell languished in enforced idleness, the diplomatic furor raged outside the walls of Fort Warren. Learning that Confederate emissaries had been taken at gunpoint from a British ship, the cabinet in Westminster wrestled with a way to avoid war, but as a precaution postponed planned reductions in military spending. Outside the corridors of Whitehall the British press concluded that the government could do no less than demand release of the commissioners and a formal apology from the American government. Some London editors (including one Karl Marx) argued that any war between Britain and the North would suit only the slave owners' purposes and for that reason must be avoided. But reinforcements sent to the British garrison in Canada reminded everyone that the incident could indeed lead to the result Mason so fervently prayed for in his cell in Boston Harbor. While in prison, the Virginia diplomat wrote afterward, he bet a fellow Southern inmate fifty barrels of corn that the British would demand his freedom.

When the American press learned of the outrage the *Trent* affair was causing in England, newspapers spread the fear of imminent conflict with Great Britain throughout the North. A prominent British correspondent in Washington wrote that if war broke out between his country and the North, "Old Nick will be unchained for some time to come." In Fort Warren, Mason and his companions read with enjoyment these reports on the apparent slide toward war their arrest had triggered.

The British cabinet finally composed an ultimatum demanding release of the diplomats and an apology. But as one of his last public acts, Prince Albert, consort of Queen Victoria, altered the text to soften it and provide the Americans with a face-saving retreat by saying the British government hoped Wilkes had not acted on higher authority. Formal presentation of the ultimatum to Secretary of State William H. Seward did not take place until December 23. A hint of the American response had been contained in earlier denials by Abraham Lincoln that his government had ordered Wilkes's action. On December 27 the crisis passed when Seward told the British ambassador that Mason and Slidell would be released without condition.

The Confederate detainees were surreptitiously bundled out of Fort Warren and transferred to a British warship that took them away in an icy gale to Bermuda and then on to London. Mason arrived to a hero's welcome in the Mayfair town houses and country homes of influential British sympathizers. Ominously, though, the government officially ignored him. Though he cultivated all the right elements in industry, press, and Parliament, Mason could not effect the goal he came to achieve—recognition of the Confederacy. In July 1862 he complained that "the Government here is tardy and supine" but hoped the success of Confederate arms and a shortage of cotton would change their minds. He wrote frequently to Lord Russell, secretary of state for foreign affairs, but could not gain an audience. Russell turned aside Mason's entreaties by writing rather offensively that if the Confederacy ever achieved "stability and permanence" it would be recognized: "That time, however, has not, in the judgment of Her Majesty's Government, yet arrived." Late in the war Mason did meet with Lord Palmerston but went away disappointed each time.

Perhaps the Confederate emissary could have achieved the diplomatic recognition Richmond desired, but Mason seems to have accepted defeat too easily. Certainly he could have shown more energy and more tenacity in pursuit of an admittedly difficult goal. Had he done so, his explanations for his failure would have sounded less like attempts to blame others for his own shortcomings.

By autumn 1862 Mason had abandoned his purely diplomatic approach and helped secure loans and facilitate commercial transactions for the South. The next August President Davis decided that because the British had refused his request for recognition, Mason should consider his mission "at an end" and leave London. Mason did as instructed but wrote a plaintive dispatch after he reached Paris saying he was "at some loss to know whether it was intended that I should remain for the present in Europe." He wrote his wife from his flat near the Arc de Triomphe, "I am plodding on in this Babel, but with little in it to interest me. . . . I have seen nothing in Paris. . . . In truth I have not the heart or spirit to gaze after new things." In the fall of 1863, however, he was appointed the Confederate commissioner on the Continent and traveled back and forth between London and Paris. He despaired of ever convincing the British of the rightness of his cause: "The so-called antislavery feeling seems to have become with them a sentiment akin to patriotism."

Up to the end of the war, even when the last Atlantic ports had fallen to Northern assaults, Mason continued to send his forlorn dispatches by blockade runner to Nassau and Bermuda in hopes that they would get through. In March 1865 he was still corresponding with Secretary of State Judah P. Benjamin about such irrelevancies as the missing Confederate seal he had dispatched the previous year. Even after learning of the evacuation of Richmond, he wrote that "the war will go on to final success." A last semiofficial act was to publish in the London *Index,* a news sheet subsidized by Confederate money, a refutation of Secretary of War Edwin Stanton's charge that the Lincoln assassination was engineered by the Confederate government.

Mason planned to sail for Canada in September 1865 after seeing Benjamin, who escaped from Richmond and made his way to London and eventual success as a barrister there. Mason did not leave as expected, however, and was not reunited with his family in Canada until the following April. Under the aegis of President Andrew Johnson's amnesty, the diplomat returned to Virginia in 1869, visibly older, his step slow and heavy. He could not return to Selma. Like the homes of many Southerners, it had been put to the torch during the war. After a long, gradual decline, Mason died on April 28, 1871, in Alexandria, Virginia.

[*See also* Trent Affair.]

BIBLIOGRAPHY

Biographical Directory of the United States Congress, 1774–1989. Washington, D.C., 1989.

Ferris, Norman B. *The Trent Affair: A Diplomatic Crisis.* Knoxville, Tenn., 1977.

Mason, Virginia. *The Public Life and Diplomatic Correspondence of James M. Mason.* New York and Washington, D.C., 1906.

Wakelyn, Jon L. *Biographical Dictionary of the Confederacy.* Westport, Conn., 1977.

NELSON D. LANKFORD

MASON-DIXON LINE. Because of disputed boundaries between English colonies in America, arising from conflicting statements in colonial charters issued by various kings of England in the seventeenth and eighteenth centuries, English surveyors and astronomers were sent to North America to locate and establish legal boundaries.

During the years 1763 through 1767, Charles Mason and Jeremiah Dixon surveyed the boundaries of three colonies, Delaware, Maryland, and Pennsylvania. The line of the latter two was surveyed westward 244 miles. Opposition by Indian tribes delayed its completion until 1784. The survey cost $75,000 and was paid by William Penn and Lord Baltimore. An eight-foot-wide vista was cut through the forests and small stone markers placed at each mile post, with larger stone markers bearing the coats of arms of Penn and Baltimore at five-mile intervals. In ensuing years many markers fell or were appropriated by settlers. In 1900 through 1902 the line was resurveyed and stabilized.

Between the Revolution and the Civil War, the line acquired additional significance as the border between Northern states that had eliminated African slavery and Southern states that retained the institution. In 1820 Missouri, west of the Mississippi River, was admitted as a slave state, with slavery prohibited in the remaining territory north of 36°30′.

Immediately prior to the Civil War, Southern slaveholding states were called "Dixie," presumably derived from the word Dixon, and popularized in a minstrel show song in 1859. The term Mason-Dixon Line has continued in use in the twentieth century to distinguish between Northern and Southern states of the American Union.

BIBLIOGRAPHY

Mason, A. Hewlett, ed. *The Journal of Charles Mason and Jeremiah Dixon, 1736–1768.* Vol. 76 of *Memoirs of the American Philosophical Society.* Philadelphia, 1969.

Matthews, Edward B., ed. *Report on the Resurvey of the Maryland-Pennsylvania Boundary Part of the Mason and Dixon Line.* Harrisburg, Pa., 1909.

Miers, Earl Schenck. *Border Romance: The Story of the Exploits of Charles Mason and Jeremiah Dixon.* Newark, Del., 1975.

Poitiaux, Robinson Morgan. *The Evolution of the Mason and Dixon Line.* Richmond, Va., 1902.

PERCIVAL PERRY

MAURY, D. H. (1822–1900) major general and U.S. diplomat. Educated at the University of Virginia and West Point, Dabney Herndon Maury had fifteen years' experience in the U.S. Army by the time the Civil War began in 1861. He had served with distinction during the Mexican War, published a tactics manual for mounted rifles, taught as an instructor at West Point, and fought Indians on the frontier. When his native state of Virginia seceded from the Union, Maury submitted his resignation papers to the U.S. Army. The army refused to accept his resignation and Maury found himself instead dismissed for his traitorous request. Nonetheless, he quickly left his post in New Mexico and arrived in Richmond in July 1861 to offer his military services to the Confederacy.

Maury's first assignment was as a cavalry captain. After a brief stint stationed on the Rappahannock River under Gen. Theophilus H. Holmes, Maury went west to join Gen. Earl Van Dorn's Trans-Mississippi Department. Maury once wrote that his only "application for services ever made during the war was for service in the field of the Army of Northern Virginia." The Confederate army never granted that request, and Maury spent the entire war far west of his native state.

At the Confederate defeat at Elkhorn Tavern, Arkansas, in March of 1862, Colonel Maury's performance in the face of failure greatly impressed Van Dorn. Promotion to brigadier general came within a week.

As a brigadier general in the Army of the West, Maury competently led Confederates through the Battles of Iuka and Corinth. During the winter of 1862–1863 he won promotion to major general. In late December 1862 his division went to the aid of Stephen Dill Lee at Vicksburg, Mississippi. On April 15, Maury received new orders to go to Knoxville, Tennessee, as commander of the Department of East Tennessee. He hoped this would keep him closer to home, but in six weeks he changed posts again.

In May 1863, Maury became commander of the District of the Gulf with headquarters in Mobile, Alabama, and he and his family settled in Mobile for the duration of the war. Maury later described this assignment as an "interesting and agreeable command." It was not an idle one. For the next two years he devoted his energy to keeping Mobile and its important bay free from Federal control. He was also responsible for diverting enemy raids sent into Mississippi and Alabama. In April 1864, Federals managed to take control of Mobile Bay, but Maury stubbornly fought to defend the city until the following spring. In April 1865 he finally acquiesced to superior forces and surrendered his command. For Dabney Maury, as for other Confederate officers, his years as a soldier had come to a bitter end.

Maury's postwar years were varied, taking him from Virginia to Louisiana before he served as the U.S. minister to Colombia. Most pertinent to the history of the Confederacy, Maury was one of the founding members of the Southern Historical Society and served as its chairman for twenty years. As part of this organization Maury joined other Southerners in working to recover and make available for publication Confederate records of the war.

BIBLIOGRAPHY

Hotchkiss, Jed. *Virginia.* Vol. 3 of *Confederate Military History.* Edited by Clement A. Evans. Atlanta, 1899. Vol. 4 of extended ed. Wilmington, N.C., 1987.

Maury, Dabney H. *Recollections of a Virginian in the Mexican, Indian and Civil Wars.* New York, 1894.

Warner, Ezra J. *Generals in Gray: Lives of the Confederate Commanders.* Baton Rouge, La., 1959.

LESLEY JILL GORDON-BURR

MAURY, MATTHEW FONTAINE (1806–1873), naval officer. Appointed an acting midshipman at the age of nineteen, Maury served for over thirty-six years in the U.S. Navy, during which time he won international recognition for his pioneering work in the fields of navigation, hydrography, and meteorology. Following Virginia's secession from the Union, Maury resigned his commission to serve in defense of his native state. He was immediately appointed by Governor John Letcher to serve on an advisory council charged with mobilizing state defenses. On April 23, 1861, Maury was commissioned a commander in the Virginia State Navy. He retained this rank when the state navy was incorporated into the Confederate navy on June 10.

In late spring 1861, Maury began a series of experiments with torpedoes, or underwater mines. He believed that, for a nation lacking the resources to construct a large navy, torpedoes offered a cheap and effective alternative for defending Southern waterways from Union warships. Although initially skeptical, Confederate Secretary of the Navy Stephen R. Mallory came to endorse Maury's ideas, and in the fall of 1861 the Confederate Congress appropriated moneys for a torpedo development program. Maury's

MATTHEW FONTAINE MAURY. Pictured with Raphael Semmes (at right), commander of the commerce raider *Alabama*.

NAVAL HISTORICAL CENTER, WASHINGTON, D.C.

researches led to building a torpedo with an improved electric detonator, the first used successfully in warfare.

Maury also advocated the construction of steam-powered gunboats to protect Southern waters. The gunboats he envisioned were shallow-draft and highly maneuverable, and mounted large-caliber rifled guns. Such vessels, Maury argued, could be quickly and economically built and, in large numbers, would be capable of driving Federal ships from the South's rivers and bays. The Confederate Congress was impressed enough with his proposal to appropriate $2 million to build one hundred of these gunboats. Yet Maury had scarcely begun supervising work on these craft when the program was abruptly canceled. The success of CSS *Virginia* against the Union blockading fleet at Hampton Roads had convinced the Confederate government that it should apply its limited resources to the building of ironclad warships.

In late summer 1862, Maury was ordered to England as a special agent with instructions to purchase ships for the Confederate government. Over the next two and a half years, he used his worldwide fame as a scientist to promote publicly the cause of Southern independence among the British people. In addition, he continued his experiments on electric torpedoes, the results of which were forwarded to the Navy Department. He also arranged for the purchase of two ships to serve as commerce raiders. One of these vessels, the screw steamer *Georgia,* made nine captures.

On May 2, 1865, knowing that the collapse of the Confederate government was imminent, Maury set sail for Texas with $40,000 worth of torpedo equipment in a last-ditch effort to help the Southern cause. Arriving in Havana twenty days later, he learned that the war was over. Because he fell into three of the six categories of Confederates exempted from the Federal government's 1863 amnesty proclamations (he was a U.S. Navy officer who had resigned and aided the South, an agent of the Confederate government, and a Confederate naval officer above the rank of lieutenant), Maury was unable to return to Virginia until July 1868. He was then appointed a professor of physics at Virginia Military Institute, a position he held until his death.

BIBLIOGRAPHY

Corbin, Diana F. M. *A Life of Matthew Fontaine Maury, U.S.N. and C.S.N.* London, 1888.

Lewis, Charles L. *Matthew Fontaine Maury: The Pathfinder of the Seas.* Annapolis, Md., 1927.

Williams, Frances L. *Matthew Fontaine Maury: Scientist of the Sea.* New Brunswick, N.J., 1963.

CHARLES E. BRODINE, JR.

MAURY, WILLIAM L. (fl. 1861), naval officer. Born in Virginia, a distant cousin of naval officer and scientist Matthew Fontaine Maury, William Lewis Maury served in the U.S. Navy and rose to the rank of lieutenant. In 1855 he was a member of the court of inquiry that recommended Matthew Maury be put on half-pay.

In April 1861, William Maury resigned his Federal commission and accepted an appointment in the Virginia State Navy. On June 10 of that year he was commissioned a first lieutenant in the Confederate navy. During 1861 and early 1862 he assisted in the placement of torpedoes, or electric mines, for the defense of the James River. For a time he commanded a battery of heavy guns on Sewell's Island and was given an army commission. Later Maury was a member of the court of inquiry into the loss of CSS *Virginia.* That court decided that *Virginia*'s commander, Josiah Tattnall, had acted properly in scuttling his ship to prevent its capture.

In the fall of 1862, Maury was listed on the rolls of the Charleston, South Carolina, Naval Station. From there, he traveled to England, delivering funds and orders to his cousin Matthew Maury, now a Confederate naval agent, in

February 1863. The funds were used to purchase the steamer *Japan,* which was transformed into the armed raider CSS *Georgia.* Under William Maury's command, the *Georgia* began its career in April 1863 and during the next six months captured or bonded Federal merchant vessels worth some $400,000. *Georgia* was not a fast ship, however, and limped into Cherbourg, France, in late October 1863 with worn-out machinery. In January 1864, Maury, pleading ill health, was replaced by Lt. William E. Evans and returned to the Confederacy via Bermuda.

Later in 1864, Maury joined the squadron commanded by Flag Officer William F. Lynch in the Carolina sounds. He then took command of the ironclad steamer *North Carolina.* Constructed in 1863, *North Carolina* was poorly built and deteriorated rapidly; it sank at its moorings in September 1864. Maury was still listed as its commander in October, and the vessel was dismantled in November. Maury apparently served ashore during the last months of the war. His activities after the war are unknown.

BIBLIOGRAPHY

Civil War Chronology, 1861–1865. Washington, D.C., 1971.

Perry, Milton F. *Infernal Machines: The Story of Confederate Submarine and Mine Warfare.* Baton Rouge, La., 1965.

Spencer, Warren F. *The Confederate Navy in Europe.* Birmingham, Ala., 1983.

Still, William N., Jr. *Iron Afloat: The Story of the Confederate Armorclads.* Nashville, Tenn., 1971.

ROBERT S. BROWNING III

SAMUEL BELL MAXEY. LIBRARY OF CONGRESS

MAXEY, SAMUEL BELL (1825–1895), brigadier general, Confederate commander in Indian Territory and superintendent of Indian affairs, and U.S. senator. Born at Tompkinsville, Kentucky, on March 30, 1825, Maxey graduated from West Point in 1846 and was assigned to the Seventh Infantry during the Mexican War. He took part in the fighting at Vera Cruz, Cerro Gordo, Contreras, Churusbusco, and Mexico City and was promoted to brevet first lieutenant for "gallant conduct." Resigning his commission in 1849, Maxey read for the law and moved to Paris, Texas.

Elected to the Texas legislature in 1861, he resigned to serve as the colonel of the Ninth Texas Infantry. After promotion to brigadier general, Maxey served in Chattanooga, Tennessee, where he commanded the observation corps that successfully harried Federal troops during the campaign. He later saw action at Port Hudson, the Big Black campaign, and the Battle of Corinth.

In 1863 Maxey was named Confederate commander in Indian Territory and appointed superintendent of Indian affairs for the pro-Confederate tribes. At the time many of the Indians were questioning their Southern allegiance, but Maxey convinced them the South was doing everything possible to honor its pledges, thereby preserving the Confederate-Indian alliance. For these efforts, Maxey was assigned to duty as major general, but his promotion was never made official. Just before the close of hostilities, he commanded a cavalry division.

After the war, Maxey resumed his legal practice. In 1875 he took a seat in the U.S. Senate where he served for twelve years with other former Confederate officers called the "Confederate Brigadiers." Maxey died in Eureka Springs, Arkansas, on August 16, 1895.

BIBLIOGRAPHY

Abel, Annie H. *The American Indian as a Participant in the Civil War.* Cleveland, Ohio, 1919.

Morton, Ohland. "Confederate Government Relations with the Five Civilized Tribes." *Chronicles of Oklahoma* 31 (1953): 189–204, 299–322.

Trickett, Dean. "The Civil War in Indian Territory." *Chronicles of Oklahoma* 17 (1938): 315–327, 401–412; 18 (1940): 142–153, 266–280; 19 (1941): 55–69, 381–396.

KENNY A. FRANKS

MAXWELL, AUGUSTUS EMMETT (1820–1903), congressman from Florida. Born in Elberton, Georgia, Maxwell graduated from the University of Virginia in 1841 and was admitted to the Alabama bar in 1843. Two years later, he moved to Tallahassee, Florida, and began a successful political career. A Democrat and a prominent vestryman in the Episcopal church, he served as attorney general of Florida (1846–1847), secretary of state (1848), and state senator (1849–1850). He was a member of the U.S. Congress from 1853 to 1857 and then returned to his law practice in Pensacola.

In 1861, Maxwell was elected to the Confederate Senate after Florida seceded. He served from 1862 to 1865 and was generally loyal to the administration, although he did support the peace movement in 1864. He was a member of the Naval Affairs, Commerce, Patents, Foreign Affairs, Indian Affairs, and Engrossment and Enrollments committees, and he strongly opposed what he considered to be excessive speculation on war goods.

After the war, Maxwell became a member of the Florida Supreme Court in 1866 but resigned to become president of the Pensacola and Montgomery Railroad and the law partner of Stephen R. Mallory, the former Confederate secretary of the navy. He resumed his public career after 1877, serving as a circuit court judge from 1877 to 1885 and as chief justice of the Florida Supreme Court from 1887 to 1891. He returned to private practice at Pensacola until his death on May 5, 1903.

BIBLIOGRAPHY

Rerick, Rowland. *Memoirs of Florida.* Atlanta, Ga., 1902.

Sifakis, Stewart. *Who Was Who in the Civil War.* New York, 1988.

Wakelyn, Jon L. *Biographical Dictionary of the Confederacy.* Edited by Frank E. Vandiver. Westport, Conn., 1977.

ARCH FREDRIC BLAKEY

MC-. Names beginning with this prefix are alphabetized as if spelled *Mac-*.

MECHANICSVILLE, VIRGINIA. Also known as Beaver Dam Creek and Ellerson's Mill, the first major confrontation of the Seven Days' Battles between Gen. Robert E. Lee's Army of Northern Virginia and Maj. Gen. George B. McClellan's Army of the Potomac took place on June 26, 1862, near the small village of Mechanicsville, east of Richmond. As McClellan brought his army within sight of Richmond, he planned to use heavy artillery to shell the Confederate capital into submission from behind well-established entrenchments. Lee refused to wait for McClellan to perfect his plans, however. Using intelligence gathered by Brig. Gen. J. E. B. Stuart, he decided to seize the initiative and attack Maj. Gen. Fitz John Porter's 30,000-man corps while the latter remained separated from the rest of the Union army by the Chickahominy River. Lee planned to supplement his forces with Maj. Gen. Thomas J. ("Stonewall") Jackson's Army of the Shenandoah Valley. If all went according to plan, Jackson would smash into the flank and rear of Porter's command while Confederates under Maj. Gens. A. P. Hill, D. H. Hill, and James Longstreet struck the Federals from the front. About one-third of Lee's army under Maj. Gens. John B. Magruder and Benjamin Huger would remain in the entrenchments to defend Richmond. Once the Federals in their front began to withdraw, they were to join the attack as well.

On June 25, the day before the Confederate offensive, Federals under Brig. Gen. Joseph Hooker clashed with Southerners under Huger at Oak Grove. Although neither side gained much advantage from the fighting, McClellan recalled Hooker when he became aware of Jackson's approach. An overwhelming sense of foreboding filled him. He informed Secretary of War Edwin Stanton: "I will do all that a General can do with the splendid Army I have the honor to command & if it is destroyed by overwhelming numbers can at least die with it & share its fate."

The fighting at Oak Grove had no effect upon the timetable for the Confederate assault on Porter, but the delay of Jackson's march threatened to wreck the schedule completely. A. P. Hill had his men ready to strike early in the day, waiting only for the flanking force to appear. As the day wore on with no word from Jackson, Hill grew impatient and decided to proceed without him. At 3:00 P.M., the Confederates swept through Mechanicsville, driving the Federals from the village. This cleared the way for D. H. Hill's and Longstreet's men to cross the Chickahominy. Under the weight of the Confederate advance, Porter's troops withdrew to geographically strong positions along Beaver Dam Creek.

Despite the strength of the Union lines, A. P. Hill sent his men against the Federals in a frontal assault. Hill first attempted to strike the Union right flank with Brig. Gen. Joseph R. Anderson's command, supported by the brigades of Gens. James J. Archer and Charles W. Field. Artillery and small arms fire hammered the Confederates and repulsed the attack. As Brig. Gen. William D. Pender's men reached the field they joined the assault, attacking the Union left flank. The Federals quickly cut Pender's command to pieces and the attack degenerated into confused, disjointed, and ineffectual stabs at the Union line.

Late in the day, Lee decided to gamble on one final assault to turn Porter out of his formidable defenses. He ordered the first of D. H. Hill's brigades, under Brig. Gen. Roswell S. Ripley, into action on Pender's right. Coincidentally, President Jefferson Davis, watching the action on the field, issued an order similar to Lee's without the latter's knowledge. Ripley's men advanced against the same strong positions opposite Ellerson's Mill and suffered the same fate as Pender's men. Darkness finally ended any further bloody assaults.

Lee had counted upon precision from his subordinates to carry out his plan. Jackson's failure to arrive in a timely manner and A. P. Hill's impetuosity cost the Confederates 1,484 casualties. In contrast, the Federals whom Lee sought to annihilate lost 361. Nevertheless, the Confederate commander had seized the initiative from his Union counterpart. McClellan would spend the remainder of the Seven Days' Battles hoping to do little more than save his army from destruction.

BIBLIOGRAPHY

Cullen, Joseph P. *The Peninsula Campaign, 1862: McClellan and Lee Struggle for Richmond.* Harrisburg, Pa., 1973.

Freeman, Douglas S. *Lee's Lieutenants: A Study in Command.* 3 vols. New York, 1942–1944. Reprint, New York, 1986.

Johnson, Robert U., and C. C. Buel, eds. *Battles and Leaders of the Civil War.* 4 vols. New York, 1887–1888. Reprint, Secaucus, N.J., 1982.

Sears, Stephen W. *George B. McClellan: The Young Napoleon.* New York, 1988.

Sears, Stephen W. *To the Gates of Richmond: The Peninsula Campaign.* New York, 1992.

BRIAN S. WILLS

MECKLENBURG COUNTY, NORTH CAROLINA. *See* Charlotte and Mecklenburg County, North Carolina.

MEDALS AND DECORATIONS. Medals and decorations, as they are understood today, had no real tradition in the American military at the time of the Civil War. Although the Congress had periodically voted to award special presentation swords or gold medals to high-ranking officers and rewarded officers' bravery with brevet rank, there were no badges of recognition for enlisted men. The Medal of Honor, the first U.S. decoration, was not established until 1862. The Confederates, raised in this tradition, which in part stemmed from American disdain of what was considered to be aristocratic European foppery, therefore had no particular reason to establish medals or decorations. As a result, although the Confederate Congress authorized the president to bestow "medals with proper devices" and "badges of distinction," little was actually done to recognize individual bravery, and the few systems that did exist were largely locally created.

A "Roll of Honor" system was implemented within the various armies, with the intention of recognizing valor and serving as a substitute until medals were issued, but the medals were in fact never struck and the Roll of Honor tended to become a quota system in which companies voted on a prescribed number of recipients for the honor. Since, in many cases, far more men were deserving of the honor than received it, most companies refused to vote at all, and the system was largely a failure.

The only medals known to have been actually presented to Confederate soldiers were what was known as the "Davis Guard Medals." This was a small round silver medal, made

DAVIS GUARD MEDALS. Silver dollar medal, designed by Charles Gottchalk and inscribed: "Wm Bailey, Sabine Pass, Sept. 8th, 1863." Photograph by Katherine Wetzel. THE MUSEUM OF THE CONFEDERACY, RICHMOND, VIRGINIA

out of Mexican silver dollars, with "Sabine Pass / Sept 8th / 1863" engraved on one side and "DG" and a Maltese cross on the other. President Davis presented forty-two of these medals to the members of the Davis Guard, a company of the First Texas Heavy Artillery, for their defense of the fortifications at Sabine Pass, Texas, in 1863.

Medallions were struck in France during the war for presentation to the members of the Stonewall Brigade, but they did not reach this country until after the war was over. They were offered for sale at veterans' reunions after 1895. All other Southern decorations, such as the United Daughters of the Confederacy's Southern Cross of Honor, were postwar decorations awarded to veterans or their families.

BIBLIOGRAPHY

Stiles, Robert. *Four Years under Marse Robert.* Washington, D.C., 1903.

Todd, Frederick P. *American Military Equipage, 1851–1872.* Vol. 2. Providence, R.I., 1977.

Les Jensen

MEDICAL DEPARTMENT. [*This entry discusses the organization of medical services in the Confederate army. For a more detailed discussion of Confederate army hospitals, see* Hospitals. *For a broader discussion of medical care, see* Health and Medicine; Nursing.] Organization of the Confederate States Medical Department began in March 1861, with the appointment of a surgeon general, four surgeons, and six assistant surgeons. The woeful inadequacy of this staff became quickly apparent, and the department was soon enlarged to meet the needs of both the field armies and the general hospitals.

The first surgeon general, David Camden De Leon, served only from May 6 to July 12, 1861. On July 30, Dr. Samuel Preston Moore, a career military surgeon, replaced him. Moore presided over the Medical Department for the remainder of the war. The surgeon general was assigned the rank of colonel (later brigadier general); surgeons, the rank of major (later colonel); and assistant surgeons, the rank of captain. Medical officer uniforms consisted of a cadet gray tunic with black facings and a stand-up collar. Trousers were dark blue with a black velvet stripe, edged with gold cord, running the length of the leg. White gloves, a star on the collar, a green silk sash, and a cap with the letters "M.S." completed the uniform. Surgeons rarely wore this dress in the field, however.

The surgeon general was responsible for the administration of the Medical Department and the hospitals; he appointed medical officers and directed their work. During the rapid expansion of the Medical Department in the early months of the war, some incompetent physicians entered the service. Moore devised a system of examinations to remove many of these dangerous individuals. He also oversaw and encouraged the publication of professional texts for use by medical personnel.

Units of the Medical Department paralleled those of the military departments. Each army had a medical director who reported to his military commander and to the surgeon general. The chief surgeon of each army division, who was free of regimental medical duties, reported to the army medical director. Brigade surgeons, who retained regimental responsibilities, reported to the chief surgeon. Finally, each regiment had a surgeon and assistant surgeon; the first reported to the brigade surgeon.

Hospital administrative districts were not necessarily the same as those of the military departments. Each hospital was supervised by a surgeon, who reported to one of eight medical directors of hospitals, who in turn reported to the surgeon general. Confusion existed during the first two years of the war because the local military commander or army medical directors could also issue orders to the hospital surgeons. But the interlocking lines of authority were separated in March 1863, so that hospital surgeons reported solely to the medical directors of hospitals who reported solely to the surgeon general.

The general hospitals, located in cities behind the lines of active campaigning, were organized so that state residents could be kept together. Although hospitals usually occupied both fixed structures and movable pavilions, in times of heavy fighting, churches, hotels, and private homes were pressed into service. Under optimal conditions, the Medical Department tried to maintain a ratio of one surgeon for 80 patients, but this sometimes had to be stretched to one surgeon for up to 250 patients. The department also established a system of "wayside hospitals" along railroads for use by furloughed and discharged soldiers returning home.

During the course of the war approximately 1,200 surgeons and 2,000 assistant surgeons served in the Confederate army, and 26 surgeons and 93 assistant surgeons served in the Confederate navy aboard ships and at five naval hospitals.

BIBLIOGRAPHY

Cunningham, Horace H. *Doctors in Gray: The Confederate Medical Service.* Baton Rouge, La., 1958.

Miller, Francis T., ed. *The Photographic History of the Civil War.* 10 vols. New York, 1911. Reprint, New York, 1957. 7:237–296, 349–352.

Herbert M. Schiller

MEDICINE. *See* Health and Medicine.

MEMMINGER, CHRISTOPHER G. (1803–1888), secretary of the treasury. Christopher Gustavus Memminger was born at Neyhinger in the Duchy of

CHRISTOPHER G. MEMMINGER. A late-nineteenth-century photograph. NAVAL HISTORICAL CENTER, WASHINGTON, D.C.

Württemberg on January 9, 1803; he was one of two foreign-born members of the Confederate cabinet. Brought to the United States in 1806, when he was orphaned, he was admitted in 1807 to the Charleston, South Carolina, Orphanage.

In 1814, he came to the attention of Thomas H. Bennett, a trustee of the orphanage and an antebellum governor of South Carolina. Bennett took Memminger into his home, assumed his guardianship, and later adopted him into his own large family. This arrangement was highly beneficial to Memminger, who gained thereby not only a happy home but the patronage of a powerful benefactor and the support of his able sons. Memminger could never have prospered to the same degree in his legal, political, and business careers or gained access to Charleston's closely knit, aristocratic society without this connection.

In 1819, Memminger graduated from South Carolina College in Charleston. Subsequently, he studied law with his uncle, Joseph Bennett, and was naturalized as an American citizen and admitted to the bar in early 1824. In his youth, Memminger displayed not only a considerable ability for hard work but also strong religious convictions. Even as a student he demonstrated a tendency toward the strict observance of rules and devotion to principles that both helped and hindered his effectiveness in public life.

Once launched on his legal career, Memminger, with his ability to present complicated legal matters in a lucid manner, soon became a leading member of the South Carolina bar. By 1860, he was a director of several companies and the owner of at least fifteen slaves, a large Charleston house, a plantation, and a summer home in Rock Hill, North Carolina. His estate, worth over $200,000, made him a Southern aristocrat.

His political career started with his serving one term as alderman in Charleston (1834–1836). During that period, he visited New England to study its educational system and on his return instituted a school board (on which he sat for many years) and free public schools for his own city. Subsequently, he served almost continuously as a member of the South Carolina Assembly (1836–1860). In that capacity he played an innovative role in promoting state support of public education, particularly the College of South Carolina.

During the nullification crisis of 1832 and 1833, Memminger had been a moderate Unionist. But he steadily became disillusioned with the Union, and by early 1860, after John Brown's raid on Harpers Ferry, he had become an advocate of secession on the basis of unified Southern action. In keeping with this plan, the South Carolina legislature sent him to Virginia to solicit the commonwealth's support for a simultaneous withdrawal of all the slave states from the Union. Because the Virginians were too badly divided to make a decision, the mission was a failure. It was significant that this reverse was attributed to Memminger's alleged lack of oratorical skills and his less than ingratiating manner.

In 1860, South Carolina seceded and Memminger was selected to go to Montgomery, Alabama, as part of the state's delegation. Before his departure, he had given some consideration to the legal needs of an independent Southern nation and had published his conclusions in "Plan of a Provisional Government for the Southern Confederacy." On the strength of this, Memminger at Montgomery was elected chairman of the committee to draft a provisional constitution. His work on that project was finished on February 8, 1861.

On February 18, Jefferson Davis arrived in Montgomery and took the oath of office as president. The next day he appointed Memminger as secretary of the treasury. The appointment was a surprise, particularly as Davis and Memminger were not acquainted. Mary Boykin Chesnut, in an addendum to her famous diary, claimed that Davis had planned to make Robert W. Barnwell, of South Carolina, secretary of state and Robert Toombs, of Georgia, secretary of the treasury. Barnwell declined the proffered honor and told Davis that the South Carolina delegation wanted Memminger at the Treasury. Davis shuffled his cabinet accordingly, moving Toombs to the State Department. Only after the appointment was announced was it discovered that the South Carolina delegation was allegedly "mortified." He was not, after all, a leading figure in South Carolina.

The new secretary's professional qualifications for his office were very limited. He was honest, hard-working, and genuinely devoted to the new country. He had been a director of the Farmers Exchange Bank of Charleston for many years and had served as a member or chairman of the South Carolina Assembly's Finance Committee from 1836 to that date. But South Carolina's finances offered an atypical experience for a man about to face record deficits, for the state budget was practically always balanced and the tax assessments on land had been frozen since 1840. Memminger thus had no experience with a modern internal revenue system of the sort that the Confederacy would need if it were to have an effective fiscal program.

Memminger was also a Jacksonian Democrat with a preference for a currency comprised solely of gold and silver coin. In two cases during the 1840s, Memminger had tried to strip some of the South Carolina banks of their charters for not paying gold or silver on their notes during a panic. His opposition to irredeemable bank notes included an emphatic distaste for a legal tender currency put out solely on the central government's credit. Yet Memminger swiftly found himself, contrary to his wishes, compelled to use Treasury notes to cover a considerable part of his expenditures.

Moreover, he had a fundamental fear of a strong central government and passionately believed in laissez-faire. He himself had voted for or moved amendments to the Constitution removing the general welfare clause and inserting a provision against government aid to any group. These restrictions were later to thwart plans for the government acquisition of or control over the cotton crop.

No less serious were his personality deficiencies. As a lawyer, he believed that all actions were either legal or illegal without any ambiguities. Still worse, he would declare a proposed solution to a problem illegal without exploring alternative approaches. When one of his proposals was rejected, he would passively accept defeat and fail to pursue the matter further. If the South were to succeed in its bid for independence, it needed to approach its problems in a pragmatic and innovative manner and with a will to persevere in the face of resistance.

Moreover, though witty and friendly within his family circle, Memminger in public life exhibited an austere personality that soon got him into trouble. He offended many members of Congress by insisting that they make appointments to see him and not just drop by. He told department employees to attend to their duties and not engage in idle conversations. His demands were reasonable enough, but he put them so tactlessly as to create much ill will.

More seriously, Memminger also quarreled with members of the cabinet. He refused to refund to Postmaster General John H. Regan the gold the post office had deposited in the Treasury until President Davis ordered him to do so. Memminger also upbraided the secretaries of war and the navy for their failure to use bonds to make payments and for their habit of making sudden demands for funds on the Treasury.

Other government officers complained that Memminger was overly preoccupied with legal technicalities, was slow and uncooperative in meeting their needs, and ungraciously acted as if he had been imposed upon whenever they requested his assistance. He also shared the public delusion that the war would not last long and was convinced therefore that no extraordinary measures were needed. His administration of the Treasury met with little approval and much condemnation both during and after the war. In retrospect he was clearly miscast for the role he was called upon to play.

Many of these problems would have been mitigated had Memminger exploited an important asset—his cordial personal relationship with the president. But Memminger apparently hesitated to invoke his chief's aid—to secure orders from Davis to other members of the cabinet requiring that they cooperate with him or support his financial proposals on the floor of Congress.

The secretary had no sooner organized his department with the help of former Washington officials than hostilities commenced on April 12, 1861. When Congress reconvened in May, Memminger laid before it a war finance plan based on suggestions made by John C. Calhoun in 1816. This program called for financing the war through the issue of Treasury notes, whose value would be sustained by making them fundable into bonds paying interest in coin. As a means of checking any redundancy of the currency thus emitted, not only would the circulation be limited by funding, but direct internal taxes were to be levied sufficient to pay the interest and the maturing principal.

The success of this plan required certain administrative actions. Among the most important was procuring the necessary Treasury notes and bonds from the printers. Memminger knew that the number of local printers was inadequate for the country's needs. Nonetheless, he opposed the creation of a Southern equivalent of the Bureau of Engraving and Printing on the doctrinaire ground that such a body would encourage the use of Treasury notes after the war, a policy he adamantly opposed. He also felt that the rights of the printers as independent contractors took precedence over the Treasury's needs. Under these circumstances, the printers were practically encouraged to do slipshod work and to be late in making deliveries. This left the entire government, particularly the army, without funds for paying the soldiers or furnishing them with essential supplies. This in turn directly promoted desertion.

Besides needing an ample supply of currency to pay the government's bills, the secretary needed a stock of coin with which to pay the interest on the public debt. Memminger failed to accumulate a reserve and refused to borrow for public use the idle coin in the banks' vaults. As a result, not only did coin payments on the debt go into default after July 1862, but bond prices in terms of gold fell, making the funding of notes financially unattractive. Thus one of the key means of sustaining the value of the Treasury notes was improvidently lost. Bond sales also depended upon opening offices to make bond purchases easy for the public. Yet prior to 1863, wanting to avoid unnecessary expense, Memminger failed to use the legal authority given to him to establish more offices. As a result, note funding and bond sales were significantly diminished.

To ensure the circulation of the Treasury notes, Memminger called together a bankers' convention in Richmond on July 24, 1861. At his suggestion, the banks agreed to receive and pay out such notes, thus making them the currency of the country. Thanks to this wise measure, the secretary secured credit for his issues without having to resort to a legal tender law as was the case in the North. This gain was unfortunately offset by the secretary's refusal to follow the advice of some bankers and others to curtail by coercion or voluntary means the issuance of rival currencies. Here again, Memminger refused to pursue the matter because it would impinge on the banks' state-granted privilege of issuing their own notes.

Another important matter was procuring from Congress adequate internal revenues. Memminger knew that the blockade would diminish customs receipts and that the cotton export duty would provide little revenue. Taxes on real estate, personal property (including slaves), incomes, and sales were clearly required.

In May 1861, Memminger asked for a direct tax, but since the president sent no message backing him, Congress put off consideration of this unpopular step until July. Then, again without support from the president or the cabinet, Memminger tried to secure the passage of a modest $25 million tax bill. Congress, after bitter debate and opposition from the large slaveholders, reluctantly complied.

Despite ample warnings from the bankers that the war tax of August 19, 1861, needed to be doubled or quadrupled in order to provide even minimal revenues, Memminger did not request any new levies in 1861. Nor did he assert himself during all of 1862. Instead, he made only weak tax proposals in very general terms. Still worse, he wasted precious time on an abortive forced-loan plan (in essence a 20 percent income tax in return for which the taxpayer would be given 6 percent bonds) and a scheme calling for a state guarantee of the Confederate debt. He did not force the tax issue until January 1863, when he belatedly procured a supporting message from President Davis. Even then, his proposals were of questionable legality and were not accompanied by draft legislation.

In consequence, the tax law of April 24, 1863, enacted two years after the war began, was seriously deficient. It did not tax slaves, despite the secretary's observation that the war was being fought to protect their $3.5 billion investment in slavery. The law also taxed other items far too lightly and ordered few collections before January 1864. As a result the currency grew to nearly $900 million and the country was overwhelmed by a disastrous inflation.

Several other economic matters also required Memminger's attention. The blockade had rendered the export of the South's cotton crop difficult, and the public was clamoring for a scheme that would harness Southern staples to the war effort.

For a while, Memminger temporized, opposing and then supporting proposals that would have the government buy the cotton crop. In October 1861, the secretary finally decided, at the behest of the bankers, to declare such a plan illegal. Had the question been reformulated as a loan by the planters to the government (the Treasury was purchasing with bonds the goods and services needed by the army), then something could have been done. As it was, a cotton purchasing operation was put off until April 1862. This resulted in planter resistance to taxation, added to the costs of acquisition, and seriously delayed shipments abroad on the government's account.

A closely related question was whether, under the King Cotton doctrine, cotton shipments should be withheld with a view to coercing Great Britain and France to recognize the Confederacy. Memminger opposed the vigilante committees that were trying to prevent cotton exports, but did so solely on legal grounds. He made no effort to check their activities and refused to make a public issue of the question. As a result, they seriously inhibited the export of cotton, which Memminger knew to be essential.

A third cotton-related question was whether the government should take an active role in organizing blockade-running operations. At George A. Trenholm's suggestion, the secretary proposed to the cabinet that the Confederacy buy two available shipping lines to promote direct trade with Europe. Thwarted by the opposition of the cabinet and his own inability to convince the president of the necessity of making this purchase, Memminger dropped any further effort to buy or lease ships on the Treasury's account. The abdication of responsibility in this area to the War Department greatly delayed cotton shipments.

Finally, given the shortage of foreign exchange from the sale of produce abroad, the secretary, who had to cover War and Navy department expenditures, realized early on that a foreign loan was urgently needed. He requested and received authority to sell bonds abroad by the act of May 16, 1861. But he failed to pursue the matter, and by 1863, when the so-called Erlanger loan was floated in Europe, the tide of battle had turned against the South. As a result, the Treasury had to borrow money on onerous terms and the funds realized were too little and too late to maintain the government's credit in London or to meet the Confederacy's pressing economic and military needs.

By February 1864, after three years in office, Memminger found himself a discredited man. Congress paid little or no attention to his recommendations. The currency had practically lost its value, the government's credit at home and abroad was badly damaged, and the tax structure was unfair and ineffective.

In May 1864, the House of Representatives passed a resolution of no confidence in the secretary, and Memminger, weary of his thankless task, promptly resigned in July after Congress adjourned. He was succeeded by his good friend and fellow South Carolinian George A. Trenholm.

With Charleston under siege and his home within the range of Union guns, Memminger retired to his summer home at Rock Hill, North Carolina, where he remained for the duration of the war. His home in Charleston was captured and pillaged in February 1865 and the property confiscated and later used as an orphanage for black children.

Unlike many of his fellow Confederate leaders, Memminger was neither arrested nor imprisoned. He procured a pardon in 1867 and resumed his business activities and law practice. He also participated in the bitter debates that followed the war, defending himself against unfair or inaccurate accusations regarding his role in the Confederacy's defeat.

In 1876, he was once again elected to the South Carolina Assembly. As part of the first legislature since the overthrow of the Radical Republicans in Columbia, he played a key role in reorganizing the state's finances. He was instrumental in preventing the government from abolishing the statewide public school system, which had been one of the major accomplishments of Reconstruction in the state. Overcoming bitter resistance, he also established with state support a college for blacks.

Retiring from public life in 1879, Memminger died in Charleston on March 7, 1888.

[*See also* Public Finance; Treasury Department.]

BIBLIOGRAPHY

Ball, Douglas B. *Financial Failure and Confederate Defeat.* Urbana, Ill., 1991.

Capers, Henry Dickson. *The Life and Times of C. G. Memminger.* Richmond, Va., 1893.

Dowdey, Clifford. *Experiment in Rebellion.* Garden City, N.Y., 1946.

Hendrick, Burton J. *Statesmen of the Lost Cause: Jefferson Davis and His Cabinet.* New York, 1939.

Lee, Charles Robert, Jr. *The Confederate Constitutions.* Chapel Hill, N.C., 1963.

Schwab, John Christopher. *The Confederate States of America, 1861–1865: A Financial and Industrial History of the South during the Civil War.* New York, 1901.

Todd, Richard Cecil. *Confederate Finance.* Athens, Ga., 1954.

Douglas B. Ball

MEMOIRS. *See* Diaries, Letters, and Memoirs.

MEMORIAL DAY. The celebration of Confederate Memorial Day, an annual ceremony honoring the Confederate dead, began in the spring of 1866. That January women in Columbus, Georgia, issued a public call to decorate Confederate graves, and for this they are sometimes credited with establishing the holiday. Jackson and Vicksburg, Mississippi, along with several other Southern communities, have challenged Columbus, Georgia's, claim. Most likely, several communities acted independently. The idea apparently grew out of the private decoration of soldiers' graves, though Southerners also borrowed from similar customs in other cultures.

During the next fifty years, more and more Southern communities celebrated the holiday, usually under the charge of a ladies' memorial association or, later, the United Daughters of the Confederacy. The date of the observance varied from place to place. In the Deep South most communities celebrated April 26, the anniversary of Joseph E. Johnston's surrender; in South and North Carolina towns more commonly chose May 10, the date of Thomas J. ("Stonewall") Jackson's death and Jefferson Davis's capture; towns in Virginia and other areas celebrated on still different dates. After Davis's death in 1889, some communities and a few states began to observe the holiday on his birthday, June 3.

As with the date, the nature of the celebration took various forms in different communities and changed over time. In the early years, citizens in some towns simply went together to the cemetery and decorated the graves. In others they held more formal programs that included hymns, prayers, and speeches in defense of the soldiers' honor and the nobility of the Southern cause. In either case, the central ritual was the placing of greenery or flowers on the Confederate graves. These ceremonies both honored the fallen soldiers and allowed survivors to mourn, thereby distancing themselves from the cause but still expressing hope for its, and their, eventual vindication. As a sense of vindication developed in the 1880s and 1890s, the tone of the celebration changed. The central ritual remained the decoration of the graves, but the occasion became somewhat less funereal and more festive. Bands now participated, often playing "Dixie," and speeches became more common. During the same years, a few cities invited Union veterans to participate with the former Confederates. The new practices reflected changes in the Lost Cause. The passions and issues of the war had begun to dissipate, and Confederate soldiers had come to serve as symbols not of rebellion but of loyalty to leaders and country.

As the veterans died and interest in the Lost Cause faded during the twentieth century, the holiday became less important in Southern culture. By the end of World War II, many communities no longer held celebrations; today only a few do. Eight Southern states still recognize Confederate Memorial Day, although not all of them close state offices on that day. Florida and Georgia observe April 26, South and North Carolina May 10, and Kentucky and Louisiana June 3. Alabama and Mississippi, making concessions to modern practices, celebrate the fourth Monday in May as Confederate Memorial Day.

BIBLIOGRAPHY

Confederated Southern Memorial Association. *History of the Confederated Memorial Associations of the South.* New Orleans, La., 1904.

Foster, Gaines M. *Ghosts of the Confederacy: Defeat, the Lost Cause, and the Emergence of the New South, 1865–1913.* New York, 1987.

Wilson, Charles Reagan. *Baptized in Blood: The Religion of the Lost Cause, 1865–1920.* Athens, Ga., 1980.

Gaines M. Foster

MEMORIAL ORGANIZATIONS. Efforts to honor the Confederate dead began shortly after the war ended. Although several groups claimed to be first, probably the earliest memorial organization was founded in Columbus, Georgia, in March 1866 by a group of women determined to decorate the graves of soldiers; in July of the same year, the women of the Soldiers' Aid Society of Wilmington, North Carolina, formed the Ladies' Memorial Association of Wilmington for the same purpose. Similar local groups developed in all parts of the South, with goals limited to decorating graves with flowers, often on a day set aside for the purpose. These efforts eventually became Confederate Memorial Day, an annual event whose date varies from state to state.

More widespread memorial organizations were founded in the later 1860s and the 1870s. Some of the organizations were military in nature, such as the Association of the Army of Northern Virginia and the Association of the Army of Tennessee. A variety of local and state organizations were formed, especially in Richmond and other cities. These groups held annual reunions, arranged for burial of soldiers, and provided benevolence for needy veterans and families. They celebrated Confederate Memorial Day throughout the South; memorials were also held on the death of Jefferson Davis and other Confederate leaders. They were joined by the Southern Historical Society (1869) and the Lee Memorial Association (1870), whose goals included preserving the Southern past and glorifying its heroes.

The Confederate Veterans, an umbrella organization of local groups, was founded in 1889 in New Orleans and quickly became a prominent Southern organization. Its first commander in chief was Gen. John B. Gordon, who retained his post until 1904. This group, which restricted membership to veterans, sought both to memorialize the war and to provide needed services to its increasingly elderly membership. Several other umbrella organizations were also formed, including the Sons of the Confederacy (1896), which allowed male descendants of veterans to join, and the United Daughters of the Confederacy (1895), which included any female relative of men who had served. The United Daughters of the Confederacy created the Children of the Confederacy (1896), a group committed to keeping the memory of the Confederacy alive among young people. The official organ for these groups and others was the *Confederate Veteran,* a periodical started in Nashville in 1893 by Sumner A. Cunningham, who remained its editor for twenty-one years.

The United Confederate Veterans was a large-scale organization: its peak membership was 80,000, about one-third of the surviving veterans in 1903. Organized along military lines, it sponsored local meetings of individual camps and annual national reunions. The organization devoted its attention to organizing public ceremonies such as dedications of monuments and Memorial Day celebrations, relief efforts for veterans and their families, drives to persuade Southern state governments to provide pensions and establish soldiers' homes, and burial societies to bury the dead from battlefields, locate and mark graves, care for cemeteries, and pay for funerals. It also boasted a Historical Committee (1892) to oversee the writing of Confederate history, aid state historical associations, and help support Confederate museums. The United Confederate Veterans met jointly with the Grand Army of the Republic in 1913 at Gettysburg, where they reenacted Pickett's charge. The group's last reunion was held in Selma, Alabama, in 1950, with one veteran in attendance.

The United Daughters of the Confederacy (UDC) shared many of the concerns of the United Confederate Veterans and added new activities of their own. Because lineal descendants of Confederate women and nieces of soldiers were included, the organization continues to the present day. In addition to raising money for monuments, caring for graves, engaging in relief work, and sponsoring local, state, and national meetings, the UDC has worked to ensure that Confederate history is taught according to its convictions. To this end it has sponsored scholarships, raised funds for libraries at home and abroad, opened "relic rooms" throughout the South to preserve Confederate artifacts, and led in the development of the Confederate Museum in the old White House of the Confederacy in Richmond. The UDC also offered the Cross of Honor beginning in 1900; this was a medal bestowed for their endurance on men who had served in the Confederate army or navy. Later, they offered the Cross of Military Service to lineal descendants of Confederate veterans who served in other U.S. wars.

The UDC had a notable ability to raise funds for monuments. Many towns owed their courthouse statue of local Confederate leaders to the UDC, which also developed many national projects, alone or in conjunction with other groups. One monument was a memorial to "the faithful slave," a massive boulder placed at Harpers Ferry in 1931 to commemorate former slave Heyward Shepherd, who refused to join John Brown's raid. Another, sponsored jointly with the United Confederate Veterans, was a memorial to the women of the Confederacy. The two groups disagreed about whether women's martial or nurturing aspects should be celebrated in the design, but the conflict was ultimately decided in favor of the men's design for a nurturing figure. The monument was dedicated in 1906. Monuments were also erected in honor of Varina ("Winnie") Davis, the original daughter of the Confederacy; Thomas J. ("Stonewall") Jackson; Robert E. Lee; Jefferson Davis; Henry Wirz, the Andersonville commandant who was executed as a war criminal; other military leaders; and various battlefields.

[*See also* Confederate Veteran; Lee Memorial Association; Memorial Day; Monuments and Memorials; Soldiers' Homes; Southern Historical Association.]

BIBLIOGRAPHY

Foster, Gaines M. *Ghosts of the Confederacy: Defeat, the Lost Cause, and the Emergence of the New South, 1865 to 1913.* New York, 1987.

Poppenheim, Mary B., et al., eds. *The History of the United Daughters of the Confederacy.* 2 vols. N.p., n.d.

White, William W. *The Confederate Veteran.* Tuscaloosa, Ala., 1962.

Wilson, Charles Reagan. *Baptized in Blood: The Religion of the Lost Cause, 1865–1920.* Athens, Ga., 1980.

MARLI F. WEINER

MEMPHIS, TENNESSEE. An important Mississippi River port, Memphis was the fastest growing and second largest city in the state in 1861. It was the sixth largest city in the Confederacy with a population of 22,263 including 3,684 slaves, 198 free blacks, and 18,381 whites. About 60 percent of the free population was American-born; the immigrant population was largely German and Irish.

The economy of the city was based primarily on the wholesale distribution of merchandise within a radius of 150 miles and the cotton market; the city was the trade center for the region's cotton planters. The delivery of merchandise into Memphis and the shipment of cotton out to textile mills, mainly in the Midwest and Northeast, made the city one of the busiest river ports in the United States. Four railroads provided overland transportation.

In addition to retail and wholesale merchants, Memphis advertised twelve wagon builders, six carriage makers, nine slave dealers, five book and job printers, four iron railing manufacturers, three flour mills, two brass and iron foundries, a railcar builder, a sugar refinery, and a brewery. The cotton trade involved approximately 125 firms that provided the services of buyers, brokers, and factors, and the facilities of gins, warehouses, oil processors, and mills.

The people of Memphis hesitated at first to join the secession movement, but when the polls opened on June 8, 1861, for a second state ballot on the question, only five Memphians cast their votes to remain in the Union. At a mass meeting a few days before, three thousand people had voted to declare the city independent of the United States and specified that if Tennessee did not follow suit, Memphis should withdraw from the state and become part of Mississippi. The young men of the city demonstrated an especially strong commitment to the South, organizing seventy-two volunteer companies for the Confederate army.

Its Mississippi River location made Memphis a target of strategic importance. The Federal high command early determined to split the South and supply its own armies in the West by controlling the river from St. Louis to the Gulf of Mexico.

In the late winter of 1862, the Union army broadened its campaign in the West by seizing control of the Cumberland and Tennessee rivers and occupying Nashville, the state capital. Just before the fall of Nashville, Memphis had welcomed Governor Isham G. Harris and a number of state officials seeking a safe haven for the seat of government. Harris convened the legislature in the city on February 20, but, in the absence of a quorum on succeeding days, he adjourned the body March 20 and departed to join Tennessee troops in the field.

Moving down the Mississippi, Union forces captured Confederate river defenses in a brisk battle at New Madrid, Missouri, on March 13. Within a month they surged farther downstream to assault and take possession of Island Number 10.

After the Union victory at the Battle of Shiloh (April 6–7), the Confederate command in the West withdrew most of its forces into northern Mississippi, leaving Memphis protected by garrisons at Forts Randolph and Pillow. When these troops were ordered to Mississippi on June 1, the city's defense was left to eight Confederate gunboats. But the gunboat defense was unsuccessful. On June 6 a Federal fleet of six gunboats and four rams challenged the defenders, and in just over an hour it controlled the river at Memphis. Only one Confederate gunboat escaped downriver; the others were sunk, burned, or run aground.

The U.S. flag was raised in Memphis the same day, and Union troops instituted military rule that lasted past the end of the war. By nightfall approximately one thousand Memphis residents, alarmed by the capture of their city, had fled southward by rail. Using impressed slave labor, the Union army hastened to erect Fort Pickering, an impressive installation that could accommodate ten thousand soldiers. Never attacked, Pickering was important primarily as a symbol of Union control.

Command of the city was held in succession by at least ten Union army officers. Generals Ulysses S. Grant, William Tecumseh Sherman, Stephen A. Hurlbut, and Cadwallader C. Washburn had the most active tenures. The administration of Military Governor Andrew Johnson at Nashville had little effect on Memphis until near the end of the war, when the governor called for statewide elections.

A flotilla of trading boats had followed the invading army into the port, bringing both new merchandise and new merchants to the city. From the first, the Federals encouraged the resumption and extension of commercial activities by businessmen old and new. With increasing success, they induced planters to bring their cotton to market in the face of Confederate insistence that it be withheld. By 1863 commerce was exceeding prewar levels.

The high levels of economic activity were due in important part to smuggling or underground trade with the Confederates, well represented in the nearby rural countryside by partisans and guerrillas. Union troops were never able to clear West Tennessee of the irregular Southern units who funneled smuggled supplies to regular army forces. The importance to the South of a Union-controlled Memphis was recognized by the various Federal commanders. They surely agreed with their colleague General Washburn when he declared in 1864, "Memphis has been of more value to the Southern Confederacy since it fell into Federal hands than Nassau." In response, Washburn clamped down on trade so stringently that commerce in Memphis came to a virtual standstill during the last few months of the war.

Although most white residents of the city were strongly sympathetic with the Confederacy, very few seemed to expect that they would be liberated by the Southern army. Hopes were raised for a few hours on August 21, 1864, when Gen. Nathan Bedford Forrest led a detachment of cavalrymen into the heart of the city to divert Federal attention from Confederate troop movements in northern Mississippi. Forrest took a number of prisoners and withdrew before the surprised enemy could offer significant resistance. The quick raid was the last combat action of the war at Memphis.

Using bluffs, threats, and intimidation, the military commanders of the city tried unendingly to return the loyalty of the populace to the Union. Recalcitrant Confederate sympathizers were sometimes jailed and often threatened with banishment. Loyalty oaths, required of merchants and other holders of privilege licenses, were pro-

MEMPHIS NAVY YARD. View from the Arkansas shore, drawn by Wade. NAVAL HISTORICAL CENTER, WASHINGTON, D.C.

moted for the entire citizenry. Although by January 1863 it was estimated that at least 15,000 citizens had taken the oath, skeptical generals tried other measures of loyalty. General Hurlbut ordered all civilians not employed by government to register either as loyal to the United States, enemy of the United States, or subject of a foreign power. In less than thirty days, 11,652 had registered as loyal, 661 as subjects of foreign powers, and 10 as enemies. General Sherman demonstrated the consequences of disloyalty when he burned the nearby town of Randolph in retaliation for its harboring Southern guerrillas who fired at Union gunboats.

Despite flight to the south by some of its citizens and the absence of a large number in the Confederate military service, the population of Memphis grew and generally prospered from 1862 to 1865. By 1866, the city held approximately 35,000 people: 21,000 whites and 14,000 blacks.

The commanding generals interfered very little in the operation of local government. They insisted that the city government fulfill its responsibilities, especially in the areas of police and fire protection, street maintenance, schools, and the administration of recorders' or police courts. An exception to this general practice of restraint was an act by General Washburn in 1864. Doubting the loyalty of a popularly elected mayor, Washburn set aside the results of the city election, declared martial law, and appointed to office all of those just elected with the exception of the mayor. A popular election a year later returned the ousted mayor to office.

Believing it to be in their best interests for life in the city to go on as normally as possible, Federal commanders usually gave free rein to educational, cultural, religious, fraternal, and social practices. One result was that public schools operated without interruption; another was that the school board incorporated schools for blacks into the city system in 1864. There were limits to freedom such as the prohibition of "treasonous" or pro-Confederate statements at all public functions, including worship, and the banning of all pro-Southern newspapers. The publisher of the *Daily Appeal* fled southward with his presses and continued to publish from points in Mississippi and Alabama. The *Appeal* was returned to Memphis after Appomattox.

The greatest change the war brought to Memphis was the unprecedented influx of blacks who first came as refugee slaves and remained to become free. Because they were runaways from neighboring plantations, the blacks had no jobs and no means of support. Some were impressed to work on military fortifications, but most eventually were placed in refugee camps just outside the city. From the camps they were employed to plant and harvest agricultural produce needed by the Union army. In November 1864, the army attempted to recruit five companies of black soldiers but at first raised only two. Other blacks volunteered soon afterward, probably attracted by a generous cash enlistment bonus put up by local whites.

Spared significant war damage, Memphis emerged from the conflict with its infrastructure largely intact and its commerce thriving. The greatest concern of the city in 1865 was the uncertainty of future relationships between the newly freed blacks and the white majority.

BIBLIOGRAPHY

Capers, Gerald M., Jr. *The Biography of a River Town; Memphis: Its Heroic Age.* Chapel Hill, N.C., 1939.

Harkins, John E. *Metropolis of the American Nile.* Edited by Charles W. Crawford. Cambridge, Md., 1982.

Hooper, Ernest Walter. "Memphis: Federal Occupation and Reconstruction, 1862–1870." Ph.D. diss., University of North Carolina, Chapel Hill, 1957.

Keating, John M. *History of the City of Memphis and Shelby County, Tennessee, with Illustrations and Biographical Sketches of Some of Its Prominent Citizens.* 2 vols. in 1. Syracuse, N.Y., 1888.

Parks, Joseph H. "A Confederate Trade Center under Federal Occupation: Memphis, 1862 to 1865." *Journal of Southern History* 7 (August 1941): 289–314.

Parks, Joseph H. "Memphis under Military Rule, 1862 to 1865." *East Tennessee Historical Society Publications,* no. 14 (1942): 31–58.

Young, John Preston, ed. *Standard History of Memphis, Tennessee, from a Study of the Original Sources.* Knoxville, Tenn., 1912.

WALTER T. DURHAM

MENEES, THOMAS (1823–1905), congressman from Tennessee. Elected in November 1861 to represent the Eighth Tennessee District in the First Congress, Menees easily won reelection two years later. During both terms he served on the Medical Department Committee—a judicious assignment, since he had been trained in medicine and possessed more than fifteen years' experience in the field. He also was appointed to the Printing and Public Lands committees.

Initially, Menees, a staunch secessionist, resisted compulsory conscription as a subversion of state rights. Yet when the spring of 1862 brought disastrous defeats to the Confederate army—especially in his home district—Menees supported the draft, even though he voted to retain state control over organization and the appointment of officers and still favored the maintenance of local defense forces. Later in the year, in the most significant of the seventeen bills he introduced while in Congress, he moved to abolish the draft exemption for employees whose businesses earned profits in excess of 25 percent. The amendment lost. By February 1864, near the end of his first term,

Menees had voted to abolish all individual exemptions and to reduce others. He also reversed himself regarding the thorny habeas corpus issue. Although he supported the 1862 measure that authorized President Jefferson Davis to suspend temporarily the privilege of the writ, he consistently opposed further authorization.

Arrested by Federal forces but paroled in late July 1865, Menees returned the following month to his home in Robertson County, Tennessee. He soon relocated to Nashville, where he later taught medicine.

BIBLIOGRAPHY

Amnesty File. Thomas Menees. Microcopy M1003, Roll 50. Record Group 94. National Archives, Washington, D.C.

Journal of the Congress of the Confederate States of America, 1861–1865. Washington, D.C., 1904–1905.

Porter, James D. *Tennessee.* Vol. 8 of *Confederate Military History.* Edited by Clement A. Evans. Atlanta, 1899. Vol. 10 of extended ed. Wilmington, N.C., 1987.

Speer, William S., ed. *Sketches of Prominent Tennesseans.* Nashville, Tenn., 1988.

Warner, Ezra J., and W. Buck Yearns. *Biographical Register of the Confederate Congress.* Baton Rouge, La., 1975.

R. B. Rosenburg

MENNONITES. Mennonites were religious pacifists who opposed participation in war, revolution, and slavery, all three of which were central to the Confederate cause. In the South they were concentrated in the militarily and economically strategic Shenandoah Valley of Virginia. Even before Virginia's secession they were pressured to vote for the secession they opposed, under threat of violence.

When the war began they were required to report for militia service; they complied reluctantly, still determined to refrain from violence, though some succumbed. By 1862 Bishop Samuel Coffman was encouraging noncooperation. Men hid in secret places in the neighborhood or the mountains or took flight northward into the Union. Two imprisoned fugitive groups were released when the Virginia legislature passed a law on March 29, 1862, that exempted members of peace churches who paid a tax penalty. One month later this state provision was superseded by a Confederate conscription law. Not until October was a similar Confederate exemption measure passed. But local conditions in the valley continued to deteriorate. In late 1864, when Gen. Philip H. Sheridan devastated the valley, many Mennonite young men, as well as families, went north with Sheridan's wagon train. Those that stayed behind eked out a meager existence.

Their contacts with the larger Mennonite group in the North and their fears generated by secession prompted a pro-Union stance. So did their inability to condone a rebellion against an established government. But Mennonites did not share the intense nationalistic fervor with which the Union pursued total victory over the Confederacy. The essential basis of their opposition was not political, but religious.

BIBLIOGRAPHY

Brunk, Harry A. *History of the Mennonites in Virginia.* Vol. 1. Harrisonburg, Va., 1959.

Horst, Samuel L. *Mennonites in the Confederacy: A Study in Civil War Pacifism.* Scottdale, Pa., 1967.

Schlabach, Theron F. *Peace, Faith, Nation: Mennonites and Amish in Nineteenth-Century America.* Scottdale, Pa., 1988.

Wright, Edward Needles. *Conscientious Objectors in the Civil War.* Philadelphia, 1931.

Samuel L. Horst

MERCER, HUGH WEEDON (1808–1877), brigadier general. Born in Fredericksburg, Virginia, Mercer, the grandson and namesake of a revolutionary war brigadier general, attended West Point, graduating third in his class

Hugh Weedon Mercer. Library of Congress

in 1828. Assigned in 1834 to quartermaster duty in Savannah, Georgia, Mercer resigned his commission in 1835 and married a local woman. He was a cashier at the Planters' Bank when the war began, although active in the militia.

Serving initially as the colonel of the First Georgia Regiment, Mercer was promoted to brigadier general on October 29, 1861, and assigned to defend the Georgia coast near Brunswick. Finding the task difficult with his limited number of troops, Mercer began the process of evacuating Brunswick in February 1862, recommending to the War Department that he be given explicit orders to burn the town for the "moral effect it would have upon the enemy."

On May 26, 1862, Mercer assumed command of the Second Military District of South Carolina. Less than two weeks later, he was sent back to Savannah ultimately to become commander of the Military District of Georgia, comprising the entire state excluding the defenses of the Apalachicola River and its main affluents. For the next two years Mercer worked to defend eastern Georgia from Federal invasion despite a dearth of manpower (troops and slaves). He complained to Secretary of War James A. Seddon that "the want of troops begets the necessity of additional works, and the want of labor renders it impossible to meet that necessity."

Mercer was relieved from command of the Military District of Georgia on April 26, 1864, and sent with his brigade to Dalton to reinforce Gen. Joseph E. Johnston, who was preparing to defend northern Georgia against Maj. Gen. William Tecumseh Sherman. Considering its inexperience, Mercer's brigade fought well during the campaign, especially at the Battle of Kennesaw Mountain. On July 22, during the opening phases of the Battle of Atlanta, Mercer assumed command of his division, replacing Maj. Gen. W. H. T. Walker who had been killed, but the division was disbanded on July 24. Although Mercer returned to brigade command, doubts about his health and fitness for field duty led to his removal the following day. He returned to Savannah, where he remained until the city was evacuated on the evening of December 20–21.

Mercer was paroled at Macon, Georgia, on May 13, 1865. After the war he lived in Savannah and Baltimore before traveling to Baden-Baden, Germany, for reasons of health. There he died and lies buried in an unknown grave.

BIBLIOGRAPHY

Derry, Joseph T. *Georgia*. Vol. 6 of *Confederate Military History*. Edited by Clement A. Evans. Atlanta, 1899. Vol. 7 of extended ed. Wilmington, N.C., 1987.

Hewitt, Lawrence L. "Hugh Weedon Mercer." In *The Confederate General*. Edited by William C. Davis. Vol. 4. Harrisburg, Pa., 1991.

Warner, Ezra J. *Generals in Gray: Lives of the Confederate Commanders*. Baton Rouge, La., 1959.

ALAN C. DOWNS

MERIDIAN CAMPAIGN. In the winter of 1863–1864, Gen. William Tecumseh Sherman decided to remove all Confederate threats to the Mississippi River. The river at Vicksburg was now under Union control, but east of Vicksburg the countryside was not secured. Of special interest was Meridian, a town in east-central Mississippi. Because two railroads—the Mobile and Ohio and the Southern—crossed there, the town was critical to Confederate communications and supply. After a visit to his home in Ohio, Sherman traveled down the Mississippi, now full of ice, to Memphis. There he gathered troops for a march to Meridian to break up the two railroads and, he hoped, "to punish the rebel General Forrest." Nathan Bedford Forrest posed a threat to the crucial Union supply routes in Tennessee.

Sherman planned to gather about 10,000 men from Gen. Stephen A. Hurlbut's forces in Memphis, journey downriver on steamers, and collect an equal number of men from Gen. James B. McPherson in Vicksburg. He would also send a force from Vicksburg up the Yazoo River to confuse the Confederates about his main goal—Meridian. Several infantry companies, under the command of Col. James H. Coates, were to leave Vicksburg on five transports, protected by five gunboats, and move toward Yazoo City. They would destroy means of crossing the river, take as much cotton as possible, and encourage the planters to cooperate with the Union in return for free access to the port of Vicksburg. In addition, Gen. William Sooy Smith was to move overland through northeast Mississippi from Memphis to Meridian with a cavalry force of 7,000. Sherman warned Smith about General Forrest and his "peculiar force."

Disembarking at Vicksburg, Sherman's forces moved on February 3 directly for Meridian. Responsible for protecting the area was Confederate Gen. Leonidas Polk, who was headquartered at Meridian. He had only 9,000 men plus Gen. Stephen D. Lee's cavalry corps of 7,500 men. Sherman had confused the Southerners by feinting an attack at Mobile, and they had located some of their resources there. General Forrest, coming from Tennessee with about 3,000 men, was in the northeastern part of the state.

As Sherman was leaving Vicksburg, Colonel Coates was receiving Confederate artillery fire on his Yazoo expedition. He disembarked to engage Gen. Lawrence Sullivan Ross's Texas Brigade. The Texans, some protected by a log fortification and some fighting on foot at twelve paces with pistols, forced the Union soldiers to fall back and move away down the river.

On February 4, Sherman's forces met General Lee's cavalry and skirmished with Gen. Wirt Adams's brigade near Jackson. The skirmishing continued almost nonstop—one skirmish on February 5 continued for eighteen miles— but the superior Union forces could not be checked.

Sherman's troops, on the morning of February 6, occupied Jackson, Mississippi's capital, about ninety miles from Meridian. Two Confederate divisions arrived too late to defend the city. As the Union troops left Jackson on the seventh, the Confederates attacked but, because of the closed ranks of the Union army, could neither inflict significant damage nor slow its progress.

Coates had occupied Yazoo City but left to go upriver to Greenwood, collecting cotton along the way. He returned downriver, and about six miles from Yazoo City went ashore. Here his forces again met General Ross's cavalry, which launched a heavy attack; one part of Coates's force was surrounded for four hours but refused three times to surrender. Eventually, after the Union soldiers were able to unite in a well-defended position, the Confederates left Yazoo City. The next day their opponents also evacuated.

Meanwhile, against lessening resistance, Sherman moved to Decatur, a hamlet about twenty miles west of Meridian, and bivouacked for the night. During the late hours, Wirt Adams's cavalry attacked, and Sherman, who had been left unguarded because of a mix-up, came close to being captured before the Southerners retreated.

By February 14, Sherman and his men had reached Meridian, having traveled 150 miles in eleven days. In Meridian they began a systematic campaign of destruction. For five days they laid waste to arms and supplies with "axes, crowbars, sledges, clawbars, and with fire." According to Sherman, "Meridian, with its depots, store-houses, arsenal, hospitals, offices, hotels, and cantonments no longer exists." His troops set to work tearing up the railroads that ran both north-south and east-west for about twelve miles each way. They also ravaged the surrounding area, destroying roads, bridges, culverts, and sawmills. With this mission fulfilled, their other goal, to destroy Forrest, remained; but in Sherman's words, "In this we failed utterly."

Gen. William Sooy Smith had been ordered to start from Memphis on February 1 to seek out Forrest, but he delayed leaving for ten days. On his way, his 7,000 men encountered Forrest's troops near West Point. On February 21 the two sides skirmished for an hour and a half. As the Union forces withdrew, moving north, Forrest and his cavalry followed. After Forrest decided that Smith and his forces "had begun a rapid and systematic retreat," he gathered reinforcements and charged their rear. The retreating men stopped their northern flight twice to resist the pursuit, but without success. In all, Forrest pursued Smith for about eighty miles. Smith's casualties (killed, wounded, and captured) were 388; Forrest's, 144. Had Forrest waited a few days before attacking, he might have been even more successful. At the time, General Lee was moving to join him but did not get to the area until February 23. Lee was disappointed at the mix-up; even with combined forces the Confederates would still have been outnumbered by Smith's command.

By February 20, Sherman had grown weary of waiting for Smith and had received no word of his misfortunes, so he and his troops started slowly back to Vicksburg. In fact, Sherman did not learn what had happened to Smith for about a week, and he never forgave Smith for his failure.

Sherman arrived back in Vicksburg at the end of February. The Meridian expedition had given him experience in the kind of warfare he would practice so successfully on his march through Georgia. His troops had proved capable of traveling great distances—in one short month they had marched from 360 to 450 miles—and they had been able to live off the land. Sherman also practiced the destructiveness for which he became renowned. The Union casualties were fairly low: of the total of 912, only 5 officers and 108 enlisted men were killed, 385 were wounded, and 414 were captured or missing. Total Confederate casualties are unknown.

BIBLIOGRAPHY

Henry, Robert S. *"First with the Most" Forrest.* Indianapolis, 1944. Reprint, Jackson, Tenn., 1969.

Lee, Stephen D. "The War in Mississippi after the Fall of Vicksburg, July 4, 1863." *Publications of the Mississippi Historical Society* 10 (1909): 47–52.

U.S. War Department. *War of the Rebellion: A Compilation of the Official Records of the Union and Confederate Armies.* Washington, D.C., 1880–1901. Ser. 1, vol. 32, pt. 1, pp. 164–391.

RAY SKATES

MERRICK, CAROLINE E. (1825–1908), suffragist and temperance advocate. Caroline Elizabeth Thomas

Merrick was born at Cottage Hall Plantation in East Feliciana, Louisiana, on November 24, 1825. As a child, she was influenced by her stepmother, Susan Brewer, a schoolteacher from Massachusetts, who insisted the Thomas children receive a rigorous and liberal education. In 1840, Merrick married Edwin Thomas Merrick, a lawyer and plantation owner considerably older than she. The plantation, Myrtle Grove in Clinton, Louisiana, was Merrick's primary residence all her life. Following her husband's appointment to the Louisiana Supreme Court in 1855, the family also maintained a home in New Orleans.

During the Civil War, Merrick and her four young children stayed at Myrtle Grove, where she continued to run the plantation and support the Confederate forces. Forced by circumstance and her husband's absence to take a day-to-day hand in the activities of the plantation, Merrick nevertheless made it a point to continue her interest in horticulture throughout the conflict. Although the war was disruptive for Merrick and her family, it proved to be less so than for others who found themselves in the path or on the fringes of battle. Following the war, Merrick became involved in women's rights and temperance. She was one of the first women in Louisiana to speak out publicly on behalf of women's rights, and in 1892 founded the Portia Club to mobilize women and study the effects of laws directed at women and children. After 1897, Merrick published many stories and sketches, and wrote her autobiography entitled *Old Times in Dixie Land: A Southern Matron's Memories* (1901), in which she recounted life on the plantation during the war. Merrick died on March 29, 1908, in New Orleans.

BIBLIOGRAPHY

James, Edward T., ed. *Notable American Women: A Biographical Dictionary*. Cambridge, Mass., 1971.

National Encyclopedia of American Biography. Vol. 10. New York, 1910.

CHRISTINE A. LUNARDINI

MERRIMACK. *See entry on the ship* Virginia.

METHODIST CHURCH. The Methodist Episcopal Church, South (MECS), which had been organized in 1844 after American Methodists split on the issue of slavery, was a bulwark of Confederate nationalism. During the war Methodists endorsed and participated in the fast days and the Confederate government's invocations of scripture to support the cause, helping to make religion the foundation of Confederate nationalism and evangelical language the metaphorical means of expressing hopes for victory and alleviating the horrors of war. In sermons and denominational publications, Methodists cast the Confederacy as the redeemer nation, the New Israel, and called on church members to sacrifice for the noble cause. Led by Methodist Bishop George Foster Pierce of Georgia, clergy emphasized moral discipline and civic duty and railed against the democratic "anarchy" of Northern society.

Methodists administered to soldiers directly by means of chaplains, semimonthly organs such as the *Soldier's Paper* (published in Richmond) for troops in Virginia and the Carolinas, and the *Army and Naval Herald* (Macon, Georgia) for those in the western theater, and numerous short, pocket-size religious tracts. The most important wartime religious events were the revivals in the ranks, beginning in 1863 and recurring in spasms thereafter. Perhaps as many as 150,000 soldiers were "born again" during the war, many of them Methodists won over by the hard preaching of Methodist chaplains or by the appeals found in Methodist devotionals and published sermons. Methodist churchmen also tried to reform soldiers' behavior. Officers otherwise indifferent to religious concerns supported moral reform efforts as a way to improve discipline. Methodists such as the Reverend R. N. Sledd, in an 1861 sermon in Petersburg, Virginia, linked personal moral victory with Southern independence. Methodists joined other Protestant denominations in stocking camp libraries with religious tracts and newspapers and running Bible classes that taught both scripture and the need to give up strong drink, cursing, and gambling.

The revivals and moral reforms among soldiers were not equaled at home, creating another gulf between soldier and citizen and, for a time, elevating the male convert-soldier to a higher spiritual and moral plane than men and women at home. The former had faced death, the latter only hardship. Such differences affected the psychological and social adjustments Southerners had to make both in and out of the church after the war.

Methodist activity and authority declined as the war disrupted the normal ecclesiastical business of the MECS. The General Conference, scheduled to meet in New Orleans in 1862, was canceled after Union troops occupied the city. Several bishops convened in Atlanta, but no important denominational business was transacted. State conferences met irregularly. Still, the MECS managed to publish its denominational papers and tracts, which became the principal means of maintaining church identity and authority.

The war affected local churches in many ways, most profoundly in the loss of ordained church leadership and the interruption of organized religious life. Preachers rushed to the colors in 1861, some enlisting as privates. Most Methodist clergy who joined the Confederate army went in either as elected officers of military units or as chaplains of regiments. Two hundred Methodists served as chaplains, more than any other single denomination. Still others, however, were drafted. The absence of ministers was disruptive enough, but the loss of stewards, class leaders, and other church officials disrupted church management in numerous congregations. Sabbath schools were suspended, and in areas close to battles, church buildings were sometimes converted to hospitals. In towns it was still possible to find Sabbath services, but in the rural areas already dependent on itinerant ministers Methodist contact ebbed. Plantation missions especially suffered. Amid such confusion, people left the church. Others found an ecumenical fellowship among other Protestants equally isolated or disrupted in their normal church practices. Such wartime unions helped build the broad Southern evangelical Protestant canopy under which common white folks gathered after the war, irrespective of denominational rivalries among ministers.

Whatever the internal confusion, Southern Methodists were galvanized in their Southern identities during the war. The war divided further the Northern and Southern Methodist churches. Northern Methodists supported the war with a fervor unmatched by any other denomination, invoking the church militant to justify a crusade to crush secession, end slavery, and remake Methodism. From the Southern perspective, it was bad enough that Union troops occupied local Methodist churches as quarters, but worse was Secretary of War Edwin M. Stanton's November 1863 directive giving Northern Methodist bishops authority over all MECS houses of worship in which "a loyal minister . . . appointed by a loyal bishop of said church does not officiate." Especially in the Gulf states, Northern clergymen pursued an aggressive takeover policy to keep Confederates from using pulpits to promulgate "treason" and to curb any "lapse into semi-barbarism" by Southerners. Embittered Southern Methodists recalled such indignities whenever talk of Methodist reunion later cropped up; indeed, the memories of wartime sufferings at the hands of Union troops and ministers became a rallying cry for continued Southern Methodist independence after the war and served also to invigorate the Lost Cause movement. Like the Old Testament Jews who had lost the temple to invaders, Southern Methodists joined other Southern Protestants in viewing themselves as a chosen people who must reclaim their holy city from infidels.

Black Methodists responded differently to wartime stresses. The absence of white ministers led to greater assertions of religious leadership among blacks in biracial churches. The collapse of slavery in the face of Union advances disordered the social relations between white and black Methodists. At the same time, Northern missionaries and teachers challenged traditional local white authority. The Northern Methodists' special effort to recruit blacks angered white Southern Methodists. So, too, did the efforts of the African Methodist Episcopal church (AME church) to educate Southern black Methodists and recruit them as members.

Black membership in the MECS fell from 207,000 in 1860 to 78,000 in 1866. Blacks left the MECS in part because of Northern recruitment efforts (which largely occurred in towns and cities) but mainly because Southern blacks had taken religious matters into their own hands. Local religious leaders led the way out of the MECS. Although black and white Southern Methodists shared a common theology and polity, blacks had chafed at their social status in and out of the church. Most black Methodists joined the AME church, which set up conferences as early as 1865 in South Carolina and then colleges and a seminary to train ministers; others formed the Colored Methodist Episcopal church in 1870 following an amicable withdrawal from the MECS; and others gravitated toward the AME Zion church. The exodus of black Methodists left the MECS almost wholly a white denomination by the 1870s and made possible the segregation of Southern churches that preceded Jim Crow law in the South. At first, the MECS bemoaned the loss, but by the 1880s it had accepted, even welcomed, the segregation.

After the war many white Southern Methodist ministers endorsed the Lost Cause movement. Former army chaplains relived the war in their sermons, recalling the religious community forged in battle and wartime revivals. The celebration of the war restored masculine authority within the church and society, and the demand for moral uprightness and integrity that accompanied ministerial claims of being God's chosen people led to an emphasis on religious, social, and political orthodoxy and attempts to enforce strict moral codes of behavior.

Methodist bishop D. S. Doggett gave the invocation at the dedication of the Stonewall Jackson statue in Richmond in 1875, the event usually regarded as the symbolic beginning of the Lost Cause movement. Extremely influential evangelist Sam Jones, a Georgia Methodist, regularly preached at veterans' reunions; Methodist bishop Atticus Haygood became a prominent booster; and Methodist publications such as the *Christian Advocate* often ran poems and paeans to the Lost Cause. For ten years from its founding in 1867, the Reverend Albert T. Bledsoe's chauvinistic *Southern Review* was the most important organ in the Lost Cause movement, and after 1890 the Methodist-controlled *Confederate Veteran* assumed that mantle. From such thinking, Methodists like Oscar Fitzgerald warned against foreign immigration and Northern influence corrupting a "new South," whereas others such as John C. Calhoun Newton, in his book *The New South and the Methodist Episcopal Church, South* (1887), feared the New South creed portended "low mammon worship."

By ennobling the memory of the war and the Old South, including slavery, the Southern Methodists played a central role in forging a regional civil religion that fused together church interest and public identity. This became the

MECS's principal legacy from the war and spoke volumes on the social and political transformation in Southern Methodism. It had metamorphosed from its inclusive, biracial, antislavery, antiestablishment colonial past into separate white and black Methodist churches and an MECS that, along with the Southern Baptist church, had come to embody the region's social and political establishment.

BIBLIOGRAPHY

Dvorak, Katharine L. *An African-American Exodus: The Segregation of the Southern Churches.* Brooklyn, N.Y., 1991.

Faust, Drew Gilpin. "Christian Soldiers: The Meaning of Revivalism in the Confederate Army." *Journal of Southern History* 53 (1987): 63–90.

Silver, James W. *Confederate Morale and Church Propaganda.* Tuscaloosa, Ala., 1957.

Sweet, William Warren. *The Methodist Episcopal Church and the Civil War.* Cincinnati, 1912.

Wiley, Bell Irvin. *The Life of Johnny Reb: The Common Soldier of the Confederacy.* Indianapolis, 1943.

Wilson, Charles Reagan. *Baptized in Blood: The Religion of the Lost Cause, 1865–1920.* Athens, Ga., 1980.

RANDALL M. MILLER

MEXICO. Confederate dealings with Mexico were influenced not by King Cotton directly but by the geographical relationship. Mexico was beyond the Union blockade. Thus, it could supply the South, particularly the Trans-Mississippi Department, with metals, saltpeter, powder, sulphur, blankets, textiles, and foodstuffs, and in turn, cotton and other Southern commodities could be exported safely. Some Confederate officials on the border noted the potential for commerce with Europe through Mexico, although with less optimism when the Mexican Liberals commanded the frontier than later when the forces of French-inspired Austrian Archduke Maximilian controlled the border. In sum, the question was whether Confederate officials in Richmond would recognize that diplomatic efforts in Mexico involved the benefits to be derived from trade with the world through Mexico and from the moral support of recognition by Mexico.

In May 1861, the Confederate government appointed John T. Pickett its minister to Mexico to stymie the expected U.S. diplomatic offensive. Many of Pickett's actions, including those that brought him criticism, were consistent with his instructions. On the one hand, he was told to proceed with convenient speed to the Republic of Mexico. On the other hand, he was allowed to converse freely with local authorities at Veracruz. This state rights view demonstrated the Confederate State Department's failure to understand the Mexican Liberals' desire to establish an effective central government. Although committed to state rights domestically, the Confederacy should have adjusted its policy for export.

BENITO JUAREZ. President of Mexico during the American Civil War. NATIONAL ARCHIVES

Once in contact with the Mexican government, Pickett was to point out that Southerners had always been Mexico's best friends and that both peoples, involved in agriculture and mining, had similar interests in obtaining cheap foreign manufactured goods and relied upon similar labor systems, slavery and peonage. He was to stress that the Confederacy expected strict neutrality in the troubles north of the border; official recognition of the Confederacy was not necessary. His instructions were open to interpretation, and Pickett carried them out in a manner that made clear his contempt for Mexico and Mexicans. His mission was also handicapped by the history of Southern slave expansionism and the filibustering expeditions of the 1850s.

During his months in Mexico, Pickett was volatile, unthinking, imprudent, hasty, a heavy drinker—all qualities that should have disqualified him for office. It was not just his personal characteristics, however, but also his instructions that contributed to the failure of his mission. The message he bore stressed the positive values of slavery, an agricultural economic system, and a decentralized state government system. It served only to persuade the Liberal government that its future was more secure in association with the North if it wished to abolish peonage, centralize government authority, create a national economic structure, attract foreign trade and investment, and end filibustering.

When King Cotton proved a weak weapon to induce European action to ensure Southern independence, a new Confederate policy in 1862 attempted to use Mexico as a pawn to be sacrificed in order to convince Napoleon III to abandon neutrality. The Confederacy was willing to overlook the Monroe Doctrine, to forgo (or at least postpone) expansion into Mexico, and to guarantee Napoleon III's position in that country against the United States in return for French recognition, which Southern leaders believed would trigger a U.S.-French military clash.

In the period from 1862 to 1865, Confederate relations with Mexico were complicated by the unstable situation in that country. A joint French, British, and Spanish intervention in 1862 quickly became a unilateral French project, and the concurrent rumors of Maximilian's pending coronation as Mexican emperor encouraged the Confederate leaders. They assumed that Maximilian's Mexico would be a sympathetic and ideologically reliable neighbor. Recognition would be forthcoming; so might a military alliance, since the South was willing to bargain away the Monroe Doctrine for an alliance. Although President Benito Juárez's government favored the North, it made no effort to block Confederate trade along the northern frontier and used every opportunity to increase its revenue from that trade.

The Confederacy sent William Preston to Mexico in 1864 on a mission to alleviate its failing fortunes. His instructions recognized the realities of the Confederate position. The touchy question of recognition was set to one side by declaring that the public reception of Preston would be equivalent to de facto recognition. But he was instructed to pursue a military alliance and commercial privileges, especially along the frontier. Maximilian, however, refused to receive Preston.

In attempting to solve their mutual border problems, Confederate and Mexican officials at the border twice came close to perfecting "treaties" (without instructions in both instances) that would have implied mutual recognition. The Hamilton P. Bee–Albino López (February 1863) and James E. Slaughter–Tomás Mejía (December 1864) accords—which regulated border relations and trade—simulated international agreements because they were enforced equally upon citizens of both nations. Still, the Confederacy's chief difficulties in obtaining desirable relations along the border lay not in the Mexican nation but within its own outlook.

The Confederacy adopted a conservative diplomatic style, when a more revolutionary, dynamic approach was required to accomplish the tasks that lay before it. It did not need the preservation of the international status quo. Its claim to existence had created a change. It needed the most favorable revision of international commerce and power that it could effect. If it were to achieve this goal, the Confederacy required trading partners and the moral and material support of recognition. Precisely these two items received low priority from the Confederate high command until near the end of the war. In Mexico, for example, Pickett and José Augustín Quintero, the Southern agent in northern Mexico, were instructed to maintain friendly relations, to seek Mexico's neutrality, and above all, to make it clear that the Confederacy would not tolerate Mexico's granting special privileges to the United States. Only if other matters went smoothly were they to seek formal trade ties. Despite these priorities, Quintero immediately pushed for close trade ties, but his labor went unrewarded because his superiors lacked interest.

Often dismissing the Confederate diplomatic failure in Mexico in terms of Pickett's personality or the ill timing of the Preston mission, historians overlook the broader aspects. Abler diplomats might have quieted the fears of Mexicans, but the conservative worldview behind the Confederacy's instructions demonstrated the inability of the South to understand its own neighbor. To instruct an agent to the Liberal government to emphasize a mutually shared interest in slavery, agriculture, and state rights was shockingly ignorant in light of the decade-long Mexican civil war during which the Liberals had fought to abolish peonage, establish a centralist government, create the basis for an industrial-commercial economy, and displace an agrarian, aristocratic elite. Furthermore, for the Confederate leadership not to focus upon drawing maximum advantage from the Texas-Mexico border reflected a mentality that was woefully out of place in the industrializing nineteenth century. In sum, the South was badly out of tune with its times, clearly in relation to Mexico and very likely elsewhere as well.

[*See also* Monroe Doctrine.]

BIBLIOGRAPHY

Daddysman, James W. *The Matamoros Trade: Confederate Commerce, Diplomacy, and Intrigue.* Newark, N.J., 1984.

Fuentes Mares, José. *Juárez y la intervención.* México, 1962.

McCormack, Richard B. "Los Estados Confederados y México." *Historia Mexicana* 4 (1966): 337–357.

Owsley, Frank. *King Cotton Diplomacy.* Rev. ed. Chicago, 1959.

Schoonover, Thomas. *Dollars over Dominion: The Triumph of Liberalism in Mexican–United States Relations, 1861–1867.* Baton Rouge, La., 1978.

Tyler, Ronnie C. *Santiago Vidaurre and the Southern Confederacy.* Austin, Tex., 1973.

THOMAS SCHOONOVER

MILES, WILLIAM PORCHER (1822–1899), mayor of Charleston and congressman from South Carolina. Born in Walterboro, South Carolina, July 4, 1822, Miles studied at Moses Waddel's Academy and in 1842 graduated from the College of Charleston. He read law with Edward McCrady, but taught mathematics at the college (1843–1855). A man of modest means, Miles by 1860 owned no slaves and property valued at only $1,800.

During a yellow fever epidemic in Norfolk, Virginia, in 1855 Miles volunteered as a hospital worker and received a gold medal. Meanwhile, the political leadership of Charleston, faced with a Know-Nothing candidate for mayor, was attracted by Miles's reputation. They decided to back him, and Miles was elected by a large majority. As mayor (1855–1857), he transformed the slave watch into a modern city police force. He attacked the problems of disease and waste disposal and inaugurated a system of tidal drainage. He consolidated the city debt and put municipal finances on a sound basis.

In 1857, in the midst of a bitter congressional campaign, the moderate candidate withdrew, and Miles entered the race. He was elected and served until he resigned with the rest of the state's delegation in 1860. Miles participated in the Washington phase of the negotiations over Federal forts in the South and signed the manifesto with other Southern congressmen declaring that a Southern confederacy was necessary.

William Porcher Miles.
Harper's Pictorial History of the Great Rebellion

Miles was elected to the secession convention and served as chairman of the Foreign Relations Committee. Gen. P. G. T. Beauregard appointed Miles a member of the delegation to arrange the surrender of Fort Sumter with Maj. Robert Anderson.

Miles was elected to the Provisional Congress and was twice reelected to Congress without opposition. He was chairman of the committee that devised the Confederate flag and the Military Affairs Committee. He became perhaps the most powerful member of the House of Representatives. His work load was staggering. He corresponded constantly with the military commanders and visited them in the field. He strongly supported Jefferson Davis's policies on the war. In 1864 when Miles supported ending all military exemptions and granting the secretary of war complete power of detail, the Richmond newspapers called him the president's "mouthpiece." But on matters not affecting the war effort directly, Miles did not always support the administration. He opposed Davis on penalties for speculation, railroad grants, a supreme court, and the suspension of the writ of habeas corpus.

In 1863 Miles married Betty Beirne, the daughter of a planter in Virginia and Louisiana. For the remainder of his life he assumed the role of a planter and country gentleman. For fifteen years after the war Miles lived in Virginia. In 1874 he was an unsuccessful candidate for the presidency of Johns Hopkins University. In 1880 he became president of the University of South Carolina after its reorganization by the white Redeemer government. Miles resigned in 1882 and moved to Ascension Parish, Louisiana, to manage his father-in-law's holdings. He lived at Houmas House and managed thirteen plantations. He was active among sugar planters and was in demand as an orator on public occasions. He died on May 11, 1899.

BIBLIOGRAPHY

Cyclopedia of Eminent and Representative Men of the Carolinas. Vol. 1. Madison, Wis., 1892.

Smith, Clarence M., Jr. "William Porcher Miles, Progressive Mayor of Charleston, 1855–57." In *Proceedings of the South Carolina Historical Association, 1942.* Columbia, S.C., 1942.

Warner, Ezra J., and W. Buck Yearns. *Biographical Register of the Confederate Congress.* Baton Rouge, La., 1975.

A. V. Huff, Jr.

MILITARY JUSTICE. The Confederate Constitution empowered Congress to establish rules for the government of Confederate soldiers. Soon there arose a system of military justice based almost entirely on the Articles of War and the army regulations of the United States, which had been derived from the system of Great Britain.

Initially, the Confederate War Department's Adjutant and Inspector General's Office was charged with review and custody of documents pertaining to military justice, but in February 1864, a new bureau, the Judge Advocate's Office under Maj. Charles H. Lee (after April under Maj. William S. Barton), assumed responsibility.

The main topics of the Articles of War adopted on March 6, 1861, were military offenses and the courts of inquiry and courts-martial that were the disciplinary procedural bodies available to deal with them. These offenses included common crimes such as insubordination, drunkenness, fighting, absence without leave, and desertion, and less common ones such as mutiny, threats or violence against superiors, cowardice, and misbehavior in action.

Courts of inquiry were fact-finding bodies ordered by President Jefferson Davis, or convened at the request of an accused, to investigate the responsibility of officers for affairs or accusations or imputations against officers or men. These courts, composed of up to three officers, plus a judge advocate to act as recorder, could summon witnesses and administer oaths, but they could not initiate an opinion and could punish only for contempt. Court findings sometimes led to the convening of courts-martial.

General courts-martial, composed of five to thirteen officers, all senior in rank to the accused, tried officers and men, as well as sutlers, drivers, and all others paid by the army. Initially, only general officers commanding field armies and colonels commanding departments could convene these courts, but by 1865 generals commanding cavalry forces not directly part of an army command, officers commanding separate departments, and generals commanding reserve forces had this authority.

Special or regimental courts-martial consisted of three officers convened to try noncapital offenses committed by soldiers or persons paid by the army. Convening authorities were officers commanding regiments or corps, or garrisons, forts, barracks, or other places where the troops were from different arms of the service.

Judge advocates prosecuted, summoned witnesses, swore in the members of the court, and were then sworn in by the court president who kept order and conducted court business. Convictions were wrought by simple majority, except death sentences which required a two-thirds majority. Sentences were carried out upon approval of the convening authority who could mitigate or suspend sentence. Only President Davis could approve sentences passed on general officers.

Once the army was on the march an expedient was the drumhead court-martial, which executed its judgments immediately. In addition, for noncapital offenses, commanding officers meted out summary justice without reference to formal judicial process. Sentences were often unfair and capricious, usually involving some form of corporal punishment, extra duty, confinement, or reduction in rank.

By 1862 Robert E. Lee and many other commanders had become convinced that the existing system was not ensuring prompt and certain punishment of offenders. The legal necessity to convene each court-martial, not always an easy or timely task during active operations, meant delays, which often resulted in witnesses being unavailable. More delay resulted from the requirements to forward charges to general headquarters before the accused could be ordered to trial and to return the findings to the convening authority for review before sentences could be executed. These shortcomings led to a sharp increase in offenses as offenders mistook the system's slowness for immunity.

The response, embodied in an act of October 9, 1862, was a new type of tribunal: a permanently open military court for each army corps in the field. These courts had three members (colonels) and a judge advocate (captain) appointed by President Davis, plus a court-appointed provost marshal to execute orders and a clerk to record decisions. By 1864, twelve corps, cavalry divisions, all military departments, northern Alabama, and each state had courts. Judges and courts could be transferred as required, and corps and department commanders could detail field officers as members. Although it was not the intent that military courts eliminate courts-martial, their inherent advantages caused a lessening of courts-martial jurisdiction.

Military courts could try all offenses against the Articles of War and the customs of war, crimes against Confederate or state law, and all cases of murder, manslaughter, arson, rape, robbery, and larceny committed by military personnel and prisoners of war outside the Confederate States, where military courts exercised powers equal to Confederate States district courts. They could summon civilian witnesses, for example, and hold them until they agreed to testify. In the case of treason, ambiguity about the applicability of the Articles of War to civilians caused disputes about the jurisdictions of civil and military courts. Military courts (and courts-martial) were not subject to appellate jurisdiction of civil courts.

One shortcoming that could not be legislated for was the tendency to leniency shown by tribunals. The long-term effect was a tide of straggling and desertion that by 1864 threatened to engulf the army. Nor did leniency help instill the desired respect for and obedience to orders that would have made best use of the experience, tenacity, and courage of the Confederate soldier. As Lee observed, many opportunities were lost and many lives uselessly sacrificed because of indiscipline.

[*See also* Desertion; Provost Marshal.]

BIBLIOGRAPHY

Confederate States War Department. *Regulations for the Army of the Confederate States, 1863.* Richmond, Va., 1863. Reprint, Harrisburg, Pa., 1980.

Robinson, William M. *Justice in Grey: A History of the Judicial System of the Confederate States of America.* New York, 1941.

Wiley, Bell I. *The Life of Johnny Reb.* New York, 1943. Reprint, Baton Rouge, La., 1971.

KENNETH RADLEY

MILITARY TRAINING. The turning of raw recruits into soldiers for the Confederacy virtually mirrored the same activity in the Union, both being based upon the system of the prewar U.S. Army. Drill and weapons training were designed to instill subordination in the soldiers, produce instant and unquestioning obedience to commands, and facilitate the orderly movement of large numbers of men quickly and effectively on the battlefield. Most officers relied on either Winfield Scott's 1835 *Infantry Tactics* or the simpler and more popular *Rifle and Infantry Tactics* written by William J. Hardee (now a Confederate general) and known simply as *Hardee's Tactics.*

Although details varied in these and the other manuals used (in volunteer regiments it was often left up to individual officers to choose whichever manual they preferred), virtually all shared features in common. Men were expected to learn to obey commands as given by bugle or drum, since a voice would not carry far in battle. As many as fifty different such commands had to be learned, not all of them applicable to all soldiers and units.

The basic drill unit was the company, though practice in squad and battalion drill was also required. Regimental drill was as large as most evolutions went, but a few brigades actually practiced full brigade drill early in the war before discovering its impracticability. In his early months in uniform, a Johnny Reb might expect to spend several hours a day practicing his evolutions. This did not include just parade ground maneuvers. Practice in line of march—usually four abreast—was also required. Separate branches like the artillery and cavalry had their own distinctive drill and training regimens.

In the early days, weapons training also occupied much time and practice until handling them became second nature. Silas Casey's 1862 *Infantry Tactics* reduced the loading and firing of the rifled musket to a dozen commands and twenty discrete actions, and Confederate manuals did much the same. Of course, the men quickly learned how to load and fire, but the object of the drill was to have them do so in unison in order to deliver a shattering volley at the command to fire. Even more time was devoted to bayonet practice, with dozens of commands and positions being studied for using the bayonet as virtually a saber at the end of the rifle. Ironically, the bayonet saw almost no practical combat use and inflicted fewer than four wounds out of a thousand.

Attempted almost universally at the outset, all but the most basic and rudimentary training disappeared from most of the Confederate forces after 1863, especially when regiments were reduced by casualties from nearly a thousand to only two hundred or so and with whole companies numbering a mere thirty to forty. Still, though haphazard and ersatz like so much else in the Southern war effort, training in the Confederate forces definitely left its mark in producing one of the most effective groups of fighting men in history.

BIBLIOGRAPHY

Davis, William C. *Fighting Men of the Civil War.* London, 1989.

Robertson, James I., Jr. *Soldiers Blue and Gray.* Columbia, S.C., 1988.

Wiley, Bell I. *The Life of Johnny Reb.* Baton Rouge, La., 1971.

WILLIAM C. DAVIS

MILLER, SAMUEL AUGUSTINE (1819–1890), major and congressman from Virginia. Born in Shenandoah County, Virginia, Miller attended Gettysburg College, traveled to Europe, and studied law in Kanawha, Virginia (present-day West Virginia). He became the law partner of his teacher, specializing in land titles, and also president of the Kanawha Salt Company.

A leading secessionist in a region that supported the Union, Miller took a commission as major in the Commissary Department of the Twenty-second Virginia Regiment. He won a special election to fill the seat in the House of Representatives vacated on the resignation of Albert Gallatin Jenkins. In 1863 he narrowly edged out his opponents, thanks to the soldier and refugee vote, in the election for the Second Congress. Miller's district was entirely in Federal hands throughout his time in the Congress. He supported most measures to expand the government's control over personal rights and the economy. He did not go as far as some, however, in giving up the prerogatives of the legislature to the executive.

After the war he returned briefly to his home in Kanawha County, but when Lincoln was assassinated, he fled to Canada, not knowing how Confederate congressmen would be treated. At the end of 1865 he returned after receiving a pardon but was not permitted to practice law again until the West Virginia Constitution was amended in 1870. Miller served in that state's legislature in 1874 and died at Parkersburg on November 19, 1890.

BIBLIOGRAPHY

Wakelyn, Jon L. *Biographical Dictionary of the Confederacy.* Edited by Frank E. Vandiver. Westport, Conn., 1977.

Warner, Ezra J., and W. Buck Yearns. *Biographical Register of the Confederate Congress.* Baton Rouge, La., 1975.

NELSON D. LANKFORD

MILLER, WILLIAM (1820–1909), brigadier general. Born in Ithaca, New York, Miller moved with his family to

WILLIAM MILLER. LIBRARY OF CONGRESS

Louisiana while still an infant. Educated at Louisiana College, he studied law prior to the Mexican War, during which he served in Zachary Taylor's army. After the war, he settled near Pensacola, Florida, operating a sawmill in Santa Rosa County.

At the outbreak of the Civil War, Miller commanded a battalion with the rank of major and participated in the Battle of Shiloh. After the battle, the battalion was consolidated into the First Florida Volunteer Regiment of Infantry, of which he was given command with the rank of colonel. He led the regiment on Braxton Bragg's Kentucky campaign and at the Battle of Perryville.

While commanding the combined First and Third Florida regiments at the Battle of Murfreesboro, Miller was severely wounded and spent nearly a year recuperating. After returning to duty, he served as commandant of the Conscript Bureau for southern Florida and Alabama. On August 2, 1864, he was commissioned brigadier general in Confederate service and received command of the reserve forces in Alabama. From September 1864 until the end of the war, he commanded the District of Florida.

After the war, Miller operated a lumber mill and farmed extensively in Washington County, Florida. He served one term in the state's lower house and in 1886 received election to the state senate, in which he served two terms. He died at Point Washington, Florida, and is buried in St. John's Cemetery, Pensacola.

BIBLIOGRAPHY

Faust, Patricia, ed. *Historical Times Illustrated's Encyclopedia of the Civil War.* New York, 1986.

Johnson, Robert U., and C. C. Buel, eds. *Battles and Leaders of the Civil War.* 4 vols. New York, 1887–1888. Reprint, Secaucus, N.J., 1982.

Warner, Ezra J. *Generals in Gray: Lives of the Confederate Commanders.* Baton Rouge, La., 1959.

CHRISTOPHER PHILLIPS

MILL SPRINGS, KENTUCKY. Kentucky was the key to the West. Events in the fall of 1861 had caused Union and Confederate armies to advance into the state, with the Federals gaining overall control. For Union planners, this conquest was a godsend. The vast Confederate border now lay open to invasion, and armies began forming across the state to carry the war south. Confederates, meanwhile, were faced with a crisis as they struggled to defend this now vulnerable line.

Union Brig. Gen. George H. Thomas advocated a prompt move into eastern Tennessee where, reports indicated, Unionists stood ready to join the colors. This plan had appeal among politicians, but was opposed by the department commander, Gen. Don Carlos Buell. Even so, he ultimately relented, and on January 1, 1862, Thomas left Lebanon, Kentucky, en route for Tennessee with an army of less than five thousand men. His first goal was to drive the remaining Confederates out of the state.

Confederate Brig. Gen. Felix K. Zollicoffer, who had been operating in southeastern Kentucky with four regiments since September, opposed the Union advance. Frequent skirmishes occurred between small mounted parties as the Union troops neared the Confederate base across the Cumberland River from Mill Springs. Heavy rains and deep mud, however, had scattered the Federal army.

In mid-January, Confederate Gen. George B. Crittenden arrived at Zollicoffer's camp with reinforcements, assumed command of the Southern forces in the area, and moved to strike the approaching Federals. Hoping to catch the enemy before he could concentrate his army, Crittenden led his four thousand troops north on January 18. At dawn the next day, amid low clouds and intermittent rain, the vanguards of the two armies clashed, nine miles from Mill Springs.

The Confederates, with more men on the field, gained an immediate advantage and drove the Federals before them. But the Union troops traded ground for time, and soon additional Federal regiments arrived. At a rail fence bordering an open field, the Union line stabilized. The

Confederates, under cover of a ravine, kept up a continuous fire. Some Northerners gave ground under the onslaught, only to be replaced in the line by fresh troops recently arrived.

Amid the fighting, General Zollicoffer fell dead and his troops wavered. As the Confederate attack stalled, Thomas ordered regiments to turn both of the Confederate flanks. Enveloped on either side, the Southerners broke and fled. Discipline and order disintegrated among the panicked Confederates, and the retreat turned to rout. Thomas pursued Crittenden to his fortified base opposite Mill Springs. The following morning, Union troops discovered that the Confederates had crossed the river overnight, abandoning all of their cannons, wagons, and heavy equipment. Among the Federals, 40 men had been killed, 207 wounded, and 15 captured. The Confederates lost 125 killed, 309 wounded, and 99 captured.

Although the Union had won, Thomas's advance into eastern Tennessee was unexpectedly canceled. General Buell, blaming bad roads and wretched weather, ordered the expedition abandoned and Thomas to rejoin the main army advancing on Nashville. The principal Southern army in the area had been essentially destroyed, but eastern Tennessee Unionists would have to wait another year and a half for an army from the North.

BIBLIOGRAPHY

Coulter, E. Merton. *The Civil War and Readjustment in Kentucky.* Chapel Hill, N.C., 1926.

Kelly, R. M. "Holding Kentucky for the Union." In *Battles and Leaders of the Civil War.* Edited by Robert U. Johnson and C. C. Buel. Vol. 1. New York, 1887. Reprint, Secaucus, N.J., 1982.

Myers, Raymond E. *The Zollie Tree.* Louisville, Ky., 1964.

DONALD S. FRAZIER

MILTON, JOHN (1807–1865), governor of Florida. Nominated for governor on the twenty-third ballot by a Democratic convention that also declared for secession, John Milton, a Jackson County planter and slave owner, defeated Constitutional Unionist Edward Hopkins in a close election in November 1860. Under Florida law he would not take office until October of the following year. Thus he had the frustrating experience of seeing his predecessor, the lame duck Madison S. Perry, with the support of the General Assembly, make critical decisions regarding the direction the state was to follow while appointing his friends and supporters to key positions, particularly in the military. Milton believed in a state militia to be controlled by the governor, whereas Perry felt the Confederate government should take full responsibility for military affairs.

Further complicating Milton's situation was the continued exercise of constituent power by the extralegal secession convention, which overrode on occasion both the executive and the legislature. The state attorney general refused to support Milton's challenge of the convention's constitutional authority, and for a while Milton had to share power with a four-man executive council. Moreover, the passage of the Confederate Conscription Act of 1862 signaled the end of Milton's state militia and left him with limited power over the meager state resources.

An ardent secessionist, a firm believer in slavery, and a particularly strong supporter of the concept of state rights, Milton nevertheless soon came to realize that it was essential during the wartime emergency that unity and harmony prevail among the central government and the states. Although he protested strongly to President Jefferson Davis over decisions and policies that he felt were invasions of state sovereignty, he nevertheless urged his fellow Floridians to acquiesce for the common good. Chief among these policies were conscription, exemptions, blockade running, and impressment. Believing conscription to be unconstitutional but a matter for a judicial body to decide, Milton supported it strongly and urged his constituents to volunteer rather than wait to be drafted. While other governors dispensed exemptions liberally, Milton felt that all men who could carry arms should be liable for military service and was much more select in allowing exemptions. He also differed with governors who attempted to evade central government regulation of blockade running by having private ships transfer their ownership to individual states. His strongest reservations were over impressment of private property for public use. He did not deny the right of Confederate government to take such property, but he continually disputed with the central government over the methods by which impressment was carried out and sought to regulate it rather than forbid it in Florida.

Governor Milton was one of the most cooperative and staunchest supporters of the Confederacy of any of the Southern governors, several of whom he criticized for placing local priorities over those of the central government. He maintained throughout his administration a continuing cordiality with Jefferson Davis, even naming one of his sons for the president.

The frustrations of his administration coupled with mounting distress over the declining fortunes of the Confederacy caused him to take his own life on April 1, 1865.

BIBLIOGRAPHY

Parker, Daisy. "Governor John Milton." *Tallahassee Historical Society Annual* 3 (1937): 14–21.

Parker, Daisy. "John Milton, Governor of Florida: A Loyal Confederate." *Florida Historical Quarterly* 20 (1942): 346–361.

Tebeau, Charlton W. *A History of Florida.* Coral Gables, Fla., 1971.

WILLIAM H. NULTY

admission of Mississippi to the Union in 1817. Yet most citizens in 1861 were immigrants, mostly from the older states of the South, for Mississippi was in many ways a frontier still growing and only beginning to develop settled institutions. In 1820 the state had had 75,448 inhabitants—42,176 whites and 33,272 nonwhites, 32,814 of them slaves. Forty years later on the eve of secession, the population had grown more than tenfold to 791,305—353,899 whites and 437,406 nonwhites, among whom 436,631 were slaves. Mississippi's whites were overwhelmingly of English and Scotch-Irish lineage. Only tiny pockets of Germans and Irish in towns like Vicksburg, Natchez, and Jackson and a few descendants of eighteenth-century French settlers living along the Gulf coast added ethnic flavor. Mississippi's slaves had largely been brought from the older states of the South to furnish labor for the booming cotton economy.

In 1860 Mississippi's society was overwhelmingly rural and the economy was almost wholly agrarian. Only 17,702 people lived in towns. Aside from some villages and hamlets, the state had only four towns of any consequence: Natchez (6,612), Vicksburg (4,591), Columbus (3,308), and Jackson (3,191). Cotton was the state's chief cash crop, and food crops, especially corn, were also produced in abundance. Most of Mississippi's planters along with their slaves lived in the western half of the state. Except for the Tombigbee Prairie, which also contained some plantations, eastern Mississippi was a land of small farmers; some owned a few slaves, and others none. This demographic division also marked a rough political division. Though never dominant, Whigs were most numerous in the plantation counties along the Mississippi River, while the small farmers and small planters were largely Democrats. Culturally in 1860, Mississippi was just emerging from its frontier past. The University of Mississippi began operation in 1848; public schools were founded in Natchez, Vicksburg, Columbus, and Jackson; a "lunatic asylum," a penitentiary, roads, and railroads had been built.

In the forty years before secession, Mississippi's slave population increased more than thirteenfold. In 1820 slaves constituted 43 percent of the population; in 1860, 55 percent. Washington and Issaquena counties on the Mississippi River counted 92 percent of their populations as slave; Jones in the southeast and Tishomingo in the northeast were respectively only 12 percent and 20 percent slave. Slave labor was considered essential for cotton production, and personal wealth of Mississippians in slave property exceeded $400 million.

Antebellum Sectional Crises. Slavery emerged as a bitterly divisive national issue in the aftermath of the Mexican War (1849–1851). Should the territories acquired from Mexico be open to slavery or not? Mississippi's governor during those years was John Anthony Quitman, a Democrat, a Southern nationalist, and a fire-eater. He counseled secession should the national government attempt to regulate slavery. Most Whigs and some Unionist Democrats, led by Senator Henry S. Foote, called for moderation and compromise. The crisis was averted when voters elected a Unionist majority to a secession convention called by Quitman. Sealing the Unionist victory, Foote narrowly defeated Jefferson Davis for the governorship in 1851.

The emotional events of the 1850s—the Kansas controversy, the rising popularity of the Free-Soil position, and the increasingly strident demands of the abolitionists—undercut the Mississippi Unionists and strengthened the appeal of fire-eaters like Quitman, Governors John Jones McRae and J. J. Pettus, and Senator Albert Gallatin Brown. The breakup of the national Whig party in the mid-1850s left many Mississippi Unionists without a party base, and the Democratic leadership was dominated by secessionists.

The crisis peaked in the presidential election of 1860. Governor Pettus, both U.S. senators (Brown and Jefferson Davis, the most moderate of Mississippi's secessionist leaders), and the entire House delegation recommended that a secession convention be called if Abraham Lincoln, a former Free-Soil Whig but now a Republican, was elected. Mississippi's delegation to the Democratic National Convention refused to support Stephen A. Douglas and walked out when the convention rejected a plank guaranteeing the rights of slavery in new territories.

Three candidates appeared on the November ballot in Mississippi: Douglas of Illinois, nominee of the Democratic party; John C. Breckinridge of Kentucky, nominee of the Southern Democrats; and John Bell of Tennessee, nominee of the Constitutional Union party. Lincoln was not on the ballot. Breckinridge had the support of the secessionist Democrats in Mississippi, and Bell was backed by Unionists and many former Whigs. The Mississippi electorate gave Breckinridge 40,464 votes, Bell 25,335, and Douglas 3,636.

Lincoln's election precipitated the state's secession. Governor Pettus called the legislature into session and recommended that it issue a call for elections to a secession convention. In the elections held on December 20, 1860, immediate secessionists won a large majority of the seats—about seventy-five out of a hundred. The delegates met on January 7, 1861, at the statehouse in Jackson and elected William Barry, an immediate secessionist, as president. Efforts by cooperationists and Unionists first to postpone secession and then to submit the question to the people in a referendum failed, and on January 9, Mississippi's ordinance of secession, drafted by L. Q. C. Lamar, was passed. Mississippi thus became the second state to secede.

Within a month all seven of the lower Southern states had left the Union, and on February 4, 1861, delegates convened

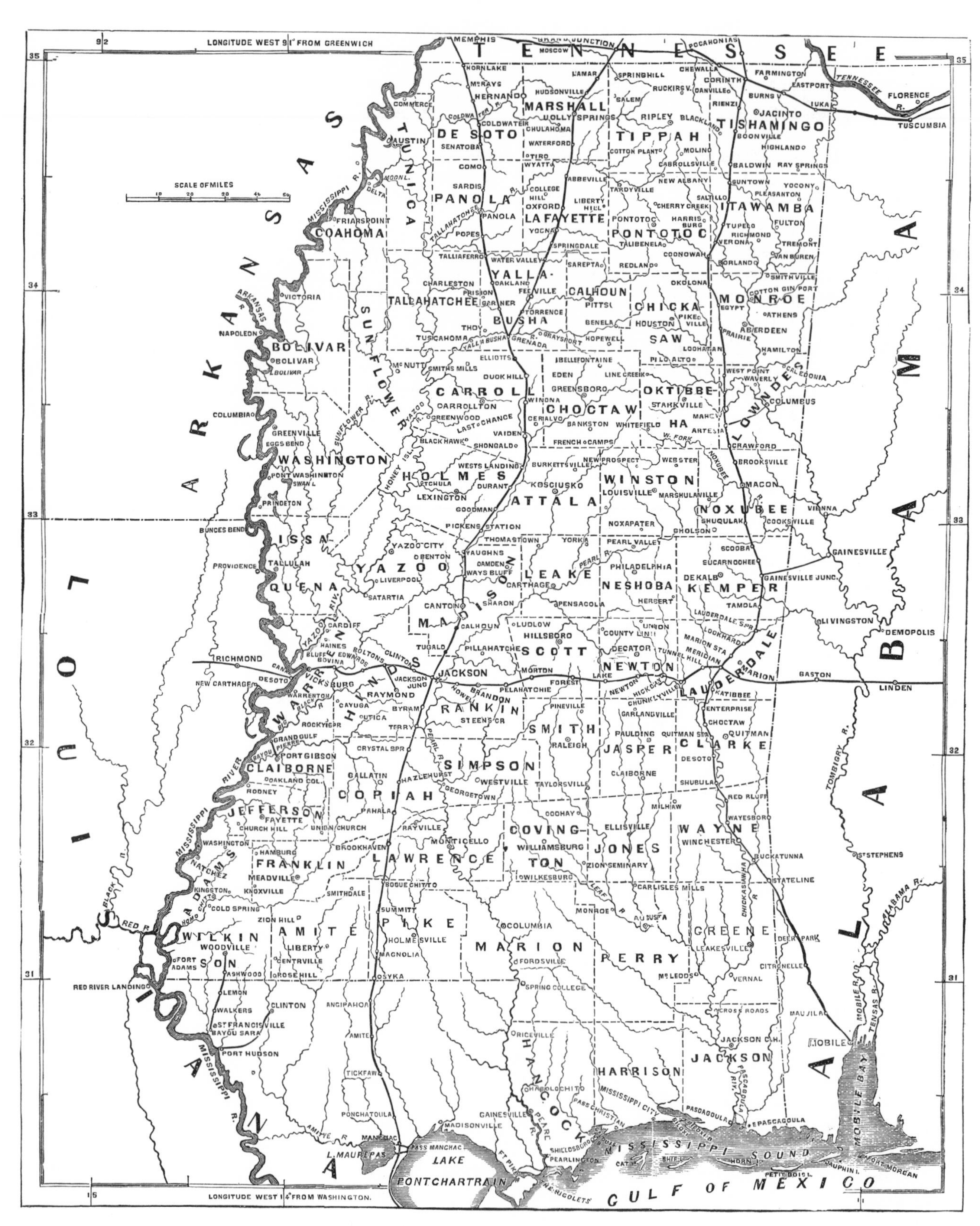

Map of Mississippi.

Harper's Pictorial History of the Great Rebellion

at Montgomery, Alabama, to form a Confederate government. The secession convention chose nine delegates to represent Mississippi. Over the next two months delegates to the Provisional Congress at Montgomery wrote a constitution and formed a government headed by Jefferson Davis of Warren County, Mississippi. In late March Mississippi's secession convention reconvened at the statehouse in Jackson and ratified the new Constitution. By then war fever was rising, and Governor Pettus had already begun to form military units, gather arms, and look to the defense of Mississippi.

The War in Mississippi. When the war began, Mississippi occupied a key place in Union strategy. The state lay in the heart of the Deep South, a strategic crossroads. The Mississippi River, a central objective for Union forces from the earliest days of the war, wound along the state's entire western border. Consequently, countless battles, raids, and skirmishes were fought within Mississippi. Nearly all the many engagements fell into three major campaigns—the campaign for Corinth in 1862, that for Vicksburg in 1862 to 1863, and that for eastern Mississippi in 1864 to 1865.

The war came to Mississippi in earnest during the early spring and summer of 1862. Having breached the South's first defensive line at Forts Henry and Donelson, Gen. Ulysses S. Grant descended the Tennessee River. Disembarking at Pittsburg Landing near a country church called Shiloh, Grant aimed his army at Corinth, twenty miles to the south. He hoped to destroy the Memphis and Charleston Railroad, a major east-west Confederate communications route. Gens. Albert Sidney Johnston and P. G. T. Beauregard had already gathered a Confederate army at Corinth. Johnston's army attacked Grant's forces around Pittsburg Landing. In two of the bloodiest days of the war, the Confederates dealt Grant a severe blow but failed to destroy him. Grant was briefly relieved, and over the next two months, the Union army, now under Gen. Henry W. Halleck, crept slowly south toward Corinth. As the Union force advanced, it grew in strength, and the Confederates, commanded by Beauregard since the death of Johnston at Shiloh, were forced to evacuate. Corinth was occupied on May 29, 1862.

Meanwhile, up from the Gulf of Mexico came a major threat to southwestern Mississippi. In early April 1862, Adm. David Farragut established a base on the Gulf coast and aimed his fleet at the lower Mississippi River. He took New Orleans on April 24, 1862, and proceeded upriver. He reached Natchez on May 12, demanded that town's surrender, and appeared off Vicksburg on May 18. In June, Farragut fought his way upriver past the Vicksburg batteries and was joined by a Union fleet from Memphis. For a month they bombarded and threatened the town. But Farragut lacked an army, and Vicksburg was well defended from the river side. Falling water in the river and the appearance of the Confederate ironclad *Arkansas* convinced Farragut he should abandon his attempt to take Vicksburg. On July 27 he weighed anchor and headed downriver.

Almost as Farragut was withdrawing, another attack on Vicksburg was being mounted, this time from upriver and with a powerful army. General Grant had barely escaped a career-ending disaster at Shiloh, while Gen. William S. Rosecrans successfully defeated a counteroffensive by Maj. Gen. Earl Van Dorn to reclaim northeast Mississippi and western Tennessee (Battle of Corinth, October 3–4, 1862). Grant then prepared to move against Vicksburg. He began his campaign in November 1862 by sending Maj. Gen. William Tecumseh Sherman downriver with forty thousand men on steamboats supported by Rear Adm. David D. Porter's fleet of gunboats. Sherman planned to tie Confederate Gen. John C. Pemberton's Confederate army to the Vicksburg defenses and make an assault on the town bluffs if possible. Meanwhile Grant would start south through central Mississippi to invest Vicksburg from the rear. Late in December, Grant's base at Holly Springs was destroyed by Van Dorn, and Sherman's assault on the Chickasaw Bluffs north of Vicksburg was repulsed by greatly inferior Confederate forces.

Sherman withdrew and established a base twenty miles north of Vicksburg while Grant retreated to Memphis. Ever tenacious, Grant then brought his forces downriver to join Sherman's force. His army reunited by the end of January, Grant determined to try again. For almost three months he tried to flank the Vicksburg defenses by sending amphibious expeditions through the tortuous, flooded waterways north of Vicksburg. Finally, on April 17 Admiral Porter ran his gunboats and steamboats by the Vicksburg batteries while Grant's army marched overland through Louisiana and recrossed the river at Bruinsburg. Grant then moved rapidly toward Jackson, hoping to keep Joseph E. Johnston's new and growing Confederate force from combining with Pemberton's army. Over the next nineteen days, Grant's army marched two hundred miles, living mostly off the country. He fought five victorious engagements at Port Gibson (May 1), Raymond (May 11), Jackson (May 14), Champion's Hill (May 16), and the Big Black River (May 17). By May 19 Pemberton was back inside the entrenchments surrounding Vicksburg. After two unsuccessful assaults on Pemberton's lines, Grant settled down for a forty-seven-day siege. Pemberton surrendered his army on July 4, 1863.

During 1864, campaigning in Mississippi shifted into the eastern and northeastern regions. Union forces had two objectives—to lay waste the economy of the unoccupied sections of Mississippi and to tie down the dangerous cavalry forces of Nathan Bedford Forrest. Sherman was beginning his campaign from Chattanooga to Atlanta, and

MISSISSIPPI DELEGATION TO U.S. CONGRESS. This group attended the Thirty-sixth Session of the U.S. Congress, March 4, 1859, to March 3, 1861. They left after January 20, 1861, when Mississippi passed its ordinance of secession. Pictured clockwise, starting from the top, are Sen. Jefferson Davis, Rep. Otho R. Singleton, Rep. John J. McRae, Rep. William Barksdale, Rep. L. Q. C. Lamar, and Reuben Davis. In the center is Sen. Albert Gallatin Brown. *HARPER'S PICTORIAL HISTORY OF THE GREAT REBELLION*

Confederate presence west of the Mississippi with diminishing success.

Two of Reynolds's notable accomplishments were his recommendations for a "Western Preferred Mail" system and a Treasury branch that could handle claims against the Confederacy without prior referral to Richmond and could engrave and sign government notes and bonds. He accompanied Sterling Price on his September 1864 raid into Missouri, hoping to reestablish his government at Jefferson City. This raid proved a dismal failure, however, and he retired with Price's force back into Arkansas.

At war's end, most of Missouri's Confederate leaders went into exile in Mexico where they joined forces with Maximilian. After his attempt to secure an empire in Mexico failed, they slowly drifted back to Missouri where many of them ultimately found prominent places in postwar Democratic politics.

All told, Missouri furnished some 30,000 men to the Confederate armed forces as opposed to the over 100,000 Missourians who served the Union. Yet there were many more unnumbered Missourians who sympathized with the Confederacy and lent it assistance through guerrilla activities within the state. Many were reluctant or unable to leave their homes to serve elsewhere, but their bitter partisanship kept Missouri in a state of turmoil whose memory lasted well into Reconstruction.

[*For further discussion of battles and campaigns fought in Missouri, see* Belmont, Missouri; Centralia Massacre; New Madrid and Island Number 10; Price's Missouri Raid; Wilson's Creek Campaign. *See also* Guerrilla Warfare; Missouri Compromise; *and biographies of numerous figures mentioned herein.*]

BIBLIOGRAPHY

Brownlee, Richard S. *Gray Ghosts of the Confederacy: Guerrilla Warfare in the West, 1861–1865.* Baton Rouge, La., 1958.

Castel, Albert. *General Sterling Price and the Civil War in the West.* Baton Rouge, La., 1968.

Fellman, Michael. *Inside War: The Guerrilla Conflict in Missouri during the American Civil War.* New York, 1989.

Kirkpatrick, Arthur R. "Missouri's Secessionist Government, 1861–1865." *Missouri Historical Review* 45 (January 1951).

Parrish, William E. *A History of Missouri. Volume III, 1860 to 1875.* Columbia, Mo., 1973.

Parrish, William E. "Missouri." In *The Confederate Governors.* Edited by W. Buck Yearns. Athens, Ga., 1985.

WILLIAM E. PARRISH

MISSOURI. In early October 1862, Lt. Jonathan Carter undertook the construction of ironclads on the Red River. On November 1, Thomas Moore and John Smoker agreed to build the first vessel for $336,500. Construction was underway at Shreveport by early 1863, and although it lacked iron cladding and machinery, the vessel was launched on April 13, 1863. Lt. Comm. Charles M. Fauntleroy was assigned to command the ship, christened *Missouri.* After inspecting the vessel, however, Fauntleroy publicly proclaimed that "he hoped the damned boat would sink . . . and that he never intended to serve on her if he could help it." Fauntleroy was transferred in June and Carter took permanent command in October.

Carter secured iron from area railroads and machinery from a steamboat slated for sinking as an obstruction, and the government accepted the one thousand-ton vessel on September 12. *Missouri,* 183 feet long with a breadth of 53 feet 8 inches, had a draft of 8 feet 6 inches and could, at best, make eight knots against the current. Its single stern-wheel was exposed and the vessel leaked badly, because the hull had been constructed of green timber caulked with cotton. It eventually mounted three guns, two forward and one aft.

Missouri was finally completed in early 1864, but low water prevented it from engaging the Union fleet during the Red River campaign. It did journey to Alexandria in the spring of 1865 before Carter surrendered it in Shreveport on June 3; it was the last such vessel in Confederate waters. Taken to Mound City, Illinois, it was eventually sold for scrap.

BIBLIOGRAPHY

Jeter, Katherine Brash. "Against All Odds: Lt. Jonathan H. Carter, CSN, and His Ironclad." *Louisiana History* 28 (1987): 263–288.

Still, William N., Jr. "The Confederate Ironclad *Missouri.*" *Louisiana Studies* 4 (1965): 101–110.

Still, William N., Jr. *Iron Afloat: The Story of the Confederate Armorclads.* Nashville, Tenn., 1971.

LAWRENCE L. HEWITT

MISSOURI COMPROMISE. When Missouri applied for statehood in 1819, Representative James Tallmadge of New York moved to amend the new state's constitution to eliminate slavery. Excepting only Louisiana itself, Missouri would be the first state to be carved out of the vast expanse of the Louisiana Purchase. Its disposition would tip the existing balance of slave and free states. Of even graver potential consequence for the South, the amendment if passed threatened to "dam up Southerners in a sea of slaves" and abrogate the understanding that underpinned the Union, that the Federal government had no constitutional right to interfere with slavery in the states.

The proposed amendment gave rise to a firestorm of public controversy, evoked virtually all the pro- and antislavery arguments that would subsequently wrack the Union, illuminated the potential of the slavery issue to divide political parties along sectional lines, and brought threats of secession. "This momentous question, like a fire bell in the night, awakened and filled me with terror," Thomas Jefferson wrote; "I considered it at once as the knell of the union." Tempers cooled only after a compromise made possible by the adept legislative maneuvering of Henry Clay: Missouri and Maine entered the Union without restriction, one slave and one free; and slavery was prohibited in the great bulk of the Louisiana territory north of 36°30′.

The controversy gave rise to a resurgent "Old Republicanism" in the South in the 1820s that helped to bring Andrew Jackson to power in 1828 and to usher in the "second party system." Dependent on support from both North and South, the Jacksonian party worked to quiet discussion of the slavery question for a generation. When abolitionist pressure and the desire to build a transcontinental railroad through the unorganized area north of 36°30′ made this no longer possible, latter-day Jacksonians repealed the territorial prohibition with the Kansas-Nebraska Act (1854), and in 1857 the Supreme Court declared in the Dred Scott decision that the prohibition had never been constitutional, ruling that Congress had no power to prohibit slavery in the territories. With the effective repeal of the Missouri Compromise the national party system collapsed, all the slavery issues came once more to the fore, and secession quickly followed.

[*See also* Dred Scott Decision; Kansas-Nebraska Act.]

BIBLIOGRAPHY

Brown, Richard H. "The Missouri Crisis, Slavery, and the Politics of Jacksonianism." *South Atlantic Quarterly* 65 (1966): 55–72.

Moore, Glover. *The Missouri Controversy, 1819–1821.* Lexington, Ky., 1953.

Richard H. Brown

MITCHEL, CHARLES BURTON (1815–1864),

congressman from Arkansas. Mitchel was born September 19, 1815, in Tennessee and settled in Washington, Arkansas, in 1836. He was a prominent physician and politician before the war. In December 1860, he was nominated in the state senate as a candidate for the U.S. Senate seat vacated by Robert W. Johnson. He stated his position on the political crisis that followed the election of Abraham Lincoln as president in a speech to the General Assembly, proclaiming his support for state rights but insisting that immediate secession was unnecessary. He was elected to the Senate and remained in Washington until April the next spring, working for a political compromise to the crisis. His telegraph to the Arkansas secession convention in March 1861, reporting that President Lincoln intended to evacuate Federal forts in Charleston Harbor, may have helped the Unionists prevent secession in the convention's first session. He was the last member of the state's congressional delegation to return home.

The state legislature elected Mitchel to the Confederate Senate in 1861. He chaired the Committee on Accounts in the First Congress and the Committee on Post Offices in the Second. Along with the rest of the state delegation, Mitchel expressed concern over the failure of the government to adequately protect his state. Generally, however, he supported the Davis administration and campaigned in Arkansas for proadministration congressional candidates in the summer of 1863. Mitchel died in office while on a trip home on September 20, 1864.

BIBLIOGRAPHY

Dougan, Michael B. *Confederate Arkansas: The People and Policies of a Frontier State in Wartime.* University, Ala., 1976.

Obituary. *Arkansas Gazette* (Little Rock), September 21, 1864.

Carl H. Moneyhon

MITCHELL, JOHN K. (1811–1889), naval officer.

Born in North Carolina, Mitchell received his midshipman's appointment to the U.S. Navy as a resident of Florida. Commissioned a commander in the Confederate navy, November 11, 1861, he was assigned to command the naval station at New Orleans, charged with the construction, provisioning, and repair of naval vessels and the recruitment, assignment, and pay of personnel.

As Union forces threatened the Confederacy from both ends of the Mississippi in 1862, the War and Navy departments, certain that Forts Jackson and St. Philip could defend New Orleans, stripped the city's defenses to counter threats on the upper river. As a Federal invasion fleet gathered below New Orleans, command of the few Confederate vessels left there fell by default to Mitchell.

Molded in the naval traditions of obedience to orders and authority through channels, Mitchell could not summon the aggressive, independent efforts required to meet the Farragut-Porter offensive successfully. His few ships fought well but were overwhelmed. The forts were bombarded into surrender on April 25, 1862, and New Orleans, perhaps the Confederacy's most important city, was lost.

Although Mitchell was cleared of blame by a court of inquiry, his accidental command in a doomed situation tainted his career and later life. Assigned to head the Bureau of Orders and Detail in Richmond, he proved an undistinguished administrator with an overdeveloped respect for paperwork. He used this office—as had all his predecessors—to lobby Navy Secretary Stephen R. Mallory for command afloat, and he finally received command of the James River Squadron. Under him, the blockaded squadron attempted a foray against the Union fleet, only to be stymied by falling water that grounded Mitchell's ironclads under the fire of shore batteries and Union monitors (January 24, 1865).

When Adm. Raphael Semmes returned from Europe on February 18, 1865, Mitchell was relieved of command afloat in favor of Semmes. The James River Squadron was Mitchell's last wartime assignment.

BIBLIOGRAPHY

Dufour, Charles L. *The Night the War Was Lost.* Garden City, N.Y., 1960.

Melton, Maurice. *The Confederate Ironclads.* South Brunswick, N.J., 1968.

Scharf, J. Thomas. *History of the Confederate States Navy.* New York, 1887. Reprint, New York, 1977.

MAURICE K. MELTON

MOBILE, ALABAMA. [*This entry includes three articles:* City of Mobile, *which profiles the city during the Confederacy;* Battle of Mobile Bay, *which discusses the naval battle of 1864; and* Mobile Campaign, *which discusses the 1865 Union campaign to capture the city.*]

City of Mobile

Mobile, Alabama, the state's only seaport and the Confederacy's second largest Gulf port, virtually lost its cotton trade during the war owing to the Federal blockade and Confederate embargo. Escaping direct attack until the end of the war, the city of 30,000 in 1860 grew to about 45,000 in 1865 as it served the Confederacy as a site for training camps, recreation, and medical care.

Before the war virtually all local commercial activities, from marketing cotton to obtaining goods for planters in the interior, served the cotton trade that undergirded Mobile's economy. The city's hinterland encompassed rich cotton-producing areas in Alabama and Mississippi. Planters in both states with access to the Alabama-Tombigbee River system that flowed into the Mobile River used Mobile as their cotton market. By 1860 Mobile had surpassed all Southern ports except New Orleans as a cotton exporter. Cotton usually made up 99 percent of the total value of exports from antebellum Mobile. Lumber and lumber products, the export ranking second in value, accounted for only 1 percent of the total value of exports.

With cotton as the basis for its economy, Mobile, as much as any other Southern port, remained essentially undiversified. Many people provided services directly related to marketing cotton or entertaining planters who visited the city, and few entered other economic pursuits. A substantial portion of profits from transactions in cotton left Mobile for northeastern American cities as well as for Liverpool and Le Havre, where international firms handled many of the transport, insurance, and market arrangements for Alabama cotton. In the 1850s, to encourage the commercial independence and diversification of the local economy, civic boosters promoted railroads, direct trade, and manufacturing. All their efforts achieved limited success. For its major lines of commerce the port still depended on its river system and Mobile Bay, which flowed into the Gulf of Mexico.

A culturally diverse work force supplied the labor for the city. Most skilled workers were white, while slaves supplied much of the semiskilled and unskilled labor. They worked as domestics, draymen, mechanics, and press hands. In 1860 half of Alabama's free blacks lived in Mobile where they constituted about 3 percent of the free labor force. Stiff competition had developed among laborers in Mobile and other Southern ports in the late antebellum years when increasing numbers of white immigrants sought jobs formerly held by slaves and free blacks. By 1860 the free male labor force of Mobile consisted of 50 percent foreign-born, 34 percent Southern-born, and 16 percent Northern-born. Irish and German workers predominated among the foreign-born. Free women, white and black, comprised about one-tenth of the total free work force in Mobile.

In the 1860 presidential election, because of their concerns for maintaining financial and commercial ties between the North and the South, Mobile's voters registered preferences for moderate candidates, with 71 percent choosing Constitutional Unionist John Bell or National Democrat Stephen A. Douglas. Of major Southern ports, only New Orleans exceeded Mobile's support for moderates. Shortly after the election, however, the citizens began shifting their sympathies from moderation to secession. In the campaign for delegates to the Alabama secession convention, both major newspapers, the *Mobile Register* and the *Mobile Advertiser,* adopted cooperationist positions, but local voters favored secessionist delegates by a two-to-one majority. Native Southerners, especially slaveholders, provided many of the votes for secessionists, while nonslaveholders born in the North gave important support to cooperationists. After the passage of Alabama's ordinance of secession on January 11, 1861, Southern loyalty for secessionists eventually overrode Unionist sentiment. Mobilians supported the Confederacy hoping that it would, among other things, end their colonial relationship to the North and spur urban growth in their city.

At the outset of the Civil War the location of Mobile made it a prime target, one of ten key Southern seaports, for Union blockaders. Initially the blockade proved ineffective, with the Federals closing off only the main entrances to Mobile; the side entrances, coast, and inlets remained unguarded. In early 1862 trade continued without much interruption between New Orleans, Mobile, and Havana by bayou and inland channels. But immediately after the capture of New Orleans in April 1862, blockade running decreased sharply, and Adm. David Farragut's capture of Mobile Bay in August 1864 essentially halted it.

Despite the blockade, Mobile's gay social life continued into the war. Residents and visitors observed local social customs such as gentlemen calling on the ladies of their acquaintance on New Year's Day. Naval officers visited fashionable homes, whose hosts and hostesses they entertained in turn with shipboard balls, dinners, and moonlight cruises. A local newspaper dubbed Mobile the "Paris of the Confederacy." Some of the most fashionable homes where Mobilians entertained visiting generals, politicians, and literary figures were those of Octavia Walton Le Vert, Mary Walker Fearn, Augusta Jane Evans, and Gen. Dabney Herndon Maury, commander of the Department of the Gulf from the summer of 1863 to the end of the war. Numerous balls and concerts benefited needy groups of soldiers and civilians. As touring companies curtailed their travels during the war, the Mobile Theatre relied heavily on local actors to maintain its offerings of plays. Visitors, particularly soldiers, composed the bulk of audiences.

A variety of local hospitals provided good medical care to soldiers and civilians. Five hospitals that were operating when the war began continued in service. From 1861 through 1864 Confederate authorities built or renovated older buildings to provide seven additional hospitals for soldiers and sailors. Local women formed charitable associations to give supplies and services to patients in the hospitals. Augusta Evans even personally established and equipped a convalescent hospital on the grounds of her home.

With the blockade cutting imports through the port and Federal occupation and Confederate impressment interfering with transport of goods from the hinterland of Mobile, food shortages and inflation troubled residents. Municipal authorities sponsored a Free Market that served hundreds of poor citizens. Private organizations labored to meet needs: the Volunteer Relief Committee solicited private funds to aid the destitute, the Mobile Military Aid Society employed soldiers' dependents to sew uniforms for Alabama companies in the Confederate army, and the Mobile Supply Association hired agents to procure foodstuffs from areas north of Mobile, ship them to the city, and sell them at cost. All of these efforts failed to avert a bread riot staged in 1863 by women who were irate at shortages and high prices. Their protest sparked municipal authorities to call for new charitable groups to canvass the city, identify needy families, and solicit donations for them; these efforts apparently succeeded in relieving many in distress.

FORT MORGAN, MOBILE POINT, ALABAMA, 1864. NATIONAL ARCHIVES

Its isolation from the war allowed Mobile to provide notable educational and publishing activities for the Confederacy. Although local public and private schools reduced operations during the war and the Medical College of Alabama in the city closed its doors, Spring Hill College continued to hold its regular sessions, even with fluctuations in numbers of students and faculty. By 1865 enrollment had reached an all-time high as parents, including high-ranking Confederate officers, placed their sons in the college to protect them against the draft. Two presses in Mobile enjoyed expansion of business because of the war. W. G. Clark and Company published the *Mobile Advertiser and Register,* as well as repeated printings of readers for Southern children by Adelaide de Vendel Chaudron. S. H. Goetzel and Company published William J. Hardee's *Rifle and Light Infantry Tactics,* Augusta Jane Evans's *Macaria,* and a variety of other books.

The Confederate embargo and the Union blockade substantially reduced the trade in cotton through Mobile for the duration of the war. Disruption of foreign trade persisted after the war as Union occupying forces, which took the city in April 1865, closed the port to foreign trade until late in August. The city survived the war intact, only to lose four-fifths of its warehouse facilities on May 25, 1865, when the ordnance depot exploded, killing as many as three hundred people and destroying more than twenty blocks. Rebuilding began in the fall.

As much as Mobilians tried to revive their prewar commerce in cotton, it failed to equal earlier volume. While agriculture adjusted to the changes brought about by war and emancipation, production of cotton in Mobile's hinterland declined. Throughout Alabama cotton production did not reach 1860 levels until the 1890s. Receipts of cotton in Mobile and exports through the port lagged far behind the boom years of the 1850s, averaging during Reconstruction about 60 percent of the 1850s average. Changes in railroad networks accounted for much of the diversion of cotton away from Mobile. The export trade in lumber, however, grew markedly.

Postwar commercial developments required extensive harbor improvements, especially the deepening of the ship channel through the bay to the city docks, and harbor improvements required substantial Federal aid. Before the Civil War the U.S. government had financed dredging the channel through Choctaw Pass to ten feet, but this channel had shoaled to seven and one-half feet by 1865. From 1870 to the mid-1890s Federal funds paid for deepening and widening the channel, and these improved port facilities served an increasingly diversified export and import trade.

Mobile in 1860 had ranked seventh in population of major Southern cities and twenty-seventh among all American cities. Disruption of the cotton trade caused by the war precipitated a decline, and Mobile never again achieved as much regional or national prominence as it had in 1860 when cotton was king.

BIBLIOGRAPHY

Amos, Harriet E. " 'All-Absorbing Topics': Food and Clothing in Confederate Mobile." *Atlanta Historical Journal* 22 (1978): 17–28.

Amos, Harriet E. *Cotton City: Urban Development in Antebellum Mobile.* University, Ala., 1985.

Amos, Harriet E. "From Old to New South Trade in Mobile, 1850–1900." *Gulf Coast Historical Review* 5 (1990): 114–127.

Bergeron, Arthur W., Jr. *Confederate Mobile.* Jackson, Miss., 1991.

McLaurin, Melton, and Michael Thomason. *Mobile: The Life and Times of a Great Southern City.* Woodland Hills, Calif., 1981.

HARRIET E. AMOS DOSS

Battle of Mobile Bay

This naval battle occurred on August 5, 1864, with Confederates fighting to retain control of Mobile Bay, Alabama. Union forces under Rear Adm. David G. Farragut led a fleet of four monitors and fourteen wooden warships into the harbor, past the formidable Fort Morgan, to engage the Confederacy's few wooden ships and single ironclad.

During the early morning hours of August 5, Union ships, fastened together in pairs, moved cautiously behind the monitors into the harbor, aware that the bay floor was lined with torpedoes. Confederates, well entrenched in Fort Morgan, quickly manned their guns and unleashed a terrific rain of fire upon the enemy. One Union ship fell victim to a mine. As four wooden Confederate ships joined the fray, Union vessels returned the deadly fire. Confederate Adm. Franklin Buchanan, famous for commanding *Virginia* at Hampton Roads, ordered *Tennessee* to head straight for the fleet as it moved out of range of Fort Morgan. Several Union ships quickly maneuvered to surround the Southern vessel, spraying its iron sides with solid shot. The effect was devastating. With the ship severely damaged and Buchanan himself seriously injured, *Tennessee* surrendered to the victorious Federals. By 10:00 A.M. the Battle of Mobile Bay was over.

The battle ended in a Federal victory with the Union losing 319 men out of a total of 3,000. Mobile itself held out for another eight months, but the battle closed the port to the outside world, led to the surrender of the ironclad *Tennessee,* and cost the South 312 men killed, wounded, or captured.

BIBLIOGRAPHY

Bergeron, Arthur W., Jr. *Confederate Mobile.* Jackson, Miss., 1991.

Bowles, R. C. "The Ship Tennessee." *Southern Historical Society Papers* 21 (1893): 291–294. Reprint, Wilmington, N.C., 1990.

Johnson, Robert U., and C. C. Buel, eds. *Battles and Leaders of the Civil War.* Vol. 4. New York, 1888. Reprint, Secaucus, N.J., 1982.

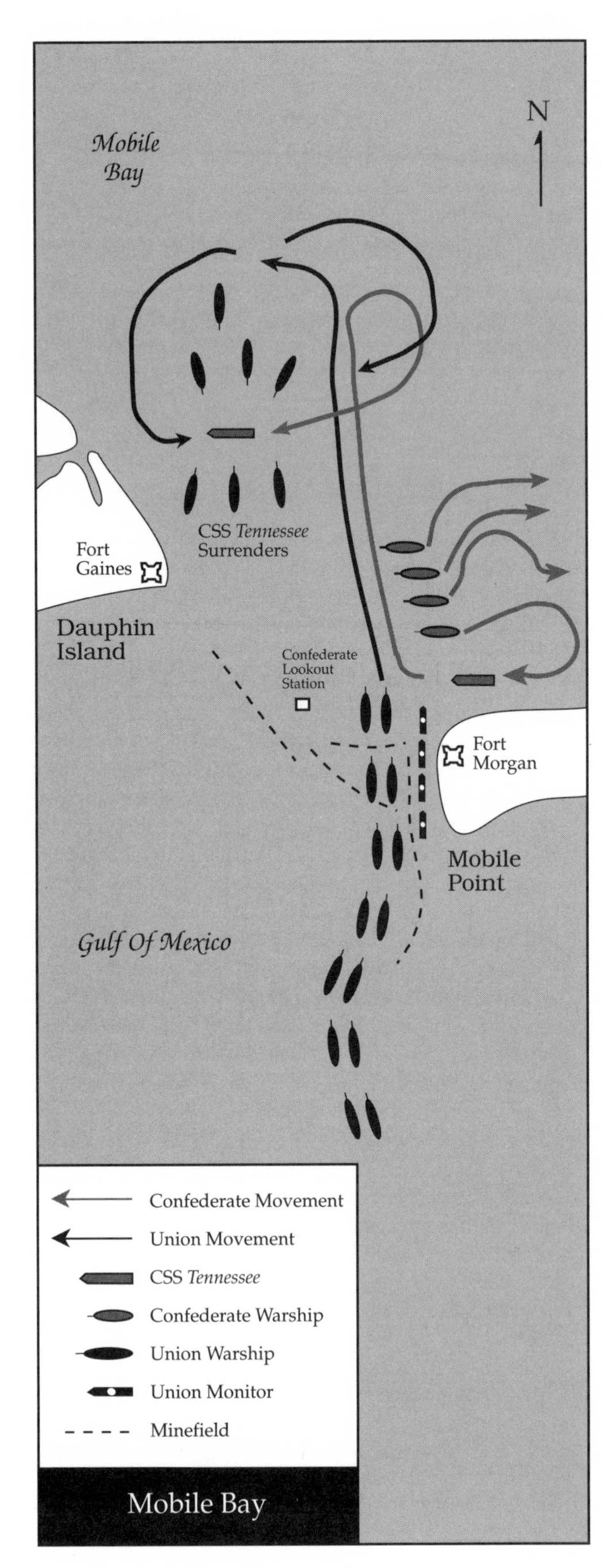

Thomas, Emory M. " 'Damn the Torpedoes': The Battle of Mobile Bay." *Civil War Times Illustrated* 16, no. 1 (1977): 5–9.

Lesley Jill Gordon-Burr

Mobile Campaign

The Mobile campaign took place from March 17 to April 12, 1865, during the final weeks of the Civil War. Mobile Bay had fallen to the Union navy in August 1864, but for eight additional months the enemy could not drive Confederates from the seaport. Thirty miles from the Gulf of Mexico, Mobile had served as a crucial port for the blockaded Confederates. It was here that Southerners built ironclads and rams to fight against the Union navy. As the Civil War entered its fourth year, a renewed Union offensive commenced in an effort to capture the city. A combined force of naval and land units laid siege to two forts surrounding Mobile. For nearly a week, Confederates offered spirited resistance but could not match the overwhelming numerical superiority of the enemy. On April 12 the Federals entered Mobile to find the city empty of Confederate soldiers. Determined and desperate, the remaining Southerners vainly sought to escape toward Montgomery. For the Confederacy the loss of Mobile was anticlimactic; three days earlier Gen. Robert E. Lee had surrendered to Gen. Ulysses S. Grant at Appomattox Courthouse in Virginia. The Confederacy would soon be no more.

After the fall of the Mississippi River to Federal control in July 1863, Union Adm. David G. Farragut had sought to wrest Mobile Bay from the Confederacy. He laid plans in January 1864 for the campaign, but it was not until early August 1864 that operations commenced against the well-fortified bay. Four hundred guns, three forts, numerous torpedoes, and floating mines defended Mobile. If an enemy invasion was going to come, Confederates were not going to make it easy. The resulting Battle of Mobile Bay was a spirited one, combining ironclad monitors and wooden vessels. Mines exploded and monitors rammed; when the smoke cleared the Confederates had lost their single ironclad *Tennessee* and the Federals had Fort Gaines and Mobile Bay.

As winter warmed to spring 1865, the city of Mobile remained in Southern hands. While Union Maj. Gen. William Tecumseh Sherman triumphantly marched through Georgia, South Carolina, and into North Carolina, and Gen. Ulysses S. Grant tightened his grip on Richmond, the scant number of defenders at Mobile poised ready for attack.

On March 17 Union troops embarked on a new mission to capture Mobile once and for all. This combined naval and land offensive included 20 ships and 45,000 men. Maj. Gen. Dabney Herndon Maury, commander of the District of the Gulf, defended Mobile with a mere 10,000 Confederates,

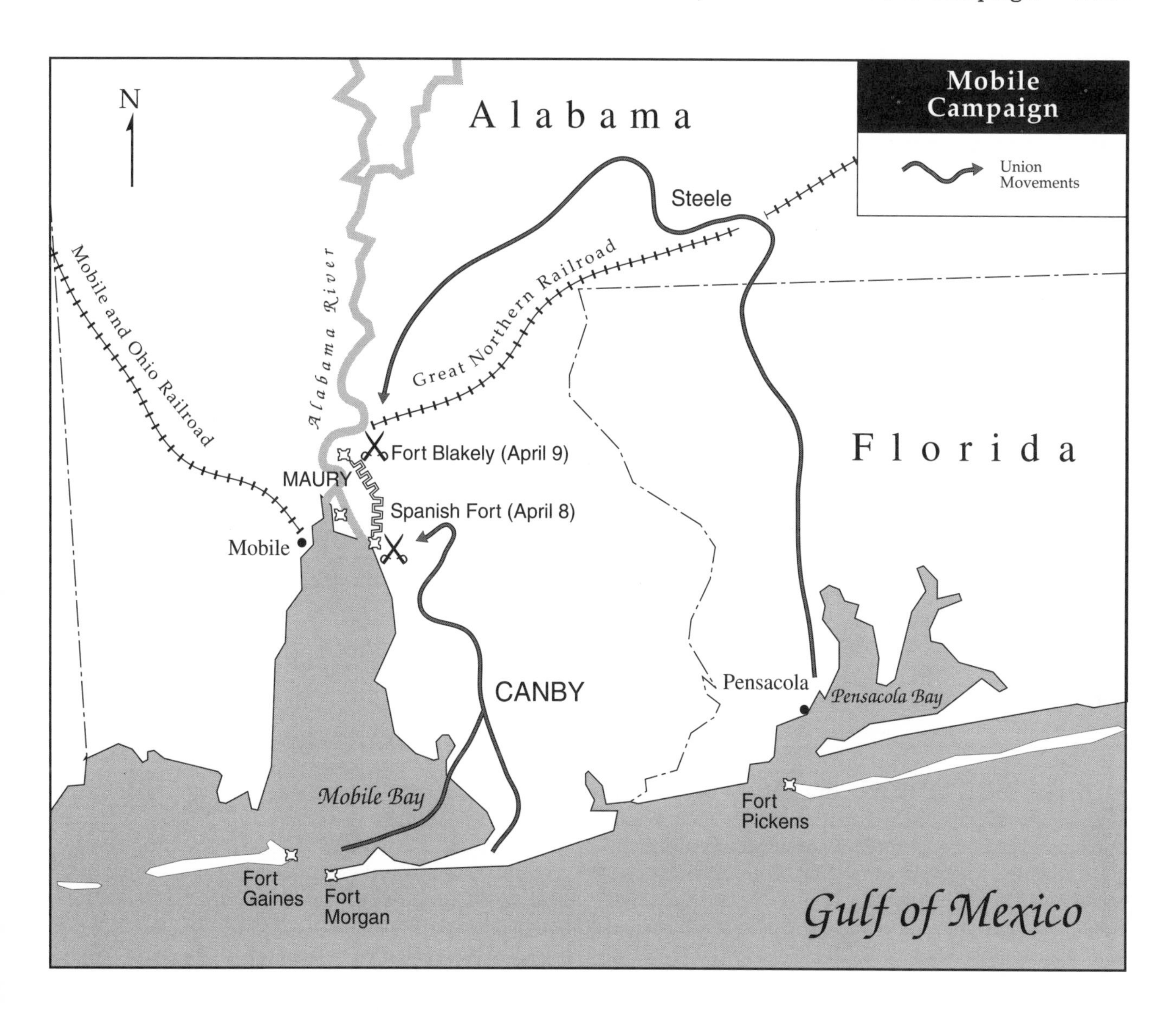

300 guns, and 5 gunboats. Federals from two directions converged on the city: 13,000 from Pensacola, Florida; the remainder, supported by gunboats, from the mouth of the bay in the east. On March 27, Federals drew near Spanish Fort, part of the inner works that defended the city from the east. From March 27 to April 8 a siege of Spanish Fort ensued. Four thousand Confederates fought eight times their strength, 32,000 Union soldiers. Over 50 siege guns and nearly 40 fieldpieces pounded into Spanish Fort's meager defenses. A final infantry assault ended the siege at midnight, April 8. Union troops captured over 3,000 prisoners and 40 guns.

Meanwhile the other contingent of Federals from Pensacola moved toward Fort Blakely, five miles north of Spanish Fort. On April 1, five miles outside of the fort, a Union cavalry detachment clashed with defending Confederates and drove them back to within a mile of the fortification. Confederates lost seventy four men while the attacking cavalrymen suffered only two casualties. Thirteen thousand enemy cavalry and infantry then laid siege to the Confederate works. A single division under Missourian Maj. Gen. Francis Marion Cockrell and a brigade commanded by William T. Thomas mustered what strength they could to fight against overwhelming odds. When Spanish Fort fell on April 8, the Federals increased their numbers at Blakely to 45,000. On April 9 the final infantry engagement of the Civil War occurred when the enemy staged a frontal assault on the besieged works. Within twenty minutes all defense had crumbled and remaining Confederates waved the white flag of surrender.

Three days later Maury evacuated Mobile, leaving 500 prisoners and 50 guns to the victorious Federals. By afternoon the mayor of Mobile had formally surrendered to Union control. Maury, with 4,500 men and 27 guns remaining, retreated with his supply train north toward Montgomery. On May 4 they too yielded to the Union.

The Mobile campaign was costly and had little effect on the war's outcome. Federals lost a total of 1,417 men; Confederate soldiers killed, wounded, missing, and captured numbered over 4,000. So many lives lost left a bitter taste in the mouth of General in Chief Grant. He later wrote:

> I had tried for more than two years to have an expedition sent against Mobile when its possession by us would have been of great advantage. It finally cost lives to take it when its possession was of no importance, and when, if left alone, it would have within a few days fallen into our hands without any bloodshed whatever.

BIBLIOGRAPHY

Johnson, Robert U., and C. C. Buel, eds. *Battles and Leaders of the Civil War.* 4 vols. New York, 1887–1888. Reprint, Secaucus, N.J., 1982.

McFeely, Mary D., and William S. McFeely, eds. *Memoirs and Selected Letters: Ulysses S. Grant.* New York, 1990.

Thomas, Emory M. " 'Damn the Torpedoes . . .': The Battle for Mobile Bay." *Civil War Times Illustrated* 16, no. 1 (April 1977): 5–9.

LESLEY JILL GORDON-BURR

MOBILE SQUADRON.

MOBILE SQUADRON. This was the Confederate naval force that defended Mobile from 1862 to 1865. It was commanded by Como. Victor M. Randolph until August 15, 1862, when he was replaced by Adm. Franklin Buchanan who served until his capture on *Tennessee* August 5, 1864. Como. Ebenezer Farrand then commanded the squadron until it surrendered May 5, 1865.

The vessels in the Mobile Squadron were either converted merchant ships or among those built in Selma and Mobile. In 1862 it included five vessels. *Baltic* was a partly armored sidewheel river towboat armed with four guns and scrapped in July 1864. *Morgan* and *Gaines,* wooden sidewheel gunboats carrying eight guns, were built in 1862. *Selma,* originally named *Florida,* was a coastal packet steamer built in Mobile in 1856. Cut down, reinforced, and partly armored, it joined the squadron in 1862. *Tennessee,* added to the squadron in July 1864, was probably the strongest ironclad built by the Confederacy. It carried six heavy guns and 6-inch armor set at a 30-degree angle.

These vessels, except for *Baltic,* formed the squadron that fought at Mobile Bay. Only *Morgan* escaped either capture or destruction. The ship's captain, Como. George W. Harrison, claimed that *Morgan* grounded in shallow water and could not rejoin the battle. As a result of this action, Adm. Franklin Buchanan accused Harrison of cowardice. He was, however, exonerated and was still in command of *Morgan* in March 1865. Other ships, most of them also built at Selma and Mobile, which joined the squadron after this were *Tuscaloosa,* a four-gun ironclad; *Huntsville,* an incomplete ironclad used as a floating battery; and *Nashville,* a heavily armored sidewheel ironclad built in Montgomery and Mobile. These vessels defended Mobile until the squadron's surrender on May 4, 1865.

[*See also* Mobile, Alabama.]

BIBLIOGRAPHY

Civil War Naval Chronology, 1861–1865. 6 vols. Washington, D.C., 1961–1966.

Jones, Virgil C. *The Civil War at Sea.* 3 vols. New York, 1961–1962.

Potter, E. B. *Illustrated History of the United States Navy.* New York, 1971.

Register of Officers of the Confederate States Navy, 1861–1865. Washington, D.C., 1931.

Scharf, John Thomas. *History of the Confederate States Navy from Its Organization to the Surrender of Its Last Vessel.* New York, 1887.

FRANK LAWRENCE OWSLEY

MONEY. *See* Currency.

MONOCACY, MARYLAND. *See* Early's Washington Raid.

MONROE, THOMAS BELL (1791–1865), congressman from Kentucky. Monroe brought a distinguished legal career to the Confederacy and provided important leadership in the Provisional Congress. A distant relative of President James Monroe, he was born in Albemarle County, Virginia, and migrated to Scott County, Kentucky, with his parents in 1793. Educated in public schools along the Kentucky frontier and later in law at Transylvania University, Monroe moved to Barren County and was elected to the Kentucky legislature in 1816.

Within several years Monroe emerged as one of the commonwealth's leading jurists and legal educators. He held various posts, including secretary of state for Kentucky (1823), reporter for the state court of appeals (1825–1828), publisher of the seven-volume *Moore's Kentucky Reports,* and professor of law at Transylvania and the University of Louisiana. In 1833 he was appointed U.S. district attorney, and in the following year, President Andrew Jackson appointed him U.S. district judge, a post he held until the start of the Civil War. He received three honorary law degrees, including one from Harvard University.

A Democrat, Monroe supported secession and fled Kentucky in 1861. The Provisional Government of Kentucky soon after appointed him a representative from the Eighth

District to the Provisional Congress. He served on the Foreign Affairs, Military Affairs, and Judiciary committees. On the latter committee Monroe helped to draft laws pertaining to sequestration, retaliation, judicial organization, and Indian rights. He favored a strong central government. One of the oldest Confederate legislators (Monroe was seventy-one years old in 1861), he elected not to run for office in either regular Congress. Monroe practiced law until he died, a refugee in Pass Christian, Mississippi, in 1865.

BIBLIOGRAPHY

Quisenberry, A. C. "The Alleged Secession of Kentucky." *Register of the Kentucky State Historical Society* 15 (1917): 15–32.

Wakelyn, Jon L. *Biographical Dictionary of the Confederacy.* Edited by Frank E. Vandiver. Westport, Conn., 1977.

Warner, Ezra J., and W. Buck Yearns. *Biographical Register of the Confederate Congress.* Baton Rouge, La., 1975.

JOHN DAVID SMITH

MONROE DOCTRINE. In 1861, Confederate diplomat John T. Pickett warned the Mexican Liberals that the Monroe Doctrine was dead, and they should not "delude themselves with the belief that North and South will combine together to resist this European Intervention in American affairs." As King Cotton proved ineffective in inducing European action to ensure Southern independence, the Confederacy was willing to overlook the Monroe Doctrine—the policy announced by President James Monroe on December 2, 1823, which had declared the New World off limits for the colonial or political ambitions of European powers. The South indicated it would guarantee French emperor Napoleon III's position in Mexico against U.S. interference in return for French recognition, which Southern diplomats believed would result in a U.S.–French military confrontation.

The Confederate leaders assumed that Archduke Maximilian's Mexico would be a sympathetic neighbor. In 1864, Confederate diplomat William Preston warned Maximilian and the French that the United States was committed to the Monroe Doctrine and the preservation of democratic government in the New World. He suggested that Maximilian should turn to the Confederacy for friendship and a barrier against the North. The South's desire for French recognition prevented any expression of concern about French intervention in Mexico until after Maximilian's refusal to receive Preston eroded Southern respect for imperial Mexico. As a result, in November 1864, Confederate Congressmen John Porry Murray and Henry S. Foote, both from Tennessee, introduced a series of joint resolutions that declared a lack of sympathy with monarchical government in the New World and asserted that the Confederacy would adhere to the principles of the Monroe Doctrine. Rather than rejecting the doctrine, the South had been offering to trade it for something it desired more—independence.

In the winter of 1864–1865, U.S. politician Francis P. Blair, Sr., schemed to preserve the Monroe Doctrine and to end the Civil War by uniting the North and South in military action against the French in Mexico. In January 1865, responding to the Blair proposal, Virginian Congressman Daniel C. de Jarnette introduced a resolution to end all "seeming violations" of the Monroe Doctrine and to pave the way for a joint military expedition to clear foreign troops from Mexico. This belated concern for the Monroe Doctrine occurred long after the Confederacy had passed up its opportunities in foreign relations.

BIBLIOGRAPHY

Fabela, Isidro. "La Doctrina Monroe y la segunda intervención Francesa en México." *Cuadernos Americanos* 16, no. 5 (1957): 210–214.

Owsley, Frank. *King Cotton Diplomacy.* Rev. ed. Chicago, 1959.

Perkins, Dexter. *The Monroe Doctrine, 1826–1867.* Cambridge, Mass., 1933. Reprint, Gloucester, Mass., 1965.

Schoonover, Thomas. *Dollars over Dominion: The Triumph of Liberalism in Mexican–United States Relations, 1861–1867.* Baton Rouge, La., 1978.

THOMAS SCHOONOVER

MONTAGUE, ROBERT LATANE (1819–1880), congressman from Virginia. Born in Middlesex County, Virginia, Montague graduated from the College of William and Mary in 1842. He owned a large farm near Saluda and practiced law in his native county, which he served for a term in the House of Delegates (1850–1851) and as commonwealth attorney (1852–1860). A Democrat and an active Baptist layman, Montague married Cordelia Gay Eubank. One of their eight children, A. J. Montague, became governor of Virginia. Robert Montague was elected lieutenant governor in 1860 and called for secession when Abraham Lincoln was elected.

Montague's oratorical skills earned him election as president of the 1861 Virginia convention. When Virginia finally followed the path Montague had urged, Governor John Letcher appointed him an ex officio member of the executive committee to prepare the state for war. The committee welcomed Jefferson Davis to Richmond in May, but friction soon developed between the committee and the Confederate government, which rapidly took over the Virginia capital. Montague won election to the Second Congress in 1863 and used his position to defend the administration fully. He believed in deferring to the president's authority in military affairs, agreed to wide-ranging impressment of goods, and urged stringent application of conscription laws. He took an interest in financial legislation and the treatment of prisoners of war and wounded soldiers. Keen to support the military effort, he opposed the right of men to contest legally their liability to conscription.

After the war Montague returned to the law and sat in the House of Delegates once more. He was elected judge of the Eighth Judicial Circuit and held that position until he died at his home on March 2, 1880.

BIBLIOGRAPHY

Gaines, William H., Jr. *Biographical Register of Members, Virginia State Convention of 1861, First Session.* Richmond, Va., 1969.

Rogers, George Wesley. *Officers of the Senate of Virginia, 1776–1956.* Richmond, Va., 1959.

Wakelyn, Jon L. *Biographical Dictionary of the Confederacy.* Edited by Frank E. Vandiver. Westport, Conn., 1977.

Warner, Ezra J., and W. Buck Yearns. *Biographical Register of the Confederate Congress.* Baton Rouge, La., 1975.

NELSON D. LANKFORD

MONTGOMERY, BENJAMIN (1819–1877), slave-born Mississippi merchant-planter and black leader. Born in Virginia, Benjamin T. Montgomery learned to read and write with his young master. When he was nineteen, Montgomery was sold to Jefferson Davis's elder brother and neighbor Joseph E. Davis, under whose tutelage he continued his literary education while learning engineering and mechanical skills useful on a large Mississippi River plantation. Davis ruled that a slave might keep any money he earned beyond his worth as a field hand. Soon Montgomery was repairing the steam gin and mill as well as planning new buildings and designing a levee system to prevent destructive floods. Shortly before the Civil War Montgomery invented an innovative boat propeller that weighed a fraction of the conventional paddle wheel. Although he never succeeded in patenting his invention, he displayed it at the Western Sanitary Fair in Cincinnati in 1863.

In 1842 Montgomery established a store on the Davis plantation, selling dry goods and staple items. Davis guaranteed his first consignment of goods, but from then on the slave maintained his own line of credit with New Orleans wholesalers. Soon he was acting as Davis's agent, buying plantation supplies and selling the huge cotton crop. From his profits Montgomery built a combined store building and living quarters for his wife, Mary Lewis Montgomery, and their children.

In 1862, when Joseph Davis and his family fled from Federal gunboats, Montgomery was left in charge of two plantations and a large slave force belonging to both Joseph and Jefferson Davis. Struggling to keep the people fed and clothed, Montgomery was befriended by Union Adm. David D. Porter who sent him and his family to safety in Cincinnati as the siege of nearby Vicksburg intensified. Porter enlisted Montgomery's young son, Isaiah, as his cabin boy and encouraged his older son, Thornton, to join the Union navy. By late 1864 all three Montgomery men were working in a canal boat yard in Cincinnati.

When the war ended, the Montgomerys returned to the Mississippi plantations and reopened Montgomery & Sons store. There Benjamin tried to create an ideal community of freedmen despite interference by agents of the Freedmen's Bureau. When Joseph Davis regained possession of his confiscated plantations in 1866, he immediately sold them to Montgomery and his sons for $300,000 with no down payment and at an annual interest rate of 6 percent. Despite floods, insect pests, falling prices, and government interference, Montgomery succeeded in building one of the largest planter-merchant operations in Mississippi, including three plantations and a mercantile commission agency with several stores. He and his family lived in the plantation home of Jefferson Davis in much the same style as the former occupants had.

As leader of the community of freed slaves at Davis Bend, Montgomery stressed self-help, industriousness, and cooperation for mutual advance. He tried to avoid involvement in politics, but the need to preserve order led him to accept the post of justice of the peace in 1867, the first black to hold public office in Mississippi.

[*See also* Davis Bend.]

BIBLIOGRAPHY

Hermann, Janet Sharp. *Joseph E. Davis, Pioneer Patriarch.* Jackson, Miss., 1990.

Hermann, Janet Sharp. *The Pursuit of a Dream.* New York, 1981.

Hermann, Janet Sharp. "Reconstruction in Microcosm: Three Men and a Gin." *Journal of Negro History* 65, no. 4 (1980): 312–335.

Litwack, Leon, and August Meier, eds. *Black Leaders of the Nineteenth Century.* Urbana, Ill., 1988.

JANET SHARP HERMANN

MONTGOMERY, ALABAMA. Montgomery became the focus of national attention in February 1861 when the city became the first capital of the Confederate States of America. Situated near the headwaters of the Alabama River, Montgomery had served as the state capital since 1849. Although Mobile was the largest city in Alabama in 1860, Montgomery claimed the next largest population, with about 9,000 citizens, of whom some 4,000 were black. Planters, lawyers, and the more successful entrepreneurs dominated the city. Often they owned slaves. That fact distinguished them from the majority of the citizens who owned no human chattel or other assets of the affluent.

Most of Montgomery's population had been born in the United States, although some were of European origin. A few free blacks (seventy in 1860) lived in Alabama's capital city, but the vast majority of blacks were slaves.

Agriculture represented the most important source of wealth, and slaves produced much of that prosperity. The river city, located in Alabama's alluvial black belt, was a center of cotton commerce. Montgomery flourished in the decade preceding the Civil War. Evidence of growth—imposing Italian-style mansions, new churches, a growing population—testified to the prosperity. A theater opened to much acclaim in 1860. By then Montgomery had ceased to be a rough frontier town.

Yet Montgomerians worried about the future. The debate over the extension of slavery threatened to break up the Union. A series of crises, climaxing with Abraham Lincoln's election in 1860, convinced most that secession was necessary, and no city in Alabama was as blatantly secessionist in outlook as Montgomery. William Lowndes Yancey, a resident and fire-eater, had advocated separation as early as 1850. John C. Breckinridge carried the city easily in the election of 1860. Relatively few Montgomerians approved the cautious course recommended by Stephen A. Douglas. Despite having spoken in Montgomery just days before the election, he received only 112 votes.

The national Republican victory led to the establishment of the Confederate States of America. At Montgomery, on January 11, a secessionist convention voted to leave the Union. That decision, rendered in the capitol building, which looked down Market Street, was anticipated, and hundreds of citizens had gathered. Cannon blasts, the raising of flags, pealing church bells, and an extended celebration followed well into the night.

Six lower South states had cut their ties with the Union by the end of January. It remained for those states to form a government. Montgomery hosted the convention that consummated the Confederacy. The city's selection was due largely to its central location and convenient river and

MONTGOMERY. View of the city celebrating its inauguration as the capital of the Confederacy, February 8, 1861.

Harper's Pictorial History of the Great Rebellion

railroad facilities. Montgomery was transformed in early February by arriving politicians, soldiers, newspaper reporters, and certainly office seekers. As a *New York Herald* correspondent observer, Montgomery had "become a focal point of interest to the whole nation" and "when the present times shall have become historic, Montgomery will be read of as the scene of one of the most wonderful revolutions." Visitors jammed the city's two hotels, the Exchange and the Madison House, crowded its dirt streets, and, pleased merchants noted, spent large sums of money.

Convening in the capitol, thirty-seven delegates began secret deliberations on February 4. Within days much of the vital work was completed: the Provisional Constitution was drafted and a vice president, Alexander H. Stephens, and a president, Jefferson Davis, were elected. The arrival of Davis several days later occasioned more festivities. That evening, at the Exchange, Yancey assured the gathered crowd, "the man and hour have met."

The Provisional Constitution provided that until otherwise decided Montgomery would be the capital, and the city took on the trappings of a government seat. A downtown building was converted into an executive complex where Davis and his cabinet members conducted government business. Varina Howell Davis arrived soon, and the first family moved into a two-story residence. The social scene reminded some of Washington. Mary Boykin Chesnut, the famous diarist, described a dinner party as "brilliant," and Howell Cobb, president of the convention, wrote after attending a ball that he had never seen "so ample a repast." In the meantime, Montgomery became the destination of some men who would soon be well known: P. G. T. Beauregard, Raphael Semmes, Joseph E. Johnston, and Braxton Bragg numbered among the visitors.

But in March, war loomed. President Lincoln stated in his inaugural address that the Union was perpetual. Compromising efforts, such as a peace convention, failed, and tension intensified at Fort Sumter when Federal forces refused to evacuate. From Montgomery, on April 12, orders were telegraphed to General Beauregard, and Confederate batteries opened fire on the fort in Charleston Harbor.

The beginning of the war forced a decision on the remaining Southern states in the Union. Within a month, five more states joined the Confederacy. Among them was Virginia and a move was soon underway to make Richmond the capital. Inadequate accommodations in Montgomery and its hot climate motivated some who favored removal. Some members of Congress argued that Virginia's safety, linked to the security of the entire Confederacy, was dependent upon locating the government there. Considerable support existed for maintaining Montgomery as the capital, but on May 20 a vote for removal barely carried.

Montgomery nevertheless remained important to the Confederacy. The city was on a major railroad thoroughfare, and thousands of troops passed through each month, with some entering one of the seven military hospitals. Montgomery also served as a major supply depot. Huge quantities of food, especially corn, were gathered there for the armies. Over the railroad lines leading in and out of the city, supplies were transported to the front. Small arms were also manufactured in Montgomery and a niter works operated.

THE WHITE HOUSE. Jefferson Davis resided in this house from February 1861 until May 1861, when the capital was moved from Montgomery to Richmond, Virginia.

HARPER'S PICTORIAL HISTORY OF THE GREAT REBELLION

In 1862, Federal troops occupied parts of northern Alabama and Montgomerians began to fear for their safety. If the enemy overran Mobile, and there was speculation of that, citizens worried about an approach from the south. But it was not until July 1864 that Federal forces threatened central Alabama. Even then Gen. Lovell Rousseau's troops only destroyed railroad track east of Montgomery, temporarily slowing the resupply of Confederate troops defending Atlanta.

A more serious threat materialized in early April 1865. Forces under Gen. James Wilson swept down from northern Alabama and defeated outnumbered Confederates at Selma. The enemy reached Montgomery on April 12. Although defensive works existed, Mayor Andrew Noble surrendered the city without a fight. The Union troops spared Montgomery but did burn some rolling mills and the small arms factory. Montgomery, where the Confederacy had been born, had fallen. On that same day, in Virginia, Robert E. Lee surrendered to Ulysses S. Grant.

[See also *Montgomery Convention.*]

BIBLIOGRAPHY

Flynt, J. Wayne. *Montgomery: An Illustrated History.* Woodland Hills, Calif., 1980.

Jones, James Pickett. *Yankee Blitzkrieg: Wilson's Raid through Alabama and Georgia.* Athens, Ga., 1976.

Napier, John H. "Montgomery during the Civil War." *Alabama Review* 4 (April 1988): 103–131.

Patrick, Rembert. *Jefferson Davis and His Cabinet.* Baton Rouge, La., 1944.

WILLIAM WARREN ROGERS, JR.

MONTGOMERY CONVENTION. Held in Alabama's capitol building from February 4 to May 21, 1861, this convention of delegates from the seven originally seceded states—South Carolina, Georgia, Florida, Alabama, Mississippi, Louisiana, and Texas (whose delegates arrived late)—launched the Confederate government. In addition to choosing a provisional president and vice president, the convention wrote provisional and permanent constitutions and, after organizing itself into a Provisional Congress, passed a spate of legislation to set the machinery of the new government in motion and gear it for war.

Each state in the convention was allowed the same number of delegates as its delegation in the Federal Congress at Washington: one for each representative and two at-large delegates. The convention operated unicamerally, however. Each state was allowed only one vote. Chosen by the secession conventions in their respective states, the vast majority of the fifty men who served in Montgomery were well-to-do planters and lawyers of considerable political experience. Sixty percent were Democrats; the other 40 percent, Whigs. All in all, they comprised a broad cross section of the South's traditional political leadership. The composition of the convention belied the revolutionary nature of the business it was about. Almost half of its delegates were Unionists or cooperationists who had been either outright opponents or at best lukewarm supporters of secession. Fire-eating radicals were distinctly underrepresented at Montgomery.

Because of the convention's decision to hold most of its sessions in secret, both contemporary observers and later historians found it difficult to learn details of the convention's actions and deliberations. Although not popular with the press, the decision for secrecy at Montgomery was never seriously questioned by the delegates. All of them recognized the need to attract foreign recognition of the Confederate States. Presenting a united and self-confident front to the world (including the United States) thus became an overriding imperative at Montgomery. The delegates naturally wanted to minimize any reports of dissension and disagreement among themselves. Equally important was avoiding any hint of precipitousness. At all costs, the Southern experiment had to appear reasoned, moderate, and justified.

It was if anything even more important that it appear this way to the border states. The slave states still remaining in the Union—who though not officially represented at the convention had all sent observers—played a crucial role in its deliberations. Devoted to the American Union, yet bound economically and temperamentally to the lower South, the border states constituted a potential infusion of vast resources for the new Southern nation if they could be induced to join it. Hence their sensitivities and desires had to be consulted at almost every turn.

The Confederate Constitution. After electing Georgian Howell Cobb as president of the convention, the thirty-seven delegates then on hand set about their work with little dissension or debate. On the convention's second day, it adopted rules drawn up by Alexander H. Stephens of Georgia and named a Committee of Twelve headed by Christopher G. Memminger of South Carolina to frame a provisional government. This committee, using a draft Memminger brought with him as a basis, produced the Provisional Constitution in only two days. The convention adopted it unanimously on February 8. On the following day, the convention, sitting now as the Provisional Congress of the Confederate States, named another committee of twelve members (chaired by Robert Barnwell Rhett, Sr., of South Carolina) to draft a permanent constitution. This committee reported its draft of the permanent Constitution to the Provisional Congress (sitting as a constitutional convention) on the last day of February. Following extensive discussion and the adoption of several amendments, the convention unanimously approved the draft on March 11.

Confronted with the immediate need to reassure the border states of the essential conservatism of their movement, the delegates adopted a fundamental law closely resembling the Constitution of the United States. Indeed, except for a few important differences, it was copied verbatim from that revered document. The main differences were features that more closely guaranteed state rights and protected the institution of slavery. Other changes made minor, but significant improvements in governmental machinery. The preamble bluntly declared that each state acted "in its sovereign and independent character" to form not "a more perfect Union" but a "permanent federal government." State legislatures were allowed to impeach agents of the federal government acting solely within the boundaries of a state. Nonetheless, state officers were bound by oath to support the Confederate Constitution, which along with Confederate laws and treaties was the "supreme law of the land." Although there was some sentiment for explicitly allowing the right of secession in the document, neither it nor John C. Calhoun's theory of state nullification of Confederate statutes was included.

Avoiding circumlocutions, the Confederate Constitution called a slave a slave. It explicitly protected the institution of slavery in the states and any territories that might be acquired. But in several ways the convention refused to adopt more radical proslavery provisions. For example, the importation of slaves from abroad was prohibited. This provision not only preserved a hallowed prohibition of the old Constitution but also indirectly endorsed the upper South's economic stake in the interstate slave trade. The convention also voted to preserve the three-fifths clause as the basis for apportioning representation in the new Congress. The Confederacy was indeed to be a slaveholding republic, but most of its founding fathers balked at stirring up needless antagonism among nonslaveholders, especially with the destiny of the border states still much in doubt. Nor were extreme Southern nationalists successful in passing an amendment barring free states from future membership in the Confederacy. Moderates led by Alexander Stephens blocked this move to limit the future expansion of the new republic.

Enshrining two long-held Southern beliefs, the Constitution allowed a tariff for revenue, but not one for protecting domestic enterprises, and it forbade central government appropriations for internal improvements. Other features of the Constitution aimed at greater economy and efficiency in the management of fiscal affairs. Congress was allowed to appropriate money only by a two-thirds vote in both houses, and the amount and purpose of each appropriation had to be explicitly spelled out. The president was allowed a single-item veto of appropriations bills. Although this provision strengthened the executive, as did another that allowed cabinet members nonvoting seats on the floor of Congress, the branch was weakened by limiting the president to a single six-year term. Interestingly, the Confederacy retained the electoral college system to elect its executive officers. Although it was widely disliked, no one could devise a suitable alternative.

Choosing a President and Vice President. The choice of president for the Confederacy engendered the most interest in Montgomery. But the overriding necessity for presenting a united front to the world dictated that the choice be unanimous and that pre-election politicking be carried out behind closed doors. The fact of secrecy not only clouded the process for contemporaries but has made it equally baffling to historians. There was no shortage of qualified candidates. As long-standing secessionists, both William Lowndes Yancey of Alabama and Rhett had good claims on the office. Georgia had three experienced, qualified politicians meriting consideration: Cobb, Stephens, and Robert Toombs. Even Robert M. T. Hunter of Virginia had some support.

For one reason or another none of these candidates was acceptable to the majority. Fire-eaters Yancey and Rhett were anathema to the border state conservatives, whom the delegates in Montgomery studiously avoided offending. The diminutive Stephens, on the other hand, had opposed secession until the very moment Georgia left the Union, and as an ex-Whig, he lacked the proper party pedigree among supporters of the movement for Southern independence. Fiery Robert Toombs suffered the same disability, although he had embraced secession earlier, and he may have further hurt his chances by gross overindulgence in alcohol at Montgomery. Cobb let it be known that he did not want the office. All three Georgians, moreover, suffered the identical stigma of lacking the unanimous endorsement of their own delegation, which was hardly surprising given the deep political and personal animosities among that state's delegates.

From the first there appears to have been a strong current in favor of Jefferson Davis of Mississippi for the presidency. A Democrat and moderate secessionist with experience in the national House and Senate as well as in the cabinet as secretary of war, Davis also had military experience, having graduated from West Point and served with distinction during the Mexican War. Besides being on almost everyone's short list of candidates, Davis had the important endorsements of Virginia's two pro-secession senators, James Mason and Hunter. When the state delegations caucused on the evening of February 8, Mississippi, Florida, and Alabama had lined up solidly behind Davis. By the following morning, only the Georgians remained divided, but to preserve harmony they promptly acquiesced. The convention elected Jefferson Davis provisional president unanimously on the afternoon of Saturday, February 9.

At the same time, it elected Alexander H. Stephens provisional vice president. The choice did not turn out to be a particularly happy one, but as in so many decisions taken at Montgomery, political imperatives overshadowed more practical alternatives. Obviously the most populous and powerful state of the Deep South could not be slighted. And as the foremost antisecessionist in the South, Stephens seemed the logical choice to attract and weld conditional Unionists and cooperationists to the new government. Stephens took the oath of office on February 11; Davis was inaugurated a week later, three days after his arrival in Montgomery.

The Provisional Congress. The Montgomery convention quickly became for the South the successor to the Federal government. After study by committee, it adopted the Stars and Bars as the national flag. It dispatched commissioners to foreign powers and to Washington to negotiate for Federal property within the Confederacy. It passed a law continuing all Federal legislation in force until November 1860, so long as these laws were consistent with the Confederate Constitution or not explicitly repealed by Congress, and it formed a committee to revise U.S. laws to fit the Confederacy. It also voted to retain the existing customs agents in the South.

The most urgent task confronting the convention was organizing and equipping an army. The Provisional Congress had initially created both a Regular Army and a Provisional Army, authorizing the recruitment of 100,000 troops who would serve either six-month or one-year enlistments. After the war started, this number was raised to 400,000 who would serve either for three years or for the duration of the conflict.

Raising money for the new government presented an almost equally pressing problem. Reluctant to strain loyalty by imposing taxes, Congress elected to rely on loans. On February 28, it passed the first major piece of financial legislation: the issue of $15 million worth of twenty-year 8 percent Treasury bonds. The onset of the war required the issue of another $50 million worth of these bonds in mid-May. Because of the dearth of hard money in the South, this law authorized payment for the bonds either in military supplies or with agricultural or manufactured products as well as specie. This so-called produce loan became a key feature of future Confederate financing. Noteworthy, too, was a provision of the law allowing the Treasury to issue $20 million worth of non-interest-bearing notes, paper currency, which would be redeemable in gold two years after the close of hostilities. This was the first wave in what became a flood of increasingly worthless paper money.

On May 21, Congress elected to move the capital of the Confederacy to Richmond, Virginia, thus bringing the Montgomery convention to a close. On balance, the convention had performed its task admirably. During its three and a half months of existence, it had in relative harmony set up a viable government, elected executive officers for it, produced its fundamental law, and begun the formidable task of setting it on a war footing. It had, in fact, formalized the South's "conservative revolution."

[*See also* Congress; Constitution; Presidency; Vice Presidency; *and biographies of numerous figures mentioned herein.*]

BIBLIOGRAPHY

Coulter, E. Merton. *The Confederate States of America, 1861–1865.* A History of the South, vol. 7. Baton Rouge, La., 1950.

Lee, Charles Robert, Jr. *The Confederate Constitutions.* Chapel Hill, N.C., 1963.

Randall, J. G., and David H. Donald. *The Civil War and Reconstruction.* 2d ed. Lexington, Mass., 1969.

Thomas, Emory M. *The Confederate Nation: 1861–1865.* New York, 1979.

Yearns, Wilfred B. *The Confederate Congress.* Athens, Ga., 1960.

Thomas E. Schott

MONUMENTS AND MEMORIALS.

[*This entry contains two articles discussing the statues, buildings, parks, and battlefields that honor and preserve the memory of the Confederacy and the Civil War:* An Overview *and* Battlefields. *For further discussion of Confederate monuments and memorials, see* Lee Monument Association; Lost Cause; *and* Memorial Organizations.]

An Overview

On a courthouse lawn stands a single stone soldier, at ease but facing north to challenge any Yankee advance. This stereotype of the Confederate monument has become one of the most common symbols of the South, especially for those from outside the region. Many Confederate monuments do look just like that, but the stereotype ignores the diversity of monument designs and oversimplifies the movement that produced them.

Southerners erected monuments not just to the common soldiers but to prominent Confederate leaders. There are several monuments to Robert E. Lee, the most honored individual, including a recumbent statue at Washington and Lee University, a towering standing figure in New Orleans, and a massive, mounted likeness on Monument Avenue in Richmond, Virginia. Monument Avenue also boasts statues to Matthew Fontaine Maury, J. E. B. Stuart, Thomas J. ("Stonewall") Jackson, and Jefferson Davis. Statues of Davis and Jackson were erected in other cities as well, and their likenesses, along with that of Lee, were carved into the face of Stone Mountain, Georgia, the most massive of Confederate monuments, which was first conceived in 1915 but not completed until 1970.

Long before, Southerners erected still other types of monuments, including a few to Confederate women and one, in Fort Mill, South Carolina, to Confederate Catawba Indians. But most Confederate monuments, as the popular stereotype suggests, honored the memory of the common soldiers. The overwhelming majority were erected in the first fifty years after the war, usually through a popular fund-raising effort led by a local women's memorial association or, later, a United Daughters of the Confederacy (UDC) chapter. The inscriptions these groups chose, of varying lengths and eloquence, praised the Confederate soldiers' honor, devotion to country, and sometimes their cause as well. The form selected for the monuments varied, too, from a towering rock pyramid in Richmond's Hollywood Cemetery to a reclining lion in Atlanta's Oakland Cemetery. Baltimore and at least two other cities chose designs that included an allegorical figure for fame. Despite some diversity, however, patterns in design and placement do emerge and help elucidate the development of the Lost Cause, which produced the monuments.

The first Confederate monument, a simple stone pillar,

JEFFERSON DAVIS MONUMENT. The monument was erected in Richmond, Virginia, in 1907. The inscription on the lower part of the column reads: "Jefferson Davis, President of the Confederate States of America, 1861–1865." On the exterior architrave is inscribed: "Erected by the People of the South in honor of their great leader, commemorating their love for the man, their reverence for his virtues, their gratitude for his services." Quotations by Davis and other inscriptions line the interior and exterior architecture.

ELEANOR S. BROCKENBROUGH LIBRARY, THE MUSEUM OF THE CONFEDERACY, RICHMOND, VIRGINIA

was erected in a cemetery in Cheraw, South Carolina, in 1867. During the following two decades most towns that dedicated Confederate monuments placed them in cemeteries and chose some sort of funereal design for them, usually an obelisk or other simple shaft, topped by an urn or a draped cloth. In placing funeral statues in cemeteries, and in celebrating the newly established Confederate Memorial Day, Southerners mourned the death not only of beloved friends and relatives but of their cause and would-be nation. Like mourning in other contexts, the process allowed them to assimilate the loss of the war and distance themselves from the failed cause.

In the late 1880s and 1890s, funereal designs became less common in Confederate monuments, and statues of soldiers, not uncommon before, became typical. Some of these statues had intricate bases. Some of the soldiers on them were cast of bronze; a few struck a heroic pose or carried a flag. But the lone marble soldier, standing at rest or even leaning on his rifle, atop a relatively simple shaft came to dominate designs. At about the same time, thoroughfares and, especially after 1900, courthouse lawns replaced cemeteries as the locations usually chosen for Confederate monuments. And the number of monuments erected increased dramatically; the overwhelming majority of Confederate monuments were dedicated between 1895 and 1915. A desire to honor aging veterans before they died no doubt contributed to the increasing pace of memorialization. But the rise in the number of monuments and, more important, the new sites and design selected for them also reflected the growing sense of vindication Southerners felt at the turn of the century. Statues honoring the Confederacy, placed not in an isolated cemetery but in the very center of the community, testified to Southerners' conviction that their cause had been noble and their soldiers heroic and manly. Through their choice of a lone soldier, in effect celebrating a representative faithful common man, Southerners may also have sought to reinforce the values of loyalty to country and deference to leaders at a time of political unrest and social change. Probably this is why there was relatively little renewed sectionalism accompanying the dedication of the monuments. The soldiers on most monuments were symbolically as well as figuratively at rest, and fewer than half of them faced North—most faced the direction the courthouse did.

Commercialism also contributed to the increase in the number of monuments and similarity in design after 1900. Two or three companies participated in this, but none more than the McNeal Monument Company. This Marietta, Georgia, firm dispatched traveling agents to drum up business, offering free marble breadboards to officers of UDC chapters who signed with them, promising easy credit terms, and advertising Confederate memorial drinking fountains that combined "Art, Sentiment, and Utility." A few towns actually erected a memorial fountain.

Such commercialization suggests that the popular need for memorialization had begun to decline; after 1915 comparatively few Confederate monuments were erected, although one was put up as late as 1980. As the twentieth century progressed, some existing monuments fell into disrepair or had to be relocated to make way for automobile traffic. More recently, a few Confederate monuments became objects of controversy when African Americans complained that they honored slavery and racism. Monuments, though, have been far less frequently embroiled in controversy than the Confederate flag, perhaps because, unlike the flag, Confederate monuments rarely became symbols of white opposition to civil rights in the 1950s and 1960s. In fact, though Confederate monuments remain prominent in the symbolic landscape of Southern literature, and are a historic part of the physical landscape of the region, and occasionally a Southern town will repair or refurbish its monument and set aside a day of celebration, they hardly seem vital symbols of the modern South.

BIBLIOGRAPHY

Davis, Stephen. "Empty Eyes, Marble Hand: The Confederate Monument and the South." *Journal of Popular Culture* 16 (Winter 1982): 2–21.

Emerson, Bettie A. C. *Historic Southern Monuments: Representative Memorials of the Heroic Dead of the Southern Confederacy.* New Orleans, 1911.

Foster, Gaines M. *Ghosts of the Confederacy: Defeat, the Lost Cause, and the Emergence of the New South, 1865 to 1913.* New York, 1987.

Widener, Ralph W., Jr. *Confederate Monuments: Enduring Symbols of the South and the War between the States.* Washington, D.C., 1982.

Wilson, Charles Reagan. *Baptized in Blood: The Religion of the Lost Cause, 1865–1920.* Athens, Ga., 1980.

Winberry, John J. "'Lest We Forget': The Confederate Monument and the Southern Townscape." *Southeastern Geographer* 23 (November 1983): 107–121.

GAINES M. FOSTER

Battlefields

Civil War monuments, memorials, and parks—much visited reminders of the war—still fire passions, as evidenced by conflicts between Civil War buffs, preservationists, and developers at Manassas and Brandy Station. The first successful effort to protect a Civil War battlefield occurred in 1864. On April 30, ten months after the battle and six months after Abraham Lincoln had spoken his immortal words at the dedication of Soldiers' National Cemetery, the state of Pennsylvania chartered the Gettysburg Battlefield Memorial Association (GBMA) to commemorate the "great deeds of valor . . . and the signal events which render these battle grounds illustrious." The association, composed of members from Northern states that had sent troops into the battle, was interested in acquiring only lands where the Army of the Potomac fought on July 1 through 3, 1863. By 1890, the association had acquired 470 acres.

JACKSON MONUMENT. Marks the spot where Thomas J. ("Stonewall") Jackson fell, Chancellorsville, May 2, 1863.

NATIONAL ARCHIVES

Civil War Battlefields and Monuments Administered by the National Park Service

Name[1]	Location	Date Established
Andersonville National Historical Site	Ga.	Oct. 16, 1970
Antietam National Battlefield Site (redesignated a national battlefield, 1978)	Md.	Aug. 30, 1890
Appomattox Courthouse Monument (redesignated a national historical park, 1954)	Va.	June 18, 1930
Arkansas Post National Memorial	Ark.	July 6, 1960
Brice's Cross Roads National Battlefield Site	Miss.	Feb. 2, 1929
Chickamauga and Chattanooga National Military Park	Ga., Tenn.	Aug. 19, 1890
Colonial National Memorial (redesignated a national historical park, 1936)	Va.	July 3, 1930
Cumberland Gap National Historical Park	Ky., Tenn., Va.	June 11, 1940
Fort Donelson National Military Park (redesignated a national battlefield, 1985)	Tenn.	Mar. 26, 1928
Fort Jefferson National Monument	Fla.	Jan. 4, 1935
Fort Sumter National Monument	S.C.	Apr. 28, 1948
Fredericksburg and Spotsylvania County Battlefields Memorial National Military Park	Va.	Feb. 14, 1927
Gettysburg National Military Park	Pa.	Feb. 11, 1895
Glorieta Pass Battlefield Unit (addition to Pecos National Historical Park)	N.Mex.	June 27, 1990
Gulf Islands National Seashore	Fla., Miss.	Jan. 8, 1971
Harpers Ferry National Monument (redesignated a national historical park, 1963)	W.Va., Md.	June 30, 1944
Kennesaw Mountain National Battlefield Site (redesignated a national battlefield park, 1935)	Ga.	Feb. 8, 1917
Manassas National Battlefield Park	Va.	May 10, 1940
Monocacy National Battlefield	Md.	Oct. 21, 1976
Pea Ridge National Military Park	Ark.	July 20, 1956
Petersburg National Military Park (redesignated a national battlefield, 1962)	Va.	July 3, 1926
Richmond National Battlefield Park	Va.	Mar. 2, 1936
Rock Creek Park (includes Fort Stevens)	D.C.	Sept. 27, 1890
Shiloh National Military Park	Tenn.	Dec. 27, 1894
Stones River National Military Park (redesignated a national battlefield, 1980)	Tenn.	Mar. 3, 1927
Tupelo National Battlefield Site (redesignated a national battlefield, 1961)	Miss.	Feb. 21, 1929
Vicksburg National Military Park	Miss.	Feb. 21, 1899
Wilson's Creek National Battlefield Park (redesignated a national battlefield, 1970)	Mo.	Apr. 22, 1960

[1]For a list of battles with dual names, see the article *Battles, Naming of.*

Civil War National Cemeteries Administered by the National Park Service

Name[1]	Location	Date Established
Andersonville	Ga.	July 26, 1865
Andrew Johnson	Tenn.	June 12, 1904
Antietam	Md.	Mar. 10, 1864
Battleground	D.C.	July 1864
Chalmette	La.	May 26, 1868
Fort Donelson	Tenn.	Mar. 9, 1867
Fredericksburg	Va.	July 15, 1865
Gettysburg	Pa.	Nov. 19, 1863
Poplar Grove	Va.	June 18, 1866
Shiloh	Tenn.	Mar. 9, 1867
Stones River	Tenn.	June 23, 1865
Vicksburg	Miss.	Oct. 27, 1866
Yorktown	Va.	July 13, 1866

[1]For a list of battles with dual names, see *Battles, Naming of.*

By the late 1870s Union soldiers and unit associations were becoming interested in memorializing themselves and their comrades on the battlefields where they had fought. The first memorials had been erected by the participants while the guns still roared. In 1861, following their victory at First Manassas, Georgia soldiers positioned a column honoring Col. Francis Barlow, killed in that battle. Twenty months later, in the spring of 1863, soldiers of Col. William B. Hazen's brigade built a monument and wall enclosing the gravesites of their comrades who had fallen in defense of the Round Forest on December 31, 1862, at Murfreesboro. Union troops posted at Vicksburg on July 4, 1864, placed a memorial at the site where on July 3, 1863, Maj. Gen. Ulysses Grant and Lt. Gen. John C. Pemberton met to discuss terms for the Confederate surrender. Then in June 1865, U.S. regulars built two pyramidal stone monuments on the Manassas battlefields—one at the Henry House and the other at the unfinished railroad grade.

Even at the time that Lincoln spoke at Gettysburg, plans

State, County, and Private Battlefield Parks

Location	Name[1]
Alabama	Fort Morgan
Arkansas	Jenkins's Ferry Battleground Marks's Mills Battleground Park Poison Spring State Park
Florida	Olustee Battleground
Georgia	Fort McAllister
Kansas	Mine Creek
Kentucky	Columbus-Belmont Battlefield State Park Perryville Battlefield State Park
Louisiana	Fort Jackson Mansfield Battle Park Port Hudson
Mississippi	Grand Gulf Military State Park
North Carolina	Bentonville Battleground Fort Fisher
Oklahoma	Honey Springs Battlefield
Tennessee	Fort Pillow State Park Nathan Bedford Forrest State Park
Virginia	New Market Battlefield Park Sayler's Creek Battlefield Park
West Virginia	Carnifex Ferry Battlefield Park Droop Mountain Battlefield Park

[1]For a list of battles with dual names, see *Battles, Naming of.*

were afoot to erect in Soldiers' National Cemetery a national monument. The proposed monument, designed by J. G. Batterson, featured a column crowned by Liberty, with four seated figures at the base representing History, Industry, War, and Prosperity. It was finally dedicated on July 1, 1870. Previous to this, two memorials had been completed and positioned in the cemetery. These were the First Minnesota Urn in 1867 and a statue of Maj. Gen. John E. Reynolds, cast from bronze cannon tubes by the sculptor John Quincy Adams Ward, in August 1872.

No monuments were erected on the GBMA's lands for some fifteen years after the battle. Meanwhile, Union veterans of Gettysburg looked back on the war as the most significant event of their lives, and they took actions to memorialize themselves and their dead comrades. The first unit to do so at Gettysburg was the Second Massachusetts Infantry in 1879, when a lettered granite block was affixed to a boulder positioned near Spangler's Spring. Other regiments and batteries rushed to emulate the Second Massachusetts, and by 1890 more than three hundred memorials and monuments had been sited on lands administered by the GBMA. Nearly $1 million had been expended on this work.

Meanwhile, veterans of the Battle of Chickamauga, following a proposal made by Union veterans H. V. Boynton and Ferdinand Van Derveer, held a reunion at Crawfish Spring in 1889. They organized the Chickamauga Memorial Association to seek the creation of a memorial park that, unlike the one at Gettysburg, would honor both armies and be administered by the U.S. government. The veterans were politically powerful, and with a spirit of reconciliation abroad, Congress acted promptly. On August 19, President Benjamin Harrison, himself a veteran of the Army of the Cumberland in its Tennessee and Georgia campaigns, signed into law a bill establishing Chickamauga and Chattanooga National Military Park, the nation's first. Under the leadership of a three-man commission, lands were purchased, troops' positions determined and marked, roads built, and state memorials and unit monuments erected. On September 18 through 20, 1895, the park was dedicated in impressive ceremonies by Vice President Adlai Stevenson before a huge audience that included forty thousand veterans.

Five years before, on August 30, 1890, Congress had authorized an Antietam National Battlefield Site to include only token tracts, scattered about the "landscape turned red," where monuments and markers were to be placed. Then, in late December 1894, President Grover Cleveland signed into law legislation creating Shiloh National Military Park to commemorate the three armies of the Southwest—two Union and one Confederate—on the ground upon which they fought. Less than two months later, on February 11, 1895, the president approved an act establishing Gettysburg National Park. The lands administered by GBMA were transferred to the United States, and the commission authorized by the legislation moved to acquire lands where both armies fought, mark and memorialize Confederates as well as Union soldiers, and restore the historic scene. On February 21, 1899, Vicksburg National Military Park was authorized.

The landscape of the five Federal Civil War parks created before 1900, unlike those established after 1916, features an unsurpassed collection of military and memorial art—statues, obelisks, temples, busts, reliefs—that date from the mid-1860s to the 1890s. These works of art, numbering in the thousands, were funded by the Federal and state governments, veterans, families and friends, and associations. Their creation provided commissions for sculptors and artists ranging from journeymen to giants such as Augustus St. Gaudens, Daniel Chester French, and Gutzon Borglun. From the 1890s through 1910, these works of art were important sources of income for bronze foundries and stonecutters.

Congress did not create another Civil War military park until 1917, when Kennesaw Mountain National Battlefield Site was established on Cheatham Hill where, three years before, veterans of "Fighting Dan" McCook's brigade had dedicated a monument funded by the state of Illinois. By that time, even the youngest of the veterans were in their midseventies and no longer had the clout to campaign and secure money for construction of battlefield monuments.

The two largest and, at the time of their construction most costly, battlefield memorials are the Illinois and the Pennsylvania memorials, the former at Vicksburg and the latter at Gettysburg. The Illinois memorial, resembling Rome's Pantheon, was dedicated in 1906 and features, on bronze and stone tablets, the names, by unit, of 36,290 soldiers from the state who participated in the Vicksburg campaign. The Pennsylvania temple, also listing its sons—approximately 33,000—who fought at Gettysburg, was dedicated in 1910.

At Shiloh in 1917, the United Daughters of the Confederacy's memorial by Frederick Hibbard was unveiled. It features two panels. In relief on the right are the heads of eleven young Southern soldiers as they march into battle, faces bright and heads held high. On the left, the relief depicts the heads of nine Confederates returning from Shiloh, their heads drooping and the fire of battle gone from their eyes. On a center pedestal are two bronze figures representing Death and Darkness snatching the laurels of victory from a third female figure, the Confederacy.

At Chickamauga, unlike the other four nineteenth-century parks, there were until the 1970s no monuments to generals, as this was deemed to be a soldiers' battle. The New York memorial, atop Chattanooga's Lookout Mountain, features a column with two soldiers, Billy Yank and Johnny Reb, with hands clasped in reconciliation. The theme of national reconciliation engendered by joint reunions, the establishment of Federal battlefields, and common sacrifices in the Spanish-American War came to fruition in the early twentieth century. Maryland at Antietam in 1900 and Missouri at Vicksburg in 1917 erected and dedicated imposing memorials honoring on the same structure their sons who fought in blue and in gray.

During the same years (1880–1917) that these major commemorative works were erected, thousands of memorials in stone and bronze appeared on courthouse squares in cities, towns, and villages, North and South, to remember local sons. A number of these—Indianapolis's Soldiers and Sailors Memorial, Boston's tribute to Robert Gould Shaw and the Fifty-fourth Massachusetts, and the memorials honoring Matthew F. Maury, Thomas J. Jackson, Jefferson Davis, Robert E. Lee, and J. E. B. Stuart on Richmond's Monument Avenue—became landmarks of late twentieth-century America, though others are too frequently looked upon merely as traffic problems. They remain, however, reminders of an era in our history when men fought to the death for principles too often out of vogue today.

BIBLIOGRAPHY

Craven, Wayne. *Sculptures at Gettysburg.* Philadelphia, 1982.

Lee, Ronald F. *The Origin and Evolution of the National Military Park Idea.* Washington, D.C., 1973.

Mackintosh, Barry. *The National Parks: Shaping the System.* Washington, D.C., 1991.

Walker, Steve, and David R. Riggs. *Vicksburg Battlefield Monuments.* Jackson, Miss., 1984.

EDWIN C. BEARSS

MOODY, YOUNG MARSHALL (1822–1866), brigadier general. Moody was born in Chesterfield County, Virginia, on June 23, 1822. After moving to Alabama as a young man, he worked as a schoolteacher, merchant, and clerk of the circuit court in Marengo County (1856–1861).

At the outbreak of the Civil War, Moody entered the Confederate army as a captain in the Eleventh Alabama Infantry. He assisted in raising the Forty-third Alabama and became the unit's lieutenant colonel under Col. Archibald Gracie, Jr. When Gracie received a promotion to brigadier general in November 1862, Moody replaced him as colonel of the regiment. He participated in Gen. Braxton Bragg's Kentucky campaign and fought at Chickamauga. In November and December 1863, he served under Lt. Gen. James Longstreet in the latter's campaign to take Knoxville. Subsequently, Moody's command transferred to Virginia under Gen. P. G. T. Beauregard. Moody suffered a severe wound in the fighting at Drewry's Bluff on May 12, 1864.

Following his recovery, Moody returned to his regiment and engaged in the siege of Petersburg. He assumed command of the brigade when his friend and commanding officer, General Gracie, was killed by a Union artillery shell. Moody received a promotion to brigadier general on March 4, 1865, and surrendered with the Army of Northern Virginia at Appomattox.

After the war, Moody moved to Alabama to start a new career. While in New Orleans on business, he contracted yellow fever and died on September 18, 1866.

BIBLIOGRAPHY

U.S. War Department. *War of the Rebellion: A Compilation of the Official Records of the Union and Confederate Armies.* Washington, D.C., 1880–1901. Ser. 1, vol. 46, pt. 3, pp. 1274, 1278, 1286–1291.

Warner, Ezra J. *Generals in Gray: Lives of the Confederate Commanders.* Baton Rouge, La., 1959.

BRIAN S. WILLS

MOON SISTERS. Virginia B. Moon (1844–1925) and Charlotte Moon Clark (1829–1895) were ardent Confederates from Oxford, Ohio, who carried dispatches between military officers in the Confederacy and Democratic dissenters in Ohio who opposed Lincoln's policies and worked in secret to aid the Confederate cause. In 1862 Lottie, who had married Judge Jim Clark of Hamilton, Ohio, relayed Confederate papers through Union lines to Kentucky; later she carried dispatches from Toronto, Canada, to Virginia, and then to Cincinnati, Ohio. Meanwhile, her younger sister, Ginnie, a resident of Memphis, Tennessee, was serving as a courier in her own right.

Early in 1863 Ginnie was arrested in Cincinnati for carrying Confederate mail and contraband. In her memoirs she proudly reports that she swallowed a secret dispatch from Confederate sympathizers in Ohio intended for Confederate authorities in Mississippi to prevent it from falling into her captors' hands. When Lottie, herself in Cincinnati at the time, heard of Ginnie's predicament, she intervened by appealing to the head of the Union Department of the Ohio, Gen. Ambrose E. Burnside, who happened to be an old suitor of Lottie's. The sisters soon after were cleared of any charges of espionage and paroled in the spring of 1863 to go to their respective homes, where they were kept under surveillance.

The Clarks eventually relocated to New York, where Lottie took up a career as a novelist and journalist. Ginnie served as a Confederate spy in Memphis for a few months after her arrest in Ohio. When Union officers ordered her to leave Memphis, she made her way to Newport News, Virginia, where she was held in custody for a month at Fortress Monroe by Gen. Benjamin Butler. She returned to Memphis after the war. Late in life, she moved to Hollywood, California, and became a motion picture actress.

BIBLIOGRAPHY

Jarecka, Louise L. "Virginia Moon, Unreconstructed Rebel." *Delphian Quarterly* 30 (1947): 17–21.

Kane, Harnett T. *Spies for the Blue and Gray.* New York, 1954.

Smith, Ophia D. *Old Oxford Homes and the People Who Lived in Them.* Oxford, Ohio, 1941.

ELIZABETH R. VARON

MOORE, ANDREW B. (1807–1873), governor of Alabama. Born March 7, 1807, in Spartanburg, South Carolina, Andrew Barry Moore moved to Perry County, Alabama, in the 1820s. There he was educated, read law, and was admitted to the bar in 1833. Moore was elected to the Alabama House of Representatives in 1839 as a Democrat but was defeated in the Whig tide of 1840. He was reelected in 1842 and served as speaker from 1843 to 1847. In 1848 he was a presidential elector on the Whig ticket. In 1851 he was appointed a circuit judge, a position he held until he resigned to run unopposed for governor in 1857. Moore was reelected in 1859. The state asylum for the insane and the school for the blind were built during his administration.

A moderate Southern rights man, Moore ordered an election for delegates to a state convention to meet in January 1861 in Montgomery to consider the secession issue. The convention passed the secession ordinance on January 11, 1861. Meanwhile, Moore had ordered the seizure of federal forts and arsenals in the state. After his term as governor ended in 1861, Moore served as adviser to the new governor, John G. Shorter, who sent Moore to northern Alabama to recruit men and supplies for Albert Sidney Johnston, to west Alabama to encourage planters to supply slave labor for work on the Alabama and Mississippi Railroad, and to the Black Belt to purchase corn for poor families of soldiers. He also supported the administration of the next governor, Thomas H. Watts, by seeking corn in the Black Belt at less than market value to distribute to the needy.

In May 1865 Moore was arrested by military officials and taken to Fort Pulaski, Savannah, where he was imprisoned with other prominent Confederate civil leaders. After his release in August 1865, he resumed his law practice in Marion in Perry County until his death there on April 5, 1873.

BIBLIOGRAPHY

Fleming, Walter L. *Civil War and Reconstruction in Alabama.* New York, 1905. Reprint, Spartanburg, S.C., 1978.

McMillan, Malcolm C. *The Disintegration of a Confederate State: Three Governors and Alabama's Home Front, 1861–1865.* Macon, Ga., 1986.

Owen, Thomas McAdory. *History of Alabama and Dictionary of Alabama Biography.* 4 vols. Chicago, 1921.

Thornton, J. Mills, III. *Politics and Power in a Slave Society: Alabama, 1800–1860.* Baton Rouge, La., 1978.

SARAH WOOLFOLK WIGGINS

MOORE, JAMES WILLIAM (1818–1877), congressman from Kentucky. Like other Confederate congressmen from his state, Moore steadfastly backed President Jefferson Davis and worked to strengthen the South's army. Born in Montgomery County, Kentucky, Moore studied in local schools, read law, and was admitted to the bar in Mount Sterling, Kentucky. A Whig, he twice was elected circuit court judge for his district but resigned in 1858 when he ran unsuccessfully for the U.S. Congress.

By 1860 Moore was a Democrat who denounced Abraham Lincoln's election and supported secession. A year later he served as a delegate from Montgomery County to the sovereignty convention in Russellville, Kentucky, and was on the Executive Council of the Provisional Government of Kentucky. In 1862 Moore was elected from the Tenth District to the First Confederate House of Representatives and was reelected in 1864. Soon after taking his seat, Moore presented a resolution censuring Secretary of War Judah P.

Benjamin for possessing neither "the confidence of the people . . . nor of the Army." Shortly after, Benjamin stepped down as secretary of war and was appointed secretary of state. Moore served on the Judiciary Committee in both Congresses. He endorsed several measures favored by Davis to increase the size of the army, including abolishing the exemption of men who hired substitutes, drafting foreigners and Marylanders, and employing blacks in a broad range of military capacities. He also proposed price limits on basic commodities to curb speculation and control the spiraling Confederate inflation.

Following Appomattox, Moore returned to Mount Sterling and practiced law.

BIBLIOGRAPHY

Quisenberry, A. C. "The Alleged Secession of Kentucky." *Register of the Kentucky State Historical Society* 15 (1917): 15–32.

Wakelyn, Jon L. *Biographical Dictionary of the Confederacy.* Edited by Frank E. Vandiver. Westport, Conn., 1977.

Warner, Ezra J., and W. Buck Yearns. *Biographical Register of the Confederate Congress.* Baton Rouge, La., 1975.

JOHN DAVID SMITH

MOORE, JOHN CREED (1824–1910), brigadier general. When the Civil War began in 1861, Moore was a college professor in Kentucky. A West Point graduate with six years of garrison duty behind him, Moore sought to put his military experience to use. He left neutral Kentucky to go farther south to Galveston, Texas, where he organized the Second Texas Infantry and became its colonel.

At the Battle of Shiloh in April 1862, Moore's regiment fled in panic when overwhelmed by the unexpected force of the enemy. In his report of the battle Gen. William J. Hardee blasted Moore and his regiment for their poor performance, but Moore defended himself and his men, attributing their action to the confusion of battle. One month later he was promoted to brigadier general. As commander of the Third Brigade in the Army of the West, Moore participated in the battles of Corinth and Iuka and the defense of Vicksburg. In July 1863, he and his brigade were captured when Vicksburg fell to the Federals. Exchanged in September, Moore returned to the Confederate army to serve under Gen. Braxton Bragg at the battles of Chattanooga and Lookout Mountain.

Moore's last assignment placed him as commander of the East and West Districts of the Department of the Gulf, primarily responsible for the defense of Mobile, Alabama. But unexpectedly, he resigned and returned to Texas to resume teaching. His desire to serve with the army may have waned because of his dissatisfaction with department responsibilities and removal from field command. Moore spent the last years of his life as a teacher and freelance writer in Mexia and Dallas, Texas.

BIBLIOGRAPHY

Faust, Patricia, ed. *Historical Times Illustrated Encyclopedia of the Civil War.* New York, 1986.

Roberts, O. M. *Texas.* Vol. 11 of *Confederate Military History.* Edited by Clement A. Evans. Atlanta, 1899. Vol. 15 of extended ed. Wilmington, N.C., 1989.

Simpson, Herald B., ed. *Texas in the War.* Hillsboro, Tex., 1965.

LESLEY JILL GORDON-BURR

MOORE, PATRICK THEODORE (1821–1883), brigadier general. Born in Galway, Ireland, on September 22, 1821, and raised in Canada as a young man, Moore moved to the United States when his father became consul in Boston. In 1850 he moved to Richmond where he worked as a merchant and served as a captain in the local militia.

Moore entered Confederate service in the spring of 1861 as colonel of the First Virginia Infantry. As part of James Longstreet's brigade, he participated and was severely wounded in the engagement at Blackburn's Ford on July 18, 1861. Unable to resume active duty, he served on Longstreet's staff as a volunteer aide during the Seven Days' Battles. From December 1862 until May 1864 Moore was a presiding judge on one of the War Department's military courts. He then assisted James L. Kemper in organizing the Virginia Reserves. Promoted to brigadier

PATRICK THEODORE MOORE. LIBRARY OF CONGRESS

general on September 30, 1864, he commanded the first brigade of the reserve forces in the Department of Richmond until the end of the war.

After the war, Moore operated an insurance agency in Richmond until his death on February 19, 1883.

BIBLIOGRAPHY

Hotchkiss, Jed. *Virginia.* Vol. 3 of *Confederate Military History.* Edited by Clement A. Evans. Atlanta, 1899. Vol. 4 of extended ed. Wilmington, N.C., 1987.

Spencer, James. *Civil War Generals.* Westport, Conn., 1986.

U.S. War Department. *War of the Rebellion: A Compilation of the Official Records of the Union and Confederate Armies.* Washington, D.C., 1880–1901. Ser. 1, vol. 2, p. 758; ser. 1, vol. 11, pt. 2, p. 462; ser. 4, vol. 2, p. 248.

MICHAEL G. MAHON

MOORE, SAMUEL PRESTON (1813–1889), surgeon general. Moore, a native of Charleston, South Carolina, graduated from the Medical College of South Carolina in 1834. In March 1835 he was commissioned an assistant surgeon in the U.S. Army, and in April 1849 he was promoted to surgeon, with the rank of major. Early in his career Moore was stationed in Missouri, Kansas, Florida, and Texas. During the Mexican War he served with troops along the Rio Grande rather than with either invading army. Following that conflict he served in Wyoming Territory; Texas again; New York, at the Military Academy at West Point; and, finally, as medical purveyor at New Orleans, a post from which he resigned in February 1861.

Although he apparently wished to avoid service on either side during the Civil War, Moore reluctantly agreed to become Confederate surgeon general and took office just after First Manassas. Moore faced an enormous task—organizing an entire medical department—and his nearly twenty-six years in the U.S. Army proved invaluable, as he drew on that model for the new department.

Moore set up examining boards to weed out unqualified physicians who had gained regimental medical posts during the first excitement of volunteering. He devised the system of individual ward buildings administered in groups, which became the five large hospitals, including Chimborazo, housing as many as twenty thousand patients in the Richmond suburbs. Concerned, too, about the restriction of medicines caused by the Federal blockade, Moore set up four laboratories to manufacture indigenous remedies to replace scarce imported drugs.

In order to encourage the spread of medical knowledge, in August 1863 Moore founded and became the president of the Association of Army and Navy Surgeons of the Confederate States, an organization that chiefly benefited doctors stationed in Richmond. He also encouraged the publication of the *Confederate States Medical and Surgical Journal* (January 1864–February 1865), as well as a book on Southern plant resources and a field surgical manual.

As surgeon general Moore supervised some three thousand surgeons and assistant surgeons in the field and in hospitals throughout the Confederacy. Their level of success depended upon the condition of transportation, communication, and supply facilities. In general, Moore was rather reserved and brusque in his dealings with his subordinates. Although considered just and fair, he was a strict disciplinarian, whom some regarded as autocratic, and a stickler about requiring absolute obedience to regulations, even the minutiae of extensive paperwork. Much about Moore's specific activities cannot be known because most of the medical department files, as well as Moore's personal papers, were destroyed in the fires when Richmond fell.

After the war Moore remained in Richmond but did not practice medicine. Instead he promoted education, serving on the Richmond school board (1887–1889), and agricultural interests, such as improving state fairs.

[*See also* Medical Department.]

BIBLIOGRAPHY

Chancellor, Charles W. "A Memoir of the Late Samuel Preston Moore, M.D., Surgeon General of the Confederate States Army." *Southern Practitioner* 25 (1903): 634–639.

Cunningham, H. H. *Doctors in Gray: The Confederate Medical Service.* Baton Rouge, La., 1958. Reprint, Gloucester, Mass., 1970.

Lewis, Samuel E. "Samuel Preston Moore, M.D., Surgeon General of the Confederate States." *Southern Practitioner* 23 (1901): 381–386.

Moore, Samuel Preston. "Address of the President of the Association of Medical Officers of Confederate States Army and Navy [1875]." *Southern Practitioner* 31 (1909): 491–498.

GLENNA R. SCHROEDER-LEIN

MOORE, THOMAS O. (1804–1876), governor of Louisiana. Moving to Louisiana in his mid-twenties, the North Carolina–born Moore had become the largest sugar planter in Rapides Parish by the eve of the Civil War. A lifelong Democrat, he served on the police jury and then represented this central Louisiana parish in both houses of the state legislature, before winning easy election to the governor's seat in 1859.

He used his office to abet the Louisiana secession movement. Declaring it dishonorable for Louisianans "to live under the government of a Black Republican president," Moore two weeks after Lincoln's election called the legislature into special session in order to prepare for a secession convention election, and he kept up the disunionist momentum by calling out the state militia and ordering it to seize Federal property before Louisiana had officially left the Union. The martial activity intimidated many Louisiana Unionists.

Until Maj. Gen. Richard Taylor (Zachary's son) was made head of the Department of Louisiana in July 1862, Moore functioned as both chief executive officer and military commander of Louisiana. After the April 1862 capture of New Orleans, however, Moore's effective authority seldom reached beyond northern Louisiana. Moore made indigent relief, especially for soldiers' families, an urgent priority of his administration. The militia and state finances also absorbed much of his attention. Like many Confederate governors, Moore wrangled with Richmond over troop deployments, military supplies, and local defenses. He once withheld arms from the Southern army. But Moore also tried to consolidate Confederate nationalism by banning illicit trade with Union-occupied territory and sponsoring "Confederate Associations" to boost morale and patriotism.

After leaving office, Moore refugeed in Texas in 1864, fled to Mexico and Cuba in 1865, returned to his devastated Rapides plantation in 1866, and died at his home in 1876.

Though ranking him below his successor, Henry Watkins Allen, historians generally believe Moore's stewardship of Confederate Louisiana deserves more credit than it has received.

BIBLIOGRAPHY

Bragg, Jefferson Davis. *Louisiana in the Confederacy.* Baton Rouge, La., 1941.

Cassidy, Vincent H. "Louisiana." In *The Confederate Governors.* Edited by W. Buck Yearns. Athens, Ga., 1985.

Davis, Edwin Adams. *Heroic Years: Louisiana in the War for Southern Independence.* Baton Rouge, La., 1964.

Odom, Van D. "The Political Career of Thomas Overton Moore, Secession Governor of Louisiana." *Louisiana Historical Quarterly* 26 (October 1943): 975–1054.

Owsley, Frank. *State Rights in the Confederacy.* Chicago, Ill., 1925. Reprint, Gloucester, Mass., 1961.

LAWRENCE N. POWELL

MORALE. Like an army that cannot fight on without rations, a new nation fighting for its very existence cannot maintain the struggle without strong, sustaining morale among its military and civilian populations. Thus morale was of vital importance to the Confederacy. The Southern nation obviously possessed spirit enough to engage in four years of a war that was the bloodiest and most destructive in U.S. history. Yet it can be said that Confederate morale proved deficient. During the Civil War the South's morale underwent a disastrous decline until ultimately, as historian Charles Wesley argued long ago, the collapse of the Confederacy came from within. Although no single factor by itself explains the South's defeat in a massive, complex, and multifaceted struggle, morale lay at the heart of the Confederacy's demise. Many scholars today view morale as the Achilles heel of the South in the grinding war it had to fight.

Before the first guns fired on Fort Sumter, Confederate morale was high, but a closer examination reveals that popular sentiments were neither uncomplicated nor untroubled. The South had traveled a long, rough, and somewhat unlikely road to secession. Throughout the 1850s only a small minority of radicals had desired the breakup of the Union, and their calls for a united stand by all the Southern states were ignored. After Abraham Lincoln won the presidential election in 1860, the strategy of separate state secession unfolded. Led by South Carolina, six Deep South states left the Union and formed a new confederacy. But even in the Deep South public opinion had been closely divided in states such as Georgia and Louisiana, and strong Unionist feelings existed elsewhere, as in Alabama. Moreover, crucial upper South states had refused to join the new nation.

Scholars have drawn different conclusions about this situation, but its significance for Confederate nationalism and unity should not be missed. Charles Roland, after surveying the secession of the lower South states, declared that they were "swept out by a great emotional folk movement. Notwithstanding the presence of large Unionist minorities in some of the states, it is doubtful that any similar political rupture in modern history has been supported by as high a proportion of the population."

Roland is probably right, yet in July of 1861 the *Richmond Examiner* stated a different and equally valid view. "Loyal as the great mass of our people are," wrote the *Examiner*'s editors, "there is yet no doubt that the South is more rife with treason to her own independence and honour than any community that ever engaged before in a struggle with an adversary." The Confederate States were in the process of forming a new government and nurturing new loyalties. Those profoundly committed to a Southern nation were few, whereas those who loved the Union and left it reluctantly were many. The solidification of Southern nationalism still lay ahead.

Regional Loyalty versus Confederate Nationalism

With the outbreak of hostilities, a large portion of the slaveholding upper South quickly entered the Confederate fold. Yet the accession of Virginia, North Carolina, Tennessee, and Arkansas to the cause only made the task of building Confederate nationalism more challenging. These states, faced by the necessity of choosing sides, had acted upon a strong sense of regional loyalty. Identification with the South, however, was not the same thing as dedication to a Confederate nation. In the upper South and elsewhere, moderate and substantially Unionist sentiments had to be turned in a new direction and harnessed for a new cause. A Confederate identity had to evolve from Southernness, and devotion to a new nation had to replace loyalty to revered American traditions.

These facts dictated the selection of moderate leaders and conservative policies at Montgomery. Fire-eating radicals, such as William Lowndes Yancey of Alabama who had pioneered in Union-hating and calls for secession, were omitted from high positions. Their day was over, and the task of consolidating a much more diverse and moderate public opinion, marked by historic affection for the Union, was at hand. President Jefferson Davis took the essential first step toward building a sense of Confederate nationalism by portraying the new Southern nation as the true carrier of American traditions. In the face of a degenerate, aggressive North, Davis argued, the Confederacy had become the guardian of the Founding Fathers' legacy. The purpose of the new Southern nation was to "perpetuate the principles" of American constitutional liberty.

This appeal to traditional national values helped unite a region faced with imminent invasion. After Lincoln called for troops, Unionists and secessionists joined together in defense of their threatened home, the South. An outpouring of regional loyalty produced 500,000 volunteers for military service in the summer of 1861—more men than the Confederate government could arm or equip and more than it would subsequently field at any one time. Morale was strong and robust.

The Phases of Morale

Yet the spirit of Confederate nationalism needed further development, or its weakness might become apparent. Events on the battlefield, on the home front, and in the halls of government would have a great effect on national unity and popular morale. To understand this process, one must consider both the phases of Southern morale and the forces that affected it positively or negatively.

Early Optimism. In the summer of 1861 the morale of the Southern people was running at high tide. Swept along by the strong wave of loyalty to their region, Southerners joined the army and prepared for their first battle. The Confederate victory at Manassas produced jubilation and some unrealistic expectations. By fall the massive preparations of the enemy had tempered overoptimistic emotions, and some disputes had arisen within the Confederacy that pointed to future difficulties. But the government of the new nation was becoming an organized fact, the South had fielded impressive armies of its own, and no major disaster had befallen the cause. Unfortunately for Confederate patriots, however, this period of enthusiasm and high hopes lasted only until the spring of 1862.

The Reality of War Intrudes. Around April of 1862 a second phase of Confederate morale began, one that would last until July 1863. In this phase unpleasant realities began to crowd out initial high hopes, and totally unexpected aspects of life in the Confederacy made themselves felt. Conscription signaled the beginning of these new facts. For the first time in American history, the central government passed laws to compel its citizens to serve in the armies. Necessity required Confederate leaders to take this step because bounties, furloughs, and other inducements had failed to lure new enlistments. Ordinary citizens who had joined the army for a year now wanted to return home and plant their crops. "The spirit of volunteering had died out," admitted Secretary of War James A. Seddon.

In this second phase other internal and external problems of fundamental importance to morale appeared. Bitter disputes over questions of policy arose, as the potent issue of state rights reared its head. A growing, activist central government displeased both planters and leaders who had expected something very different in a Southern government. At the same time, Confederate policies generated deep divisions in the population along class lines. Financial and economic difficulties deepened, and the first food riots occurred in Southern cities.

On the battlefield Southern troops won some victories, but Union forces made significant territorial gains, especially with the fall of New Orleans and Forts Henry and Donelson. Any hope for a brief war was fading, and reasons to doubt the Confederacy's staying power were multiplying. When Confederate offensives into Maryland and Kentucky both failed in the fall of 1862, Jefferson Davis had cause to remark that Southerners were entering "the darkest and most dangerous period we have yet had."

Thus from April 1862 to July 1863 the skies over the new nation were darkening. Yet in this period the Confederacy also marshaled its strength and resisted the forces weakening it. Government measures largely stemmed desertion from the armies, and the military situation was far from hopeless. On occasion, a notable success, such as the victory at Chancellorsville, stimulated hopes for a revival of Confederate fortunes. The decline in morale had not become uncontrollable.

Impact of Vicksburg and Gettysburg. A third and far more ominous phase in Confederate morale arrived with the shocking defeats at Vicksburg and Gettysburg in July 1863. It took some days for accurate news of these disasters to reach the population, but once they did, no one could deny their depressing significance. Robert E. Lee's defeat in Pennsylvania shattered all hopes of winning Confederate independence through successful offensive action. The strongest Southern army had been driven back and had no option thereafter but to assume a defensive posture. Any realistic hope of foreign recognition and aid, long sought but already unlikely, had to be given up. With the capture of

Vicksburg, the Confederacy itself was cut in two. The resources of the Trans-Mississippi West fell out of reach, and the Gulf states lay open to Federal invasion from armies in Mississippi or Tennessee. Jefferson Davis admitted that these defeats submerged him "in the depths of . . . gloom," and so dedicated a Confederate as Josiah Gorgas confided to his diary, "Today absolute ruin seems our portion. The Confederacy totters to its destruction."

After this turning point, internal forces of disintegration outpaced the government's efforts to hold the Confederacy together. On the home front, resistance to conscription and impressments grew rapidly. As poverty deepened, thousands of suffering yeoman families quietly withdrew their support from the cause, and more politically active Confederates, particularly in North Carolina and Georgia, began to agitate openly for peace. The army's strength, which had already begun to fall, now plunged sharply downward as the flow of deserters widened into a racing stream. The government began using detachments of seasoned troops to round up concentrations of deserters, but without permanent effect.

The words of Confederate officials documented this increasingly desperate, third phase of morale. Assistant Secretary of War John A. Campbell asked on July 25, 1863, whether "so general a habit" as desertion should be considered a crime when some 40,000 to 50,000 men were absent without leave and 100,000 evaded duty in some manner. On November 26, 1863, Secretary of War Seddon reported that "the effective force of the Army is generally a little more than a half, never two-thirds, of the numbers in the ranks." By the middle of 1864 the army's strength had fallen to 195,000 present out of 316,000 enrolled. Senator Herschel Johnson of Georgia advised Jefferson Davis in 1864 that "the disposition to avoid military service is . . . general," and Maj. S. B. French reported at the end of this period that "in all the States impressments are evaded by every means which ingenuity can suggest, and in some openly resisted."

Morale was very low, but the Confederate cause was not yet seen as hopeless, for the North also was war-weary and staggering beneath the conflict's heavy burdens. Abraham Lincoln sometimes despaired of his reelection, and propeace elements in the Democratic party were working hard to control their party's platform and presidential nomination. Jefferson Davis pursued a strategy of encouraging Northern peace advocates while doing everything that could be done to present the stiffest possible resistance on the battlefield. State leaders joined Davis in predicting extermination and degradation at the hands of a depraved enemy unless the South prevailed. The end of this policy, and of the third phase in Confederate morale, approached as William Tecumseh Sherman's troops neared Atlanta.

Morale at Low Tide. "Our all depends on that army," wrote Mary Boykin Chesnut. "If that fails us, the game is up." Unfortunately for Confederates, she was right. Atlanta fell, and the Richmond war clerk J. B. Jones lamented that "our fondly-cherished visions of peace have vanished like a mirage of the desert." Although Jefferson Davis exhorted his countrymen to fight on, he had to admit that "two-thirds of our men are absent . . . most of them absent without leave." Not long after Sherman's strategic breakthrough, Lincoln won reelection, and Southerners knew that Confederate defeat was only a matter of time.

In this final phase in the level of morale, most sources of support for the Confederacy were evaporating. Only the central government and those determined soldiers who stayed with the armies remained resolute. For a few more months the government tried desperate expedients and brave men in gray fought on, but most Southerners were resigned to defeat before Lee arrived at Appomattox.

Forces Affecting Morale

The spirit of Confederates was tested in many ways during the Civil War. Events naturally affected morale as Southern armies met defeats in battle and as Union pressure helped damage a mismanaged economy. But internal forces also had a serious impact on morale. Opposition to the government flourished among both planters and small farmers, and class resentments among the poor caused a steadily increasing number to withdraw their support from the war effort.

The Effect of the War. It is self-evident that defeats on the battlefield worked powerfully to depress Confederate morale. The Confederacy was a beleaguered new nation, and after the first year no Southerner could deny that the cause was losing ground. As time went on, the lengthening litany of defeats eroded confidence among even the stoutest patriots. The connection between military reverses and declining morale is manifest in the correlation between key defeats and trends in desertion. Moreover, it was inevitable that the human cost of the South's struggle for independence would produce a reaction. As the world marveled at the unprecedented carnage Americans were inflicting on one another, hundreds of thousands of Southern homes went into deep mourning. In America's bloodiest war, the South bore the brunt of destruction.

There was another, paradoxical side, however, to the effects of war. Armed conflict strengthened Southern morale by creating an intense and unifying hatred of the enemy. War always forces its combatants to depersonalize the foe in order to cope with the psychological trauma of killing, and civilians share in this process. Moreover, hostile images of the Yankee had long been current in Southern culture. The Civil War provided reason to magnify these negative images enormously. Cultural conceptions of honor contributed to the process, as Southerners judged their opponents by standards the latter did not share.

Confederate political leaders did all they could to intensify these attitudes. From the first days of the Confederacy, Jefferson Davis depicted the United States as a consolidated despotism where corruption reigned and freedom was extinguished. Soon after the fighting started, he began a steady practice of denouncing the Union as an uncivilized, inhuman, and brutal foe. Governors and state legislators added bitter criticisms of the "ruthless barbarity" of an enemy that intended to impose the vilest forms of subjugation upon the South. To the *Charleston Mercury,* Northerners were "civilized savages . . . plunderers, liars, fanatics." When other newspapers, such as the *Richmond Enquirer,* spoke of Northerners' "extreme malignity toward us," they were accelerating a potent social process. Southerners were unifying themselves by defining their foe as so hateful and despicable that no thought of reunion could be entertained. In this way, the war generated feelings that supported Confederate morale and endured long after the Confederate government disappeared.

Confederate Policy and Planters. Another factor affecting morale involved fundamental problems related to the class system and the economy. These caused so much frustration and resentment that many questioned whether the government deserved their support. An indicator of the severity of the Confederacy's social problems is the fact that dissatisfaction appeared from an early date at the two extremes of the social scale. For differing reasons, both wealthy planters and small yeoman farmers became alienated from the cause.

The large plantation owners discovered that life under the Southern government was shockingly different from their expectations. They had sought to insulate their holdings from change, to guard their world against the intrusions of "Black Republicans." In order to shield slavery and plantation agriculture, they had embarked on a quest for independence that involved them in a massive war. But soon it became evident that the necessities of fighting the war clashed radically with the ends they pursued.

Davis's administration sought firmly and resolutely to build the strong central government needed to fight the North. Control of the armies, conscription of men, impressment of supplies, and suspension of the writ of habeas corpus showed by early 1862 that the Confederate government was going to lead with a strong hand. Davis sincerely believed that all his measures were constitutional, especially given the government's powers to make war and raise armies. But such steps surprised many in the planter class. They had expected a weak and limited central government in a nation devoted to state rights. Instead they saw a behemoth in Richmond whose bureaucracy became larger, in proportion to population, than the government of the North.

Moreover, this central government adopted policies that intruded directly into the affairs of each plantation. Not content with impressing goods, the Confederacy began to impress slaves. Despite the fears of slave owners concerning the treatment of their valuable property, the government commandeered slave labor to dig trenches, build fortifications, and otherwise assist the armies. Davis supported efforts to change what the planters grew by urging them to shift from cotton to food crops. Whenever Federal forces moved deeper into the Confederacy, army officers confiscated planters' stores of cotton and burned it to keep it from falling into the hands of the enemy. By 1863 the tax-in-kind was taking from planters and other farmers a portion of all their food crops. In 1864 new legislation required planters, as a means of keeping their overseers, to promise under bond to provide one hundred pounds of bacon and one hundred pounds of beef for each able-bodied slave. The government had become directly involved in plantation affairs.

These policies caused consternation and provoked harsh attacks on the government in the political arena. Early in the war representatives of the planter class began to express profound ideological dissatisfaction with the central government. Georgia's governor, Joseph E. Brown, who charged that conscription controverted "all the principles for which Georgia entered into this revolution," was the policy's most outspoken critic, but he was not the only one. Congressmen and newspaper editors joined in denouncing the South's new government as traitorous to the Confederacy's basic purposes. The *Charleston Mercury,* for example, quoted Linton Stephens with approval in 1862 when he condemned conscription as "the very embodiment of Lincolnism, which our gallant armies are today resisting."

Jefferson Davis defended his policies and put them into operation despite the opposition. Eventually, as the Confederacy's situation became more desperate, a few critics realized that Davis and the South had no alternative and dampened their criticism. But much damage had been done to Confederate morale. Leaders of public opinion had questioned the legitimacy of their new government and argued, in effect, that it was unworthy of the people's allegiance. Such criticism did more than express planters' dissatisfaction. It depressed morale generally and impeded the process of building support for the new nation.

The Deteriorating Economy. The serious financial and economic problems of the Confederacy also damaged morale for common citizens as well as planters. The government held little specie, raised very little revenue through taxes (partly because planters objected to them), and printed far too much money. As a result uncontrollable inflation ravaged the economy. Moreover, shortages of many commodities that the South was accustomed to buy from Europe or the North quickly developed. Hoarding made shortages worse, and profiteering aggravated the inflation of prices. The economic situation deteriorated steadily and caused many in disgust to condemn the government.

If these economic setbacks were inconvenient for wealthy planters, they were devastating to poorer white citizens. Although small farmers were largely self-sufficient in normal times, most needed a few essential items they could not produce. Salt was a vital preservative for meat, and most families also purchased such items as coffee, sugar, some clothing, and tools. Inflation and shortages quickly drove prices of these commodities out of reach, and instances of hoarding enraged the citizenry. The governors of several states denounced speculation, and newspapers joined in the outcry over greed and the lack of patriotism. In 1861 the *Richmond Examiner* declared, "This disposition to speculate upon the yeomanry of the country . . . is the most mortifying feature of the war." One year later it judged "native Southern merchants" as worse than Yankees and lamented, "The whole South stinks with the lust of extortion." The Rome, Georgia, *Weekly Courier* quoted the Bible against extortioners, and the *Atlanta Daily Intelligencer* warned that because of extortion, "want and starvation are staring thousands in the face."

In fact, the causes of hunger went beyond hoarding and profiteering. Drought or crop failures occurred in years of war as well as peace and naturally depressed morale. But in addition the Confederacy itself sometimes seemed responsible for suffering, as families were victimized by impressment or abuses by the military. Florida's governor complained that soldiers had taken the last milk cows from starving families of soldiers, and in 1864 Secretary of War Seddon admitted that "the most scandalous outrages" had occurred in Mississippi. One woman wrote that the troops camped on her land had not hesitated to "catch up the fowls before my eyes." Commenting in 1862, the *Richmond Enquirer* reported, "We often hear persons say, 'The Yankees cannot do us any more harm than our own soldiers have done.' "

Even more serious was the shortage of labor on small farms caused by volunteering and conscription. An early warning sign of this problem was the flood of letters in 1861 from rural districts lamenting the absence of blacksmiths and other artisans. Soon thereafter many more nonslaveholding families began to appeal for exemptions or furloughs of the husbands or sons who were their chief source of labor. Increasingly on one-man farms, wives and children found that they could not keep up the work of cultivation unaided. As the Edgefield, South Carolina, *Advertiser* explained, "The duties of war have called away from home the sole supports of many, many families. . . . Help must be given, or the poor will suffer." A desperate woman named Elizabeth Leeson wrote to Secretary of War Seddon in 1863: "I ask [you] in the name of humanity to discharge my husband[;] he is not able to do your government much good and he might do his children some good. . . . The rich has aplenty to work for them." The suffering of soldiers' families was a critical danger to the Confederacy. Military and political officials agreed that letters from suffering loved ones led to many desertions. As an anonymous Virginian wrote to Secretary of War Seddon, "What man is there that would stay in the armey and [k]no[w] that his family is sufring at home?"

Hunger and speculation were destroying people's morale. One acquaintance of Jefferson Davis advised the president that speculation was "the cause of thousands of good men leaving their posts." In 1863 an enrolling officer reported from the hill country of South Carolina that previously loyal citizens were supporting deserters. Citing "the speculations and extortions so rampant throughout the land," he wrote that these civilians "swear by all they hold sacred that they will die at home before they will ever be dragged forth again to do battle for such a cause."

Class Resentment. The most corrosive factor in the decline of yeoman morale was class resentment, a sense of class injustice. Elizabeth Leeson had voiced the feeling that her family was sacrificing heavily while rich slaveholders had "aplenty to work for them." Perhaps this aspect of "a rich man's war and a poor man's fight" was unavoidable, given the fact that most Southern whites did not own slaves. But Confederate laws and policies magnified the advantage possessed by slaveholders and convinced many nonslaveholders that they were being asked to do much more than their fair share. Nothing damaged Confederate morale more than this conviction of class discrimination and social injustice. The outcry against unfair government policies was intense.

Objections to favoritism in the raising of troops arose in the summer of 1861. After volunteers began to exceed the Confederacy's supply of arms, the government announced that it would arm and accept only long-term volunteers. Companies that could arm and equip their own men, however, were still allowed to enroll for only twelve months' service. In practice, only wealthier men could bear the costs of raising twelve-month units. This policy, admitted Albert T. Bledsoe, chief of the Bureau of War, created "no little dissatisfaction in the country." William Brooks, the presiding officer at Alabama's secession convention, reported that leading men had struggled to encourage enlistments among nonslaveholders in Perry County. Just when leaders had "partially" changed the sentiments of men who "not unfrequently declared that they will 'fight for no rich man's slaves,' " the Confederacy declared its new policy. These "poor laboring men," Brooks pointed out, compared their lot to "slaveholders [who] can enter the army and quit it at the end of twelve months. . . . I leave you to imagine the consequences."

Angry feelings proliferated with the adoption of conscription. The law provided for exemptions for the disabled or unfit and for a variety of occupations, such as transportation workers, miners, and state and Confederate officials. Complaints of favoritism in the application of the law arose almost immediately. Officeholders tended to be from the upper classes, and some states declared that thousands of them were essential to the operation of the government. Careless administration of the law also produced inequities. An anonymous Georgian, for example, complained to the War Department that it was "a notorious fact if a man has influential friends—or a little money to spare he will never be enrolled." Judge Robert S. Hudson of Mississippi warned President Davis that incompetence or favoritism by enrolling officers had created much "disloyalty, discontent, and desertions." In 1864 Congressman Robert Henry Whitfield of Virginia urged an investigation of exemption boards in the name of "common justice to the poor and uninfluential."

Far more serious was the resentment created by two other features of the conscription law: substitution and the exemption of overseers. The government permitted a conscript, if he had the means, to hire someone to go to war in his place. To the *Richmond Examiner* this ability to pay for a substitute was "the best proof of the citizen's social and industrial value," but, needless to say, many poorer citizens regarded it as an unjust privilege for the rich. Mary Boykin Chesnut wrote in her diary about planters' sons who had "spent a fortune in substitutes," and Confederate documents recorded that at least fifty thousand men escaped the dangers of battle by hiring a substitute. As early as 1862 Secretary of War George Wythe Randolph condemned the "great abuses" of substitution, which had become "a regular business," but not until the beginning of 1864 did Congress end this divisive and unpopular system.

The exemption of overseers, which had been demanded by planters and state officials, created an even greater storm of protest. Because Congress, in October 1862, exempted one white man for every twenty slaves under his supervision, this statute soon was denounced as the "twenty-nigger law." Many nonslaveholders already believed that the war's benefits would accrue primarily to slaveholders; now it seemed that slaveholders would also avoid the war's dangers. "Never did a law meet with more universal odium," observed one congressman, "than the exemption of slave-owners. . . . Its influence upon the poor is most calamitous, and has awakened a spirit and elicited a discussion of which we may safely predict the most unfortunate results." The legislature of North Carolina soon bowed to popular pressure and protested to Congress about the "unjust discrimination" of the law, but Congress enacted only mild restrictions on the exemption of overseers. Planters gladly paid a tax imposed on overseers, who thus continued to enjoy safety in a war that was killing unprecedented numbers of Southerners. The situation fed a popular impression, as Senator James Phelan of Mississippi observed, that "nine tenths of the youngsters of the land whose relatives are conspicuous in society, wealthy, or influential obtain some safe perch where they can doze with their heads under their wings."

Meanwhile, the families of nonslaveholding soldiers faced grinding poverty and suffering. The Confederate government, struggling against enormous problems, was not providing the essentials of economic or physical security. Moreover, as the conviction spread that government policies were discriminatory and unjust, the Confederacy's demands for sacrifice increased. These pressures on morale became insupportable. Coupled with growing evidence of defeat on the battlefield, class resentments and the sheer difficulty of surviving in the Confederacy caused hundreds of thousands of citizens to withdraw their active support from the war effort.

In March 1864, an impressment officer in South Carolina encountered an uncooperative and frustrated citizen. "The sooner this damned Government [falls] to pieces," he said, "the better it [will] be for us." He was ready to compromise and "get back into the old Union." Like most Southerners, this man had sacrificed much for the cause, and he probably had little love for Yankees. But he was one of many whose patience was exhausted. He was angered by the unexpected or unfair policies of his government and disgusted by its inability to provide basic economic or physical security. For him, as for most Southerners, loyalty to his region had not grown into a sustaining devotion to Confederate nationalism. The corrosive and depressing forces that sapped morale had proven too great.

[*See also* Bread Riots; Class Conflict; Conscription; Desertion; Extortion; Impressment; Inflation; Nationalism; Poverty; Speculation; Taxation.]

BIBLIOGRAPHY

Beringer, Richard, Herman Hattaway, Archer Jones, and William N. Still, Jr. *Why the South Lost the Civil War*. Athens, Ga., 1986.

Escott, Paul D. *After Secession: Jefferson Davis and the Failure of Confederate Nationalism*. Baton Rouge, La., 1978.

Lonn, Ella. *Desertion during the Civil War*. New York, 1928. Reprint, Gloucester, Mass., 1966.

Owsley, Frank L. *State Rights in the Confederacy*. Chicago, 1925. Reprint, Gloucester, Mass., 1961.

Ramsdell, Charles W. *Behind the Lines in the Southern Confederacy*. Edited by Wendell H. Stephenson. Baton Rouge, La., 1944.

Silver, James W. *Confederate Morale and Church Propaganda*. Tuscaloosa, Ala., 1957.

Tatum, Georgia Lee. *Disloyalty in the Confederacy.* Chapel Hill, N.C., 1934. Reprint, New York, 1970.
Thomas, Emory M. *The Confederate Nation, 1861–1865.* New York, 1979.
Wesley, Charles H. *The Collapse of the Confederacy.* Washington, D.C., 1937.
Wiley, Bell Irvin. *The Plain People of the Confederacy.* Baton Rouge, La., 1943. Reprint, Gloucester, Mass., 1971.

PAUL D. ESCOTT

MORAVIAN CHURCH. The foundations of the Moravian church in the South were laid in 1752 when an advance party from Pennsylvania acquired a large tract of land they called Wachovia in the Yadkin River valley of North Carolina. The town of Salem, laid out in 1766, became a significant center of culture, music, trade, and religious activity. It was a church-oriented community in which property was owned by the church and both civic and religious affairs were tightly controlled. Schools were operated by the church; businesses, crafts, and professions were regulated; marriages were arranged or approved by the church governing body; and though married couples occupied their own homes, dormitorylike living quarters were provided for those who were single.

In 1860 Moravian missions in Florida, Georgia, and Arkansas were staffed and largely supported by the Salem congregation. In many instances they served Creek and Cherokee communities and in Florida operated one for blacks. With the beginning of the Civil War, contact was largely broken, but the missionaries remained. The loyalty of Cherokees in Arkansas was split between the Confederacy and the United States; those remaining loyal to the Union seized several missionaries, one of whom they murdered.

Although not totally prohibited, slavery was looked upon with disfavor, yet slaveholding was permitted and blacks lived in the community. The church itself occasionally held one or more slaves who were assigned work in the community until arrangements could be made for their manumission. Blacks attended church with whites, and it was natural that funerals for blacks should be held there. In 1856, following the funeral of a highly respected black man, some members voiced opposition to this practice. A short while later it was decided that henceforth blacks would be seated in the back rows as was the custom in the region, and in 1860 a church for blacks was erected in Salem.

With the growing anticipation of war, Moravians became concerned about their young men attending school in Pennsylvania. Several parents ordered them to come home, but others permitted theirs to stay. A male teacher in the Salem Academy went home to Virginia, but a female teacher continued her duties. Some students in the academy from distant Southern states remained in Salem and were stranded until the war ended. Frequently between 1861 and 1865 school officials were obliged to raise fees because of inflation. Despite the disruption of war, the scarcity of goods, and increased costs, their fears that enrollment would drop proved groundless.

Salem had two newspapers—one urged moderation in the North-South dispute while the other prodded the South to resist Northern "aggression." In November 1860 voters among the Moravians, like a majority of others in the state, rejected secession. Yet on May 20 the next year, in a convention to which no Moravians were delegates, North Carolina seceded from the Union. On June 19 the church fathers took note of their state's having "joined the southern confederation, the Confederate States," and directed that prayers in the church litany henceforth "be consistent with our present circumstances."

Initially Moravians had opposed the bearing of arms, but by 1831 this sentiment had disappeared and a military company was organized. When the Civil War opened, men among the Moravians were organized, equipped, and trained for service. On the morning of June 17, 1861, three companies gathered in Salem Square, and following a solemn service, a short address, and prayers by the bishop, they left for Virginia to join the army being formed there. A month later, at the request of many members, the church began a daily service of prayer at 8:00 each evening "to intercede at the throne of grace for friends and relatives." These events, marked by the prayers of Bishop George F. Bahnson, heralded the end of a long practice of nonviolence by Moravians.

Large numbers of men from Salem and other Moravian communities served faithfully and effectively, largely in Virginia and North Carolina. The village band, the pride of the community, was in the midst of the action. There were fatalities in battle, of course, and one was particularly moving. Litter bearers found the body of a Salem youth after the Battle of Fredericksburg with his Bible open on his breast. Many also died of disease. By late 1864 younger men, and older men who had heretofore been passed over, were volunteering. Throughout the four years people at home provided such supplies as they could. The owner of the local woolen mill generously clothed many of the men who enlisted early; from tables at Salem Square residents regularly offered food to soldiers who passed by.

With the end of the war church officials resumed their correspondence with their counterparts in Pennsylvania. Former Confederates were urged to banish all resentments. Those who chose to cherish the deeds of the immediate past, it was suggested, should do so among themselves. Veterans were welcome to talk of their valor and the cause for which they had fought and encouraged to discuss the war with young people; but they were admonished to lay aside all bitterness.

BIBLIOGRAPHY

Clewell, John Henry. *History of Wachovia in North Carolina.* New York, 1902.

Fries, Adelaide L., and J. Kenneth Pfohl. *The Moravian Church, Yesterday and Today.* Raleigh, N.C., 1926.

Hamilton, Kenneth G., ed. *Records of the Moravians in North Carolina.* Vol. 11 (1852–1879). Raleigh, N.C., 1969.

Wellman, Manly Wade. *The War Record.* Vol. 2 of *Winston-Salem in History.* Winston-Salem, N.C., 1976.

WILLIAM S. POWELL

MOREHEAD, JOHN MOTLEY (1796–1866), North Carolina governor and congressman. Morehead was born in Pittsylvania County, Virginia, July 4, 1796. In his infancy he moved with his family to Rockingham County, North Carolina, and graduated in 1817 from the University of North Carolina, where he demonstrated a remarkable flair for scholarship. Two years later he was licensed to practice law and was elected from Rockingham County to serve in the Virginia House of Commons in 1821 and 1822. Upon moving to Guilford County to practice law, he represented Guilford in the House from 1826 to 1828.

In 1835 he sat as a delegate to his state's constitutional convention where he worked on behalf of efforts to reform the system of representation in order to promote greater equality between eastern and western sections of the state. His early identification with the stimulation of railroad building and other internal improvements—particularly for the western counties—drew him from the Jacksonian wing of the Democratic party into a position of leadership in the Whig party. In 1840 and 1842 he was elected to two terms as governor. Again, he gave his best efforts to foster railways and waterways against the strong (and sometimes successful) opposition of his Democratic foes.

After retiring from the governorship, Morehead again devoted himself to business and his law practice, serving for several years as president of the North Carolina Railroad and as an organizer of the Western North Carolina Railroad. From 1859 to 1861 he was returned to the general assembly.

A slave owner himself, he candidly expressed disapproval of the institution on moral grounds but shrank from association with abolitionists because, he was at pains to point out, the system was an existing fact, recognized by federal and state constitutions and statutes, and because, he warned, the hasty and forced liquidation of slavery would produce civil, social, and economic convulsions.

In the presidential election of 1860 Morehead supported John Bell, the nominee of the Constitutional Union party, and upon Abraham Lincoln's election denied that this turn of events in and of itself justified secession of the slave states. Indeed, as the crisis deepened he still declared himself a conservative, opposed to the dissolution of the Union. He gladly accepted appointment to serve as the head of North Carolina's five-man delegation to the Washington peace conference of February 1861. "I came here to act for the Union—the whole Union," he said upon his arrival. "I recognize no *sides,* no party."

While he was in Washington, his state voted on February 28 on the question of calling a convention to consider secession. His own county voted 2,771 to 113 against holding a convention, and the state at large, though by a much smaller majority, also voted in the negative. Tempers continued to rise, however, and a special session of the legislature on its own motion voted to convoke a convention to meet on May 20. There an ordinance of secession was adopted and the state ratified the Constitution of the Confederate States.

The failure of the Washington conference to achieve an accommodation was a heavy disappointment to Morehead. Though he continued to resist the secession movement, nevertheless when his state did secede he became a sturdy Confederate loyalist and remained so throughout the war.

Before the legislature adjourned on May 28, it elected eight delegates, including State Senator Morehead, to sit in the Provisional Congress. That body had, by this time, already completed two sessions in Montgomery, Alabama. It was not until the next session commencing on July 20 in Richmond that Morehead and his North Carolina associates took their seats. The Provisional Congress ceased to exist on February 17, 1862, and with that, Morehead's formal political career closed after forty years of public life. He died in 1866 and was buried in the Greensboro, North Carolina, First Presbyterian Church, which later became the Greensboro Historical Museum.

Some authorities argue that though Morehead's brief participation in the Confederate Congress was relatively obscure, he exerted real influence unofficially through his personal association with President Jefferson Davis, who looked upon him as a trusted friend and adviser. He also served as North Carolina's member of the Congress's Committee on the Financial and Commercial Independence of the Confederate States, and it was in that capacity that he played an important role in securing the extension of the Richmond and Danville Railroad from the Confederate capital to Greensboro, North Carolina.

Perhaps Morehead's principal service to the Confederacy was rendered long before the secession crisis, in the form of his sponsorship of internal improvements, especially railroads, in North Carolina in the 1840s and 1850s. These provided crucial links in the future Confederacy's transportation lines, which proved in time to be of critical importance in shaping the Confederacy's economic and social development and in adding to its ability to wage war.

Morehead was, by contemporary accounts, a man of

impressive persona, with a gift for persuasive oratory. He is usually ranked as one of the state's strongest nineteenth-century governors, and his principal biographer has characterized him as the "Father of Modern North Carolina."

BIBLIOGRAPHY

Konkle, Burton Alva. *John Motley Morehead and the Development of North Carolina.* Raleigh, N.C., 1922.

Powell, William S., ed. *Dictionary of North Carolina Biography.* Vol. 4. Chapel Hill, N.C., 1990.

RICHARD BARDOLPH

MORGAN, JOHN HUNT (1825–1864), brigadier general and guerrilla raider. Born June 1, 1825, in Huntsville, Alabama, Morgan grew up in Lexington, Kentucky, where he attended Transylvania University. In the Mexican War he fought as a first lieutenant in the Kentucky cavalry, participating in the Battle of Buena Vista, February 23, 1847. A manufacturer of hemp in Lexington, Morgan organized and commanded an artillery company in the state militia from 1852 through 1854. In 1857 he formed the Lexington Rifles, a volunteer infantry company that joined the pro-Southern state guard militia in 1860. A Confederate from the beginning, he wired President Jefferson Davis on April 16, 1861, offering to serve as a recruiter. He raised a Confederate flag on his woolen factory, declaring that henceforth he would sell only uniforms of Confederate gray. When Kentucky decided to stay in the Union, he and the Lexington Rifles left for the war on September 20, 1861, rendezvousing with two hundred other men at Bloomfield, Kentucky. The group elected Morgan to lead them to Confederate lines in western Kentucky.

JOHN HUNT MORGAN. LIBRARY OF CONGRESS

From October 1 to October 27, 1861, he conducted raids behind the lines on his own authority. Then, on October 27, he was sworn in and elected captain of a cavalry company. Continuing guerrilla warfare, he had, by March 1862, achieved many small victories that made him a famous folk hero, the "Francis Marion of the war." To many Southerners he represented the ideal of the romantic cavalier. His success inspired the popular movement for guerrilla war that culminated in the Partisan Ranger Act of April 21, 1862, which authorized the president to commission companies, battalions, and regiments to conduct guerrilla war behind enemy lines.

Promoted to colonel on April 4, 1862, he commanded a squadron at Shiloh. Gen. P. G. T. Beauregard increased his command to 325 men, and by the time of Morgan's promotion to brigadier general on December 11, 1862, it had grown to a division of 3,900. Discarding the saber, Morgan armed his raiders with infantry rifles and Colt revolvers. They lived off the land and traveled light; their only wheels were two mountain howitzers for each brigade. He used horses to provide mobility, to hit and run. In skirmishing, he deployed the artillery and dismounted the men to fight as infantry. For intelligence, he sent out scouts and intercepted telegraph messages. On the march, he used a system of rolling guards protecting the flanks and leapfrogging to the front when the column passed. He usually kept his opponents confused by sending out feints and fake telegrams.

In the first two years of the war, Morgan's raids made a mockery of Federal attempts to protect border state Kentuckians. After the first Kentucky raid, General in Chief Henry W. Halleck admitted, "The stampede among our troops was utterly disgraceful." Andrew Johnson, military governor of Tennessee, concluded that Morgan's raids undermined Federal authority and the efforts to strengthen loyalty to the Union. William Tecumseh Sherman proclaimed that Morgan and the other Confederate raiders were the most dangerous men of the war and would have to be killed or captured.

In reaction to a raid at Gallatin, Tennessee, Union Gen. Don Carlos Buell concentrated his entire cavalry force of 700 men under Gen. Richard W. Johnson and ordered them to seek out and destroy Morgan. Johnson boasted that he would return "with Morgan in a bandbox." On August 21, 1862, he located Morgan near Gallatin, but after two mounted assaults with sabers, the Union cavalry scattered in wild retreat, losing 21 dead, 47 wounded, and 176 missing, including General Johnson, who was captured by his prey.

Morgan's greatest contribution to the Confederate war effort was the diversion of Union troops and resources to defend against his raids. By mid-December 1862, the Union army had 20,357 men guarding communication lines and supply depots in the West. Morgan and other raiders forced the Union to channel men and resources into the construction of stockades to defend railroad trestles and the reconstruction of tunnels, bridges, track, and telegraph lines. But because of Morgan, the Union commanders strengthened their cavalry and organized mounted infantry, and by the summer of 1863, the stronger Union cavalry ended the advantage the Confederate raiders had enjoyed. Morgan's men now suffered a series of defeats.

Attempting to restore morale and efficiency, Morgan marched into Indiana and Ohio without authority and was captured and imprisoned. Many Southerners nevertheless praised him for carrying the war to the enemy. He escaped from the Ohio penitentiary on November 27, 1863, and served as commander of the Department of Western Virginia and East Tennessee from June to August 22, 1864. He was killed on September 4 in Greeneville, Tennessee, attempting to escape from Federal cavalry under Gen. Alvan C. Gillem. Given a state funeral in Richmond, Virginia, he was buried in Hollywood Cemetery and then reinterred with honor in 1868 in Lexington, Kentucky.

[*See also* Guerrilla Warfare; Morgan's Raids.]

BIBLIOGRAPHY

Ramage, James A. *Rebel Raider: The Life of General John Hunt Morgan.* Lexington, Ky., 1986.

Thomas, Edison H. *John Hunt Morgan and His Raiders.* Lexington, Ky., 1975.

JAMES A. RAMAGE

MORGAN, JOHN TYLER (1824–1907), brigadier general and U.S. senator. Prior to the Civil War, Morgan practiced law in Alabama and was an elector on the Breckinridge ticket in 1860. He attended Alabama's secession convention in January 1861 and then enlisted in the Cahaba Rifles, later incorporated into the Fifth Alabama Volunteers.

After participating in First Manassas, Morgan returned to Alabama to recruit a regiment of cavalry. As colonel of the Fifty-first Alabama, he served under Nathan Bedford Forrest at Murfreesboro and during the Tullahoma campaign. Transferred to the command of Joseph Wheeler, he led a brigade of cavalry at Chickamauga and took part in the operations against Knoxville. Promoted to brigadier general on November 17, 1863, Morgan later participated in several cavalry engagements in Tennessee, including the famous raid in the Sequatchie Valley, where a thousand wagons loaded with provisions were destroyed. He continued his

JOHN TYLER MORGAN. NATIONAL ARCHIVES

fine service during the Atlanta campaign by attacking William Tecumseh Sherman's lines of communication and supply. When John Bell Hood abandoned Atlanta, Morgan remained behind to observe and harass the enemy as best he could. At the close of the war, he was in Mississippi recruiting black troops for the Confederate army.

After the war, Morgan served five terms in the U.S. Senate (1877–1907). He died in Washington, D.C., on June 11, 1907.

BIBLIOGRAPHY

U.S. War Department. *War of the Rebellion: A Compilation of the Official Records of the Union and Confederate Armies.* Washington, D.C., 1880–1901. Ser. 1, vol. 2, p. 446; ser. 1, vol. 23, pt. 2, pp. 923, 960.

Wakelyn Jon L. *Biographical Dictionary of the Confederacy.* Edited by Frank E. Vandiver. Westport, Conn., 1977.

Wheeler, Joseph. *Alabama.* Vol. 7 of *Confederate Military History.* Edited by Clement A. Evans. Atlanta, 1899. Vol. 8 of extended ed. Wilmington, N.C., 1987.

MICHAEL G. MAHON

MORGAN, SIMPSON HARRIS (1821–1864), congressman from Texas. Born in Rutherford County,

Tennessee, Morgan attended the local public schools and no other. He moved to Texas in 1844 with R. K. Clark, an attorney. He settled briefly in Paris, Lamar County, where Clark had determined to practice law. From there Clark wrote to his brother and sister in Illinois on November 17, 1844, that Simpson Morgan was still with him and that "a truer and better friend never lived. He is doing well." Morgan did not stay long in Paris, but moved southeasterly to the adjoining county of Red River and settled in Clarksville or its vicinity, where he farmed and was admitted to the practice of law.

The Federal Census, taken on December 16, 1850, showed Morgan as being twenty-nine years of age, a practicing attorney, and the owner of $500 in real property.

He married into the family of Augustus H. Garland, of Lafayette County, Arkansas, who later became a member of the House of Representatives of the Confederate Congress from Arkansas. The census taker on August 22, 1860, found Morgan living in Clarksville with his wife Laura A., age nineteen, born in Tennessee, and as having a one-month-old son, born in Texas. In his household in 1860 lived A. Glawson Morgan, a sister-in-law, age thirty, born in Texas, and her son William Boyd, age 11, born in Arkansas. At that time, Simpson H. Morgan was listed as thirty-eight years of age, and the owner of $18,150 in real estate and eight thousand dollars in personal property. He was one of the promoters and, for a while, president of the Memphis, El Paso, and Pacific Railroad chartered in 1853, which later became a part of the Texas and Pacific Railroad.

During the Civil War Morgan was elected in November, 1863, to the House of Representatives of the Second Confederate Congress (May 2, 1864–March 18, 1865) from the Sixth Congressional District of Texas, defeating William B. Wright, and took his seat on May 21. He served on the Select Impressment, the Judicial, and the Select Compensation and Mileage committees of the House. He supported measures to give the central Confederate government a stronger hand in conducting the war and opposed the imposition of special taxes on agriculture. His political affiliation is unknown, but during his brief service in Congress he gave steady support to the administration of President Jefferson Davis.

While on his way to attend the Second Session of the Second Congress, Morgan died of pneumonia at Monticello, Arkansas, on December 15, 1864. His body was returned to Clarksville for burial in the family cemetery on his property, now the Simpson H. Morgan Memorial Park. Memorial resolutions were adopted in the House of Representatives and in the Senate of the Confederate Congress on January 17, 1865, and the two houses adjourned for the remainder of the day as a "mark of respect for the memory of the deceased."

BIBLIOGRAPHY

Clark, R. K. "To Dear Brother and Sister, Paris, Lamar County, Texas, Nov. 17th 44." *Southwestern Historical Quarterly* 53 (1949–1950): 86–87.

Journals of the Congress of the Confederate States of America, 1861–1865. 7 vols. Washington, D.C., 1904–1905.

Reed, St. Clair Griffin. *A History of the Land Grants and Other Aids to the Texas Railroads by the State of Texas.* Houston, Tex., [c. 1942].

U.S. Bureau of the Census. *Population Schedules, 1850, 1860. Texas.* National Archives, Washington, D.C.

Wakelyn, Jon L. *Biographical Dictionary of the Confederacy.* Edited by Frank E. Vandiver. Westport, Conn., 1977.

Warner, Ezra J., and W. Buck Yearns. *Biographical Register of the Confederate Congress.* Baton Rouge, La., 1975.

JOSEPH MILTON NANCE

MORGAN'S RAIDS. Col. John Hunt Morgan, with a brigade of 867 cavalrymen, marched from Knoxville, Tennessee, to Cynthiana, Kentucky, on the first Kentucky raid, July 4 through 28, 1862, recruiting 300 men and eluding a Union force of 3,000 under Gen. G. Clay Smith. President Abraham Lincoln wired: "They are having a stampede in Kentucky. Please look to it!" Morgan exaggerated Southern sympathy and encouraged the Confederate high command to assume that the people of Kentucky would rise in support of an invading Confederate army.

In early August 1862 civilian informers reported that the twin tunnels behind enemy lines on the Louisville and Nashville Railroad seven miles north of Gallatin, Tennessee, were weakly guarded by 375 infantrymen under Union Col. William P. Boone. Morgan prepared for a raid on Gallatin by sending teenage couriers to arrange for food and forage along the seventy-five-mile passage from Sparta to Gallatin. Marching light and under cover of darkness, the raiders reached Gallatin before dawn on August 12, and learned from civilians that Boone's 124 guards were asleep on the courthouse lawn and Boone was sleeping in the hotel with his wife. Morgan's men surprised the Federals and captured them, including Boone, without firing a shot. The soldiers defending the tunnels surrendered with no resistance, and civilians participated in the destruction of the tunnels. The Louisville and Nashville Railroad was Gen. Don Carlos Buell's main artery of supply, and this, the most strategic guerrilla raid of Morgan's career, shut it down, suspending Buell's advance on Chattanooga for ninety-eight days and giving the initiative to Gen. Braxton Bragg for the invasion of Kentucky.

Morgan commanded 2,140 men in a raid on Union Col. Absalom B. Moore's brigade of 2,100 at Hartsville, Tennessee. In a frontal assault on December 7, 1862, Morgan lost 21 men and another 104 were wounded, but the raiders

MORGAN'S RAIDERS. *HARPER'S PICTORIAL HISTORY OF THE GREAT REBELLION*

killed 58, wounded 204, and captured 1,834. The purpose of the Christmas raid, December 22, 1862, to January 1, 1863, was to destroy the two Louisville and Nashville Railroad trestles north of Elizabethtown, Kentucky. Morgan's division of 3,900 succeeded, closing the railroad for five weeks and diverting 7,300 troops from the Union army in the Battle of Murfreesboro.

On the "Great Raid," July 1–26, 1863, Morgan's 2,500 men raided through Indiana and Ohio. On July 19, at Buffington Island, Ohio, the pursuing Union cavalry organized by Gen. Ambrose Burnside and commanded by Generals Edward H. Hobson and Henry M. Judah, captured 700 of Morgan's men. Morgan retreated and was captured on July 26 near West Point, Ohio. The raid delayed Burnside's advance into East Tennessee for one month and boosted Southern morale.

Morgan was incarcerated in the Ohio State Penitentiary. He escaped on November 27, 1863, and with two thousand men, raided from southwestern Virginia into Kentucky from May 30 to June 12, 1864, confiscating horses in Lexington and advancing to Cynthiana. There, on June 12, his command was defeated by the cavalry brigade of Stephen G. Burbridge.

Discipline broke down, and after the raid the Confederate War Department charged Morgan with allowing "excesses and irregularities" relating to the armed robbery of the Farmer's Bank of Kentucky in Mount Sterling and other banks. The men who robbed the banks distributed the money among themselves. Robbery of nongovernmental funds was illegal, as was withholding stolen funds from the Confederate government. Morgan was charged with allowing bank robbery in the Union state of Kentucky, and on August 30, 1864, he was suspended, pending a court of inquiry scheduled for September 10. Six days before the inquiry was to commence, Morgan was killed in Greenville, Tennessee, while attempting to escape from Union cavalry that had surrounded his headquarters and separated him from his men.

[*See also* Morgan, John Hunt.]

BIBLIOGRAPHY

Duke, Basil W. *History of Morgan's Cavalry.* Cincinnati, Ohio, 1867.

Ramage, James A. *Rebel Raider: The Life of General John Hunt Morgan.* Lexington, Ky., 1986.

JAMES A. RAMAGE

MORRIS, AUGUSTA HEWITT (1833 or 1834–?), spy. A baker's daughter from Alexandria, Virginia, Morris acquired a reputation among Federal authorities as "a second Mrs. [Rose O'Neal] Greenhow." As a boarder at Brown's Hotel in Washington, D.C., Morris, who was estranged from her husband, John Francis Mason, collected information on the position and strength of Federal troops and fortifications in the capital. This information she transmitted to Col. Thomas Jordan, who ran the Confederacy's principal spy ring in Washington.

On February 7, 1862, Morris was arrested by order of Maj. Gen. George B. McClellan and confined, along with her son Frank, in Old Capitol Prison. Her fellow inmates at Old Capitol included two other female operatives, Rose O'Neal Greenhow and Catherine Baxley. Morris and Greenhow took an instant dislike to each other. Morris accused the "Rebel Rose" of "mean ambition," and Greenhow claimed that Morris specialized in scandalous behavior, not espionage.

The rival spies were paroled, along with Baxley, in June 1862 and sent to Richmond. Although Greenhow and Baxley were paid for their services by the Confederate government, Morris, tainted by the rumor that she had once tried to sell a key to Confederate army signals to Federal authorities for $10,000, seems never to have received remuneration. No traces remain of Morris's activities after the war.

BIBLIOGRAPHY

Axelrod, Alan. *The War between the Spies: A History of Espionage during the American Civil War.* New York, 1992.

Ross, Ishbel. *Rebel Rose: Life of Rose O'Neal Greenhow, Confederate Spy.* New York, 1954.

Sigaud, Louis A. "Mrs. Greenhow and the Rebel Spy Ring." *Maryland Historical Magazine* 41 (1946): 173–198.

ELIZABETH R. VARON

MORTON, JACKSON (1794–1874), congressman from Florida. Born in Fredericksburg, Virginia, Morton was orphaned at a young age, and an uncle, William Mogen, took care of him. He enrolled at Washington College in 1814 and graduated from the College of William and Mary in 1815. He moved to Pensacola, Florida, and by 1820 was a prominent sawmill operator and later a wealthy planter. His public career began in 1836 when he served in the territorial legislature as a Whig and from 1848 to 1855 as a U.S. senator. He most often voted with his Democratic counterpart, the radical David Levy Yulee, but became more moderate in his views at the end of the decade.

In 1861, Morton was a cooperationist who urged that Florida not secede unless Alabama did, but after the vote he volunteered for military service. He did not serve in the army because he was elected to the Confederate House of Representatives for the duration. He helped write the Confederate Constitution and served on the Commercial Affairs, Inauguration, Flag and Seal, and Indian Affairs committees. He was critical of President Jefferson Davis for leaving Florida defenseless but continued to support the war effort.

After the war Morton returned to his plantation, Mortonia, near Pensacola, and retired from public service. He died at home on November 20, 1874.

BIBLIOGRAPHY

Davis, William Watson. *The Civil War and Reconstruction in Florida.* New York, 1913.

Sifakis, Stewart. *Who Was Who in the Civil War.* New York, 1988.

Wakelyn, Jon L. *Biographical Dictionary of the Confederacy.* Edited by Frank E. Vandiver. Westport, Conn., 1977.

ARCH FREDRIC BLAKEY

MOSBY, JOHN S. (1833–1916), partisan officer. Enlisting as a private in the First Virginia Cavalry in May 1861, Mosby eventually became a scout for J. E. B. Stuart. In January 1863, with Stuart's approval, Mosby began guerrilla operations in northern Virginia. For the next two years the Forty-third Battalion of Virginia Cavalry, or Mosby's Rangers, waged partisan warfare against Union troops and supply lines.

A small, thin, restless man of absolute fearlessness, Mosby, called the "Gray Ghost," was a natural guerrilla leader. He recruited and organized his command, disciplined its youthful members, and plotted the raids. He possessed a keen intellect, an untiring energy, and an iron will. Few, if any, Confederate units reflected its leader more than Mosby's Rangers.

Mosby operated from the counties of Fauquier and Loudoun that became known as "Mosby's Confederacy." From this base, the Rangers attacked Union wagon trains, railroad lines, and troop detachments. His mission, as he said, was "to weaken the armies invading Virginia by harassing their rear."

Wounded three times, Mosby forged the battalion into one of war's finest commands. Robert E. Lee regarded him highly and cited him more often in reports than any other officer. Mosby provided Lee with valuable information and seized hundreds of prisoners and large quantities of arms, equipment, horses, and supplies.

Mosby rose to the rank of colonel and, at war's end, commanded two battalions of eight companies. Refusing to surrender, he disbanded his command on April 21, 1865. His record was unmatched by any other Confederate partisan officer.

Unlike many Southerners, Mosby accepted the defeat of the Confederacy. He resumed his legal practice and eventually worked in the Federal government. He served under Republican administrations as a consul in Hong Kong, in the General Land Office, and as an attorney in the Department of Justice. Mosby died in the nation's capital and was buried in "Mosby's Confederacy," in Warrenton, Virginia.

[*See also* Mosby's Rangers.]

BIBLIOGRAPHY

Jones, Virgil Carrington. *Ranger Mosby.* Chapel Hill, N.C., 1944.

Siepel, Kevin H. *Rebel: The Life and Times of John Singleton Mosby.* New York, 1983.
Wert, Jeffry D. *Mosby's Rangers.* New York, 1990.

JEFFRY D. WERT

MOSBY'S RANGERS. Officially designated the Forty-third Battalion of Virginia Cavalry, Mosby's Rangers was a guerrilla unit under the command of John S. Mosby; it operated in northern Virginia from the winter of 1863 until the end of the war. During that twenty-eight-month span, the rangers became the most effective and feared partisan command in the Confederacy.

In January 1863, Mosby, a cavalry officer, and fifteen men undertook guerrilla operations in the Virginia counties south and west of Washington, D.C. Within five months, so many volunteers had joined the unit that Mosby received permission to organize the command into a unit of the Army of Northern Virginia. At Rector's Cross Roads on June 10, Mosby organized Company A, Forty-third Battalion of Virginia Cavalry. By war's end, the command consisted of two battalions of eight companies, and at least 1,900 men had served in the unit.

Mosby's Rangers operated from a base in the counties of Fauquier and Loudoun, which became known as "Mosby's Confederacy." There civilians concealed, sheltered, and fed the rangers while acting as an information and warning network. From this base, the guerrillas operated eastward toward the Union capital, westward across the Blue Ridge Mountains into the Shenandoah Valley, and northward across the Potomac River into Maryland.

From Mosby's Confederacy, the rangers stood across the supply and communication lines of invading Union armies. Union wagon trains, railroad cars, outposts, and troop detachments became the rangers' targets. Each raid was plotted carefully by Mosby, and when his men struck, they did so swiftly in daylight or darkness. By forcing Federal officers to guard the wagons and railroads, the rangers drained the strength of the invading enemy and became a constant factor in Union campaign strategy.

Although Mosby had hundreds of men at hand, he seldom took more than several dozen with him on a raid. The nature of the warfare demanded secrecy and celerity, and small bodies of mounted men were most effective. Raids lasted usually two or three days, with the rangers returning to their base before dividing the spoils and disbanding. The

GROUP OF MOSBY'S RANGERS. LIBRARY OF CONGRESS

unit's successes came at a high cost, however: the rangers incurred casualties of between 35 and 40 percent, with nearly five hundred rangers spending some time in Federal prisons.

Their various exploits and raids brought the rangers wartime fame and an enduring legacy—the capture of a Union general at his headquarters; the seizure of a railroad train and $178,000 in Union greenbacks; and the relentless campaign against Philip H. Sheridan's Union army in the Shenandoah Valley.

On April 21, 1865, Mosby disbanded the command, refusing to surrender it. The rangers had provided Robert E. Lee with valuable intelligence and captured hundreds of enemy soldiers and hundreds of thousands of dollars worth of material, but they did not lengthen the war in Virginia or alter its basic nature.

BIBLIOGRAPHY

Jones, Virgil Carrington. *Ranger Mosby.* Chapel Hill, N.C., 1944.

Wert, Jeffry D. *Mosby's Rangers.* New York, 1990.

JEFFRY D. WERT

ALFRED MOUTON. LIBRARY OF CONGRESS

MOURNING. *See* Death and Mourning.

MOUTON, ALFRED (1829–1864), brigadier general. The son of Alexander Mouton, governor of Louisiana and a U.S. senator, Jean Jacques Alfred Alexander Mouton graduated from West Point in 1850, but resigned from the army soon after. Afterward, for a short time he worked as an assistant engineer on the New Orleans and Opelousas Railroad founded by his father. He gave this up to manage the family plantation and then started a plantation of his own. In 1856, he was appointed a brigadier general in the Louisiana militia. He also led a vigilante committee ("comité de vigilance") fighting against local outlaws and thieves.

At the start of the Civil War, he raised a regiment and was elected colonel in the Eighteenth Louisiana Infantry (October 1861). During a skirmish at Pittsburg Landing (February 28, 1862), he caught the attention of Gen. P. G. T. Beauregard. On April 6 at Shiloh, his charge against Union lines cost his regiment 207 casualties, and Mouton's horse was shot out from under him. The next day he was severely wounded and had to give up his command. While recuperating, he was promoted to brigadier general (April 16). That fall he was back in action, fighting in the La Fourche District, Louisiana, under Richard Taylor, who praised his gallantry. He commanded a brigade at Irish Bend and Fort Bisland (April 12–14, 1863) and again received praise. Taylor, however, noted that Mouton was "unequal to the task of handling and disposing of any large body of troops."

During the Red River campaign of 1864, Mouton commanded a division, holding the Confederate left on the afternoon of April 8. After retreating for some weeks, Taylor decided to attack, and Mouton led the charge that routed the Union right at Mansfield. There he was killed on April 8. Taylor observed that despite "heavy losses of officers and men, the division never halted for a moment, nor ever fell into confusion." This assault halted Nathaniel P. Banks's advance up the Red River.

BIBLIOGRAPHY

Arceneaux, William. *Acadian General: Alfred Mouton and the Civil War.* Lafayette, La., 1981.

Kerby, Robert L. *Kirby Smith's Confederacy: The Trans-Mississippi South, 1863–1865.* New York, 1972.

THOMAS J. LEGG

MULES. *See* Horses and Mules.

MUNFORDVILLE, KENTUCKY. This town, located about thirty-five miles northeast of Bowling Green, covered an important bridge of the Louisville and Nashville Railroad on the southwesterly flowing Green River. During mid-September 1862 it was garrisoned on both sides of the river by approximately 4,000 Federal troops and four fieldpieces in earthworks and forts south and west of Munfordville, which defended the railroad and its bridge.

The force was commanded by Col. John T. Wilder of the Seventeenth Indiana Infantry.

In August, Confederate Gens. Braxton Bragg, with 30,000 troops in Chattanooga, and E. Kirby Smith, with 10,000 men in Knoxville, began a combined invasion of Kentucky, with the main object of securing that state for the Confederacy. By September 13, although pursued by a slow-moving Union army of 55,000 soldiers commanded by Gen. Don Carlos Buell, Kirby Smith had captured and occupied Frankfort and Bragg was moving in the direction of Munfordville.

That same day, determined to destroy the railroad bridge and sever Buell's lines of communication with Louisville, Bragg sent forward a brigade of Mississippi infantry, commanded by Gen. James Ronald Chalmers, and a detachment of cavalry to force the Federals to capitulate. Col. John S. Scott, commanding the Confederate cavalry, arrived ahead of the infantry and demanded that Wilder surrender unconditionally. He refused, and the next morning at dawn, Chalmer's Mississippians made a futile assault on the Federal positions, losing over 200 men. Nevertheless, the Southerners once more demanded surrender, telling Wilder his position was hopeless. Again Wilder refused.

That night, a small number of reinforcements under Col. Cyrus L. Dunham came to Wilder's aid from Louisville, but they were too few to make much difference in the Federal force. Dunham, however, was Wilder's superior, and Wilder offered to relinquish the command to him; Dunham at first declined.

On September 15, fearing an attack on his western flank by Buell's superior army, Bragg moved his entire force north from Glasgow to take Munfordville quickly and then march on Louisville or join Kirby Smith. Arriving at Munfordville that same day, Bragg planned an immediate assault. But division commander Gen. Simon Bolivar Buckner, apprehensive for the safety of the town's citizens—many of whom he knew personally—persuaded Bragg to postpone the action. Bragg then ordered two of his division commanders, Gen. William J. Hardee and Gen. Leonidas Polk, to surround the town and its garrison—Polk north of the river and Hardee south of it. At six o'clock the following evening, September 16, Bragg again demanded Wilder's surrender.

Meanwhile, though, Dunham had taken command of the Union troops at Munfordville, and he at first refused to strike his colors, but then requested, and received, time to consider Bragg's demands. During this interval, Dunham was relieved of command by orders from Louisville, and Wilder assumed his former position. Wilder was then taken on an inspection tour of the Confederate positions by Buckner, and after concluding that he could not win a battle, he formally surrendered his garrison early on the morning of September 17. After paroling the Federal captives, Bragg stayed at Munfordville until September 20, when he continued moving north to confront Buell, who had taken his army to reinforce Louisville.

BIBLIOGRAPHY

Faust, Patricia L., ed. *Historical Times Illustrated Encyclopedia of the Civil War.* New York, 1986.

Harrison, Lowell H. *The Civil War in Kentucky.* Frankfort, Ky., 1975.

Stickles, Arndt M. *Simon Bolivar Buckner: Borderland Knight.* Chapel Hill, N.C., 1940.

U.S. War Department. *War of the Rebellion: A Compilation of the Official Records of the Union and Confederate Armies.* Ser. 1, vol. 16, pts. 1–2. Washington, D.C., 1886.

Woodworth, Steven E. *Jefferson Davis and His Generals: The Failure of Confederate Command in the West.* Lawrence, Kans., 1990.

WARREN WILKINSON

MUNITIONS. *See* Artillery; Naval Guns; Niter and Mining Bureau; Ordnance Bureau; Small Arms.

MUNNERLYN, CHARLES JAMES (1822–1898), congressman from Georgia and lieutenant colonel. Munnerlyn was born in Georgetown, South Carolina, on February 14, 1822, and spent his early youth there. When he was eleven, his family moved to Florida for several years before settling in Bainbridge, in southwest Georgia, in 1837, where his father became a wealthy landholder and slave owner. Charles was educated at Emory College in Oxford and studied law under its president, Augustus Baldwin Longstreet, better known for his humorous frontier sketches. Though admitted to the bar, Munnerlyn never actively practiced law; instead he took over management of his father's plantation and over five hundred slaves. He married Eugenia Shackleford of Charleston and fathered nine children.

Though he had no previous political experience, Munnerlyn was elected to represent Decatur County at Georgia's secession convention in January 1861, where he supported the state's immediate secession. Once the war broke out, he enlisted as a private in the First Georgia Volunteers but served only briefly at Pensacola, Florida, and in West Virginia before resigning because of poor health in November 1861. He had by that time been elected to the First Congress from Georgia's Second District and took his seat in Richmond in February 1862. He made little active contribution, but his votes indicate that he was a strong supporter of Davis administration policies, despite Governor Joseph E. Brown's increasing opposition to them. Like several of his Georgia colleagues, he voted for conscription and paid the price for support of this very unpopular measure by losing his bid for reelection in 1863.

Munnerlyn immediately reenlisted as a private, until Jefferson Davis rewarded him for his loyalty to the administration by giving him a major's commission and sending him to Florida to organize a reserve regiment, the primary function of which was to protect and facilitate the movement of supplies to the Army of Virginia. Despite difficult circumstances involving widespread desertion, lack of discipline, and inadequate armaments among his Florida troops, he was effective in keeping supply lines open and moving. In 1864 alone, he supplied Confederate armies to the north with over a hundred thousand head of cattle. He was rewarded with promotion to lieutenant colonel.

After the war, Munnerlyn remained in Florida where he worked to facilitate the flight of Confederate officials from the country. Secretary of War Judah P. Benjamin was among those whose escape to the Bahamas Munnerlyn helped arrange. By the end of 1865, Munnerlyn returned home, and despite the tremendous financial loss resulting from emancipation, he managed to rebuild his plantation with a tenant labor force. He invested heavily in railroads and was instrumental in the construction of the Atlantic and Gulf Railroad linking Savannah with Pensacola and Mobile. In 1884 he was elected to the first of several terms as Decatur County ordinary. He died on his plantation on May 17, 1898.

BIBLIOGRAPHY

Northen, William J., ed. *Men of Mark in Georgia*. Vol. 3. Atlanta, 1908. Reprint, Spartanburg, S.C., 1974.

Warner, Ezra J., and W. Buck Yearns. *Biographical Register of the Confederate Congress*. Baton Rouge, La., 1975.

JOHN C. INSCOE

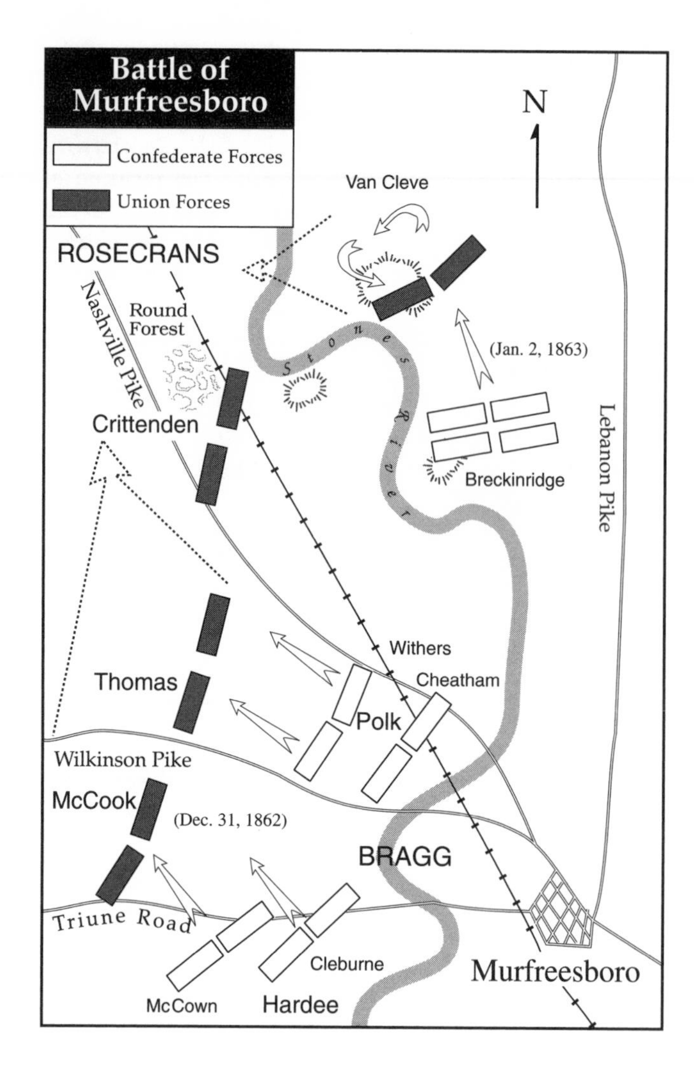

MURFREESBORO, TENNESSEE.

In early December 1862 the Lincoln administration urged the new commander in middle Tennessee, Gen. William S. Rosecrans, to start a campaign against Braxton Bragg's 37,700-man Army of Tennessee at Murfreesboro. Though still exhausted by the long Perryville, Kentucky, campaign of October and weakened by the detachment of 7,500 men to Vicksburg under Gen. Carter Stevenson, Bragg's army was still a formidable fighting force. On December 26, Rosecrans marched the three wings of his 43,400-man army out of Nashville toward the Confederates at Murfreesboro. Because of bad weather and the delaying attacks of Confederate cavalry under Gen. Joseph Wheeler, Rosecrans's army took until December 30 to cover the thirty-mile route.

On the morning of December 31, Rosecrans hoped to hold with his right wing under Gen. Alexander McCook while his left under Gen. Thomas Crittenden advanced at 8:00 A.M. across the fords of Stones River to crush the Confederate right. McCook's wing had not prepared any defenses and were poorly positioned to repulse a Confederate attack. Bragg planned to launch an all-out assault with two of Gen. William J. Hardee's divisions (under Gen. Patrick Cleburne and Gen. John P. McCown) against the Union right. Gen. Leonidas Polk's corps would advance simultaneously, with the units joining in a giant wheeling movement to roll up the Union center. Prior to battle, Polk's command was reorganized. Two of Gen. B. Franklin Cheatham's brigades were exchanged for two of Gen. Jones Mitchell Withers's, which resulted in poorly coordinated attacks along that front. Gen. John C. Breckinridge's division of Hardee's corps was to hold east of Stones River to guard the Confederate right and act as a reserve to exploit any Confederate successes.

Before the Union advance began, Hardee's forces struck McCook's wing at 6:00 A.M. McCown's division quickly routed two Union brigades, capturing one general (August Willich) and mortally wounding another (Edward Kirk).

THE TOWN OF MURFREESBORO, TENNESSEE. *HARPER'S PICTORIAL HISTORY OF THE GREAT REBELLION*

Cleburne's division soon followed, moving into the Union rear and forcing back two of the Federals' brigades. Two brigades of Gen. Jefferson C. Davis's division joined with Gen. Philip Sheridan's division in successfully resisting the initial uncoordinated attacks of Polk's corps.

Hardee's command had broken into the Union rear and captured McCook's headquarters and the Gresham House, field hospital for the right wing. Confederate cavalry under Gen. John Austin Wharton also rode into the area, chasing off Union ammunition wagons and threatening the Nashville Pike. With ammunition running low and under mounting pressure from front and rear, Davis's and Sheridan's divisions retreated toward the pike.

By 9:00 A.M. it was obvious to Rosecrans that his right had been pushed back and his last supply route, the Nashville Pike, was threatened. He countered by calling off his attack and sending Gen. Lovell Rousseau's division into a cedar forest north of the Wilkinson Pike to link up with Sheridan and protect the rear of Gen. James Negley's division. Two of Gen. Horatio Van Cleve's brigades and one of Gen. Thomas Wood's were to hold the area farther west along the Nashville Pike.

The Confederates continued their advance into the Union rear. McCown's division of three brigades, which had advanced farther west than planned, now turned east in an uncoordinated attack and was repulsed by Union reserve infantry and artillery. This action resulted in the death of one brigade commander, Gen. James Edwards Rains, who was shot through the heart, and temporarily destroyed the effectiveness of these units.

Negley's division and parts of Sheridan's and Rousseau's division were soon caught in a pocket just north of the Wilkinson Pike with the Confederates on three sides. Sheridan's exhausted division pulled out, followed by Rousseau. Pressure from Gen. Patton Anderson's Mississippi brigade forced Negley's units, which were in danger of being cut off, back to the Nashville Pike. By noon, despite a spirited defense by Col. Oliver Shepherd's regular brigade, the Confederates of Polk's corps had driven through the forest of cedars to a large cotton field bordering the Nashville Pike. But there the drive stalled, owing to lack of artillery support to counter the Union batteries along the pike. The Confederates' artillery had been unable to follow through the dense cedar woods and limestone outcroppings. Col. Francis Walker of the Nineteenth Tennessee later claimed that if even one battery could have been brought up, the South would have won the day completely.

Cleburne's division, farther west, continued pushing the Union forces toward the Nashville Pike. At one point in the afternoon Gen. Bushrod Rust Johnson's brigade had captured the pike but was repulsed by a Union counterattack by re-formed units. Johnson complained, "At the moment in which I felt the utmost confidence in the success of our arms, I was almost run over by our retreating troops. Our men were in sight of the Nashville Pike. . . . Had we held this position the line of communication of the enemy would have been cut." By 3:00 P.M. the Confederate attacks in the area faltered, with the men exhausted and lacking support.

While Confederate attacks on the left enjoyed some success, Withers's advances along the Nashville Pike made little progress against the Union line at the Round Forest, a half acre of mature hardwoods along the Nashville and Chattanooga Railroad. Earlier, at approximately 10:00 A.M., Col. James Chalmer's brigade of Mississippians had advanced against the Round Forest position held by Col. William Hazen's brigade. But Chalmers's unit retreated when its line was broken by the ruins of the Cowan House and it tried to re-form under a deadly Union crossfire. Gen. Daniel Smith Donelson's Tennessee brigade immediately advanced against the same position, but their attack on the Round Forest also faltered.

Bragg asked Breckinridge at 10:00 A.M. for two brigades to reinforce Hardee's drive farther west, but they were delayed as a result of what they thought was a Union threat from the north. When they finally arrived at 1:00 P.M., they were thrown instead against the Union line at the Round Forest, which had been reinforced. After these two brigades failed, Bragg called for Breckinridge to send two more against the same position. At about 3:30 P.M. Gen. William Ballard Preston's and Col. Joseph Palmer's brigades advanced. Union Colonel Hazen was impressed by the "dreadful splendor" of the Confederate line stretching into the distance. These units too were repulsed by the deadly Union fire in the last major Confederate attack of the day.

Overall, however, the first day of fighting at Murfreesboro had ended in a Confederate victory. The Federals' right and center had been crushed and only their Round Forest position on the left had held. Rosecrans could barely hold on to his last supply line, the Nashville Pike. Casualties on both sides had been high (approximately 17,000), making December 31, 1862, the bloodiest single day of the war in Tennessee.

For Bragg, nightfall ushered in a happy new year, and he sent an exultant victory telegram to Richmond: he had driven the Union forces from nearly every position, inflicted heavy casualties, and captured supply wagons, thousands of soldiers, and thirty-one pieces of artillery. The Confederates expected the Union army to retreat to Nashville and lick its wounds. The fighting, however, was not yet over, for that evening Rosecrans determined to make a stand. He pulled back from the Round Forest and ordered the battered Union army to dig in along the Nashville Pike.

January 1, 1863, saw only minor action as Bragg waited for the supposedly defeated Union force to retreat. Rosecrans sent three brigades of Van Cleve's division and one of Gen. John Palmer's division across the river at McFadden's Ford to a position that threatened Bragg's right.

Bragg ended the period of inactivity the next day at 4:00 P.M., ordering four brigades of Breckinridge's division to attack the Union units east of the river. Breckinridge argued with Bragg against making the charge, which he considered suicidal, and Gen. Roger Hanson of the Orphan Brigade reportedly volunteered to shoot Bragg instead of attacking. Despite the protests, the attack went forward. After initial success in routing two Union brigades, the Confederate line advanced toward McFadden's Ford. Although the Confederates pushed the second Union line across the river, they soon ran into the massed fire of fifty-seven Union artillery pieces on the west side. The artillery fire caused many casualties, including Hanson, who fell mortally wounded. Negley's division made a successful counterattack, which was joined by other Union units.

Breckinridge's attack had resulted in about 1,700 casualties, representing 38 percent of those who advanced. For this sacrifice Bragg had nothing to show, but had actually lost ground as well as three Confederate cannons. Breckinridge, upon seeing the gaps in the ranks of his old unit, cried out, "My poor Orphans! My poor Orphan Brigade! They have cut it to pieces!"

The day's outcome left the Army of Tennessee disheartened. Polk complained to Bragg in a letter, "I greatly fear the consequences of another engagement at this place." With the rain increasing and his army exhausted, Bragg decided to abandon Murfreesboro and retreat south to Shelbyville and Tullahoma on January 3. Two days later, Rosecrans's army occupied Murfreesboro.

Both armies suffered high casualties. Union losses were 12,700, or 29 percent of those engaged, while the Confederates lost 9,870, representing 27 percent of their force. Although the Union victory was not decisive, it gave a psychological boost to a war-weary North. Bragg's staff blamed him for turning a hard-fought victory into defeat by retreating. The bickering and morale problems that plagued Bragg and his command continued to fester as a result of this lost opportunity.

BIBLIOGRAPHY

Cozzens, Peter. *The Battle of Stones River: No Better Place to Die.* Chicago, 1990.

Davis, William C. *The Orphan Brigade.* Garden City, N.Y., 1980.

Johnson, Robert U., and Buel, C. C., eds. *Battles and Leaders of the Civil War.* Vol. 3. New York, 1888. Reprint, Secaucus, N.J., 1982.

McDonough, James Lee. *Stones River: Bloody Winter in Tennessee.* Knoxville, Tenn., 1980.

Spearman, Charles M. "The Battle of Stones River." *Blue and Gray Magazine* 6, no. 3 (1988): 8–30, 36–45.

Stevenson, Alexander. *The Battle of Stones River near Murfreesboro, Tennessee.* Boston, 1884. Reprint, Gettysburg, Pa., 1983.

U.S. War Department. *War of the Rebellion: A Compilation of the Official Records of the Union and Confederate Armies.* Washington, D.C., 1880–1901. Ser. 1, vol. 20, pt. 1, pp. 166–979.

CHARLES M. SPEARMAN

MURPHY, ISAAC (1799–1882), Unionist governor of Arkansas. Murphy was born in Pennsylvania on October 16, 1799, and settled in northwestern Arkansas in 1834. He was an educator, attorney, and politician in Washington and Madison counties prior to the Civil War. He opposed secession in 1861 and was elected to the state secession convention as a Unionist. With other Unionists, Murphy helped prevent secession in the first session of that convention in March 1861. Following President Abraham Lincoln's call for volunteers after Fort Sumter, the convention reconvened and passed a resolution of secession. Murphy remained opposed to the measure and ultimately was the only member of the body to vote against it. In a statement that challenged the secessionist passion of the gallery, Murphy told the delegates that he was aware of the consequences of his vote, but that he could not in good conscience change it.

Murphy returned to Madison County following the convention. Unpopular and suffering from persecution because of his pro-Union stance, Murphy joined the staff of Gen. Samuel R. Curtis as a volunteer when the Union army moved into northwestern Arkansas in the spring of 1862, and he left the state when Curtis withdrew after the battle of Elkhorn Tavern. Murphy moved for a time to St. Louis where he may have been active in Unionist politics. In September 1863 he accompanied Gen. Frederick Steele's expedition against Little Rock and entered the capital with Union troops when it fell. Murphy was a prominent leader of Unionists in Little Rock and worked to reconstruct the state under President Lincoln's Ten Percent Plan. He was elected governor of a Unionist state government established at Little Rock in January 1864 and remained in that role until July 1868. With inadequate funds and little real power to enforce its will, the Murphy government was able to achieve little. Unionist civilians were unprotected except at the whim of Federal military commanders. Although Murphy acted as governor until 1868, his government was never recognized fully by the U.S. Congress.

He returned to Huntsville after stepping down as governor and was a farmer and attorney there until his death on September 8, 1882.

BIBLIOGRAPHY

Obituary. *Arkansas Gazette* (Little Rock), September 12, 1882.

Shea, William L. "Isaac Murphy." In *The Governors of Arkansas.* Edited by Timothy P. Donovan and Willard B. Gatewood, Jr. Fayetteville, Ark., 1980.

Smith, John I. *The Courage of a Southern Unionist: A Biography of Isaac Murphy, Governor of Arkansas, 1864–68.* Little Rock, Ark., 1979.

CARL H. MONEYHON

MURRAH, PENDLETON (1826–1965), governor of Texas. Following his probably illegitimate birth during 1826 in Alabama, Murrah lived for a time in a home for orphans before a Baptist group financed his college education. In 1848 he received a degree from Brown University and then read for the law in Alabama. After developing tuberculosis, he migrated to what he hoped would be a healthier climate in Texas in 1850.

Murrah became a lawyer at Marshall, where he married into one of the prominent plantation families. He became active in the Democratic party and lost in an 1855 legislative election to a man favored by the American, or Know-Nothing party, though Murrah won two years later. The Democratic party in Texas placed him on its executive committee in 1858. During the 1860 presidential election he served as an alternate Breckinridge elector for his district. In 1861 Murrah was considered for but not elected by the Texas secession convention to membership in the Provisional Congress that created the Confederacy. Health problems that same year caused him to drop out of a congressional campaign and limited his quartermaster service with the Fourteenth Texas Infantry.

When the Texas gubernatorial election approached in 1863, Murrah joined several possible candidates. The race narrowed to Murrah and Thomas Jefferson Chambers, a flamboyant and uncooperative figure who had been defeated in earlier races for the state's highest office. Because Chambers had been a critic of the Confederate government and President Jefferson Davis, Murrah received support from a majority of Texas political figures and voters.

As Murrah assumed office in the fall of 1863, Texas faced growing economic problems and the threat of Union invasion. The governor found himself in disagreement with Gen. John B. Magruder, district commander for Texas, over how to meet these pressures. Murrah opposed extensive impressment of slave labor by the army and urged payments for use of bondsmen. Whether new draft-age soldiers should serve in the Confederate army or the state military stirred another clash between the governor and the general. The Trans-Mississippi Department commander, Gen. E. Kirby Smith, arranged for Murrah to keep the state soldiers unless a crisis arose, as in the Red River campaign of 1864. Differences lingered about control over men in units organized for frontier protection. Competition between policies and efforts of the Confederate Cotton Office in Texas and state cotton buyers for control of the cotton trade led to tension that Murrah and Smith resolved during the summer of 1864 in favor of the army's need to trade for war necessities. The governor also struggled with increasing inflation that limited the state's finances and its ability to aid destitute relatives of soldiers.

When the Confederate army in the Trans-Mississippi region surrendered in June 1865, Murrah and other officials who feared punishment left for Mexico. The difficult overland travel weakened his already delicate health and led to his death on August 4 at Monterrey.

BIBLIOGRAPHY

Deuson, Benny E. "Pendleton Murrah." In *Ten Texans in Gray.* Edited by W. C. Nunn. Hillsboro, Tex., 1968.

Pendleton Murrah File. Southwest Collection, Texas Tech University, Lubbock.

Wooster, Ralph A. "Texas." In *The Confederate Governors.* Edited by W. Buck Yearns. Athens, Ga., 1985.

ALWYN BARR

MURRAY, JOHN PORRY (1830–1895), colonel and congressman from Tennessee. Murray was born and reared in Gainesboro (Jackson County), Tennessee, and began the practice of law there in 1852. He soon established a widely recognized reputation as a trial lawyer and leader in the Democratic party. In 1857, he was appointed circuit judge of the Sixth District, becoming one of the youngest judges in the state.

Four years later, after Tennessee joined the Confederacy, Murray helped organize an infantry company in his county and soon became commandant of the Twenty-eighth Tennessee Infantry. In the following year he was promoted to colonel and participated in several engagements until he was wounded at the Battle of Shiloh in June 1862. Because of his disability, he retired to the practice of law in Gainesboro and in 1863 was elected to the Second Congress for the Fourth District.

As congressman, Murray voted with other nationalists who emphasized the maintenance of a strong military force, and he was always interested in the lot of the common soldier. He spoke frequently on this and other matters on the floor of Congress. Well informed generally, Murray was disturbed when the Maximilian regime was established in Mexico, and he sponsored a resolution condemning the action.

Murray's ardor for the Confederate cause is interesting in view of his strong position earlier against secession. His county was far below the state average in natural wealth, and there were very few slaveholders in Jackson County and those immediately surrounding. But when Abraham Lincoln invaded the South, Murray joined with a majority of his fellows in support of Tennessee and the Southern states.

Having led the forces for Andrew Johnson in the gubernatorial campaigns of 1853 and 1855, Murray considered Johnson a personal friend and was among the first high ranking Confederates from Tennessee to call upon the president after the war ended. Murray continued in the practice of law in Gainesboro until his death on December 21, 1895. He was buried in the family cemetery there.

BIBLIOGRAPHY

Journal of the Congress of the Confederate States of America, 1861–1865. 7 vols. Washington, D.C., 1904–1905.

Moore, John T., and A. P. Foster. *Tennessee: The Volunteer State.* Vol 2. Nashville, Tenn., 1923.

Warner, Ezra J., and W. Buck Yearns. *Biographical Register of the Confederate Congress.* Baton Rouge, La., 1975.

Vandiver, Frank E. "Proceedings of the Second Confederate Congress." *Southern Historical Society Papers* 51–52 (1958). Reprint, Wilmington, N.C., 1992.

ROBERT E. CORLEW

MUSCOGEE. *See entry on the ship* Jackson.

MUSEUMS AND ARCHIVES. Studying and interpreting Confederate history is a fascinating and time-consuming process. Important research collections are housed in numerous archives, libraries, and museums across the United States, many of which are located in the Southern states that once formed the Confederacy. Resources such as manuscripts, printed works, photographs, other artwork, and contemporary physical artifacts are equally important components in the research process. To contact the public or private facilities that specialize in Confederate history, consult the published directories that describe historical agencies in general, or consult any of the several published catalogues and guides to specific collections.

The largest and most important archival collections are housed in the National Archives and the Library of Congress, both of which are located in Washington, D.C. These facilities have vast quantities of materials related to Confederate civil and military affairs, as well as the papers of prominent politicians and military leaders. Both institutions have published guides to their collections, Henry Putney Beers's *The Confederacy: A Guide to the Archives of the Government of the Confederate States of America* (1968, 1986) and John R. Sellers's *Civil War Manuscripts: A Guide to Collections in the Manuscript Division of the Library of Congress* (1986). Another essential access tool is the *National Union Catalog of Manuscript Collections (NUCMC)* and its index, copies of which are at all major research libraries around the country.

Visual images of the Confederacy, including photographs, paintings, prints, drawings, and portraits, are available at the National Archives, the Library of Congress, and the National Portrait Gallery. Access to the latter two collections is available through Hirst D. Milhollen and Donald H. Mugridge's *Civil War Photographs, 1861–1865: A Catalog of Copy Negatives Made from Originals Selected from the Mathew B. Brady Collection in the Prints and Photographs Division of the Library of Congress* (1961) and the Smithsonian Institution's *National Portrait Gallery Permanent Collection Illustrated Checklist.* Other important photograph collections are housed at the United States Army Military History Institute, Carlisle Barracks, Pennsylvania, and the Valentine Museum in Richmond, Virginia. In addition, numerous examples of Confederate artwork are housed in other facilities in the United States. For an example, consult Virginius C. Hall, Jr.'s, *Portraits in the Collection of the Virginia Historical Society: A Catalogue* (1981).

Maps, atlases, and related cartographic items are especially important to the study of military history. Guides to the collections in Washington, D.C., are Richard W. Stephenson's *Civil War Maps: An Annotated List of Maps and Atlases in the Library of Congress,* 2d ed. (1989), and *A Guide to Civil War Maps in the National Archives* (1986). Other maps are more readily available in the *Atlas to Accompany the Official Records of the Union and Confederate Armies* (1891–1895) and in the numerous secondary sources that are at most research facilities.

State-run libraries and archives and historical societies in those states that once formed the Confederacy also have significant collections. An overview of this level of the study of Confederate history is found in James C. Neagles's *Confederate Research Sources: A Guide to Archive Collections* (1986). Many of the state-run collections have individually published guides; for an example, see the Florida Department of State, Division of Library and Information Services, Bureau of Archives and Records Management, *Guide to the Records of the Florida State Archives* (Tallahassee, Fla., 1988).

Other materials at state facilities concentrate on the Confederate period of individual state governments, the state military regiments that constituted the Confederate army, and the compiled service and pension records of individual soldiers and their widows. The state of North Carolina, for example, has an extensive regimental history and troop roster publication begun in 1966, *North Carolina Troops, 1861–1865,* covering the artillery, cavalry, and infantry. State facilities often contain the papers and diaries of prominent citizens and military men as well as those of ordinary citizens. Many house collections of wartime newspapers and Confederate imprints. Their collections of related photographs and artwork capture the wartime life and surroundings of the individual states.

Other important primary source collections are in the custody of major state and private university libraries, large city or county governments, independently operated historical societies and libraries, or in private collections.

The Southern Historical Collection, which covers the whole of Southern history, is housed at the Wilson Library at the University of North Carolina at Chapel Hill. It features *A Guide to Manuscripts* (1970) and a supplement (1976).

The Virginia Historical Society in Richmond, the center for the study of Virginia history, features Waverly K. Winfree's *Guide to Manuscript Collections of the Virginia Historical Society* (1985). The society's Confederate collections include the bulk of Robert E. Lee's papers and papers of military notables Thomas J. ("Stonewall") Jackson, J. E. B. Stuart, A. P. Hill, and Jubal Early, and materials on various Virginia military regiments.

Items related to Jefferson Davis, Albert Sidney Johnston, and postwar veterans' organizations are on deposit in the Howard-Tilton Memorial Library at Tulane University and are accessed through the *Inventory of the Louisiana Historical Association Collection* (1983).

The Huntington Library in San Marino, California, houses a valuable Civil War collection including papers of Joseph E. Johnston and Stuart that are described in the *Guide to American Historical Manuscripts in the Huntington Library* (1979).

The Eleanor S. Brockenbrough Library at the Museum of the Confederacy in Richmond has an important postwar collection of Davis materials; papers of Lee, Jackson, and Stuart; regimental items pertaining to the theater of operations of the Army of Northern Virginia; and a fine collection of Confederate currency and bonds.

The William Stanley Hoole Special Collections Library at the University of Alabama has a collection of Davis papers, the diaries and papers of Josiah Gorgas, the records of the Shelby Iron Works, and materials related to the wartime history of the state as a whole.

The Hargrett Rare Book and Manuscript Library at the University of Georgia houses the Permanent Constitution of the Confederacy, the papers of Howell Cobb, and a large collection of Confederate imprints.

Confederate artifacts reflecting the material culture of the wartime South are housed in museums throughout the United States. In some instances institutions that are not formally designated as museums, such as state-run historical agencies, will have collections of three-dimensional objects that date from the Confederate years. In addition, there are fine collections in the possession of private citizens.

Some Confederate museums have direct ties to the wartime years, in that the particular facility may have served as a residence of a prominent citizen, a military headquarters, or a postwar veterans' meeting hall. In turn, this added significance often helped with the acquisition of artifacts. During the 1890s, certainly prompted by the twenty-fifth anniversary of the war years, Confederate museums were established in Richmond, New Orleans, Charleston, and other cities. Former Confederates, from individuals in the top ranks of government down to ordinary soldiers or their descendants, began donating wartime possessions to these and other custodial institutions for posterity. The practice continued well into the twentieth century, and the verbal anecdotes that often accompanied the donations add as well to the store of narrative histories concerning the Confederate experience. Today, the museums that study the Confederacy are more than relic halls, and they are actively engaged in the preservation, study, and interpretation of the wartime South for national audiences.

The Museum of the Confederacy in Richmond houses one of the nation's largest Confederate collections. Founded in 1890 and opening in 1896, the museum features collections of flags, uniforms, edged weapons, firearms, and a variety of other wartime military and domestic effects. Also housed there are personal effects of Davis, Lee, Jackson, and Stuart. The monumental oil painting *The Last Meeting of Lee and Jackson,* by E. B. D. Julio, is on display. Adjacent to the museum is the White House of the Confederacy, the wartime residence of Davis and his family. Fully restored to its mid-nineteenth-century appearance, the building features a fine collection of furniture and decorative arts, many of which were used by the Davis family. In addition, the museum also houses the Eleanor S. Brockenbrough Library, which is its research facility.

Other important and historic buildings associated with the Confederacy include the First White House of the Confederacy and the Alabama Capitol, both in Montgomery. Jefferson Davis's last home, Beauvoir, in Biloxi, Mississippi, is where he wrote his two-volume memoir, *The Rise and Fall of the Confederate Government.*

The Confederate Museum in New Orleans was founded in 1891 and is located in the former meeting hall of the city's United Confederate Veterans. The featured holdings include possessions of Davis, uniforms of P. G. T. Beauregard and Braxton Bragg, flags, weaponry, and oil paintings. The museum's archival and manuscript holdings are on deposit at the Howard-Tilton Memorial Library at Tulane University.

The Confederate Museum in Charleston was opened in 1894 by Confederate veterans, and today the facility is operated by their descendants. The museum's holdings include both military and civilian artifacts from the firing on Fort Sumter to William Tecumseh Sherman's March to the Sea.

The Virginia Historical Society in Richmond, founded in 1831, houses the Maryland-Steuart Collection, one of the nation's finest collections of Confederate firearms, edged weapons, and military accoutrements. The *Four Seasons of the Confederacy,* a series of military murals painted by Charles Hoffbauer, is another of the society's many treasures. The research arm of the society is nationally renowned for its holdings on the Civil War in Virginia.

The Confederate Naval Museum in Columbus, Georgia, houses the remains of CSS *Jackson (Muscogee)* and the remains of CSS *Chattahoochee.* Both vessels were in active service before being destroyed to avoid capture by Union forces. The museum holds other naval artifacts and ship models and features exhibitions on the Confederate navy and marine corps.

Museum of the Confederacy, Richmond, Virginia.

[*See also* Beauvoir; Memorial Organizations; White House.]

BIBLIOGRAPHY

American Association for State and Local History. *Directory of Historical Organizations in the United States and Canada.* 14th ed. Edited by Mary Bray Wheeler. Nashville, Tenn., 1990.

American Association of Museums. *The Official Museum Directory, 1992.* Wilmette, Ill., 1991.

National Historical Publications and Records Commission. *Directory of Archives and Manuscript Repositories in the United States.* 2d ed. Phoenix, Ariz., 1988.

National Park Service, U.S. Department of the Interior. *The National Parks: Index 1985.* Washington, D.C., 1985.

Guy R. Swanson

MUSIC. The music of the Confederacy was in part a distinct cultural flowering and in part a reflection of the national musical trends of the 1860s. It included songs and tunes actually performed by soldiers in the field, military and marching music, concert music that entertained the troops, sentimental parlor songs popular on the home front, and rousing patriotic songs designed to rally support for the cause. Some songs dealt with specific topics from the war, but far more dealt with the ageless and universal subjects of love, death, family, and separation.

Sheet Music

The primary medium for popular songs during the war was, for both North and South, sheet music. Well before the war, the music publishing industry had become surprisingly sophisticated in marketing and promoting hit songs, and though it was still centered in New York, dozens of independent publishers had sprung up in smaller cities around the country. This meant that the South had in place a network of publishers on the eve of the war, and that throughout the four years of the conflict a steady stream of Confederate imprints flowed forth. Over 650 different pieces of sheet music have been identified as items published by Confederate presses from venues not under Federal occupation. Most of the pieces came from New Orleans (167), Augusta (137), Richmond (91), Macon-Savannah (73), and Macon (60), though cities like Charleston, Nashville, Columbia, Danville, Memphis, Mobile, and Wilmington also boasted some publications.

Not all these songs were originals written by Confederate composers; many were Southern editions of songs that had nationwide popularity. Blackmar and Brother, for instance, issued a series called "The Exotics: Flowers of Song Transplanted to Southern Soil," which included Northern favorites like "What Is Home without a Mother" and "Cottage by the Sea." John Schreiner and Son of Macon had a similar series called "The Southern Musical Bouquet" that included "Her Bright Smile Haunts Me Still" and Mrs. Norton's "Juanita." As the war dragged on, many of these publishers found it hard to get quality paper, and this led to a downsizing of the sheet music and, later, publication on inferior paper that quickly deteriorated.

The two most prolific New Orleans publishers were the firms of P. P. Werlein and Halsey, and the brothers Armand Edward and Henry Clay Blackmar. Werlein, the city's leading firm since 1854, had established a cadre of his own engravers and printers. A. E. Blackmar, originally from Vermont, was a graduate of Western Reserve College in Cleveland who had taught music in Huntsville, Alabama, and at Centenary College in Jackson, Louisiana. He and his brother opened a music store and publishing business in New Orleans in 1860. One of their most spectacular successes was a song that would become, next to the well-known "Dixie," the best remembered of all the Confederate songs: "The Bonnie Blue Flag." From 1861 to 1864 the Blackmars published no fewer than six different editions of the song. The title came from a flag used by South Carolina after the state's secession in 1860; it was a plain blue flag with a single white star in its center, and it became the temporary banner for the seceding states. Different verses of the song, in fact, listed the states of the Confederacy, with new verses added as new states joined the cause.

The words to the song were written by Harry Macarthy, a singer who was born in England in 1834 and came to America when he was fifteen. Described by a contemporary as "a good vocalist as well as protean actor," Macarthy was noted for his "impersonation concerts," which featured songs in dialect and in which he billed himself (for obscure reasons) as "The Arkansas Comedian." In September he grafted his words to an old melody called "The Irish Jaunting Car" and premiered the song in New Orleans before an audience of soldiers on their way to the Virginia front. It was an immediate success, and Macarthy's friend A. E. Blackmar arranged not only to publish it but to help Macarthy further popularize it. Soon the singer was the most popular entertainer in the South; his fellow songwriter Will S. Hays dedicated "The Drummer Boy of Shiloh" to him. The song was so potent that when New Orleans was captured by Northern forces in April 1862, Union commander Gen. Benjamin F. Butler tried to suppress the song by destroying all copies of the sheet music, fining Blackmar, and threatening a fine of twenty-four dollars for anyone caught singing or even whistling the song.

With the fall of New Orleans, the center for Confederate music publishing moved to Georgia. The Blackmars relocated in Augusta, where they continued to sell their hit songs like "Bonnie Blue Flag," Macarthy's "The Volunteer," "The Confederate Flag," and "Maryland, My Maryland." Also located in Georgia was the firm of Herman L. Schreiner, a German immigrant who arrived in the United States in 1849, settling in Macon and doing business as John Schreiner and Sons. After the fall of New Orleans, he made his way north, purchased a font of music type, and smuggled it back through Union lines to Georgia. This gave the firm a major advantage in the Confederate publishing scene—some historians have said that for a time it was the only publishing house active in the Confederacy—and its headquarters in Macon and Savannah produced over seventy pieces. Schreiner himself often gave concerts for hospitals and relief societies, and did musical scores for songs like "The Mother of the Soldier Boy."

Schreiner often worked with John Hill Hewitt, a dramatist, poet, historian, publisher, and songwriter par excellence. Before the war, Hewitt had won a national reputation as a writer of what many consider to be America's first native ballad, "The Minstrel's Return from the War" (1827). A student at West Point, an acquaintance of Edgar Allan Poe, and a magazine editor and playright active in the upper South through the 1850s, Hewitt spent the first part of the war managing a theater in Richmond and then moved to Augusta. He continued to write musical plays and operettas, but won most fame with songs like "All Quiet along the Potomac Tonight" (1862), "Rock Me to Sleep, Mother" (1862), and "Somebody's Darling" (1864).

SHEET MUSIC COVER OF "OUR NATIONAL CONFEDERATE ANTHEM." One of numerous Confederate national anthems. Lithograph on wove paper by Ernest Crehen, published by the composer in Richmond, Virginia, 1862. LIBRARY OF CONGRESS

In addition to Macarthy and Hewitt, the third major Confederate songwriter was a colorful Louisville newspaperman and riverboat captain named William Shakespeare Hays. Hays would eventually publish over three hundred songs, some of them among the best-selling sheet music editions in history. Hays appears not to have had strong sympathies with either side in the war—he wrote a campaign song for George B. McClellan—but many of his songs, such as "The Old Sergeant," have a distinct pro-South tone. "The Drummer Boy of Shiloh" (1862), Hays's memorable account of a dying drummer boy on "Shiloh's dark and bloody ground," was published repeatedly throughout the war and inspired a flood of imitative pieces. When Blackmar issued later editions of the song, the music credit was given to "the First Tennessee Concert troupe."

Some songs were so popular that their fame transcended any association with publisher or even composer. One of these, of course, was "Dixie." Another, only slightly less popular, was "Maryland, My Maryland," written by James Ryder Randall in April 1861 at Poydras College in Pointe Coupee, Louisiana. Randall was a native of Baltimore who wrote the song after hearing about a clash between the city's residents and the Sixth Massachusetts Regiment; a Baltimore musician named Charles Ellerbrock later grafted to it an arrangement of the tune to the German Christmas song "Tannenbaum, O Tannenbaum." The South's favorite marching song became "The Yellow Rose of Texas," a minstrel song from the decade before the war. "Stonewall Jackson's Way" was first published in Baltimore in 1862 (before Jackson's death) and was banned by Union occupation troops; the song made its way South and enjoyed renewed popularity after its subject's death.

Probably the best loved of all sentimental songs was "Lorena," written by a Massachusetts minister named H. D. L. Webster in 1857. It was published by several publishers in both Northern and Southern cities and was sung, according to Brander Matthews, "until the last musket was fired and the last camp fire grew cold." The song remained indelibly etched in the public image of the Confederacy for decades after—even to the point of being used in both the novel and the film of *Gone with the Wind.*

Since very few Confederate music business records survived, it is hard to know what songs were most popular during the war or which ones the soldiers sang the most. The best attempt to ascertain the latter is found in historian Bell Irwin Wiley's *The Life of Johnny Reb,* in which he surveyed hundreds of soldiers' letters and diaries and compiled a list of the songs most frequently mentioned. In addition to well-known songs like "Home Sweet Home," "Lorena," "Just Before the Battle, Mother," and "All Quiet along the Potomac Tonight," the list was composed almost entirely of songs from Northern sources that were popular before the war. These included "Annie Laurie" (an 1838 song popularized by British soldiers during the Crimean War); "Lily Dale" (a morose 1852 ballad popularized by the Continental Vocalists, a rival to New England's famed Hutchinson Family singing group); "Bell Brandon" (an 1854 song by T. Elwood Garrett and Francis Woolcott); and "Listen to the Mocking Bird" (an 1855 tune by veteran songsmith Septimus Winner, writing under the name "Alice Hawthorne"; this song was a favorite of Abraham Lincoln's).

Two of the songs on Wiley's list were published during the war: "Annie of the Vale," an 1861 song by New Yorker H. S. Thompson, composer of "Woodman, Spare That Tree," and "Her Bright Smile Haunts Me Still," a sailor's song that originated in England and bore composer credits of J. E. Carpenter and W. T. Wrighton. Two of the songs, "Sweet Evelina" and "The Girl I Left behind Me," probably came from folk tradition; the latter song was a special favorite with brass bands and fiddlers alike and appears to have derived from an English tune called "Brighton Camp" dating from the 1770s. Wiley's list shows the extent to which Confederate and Union troops shared a common heritage of popular songs, and the extent to which soldiers in the field favored older, sentimental songs that reminded them of happier times before the war.

Slave Spirituals and Folk Music

One musical genre from the war that was to have a profound impact on later American music was the slave spiritual. Though these unique songs had been part of plantation life for decades, it was only after the war started that missionaries, educators, and aid society workers began to collect and publish them and introduce them to the rest of the nation. Not long after the firing on Fort Sumter, refugee slaves began streaming into the Union's Fortress Monroe in Virginia; here the commander, General Butler, declared them "contraband of war" so he would have a legal reason for not returning them to their owners. Newspapers picked up the phrase, and soon "contraband" became a new Northern synonym for "slave." As more and more ex-slaves arrived at the Chesapeake Bay fort, and Butler's resources were stretched to the breaking point, Northern churches and missionary societies began to organize relief drives and sent representatives down to assess the situation.

On September 3, 1861, the Reverend Lewis C. Lockwood arrived at the fort from the New York YMCA; that night, from the piazza of his hotel, he heard a strange new music coming from "a long building just outside the entrance of the Fortress" where a number of "colored people" had assembled for a prayer meeting. Lockwood listened to a song he later learned was "Go Down, Moses," a spiritual that had been sung for "at least fifteen or twenty years in Virginia and Maryland, and perhaps in all the slave states, though stealthily, for fear of the lash." Lockwood eventually copied the words to the song and sent them to the *New York Tribune,* where they caused a stir when published there in December 1861. Two weeks later a piece of sheet music entitled "The Song of the Contrabands: O Let My People Go" was published by the Horace Waters Company on Broadway, with a note that read, "words and music obtained through the Rev. L. C. Lockwood, Chaplain of the Contrabands at Fortress Monroe." Soon the song—apparently the first published spiritual—was being sung at antislavery meetings and even at the first White House emancipation signing in 1863. It has remained popular ever since, enjoying renewed popularity during the civil rights movement of the 1960s.

The first real description of African American spiritual singing came from a woman named Lucy McKim, the nineteen-year-old daughter of a noted abolitionist; she had spent three weeks collecting songs on the Sea Islands off the South Carolina coast. A formally trained musician, she understood the musical content of what she heard; in a famous letter to Dwight's *Journal of Music* (November 8, 1862), she called attention to the unique qualities of the spirituals, admitting that the classical European musical notation system had no way to accommodate the "odd turns" and "irregular intervals" of the songs. She planned a series of sheet music editions of eight of the songs she collected, but apparently only two of these came out. As "Songs of the Freedmen of Port Royal," two titles, "Roll Jordan Roll" and "Poor Rosy, Poor Gal," were issued in November 1862, probably more accurate with transcriptions of words and music than those of Lockwood.

In the meantime, Charles Pickard Ware, a Harvard graduate, began working on the Sea Islands for the Educational Commission, and he too became interested in the songs he found there. He soon had "175 pages of Negro melodies" and by 1865 had joined forces with his cousin William Allen, a trained historian and accomplished musician who had spent two years in Arkansas collecting songs. At the instigation of Wendell Phillips Garrison, editor of the *Nation* magazine, the cousins pooled their collections, added songs from Lucy McKim, and produced one of the most important cultural documents to come out of the war, *Slave Songs of the United States* (1867). This volume contained both words and music to some 136 songs and became the first serious collection of African American folk culture.

Throughout the war, and in the months after it, various magazine letters and journal entries continued to describe the music of the freed slaves, and evidence emerged that such spirituals had played a significant role in the war. Songs like "Go in the Wilderness" became favorite marching songs of black regiments. Thomas Wentworth Higginson, the Unitarian clergyman who commanded one of the Union's first black regiments, described this as "their best marching song." After the war, African American groups like the Fisk Jubilee Singers took the spirituals across the nation and, indeed, around the world.

The war was also the subject of a rich variety of other types of folk music, from ballads to fiddle and banjo tunes. Though they have been much more sparsely documented—there has never been a major collection of them—folk ballads of the South often dealt with specific battles. Ballads have been collected about Sharpsburg (Antietam), Shiloh, Manassas (Bull Run), the Battle of the Wilderness, Wilson's Creek, Murfreesboro (Stones River), and the *Cumberland-Virginia* encounter; others tell of how "Booth Killed Lincoln," how Sherman marched to the sea, or the monotony of eating "Goober Peas." Most of these songs circulated by word of mouth and were kept alive for generations before they were collected or published. Other songs came from cheap pocket "songsters"—tiny books sold and passed around that contained words, but no music. *The Stonewall Songbook* (Richmond, 1864) was one of the most popular of these; others bore titles like *The Gen. Lee Songster* (1865), *The Dixie Land Songster* (1863), and *Hopkins' New Orleans 5 Cent Song-Book* (1861).

Most instrumental music was the province of the fiddle and banjo—the guitar was still a rare instrument in the South, and cheap, mass-produced harmonicas were just starting to filter into the country. Even more than ballad singers, fiddlers both North and South shared a common repertory of tunes often borrowed from Scotch and Irish sources. Tunes mentioned as favorites among Confederate soldiers included not only predictable fare such as "Dixie" and "My Old Kentucky Home" but also numbers like "Hell Broke Loose in Georgia" (which is still played by Georgia fiddlers today), "Billy in the Low Ground," "Natchez under the Hill," "The Goose Hangs High," "Oh Lord Gals One Friday," and "Arkansas Traveler." Many tunes were fiddled unaccompanied, as they had been for decades in the rural South, but occasionally a camp would boast of a string band that might include one or more fiddles accompanied by a banjo, or somebody "beating straws" on the fiddle bridge to accompany the fiddler's bowing.

Military Music

In the two decades before the war, the mass production of rotary valve instruments had created a national boom in the popularity of the community brass band. Even small towns often boasted an amateur brass band, and when fighting began, some of these bands enlisted en masse; other individual musicians found their way to newly formed regimental bands. Bands played at the train stations as recruits left town for the front; later they played for ceremonies, during the interminable inspections of camp life, at funerals and some church services, and even during battles. Many of them featured a selection of instruments seldom heard today: E-flat cornets and alto horns, ophicleides, and keyed bugles. Since instrument makers had not yet agreed on a standard pitch for the basic "concert A" note, keeping in tune was always a problem. Confederate bands were generally smaller than their Union counterparts; some of them would have as few as ten or twelve members, whereas the Union bands often boasted of twenty or more.

Most of the bands had their own "band books," which contained their basic repertoires: sixty to eighty selections drawn from the full range of nineteenth-century sources. These included patriotic airs and marches such as "Colonel Kirkland's March," "Garry Owen," and "La Marseillaise"; pieces adapted from current or recent popular songs, such as "Juanita," "My Old Kentucky Home," "Lorena," and "Come Dearest, the Daylight Is Gone"; quicksteps and dance tunes like "Mockingbird Quickstep," "Slumber Polka," "Jenny Lynd Polka," "Hurrah Storm Galop," and "Martha Quickstep"; waltzes, used both for dances and for long inspections on the parade grounds; religious music used for funerals and solemn occasions; and adaptations of both light and serious classics, such as "Anvil Chorus" (which was played during the burning of Atlanta), "Schubert's Serenade," and "In Happy Moments" from the opera *Maritana.*

The other major type of military music was that of the fife and drum corps. Though the war generated one of the most famous bugle pieces, "Taps," most of the day-to-day functions of a camp were regulated by the sound of the fife and drum. These calls and tunes were codified in books like *The Drummers and Fifers Guide,* compiled by George B. Bruce and "Dixie" composer Dan Emmett; it contained the music for the camp duty, as well as a selection of marches and quicksteps and "side-beats."

INSTRUMENTS FROM A CIVIL WAR MILITARY BAND. Pictured from left to right are a brass cornet, bugle, and snare drum.

CIVIL WAR LIBRARY AND MUSEUM, PHILADELPHIA

Many fifers and drummers—often the youngest men in a company—had to learn the bulk of the pieces by heart. Each call had a specific function in camp routine: "drummer's call," often played at 5:45 A.M., signaled the other musicians to assemble; a "second call," by drummers alone, told the troops to fall out and form up. After roll call and announcements came "Reveille," not a single call but a series of six pieces with names like "Three Camps," "Slow Scotch," "Austrian," and "The Dutch." Then, around 6:15, came "pioneer's call" or "fatigue call" to summon work parties and invite any camp followers to leave. "Surgeon's call" was sounded for the sick or lame to report to the hospital, and finally, at around 7:00, a tune called "Peas on a Trencher" was often sounded as breakfast call. Similar calls were heard throughout the day, marking the various stages of camp duty. Fifers were used also on special occasions; men who had been found guilty of desertion or any misdemeanor were often drummed out of a unit to the playing of the "Rogue's March."

Drummers especially were often used in actual battles, and more than a few were killed or captured. Thomas J. ("Stonewall") Jackson used a young drummer boy to "beat the rally" at Fredericksburg. Another well-known story involves Pvt. David Scantlon, a drummer with the Fourth Virginia Regiment of the same Stonewall Brigade, who beat the rally at the height of the Battle of First Manassas by turning his back to the enemy so they could not shoot a hole in his drum. Such stories doubtless inspired comments like that of Gen. Robert E. Lee, who said, "I don't believe we can have an army without music."

[*See also* Broadsides; Discography; Dixie; Folk Narratives.]

BIBLIOGRAPHY

Allen, Francis William, Charles Pickard Ware, and Lucy McKim Garrison, eds. *Slave Songs of the United States.* New York, 1867. Reprint, with new introduction by William K. McNeil, Baltimore, 1992.

Crawford, Richard, ed. *The Civil War Songbook.* New York, 1977.

Emurian, Earnest K. *Stories of Civil War Songs.* Natick, Mass., n.d.

Epstein, Dena J. *Sinful Tunes and Spirituals: Black Folk Music to the Civil War.* Urbana, Ill., 1977.

Glass, Paul, and Louis G. Singer. *Singing Soldiers: The Spirit of the Sixties.* New York, 1968.

Harwell, Richard B. *Confederate Music.* Chapel Hill, N.C., 1950.

Hoogerwerf, Frank W. *Confederate Sheet-Music Imprints.* Brooklyn, N.Y., n.d.

Olson, Kenneth. *Music and Muskets: Bands and Bandsmen of the American Civil War.* Westport, Conn., 1981.
Our War Songs, North and South. Cleveland, Ohio, 1887.
Silber, Irwin. *Songs of the Civil War.* New York, 1960.
Songs of Dixie: A Collection of Camp Songs, Home Songs, Marching Songs, Plantation Songs. New York, 1890.
Wellman, Manly Wade. *The Rebel Songster: Songs the Confederates Sang.* Chapel Hill, N.C., 1959.
Wiley, Bell Irwin. *The Life of Johnny Reb.* New York, 1943.

CHARLES K. WOLFE

MYERS, ABRAHAM C. (1811–1898), colonel and quartermaster general. Myers was born in Charleston, South Carolina, a descendant of Moses Cohen, the city's first rabbi. After graduating from West Point in 1833, he served as a quartermaster in western posts and saw service in the Mexican War for which he received two brevets. Myers was a brevet lieutenant colonel quartermaster in New Orleans in 1860 and adopted Louisiana as his home state. He resigned from the U.S. Army on January 21, 1861, after reporting that Louisiana was seizing Federal property in New Orleans.

Myers was a welcome addition to the fledgling Confederate army being formed at Montgomery. On March 25, 1861, President Jefferson Davis appointed him a lieutenant colonel and quartermaster general of the army. He was nominated to colonel and approved by the Confederate Congress on February 15, 1862. Davis justified the selection on the grounds that Myers had held numerous positions of trust in the U.S. Army and that his experience was needed. Myers, however, soon lost favor with Davis for two reasons. He proved inadequate for the job of supplying the army with uniforms and nonordnance equipment, and rumors circulated that his wife had called Mrs. Varina Davis a "squaw" because of her dark complexion.

Myers's job became steadily more difficult because of spiraling wartime inflation and the obstructions caused by governors who kept war supplies and raw materials for their own states' use. He nevertheless tried his best, occasionally attempting innovative techniques to acquire supplies. When the army needed blankets that were in Memphis, for example, Myers recommended that cotton be traded for them. Davis refused because Memphis was in Federal hands. Although Myers became a target of constant criticism, he had supporters in Congress who attempted to get him promoted from colonel by passing legislation to upgrade the rank of his position to brigadier general. Davis, irked with Congress, approved the legislation but assigned Alexander R. Lawton, already a brigadier general, to the job. Myers then resigned on August 10, 1863.

Myers moved to Georgia after he resigned and lived in poverty, mostly on the charity of friends. He subsequently moved to Maryland and was in Washington when he died on June 20, 1889. To his death he maintained that Jefferson Davis had treated him unfairly.

BIBLIOGRAPHY

Coulter, Merton E. *The Confederate States of America, 1861–1865.* A History of the South, vol. 7. Baton Rouge, La., 1950.
Davis, Jefferson. *Jefferson Davis, Constitutionalist: His Letters, Papers and Speeches.* Jackson, Miss., 1923.
Eaton, Clement. *A History of the Southern Confederacy.* New York, 1954.
U.S. War Department. *War of Rebellion: Official Records of the Union and Confederate Armies.* Washington, D.C., 1880–1901. Ser. 4, vol. 2, p. 188; ser. 4, vol. 3, p. 318.
Vandiver, Frank E. *Rebel Brass: The Confederate Command System.* Baton Rouge, La., 1956.
Weinert, Richard P. *The Confederate Regular Army.* Shippensburg, Pa., 1991.

P. NEAL MEIER

NAMES OF BATTLES. *See* Battles, Naming of.

NASHVILLE, TENNESSEE. When Tennessee voted on June 8, 1861, to leave the Union, Nashville was its capital city with a population of approximately thirty thousand. There were about twenty-four thousand whites, one thousand free blacks, and five thousand slaves in the city and its suburbs. The vast majority of the whites were immigrants or descendants of immigrants from England, Scotland, and Ireland.

Located on the banks of the Cumberland River, the Tennessee capital was one of the largest and most important American cities south of the Ohio River. A busy user of river transportation since its settlement in 1780, Nashville had expanded its commerce in the 1850s through the construction of five railroads that connected to most of the major markets in the South and East.

The principal economic activity was the importation and wholesale distribution of goods. From their location at the center of several neighboring towns, wholesalers distributed groceries, liquors and wines, boots and shoes, dry goods, hardware, and other farm and home supplies. Commission merchants shipped agricultural produce of the region to Southern and Midwestern markets.

Manufacturing was important to the city, with $1,520,000 invested in 73 factories that employed 1,318 workers. Notable manufactures were lumber and wood products, leather goods, stoves, carriages, rail cars, castings, farm implements, and tobacco products.

The intellectual life of Nashville was nurtured by three outstanding educational institutions with a combined enrollment of approximately 1,150 students: the Shelby Medical College, the University of Nashville and its medical college, and the Nashville Female Academy. There were more students enrolled in the two Nashville medical colleges than in the medical schools of any other city in the United States with the exception of Philadelphia.

The religious preference of the citizens was overwhelmingly Protestant Christian. There were two Catholic churches, two Jewish congregations, and numerous churches of the various Protestant denominations, including four for blacks. The Methodists and Baptists published tracts, periodicals, and books in Nashville and distributed them throughout the Southeast.

Nashville was headquarters for all the branches of the state government. Most offices were in the new capitol, completed only a short time before war broke out. The state maintained a school for the blind, an asylum for the insane, and a penitentiary in the city.

Before Union occupation, Nashville was a major supply center for the Southern army. Local plants produced cannons, muskets, ball and shot, percussion caps, friction primers, swords, saddles, harnesses, carriages, and gray uniform cloth.

To protect Nashville, the Confederate army depended on a defensive line across southern Kentucky and two forts on the Cumberland River. Forts Henry and Donelson, overlooking the river about sixty-five miles northwest of Nashville, guarded against invasion of the city by water. Seemingly secure behind these defenses, Nashvillians were stunned on February 16, 1862, by the unexpected surrender of the forts on the third day of siege by Union forces. Southern troops simultaneously abandoned the defense line in Kentucky, and by nightfall many of those troops had passed through Nashville toward Murfreesboro. The capital city was no longer defended.

Terror gripped the populace. Many fled south by train to Alabama and Georgia and some took to the country, but most remained behind. From February 16 until February

THE STATE CAPITOL AT NASHVILLE, LOOKING NORTHWEST. LIBRARY OF CONGRESS

25, a bizarre period known locally as "the great panic," Nashville was engulfed by rumors and false reports that Federal gunboats were about to level the city. Convinced they were facing starvation, fearful mobs pillaged Confederate army supplies even as they were being loaded on trains for shipment to the South. After a few days of chaos, order was restored by the arrival of Col. Nathan Bedford Forrest's regiment, which had escaped capture at Fort Donelson.

On February 25, 1862, Nashville became the first Confederate state capital to fall. The mayor surrendered the city to Gen. Don Carlos Buell, and Union troops began a military occupation that lasted until after the war. It was the longest uninterrupted wartime occupation experienced by any Confederate city.

Nashville quickly became the principal supply center for the western operations of the Union army, and to protect it, army engineers erected forts and other defenses along its southern perimeters. Within the city, the quartermaster seized schools, churches, and public and private buildings for use as offices, hospitals, barracks, and warehouses.

Immediately after occupation, Nashville received the war's first military governor. President Abraham Lincoln sent Andrew Johnson, governor of Tennessee from 1853 to 1857 and staunch Unionist U.S. senator when the war erupted. Although popular during his earlier term as governor, Military Governor Johnson found most of his old friends hostile to him and the Union.

At once the governor undertook the task of reconstructing the state into a viable member of the Union. Finding that loyalists were a small minority, Johnson implored the majority to return their allegiance to the Union. Responses to his pleas were so negative that he arrested three prominent Confederate sympathizers and dispatched them to prison in northern Michigan as an example. Although the citizens were neither intimidated nor persuaded, Johnson continued to threaten, arrest, and imprison leading Confederate supporters.

The city's white population was slow to recommit its loyalty because they believed they would be liberated by the

Southern army. Confederate raiding parties frequently threatened the city, and letters home from Nashville soldiers in gray promised that the Northerners would soon be driven out. Citizens feared, in that event, of being accused of having collaborated with the enemy.

Slaves in the city were thoroughly confused. When the Union army came in, many left their owners, thinking they were free, only to discover they were not. Later when the first Emancipation Proclamation was issued, most believed they had been freed by the president but then learned that, at Governor Johnson's behest, Tennessee had been excluded from the provisions of the proclamation.

Upon its arrival, the Union army established several hospitals, many of them in schools and churches. Soon afterward, their successful treatment of the heavy casualties from the battles of Murfreesboro and Shiloh prepared the way for Nashville to become the major hospital center for the Union army in the West.

Pioneering in the wartime use of railroads to move men and matériel, the Union command built extensive machine shops to maintain and repair rolling stock. The government brought in additional locomotives and freight cars and rushed the completion of the Nashville and Northwestern Railroad to Johnsonville, a military port established on the Tennessee River. The connection provided a route into the city for military supplies when navigation on the Cumberland was halted by low water. Gunboats regularly patrolled the Cumberland River and often escorted cargo and troop carriers up and down its waters. To maintain the various river craft, the U.S. Navy set up a navy yard just downstream from the Nashville public square on the opposite bank of the river.

The Union quartermaster found the many wholesale distribution warehouses made to order for storage of military supplies. His department operated shops to manufacture and repair harnesses, carts, wagons, and other carriages, and to repair weapons.

By the middle of 1864, approximately ten thousand persons were employed by the government to assist the army at Nashville, and nearly all of them had been imported from the North. Several local whites and free blacks were among their numbers, however. Frequently, the occupying army impressed slaves to work on construction projects. Hundreds of slaves built Fort Negley, the city's largest bastion. Other blacks who had walked away from slavery worked as laborers, servants, cooks, and maids in hospitals and camps. Their numbers were constantly augmented by the arrival of refugees from the surrounding countryside.

The appearance of the city was militaristic in the extreme. Fort Negley dominated the skyline south of the capitol and other forts were under construction. Even the proud new capitol was fortified. Heavy military traffic clogged the streets. Uniformed men were everywhere as fresh troops arrived from the North and those they were to replace returned from duty in the South. Army tent cities appeared and disappeared on all sides.

The soldiers and the sizable corps of male government employees provided a ready clientele for prostitutes. These women flowed into the city, and venereal disease became rampant, especially among the soldiers. Recognizing prostitution as a major problem, civil and military authorities tried to exile the women. In 1863, they sent many of them northward on riverboats destined for Louisville or Cincinnati, but these cities would not accept them and they were returned to Nashville. Army medical officers then attempted to control the problem by permitting women to practice prostitution but only with a license that required an initial physical examination and periodic reexaminations. The army maintained a hospital for the diseased prostitutes, and the licensing procedure was continued during the remaining years of the war.

The occupying army dominated the city's economy. The quartermaster purchased large quantities of locally produced goods. Logs and lumber were in great demand, but the largest purchases were of farm produce, especially foodstuffs and forage. Hotels, boardinghouses, restaurants, theaters, and saloons thrived. Although several local merchants closed their stores rather than sign a loyalty oath, new retailers appeared often among people arriving from the North.

The presence of the Union army left no aspect of life in the city untouched. At various times most houses of worship were in the hands of the army, and congregations gathered in private homes or wherever space could be found. The large public and private schools were closed during much of the occupation, their facilities in use by the army. Only the medical school of the University of Nashville was able to continue without major interruption, though on a much reduced scale.

At first most white citizens were hostile to Union soldiers, but their attitude gradually mellowed. While they retained their bitterness toward the military governor, significant numbers had declared their loyalty to the Union by the summer of 1864. With national elections scheduled for the autumn, Governor Johnson issued an amnesty oath that was required of all voters. Even many of his Union friends were outraged. Citizens quickly dubbed it "the Damnesty Oath" and vented their wrath on the governor, by then the Republican party's nominee for vice president on the ticket with President Lincoln. Few Nashvillians went to the polls that fall.

By the autumn of 1864, most Nashvillians—old and new—had concluded that the Confederacy could not win the war. Consequently, the city was shocked when news was received in the latter part of October that Gen. John Bell Hood had disengaged his army from operations near Atlanta and was sweeping northward toward middle Tennessee. Thirty days later, it was clear that he was moving on Nashville.

Although Hood took staggering losses at the Battle of Franklin on November 30, the Union army also suffered heavily and fell back to Nashville twenty-five miles away. The Confederates followed, but stopped about three miles south of the city. Unable to build up his forces, Hood remained immobile for two severely cold weeks while Union Gen. George H. Thomas accumulated a force twice the size of Hood's.

The Battle of Nashville was swift and decisive. On December 15, Union forces drove the Confederates out of their dug-in positions, and by nightfall of the second day, the Southerners were in full retreat. General Thomas pursued them for about one hundred miles before breaking off contact. By that time the shattered enemy had divided into several small detachments, making their ways eastward to join other forces still in the field. The Union victory at Nashville eliminated the last vestiges of a Confederate army in the area between the Appalachians and the Mississippi River. The battle destroyed the last hope the Confederates had for sending a strike force into the undefended midwestern states. Had such a maneuver been successful, it could have led to a negotiated settlement of the war.

On February 24 Andrew Johnson left Nashville to be inaugurated vice president of the United States. Before leaving, he had set the stage for a tightly controlled election in which the only candidate, William G. Brownlow, Knoxville Methodist preacher, editor, and abolitionist, would be elected governor on March 4, 1865. The Confederacy capitulated April 9 at Appomattox, Lincoln was assassinated on April 14, and Andrew Johnson succeeded to the presidency on April 15.

In Nashville military installations were speedily dismantled, and soldiers and most civilian employees of the army soon departed. Yet converting to a peacetime economy was difficult for those left behind, especially for former slaves who were now free and adrift. Like the slaves, most whites were unsure of their roles in the postwar era. Only the Nashville planters and businessmen who had become reluctant partners with the Union and had prospered during the latter years of the conflict found the adjustment to peace relatively easy.

[*For further discussion of the fall of Forts Henry and Donelson, see* Henry and Donelson Campaign. *See also* Franklin and Nashville Campaign.]

BIBLIOGRAPHY

Crabb, Alfred Leland. "The Twilight of the Nashville Gods." *Tennessee Historical Quarterly* 15 (December 1956).

Durham, Walter T. *Nashville, the Occupied City.* Nashville, Tenn., 1985.

Durham, Walter T. *Reluctant Partners—Nashville and the Union.* Nashville, Tenn., 1987.

Fitch, John. *Annals of the Army of the Cumberland.* Philadelphia, 1864.

Graf, Leroy P., and Ralph W. Haskins, eds. *The Papers of Andrew Johnson.* 9 vols. to date. Knoxville, Tenn., 1967–1991.

Horn, Stanley F. *The Decisive Battle of Nashville.* Knoxville, Tenn., 1968.

Maslowski, Peter. *Treason Must Be Made Odious.* Millwood, N.Y., 1978.

WALTER T. DURHAM

NASHVILLE. A commerce cruiser, CSS *Nashville* was a square-rigged passenger steamer running between New York and Charleston, South Carolina, before the outbreak of the Civil War. After the firing on Fort Sumter the Confederates seized her at Charleston and fitted her out as a cruiser. She was a 1,221-ton side-wheeler with a complement of forty officers and seamen and carried a battery of two 6-pounder smoothbore guns.

On the night of October 26, 1861, under the command of Lt. R. B. Pegram, a former officer in the U.S. Navy, *Nashville* ran the blockade off Charleston. She took on coal at Bermuda on November 5 and two weeks later captured and burned the 1,482-ton clipper *Harvey Birch,* the first prize taken by a Confederate raider in the North Atlantic. Two days later *Nashville* arrived in Southampton, England, the first ship of war to fly the Confederate flag in English waters. As a result of damage sustained in the crossing, *Nashville* was placed in dry dock. While she was being repaired, USS *Tuscarora* entered the port with the objective of attacking the Confederate warship if she attempted to leave Southampton. Nevertheless, on February 3, 1862, *Nashville* successfully eluded the Federal ship and disappeared into the Atlantic. On February 26, the Confederate cruiser captured her second merchant vessel, the schooner *Robert Gilfillan.* This was her last prize. On March 17, *Nashville* once again slipped through the Union blockade and entered the port of Morehead City, North Carolina. This ended her career as a cruiser.

The steamer was sold to Fraser, Trenholm, and Company and converted to a blockade runner named *Thomas L. Wragg.* She made several successful runs through the blockade from Georgetown, South Carolina, to Nassau before being chased into Warsaw Sound, Georgia. There she was blockaded by Union warships for more than eight months. On November 8, 1862, she was commissioned as the privateer *Rattlesnake.* While trying to slip past Union warships, she was destroyed by the monitor *Montauk* on the last day of February 1863.

CSS *Nashville* (1861–1863). Wash drawing by R. G. Skerrett, 1901. NAVAL HISTORICAL CENTER, WASHINGTON, D.C.

BIBLIOGRAPHY

Chance, Franklin N., Paul C. Chance, and David L. Topper. *Tangled Machinery and Charred Relics: The Historical and Archaeological Investigation of the C.S.S. Nashville.* Orangeburg, S.C., 1985.

Dalzell, George W. *The Flight from the Flag.* Chapel Hill, N.C., 1940.

WILLIAM N. STILL, JR.

NATIONALISM. The discussion of nationalism and the Confederacy can be divided usefully into two parts: a discussion of the Old South, Southern nationalism, and secession, and a discussion of Confederate nationalism. Inevitably, questions about the existence of Southern nationalism also become questions about the coming of the Civil War. If the South was so distinct and distinctive from the North as to be its own nation, then secession can be easily explained, if not the war itself. (Indeed, then the question becomes, if the South was so different, why did the rest of the country fight to keep it?) If the South was more a region than a nation, what did provoke secession and the ensuing war?

Historian David M. Potter, who long considered the question of Southern nationalism, wrote that

students of the theory of nationalism generally agree that while nationalism itself is a subjective, psychological phenomenon—a matter of sentiment, will, feeling, loyalty—and not an objective phenomenon, capable of being measured by given ingredients, it is nevertheless true that a certain core of cultural conditions is conducive to the development of nationalism, and that among these conditions are "common descent, language, territory, political entity, customs and tradition, and religions."

Antebellum Nationalism

Many have argued—at the time and later—that the antebellum South did possess the "core of cultural conditions" necessary to maintain a sense of separate nationhood. If this was the case, then Southern secession was primarily the product of Southern nationalism. If not, then Southern secession might be explained in various other ways, such as a breakdown of the political system, hysteria over real or perceived threats to slavery, or even as a ruse intended to gain the South more advantages within the Union. Those who believe in antebellum Southern nationalism point to the Old South's ethnic and religious homogeneity, its agrarian society, its economic system, and its aristocracy as factors in creating a viable nationalism. Others argue that the existence of antebellum differences has been exaggerated.

Ethnically—if one ignores the obvious presence of a sizable African American minority and focuses on the political community—the South was more homogeneous than the North. Most Southern white people were of British descent. Some have seen the Old South as more unified than the North religiously. Most Southerners were orthodox Protestants. Presbyterians and Episcopalians dominated the upper classes, while the bulk of the population—white and black—were Methodist and Baptist. Thus religion contributed to the homogeneity of the Old South.

Southern nationalists also manufactured imaginary ethnic differences. White Southerners were told that they were descended from Cavaliers, English gentlemen who had fought for Charles I. Northerners, on the other hand, were held to be the descendants of Roundheads, Puritan supporters of Oliver Cromwell who were not gentlemen at all. The Cavalier-Roundhead myth invoked both ethnicity and class to postulate a hereditary Southern distinctiveness. This myth—which had very little in the way of hard evidence behind it—proved remarkably durable, perhaps because it succeeded in flattering the self-images of both Northerners and Southerners.

The ethnic thesis has reemerged in recent years, although in very different form. One interpretation advanced for Southern distinctiveness is the so-called Celtic thesis. This postulates that most Southern white people were of Celtic stock—Irish or Scottish or Scotch-Irish—and those that were not had been Celticized by intimate contact with Southern Celts.

The most obvious ethnic difference between the North and South was one that Southern nationalists could not exploit. The North was fundamentally European American; the South was European African American. If the presence of slavery set the South apart legally and economically, the presence of a large African population set it apart ethnically. And although the laws of Southern states defined them as black, many Southerners had both European and African ancestry. Nobody, however, proposed that this crucial ethnic difference justified the creation of a Southern nation. (Abolitionist John Brown, however, did envision a revolutionary government of freed slaves fortified in the Appalachian Mountains, and in the twentieth century, the Communist party advocated the creation of a black socialist soviet republic in the Deep South.)

Ignoring the black presence in the Old South, though difficult, was probably reassuring to the not overwhelming white majority. That Southern nationalists left black Southerners—but not the enormous fact of slavery—out of their calculations is also understandable. But for anyone since then seeking to understand the nature of Southern distinctiveness, ignoring the black presence would be blind folly. Surely one of the things that set the Old South apart from the rest of the nation was its African American community. Southern culture itself is a product of the interaction between African Americans and European Americans. Just as significant for the course of events that led to the Civil War and its conclusion, only the South, among all American regions, based its political, social, and political order on the systematic denial of rights to large numbers of people defined as racially distinct. The white South lived in constant fear of insurrection on the part of the black South. Its response was oppression. This oppression, being at the heart of Southern society, really did make the Old South different.

There is also the question of the relationship of the Old South to capitalism. Some have boldly argued that the Old South's planter class was precapitalistic and even anticapitalistic. Others have seen the planters as a historic anomaly—slaveholding capitalists, as much bent on maximizing profits as any Northerner. Whether or not planters should be viewed as capitalist, what is undeniable is that the Southern slave economy emerged within the context of a capitalist Atlantic economy.

Slavery increasingly set off the South not only from the North but from the rest of the world. The fact that slavery was globally a dying institution by the mid-nineteenth century made Southern defensiveness all the greater. Yet if slavery set off the South, the products of slavery linked it thoroughly to the capitalist world. The plantation may have seemed to be a little world of its own, one in which the owner was master not only of his slaves but of his fate, but in fact the plantation depended on the world market. Both the North and Britain purchased Southern cotton. Yet Southerners, proclaiming that Cotton was King, reversed the dependency. They argued that the rest of the world depended on them for its raw material. These economic interdependencies argued neither for a separate Southern nation nor against it. Economic forces routinely cross national boundaries. An independent South probably would have been as dependent on trade with the North and the rest of the world as it had been as a region of the United States.

Proponents of Southern nationalism also argue that the South's agrarian economy was key to its identity. They contrast an industrial North with an agrarian South. Southern reliance on agriculture created a separate set of economic interests. It also, they argue, created a Southern way of life. Oddly enough, this argument is most frequently evoked not by those who ground Southern distinctiveness in slavery and the production of staple crops but by those who seek an alternative to slavery to explain why the Old South was different.

Another common conception is that the Old South was "aristocratic" in comparison with a "democratic North." This view generally is sustained by ignoring the actual politics of the Old South and focusing on the pretensions of

Southern planters. It is also sustained by a failure to consider the nature of a real aristocracy on the European model, whose power was maintained by an elaborate system of legal privilege. Instead, what is too frequently offered is a description of a cosmetic aristocracy—people living in big houses with lots of servants and lots of leisure. More sophisticated analysis suggests that the dominance of the planter image in the Old South helped organize the aspirations of Southern white men so that ambition was channeled into replicating the existing social structure rather than transforming society, and that within a democratic political structure, the planters exerted a disproportionate political power. Of course, the same might be said of rich capitalists in the Northeast. It is, however, undeniable that the Old South was led by a planter class, which, if not an aristocracy, had no counterpart in the rest of the United States.

The problem is that most of the things that united Southern white people were shared by most other Americans, too. If most white Southerners were of British origins, so were most white native-born Americans. Both North and South were predominantly Protestant. Immigrants and their children, to be sure, were often Irish or German and frequently Catholic. But the antebellum North hardly welcomed these new Americans with open arms. As for the contrasting images of the agrarian South and the industrial North, these too have been exaggerated. The antebellum North was industrializing, not industrialized. The South, while by no means as industrial as the North or Great Britain, had more factories than most existing nations—although a large percentage of them were in Virginia, where agriculture had become less profitable. North and South shared common political institutions. Suffrage for white men—and white men only—characterized both sections of the country. The political subdivisions of town, county, and state organized government North and South, and the regions shared a similar system of legislature, governor, and courts. Both revered the U.S. Constitution, even while reading it in different ways.

Even the greatest unifying force the white South possessed—racism, with its devotion to white supremacy—was something they shared with the North. Some historians have pointed to the prevalence of racism to explain why white nonslaveholders supported slavery, arguing that the white South was a "herrenvolk democracy," in which all white people acquired status from the simple fact that they were white. Ulrich B. Phillips went so far as to identify white supremacy as the unifying theme in Southern history. Other white Americans shared the racism. They did not, however, share Southern white fears that "the white man's country" might become "the black man's country." Other white Americans also had become less convinced that what they too perceived as black inferiority required or justified the institution of slavery.

Southern Nationalists

Whether or not there was a distinct Southern nation, there were certainly Southern nationalists in the Old South. These were Southerners whose political and cultural goal was to create a widespread belief in a separate Southern destiny and then to encourage the establishment of a separate Southern nation. As historian John McCardell points out, several movements in the Old South contributed to a belief in separate Southern identity. Southern nationalism is sometimes traced to the doctrine of nullification, as espoused by John C. Calhoun in the 1830s. Calhoun and many of his supporters saw nullification as a means to preserve the Union, not break it up. But there was a tiny group of South Carolina nullifiers, led by Thomas Cooper, the president of South Carolina College, who looked to the eventual creation of a Southern nation. Both nullification and Southern nationalist thinking was inevitably linked with proslavery thought. It was slavery that set the South apart from the rest of the nation. Slavery was the interest that Southern politicians most wished to defend, and it was the basis of the distinctive Southern society that nationalists wanted to incorporate as an independent nation. Initially, however, proslavery thought was reactive; it appeared in response to the heightened abolitionist attacks on slavery in the 1830s. Yet the desire to maintain slavery did not require the desire for an independent Southern nation. Many slavery advocates believed that the institution would best be protected within the Union—and events proved them right. As John McCardell observed, "To support slavery, then, did not alone make a man a Southern nationalist."

The antebellum South also witnessed a series of commercial conventions dedicated to eliminating the section's economic dependence on the North. Northern merchants marketed the Southern cotton crop; Northern and British factories bought the crop; and Northern and British factories provided the South with its manufactured goods. These conventions called upon Southerners to invest not just in land and slaves but in banks, steamships and railroads, and factories. Although advocates of Southern nationalism welcomed the call for Southern economic independence, one question troubled them. Was economic diversification compatible with the distinctiveness that other antebellum nationalists claimed for the South? The worry was theoretical: the principal product of the commercial conventions was rhetoric. In the 1850s, Southerners continued to put the bulk of their capital into the production of cotton. They did so less because of a commitment to Southern distinctiveness than of a commitment to high profits.

For slavery expansionists, the key issue for Southern nationalism was not so much a Southern civilization as a Southern government. The U.S. government was increasingly reluctant to admit new slave states. This threatened to decrease the Southern side of the sectional balance of power and to prevent the spread of slavery. Slavery expansionists looked not just to the territories already owned by the United States but to the Caribbean and Latin American nations as well. Presumably, a Southern government would at the most aid and encourage the territorial expansion of slavery and at the least not hinder it. In October 1860, a pro-secession Mississippi newspaper claimed that "the acquisition of Mexico, Central America, Cuba, Santo Domingo, and other West India Islands would follow as a direct and necessary result" of the establishment of a Southern nation.

For much of the antebellum period, most Southern white people seem to have regarded the vocal Southern nationalists as quasi lunatics. But if they were fools, they were licensed fools. Some were persuaded of their ideas by argument and others by reiteration. However the nationalists themselves were viewed—and they would not obtain high office within the Confederacy—they put their ideas into circulation; their rhetoric became part of the common political discourse. They made secession and Southern independence thinkable.

Sectionalism

Arguably more important than the movement for Southern nationalism was the rise of political sectionalism in the antebellum era. Sectionalists were those concerned with maintaining the region's balance of power within the United States. They viewed the South as having interests distinct from the rest of the country, although they often hoped to make common cause with the West against the Northeast. One such interest, the most important one, was slavery. Its expansion, the return of fugitive slaves, the possibility of reopening the international slave trade, even its very existence—all might be determined by national policy. But there were other political interests that sectionalists believed the South must protect. As a staple-producing region, for example, the South preferred free trade; the tariff was a source of constant grievance to most Southern farmers.

As the nineteenth century wore on, Southern politicians were increasingly aware that the South was becoming a minority section within the United States as a whole. Its control over first the House of Representatives and then the presidency and the Senate diminished. Sectionalists desperately wanted to halt this trend, and they had hopes to reverse it. Both proslavery ideologues and practical sectionalists could agree that extending slavery into the territories was crucial. For apologists, a national prohibition on slavery in the territories would indicate a condemnation of an institution they believed righteous. For sectionalists, the failure of slavery to reach the West meant the South's accepting a minority status within the Union—and within Congress. Thus the struggle between North and South developed first over the status of the West.

As a political solution, secession had its drawbacks. Although it opened the possibility that the new Confederacy might expand southward, it would not gain slaveholders access to the disputed western territories. Why should the remaining still-united states let foreigners bring slaves into U.S. territories? Nor would any future treaty provisions really make the return of fugitive slaves to the South any more likely. Many of the irritants of the sectional conflict would have remained in place even had peaceable secession occurred.

What would secession accomplish? It would allow the Confederacy to try to colonize Latin America. It would permit the Confederacy to become a free-trade zone. If successful, it would prevent the U.S. government from abolishing slavery within the Southern states.

In 1860, many advocates of secession viewed it as a last resort. The withdrawal of the Southern states and the establishment of an independent Confederacy was a refuge to which they felt driven, not a national destiny that they eagerly embraced. Southern nationalists had succeeded in making secession an acceptable recourse in the Southern mind; they had generally failed in creating a regionwide desire for a Southern nation. For many, secession would be not the beginnings of a glorious national destiny but a defensive move in an increasingly hostile world.

Confederate Nationalism

Nationalism—or its failure—has been invoked to explain the causes, the course, and the conclusion of the Civil War. There are two distinct lines of thought about the relationship of nationalism to the Confederate experience. Some invoke nationalism to explain how the Confederacy fought as long and as hard as it did; others to explain why the Confederacy was defeated—or, as they would have it, why the Confederate people gave up.

Historian Emory Thomas has been one of the leaders in finding within the Confederacy a nationalism so strong that it was willing to embrace revolutionary means to achieve independence. He points to the fact that the Confederacy centralized its government, subjected its economy to government control, sponsored industrialization, instituted the first national draft in America, and finally agreed to recruit slaves into its army. All of this unprecedented innovation, he argues, constituted a revolution—not one intended by Southern nationalists but one into which Confederate nationalists were forced. For Thomas, their willingness to advocate and implement these measures, however falteringly, proves the existence of a strong nationalism—although he admits that for many white Southerners, black enlistment was going too far.

For other historians, Confederate defeat itself undermines the notion of thoroughgoing Confederate nationalism. They argue that in April 1865 the Confederacy still had the means to continue the fight against the Union forces. If Confederates chose surrender over struggle, then their desire for independence was insufficient. For them, nationalism implies a will to achieve and maintain nationhood on the part of a majority of citizens so great that they would accept death more readily than the end of national identity.

Of course, if this standard is applied, there are probably few nations. The South endured a great deal in its fight for independence—social dislocation followed by social revolution, a death toll on the order of France's in the First World War. Another viewpoint might be offered by the military historian. Nationalism in military history is usually associated with the French Revolution and the Napoleonic Wars. In that context, nationalism implies citizen armies, the levee en masse, and patriotically motivated soldiers. If this definition of nationalism is employed, there can be no question that the Confederacy was nationalistic. It raised mass armies—approximately four of every five white men of military age served—its government took unprecedented control of the economy to shift it to war production, its popular press supported the war passionately, its soldiers, initially, were volunteers. If the French Revolution and the Napoleonic Wars had created new rules of patriotism and nationalism for warfare, the Confederacy played by them.

But a military historian would never assume that the presence of nationalism would be decisive on the battlefield. The nineteenth and twentieth centuries have been periods of nationalistic wars, where two or more nation-states battled with one another. Nobody suggests that the France that lost the Franco-Prussian War was not a nation; it clearly was, but it was a nation defeated by a more militarily adept nation. Nations routinely make war against one another and lose. Nationalism is not a magic potion that conveys invulnerability on those who drink it.

Southern nationalists presented the new Confederacy with a contradictory agenda. The Confederacy was to become a "nation among nations"—a powerful, respected force in world politics. As such, it would have to industrialize, raise armies and navies, establish a vigorous government. But the Confederacy was established to resist what Southerners viewed as potential tyrannies of the Federal government; it was established in rebellion against a vigorous government and against an industrializing region. From that point of view, the Confederacy should celebrate diversity, strong state governments and a weak central government, and an agrarian, not an industrial, way of life. The problem with this vision of the new nation was that it seemed inadequate for establishing the Confederacy's very existence.

Another part of Southern political culture said to set it off from the rest of the United States was its devotion to the concept of state rights. But zeal in defense of state rights, though a potent motive for secession, was hardly a desirable passion for nation-building. If the South's state rights ideology helped create the Confederacy, it also helped destroy it. Indeed, Frank Oswley suggested that "Died of States Rights" was the most appropriate epitaph for the Confederacy. Yet it must also be acknowledged that in many ways the Confederacy went further overturning state rights than did its opponent to the north.

One thing was clear: if the Confederacy failed to defeat the Union, Confederate nationalism would be meaningless. Even if antebellum Southern nationalism had been widespread and deeply felt, even if the Confederacy embodied white Southerners' sincere desire for an independent nation, its existence depended on practical success, both military and political. A genuine nationalism can be suppressed by force. The Union planned to crush the rebellion. If the Confederacy did not win, Southern nationalism would have produced, most notably, dead Southerners. So the cause of Confederate nationalism became one with the cause of the Confederate army.

At the time, the relationship between military events and Confederate nationalism raised the issue of what it sometimes called national strategy. How the Confederacy should fight its war could not be divorced from the question of its war aims and national identity. Was the ultimate aim of the South a Confederate nation, or was the Confederate nation itself primarily a means to some other end—such as the preservation of slavery? If the latter was the case, what would happen to support for the new nation if it failed to serve its ends?

The Confederacy had to do more than simply defeat the Union armies. It had to persuade Southerners that the new nation and its government served them well enough to justify the demands it placed on them. It had to do this because without ongoing popular support, Confederate victory was unlikely. Historian Drew Gilpin Faust observes that "the ideological foundations of nationalism required popular consent; nationalism, not to mention total war, necessarily involved and thus empowered the people at large." But here the diversity that underlay the South's vaunted homogeneity made the political problems extremely difficult. Policies that pleased slaveholders might not please nonslaveholders, nor would they necessarily please the slaves themselves.

How successful was the Confederacy in building a national consensus? That depends on at what point in the Confederacy's brief existence the question is asked. Among the white population, perhaps 10 percent were still Unionist after secession took place and the war began. The other 90 percent of new Confederates seemed to be wildly enthusiastic in their support of the war for independence. As Union armies penetrated the South, as demands made by the war became more extreme, as Confederate victory became less likely, and as suffering became commonplace throughout the South, the enthusiasm dwindled. Disaffection with the Confederacy was hardly limited to any single group in society. Women wanted their sons and husbands home. Both planters and yeomen grew disillusioned. Even the army was not immune: by 1865, desertion was crippling the war effort.

Perhaps the most significant Confederate failure is one that was predestined: the Confederacy could not persuade slaves that the creation of a nation based on their continued slavery was desirable. Confederate nationalism could not be a cause backed by the South's substantial black minority. Black Southerners were instinctive Unionists. During the war, they slowed the pace of their labor and sabotaged much of the war effort, they fled Confederate areas of the South to enter the lines of the Union army and so gain their freedom, and they enlisted in that army to fight for freedom and for Union. If black Southerners had accepted their enslavement, the Confederacy probably would have established its independence.

One problem with most approaches to Southern nationalism is that they treat nationalism as a thing, as an inherent quality, indeed as a measurable quality. It is almost as though historians have tried to count how many "nationalism units" the Confederacy had. This approach to nationalism stems from the nineteenth century, the era in which the notion of nationalism itself was invented. The initial theorists of nationalism—not surprisingly, nationalists themselves—saw it as something inherent among peoples, a force, sometimes latent, that existed in the souls of a people. If a people were a nation, it gave legitimacy to that people's aspirations to be free. Needless to say, this way of thinking is troublesome when applied to the Confederacy, as it suggests that the South had a moral right to independence, which in turn seems to deny any right of nationhood to black Southerners.

The question of Southern nationalism is, for many, really a moral question. "Was the South a nation?" is often a cover for the question "Did the South deserve to be a nation?" As its nineteenth-century theorists desired, nationalism is still seen as giving moral legitimacy. In this regard, the question of Southern nationalism is linked to the question of Confederate defeat; as Drew Gilpin Faust has pointed out, "Confederate defeat became for many southerners an expression of the region's moral inadequacies."

It might be better to think of nationalism as not a thing but a process. If we do think of nationalism as a process, how successful was Confederate nationalism? The instinctive answer is, not very—there is no Confederate nation. But that is the result of military defeat. Military defeat is not the same as a failure of the nationalistic process.

If the Confederacy had succeeded, would the new political reality of an independent state have created a sense of nation among at least white Southerners? And if Confederate independence had been established by a war of secession, would the war itself have helped create that sense of nation? Any answer is speculative. Mine is "probably."

What is clear is that the Confederate experience itself created "the South" as nothing had done before it. Now white Southerners had a new set of heroes, a new series of grievances and griefs, a new history that united them at the same time it set them apart from the rest of the nation. If nationalism is primarily an emotional response, it was one deeply felt after 1865 as Southerners created the mythology of the Lost Cause. One final product of the Civil War, one final product of Confederate nationalism, was loyalty to a dead nation.

[*See also* Civil War, *articles on* Causes of the War, Strategy, *and* Causes of Defeat; Economy; Expansionism; Fire-eaters; Honor; Morale; Population; Proslavery; Religion; Slavery.]

BIBLIOGRAPHY

Beringer, Richard E., Herman Hattaway, Archer Jones, and William N. Still, Jr. *Why the South Lost the Civil War.* Athens, Ga., 1986.

Escott, Paul D. *After Secession: Jefferson Davis and the Failure of Confederate Nationalism.* Baton Rouge, La., 1978.

Faust, Drew G. *The Creation of Confederate Nationalism: Ideology and Identity in the Civil War South.* Baton Rouge, La., 1988.

Genovese, Eugene. *The Political Economy of Slavery: Studies in the Economy and Society of the Slave South.* New York, 1965.

McCardell, John. *The Idea of a Southern Nation: Southern Nationalists and Southern Nationalism, 1830–1860.* New York, 1979.

McWhiney, Gray, and Perry D. Jamieson. *Attack and Die: Civil War Military Tactics and the Southern Heritage.* University, Ala., 1982.

Owsley, Frank L. *States Rights in the Confederacy.* Chicago, 1925.

Potter, David M. *The Impending Crisis, 1848–1861.* New York, 1976.

Powell, Lawrence, and Michael Wayne. "Self-Interest and the Decline of Confederate Nationalism." In *The Old South in the Crucible of War.* Edited by Harry Owens and James Cooke. Jackson, Miss., 1983.

Stampp, Kenneth M. "The Southern Road to Appomattox." In *The Imperilled Union: Essays on the Background of the Civil War.* New York, 1980.

Thomas, Emory M. *The Confederate Nation, 1861–1865.* New York, 1979.

REID MITCHELL

NAVAL GUNS. [*This entry is composed of four articles:* Confederate Naval Guns; Captured U.S. Naval

Guns; European Naval Guns; *and* Naval Munitions. *See also* Charlotte Navy Yard; Columbus Naval Ironworks; Gosport Navy Yard; Munitions, *article on* Naval Munitions; Selma Naval Ordnance Works; Tredegar Ironworks.]

Confederate Naval Guns

The Confederacy faced serious problems in securing naval ordnance. Its sole prewar source for the manufacture of heavy guns was the Tredegar works (J. R. Anderson and Company) at Richmond. During the conflict Tredegar produced the bulk of ordnance for the Confederacy: between 1,043 and 1,099 pieces of all types, an output equal to the total of 1,050 guns produced by the eleven other Southern firms during the same period. Tredegar, however, was not able to cast heavy guns hollow on the Rodman method, which cooled the gun from the interior by means of water passed through a hollow core. This process produced guns of greater strength. Anderson's refusal to adopt the Rodman method in the years before the war had a profound impact on the Confederate ability to cast heavy guns during the conflict, and no Rodman-method guns were finished in time for actual service on the Confederate side.

In February 1863, the Confederate government purchased a new facility, which became the Selma, Alabama, Naval Works. It cast ordnance, chiefly for use against Union ironclads, but as of February 1865, it had produced less than two hundred guns. Other heavy guns were also manufactured at the Bellona Foundry near Richmond.

Despite problems, Confederate naval ordnance production was sufficient to meet the Confederacy's more modest requirements, although the lack of manufacturing facilities and skilled labor led to difficulties in mounting guns and shortages in shells and wrought-iron bolts.

Most Confederate naval ordnance consisted of captured Union pieces, but some excellent pieces were designed by John M. Brooke. A lieutenant in the U.S. Navy, Brooke resigned his commission upon the secession of Virginia. He was in charge of naval ordnance experiments and later was chief of naval ordnance for the Confederacy. Brooke developed shells, fuses, a flat-headed bolt for use against ironclads, and submarine mines, but he is best known for his naval ordnance.

Brooke designed 32-pounder and 10- and 11-inch smoothbores, all based on standard U.S. Navy patterns. An 1863 design for a 10-inch smoothbore gun was double-banded and 158.5 inches in length. Brooke, however, is best known for his rifled guns. The Union navy favored Dahlgren smoothbores in turreted ironclads, but the Confederate navy embraced rifled guns in ironclad, casemated vessels. Brooke's rifles, in 6.4-, 7-, and 8-inch sizes, were the most accurate and powerful guns developed in the Confederacy and quite possibly the best naval weapons on either side in the war. The guns greatly resembled the Union Parrott rifled gun in form, but differed from it in having a second and even third ring of reinforcing bands. Instead of being solid, these bands, approximately six inches wide, were made up of a succession of rings. Brooke's rifled guns weighed more than comparable Union Parrott rifles.

The first Brooke rifle was a 7-inch. It was essentially the 9-inch Dahlgren pattern gun, bored out to only 7 inches and then rifled. From 143 to 147.5 inches long, it weighed 15,000 pounds, was designed for pivot use, and was produced in four patterns. It took shells of 110 pounds and bolts of 120 pounds. Brooke 7-inch rifled guns firing armor-piercing bolts were responsible for much of the damage on Union monitors attacking Charleston in 1863.

The 6.4-inch Brooke rifle, based on the standard U.S. Navy 32-pounder design, was from 141 to 144 inches long, weighed 9,000 pounds, and was intended as a broadside gun only. It was produced in two patterns. It took shells of 65 pounds and bolts of 80 pounds.

Little is known of the 8-inch Brooke, which was produced in only one pattern. Some Brooke rifles were later reamed

BROOKE DOUBLE-BANDED RIFLE. Detailed plan of a gun and carriage intended for a Confederate ironclad, designed by George T. Gery, Richmond, Virginia, 1864.
NAVAL HISTORICAL CENTER, WASHINGTON, D.C.

up to make larger smoothbores: the 6.4-inch rifle, for example, became an 8-inch piece, and the 8-inch rifle a 10-inch smoothbore.

The output of Brooke guns during the Civil War was quite small. Tredegar cast no more than eighty-three rifled guns; most were 7-inch types, and only one was an 8-inch. The same foundry cast sixteen Brooke smoothbores. But these were only a small amount of the total produced by Tredegar. At Selma an additional fifty-five Brooke rifles and eighteen smoothbores were cast from January 1864 to March 1865.

A principal difference between Union and Confederate naval guns was that Confederate pieces were not given a smooth exterior finish. "Turning smooth" contributed nothing to the functioning of the gun and was a costly operation; the exteriors of Confederate guns were often the same as when they left the molds.

Tennessee, most powerful of all Confederate ironclads, mounted two 7-inch Brookes in pivot and four 6.4-inch rifled guns in broadside on two-truck Marsilly carriages. The two 7-inch pieces are now at the Washington Navy Yard. Among Confederate vessels mounting Brookes were the ironclads *Virginia* and *Nashville* and gunboats *Gaines, Morgan, Selma, Peedee, Muscogee,* and *Chattahoochee.*

Confederate navy ordnance practices were essentially those of the U.S. Navy, and the 1864 Confederate navy ordnance manual is an almost word-for-word copy of that of the U.S. Navy.

Contrary to what some Union naval officers thought at the start of the conflict, Confederate naval ordnance arrangements were on a par with their own. As Rear Adm. Louis Goldsborough, commander of the Union North Atlantic Blockading Squadron, noted regarding Confederate vessels in early 1862: "His ordnance arrangements take us quite by surprise. They are really excellent, if not admirable. We have captured quite a large number of his

Loading a fifteen-inch gun of an ironclad.

Frank Leslie's Illustrated Famous Leaders and Battle Scenes of the Civil War

Gun from *Virginia.* U.S. Dahlgren shell gun with a burst muzzle. British and other Civil War relics are in the background. Photographed at the Washington Navy Yard on April 27, 1933.

Naval Historical Center, Washington, D.C.

guns & fixings, & are mounting some of the former on board our own vessels."

BIBLIOGRAPHY

Tucker, Spencer C. *Arming the Fleet: U.S. Navy Ordnance in the Muzzle-Loading Era.* Annapolis, Md., 1989.

Tucker, Spencer C. "Confederate Naval Ordnance." *Journal of the Confederacy* 4 (1989): 133–152.

SPENCER C. TUCKER

Captured U.S. Naval Guns

The Confederacy was fortunate in that Virginia's secession gave it access to the largest prewar U.S. Navy Yard, that of Gosport, also known as the Norfolk Navy Yard. There the Confederates captured 1,198 heavy guns, ranging from carronades to modern shell guns and including fifty-two 9-inch Dahlgrens. They also took three Dahlgren boat howitzers, as well as large quantities of powder and shell. The frigate *Merrimack* alone yielded 2,200 powder cartridges stored in her magazines in watertight tanks. Within a few months the yard had shipped 533 guns all over the Confederacy. Most went to arm fortifications, but a number saw service afloat. In addition, the Confederacy obtained thirty-three cannon and some ordnance stores at Pensacola.

Throughout the war, the Confederates made excellent use of their captured Union ordnance. For example, two 9-inch Dahlgrens were mounted in pivot on board *Charleston,* along with four Brookes in broadside. *Virginia* mounted six 9-inch Dahlgrens in broadside along with two Brookes in pivot. The Confederacy modified a number of the captured pieces by giving them rifling and banding. Usually these were single-banded, but there were also double-banded pieces.

At the beginning of the war, the U.S. Navy employed a mix of old-system and new Dahlgren-system guns. It is safe to assume that all old-system guns were employed by both sides during the war. The U.S. Navy's Dahlgren pieces had been introduced in the 1850s. They were instantly recognizable by their heavier weight of metal around the breech, leading them to be known as "soda bottles." The mainstay of the Dahlgren system was the 9-inch smoothbore, introduced in 1850, which was designed for both pivot and broadside use. It weighed 9,200 pounds and was 107 inches in length of bore. Both sides used it during the war.

BIBLIOGRAPHY

Tucker, Spencer C. *Arming the Fleet: U.S. Navy Ordnance in the Muzzle-Loading Era.* Annapolis, Md., 1989.

Tucker, Spencer C. "Confederate Naval Ordnance." *Journal of the Confederacy* 4 (1989): 133–152.

SPENCER C. TUCKER

European Naval Guns

Because the Confederacy lacked facilities to manufacture sufficient guns for its needs, the government sought to purchase them abroad. Virtually all ordnance obtained from overseas was of English manufacture, and the most highly prized were rifled guns. Three were successful: the Armstrong, Whitworth, and Blakely. A fourth, the Clay, was a failure.

William G. Armstrong produced his first breech-loading

Old-system U.S. Naval Guns[a]

CALIBER	WEIGHT	BORE	CHAMBER	CHAMBER	SLOPE	GUN	BORE
	in hundred weight (772 lbs.)	diameter in inches		length in inches			
10-inch	89 cwt	10.0	7.00	9.50	5.5	112	106.00
8-inch	90 cwt	8.0	6.40	13.20	5.0	114	111.00
8-inch	63 cwt	8.0	6.40	7.45	5.0	106	102.00
8-inch	55 cwt	8.0	5.40	7.00	4.0	100	95.40
64-pdr	106 cwt	8.0	–	–	–	130	124.50
32-pdr	61 cwt	6.4	–	–	–	112	105.60
32-pdr	57 cwt	6.4	–	–	–	111	107.90
32-pdr	51 cwt	6.4	–	–	–	108	104.00
32-pdr	46 cwt	6.4	–	–	–	102	98.00
32-pdr[b]	42 cwt	6.4	5.82	7.25	3.5	96	90.50
32-pdr[b]	33 cwt	6.4	5.82	7.00	2.5	79	75.00
32-pdr	27 cwt	6.4	5.82	6.00	2.5	72	67.65, 68.84, 70.0

[a]Also aboard U.S. Navy vessels were 24-pounders (5.82″ bore), 18-pounders (5.3″), 12-pounders (4.62″) and 9-pounders (4.2″).

[b]These guns were given chambers at the bottom of the bore.

ONE HUNDRED-POUNDER ARMSTRONG BREECH-LOADING RIFLES. Engraving entitled "The Gun Deck of the *Merrimack*" from *Illustrated Times,* May 31, 1862. In actuality, CSS *Virginia* (built on the hull of the ex-Union steam frigate *Merrimack*) carried no guns of this type.
NAVAL HISTORICAL CENTER, WASHINGTON, D.C.

rifled gun in 1855. Armstrongs were built-up guns of wrought-iron tubes from spiral coils; some had a main tube of steel. The breech unscrewed for loading. Armstrongs were also made as muzzleloaders and came in a variety of calibers from 6- to 600-pounders. *Stonewall,* constructed for the Confederacy in France, mounted three: a 300-pounder in a casemate forward and two 70-pounders aft. There may have been attempts to produce Armstrongs at New Orleans and Norfolk during the war.

The Whitworth rifled gun, designed by Joseph Whitworth, was also both a breechloader and a muzzleloader. Its unique feature was a hexagonal spiral bore. Its delicate mechanisms were prone to jam, however, and projectiles sometimes lodged in the bore and could be freed only by heavy blows, with occasional fatal results. The Whitworth was made both of cast iron bored from the solid, and of steel, with wrought-iron rings shrunk on. By 1862, Whitworth guns were of 3-, 12-, and 80-pounder sizes and ranged in weight from 208 pounds to 4 tons. The Union navy captured four 5-inchers on the blockade runner *Princess Royal* near Morris Island in January 1863, two of which were part of the Union battery on Morris Island.

The Blakely was constructed on the same built-up principle as the Armstrong and Whitworth, with wrought-iron rings shrunk around a cast-iron core. It appeared only as a muzzleloader. Because Alexander T. Blakely had no manufacturing facilities of his own, his designs were cast by others in a variety of sizes and configurations. *Alabama,* constructed in England under the name *Enrica,* mounted a 7-inch Blakely in pivot, as well as other English-manufactured guns: a 68-pounder pivot gun and six long 32-pounder smoothbores in broadside. (To satisfy Britain's Foreign Enlistment Act, *Enrica,* like other English-made Confederate ships, had to be sent out of the country unarmed. Its armament was sent on another vessel and transferred at the Portuguese island Terceira after the Confederates had taken possession of *Enrica.*) A 7-inch Blakely rifle, mounted in pivot on *Florida,* may be seen at the Washington Navy Yard.

BIBLIOGRAPHY

Ripley, Warren. *Artillery and Ammunition of the Civil War.* New York, 1970.

Tucker, Spencer C. "Confederate Naval Ordnance." *Journal of the Confederacy* 4 (1989): 133–152.

SPENCER C. TUCKER

Naval Munitions

Confederate warships were equipped with a wide variety of artillery projectiles, depending on the type of ordnance carried aboard. Smoothbore cannons were usually supplied with spherical solid shot and explosive shell, grapeshot, and canister. Late in the war, particularly with the advent of the large-caliber Brooke smoothbores, wrought-iron bolts were issued in limited quantities for use against ironclads at close range. Rifled cannons, especially the much-favored Brooke rifles, could be provided with some or all of the following projectile types: cast-iron bolts, chilled-iron bolts, wrought-iron bolts (the latter two for use against ironclads), percussion- and time-fused shell, grape, canister, and shrapnel. In addition, incendiary shell were sometimes furnished in small numbers to both types of cannons.

The navy initially procured projectiles from numerous government and private sources, but by 1864 naval ordnance works at Atlanta, Charlotte, Richmond, and Selma were the principal suppliers. A considerable amount of ordnance was also brought in through the blockade.

To satisfy propellant needs, the navy established a powder mill at Petersburg, Virginia, but removed it to Columbia, South Carolina, in mid-1862. Army and imported powder supplemented the facility's output, even after production was able to meet the navy's demands in 1864.

The Confederate navy's Bureau of Ordnance and Hydrography was progressive and innovative. Under the guidance of Comdr. John Mercer Brooke through most of the war, the bureau developed new types of fuses and projectiles and experimented extensively with others. It was particularly interested in developing projectiles able to penetrate the thick-skinned armor of Union monitors and tested such modern designs as an armor-piercing rifle shell with a delayed action fuse that caused detonation only after penetration was achieved. Although the Confederate navy never gained parity with its foe in the quantity of ordnance produced, the technology it employed was often superior.

BIBLIOGRAPHY

Dickey, Thomas S., and Peter C. George. *Field Artillery Projectiles of the American Civil War.* Atlanta, Ga., 1980.

Kerkis, Sidney C., and Thomas S. Dickey. *Heavy Artillery Projectiles of the Civil War, 1861–1865.* Kennesaw, Ga., 1972.

Ripley, Warren. *Artillery and Ammunition of the Civil War.* 4th ed. rev. Charleston, S.C., 1984.

Still, William N. *Confederate Shipbuilding.* 2d ed. Columbia, S.C., 1987.

Wells, Tom H. *The Confederate Navy: A Study in Organization.* University, Ala., 1971.

A. Robert Holcombe, Jr.

NAVAL ORDNANCE WORKS. The Confederacy's attempt to equip a navy joined two of its weaker characteristics: lack of industry and lack of a seafaring tradition. In spite of great difficulties, the creation of an industrial base for naval warfare was an impressive accomplishment. Even with losses, by war's end the Confederate navy operated five ordnance works, including two marine machinery shops. These facilities were supported through contracts with private ironworks and foundries. Two principal suppliers, the Tredegar Iron Works in Richmond and the Shelby Iron Company in central Alabama, were contractors, not governmental facilities.

When the war began, the Confederacy held the former U.S. facility at Norfolk, a major ordnance complex with capacity to forge large castings and to produce cannons, projectiles, and gun carriages. The navy immediately sought to develop additional ordnance works in Atlanta and New Orleans.

Both Norfolk and New Orleans were threatened early in the war by Federal military operations. Much of the equipment at Norfolk, including a large steam hammer, was evacuated to Charlotte, and some was sent to Richmond. By the spring of 1862, Norfolk and New Orleans were lost to the Confederacy. These losses, plus that of the iron furnaces

Confederate Naval Ordnance Works

Name	Location	Years	Principal Functions
Gosport Navy Yard	Norfolk, Va.	1861–1866	Gun carriages, shot, shells, cannons
New Orleans Naval Ordnance Works	New Orleans, La.	1861–1862	Shot, shells
Atlanta Naval Ordnance Works*	Atlanta, Ga.	1861–1864	Gun carriages, sights
Richmond Naval Ordnance Works (Shockhoe Foundry)	Richmond, Va.	1862–1865	Marine machinery
Charlotte Naval Ordnance Works (Mecklenburg Iron Works)	Charlotte, N.C.	1863–1865	Heavy forging of shafts & anchors, shot, shells, cannons, gun carriages
Columbus Naval Ordnance Works (Columbus Iron Works)	Columbus, Ga.	1862–1865	Cannons, marine machinery
Selma Naval Ordnance Works (Selma Foundry)	Selma, Ala.	1863–1865	Brooke guns, cannons

*The Atlanta facilities were evacuated in the summer of 1864 and machinery moved to Augusta, Georgia; Charleston, S.C.; and Fayetteville, N.C.

of eastern Tennessee, forced the Confederacy to reorganize its iron production.

Facilities were established at Richmond, Charlotte, and Atlanta. The Richmond complex depended heavily upon Tredegar and the Bellona Iron Works as private contractors, but it also included governmental facilities: the Rocketts Shipyard and the Shockoe Foundry. The latter was leased in February 1862 to construct marine machinery. Charlotte was not well developed until the end of 1863. By late 1864, it was the South's only facility for heavy forging. Atlanta possessed foundries and a rolling mill at the beginning of the war, and it quickly became an important navy facility.

Rolling mill capacity for armor plate was limited. Only Tredegar in Richmond and Scofield and Markham Iron Works in Atlanta were able to roll two-inch armor plate in 1861. The Shelby Iron Company rolling mill reached this capacity in 1863.

In 1862, the navy acquired the Columbus (Georgia) Iron Works and the Selma (Alabama) Foundry. Columbus became the Confederacy's second and most important plant for manufacturing marine machinery. It produced at least eleven large engines and boilers for six steam vessels, repaired others, and made spare parts. The Selma facility was beset with problems and did not become productive until January 1864, but it produced over a hundred Brooke guns by war's end.

All facilities suffered shortages of iron and skilled labor. All competed for both resources with each other, the army, the railroads, and other private manufacturers. The army controlled the acquisition of iron, most of the skilled manpower, and the use of transportation. Lack of an integrated transportation system was very troublesome. By war's end, the navy's facilities were operating at half capacity before being occupied by Federal troops.

[*See also* African American Forgeworkers; Charlotte Navy Yard; Columbus Naval Ironworks; Gosport Navy Yard; Selma Naval Ordnance Works.]

BIBLIOGRAPHY

Still, William N., Jr. *Confederate Shipbuilding.* Athens, Ga., 1969.

Wells, Tom H. *The Confederate Navy: A Study in Organization.* University, Ala., 1971.

Robert H. McKenzie

NAVAL STATIONS. Confederate naval stations were administrative and logistical units occupying specific geographical areas defined by the secretary of the navy. The station commander, often assisted by an ordnance officer, a surgeon, a paymaster, and an engineer, was responsible for recruiting, ordnance works, naval storehouses, hospitals, marine detachments, and sometimes naval construction in his district. He also inspected commissioned vessels in port and reported their conditions to the department, and he received all reports and requisitions from the commanders of vessels within the limits of his station. By regulation he exercised no authority or control over the commanding officer of a navy yard without the express permission or order of the secretary of the navy. In practice, however, the administrative distinction between station and yard was often ambiguous, and many stations and yards within the same area were under the command of a single officer.

Prior to the spring of 1863 the station commander had operational control of warships within his territorial limits. Afterward, in an effort to have younger, more aggressive officers in control of the naval forces afloat, he was taken out of the operational chain of command and placed in a logistical support role.

Although the imprecise terminology used in contemporary records often makes it difficult to distinguish between various types of naval establishments, the Confederate navy operated at least fourteen stations during the course of the war: Richmond, Virginia; Halifax, Kinston, Charlotte, and Wilmington, North Carolina; Marion Court House and Charleston, South Carolina; Savannah and Columbus, Georgia; St. Marks, Florida; Mobile, Alabama; Jackson, Mississippi; and New Orleans and Shreveport, Louisiana. Additionally, some sources consider the installations at Little Rock, Arkansas; Selma, Alabama; and Yazoo City, Mississippi, as naval stations.

BIBLIOGRAPHY

C.S. Navy Department. *Regulations for the Navy of the Confederate States, 1862.* Richmond, Va., 1862.

Still, William N. *Confederate Shipbuilding.* 2d ed. Columbia, S.C., 1987.

Wells, Tom H. *The Confederate Navy: A Study in Organization.* University, Ala., 1971.

A. Robert Holcombe, Jr.

NAVY. [*This entry is composed of four articles:* Confederate Navy, *which overviews the creation and activities of the Confederate Navy;* Navy Department, *which discusses the organization and leadership of the cabinet-level department overseeing the navy;* Manpower, *which discusses the demographic makeup of the navy; and* African Americans in the Confederate Navy, *which examines the role of African Americans in the construction, maintenance, and operations of the navy. For further discussion of naval ordnance, shipbuilding, and ships, see* Arms, Weapons, and Ammunition, *article on* Naval Ordnance; Blockade, *article on* Blockade Runners; Commerce Raiders; Cottonclads; Davids; Ironclads; Naval Ordnance Works; Powder Works; Rams; Shipyards; Submarines; *and entries on particular* *ships. See also* Anglo-Confederate Purchasing; Marine Corps; Naval Stations; State Navies; Uniforms, *article on Navy and Marines Uniforms;* Waterways; *and entries on particular naval battles and on biographies of numerous figures mentioned herein.*]

Confederate Navy

On February 20, 1861, delegates from the seven Southern states that had proclaimed their secession from the Union passed an act to establish a Navy Department. The act provided for the appointment of a secretary, a chief clerk, and other minor officials. The following day Stephen R. Mallory of Florida was designated secretary of the Confederate States Navy. The organization of the Confederate navy was patterned after that of the U.S. Navy. A congressional act created four bureaus: Ordnance and Hydrography, Orders and Details, Medicine and Surgery, and Provisions and Clothing. The act also established a Marine Corps. Later a chief constructor and chief engineer were added.

MEN WANTED
FOR THE
NAVY!
All able-bodied men not in the employment of the Army, will be enlisted into the Navy upon application at the Naval Rendezvous, on Craven Street, next door to the Printing Office.
H. K. DAVENPORT,
Com'r. & Senior Naval Officer.
New Berne, N. C.,
Nov. 2d, 1863.

NAVAL RECRUITMENT POSTER. Issued at New Berne, North Carolina, 1863. NATIONAL ARCHIVES

Building the Navy. The newly organized navy needed ships and personnel to man them. Some 343 officers, approximately 24 percent of the 1,554 officers who were serving in the U.S. Navy as of December 1, 1860, resigned their Union commissions and joined the Confederate navy. Of this number about a third would in time actually serve. The majority of the remainder accepted appointments with the Confederate army or state military forces or were too old and unfit for active duty. The navy's officer corps would reach a maximum number of 753.

Enlisted personnel were more difficult to acquire. Few left the U.S. Navy for Confederate service. Through volunteering, conscription, and transfer from the army, 3,674 were on active duty by the beginning of 1865.

Confederate Marines numbered 539 officers and men in October 1864. Detachments served on various warships including commerce cruisers, as well as stations and other shore facilities and fortifications.

Ships were equally scarce. The Confederate navy inherited five small vessels from the seceded states. In addition, four revenue cutters, three slavers, two privately owned coastal steamers, and *Fulton,* an old side-wheeler laid up in the Pensacola Navy Yard, were purchased or seized. As a stopgap measure the Navy Department continued purchasing merchant steamers for conversion, but Secretary Mallory determined to initiate a warship construction program at home and abroad.

In May 1861 naval agents were sent to Great Britain and France to obtain vessels that could be used for commerce raiding. Later the department contracted for the construction of armored warships. *Stonewall,* however, was the only one of these ironclads to reach Confederate hands. The South was more successful in obtaining wooden cruisers. Commerce raiding has traditionally been a strategy of nations with weak navies, and the Confederacy, with its limited warship building expertise and facilities, could not create a navy strong enough to challenge Union seapower. Also, Mallory hoped to weaken the blockade by forcing the Union navy to convoy merchant ships and seek out and destroy the raiders in various parts of the world. Finally, commerce raiding might disrupt Union shipping to the point where Abraham Lincoln's government would have to negotiate an end to the conflict in order to prevent economic disaster.

The Confederate government built or purchased at home and abroad more than a dozen raiders including *Alabama, Florida,* and *Shenandoah.* Together they destroyed some 5 percent of the Union merchant fleet and seized or destroyed millions of dollars in cargo. For every vessel the Confederate raiders destroyed or seized, the Union merchant fleet lost eight others as an indirect result. Exorbitant insurance rates caused by war risks resulted in hundreds of vessels remaining in port. In addition nearly a thousand were transferred to other flags, principally British. Altogether, more than 1,616 vessels, with a total tonnage of 774,000 tons, were lost to the American merchant marine during the war. Nevertheless, the Confederate raiders had little of the hoped-for influence on Union policy; the blockade was not weakened and Lincoln and his advisers gave no thought to a negotiated peace.

In contrast to the raiders, ironclad warships built by the Confederate government played a more useful role in the war. Secretary Mallory emphasized armored vessels in his construction program. On May 9, 1861, he wrote: "I regard the possession of an iron armored ship as a matter of the first necessity. . . . inequality of numbers may be compensated by invulnerability; and thus not only does economy but naval success dictate the wisdom and expediency of fighting with iron against wood." Initially, the secretary concentrated on obtaining armored warships in Europe but in the summer he ordered the conversion of *Merrimack* into *Virginia* and contracted for the building of two ironclads in New Orleans (*Mississippi* and *Louisiana*), and two in Memphis (*Arkansas* and *Tennessee*). These five ironclads were all unusually large and were designed to operate on the open sea as well as on inland waters. They were intended not only to break the blockade but also, as Secretary Mallory wrote, to "traverse the entire coast of the United States . . . and encounter, with a fair prospect of success, their entire Navy."

By 1862 Mallory abandoned his decision to build large seagoing ironclads within the Confederacy and instead concentrated on small, shallow-draft, harbor-defense armored vessels. Various factors influenced this change in policy: the apparent unseaworthiness of *Virginia* and the ironclads built in New Orleans and Memphis, the belief that the South would be able to obtain powerful seagoing armored ships in Europe, and the pressing need for defensive vessels. Because of the continuing success of the Union's combined operations along the Southern coastline as well as the ineffectiveness of the blockade, Confederate naval strategy emphasized defense. Naval forces were organized to guard ports and rivers and inlets that opened the interior to invasion. The small ironclads were designed to be the nucleus of these naval forces.

Approximately forty were laid down within the Confederacy and half of them completed and placed in operation. The James River Squadron included *Virginia II, Richmond,* and *Fredericksburg;* the Wilmington Squadron, *North Carolina* and *Raleigh;* the Charleston Squadron, *Chicora, Palmetto State, Charleston,* and *Columbia;* the Savannah Squadron, *Atlantic, Georgia,* and *Savannah;* and the Mobile Squadron, *Tennessee* (II), *Nashville, Tuscaloosa,* and *Huntsville.* A number of ironclads were constructed on the rivers: *Albemarle* on the Roanoke, *Neuse* on the Neuse, *Jackson* on the Chattahoochee, and *Missouri* on the Red. In cooperation with wooden gunboats, forts, and other land and water defenses, these armored warships played a major role in Confederate defense efforts, and they contributed significantly to the defense of Richmond, Charleston, Savannah, and Mobile. *Albemarle* was instrumental in the recapture of Plymouth, North Carolina, in April 1864.

The Confederate government also contracted for a large number of wooden gunboats, many of which were completed and joined the various squadrons. Several experimental vessels such as the submarine *H. L. Hunley* and the semisubmergible *David* were completed. Both *Hunley* and *David* successfully attacked Union warships. Other vessels similar to *David* were laid down but never became operational.

Gun foundries, machine shops, rolling mills, and other manufacturing facilities needed to outfit warships were established in the Confederacy, but these industries were severely handicapped by the lack of labor. Nevertheless, ordnance works in Richmond and Selma, Alabama, cast hundreds of guns, the majority designed by John Mercer Brooke, chief of the Bureau of Ordnance and Hydrography. Armor plate was rolled by Tredegar in Richmond, the Shelby Iron Works in Alabama, and the Atlanta Rolling Mill. Machinery was manufactured in Columbus, Georgia.

The Naval War. The Confederacy suffered setbacks before the new warships were ready for active service. In November 1861, a combined Union army and naval force captured Port Royal, South Carolina, despite Confederate defenses including a small naval squadron of converted steamers. In the winter and spring of 1862, Federal forces occupied much of coastal North Carolina, defeating a number of small Confederate gunboats in the process. During this period Confederate naval forces were also involved in combat in Virginia waters.

The James River Squadron was established in 1861 and consisted of the small gunboats *Patrick Henry, Jameston, Teaser, Raleigh,* and *Beaufort.* In early March 1862, the ironclad *Virginia* converted from *Merrimack* joined the small naval force. *Virginia* encountered the Union ironclad *Monitor* in an indecisive engagement that lasted nearly four hours. Both vessels, damaged but intact, withdrew. In May with the capture of Norfolk by Union forces, *Virginia* was blown up by its crew, and the remainder of the James River Squadron withdrew up the James.

In the West, the year 1862 was equally disastrous for Confederate naval forces. On April 24 a Union fleet under Flag Officer David Farragut ran past two forts guarding the Mississippi River below New Orleans and engaged more than a dozen Confederate vessels. All were destroyed or surrendered including the ironclad *Manassas. Mississippi* and *Louisiana,* two large ironclads under construction in

CONFEDERATE NAVAL BATTERY. At Manassas Junction, Virginia, late 1861. NAVAL HISTORICAL CENTER, WASHINGTON, D.C.

New Orleans, were also destroyed by the Confederates to prevent their capture.

Although the Confederate government would lay down additional warships in the Yazoo and Red rivers, including the ironclad *Missouri* at Shreveport, Louisiana, none would be combat-tested. By late 1862, however, the first of the harbor defense ironclads were approaching completion. *Palmetto State* in Charleston and *Georgia* in Savannah, were commissioned in the fall. Sixteen additional armored vessels would be added to the fleet in the following two years and would become the nucleus of the various Confederate squadrons. More than a dozen would never be completed because of the lack of iron and the scarcity of workers.

Newly built wooden gunboats were also joining the fleet. *Morgan* and *Gaines* in Mobile and *Hampton* and *Nansemond* in Norfolk, Virginia, were completed and commissioned in the fall of 1862. The latter two were "Maury gunboats," named after Matthew Fontaine Maury, famous oceanographer and father of hydrography in the U.S. Navy, who resigned his commission to join the Confederate navy. One hundred of these small wooden gunboats were planned, but very few were actually finished. *Chattahoochee* was completed on the Chattahoochee River in 1863, and the *Pee Dee* on the Pee Dee in 1864.

By 1863 Union blockading squadrons along the Atlantic and Gulf coasts had increased to more than three hundred ships including several of the recently completed monitors. Confederate military officials in Charleston determined to attack the Federal naval force off the port before it was closed. On the last day of January 1863 two Confederate ironclads, *Chicora* and *Palmetto State,* steamed out of the harbor and forced the surrender of two blockaders, *Mercedita* and *Keystone State*. Efforts to bring other Union warships under fire were unsuccessful, and in fact the two that surrendered took advantage of the confusion to rejoin the retiring Union naval force. The two Confederate ironclads returned to the harbor. For the remainder of the war the Charleston Squadron guarded the channels and cooperated with the forts and batteries in defending the port. The Confederate vessels were destroyed by their crews as Gen. William Tecumseh Sherman's army approached the city.

In the spring of 1862 Federal forces took Fort Pulaski, guarding the river entry to Savannah, Georgia. The combined forces, however, were unable to capture the port. Confederate defenses included a squadron of ironclads and wooden gunboats. The first ironclad in the squadron, *Georgia,* was moored in the Savannah River where it could fire down either channel. Later the ironclad *Savannah* and the wooden gunboats *Isondiga* and *Macon* reinforced *Georgia*. The squadron included a third ironclad, *Atlanta*. It was converted from the blockade runner *Fingal* and when completed was probably the most powerful armored warship in Confederate service. In July 1863 it attempted to evade blockaders off the port but ran aground in the river and surrendered to two monitors. As in Charleston the approach of Sherman's army resulted in the destruction of the Confederate naval vessels by their crews.

Richmond, Virginia, the capital, was also defended by a Confederate naval squadron. After the fall of Norfolk in May 1862, the James River Squadron retired up the James above obstructions at Drewry's Bluff. There the ships remained throughout the war, venturing below the obstructions only twice. The nucleus of the Confederate naval forces in the James were the ironclads *Virginia II, Richmond,* and *Fredericksburg*. This force exchanged gunfire with Federal land batteries and warships below the obstructions until Richmond was evacuated in April 1865. The decision to evacuate led to the destruction of the ironclads, the wooden gunboats, and the training ship *Patrick Henry* by their crews. They then joined other naval personnel and Marines who had manned batteries along the river and retired from the abandoned capital.

In North Carolina Flag Officer William F. Lynch commanded the naval forces. His force consisted of a small squadron of ironclads and wooden vessels in the Cape Fear River guarding Wilmington and two ironclads constructed on the Neuse and Roanoke rivers. These two warships were built to cooperate in the recapture of eastern North Carolina including the sounds. In April 1864 *Albemarle*, constructed on the Roanoke River, successfully cooperated in a combined attack against Federal forces at Plymouth. The Confederate attempt to enter the sound was repulsed by Union warships. Later *Albemarle* was sunk at its moorings by a Union raiding force in a small boat. In May the ironclad *Raleigh* attacked blockaders off the Cape Fear River. After a futile effort to destroy the Union ships, the Confederate ironclad grounded while attempting to reenter the river. With the exception of *Albemarle*, which was raised and towed to Norfolk by Union personnel, all Confederate naval vessels in North Carolina waters were destroyed by their own crews, the Cape Fear Squadron upon the fall of Fort Fisher in February 1865 and the ironclad *Neuse* in the Neuse River in April.

The Mobile Squadron was commanded by Adm. Franklin Buchanan. In 1864 it consisted of four ironclads and wooden gunboats. On August 5, 1864, units of the squadron engaged a Federal fleet under Adm. David Farragut. Buchanan's force was defeated: the ironclad *Tennessee* and wooden gunboat *Selma* were captured, the gunboat *Gaines* ran aground, and the gunboat *Morgan* escaped. In the months that followed, *Morgan* along with the ironclads *Huntsville, Tuscaloosa,* and *Nashville* defended the river approaches to Mobile in cooperation with land forces. The capture of Mobile on April 12, 1865, resulted in the destruction of these ships by their crews.

Mobile was the last important port in the Confederacy to surrender. In all the ports, except Galveston, naval units contributed to their defense. Nonetheless, the Confederate navy had limited success against Federal warships. Only a half-dozen Union vessels of war were actually sunk in action by Confederate warships. This includes *Underwriter*, destroyed in a small-boat engagement. Torpedoes (mines) proved to be the most successful weapon used against Union ships. More than sixty ships including armored vessels were sunk by Confederate torpedoes during the war. In the final analysis, however, the Confederate navy had little chance against its more formidable opponent.

[*For further discussion of particular naval squadrons, see* Charleston Squadron; James River Squadrons; Mobile Squadron; River Defense Fleet; Savannah Squadron.]

BIBLIOGRAPHY

Merli, Frank J. *Great Britain and the Confederate Navy.* Bloomington, Ind., 1970.

Perry, Milton F. *Infernal Machines: The Story of Confederate Submarine and Mine Warfare.* Baton Rouge, La., 1965.

Scharf, J. Thomas. *History of the Confederate States Navy.* New York, 1887. Reprint, New York, 1977.

Spencer, Warren F. *The Confederate Navy in Europe.* University, Ala., 1983.

Still, William N., Jr. *Confederate Shipbuilding.* Columbia, S.C., 1987.

Still, William N., Jr. *Iron Afloat: The Story of the Confederate Armorclads.* Columbia, S.C., 1986.

Wells, Tom H. *The Confederate Navy: A Study in Organization.* University, Ala., 1971.

WILLIAM N. STILL, JR.

Navy Department

On February 20, 1861, the Confederate Congress meeting in Montgomery enacted legislation creating the Confederate Navy Department. To head this department President Jefferson Davis turned to Stephen R. Mallory. Born on the island of Jamaica, Mallory moved as an infant to Key West, Florida, a place he would always cherish as home. A successful lawyer, he entered the U.S. Senate in 1851 and served on the Naval Committee, becoming chairman in 1855. Thanks to his position, Mallory was without doubt well informed on naval matters. When Florida left the Union in January 1861, Mallory resigned from the Senate and returned home until summoned by Davis to his new post.

CONFEDERATE NAVAL LEADERS. Seated from left to right are Franklin Buchanan, Josiah Tattnall, and Matthew Fontaine Maury. Standing from left to right are George N. Hollins, Raphael Semmes, and Stephen R. Mallory. Painted by Creative Arts Studio for *Naval History Film,* part 1. NAVAL HISTORICAL CENTER, WASHINGTON, D.C.

Under the legislation of February 20 the Navy Department's administrative structure consisted of the secretary, two chief clerks, three additional clerks, and a messenger. Initially the department had its offices in Montgomery, but during May and June 1861 it moved with the rest of the Confederate government to Richmond. The Navy Department's offices were located in the Mechanics Institute on Ninth Street between Main and Franklin. Here Mallory and his staff wrestled with the problems of creating and managing a navy.

For the most part matters of policy and strategy were decided by the secretary and his two chief clerks, French Forrest and E. M. Tidball. Forrest was an old navy veteran who had joined the service shortly before the War of 1812. He detested bureaucratic routine, and after importuning the secretary, he was assigned to more active duty. Tidball was not an officer but a bureaucrat who brought to the office political and managerial skills the secretary would find useful.

Despite the tidal wave of problems the department encountered, its employees were fortunate in one respect: they did not have to contend with constant meddling from the president. As a West Point graduate and former secretary of war, Jefferson Davis felt competent to intrude into matters of Confederate military policy and strategy, a habit that often proved troublesome. Having virtually no background in naval matters, however, he rarely interfered in that department's affairs. On the other hand, although this hands-off policy was generally positive, it did have some negative impact. Davis's lack of appreciation for naval power bordered at times on indifference, a common characteristic among Confederate leaders. As secretary, one of Mallory's chief tasks was simply to make the president and his colleagues aware of the value of the Confederate navy in order to garner support.

Organization

To assist the secretary in formulating and executing policy, four offices were created, all located at the general headquarters on Ninth Street. The organization closely resembled the one Mallory had helped fashion to administer the Federal navy in the antebellum years.

J. K. Mitchell was in charge of the Office of Orders and Detail, which held primary responsibility for matters of personnel, including the recruiting, promotion, and assignment of officers and crews. The office also had logistical responsibilities that included procurement and distribution of coal and operations at the naval ropewalk in Petersburg.

The Office of Ordnance and Hydrography was in the hands of John M. Brooke, an Annapolis graduate. As its name implies, Brooke's department was responsible for obtaining and distributing to the fleet ordnance and munitions. It was also the duty of this office to provide navigational equipment including instruments and charts as well as to oversee the maintenance of docks and yards.

Medicine and Surgery was under the direction of W. A. W.

Spotswood and was charged with providing medical service to the navy. The department administered a hospital in Richmond and smaller institutions at various ports. Providing sufficient quantities of drugs was a particular problem: the department was forced to place an inordinate reliance on costly supplies delivered by blockade runners.

The fourth principal office was that of Provisions and Clothing under the command of John De Bree. Acting much like a quartermaster corps, the men under De Bree were responsible for delivering food, clothing, and other such items to the men in the fleet. Key to the functioning of this office were the paymasters and assistant paymasters, who dealt both with officers and enlisted men of the navy and with civilian contractors and suppliers.

Although these four offices handled the bulk of the affairs of the Navy Department, there were other places of power that, because they did not fall neatly under these offices, enjoyed a fair degree of autonomy. Among them were Steam Engineering, Naval Constructor, Torpedo Bureau, and the Marine Corps. In addition there were floating forces under army command, most notably the Mississippi River Defense Force in 1862 and the Texas Marine Department.

Mallory's organization had much to recommend it, but it suffered from two chronic weaknesses of the Confederacy itself: poverty and state rights, or decentralization. Problems arising from an inadequate budget were compounded by the independent attitudes of the Confederate states. Having left the Union in the name of state rights, the members of the Confederacy were reluctant to grant another central government, this one in Richmond, power over them. The result for the navy was a high degree of decentralization that often resulted in poor planning and control.

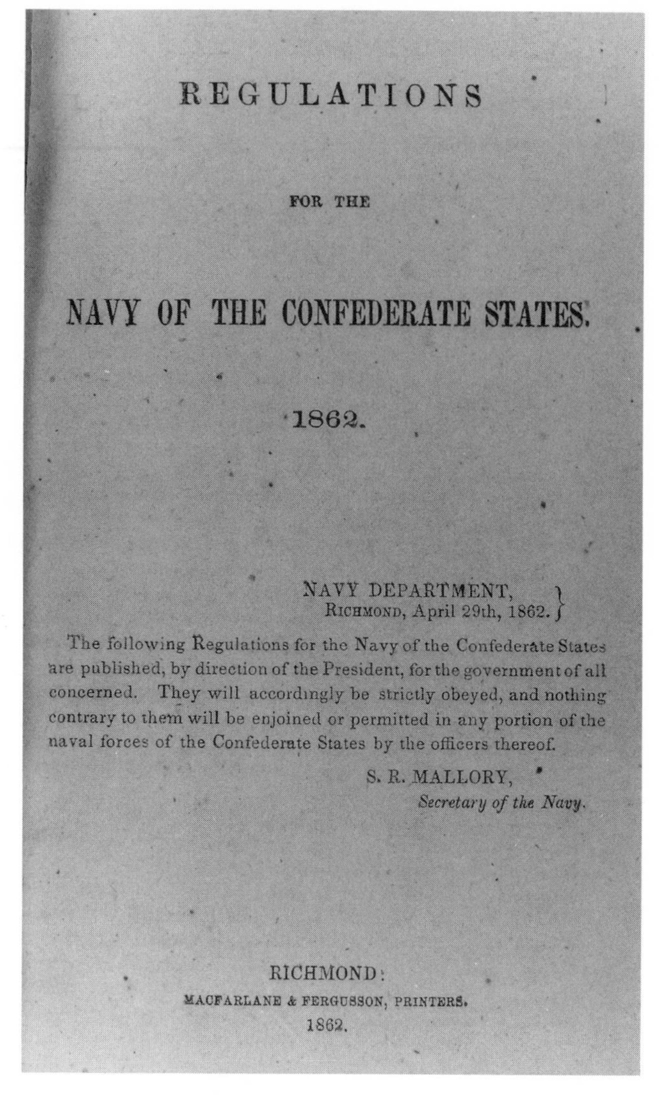
REGULATIONS

FOR THE

NAVY OF THE CONFEDERATE STATES.

1862.

NAVY DEPARTMENT,
RICHMOND, April 29th, 1862.

The following Regulations for the Navy of the Confederate States are published, by direction of the President, for the government of all concerned. They will accordingly be strictly obeyed, and nothing contrary to them will be enjoined or permitted in any portion of the naval forces of the Confederate States by the officers thereof.

S. R. MALLORY,
Secretary of the Navy.

RICHMOND:
MACFARLANE & FERGUSSON, PRINTERS.
1862.

NAVY REGULATIONS. A standard handbook of rules for naval personnel. CIVIL WAR LIBRARY AND MUSEUM, PHILADELPHIA

Outfitting the Navy

Although shortages of nearly everything would greatly hamper the Confederate navy, at the beginning of the war it was ironically a surplus that proved nettlesome. When confronted with the need to decide where their loyalty lay—with the Union or with their home state—many Federal naval officers chose their state. These men who "went south" either wrote to or showed up at the offices on Ninth Street to offer their services. To accommodate these officers, at least on paper, the Confederate Congress in April 1862 authorized the appointment of nine admirals, six commodores, twenty captains, twenty commanders, twenty first lieutenants, sixty-five second lieutenants, and sixty masters.

Finding berths for all these men was impossible, and few of these billets were actually filled. At its height the Confederate navy never had more than forty vessels in service. Most of the officers who volunteered their services either ended up on furlough awaiting orders or were directed to the army where they were often attached to a heavy ordnance unit. Those for whom berths were found, however, generally proved to be able and courageous officers.

Under Mallory's direction, the department focused on three strategic goals: the harassment of Union shipping; protection of the Atlantic and Gulf ports; and defense of the Mississippi and its southern tributaries. Each of these tasks presented special problems, but they shared a common requirement—ships.

From the outset Mallory appreciated that it would never be possible for the Confederacy to outbuild the Union; Southerners had neither the shipyards nor the resources to win a race against the North. Driven by that constraint, Mallory opted to build ironclads, hoping that a superior weapons system would compensate for numbers. His prescience in this matter helped make the Confederate States Navy far more effective than it might otherwise have been. Despite critical shortages of nearly everything necessary for the construction of modern ironclad warships, the South managed to launch a goodly number, enough at least to keep a vastly superior Union navy busily engaged. Altogether during the war the Confederate Navy Department built at least twenty ironclads.

Some of the ironclads, as well as conventional vessels, were built at private yards in the South. Others, however, were built in facilities under direct Department of the Navy control. During the war the department had in operation at one time or another twenty yards, one powderworks, two shops for constructing marine engines, five ordnance manufactories, and the ropewalk in Petersburg. Given the general lack of shipbuilding resources, the Confederacy did remarkably well to build as many warships as it did.

Because Mallory understood the domestic limitations on construction, he looked abroad for assistance. In May 1861 he dispatched a secret naval agent, James Dunwoody Bulloch, to England to procure suitable war vessels. Over the next four years Bulloch played a central role in the intrigue designed to evade laws of neutrality so that the Confederacy might obtain warships. Although Bulloch did contract for the construction of two ironclad rams with which Mallory hoped to attack Union blockaders, his work for the secretary for the most part was aimed at obtaining fast vessels designed to raid Union commerce. In this he was very successful.

Mallory believed that by sending raiders to sea he could accomplish two tasks—wreak havoc on Union commerce and at the same time force the Federal navy to withdraw vessels from blockade duty to chase down *Alabama, Florida,* and their sister ships. This did not prove to be the case. The raiders provided an aura of adventure and romance, but the damage they inflicted, although harmful to Union commerce, was nonetheless tolerable. Furthermore, the Union navy had sufficient vessels available to both chase the raiders and maintain the blockade. Eventually, because no European nation was willing to risk the wrath of the Union, they allowed the raiders to remain in their ports only long enough to make essential repairs and to take on enough fuel to reach the next port. Alone and isolated, unable to find safe ports for resupply and refitting, the raiders found themselves hunted down and either captured or destroyed.

Mallory believed that large ironclads were indispensable for defending Southern ports, a conviction that was reinforced in November 1861 when Port Royal, South Carolina, was attacked by a Federal fleet commanded by Samuel Francis DuPont. Confederate Commodore Josiah Tattnall sortied to defend the port with an assortment of ragtag converted wooden gunboats. A few Federal broadsides sent them scurrying. Unless the Confederacy built vessels more substantial than these cockleshells, Tattnall's rout was likely to be repeated at every Confederate port.

Under the secretary's direction, considerable resources were gathered at New Orleans to build ironclads. The money seems not to have been well spent, however, and during the summer of 1861 the Navy Department was being heavily criticized for its wasteful practices by, among others, Louisiana's governor. Mallory dispatched officers to the Crescent City to clear up the mess and get the ironclads built. Adding to the department's woes was the difficulty of securing sufficient funds for construction from the Confederate Treasury Department and a disagreement within the local army command as to responsibilities for the defense of the city.

The fall of New Orleans in April 1862 sparked numerous investigations within the Confederate government. The Navy Department was not spared. For more than six months a congressional committee took testimony in its inquiry into the administration of the department. In the end Mallory was exonerated from any misconduct; nonetheless, it was a humiliating experience and one that damaged his and the department's reputation.

With New Orleans in Union hands, the Confederate Navy Department was deprived of its only significant shipbuilding facility on the Mississippi. Although the department was able to take into service a variety of rivercraft, these were lightly built vessels that would prove no match for the heavily armed and armored Union squadrons. Mallory's greatest success on the rivers was *Arkansas,* an ironclad built at Yazoo City. It came down the Yazoo in July 1862 and blazed its way through the somnolent Union fleet at anchor near Vicksburg. But it later suffered engine problems and had to be scuttled to avoid capture. The Confederate navy had little impact on the war in the West.

The Navy in Action

Mallory's commitment to ironclads could be most clearly seen along the Atlantic coast. The appearance of *Virginia* on March 8, 1862, demonstrated his belief that large ironclads could both aid in defending the ports and on occasion interrupt the Union blockade. Under his authority other ironclads were built to defend Savannah, Charleston, and the North Carolina sound. At each of these ports Mallory's ironclads posed a threat that the Union forces could not ignore. At the same time, however, with the exception of those at Charleston these ironclads remained only a potential force and never succeeded in attacking and inflicting damage on the enemy. Their inactivity was the object of considerable criticism.

At Charleston Mallory endured an uncomfortable relationship with the army commander Gen. P. G. T. Beauregard. Under the Navy Department's direction two ironclads, *Palmetto State* and *Chicora,* had been built at Charleston for the defense of that port. (In 1864 they were joined by a third, *Charleston.*) To the dismay of Mallory and his department, these ironclads in practice came under the operational authority of Beauregard. At the general's orders in January 1863 these two vessels steamed out of the harbor and drove off the blockaders. It was only a temporary victory, however, for soon the Federals were back with a force sufficient to demolish the Confederates should they make a similar attempt again. Despite the danger, Beauregard urged repeatedly that the ironclads sortie. Mallory would not permit it. The same situation existed at Savannah where the ironclads *Atlanta* and *Savannah* were stationed. Mallory's argument was that sending these vessels out to engage a vastly superior Union force was suicide. He was right; however, the fact that the navy's ironclads remained snug in the harbor angered some and presented a sorry picture to the Southern public. *Atlanta* was run aground and then captured by Union forces in Wassaw Sound, while *Albemarle* was destroyed by Union Navy Lt. William Cushing in one of the great tales of the war. All the Confederate ironclads on the Atlantic coast were destroyed or captured.

One of the arguments Beauregard persisted in making was that the Navy Department ignored the value of torpedoes (underwater mines). Under Mallory's direction the department had established a Torpedo Bureau. Although often unreliable, these weapons had been employed with success on the western rivers, but the department was slow to use them to advantage in the East.

It was at Charleston that the Confederate Navy employed *H. L. Hunley,* a submarine built at Mobile but brought to Charleston in the summer of 1863 on the orders of Beauregard. *Hunley* proved exceedingly unreliable. On two dives it failed to return to the surface with a heavy loss of life. Desperate to find some way to drive the blockaders away, the Confederates on the night of February 17, 1864, sent *Hunley* to attack the Union frigate *Housatonic.* It succeeded in its mission but then went down with all hands lost.

On the Gulf coast at Mobile, the Navy Department placed under construction four ironclads for that port's defense. It was an overly ambitious program that went beyond what local resources could sustain. Only one of the ironclads, *Tennessee,* was completed to the point where it could play a role in defending against the Union attack in August 1864 commanded by Adm. David Farragut. The Confederate naval forces under Franklin Buchanan put up a stiff resistance against a much superior Federal force. *Tennessee* steamed bravely into the middle of the fray only to be sent to the bottom. The remaining unfinished ironclads played no role in the fight.

In addition to building and managing fighting ships, the Navy Department also had under its jurisdiction several blockade runners. Many of these were specially built for the trade under the direction of Bulloch operating under various guises. Altogether about twenty of these vessels served the Confederacy, bringing in much needed supplies, particularly munitions and medicines. On the outward voyage they generally carried cotton. The success of the department's blockade runners is attested to by the fact that Bulloch seemed always to have sufficient cash and credit to carry on his business of ship buying and building. His principal source of income was the sale of cotton run out of the South.

As the war dragged to its climax, Mallory watched unhappily as his ships were captured, scuttled, or destroyed. Some of his vessels participated in the defense of Richmond by trying to hold on to the James River. But the situation was hopeless, and on Sunday evening April 2 Mallory joined Jefferson Davis and the remainder of his cabinet on a train out of Richmond. The withdrawal of the Confederate government soon turned into flight. On May 2 Mallory resigned from the government and a few days later was captured. After an imprisonment of less than a year he was released. He returned to Florida and settled in Pensacola where he remained until his death in November 1873.

Given the resources at hand, the Confederate Navy Department accomplished a great deal. Although Mallory may be faulted for too heavy a reliance on large ironclads and high seas raiders, and inattention to torpedoes, overall he and his department were remarkably effective under the circumstances.

BIBLIOGRAPHY

Anderson, Bern. *By Sea and by River: A Naval History of the Civil War.* New York, 1962.

Bulloch, James D. *The Secret Service of the Confederate States.* 2 vols. New York, 1884.

Durkin, Joseph T. *Stephen R. Mallory: Confederate Navy Chief.* Chapel Hill, N.C., 1954.

Fowler, William M. *Under Two Flags: The American Navy in the Civil War.* New York, 1990.

Sharf, J. Thomas. *History of the Confederate States Navy from Its Organization to the Surrender of Its Last Vessel.* New York, 1887. Reprint, New York, 1977.

U.S. War Department. *Official Records of the Union and Confederate Navies in the War of the Rebellion.* 30 vols. Washington: Government Printing Office, 1892–1921.

William M. Fowler, Jr.

Manpower

From the very beginning of the Civil War, Southern naval authorities struggled to acquire adequate personnel, for the navy had no pool of trained seamen to augment its enlisted force. Throughout four years of war, and in the face of overwhelming personnel and material shortages, the navy nevertheless amassed an honorable record. By 1864, its strength was almost four thousand officers and men.

President Jefferson Davis in his inaugural address called upon the Provisional Congress to establish a navy to protect the harbors and commerce of the Southern states, and on February 20, 1861, the Confederate States Navy came into being. Stephen R. Mallory of Florida was appointed secretary of the navy and given a clerical force consisting of a chief clerk, a correspondence clerk, and a messenger. The secretary was charged with administering the various bureaus, which included Ordnance and Hydrography, Orders and Details, Medicine and Surgery, and Provisions and Clothing.

On March 16, an act of Congress established manpower limits for the navy and authorized President Davis to create the posts of four captains, four commanders, thirty lieutenants, five surgeons, five assistant surgeons, six paymasters, and two chief engineers. He was also empowered to employ as many as three thousand masters, midshipmen, engineers, naval constructors, boatswains, gunners, carpenters, sailmakers, warrant and petty officers, and seamen. The act made provisions for a marine corps to consist of one major, one quartermaster, one paymaster, one adjutant, one sergeant major, and six companies of marines. In turn, each company was to have a captain, a first and a second lieutenant, four sergeants, four corporals, one hundred men, and ten musicians.

The navy benefited from the 332 officers who resigned from the Federal navy and returned to their native states. Eventually, they transferred from state service to the Confederate States Navy, carrying the same rank they had held in the "old" service. To accommodate this large increase in officers, the Amendatory Act of April 21, 1862, increased the number of officers authorized for the navy.

To train additional officers the navy founded an academy on March 23, 1863, at Drewry's Bluff, Virginia, on the James River. The steamship *Patrick Henry* was the school's ship. Cabins were built on shore for the midshipmen, who were expected to spend half their time ashore and the other half aboard the training ship. The academy did not have sufficient longevity to graduate any cadets; the first class of 1863 contained fifty acting midshipmen.

The experience of naval administrators in obtaining qualified officers was duplicated in their attempts to recruit enlisted men. The South's lack of a seafaring tradition limited opportunities for finding trained seamen. To encourage enlistments, the navy opened rendezvous stations (recruiting stations) in all major Southern cities and towns, a practice long followed by the U.S. Navy. At the rendezvous, the recruit was interviewed and given a physical. Upon passing the tests, the recruit signed shipping articles that corresponded with the descriptive roll used by the army and was assigned to a receiving ship for training.

The navy also followed the U.S. Navy practice of stationing receiving ships at major ports. These ships served as barracks and training areas for the sailors before they shipped off to a regular assignment. Each receiving ship had a small complement of officers and petty officers to act as instructors. Here the new sailor literally "learned the ropes." The basic rank assigned a raw recruit was landsman; after some training he was promoted to ordinary seaman and then to seaman—the same enlisted rank structure used by the Union navy. The initiate received instruction in seamanship, gunnery, naval regulations and discipline, and a seaman's life in general. The Confederate navy had receiving ships, at one time or another, at Wilmington, North Carolina, Mobile, Alabama, Charleston, South Carolina, Savannah, Georgia, New Orleans, Louisiana, and Norfolk, Virginia.

In an effort to increase its strength, the navy frequently requested men from the army, but the army was reluctant to release any. In early 1862, the navy offered a bounty of fifty dollars to any man who enlisted for three years. This offer met with only limited success. One source of manpower overlooked by the navy was the slave population. The Confederate navy did not enlist African Americans in any large numbers, unlike the Federal navy, which recruited nearly nine thousand black sailors.

The Confederate conscription acts of April 1862, October 1862, and May 1863 allowed men with seafaring experience who had enlisted in the army to transfer to the navy. In March 1864 Congress passed the General Conscription Law, which ordered the army to release 1,200 men to the navy; 960 men were transferred. By the end of 1864 the Confederate navy had reached its manpower peak of 3,674 enlisted men, but more were still needed, and convicts were ordered to serve aboard warships.

The one area in which recruitment went well was the oceangoing navy. The raiding cruisers that sailed the high seas interdicting Union shipping had little trouble acquiring personnel. Most of these seamen were of foreign birth and signed on for the prize money.

The navy had started with a dearth of men and ships, but within four years it had made some progress in creating a viable naval force. The officers and men served their cause well and earned the respect of their adversaries.

BIBLIOGRAPHY

Jones, Virgil Carrington. *The Civil War at Sea.* 3 vols. New York, 1960.

Scharf, John Thomas. *History of the Confederate States Navy.* 2 vols. New York, 1887. Reprint, New York, 1977.

Spencer, Warren F. *The Confederate Navy in Europe.* University, Ala., 1983.

QUARTERMASTER'S WHARF, ALEXANDRIA, VIRGINIA. African American dockworkers crowding a wharf on the James River. Photograph by Mathew Brady, c. 1863. NATIONAL ARCHIVES

Turner, Maxine T. *Navy Gray: The Story of the Confederate Navy on the Chattahoochee and Apalachicola Rivers.* Tuscaloosa, Ala., 1988.

DAVID L. VALUSKA

African Americans in the Confederate Navy

The Confederate navy never adopted a policy comparable to the Federal navy regarding the utilization of blacks in the naval service. From the outset of the war the Union navy employed African Americans aboard ship in an integrated fashion, and approximately 9 percent of the Federal navy was black. These men could be recruited in the ranks of landsman, ordinary seaman, and seaman, and by 1863, they were also receiving pay equal to that of white shipmates. There was no similar program in the Confederate navy, and any blacks brought on board were slaves. It is difficult to find any record of free blacks serving aboard ship.

The Southern navy employed slaves in many different ways within the service: they worked in navy yards and armament factories, constructed naval land batteries, and filled noncombat roles on board ships. In an act passed on February 17, 1863, the Confederate Congress authorized the rental of 20,000 slaves for service in workshops and hospitals run by the military. The Selma Naval Ordnance Works, among other such plants, augmented their work force with rented slaves.

On March 13, 1865, less than a month before Appomattox, President Jefferson Davis signed an act providing for the recruitment of 300,000 slaves into the military. But it was too late for the Confederate navy to benefit from the act.

BIBLIOGRAPHY

Turner, Maxine T. *Navy Gray: A Story of the Confederate Navy on the Chattahoochee and Apalachicola Rivers.* Tuscaloosa, Ala., 1988.

Wells, Tom Henderson. *The Confederate Navy: A Study in Organization.* University, Ala., 1971.

DAVID L. VALUSKA

NELSON, ALLISON (1822–1862), brigadier general. Nelson was born March 11, 1822, in Fulton County,

Georgia. After studying law, he was admitted to the Georgia bar. He served as mayor of Atlanta in 1844 and as a member of the Georgia legislature from 1849 to 1853. When war broke out with Mexico, Nelson raised a volunteer company and was elected its captain. In 1855, he moved to Texas and became an Indian agent there under Lawrence Sullivan Ross. Commissioned a captain in the Texas State Forces during the Indian campaigns just prior to the Civil War, Nelson distinguished himself as an able and aggressive commander. His gallantry won him a seat in the legislature in 1860, and he participated in the secession convention, voting for secession.

When Texas seceded, Nelson was instrumental in raising the Tenth Texas Infantry Regiment and was elected colonel. After being accepted into Confederate service, the Tenth Texas reported to Gen. Thomas C. Hindman in Arkansas. Nelson participated in a planned amphibious operation against St. Charles, Arkansas, on June 17, 1862, but it was halted at the last moment when it was learned that the Federals had occupied the town. Nelson's aggressiveness in the St. Charles operation led General Hindman to appoint him to brigade command in his newly organized division. Nelson's brigade consisted of his own Tenth Infantry plus three dismounted Texas cavalry regiments and an Arkansas regiment. In the engagement at DeVall's Bluff, July 6, 1862, his bravery and aggressiveness caused both Hindman and Maj. Gen. Theophilus H. Holmes, the Trans-Mississippi Department commander, to recommend him for promotion to brigadier general. The Confederate government promoted him effective September 12, 1862. But on the twenty-eighth, the day after he received his command, the Second Division of Holmes's infantry, Nelson became ill with typhoid fever. He died in camp near Austin, Arkansas, on October 7 and was buried in Little Rock.

BIBLIOGRAPHY

Fitzhugh, Lester N., comp. *Texas Batteries, Battalions, Regiments, Commanders, and Field Officers, Confederate States Army, 1861–1865.* Midlothian, Tex., 1959.

Roberts, O. M. *Texas.* Vol. 11 of *Confederate Military History.* Edited by Clement A. Evans. Atlanta, 1899. Vol. 15 of extended ed. Wilmington, N.C., 1989.

ROY R. STEPHENSON

NEUSE. A light-draft *Albemarle* class ironclad ram, the *Neuse* was 158 feet long and 37 feet wide, and drew nearly 8 feet of water. It carried two 6.4-inch Brooke rifles in a 22-inch-thick wooden casemate covered with 4 inches of rolled iron plate.

Pursuant to an October 17, 1862, contract between the Navy Department and Thomas S. Howard and Ellizah W. Ellis, *Neuse* was laid down at White Hall, North Carolina, on the banks of the river for which it was named. Launched in March 1863, the flat-bottomed ironclad was taken downriver to Kinston to be equipped with machinery, armament, iron plate, and other necessary fittings. Delays in receiving various materials prevented *Neuse's* completion for another year.

On April 22, 1864, *Neuse* ran fast aground on a sandbar barely one-half mile from Kinston after being ordered to take part in an attack on the nearby port of New Bern. Freed by rising waters the following month, *Neuse* returned to its familiar moorings at Kinston where it remained until fired by its crew to prevent capture March 12, 1865. Efforts to recover the ship's hull began in 1961 and were successfully completed in 1963. The hull is on display at the Caswell-*Neuse* State Historic Site in Kinston.

[*See illustration on next page.*]

BIBLIOGRAPHY

Bright, Leslie S., William H. Rowland, and James C. Bardon. *C.S.S. Neuse: A Question of Iron and Time.* Raleigh, N.C., 1981.

Still, William N. "Career of the Confederate Ironclad *Neuse.*" *North Carolina Historical Review* 43 (January 1966): 1–13.

Still, William N. *Iron Afloat: The Story of the Confederate Armorclads.* 2d ed. Columbia, S.C., 1985.

A. ROBERT HOLCOMBE, JR.

NEW MADRID AND ISLAND NUMBER 10. An operation at New Madrid and Island Number 10 in March and April 1862 opened to Union forces the Mississippi River up to Fort Pillow, Tennessee. In April 1861, Brig. Gen. Gideon Pillow began fortifying the Tennessee bluffs overlooking the Mississippi River and the eastern side of Island Number 10 to halt Union navigation. Ten miles downriver, at New Madrid, Missouri, Confederate warships supported a substantial redoubt that guarded the western approaches to New Madrid Bend, an elongated, crescent-shaped peninsula that cradled Island Number 10.

When Maj. Gen. Leonidas Polk abandoned Columbus, Kentucky, February 29 through March 2, 1862, he sent John Porter McCown (promoted to major general March 10) with 5,000 men and numerous cannons to reinforce the 2,000 soldiers already garrisoning New Madrid and Island Number 10. A floating battery augmented the defenses, now the uppermost on the Mississippi.

Opposing McCown was Maj. Gen. John Pope's Army of the Mississippi and Flag Officer Andrew H. Foote's six gunboats and eleven mortar boats. On March 3 Pope surrounded New Madrid with 18,000 soldiers, but fifty heavy guns ashore supported by gunboats necessitated a siege. While awaiting the arrival and deployment of siege cannons, the Federals fended off M. Jeff Thompson's troopers in their rear. On March 13 Pope commenced a massive bombardment that quickly convinced Confederate

CSS *Neuse* (1864–1865). A bow view of the ship's hull, displayed at Kingston, North Carolina, c. 1964.

Naval Historical Center, Washington, D.C.

navy Capt. George N. Hollins to withdraw his gunboats. That night McCown ordered the evacuation of New Madrid and transferred his garrison to the peninsula across the river to avoid being trapped on the north shore.

McCown's abandonment of the west bank severed river communication with and supply of Island Number 10 and that, coupled with the virtually impassable swamps east of New Madrid Bend, effectively trapped the garrison on the peninsula and island, from which McCown nevertheless refused to withdraw. Abandonment of New Madrid cost McCown his command on March 31. His successor, Brig. Gen. William W. Mackall, also chose not to withdraw.

Pope's men occupied the deserted New Madrid fortifications on March 14. A few days later Foote's flotilla proved unable to silence the batteries upriver. Pope now determined to isolate the entire Confederate garrison. He set his men to cut a canal through the swamps on the west bank so that shallow-draft steamboats could bypass the Confederate river batteries.

To enable the gunboats to run the gauntlet, forty-five volunteers landed near the uppermost battery. They dispersed its guard, spiked six guns, and escaped safely. The canal was finished April 4 and that night during a storm *Carondelet* successfully passed the island. At 2:00 A.M. on the seventh, *Pittsburg* ran the batteries. By noon, four steamers were landing four regiments on the east bank. While the infantry cut Mackall's only line of retreat via the road to Tiptonville, Union sailors silenced the river batteries upstream.

Trapped, Mackall on April 8 surrendered some 6,000 men, including over 1,500 sick, with all their equipment and ordnance; the balance of the garrison escaped through the swamps. The combined operations cost the Federals 17 killed, 34 wounded, and 3 captured or missing; the Confederates had 17 killed and 6,976 captured, of whom a few were wounded. This Union success convinced President Abraham Lincoln to select Pope to command the newly formed Army of Virginia.

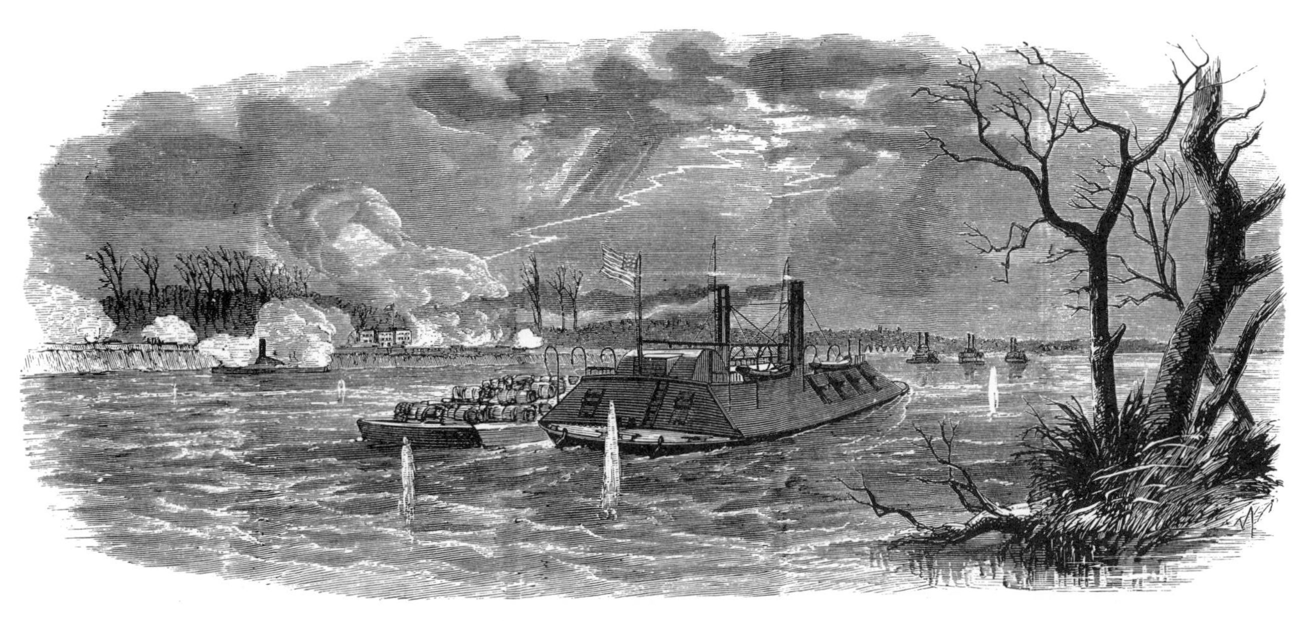

THE FEDERAL SHIP *CARDONDELET* RUNNING CONFEDERATE BATTERIES AT ISLAND NUMBER 10.

HARPER'S PICTORIAL HISTORY OF THE GREAT REBELLION

BIBLIOGRAPHY

Greene, Francis V. *The Mississippi*. Vol. 8 of *Campaigns of the Civil War*. New York, 1885. Reprint, Wilmington, N.C., 1989.

Mullen, Jay C. "Pope's New Madrid and Island Number Ten Campaign." *Missouri Historical Review* 49 (1965): 325–343.

Schutz, Wallace J., and Walter N. Trenerry. *Abandoned by Lincoln: A Military Biography of General John Pope*. Champaign, Ill., 1990.

White, Lonnie J. "Federal Operations at New Madrid and Island Number Ten." *West Tennessee Historical Society Papers* 17 (1963): 47–67.

LAWRENCE L. HEWITT

NEW MARKET, VIRGINIA. The little town of New Market was the site of an important Confederate victory on May 14, 1864, that kept the vital Shenandoah Valley in Southern hands most of the last summer of the war. Federal plans for the spring of 1864 called for a three-pronged operation against Confederate positions in Virginia. While large Union armies moved on the Southerners in southeastern and central Virginia, a third invasion menaced the strategic Shenandoah Valley, an agriculturally important area between the Blue Ridge and Allegheny mountain ranges.

This third thrust into the Old Dominion consisted of two parts. One force would move from West Virginia into the upper (southern) Shenandoah Valley to cut the Virginia and Tennessee Railroad, damage the saltworks at Saltville and the lead mines at Wytheville, and then move on Lynchburg or Staunton. Meanwhile, another column, some 9,000 men under Maj. Gen. Franz Sigel, would march into the lower (northern) part of the valley to distract the Confederates, keep them from sending reinforcements to other points, and perhaps meet the column from the west. Sigel's advance got underway in late April.

The Confederates defending the area were also divided. Brig. Gen. John D. Imboden commanded 2,000 men in the lower Shenandoah Valley; Maj. Gen. John C. Breckinridge with 6,700 men was charged with defending the upper valley. In early May Breckinridge was given authority over all Confederates in the valley. Wisely, the Southerners chose to concentrate the bulk of their available forces against Sigel. His advance menaced the lower and middle valley, and he might turn east, cross the Blue Ridge, and join in the attack on the main Southern army in central Virginia.

Leaving some of his men to guard key areas in southwestern Virginia, Breckinridge hurried to unite with Imboden. As he went, he called out local reserve forces, including the 250 members of the Corps of Cadets from the Virginia Military Institute in Lexington. When he got all his available force together, Breckinridge had about 5,300 men with whom to meet Sigel's column. On the rainy day of May 15 the two forces collided at New Market.

The battle was a simple one, fought in a small area between the North Fork of the Shenandoah River on the west and Smith's Creek to the east. Breckinridge deployed his small army on an east-west line across the southern part of the battlefield. The Federals occupied a parallel line to the north, though not all their units had reached the field.

Breckinridge originally planned to fight a defensive battle. He hoped to lure Sigel into attacking a strong fortified position and trusted that the usual advantage enjoyed by the defense over the offensive would offset the numerical superiority of the Federals. When they refused to take the bait, Breckinridge decided to strengthen the left of his line and attack at the spot where the terrain offered some advantage to his men. At about 11:30 A.M. the Confederate advance lurched forward. By that time Sigel had begun to pull back to a position north of New Market.

In midafternoon, as Breckinridge pushed ahead, his men began to take heavy casualties. A gap opened in his line, and the Southerners feared that Sigel would see it and launch a countercharge. The only reserve was the Corps of Cadets, and Breckinridge reluctantly threw it into the line. The gap was plugged, and Confederate fire soon halted feeble Federal efforts at a counterblow. Sigel began to withdraw from the field. By 3:00 P.M. momentum had shifted to the Southerners, and they began the final charge of the day. As the Federals withdrew, the Confederates occupied the field.

About 6,300 Union troops had fought at New Market; 96 had been killed, 520 wounded, and 225 captured or missing. Breckinridge had sent about 4,100 men into the fight. Partial reports indicate that he lost at least 43 killed, 474 wounded, and 3 captured.

After the battle Breckinridge transferred most of his little command across the Blue Ridge to reinforce the main Confederate army then engaged in desperate fighting north of Richmond. By the time the Federals in the Shenandoah Valley managed to get themselves organized for another advance, the situation near Richmond had stabilized, and the Southerners were able to dispatch enough reinforcements to hold the valley through the summer of 1864.

Had New Market been a Federal victory, the Confederates would have lost control of the Shenandoah Valley in the spring of 1864. Deprived of the valley and its agricultural produce, they probably would have been unable to hold out as long as they did. Because it enabled the Southerners to retain possession of the valley, New Market has been called "the biggest little battle of the war."

BIBLIOGRAPHY

Davis, William C. *The Battle of New Market.* New York, 1975.

Davis, William C. *Breckinridge: Statesman, Soldier, Symbol.* Baton Rouge, La., 1974.

Turner, E. Raymond. *The New Market Campaign, May, 1864.* Richmond, Va., 1912.

RICHARD M. MCMURRY

NEW MEXICO. War between North and South profoundly affected the region between Texas and California. In 1860, little more than a decade after the United States seized the area from Mexico, census takers reported 93,516 residents in New Mexico Territory, most in the northeastern quarter, around Santa Fe. The number included no slaves, only 85 free blacks, and only a small number of settlers from any American state, North or South.

Beginning in July 1861, Confederate forces from Texas under Lt. Col. John R. Baylor and Brig. Gen. Henry H. Sibley moved up from El Paso to take control of the territory. In the months that followed, they gave the Union commander, Lt. Col. Edward R. S. Canby, all he could handle and swept all the way to Albuquerque and Santa Fe. In early 1862, Confederate and Union forces clashed in two major battles. One (February 21, 1862), a Confederate victory, took place near the Rio Grande at Valverde, between Fort Craig and Socorro. The second, and deciding, one (March 26 and 28, 1862) was at Glorieta Pass, on the Santa Fe Trail, southeast of Santa Fe. When Union forces, most of them from Colorado Territory, destroyed the Confederate supply train, the fighting at Glorieta resulted in a Union victory sometimes termed "the Gettysburg of the West." The Confederacy found itself forced to give up its dreams of controlling the area and using it as a route to southern California and the Pacific Ocean.

In February 1863, the U.S. Congress enacted a bill establishing Arizona as a separate territory, one that, unlike the Confederacy's counterpart measure the previous year, comprised the western half of the area rather than the southern half. At first, war among whites only encouraged the Navahos' raiding parties, but Kit Carson led a force that, through 1864, defeated the Navahos, burned their fields, slaughtered most of their sheep, and forced the "Long Walk," an evacuation from the Four Corners area to an exile at Bosque Redondo in eastern New Mexico.

[*See also* Glorieta Pass, New Mexico.]

BIBLIOGRAPHY

Colton, Ray C. *The Civil War in the Western Territories: Arizona, Colorado, New Mexico, and Utah.* Norman, Okla., 1959.

Hall, Martin Hardwick. *Sibley's New Mexico Campaign.* Austin, Tex., 1960.

Josephy, Alvin M., Jr. *The Civil War in the West.* New York, 1991.

Lamar, Howard Roberts. *The Far Southwest, 1846–1912: A Territorial History.* New Haven, Conn., 1966.

PETER WALLENSTEIN

NEW ORLEANS, LOUISIANA. [*This entry includes two articles,* City of New Orleans, *which profiles the city during the Confederacy, and* Capture of New Orleans, *which discusses the Federal capture of the city in 1862.*]

City of New Orleans

The South's largest and most cosmopolitan city, New Orleans had the briefest of stints under Confederate

THE FRENCH QUARTER IN NEW ORLEANS AROUND THE MIDDLE OF THE NINETEENTH CENTURY.

HARPER'S PICTORIAL HISTORY OF THE GREAT REBELLION

authority. Fifteen months after Louisiana seceded, the Crescent City was back under Union rule after Adm. David G. Farragut dropped anchor outside the levee on April 25, 1862.

Pinched into a shallow clay saucer between Lake Pontchartrain and the Mississippi, New Orleans derives its nickname from the huge crescent bend that the river describes near the French Quarter. Most of the city's 168,000 residents in 1860 hugged the high ground near the river levee, on either side of Canal Street, which historically separates Gallic downtown and Anglo uptown. It was a population of infinite ethnic variety and romantic charm. To the original white creole population (of mixed French and Spanish ancestry) were added, during the antebellum period, heavy infusions of Protestant Americans from both North and South, continuing inputs of foreign French—often refugees from the French and Haitian revolutions—and a huge influx of German and Irish immigration. Even driblets of Italian settlement had reached the Crescent City prior to the Civil War. Comprising nearly 40 percent of the 1860 population, New Orleans's foreign-born community loomed larger than any other Southern city's at the time. Although only one-sixth the size of the white population, the black population in 1860 was also ethnically diverse. In addition to slaves, New Orleans was home to the most prosperous and sophisticated free black community in the United States, which itself was split between the more numerous Francophone Catholics and a small coterie of Protestant African Americans.

New Orleans's heterogeneity, plus the city's historic trade ties with the upper Mississippi valley, rendered secession difficult. John C. Breckinridge, the Southern rights candidate in 1860, ran third in every district of the city. John Slidell, one of New Orleans's two Democratic U.S. senators, blamed Breckinridge's poor showing on the fact that "here in the city seven-eighths of the vote for [Stephen] Douglas were cast by the Irish and Germans." The Crescent City's business community, a substantial element of which hailed from the Northeast, was also tugged toward Unionism by trade and shipping connections with the free states. But for the hysteria aroused by well-organized Southern nationalist groups—helped by Presbyterian minister Benjamin M. Palmer's fire-breathing Thanksgiving Day sermon—the city's immediate secessionists, in the January 7, 1861, election, might not have won a 52 to 48 percent victory for their delegate slate to the state's secessionist convention. Voter turnout was noticeably lower than it had been in the presidential election two months earlier.

Although divided in secession, New Orleans was momentarily united in war. Some of the contagion of the city's being a troop-mustering center spread to the local population. Uptown New Orleans's famed Washington Artillery, which traced its military tradition back to the Mexican War, entrained for Virginia in May to a citywide send-off. A variety of privately outfitted Zouave units also enlisted in the Confederacy. So did assorted ethnic regiments: the French and creole populations set the pace, but various German and Irish units followed close behind. Polyglot New Orleans also furnished a Garibaldi Legion, a Spanish Legion, a Scandinavian Guard, a Polish Brigade, a Scotch Rifle Guard, a Belgian Guard, two companies of Slavonian Rifles, and a company of Greek citizens wearing the national Albanian uniform. Tracing its military tradition back to the colonial period, the city's Franco-African population also offered its services to the Confederacy, but because the idea of black soldiers contradicted Confederate racial nationalism, their Native Guard was mustered into the state militia only.

As the gateway to the Mississippi valley, the country's second leading port early on felt squeezed by the Union blockade. After May 26, 1861, when the USS *Brooklyn* anchored off the mouth of the Mississippi, ocean vessels ceased docking in the Crescent City, although some coastal shipping slipped into the city through the lake. From the summer onward, trade stagnated, prices soared, and necessities like coal and food grew scarce. The city council tried to fend off destitution by establishing a free market in the new ironworks building at the foot of Canal Street, where foodstuffs supplied by local planters were distributed to poor families. In September the banks, by order of the Confederacy, suspended specie payments, drying up the supply of small change and giving rise to a variety of makeshift expedients (like streetcar tickets). Meanwhile, military recruiters siphoned some of the unemployed, mainly the Irish poor, into Confederate armies.

Because the Union brass was determined to split the Confederacy by seizing the Mississippi, it was only a matter of time before a joint army-navy expedition took aim at the Crescent City. The War of 1812 had made local authorities conscious that such an attack was likely, but work on local defenses lagged under Maj. Gen. David Twigg, who was in command of New Orleans and vicinity until October 1861. Twigg's replacement, Mansfield Lovell, who had been a New York City street commissioner only weeks before moving to the South (he was an unpopular choice because favorite sons like P. G. T. Beauregard had been passed over), invigorated the work of military preparedness, creating powder works, helping local foundries convert to armament production, supervising naval shipbuilding, and completing work on exterior entrenchments. The press extolled his "restless activity." One item of local defense that Lovell pushed to conclusion was the cypress log raft, tied together with chains and huge timbers, that reached between opposite banks of the Mississippi, near Fort Jackson and Fort St. Phillip, seventy-five miles downriver from New Orleans.

This manmade invasion barrier proved porous. Proceeding from their staging area at Ship Island (which guarded the approaches to the lake), Union Adm. David G. Farragut's seventeen-ship fleet, together with twenty mortar schooners under Como. David Porter, and a fifteen-thousand-man army recruited in New England by Maj. Gen. Benjamin F. Butler, reached the two forts by mid-April, and, after a five-day mortar bombardment, cut the river chain and ran the gauntlet on April 24. The following day Farragut's naval guns were peering over the levee of a panic-stricken city, many of whose defenders had just been sent to reinforce the collapsing Confederate line in Tennessee and Mississippi.

For a few days Mayor John Monroe defied Farragut's surrender order, galvanizing some of the nativist thugs whose votes and fists had put him into office. "We don't want you here, damn it!" a menacing mob yelled at the first Union officers to come ashore. Farragut threatened to cannonade the city into submission, despite pleas from foreign consuls. In the meantime, General Lovell had evacuated his troops from the city, and drayloads of cotton and sugar, corn and rice, were brought to the riverfront and set afire. Monroe capitulated when word arrived that the downriver forts had surrendered on April 28 (in part because immigrant troops from New Orleans had mutinied). When Ben Butler's troops clambered down the gangplank on May 1, 1862, New Orleans joined New York as one of only two major cities in U.S. history to undergo enemy occupation for an extended period. For the next three years Union-occupied New Orleans served as the nerve center of the newly formed Department of the Gulf.

Because the Crescent City was a command headquarters in a combat zone, military security took first priority, and Ben Butler wasted little time in bringing the turbulent population to heel. He hanged a professional gambler, William Mumford, for lowering the U.S. flag that Farragut had hoisted over the Federal mint. He silenced females who acted insultingly toward Union soldiers by issuing an edict directing that they be treated as streetwalkers—and acquired the nickname "Beast." (The Davis government in retaliation placed a bounty on Butler's head.) He seized newspapers, censored sermons, and made schoolteachers swear allegiance to the Union. He even threatened to confiscate the hotel where he made his headquarters when the proprietor refused to serve him breakfast. And when Mayor Monroe kept up his obstructionism, Butler had him incarcerated for the duration of the war. Thereafter New Orleans's municipal affairs were administered by a succession of military-appointed mayors.

In local legend Butler was also known as "Spoons" for allegedly helping himself to family silver (the corruption charge is probably truer of his brother). But historians better remember Butler, a skillful Massachusetts politician, for sponsoring a new political and social order in the Crescent City. President Lincoln looked on New Orleans as a promising location in which to field-test various emancipation and Reconstruction experiments. Butler galvanized working-class immigrant Unionism by putting destitute Irish and Germans to work cleaning canals and streets, which he financed by taxing wealthy Confederates. He accommodated the slaves' yearning for freedom by ordering that they be paid wages. He accepted the military services of a black creole regiment (the Corps d'Afrique, which was disbanded by Butler's successor), thereby encouraging the city's influential free people of color to follow the lead of its philosophical radicals, men like the Roudanez brothers, Charles and Louis, and Paul Trevigne. By the time Butler was replaced seven months later, the nucleus of an interracial political party called the Free State movement had taken shape in New Orleans.

A Massachusetts politician like his predecessor, Maj. Gen. Nathaniel P. Banks extended and modified Butler's race and Reconstruction policies after taking command of the Department of the Gulf in December 1862. But Banks sought to conciliate upper-class conservative Unionists by clamping down on the black population, both freeborn and slave, and dampening the indigenous drive to extend the vote to creoles of color. When Lincoln's Ten Percent Plan took effect in December 1863—restoring civil government whenever one-tenth of the 1860 voting population resumed their Unionist allegiance—Banks helped ensure that a top-down coalition of white Unionists took control. Although the state was returned to civil rule (albeit under military supervision) in 1864, New Orleans continued to be administered by occupying authorities for the duration of the war.

New Orleans's status as an occupied city officially ended when John Monroe was reelected mayor in March 1866. It was under Monroe's administration that the police massacre known as the New Orleans Riot of 1866 occurred. Many of the policemen were probably the same plug-uglies who had jeered Farragut's officers when they first stepped ashore four years earlier.

[*See also* Butler's Woman Order; Creoles.]

BIBLIOGRAPHY

Bragg, Jefferson Davis. *Louisiana in the Confederacy.* Baton Rouge, La., 1941.

Capers, Gerald M., Jr. "Confederates and Yankees in Occupied New Orleans, 1862–1865." *Journal of Southern History* 30 (November 1964): 405–426.

Dufour, Charles L. *The Night the War Was Lost.* New York, 1960.

McCrary, Peyton. *Abraham Lincoln and Reconstruction: The Louisiana Experiment.* Princeton, N.J., 1978.

Ripley, C. Peter. *Slaves and Freedmen in Civil War Louisiana.* Baton Rouge, La., 1976.

Winters, John D. *The Civil War in Louisiana.* Baton Rouge, La., 1963.

LAWRENCE N. POWELL

Capture of New Orleans

Despite the strategic and commercial importance of New Orleans, Union authorities did not turn their attention to the Crescent City until November 15, 1861. Although his Southern heritage raised doubts about his loyalty, Capt. David G. Farragut was assigned to command the naval forces; Maj. Gen. Benjamin F. Butler led the army contingent. Union forces first concentrated on Ship Island in the Gulf of Mexico, which led Confederate officials to conclude that their objective was Mobile or Pensacola, not New Orleans. By early April 1862, when Farragut's ships entered the Mississippi River, troop transfers had reduced the defenses of New Orleans to little more than 4,500 militia scattered among the masonry forts that protected the city.

Two forts, eighty miles downriver, guarded the Mississippi: Jackson on the west bank and St. Philip, eight hundred yards north, on the east bank. A chain floated on barges barricaded the river, although high water had partially destroyed this obstacle in late February and again on April 11. An unusual fleet supported the five hundred men and eighty cannon in the forts: three ironclads (the ram *Manassas,* the underpowered *Louisiana* anchored above St. Philip as a floating battery, and the unfinished *Mississippi*), fire barges, and nine other vessels divided

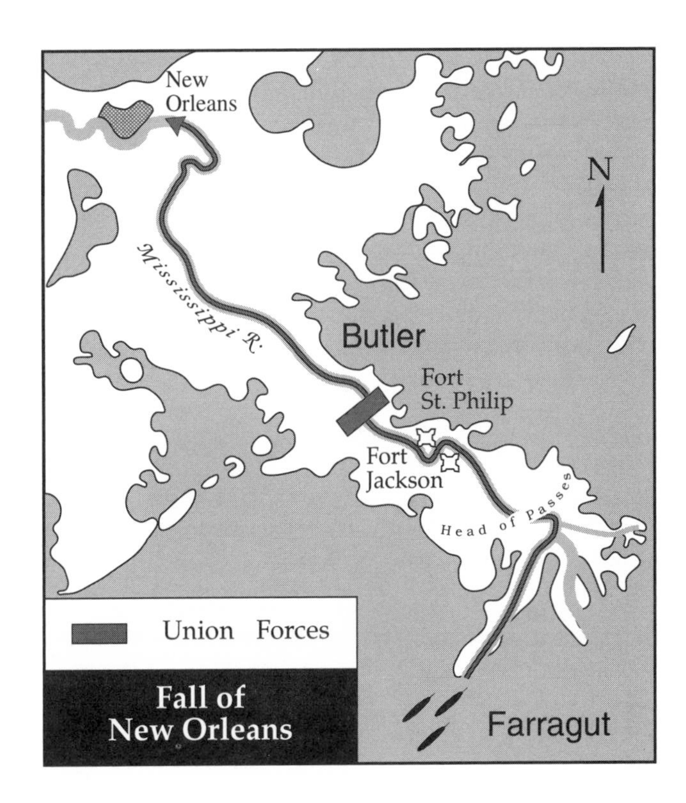

Fall of New Orleans

among the Confederate navy, the Louisiana navy, and the river defense fleet.

Just above Head of Passes on April 8 Farragut assembled twenty-four wooden vessels, mounting about two hundred guns, and Commdr. David D. Porter's nineteen mortar schooners, each carrying one 13-inch mortar. On April 18 the mortars began a bombardment that Porter believed would silence the forts, thus permitting Farragut's ships to pass them safely. During an eight-hour period that day, Porter fired 2,997 rounds into Fort Jackson. But Farragut, lacking faith in the mortars, had his vessels open a channel through the barricade during the night of April 20. Although the mortars failed to silence Jackson, at 2:00 A.M. on the twenty-fourth, Farragut's fleet steamed upriver. By dawn, twenty-one of his vessels had successfully passed the barricade and the forts. Then, in a free-for-all, Farragut's ships avoided the bull-like charges of *Manassas* and the fire rafts and destroyed the enemy's flotilla. Farragut lost the converted merchantman *Varuna,* and 171 sailors were killed or wounded. The forts' defenders had sustained fewer than 50 casualties.

Leaving two gunboats above the forts to support Butler's troops marching overland from their gulf landing toward the rear of St. Philip, Farragut continued upriver to New Orleans. The city, now undefended since Confederate Maj. Gen. Mansfield Lovell had evacuated it, fell on April 25. Civilian authorities formally surrendered on the twenty-eighth. With the city lost and Union infantry closing in, most of Brig. Gen. Johnson Kelly Duncan's men in the forts mutinied, and he surrendered the same day. Butler occupied New Orleans on May 1. A court of inquiry cleared Lovell on July 9, 1863, of any responsibility for the loss of the city. The onus fell upon the Richmond government for having stripped the garrison of its troops and having failed to place Lovell in command of all naval forces. In all, the Federals had lost 39 men killed and 171 wounded while taking the city. The Confederates had lost 85 men killed, 113 wounded, and approximately 900 captured.

BIBLIOGRAPHY

Dufour, Charles L. *The Night the War Was Lost.* Garden City, N.Y., 1960.

Heleniak, Roman J., and Lawrence L. Hewitt, eds. *The 1989 Deep Delta Civil War Symposium: Leadership during the Civil War.* Shippensburg, Pa., 1992.

Lewis, Charles L. *David Glasgow Farragut.* 2 vols. Annapolis, Md., 1941–1943.

Mahan, Alfred T. *Admiral Farragut.* Great Commanders Series. New York, 1892.

LAWRENCE L. HEWITT

NEW PLAN. The *New Plan* was the name given to a series of administrative actions and congressional laws whose object was to evade the blockade and put Confederate finances abroad on a cash basis. President Jefferson Davis authorized this program in 1863 and 1864. The indispensable first step was the appointment of an agent to supervise fund-raising abroad. Colin J. McRae, a former Confederate congressman, accepted this appointment and went to Paris. In September 1863, after carefully surveying the situation, he sent President Davis a series of recommendations that became the New Plan.

First, McRae suggested that he be given full authority to allocate scarce Confederate funds abroad among the conflicting claims of the War and Navy departments' procurement offices. In addition, no agents were to sign contracts without securing McRae's approval for the payment terms.

Second, the government should stop making contracts payable in cotton. The Confederacy was spending six hundred dollars in cotton to get one hundred dollars worth of goods. If the contractors could ship cotton out of the country, there was no reason the government could not do so on its own account.

Third, McRae urged that the government employ its powers over foreign commerce to regulate imports and exports. The practice of blockade runners bringing in luxury goods and refusing to take government cotton cargoes had to be stopped.

Fourth, McRae asked that he be appointed a Confederate Depositary at Paris and that as bursar he alone be authorized to make payments for goods purchased by government procurement agents.

McRae's suggestions met with President Davis's approval. Davis then authorized Secretary of State Judah P. Benjamin to arbitrate the differences among the War, Navy, and Treasury departments and to formulate a specific program to implement McRae's recommendations. Meanwhile, in late 1863, the War Department empowered its officers to preempt a third of all outbound cargo space for the export of government cotton.

Secretary Benjamin swiftly carried out his mandate. Acting on the suggestions of John Slidell, the Confederate commissioner to Paris, which largely coincided with McRae's views, he armed McRae with full powers to supervise other agents, to coordinate their actions, and to control all payments. Benjamin then drafted an agreement and got his cabinet colleagues' assent to coordinate their policies and not to enter into any more agreements with private contractors. It then proved an easy matter to induce a lame-duck Congress to enact other key parts of the government plan.

By one act passed on February 6, 1864, Congress empowered the president to prohibit the exportation of staple produce except under regulations of his own devising. The only exemption (in deference to state rights sentiment) was for state-owned blockade runners. A second act, passed the same day, expressly prohibited the importation of items "not of common necessity and use." This put a stop to the cargoes of brandy, silks, and jewelry that did little to feed or clothe the army or the people.

Finally, President Davis promulgated a whole series of regulations to put the plan into effect. All government cotton became the property of the Treasury Department, and the War Department was empowered to collect Treasury cotton and export it. To finance this effort, $20 million was appropriated, Lt. Col. Thomas L. Bayne was made bureau chief, and half of all incoming and outgoing cargo space was reserved for the government. In addition, McRae was authorized to purchase a fleet of blockade runners.

These measures encountered considerable opposition. Resistance centered on the government's control of cargo space. State rights advocates were alienated because state sovereignty did not protect ships leased by state governments. Blockade-running firms attempted to exempt themselves from the regulations by leasing their ships to the states or by refusing to sail. President Davis, however, remained adamant. Ships not authentically operated under state authority were compelled to follow the new rules, and ultimately the shippers yielded.

Government finances abroad were greatly improved. By December 1864, James Seddon, the secretary of war, reported that over 27,299 bales of cotton had been exported, for $5.3 million of sales. Only 1,272 bales were lost, despite

Wartime Press." In *South Carolina Journals and Journalists.* Edited by James B. Meriwether. Spartanburg, S.C., 1975.
Griffith, Louis Turner, and John Erwin Talmadge. *Georgia Journalism, 1763–1950.* Athens, Ga., 1951.
Jobe, Nat. "Edward Alfred Pollard: Symbol of Opposition." In *Divided We Fall: Essays on Confederate Nation Building.* Edited by John M. Belohlavek and Lewis N. Wynne. Saint Leo, Fla., 1991.
Trexler, Harrison A. "The Davis Administration and the Richmond Press, 1861–1865." *Journal of Southern History* 16 (May 1950): 177–195.

CHARLES MCARVER

NICARAGUA. At independence in 1823, Nicaragua's population was about 84 percent ladino (Hispanicized people of mixed racial origins, most commonly Spanish and Indian), 2 or 3 percent Spanish or European stock, and about 12 percent Indian or black (most of whom lived on the Mosquito Coast). Slavery was abolished in the Central American Constitution of 1824, but coerced labor remained prevalent. In 1861 Nicaragua had a population of about 320,000. Gen. Tomás Martínez was president from 1857 until 1867.

The Confederacy had received a legacy of political involvement in Central America from filibusterer William Walker (seized and shot during his fourth expedition to Central America in September 1860) and Southern expansionists. Confederate leaders recognized that the isthmus was of strategic importance because it contained the only transcontinental railroad (in Panama) and a second transit route in the waterways of Nicaragua. So, while the expansionist efforts of the prewar years helped turn Confederate eyes southward, it was the imperatives of the world economic system that made that region a target of Confederate activity during the Civil War.

Andrew B. Dickinson, U.S. minister to Nicaragua, cultivated the country's friendship and labored hard to alter Nicaraguan anti-Americanism rooted in Walker's filibustering. When cotton prices rose dramatically after 1861, Nicaragua increased its cotton exports significantly. Between 1861 and 1865, its customs revenues rose markedly as trade with the United States increased. Dickinson believed that secessionist influence was responsible for an objectionable decree in November 1861 that authorized privateers to stay twenty-four hours in its ports and take on "very necessary" articles. In June of 1862, in response to his efforts, a second Nicaraguan decree permitted entry of privateers only in cases of overriding necessity and, even then, did not allow for provisioning.

The Confederate government never sent an official agent to Nicaragua, but John P. Heiss, a Southern businessman who had moved to Nicaragua in the 1850s, and Ran Runnels, U.S. consular agent in Corinto, were rumored to be serving Confederate interests. Heiss played a major role in persuading his friend President Martínez to oppose a Union project to colonize freed slaves in Central America. U.S. officials in Panama and Nicaragua were convinced that Runnels was opening U.S. mail passing through Corinto and reporting to Confederate agents about U.S. naval and diplomatic activity.

[*See also* Expansionism; Imperialism.]

BIBLIOGRAPHY

Bermann, Karl. *Under the Big Stick: Nicaragua and the United States since 1848.* Boston, 1986.
Lanuzo, Alberto, Juan Luis Vázquez, Amaru Barahona, and Amalia Chamorro. *Economía y sociedad en la construcción del estado en Nicaragua.* San José, Costa Rica, 1983.
Schoonover, Thomas. "The Confederates in Central America: Coming to Grips with the World System." In *The United States in Central America, 1860–1911: Episodes of Social Imperialism and Imperial Rivalry in the World System.* Durham, N.C., 1991.
Schoonover, Thomas. "Misconstrued Mission: Expansionism and Black Colonization in Mexico and Central America during the Civil War." *Pacific Historical Review* 49 (1980): 607–620.
Woodward, Ralph Lee, Jr. *Central America: A Nation Divided.* 2d ed. New York, 1985.

THOMAS SCHOONOVER

NICHOLLS, FRANCIS (1834–1912), brigadier general and postwar governor of Louisiana. Born August 20, 1834, at Donaldsonville, Louisiana, Francis Redding Tillou Nicholls graduated from West Point in 1855, twelfth out of thirty-four. He resigned from the army in 1856 and attended the University of Louisiana, now Tulane.

He gave up his law practice at Napoleonville when the Civil War began and entered the Confederate army as a captain in the Phoenix Guards. Selected as lieutenant colonel of the Eighth Louisiana, Nicholls fought with this regiment at First Manassas and under Thomas ("Stonewall") Jackson in the Shenandoah Valley. He lost his left arm and was taken prisoner at Winchester. Promoted to brigadier general on October 14, 1862, he returned to the army in time to lead a Louisiana brigade at Chancellorsville where his left foot was blown off by an artillery shell. Now unfit for active service, Nicholls was sent to Lynchburg, Virginia, where he commanded from August 1863 until June 1864. He was then transferred to the Trans-Mississippi Department to replace Brig. Gen. Elkanah Brackin Greer as commandant of conscripts, but E. Kirby Smith refused at first to recognize the orders. The department insisted upon the change, however, and Nicholls replaced Greer in December 1864.

Following the war, Nicholls was elected governor of Louisiana in 1876 and 1888. (It was said of his 1876 race that "all that was left of Nicholls" campaigned dutifully.) In

FRANCIS NICHOLLS. LIBRARY OF CONGRESS

his later life he served on the Louisiana supreme court. He died on January 4, 1912, and is buried at Thibodeaux.

BIBLIOGRAPHY

Dawson, John G., III. *Army Generals and Reconstruction: Louisiana, 1862–1877.* Baton Rouge, La., 1982.

Jones, Terry L. *Lee's Tigers: The Louisiana Infantry in the Army of Northern Virginia.* Baton Rouge, La., 1987.

Kerby, Robert L. *Kirby Smith's Confederacy: The Trans-Mississippi South, 1863–1865.* New York, 1972.

ANNE J. BAILEY

NISBET, EUGENIUS ARISTIDES (1803–1871), congressman from Georgia. Born in Greene County, Georgia, Nisbet was the son of an affluent physician and plantation owner. Educated at the College of South Carolina, the University of Georgia, and the law school at Litchfield, Connecticut, Nisbet settled in Madison, Georgia, where he opened a law practice in 1823. There he met and married Amanda Battle, who bore his twelve children. He became active in Whig politics, was elected to the Georgia General Assembly in 1827 and served in both houses over the next decade. He promoted prison and educational reform and pushed for the establishment of a state supreme court. In 1837, Nisbet moved to Macon and was elected to two terms in Congress in 1838 and 1840. He returned to Macon halfway through his second term to resolve financial problems. When Georgia established its state Supreme Court in 1845, he became one of its three judges, serving until 1853.

In 1855 despite his support of the state Know-Nothing movement, Nisbet began a gradual shift to the Democratic party and became an increasingly strong advocate of secession. At Georgia's secession convention in January 1861, Nisbet chaired the committee that drew up the articles of secession. He was one of ten Georgians elected to the Confederacy's Provisional Congress and served as a member of the committee to draw up the new nation's Constitution, where he was instrumental in incorporating a single presidential term of six years. He proposed Alexander H. Stephens for the vice presidency. Pushing for an export duty on cotton as the primary means of funding the Treasury, he traveled through Georgia in July to gain support for the proposal. In November 1861 he ran for governor against incumbent Joseph E. Brown, after being drafted as a candidate by an anti-Brown Know-Nothing convention. Despite his bipartisan popularity and the support of most of Georgia's newspapers, Nisbet lost the election by over fourteen thousand votes. In December, poor health forced him to resign from Congress and retire from public life.

After the war, Nisbet continued to practice law, lectured, and wrote on a variety of legal issues. In 1868 he was awarded an honorary doctorate from the University of Georgia, which he had served in a variety of capacities. He died in Macon on March 18, 1871, as the result of a cold contracted while laying the cornerstone of the city's new courthouse.

BIBLIOGRAPHY

Coleman, Kenneth, and Charles Stephen Gurr, eds. *Dictionary of Georgia Biography.* Vol. 2. Athens, Ga., 1983.

Knight, Lucian Lamar. *Reminiscences of Famous Georgians.* Vol. 1. Atlanta, 1907.

Northen, William W. *Men of Mark in Georgia.* Vol. 3. Atlanta, 1908. Reprint, Spartanburg, S.C., 1974.

Parks, Joseph. *Joseph E. Brown of Georgia.* Baton Rouge, La., 1977.

JOHN C. INSCOE

NITER AND MINING BUREAU. At the instigation of Josiah Gorgas, head of the Ordnance Department, the Confederate Congress, on April 11, 1862, passed an act establishing a niter corps as a branch of the Ordnance Department. This corps was to be composed of a superintendent, four assistants, and eight subordinates with the rank, pay, and allowances of majors, captains, and first lieutenants of artillery respectively. The primary responsibility of these officers was to procure niter (saltpeter), a mineral that comprised about 75 percent of gunpowder. To head the corps, Gorgas chose Isaac M. St. John, an able civil engineer who had supervised the construction of defenses in the Yorktown, Virginia, area.

In April 1863 the Congress passed another act that separated the corps from the Ordnance Department and made it an independent bureau, directly responsible to the War Department, under the new name of the Niter and Mining Bureau. In addition to procuring niter, the new bureau was responsible for mining or otherwise collecting and purchasing iron, copper, lead, coal, and zinc for military uses. In order to allow the bureau to perform these tasks more efficiently, the act provided for more officers and increased their rank to one lieutenant colonel, three majors, six captains, and ten lieutenants, with rank and pay equivalent to that of cavalry officers. Finally, in June 1864, a third act allowed a maximum of six chemists and six professional assistants to be attached to the bureau to aid it in the scientific aspects of mineral collection.

The Confederacy was divided into about fourteen niter and mining districts, smaller administrative units supervised by bureau officers who were responsible for the production of minerals in their area. Most of the districts were east of the Mississippi River, but the Trans-Mississippi district did provide a substantial amount of some materials, at least for its own use.

Niter could be procured by four methods. The first was importation, a means quickly jeopardized by the Union blockade, causing the bureau to seek to expand domestic production. Second, niter could be mined from certain caves with particular geologic and climatic characteristics, generally located in the mountains of Tennessee, Arkansas, Virginia, Georgia, and Alabama. Third, it could be gathered from the dirt under old buildings. Finally, niter could be manufactured artificially in carefully tended niter beds containing decomposing vegetable, animal, and human waste products. At least thirteen "nitriaries" were established in the eastern Confederacy near major cities such as Richmond, Virginia, Selma, Alabama, and Augusta, Georgia, but they required months of preparation before the beds produced much niter. Private citizens were encouraged to produce niter, and several instruction pamphlets were published to assist them. Records show that by September 30, 1864, government workers and private contractors, working caves as well as other deposits, had delivered 1,735,531.75 pounds of niter to the bureau, just slightly more than the 1,720,072 pounds that had been imported. Of this total amount, 408,905 pounds were procured in Arkansas and Texas.

Copper, to make percussion caps for firing guns as well as bronze for cannons, was another necessity. This mineral was found in few places in the Confederacy, and the bureau relied on several mines near Ducktown in Polk County, Tennessee. Incomplete reports indicate that these mines produced at least 775,000 pounds of copper before the Confederates lost control of the area in late 1863.

Niter Production to September 30, 1864

State	Total Receipts in Pounds
Virginia (5 districts)	505,584.25
North Carolina	238,907.50
South Carolina	2,008.00
Tennessee	190,307.00
Tennessee and Georgia	85,706.00
Georgia	29,913.00
Alabama (2 districts)	260,381.00
Florida	820.00
Texas and Arkansas	408,905.00
Other Virginia and Tennessee districts	13,000.00*
	1,735,531.75
Imported	1,720,072.00
Total	3,455,603.75

*Made but not delivered.

SOURCE: U.S. War Department. *War of the Rebellion: A Compilation of the Official Records of the Union and Confederate Armies.* Washington, D.C., 1880–1901. Ser. 4, vol. 3, pt. 4, pp. 698–699.

The Union Lead Mines, usually called the Wytheville Mines, in Wythe County, Virginia, were the major domestic source of lead for the Confederate states. Including materials from the Silver Hill Mines in North Carolina and the collection of scrap lead, the Confederates produced at least 2,508,079 pounds and imported about 1,368,125 pounds more by September 30, 1864. The Trans-Mississippi Department contributed 897,815 pounds of lead from Mexico and Arkansas, as well as scrap lead, to these figures.

Iron, critical not only for armaments but also for railroad repair, plating iron-clad ships, making agricultural implements, and numerous other military and civilian uses, was always in very short supply. Alabama and Virginia had the most mines and blast furnaces, but some iron was also manufactured in North Carolina, South Carolina, Tennessee, Georgia, and the Trans-Mississippi West. By September 30, 1864, the bureau had received a total of 25,354.6 tons of iron, which it carefully dispensed to what seemed the most crucial projects.

Sulphur and sulphuric acid (the latter manufactured at Charlotte, North Carolina) were being produced on a small scale of about 4,000 pounds per month by late 1864. By this time the single zinc factory, near Petersburg, Virginia, had been closed because of the proximity of Union forces.

Although all the minerals and metals to be gathered by the bureau also came through the blockade in limited quantities, most blockade runners were reluctant to bring in products such as niter and lead, which consumed

Iron Production to September 30, 1864

State	Total Receipts in Tons
Virginia	10,150.0
North Carolina	1,620.2
South Carolina	170.0
Alabama	12,405.0
Georgia	685.4
Mississippi	30.1
Tennessee	293.9
Trans-Mississippi	no records received
Total	25,354.6

SOURCE: U.S. War Department. *War of the Rebellion: A Compilation of the Official Records of the Union and Confederate Armies.* Washington, D.C., 1880–1901. Ser. 4, vol. 3, pt. 4, pp. 700–701.

considerable space and weight. In case of pursuit, the blockade runner would throw these supplies overboard first to lighten the ship. As the war progressed and greater shortages resulted, the Niter Bureau was authorized to impress raw materials as well as railroad tracks no longer in service and copper tubing from turpentine and apple brandy stills in North Carolina. After the battles around Atlanta, bureau workers scoured the battlefields collecting lead to be recycled into new bullets.

In its various endeavors the bureau employed a great many workers of different types. Exempted from military service, civilians worked as miners, carpenters, and wagon drivers, or contracted to provide livestock, other foodstuffs, or necessary construction materials. A number of the workers were men detailed from the army, in some cases because of useful prewar experience or skills. In March 1864, for example, at least 2,783 men were detailed for bureau jobs. The bureau also hired many slaves from their owners and impressed free blacks to do most of the hard labor. In September 1864, 4,557 blacks were employed at the iron mines and foundries, 1,252 mined niter, and 490, the entire nitriary staff except for superintendents, cared for the niter beds.

In addition, the bureau employed several notable chemists and geologists including John and Joseph LeConte in Columbia, South Carolina, and Nathaniel A. Pratt, the bureau chemist at the laboratory in Augusta, Georgia. These men made geological maps, sought to speed up the formation of niter in nitriaries, produced various chemicals, and inspected niter and other mines and works.

The location of most of the Confederate mines in the mountainous areas of western Virginia, eastern Tennessee, and northern Georgia and Alabama led to several types of problems. Since many of the local residents were outright Unionists or only marginally loyal to the Confederacy, they were often not very reliable workers. Conscripts and detailed men deserted and slaves ran away into the wild hilly areas near the mines. Union troops also raided the mines with increasing frequency as the war progressed, destroying equipment, capturing workers, and causing many of the installations to cease production. Finally, threats of raids and the general manpower shortage forced bureau workers into active military service, either temporarily or permanently, despite vigorous protests from bureau officers. All of these factors combined to decrease the production of niter and other necessary minerals, but the resources of the bureau were not exhausted before the war ended.

Isaac M. St. John remained in charge of the bureau until February 16, 1865, when he was promoted to brigadier general and replaced Lucius B. Northrop as commissary general. Richard Morton, who succeeded St. John on February 22, had served with St. John as an engineer on the Virginia peninsula and then as second in command of the Niter Bureau, so he was well-prepared to assume his responsibilities, which, however, lasted only a few more weeks.

[*See also* Lead; Mining; Saltpeter; St. John, Isaac M.]

BIBLIOGRAPHY

Donnelly, Ralph W. "The Bartow County Confederate Saltpetre Works." *Georgia Historical Quarterly* 54 (1970): 305–319.

Donnelly, Ralph W. "Confederate Copper." *Civil War History* 1 (1955): 355–370.

Donnelly, Ralph W. "The Confederate Lead Mines in Wythe County, Virginia." *Civil War History* 5 (1959): 402–414.

Donnelly, Ralph W. "Scientists of the Confederate Nitre and Mining Bureau." *Civil War History* 2 (1956): 69–92.

Schroeder, Glenna R. " 'We Will Support the Govt. to the Bitter End': The Augusta Office of the Confederate Nitre and Mining Bureau." *Georgia Historical Quarterly* 70 (1986): 288–305.

Sheridan, Richard C. "Production of Saltpetre from Alabama Caves." *Alabama Review* 33 (1980): 25–34.

Smith, Marion O. "The Sauta Cave Confederate Niter Works." *Civil War History* 29 (1983): 293–315.

U.S. War Department. *War of the Rebellion: A Compilation of the Official Records of the Union and Confederate Armies.* Washington, D.C., 1880–1901. Ser. 4, vols. 1–3.

Vandiver, Frank E. *Ploughshares into Swords: Josiah Gorgas and Confederate Ordnance.* Austin, Tex., 1952.

Glenna R. Schroeder-Lein

NORFOLK, VIRGINIA. Situated near the Elizabeth River's confluence with the James River at Hampton Roads, Norfolk proved important militarily in the early stages of the Civil War.

In 1860 Norfolk contained 14,620 people, of whom 3,284 were slaves. Of the free inhabitants, about 10 percent were of African descent and another 7 to 8 percent had been born in states north of Virginia. Natives of North Carolina and Ireland composed about 6 percent each, and a smaller percentage came from Germany. The majority of the population were native Virginians. Directly across the Elizabeth River lay Portsmouth, with 9,496 residents. The population of the two cities rose during the 1850s despite an 1855 epidemic of yellow fever that killed several thousand people.

Although secession sentiment surfaced in the city before the Civil War, support for preserving the Union was dominant until after the fall of Fort Sumter. The existence of the Gosport Shipyard (Norfolk Navy Yard), a Federal facility located just south of Portsmouth on the southern branch of the Elizabeth River, and the presence of the U.S. Navy throughout Hampton Roads, especially in Norfolk's harbor, encouraged the Union sentiment. On the eve of the Civil War, the Navy Yard, the biggest single employer in the district, provided work for about 1,400 local people. Its size and importance were magnified because of the relatively small manufacturing base of the private sector.

In addition, overseas exports and imports in the district totaled barely 100,000 tons in 1860—far less than the amount for the Richmond district. Coastal commerce included cotton from North Carolina, corn from eastern Virginia and North Carolina, oysters from local waters, and a wide variety of truck crops from small farms on the outskirts of the two cities. Norfolk's waterfront contained over forty warehouses and numerous wharves and piers, including stations for steamboats plying Virginia's rivers, the Chesapeake Bay, and the Atlantic Ocean. Near its wharves over seventy wholesalers and retailers conducted business. Two canals connected Norfolk and Portsmouth with northeastern North Carolina. A railroad tapped the Roanoke River at Weldon, North Carolina, and another rail line reached Petersburg, Virginia, just before the Civil War.

In 1860 Norfolk had a public school system, a large private library, three major newspapers, many churches, and several charitable associations such as the Humane Society, the Dorcas Society, and the Howard Association (founded as a result of the 1855 epidemic). With municipal gaslighting and street improvements, the city had countered negative publicity regarding its earlier backwardness.

Early in the war, Confederate troops occupied the Gosport Shipyard, partially destroyed by departing Union forces. After restoring a stone drydock, the Confederates salvaged the Federal ship *Merrimack,* rebuilt it as an ironclad, and renamed it *Virginia.* In March 1862, *Virginia* engaged in an inconclusive duel with the Federal ironclad *Monitor* in Hampton Roads.

In January and February 1862, Federal troops under Gen. Ambrose Burnside threatened the Elizabeth River cities from the south. In May, Federals under Gen. John Wool, along with President Abraham Lincoln and other officials, crossed Hampton Roads from Fort Monroe (which remained in Union hands throughout the war) and landed at Ocean View in the northern part of Norfolk County. Confederate forces then abandoned the forts protecting Norfolk and Portsmouth, severely damaging the shipyard as they departed.

Norfolk's mayor William Lamb and a delegation of city fathers met the Federal entourage outside the city and surrendered it to General Wool. When the civilians refused to take an oath of allegiance to the Union, Wool imposed martial law and placed Gen. Egbert Viele in command. During his tenure, Dr. David Wright, a hero during the yellow fever outbreak, killed a white Union officer who commanded black troops. Tried by a military court, Wright was convicted and, despite numerous appeals, executed.

Civilian government returned in June 1863, composed of those who would take the oath of allegiance. But the Union government of Francis H. Peirpoint, located in Alexandria,

Hoisting the U.S. flag over the Norfolk customs house.
Harper's Pictorial History of the Great Rebellion

claimed jurisdiction over the local civilians, and a year later Gen. Benjamin F. Butler, the new commandant of the district, took over the operations of the civil court and issued a series of orders aimed at controlling the population. Although many Confederate sympathizers complained about the general, Butler restored gaslighting, cleaned the streets, and opened up commerce with the outside world. Under Union occupation freed slaves worked some thirty-five farms owned by Confederates, including one located east of Norfolk, the property of Gen. Henry A. Wise, a former Virginia governor. On that plantation was a school for black children, one of several in the district.

All prewar newspapers stopped publication during the war, and the Federals put out their own, the *New Regime*. African American fraternal associations such as the Freemasons, which had operated clandestinely before the war, appeared openly by the end.

When the fighting ceased in 1865, Norfolk had an expanded population of African Americans and an improving economy. In 1870, the number of whites in the town was slightly less than it had been in 1860, but the number of blacks had more than doubled. John Lonsdale Roper, a Union officer stationed in Norfolk, remained after the war and developed a lumber business in the 1870s and later a major shipbuilding company. Norfolk's residents also began processing peanuts, a local product whose fame had spread during the war. Cotton flowed directly to Europe in considerable quantities as local businessmen erected cotton compresses. With ships becoming ever larger, Norfolk replaced Richmond as the state's major seaport for overseas commerce.

[*See also* Gosport Navy Yard.]

BIBLIOGRAPHY

Dabney, Virginius. *Virginia: The New Dominion.* Garden City, N.Y., 1971.

Wertenbaker, Thomas J. *Norfolk: Historic Southern Port.* 2d ed. Edited by Marvin W. Schlegel. Durham, N.C., 1962.

PETER C. STEWART

NORTH, JAMES H. (1813–1893), naval purchasing agent in Europe. North was born on September 17, 1813, into a seafaring family of Charleston, South Carolina. By the age of sixteen he was a midshipman in the U.S. Navy, and he achieved the rank of lieutenant in 1841. Within a month of South Carolina's secession, North had resigned his U.S. commission, and in March 1861 he was commissioned a lieutenant in the Confederate navy. The Department of the Navy, directed by Secretary Stephen R. Mallory, commissioned North as naval purchasing agent on May 17, 1861, and he was sent to Europe, backed by funds from the Confederate Congress, to purchase or have constructed the kinds of armored gunboats and ironclads the Confederacy could not build in its own ports. In Europe the finest up-to-date naval ships could be acquired as long as they were not obviously equipped with weapons or in violation of neutrality laws.

North's slowness in initiating construction irked Mallory and contrasted with Lt. James Dunwoody Bulloch's quick action in commissioning such gunboats as *Florida* and *Alabama* at Liverpool, and later, the Laird rams. Thus North was ordered to deal with Bulloch as chief agent for European naval purchases.

By spring 1862, North had arranged with Thompson Brothers, on the Clyde in Glasgow, for the construction of a 270-foot armored frigate, called *No. 61.* North was promoted to commander on May 2, 1862, and he looked forward to taking command within the year of what he said would be a "noble" ship, slated to be the largest warship ever built.

By 1863, however, Confederate difficulties in making financial payments as well as Britain's more rigorous surveillance, under Union pressure, of what was going on in its shipyards, convinced Bulloch and Confederate emissaries James Mason and John Slidell that *No. 61* would never make it out of its Scottish port. They urged North to sell his ship. North turned his "fine specimen" over to the builders, who arranged its sale to the Danish government at the end of 1863. North moved to France, hoping to command some ship under French construction. But on January 2, 1865, Commander North was relieved of his duties in Europe and returned to Richmond. En route for home he learned of the Confederacy's fate, so he returned to England from Havana to remain with his family for some time. Finally, he returned to the United States to engage in farming in northern Virginia where he died on August 18, 1893.

BIBLIOGRAPHY

Bulloch, James D. *The Secret Service of the Confederate States in Europe.* 2 vols. London, 1883. Reprint, New York, 1959.

Merli, Frank J. *Great Britain and the Confederate Navy, 1861–1865.* Bloomington, Ind., 1970.

Spencer, Warren F. *The Confederate Navy in Europe.* Tuscaloosa, Ala., 1983.

FREDERICK SCHULT and CHARLES V. PEERY

NORTH CAROLINA. In 1860 North Carolina's voters gave a narrow majority to John C. Breckinridge, the candidate of the Southern Democrats, but popular sentiment differed sharply from the secessionist mood of the Deep South states. Both Unionism and competitive two-party politics remained strong in North Carolina, and the dominance of nonslaveholding small farmers in the white population posed a potential challenge for the Confederacy. When war came, North Carolinians made exceptional sacrifices for the Southern cause, but unusually strong protests and opposition to the Confederacy also developed. The burdens of the Civil War severely tested Confederate loyalties, and the internal problems that plagued the Confederacy were especially salient in this upper South state.

The Secession Crisis

When the crisis of 1860–1861 arrived, it affected a people whose material circumstances were quite different from those in the Deep South. Of North Carolina's population of 992,622 people, 631,100 were white. There were 331,059 slaves in the Tarheel State, and 30,463 free African Americans. Overwhelmingly rural, North Carolina had few towns or cities of any size—Wilmington was the largest with only 10,000 residents. For decades economic growth had been comparatively slow, and as a result the state had attracted few immigrants. Less than 1 percent of the population was foreign-born, and most of these individuals came from the British Isles. Mixed farming was the rule, even for many of the largest slaveholders, and plantation districts were rare. The influence of the market economy remained weak, although tobacco flourished in a line of counties along the Virginia border, some eastern counties grew substantial amounts of cotton, and rice plantations existed near Wilmington. Seventy-two percent of the white families in the state owned no slaves, and most farms were small, self-sufficient operations encompassing no more than fifty or one hundred acres.

Few leaders of the state shared secessionists' alarm about Southern rights. Charles Manly, former Whig governor, condemned the "fanatics" on both sides and fervently hoped that "the People will save" the nation. Democrat Rufus Lenoir Patterson fumed about the influence of fire-eaters like William Lowndes Yancey of Alabama who were pursuing "ulterior objects in which the *citizens of N.C.* cannot be interested." The state treasurer, Jonathan Worth, similarly declared that if Abraham Lincoln "should pledge himself to execute the Fugitive Slave Law, and do it, I care nothing about the question as to Squatter Sovereignty."

The vote for Breckinridge was a vote for the candidate of the regular Democratic organization, and most voters, whether supporters of the Democrats or of the (formerly Whig) Opposition party, hoped the Union would be preserved. As the lower South seceded and organized the Confederate States of America, even large slaveholders felt dismay. Paul Cameron, the wealthiest planter in the state, wrote: "I try to keep myself employed, but I find my mind nearly all the time occupied with the State of the Country and it makes me very unhappy. I love the Union."

On February 28, 1861, voters cast ballots on the question of calling a convention to consider secession. Although Governor John W. Ellis favored and was working for secession, the voters refused to hold a convention. The drift of events toward war, however, steadily affected North Carolinians. As one man wrote to future governor Zebulon Vance, "I am a Union man but when they send men South it will change my notions." Vance himself was speaking for the Union and gesturing with upraised hand when word of the firing on Fort Sumter reached him. His hand fell "slowly and sadly by the side of a Secessionist." With war a reality, the North Carolina General Assembly passed a bill for a convention, and on May 20 this body took the state out of the Union and into the Confederacy.

Contributions to the War

Immediately, Tarheel citizens began to make unusually large contributions and sacrifices for the Confederate cause. In fact, the First North Carolina Regiment boarded trains for Virginia on May 11, nine days before the state formally left the Union. The initial excitement and romance of military service faded quickly before the grim tragedies of war, but North Carolina continued, through volunteering and conscription, to furnish a disproportionate number of soldiers to the Confederacy.

Before the war was over the state provided thirty-six generals to the armies, including Theophilus H. Holmes, D. H. Hill, William Dorsey Pender, and Dodson Ramseur. Among the state's naval officers were Capt. James W. Cooke of the ram *Albemarle* and Capt. James Waddell of *Shenandoah,* which destroyed more Union commerce than any ship save *Alabama.* But the greatest contributions were made by the common soldiers and their immediate superiors, who fought and died in substantial numbers in every theater east of the Mississippi.

The heaviest fighting for the state's troops took place on the battlefields of Virginia. George E. Pickett's famous charge on the third day at Gettysburg is identified with his gallant Virginia troops, but four brigades under Gen. J. Johnston Pettigrew also answered the call to advance "for the honor of the good Old North State." They, too, fell in large numbers before the withering Union fire. Only three of Pettigrew's field officers returned from that charge, and of the 15,301 Confederates killed or wounded at Gettysburg, 4,033 were North Carolinians. Many other battles in the Old Dominion exacted heavy Tarheel casualties.

Although North Carolina contained only about one-ninth of the Confederacy's white population, it supplied nearly one-sixth of the Southern nation's fighting men. Nearly one-fourth of all Southern conscripts, 21,348 men, came from North Carolina. The normal military population of the state (white males between the ages of eighteen and forty-five) has been estimated at 116,000, yet 120,000

North Carolinians served in the Confederate armies before the war was over. Of these, 40,275 died, falling in roughly equal numbers to battle and disease. These statistics represented one-quarter of all Confederate battle deaths and the largest death toll of any Southern state. (Only a few white citizens fought for the North, but 7,000 black Tarheels joined the Union army.)

North Carolina also made unusual efforts to supply and support its Confederate troops. In the first year of the war, as state officials struggled to clothe volunteers, they ordered the entire output of the state's thirty-nine cotton mills and nine woolen mills for manufacture into uniforms. This became a continuing practice, and as time went on the state undertook to clothe all its troops and, after buying up all cloth produced in the state, sent purchasing agents into other Southern states. In the final years of the war, Governor Vance, who was first elected in 1862, used state-chartered blockade runners to exchange cotton for blankets, shoes, and uniforms.

Military Operations in the State

Military operations within North Carolina were comparatively minor through most of the war, although they always aroused anxiety among the population. The first threat came in the form of Federal invasion of the coast, beginning with the capture of Fort Hatteras in August 1861. Next Union forces under the command of Gen. Ambrose Burnside captured Roanoke Island on February 8, a defeat that dismayed many Tarheels. At his post in Richmond, Attorney General Thomas Bragg heard of complaints that "No. Ca. has been neglected, her troops sent to other points, while she is left to the tender mercies of the enemy." General Burnside followed up his victory with raids on Elizabeth City and Edenton and the capture of New Bern on February 14. Morehead City and Beaufort fell in March, and Fort Macon surrendered on April 25, 1862. From this point onward the Union forces controlled most of North Carolina's coastline north of Wilmington.

Occasional Federal raids and Confederate counterstrikes occurred thereafter in the eastern part of the state without a substantial occupation of territory. Unionist sympathizers and "Buffaloes," who were generally poorer whites, often preyed on the property of large planters. The major Federal presence was in New Bern, where large numbers of runaway slaves arrived in search of freedom. Freedmen's Bureau officials later organized their settlement in a community known as James City. Meanwhile, President Lincoln appointed Edward Stanly, an old-line Whig, as the military governor of North Carolina. On May 26 Stanly assumed jurisdiction in New Bern, but he found that a groundswell of pro-Union sentiment was not forthcoming and resigned following issuance of the Emancipation Proclamation.

In 1864 Confederate forces recaptured, and then lost again, the eastern town of Plymouth, and there were some small-scale Union raids in the western mountains. Major military operations, however, did not occur until the closing months of the war. The first of these focused on Wilmington, a favorite base for blockade runners and the last major port open for the Confederacy, and on Fort Fisher, the massive earthwork structure that guarded the approaches to Wilmington.

In December 1864 Union naval and infantry forces under Rear Adm. David D. Porter and Gen. Benjamin F. Butler attacked Fort Fisher without success. Despite a lengthy bombardment by Porter's massive armada, Butler's men were turned back within fifty yards of the fort. In January Porter tried again with troops commanded by Maj. Gen. Alfred H. Terry. This time the fort and its outnumbered defenders, commanded by Col. William Lamb, fell after vicious hand-to-hand combat. Wilmington was captured by the Federals on February 22, 1865.

Early in March 1865 the army of Gen. William Tecumseh Sherman entered the state. After his destructive march through Georgia, Sherman had paused at Savannah and then headed north through Columbia, South Carolina. His objective in North Carolina, besides the continued destruction of Southern resources and spirit, was the town of Goldsboro, where there were important railroad connections to the coast. Sherman's army of sixty thousand men traveled in two columns. Opposing them were no more than thirty thousand Confederates under the command of Gen. Joseph E. Johnston.

The challenge for Sherman was to keep the two wings of his army in close communication, while Johnston sought to fall upon one or the other column separately. On March 15 a sharp engagement took place at Averasboro, which allowed Johnston to slow Sherman's left wing and separate it farther from the other Federal column. Four days later at Bentonville the Confederates attacked Gen. Henry W. Slocum's forces in a day of heavy fighting. But Sherman reinforced Slocum during the next two days, and Johnston had to withdraw. On March 23 Sherman entered Goldsboro.

The next day Maj. Gen. George H. Stoneman left Tennessee and initiated a highly destructive cavalry raid through southwestern Virginia and western North Carolina. Commanding a veteran cavalry division of approximately six thousand men, Stoneman encountered little serious opposition. In North Carolina his forces struck at Boone, Wilkesboro, Elkin, High Point, Salisbury, Statesville, Lincolnton, Morganton, and other places. They cut railroad lines near Greensboro, burned factories anywhere they found them, and in Salisbury destroyed the Confederate prison and a large quantity of food and supplies. After ransacking Asheville on April 26, they left the state.

Meanwhile, General Johnston had surrendered the last

FORT FISHER, NORTH CAROLINA. View from the second traverse of the northwest salient, January 1, 1865. Sketch from a photograph taken after the fort's capture. NATIONAL ARCHIVES

major Confederate army to General Sherman. After resting at Goldsboro, Sherman's men had moved west, rejoicing at news of the fall of Richmond, and occupied Raleigh on April 13. General Johnston, recognizing the futility of further resistance, met Sherman on April 17, 1865, at the farmhouse of James and Lucy Bennett near Durham. Sherman had just learned of President Lincoln's assassination, which he announced that night. On the eighteenth he concluded terms of surrender with Johnston, but his political superiors rejected these as too liberal, for they included recognition of existing state governments and a guarantee of property rights that could be interpreted to include slaves. On April 26, 1865, Sherman and Johnston met again at the Bennett farmhouse and signed a document based on the terms agreed to at Appomattox. By early May minor skirmishes in the mountains had ceased, and the fighting was over.

Burdens on the Home Front

North Carolina's large contributions of fighting men had their counterpart in the heavy burdens borne by citizens on the home front. Shortly after the Union navy imposed its blockade, citizens began to experience shortages of both imported luxury items and essentials such as salt. Inflation and speculation or extortion aroused much concern as ordinary Tarheels wondered how they could pay the skyrocketing prices of goods. The burden felt most widely, however, was the shortage of labor in nonslaveholding families. Because most farms in the state were small, subsistence operations lacking any slave labor, the absence of men in the armies quickly affected the women and children left behind. North Carolina's large contribution of soldiers threw heavy burdens on families that were ill-equipped to carry them.

On numerous occasions Governor Vance pleaded with the War Department to suspend conscription in hard-pressed localities or to allow men to return home for a few weeks to help with the harvest. Officials in Richmond complied with his requests as far as they could, but their attempts to cooperate could not remove the problem. By March of 1863 Vance was protesting that conscription had swept off "a large class whose labor was, I fear, absolutely necessary to the existence of the women and children left behind."

Impressment also deprived citizens of valuable food or supplies, and, as Secretary of War James A. Seddon once admitted, it did so in an unequal manner that was much resented. Governor Vance often protested against impressment, but he reserved his hottest denunciations for the depredations of Confederate cavalry forces. "If God Almighty had yet in store," Vance once thundered, "another plague [for the Egyptians] worse than all others . . . I am sure it must have been a regiment or so of half-armed, half-disciplined Confederate cavalry." Had God turned the Confederate cavalry "loose among Pharaoh's subjects . . .

he never would have followed the children of Israel to the Red Sea! No sir; not an inch!"

The geographical position of North Carolina exacerbated these difficulties. As the Confederacy lost territory around its periphery, government officials had to draw more and more heavily upon the regions that remained under their control. Most of North Carolina remained firmly under Confederate authority throughout the war, and to many Tarheel citizens it appeared that the Richmond administration relentlessly increased its demands for men, money, and supplies. Records of the tax-in-kind are incomplete, but surviving statistics suggest that substantial collections of farm produce were made in 1863 and 1864. North Carolina farms, because they were available to government officials, figured prominently in these levies.

The burdens of the home front produced a great deal of human suffering. In the early months of the war, many North Carolinians petitioned the War Department (usually in vain) for the exemption of craftsmen who were needed in rural districts, especially those who could repair farming tools. "We are getting scarce of almost every article of necessity, from a needle to a scythe blade," wrote one citizen in 1862. As prices rose, Zebulon Vance observed that "the cry of distress comes up from the poor wives and children of our soldiers . . . from all parts of the State." Shortage of provisions became the most serious problem, caused not only by bad weather and crop failures but also by the government's policy of "taking too many men from their farms," as one private described it.

Even conservative members of the political elite, who for decades had controlled local government from appointive, rather than elected, positions, grew alarmed at the deteriorating conditions of life among the common people. As early as June of 1862 Walter Gwynn wrote to former state Supreme Court justice Thomas Ruffin, "I have witnessed great distress, among the lower and poorer classes." He added, "I fear . . . starvation." Kenneth Rayner, a planter from Hertford County, agreed that the "suffering among the poor . . . is dreadful to contemplate." In January 1863 Joseph A. Worth wrote to his brother Jonathan, the state treasurer, that "if more men are called to the field, . . . many *must* starve." A year later he reported that "much suffering among the people exists. . . . In Chatham county one of the best counties in the state for provisions a great many have not had any meat for months. Clothing is very scarce. People known as the poorer class are almost destitute."

Members of "the poorer class" also spoke up about their own plight. Among the hundreds of wives who wrote to Governor Vance was one who explained, in a direct manner, "I want you . . . and Mr. Davis to . . . send home the poor solgers." Another noted that she was one of the many "who have neither brother, husband, nor Father at home . . . and no slave labor to depend on." A soldier let Vance know that "I have received a letter from home yesterday and [my family] are sufering very much for the want of provisions or money to b[u]y with." Another soldier, Private O. Goddin, pointedly asked the governor: "Now Govr. do tell me how we poor soldiers who are fighting for the 'rich man's negro' can support our families at $11 per month? How can the poor live?"

Survival became increasingly difficult for large segments of the population who felt the grip of poverty and hunger. County courts scrambled to find cornmeal and pork for distribution to the hungry. Newly appointed county corn agents traveled far within North Carolina and outside the state trying to buy provisions. Surviving county records give some evidence of the extent of the problem. In Orange County, 19.7 percent of the adult white women and 35 percent of the white children depended on county relief for food. In Randolph County 34.4 percent of the adult white women were on relief; in Duplin County the figure was 32.9 percent, and in Cumberland it was 40.7 percent. Such need often overwhelmed the resources of local government, and although the state appropriated more than $6 million to buy food for the poor, much of this aid was never more than a figure on a piece of paper.

Disaffection and Unionism

Suffering on this scale was bound to strengthen the disaffection that had always been latent in the state. Unionism was real but a comparatively small part of the problem. Class resentments and a sense of injustice motivated many more Tarheels to withdraw their support from the government. As the conditions of life deteriorated and the failure of government to provide the basic necessities for security became manifest, more and more ordinary people turned against the war.

Unionism in the state was real and sometimes ran deep. In the weeks after secession, individuals who loved the Union mounted a small number of scattered protests in every part of the state. As the Confederate government became more unpopular and adopted objectionable policies, some of these people became more outspoken or determined about their feelings of opposition. The Heroes of America, a secret organization also known as the Red Strings (for an identifying red string worn in the lapel), organized in 1861 and sought to aid draft resisters and deserters and oppose the Confederacy. The HOA was especially active in the "Quaker-belt" counties of Randolph, Davidson, Forsyth, and Guilford, but by 1863 its influence had begun to spread beyond the Piedmont. Working actively behind the scenes, the HOA elected some of its members to office and aided peace candidates. According to the closest students of the organization, it "counted perhaps 10,000 members in North Carolina and . . . played an active part not only in resisting the Confederacy but also in wartime and Reconstruction politics in the state."

Nevertheless, the Heroes of America were a minor, and not typical, part of the serious disaffection that grew in North Carolina. It was a combination of suffering and class resentments that usually caused people's discouragement to ripen into disaffection. Private O. Goddin, who had asked Governor Vance how the families of poor soldiers could live, also made an ominous and insightful prediction. "We will have a revolution," Goddin wrote in February 1863, "unless something is done." The potential for revolution, to which Goddin referred, was rooted in class and in perceptions of class favoritism by the government. "The majority of our soldiers," Goddin explained, "are poor men with families who say they are tired of the rich mans war & poor mans fight."

Goddin enumerated some of the governmental policies that had aroused class resentment. At the top of his list were the army's acceptance of substitutes (which only the rich could afford to hire) and the exemption of overseers. Many nonslaveholding small farmers had volunteered for the cause only to find, Goddin charged, that "the Govt. has made a distinction between the rich man (who had something to fight for) and the poor man who fights for that he never will have. The exemption of the owners of 20 negroes & the allowing of substitutes clearly proves it." In this statement Goddin surely reflected the feeling of thousands of the state's yeoman farmers, for the exemption of overseers detonated such loud protests that the General Assembly felt compelled to pass resolutions criticizing the Confederate law.

Many also shared Goddin's perception that "healthy and active men who have furnished substitutes are grinding the poor by speculation while their substitutes have been discharged after a month's service as being too old or invalids." A woman in the mountains complained that well-to-do, privileged men in the home guards rounded up draftees with alacrity but fled to Tennessee when drafted themselves. Another woman charged that militia officers and magistrates who "remained at home ever since the war commenced" devoted themselves to arresting "old grey headed fathers" and "shooting down without halting them . . . [men] that has served in the army, some of them for 2 or 3 years." Upper-class status did convey benefits in Southern society, and one patriotic planter lamented that too few "young men of wealth . . . are facing danger and enduring privations." Every instance of a wealthy man who evaded service attracted attention and aroused resentment among the hard-pressed nonslaveholders.

As destitution tightened its grip on the state, desertion from the armies grew rapidly. Sharing Private Goddin's belief that "a man's first duty is to provide for his own household," hundreds of North Carolina soldiers left the armies and, if challenged, merely patted their rifles and said, "This is my furlough." By April 1863 General Pender was expressing alarm at the rate of desertion from "the North Carolina regiments of the army." The men were receiving letters from home "urging them to leave," explained Pender, and he feared that "the matter will grow from bad to worse." Pender was right, and desertion received further encouragement when North Carolina Chief Justice Richmond Pearson issued a decision against the Conscription Act.

From 1863 to the end of the war large numbers of deserters gathered in the western and Piedmont sections of North Carolina, despite periodic efforts by the Confederate army to collect them. Soon after deserters arrived home, events took place that drove many from a quiet withdrawal of support from the Confederacy in order to help their families to open opposition to constituted authority. Local officials decided that they could not tolerate the situation and launched efforts to arrest the deserters, who then had to choose a career as outlaws if they were going to remain near home and benefit their loved ones. In this way thousands of Tarheel deserters became "outliers" or "bushwhackers," men who lived in small bands, hiding in the countryside and stealing from the homes and storehouses of the rich in order to feed themselves and their families.

In the final months of the Civil War, disorder spread alarmingly across North Carolina. Bands of deserters often controlled roads, outnumbered the home guards, and overawed the courts. The situation was so far out of hand that some of the county courts attempted to negotiate a truce with the deserters, or recusant conscripts, as they also were called, in order simply to restore some security to property. Local officials often reported that the general population gave "aid and comfort" to the deserters and refused to muster with the home guards to oppose them. A colonel in Wilkes County pronounced himself "satisfied" that militia and home guard officers were "encouraging desertion and have gone under with the disloyal sentiment with at least one-half of the people of the county." By the time the war ended, Confederate authority as a practical matter had been severely undermined in many parts of the state.

Political Protest and Opposition

Because the Civil War brought such severe sacrifice and suffering to a people who had not been eager to leave the Union, it is not surprising that political protests were frequent and that opposition became strong enough to generate the only open and avowed peace movement in the Confederacy. Political discontent sprang from the ranks of the elite as well as the common people and grew steadily. It was fortunate for the Confederacy that in Zebulon Vance North Carolina had a leader who could express public discontent effectively without destroying cooperation with the central government.

Secession had produced some change in the state's political parties. Secessionists promptly organized a "Confederate" party that consisted mostly of former Democrats. In place of the old Opposition party, a "Conservative" party emerged that was composed of former Whigs and Democrats who had clung to the Union as long as possible. The Confederate party remained a viable organization for only about a year.

The tide of public opinion in the state is indicated by the fact that Conservatives soon branded their opponents as the "Destructives," and the name stuck. As the policies of the central government became more demanding, Conservatives condemned the Destructives and blasted their support of the Davis administration as another sign of their recklessness and irresponsibility. In the spring of 1862 a gubernatorial election took place to elect a successor to Henry T. Clark, who had served for about a year after the death of John Ellis. William W. Holden, the powerful editor of the *Raleigh Standard,* attacked Clark's policies on behalf of the Conservatives, charging that Clark wanted to waste "the last man and the last dollar" to fight the war. Holden supported Zebulon Vance, a colonel in the Twenty-sixth North Carolina, against the Destructives' candidate, William J. Johnston, and Vance rolled up a victory margin greater than five to two. Thereafter the spectrum of politics in the state shifted to the left; the Confederate party virtually disappeared, except as a whipping boy, and the Conservative organization of Vance fought out the next gubernatorial election against a growing peace movement.

Some of the earliest protests against the Richmond government came from upper-class North Carolinians. The resolutely nationalist policies of Jefferson Davis were a shock to many Tarheel politicians. Higher taxes, impressment, conscription, and government-ordered destruction of cotton that was threatened by the enemy were just a few of the policies that offended their state rights principles. They protested most bitterly against suspension of the writ of habeas corpus and fulminated against the Davis government as a despotism. Many of North Carolina's traditional leaders also chafed under the minor role they were called upon to play in the new nation. Feeling that they were overlooked and the state unrepresented in the highest councils of the government, they charged that North Carolina had been taken for granted and neglected. This chorus of protests strengthened discontent and placed the governor under the political necessity of appearing always to defend the interests of the state.

Zebulon Vance had announced before his election that he favored prosecution of the war until independence was achieved. Although he never abandoned his support for independence, he quickly learned that as governor his actions had to reflect the unpopularity in his state of many Confederate policies. In October 1862 he warned Jefferson Davis that "the original advocates of secession no longer hold the ear of the people" and that, despite "all the popularity with which I came into office, it will be exceedingly difficult for me to execute" the conscript law. This statement prefigured Vance's course as governor, for he balanced sensitivity to his constituents with concern for the national cause. Vehemently protesting against many government policies, Vance also attempted to support the war effort.

Frequently the governor interceded with Richmond authorities on behalf of his citizens, and when a native of another state was sent to enforce the Conscription Act, Vance voiced his own state's feeling of neglect. On many occasions he criticized impressment, conscription, the consumption of corn by Confederate distilleries, and other policies, but he usually avoided prolonged confrontations. On one point, however, Vance stood firm. Officials and employees essential to the state government had to be exempted from conscription, he insisted. Acting on this claim, Vance exempted 14,675 men—an unusually large number, but one perceived as justified in a state that was making great sacrifices.

Where the welfare of North Carolinians was directly concerned, Vance had to stand up to Richmond, and this political reality explains a bizarre situation that developed near the end of his term in office. As Lee's tattered and hungry soldiers fell back toward Appomattox, state warehouses bulged with supplies for North Carolina troops. Vance controlled 40,000 blankets, 150,000 pounds of bacon, cloth for 100,000 uniforms, leather for 10,000 pairs of shoes, plus other supplies, and he refused to relinquish them. The Confederacy needed these goods desperately, but it was impolitic in North Carolina to give them up as long as there was a chance they would be needed by Tarheels.

This reality also explains Vance's challenge to the Confederacy's control of international shipping in the closing months of the war. Using a steamer dubbed *Advance,* the governor was running the blockade and importing essential supplies for the soldiers and people of his suffering state. When the central government tightened regulations and tried to take over most cargo space for Confederate purposes, Vance organized a constitutional protest by other governors. Unless he fought for the welfare of his hard-pressed constituents, he could not keep them in the war.

Maintaining North Carolina's support for the war effort grew increasingly difficult. In January 1863 State Treasurer Jonathan Worth reported that "nearly every man I saw . . . is openly for re-construction on the basis of the Constitution of the U.S., if these terms can be obtained." That fall's congressional elections showed how far discontent and peace sentiment had advanced. Eight of the state's ten newly elected congressmen opposed the administration. No original secessionists and only one Democrat triumphed, and five of the victorious candidates ran on a peace platform.

William W. Holden, the influential Raleigh editor, had organized a popular campaign for peace in the summer of 1863. Approximately one hundred public meetings called for a peace convention and an immediate armistice. Holden then announced that he would challenge Vance in the 1864 gubernatorial elections.

Vance believed that honor required him and his state to stay in the war to the end, but he knew that Holden read the popular sentiment correctly. Independence would require more "blood and misery," Vance wrote, "*and our people will not pay this price* . . . I am convinced of it." Nevertheless he fought Holden shrewdly, emphasizing the efforts that he and the Confederate government had made for peace. He also branded Holden as "the *war* candidate," charging that Holden's plans would embroil North Carolina in war with its neighbors, "a bloodier conflict than that you now deplore."

These tactics, plus Vance's immense personal popularity, carried him to victory and kept North Carolina in the war to the bitter end. But the governor's political adroitness could not remove his people's travail. Thus, it was natural that a state that sacrificed and suffered much for the cause also protested greatly.

[*For further discussion of battles fought in North Carolina, see* Burnside's Expedition to North Carolina; Carolinas Campaign of Sherman; Stoneman's Raids. *For further discussion of North Carolina cities, see* Charlotte and Mecklenburg County, North Carolina; Greensboro, North Carolina; Raleigh, North Carolina; Wilmington, North Carolina. *See also* Heroes of America *and biographies of numerous figures mentioned herein.*]

BIBLIOGRAPHY

Auman, William T., and David D. Scarboro. "The Heroes of America in Civil War North Carolina." *North Carolina Historical Review* 58, no. 4 (1981): 327–363.

Barrett, John G. *The Civil War in North Carolina.* Chapel Hill, N.C., 1963.

Durrill, Wayne K. *War of a Different Kind.* New York, 1990.

Escott, Paul D. *Many Excellent People: Power and Privilege in North Carolina, 1850–1900.* Chapel Hill, N.C., 1985.

Kruman, Marc W. *Parties and Politics in North Carolina, 1836–1865.* Baton Rouge, La., 1983.

Mobley, Joe A. *James City: A Black Community in North Carolina, 1863–1900.* Raleigh, N.C., 1981.

Paludan, Phillip Shaw. *Victims.* Knoxville, Tenn., 1981.

Yearns, W. Buck, and John G. Barrett. *North Carolina Civil War Documentary.* Chapel Hill, N.C., 1978.

Paul D. Escott

NORTH CAROLINA. *For discussion of the ship* North Carolina, *see* Laird Rams.

NORTHERNERS. One would not expect to find a significant number of Northerners in either the antebellum or the Confederate South. Yet the census of 1860 indicates that there were approximately 360,000 Northerners residing in the Old South; some estimates place that number as high as 500,000. Many Northerners, of course, found an inhospitable environment in the South and returned to their native states. But a surprising number of Northerners remained in the South and made their life's work there.

Northerners living in the South spanned the entire socioeconomic spectrum. Some were farmers, planters, or overseers; others were common laborers or skilled artisans; many became merchants, shippers, bankers, industrialists, or railroad magnates. A number of Northerners found a rewarding professional life in the South as tutors, college professors or presidents, lawyers, doctors, ministers, and scientists; still others became journalists, politicians, and diplomats.

Some fifty Northern-born men rose to the rank of general in the Confederate army, and many others filled the muster rolls at lesser ranks. Indeed, some of the most vituperative comments directed at Northerners were a consequence of their successful status in the Confederacy. For example, a Richmond editor charged in 1862 that "all the officials, who constitute the very pivot on which the whole war hinges are either Yankees, or foreigners, or Jews."

Several months later, that same editor spoke for many of his fellow Southerners when he became more specific in his vitriol. Judah P. Benjamin, a man who would occupy three cabinet-level positions (in the War, State, and Justice departments) was a "foreigner and a Jew"; Adj. Gen. Samuel Cooper was a "New Yorker"; Secretary of the Navy Stephen R. Mallory was "born in the West Indies of Yankee parents, and educated in Connecticut"; Quartermaster General Abraham C. Meyers was a "Pennsylvanian and a Jew"; and Chief of Ordnance Josiah Gorgas was "a Northern man of an unknown state."

Although they had resided in the South for quite some time, the most prominent native Northerners to become generals in the Confederate army were Gorgas, Cooper, Mansfield Lovell, John C. Pemberton, Daniel Ruggles, and Samuel G. French. Antipathy toward important Northerners in the Confederacy was exacerbated when Lovell and Pemberton, commanding the defenses of New Orleans and Vicksburg, respectively, were forced to surrender to the Federals.

In this regard, President Jefferson Davis became a focal point for criticism of southernized Northerners by appointing them to office and command. Davis and others, however, defended the contributions of the Northerners to the Confederate war effort. "Casting imputations of disloyalty upon those of Northern and Foreign birth because of that fact alone," wrote the editor of the *Macon Telegraph,* "is a poor way of displaying zeal in behalf of the Southern Confederacy." The editor went on to remind his Southern brethren that there had "been as many traitors to our cause of Southern birth as of Northern birth."

In short, Northerners in the Confederacy exerted an influence on Confederate life far more than hitherto believed and certainly disproportionate to their numbers.

BIBLIOGRAPHY

Coulter, E. Merton. *The Confederate States of America, 1861–1865.* A History of the South, vol. 7. Baton Rouge, La., 1950.

Green, Fletcher M. *The Role of the Yankee in the Old South.* Athens, Ga., 1972.

Thomas, Emory M. *The Confederate Nation, 1861–1865.* New York, 1979.

JASON H. SILVERMAN

NORTHROP, LUCIUS B. (1811–1894), colonel and commissary general. One of the most disliked of all Confederate officials, Lucius Bellinger Northrop was born September 8, 1811, of well-to-do parents in Charleston, South Carolina. He graduated in 1831 from West Point. Among his closest army friends was Jefferson Davis. While campaigning against Indians in the territories in 1839, Northrop accidentally shot himself in the knee. He received permanent sick leave from the army because of the crippling wound. Northrop then studied medicine and maintained a practice in Charleston until his 1861 appointment by President Davis as commissary general.

In many respects, this was the worst presidential assignment that Davis made during the war. Northrop's responsibility was to provide food for Southern soldiers and, beginning in August 1863, Federal prisoners of war. It was an exceedingly difficult task because of a number of factors: inflation, hoarding, slow collapse of railroad transportation, shortage of wagons and teams, military reverses, dishonest agents, public antagonism toward impressment, price-fixing, and the steady loss of Southern territory where food was most plentiful. Yet Northrop brought much of his failure on himself.

Davis's praise of him as a man of "strong political sense and incorruptible integrity" was true, but it ran completely counter to popular opinion in the South. In a position that required tact and patience, Northrop brought pettiness, rigidity, blind devotion to bureaucracy, and the personality of a malicious old man.

War Department clerk J. B. Jones observed that when something went wrong in Northrop's agency, he "splutters over it in his angular chirography at a furious rate." Famous diarist Mary Boykin Chesnut called him "the most cussed and vilified man in the Confederacy." To contemporaries Northrop was "an old stoic," "an eccentric creature," "the hated," and "peevish, obstinate, condescending, and fault-finding." When Northrop reportedly voiced the opinion that soldiers should learn to eat less meat, he was widely accused of attempting to convert the Southern armies to vegetarianism.

In 1864 the Confederate Senate attempted in vain to have him removed from office. Davis responded on November 26 by appointing Northrop a brigadier general—but the president did not submit the promotion for Senate confirmation because of a certainty of rejection. On February 15, 1865, with Southern armies starving in the field, and in the face of overwhelming criticism, Northrop relinquished his duties. Federals arrested him on June 29 and charged him with deliberately starving captured Union prisoners. The charges were dropped in October and Northrop was released from Castle Thunder Prison.

For twenty-five years thereafter, he lived on a farm near Charlottesville, Virginia. He was openly resentful and venomous toward a number of generals, including Robert E. Lee. A stroke in 1890 left Northrop partially paralyzed. He died February 9, 1894, in a Maryland veterans' home. He is buried in Baltimore's New Cathedral Cemetery.

Northrop held the commissary general's post for almost four years. He did extensive damage to the Confederate cause because he was Davis's friend and in that situation could do no wrong. A thoroughgoing bureaucrat, the crippled colonel brought limited vision to his office and little food to the armies. The passage of time has done little to salvage his reputation.

[*See also* Commissary Bureau.]

BIBLIOGRAPHY

Felt, Jeremy P. "Lucius B. Northrop and the Confederacy's Subsistence Department." *Virginia Magazine of History and Biography,* April 1961.

Goff, Richard D. *Confederate Supply.* Durham, N.C., 1969.

Hay, Thomas Robson. "Lucius B. Northrop: Commissary General." *Civil War History,* March 1963.

Wright, Willard E., ed. "Some Letters of Lucius Bellinger Northrop, 1860–1865." *Virginia Magazine of History and Biography,* October 1960.

JAMES I. ROBERTSON, JR.

NORTHWESTERN CONSPIRACY. Even before the Civil War reached the halfway mark, Governor Oliver P. Morton of Indiana expressed fears that Democrats dissenting from the war effort were planning to revolutionize the upper Midwest. He claimed that certain groups intended to free Confederate prisoners held in Camp Morton near Indianapolis and establish a Northwest confederacy allied with the South. In the fall of 1864 a Morton protégé raided the quarters of Harrison H. Dodd and seized papers that enabled him to concoct an exposé of the Sons of Liberty and publicize Morton's conspiracy theory. Dodd, a printer and Democratic activist, had founded the Sons of Liberty as a secret order to promote conservative measures and win elections.

Just prior to the November 1864 elections soldiers seized some revolvers shipped to Dodd's printing plant from New York and made a round of arrests, including Dodd and Joseph J. Bingham, editor of the Democratic-oriented *Indianapolis State Sentinel*. Governor Morton parlayed the arrests into "a gigantic Northwestern conspiracy." Later Dodd and four others were tried by a military commission in the Indianapolis treason trials. Actually, Morton's molehill-to-mountain plot consisted of a few facts and much conjecture—there was no overt act.

In Illinois, too, on the eve of the 1864 elections, an editor of the *Chicago Tribune* and the commandant at Camp Douglas (a compound holding eleven thousand Confederate prisoners) claimed that secret society members and Copperheads intended to free the prisoners, burn Chicago, take over the polls, and establish a Northwestern confederacy. Authorities made a number of arrests and the "Camp Douglas conspiracy," or "Chicago conspiracy," received national publicity. A military commission conducted a treason trial in Cincinnati the next year.

A few Confederate officials at the time convinced themselves that there was a possibility of dissenters establishing a separate confederacy in the upper Midwest. But some present-day historians have debunked the Chicago and Indianapolis conspiracies, contending they were little more than fantasies devised to discredit Democrats and influence the 1864 elections.

[*See also* Copperheads.]

BIBLIOGRAPHY

Klement, Frank L. *Dark Lanterns: Secret Political Societies, Conspiracies, and Treason Trials in the Civil War.* Baton Rouge, La., 1984.

Milton, George Fort. *Abraham Lincoln and the Fifth Column.* New York, 1942.

Tredway, Gilbert R. *Democratic Opposition to the Lincoln Administration in Indiana.* Indianapolis, 1973.

FRANK L. KLEMENT

NORTON, NIMROD LINDSAY (1830–1903),

colonel and congressman from Missouri. Norton was born April 13, 1830, in Nicholas County, Kentucky. He studied at Fredonia Academy in New York State and at the Kentucky Military Institute. In 1853, he married and moved to Callaway County, Missouri, where he engaged in farming.

Although opposed to secession, Norton believed in state rights and sided with the South. In 1861 he was captain of a company of volunteers that formed at Millersburg, Missouri, and participated in a skirmish at Overton Run, near Fulton. After the Battle of Wilson's Creek, Norton resigned from the company to serve on Gen. Sterling Price's staff, eventually attaining the rank of colonel.

During the spring of 1864, the staid Norton, who championed morality and sobriety, challenged Thomas A. Harris in his reelection bid for Congress. Harris, noted for his hearty lifestyle, garnered only 20 percent of the soldier and refugee vote, and the straight-arrow Norton began his term in Congress on November 21. Norton served on the Territories, Claims, and Public Land committees. During his brief time in Congress, he voted for most of the emergency legislation, although he opposed requiring certain workers and slaves to join the army. Norton viewed much of the legislation in terms of how it would affect Missouri.

After the war Norton settled in southern Texas. In 1870 he moved to Austin and served as one of the state capitol building commissioners. He died in Austin on September 28, 1903.

BIBLIOGRAPHY

Brown, John Henry. *Indian Wars and Pioneers of Texas.* Austin, Tex., n.d.

Carter, R. C. "A Short Sketch of My Experiences during the First Stages of the Civil War." Western Historical Manuscript Collection. University of Missouri, Columbia.

Wakelyn, Jon L. *Biographical Dictionary of the Confederacy.* Edited by Frank E. Vandiver. Westport, Conn., 1977.

Warner, Ezra J., and W. Buck Yearns. *Biographical Register of the Confederate Congress.* Baton Rouge, La., 1975.

JAMES W. GOODRICH

NULLIFICATION CONTROVERSY.

During the late fall and winter of 1832 and 1833, the nullification controversy, the most important constitutional crisis between the adoption of the Constitution and the secession of the South, took place.

The controversy had its origins in the passage of the highly protective Tariff of Abominations in 1828, which many in South Carolina believed to be unconstitutional. Over the next several years, radicals led by James Hamilton and Robert Barnwell Rhett, Sr., effectively organized and enlarged their following. When President Andrew Jackson refused to push very hard for a reduction of the tariff and in 1832 signed into law a new measure that only partially reduced duties and did not abandon the principle of protection, South Carolina proceeded to implement the doctrine of nullification as it had been developed by John C. Calhoun in his "South Carolina Exposition and Protest" (1828) and in several important speeches.

Governor Hamilton convened a special session of the state legislature on October 22, 1832, which immediately called a convention to meet at Columbia on November 19. This convention adopted an ordinance declaring the tariffs of 1828 and 1832 unconstitutional and prohibited the collection of Federal duties within the state beginning on February 1, 1833. It also prescribed a test oath for all military and civil officers of the state, except members of the legislature, and forbade any appeal to the U.S. Supreme Court in cases arising under the ordinance. The convention also warned that any attempt by the Federal government to use force would be cause for South Carolina to secede from the Union. The legislature immediately adopted laws to enforce the ordinance, which included the establishment of a military force and the distribution of weapons.

As these events unfolded, President Jackson's rage mounted. Throughout his first term in office he had made clear his dislike of nullification: it was an illegitimate form of state rights, an assault on the doctrine of majority rule, and a threat to the continued existence of the Union. On December 10 he issued his "Proclamation to the People of South Carolina" making clear his intention to uphold the supremacy of the Federal government even if it meant the shedding of blood. Jackson then ordered a variety of military activities and on January 16, 1833, sent a special message to Congress asking for a Force Bill authorizing him to use the military to collect the Federal revenues.

Most people believed South Carolina had acted rashly. No other state formally endorsed the doctrine of nullification and many condemned it. But there was also, especially in the South, widespread opposition to Jackson's desire to use force and to hang the nullifiers for treason, and a number of states rejected the nationalist principles contained in the president's nullification proclamation. Fearful of civil war, Congress, under the leadership of Henry Clay, formulated a compromise: a new tariff that provided for a gradual reduction of duties over the next decade and that abandoned the principle of protection. As a sop to the president the Force Bill was also adopted. Jackson signed both into law on March 2, 1833.

Upon learning that a compromise was likely, South Carolina suspended its ordinance on January 21. Shortly after the adoption of the congressional compromise, the state reconvened its convention and rescinded its ordinance, but in a final act of defiance it nullified the Force Act. Both sides claimed victory. The most important result of the controversy was that over the next three decades the idea of secession became increasingly enmeshed with the doctrine of state rights and the South's defense of slavery.

BIBLIOGRAPHY

Ellis, Richard E. *The Union at Risk: Jacksonian Democracy, States' Rights and the Nullification Crisis.* New York, 1987.

Freehling, William W. *Prelude to Civil War: The Nullification Controversy in South Carolina, 1811–1836.* New York, 1965.

RICHARD E. ELLIS

NUMISMATICS. *See* Currency, *article on* Numismatics.

NURSING. At the outbreak of the Civil War, the only professional nurses in the South were Roman Catholic nuns of the Sisters of Mercy and the Sisters of Charity. Few other nineteenth-century women ventured into medicine except in the field of midwifery. Nursing took place in the home and was the duty of women in the family. Public nursing practice was viewed as too arduous and unfeminine. One Confederate soldier summed up many soldiers' feelings when he wrote to his wife and cautioned her, "Do not think of coming here as a nurse. It is no place for a young and inexperienced lady. . . . You cannot imagine the labor you would have to undergo, and disgusting much of it is."

But in early June 1861, Mary Boykin Chesnut commented in her diary that "every woman in the house is ready to rush into the Florence Nightingale business." As men answered the call to arms, women expressed their patriotism by establishing hospitals and tending wounded soldiers. Many nursed the injured in their own homes with their personal physicians in attendance.

As wounded from the Battle of First Manassas flooded into Richmond, it became evident that the government's medical facilities were extremely inadequate and that private resources needed to be pressed into service. Sally L. Tompkins took the lead in establishing and supervising the highly successful Robertson Hospital in Richmond. Operating throughout the war, it served 1,333 patients with only 73 deaths. Juliet Ann Opie Hopkins traveled from Alabama to organize and operate hospitals for her state's wounded soldiers. Using donations from home and $500,000 of her personal funds, she founded the First, Second, and Third Alabama Hospitals. Taking her medical knowledge onto the battlefield, Hopkins was wounded twice at the Battle of Seven Pines, and her injuries left her lame for life. In Williamsburg, Letitia Tyler Semple organized that city's first hospital, staffed in part with visiting North Carolina women as volunteer nurses.

Throughout the South, other women rallied to the cause. Over one thousand women, assigned to duty or as volunteers, served alongside thousands of their male counterparts. Felicia Grundy Porter headed the Women's Relief Society of the Confederate States. This Tennessee native started in her home state and expanded her hospitals throughout the Confederacy. She also sought funds to purchase artificial limbs for the poor. Mrs. Frank Newsone, a doctor's widow, continued his work by administering his hospitals. Others renowned for their dedication were Betsy Sullivan, the "Mother of the First Tennessee Regiment"; Betsy T. Philips, the "Mother of the Orphan Brigade"; and Ella K. Trader, the "Florence Nightingale of the South."

Women first entered hospitals to visit friends and relatives, and remained as volunteers. Their presence was regarded as a mixed blessing. Occasionally, an overly zealous volunteer would try to feed a heavy meal to a patient recovering from surgery. Once a volunteer confused the prescriptions that a surgeon had allowed her to administer. Sometimes volunteers played favorites. In the case of Mary Chesnut, she was reprimanded by Tompkins when she tried to provide special treats to the South Carolina wounded in Robertson Hospital. Young, handsome patients received more attention than older, less attractive men. The nurses in one Georgia hospital were chagrined to discover that the handsome, precariously ill soldier they had watched over so diligently was a Northerner.

Six months after First Manassas, a committee in the Confederate Congress examined the overall state of hospitals in the Confederacy. They found mismanagement, lack of supplies, materials of inferior quality, unsanitary conditions, and unqualified surgeons. Because of a high turnover in wounded soldiers detailed to act as nurses, the committee recommended that females be hired to serve in field and general hospitals as nurses. They authorized each hospital to employ a staff of two matrons in chief, two assistant matrons, and two matrons for each ward. They were to receive food and lodging and monthly stipends of $40, $34, and $30, respectively.

The matrons' duties were limited. They did not give medications, assist in the operating room, or provide routine medical attention, although these restrictions were lifted in the face of emergencies. Matrons then assisted in surgery, administered chloroform, and dressed wounds. Under the law, the domain of the matrons was to oversee the hospital's use of money for quality food and the proper preparation of patients' diets.

As chief matron of Division No. 2 of Chimborazo Hospital in Richmond, Phoebe Yates Pember focused on arranging the daily diet list, making sure that no ward was treated differently from another. Surgeons' as well as her own special instructions helped tailor diets to individual needs. She described the daily fare as "chicken soup for twenty—beef tea for forty—tea and toast for fifty." As food grew short in the course of the war, patients subsisted on salt pork, corn meal, and dried peas. At Chimborazo, the men finally rebelled when the menu consisted of pea soup, cold peas, fried peas, and baked peas on a rotating basis. An important duty of the matron was controlling the whiskey supply and restricting it to medical usage.

Matrons worked hard to be accepted, to introduce new ideas in patient care, and to bring order. But visitors to the hospital wards disrupted the daily routine. In one instance, a well-intentioned visitor loosened the compression bandage on an amputated arm, and the patient bled to death. In another case, a Mrs. Daniells from West Virginia visited her hospitalized husband. She displaced her husband in his bed in order to give birth to their daughter, placing Pember in the awkward position of caring for mother and child. Trouble followed when the mother returned home and left little "Phoebe" with Pember. A furlough had to be arranged for the father to take the child home.

According to Kate Cumming, a matron with the Army of Tennessee, a typical nurse's day started at 4:00 A.M. and continued until midnight. Breakfast was eaten with the staff or in their rooms. In addition to their regular assignments, performing personal tasks for patients such as mending, and writing or reading letters, wore the women down. Little respite was found at the day's end. If fortunate, the matron retired to an area of the ward where a bed, table, and chest were her private accommodations.

Matrons, over the objections of surgeons, introduced home remedies, airing of the wards, and simple cleanliness. They became the link between hospital and home for their patients. It was through their persistence and dedication that many a soldier survived his wounds and lived to see his family again.

[*See also* Health and Medicine, *article on* Medical Treatments; Hospitals; Medical Department; *and biographies of numerous figures mentioned herein.*]

BIBLIOGRAPHY

Buck, A. T. "Founder of the First Confederate Hospital." *Confederate Veteran* 2 (May 1894): 141. Reprint, Wilmington, N.C., 1985.

Cumming, Kate. *A Journal of Hospital Life in the Confederate Army of Tennessee.* Louisville, Ky., 1866.

Cunningham, Horace H. "Confederate General Hospitals: Establishment and Organization." *Journal of Southern History* 20 (1954): 376–394.

Hall, Courtney R. *Medical Life.* New York, 1935.

Harwell, Richard B., ed. *Kate: The Journal of a Confederate Nurse.* Baton Rouge, La., 1959.

Pember, Phoebe Yates. *A Southern Woman's Story: Life in Confederate Richmond.* Edited by Bell I. Wiley. New York, 1959.

Simkins, P. B., and J. W. Patton. *The Women of the Confederacy.* Richmond, Va., 1936.

Sterky, H. E. *Some Notable Alabama Women during the Civil War.* Montgomery, Ala., 1962.

SANDRA V. PARKER

OAK HILLS, MISSOURI. *See* Wilson's Creek Campaign.

OATH OF ALLEGIANCE. One of the primary problems facing the Federal government when the Civil War began was ensuring that its employees and military men were loyal. Over three hundred U.S. officers resigned to join the Confederacy, as did numerous government clerks and officials. Fearful of disloyalty among those who remained, President Abraham Lincoln on April 30, 1861, ordered all military personnel to retake an oath of allegiance. And Congress, on August 6, 1861, passed legislation requiring civil servants also to take or retake an oath of allegiance.

Even though these regulations were rigidly enforced, fears of disloyalty remained, and numerous ad hoc oaths of allegiance were used as a means of testing and ensuring loyalty. By the summer of 1862, most of the oaths, civil and military, were combined under one oath, the Ironclad Test Oath of Loyalty. The Ironclad Oath was so named because it required the oath taker to swear that "I have never voluntarily borne arms against the United States." In addition, the person had to forsake any allegiance to state authority and swear to "support and defend the Constitution of the United States against all enemies foreign and domestic; . . . bear true faith and allegiance to the same."

An oath of allegiance rapidly became a test of loyalty for common citizens. Maj. Gen. Benjamin F. Butler as military governor of New Orleans required that after October 12, 1861, anyone who wanted to do business in the city or with the U.S. government had to take an oath of allegiance to the United States. As stated by Butler, "It enables the recipient to say, 'I am an American citizen,' the highest title known."

Butler's practice became commonplace as the war progressed, and the Ironclad Oath or a variant thereof was required of thousands of Federals and Southerners. People who wanted to do business with the government, Confederate prisoners of war who wanted parole, Southerners who wanted to be reimbursed for goods taken by foraging Federal troops, and Union sympathizers in the South who wanted to govern themselves—all took the oath. Some took it numerous times: the record might have been set by Robert J. Breckinridge who took the oath nine times between June and December 1865.

After the war the oath presented an immediate problem for both the North and the South. Since its provisions remained in effect, no former Confederate soldier or any Southern citizen who had assisted in the South's war effort could hold a Federal, state, or local office or serve in the

I, John James, of Stokes County, State of North-Carolina, do solemnly swear or affirm, in presence of Almighty God, that I will henceforth faithfully support, protect and defend the Constitution of the United States and the Union of the States thereunder; and that I will, in like manner, abide by and faithfully support all laws and proclamations which have been made during the existing rebellion with reference to the emancipation of slaves. So help me God.

John James

Sworn and subscribed to this the 15 day of September, A. D., 1865, before C J Carrell, J. P.

It is hereby certified that the above is a true copy of the original oath taken and subscribed by

C J Carrell, J. P.
J E Gentry, J. P.
, J. P.

OATH OF ALLEGIANCE. An example of one of the many oaths of allegiance used during and after the Civil War. This oath was signed by John James of Stokes County, North Carolina, on September 15, 1865. CIVIL WAR LIBRARY AND MUSEUM, PHILADELPHIA military. To evade the "ironclad" portion of the oath concerning bearing arms against the United States, former Confederates had to petition the president of the United States for a pardon, and the presidents immediately after the war approved many such requests.

In 1884 Congress removed all the iron from the Ironclad Oath when it passed into law a new Oath of Allegiance. The 1884 oath removed all the restrictive portions of the older oaths and left it in its current form—an oath to support and defend the Constitution.

BIBLIOGRAPHY

Hyman, Harold M. *Era of the Oath*. Philadelphia, 1954.

Nevins, Allen. *Ordeal of the Union: The Emergence of Lincoln*. Vol. 2. New York, 1950.

Statutes at Large of the United States of America, 1789–1873. Washington, D.C., 1850–1873. Vol. 12, pp. 326–327, 502–503; vol. 23, pp. 21–22.

Tarhane, A. C. "Robert J. Breckinridge." *Confederate Veteran* 23 (May 1915): 215. Reprint, Wilmington, N.C., 1985.

U.S. War Department. *War of the Rebellion: A Compilation of the Official Records of the Union and Confederate Armies*. Washington, D.C., 1880–1901. Ser. 1, vol. 15, p. 483; ser. 3, vol. 2, p. 227.

P. NEAL MEIER

OCHILTREE, WILLIAM B. (1811–1867), congressman from Texas and colonel.

Born in North Carolina on October 18, 1811, William Beck Ochiltree moved to Texas in 1839. He settled in Nacogdoches, where he became an attorney and judge. He was a prominent officeholder in the Republic of Texas, a member of the state constitutional convention of 1845, and a member of the Texas legislature. He moved to Marshall, Harrison County, Texas, in 1859.

During his early political career, Ochiltree was a Whig. In 1859, however, he ran unsuccessfully for Congress as a representative of the ultra-Southern wing of the Democratic party against John H. Reagan, whose opposition to reopening the slave trade had lost that group's support. In November 1860, he was active in local meetings that demanded that state leaders not submit to the election of Abraham Lincoln, arguing that his election threatened slavery and a loss of Southern equality in the Union. He ran as a secessionist for the state convention of February 1861 and was elected. As one of the best-known members of the convention, Ochiltree was chosen as a delegate to the Provisional Congress. Ochiltree was an active member, supporting measures that would be to the advantage of his state, including the construction of fortifications at Sabine Pass, limiting the power of the central government to remove local militia forces from the state, and settling affairs with Indians along the Texas frontier. He also backed legislation designed to help the local economy, such as tax exemptions for railroads, the construction of a railroad tie between his state and the East, the establishment of new ports of entry, the suppression of import duties, and attempts to limit regulation restricting planters from freely marketing their cotton crops. He announced at an early date that he had no intention of serving in the regular Congress and gave up his seat when the Provisional Congress adjourned in February 1862.

Returning to Texas, he organized the Eighteenth Texas Infantry and was elected its colonel. Ochiltree was with this unit until 1863, when he resigned his commission because of ill health and returned to Jefferson where he practiced law.

Ochiltree ran for Congress as a conservative in 1866 but was not seated. He died at Marshall on December 27, 1867.

BIBLIOGRAPHY

Lynch, James D. *The Bench and Bar of Texas*. St. Louis, Mo., 1885.

Warner, Ezra J., and W. Buck Yearns. *Biographical Register of the Confederate Congress*. Baton Rouge, La., 1975.

CARL H. MONEYHON

OLDHAM, WILLIAMSON S. (1813–1868), congressman from Texas.

Born June 19, 1813, in Tennessee, William Simpson Oldham moved to Arkansas in 1836 and became a prominent politician there. He moved again to Austin, Texas, in 1849 and worked as a railroad developer, attorney, editor of the *Texas State Gazette,* and publisher of *A Digest of the General Statutes of the State of Texas* (1859). In the antebellum period he was a political enemy of Sam Houston and a perennial candidate for public office.

In the 1860 presidential election Oldham supported John C. Breckinridge. An advocate of secession, he was elected to the state convention in February 1861 and then was sent to the Arkansas convention in March to urge that state's secession. Oldham was chosen by the Texas convention as a member of the Provisional Congress and attended its sessions at Montgomery and Richmond.

In November 1861, the state legislature elected Oldham to the Senate in the First Congress. Although a friend of Jefferson Davis, he was a strident supporter of state rights and opposed the president's policies on conscription and suspension of the writ of habeas corpus. He also opposed all efforts to restrict the planting of cotton in favor of grains. On the other hand, he was willing to take extreme measures in support of the Confederacy and backed high taxes, efforts to control inflation, and ultimately even arming slaves.

Following the war, Oldham fled to Mexico and then moved to Canada. He worked as a photographer and wrote *The Last Days of the Confederacy* (1868). He returned to Texas in 1866 but refused to take the loyalty oath. He died at Houston from typhoid fever on May 8, 1868.

BIBLIOGRAPHY

King, Alma D. "The Political Career of William Simpson Oldham." *Southwestern Historical Quarterly* 33 (October 1929): 112–133.

Warner, Ezra J., and W. Buck Yearns. *Biographical Register of the Confederate Congress.* Baton Rouge, La., 1975.

Carl H. Moneyhon

OLUSTEE, FLORIDA. Thirteen miles east of Lake City, Florida, on the Florida Atlantic and Gulf Central Railroad, Olustee was the site of the February 20, 1864, battle that was a decisive victory for Confederate Gen. Joseph Finegan. It was decisive in that the interior of Florida remained in Confederate hands for the duration of the conflict, enabling shipments of foodstuffs from Florida, largely cattle and hogs, to continue to feed Confederate armies. It cost the Confederates 946 men dead, wounded, or missing; the Federals suffered a total of 1,861 casualties.

The Federals made no serious effort to invade and occupy the interior of Florida until February 1864. An abrupt reversal of this policy came that month when 5,000 Federal troops from lower South Carolina and upper Georgia embarked aboard transports for an invasion of northeast Florida. A major invasion objective was political. President Abraham Lincoln doubted that he would be the Republican nominee to succeed himself in 1864. Salmon P. Chase, secretary of the treasury in Lincoln's cabinet, was his major challenger. Lyman P. Stickney, Chase-appointed tax collector, had served in Union-occupied sections of eastern Florida since 1862. He advised Chase that many Union supporters would assist Federal troops in restoring Florida to the Union and would provide a Chase delegation to the Republican National Convention. Lincoln, aware of these activities, sent his personal secretary, John Hay, to Florida, and he reported that the Unionists were friendlier to Lincoln than to Chase. Thus, Lincoln approved of the Federal invasion of February 1864 as a measure to restore Florida to the Union. His advisers were confident that the invasion would encounter little resistance, Floridians would accept Lincoln's generous plan for reconstruction, and the reconstructed state would send a Lincoln delegation to the Republican National Convention.

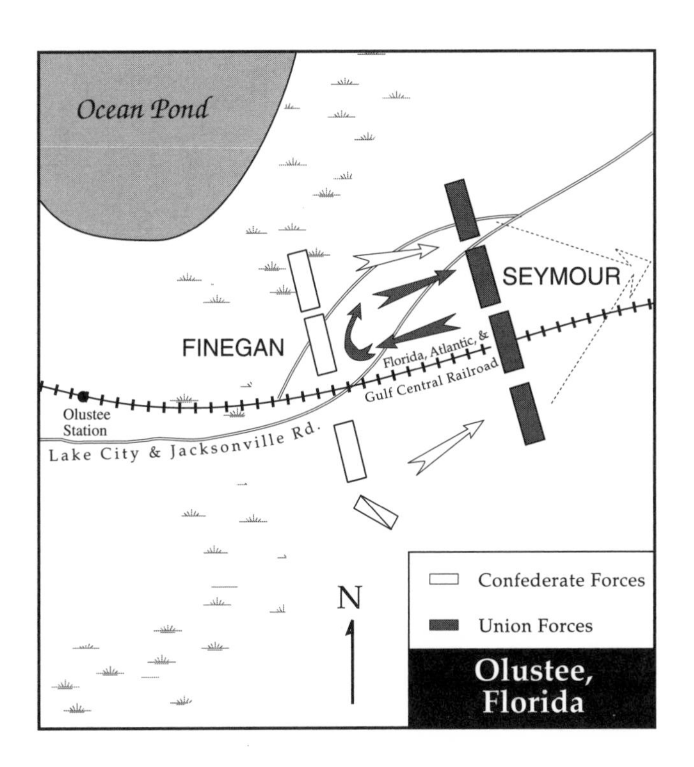

A second, and more obvious, reason for the invasion was to halt the movement of cattle, hogs, salt, and sugar from Florida that supplied Confederate armies to the north. The capture of Vicksburg by Union forces in 1863 had cut off the supplies of foodstuffs from Texas; the Confederacy needed Florida cattle and hogs to continue the war. A third objective was to free the slaves and enlist them as soldiers in the Union armies.

The Federal forces, commanded by Gen. Truman A. Seymour, reached Jacksonville on February 7, 1864. They moved westward following the route of the Florida Atlantic and Gulf Central Railroad in the direction of Lake City. Finegan, commander of the East Florida Military District, was ordered to halt the invaders and engage them in battle. Despite critical needs for troops elsewhere, Gen. Robert E. Lee ordered reinforcements from Georgia to join Finegan's command. Finegan withdrew his forces ahead of the Union advance in search of a better defensive position and to await the reinforcements. Confederate and Union commanders both overestimated the other's strength. Finegan's reinforced units numbered 5,000. After Seymour enlisted about 500 freed slaves for combat duty, his forces numbered about 5,500. Finegan called his withdrawal to a halt thirteen miles east of Lake City and found a defensive position near the village of Olustee—a rail embankment about a mile and a half long facing an open field. The embankment extended from Ocean Pond on the north to a large cyprus swamp on the south.

About noon on February 20, Union forces approached the Confederate defenses. The Southerners, aware that the Union men were tired from their long march and that many Federals had not yet reached the battle scene, ventured out of their prepared defenses and attacked the vanguard of the Union forces in an open field. When the Confederate cavalry and infantry attack was repulsed and driven back to the defenses, Seymour ordered the Federals to attack. Artillery prepared the way. Infantry and cavalry fired at a close range of about a hundred yards and then lunged forward. The defenders responded with a curtain of fire that turned back three Federal offensives.

A little after six in the evening, Seymour, responding to extremely high casualties and the stubborn resistance, ordered his units to retreat. He left behind some of the 1,861 dead and wounded. The Confederates, who captured 5 cannons, 1,600 small arms, and 130,000 rounds of ammunition, lost 93 killed, 847 wounded, and 6 missing. Though the battle at Olustee was minor in regard to the number of men engaged, both Confederate and Union forces suffered the highest percentage of casualties of any battle in the Civil War: the Union, about 37 percent and the Confederates, almost 20 percent.

The heavy Confederate casualties persuaded Finegan to halt the pursuit of retreating Federals about twelve miles west of Jacksonville. In April the Union strategy called for withdrawal of military forces from Florida to strengthen attacks to the north.

Olustee was a decisive victory for the Confederacy, and Finegan received a vote of thanks from Congress. Seymour was bitterly criticized by his own troops and by the Northern press. The supply lines to the Confederate armies remained open. Historian Rembert Patrick estimates that these foodstuffs enabled Lee to continue the war for another year. Tallahassee was the only Confederate capital in Confederate hands when the war ended. It was victories elsewhere, not a victory at Olustee, that renominated Abraham Lincoln for the presidency.

BIBLIOGRAPHY

Baltzell, George F. "The Battle of Olustee (Ocean Pond), Florida." *Florida Historical Quarterly* 9 (1930–1931): 199–223.

Johns, John E. *Florida during the Civil War.* Gainesville, Fla., 1963.

Tebeau, Charlton. *A History of Florida.* Coral Gables, Fla., 1980.

MERLIN G. COX

OLUSTEE. *See entry on the ship* Tallahassee.

O'NEAL, EDWARD ASBURY (1818–1890), brigadier general and postwar governor of Alabama. In the first days of the war many public figures raised volunteer units and owed their commissions to local prominence rather than to any military merit. Though some received subsequent promotions, they did not always perform well at higher grades. O'Neal was one of those in the Army of Northern Virginia who succeeded as a field officer but failed badly as a brigadier.

O'Neal was born in Madison County, Alabama, on September 20, 1818, was educated at La Grange College, and practiced law in Alabama for many years. He organized a company in the Ninth Alabama Infantry when the war began and had risen to lieutenant colonel by October 1861.

Appointed colonel of the Twenty-sixth Alabama Infantry in the spring of 1862, O'Neal was wounded at Seven Pines in May and was praised for his performance during the Seven Days' campaign. He was wounded twice at Sharpsburg and commanded a brigade, as senior colonel, by the spring of 1863. His reputation was somewhat diminished when he left the field with a slight wound at Chancellorsville, and his superiors recommended his promotion only reluctantly. O'Neal's appointment to brigadier general was dated June 6, 1863, but was canceled after he badly mishandled his brigade at Gettysburg. He attempted to resign, but was transferred to the Army of Tennessee in July 1864 and was a disappointment there as well. By early 1865 he was collecting absentees and deserters in northern Alabama.

O'Neal resumed his public career after the war, practicing law and serving two terms as governor of Alabama in the 1880s. He died at Florence, Alabama, on November 7, 1890.

BIBLIOGRAPHY

Compiled Military Service Records. Edward A. O'Neal. Microcopy M331, Roll 190. Record Group 109. National Archives, Washington, D.C.

Wheeler, Joseph. *Alabama.* Vol. 7 of *Confederate Military History.* Edited by Clement A. Evans. Atlanta, 1899. Vol. 8 of extended ed. Wilmington, N.C., 1987.

J. TRACY POWER

OPEQUON CREEK, VIRGINIA. *See* Winchester, Virginia.

OPOTHLEYAHOLA (c. 1790–1863), leader of the Unionist Creek (Muscogee) Indians. Born in the late 1790s in Tuckabatchee Town on the Alabama River, Opothleyahola was said to be the son of a leader of mixed ancestry named David Cornell. Cornell was murdered by Georgia militiamen when the boy was young. By the 1820s Opothleyahola had emerged as one of the most respected leaders of the traditionalist Creeks. He strongly opposed the Federal Indian removal policy but in 1832 reluctantly signed the final treaty to remove the last Creeks from Alabama and Georgia and to resettle the tribe in Indian Territory (present-day Oklahoma).

At the outbreak of the Civil War, Opothleyahola was a slave owner who farmed some two thousand acres of cotton near North Fork Town, but he opposed a Creek alliance with the Confederacy. In attempting to remain neutral in the struggle, he led more than five thousand loyalist Creeks and about one thousand other loyalist Indians of various tribes to the safety of Kansas in the winter of 1862–1863. During the difficult trek, a Confederate force of whites and Indians under the command of Col. Douglas Cooper and a Creek leader, Col. Daniel N. McIntosh, attacked the neutral party in three battles.

Although routed in the final battle (Chustenahlah) on December 26, Opothleyahola and the survivors completed the journey to Kansas where they encamped on the upper Verdigris River near Fredonia. The Federal government later moved them to the Sac and Fox Reservation in southeastern Kansas. Many of the loyalists returned to Indian Territory to fight in a Union detachment.

The old leader was never able to return to his Creek Nation. He died in Kansas some time during the spring of 1863 and was buried near Belmont.

BIBLIOGRAPHY

Bearss, Edwin C. "The Civil War Comes to Indian Territory, 1861: The Flight of Opothleyahola." *Journal of the West* 11 (January 1972): 9–42.

Clark, Carter Blue. "Opothleyahola and the Creeks during the Civil War." In *Indian Leaders: Oklahoma's First Statesmen.* Edited by H. Glenn Jordan and Thomas M. Holm. Oklahoma City, 1979.

Franks, Kenny. "Operations against Opothleyahola, 1861." *Military History of Texas and the Southwest* 10 (1972): 187–196.

Meserve, Bartlett. "Chief Opothleyahola." *Chronicles of Oklahoma* 9 (1931): 428–453.

DONALD E. GREEN

ORAL HISTORY. *Oral history* is a term used to refer to both a topic of study and the methodology used to record the information studied. An example of this technique are the seven interviews collected by Kate Cashman Conway from survivors of the Civil War and published in the *Vicksburg Evening Post* in 1906. All those who lived in the South during the Civil War are long dead, of course, but in most instances, their families still exist and are one of the prime conduits through which historical traditions concerning the war have survived to the present.

There are several reasons oral history is valuable for researchers interested in the Confederacy. Chief among these is that oral historical traditions preserve information not available in written sources. For example, the activities of Beanie Short, a guerrilla active in the Cumberland region of northern Tennessee and southern Kentucky, would be unknown today if it weren't for oral tradition. No newspapers in the area recounted his exploits, and there is no mention of him in court records, because few guerrillas stood trial for their crimes during the war. Oral historical narratives also often preserve what is psychologically true, and that can be as important as what is factually true. A South Carolina family still tells a story about two ancestors that explains why they left the Confederate forces to join the Union side. The brothers were part of a band of Confederates traveling through Virginia during the first half of the war. Although they were starving, they were given strict orders by their commanding officer not to steal apples from a nearby orchard. One of the brothers disobeyed, and the commander shot him in the arm. As a result the brothers left and joined the opposing side. Whether or not such an incident ever occurred is less important than the fact that the family today thinks it did. The story enables family members to regard their ancestors in a positive light rather than think of them as merely deserters.

Information gleaned from oral history interviews often humanizes the Civil War. One may read accounts of noted generals and battles without understanding what life during the conflict was like for most people. Orally preserved accounts of families living for weeks on roasted cottonseed or killing their only mule for food make the difficulty of the times more vivid.

Oral histories also often provide a source for popular beliefs and attitudes. A legend common in the southern Appalachians maintains that Abraham Lincoln was the illegitimate son of a Southerner—in some accounts of John C. Calhoun, in others of an unheralded North Carolina mountaineer named Abraham Enloe. Although those who keep such traditions alive take them seriously, they are probably dismissed by most professional historians. They remain alive mainly because of the mountaineers' pride in having Lincoln as one of their own. Another traditional account preserved in some areas is that Lincoln and Jefferson Davis were half-brothers, which can be seen as symbolizing the healing of political divisions among the American people. Moreover, for some people Lincoln's illegitimacy explains his presumed persistent melancholy.

Other positive features of oral history include the possibility of verifying incidents and the provision of information concerning minority groups who, during the war, were more dependent on the spoken than on the written word. Yet, despite its advantages, oral history and the related field of folklore have not been used to their fullest potential by historians studying the Confederacy.

[*See also* Folk Narratives.]

BIBLIOGRAPHY

Alley, Judge Felix E. *Random Thoughts and the Musings of a Mountaineer.* Salisbury, N.C., 1941.

Cotton, Gordon A. *Yankee Bullets, Rebel Rations.* Vicksburg, Mississippi, 1989.

Deering, Mary Jo, and Barbara Pomeroy. *Transcribing Without Tears: A Guide to Transcribing and Editing Oral History Interviews.* Washington, D.C., 1976.

Dorson, Richard M. *American Folklore and the Historian.* Chicago, 1971.

Hoopes, James. *Oral History: An Introduction for Students.* Chapel Hill, N.C., 1979.

W. K. McNeil

ORDER OF AMERICAN KNIGHTS. *See* Copperheads.

ORDNANCE BUREAU. The Ordnance Bureau of the Confederate army functioned as a subsection of the Artillery Corps, but achieved status as one of the most important and successful supply agencies in the Confederacy. The tasks facing the bureau were formidable. All war munitions would have to be provided as state and Confederate forces came into being, but each state worked to provide for its own troops, so that the bureau encountered proprietary and patchwork efforts across the country.

Fortunately for the bureau, Maj. (later Brig. Gen.) Josiah Gorgas, a Pennsylvanian turned Southerner, became its chief on April 8, 1861. A sober, quiet man, Gorgas after graduating from West Point had distinguished himself in the U.S. ordnance service for his ability, although he chafed at his subordinate role. While serving at Mount Vernon Arsenal in Alabama, he met his future wife, Amelia Gayle, daughter of a former Alabama governor, and became converted to the Southern way of life.

With characteristic energy, Gorgas surveyed his bureau and his new country. On May 7, 1861, he reported to Congress that the South had 164,010 small arms ranging from U.S. rifled muskets to .69-caliber muskets, new and altered percussion and flint muskets, Harpers Ferry rifles, Colt rifles, Hall rifles, varied carbines, and Colt and percussion pistols. He discovered some 3.2 million small arms cartridges, along with 168,000 pounds of musket and rifle powder—enough for another one and a half million cartridges. Cannon powder was located at permanent fortifications. Percussion caps, a vital ingredient in modern weaponry, numbered about 2 million, with "a good many at the arsenals and bundled with the cartridges." Georgia was rumored to have 150 tons of saltpeter, with sulphur enough to make another 200 tons of powder. The question was, would fervent state rights Governor Joseph E. Brown contribute these ingredients to the Confederacy?

Gorgas knew many of the arsenals in the South well, and he worked quickly to revamp and modernize several. Charleston's arsenal received steam power; Montgomery's shops were upgraded to repair small arms and manufacture leather goods. Small works were established at Knoxville, Tennessee, Jackson, Mississippi, and Dublin, Lynchburg, and Danville, Virginia. Nashville had extensive shops already, and they became a mainstay for forces assembling under Gen. Albert Sidney Johnston.

From the beginning, the Ordnance Bureau faced serious procurement, collection, and distribution problems. Gorgas decided early to try to centralize manufacturing in Georgia and use the Atlanta rail hub as well as river arteries to distribute the products. Major manufacturing plants were established at Augusta and Macon. The Augusta Powder Works became one of the best in the world, and the Macon Arsenal and Armory ranked among the most efficient installations, along with that town's Confederate States Central Laboratory.

The success of these plants derived from Gorgas's leadership. Because he himself did not work well under authority, he understood the need for freedom in others. And as high responsibility soothed his own abrasiveness, he cherished independence in his subordinates. Careful searching found the right men. From the start he knew that a gifted scientist was needed in the bureau, and he found John W. Mallet, an Englishman serving on the field staff of Brig. Gen. Robert Rodes. Mallet, a member of Great Britain's Royal Society, had been chemist to the Alabama Geological Survey when the war started. His appointment filled a vital niche in the ordnance technological staff. Assigned as chief of the Central Laboratories, Mallet brought standardization to the maze of calibers in small arm ammunition production, invented new and impressive weapons (the "polygonal shell" broke into a predetermined number of pieces), and worked to institutionalize quality in ammunition production.

James H. Burton, who became superintendent of armories, possessed a complete set of English Enfield rifle plans and put them to good use in making a passable Confederate copy. But George Washington Rains stands out as the most successful of Gorgas's stellar subordinates. On April 10, 1862, his Augusta Powder Works began operations. Rains had found the site, secured the Confederate title, and supervised construction of a plant to rival the famous Waltham Abbey Works in England. The Augusta facility, plus others directed by Rains, provided sufficient powder for the war.

Niter was an essential ingredient in powder manufacture, but neither Gorgas nor Rains could devote time to locating sources of the component. Gorgas pushed for a separate Niter and Mining Bureau, attached to the Ordnance Bureau, to find this necessity. Maj. Isaac M. St. John took charge of this bureau in April 1862, and it grew into an indispensable agency. St. John used human urine to leach niter beds across the South.

Ordnance officers became involved in all kinds of activities. Since they served the artillery, leather harnesses, traces, and caissons were among their concerns. Moreover, supplies for ordnance workers increasingly had to come from ordnance establishments. So the bureau became a small "vertical combine," supplying its workers with food, clothing, shoes, medical services, and other needs.

From the outset ordnance officers counted on three sources for arms and munitions: battlefield captures, home manufacturing, and blockade running. Captures provided early supplies; manufacturing, heavily pressed, took time and resources to reach production; and though organization of blockade running also took time and resources, the Ordnance Bureau—chiefly because of Gorgas's personal attention—quickly assumed a key role in importing supplies from abroad. Relying as always on talent, Gorgas sent Maj. Caleb Huse to Europe, charged with the purchase and shipment of arms and munitions. Energetic, sometimes recklessly eager, Huse did admirable work—his astronomical debts were the best proof of his ability.

Funds were always a problem in foreign purchasing, and Gorgas, working with the quartermaster general and the surgeon general, sought innovative ways to provide money. The best system proved to be the exportation of Confederate cotton for exchange in England or other European countries. Various private firms were involved as cotton brokers. Among the most important were Saul Isaac, Campbell and Co.; Collie, Crenshaw, and Co.; and Fraser, Trenholm, and Co. These and other firms not only traded cotton for funds, but many bought and ran blockade runners to and from the embattled South. Gorgas and other supply chiefs tried various schemes for exporting government bales: space on runners was usually purchased on a bale-for-bale basis—that is, one government bale transported along with one bale paid for the privilege.

Complaints of high costs abroad, even of fraud in the blockade-running business, were hardly unexpected. So profitable a business (a successful run might well pay for a private vessel twice over) and so vital a venture for the Confederacy could not escape some excesses. But gradually Gorgas and other bureau chiefs managed the effort efficiently. A new system went into effect in 1863 when Colin J. McRae, an Alabama businessman, went abroad to take charge of foreign purchasing under proceeds of the $15 million Erlanger loan. Although not as helpful as hoped, the loan nonetheless did finance the purchase of blockade runners as well as myriad supplies.

Once purchased, supplies had to reach the South. Freighters could not elude the Federal blockade, so they took their cargoes to transshipment harbors in Nassau, Bermuda, and Cuba. From those ports swift, light-draft blockade runners took the cargo on to the Confederacy. These vessels were always at high risk. The derring-do of blockade runners fills some of the most exciting pages of Civil War history. The Ordnance Bureau shared some five runners with the Quartermaster and Medical Departments.

As private vessels entered the trade, Gorgas took charge of managing the government's program. He shifted the duty to Maj. Thomas L. Bayne, head of the Bureau of Foreign Supplies in 1862, but kept pushing foreign operations. He achieved a complete change in government blockade running early in 1864 with the passage of two important laws that partly nationalized space on outgoing and incoming vessels and limited importation of luxury goods.

Blockade running proved highly successful, despite increased captures. In the course of the war the Ordnance Bureau imported no less than 330,000 arms, mostly Enfield rifles (state and private ventures brought in at least 270,000 more) and from December 1863 to December 1864, 1,933,000 pounds of saltpeter and 1,507,000 pounds of lead.

Domestic production grew apace but suffered the vagaries of poor transportation, enemy incursions, and dwindling supplies of lead, powder, copper, and saltpeter. By the end of 1862 monthly small arms ammunition production from eight important arsenals totaled 170,000 rounds. But as the war continued, shortages increased. Copper became so scarce that whiskey stills in mountain country were confiscated, and when lead ran short, window weights were taken from buildings in major cities.

As conscription tightened across the South, skilled ordnance workers often were called up for general service or for local defense. Gorgas pointed out the damage done by the loss of one barrel straightener at the Richmond armory—production dropped 360 rifles per month! Ordnance workers were national resources and the bureau chief strenuously fought to keep them at work.

The various makeshifts did the job. The Ordnance Bureau continued providing munitions to Confederate forces until the end of the war. No other Southern supply bureau achieved so much with so few resources. Gorgas ranks as a logistical genius and a management wizard who picked the right men for the field armies and for production, distribution, and foreign operations.

On April 8, 1864, Gorgas wrote in his diary an assessment of his bureau:

> It is three years ago today since I took charge of the Ordnance Department. . . . I have succeeded beyond my utmost expectations. From being the worst supplied of the Bureaus of the War Department it is now the best. Large arsenals have been organized at Richmond, Fayetteville, Augusta, Charleston, Columbus, Macon, Atlanta and Selma, and smaller ones at Danville, Lynchburgh, and Montgomery, besides other establishments. A superb powder mill has been built at Augusta. . . . Lead smelting works were established . . . at Petersburgh. . . . A cannon foundry established at Macon for heavy guns, and bronze foundries at Macon, Columbus, Ga., and Augusta; a foundry for shot and shell at Salisbury, N.C.; a large shop for leather work at Clarksville, Va.; besides the Armories here [Richmond] and at Fayetteville, a manufactory of carbines has been built up here; a rifle factory at Ashville (transferred to Columbia, S.C.); a new

> and very large armory at Macon, including a pistol factory, built up under contract here and sent to Atlanta, and thence transferred under purchase to Macon; a second pistol factory at Columbus, Ga.;— All of these . . . have borne such fruit as relieves the country from fear of want in these respects.

Gorgas was right. When Robert E. Lee took his army toward Appomattox Courthouse in April 1865, he stuck to a rail line looking for a ration train. No ration train came, but an ammunition train did.

[*See also* Arsenals and Armories; Artillery; Edged Weapons; Hand Grenades and Mines; Munitions; Niter and Mining Bureau; Powder Works; Small Arms.]

BIBLIOGRAPHY

Broun, W. LeRoy. "The Red Artillery." *Southern Historical Society Papers* 26 (1898): 365–376. Reprint, Wilmington, N.C., 1991.

Goff, Richard D. *Confederate Supply.* Durham, N.C., 1969.

Gorgas, Josiah. *The Civil War Diary of General Josiah Gorgas.* Edited by F. E. Vandiver. University, Ala., 1947.

Gorgas, Josiah. "Ordnance of the Confederacy, I, II." *Southern Historical Society Papers* 12 (1884): 67–94. Reprint, Wilmington, N.C., 1990.

Huse, Caleb. *The Supplies for the Confederate Army, How They Were Obtained in Europe and How Paid For. Personal Reminiscences and Unpublished History.* Boston, 1904.

Thompson, Samuel B. *Confederate Purchasing Operations Abroad.* Chapel Hill, N.C., 1935.

Vandiver, Frank E. *Ploughshares into Swords: Josiah Gorgas and Confederate Ordnance.* Austin, Tex., 1952.

Frank E. Vandiver

ORPHAN BRIGADE. Officially designated the First Kentucky Brigade, this most famous of Confederate organizations from the Bluegrass State had its origins in the pro-secessionist prewar state guard. In the spring and summer of 1861, while Kentucky remained neutral, secessionist sympathizers gathered across the line at Camp Boone, Tennessee, to enlist with the Confederacy. The Second Kentucky Infantry organized on July 13, followed by the Third Infantry a few days later. The Fourth Infantry followed on September 1, along with Edward Byrne's battery of artillery. That fall, through an administrative confusion, two Fifth Kentucky Infantries were organized, one later being designated the Ninth. On November 19, 1861, the Sixth Infantry organized, and two more batteries, H. B. Lyon's and Rice E. Graves's, were added. For a time the First Kentucky Cavalry and a squadron of horsemen led by John Hunt Morgan were also a part of the brigade, making it more of a "legion" in the then-current definition. During the course of the war there would be several cases of tampering with the brigade's organization, but eventually it came down to the Second, Fourth, Fifth, Sixth, and Ninth Infantries, and Robert Cobb's and Graves's batteries.

Simon Bolivar Buckner briefly commanded the brigade as it was forming, but John C. Breckinridge soon superseded him, commencing a long association with the Kentuckians. In turn, he yielded command to Col. Roger W. Hanson, who was captured along with the Second Kentucky in the fall of Fort Donelson. Thus Col. Robert P. Trabue led the men in their first battle at Shiloh, where they distinguished themselves in the taking of the Hornet's Nest. After covering the Confederate retreat from Shiloh, the Kentuckians went on to serve at Vicksburg that summer and then participated in the August 5, 1862, attack on Baton Rouge.

They probably acquired their nickname in the carnage of the abortive January 2, 1863, assault on the Federal left at Murfreesboro. Breckinridge, now division commander, opposed the attack, as did Hanson, who had been exchanged and was back in command of the brigade. Hanson took a mortal wound, and the brigade suffered more than 25 percent casualties. Breckinridge wept, crying "My poor Orphans! My poor Orphan Brigade!" He was presumably referring to the fact that Kentucky never left the Union, leaving its Confederate soldiers cut off from succor and support, material and moral, from home. The nickname stuck, acquiring limited use during the war and universal adoption by the 1880s.

Following Murfreesboro, the brigade returned to Mississippi in the failed attempt to relieve Vicksburg and then fought with the Army of Tennessee at Chickamauga, where commander Ben Hardin Helm fell and Col. Joseph Lewis took command for the balance of the war. The Orphans served through the Atlanta campaign until heavy losses at Jonesboro on September 1, 1864, practically destroyed the brigade. Some of those left were given horses to finish out the war as mounted infantry, operating with Confederate cavalry in Georgia and South Carolina. Of the four thousand who had enlisted in 1861, barely six hundred were left to give their parole at Washington, Georgia, on May 7, 1865.

Joseph E. Johnston, William J. Hardee, and other leading generals pronounced the Orphans the finest brigade in the Army of Tennessee. Even allowing for hyperbole, the Kentuckians remain one of the most colorful, hard-fighting, and dedicated units of the Confederate service.

BIBLIOGRAPHY

Davis, William C. *The Orphan Brigade.* New York, 1980.

Jackman, John S. *Memoirs of a Confederate Soldier: Soldiering with the Orphan Brigade.* Edited by William C. Davis. Columbia, S.C., 1990.

Thompson, Ed Porter. *History of the First Kentucky Brigade.* Cincinnati, 1868.

William C. Davis

BIBLIOGRAPHY

Breeze, Donald H. "James L. Orr, Calhoun, and the Cooperationist Tradition in South Carolina." *South Carolina Historical Magazine* 80 (1981): 273–285.

Cauthen, Charles E. *South Carolina Goes to War, 1860–65.* Chapel Hill, N.C., 1950.

Cyclopedia of Eminent and Representative Men of the Carolinas. Madison, Wis., 1982.

Leemhuis, Roger P. *James L. Orr and the Sectional Conflict.* Washington, D.C., 1979.

Warner, Ezra J., and W. Buck Yearns. *Biographical Register of the Confederate Congress.* Baton Rouge, La., 1975.

A. V. HUFF, JR.

ORR, JEHU AMAZIAH (1828–1921), colonel and congressman from Mississippi. Orr was born in South Carolina and attended Erskine College there before graduating from what is now Princeton University. Orr then set up a law practice in Houston, Mississippi. In 1850 he was named secretary of the state senate and two years later was elected to the state house of representatives. From 1854 to 1855 he was a U.S. district attorney and the next year served as a presidential elector for James Buchanan.

Although opposed to secession and a supporter of Stephen A. Douglas in the Democratic National Convention of 1860, he eventually came to view secession as inevitable and voted for it in the Mississippi secession convention in 1861.

Orr succeeded William Sydney Wilson as a member of the Provisional Congress and served until 1862 when he became commander of the Thirty-first Mississippi Regiment. In that role he participated in many battles—among them, Coffeeville, Baton Rouge, Vicksburg, and Jackson. At the Battle of Harrisburg, he served as the volunteer aide to Gens. Nathan Bedford Forrest and Stephen D. Lee.

Orr lost the election for the First Congress at Richmond. He was defeated by J. W. Clapp, the man whom he in turn defeated two years later for a seat in the Second Congress. While in Congress, Orr opposed most of the powers and policies of Jefferson Davis, working to help the economy of the Southern states and to promote an end to the war through negotiation. As a member of the Committee on Foreign Affairs, he was appointed to report to the Congress on resolutions that sought "to see if the matters in controversy" could be "adjusted by negotiation, without further effusion of blood." His committee suggested that three people be selected to meet with Abraham Lincoln to negotiate for peace. After Orr reported the resolution, the Hampton Roads Conference subsequently took place, but the negotiations failed because of language calling for recognition of the independence of the Confederacy. Orr blamed the failure of the conference on Jefferson Davis's inflexibility.

After the war Orr sought to mend sectional fences and to facilitate Southern recovery. From 1870 to 1876, he served as circuit judge and continued working to rescue the state from the disorder brought on by the war and Reconstruction. Orr lived to the age of ninety-three and actively practiced law until he died.

BIBLIOGRAPHY

Alexander, Thomas B., and Richard E. Beringer. *The Anatomy of the Confederate Congress: A Study of the Influences of Member Characteristics on Legislative Voting Behavior, 1861–1865.* Nashville, Tenn., 1972.

Warner, Ezra J., and W. Buck Yearns. *Biographical Register of the Confederate Congress.* Baton Rouge, La., 1975.

RAY SKATES

OSAGES. The Osages, a Dhegiha Siouan tribe originally located in what is now Missouri, were occupying a large reservation in Kansas when the Civil War began. The majority of this fringe Plains tribe lived along the Verdigris and Neosho rivers that flowed through the extreme eastern portion of the reservation whose southern border was Indian Territory and the lands of the Five Civilized Tribes. Unlike their southern neighbors, the Osages were not slave owners and knew little of the black men they called *nika-sabe;* thus their participation in the war was based on personal, not tribal loyalties.

In July and August 1861, Confederate sympathizer and Indian trader John Mathews led joint forces of pro-Southern whites and Osages in several skirmishes against local settlers supporting the Union. Father Schoenmakers, a Unionist and head of the Osage Mission, was forced to flee the region. In September the Sixth Kansas Cavalry routed Mathews's company. Mathews was killed and his death left the Confederate cause without a local leader.

Albert Pike persuaded the Osages to sign a treaty with the Confederate government on October 2, 1861. Fifty-seven Osage chiefs and counselors signed the treaty of amity and a promise by the Osages to furnish five hundred warriors to the war effort and allow a fort to be built on tribal land. Only a band led by Black Dog and Big Chief actively supported the Confederacy, however, fleeing their reservation to live among the Creeks and Cherokees. Some of their warriors fought individually in minor engagements in Indian Territory. Osages supporting the Union attacked twenty-two Confederate officers, disguised as civilians, crossing the Kansas reservation on a spying expedition in May 1863. Only two officers escaped death and the scalping knife.

BIBLIOGRAPHY

Mathews, John Joseph. *Osages: Children of the Middle Waters.* Norman, Okla., 1961.

Wilson, Terry P. *The Osage.* New York, 1988.

TERRY P. WILSON

OURY, GRANVILLE H. (1825–1891), congressional delegate from Arizona Territory. Born March 12, 1825, in Abingdon, Virginia, Oury moved to Missouri in 1836. Here, in 1848, he passed the bar. The following year, on his brother's advice, Oury went to Texas. After arriving in San Antonio, the adventurous lawyer joined a party of California gold seekers. After several years on the Pacific coast, Oury abandoned the gold fields in 1856 and moved to Tucson.

In 1857, Oury supported Henry Crabb's disastrous filibustering expedition into Sonora. He subsequently became active in Tucson politics, advocating a separate territory called Arizona to be created out of the Gadsden Purchase. With the arrival of the secession crisis in 1860, Oury and the citizens of Arizona sided with the Confederacy. On March 23, 1861, a convention of sixty-eight voters in Tucson endorsed secession and elected Oury to represent the new territory in Richmond.

Oury made the difficult trip to Virginia and took office as a nonvoting delegate in January 1862. Political infighting soon led the temperamental governor of Arizona, John Robert Baylor, to replace Oury with Marcus (or Malcolm) Macwillie. Before Macwillie could arrive, Arizona was overrun by Union troops from California and New Mexico Territory. Oury returned to Texas, where he served as a volunteer aide-de-camp in the Confederate army.

After the war, Oury returned to his Tucson law practice and politics. He served in various territorial posts, including attorney general, as well as serving two terms in the U.S. House of Representatives. He died on January 11, 1891.

BIBLIOGRAPHY

Ganaway, Loomis Morton. *New Mexico and the Sectional Controversy, 1846–1861.* Albuquerque, N.M., 1944.

Smith, Cornelius C., Jr. *William Sanders Oury: History-Maker of the Southwest.* Tucson, Ariz., 1967.

Stout, Joseph Allen, Jr. *The Liberators: Filibustering Expeditions into Mexico, 1848–1862, and the Last Thrust of Manifest Destiny.* Los Angeles, 1973.

DONALD S. FRAZIER

OVERSEERS. Employed on virtually all rice and sugar plantations, on most cotton plantations with twenty or more adult field hands, and on many smaller units in the tobacco and grain regions, overseers were essential functionaries in managing Southern plantations and controlling the slave population. The overseer, usually a white man of yeoman farmer antecedents, was the link in the managerial chain between the plantation owner or his agent and the black slave drivers. Chiefly responsible for slave welfare and discipline as well as crop production, he assigned gangs to work, apportioned tasks, supervised field labor, administered punishment, enforced curfews, distributed food and clothing, periodically inspected slave cabins, treated minor medical ailments, and maintained various record and account books. In areas of the plantation South where blacks heavily outnumbered whites—most notably along the rice coast of South Carolina and Georgia and in the Yazoo, Mississippi, delta—overseers provided the sparse white population with its principal security against slave misconduct and possible insurrection.

With the continuing expansion of the plantation system into the Southwest along with a concomitant trend toward consolidation of existing units, the number of overseers doubled during the decade of the 1850s, reaching a total of nearly 38,000 on the eve of the Civil War. Of that number, more than two-thirds were located in the leading plantation states of Alabama, Georgia, Louisiana, Mississippi, North and South Carolina, and Virginia. Although the incidence of overseer utilization was highest on the vast sugar and rice estates of Louisiana and South Carolina, respectively, the majority of plantation superintendents were employed on cotton plantations from southern Virginia to eastern Texas. The ratio of overseers to total slave population within different staple regions ranged from a low of one overseer for every seventy-five to one hundred slaves in the cotton, grain, and tobacco counties to a high of one manager for more than three hundred slaves in the heavily black rice districts between Charleston and Savannah. Clearly, the presence of white overseers in such areas as the latter became more crucial than ever following the outbreak of the Civil War.

When hostilities erupted in April 1861, the relative youth and physical hardiness of overseers made them prime candidates for military service. Although many plantation managers responded enthusiastically to the call of their nascent country, their employers manifested almost universal reluctance to dispense with their services. Indeed, efforts by Confederate authorities to enroll overseers in the military provoked a veritable storm of protest from members of the planter class, who, ironically, had previously berated their subordinates for a variety of alleged shortcomings and transgressions. Now they were suddenly considered indispensable—not only to individual proprietors but to the entire white community. Praising "the Overseer system as the best civil police system that can be invented," South Carolina rice magnate James Barnwell Heyward pleaded for the exemption of overseers in his district both to police the slave population and to render the plantations more effective in furnishing "supplies for the army." Such appeals, with similar reasoning, became general throughout the South.

The exemption of plantation managers proved to be one of the most controversial domestic issues during the war, spawning bitterness and disaffection among small farmers and nonslaveholders. Surprisingly, overseers were not among the occupational groups initially exempted from military service under legislation enacted by the Confederate Congress pursuant to the Conscription Act of April 1862. But in October of that year, in order "to secure the proper police of the country," Congress provided for the exemption of "one person, either as agent, owner or overseer" on each plantation with twenty or more slaves. Subsequent revisions of this statute in May 1863 and in February 1864 substantially reduced the number of overseer exemptions. Thus, by the end of 1863 the number of overseers exempted by authority of Congress had dwindled to approximately three hundred in South Carolina and a mere two hundred each in Georgia and Virginia. It should be noted, however, that regulations governing the exemption of overseers varied considerably from state to state, and additional exemptions were granted by governors and local military commanders as circumstances dictated.

Despite efforts by both Confederate and state officials to respond to planters' concern for the security of their chattel, a severe shortage of overseers developed during the war. Various expedients were devised to combat this shortage. Perhaps the most obvious was that of simply getting along without an overseer, a viable option for many smaller planters. On other units women assumed the unaccustomed role of superintending planting operations, frequently with inauspicious results. In some localities proprietors joined forces and entrusted a single overseer with the oversight of multiple properties. Other planters hired novice overseers from other occupational groups or retained in their employ mediocre managers who, in normal times, would have been summarily discharged. As the war continued, the deficiency in experienced plantation managers became more acute, and Southern agricultural production suffered accordingly.

Malingering as well as more serious violations of plantation regulations became more common in the absence of an overseer, who had enforced discipline primarily through close surveillance of the slave force and by administering corporal punishment to offenders within parameters specified by his employer. Although violent acts of insubordination were rare, at least before Federal troops arrived in their immediate vicinity, slaves took advantage of relaxed supervision to work at a more leisurely pace, to demand additional privileges, and to augment their food supply with more frequent raids upon their owners' larders.

Even for those planters able to secure competent overseers, the war exacerbated long-standing animosities and rendered more difficult the control of the slave population. Always ready to exploit to their own advantage the inherent conflict between the interests of owner and overseer, the slaves found wartime conditions particularly congenial to such efforts to ameliorate their situation. Moreover, relations between overseers and slaves, at best tenuous in normal times, were further inflamed during the war. The problems became most critical in those portions of the plantation South—especially Virginia and Louisiana—that were subjected to repeated Federal incursions. The presence of Union troops frequently engendered disruptive conduct by overseers and slaves alike, thereby resulting in a total failure of agricultural operations in the occupied area.

It seems fair to conclude that Southern agriculture was severely impaired during the war by a scarcity of able plantation managers, by the unsatisfactory performance of their substitutes, and by the resulting insubordination of the laboring force. This failure to solve the problem of controlling slaves had a demoralizing impact on the home front and was therefore a significant factor in the demise of the Confederacy.

[*See also* Conscription; Slave Drivers.]

BIBLIOGRAPHY

Easterby, James H., ed. *The South Carolina Rice Plantation as Revealed in the Papers of Robert F. W. Allston.* Chicago, 1945.

Roark, James L. *Masters without Slaves: Southern Planters in the Civil War and Reconstruction.* New York, 1977.

Roland, Charles P. *Louisiana Sugar Plantations during the American Civil War.* Leiden, 1957.

Scarborough, William K. *The Overseer: Plantation Management in the Old South.* Baton Rouge, La., 1966. Reprint, Athens, Ga., 1984.

Wiley, Bell I. *Southern Negroes, 1861–1865.* New Haven, 1938.

WILLIAM K. SCARBOROUGH

OWENS, JAMES B. (1816–1889), congressman from Florida. Born in Barnwell District, South Carolina, Owens graduated from Furman College and moved to Marion County, Florida, in 1853. He and his brothers, William and Samuel, became wealthy cotton planters, and Owens was active in politics. A delegate to the Democratic convention at Charleston in 1860, he supported John C. Breckinridge but also tried to prevent the party split between his wing and those committed to Stephen A. Douglas. He represented Marion County at the state secession convention and voted for secession.

Owens was elected to the Provisional Confederate Congress and was on the committee that drafted the Permanent

Constitution. A strong advocate of state rights, he opposed the Davis administration, and took no part in the war after his term ended.

Owens was also a Baptist minister who preached all over Marion County during the war. Although he had owned large slaveholdings, after the surrender he worked hard to resettle and improve the lives of black freedmen during Reconstruction. He became a successful citrus grower and a prominent citizen until his death in Ocala on August 1, 1889.

BIBLIOGRAPHY

Ott, Eloise R., and Louis Hickman Chazal. *Ocali Country, Kingdom of the Sun: A History of Marion County, Florida, 1559–1965.* Ocala, Fla., 1966.

Sifakis, Stewart. *Who Was Who in the Civil War.* New York, 1988.

Wakelyn, Jon L. *Biographical Dictionary of the Confederacy.* Edited by Frank E. Vandiver. Westport, Conn., 1977.

Arch Fredric Blakey

PADUCAH, KENTUCKY. This town, located on the Ohio River at the mouth of the Tennessee River, was the site of a Confederate raid by Gen. Nathan Bedford Forrest on March 25, 1864. It cost the Confederates twenty-five men killed or wounded; the Union forces reported casualties of fourteen killed and forty-six wounded.

Because of its strategic location, Gen. Ulysses S. Grant had occupied the town of Paducah on September 6, 1861. Since the loyalty of the town was in question, military rule was established under successive Union Gens. E. A. Paine, Charles F. Smith, Lew Wallace, and Sol Meredith, and Col. Stephen G. Hicks. The town was defended by Federal gunboats and an earthwork fort surrounded by deep ditches. Fort Anderson was defended by some 665 men from the 122d Illinois Infantry, the 16th Kentucky Cavalry, and the 1st Kentucky Artillery, and the 8th U.S. Heavy Artillery. The latter was a black regiment that was unpopular with the townspeople.

On March 25, 1864, with about 2,700 troops (Forrest's three regiments of 700 men and Gen. Abram Buford's two brigades of 2,000 men), Forrest advanced toward Paducah from Mayfield, Kentucky. When he arrived around two o'clock in the afternoon, Colonel Hicks immediately withdrew into the fort and ordered the Federal gunboats, *Poesta* and *Paw Paw,* to open fire upon the invaders. When Forrest requested the surrender of the fort, Hicks refused, whereupon Forrest gave the order to advance. Led by Col. Albert P. Thompson, the Confederates charged but they were driven back and Thompson was killed. Using nearby residences, Confederate sharpshooters opened fire upon the Union soldiers. Because Hicks's troops were running short of ammunition, he ordered them to fix bayonets, expecting Forrest to charge. After three attempts to reduce the fort, Forrest ordered his troops to cease firing.

The Confederate forces remained in the town until near midnight, seizing Union stores, military supplies, and some 400 horses and mules. According to Forrest, they burned 60 bales of cotton, the steamer *Dacotah,* and a dry dock, and took 50 prisoners. With the withdrawal of the Confederates, Hicks ordered the burning of some 60 houses they had used to fire upon the fort, which aroused the anger of the residents. On the morning of March 26, under a flag of truce, Forrest offered a prisoner exchange, which Hicks refused since he lacked the authority.

When Hicks reported that the Confederates had stolen private property rather than the well-hidden Union mules and horses, Confederate General Buford, with 800 men, returned to Paducah on April 14 and, despite the fire from Federal gunboats, drove the Union forces back into the fort and seized Union stores and supplies together with a large number of horses and mules (Forrest claimed to have taken 140 horses, Hicks, 411). The Confederates remained in Kentucky and Tennessee for more than a month, recruiting and sequestering supplies.

As a result of these raids, there was a change of Union military command, martial law was proclaimed, and the writ of habeas corpus was suspended in Kentucky.

BIBLIOGRAPHY

Harrison, Lowell H. *The Civil War in Kentucky.* Lexington, Ky., 1975.

Jordan, Thomas, and J. P. Pryon. *The Campaigns of Lieut.-General Forrest, and of Forrest's Cavalry, with Portraits, Maps, and Illustrations.* New Orleans, La., 1868.

Neuman, Fred G. *The Story of Paducah (Kentucky).* Paducah, Ky., 1927.

Robertson, John E. L. *Paducah 1830–1980.* Paducah, Ky., 1980.

Ross A. Webb

PAGE, RICHARD L. (1807–1901), naval officer and brigadier general. Page was ordnance officer at the Norfolk navy yard when he resigned from the U.S. Navy in 1860. Joining the Virginia navy first, he helped plan the defenses of the James River. In June 1861, he joined the Confederate navy and once more served as ordnance officer at the Norfolk navy yard. When Norfolk was evacuated in May 1862, Page supervised the movement of machinery and workers to Charlotte, North Carolina. During his two-year administration, Charlotte became a major production center. In the course of these years, Page also joined Como. Josiah Tattnall aboard *Savannah* in defense of Port Royal. He was second in command of the squadron under Tattnall, and during the battle he commanded *Savannah's* forward gun.

In 1864 Page was sent to Mobile to command that port's outer defenses. In line with his new duties, he was transferred to the Confederate army and appointed brigadier general. He was given command of Fort Morgan because of his expertise in ordnance. Page augmented the defenses in Mobile Bay, making it one of the best fortified points in the Confederacy. After the Union navy defeated Confederate forces in the bay in August 1864, Page was cut off from resupply and had no choice but to surrender Fort Morgan. He had held his position as long as he could. Taken prisoner, he was not released until September 1865.

RICHARD L. PAGE. LIBRARY OF CONGRESS

Page spent his later years in Norfolk, where he served in several positions including that of superintendent of the city's public schools.

BIBLIOGRAPHY

Civil War Naval Chronology. 6 vols. Washington, D.C., 1961–1966.

Jones, Virgil C. *The Civil War at Sea.* 3 vols. New York, 1961–1962.

Register of Officers of the Confederate States Navy, 1861–1865. Washington, D.C., 1931.

Scharf, John Thomas. *History of the Confederate States Navy from Its Organization to the Surrender of Its Last Vessel.* New York, 1887. Reprint, New York, 1977.

FRANK LAWRENCE OWSLEY

PALMER, JOSEPH BENJAMIN (1825–1890), brigadier general. Palmer was born November 1, 1825, in Rutherford County, Tennessee. Raised by his grandparents, he was educated at Union University (Murfreesboro, Tennessee) and in 1848 began the practice of law. A Whig, he served in the state legislature and from 1855 to 1859 was mayor of Murfreesboro.

Although opposed to secession, Palmer helped organize what became Company C of the Eighteenth Tennessee Infantry Regiment and was elected its captain. The Federals captured the regiment at Fort Donelson in February 1862 and imprisoned Palmer at Fort Warren, Massachusetts. Exchanged in August 1862, the regiment reorganized, and Palmer was elected colonel.

Palmer suffered three wounds in the Battle of Murfreesboro (December 31, 1862–January 2, 1863) but refused to leave the field until the battle ended. After a long recuperation, he returned to duty only to be seriously wounded again at Chickamauga (September 19–20, 1863). Palmer did not rejoin the army until the summer of 1864. He then commanded what had been John C. Brown's brigade in the last weeks of the Atlanta campaign and through the Franklin and Nashville campaign.

In December 1863 Maj. Gen. B. Franklin Cheatham had written that Palmer was "one of the best Cols. now in the army." On December 7, 1864, Palmer was promoted to brigadier general with date of rank set at November 15. He participated in the Carolinas campaign of 1865 and was paroled at Greensboro, North Carolina, May 1, 1865.

After the war Palmer resumed his law practice. He died November 4, 1890, and is buried in Evergreen Cemetery, Murfreesboro.

BIBLIOGRAPHY

Bearss, Edwin C. "Joseph Benjamin Palmer." In *The Confederate General.* Edited by William C. Davis. Vol. 5. Harrisburg, Pa., 1991.

JOSEPH BENJAMIN PALMER. LIBRARY OF CONGRESS

Warner, Ezra J. *Generals in Gray: Lives of the Confederate Commanders*. Baton Rouge, La., 1959.

RICHARD M. MCMURRY

PALMETTO ARMORY. The Militia Act of 1808 authorized distribution of arms by the Federal government to state militias on an annual basis, but South Carolina, after the nullification movement began in 1832, desired to acquire or build its own arms with which to defend state interests. Stimulated by the secession crisis, William Glaze and Thomas W. Radcliffe, both of Columbia, South Carolina, approached state politicians proposing arms procurement. A Board of Ordnance was established in 1850, and $350,000 was authorized by the General Assembly for purchases. Glaze, selected as agent, procured arms during this period from various sources outside the state, including a firm headed by Benjamin Flagg in Millbury, Massachusetts.

Glaze earlier had entered into a partnership with James Boatwright of Columbia, and about 1850, Glaze, Boatwright, and Flagg founded the Palmetto Armory, with Flagg moving his gun-making machinery to Columbia.

The act of 1850 to build up the South Carolina militia set the stage for the Palmetto Armory's greatest success. The initial contract called for 6,000 muskets with bayonets (.69 caliber smoothbore) at $14.50 each; 1,000 rifles (.54 caliber rifled) at $15.50; 1,000 pair of pistols (.54 caliber smoothbore) at $14.50 per pair; 1,000 cavalry sabers with scabbards at $6.50 each; and 1,000 light artillery sabers with scabbards at $6.50 each. All were to be totally manufactured within the state, but problems arose and some component parts were purchased out of state and the contract altered to permit modifications. In addition, the armory received a contract to alter the state's obsolete flintlock arms to the new percussion system. The arms manufactured in 1852 and 1853 are readily identified. The firearms are marked on the lockplate "Palmetto Armory SC" in a circle surrounding a palmetto tree and on the breech of the barrel either "Wm. Glaze & Co." or "W. G. & Co." The edged weapons are usually marked "Wm. Glaze & Co." on the reverse ricasso and "Columbia, S.C." on the obverse. As martial arms these are some of the most pleasing to the eye with their brass mounts. There have been numerous modern efforts to copy them. Specimens of these arms, which were issued primarily to South Carolina state troops, have been excavated at Civil War battle sites.

With no further arms contracts in sight, the Palmetto Armory became the Palmetto Iron Works manufacturing a variety of engines, boilers, iron and brass castings, ornamental iron, farm machinery, and sugar mills. By 1860 Glaze was a wealthy man owning substantial acreage and a successful business.

As soon as the Civil War began, Glaze again offered his state the benefits of his firearms manufacturing expertise. Two of his initial proposals were rejected, but in January 1861, the firm received a contract to produce 10-inch shells and 24-pound shot, which was completed April 8, 1861. Glaze also received a contract to rifle some of the brass-mounted .69 caliber smoothbore muskets that he had manufactured in 1852 and 1853, and he seems to have altered 3,720 of these rare arms. The company also produced bayonets, some of which the state accepted and others of which were sold to Georgia for its state forces. Subsequent efforts to obtain state arms contracts were unsuccessful. In late 1862 Glaze was involved in producing a prototype of the George revolving cannon, which, though marginally effective, never reached production.

When William Tecumseh Sherman occupied Columbia on February 17, 1865, the Palmetto Iron Works, with its vast arms-making potential, was among the first structures burned to the ground. Glaze tried to rebuild after the war, but in April 1868 he went bankrupt and all his property including the ironworks was sold.

BIBLIOGRAPHY

Albaugh, William A., III, and Edward N. Simmons. *Confederate Arms.* Harrisburg, Pa., 1957.

Fuller, Claud E., and Richard D. Steuart. *Firearms of the Confederacy.* Huntington, W.Va., 1944.

Meyer, Jack Allen. *William Glaze and the Palmetto Armory.* Columbia, S.C., 1982.

Reilly, Robert M. *United States Military Small Arms, 1816–1865.* Baton Rouge, La., 1970.

Steuart, Richard D. "A Pair of Navy Sixes." *Confederate Veteran* 33 (1925): 92–95. Reprint, Wilmington, N.C., 1985.

RUSS A. PRITCHARD

PARKER, WILLIAM (1826–1896), naval officer. An 1848 graduate of the U.S. Naval Academy, William Harwar Parker resigned his commission in 1861 to serve in the Confederate navy even though his older brother, Foxhall Parker, remained loyal to the Union. In command of the gunboat CSS *Beaufort,* William took part in the unsuccessful defense of Roanoke Island in February 1862. Afterward, he commanded the same vessel during the Battle of Hampton Roads and witnessed the duel between CSS *Virginia* and USS *Monitor.* After the Confederates abandoned the James River during George B. McClellan's peninsular campaign, Parker was transferred to Charleston Harbor where he became executive officer of the ironclad CSS *Palmetto State.* On January 31, 1863, *Palmetto State* and CSS *Chicora* sortied from Charleston Harbor to attack the Federal blockading fleet. *Palmetto State* rammed USS *Mercedita* and forced its surrender, though later the Federal vessel rehoisted its flag and limped away. In April Parker's vessel participated in the successful defense of Charleston Harbor against an attack by Rear Adm. S. F. Du Pont's Federal squadron.

In the fall of 1863, Parker was appointed superintendent of the Confederate Naval Academy, which consisted of the training ship *Patrick Henry,* a former passenger steamer. *Patrick Henry* participated in the defense of Richmond and Petersburg in 1864 and 1865, and when Grant's armies broke through the Petersburg defense lines in April 1865, Parker and his midshipmen were ordered to guard the Confederate treasury during the evacuation. For thirty days, Parker's midshipmen acted as an escort for the treasure train as it traveled southward through the Carolinas into Georgia. On May 2, Parker transferred the treasure to the care of Gen. Basil Wilson Duke at Abbeville, Georgia, and in response to the orders of Confederate Navy Secretary Stephen R. Mallory, he mustered the midshipmen out of service. After learning of the surrender of Joseph E. Johnston, Parker accepted parole from the nearest Federal forces and made his way back to Virginia.

After the war, Parker served as a merchant steamer captain, president of the Maryland Agricultural College (later the University of Maryland), and briefly as U.S. minister to Korea (1886).

BIBLIOGRAPHY

Parker, William H. *Recollections of a Naval Officer, 1841–1865.* New York, 1883. Reprint, Annapolis, Md., 1985.

Scharf, Thomas J. *History of the Confederate States Navy.* New York, 1887.

CRAIG L. SYMONDS

PARSONS, MOSBY MONROE (1821–1865), brigadier general and acting major general. Parsons was born May 21, 1821, at Charlottesville, Virginia. As a young man he moved to Missouri where he studied law and was admitted to the bar. In the war with Mexico, Parsons led a mounted volunteer company. After the war, he served in the state senate and as attorney general.

An active supporter of Governor Claiborne F. Jackson's efforts to bring Missouri into the Confederacy, Parsons was rewarded with an appointment to command of the Sixth Division of the Missouri State Guard. During Sterling Price's 1861 retreat before Unionist Nathaniel Lyon's advance, Parsons fought at Carthage, helping drive Franz Sigel from the field. He received a Confederate brigadier commission in November 1862. At Wilson's Creek, Parsons commanded a brigade of Price's army and participated in the Arkansas campaigns of 1862 and 1863, moving up to division command the latter year. During the Red River campaign, his division reinforced Richard Taylor's command and fought at Mark's Hill and Jenkins's Ferry. Parsons, appointed major general on Trans-Mississippi orders on April 30, 1864 (never officially recognized), participated in Price's raid that year into Missouri.

With the surrender of the Trans-Mississippi Department, Parsons went to Mexico to join the imperialist forces. He was killed in August 1865 in Nuevo León by Mexican irregulars.

Because Parsons served in the Trans-Mississippi, the Confederate government never gave him the recognition he deserved. His progress to the rank of major general stalled because the War Department resisted the promotion requests of Gen. E. Kirby Smith, commander of the Trans-Mississippi Department. Nevertheless, Parsons was an aggressive and capable commander, clearly the equal to many who received promotions for service east of the Mississippi River.

BIBLIOGRAPHY

Kerby, Robert L. *Kirby Smith's Confederacy: The Trans-Mississippi South, 1863–1865.* New York, 1972.

Shoemaker, Floyd Calvin. *Missouri and Missourians.* 5 vols. Chicago, 1943.
Warner, Ezra J. *Generals in Gray: Lives of the Confederate Commanders.* Baton Rouge, La., 1959.

ROY R. STEPHENSON

PATENT OFFICE. Established informally by resolution of the Provisional Congress on March 4, 1861, the Patent Office was officially the product of an act of the Provisional Congress passed May 21, 1861. In accordance with the provisions of the law, the president appointed Rufus R. Rhodes as commissioner of patents on May 22. Rhodes reported to the attorneys general, spent two appropriations of $500 each on a technical library, and by authority of an act of the Provisional Congress passed August 30, 1861, appointed a staff that in February 1862 numbered six people.

The Patent Office examined applications and issued patents for a variety of inventions and devices in classes ranging from "manufacture of fibrous tissues" to "fine arts." Particularly brisk, however, were entries in the "firearms" and "surgical instruments" categories. As the war continued, battle wounds generated developments in prosthetics, and naval officer John M. Brooke secured Patent No. 100 for his design of the ironclad warship *Virginia.* Other examples of patents include "an improvement in torpedoes," a revolver, and "an improved instrument for measuring distances."

BIBLIOGRAPHY

Beers, Henry Putney. *Guide to the Archives of the Government of the Confederate States of America.* Washington, D.C., 1968.
Robinson, William M., Jr. *Justice in Grey: A History of the Judicial System of the Confederate States of America.* Cambridge, Mass., 1941.

EMORY M. THOMAS

PATRICK HENRY. The wooden side-wheel steamer *Patrick Henry* displaced 1,300 tons and was 250 feet in length, with a crew of 150 officers and men. It was armed with ten 32-pounders in broadside, one 10-inch shell gun pivoted fore, and an 8-inch solid-shot gun pivoted aft. Originally *Yorktown,* a freight and passenger vessel built in 1859 for the New York and Old Dominion Steamship Line, *Patrick Henry* was seized by Virginia authorities on the James River in April 1861 and converted to a war steamer under the direction of Comdr. John Randolph Tucker. The upper passenger decks were removed and a battery of guns was mounted; the steamer's boilers and engines were shielded by iron plates of 2 and 3¾ inches, perhaps the earliest use of armor in the Confederate navy.

Patrick Henry served as flagship of Tucker's James River Squadron, a small flotilla of gunboats guarding the river route to Richmond. Between March and May 1862 this vessel fought in the Battle of Hampton Roads, evacuated war matériel from Norfolk, and supported the army's defense of the Virginia peninsula against Gen. George B.

CSS *PATRICK HENRY.* Sketched during its service as the school ship for the Confederate States Naval Academy.
NAVAL HISTORICAL CENTER, WASHINGTON, D.C.

McClellan's Army of the Potomac. Guns removed from *Patrick Henry* and manned by that vessel's crew turned back a Union navy flotilla at the Battle of Drewry's Bluff on May 15, 1862. Thereafter, *Patrick Henry,* berthed at Drewry's Bluff, became the floating campus of the Confederate States Naval Academy. The Confederates destroyed the vessel on April 3, 1865, during the evacuation of Richmond.

BIBLIOGRAPHY

Parker, William Harwar. *Recollections of a Naval Officer, 1841–1865.* New York, 1883. Reprint, Annapolis, Md., 1985.

Rochelle, James Henry. "The Confederate Steamship 'Patrick Henry.'" *Southern Historical Society Papers* 14 (1886): 126–136. Reprint, Wilmington, N.C., 1990.

Werlich, David P. *Admiral of the Amazon: John Randolph Tucker, His Confederate Colleagues, and Peru.* Charlottesville, Va., 1990.

DAVID P. WERLICH

PAXTON, ELISHA FRANKLIN (1828–1863), brigadier general. "Bull" Paxton and "Stonewall" Jackson were fellow townsmen, fellow Presbyterian worshipers, and dead within a week of each other.

Born March 4, 1828, in Rockbridge County, Virginia, Paxton graduated from Washington College at the age of seventeen and subsequently obtained degrees from Yale and the University of Virginia. He practiced law in Ohio before returning in 1854 to Lexington. Five years later, he abandoned the legal profession because of weak eyesight. Although he and Jackson had become close friends, the events of 1860 and 1861 so strained their relations that, at Virginia's secession, the two men were not on speaking terms. In the initial stages of the crisis, Jackson remained a Unionist while Paxton did not.

Bull Paxton, heavy of build and strong of opinion, entered Confederate service as a lieutenant of a Rockbridge County infantry company. He became major of the Twenty-seventh Virginia but lost his position in the spring 1862 army elections. Jackson promptly named him his chief of staff. On November 1, 1862, at Jackson's recommendation and to the dissatisfaction of senior and more qualified officers, Paxton jumped three ranks to brigadier general and took command of the Stonewall Brigade.

He performed competently at Fredericksburg and worked hard to increase the efficiency of his brigade. At Chancellorsville, on the evening of May 2, 1863, Jackson fell wounded. Before battle resumed the next morning, Paxton had a premonition of death. He made hasty arrangements, donned his best uniform, and was killed in the first minutes of the action. Paxton was buried at Guiney's Station, only yards from where Jackson lay dying. His remains are now in Lexington, appropriately close to those of his friend and benefactor.

BIBLIOGRAPHY

Douglas, Henry Kyd. *I Rode with Stonewall.* Chapel Hill, N.C., 1940.

Paxton, Elisha F. *The Civil War Letters of General Frank "Bull" Paxton.* Hillsboro, Tex., 1978.

Robertson, James I., Jr. *The Stonewall Brigade.* Baton Rouge, La., 1963.

JAMES I. ROBERTSON, JR.

PAYNE, WILLIAM HENRY FITZHUGH (1830–1904), brigadier general. Payne was born on January 27, 1830. After attending the Virginia Military Institute and the University of Virginia, he practiced law in Warrenton, where he cofounded the Black Horse Troop in 1859. Payne's men were sent to Harpers Ferry in response to John Brown's raid.

In April 1861 Payne became the company's captain and was named major in the Fourth Virginia Cavalry when the Black Horse became Company H of that regiment in September 1861. On May 5, 1862, while commanding the Fourth Virginia at Williamsburg, Payne was shot in the face. Being too injured to move, he was captured from a field hospital when the Confederates withdrew up the peninsula to Richmond. Payne was paroled on July 24 and returned to

WILLIAM HENRY FITZHUGH PAYNE. LIBRARY OF CONGRESS

propelled Peirpoint to leadership among the Opposition, a group that carried on a campaign, largely through the small independent newspapers of northwestern Virginia, alleging the dominance of the "slave power" over Virginia.

Although Peirpoint did not condone John Brown's raid on Harpers Ferry, he was incensed by what he believed was the demagoguery in Richmond in the aftermath of the incident. Peirpoint rejoiced that John Bell and the Constitutional Union party won a plurality of Virginia's votes in the presidential election of 1860, but he believed that the disruption in the Democratic party made civil war inevitable.

After the Virginia convention adopted an ordinance of secession on April 17, 1861, mass meetings throughout northwestern Virginia expressed opposition. Peirpoint was among the 436 delegates representing twenty-seven counties who met in Wheeling on May 13 to determine what action northwestern Virginia should take. Members at the meeting, known as the First Wheeling Convention, tabled a new state proposal, as Peirpoint urged, and agreed to campaign against approval of the secession ordinance, scheduled for a popular vote on May 23. They also agreed that if the ordinance passed, they would elect delegates to a second Wheeling convention. In the interim, a central committee, including Peirpoint as one of its nine members, served as a temporary authority in northwestern Virginia.

The popular vote having approved the secession ordinance (although voters in western counties voted nearly two to one against it), the Second Wheeling Convention convened on June 11, 1861, and adopted Peirpoint's proposal to set up a loyal government to be called the Restored Government of Virginia. The convention elected Peirpoint governor to serve until "an election can be properly held."

FRANCIS H. PEIRPOINT. *THE SOLDIER IN OUR CIVIL WAR*

Peirpoint took the job of governor seriously, establishing headquarters in Wheeling, raising money and troops, and cooperating with military authorities in establishing Union control of northwestern Virginia. Both President Abraham Lincoln and Congress recognized the Restored Government of Virginia, accepting its military appointments and the senators elected by the Restored General Assembly to replace the expelled senators of Virginia's Confederate government.

In spite of the successful establishment of a Unionist alternative to the Confederate state government, the idea of creating a separate state in western Virginia continued to grow. The Second Wheeling Convention reconvened in August 1861 and moved quickly to establish a new state. Because Peirpoint cooperated with the statehood movement by securing the consent of the Restored General Assembly of Virginia and by actively lobbying both president and Congress for its success, he has been called "the Father of West Virginia." But though he was offered leadership in the new state, he chose to remain the governor of Restored Virginia.

With the creation of the new state, Peirpoint's government moved to Alexandria, where he and other officials of his government struggled to be taken seriously. Though still claiming to represent loyal Virginia, the Peirpoint government controlled only Alexandria and a few nearby counties, the eastern shore, and areas under Union military control around Norfolk. Congress would seat neither representatives nor senators of the Alexandria administration, and Peirpoint no longer enjoyed the close cooperation of military officials as he had in Wheeling.

In May 1865, under the authority of an order by President Andrew Johnson, Peirpoint and his restored government moved to Richmond, but his hopes for a quick and painless reconstruction proved naive. He assumed that the main issues—the preservation of the Union and the end of slavery—had been settled and that the former Confederates would now cooperate in building a new order based on free labor. In June 1865, with Peirpoint's urging, the Restored General Assembly restored voting and officeholding privileges to former Confederates. When elections were held in October, they won with ease, embittering Unionists and Republicans and alerting moderate Republicans in Congress to the need for strong congressional guidance in Reconstruction.

When the new General Assembly ignored Peirpoint and passed many reactionary measures, he found himself without significant support. Former Confederates could not forgive his wartime role, and he had alienated strong Unionists and Republicans with his lenient policy toward former Confederates. The coming of Congressional Reconstruction in March 1867 left him in office but powerless as martial law was imposed. He continued his efforts to build a moderate political base, but few rallied to his cause. The Union general in charge of Reconstruction, John M. Schofield, dismissed Peirpoint on April 4, 1868.

Peirpoint returned to Fairmont, West Virginia, in 1868. He served one term in the West Virginia House of Delegates, but after 1869 he concentrated on his business and legal activities in Fairmont.

Believing that he was correcting errors that had crept into the spelling of his family name, he changed the spelling from "Peirpoint" to "Pierpont" in 1881. This is the spelling that historians and biographers have generally followed since.

BIBLIOGRAPHY

Ambler, Charles H. *Francis H. Pierpont: Union War Governor of Virginia and Father of West Virginia.* Chapel Hill, N.C., 1937.

Lowe, Richard G. "Francis Harrison Pierpont: Wartime Unionist, Reconstruction Moderate." In *The Governors of Virginia, 1860–1978.* Edited by Edward Younger and James Tice Moore. Charlottesville, Va., 1982.

JERRY BRUCE THOMAS

PEMBER, PHOEBE YATES (1823–1913), chief matron, Chimborazo Hospital. During the first year of the Civil War, recently widowed Phoebe Yates Pember expressed dissatisfaction with the inactivity and personal tensions of living with relatives who had fled from Charleston, South Carolina, to Marietta, Georgia. Her connections with the Confederate elite, however, soon changed all that. The wife of Secretary of State George W. Randolph suggested that Pember be considered for the position of chief matron of the second division of Chimborazo hospital in Richmond, Virginia. Pember was stunned by the offer; Chimborazo was the largest military hospital in the world at the time and subsequently provided treatment for over 76,000 Civil War patients. Highly educated and competent, she impressed the Chimborazo surgeon in chief, Dr. James B. McCaw, who gave final approval for the appointment.

Like many other Civil War nurses, Pember faced numerous professional barriers and regularly endured insults from both inferiors and superiors who believed that no respectable woman could (or should) minister to the needs of wounded and dying soldiers. A strong-minded, self-possessed woman, Phoebe Pember cared for them anyway; after the war, she wrote a surprisingly unsentimental account of her wartime nursing experiences. Her memoirs, *A Southern Woman's Story,* first published in 1879, provide much more, however, than an account of the upheaval in gender relations brought by the war. She gave a vivid personal account of the conditions in a major Confederate hospital, provided a sympathetic and humane portrait of the common soldier, and illuminated the ongoing problems of scarcity and inflation in the Confederacy. According to its editor, Bell Irvin Wiley, Pember's book "is rated as one of the very best Confederate memoirs" ever published. In later years, Phoebe Pember chose extensive travel in America and Europe over a career as a writer.

BIBLIOGRAPHY

Pember, Phoebe Yates. *A Southern Woman's Story: Life in Confederate Richmond.* New York, 1879. Reprint, edited by Bell I. Wiley. Jackson, Tenn., 1959.

Simkins, Francis Butler, and James Welch Patton. *The Women of the Confederacy.* New York, 1936.

Wiley, Bell I. *Confederate Women.* Westport, Conn., 1975.

VICTORIA E. BYNUM

PEMBERTON, JOHN C. (1814–1881), lieutenant general. Born August 10, 1814, in Philadelphia, Pennsylvania, John Clifford Pemberton's marriage to a Virginia woman influenced him to fight for the South. By war's end, he had become one of the Confederacy's most controversial generals.

JOHN C. PEMBERTON. NATIONAL ARCHIVES

An 1837 graduate of the U.S. Military Academy, Pemberton saw action in the Second Seminole War and was decorated for bravery in the Mexican War. In peacetime, he proved to be an effective administrative officer. Though his defenders would later claim that Pemberton frequently exhibited antebellum pro-Southern sentiments, there is much evidence to the contrary. When war broke out in 1861, he agonized for weeks before coming to Virginia to fight for his wife's native land.

Pemberton's first significant duty came in March 1862, when he was promoted to major general and took command of the Department of South Carolina and Georgia. Always adept at military politics, he had moved rapidly upward in rank despite a lack of accomplishments.

The new commander soon was embroiled in controversy. Many South Carolinians feared that the Northern-born general was not dedicated to an all-out defense of the department. Pemberton added to their fears by declaring that, if he had to make a choice, he would abandon the area rather than risk losing his outnumbered army. When state officials complained to Robert E. Lee, Pemberton's predecessor and now adviser to Confederate President Jefferson Davis, Lee told Pemberton that he must defend the department at all cost. Pemberton was eventually relieved from command, but he had learned a fateful lesson from Lee.

Despite Pemberton's preference for administrative duties and his problems in South Carolina, Davis promoted him to lieutenant general and gave him arguably the most difficult command in the Confederacy. Pemberton was to defend Vicksburg, a Mississippi city standing on high bluffs above the Mississippi River. Its defenses were the last major river obstacle to Union shipping.

Taking command of the Department of Mississippi and East Louisiana on October 14, 1862, Pemberton immediately set to work solving supply problems and improving troop morale. For several months he enjoyed remarkable success, defeating attempts by Union Gen. Ulysses S. Grant to take Vicksburg in the winter of 1862–1863.

In the spring, however, Grant confused Pemberton with a series of diversions and crossed the Mississippi below Vicksburg practically unnoticed. Grant was free to maneuver because Pemberton had remembered Lee's admonishment and had fought to hold Vicksburg at all cost. Jefferson Davis reinforced Pemberton's thinking with an order not to give up the river city "for a single day." Now that Grant had successfully crossed the Mississippi, Pemberton determined to stay close to Vicksburg. Davis complicated matters by sending Gen. Joseph E. Johnston to Mississippi to try to reverse declining Confederate fortunes. Johnston ordered Pemberton to unite his forces and attack Grant, if practicable, even if that meant abandoning the defense of Vicksburg.

Torn by conflicting orders, Pemberton marked time while Grant swept inland scoring a series of quick victories at Port Gibson, Raymond, and Jackson. Pemberton finally tried to please both Davis and Johnston. He moved his army east from Edwards Station, all the while maintaining close contact with Vicksburg. A new order from Johnston forced Pemberton to reverse his course and unite with Johnston's forces that had been defeated at Jackson. Before the order could be carried out, Pemberton's army bumped into Grant's forces at Champion's Hill and suffered a major defeat. Pemberton retreated to the Big Black River where he suffered more heavy losses. Remembering Lee's and Davis's orders, Pemberton chose to ignore another order from Johnston to evacuate Vicksburg. He would try to save the city even if that meant risking the loss of his army. He retreated into the city where he and his men endured a forty-seven day siege before surrendering on July 4, 1863. Pemberton became a pariah in the South and was accused by his immediate superior, General Johnston, of causing the Confederate disaster by disobeying orders.

John Pemberton might have made a positive contribution to the Confederate war effort had his talents been properly used. An able administrator, he was uncomfortable in combat. He had demonstrated his weaknesses in South Carolina, yet Davis had sent him to Mississippi anyway. A few months after Vicksburg, Pemberton displayed his loyalty to the Confederate cause by requesting a reduction in rank. He served the remainder of the war as a lieutenant colonel of artillery in Virginia and South Carolina.

After the war, Pemberton lived in Virginia and Pennsylvania. He died August 14, 1881, and is buried in Laurel Hill Cemetery in Philadelphia.

BIBLIOGRAPHY

Ballard, Michael B. *Pemberton: A Biography.* Jackson, Miss., 1991.

Bearss, Edwin Cole. *The Campaign for Vicksburg.* 3 vols. Dayton, Ohio, 1985–1986.

Pemberton, John C. [III]. *Pemberton: Defender of Vicksburg.* Chapel Hill, N.C., 1942. Reprint, Wilmington, N.C., 1987.

MICHAEL B. BALLARD

PENDER, WILLIAM DORSEY (1834–1863), major general. Pender was born February 6, 1834, in North Carolina and was educated at the U.S. Military Academy. He graduated nineteenth in the class of 1854. As a lieutenant of artillery and then of dragoons, Pender served on frontier duty in New Mexico and on the west coast. He saw enough fighting to be able to report with pride having been "mentioned three times [in reports] for conduct in Indian engagements."

Lieutenant Pender resigned from the U.S. Army in March 1861 and immediately received a Confederate commission as captain of artillery. Two months later Pender was elected colonel of the Third (later the Thirteenth) North Carolina Infantry. He assumed command of the Sixth North Carolina in August 1861 and led that regiment with such élan at Seven Pines the following spring that President Jefferson Davis commended him on the field and promoted him to brigadier general to date from June 3, 1862. General Pender took command of a brigade of North Carolina regiments, including his old Thirteenth, in A. P. Hill's division. He led the brigade through the heaviest fighting during the Seven Days' Battles with notable success and suffered in the process the first of a series of slight wounds incurred in battles. Pender and his men also fought at the heart of the battles of Second Manassas and Ox Hill and participated in the Maryland campaign. At Fredericksburg his North Carolinians stood on the far left of Hill's division.

Pender earned a reputation for stern, even brutal, discipline as a result of his ardent efforts to reduce the desertion rate that bedeviled North Carolina units. According to J. R. Boyles, a Confederate soldier at the time, troops of adjacent brigades "had a perfect horror" of Pender "as being such a strict disciplinarian." Although Pender was of very slight build (about 135 pounds), a member of J. E. B. Stuart's staff declared that the North Carolinian was one of the two "most splendid looking soldiers of the war." His ability to hold his troops to their duty appealed strongly both to units that served near them and to the army high command. Late in 1862 Hill commended Pender as "one of the very best officers I know" and in January 1863 again recommended promotion for him. In the reorganization after Chancellorsville, where he had again performed brilliantly, Pender won promotion to major general.

Pender's new division included the best troops of Hill's old command. The men who had feared him soon discovered Pender to be "quite humane, [he] treated us kindly," as long as no one deserted. Major General Pender's only day in combat was July 1, 1863, when he pushed his command through bitterly contested ground just west of Gettysburg and onto Seminary Ridge at the climax of that day's fighting. The next day a piece of shell wounded Pender in the thigh, though not in a fashion to prompt concern for his recovery. A sudden hemorrhage, however, led to amputation of the leg on July 18, and the general died a few hours later. Pender's solid contributions to the Army of Northern Virginia as one of its most able brigadiers are a matter of clear record. His further potential seemed large, as attested by several wistful comments by both Hill and Lee after Pender's death.

BIBLIOGRAPHY

Hassler, William W., ed. *The General to His Lady.* Chapel Hill, N.C., 1965.

Montgomery, Walter A. *Life and Character of Major-General W. D. Pender.* Raleigh, N.C., 1894.

ROBERT K. KRICK

PENDLETON, WILLIAM N. (1809–1883), brigadier general. The future father of Col. Alexander ("Sandie") Pendleton and father-in-law of Brig. Gen. Edwin G. Lee was born in Richmond, Virginia, December 26, 1809. He graduated from the U.S. Military Academy in 1830, ranking fifth in a class of forty-two that also included John B. Magruder. Pendleton resigned from the army after three years to accept a college professorship in Pennsylvania. He then became principal of Episcopal high schools in Alexandria and Baltimore before accepting the rectorship of, first, All Saints Church, Frederick, Maryland, and in 1853, of Grace Church, Lexington, Virginia.

When the Civil War broke out, Pendleton was elected captain of the Rockbridge Artillery, which was attached to the brigade of Thomas J. ("Stonewall") Jackson. The battery consisted of four guns that were christened "Mathew," "Mark," "Luke," and "John" in tribute to the clergyman-commander. At First Manassas, by which time Pendleton had been promoted to colonel, the battery figured prominently in the repulse of the Federal attack on the left of the Confederate line. Pendleton also served as chief of

WILLIAM N. PENDLETON. LIBRARY OF CONGRESS

artillery on the staff of Joseph E. Johnston. He was appointed brigadier on March 26, 1862.

Pendleton continued as artillery chief under Robert E. Lee, always mingling his military and ecclesiastical fervor. Once, while directing artillery fire against the enemy, he shouted, "Lord have mercy on their souls!"

Pendleton suffered his most humilitating embarrassment on the retreat from Sharpsburg. Commanding the army's rear guard to dispute the enemy's crossing of the Potomac, he mismanaged his task so egregiously that, he reported to Lee, he had lost his 44 guns. The next day, however, he escaped a possible court martial when Jackson recaptured all but four of the field pieces.

Dissatisfaction over Pendleton's performances mounted, and for the last two years of the war his duties were chiefly administrative. In March 1864, Adjutant General Samuel Cooper ordered Pendleton to Dalton, Georgia, to inspect Johnston's artillery. When Pendleton dallied, a second order was issued a month later. By November, strained relations existed between Cooper and the brigadier. Pendleton complained about the "exclusive & extremely invidious obstruction placed at the door of your Dept." for field officers wishing to see the adjutant.

Paroled at Appomattox, Pendleton resumed his rectorship in Lexington, where he died January 15, 1883. He was buried in the town cemetery.

BIBLIOGRAPHY

Bean, William G. *Stonewall's Man, Sandie Pendleton.* Chapel Hill, N.C., 1959. Reprint, Wilmington, N.C., 1987.

Compiled Military Service Records. William Nelson Pendleton. Microcopy M331, Roll 196. Record Group 109. National Archives, Washington, D.C.

Hotchkiss, Jed. *Virginia.* Vol. 3 of *Confederate Military History.* Edited by Clement A. Evans. Atlanta, 1899. Vol. 4 of extended ed. Wilmington, N.C., 1987.

Lee, Susan P. *Memoirs of William Nelson Pendleton.* Philadelphia, 1893.

Warner, Ezra J. *Generals in Gray: Lives of the Confederate Commanders.* Baton Rouge, La., 1959.

LOWELL REIDENBAUGH

PENINSULAR CAMPAIGN. The Peninsular campaign lasted nearly four months, from March to July 1862, and stretched across the southeastern Virginia Peninsula from the Chesapeake Bay to the suburbs of Richmond. Union Maj. Gen. George B. McClellan had planned to advance his Army of the Potomac triumphantly up the stretch of land between the York and James rivers and capture Richmond. With the Confederate capital taken, the Federal government hoped to bring the year-old Civil War to a swift and decisive end. Throughout the spring and early summer months of 1862 approximately 60,000 Confederates doggedly fought nearly double that number of Federals. After several weeks of mud-drenched marches and siege warfare, several bloody battles ensued, which cost the Union army over 15,000 soldiers; the defending Confederates lost 20,000 men killed, wounded, and missing. Richmond was free from capture, the Union suffered another embarrassing setback, and the war dragged on for three more years.

Two divisions from McClellan's army landed at Federally held Fort Monroe at the tip of the peninsula in mid-March. As scores of bluecoats debarked from vessels onto Southern soil, Maj. Gen. John B. Magruder, commander of the Confederate defenses at Yorktown, readied his scanty force of 10,000 men for combat. Magruder's Army of the Peninsula lay directly in McClellan's path up the peninsula. Luckily for the Confederates, McClellan severely overestimated Confederate strength—he thought it to be nearly ten times as strong as it was. Magruder added to the Federals' confusion by marching his men through clearings in circles to give the impression of many more troops. Instead of attacking frontally, which would have crumbled Magruder's meager force, McClellan began to amass artillery to pound Yorktown into submission. All through April, McClellan pressed his siege of Yorktown.

Meanwhile, Joseph E. Johnston and his Army of Northern Virginia had lain idle following the Confederate victory at the Battle of Manassas in July 1861. Johnston did not wish to engage McClellan's formidable forces head on and remained content waiting for the enemy's attack. But on April 14, Confederate President Jefferson Davis held a special council of war to determine Johnston's next move. For fourteen hours, Johnston, Maj. Gen. James Longstreet, Secretary of War George Wythe Randolph, Maj. Gen. Gustavus W. Smith, and Davis's military adviser, Gen. Robert E. Lee, discussed how to deal with the growing Union threat at Yorktown. Johnston suggested that his army move inland and await McClellan's approach to Richmond before fighting. Lee, fearful to allow this undetermined force of Federals to move so close to the capital, argued that the peninsula offered numerous defensive positions from which the Confederates could derive advantage. At 1:00 A.M. on April 15, President Davis came to a decision. He ordered Johnston to move his army to Yorktown to reinforce Magruder and fight back the enemy on the peninsula. Johnston abandoned central Virginia to the Union and grudgingly joined Magruder at Yorktown. His men settled into the flooded trenches, unsure how long they would have to remain.

On May 4, McClellan deemed himself ready to do battle. But on that same day, Johnston left, intending to follow his original plan to fight outside of Richmond. On May 5, 1862, the rear guard of Johnston's retreating army turned to fight pursuing Federals near the old colonial capitol of Williams-

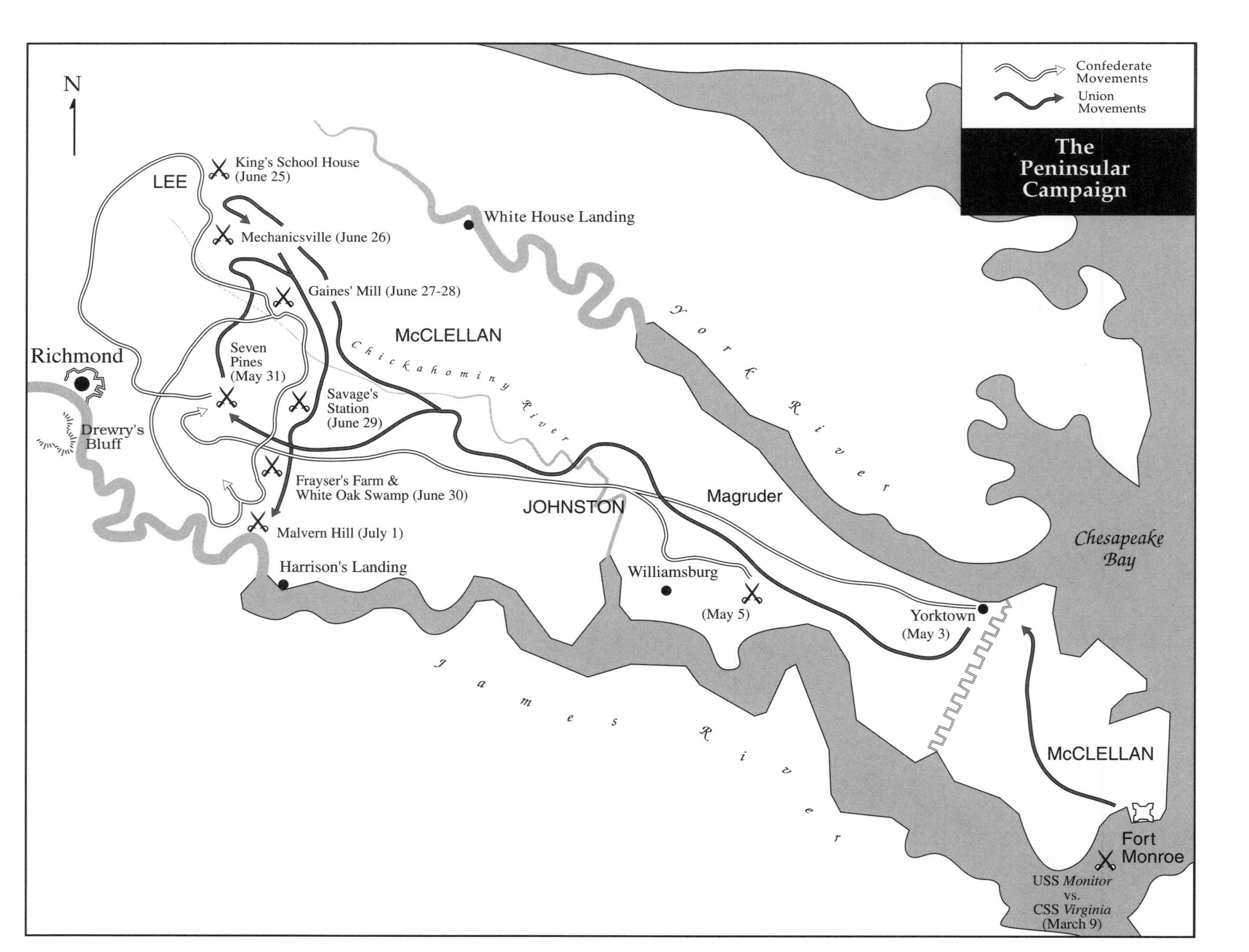

Confederate Movements
Union Movements
The Peninsular Campaign
N
LEE
King's School House (June 25)
Mechanicsville (June 26)
White House Landing
Gaines' Mill (June 27-28)
McCLELLAN
Richmond
Seven Pines (May 31)
Savage's Station (June 29)
Drewry's Bluff
Chickahominy River
York River
Frayser's Farm & White Oak Swamp (June 30)
Malvern Hill (July 1)
JOHNSTON
Magruder
Harrison's Landing
Williamsburg
(May 5)
Yorktown (May 3)
Chesapeake Bay
James River
McCLELLAN
Fort Monroe
USS Monitor vs. CSS Virginia (March 9)

burg. Six brigades of James Longstreet's division fought to gain needed time for the fleeing Confederates. The Battle of Williamsburg yielded 2,239 Federal casualties and 1,603 Confederate. Many more would soon follow.

Johnston's movement up the peninsula required the abandonment of the seaport town of Norfolk, Virginia. The famed Southern ironclad CSS *Virginia* would be without a port. Rather than leave the ship to the enemy, Confederates burned the vessel. Soon Union troops moved in and spread to nearby Suffolk. Seven miles of the James River below Richmond were now open to Federal forces. A Union fleet attempted to move up the James, but on May 15, Confederates fired on the Federal ships at Drewry's Bluff. The orphaned crew of *Virginia,* a detachment of infantry, and a slew of heavy artillery guns mustered enough resistance to spoil the enemy's plans.

Outside of Richmond, three corps of McClellan's large force positioned themselves south of the swollen Chickahominy River; the other two were on the northern side. When word reached Johnston that McClellan might soon receive reinforcements from Maj. Gen. Irvin McDowell's corps, he concluded that quick, decisive action was in order. On May 31 incessant rains washed away bridges connecting McClellan's corps, leaving two isolated and vulnerable corps north of the Chickahominy. The Battle of Seven Pines was an embarrassing Confederate failure. Johnston's officers bungled orders and moved sluggishly. When fighting finally began, it was heavy but the Southerners failed to gain any ground. Johnston fell severely wounded and Gustavus W. Smith briefly took command. The next day a renewed offensive by the Confederates again failed. By afternoon Robert E. Lee had arrived on the field to take command and order a withdrawal. The Confederate failure cost over 6,000 casualties; the Federals suffered over 5,000. During the next three weeks both armies waited and watched for new bloodletting.

Lee's first concern as commander was to bolster Richmond's defenses. He soon had his men digging field fortifications outside the city. On June 12, Lee sent Maj. Gen. J. E. B. Stuart on a reconnaissance mission into Union lines to determine enemy strength. Stuart rode entirely around McClellan's army in a dramatic cavalry sweep. In the process his troopers discovered that the right flank of McClellan's army stood vulnerable to attack. Upon receiving this information, Lee quickly laid plans to strike at McClellan's weakness. But the Federals were not unaware; Stuart's ride prompted McClellan to execute a "change of base" southward from his vulnerable position on the York to the James River.

Lee hurried to attack. Leaving a mere 25,000 men between Richmond and the Federal army, Lee moved his remaining 47,000 soldiers to assault the Union flank. With the aid of Maj. Gen. Thomas J. ("Stonewall") Jackson's Army of the Valley, Lee planned to surprise the exposed Federals. The subsequent battles at Mechanicsville on June 26 and Gaines' Mill on June 27 were indecisive. Unfulfilled was Lee's primary objective of destroying the isolated corps and seriously damaging McClellan's strength. Stonewall Jackson's poor performance was especially disappointing. At both of these engagements his delay undeniably contributed to the Confederate failures. But Lee was undaunted. The next day he continued in bold pursuit while McClellan, stunned by the Confederates' continued aggressiveness, retreated. He was now even more convinced that his men faced superior numbers.

Beginning with a brief engagement at King's School House on June 25, the Seven Days' Battles consisted largely of Lee's dogged attempts to corner and destroy pieces of McClellan's army. Mechanicsville and Gaines' Mill were followed by Savage's Station on June 29, Frayser's Farm on June 30, and finally Malvern Hill on July 1. Similar to Johnston's mishap at Seven Pines, Lee's ambitious plans went awry owing to failed coordination between units, misunderstood orders, and poor staff performance. Savage's Station yielded 626 Confederate casualties and 1,590 Federals; Frayser's Farm cost 2,853 Federal casualties and 3,615 Confederate. At Malvern Hill, Lee suffered a severe defeat when he ordered his troops to charge the enemy's nearly impregnable position atop the hill. When Union artillery unmercifully poured into the infantrymen attempting to charge forward, 5,355 Confederates were lost; Federal casualties numbered 3,214. Confederate Maj. Gen. D. H. Hill later remarked that Malvern Hill was "not war—it was murder."

With this Union victory, McClellan completed his retreat to Harrison's Landing on the James River. He soon turned north to Washington, and the threat to Richmond had passed.

General Lee did not write his report of the Peninsular campaign for two years. Citing a lack of maps and information, he admitted his failure to destroy or even weaken the Union army. But Lee had successfully managed to take advantage of McClellan's overcautiousness and halt the enemy movement toward Richmond. For two full years the Federals would not attempt such an operation again. The Peninsular campaign also cemented Lee's reputation as an aggressive and stubborn fighter. For the next two years of war, Lee showed this ability again and again in the face of Union commanders more talented than McClellan.

[*See also* Drewry's Bluff, Virginia; Seven Pines, Virginia; Seven Days' Battles; Stuart's Raids; Williamsburg, Virginia; Yorktown, Virginia.]

BIBLIOGRAPHY

Cullen, Joseph P. *The Peninsular Campaign.* Harrisburg, Penn., 1973.

Dowdey, Clifford. *The Seven Days: The Emergence of Lee.* Boston, 1964.
Freeman, Douglas S. *Lee's Lieutenants: A Study in Command.* Vol. 1. New York, 1942. Reprint, New York, 1986.
Sears, Stephen W. *The Peninsula Campaign.* New York, 1993.
Thomas, Emory M. "The Peninsular Campaign: Parts I-II." *Civil War Times Illustrated* 17, no. 10 (February 1979): 4–9; 18, no. 1 (April 1979): 28–35; 18, no. 2 (May 1979): 12–18; 18, no. 3 (June 1979): 10–17; 18, no. 4 (July 1979): 14–24.

LESLEY JILL GORDON-BURR

PERKINS, JOHN, JR. (1819–1885), congressman from Louisiana. Born in Natchez, Mississippi, on July 1, 1819, John Perkins, Jr., grew up among the great slaveholders of the Natchez district. Like many planters' sons, Perkins had private tutors in his boyhood and was sent to Yale, from which he graduated in 1840. To complete his education, Perkins attended Harvard Law School, distinguishing him from the average Southern lawyer. In 1843, he was admitted to the Louisiana bar and began to practice law in New Orleans. His inherited wealth permitted him the leisure to dabble in scholarly pursuits that led him to take part in the founding of the Louisiana Historical Society in 1846. Out of recognition of his legal background, Perkins was appointed a circuit judge in 1851. By this time he had moved to Madison Parish where he owned a plantation called Ashwood. Perkins, a Democrat, served one term in the House of Representatives (1853–1855) and then returned to his position as circuit judge. By 1860 he had also taken over the management of his father's plantation, Somerset.

Perkins's deep involvement within the plantation economy of the South influenced him to side with the immediate secessionists during the crisis of 1861. Not only did he take part in the Louisiana secession convention, but he also served as chairman of the committee that drafted the Louisiana secession ordinance. Perhaps as a reward for his ardent support of the state's withdrawal from the Union, the convention nominated Perkins as one of six delegates to the Montgomery convention. In November 1861, the Sixth Congressional District, which comprised northeastern Louisiana, elected him to the House of Representatives, and he was reelected in 1863.

Throughout his service to the Confederacy, Perkins generally supported the Davis administration, but he was known to have some independent views. He believed that conscription was unconstitutional. He opposed the arming of the slaves, a policy favored by the Davis administration toward the end of the war. He was also convinced of the possibility of negotiating peace with the Union on terms favorable to the South. And, like many other Confederate congressmen, he opposed several of Davis's advisers. Perkins exhibited his bias in favor of slave owners in two actions. During the constitutional convention he proposed an amendment prohibiting any nonslaveholding state from joining the Confederacy, and after the war's commencement, he introduced a bill that required the government to compensate the owners of slaves who were killed in battle while in the service of the Confederacy. Such measures reflected his background as the owner of over three hundred slaves.

Perkins's principal interests, though, lay in the realms of commerce and foreign affairs. By serving on both committees during his first term, Perkins had ample opportunity to influence Confederate policy. He successfully persuaded Congress to pass a bill establishing a bureau of foreign supplies, but the measure was vetoed by Davis. He then went on to push for the government policy of buying up all of the South's cotton and tobacco crops, which were used as a basis for obtaining cash and foreign credit. In order to discourage the inflationary and widespread circulation of state and U.S. currency, he supported a measure that made Confederate Treasury notes legal tender, and he favored the imposition of a tax-in-kind that allowed people to pay their taxes in livestock or produce. Perkins also opposed cotton diplomacy, a policy originating in 1861 that encouraged planters to voluntarily withhold their cotton from overseas markets. Instead, he advocated free trade with Europe, arguing that this would induce France and England to break the Union blockade in order to acquire cheap cotton; his opponents countered that Europe would not risk war for cotton. By late 1862, however, the combination of Lincoln's preliminary Emancipation Proclamation and the effectiveness of the Union blockade, especially after the capture of New Orleans, made Perkins's argument a moot point.

After the war's end, Perkins—conscious of his conspicuous role in Louisiana's secession—decided to flee from the United States and made his way to Mexico with several other former Confederates. From there he went to Europe and for a while attempted to establish a coffee plantation in Córdoba, Spain. Although Perkins reportedly had incurred heavy debts during the war, he eventually returned to Madison Parish in 1878. Having resumed his former life as a cotton planter, he resided in Louisiana, traveling to Virginia during the summers. He died in Baltimore, Maryland, on November 28, 1885.

BIBLIOGRAPHY

Alexander, Thomas B., and Richard E. Beringer. *The Anatomy of the Confederate Congress: A Study of the Influences of Member Characteristics on Legislative Voting Behavior, 1861–1865.* Nashville, Tenn., 1972.
Wakelyn, Jon L. *Biographical Dictionary of the Confederacy.* Edited by Frank E. Vandiver. Westport, Conn., 1977.

Warner, Ezra J., and W. Buck Yearns. *Biographical Register of the Confederate Congress.* Baton Rouge, La., 1975.
Yearns, Wilfred B. *The Confederate Congress.* Athens, Ga., 1960.

LESLIE A. LOVETT

PERRIN, ABNER MONROE (1827–1864), brigadier general. Born in Edgefield District, South Carolina, on February 2, 1827, Perrin later served in the Mexican War as a first lieutenant. A lawyer before the war, Perrin began his Confederate service as a captain in the Fourteenth South Carolina Infantry. Assigned to garrison duty along the South Carolina coast, he participated in the engagement at Port Royal Ferry on January 1, 1862. Transferred to Richmond in the spring of 1862, he fought in the Seven Days' Battles and at Cedar Mountain, Second Manassas, Harpers Ferry, Sharpsburg, and Fredericksburg. Promoted to colonel on February 20, 1863, Perrin led a regiment in Samuel McGowan's brigade at Chancellorsville, taking command when McGowan fell wounded during the second day of fighting. He presided over the brigade at Gettysburg, and in the retreat his men served as rear guard, beating off a cavalry attack near Falling Waters. Appointed brigadier general on September 10, 1863, he remained in temporary command of the brigade during the fighting at Bristoe Station and Mine Run. When McGowan returned to active duty in the spring of 1864, Perrin assumed command of a brigade in Richard Anderson's division and fought at the Wilderness. In the fighting at the Bloody Angle at Spotsylvania on May 12, while leading a counterattack against the Federal advance, he was shot several times and fell dead from his horse.

ABNER MONROE PERRIN. LIBRARY OF CONGRESS

BIBLIOGRAPHY

Capers, Ellison. *South Carolina.* Vol. 5 of *Confederate Military History.* Edited by Clement A. Evans. Atlanta, 1899. Vol. 6 of extended ed. Wilmington, N.C., 1987.
Spencer, James. *Civil War Generals.* Westport, Conn., 1986.
U.S. War Department. *War of the Rebellion: A Compilation of the Official Records of the Union and Confederate Armies.* Washington, D.C., 1880–1901. Ser. 1. Vol. 25, pt. 1, pp. 907–908, 911; vol. 27, pt. 2, p. 664; vol. 29, pt. 2, pp. 739–740.

MICHAEL G. MAHON

PERRY, EDWARD AYLESWORTH (1831–1889), brigadier general and governor of Florida. Perry was born in Richmond, Massachusetts, on March 15, 1831. He entered Yale in 1850, but remained only a year before moving to Alabama to teach school and study law. In 1857 he moved to Pensacola, Florida, setting up a law practice there.

In 1861, Perry raised Company A of the Second Florida Infantry and served as the unit's captain. He became colonel in May 1862 and was badly wounded in the fighting at Frayser's Farm during the Seven Days' Battles. He received a promotion to brigadier general August 28, 1862, and led the Florida brigade at Chancellorsville. Soon after, he contracted typhoid fever and was too sick to participate in the Gettysburg campaign.

Perry recovered from his illness and returned to active duty in Virginia. He fought at the Wilderness in 1864, where again he was severely wounded. Afterward, he accepted an assignment with the reserve forces of Alabama, serving until the end of the war.

Following the war, Perry returned to his law practice and became active in Democratic politics in Florida. He became governor of the state in 1884 and served for one term. Shortly after, on October 15, 1889, he died of a stroke while in Kerrville, Texas.

BIBLIOGRAPHY

Johnson, Allen, and Dumas Malone, eds. *Dictionary of American Biography.* New York, 1937–1964.
Scott, Robert Garth. *Into the Wilderness with the Army of the Potomac.* Bloomington, Ind., 1985.
U.S. War Department. *War of the Rebellion: A Compilation of the Official Records of the Union and Confederate Armies.* Wash-

ington, D.C., 1880–1901. Ser. 1, vol. 21, p. 618; ser. 1, vol. 35, pt. 1, pp. 874–1877.
Warner, Ezra J. *Generals in Gray: Lives of the Confederate Commanders*. Baton Rouge, La., 1959.

BRIAN S. WILLS

PERRY, MADISON S. (1814–1865), governor of Florida and colonel. Born in South Carolina in 1814, Madison Starke Perry moved to Florida as a young man and became a prosperous planter in the area of present-day Rochelle about six miles east of Gainesville. After gaining a reputation as an orator, he was elected to the Florida legislature in 1849 and the Florida Senate in 1850. He was elected the fourth governor of Florida on the Democratic ticket on October 6, 1856. Governor Perry's administration (1857–1861) was notable for construction of new railroads that opened the interior of Florida to development. Mindful of the impending conflict, Perry strengthened the state militia and upgraded military resources within the state.

On November 26, 1860, the governor urged immediate secession in his message to the legislature. Abraham Lincoln's election, he argued, meant that the only hope of the Southern states for domestic peace and safety lay in their seceding. Florida and other Southern states, he said, "must not be subservient to the Northern industrial powers." The Florida secession convention, meeting in Tallahassee, voted to withdraw Florida from the Union on January 10, 1861. Governor Perry quickly ordered the evacuation of all U.S. troops from military installations within Florida and directed that they be taken over by state militia troops. In October 1861, he turned the reins of government over to John Milton.

Very loyal to the Confederacy, Perry volunteered for active service and was elected colonel of the Seventh Florida Infantry Regiment in April 1862. He served with his troops in Tennessee until he contracted a fever. Resigning his commission in June 1863, Perry returned to his plantation in Alachua County, where his condition worsened and he died in March 1865, a month before the war ended.

BIBLIOGRAPHY

Davis, William Watson. *The Civil War and Reconstruction in Florida*. New York, 1913.
Morris, Allen. *The Florida Handbook*. Tallahassee, Fla., 1989.
Johns, John E. *Florida during the Civil War*. Gainesville, Fla., 1963.
Hildreth, Charles H., and Merlin G. Cox. *History of Gainesville, Florida, 1854–1979*. Gainesville, Fla., 1981.

MERLIN G. COX

PERRY, WILLIAM FLANK (1823–1901), brigadier general. Many colonels in the Army of Northern Virginia were qualified for advancement but could not be promoted because there were no vacancies. A notable example was William Flank Perry, one of the last officers promoted to brigadier general before Appomattox.

Perry was born March 12, 1823, in Jackson County, Georgia, and grew up in Alabama. He was a lawyer and state superintendent of education before the war; when he enlisted in May 1862, he was president of East Alabama Female College. Perry was elected major of the Forty-fourth Alabama Infantry when it organized and was with it in its first battle at Second Manassas. He was appointed lieutenant colonel just after the campaign, and when the colonel of the regiment was killed at Sharpsburg in September 1862, Perry succeeded him.

Superiors recognized Perry in reports and recommended his promotion, which was endorsed by many of his men, after he led a brigade at Chickamauga in September 1863. He also commanded his brigade in the winter of 1863–1864 and after permanent commander Evander McIvor Law was wounded at Cold Harbor in June 1864. Perry was finally appointed brigadier general on March 16, 1865, and surrendered his brigade three weeks later at Appomattox.

After the war, Perry moved to Kentucky and served for many years as an educator. He was a professor at Ogden College when he died at Bowling Green on December 18, 1901.

BIBLIOGRAPHY

Perry, William Flank. "The Devil's Den." *Confederate Veteran* 9 (1901): 161–163. Reprint, Wilmington, N.C., 1985.
Perry, William Flank. "Reminiscences of the Campaign of 1864 in Virginia." *Southern Historical Society Papers* 7 (1879): 49–63. Reprint, Wilmington, N.C., 1990.
Wheeler, Joseph. *Alabama*. Vol. 7 of *Confederate Military History*. Edited by Clement A. Evans. Atlanta, 1899. Vol. 8 of extended ed. Wilmington, N.C., 1987.

J. TRACY POWER

PERRYVILLE, KENTUCKY. On October 8, 1862, the town of Perryville was the site of an indecisive battle that marked the turning point in Gen. Braxton Bragg's ill-starred Kentucky campaign. After taking most of the state and inaugurating a Confederate state government, Bragg faced a perilous strategic situation. Arrayed against his 48,776 men was a Union army of over 80,000 troops centered at Louisville and another 45,000 at Cincinnati. To complicate matters, Bragg's divisions were scattered in garrisons across central Kentucky.

In the first week of October 1862, Union Gen. Don Carlos Buell and 61,000 men moved away from the Ohio River in four corps on separate roads a day's march apart. Confederate cavalrymen under Col. Joseph Wheeler reported

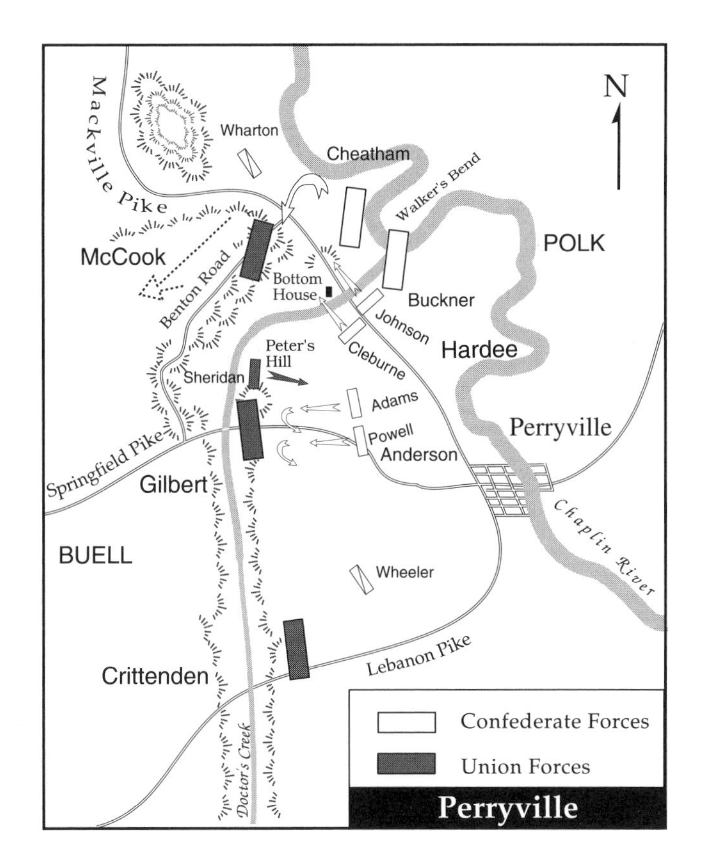

Federal troops moving toward Versailles and Perryville, threatening Confederate depots. Bragg reacted by dispatching troops to both points. On October 7, near the hamlet of Perryville, Southern horsemen skirmished with the advance elements of Buell's army along the Springfield and Mackville pikes. Confederate infantry under Maj. Gen. William J. Hardee hurried forward, forming a battle line east of town.

Hardee soon ascertained that the main Union blow would fall against him. He called for his divisional commander, Simon Bolivar Buckner, to bring his men up. Bragg, too, left Lexington for Perryville, ordering Maj. Gen. Leonidas Polk, commander of the Confederate troops in the vicinity, to "attack the enemy immediately," defeat him, and then join Maj. Gen. E. Kirby Smith.

In early morning darkness the following day, Union skirmishers, who were desperate for water, moved toward Doctor's Creek and ran into Confederate pickets at Peter's Hill. Both sides called for reinforcements. The Union brigade of Brig. Gen. Philip Sheridan pushed the Southerners down the Springfield Pike, but by daybreak the fighting had lulled and the Federal advance stalled.

The Confederates responded, though Polk hesitated despite General Bragg's orders for an attack at dawn. As additional Federals arrived, the Southerners deployed their 16,000 men in three divisions along the banks of Doctor's Creek in a battle line facing west. Maj. Gen. B. Franklin Cheatham's men occupied the Confederate right, anchored on Walker's Bend of the Chaplin River. In the center was Buckner's division, with Brig. Gen. James Patton Anderson's troops on its left. On the Confederate extreme right rode the cavalry of Col. John Austin Wharton, searching for the enemy flank, while Wheeler's troopers covered the left. By midday, Confederate cavalry reported the Union left flank to be farther north than expected. Accordingly, Cheatham ordered his men across the Chaplin River and into Walker's Bend to gain more room to launch an assault.

At 2:00 P.M. on October 8, the Confederate troops finally splashed across the stream and directly into the front of Union Maj. Gen. Alexander McCook's First Corps of the Army of the Ohio. Having missed the flank, Cheatham's infantry fought desperately while Buckner and Anderson added their troops to the fight, advancing obliquely to the right. With increasing pressure upon their front and left, McCook's men gave ground. Two Union brigadier generals, James S. Jackson and William R. Terrill, fell dead as the battle intensified.

On Buckner's front, the Confederate brigade of Brig. Gen. Bushrod Rust Johnson ran into heavy fire near the H. P. Bottom house on Doctor's Creek, forcing the Southerners to take cover behind a stone fence. Reinforcing brigades under Patrick Cleburne and Daniel Adams pushed beyond the stalled Confederate line and advanced up the slopes overlooking the creek, driving the Federals before them along the Mackville Pike. The Confederate push continued as Bragg's generals concentrated the major portion of his army against McCook's corps. One by one the Northern brigades broke and retreated before the onslaught. To the south, the Union troops of Maj. Gen. Charles C. Gilbert's corps nervously watched the disaster to their left—Buell had issued orders for no other troops to engage. By 4:00 P.M., however, the Confederate advance slowed as McCook's men formed a tattered but intact line.

The fighting now shifted to the Confederate left as Col. Samuel Powell's advancing brigade collided with Gilbert's untested corps. After a severe exchange, the outnumbered Southerners gave way, pursued down the Springfield Pike by Sheridan's Federals. Soon the fighting moved into the streets of Perryville. As the Confederates gave ground, Sheridan grew uneasy about his exposed position and ordered a withdrawal back to his original lines. This ended the fighting for the day.

Bragg had committed all of his available troops at Perryville. Almost 3,100 men had been killed, wounded, or captured—nearly 20 percent of the Confederates involved. Buell, however, had used only half of his men. About 25,000 of his 61,000 troops fought at Perryville, of which nearly 3,700 became casualties. The untested portion of the

Federal army appeared ready to continue the fight the following morning.

That evening, as additional Union divisions moved into place, Bragg ordered a withdrawal. Badly outnumbered, the Southern leader hastened to concentrate his troops with the balance of the Confederate army under Kirby Smith at Harrodsburg. The battle had had a potential for disaster, as unsupported elements of the Confederate army had met the bulk of Buell's force; only the lack of decisive Union leadership and aggressive pursuit had spared the Confederates.

Tactically, the Battle of Perryville was a draw. McCook's corps had been roughly treated and had given ground but still managed to hold off the repeated Confederate attacks. Elsewhere on the battlefield, however, the outcome had been different. Nightfall and lack of adequate support were all that kept Sheridan from inflicting a disaster on the Confederate left.

The Battle of Perryville ended Bragg's campaign in Kentucky. The concentration of Federal forces against him, plus his lackluster reception by the citizens of the state, compelled him to withdraw. After combining with Kirby Smith's forces, the Confederate army marched through Cumberland Gap into Tennessee, leaving Kentucky behind.

BIBLIOGRAPHY

Connelly, Thomas L. *Army of the Heartland: The Army of Tennessee, 1861–1862.* Baton Rouge, La., 1967.

Coulter, E. Merton. *The Civil War and Readjustment in Kentucky.* Chapel Hill, N.C., 1926.

Gilbert, Charles C. "On the Field of Perryville." In *Battles and Leaders of the Civil War.* Edited by Robert U. Johnson and C. C. Buel. Vol. 2. New York, 1888. Reprint, Secaucus, N.J., 1982.

Hawke, Paul. "Perryville Kentucky." In *The Civil War Battlefield Guide.* Edited by Francis H. Kennedy. Boston, 1990.

McWhiney, Grady. *Braxton Bragg and Confederate Defeat.* Vol. 1. New York, 1968. Reprint, Tuscaloosa, Ala., 1991.

Wheeler, Joseph. "Bragg's Invasion of Kentucky." In *Battles and Leaders of the Civil War.* Edited by Robert U. Johnson and C. C. Buel. Vol. 2. New York, 1888. Reprint, Secaucus, N.J., 1982.

DONALD S. FRAZIER

PETERSBURG CAMPAIGN. For ten grinding months—from June 15, 1864, to April 3, 1865—Confederate forces under Gen. Robert E. Lee conducted the longest sustained defensive operation of the war in the works surrounding Petersburg, Virginia. All but one of the railroads that connected Richmond to remaining Confederate supplies passed first through Petersburg. Both Lee and Lt. Gen. Ulysses S. Grant, commander of all Federal armies, recognized that Union possession of the city would force the evacuation of Richmond and shorten the war.

By early June, Grant's strategy had failed to capture Lee's army northeast of Richmond. Maj. Gen. Benjamin Butler's Army of the James was ignominiously bottled up by Confederate forces near Bermuda Hundred, unable to threaten either Richmond or Petersburg. Maj. Gen. George G. Meade's Army of the Potomac incurred huge casualties in the Overland campaign, leaving the Army of Northern Virginia damaged but not destroyed. In an effort to break the stalemate near Cold Harbor, Grant looked south to Petersburg. If he could sever Confederate supply lines, Lee's army would have to leave entrenchments for open combat.

On June 12 Grant's army slipped away from Cold Harbor and began an audacious turning movement. Maj. Gen. William Smith's Eighteenth Corps went by ship to Bermuda Hundred while the Army of the Potomac marched through fifty miles of enemy territory to the James River. Transports and the 2,100-foot-long James River pontoon bridge, a marvel of combat engineering, placed Federal units a day's march from Petersburg.

Through rapid movement and a convincing feint against Richmond, Grant had frozen Lee north of the James. In Petersburg, Brig. Gen. Henry A. Wise's patchwork force of 2,200 Confederates faced the arrival of Smith's 12,500 men. Despite delays and command mistakes, Union attackers quickly overwhelmed three and one-half miles of the imposing Dimmock Line that surrounded the city. As darkness fell on June 15 and Maj. Gen. Winfield S. Hancock's Second Corps arrived, Smith exercised caution and stopped his advance within sight of Petersburg's spires. Confederate Gen. P. G. T. Beauregard took advantage of this delay to reinforce Petersburg with units from the Bermuda Hundred lines. By June 16 Beauregard had marshaled 14,000 men to face Federal troops that would number between 63,000 and 80,000 men on June 17.

On June 16, 17, and 18, Federal forces continued pouring into the Petersburg area. Each day witnessed piecemeal Union attacks against strongly entrenched Confederate lines. Petersburg might have fallen on June 17 when Confederate lines were twice shattered, but heroic Confederate counterattacks by Maj. Gen. Bushrod Rust Johnson's division closed the gaps when Union reinforcements failed to arrive.

Beauregard fought his finest battle at Petersburg, while the Union army suffered from a combination of poor leadership and extreme combat exhaustion. After four days of fighting, Federal losses totaled 10,586 compared to an estimated 4,000 Confederate casualties. With the arrival of Lee's forces on June 18, Grant halted frontal attacks and chose instead "to use the spade."

On June 19 Lee and Grant found themselves in a position neither wanted. For Grant, siege tactics meant slow progress and dwindling morale, something Abraham Lincoln's party could ill-afford in an election year. Lee likewise

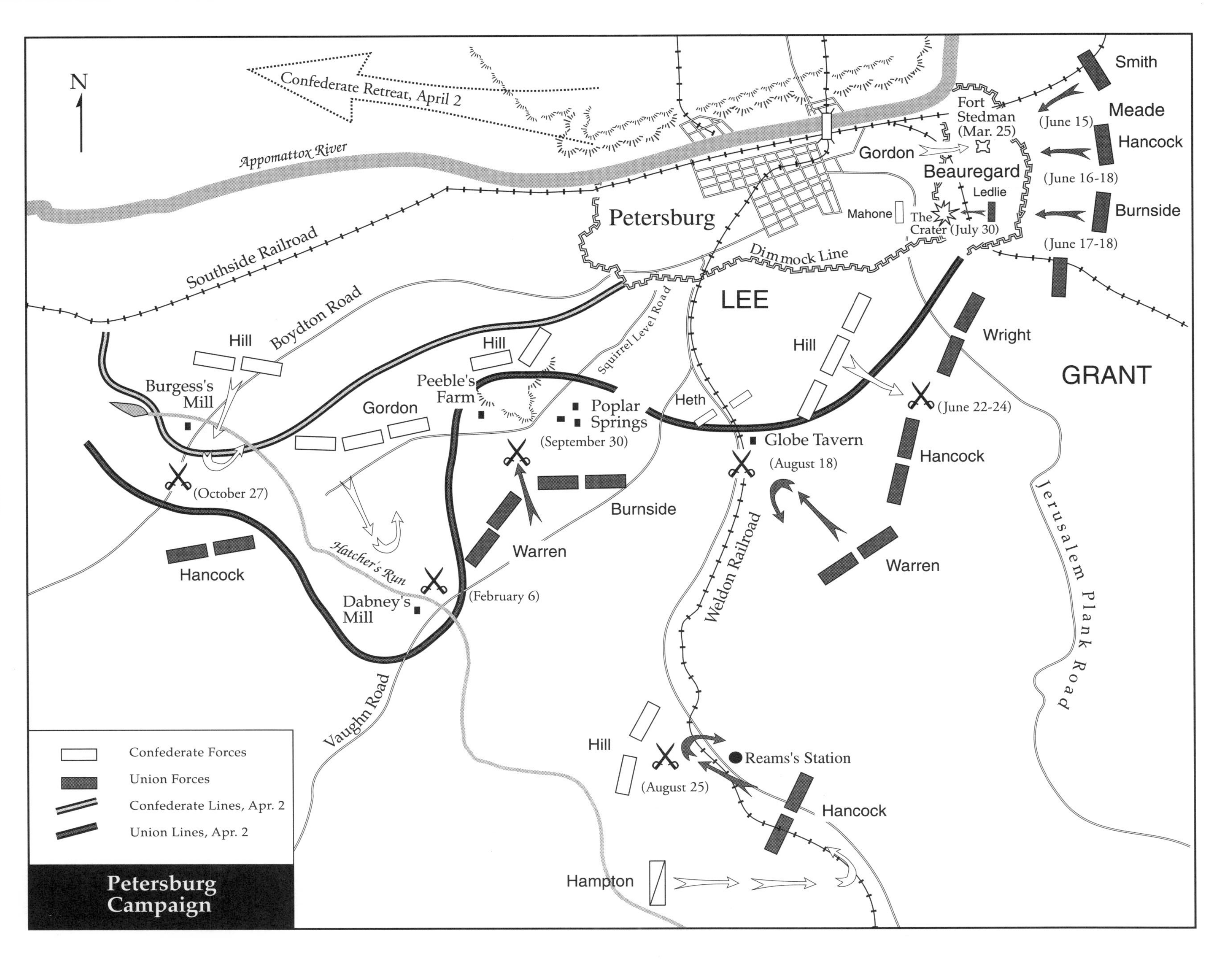
Confederate Retreat, April 2
N
Appomattox River
Southside Railroad
Petersburg
Fort Stedman (Mar. 25)
Gordon
Beauregard
Ledlie
Mahone
The Crater (July 30)
Dimmock Line
Smith
Meade
(June 15)
Hancock
(June 16-18)
Burnside
(June 17-18)
LEE
GRANT
Wright
Hill
(June 22-24)
Hancock
Globe Tavern
(August 18)
Warren
Heth
Weldon Railroad
Jerusalem Plank Road
Boydton Road
Hill
Burgess's Mill
Hill
Peeble's Farm
Gordon
Squirrel Level Road
Poplar Springs
(September 30)
(October 27)
Burnside
Warren
Hatcher's Run
Dabney's Mill
(February 6)
Hancock
Vaughn Road
Hill
(August 25)
Reams's Station
Hancock
Hampton
Confederate Forces
Union Forces
Confederate Lines, Apr. 2
Union Lines, Apr. 2
Petersburg Campaign

recognized that the offensive skills of his smaller army would mean little in a campaign of attrition. By late June, Lee's 50,000 men had covered a twenty-six-mile line from Richmond to Petersburg and faced a Federal host that hovered around 112,000 troops.

Drawing upon his Vicksburg experience, Grant began a two-pronged strategy designed to encircle Petersburg while cutting Lee's supply lines. On June 22 through 24, the Second and Sixth Corps challenged Maj. Gen. A. P. Hill's corps for possession of the Weldon Railroad. Hill, however, exploited a gap that developed between the two corps and inflicted 2,962 casualties while maintaining control of the railroad. The Battle of Jerusalem Plank Road (or Weldon Railroad) foreshadowed the coming nine months of action. With each Federal movement westward, Lee launched increasingly desperate counterattacks to prevent the extension of earthworks while preserving connections with Southern supplies.

In late July, Grant hesitantly moved the focus of his strategy from the left flank to an attack in the center of the Confederate line opposite Maj. Gen. Ambrose Burnside's Ninth Corps. Coal miners from the Forty-eighth Pennsylvania tunneled 511 feet to the Confederate line and packed eight thousand pounds of black powder into a gallery under Brig. Gen. Stephen Elliot's salient. Brig. Gen. Edward Ferrero's large, fresh division of black soldiers had been carefully trained to spearhead the attack through the breach made by "springing the mine." Meade, however, had reservations about the black division's inexperience and about potential political fallout should heavy casualties lead to charges that the army deliberately sacrificed black soldiers. With Grant's approval, Meade ordered an enraged Burnside to choose a new lead division only one day before the assault. The job fell by lot to the division of Brig. Gen. James Ledlie, an incompetent officer who was to spend the attack hiding in a bombproof.

At 4:40 A.M. on July 30 a spectacular explosion blasted a hole 170 feet long, 60 feet wide, and 30 feet deep in the Confederate line. Defenders were thrown into disarray, and despite a late start more than 15,000 troops from the Ninth Corps rushed into the Crater and adjacent works. Lacking leadership, the men milled about in the captured line and failed to gain the high ground just beyond.

Confederate counterattacks, led by Brig. Gen. William Mahone's division, drove Federal troops from the captured works and slaughtered those trapped in the Crater. By 1:00 P.M. the attack was over. The Union army lost an estimated 4,000 men against just 1,500 for the Confederates in a fiasco that prompted a congressional investigation and a military court of inquiry. Grant called the Battle of the Crater "the saddest affair" of the war and resigned himself to a strategy of exhaustion.

In mid-August Federal forces moved again to extend their lines westward. On August 18, as the Union Second and Tenth Corps attacked north of the James near Fussell's Mill, Maj. Gen. Gouverneur Warren's Fifth Corps struck the Weldon Railroad near Globe Tavern, about four miles south of Petersburg. Warren's soldiers moved north from the tavern for a mile, ripping up track as they marched. Two Confederate brigades under Maj. Gen. Henry Heth responded promptly to contest the railroad's destruction. The next day Hill's corps joined the fight and captured more than 2,500 prisoners while driving the Federal line south. Warren's corps regrouped and dug in around Globe Tavern, and on August 21 Hill's men attacked but failed to carry the Union line. Lee then arrived on the field from north of the James and called a halt to assaults against the Union position. Federal losses in the Battle of Globe Tavern (or Weldon Railroad) totaled 4,455, well in excess of the Confederate's estimated 1,600 casualties, but the railroad was cut. Confederate teamsters now had to supply Petersburg by wagon from Stony Creek Depot, twenty miles south of Petersburg. In December a Federal raid at Hicksford destroyed another sixteen miles of the Weldon Railroad and forced an even longer wagon supply route.

Confederate forces did enjoy some success in late summer. On August 25 Hancock's Second Corps was five miles south of Globe Tavern, destroying track at Reams's Station, when a vigorous attack by Hill's corps stampeded raw Union recruits and crumpled Hancock's left. Confederate forces captured 9 guns, 12 flags, and more than 2,150 men. And between September 11 and 17, Maj. Gen. Wade Hampton's horsemen rode into the rear of the Union army and captured about 300 men and 2,400 head of cattle. Reams's Station and the Beefsteak Raid improved Confederate morale, but the Federal army missed neither the men nor the meals.

Grant's inexorable strategy continued in late September. As part of a major thrust north of the James at Fort Harrison, elements of the Fifth and Ninth Corps near the Weldon Railroad staged a reconnaissance in force north and west toward the Southside Railroad. On September 30 Union forces captured trenches and a Confederate redoubt at Peeble's Farm near Squirrel Level Road. With characteristic combativeness, Hill attacked the Union position with two divisions and temporarily drove the Federals south. Union counterattacks reestablished the line near Peeble's Farm, and by October 2 Federal troops had extended their line more than a mile west of Globe Tavern. The Battle of Peeble's Farm (or Poplar Springs Church) cost Grant another 2,889 casualties, but it forced Lee to match the extended line or risk envelopment.

In a final attempt to capture the Southside Railroad before winter, Grant employed elements of three corps and on October 27 gained control of the Boydton Road near Burgess's Mill. Hill responded immediately. Confederate

Born in Tyrrell County, North Carolina, on July 4, 1828, Pettigrew graduated first in the class of 1847 at the University of North Carolina. He later moved to South Carolina, where he practiced law, served in the legislature, and was an officer in the militia.

After serving as military adviser to the governor and colonel of a state regiment from South Carolina's secession to the fall of Fort Sumter, Pettigrew became colonel of the Twenty-second North Carolina Infantry in July 1861. He was promoted to brigadier general in February 1862. At Seven Pines, on May 31, 1862, Pettigrew was severely wounded and captured in his first battle.

When he returned to duty Pettigrew commanded a newly formed brigade which saw service on the North Carolina and Virginia coasts and joined the Army of Northern Virginia for the Gettysburg campaign. On July 1, 1863, his brigade suffered heavy casualties but fought brilliantly. Pettigrew, in temporary command of the division on July 3, led it and was wounded in the assault popularly known as Pickett's Charge. On July 14, during the retreat through Maryland, Pettigrew was mortally wounded at Falling Waters; he died July 18, 1863.

He was one of the best educated and most intellectual Southern generals. Lee called him "an officer of great promise" and observed, "his loss will be deeply felt by the country and the army."

BIBLIOGRAPHY

Freeman, Douglas S. *Lee's Lieutenants: A Study in Command.* 3 vols. New York, 1942–1944. Reprint, New York, 1986.

U.S. War Department. *War of the Rebellion: A Compilation of the Official Records of the Union and Confederate Armies.* Washington, D.C., 1880-1901. Ser. 1, vol. 11, pts. 1–2.

Wilson, Clyde N. *Carolina Cavalier: The Life and Mind of James Johnston Pettigrew.* Athens, Ga., 1990.

J. TRACY POWER

PETTUS, EDMUND WINSTON (1821–1907),

brigadier general and U.S. senator. Born July 6, 1821, in Limestone County, Alabama, Pettus studied at Clinton College in Tennessee and read law in Tuscumbia, Alabama. In 1842 he moved to Gainesville, Alabama, and began to practice law. He held several minor political offices in the 1840s and 1850s.

In 1861 Pettus served as an Alabama commissioner to Mississippi (of which his brother J. J. Pettus was then governor). After that mission he helped raise the Twentieth Alabama Infantry Regiment. On September 9 he was appointed major of that unit and a month later became the regiment's lieutenant colonel. He was captured at Port Gibson, Mississippi, May 1, 1863, but soon escaped. Rejoining his regiment, he fought through the Vicksburg campaign, and on May 28 he was promoted to colonel. He surrendered with the Vicksburg garrison (July 4) and was exchanged in late 1863.

Promoted to brigadier general September 19, 1863, Pettus took command of a brigade in the Army of Tennessee. He fought doggedly through the Atlanta, Franklin and Nashville, and Carolinas campaigns of 1864–1865. At the Battle of Bentonville, North Carolina (March 19–21, 1865), he was wounded in the right leg.

After the war Pettus settled in Selma, Alabama, and resumed his law practice. A Democrat, he was elected to the U.S. Senate in 1896 and held that post until his death on July 27, 1907. He was buried in Old Live Oak Cemetery in Selma. He was the last Confederate brigadier to serve in the U.S. Senate.

BIBLIOGRAPHY

Jones, Terry L. "Edmund Winston Pettus." In *The Confederate General.* Edited by William C. Davis. Vol. 5. Harrisburg, Pa., 1991.

Warner, Ezra J. *Generals in Gray: Lives of the Confederate Commanders.* Baton Rouge, La., 1959.

RICHARD M. MCMURRY

PETTUS, J. J. (1813–1867), governor of Mississippi.

John Jones Pettus moved to Mississippi from Tennessee as a youth and became a lawyer and cotton planter in Kemper County. Throughout his life, Pettus never lost his identification with his roots and his frontier simplicity. From 1846 to 1848, Pettus served in the state house of representatives, and from 1848 to 1858, in the senate. For five days in 1854 he served as acting governor, when Governor Henry S. Foote resigned in a feud with Senator Jefferson Davis. In 1859, he was elected governor, beating his opponent 34,559 to 10,308 on the issue of taking decisive action to protect the rights of slave-owning states if a Republican was elected president. He pledged he would ask the legislature "to fill the arsenal with arms that the state might be prepared for the worst."

Soon after Pettus took office John Brown raided the arsenal at Harpers Ferry, and Pettus's views became more extreme. He envisioned a South united under the motto "Superiority and Supremacy of the White Race" and believed that whites in the North would seek union with the South. He began to arm the state as early as 1860, using a legislative appropriation of $150,000 to purchase several thousand rifles with bayonets. He also encouraged the organization of many volunteer companies.

Mississippi at this time was split between the cooperationists and the secessionists. Although agreeing with the secessionists that the South had grievances against the Northern states, the cooperationists wanted to fight for their rights within the Union. The extreme secessionists, of course, favored immediate separation, and Pettus was a member of this group. (At one point, a short play was staged in which Pettus was portrayed as an inmate of a "lunatic asylum"; he was described as sensible on many subjects, but if anyone said to him the word *abolition,* "you will see his knees tremble, the color leave his cheeks, his eye-balls start, his whole countenance become distorted with fear.")

After Abraham Lincoln's election, Pettus called a special session of the Mississippi legislature to debate the best course for the state. The legislature ordered elections to a state convention, and on January 9, 1861, the members voted 84 to 15 to pass an ordinance of secession. In a message to the legislature on January 18, Pettus reported that the state had sent seven companies to assist in the Fort Pickens siege at Pensacola and predicted the likely approach of "open war."

Pettus was optimistic when the war began. In a special session of the legislature soon after the Confederate victory at Manassas, he announced that the revolution was "prosperous and successful." Financial problems, however, immediately surfaced, and Pettus had to suspend all payments of state debts, call for private donations to the military, and request increased taxes.

In October 1861, Pettus was reelected governor with little opposition. Problems intensified, and early in 1862, the war reached Mississippi. The governor called for all males to enroll in the militia, and after the Confederate defeats at Corinth, Memphis, and New Orleans, he decided to use the state troops to defend Vicksburg. This action was criticized as a feeble resistance that could backfire, and the militia in 1863 got restive in camp. But Pettus refused to disband the militia or place it under Confederate control. Newspapers attacked him as "Pettus the Firm."

During the remainder of his term, Pettus struggled with the lack of adequate provisions, with inflation, with conscription, with finances, and with the impossibility of holding back the invading forces. As Ulysses S. Grant closed in on Vicksburg, Pettus, in desperation, proclaimed to the people of Mississippi that the state battle flag could not be "dragged to the dust by barbarian hordes on her own soil." At the same time he was calling the state to action, he was preparing to flee the capital. After battles at Raymond and Jackson, the state government was moved to Enterprise and later to Macon. In October 1863, in the regular biennial elections, Gen. Charles Clark won the governorship. Under the state constitution Pettus was ineligible for another term.

After the fall of the Confederacy, Pettus's political career was over. He was even rumored to have had some part in Lincoln's assassination. According to one account, he fled to the swamps to hide until he escaped to Arkansas, traveling under a pseudonym. There he died in 1867.

BIBLIOGRAPHY

Dubay, Robert W. *John Jones Pettus, Mississippi Fire-Eater: His Life and Times, 1813–1867.* Oxford, Miss., 1975.

Yearns, W. Buck, ed. *The Confederate Governors.* Athens, Ga., 1985.

RAY SKATES

PEYTON, ROBERT LUDWELL YATES (1822–1863), colonel and congressman from Missouri. Born in Loudon County, Virginia, February 8, 1822, Peyton was the descendant of a prominent Virginia family. While he was still a child his parents moved to Oxford, Ohio, where he graduated from Miami University in 1841. After graduation he earned a law degree from the University of Virginia. Apparently disappointed by an early romance, he left for Missouri, settling in Harrisonville, Cass County, prior to 1844. Peyton was described as a procrastinator who had few wants and was inattentive to detail. His excellent intellect and oratorical skills, however, made him a formidable legal opponent. He served in the state senate in 1858.

A state rights Democrat and secessionist, Peyton was elected by the rump Neosho legislature as one of Missouri's senators in the Provisional Congress. He was also a colonel in the Third Missouri Cavalry and saw action in several military engagements.

As a senator in the First Congress, Peyton served on the Indian Affairs, Claims, Commerce, and Engrossment and Enrollment committees. He was appointed to a special committee to investigate the Confederate navy. With the exception of policies directly affecting the war effort, Peyton seldom sided with the Davis administration, although he affirmed the government's emergency control over the South's resources.

Peyton died on September 3, 1863, in Bladon Springs, Alabama.

BIBLIOGRAPHY

Glenn, Alan. *History of Cass County, Missouri.* Topeka, Kans., 1917.

History of Cass and Bates Counties, Missouri. St. Joseph, Mo., 1883.

Wakelyn, Jon L. *Biographical Dictionary of the Confederacy.* Edited by Frank E. Vandiver. Westport, Conn., 1977.

Warner, Ezra J., and W. Buck Yearns. *Biographical Register of the Confederate Congress.* Baton Rouge, La., 1975.

JAMES W. GOODRICH

PHELAN, JAMES (1820 or 1821–1873), congressman from Mississippi. James Phelan's father emigrated from Ireland to New York and New Jersey, but eventually moved south to Alabama, where Phelan was born. At the age of fourteen, Phelan went into the newspaper business as a printer and soon began writing editorials, first at the *Huntsville Democrat* and later in Tuscaloosa at the *Flag of the Union,* the organ of the Democratic party. Phelan then changed to a legal career with the help of a brother, Judge John D. Phelan.

In 1849 Phelan moved to Aberdeen, Mississippi, where he became a vigorous defender of state rights. In 1860 he was elected to the state senate, and in 1861 he was chosen as senator in the First Congress, but only for a two-year term.

During his term, he followed Jefferson Davis's position without any significant dissent; in fact, he felt that dissension would weaken the Confederacy. Phelan's pugnacity and antipathy toward Northern policy, especially toward freeing slaves, are apparent in his emotional speeches. In one he labeled Northerners "our brutal foes" and accused them of seeking "to light in our land the baneful fires of servile war, by emancipating amongst us four million of negro slaves, with the design of effecting an indiscriminating slaughter of all ages, sexes and conditions of our people." He called emancipation an "atrocious and infernal" scheme that "surpasses in atrocious cruelty the most signal despotism that ever disgraced the earth." He insisted that the Northerners were seeking "the subjugation or the annihilation of the people of these United States."

In the Senate Phelan consistently opposed military substitution and draft exemptions. On December 9, 1862, he wrote to President Davis opposing exemptions for the wealthy and influential, who were able to "obtain some safe perch where they can doze with their heads under their wings." He supported a very strong central government for the Confederacy. In 1863 he introduced a bill to seize all cotton in the South so that it could not fall into enemy hands and could serve as the basis for foreign loans. Those who refused to hand over the cotton for fifteen cents a pound, payable in Confederate bonds, would be punished by death. Because of the controversy stirred by this proposal, Phelan was burned in effigy and then defeated in 1863 by John W. C. Watson, who remained a senator for the duration of the Congress. After Phelan's brief senatorial stint, he was appointed a military judge and served until the end of the war.

After the war Phelan suffered economic destitution and traveled to Washington, D.C., where he met with President Andrew Johnson to plead for permission to work. Johnson consented to recommend a work permit despite Phelan's refusal to apologize for his wartime positions. Phelan returned to the law in Aberdeen and in 1867 moved to Memphis, where he died in 1873.

BIBLIOGRAPHY

Alexander, Thomas B., and Richard E. Beringer. *The Anatomy of the Confederate Congress: A Study of the Influences of Member Characteristics on Legislative Voting Behavior, 1861–1865.* Nashville, Tenn., 1972.

Warner, Ezra J., and W. Buck Yearns. *Biographical Register of the Confederate Congress.* Baton Rouge, La., 1975.

RAY SKATES

PHOTOGRAPHY. When the Civil War commenced, there were in the United States more than 3,100 ambrotypists, daguerreotypists, calotypists, melainotypists, and others, all of whom were, by one process or another, photographers. Of their number, only a fraction practiced their trade in the seceded states. New York City alone boasted more artists than almost the entire Confederacy. Arkansas, by contrast, had a mere nineteen. Moreover, while the number of photographers grew in the North during the war, it shriveled in the South, where demands for manpower took many artists into the armies and the ever-increasing shortage of chemicals, paper, and other necessaries simply put others out of business.

Still the Confederate photographers did create and leave behind an indelible record of several aspects of their side of the conflict. Indeed, the first war photographer was a Confederate, J. D. Edwards. A thirty-year-old New Hampshire native, he was working in New Orleans when the secession crisis erupted. Perhaps as early as January 1861 he was taking images of local volunteers, including excellent outdoor group portraits of members of New Orleans' colorful Washington Artillery (local artist J. W. Petty would also do a series on this unit). Then in April he took his camera to Pensacola, Florida, to produce what still remains the finest body of outdoor work by any Southern photographer. He made at least sixty-nine images of Fort Pickens, Fort Barrancas, Fort McRee, the navy yard, and the dozens of volunteer units there mustered. Many have since been lost, but about fifty are known to survive, constituting nearly half of the extant body of Confederate outdoor views.

Edwards, like all other artists at the war's outset, viewed his work as a commercial enterprise, not a historical record. He advertised his prints in the New Orleans press and sold copies, as did other artists as long as their supplies held out. While Edwards worked in large format, the South's other war artists took another direction. Just three days after the fall of Fort Sumter, the business team of James M. Osborn and F. W. Durbec of King Street, Charleston, took a camera and portable darkroom inside the still smoldering ruins of the fort to make over forty images of it and the Confederate batteries that forced it to submit. Theirs is still the most complete contemporaneous record of any Civil War event, North or South.

Edwards worked in the wet plate process, making a negative in emulsion on glass. Osborn and Durbec made stereo views, nearly duplicate images placed side by side

Confederate battery at Pensacola, Florida. One of the many outdoor photographs of the Pensacola area produced by New Orleans photographer J. D. Edwards in early 1861. Pictured are Confederates manning 32-pound model 1829 guns. A substantial number of these iron seacoast guns were captured when Confederate forces occupied Federal installations in the South.

National Archives

that, when viewed in a stereo viewer, gave a three-dimensional effect. They were probably the only Confederate photographers to do so. Virtually all the rest used the wet plate process, or else made tintypes on sensitized iron plates. None was successful in marketing this work extensively. The real demand in the Confederacy was for soldier portraits, and consequently, the photographers husbanded their precious raw materials for this more lucrative trade. By comparison with barely more than 100 outdoor views of scenes and soldiers in the field that are known to have been taken, probably 100,000 or more studio portraits were made of individual Confederates.

The Confederates rarely attempted to put the camera to military use. A. D. Lytle of Baton Rouge has long been believed to have made images of Federal troops to send to Confederate leaders, but there is nothing in his surviving images that would have any military value. Richmond's David Rees did make a few 1863 images of the infamous Libby Prison, and on August 17, 1864, Georgia photographer A. J. Riddle made a series of photos of Camp Sumter at Andersonville. None of this work appears to have been inspired by anything more than commercial motivation or curiosity.

George Cook, who lived in Charleston at the beginning of the war, eventually moved to Richmond, but not before making a memorable series of prints of the interior of Fort Sumter on September 8, 1863, while the Northern fleet bombarded the garrison. He caught the only known image of a shell bursting and soon afterward made an image of three Union ironclads as they were firing. They are the only action images of the war, North or South.

By the last months of the war, most photographers were out of materials and out of business. Those who continued to operate were located in areas occupied by the Federals. With a free flow of supplies to these areas, such artists could resume their craft, and many made a lucrative business from their one-time enemies, especially in New Orleans, Baton Rouge, Nashville, Memphis, and other larger cities. Ironically, then, the largest remaining output from the Confederate photographers as a whole is pictures of Union soldiers and officers. Some of their work even found its way into the North's illustrated press via woodcuts. The

INTERIOR OF FORT SUMTER. View of the eastern barracks after bombardment by the Union fleet. Photographed by George Cook as part of his series of images of the fort, September 8, 1863.

LIBRARY OF CONGRESS

Confederacy's one such newspaper, the *Southern Illustrated News,* died early and made little use of Confederate photographers' work.

Unfortunately, after the war hundreds—maybe thousands—of Confederate images disappeared, lost or destroyed as baleful reminders of defeat and devastation.

BIBLIOGRAPHY

Davis, William C., ed. *The Image of War.* 6 vols. New York, 1981–1984.

Roberts, Bobby, and Carl Moneyhon. *Portraits of Conflict.* Fayetteville, Ark., 1987.

WILLIAM C. DAVIS

PICKENS, FRANCIS W. (1807–1869), U.S. congressman, diplomat, and governor of South Carolina. Born on April 7, 1807, in St. Paul's Parish, near Charleston, Pickens was the grandson of Revolutionary Gen. Andrew Pickens and son of Governor Andrew Pickens, Jr., and Susan Wilkinson. He grew up near Pendleton until his family moved to Edgefield and to Alabama. He attended South Carolina College and then practiced law and managed six plantations with 417 slaves.

In 1832 Pickens was elected to the state legislature and was prominent in the nullification crisis. In 1834 he went to Congress and was John C. Calhoun's spokesman. He urged his state to reject the Compromise of 1850 and secede, but in 1852 he supported cooperation with other states. In 1858, he became minister to Russia.

In 1860, Pickens returned home, still a cooperationist. But in November he urged secession at a rally in Edgefield. A few days later, before the legislature, he "appeal[ed] to the god of battles—if need be [to] cover the state with ruin, conflagration and blood rather than submit." Mary Boykin Chesnut called him "a fire-eater down to the ground." On December 12, he was elected governor. Aloof and overbearing, Pickens was not popular. He was elected because he had not been involved in the disputes of the past two years. Pickens wrote, "I believe it my destiny to be disliked by all who know me well."

After secession, the convention assumed extraordinary powers. It ordered Pickens to prevent the garrisoning of Federal forts in Charleston. Despite his efforts, Maj. Robert

FRANCIS W. PICKENS.

HARPER'S PICTORIAL HISTORY OF THE GREAT REBELLION

Anderson occupied Fort Sumter, and on December 30, the governor ordered the occupation of Federal property. The convention created a five-member Executive Council as a cabinet for Pickens as the head of state. It was advisory, but served as a check on the governor.

Meanwhile Pickens refused to move against Sumter. Not until the Confederacy decided to act did he demand the fort be taken. When Pickens authorized volunteers to leave the state without council approval, he was severely criticized. The council ceased to function after April 1861.

In his address to the legislature on November 5, 1861, Pickens only revived the glories of secession. When a Federal force occupied Beaufort two days later, there was a chorus of criticism regarding his lack of preparation. The convention reconvened on December 27 and ordered improvement of the state's defenses and the creation of a new Executive Council. This time the council became a plural executive, with the governor casting one vote. Pickens was furious.

The council ruled dictatorially, conscripted troops, and impressed slaves. It became increasingly unpopular, although Mary Chesnut blamed its reputation on "Pickens' miserable jealousy." In addressing the legislature in November 1862, the governor attacked the council, and it was abolished. In the closing weeks of his term, Pickens's popularity increased. He returned to Edgefield on December 18 and resumed planting.

By 1864 Pickens was "patiently waiting the catastrophe," as he wrote to Governor Andrew G. Magrath. He served as a delegate to the state constitutional convention of 1865 and died without a pardon in Edgefield on January 25, 1869.

BIBLIOGRAPHY

Edmunds, John B., Jr. *Francis W. Pickens and the Politics of Destruction.* Chapel Hill, N.C., 1986.

Yearns, W. Buck, ed. *The Confederate Governors.* Athens, Ga., 1985.

A. V. HUFF, JR.

PICKETT, GEORGE E. (1825–1850), major general. George Edward Pickett was born into the Virginia aristocracy on January 28, 1825, and grew up on the family plantation on the James River. He attended Richmond Academy and in 1824 received an appointment to West Point. Four unhappy years later, he graduated at the bottom of his class but fought the Mexican War with the Eighth Infantry Regiment and received two brevets for bravery. From 1849 through 1861 he served on frontier duty, first in Texas and then in Washington Territory, where in 1859 he helped provoke a near-war with the British over the possession of San Juan Island.

When the Civil War started, Pickett resigned his commission in the U.S. Army and returned to Virginia. His first commission in Confederate service was as a captain of infantry in the Provisional Army. He was quickly promoted to colonel and posted on the Rappahannock front under Theophilus H. Holmes. Although he was the most junior of all the colonels in his district, he was promoted to brigadier general in 1862, reflecting more the need for experienced officers than a high regard for his services.

The spring of 1862 found him on the peninsula as part of Joseph E. Johnston's army, James Longstreet's division. Pickett led his brigade ably at Seven Pines and (after Robert E. Lee took over) during the Seven Days' Battles, where he reported "quite severe" losses. In the Battle of Gaines' Mill, Pickett suffered his first wound, a severe shoulder injury that put him out of combat for three months. When he returned in October 1862, he became a major general in Longstreet's First Corps. His division was in reserve at the Battle of Fredericksburg. In the spring of 1863 when two of Longstreet's divisions were detached for service in the Suffolk campaign in southeastern Virginia, Pickett went along but spent more time courting LaSalle Corbell than fighting Yankees.

Pickett did not reach the battlefield at Gettysburg until late on the second day. The next afternoon he led his division forward as part of the assault that bears his name.

Three-fourths of his command became casualties in less than an hour, although Pickett himself emerged unscathed, raising questions about his whereabouts at the height of the charge. His moment of glory had come and gone.

After the army returned to Virginia he was assigned to garrison duty south of Richmond during the early part of 1864. He organized an unsuccessful attack on New Bern, North Carolina, in February 1864, which led to charges of murder of Carolina Unionists. Twenty-two prisoners from the Second U.S. North Carolina Volunteers were accused of being deserters from Confederate service and were hanged under Pickett's orders. After the war when the U.S. secretary of war and the judge advocate recommended filing formal charges against Pickett, only Ulysses S. Grant's personal intervention prevented any action from being taken.

In May 1864 Pickett distinguished himself for the last time in the war by helping "bottle up" Gen. Benjamin Butler at Bermuda Hundred. After stopping Butler, he seems to have suffered a mental breakdown in May 1864, for he took to his bed for a week or more and was relieved of duty. He returned to his command in June, after the siege of Petersburg had already started, but little was heard of him until March 1865 when Gen. Robert E. Lee sent him to hold the strategic junction at Five Forks. On April 1 his division was destroyed while he was enjoying himself at an impromptu shad-bake with Gens. Fitzhugh Lee and Thomas Lafayette Rosser two miles behind the lines. In the confusion of the retreat to Appomattox he remained with the army, although Gen. Robert E. Lee pointedly dismissed him just one day before the surrender.

After the war he fled to Canada to escape prosecution for war crimes. He returned to Virginia in 1866, sold life insurance, and participated in veterans' activities. He died suddenly on July 30, 1875, in Norfolk, Virginia, a prematurely old and embittered man. He is remembered as a giant of Confederate history, but that mythic reputation rests on the events of one afternoon, July 3, 1863. His career up to that date had been unremarkable, and afterwards it was marred by disasters and doubts.

BIBLIOGRAPHY

Freeman, Douglas S. *Lee's Lieutenants: A Study In Command.* 3 vols. New York, 1942–1944. Reprint, New York, 1986.

Harrison, Walter. *Pickett's Men: A Fragment of War History.* New York, 1870. Reprint, Gaithersburg, Md., 1984.

Hotchkiss, Jed. *Virginia.* Vol. 3 of *Confederate Military History.* Edited by Clement A. Evans. Atlanta, 1899. Vol. 4 of extended ed. Wilmington, N.C., 1987.

Pickett, LaSalle Corbell. *Pickett and His Men.* Atlanta, 1899.

Stewart, George R. *Pickett's Charge: A Microhistory of the Final Attack at Gettysburg, July 3, 1863.* Boston, 1959.

RICHARD SELCER

PICKETT, JOHN T. (1823–1884), special agent to the Mexican government. Pickett was born in Maysville, Kentucky. He attended West Point in the early 1840s, but did not graduate. He studied at the Lexington Law School and passed the bar examination. At one time a newspaper writer, Pickett, more a man of action than words, served many causes prior to 1861. He soldiered with Louis Kossuth in the Hungarian insurrection (1849), with Narciso López in Cuba (1850), and with William Walker. He served as U.S. consul at Turk's Island (Jamaica jurisdiction) from 1845 to 1849 and as U.S. consul at Vera Cruz from 1853 until February 1861. He also served as secretary to the Confederate commissioners sent to treat with the U.S. government in March and April 1861.

In early March 1861, Pickett argued that the appointment of Thomas Corwin as U.S. minister to Mexico revealed that U.S. policy intended to block any Confederate expansion southward. In 1861, Pickett analyzed the future struggle in Mexico in terms of competing systems, one of which he defined as the "free-soil" group. The other consisted of the Confederacy allied with the Mexican conservative faction, which was Catholic, agriculturalist, in favor of peonage, and willing to make concessions on transit rights, perhaps even to sell land to the Confederacy. Because of his analysis of Union policy in Mexico, Pickett was commissioned to serve as special agent to the Mexican government on May 17, 1861.

Once in Mexico, Pickett hastened to the capital when he heard that the government might permit Union troops to cross Mexican soil to invade the Confederacy. He informed the Mexican government that the Confederacy sought peaceful relations, "the strictest neutrality," and "full belligerent rights." His mission was burdened by Southern slave expansionism and filibustering.

Pickett was contemptuous of Mexicans and often sarcastic and bitter in his conversations with them. He considered Benito Juárez's government weak and unstable. Dissatisfied with the negotiations, he planned to sever Confederate-Mexican relations by sending an insulting dispatch to Foreign Minister Manuel María Zamacona and by fighting with a Northern sympathizer at the latter's place of business. He was arrested and expelled. He regarded his ejection from Mexico as a clever diplomatic victory: "It was my object . . . to fasten a diplomatic question on a Government which, whilst openly professing friendship and neutrality had at times already clandestinely violated that neutrality, and was secretly intriguing against and wholly unfriendly to . . . the Confederate States." Pickett's dispatches carry heavy post hoc explanations that make the separation of reality and imagination nearly impossible.

Pickett was volatile, imprudent, hasty, a heavy drinker, and much more that should have disqualified him for office. Not just these personal characteristics, however, but also the guidelines of his instructions contributed to the failure of his mission. Instructions insisting upon the positive values of slavery, an agricultural economic system, and a decentralized state government encouraged actions by Pickett that alerted the Liberal government that its future was more secure in association with the North if it wished to abolish peonage, centralize government authority, create a national economic structure, attract foreign trade and investment, and end filibustering.

After leaving Mexico, Pickett served briefly as chief of staff to Gen. John C. Breckinridge. In 1865 and 1866, when Secretary of State William Seward schemed with the former president of Mexico, Antonio López de Santa Anna, to oust Archduke Maximilian, Pickett was selected as Santa Anna's chief of staff. The scheme collapsed when Santa Anna was arrested in Yucatán. Pickett was associated with a railroad project of the Louisiana Tehuantepec Company in 1866 and 1867, which failed because the Mexican government considered it a speculative venture rather than a serious effort to construct a railroad.

As the Confederacy collapsed, Pickett obtained control of five trunks of Confederate State Department records, which he later sold to the U.S. government for $75,000 in 1870. The records rest in the Manuscript Division of the Library of Congress. Pickett practiced law in Washington, D.C., until he died in 1884.

BIBLIOGRAPHY

Daddysman, James W. *The Matamoros Trade: Confederate Commerce, Diplomacy, and Intrigue.* Newark, N.J., 1984.

Hendrick, Burton J. *Statesmen of the Lost Cause: Jefferson Davis and His Cabinet.* New York, 1939.

Owsley, Frank. *King Cotton Diplomacy.* Rev. ed. Chicago, 1959.

Schoonover, Thomas. *Dollars over Dominion: The Triumph of Liberalism in Mexican–United States Relations, 1861–1867.* Baton Rouge, La., 1978.

Tyler, Ronnie C. *Santiago Vidaurre and the Southern Confederacy.* Austin, Tex., 1973.

THOMAS SCHOONOVER

PIEDMONT, VIRGINIA. This village located in the Shenandoah Valley approximately five miles northeast of Staunton was the site of a battle fought on June 5, 1864. After the battle the Union army occupied the Shenandoah Valley of Virginia for the first time during the war.

The defeat of the Union army under Gen. Franz Sigel at New Market three weeks earlier had convinced Gen. Robert E. Lee that the Shenandoah Valley was no longer in danger of a Northern invasion. But Sigel had been replaced by Gen. David Hunter who began to advance up the valley. The Confederate troops who had defeated Sigel had been transferred to Richmond, and a makeshift force under Gen. William E. ("Grumble") Jones was now rushed to the valley from southwestern Virginia.

Jones placed his troops, some six thousand men, just north of the village. His infantry was positioned with its right flank near the East Road and the left flank along the Middle River. Jones had his back to a stand of woods as he prepared to meet the nearly ten thousand troops under Hunter. The village of Piedmont created a gap in the Southern line for several hundred yards and separated Jones's infantry from his cavalry, which stretched along the hillside to the east of the village.

The cavalry skirmished in the early morning hours to begin the fighting. Hunter began the actual battle at 9:00 A.M. with an artillery barrage that was followed by an assault on the Southern left. The Union attack was repulsed and Jones ordered a counterattack. The Southern troops were forced back to a line of rail fences where the fighting continued for several hours. Jones ordered his infantry to pull back to realign with the cavalry, thus removing the gap in his line. But before the movement could be completed, Hunter attacked at the gap and soon had the right flank of the Southern infantry in disarray. The Federals forced back the Southern flank and moved into the woods where hundreds of Confederate soldiers were captured.

As the Union troops began to cut through the confused Confederates, the Southern cavalrymen under Gen. John Crawford Vaughn pleaded with their commander to let them attack the advancing Federals. Vaughn, who had been ordered to hold his position, refused to move and merely watched as the Southern infantry was routed.

When the fighting was over the Confederates had suffered nearly a thousand casualties, including General Jones who was killed as he attempted to rally his troops. Hunter's losses were approximately eight hundred.

Hunter continued up the Shenandoah Valley until he was stopped on June 18 by Gen. Jubal Early. He then retreated into the hills of West Virginia.

BIBLIOGRAPHY

Brice, Marshall Moore. *Conquest of a Valley.* Verona, Va., 1965.

Humphreys, Milton. *History of the Lynchburg Campaign.* Charlottesville, Va., 1924.

Lewis, Thomas A. *The Shenandoah in Flames.* Alexandria, Va., 1987.

J. L. SCOTT

PIERPONT, FRANCIS H. *See* Peirpoint, Francis H.

PIKE, ALBERT (1809–1891), brigadier general. Born December 29, 1809, in Boston, Massachusetts, Pike was accepted at Harvard but did not attend for financial reasons. He moved to Arkansas and served in the Mexican War. After he returned to Arkansas, a controversy over the Battle of Buena Vista led to a duel between Pike and future Confederate brigadier general John Selden Roane in which neither man was injured. During the 1850s Pike earned a reputation as an outspoken lawyer and took Indian grievances as far as the U.S. Supreme Court.

When the Civil War began, Pike sided with his adopted state and was commissioned a brigadier general on August 15, 1861. Assigned to negotiate with the Indians, he commanded the Department of the Indian Territory and took Indian troops to fight at Elkhorn Tavern. Unfortunately, the Indians' conduct reflected poorly on Pike. Because of problems with other commanders, particularly Thomas C. Hindman, Pike resigned on July 12, 1862. He withdrew his resignation, however, and charged that other generals were stealing supplies from him. Brig. Gen. Douglas Hancock Cooper believed that Pike was "partially deranged, and a dangerous person," even telling Jefferson Davis that Pike was mad. Richmond, therefore, accepted his original resignation on November 5, 1862. Untrusted by both sides, Pike took no further part in the war.

When it ended, he moved to Washington, D.C., and became known as a poet and author. He wrote much about Freemasonry and died in the house of the Scottish Rite Temple in Washington on April 2, 1891. He is buried in Oak Hill Cemetery.

BIBLIOGRAPHY

Allsop, Frederick W. *Albert Pike: A Biography.* Little Rock, Ark., 1928.

Duncan, Robert Lipscomb. *Reluctant General: The Life and Times of Albert Pike.* New York, 1961.

ANNE J. BAILEY

PILLOW, GIDEON (1806–1878), brigadier general. A native of Williamson County, Tennessee, law partner to James K. Polk, and active in prewar state and national Democratic politics, Gideon Johnson Pillow had ignominiously commanded a volunteer division during the Mexican War. Although initially opposed to secession, he remained loyal to his state when it left the Union and so earned a senior major generalship in Tennessee's provisional army. He combined patriotism, oratorical zest, and organizational talents to mobilize state forces in 1861. Pillow commanded a division as Confederate brigadier at Belmont, Missouri, in November 1861 and at Fort Donelson (February 13–16, 1862). He successfully led a breakout attempt from Ulysses S. Grant's investment of the fort, but he and his fellow brigadiers John B. Floyd, Simon Bolivar Buckner, and Bushrod Rust Johnson subsequently yielded the initiative, directly contributing to the inglorious surrender of the fort and over fifteen thousand men. Roundly condemned by press and public, he spent six months explaining his action. The loss of Fort Donelson cost the Confederacy the upper heartland, which it never recovered.

GIDEON PILLOW. LIBRARY OF CONGRESS

Although he returned to brigade command at Murfreesboro in 1863, he never regained the trust of Confederate leaders. Relegated to conscription duty, he ended the war as the last commissary general of prisoners. A tragic figure, impoverished by his contribution to the Confederate cause, he joined former Tennessee governor Isham G. Harris in postwar law practice at Memphis and sought to rebuild his plantation empire in Tennessee and Arkansas. The remainder of his life, however, was spent under the cloud of the Fort Donelson debacle for which he was largely responsible. Polk termed him the "shrewdest man you ever knew," but William Tecumseh Sherman characterized him as "a mass of vanity, conceit, ignorance, ambition, and want of truth"—an image that has prevailed. Pillow epitomized the nineteenth-century amateur soldier or politician in uniform, who lusted for martial fame, but whose talents truly lay in mobilizing public opinion and the sinews of war.

BIBLIOGRAPHY

Bell, Patricia. "Gideon Pillow: A Personality Profile." *Civil War Times Illustrated* 6 (October 1967): 13–19.

Cooling, Benjamin Franklin. "Lew Wallace and Gideon Pillow: Enigmas and Variations on an American Military Theme." *Lincoln Herald* 84 (Summer 1981): 651–658.

Stonesifer, Roy P., Jr. "Gideon J. Pillow: A Study in Egotism." *Tennessee Historical Quarterly* 25 (Winter 1966): 340–350.
Warner, Ezra J. *Generals in Gray: Lives of the Confederate Commanders.* Baton Rouge, La., 1959.

B. Franklin Cooling

PITTSBURG LANDING, TENNESSEE. *See* Shiloh Campaign.

PLAIN FOLK. Plain folk formed the core of the South's rural middle class. Neither rich nor very poor, they were the self-sufficient farming and herding families that defined Southern agriculture. Their social and economic condition ranged from tenant farmers to middling landowners who might own as many as two hundred acres. Few plain folk owned or rented slaves, and those who did generally kept fewer than six.

Most plain folk inhabited three distinct parts of the South: the upper South, where they benefited from agricultural diversification; Piedmont regions of the lower South, where they did not have to compete directly against low-country planters; and the backwoods, areas particularly suited to open-range herding and subsistence farming. Everywhere they lived in log or plank dwellings, sparsely furnished and largely unkempt. Most houses contained only one or two rooms, although a few ambitious people had as many as seven or eight. A farmer in the latter group might even own a clock, a half dozen books, or a piano. Most plain folk achieved only an elementary ability to read and write. Their schools operated on a subscription basis, tuition often payable in farm products. The school year lasted only a few months during the winter, when it would not interfere with planting and harvesting. Socially, plain folk exhibited a cordiality and friendliness that bade all welcome to bed and board, whether strangers or neighbors. Dancing (to fiddles and banjos), drinking, gambling, and storytelling constituted their favorite social activities.

Depending on whether they relied more heavily on crops or livestock for a living, some plain folk enjoyed more leisure than others, but none seemed to labor very hard. Plain folk—and to some degree all Southerners—prized their freedom and leisure time. Most were not acquisitive, and they worked only enough to secure life's necessities. Those dependent largely on livestock let their hogs and cattle run free most of the year while they devoted minimal energy to their crops. Corn reigned as the universal crop, but, where geography allowed, tobacco or cotton also served personal and market needs. Only those plain folk who lived in regions dominated by planters had very strong ties to a market economy. Nearly all plain folk tended small vegetable patches in addition to their tilled fields, and they spent a good deal of time hunting and fishing. Some farmers achieved this balance between leisure and survival by owning or hiring slaves. Others planted only enough land to meet their needs and secure some ready cash. Even at that, much rural trade utilized barter rather than money.

Political and social tensions existed between planters and plain folk, but they were not intense or terribly divisive. The strong kinship bonds that defined Southern society preempted much potential class tension. Also, Southern families frequently ran the gamut from nonslaveholder to planter, a circumstance that produced some degree of sympathy and understanding between social classes. Equally important was the communal power of rural society. In mixed planter–plain folk neighborhoods, landholdings and wealth varied widely, and ties of mutual political and economic dependency generally outweighed class resentment. Most rural Southerners, particularly in up-country and backwoods neighborhoods, remained geographically isolated from regions dominated by the plantation economy. The resulting sense of independence and liberty defused tensions and minimized the threat of planter dominance.

White Southerners also enjoyed a common ethnic heritage and a number of shared cultural traits, including heightened sense of honor, the Protestant religion, and an interest in black slavery. Slaveholders prized the latter institution for its economic benefits, but even nonslaveholders viewed slavery as a means of controlling a potentially dangerous portion of the South's population. As abolitionist attacks increased after 1830, and as political reform provided nearly all white adult males with the vote by the 1850s, most white Southerners could rally together in a common cause.

Plain folk played a pivotal role in the history of the Confederacy, beginning with the secession crisis. Plain folk divided on that heart-wrenching issue, as did planters, poor whites, merchants, and craftsmen. Allegiance to class or vocation became less important than kinship, age, economic interests, political affiliation, and a community's racial composition when deciding whether to support or resist disunion. For instance, in those parts of the South where railroads, a market economy, and industry had gained a foothold, many plain folk endorsed secession because they believed Northern economic imperialism threatened their independence. On the other hand, the strongest resistance to secession came in the upper South, where plain folk did not believe that Abraham Lincoln's election posed an immediate threat to local autonomy and security. They became alarmed only when Lincoln, following the attack on Fort Sumter, declared the South to be in rebellion. Upper South plain folk then cursed Lincoln for embarking on "a war of conquest" and forcing them to choose between the Union and the South. Interestingly, 52 percent of the

Confederacy's white population, and the majority of its plain folk, resided in the upper South states of Arkansas, North Carolina, Tennessee, and Virginia, the last four states to secede. It is thus conceivable that war could have been avoided, or vastly shortened, had not those key states been driven out of the Union.

Plain folk initially flocked to the Stars and Bars, but their loyalty became severely tested. Young men spoke excitedly about maintaining Southern honor, defending their homes, and preserving the Southern way of life. Their enthusiasm stemmed, in part, from a romantic image of war, but they also believed that the war would be short and hugely successful. As the war bogged down and as common soldiers witnessed the slaughter and suffering of the battlefield, they lost much of their zeal. Once experiencing the exhaustion, discomfort, and sickness of campaigning and camp life, some men declined to reenlist and drifted home.

Others received pitiful pleas from their families, begging them to return. Southern women spun cloth, tended crops, and did all they could to further the war effort, but their resilience had limits. "Unless you come home," warned one hard-pressed soldier's wife, "we must die. Last night I was aroused by little Eddie's crying . . . 'O mamma! I am so hungry!' " Such laments naturally affected soldiers. One Confederate wrote in 1863, "Our men have stayed here till they are very anxious to go home and anxious for the war to end a heap of them says there famileys is out of provisions."

Regions of the South first scorched by the flames of war—Tennessee and northern Virginia in particular—suffered much destruction, confiscation, and social upheaval. Black and white refugees flooded the South as slaves fled their masters and whites fled contesting armies. Whether staying or fleeing, plain folk lost much of their property. "In every direction there appeared a frightful scene of devastation," confessed a Union cavalryman as he surveyed the wreck of one Virginia farming community. "Furniture . . . was mutilated and defaced; beds were defiled and cut to pieces . . . windows were broken, doors torn from their hinges, houses and barns burned down." Federal forces "plundered" another farmer "of all he had, his corn, wheat, and pork, killed his hogs, drove off his beef cattle and even his milch cows." As a Northern policy of "total war" emerged after mid-1862, Southern civilians suffered increasingly greater deprivation over an ever-broadening area.

The growing centralization of the Confederate government also sapped confidence. By 1863, military conscription, suspension of habeus corpus, increased taxes, impressment of farm products and livestock, and a passport system for travel seemed to make a mockery of the doctrine of state rights. Likewise, local communities, jealous of their autonomy, believed the authority of state government far exceeded prescribed bounds. Conscription became a particular sore point as plain folk saw many professional people, skilled urban workers, and planters exempted from military service. Cries were heard of a "rich man's war and a poor man's fight."

Making matters worse was a belief that government sought greater power while shirking its responsibility. Neither state nor national government seemed to concern itself with the suffering and privation of civilians. Complaints about hunger, labor shortages, and insufficient military defenses seemed to draw little sympathy from the governments the plain folk supported with their blood and toil. As more areas of the South fell under Federal control, discontent, caused by physical suffering and hardship, produced widespread grumbling. Politicians seemed unable or unwilling to shore up the Confederacy's flagging economy. Rampant inflation, price gouging, and illegal hoarding wreaked havoc on plain folk.

Some parts of the Confederacy populated largely by plain folk became notorious Unionist strongholds. Northwestern Arkansas, eastern Tennessee, western Virginia, and the upcountry of North Carolina, Georgia, and Alabama opposed Confederate rule throughout the war. Many communities in those places offered havens to deserters, conscripts, and tax evaders. West Virginia rejoined the Union, and vocal peace organizations thrived in Arkansas and North Carolina.

Yet, despite the steadily declining fortunes of the Confederate nation and the increased suffering of families and soldiers, most plain folk supported the Confederacy to the bitter end. The explanations are several. First, plain folk became not so much disloyal as disillusioned and discouraged, not so much anti-Confederacy as anti-authoritarian. Thousands of men deserted the Confederate army, particularly after 1863, and, insofar as plain folk comprised most of the army, it is safe to say that they supplied most of the deserters. They left the army in response to pleas from their families, and because they were worn out and discouraged. "I have a very large family of whites consisting of a wife and 10 children," wrote a Virginian seeking exemption from further military service. "I feel that I am willing to bear my full part in this struggle but having served 16 mos . . . I feel that I am worth more to the government at home to raise meat and bread." The principal complaint of this man and many like him was the power of the government to interfere in his life and challenge his independence.

Plain folk also remained loyal advocates of slavery, the existence of which was starkly challenged after 1862. Plain folk became increasingly resentful of slaveholders as the war progressed, yet they seldom renounced slavery or advocated its abolition. They supported slavery for the same reasons they had always supported it; it was part of the Southern way of life, and plain folk were not social revolutionaries. They feared that should the Confederacy fail, over 3 million freed blacks would lead the South to chaos and ruin.

Thus plain folk played a critical role in the life and death of the Confederacy. Without their consent, secession would have failed. Without their presence in army ranks, the Confederacy would have collapsed far sooner. A sense of class resentment emerged as the war dragged on, a more visible and divisive variety than anything that had preceded the war, but this was not the ultimate reason that plain folk loyalty wavered. Their will to fight faded only after they and their families had been battered into submission by hunger and a stronger military force, and after their own government had initiated policies that left little to choose between the Confederate States and the United States.

[*See also* Class Conflicts; Desertion; Farming; Honor; Morale; Poverty; Unionism.]

BIBLIOGRAPHY

Escott, Paul D. *After Secession: Jefferson Davis and the Failure of Confederate Nationalism.* Baton Rouge, La., 1978.

Genovese, Eugene D. "Yeomen Farmers in a Slaveholders' Democracy." *Agricultural History* 49 (1975): 331–342.

Harris, J. William. *Plain Folk and Gentry in a Slave Society: White Liberty and Black Slavery in Augusta's Hinterlands.* Middleton, Conn., 1985.

McWhiney, Grady. *Cracker Culture: Celtic Ways in the Old South.* Tuscaloosa, Ala., 1988.

Owsley, Frank L. *Plain Folk of the Old South.* Baton Rouge, La., 1949.

Thomas, Emory M. *The Confederate Nation: 1861–1865.* New York, 1979.

Watson, Harry L. "Conflict and Collaboration: Yeomen, Slaveholders, and Politics in the Antebellum South." *Social History* 10 (1985): 273–298.

Wiley, Bell I. *The Plain Folk of the Confederacy.* Baton Rouge, La., 1944. Reprint, Gloucester, Mass., 1971.

Daniel E. Sutherland

PLANTATION. A large plantation was not just cotton fields and a stately mansion approached along an oak-lined drive. A plantation included many other buildings: the smokehouse where meat was preserved, the henhouse where poultry was raised, stables where thoroughbreds were tended, the barn where dairy cows and work animals were housed, and sheds and silos for tools, grain, and other farm necessities. In workshops scattered near the barnyard, slave artisans might craft barrels, horseshoes, furniture, and cloth for use on the plantation. Gardens were cultivated to supply herbs and vegetables. Larger plantations might also maintain a schoolhouse for white children. Some planters built chapels for family worship, and some allowed religious services for slaves as well. More commonly, large plantations included slave infirmaries and nursery facilities where older slave women tended the children of women who worked in the fields. As a safety precaution, almost all plantations had kitchen structures separate from the "big house," the main mansion that housed the planter family.

The big house, usually a two or three-storied mansion, was a visible symbol of the planter's wealth. Coming in from the front porch, a wide entrance hall might lead into a dining room, a parlor, a library, and one or more sitting rooms. In these rooms a planter could display his wealth with European furnishings and imported artwork. On the upper floors, bedrooms for family members and guests were maintained with the most comfortable and luxurious decor available. Nurseries for planters' children were located on the uppermost floors and could be reached by the servants' stairs at the back of the house.

The big house, the centerpiece of the entire plantation, might have formal flower gardens, like the famed plantings at Middleton Place outside Charleston, which took nearly ten years to complete. A separate office for the planter or overseer might be attached to the main house. Slave cabins were often built not far from the big house. Overseers sometimes lived on the plantation, in which case their modest homes might also be found not far from the slave cabins, especially in the case of absentee planters. But economic studies indicate that fewer than 30 percent of planters employed white supervisors for their slave labor. Although not all plantations contained every element listed above, the crucial components were the master's home and the slaves' domiciles, reflecting the difference in status between the black and white worlds on the plantation.

Plantations in Antebellum Society. These large plantations were not the average, but the model to which the majority of white Southerners—owners of small slaveholdings and yeomen farmers—might aspire. On the eve of the Civil War, approximately 400,000 masters owned slaves, but only 50,000 boasted plantations—farms with 20 slaves or more—and only 2,300 planters owned holdings of over 100 slaves. Yet almost all slave owners followed the planters' lead and subscribed to the cash crop system, devoting a majority of arable land to a single crop to be sold at market. And in the case of the Confederate South, cotton was king. In the border states as well as Virginia, tobacco cultivation still employed slave labor. In Missouri and Kentucky hemp growers also supplied an eager market, but these crops involved only a small proportion of slave labor. More commonly, coastal planters in the Deep South might plow and irrigate rice fields to harvest their profitable crop, and Louisiana planters could and did put slaves to use in the back-breaking cane field to produce sugar. In all areas, corn was grown to supplement these cash crops and to feed the slave work force.

Because slaves were considered property, the per capita

wealth of Southern whites was nearly double that of Northern whites in 1860. With only 30 percent of the nation's free population, the South boasted 60 percent of the nation's wealthiest men. Income levels were lower for Southern whites than for Northern whites, however, and many economists continue to wrangle over the figures and their meaning.

Plantations Mobilize for War. From Abraham Lincoln's election onward, secession fever propelled the South into war. Once South Carolina broke with the Union and the rest of the Southern states fell like dominoes in the early part of 1861, war appeared inevitable. Mary Boykin Chesnut saw the handwriting on the wall: "These foolish, rash, harebrained southern lads . . . are thrilling with fiery ardor. The red-hot Southern martial spirit is in the air," she wrote in her diary.

Southern gentlemen, especially the young, knew their choices and, buoyed by secessionist bravado, enlisted when the war broke out. Confederate manhood ironically required husbands and fathers to leave the very home and loved ones they were pledging to protect. Slave-owning patriarchs had to abandon their beloved plantations. Loyal Confederate plantation mistresses had to hammer home the necessity of fighting, in case men might falter in their duty. The press and private correspondence overflowed with parables of strident patriotic females: the belle who broke an engagement because her fiancé did not enlist before the proposed wedding day, the sweethearts who sent skirts and female undergarments to shirkers.

The formation of many Confederate units demonstrated the resolve of the planter class to serve. In Selma, Alabama, the Magnolia Cadets assembled, manned entirely by local gentry. In Georgia, the Savannah Rifles, the Blue Caps, the Rattlesnakes, and many other colorful groups closed ranks against the charge that the battle would be a "rich man's war and a poor man's fight."

Class solidarity was built on the bedrock of white superiority to which most white Southerners subscribed. As contemporary Southerner William Cabell Rives proclaimed, "It is not a question of slavery at all; it is a question of race." Therefore planters necessarily blurred class lines for whites by engaging in cooperative ventures during wartime. Parthenia Hague described the way in which Alabamians forged alliances during war: "We were drawn together in a closer union, a tenderer feeling of humanity linking us all together, both rich and poor; from the princely planter, who could scarce get off his wide domains in a day's ride, and who could count his slaves by the thousand, down to the humble tenants of the log cabin on rented or leased land."

The blockade, of course, threw all within the Confederacy's borders back on their own resources. Plantations were not the hardest hit, but they did have to modify long-established patterns of production and consumption. Most significantly, the Confederate government wanted planters to switch voluntarily from the cash crop system to a more diversified subsistence strategy, which would include the planting of crops that could feed the army and civilian populations. A slogan that appeared in the press captured Confederate philosophy: "Plant Corn and Be Free, or plant cotton and be whipped."

Many planters in the Deep South, which was more dependent upon food imports than the upper South border states, adopted the "corn and bread" ideology early on. Cotton production was severely curtailed, dramatically so in the first year of the war. The South's output, 4.5 million bales in 1861, was cut to 1.5 million in 1862. Some states complied more than others; indeed, Georgia reduced its cotton output by nine-tenths from 1861 to 1862. In the coastal regions, especially Louisiana, sugar planters responded to the call, with a decline from 459 million pounds in 1861 to 87 million in 1862.

Many planters were concerned about this move and wondered how they could keep their slaves occupied and afford their upkeep under such conditions. The more conservative decided to reverse the traditional proportion of cash crops to foodstuffs; instead of the usual 600 acres of cotton to 200 acres of corn, they planted 200 acres of cotton to 600 acres of corn. A high rate of cotton production was nevertheless maintained by a minority of planters who refused to toe the patriotic line. As private speculators sought out cotton to store for future sale, a number of planters were happy to supply them, viewing war as an opportunity for profit. Indeed, many smuggled their cotton to Europe through Texas and Mexico, ignoring the government proscription. A handful of planters, oblivious to the charge of treason that could be brought against them, sought out Northern buyers. They hid their bales in remote warehouses or buried the cotton on their plantations until safe passage might be secured.

One such manipulator, James Alcorn, whose plantation was in the fertile Mississippi Delta, owned a hundred slaves and property worth nearly $250,000. When war broke out, Alcorn sent his family to Alabama and continued his prosperous trade in cotton, hiding and selling it, and avoiding both armies. In 1862 he reported that he had sold over a hundred bales, with another ninety ready to ship. Greed was his motive: "I wish to fill my pockets," he said, and boasted, "I can in five years make a larger fortune than ever. I know how to do it and will do it." At war's end, however, Alcorn decided to cater to loyalist dictates rather than side with the enemies with whom he had collaborated in matters of business. Although he had traded with Northerners, after the surrender at Appomattox he refused to take the oath of allegiance to the Union and was credited with being a great Southern patriot, much to the mystification of his former slaves.

Planters and Conscription. Planters were divided on the subject of cotton policy and many other issues, but the question that seemed to dominate the Cotton Planters Convention in Memphis during their meeting in February 1862 was not agriculture but politics. And many expressed doubt that their revolution, Confederate independence, would succeed. The intertwining of economics and politics was too tied to the fortunes of war.

When in September 1862 the Confederate Congress raised the upper age limit of conscription from thirty-five to forty-five, heads of many poor families were for the first time subject to the draft. This legislation appeared just at a time when that summer's drought had ruined most harvests. Compounding the difficulties, the Confederate Congress in October passed an even more unpopular statute that became known as the Twenty-Slave Law, which exempted from army service any white man who could demonstrate that he was in a managerial role on a plantation with twenty slaves or more; both owners and overseers qualified. This law was intended ostensibly both to control the slave population and to keep the Confederacy fed. But the argument that the law would benefit all whites stuck in the craw of most white Southerners. Even when in May 1863 exempted slaveholders were taxed $500 (to fund the distribution of food for soldiers' families), civilians and especially soldiers were not mollified.

Throughout the war, only 4,000 to 5,000 men received exemptions under this law; indeed, only 3 percent of those men who claimed exemptions took them on the basis of the Twenty-Slave Law. On 85 percent of those plantations that qualified for exemptions, none was taken. Nevertheless, the perception of favoritism rankled. Members of the planter class already could afford to buy substitutes, and now any choice to sit out the war was ratified by government legitimation. Attitudes may have been regionalized: within the Deep South more planters perhaps took advantage of the system, sparking more resentment. There were 1,500 exemptions issued in Alabama alone and of the nineteen categories of exemption, only medical disability was employed more often than the Twenty-Slave Law. Thus, the law was a public relations disaster, to say the least. Mississippian James Phelan wrote a warning to Jefferson Davis: "It has aroused a spirit of rebellion in some places, I am informed, and bodies of men have banded together to resist; whilst in the army it is said it only needs some daring men to raise the standard to develop a revolt."

White women, too, voiced their alarm over conscription. Many left behind in parishes and counties without adequate male assistance appealed to their government. Late in the war a group of women in South Carolina sent a plaintive letter to the governor:

> We are personally acquainted with Erwin Midlen for over three years and do no that he is a sickly and feeble man and we do Believe that he is not able for service in the field. We are informed that he is in the 56th year of his age. And we do further sware that he has done all our hawling for the last three years and attended to all our domestic business as we could not Procure any other man to do—see to our hawling and other business as our Husbands are all in the army and some of them killed and some died in service.

The seventeen women who signed begged that Midlen be spared military service. The governor's ruling on the matter remains unknown.

The Decline of Plantation Agriculture and Planter Morale. Even more disheartening to both the Confederate government and the Southern farmer was the fact that all agricultural indicators in the South spelled decline, while prosperity reigned in the fertile regions of the Midwest. Although over 75,000 farm boys left Iowa for Union service and over 90,000 came from Wisconsin, Northern agriculture did not suffer. Iowa and Wisconsin both reported improved acreage and grain production as well as a rise in farm income during the war.

The South's declining agriculture created a dilemma. The army needed fresh troops, but the home front required care as well. President Davis, among others, harped on the dangers of deserted or unproductive plantations; these Cassandras were unpopular yet prophetic. One advised: "We are today in greater danger of whipping our selves than being whipped by our enemy." Sinking morale and declining food supplies contributed to gloomy predictions of further degradation. The crippling of cotton production undermined the ruling elite's sense of mastery and helped pave the way for defeat. There were countless examples of reduced fortunes: by 1864 James Heyward of South Carolina planted only 330 acres in rice and 90 in provisions; a mere one-tenth of his land holdings were under cultivation.

Heyward at least was able to continue planting. Many slave owners were driven off their plantations, losing homes and livelihoods in one fell swoop. Some former mistresses, hoping to elude Federal troops, were reduced to living in cabins in the woods. In the first few months of the war, Confederates feared the unknown threat of a Union army, but by 1862 too many Southerners knew firsthand the toll such an invasion extracted. In December 1863 the Confederate Congress railed against the enemy:

> Houses are pillaged and burned, churches are defaced, towns are ransacked, clothing of women and infants is stripped from their persons, jewelry and momentoes of the dead are stolen, mills and implements of agriculture are destroyed, private salt works are broken up, the introduction of medicines is forbidden.

Indeed, plantation mistresses turned to the woods as "nature's drugstore" and for other necessities of life. One woman reported that after the enemy left her home she was "forced to go out into the woods nearby and with my two little boys pick up fagots to cook the scanty food left to me." The scorched-earth policy of William Tecumseh Sherman and other Union generals reduced many plantations to ashes and permanently impaired the planters' ability to recover.

Morale was at a low ebb and hopes were being steadily dashed against the shoals of wartime reality. Those planters who stockpiled their cotton crop were in as much danger of losing it to the Confederate cause as to invading Northerners. It was the policy of the Confederate army to burn cotton whenever Federals moved within striking distance. This was an unpopular measure, to say the least, especially at a time when planters were pressing the government to buy their unsold crops. To have their hopes go up in smoke at the hands of soldiers in gray rather than the hated Federals created conflicting loyalties.

Some of these policies alienated planters to the point of political disaffection. In the 1870s the Southern Claims Commission was empowered to rule on the petitions of planters who declared both their pro-Union sympathies during wartime and the destruction of property by Union troops. Of the 700 claims filed to obtain damages of over $10,000, only 191 were successful, and a mere 224 of the 800 and more who complained of property losses of less than $10,000 were granted.

Perhaps no more than 5 percent of the planter class were Union loyalists during wartime. But many more simply resisted the entreaties of the Confederate government to perform patriotically. As many as 25 percent of the slaveholders in Virginia refused to comply with the government's requisition of their property—slaves—in 1864. Both the loss of labor and the strong resistance combined to weaken the Confederacy's ability to win its war for independence.

The End of Slavery and the Plantation System. The dangers within arose not only from recalcitrant planters but from the omnipresent threat of slave resistance. John Edwin Fripp of Saint Helena Island off the coast of South Carolina was able to write: "I am happy to say my negroes have acted orderly and well all the time, none going off excepting one or two Boys who accompanied the yanks for plunder but have returned home and appear quite willing to work." Nevertheless, Fripp's experience was the exception rather than the rule. The majority of planters made careful notations in their logs about African Americans deserting plantations. Whenever Union troops moved into a region, slaves fled behind enemy lines. Many, if not most planters, felt wounded when their slaves abandoned the plantation for "Lincoln land." They were especially angered by those African Americans who led Federal troops to storehouses of food and buried treasure—the family silver and other heirlooms. Even after the issuance of the Emancipation Proclamation in January 1863, slave owners mistakenly placed their faith in paternalism. As one woman complained bitterly, "Those we loved best, and who loved us best—as we thought—were the first to leave us."

Planters who feared insurrection, however, were pleasantly surprised, in contrast to those whose cherished notions of slave loyalty were disappointed. Historian James Roark has suggested: "Slavery did not explode; it disintegrated . . . eroded plantation by plantation, often slave by slave, like slabs of earth slipping into a Southern stream." Some planters responded by moving their slaves away from approaching Federal troops, but as the war dragged on, there was nowhere left to hide and hundreds of thousands of African Americans made their way to freedom.

During the fall of 1863 over 20,000 slaves were recruited for service in the Union army in the Mississippi valley alone. Jane Pickett, a plantation mistress and a refugee, recounted the planters' predicament: "The negroes in most instances refused to leave with their masters, and in some cases have left the plantations in a perfect stampede. Mississippi is almost depopulated of its black population." By the winter of 1864–1865, slave owners were reduced to a lengthy process of negotiation with those African Americans who remained. Emma LeConte of Berkeley County, South Carolina, lamented: "The field negroes are in a dreadful state; they will not work, but either roam the country, or sit in their houses. . . . I do not see how we are to live in this country without any rule or regulation. We are afraid now to walk outside of the gate."

The fall, then, came from within, as historian Armstead Robinson has argued, as well as from without. The plantation South simply crumbled, unable to withstand African American challenges to slavery as well as the burdens of blockades, wartime production, and invading armies. The superhuman task of retaining the illusion of white superiority in the face of black resistance, African American independence, and the final blow—the full-blown glory of black manhood in the form of African American Union soldiers—combined to destroy Confederate dreams. Economic ruin further eroded the fragile leadership of the struggling nation. Confederate wealth (excluding slave property) declined nearly 45 percent during the war.

In February 1864 the Confederate Congress authorized impressment of free blacks and slaves for noncombatant military roles, and by November 1864 President Davis was advocating gradual emancipation and military use of African Americans. Davis wrongly assumed that Southerners would choose to give up slavery rather than go down to defeat. But slaveholders stuck to their guns. The Confederacy had been founded because of the perceived threat that Northern Republicans presented to the institution of slavery, and proslavery stalwarts stayed the course: "We want no confederate Government without our institutions." These and other sentiments have prompted historian David Herbert Donald to suggest that the Confederacy might ironically have "died from democracy." Whatever the cause, the plantation system, with its fortunes so tied to black labor, died along with slavery.

The surrender at Appomattox triggered a long, slow process of recovery, but planters never actually recovered. Rather, they devoted their time and energies to promoting romantic legends of the Lost Cause—seeking historical justification rather than economic recovery. Planters' devotion to an imagined past was embodied in Margaret Mitchell's mythic re-creation of Tara and Twelve Oaks, perhaps the most famous plantations of all, in her 1936 novel, *Gone with the Wind.* Despite such fictional exaggerations, most plantations were scarred visibly by the war. And even those not damaged by wartime destruction indisputably suffered a permanent stain—the psychic blight of Confederate defeat.

[*See also* Class Conflict; Conscription; Cotton; Impressment; Plantation Mistress; Planters; Rice; Slavery; Sugar; Tobacco.]

BIBLIOGRAPHY

Clinton, Catherine. *Tara Revisited: Women, War, and the Plantation Legend.* New York, forthcoming.

Durden, Robert. *The Gray and the Black: The Confederate Debate on Emancipation.* Baton Rouge, La., 1972.

Massey, Mary Elizabeth. *Refugee Life in the Confederacy.* Baton Rouge, La., 1964.

Mohr, Clarence. *On the Threshold of Freedom: Masters and Slaves in Civil War Georgia.* Athens, Ga., 1986.

Roark, James L. *Masters without Slaves: Southern Planters in the Civil War and Reconstruction.* New York, 1977.

CATHERINE CLINTON

PLANTATION MISTRESS. The plantation was generally defined in the antebellum South as an estate run by a planter who owned twenty slaves or more. The wife of the slave owner, the plantation mistress, was an important component within this complex economic system. During wartime, her significance increased dramatically as men marched off to war, leaving slaves and families behind and expecting wives to manage the home front while Confederate soldiers battled for independence.

Even before the war most plantation mistresses played key roles in the running of their husbands' estates. Wives of planters were charged with slaves' well-being in four critical areas: food, shelter, clothing, and medical care. The degree of caregiving and the responsibilities of mistresses varied from plantation to plantation. But the majority of plantations did not employ an overseer, so that women's roles were central to managing the slave workforce. In addition, the female head of household was expected to undertake a wide range of arduous tasks associated with her own family as well as her husband's slaves: growing herbs, planting gardens, blending medicines, spinning thread, weaving cloth, knitting socks, sewing clothes, supervising the slaughtering of hogs, processing and curing meats, scouring copper utensils, preserving vegetables, churning butter, dipping candles, and a host of other challenging tasks. Often as not the plantation mistress was more of a producer than a consumer, despite her wealth and status.

Although their duties might not necessarily have increased dramatically during wartime, planter wives' roles altered significantly. Before battle broke out, the majority of mistresses who managed plantations during a husband's absences were confident of his return. With the war none was assured of this peacetime luxury, and women faced the constant threat of widowhood; they conducted plantation affairs in fear they would become sole parent instead of surrogate head of household. Women managed their husbands' estates despite the increasing incidence of slave unrest and wartime disruption. One mistress, Susanna Clay, found her slaves less and less willing to undertake the work she demanded; by the fall of 1863 she complained: "We cannot exert any authority. I beg ours to do what little is done."

This resistance and the scores of slaves who ran away were viewed by the majority of mistresses as a betrayal, and they prepared themselves for rebellion on the plantation as well as invasion by Northern forces. Bess Dell was part of a group of nine women who met on Wednesdays and Saturdays in Bascom, Georgia, for target practice. She reported: "You know how nervous and timid Millie was. Well now she can load a gun and fire and hit a spot at a good distance." Arming, however, was hardly the solution sought by most planter women. Rather, they might petition the government to let their men return home—or more often send a plea to the governor begging him to reverse a conscription order for one of the few remaining males left in the county.

As the Northern onslaught continued, many more plantation mistresses were subjected to the two final indignities of war—evacuation and occupation. Judith McGuire bemoaned: "With a heavy heart I packed trunks and boxes, as many as our little carriage would hold. . . . In bitterness of heart I exclaimed, 'Why must we leave thee, Paradise!' and for the first time my tears streamed." Cornelia Peake McDonald bitterly described her home's invasion in May 1862:

> The hall, the rooms and even the kitchen was thronged. I tried to get into the kitchen to get some supper for the children, but had to give it up. So Mary and I took our little ones and went up stairs for the night, leaving the invaders possession of the lower floor. The next morning I went down, determined at all hazards to have some breakfast for my family. My heart sunk as I beheld

the scene that waited me downstairs. Mud, mud, mud—was everywhere, over, and on and in everything.

Nevertheless, McDonald—able to feed her family, her house relatively unplundered, and allowed to remain rather than being evicted—must be counted among the lucky. When Sarah Morgan returned to her home following its occupation by enemy troops, she despaired:

> I stood in the parlor in silent amazement; and in answer to Charlie's "Well?" I could only laugh. . . . The papier-mache workbox Miriam had given me was gone. The baby sacque I was crocheting, with all knitting needles and wools, gone also. . . . Not a book remained in the parlor. . . . Precious letters I found under heaps of broken china and rags.

Morgan's desolation, however, has to be measured alongside those women who returned home to find houses burned to the ground.

BIBLIOGRAPHY

Clinton, Catherine, and Nina Silber, eds. *Divided Houses: Gender and the Civil War.* New York, 1992.

Rable, George. *Civil Wars: Women and the Crisis of Southern Nationalism.* Urbana, Ill., 1989.

Scott, Anne. *The Southern Lady: From Pedestal to Politics, 1830–1930.* Chicago, 1970.

CATHERINE CLINTON

PLANTERS. Although plantation slavery never dominated the entire South, the plantation belt contained the region's best farmland, the major portion of its wealth, and the majority of its slaves. It gave rise to a planter class that, though less than 5 percent of the white population, dominated local and state governments and shaped regional institutions in its own interests. The sprawling plantation South was vast enough to encompass a variety of planter types and personalities. Whether old money or new, paternalist or pure capitalist, planters (owners of twenty or more slaves) formed a distinctive and self-conscious elite that was united in its commitment to preserving slavery as the basis of its power, wealth, and identity. From the moment of secession to the end of the Civil War, plantation slavery remained the touchstone of planters' existence.

During the secession crisis of 1860 and 1861, planters divided on whether the defense of slavery required the destruction of one national government and the creation of another. Those who resisted Southern independence showed no less dedication to slavery. They argued that slavery was safer—for the moment, at least—within the Union than out of it. Still, there was a strong correlation between slavery and support for secession. In general, the greater the density of slaves and slaveholders in a state's population, the greater the support for Southern independence. By spring 1861, planters had led eleven states out of the Union. The Confederate States of America became home to some 43,000 planters (plus those in Arkansas, for which the census returns are incomplete), and no more than a tiny fraction, perhaps one in twenty, remained loyal to the United States.

Planters greeted war with a burst of Confederate patriotism. They rushed to buy Confederate bonds and marched off at the head of regiments they organized and often outfitted with their own money. They eagerly assumed prominent positions in their new nation's government. Confident that cotton was king, they looked forward to bringing the North to its knees and cotton-importing Europe to their side. Victory would secure both the preservation of slavery and Southern independence. To planters, it was obvious that slavery and Southern nationhood went hand in hand.

But mobilization for war required that the government in Richmond build armies and regiment the home front. Government, which traditionally had borne lightly on the people, reached more and more deeply into civilian life, restricted personal freedom, imposed unprecedented burdens, and demanded unimaginable sacrifices. As the war lengthened, Richmond grew increasingly single-minded in its commitment to political independence and more and more willing to subordinate all other interests to that goal. Confederate action forced planters to reveal that they assigned different values to independence and slavery.

At first, Richmond was sensitive to the interests of the planter class, which had brought the new nation into being. A raft of class legislation favored the elite. The Conscription Act of 1861 provided for hiring substitutes, but the cost put the option beyond the reach of most nonslaveholders. The Twenty-Slave Law exempted one able-bodied white male from military service for every twenty slaves on a plantation. Nonslaveholders were quick to point out that the provision allowed many overseers and planters' sons to escape the fighting. The gentry defended the government's favoritism, arguing that without white men to supervise slaves, they would refuse to work, run off, and threaten white women. Only well-ordered plantations could provide the Confederacy with the food and fiber necessary for victory.

In time, however, the elite experienced the rigors of war and the sting of intrusive Confederate policy. Large slaveholders suffered less than plain folk, but they yelled louder. At first, privation meant no more than learning to live without luxuries, but in time necessities such as salt and medicines grew scarce. Planters tolerated privation better than the growing government intervention into plantation affairs. Before the war, as the daughter of a Mississippi planter put it, "each plantation was a law unto itself." Laws had existed to regulate slaves, rarely planters. But as

Richmond centralized power in order to fight efficiently, it increasingly ran roughshod over prewar notions of the proper relationship between government and citizens. Jealous of their prerogatives, large slaveholders fought fiercely to maintain their authority, even against their own government, the cornerstone of which, Vice President Alexander H. Stephens had said, was slavery.

Early in the war, state governments and public opinion demanded that planters cease growing cotton, perceived as a selfish act, and start growing corn, vital to the Confederate war effort. Some complied voluntarily, but others resisted. Later, when the Federal blockade choked cotton exports, planters had little choice but to switch to food production. With most white men away at war, responsibility for supervising the transformation often fell to white women. Female planters were not unknown before the war—thousands of women legally owned plantations—but few actually managed their estates. Planters kept up a heavy correspondence with their wives, and plantation women successfully oversaw the formidable adjustment from staples to food crops. But without cotton, planters' incomes shriveled.

With every passing month, Richmond became more entangled in plantation affairs. Confederate officials told planters what and with whom they could trade and took or burned the cotton or sugar crops when they deemed it prudent. Officials dragged white men away from the plantation and impressed food, livestock, tools, animals, and wagons, paying whatever prices they saw fit in notes. The government created currency and tax systems that planters perceived as discriminatory, even though Richmond never taxed slaves. Confederate troops raided plantations, picking them as clean as Federal soldiers did. Hatred of the North soared, but with few Southern military victories or diplomatic successes, love of the Confederacy did not blossom correspondingly. Instead, planter support for Richmond faded.

Planters found Confederate impressment of slaves particularly troubling. Although slaves were barred from combat, they were theoretically available for military labor. But slaveholders resisted giving up their bondsmen to build fortifications, standing on principle—they felt a man had a right to control his slave property—and complaining that the military mistreated slaves and returned them in poor health and recalcitrant. Planters believed they had enough difficulty maintaining control without the government adding to their troubles. When the war began, they made every effort to tighten controls over slaves and those who came into contact with them. They buttressed slave patrols and canceled exemptions from duty. They called home slaves who were on hire in cities and voided their passes to travel and visit families. But nothing they could do restored the stable order upon which slavery depended.

When the war reached the plantations, it sent slavery into a spiral of disintegration. As traditional routines crumbled, planters complained that slaves were "demoralized," a generic term that referred to every sort of misbehavior from rudeness to outright rebellion. Accustomed to respect and obedience from servants they had convinced themselves were loyal and loving, planters were beset by insolence, disobedience, theft, and malingering. Moreover, whenever proximity to Union soldiers made escape possible, the slaves ran away. As their owners' power eroded, they claimed their freedom bit by bit. On many estates, effective control shifted from the "big house" to the slave quarters. Before the war ended, the master-slave relationship was in tatters.

Slavery died for many reasons, but planters pointed the finger of blame at Richmond almost as often as at Washington. On January 1, 1863, Abraham Lincoln issued the Emancipation Proclamation, which planters denounced as an invitation to slaves to rise up in bloody "servile insurrection." Less than two years later, Jefferson Davis, in an equally revolutionary move, proposed that the Confederacy itself arm and free its slaves. The government had concluded that only by sacrificing slavery could the South win its independence. Planters branded Richmond's plan an outrageous betrayal. A partial version of the plan became law on March 13, 1865, but planters gave up their slaves only when Union soldiers appeared at their gates.

In parts of the Confederacy, however, Federal troops arrived long before the war ended, freeing the slaves in each area they occupied. Planters often fled before their arrival, taking their slaves with them to refugee elsewhere. But in the lower Mississippi valley, many stayed and participated in federally sponsored wartime experiments with free black labor. Union officials sought to resurrect the devastated sugar and cotton economies and to restore the link between planter self-interest and political loyalty. Because the system of contract labor they initiated resembled the South's prewar labor system, some planters found reason for hope. But Federal efforts to maintain control of blacks and to stabilize agriculture did not revive planters' material fortunes. Most plantation owners saw little value in free black labor and no reason to pledge allegiance to a government that had made black freedom a war aim.

On the other hand, planters no longer sympathized with Richmond either. They were unwilling to defend a government that, for whatever reason, did not defend them. Indeed, complying with government policy meant collaborating in their own destruction. Yeomen also felt alienated from their government, but they believed that Richmond favored the wealthy and failed to make them carry their fair share of the burden. Planters judged the matter of sacrifice differently. No longer loyal to Richmond and unable to transfer loyalty to Washington, they withdrew to their plantations and did what they could to help themselves. They grew increasingly ready to evade conscription, desert from the army, plant cotton rather than corn, and engage in cotton trading with whomever would buy. In the end, they chose the homestead over the homeland.

By the time of the surrender at Appomattox, the planters' world lay in shambles. The North had triumphed over the South, free labor had triumphed over slave labor, and industrial capitalism had triumphed over the political economy of slavery. Because of remarkable miscalculation, the South's planters went from being one of the strongest agrarian classes in the western world to being the weakest. War had destroyed the very institution that secession was intended to secure. Armies had turned plantations into battlefields, hospitals, barracks, feed and fuel centers, and labor pools. Large slaveholders had been devastated physically, economically, and psychologically. Thousands had died; thousands more had lost their sons, their slaves, their life savings. A few planters weathered the storm—those who had extensive Northern investments, those who had hidden away cotton and could reap dollar-a-pound prices, those who could attract rich Northerners to lease their plantations. But war had impoverished the overwhelming majority. Stripped of slaves, wealth, and power, hundreds fled the region, although most saw no choice but to remain.

Planters understood that defeat and emancipation meant a revolution in their lives. They were painfully aware of what Jefferson Davis called a "break in time." The old order was gone, but the new had not yet emerged. Proslavery doctrine had predicted that emancipation would lead to racial warfare, social anarchy, and economic collapse, and, indeed, planters found themselves surrounded by devastation. Northern radicals demanded even more: confiscation and perhaps banishment to stamp out the South's aristocratic "traitors." Planters welcomed peace, but they found little reason for optimism. In their minds, defeat had not invalidated the basic assumptions that had undergirded their belief in slavery: that blacks were inherently and immutably lazy, that without total subordination they were dangerous and destructive, and that without coercion they would not work. "Nothing could overcome this rooted idea," a visiting newspaper man noted in 1865, "that the negro was worthless, except under the lash." Unwilling to admit that they had been wrong about slavery or about the nature of the Union, planters had little choice but to give up their dream of an independent slaveholders' republic and to go on farming in a slaveless South.

[*See also* Class Conflict; Conscription; Cotton; Currency, *overview article;* Impressment; Plantation; Plantation Mistress; Rice; Slavery; Sugar; Taxation; Tobacco.]

BIBLIOGRAPHY

Ash, Stephen W. *Middle Tennessee Society Transformed, 1860–1870: War and Peace in the Upper South.* Baton Rouge, La., 1988.

Escott, Paul D. *After Secession: Jefferson Davis and the Failure of Confederate Nationalism.* Baton Rouge, La., 1978.

Foner, Eric. *Reconstruction: America's Unfinished Revolution, 1863–1877.* New York, 1988.

McPherson, James M. *Battle Cry of Freedom: The Civil War Era.* New York, 1988.

Owens, Harry P., and James J. Cooke, eds. *The Old South in the Crucible of War.* Jackson, Miss., 1983.

Potter, David M. "The Historian's Use of Nationalism and Vice Versa." In *The South and the Sectional Conflict.* Baton Rouge, La., 1968.

Roark, James L. *Masters without Slaves: Southern Planters in the Civil War and Reconstruction.* New York, 1977.

Thomas, Emory M. *The Confederate Nation, 1861–1865.* New York, 1979.

Wayne, Michael. *The Reshaping of Plantation Society: The Natchez District, 1860–1880.* Baton Rouge, La., 1983.

JAMES L. ROARK

POINT LOOKOUT PRISON. After the Battle of Gettysburg, the United States provided for the sudden increase of prisoners by opening a depot on Point Lookout, Maryland, the peninsula formed where the Potomac River joins Chesapeake Bay. The land was flat, mostly sandy with some marsh, and barely above the water. Because of the Point's proximity to the eastern battlefields, the government had already found it convenient to lease this prewar resort locale for a hospital that was subsequently used, in part, for wounded Confederates.

In late July 1863, quartermaster officers opened a camp for 10,000 men to be housed in old tents. Though the War Department rejected later proposals for barracks, there were wooden cookhouses. The camp consisted of two pens surrounded by fourteen-foot high fences, one for enlisted men of about twenty-three acres and a smaller one for the officers infrequently and temporarily held at the prison. With 14,489 inmates in July 1864 and an exceptionally large population of 19,786 during the exchange of prisoners in May 1865, this was the largest Union prison and with its overall total of some 52,000 was probably the largest prison of either side. Officially called Camp Hoffman after Commissary General of Prisoners William Hoffman, the prison was usually referred to by the name of its location.

Point Lookout's first commander was Brig. Gen. Gilman Marston. There were complaints, even from Union inspectors, about physical conditions under his and his successors' management. In July 1864, Brig. Gen. James Barnes, a Massachusetts-born West Pointer, took command, and he and his provost marshall, Maj. Allen G. Brady, made some improvements. The guard force at first consisted of troops drawn from the field, but these were rapidly succeeded by white semidisabled troops from the Veteran Reserve Corps and newly recruited blacks, often recent slaves. To the latter the Confederates usually reacted contemptuously and hostilely, feelings frequently returned by the black soldiers. With occasional exceptions, relations between the races were unfriendly. Partly because of the prisoners' unhappiness, the Federal authorities were able to recruit over a thousand of them who became "galvanized Yankees" to fight the western Indians.

Far more prisoners continued to endure the hardships of a pen unshaded in summer and frigid in winter. The wood needed to heat the tents was limited in quantity as were blankets and clothing. The United States attempted simply to prevent nakedness and often discouraged outsiders from sending such items. The official ration of food was also limited, and prisoners caught crabs and made jewelry, fans, and even pictures of the prison to trade for additional food. A particular grievance concerned the quality of the water. Some was shipped in, but much came from shallow wells that rapidly became polluted by sewage from the camp's surface. This contributed to diseases, which, along with less common causes like shootings by guards, accounted for 3,584 deaths, according to Federal records, or in the opinion of a recent historian, over 4,000. Such mortality and the hunger and cold experienced by the prisoners left a postwar legacy of bitterness.

Inevitably some prisoners attempted escape. Prior to the completion of the fence it was possible with luck to run the sentry line at night and get away with help from the strongly pro-Southern inhabitants of the vicinity. After the prisoners were surrounded by boards, the river offered an alternative for those willing to risk swimming with the help of some form of flotation device. From the beginning, Federal authorities stationed naval vessels in the river to forestall any attempt to use boats for escape or rescue.

The accessibility of the equivalent of a small army of reinforcements tempted the Confederates to try to recover the captives. In the winter of 1863–1864, Robert E. Lee formulated a scheme to throw across the Potomac a force of Marylanders drawn from his army to free the prisoners. In July 1864, he added the release of the prisoners to the mission of Jubal Early's Maryland raid. But the partial failure of Early's raid caused the abandonment of the plan. The alarmed Federals immediately built earthworks mounting cannons and a stockade to cut off either attack from the mainland or an uprising from within the prison. They also reduced the temptation for a rescue by moving half of the prison population farther north.

The prison camp continued to operate on a reduced scale until February 1865, when exchange resumed. Union authorities wished to send troops from western states to be exchanged in the East (believing that these would be least likely to retake the field for the Confederates) and hence began to accumulate such troops at Point Lookout. When the fall of Richmond disrupted exchange, the Union retained additional prisoners at Lookout, crowding the prison to its utmost. But the end of the war produced a speedy exodus of prisoners who took the oath of allegiance. By July 1865, the last were gone and the prison was abandoned.

The government preserved the camp's graves, which were moved several times to a nearby national cemetery containing both U.S. and Maryland monuments. The prison site reverted to recreational purposes with considerable portions vanishing through erosion. The remainder is today a Maryland state park.

[*See also* Early's Washington Raid.]

BIBLIOGRAPHY

Beitzell, Edwin W. *Point Lookout Prison Camp for Confederates.* Abell, Md., 1972.

Byrne, Frank. "Prison Pens of Suffering." In *Fighting for Time.* Edited by William C. Davis. Vol. 4 of *The Image of War, 1861–1865.* Garden City, N.Y., 1983.

Hesseltine, William B. *Civil War Prisons: A Study in War Psychology,* Columbus, Ohio, 1930. Reprint, New York, 1964.

Maryland State Park Foundation, Inc. *Sketches from Prison: A Confederate Artist's Record of Life at the Point Lookout Prisoner-of-War Camp.* Baltimore, Md., 1990.

FRANK L. BYRNE

POLIGNAC, CAMILLE J. (1813–1913), major general. Born near Paris, Camille Armand Jules Marie Prince de Polignac was the only noncitizen to achieve the rank of major general during the Civil War. Son of a

CAMILLE J. POLIGNAC. LIBRARY OF CONGRESS

minister to King Charles X, Polignac won acclaim in the Crimean War.

When the Civil War began, he offered his services to the Confederacy and was made a lieutenant colonel on the staff of P. G. T. Beauregard. After promotion to brigadier general January 10, 1863, he was transferred to the Trans-Mississippi Department in March. In the Battle of Mansfield (April 8, 1864), he commanded a brigade in Alfred Mouton's division, which routed the Union forces under Nathaniel P. Banks. Because Polignac took command of the division when Mouton was killed, Gen. Richard Taylor credited him with the victory. On the ninth, Polignac commanded the division at the Battle of Pleasant Hill. Here the Confederates were repulsed, but despite his tactical victory, Banks retreated down the Red River Valley. Gen. E. Kirby Smith ordered Polignac to harass Banks as he went, which he did for more than a month. Polignac was promoted to major general to date from the action at Mansfield.

In January 1865, he was granted a leave of absence to travel to France to promote the interests of the Confederacy with the French government, but he arrived too late to fulfill his mission. After the war Polignac remained in Europe; he fought in the Franco-Prussian War and was awarded the Legion of Honor. He died in Paris on November 15, 1913, the last surviving major general of the Confederacy.

BIBLIOGRAPHY

Kerby, Robert L. *Kirby Smith's Confederacy: The Trans-Mississippi South, 1863–1865.* New York, 1972.

Pierredon, Count Michelde. "Major General C. J. Polignac." *Confederate Veteran* 22 (1914): 389. Reprint, Wilmington, N.C., 1985.

Polignac, C. J. "Polignac's Mission." *Southern Historical Society Papers* 35 (1907): 326–334. Reprint, Wilmington, N.C., 1991.

THOMAS J. LEGG

POLITICS. Like most aspects of life in the South, politics underwent profound changes during the Civil War. The predominant issues of the prewar period, secession and union, were supplanted by war-related controversies. Parties disappeared, replaced by a wartime unity that only barely masked a continuation of antebellum partisan hostility. Elections changed as well, as politicians adopted new standards of campaigning that seemed more appropriate for a nation at war. The electorate, of course, remained the same, as did most of the prominent personalities involved in politics. But even these groups would be permanently altered by the War between the States.

Political Issues

The greatest political changes in the South during the Civil War concerned issues debated by politicians and voters. In the 1840s and 1850s, a variety of national and local issues determined the tenor of Southern political discourse. Most Southerners in the antebellum period believed that state rights were paramount, that the right to hold slaves in the territories could not be abridged by Congress, and that tariff rates ought to be lower. They disagreed, however, about issues such as temperance, government subsidies for railroads, and whether secession was the best way to guarantee the South's rights.

The creation of the Confederacy rendered these issues either moot or insignificant. At first, there were no questions of importance to fill this void. Believing it necessary to present a united front to the enemy, candidates in the elections for the First Confederate Congress conducted virtually no campaigns. Office seekers often placed notices in the local press informing the public of their candidacy, but these announcements rarely differed from one aspirant to another. They uniformly proclaimed themselves to be ardent supporters of Southern independence, proponents of a vigorous prosecution of the war, and so forth.

After the Confederate war effort began to falter, differences concerning the conduct of the war became the focus of political contention. One of the most hotly debated issues concerned the Confederate government's conscription system. Sensing their constituents' displeasure with this "horror of conscription," many candidates running for seats in the Second Congress condemned the policy. Some did so on the grounds that it detracted from state and local defense efforts, while others argued that it placed too much power in the hands of President Jefferson Davis. Even more controversial was the provision added to the law in September 1862 that exempted from military duty one white man on every plantation containing twenty or more slaves. Administration defenders insisted that the clause was necessary in order to maintain agricultural production as well as to prevent disciplinary problems with slaves. Nonetheless, by pointing out that the exemption provisions of the conscription law "made a broad and degrading line of distinction between . . . the silken son of pleasure and the hardy son of the soil," many candidates for the Second Congress were able to defeat incumbents who supported the administration's conscription policy.

Another issue that sparked controversy was the suspension of habeas corpus. Local judges were enabling army deserters to avoid prosecution by issuing writs for those held under Confederate authority. Congress attempted to eliminate this practice by granting Davis the power to suspend the writ and declare martial law as well if necessary, and it was primarily a perception of the overzealous use of this latter proviso that brought about the preponderance of disaffection. As with the conscription issue, most of the outcry against suspending habeas corpus came from radical state rights advocates. Among the most vociferous critics of the suspension were Georgia Governor Joseph E. Brown, North Carolina Governor Zebulon Vance, and Vice President Alexander H. Stephens. "Away with the idea of getting independence first, and looking for liberty afterwards," Stephens declared. "Our liberties, once lost, may be lost forever." Davis, however, suspended the writ for only sixteen months in all, and his abridgments of civil liberties were never as frequent or severe as those carried out by his counterpart in Washington.

The government's taxation policies also caused political divisions. Runaway inflation had by the spring of 1863 forced Congress to find alternative means of financing the war. Although a variety of taxes was imposed, the one that generated the most discontent was the 10 percent tax-in-kind levied on agricultural products. Poor yeoman farmers complained that it was unfair for the government to take 10 percent of their meager surpluses, while city dwellers such as clerks and teachers paid only 2 percent of their income. Moreover, the legislation left the principal possession of the wealthy—slaves—untaxed. The administration's advocates argued that slaves could not be taxed without a census, something that could not be undertaken during a war, but this provided little comfort to the impoverished farmer whose produce was hauled away while his rich neighbor's slaves escaped taxation. The army's impressment policy, by which it purchased whatever supplies it wanted from nearby farmers in exchange for worthless promissory notes, also bred resentment toward the Richmond government. Many Southerners harboring political ambitions used opposition to the tax-in-kind and impressment policies to unseat incumbents in the 1863 elections.

As the war grew longer and hopes of victory became increasingly remote, peace became the overriding political issue in the Confederacy. At first, peace proponents sought to win independence simply by negotiating with the U.S. government. They asserted that Davis was stubbornly continuing the fighting even though the South might gain its sovereignty at the negotiating table. The president argued, however, that a peace overture would be fruitless and would irreparably damage public morale as well. Later on, and especially after the defeats at Gettysburg and Vicksburg, the peace movement became a haven for a wide variety of politicians. Some, such as W. W. Boyce of South Carolina, merely believed that a well-defined peace policy would bring about Southern independence more quickly by making it easier for Peace Democrats in the North to oust Abraham Lincoln. Others, such as William W. Holden of North Carolina, seemed to favor peace even if Southern independence had to be sacrificed, and he proposed that North Carolina initiate its own negotiations if Davis refused to do so. "We would prefer our independence, if that were possible," one of Holden's followers stated, "but let us prefer *reconstruction* infinitely to *subjugation*." Campaigning primarily on this issue and holding election rallies that administration supporters characterized as treasonous (the Stars and Stripes were supposedly flown at some of these gatherings), Holden's "Conservative party" won widespread support, especially in western North Carolina, and captured at least five, and perhaps as many as eight, of the state's ten seats in the 1863 congressional elections. In Georgia and Alabama, as well as the more isolated upcountry regions of other states, candidates for the Second Congress managed to defeat incumbents by stressing the peace issue.

Disappearance of Parties

Ordinarily, political parties would have served as the conduit through which voters would express their opinions on these issues. In the Confederacy, however, there were no formal parties. This resulted in part from the belief that a political process unencumbered by partisan squabbling would best aid the war effort. Yet while the same belief pervaded the North, partisanship there subsided only temporarily, and the parties themselves never ceased operations. Why, then, did parties so abruptly disappear in the Confederacy?

The answer lies primarily in the decline of the two-party system in the South during the 1850s. After the demise of the Whig party in 1854 and 1855, Southerners who opposed the "Democracy" sought alternative affiliations. At first, it appeared as if the anti-immigrant Know-Nothing movement, which eventually became known as the American party, might win the loyalty of former Whigs, but the dismal performance in 1856 of its presidential candidate, Millard Fillmore, doomed that party to extinction. The Constitutional Union party captured a respectable 39 percent of the Southern vote in the presidential election of 1860, but because that organization had opposed secession as a means to guarantee the South's rights, it too disintegrated soon after the canvass. Recognizing no further reason to continue operations and believing that the energy previously exerted on its behalf would better serve the war effort, the Democratic party ceased functioning soon after the completion of the secession process.

Southerners were proud of the fact that their nation contained no political parties. Like those who had started the previous American revolution, most Southerners believed that in an ideal society there would be no parties, because more often than not these organizations degenerated into self-serving associations that placed the perpetuation of their own power ahead of the public good. Thus, the president pro tem of the First Confederate Congress congratulated legislators that "the spirit of party has never shown itself for an instant in your deliberations." Parties were not merely absent from the floors of Confederate legislative bodies. Party offices closed and officials found new work. In addition, no caucuses were held, no fund-raising took place, no propaganda was distributed, and no party committees directed communications from the electorate to the officeholders and back.

Although Southerners were proud that their nation lacked partisan political organizations, there were drawbacks to this state of affairs that became clear only in retrospect. For example, the lack of parties created a major impediment to the smooth and successful implementation of Davis's legislative agenda. In the North, Republican congressmen and governors understood that publicly opposing Lincoln's policies would make them pariahs within the Republican party and doom their political careers, convincing most of them that they should support the president even if they privately harbored doubts about his proposals. For the same reasons, party members were obligated to support their organization's policies after the legislation was implemented. In the South, however, obstructionist governors such as Brown and Vance were able to paralyze the war effort because, as historian James M. McPherson has noted, "the centrifugal tendencies of state's rights were not restrained by the centripetal force of party."

The lack of organized parties created other difficulties as well. For example, without the existence of a unified opposition party, Davis could not convincingly argue that his policies were superior to the program of his opponents, because he could not focus on a single opposition agenda with which to compare his own. In addition, the absence of parties created frustration for voters, because they could not identify those responsible for the government's program and register approval or disapproval on election day by voting a party's ticket. Finally, without parties to oversee the distribution of patronage, these appointees could no longer be used as a means to mobilize support for either the administration's policies or friends.

Despite the absence of formal political parties, historians have noted an "unconscious spirit of party" in the national and state governments of the Confederacy. Each of Davis's original cabinet nominees, for example, had been Democrats before the war. Furthermore, many states made deliberate decisions to send one ex-Democrat and one ex-Whig to the Confederate Senate. Nonetheless, statistical studies of the Confederate Congress have demonstrated that an officeholder's stance on secession and the proximity of his district to the war zones tended to play a larger role than prior party affiliation in determining the representative's stance on the measures before him. Yet even these factors were far from reliable predictors of congressional voting behavior. To a much greater extent than perhaps at any previous time in American history, congressmen seem to have genuinely voted according to their consciences on most issues before the Confederate Congress, and as a result no single consistently identifiable opposition grouping ever emerged.

Nonetheless, the public noticed the formation of a number of small opposition factions in Congress. One, which concentrated its attention on the peace issue, coalesced around the leadership of Boyce. The bulk of the Second Congress's North Carolina delegation, which seemed to oppose virtually everything proposed by the administration, was another such faction. The single individual most commonly identified as the leader of the opposition in Congress, however, Senator Louis T. Wigfall of Texas, belonged to neither of these groups. Formerly a fire-eating Democrat, Wigfall had initially supported Davis's most controversial proposals. It seems to have been a perceived insult concerning Wigfall's advice on a cabinet selection, combined with his admiration for another emerging foe of Davis, Gen. Joseph E. Johnston (under whom Wigfall had served during the first year of the war), that pushed the Texan into the opposition camp. Outside of Congress, many of Davis's opponents took their cues from a triumvirate of Georgians: Stephens, Brown, and ex-general and Confederate secretary of state Robert Toombs, who did everything in their power to embarrass the president and discredit his policies. These groupings, however, never assumed the official trappings of prewar political organizations; they more closely resembled the cliques and factions of the pre-Jacksonian era.

These opposition groups always constituted a small minority in the Confederate Congress. The administration's supporters, like the Southern Democratic party that had preceded them, were dominated by the same prominent personalities and families that had taken the lead in politics before the war. Robert M. T. Hunter of Virginia and Robert Barnwell Rhett, Sr., of South Carolina, as well as Stephens and Toombs, continued to play leading roles as they had before secession. These personalities remained in the forefront of Southern politics in part because ambitious young men who would ordinarily have entered politics instead chose to make their names in the military. Consequently, newspapers complained throughout the war that the state legislatures were filled with amateurs and incompetents, and although this resulted to some extent from the press's dissatisfaction with the legislators' inability to remedy the problems caused by the war, such comments also reflected a very real vacuum of experience and talent in state and local politics.

Other Political Voices

Although prominent politicians and families continued to dominate national political life in the Confederacy as they had in the antebellum period, the war did provide some unique opportunities for poor whites to exert political influence. For example, the belief that the conflict represented a "rich man's war and a poor man's fight" prompted many poor whites to funnel their energy into electing representatives who better reflected their socioeconomic outlook. In addition, poor yeoman farmers dominated the Unionist organizations that began proliferating in the up-country in late 1863. These associations, such as the Heroes of America in western North Carolina and eastern Tennessee, the Peace Society in northern Georgia and northern Alabama, and the Peace and Constitution Society in Arkansas, served as incubators for the Southern Republican party, in which poor whites would exert far more influence than they had in the South's prewar parties. Poor whites did not necessarily have to wait until after the war to wield this political power. The eventual Union occupation of areas such as West Virginia, eastern Tennessee, the Sea Islands of South Carolina, and Louisiana enabled poorer politicians such as Andrew Johnson to gain significant political clout in these regions well before the war had ended. With the reconstruction of each state government in the South, poor whites gained power that had been unattainable under a political system previously weighted in favor of slaveholders.

Like the South's poor white inhabitants, women also enjoyed increased political power during the Civil War. The most common method by which women made their influence felt in politics was still, as it had been before the war, through their politically active husbands. The diary of Mary Boykin Chesnut documents the efforts of these "female politicians" to have their concerns addressed by their male counterparts. Yet these well-to-do women were not the only ones whose voices were heard in political circles during the war. The correspondence of wartime governors contains an unprecedented number of letters from women, especially those running family farms while their husbands served in the army, concerning political issues. These women often explained in their letters that although they preferred to avoid politics, conditions in the countryside had become so unbearable (usually because of the tax-in-kind or impressment policies) that they felt obligated to inform government officials of the situation and seek redress.

Women may have exercised the most political clout during the Civil War through their participation in civil unrest. On April 2, 1863, for example, several hundred women in Richmond marched to the state capitol to complain that the price and supply of bread had reached intolerable levels. When Governor John Letcher told the protesters that he was incapable of remedying the situation, the crowd took matters into its own hands. Pulling knives, hatchets, and a few pistols from their skirts and pocketbooks, the women proceeded to loot the commercial district of whatever bread and other food items they could find. The events in Richmond were far from unique, as bread riots instigated wholly or in part by women also broke out in Atlanta, Macon, Augusta, Mobile, and a half-dozen other towns. Although the bread riots accomplished little in terms of increasing the supply of food in urban areas, they served as a warning that even without the vote, women were determined to make politicians act upon their concerns.

As the unprecedented role of women in the civil unrest in Richmond demonstrates, politics underwent significant change during the Civil War. Issues were transformed, parties disappeared, and many constituencies learned to wield unprecedented political power. Although it might be argued that the political revolution wrought by Reconstruction would prove even more profound, it was during the Civil War that Southern politicians abandoned the two-party system of politics, and this innovation laid the groundwork for the one-party system that would characterize the region's politics for the succeeding century.

[*See also* American Party; Bread Riots; Class Conflict; Congress; Conscription; Constitutional Union Party; Democratic Party; Election of 1863; Habeas Corpus; Judicial System; Peace Movements; Presidency; Public Finance; State Rights; Unionism; Vice Presidency; Whig Party; *and biographies of numerous figures mentioned herein.*]

BIBLIOGRAPHY

Alexander, Thomas B. "Persistent Whiggery in the Confederate South, 1860–1877." *Journal of Southern History* 27 (1961): 305–329.

Alexander, Thomas B., and Richard E. Beringer. *The Anatomy of the Confederate Congress: A Study of the Influences of Member Characteristics on Legislative Voting Behavior, 1861–1865.* Nashville, Tenn., 1972.

Beringer, Richard E. "The Unconscious 'Spirit of Party' in the Confederate Congress." *Civil War History* 18 (1972): 312–333.

McKitrick, Eric L. "Party Politics and the Union and Confederate War Efforts." In *The American Party Systems: Stages of Political Development.* Edited by William N. Chambers and Walter D. Burnham. New York, 1967.

McPherson, James M. *Battle Cry of Freedom: The Civil War Era.* New York, 1988.

Ringold, May. *The Role of State Legislatures in the Confederacy.* Athens, Ga., 1966.

Yearns, Wilfred B. *The Confederate Congress.* Athens, Ga., 1960.

Yearns, W. Buck, ed. *The Confederate Governors.* Athens, Ga., 1985.

TYLER ANBINDER

POLK, LEONIDAS (1806–1864), lieutenant general. Born April 10, 1806, at Raleigh into a prominent North Carolina family, Polk was educated by private tutors before entering the University of North Carolina in 1821. He wanted to be a soldier, however, and in 1823 he received an appointment to the U.S. Military Academy.

Polk did well in his West Point studies and at his 1827 graduation stood a respectable eighth in a thirty-eight-man

LEONIDAS POLK.

HARPER'S PICTORIAL HISTORY OF THE GREAT REBELLION

class. While at the academy he formed two friendships that were to be of great importance to his Confederate career—one with Albert Sidney Johnston (class of 1826); the other with Jefferson Davis (class of 1828).

Around 1826 Polk underwent a religious experience that convinced him to enter into the ministry. On December 1, 1827, therefore, he resigned his artillery lieutenant's commission and began studies for the Episcopal ministry. In April 1830 he was ordained a deacon and in 1838 missionary bishop of the Southwest (then Louisiana, Arkansas, Texas, Mississippi, and Alabama). In 1841 Polk was chosen bishop of Louisiana.

Meanwhile, he married Frances Anne Devereux and through his wife and her family acquired land and slaves in Tennessee. In 1841 he purchased a sugar plantation in Louisiana and in 1847 sold his Tennessee property. In 1854 he moved to New Orleans. He was also a leader in the movement to create a university of the South where Southern boys could be educated without the "contaminating" influence of Yankee ideas.

When disunion came in 1861, Polk hastened to offer his services to the Confederacy. President Jefferson Davis commissioned Polk major general and sent him to command Department No. 2, consisting of western Tennessee and eastern Arkansas.

Establishing his headquarters in Memphis, Polk quickly fell under the influence of locals who believed that the major threat to the South would come from a Federal thrust down the Mississippi River. They thought that the Confederates should build up their defenses in the Mississippi Valley at the expense of less important areas. Polk, thoroughly under their sway, tended to neglect all but the Mississippi River route into the Confederacy.

In early September Polk—acting without the approval or knowledge of the government—sent troops to occupy Columbus, Kentucky, on the Mississippi a few miles north of the Tennessee-Kentucky border. Since Polk did not push on to seize Paducah, Kentucky, at the mouth of the Tennessee River, occupation of Columbus was of no benefit to the South. (Whoever held Paducah controlled the Tennessee River; whoever controlled that river could easily outflank Columbus and force its evacuation.) Historian Steven Woodworth has called Polk's action "one of the most decisive catastrophes the Confederacy ever suffered" and notes that "Polk's presence in Kentucky was a political disaster" for the South because it drove the state—which had been trying to remain neutral—into the arms of the Federal government.

In early 1862 the Northerners moved up the Tennessee River and forced the Confederates to evacuate Columbus along with most of western Tennessee. Polk and his troops joined the force Gen. Albert Sidney Johnston was organizing at Corinth, Mississippi, that eventually became the Army of Tennessee. When that army was divided into corps, Polk was given command of the First Corps, which he led at the Battle of Shiloh.

In the summer of the same year the army was informally organized into wings, and Polk commanded one of them. In October he was promoted to the newly created grade of lieutenant general and assigned to command a corps.

During those same months, Polk became embroiled in numerous petty quarrels. He developed a consuming hatred for his commander, Braxton Bragg, and quickly became the leader of what amounted to an anti-Bragg clique within the army. For more than a year Polk waged a more or less open campaign to discredit Bragg and have him removed from command. Polk bombarded the government with criticism of Bragg, and on several occasions he and other anti-Bragg officers simply refused to obey that general's orders. Bragg, meanwhile, distrusted Polk's ability and tried to replace him with some better general. Polk's high rank, his close friendship with Davis, and what historian Thomas Connelly called his "remarkable ability to evade the blame for situations that were the result of . . . flaws in his character" all combined to nullify Bragg's efforts.

Polk remained in command of his corps until after the Battle of Chickamauga. Then Bragg, angered because several officers had again disobeyed orders, brought matters to a head by relieving Polk from command. He charged Polk himself with disobeying orders on September 20, 1863, and sent him away from the army. Bragg's action forced Davis to try to deal with the command crisis in the Army of Tennessee. As part of his "solution" to the problem, Davis transferred Polk to take charge of the Department of Alabama, Mississippi, and East Louisiana.

Polk remained in Mississippi until May 1864 when he was ordered to North Georgia to reinforce the Army of Tennessee, then under Gen. Joseph E. Johnston. The troops who accompanied Polk to Georgia, although technically an independent army, became in effect a corps in the Army of Tennessee. They and Polk took part in the early battles of the Atlanta campaign.

In June the Confederates occupied a position above Marietta, Georgia, some twenty-five miles north of Atlanta. On the fourteenth Polk went with a group of officers to Pine Mountain to observe the area. The group attracted the attention of Federal troops, and a Northern artillery battery opened fire. One of the shells hit Polk, killing him instantly. He was buried in Augusta, Georgia, but in 1945 his remains were removed to Christ Church Cathederal in New Orleans.

Polk had some popular appeal, but his military ability was very limited. His 1861 seizure of Columbus was a geopolitical mistake of the first magnitude, and his vendetta against Bragg weakened the Army of Tennessee. It is certain that President Davis's unwillingness to remove Polk or to curb his insubordination greatly damaged the Confederate cause.

BIBLIOGRAPHY

Connelly, Thomas L. *Army of the Heartland: The Army of Tennessee, 1861–1862.* Baton Rouge, La., 1967.

Connelly, Thomas L. *Autumn of Glory: The Army of Tennessee, 1862–1865.* Baton Rouge, La., 1971.

Parks, Joseph H. *General Leonidas Polk, C.S.A.: The Fighting Bishop.* Baton Rouge, La., 1962.

Polk, William Mecklenburg. *Leonidas Polk: Bishop and General.* 2 vols. Rev. ed. New York, 1915.

Woodworth, Steven E. *Jefferson Davis and His Generals: The Failure of Confederate Command in the West.* Lawrence, Kans., 1990.

RICHARD M. MCMURRY

POLK, LUCIUS EUGENE (1833–1892), brigadier general. Born July 10, 1833, at Salisbury, North Carolina, Polk was the nephew of Confederate Lt. Gen. Leonidas Polk. Lucius Polk grew up in Tennessee, studied at the University of Virginia, and settled near Helena, Arkansas, where he became a planter.

In 1861 Polk joined the First (later designated the Fifteenth) Arkansas Infantry Regiment of which his friend Patrick Cleburne was colonel. Polk was soon elected lieutenant. Wounded at Shiloh (April 6–7, 1862), Polk was promoted to colonel on April 11, 1862. He was wounded again at Richmond, Kentucky (August 29–30). In December he was promoted to brigadier general and assigned to command what had been Cleburne's Brigade. Polk served with the brigade in the 1863 campaigns of the Army of Tennessee. On June 17, 1864, during the Atlanta campaign, Polk was so seriously wounded that his leg had to be amputated, and he retired from the army.

After leaving the army, Polk moved to Columbia, Tennessee, where his family had long owned property, and lived there for the remainder of his life. He was a delegate to the Democratic National Convention in 1884, and three years later he was elected to the Tennessee State Senate.

Polk died December 1, 1892, and was buried in St. John's Churchyard, Ashwood, Tennessee. His friend and commander Cleburne had been buried there after his death at Franklin November 30, 1864. In 1870 when Cleburne's remains were moved to Helena, Arkansas, Polk was among those involved in the procession through Columbia.

BIBLIOGRAPHY

Hewitt, Lawrence L. "Lucius Eugene Polk." In *The Confederate General.* Edited by William C. Davis. Vol. 5. Harrisburg, Pa., 1991.

Warner, Ezra J. *Generals in Gray: Lives of the Confederate Commanders.* Baton Rouge, La., 1959.

RICHARD M. MCMURRY

POLLARD, EDWARD A. (1832–1872), journalist and contemporary historian of the Confederacy. Pollard, a descendant of the Rives family, grew up on its Oakridge estate in Nelson County, Virginia. Educated at Hampden-Sydney College and the University of Virginia, he was expelled from law school at the College of William and Mary for misconduct. In the early 1850s he prospected for gold in California, became a journalist in San Francisco, and traveled in eastern Asia. Returning to the eastern states in 1856, he became a publicist for Southern rights causes, including William Walker's projects in Nicaragua and reopening of the African slave trade. In *Black Diamonds* (1859), he combined such arguments with sketches of plantation life and master-slave relations.

The attempt to resupply Fort Sumter in 1861 impelled Pollard (then living in Washington) to join the Southern Confederacy. After a brief advocacy of secession in Maryland, he and his brother H. Rives Pollard joined the staff of the *Richmond Examiner.* Many have had the mistaken impression that Pollard was its wartime editor. He was acting editor only in the summer of 1862 during the absence of editor John Moncure Daniel. He and others contributed draft editorials, but Daniel thoroughly rewrote them before publication. Pollard shared the *Examiner*'s extreme Southern-rights views and its animus against Jefferson Davis's administration.

Pollard resolved in 1861 to be the contemporary historian of the war for Confederate independence. He published *The First Year of the War* in 1862 and followed it with annual volumes thereafter. In 1864 the Federal navy captured him trying to travel through the blockade to Europe. He was imprisoned in Boston, then paroled in Brooklyn and exchanged from Fortress Monroe in January 1865. Back in Richmond, he exhorted Confederates to fight on until victory.

After the surrender, Pollard continued his laudatory histories of the Confederacy. He completed his annual series and published it as *Southern History of the War* (1865) and followed it with his most famous work, *The Lost Cause* (1866), and *Lee and His Lieutenants* (1867). Those works embroiled him in historical controversy with D. H. Hill and other Confederate generals and with admirers of Jefferson Davis about those leaders' wartime performance.

In 1868 Pollard, who had hoped for a renewed Confederate struggle, became reconciled to the national conservative politics of President Andrew Johnson and the Northern Democrats. In *The Lost Cause Regained,* he interpreted their effort for white supremacy and state rights as the substance of what Southerners had sought in the Confederacy. That winter he returned to Richmond to seek judicial vengeance for the murder of Rives Pollard there. In 1869 he wrote his hostile *Life of Jefferson Davis, and Secret History of the Southern Confederacy.*

After that Pollard settled with relatives in Lynchburg and (except for a travel guide) directed his writing to articles. He continued to discuss Confederate history but became a "reconstructed" Southern conservative, urging national reconciliation, economic development, and benevolence toward blacks. He died in 1872, but his writings continued to influence Southern thought about the Lost Cause.

BIBLIOGRAPHY

Davidson, James Wood. "Edward A. Pollard." In *The Living Writers of the South.* New York, 1869.

Maddex, Jack P., Jr. *The Reconstruction of Edward A. Pollard: A Rebel's Conversion to Postbellum Unionism.* Chapel Hill, N.C., 1974.

Wilson, James Southall. "Edward Alfred Pollard." In *Library of Southern Literature.* Edited by Edward A. Alderman, Joel Chandler Harris, and Charles W. Kent. New Orleans, 1907.

JACK P. MADDEX, JR.

POOR RELIEF. The unexpected and unprecedented poverty that afflicted the Confederacy provoked innovative but inadequate responses. In a region that had never employed extensive means of poor relief, substantial new initiatives came from individuals and from local and state governments. Ultimately, however, the scope of the war effort required Confederate involvement if aid to the poor was to be effective. Despite some relief activities by the Richmond administration, the problems of poverty and hunger remained unsolved and severely eroded support for the government among the common people.

Poor relief had been a modest affair before the war. The states employed a variety of means to assist the poor, but all were on a small scale. A stigma attached to the recipients of aid; healthy children usually were apprenticed rather than supported as paupers. Government-sponsored poor farms or poorhouses sheltered many of the destitute, and local authorities entrusted others (often elderly persons) to the care of some responsible person who agreed to maintain them for a modest fee. The counties of North Carolina, for example, practiced all these methods and levied taxes at varying levels to defray costs. In Southern cities charitable organizations had developed to give some aid to the destitute. In the words of one writer, poverty was "associated in public opinion with illness and petty crime." An antebellum North Carolinian observed that "the poor will suffer almost any privations before" accepting public relief.

The war forced enormous changes in these practices and public attitudes, but the experience of poverty remained physically harsh and psychologically painful for thousands of yeoman families. In the early days of the conflict there was a widespread recognition that soldiers and their families might need—and deserved—support. Governor Joseph E. Brown of Georgia appealed in May 1861 for contributions to aid soldiers' families and offered prizes to recognize those citizens who did the most to contribute. Artisans, such as tanners or millers, offered their services free to soldiers' families, and some merchants invited local troops to select the goods they needed. Many companies and factories contributed money or donated some of their products. As the war went on, "free markets" came into being in the cities. Tickets were distributed to the poor in New Orleans, Mobile, Charleston, and Richmond; ticket holders then could visit the market to obtain free supplies. Macon, Atlanta, Savannah, Shreveport, and other cities had stores that sold goods to the needy at cost. In Richmond the Union Benevolent Society received aid from the city government and fed 4,500 people by the end of the war.

As the size of the conflict became apparent, local and state governments became more heavily involved. Most states passed laws early in the war to suspend the collection of debts ("stay laws") or exempt soldiers' families from certain taxes. Between November 1861 and March 1862, seven states formulated relief laws, which typically gave county governments responsibility for using the funds raised by a special tax. With hunger spreading, a corps of county officials came into being who scoured their region, or even distant areas, seeking to buy foodstuffs and distribute them to the poor. To assist the county officials, state lawmakers appropriated as much as $6 million at one time for poor relief, in addition to buying and distributing items such as salt, medicines, cloth, and cotton and wool cards. In 1863 the Georgia legislature bought 97,500 bushels of corn for the poor in sixteen suffering counties of that state.

These impressive efforts did not solve the problem, however. Many of the larger state appropriations never existed except on paper, and county purchasing agents increasingly came into competition with the Confederacy's efforts to supply the armies. Only the Confederate government was large enough to cope with the problem of hunger. What, then, did the Confederacy do?

Occasionally the Confederate government cooperated with private charities by exempting their goods from impressment or encouraging the railroads to arrange transportation. In especially deserving cases, under the Exemption Act of May 1, 1863, the Davis administration allowed individual soldiers to return home to their families. Under the Exemption Act of February 17, 1864, Congress required planters who wished to retain their overseers to promise under bond to raise stated amounts of meat and food for the government. These foodstuffs were sometimes sold to soldiers' families at below-market prices. In August 1864, the War Department instructed its commissaries to leave one-half of the surplus raised by bonded planters for "persons who purchase on behalf of the families of soldiers." Records of bonded farmers also show that a small proportion of them were small farmers exempted for "Care of Private Necessity."

The greatest potential for relieving hunger, however, lay with the Confederate tax-in-kind. In 1863, as the central government began to collect large quantities of crops in depots, county relief agents sought help, asking to buy back the crops from poverty-stricken counties at the low prices set by local boards under the Impressment Act. Records show that for a year the Confederacy extended some aid in this way, but the military's needs soon precluded assistance to civilians.

Thus the problem of poverty in the Confederacy remained unsolved. It brought physical and mental suffering to proud, independent yeoman families that had never before needed aid. In 1862 some nonslaveholding citizens of Smith and Scott counties, Mississippi, had petitioned Congress for a law to aid the poor. Although they expressed a willingness to defend slave property, these petitioners warned that they were "not willing to sacry fize our wives and childron and leave them to starve for bread and clothing." As poverty spread and poor relief proved inadequate, discontent, disaffection, and desertion grew. Commanders recognized that despairing letters from home caused many men to leave the armies. Poverty influenced many others to turn against the cause. The inadequacy of poor relief, and the fact that it had become necessary, did great damage to the Confederacy.

[*See also* Free Markets; Poverty; State Socialism; Tax-in-Kind.]

BIBLIOGRAPHY

Coulter, E. Merton. *The Confederate States of America, 1861–1865.* A History of the South, vol. 7. Baton Rouge, La., 1950.

Escott, Paul D. *After Secession: The Failure of Confederate Nationalism.* Baton Rouge, La., 1978.

Escott, Paul D. " 'The Cry of the Sufferers': The Problem of Welfare in the Confederacy." *Civil War History* 23, no. 3 (September 1977): 228–240.

Escott, Paul D. "Poverty and Governmental Aid for the Poor in Confederate North Carolina." *North Carolina Historical Review* 61, no. 4 (October 1984): 462–480.

Massey, Mary Elizabeth. *Ersatz in the Confederacy.* Columbia, S.C., 1952.

Thomas, Emory M. *The Confederate State of Richmond: A Biography of the Capital.* Austin, Tex., 1971.

PAUL D. ESCOTT

POPULAR CULTURE. In September 1861 the *Southern Literary Messenger* pointed with excitement to the "splendid opening which the impending Revolution secures to every Southern enterprize," not the least of which was the evolution of a Confederate popular culture. Not necessarily distinct from that of the antebellum South's, it at least "should occupy, in some respects," as an 1864 broadside remarked, "a different sphere of usefulness." Thus traditional pastimes, fetes, and other entertainments were adapted to wartime civilian and military society, particularly so "for the benefit of the soldiers" and "their wives and children."

Enormously popular, for example, were cartes de visite, small photographic images mounted on heavy card stock usually measuring two and a half by four inches. Easily carried in a pocket or haversack and cheap to produce—created from a negative from which any number of reproductions could be made—they provided accessible and affordable mementos or keepsakes for soldiers and their families. Despite paper shortages, photo studios such as Minnis and Cowell in Richmond and the Metropolitan Gallery in Nashville did a brisk business in marketing carte de visite likenesses of famous individuals as well. Period scrapbooks thus abound with pictures of family members alongside images of Robert E. Lee, Jefferson Davis, and other Confederate leaders. Somewhat more expensive were daguerreotype, ambrotype, and ferrotype images. An ambrotype, for example, cost from one dollar for a small image to several dollars for a larger one. Whereas the cards could be copied in any number, the more elaborate likenesses were one-of-a-kind positive images, often hand-tinted, mounted under plush velvet in elaborate decorative frames, and available in a variety of sizes.

Prints and engravings proved far more difficult to produce. With the fall of New Orleans, the South lost much of its printing expertise. And whereas Northern printers produced several Confederate scenes—a Baltimore firm, for example, published a series of pro-Confederate etchings by Adalbert J. Volck in 1863 and 1864—such pictures remained largely unseen in the South until after the war. Plagued also by shortages of skilled craftsmen, inadequate paper supplies, and a more pressing need for stamps and currency, graphic art thus remained rare in the Confederacy. There were exceptions, though. In 1861 both Pessou and Simon, of New Orleans, and R. H. Howell, of Savannah, issued handsome lithographs of early Confederate scenes; Tucker and Perkins of Augusta, Georgia, that same year published a finely rendered print of Jefferson Davis, copied from a prewar Mathew Brady photograph; and Ernest Crehen in Richmond as late as 1863 published a striking portrait of J. E. B. Stuart. By and large, however, popular prints were infrequent and poorly produced. Hoyer and Ludwig's highly fanciful 1861 lithograph of an oddly uniformed Jefferson Davis is far more representative. Cartoons were somewhat more forgiving of style and quality. The four lithographed *Dissolving Views of Richmond,* published by Blanton Duncan in Columbia in 1862, ridiculed George B. McClellan's Peninsula campaign, and Richmond's George Dunn and Company issued a biting series of caricatures aimed at shirkers, hoarders, and doomsayers.

Painters, too, suffered from scant supplies. With no canvas available, artist John R. Key, nephew of Francis Scott Key, resorted to using burlap for his painting of Fort Sumter. Such topical work was nevertheless eagerly awaited. In Richmond, William D. Washington attracted considerable attention with his masterwork, *The Burial of Latané,* depicting Southern women and their slaves mourning the death of the sole Confederate casualty of Stuart's 1862 ride around McClellan's army. In 1865, soldiers and civilians crowded through the Virginia capitol to view Edward Caledon Bruce's monumental portrait of Lee, since disappeared. Bruce, deaf since the age of fourteen and thus unable to enlist, was unique. Louis M. Montgomery, of the famed Washington Artillery, completed nearly two hundred sketches of military life, but like most other Southern artists—Conrad Wise Chapman, John Elder, Alan Christian Redwood, and William Ludwell Sheppard, for example—he was unable to exhibit much work while actively serving in the army.

Confederate theaters offered artwork of a sort. One Richmond playhouse featured the "Southern Moving Dioramic Panorama," a canvas eight feet high and seventy-five feet long filled with historical scenes. The nearby Metropolitan Theater presented a massive "scenic and automatic spectacle" of wartime illustrations, accompanied by animated "miniature moving, life like figures" and an explanatory lecture. Usually the plays alone were enough to bring in large audiences. Theater provided a vibrant source of entertainment in each of the Confederacy's major cities, although, after the fall of New Orleans in 1862, Charleston's Hibernian Hall and Richmond's Metropolitan, New Richmond, and Varieties theaters remained the most active. Besides Charles Morton, the "most versatile and popular Comedian and Vocalist in the Confederacy," and Ella Wrenn, the "accomplished Tragedienne and Prima Donna," other popular actors included E. R. Dalton, Walter Keeble, D'Orsay Ogden, Harry Macarthy, Mary Partington, Jennie Powell, and Ida Vernon. Easily the most famous of the many traveling companies was the W. H. Crisp troupe, its male members all honorably discharged Confederate veterans.

In the press of wartime, however, performances often degenerated into rowdy brawls. Soldiers on leave, civilian workers, and drunken troublemakers all eager for a good time filled the cheaper seats, often firing pistols and otherwise disturbing the more cultured theatergoers in the lower tiers. So bad did the situation become that the gentler sort regularly urged theater owners to close down their saloons and upper tiers—hardly a likely prospect in the face of an overwhelming demand from all quarters for entertainment. Theaters presented an array of productions, from traditional operas such as *Il Trovatore* and Shakespearean plays to the melodramatic *Corsican Brothers* and *The Marbled Heart.*

Many more dramas—such as *The Ticket-of-Leave Man, The Capture of Courtland, Alabama,* and *Miscegenation; or, A Virginia Negro in Washington*—reflected the times. In 1864, the New Richmond Theater introduced *The Ghost of Dismal Swamp; or, Marteau, the Guerrilla* with special effects so realistic that critics called it "the great Spectral wonder of the nineteenth century." Most of the productions were abysmally written but were at least presented with unflagging enthusiasm; actors often perceived of themselves as charged with a patriotic duty to bolster morale. Minstrels such as Tom Morris, "the renowned negro delineator," and his Iron-Clad Ethiopian Troupe were especially popular, although keeping any acting company intact was always difficult. Morris and his minstrels were drafted in 1864.

Like theater, music attracted the broadest possible audience. In the first year of the war alone the public could buy the eighteen-page *New-Orleans 5 Cent Song-Book,* the sixteen-page *Original Songs of the Atlanta Amateurs* ("containing more truth than poetry"), or, the next year, the massive two-hundred-page *War Songs of the South.* Until 1865, despite the shortages that so plagued every printer, song sheets and collections remained available. A Charleston publisher as late as 1864 issued a monthly pocket-size *Taylor's Southern Songster.* As expected, many of the titles honored the ordinary Confederate soldier, various generals, or Southern sentiments. There were nearly fifty musical selections published on Stonewall Jackson's death alone. Popular music titles included "Dear Mother, I'll Come Home Again," "Boys, Keep Your Powder Dry," "The Murmur of the Shell," and "Adieu to the Star Spangled Banner Forever."

Although attracting a smaller segment of the Confederate public, magazines were also part of wartime popular culture. But of the approximately one hundred Southern periodicals in business in 1861, only a few survived the war. The *Southern Literary Messenger* lasted until 1864, as did the *Southern Literary Companion* and *Southern Field and Fireside,* both published in Georgia; *De Bow's Review,* except for a single issue, suspended publication in 1862 until after the surrender. The *Southern Monthly,* with hopes of becoming a Confederate *Harper's,* lasted only for several issues. Richmond's *Southern Punch,* Mobile's *Confederate Spirit and Knapsack of Fun,* and Atlanta's *Hard Tack* were game attempts at Confederate, especially military, humor. Two new periodicals published in Richmond, the *Southern Illustrated News* and *Magnolia,* a literary magazine, by 1863 were forced to charge twenty dollars for a year's subscription; neither lasted out the war. One that did, the *Countryman,* published in Eatonton, Georgia, employed a young typesetter and writer named Joel Chandler Harris. For children, there were the *Portfolio,* published in Charleston and later Columbia, and the *Child's Index,* printed in Macon.

Popular fiction fared little better than the magazine. Printers issued barely more than a hundred literary titles during the war years. In 1861 Strother and Marcom in Raleigh published a collection of poetry, Hunter Hill's *Hesper;* a Charleston printer that same year issued Claudian B. Northrop's *Southern Odes.* West and Johnston in Richmond and Goetzel and Company in Mobile produced nine literary titles each, the most of any single printer. Both issued editions of two of the war's most popular titles, Victor Hugo's *Les Misérables* (1863–1864) and Augusta Evans Wilson's stilted romance, *Macaria* (1864). Sigmund Goetzel's firm also published two stories by Charles Dickens, George Eliot's *Silas Marner,* and Julian Fane's *Tannhauser.* It was Goetzel too who, faced with the shortage of paper, resorted to printing book covers on sample sheets of wallpaper. Some Confederate fiction, such as Sallie Rochester Ford's *Raids and Romance of Morgan and His Men,* proved popular enough to be pirated in the North. Other works—such as W. D. Herrington's *The Captain's Bride* or Braxton Craven's *Mary Barker*—were but cheap novelettes, worthy of only a moment's attention.

The same might be said of many Confederate broadsides, posters, newspaper notices, and other forms of advertising. While educational, religious, and civic organizations usually struck a serious tone, many merchants and other entrepreneurs were seldom timid in touting their products. A grocery in Cold Springs, Texas, for example, boasted of its "largest and best" inventory, adding that "If you want the worth of your money, call and see us!" In Greensboro, North Carolina, the locally produced Tarpley Rifle was "the best . . . introduced in the country." Some notices were practical: a New Orleans company in late 1861 finally bowed to the inevitable and agreed to accept Confederate currency in order "to facilitate the efforts of our customers."

That some vestiges of Confederate popular culture were less than ideal was not significant, however. As the editor of a leading Southern newspaper put it, for many citizens it was equally important that the South "along with her political independence" achieve an "independence in thought and education, and in all . . . forms of mental improvement," whether they were extraordinary or mundane.

[*See also* Broadsides; Literature, *article on* Literature in the Confederacy; Lost Cause, *article on* Iconography of the Lost Cause; Magazines; Music; Newspapers; Photography; Printmaking; Theater.]

BIBLIOGRAPHY

Albaugh, William A., III. *Confederate Faces: A Pictorial Review of the Individuals in the Confederate Armed Forces.* Solana Beach, Calif., 1970.

Harwell, Richard B. *Brief Candle: The Confederate Theatre.* Worcester, Mass., 1971.

Harwell, Richard B. *Confederate Belles-Lettres: A Bibliography and a Finding List of the Fiction, Poetry, Drama, Songsters, and Miscellaneous Literature Published in the Confederate States of America.* Hattiesburg, Miss., 1941.

Harwell, Richard B. *Confederate Music.* Chapel Hill, N.C., 1950.

Kennerly, Sarah Law. "Confederate Juvenile Imprints: Children's Books and Periodicals Published in the Confederate States of America, 1861–1865." Ph.D. diss., University of Michigan, 1956.

Neely, Mark E., Jr., Harold Holzer, and Gabor S. Boritt. *The Confederate Image: Prints of the Lost Cause.* Chapel Hill, N.C., 1987.

Parrish, T. Michael, and Robert M. Willingham, Jr., comps. *Confederate Imprints: A Bibliography of Southern Publications from Secession to Surrender.* Austin, Tex., and Katonah, N.Y., 1987.

EDWARD D. C. CAMPBELL, JR.

POPULATION. The eighth census of the United States reported that, as of June 30, 1860, the total population of the United States of America was 31.18

1860 Population Distribution of the Border Slaveholding States[1]

	White	Slave	Free Black[2]	Total
Delaware	90,589 (80.7%)	1,798 (1.6%)	19,829 (17.7%)	112,216
Kentucky	919,484 (79.6%)	225,483 (19.5%)	10,684 (0.9%)	1,155,651
Maryland	515,918 (75.1%)	87,189 (12.7%)	83,942 (12.2%)	687,049
Missouri	1,063,489 (90.0%)	114,931 (9.7%)	3,572 (0.3%)	1,181,992
Total	2,589,480 (82.5%)	429,401 (13.7%)	118,027 (3.8%)	3,136,908

[1]All percentages are rounded to the nearest tenth.
[2]Includes all free persons of African descent.
Source: U.S. Census Office, Eighth Census [1860], *Population*, Washington, D.C., 1864.

1860 Population Distribution of the Eleven Future Confederate States[1]

	White	Slave	Free Black[2]	Total
Alabama	526,271 (54.6%)	435,080 (45.1%)	2,690 (0.3%)	964,041
Arkansas	324,143 (74.4%)	111,115 (25.5%)	144 (0.1%)	435,402
Florida	77,747 (55.4%)	61,745 (44.0%)	932 (0.7%)	140,424
Georgia	591,550 (56.0%)	462,198 (43.7%)	3,500 (0.3%)	1,057,248
Louisiana	357,456 (50.5%)	331,726 (46.9%)	18,647 (2.6%)	707,829
Mississippi	353,899 (44.7%)	436,631 (55.2%)	773 (0.1%)	791,303
North Carolina	629,942 (63.5%)	331,059 (33.4%)	30,463 (3.1%)	991,464
South Carolina	291,300 (41.4%)	402,406 (57.2%)	9,914 (1.4%)	703,620
Tennessee	826,722 (74.5%)	275,719 (24.9%)	7,300 (0.7%)	1,109,741
Texas	420,891 (69.7%)	182,566 (30.2%)	355 (0.1%)	603,812
Virginia	1,047,299 (65.6%)	490,865 (30.8%)	58,042 (3.6%)	1,596,206
Total	5,447,220 (59.9%)	3,521,110 (38.7%)	132,760 (1.5%)	9,101,090

[1]All percentages are rounded to the nearest tenth.
[2]Includes all free persons of African descent.
Source: U.S. Census Office, Eighth Census [1860], *Population*, Washington, D.C., 1864.

million people. Just over 9 million of these people lived in the states that formed the Confederate States of America in the spring of 1861, and another 3.1 million, many of them sympathetic to the Confederate cause, lived in the border states of Delaware, Kentucky, Maryland, and Missouri. The census numbers confirmed that the slaveholding states of the Union were a distinct minority of the total population of the United States. Not counting slaves, the free population of the Confederacy represented only about one-fourth of all free Americans.

This had not always been the case. In 1790, the population—including slaves—of the Southern states approximately equaled that of the North. But while the population of the North had increased by a factor of about five between 1790 and 1860, that of the South had only doubled. This growing demographic imbalance posed a major dilemma for the political leaders of the South in 1860. On the one hand, the realignment of congressional seats in the House of Representatives following the 1860 census would further increase the power of Northern interests in the Federal government, and the election of Abraham Lincoln—who was not even on the ballot in the Deep South—underscored the fact that Southerners could no longer block the choice of a president opposed to their interests. In this respect, the demographic imbalance supported a political argument favoring secession. On the other hand, the population figures meant that, should the North contest secession, the South would find itself at a considerable disadvantage in terms of military manpower. In this respect, demographic considerations urged caution.

The manpower disadvantage became evident once war broke out. Since slaves were not allowed to fight, the primary pool of manpower for the Confederate army was the 1.1. million white males aged fifteen to thirty-nine who lived in the eleven states of the Confederacy. This pool was augmented by volunteers from the slaveholding border states who joined the South's cause and by enlistment of younger and older men as the war continued. A maximum estimate of men available to serve in the Confederate army would be 1.75 million men. By comparison, the Union army could draw upon a pool of over 6 million men. Thus, the Confederacy began the war with a disadvantage of more than three to one in terms of military manpower.

Numbers alone do not tell the full story. An examination of the reasons for the divergent patterns of regional population growth reveals the fundamental differences in economic and social structure of the Northern and the Southern societies. In the states that formed the Confederacy, population growth before 1860 was largely the result of a high birthrate among both the native population of free whites and black slaves. One consequence of this pattern of natural increase was that, despite the settlement of a vast territory of western lands and the emergence of cotton to replace tobacco and rice as the major staple crops of Southern agriculture, the social and demographic contours of Southern society remained essentially unchanged.

On the eve of the Civil War, most Southerners farmed their land much as their grandfathers had seventy years earlier. Indeed, a visitor from 1790 would have felt quite at home in the South of 1860. Slave owners cultivated cash crops with slave labor on their plantations. Most other whites lived on family farms, where they produced a modest surplus of staple crops for the market. Slaves toiled under the control of their owners as they had in colonial times.

A visitor from 1790 to the Northern states, on the other hand, would have noticed enormous changes in the everyday life of people. Population growth in the free states reflected not only a high birthrate among the native population but also the effects of immigration. In the three decades before the Civil War, nearly 5 million people emigrated from Europe to the United States. Most of these newcomers stayed north of the Ohio River, claiming land to farm or settling in the growing urban centers of the North. As a consequence of this immigration, one out of six persons living in the free states in 1860 was foreign-born, and an equal fraction was composed of first-generation Americans whose parents had immigrated to the United States.

By contrast, only one in thirty individuals living in the Confederacy was born outside the United States. (Since very few black slaves were brought into the United States after the closure of the Atlantic slave trade in 1809, by the time of the Civil War almost all slaves were native-born.) The presence of foreign-born residents in rural areas of the South was particularly rare. Compared to the North, where ethnic diversity was an important influence in virtually every sphere of life, Southerners lived in a world where values and institutional arrangements—especially their peculiar institution of slavery—reflected a uniquely *American* experience.

The influx of European immigrants was not the only change in the Northern states that would have struck a visitor from 1790. Equally evident would be the growth of urban centers. Only one city in the Confederacy—New Orleans—had a population over 175,000 in 1860, and two others—Richmond, Virginia, and Charleston, South Carolina—had populations approaching 50,000. In all, only nine cities in the Confederacy had populations in excess of 10,000 people. The presence of many times that number of urban areas in the North reflected the greater role of commerce and manufacturing. In 1860 more than a million men and women were employed in Northern factories. Barely one-tenth that number were factory workers in the Confederacy. Only Virginia, which accounted for one-third of all manufacturing employment in the Confederacy, could boast of a city—Richmond—with any significant industrial employment.

Equally striking was the absence of smaller towns in the South. Southern families lived on self-sufficient farms and sent their cash crops directly to the cotton brokers located along the major rivers or on the seacoast. They had little need for the commercial services provided by small towns that were an essential part of agriculture in the North and West. Thus, whereas villages and towns dotted the landscape of New England, the Mid-Atlantic states and the Old Northwest Territory, visitors to the South consistently complained of the long distances traveled without encountering any towns.

The Confederacy, in short, was a rural society of 9.1 million people scattered over a vast territory that stretched from the Atlantic Ocean to the Gulf of Mexico. It was a class society where economic and social power rested primarily on the ownership of two assets—land and slaves. There were basically three classes of people in the Confederacy: slaveholders, nonslaveholding whites, and black slaves.

The most powerful class comprised the 300,000 slave owners. Together with their family members, this group numbered some 1.7 million individuals, or about 30 percent of the total free population. The basis of these people's power stemmed from the enormous wealth represented by the land and slaves they owned. The average slaveholder in the Confederacy owned eleven slaves and farmed more than ten thousand acres of land. These statistics do not reveal the enormous range in the size of slaveholdings. In areas such as the alluvial regions of the Mississippi River or the rice regions of South Carolina or Louisiana, planters often owned several hundred slaves. The wealth of these families rivaled that of anyone in the United States. Yet 30 percent of all slaveholders owned only one or two slaves and operated modest-sized farms. Though they could hardly claim to be "planters," this group of farmers was very well off by contemporary standards. In 1860 a single male slave field hand was worth between $1,500 and $2,000, a sum nearly equal to the total value of a farm reported to the census by the average family in the Old Northwest.

Slaveholders were instrumental in the formation of the Confederate States of America, and they dominated the politics of the new nation from its birth until its collapse in 1865. The planter-aristocrats of the South felt that breaking away from the Union in 1860 was the best way to protect the system of slavery. But they also had the most to lose should the Confederacy be defeated. The emancipation of slaves in 1865 brought huge financial losses to those who owned large numbers of slaves. Their financial woes did not, however, mean total ruin. Thanks to their vast holdings of land, many of the prominent families retained their dominant social and economic position in the postbellum period despite the impact of the war.

At the other end of the economic and social spectrum in the Confederacy were the 3.5 million black slaves. By law, these people were the personal property of their owners. Despite the fact that almost one-half of all slaveholdings were of five or less slaves, nine out of ten slaves lived on farms or plantations with five or more slaves. Few were skilled. Apart from a small fraction of overseers, craftsmen, and house servants, slaves—men, women, and children—worked in the fields. Slaves clearly had the most to gain from a Confederate defeat—their freedom. As the war progressed, thousands of blacks responded to the promise of freedom by leaving their plantation to seek refuge behind the Union lines. When Union victory became more certain and the Confederate government's control weakened, an increasing number of blacks left their owner's plantation to search for family, friends, and a better life. This migration, which swelled to very large numbers of people near the end of the war, created considerable stress on cities, which offered refuge for blacks who were seeking a new start under freedom.

The largest single class of people in the Confederacy were the 3.9 million whites who owned no slaves at all. Most of these people operated farms that relied entirely on family labor. They devoted their attention primarily to the production of the corn, poultry, and pork that ensured food for the family and farm animals. They grew cotton or tobacco to earn cash for the modest supplies they had to purchase.

A substantial majority of these people probably supported the idea of secession from the Union in 1861. They were, however, much less enthusiastic about the war that followed. In the western regions of Virginia and the Carolinas, or the hills of northern Georgia, Alabama, and Mississippi, many people were at best ambivalent about the war. There were few slaves in these areas, and as the cost of the war mounted in both human and economic terms, opposition to the war effort became more pronounced. But their opposition to the war did not mean they embraced the Union cause. Although most of these people had only a limited interest in the protection of slavery, they were not eager to see blacks freed through emancipation, and they deeply resented the invasion of their territory and the deprivations brought by the Federal army. If forced to choose between the invading Northerners or the Confederate cause, these people tended to side with the South. It was men from this class throughout the South who formed the backbone of the Confederate armies in Virginia and Tennessee.

The Civil War brought vast changes to Southern society with the emancipation of slaves. Yet it did not produce major changes in the demographic patterns of the Southern population. The birthrate remained high, which helped to offset the loss of a quarter of a million young men as casualties in the war. Plantations disappeared, but blacks remained in the cotton belt as sharecroppers and tenant farmers. Immigrants continued to flow into the United States, but they still settled mostly in the North and West. Perhaps the most significant impact of the war was the impetus it gave to growth of the larger urban centers in the South. The war stimulated economic activity in such cities as Richmond, Atlanta, Augusta, and Selma. Though these cities suffered considerable destruction toward the end of the war, the economic stimulus for growth remained. A second source of urban growth was the flight of refugees—whites as well as freed blacks—to cities. Most of the urban centers of the South experienced significant population growth after the war.

Still, the South remained essentially a rural, agrarian society. The destruction of slavery had momentarily altered the political balance of power in the South, but there remained three basic classes of people: white planters (now using tenant or wage labor); white farmers (many now tenants), and free blacks (who at least had gained freedom).

[*See also* African Americans in the Confederacy; Army, *article on* Manpower; Creoles; Civil War, *article on* Losses and Numbers; Foreigners; Germans; Indians; Irish; Jews; Navy, *article on* Manpower; Urbanization; Women.]

BIBLIOGRAPHY

Cooper, William J., Jr., and Thomas E. Terrill. *The American South: A History.* 2 vols. New York, 1991.

Gray, Lewis Cecil. *History of Agriculture in the Southern United States to 1860.* 2 vols. Pittsburgh, 1933. Reprint, Gloucester, Mass., 1958.

Olmsted, Frederick Law. *The Cotton Kingdom.* Edited by Lawrence Powell and Arthur M. Schlesinger, Sr. New York, 1983.

Ransom, Roger L. *Conflict and Compromise: The Political Economy of Slavery, Emancipation, and the American Civil War.* New York, 1989.

Stampp, Kenneth. *The Peculiar Institution: Slavery in the Antebellum South.* New York, 1956.

ROGER L. RANSOM

PORTER, JOHN L. (1813–1893), chief naval constructor. Remembered principally as codesigner and constructor of CSS *Virginia* (USS *Merrimack*), Porter conceived the majority of the gunboats and ironclad warships built in the Confederacy. Prominent among his designs are *Albemarle, Arkansas, Columbia, Richmond,* and *Tennessee.*

Son of a Portsmouth, Virginia, shipwright, Porter by 1846 had secured a civilian position with the U.S. Navy and was superintending the construction of *Allegheny* at Pittsburgh. He developed drawings of an armor-plated warship propelled by the unorthodox Hunter horizontal paddlewheel system. Although this plan was never accepted by the navy, it served as the basis for his later Civil War designs powered by more conventional screw and paddlewheel arrangements. Porter, appointed a U.S. naval constructor in 1859, was charged in 1860 with neglect of duty in the construction of USS *Seminole* but was acquitted.

On May 1, 1861, Porter resigned from the U.S. Navy and was appointed a naval constructor in the fledgling Confederate navy in June. That same month he, Lt. John M. Brooke, and Chief Engineer William P. Williamson were assigned the task of converting the burned-out remains of USS *Merrimack* into an armored warship, named CSS *Virginia.* After the fall of Norfolk he moved to Richmond where he supervised naval construction at Rocketts Navy Yard and served as an adviser to Navy Secretary Stephen R. Mallory. On January 7, 1864, he was formally appointed chief naval constructor, although he had been acting in that capacity for at least two years. In May 1864 he went to Wilmington, North Carolina, to expedite the construction of a twin-casemated ironclad intended for the defense of that port. He was paroled at Greensboro, North Carolina, April 28, 1865.

After the war Porter worked in several shipyards and an ironworks before becoming superintendent of the Norfolk County, Virginia, ferries in 1883. He died December 14, 1893, and is buried in Cedar Grove Cemetery, Portsmouth, Virginia.

BIBLIOGRAPHY

Baxter, James P. *Introduction of the Ironclad Warship.* Cambridge, Mass., 1933.

Porter, John W. H. *Record of Events in Norfolk County, Virginia, from April 19th, 1861, to May 10th, 1862.* Portsmouth, Va., 1892.

Still, William N. *Iron Afloat: The Story of the Confederate Armorclads.* 2d ed. Columbia, S.C., 1985.

Wells, Tom H. *The Confederate Navy: A Study in Organization.* University, Ala., 1971.

A. ROBERT HOLCOMBE, JR.

PORT GIBSON, MISSISSIPPI. Nestled along the south bank of Little Bayou Pierre, thirty-five miles south of Vicksburg, the town of Port Gibson witnessed the horrors of war on May 1, 1863, as opposing armies battled

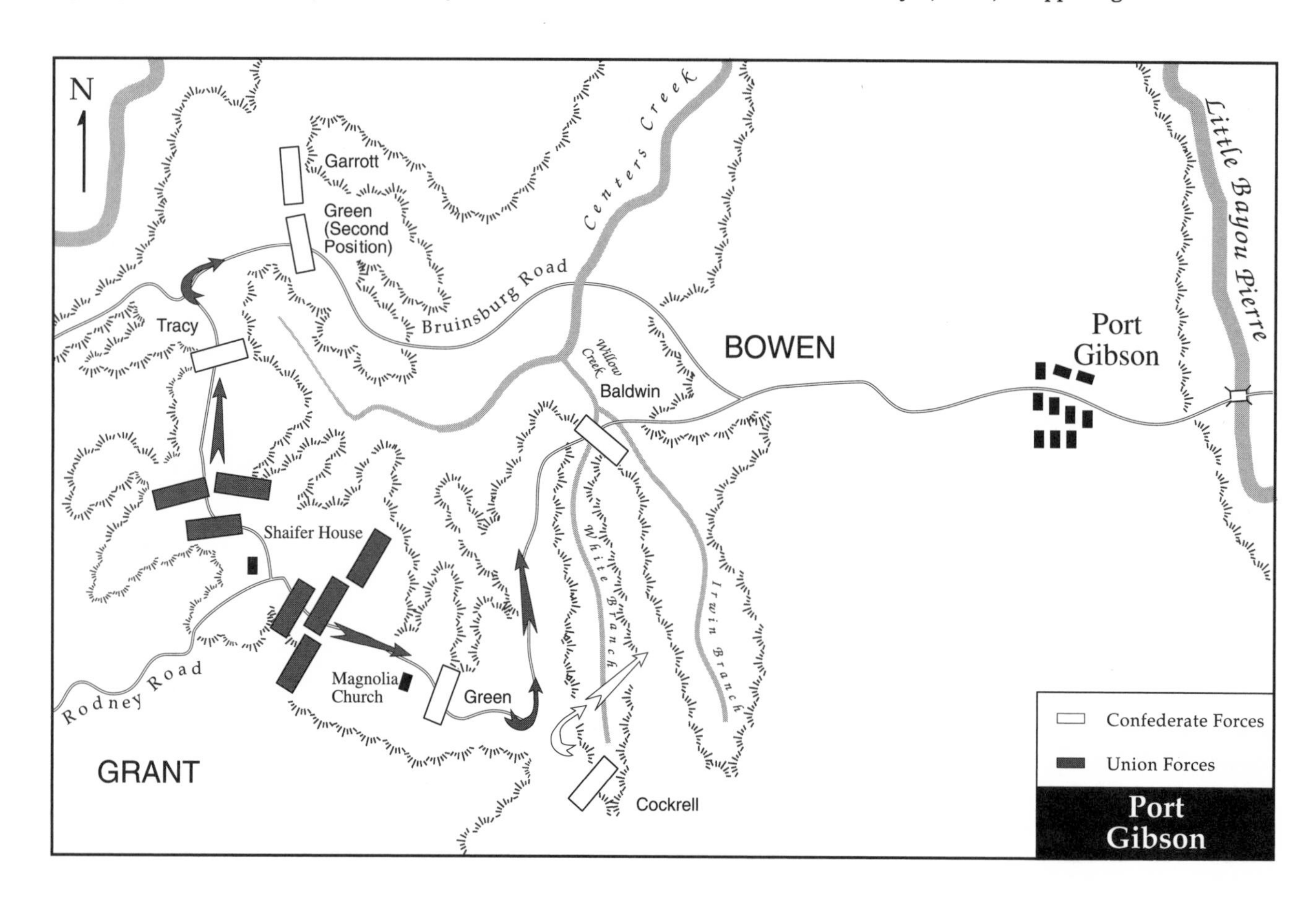

for control of the fortress city on the Mississippi River. At stake was the "Gibraltar of the Confederacy," Vicksburg, one of the last Confederate strongholds on the Mississippi River and the connecting link between the eastern and western parts of the Southern nation. Its defense was seen as vital.

The final campaign for Vicksburg began to unfold in the spring of 1863 as Maj. Gen. Ulysses S. Grant launched his Army of the Tennessee on a march down the west side of the Mississippi River from Milliken's Bend to Hard Times, Louisiana. It was Grant's intention to force a crossing of the river at Grand Gulf and move on "Fortress Vicksburg" from the south. The battle-tested division of Confederate Brig. Gen. John S. Bowen, however, was poised at Grand Gulf to meet such an invasion attempt.

When the combined Union land and naval force appeared opposite the Grand Gulf defenses on April 28, Bowen sent an urgent plea requesting "that every man and gun that can be spared from other points be sent here." Lt. Gen. John C. Pemberton immediately ordered two brigades, those of Brig. Gens. Edward Dorr Tracy and William Edwin Baldwin, dispatched from the Vicksburg defenses.

As the soldiers headed south from Vicksburg, the Union fleet bombarded the fortifications at Grand Gulf in an attempt to silence the Confederate guns and clear the way for a landing by Grant's troops. For five hours on April 29, Bowen's gunners stood at their posts and fired their guns, inflicting heavy damage on the fleet. Having successfully thwarted a landing at Grand Gulf, however, the Confederates could only watch helplessly as the enemy fleet passed their batteries and headed south toward a rendezvous with Grant.

Bowen moved quickly to redeploy his men as Grant's army stormed ashore at Bruinsburg on April 30. He moved two brigades into the woods west of Port Gibson and deployed Brig. Gen. Martin E. Green's brigade of Missourians and Arkansans astride the Rodney Road. Tracy's brigade assumed position athwart the Bruinsburg Road. The two wings were widely separated by the densely wooded valley of Centers Creek, but terrain favored the defenders.

Elements of the Union army pushed inland and took possession of the bluffs, thereby securing the landing area. By late afternoon, April 30, seventeen thousand men were ashore and the march inland began. Instead of taking the Bruinsburg Road, which was the direct road from the landing area to Port Gibson, Grant's columns swung into the Rodney Road and marched through the night. Shortly after midnight Green's outpost near the A. K. Shaifer house opened fire. A spirited skirmish ensued that lasted until 3:00 A.M. The Confederates, however, held their ground. For the next several hours an uneasy calm settled over the woods and scattered fields. Throughout the night the Federals gathered their forces in hand, and both sides prepared for the battle that was to come at sunrise.

Green watched at dawn as Union troops deployed in battle formation and moved in force along the Rodney Road toward Magnolia Church. One Union division was sent along a connecting plantation road toward the Bruinsburg Road and the Confederate right flank. With skirmishers well in advance, the Federals began a slow and deliberate advance around 5:30 A.M. On both fronts the Confederates contested the advance, and the battle began in earnest.

Most of the Union forces moved along the Rodney Road toward the Confederate left held by Green's brigade. Heavily outnumbered and hard-pressed, Green's men gave way shortly after 10:00 A.M., falling back a mile and a half. Here the infantrymen of Baldwin's and Col. Francis M. Cockrell's brigades, recent arrivals on the field, established a new line between the White and Irwin branches of Willow Creek, and reestablished the Confederate left flank. Exhausted and badly shaken, Green's brigade was ordered to re-form on the march and move to support the Confederate right along the Bruinsburg Road.

The morning hours witnessed Green's brigade driven from its position by the principal Federal attack. Ed Tracy's Alabama Brigade, astride the Bruinsburg Road, also experienced hard fighting. Tracy watched with anxiety as the Federal line crept toward his position. Sgt. Francis G. Obenchain of the Botetourt (Virginia) Artillery recalled that while speaking to the general, "a ball struck him on back of the neck passing through. He fell with great force on his face and in falling cried 'O Lord!' He was dead when I stooped to him."

Although Tracy was killed early in the action, his brigade managed to hold its tenuous line. It was clear, however, that unless the Confederates received heavy reinforcements they would lose the day. Bowen wired his superiors: "We have been engaged in a furious battle since daylight; losses very heavy—The men act nobly, but the odds are overpowering."

Early afternoon found the Alabamians, now under the command of Col. Isham Garrott, slowly giving ground. Green's weary soldiers arrived to bolster the line on the Bruinsburg Road. Even so, late in the afternoon, the Federals advanced all along the line in superior numbers. As Union pressure built, Cockrell's Missourians unleashed a counterattack near the Rodney Road, which began to roll up the blue line. The Sixth Missouri also counterattacked, hitting the Federals near the Bruinsburg Road. But all this was to no avail. On both fronts the Confederates were checked and driven back.

At 5:30 P.M., as the Confederates began to retire from the field, Pemberton notified the authorities in Richmond of the day's events. He implored them, "Large reenforcements should be sent me from other departments. Enemy's movement threatens Jackson, and, if successful, cuts off

Vicksburg and Port Hudson from the east." The inland campaign for Vicksburg had begun.

In the Battle of Port Gibson, the Southerners inflicted 131 killed, 719 wounded, and 25 missing on Grant's force of 23,000 men. Bowen's command suffered 60 killed, 340 wounded, and 387 missing out of 8,000 men engaged. In addition, four guns of the Botetourt Artillery were lost. The action at Port Gibson underscored Confederate inability to defend the line of the Mississippi River and to respond to amphibious operations. The defeat not only secured Grant's position on Mississippi soil but opened the road to Raymond, Jackson, Champion Hill, Big Black River Bridge, and, ultimately, Vicksburg.

BIBLIOGRAPHY

Bearss, Edwin C. *Grant Strikes a Fatal Blow.* Vol. 2 of *The Vicksburg Campaign.* Dayton, Ohio, 1986.

Johnson, Robert U., and C. C. Buel, eds. *Battles and Leaders of the Civil War.* 4 vols. New York, 1887–1888. Reprint, Secaucus, N.J., 1982.

TERRENCE J. WINSCHEL

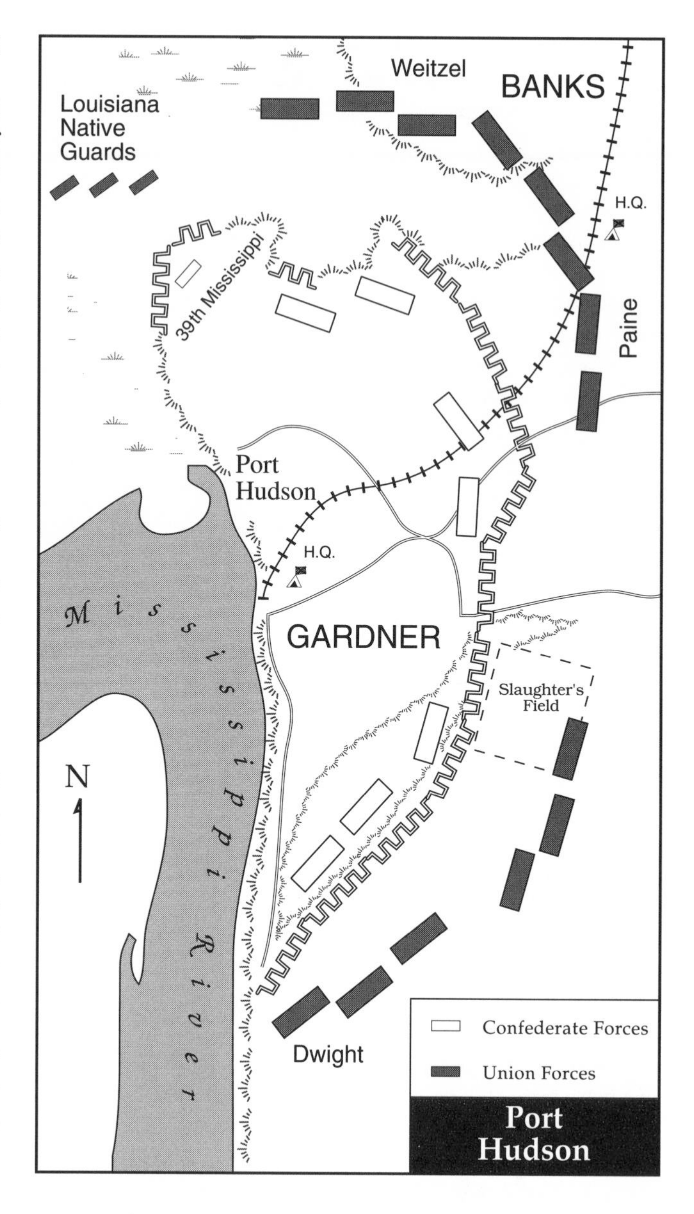

PORT HUDSON, LOUISIANA. Located 25 miles up the Mississippi River from Baton Rouge, Port Hudson was the site of the longest true siege in American military history. Some 7,500 Confederates resisted more than 40,000 Union soldiers for nearly two months. Confederate casualties included 750 killed and wounded, 250 dead of disease, and 6,500 captured. The Federals lost nearly 10,000, almost evenly divided between battle casualties and disease.

Control of the Mississippi River was a key objective of Union strategists at the outset of the Civil War. Aware of this, the Confederacy, in August 1862, had its forces under Maj. Gen. John C. Breckinridge begin erecting earthworks at Port Hudson. Within six months the bastion was as formidable as Vicksburg.

In March 1863 Union Rear Adm. David G. Farragut attempted to force the Confederates to evacuate Port Hudson by cutting off their provisions from the Trans-Mississippi. Seven Union vessels tried to steam past Port Hudson on March 14. But only two succeeded, and they proved insufficient to enforce an effective blockade of the Red River. Later that month, Union Maj. Gen. Nathaniel P. Banks advanced west of the Mississippi to achieve Farragut's objective by land. Although he severed Port Hudson's Trans-Mississippi supply line, the Confederate garrison refused to capitulate.

In mid-May Banks finally moved against the bastion. While three divisions came down the Red River to assail Port Hudson from the north, two others advanced from Baton Rouge and New Orleans to strike from the east and south. By May 22, 30,000 Union soldiers, assisted by Farragut's fleet, had isolated 7,500 Confederates behind 4½ miles of earthen fortifications.

On May 26 Banks issued orders for a simultaneous attack all along the Confederate perimeter the following morning. But the vagueness of the orders, uncooperative subordinates, and the terrain rendered a coordinated effort impossible. First assailed was the Confederate left wing, which guarded the northern approaches. Timely reinforcements from the Confederate center enabled the defenders to repulse several assaults. Except for sporadic sharpshooting and artillery fire, the fighting in this sector ended before Banks's remaining two divisions advanced against the Confederate center. This delay enabled the Confederates to virtually abandon their center and replace those departing from the center with men from the right. When the Federals finally advanced across Slaughter's Field toward the Confederate center, they were easily repulsed. Approximately 2,000 Union soldiers had been killed or wounded; Confederate casualties were less than 500. That evening, both sides were amazed that the Confederate lines remained unbreached.

Union casualties included 600 African Americans of the First and Third Louisiana Native Guards who had advanced across the flooded batture (the land between the river and the levee) against the extreme left of the Confederate line, where the Thirty-ninth Mississippi was deployed along the edge of a sixty-foot bluff and supported by several cannon. Wealthy, well-educated, free blacks from New Orleans composed a majority of the First Louisiana Native Guards, including the line officers. Former slaves commanded by white officers composed the Third Louisiana Native Guards, which had been organized in late 1862.

A free black from New Orleans, Capt. Andrew Cailloux, shouted his orders in both English and French until a shell struck him dead. A few of the assailants managed to reach the fortifications before they were killed. Although quickly repulsed, the black soldiers had demonstrated both their willingness and their ability to fight.

Unwilling to withdraw, Banks brought up additional troops and cannon and commenced siege operations. Finally, on June 13, he believed he could breach the fortifications. After terrorizing the Confederates with a one-hour artillery bombardment, Banks demanded that they surrender. Northern-born and Southern-wed Maj. Gen. Franklin Gardner declined. Banks resumed the bombardment and deployed for an assault the next day.

Brig. Gen. Halbert E. Paine's division then spearheaded the main assault against the Confederate center on June 14. Diversionary attacks were made against the extreme Confederate right by Brig. Gen. William Dwight's division and, just west of Paine, by the division of Brig. Gen. Godfrey Weitzel. Paine's assault, supported by Weitzel, began at 4:00 A.M., with Dwight contributing little assistance. The few Federals who managed to breach the fortifications quickly surrendered and by 10:00 A.M. the assault had failed. The Union had suffered 1,805 casualties; the Confederates less than 200.

Banks resumed siege warfare, devoting the remainder of June and early July to digging approach saps and advancing his artillery. Although reduced to eating rats and mules, the Confederates held out until Gardner learned of the surrender of Vicksburg. Without its upriver counterpart, Port Hudson lacked strategic significance. The Confederate garrison surrendered on July 9.

BIBLIOGRAPHY

Hewitt, Lawrence Lee. *Port Hudson, Confederate Bastion on the Mississippi.* Baton Rouge, La., 1987.

Wright, Howard G. *Port Hudson: Its History from an Interior Point of View, as Sketched from the Diary of an Officer, Howard G. Wright, 1863.* Baton Rouge, La., 1961.

LAWRENCE L. HEWITT

PORT REPUBLIC, VIRGINIA.

See Cross Keys and Port Republic, Virginia.

PORT ROYAL, SOUTH CAROLINA.

Located thirty miles north of Savannah, Georgia, Port Royal was the scene of a battle on November 7, 1861, between a Union flotilla and the Confederate forts guarding the harbor's entrance. The Union victory gave the Federals control of what was considered one of the finest natural harbors on the southern Atlantic seaboard.

The task force for this expedition, under the command of Flag Officer Samuel F. Du Pont, included seventeen warships, as well as transport and supply vessels, carrying 12,000 infantry and 600 marines. On October 31, the flotilla encountered gale force winds and rough water off Cape Hatteras, which threatened the less seaworthy vessels, sinking or disabling several. But as the weather cleared,

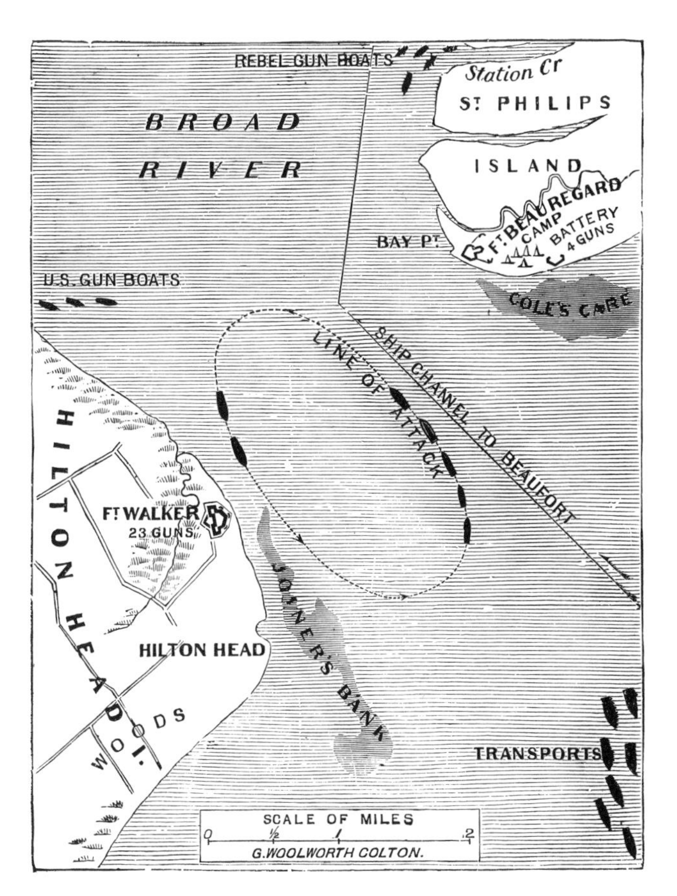

MAP OF THE BATTLE OF PORT ROYAL, NOVEMBER 7, 1861.

THE SOLDIER IN OUR CIVIL WAR

the fleet reassembled and continued toward Port Royal.

Upon his arrival off Hilton Head Island, Du Pont met with his commanders and laid out his plan for attacking the two forts confronting them: Fort Walker on Hilton Head and Fort Beauregard at Bay Point on Phillips Island. The Union warships were to enter the harbor in two lines, midway between the forts. As the vessels passed they could bring maximum firepower upon the Confederates. Then the ships would circle back, repeating this series of turns until they had silenced the forts' guns.

Du Pont had hoped to begin the operation on November 6, but heavy winds delayed the attack. By the time the winds subsided, the light was so poor that the lead ship, USS *Wabash,* ran aground. Although the crew freed it from the shoals, there was no longer enough light to operate effectively.

Early the next morning, the Federals finally launched their assault. About 9:30 A.M., the Confederates from the forts and three gunboats, under Flag Officer Josiah Tattnall, opened fire on the lead vessels. As the line of Union warships advanced, the Confederate gunboats withdrew, leaving the defense to the gunners in the forts. The ships in the main line passed the forts in good order and then headed back for the sea, completing the operation as planned. The Union fleet repeated the maneuver, the warships pouring their fire once again into the forts. Ironically, some of the most destructive fire came from a vessel skippered by Comdr. Percival Drayton, brother of the commander of the Confederate land forces, Brig. Gen. Thomas F. Drayton.

A little after 1:00 P.M., the Southerners in Fort Walker, with their ammunition running low and many of their artillery pieces dismounted or unserviceable, abandoned their positions. The Federals sent troops ashore to secure the earthwork. In the meantime, the Confederates in Fort Beauregard, hearing the cheers of the Union sailors instead of the guns of Fort Walker, determined that their companion fort had fallen and decided to retreat as well. The Federals had won the victory at a cost of eight killed and twenty-three wounded; the Southerners lost eleven killed, forty-eight wounded, and seven missing.

The loss of Port Royal and Hilton Head proved a severe blow to the defense of the Southern seaboard. The Federals obtained the valuable coaling and supply station they needed for the blockade and a base from which to menace other ports on the Confederacy's lower coastline.

Port Royal and the South Carolina Sea Islands also became famous as a laboratory for Reconstruction when fleeing white inhabitants abandoned their plantations and left behind some 10,000 slaves. The slaves and the Northern missionaries, teachers, military officers, government officials, and speculators that descended upon the region engaged in a vigorous debate over labor and land redistribution. The disagreement underscored the diversity of interests and the aspirations of the groups. Blacks demonstrated little concern for wages and cotton production for the marketplace, preferring instead to grow crops for themselves and to own their own plots of land.

BIBLIOGRAPHY

Johnson, Robert U., and C. C. Buel, eds. *Battles and Leaders of the Civil War.* 4 vols. New York, 1887–1888. Reprint, Secaucus, N.J., 1982.

Rose, Willie Lee. *Rehearsal for Reconstruction: The Port Royal Experiment.* Indianapolis, 1964. Reprint, New York, 1976.

U.S. Naval War Records Office. *Official Records of the Union and Confederate Navies in the War of the Rebellion.* Washington, D.C., 1894–1927. Ser. 1, vol. 12, pp. 262–292.

U.S. War Department. *War of the Rebellion: A Compilation of the Official Records of the Union and Confederate Armies.* Washington, D.C., 1880–1901. Ser. 1, vol. 6, pp. 3–30.

BRIAN S. WILLS

POSEY, CARNOT (1818–1863), brigadier general. An indication of the personal leadership displayed by Confederate generals is that nearly one-fifth of them were killed or mortally wounded. One such officer in the Army of Northern Virginia was Carnot Posey.

CARNOT POSEY. LIBRARY OF CONGRESS

Posey was born in Wilkinson County, Mississippi, on August 5, 1818, and studied law at the University of Virginia. He was a lawyer and planter in Mississippi in the antebellum period and also saw service during the Mexican War as a lieutenant in Jefferson Davis's First Mississippi Rifles. Posey organized a company when the Civil War began and soon became colonel of the Sixteenth Mississippi Infantry.

He fought at First Manassas and Ball's Bluff in 1861 and in June 1862 was wounded at Cross Keys, during the first Shenandoah Valley campaign. After commanding a brigade at Second Manassas and Sharpsburg, Posey was promoted to brigadier general on November 1, 1862, though his appointment was not permanent until January 1863. At Chancellorsville, his first battle as a brigadier, Posey's conduct was praised by his superiors. His Mississippians saw limited combat at Gettysburg. Posey was wounded in the left thigh on October 14, 1863, at Bristoe Station, a minor engagement, but one in which the Confederates suffered heavy losses. Though the wound was not thought to be a mortal one, infection set in and Posey died at Charlottesville, Virginia, on November 13, 1863. He is buried in the University of Virginia's cemetery.

BIBLIOGRAPHY

Compiled Military Service Records. Carnot Posey. Microcopy M331, Roll 200. Record Group 109. National Archives, Washington, D.C.

Hooker, Charles E. *Mississippi*. Vol. 7 of *Confederate Military History*. Edited by Clement A. Evans. Atlanta, 1899. Vol. 9 of extended ed. Wilmington, N.C., 1987.

J. Tracy Power

POST OFFICE DEPARTMENT. Created on February 21, 1861, the Post Office Department of the Confederacy became one of Jefferson Davis's triumphs. Davis benefited by the seventy-year-old in-place system constructed by the Federal government. Even after the firing on Fort Sumter, the U.S. Post Office continued to provide uninterrupted service in the South, and Southerners still attached U.S. stamps to their local, intra-Confederacy, and foreign letters. On June 1, 1861, the postal system ceased to be Federal and became Confederate.

Creation of the Post Office Department. Davis insisted that the new post office be self-sufficient, unlike the old system, which had never paid for itself since its establishment in 1789. In 1860, mail service in the eleven states that would form the Confederacy cost $2,897,530.77, with receipts of $938,105.34, leaving a deficit of nearly $2 million. In February 1861, the Confederate Congress passed an act calling for a balanced operation by March 1, 1863, and raised the postage rate from three cents to five cents on a half-ounce letter for the first five hundred miles, with double rates thereafter. One year later, when that increase failed to cover costs, Congress doubled the standard rate to ten cents to be effective on July 1, 1862. Newspaper and book rates were set by the number of papers and weight to be sent. Further, the congressional Committee for Postal Affairs called upon the still-to-be-named postmaster general to discontinue unprofitable routes, to eliminate duplicate routes, and to replace daily with triweekly service in most areas.

On March 6, 1861, Davis asked forty-three-year-old John H. Reagan to head the Confederate Post Office. Reagan, who had represented Texas in the U.S. Congress (1857–1861) and in the Provisional Government of the Confederacy, was Davis's third choice after fellow Mississippians Henry T. Ellet and William Wirt Adams declined the position. Reagan himself twice turned down the job before deciding it was his patriotic duty to accept. Reagan feared the enormity of the job and worried that in its frustration, the public would criticize the department and focus its contempt on the postmaster general.

The day he took the office, Reagan sent a friend to Washington, D.C., to persuade Southern sympathizers in the U.S. Post Office to abandon their jobs and accept new posts with the Confederacy. Reagan wrote a letter to each of these men and asked them to bring reports, route maps of the Southern states, forms, and other useful administrative materials when they relocated to the South. Within a fortnight, Reagan had an experienced staff and the requisite materials to organize his charge. The U.S. postmaster general's appointment book gave Reagan the name of every postmaster in the South. To house the department, he rented a three-story building on Bibb Street in downtown Montgomery and oversaw the training of

Postmaster General John H. Reagan.

Harper's Pictorial History of the Great Rebellion

new employees at an evening school in the building. By April 2, Reagan was advertising for company bids to provide stamps and postal supplies such as mail bags, forms, paper, and wax.

From the beginning, Reagan tried to keep costs low so that he could comply with the administrative and legislative mandates for a balanced budget. He expeditiously cut weight and volume by inducing Congress to eliminate the franking privilege—marking letters with official signatures of officeholders so that mail goes postage-free—except for postal business. He cut the number of employees by one-half and implemented the recommendations of Congress concerning superfluous, unprofitable routes. Of course, he did not have to deal with the costs of modern mail delivery to private houses or corner boxes because everyone deposited and inquired for mail at the central post office, which occupied either its own building or, more commonly, a corner of the local general store.

The biggest costs, comprising two-thirds of antebellum postal expenses, were transportation charges. On April 16, 1861, Reagan sent a circular letter to railroad executives and asked them to meet him in Montgomery on April 26 to discuss hauling rates. Thirty-five managers came to the meeting. Reagan appealed to their patriotism to help the new country through its emergency. He suggested one daily haul instead of two, and he got the executives to agree to cut their rates in half by promising that once the war was won, they could again ask for premium prices. Later, as the conflict dragged on, as inflation devoured profits, and as war damage brought increased costs, many felt less patriotic and pressed for higher rates.

Postal Service in the Confederacy. By April 29, Reagan had organized the Confederate Post Office and was ready to inaugurate service. After the government relocated to Richmond, the Post Office Department established itself in Goddin Hall near the capitol. On May 13, Reagan issued orders to Southern postmasters to continue to work under the U.S. government until June 1, when they would come under control of the Confederacy. He instructed his men to close accounts on May 31 and to forward moneys, stamps, and stamped envelopes to Washington. Lincoln's Postmaster General Montgomery Blair issued similar orders to cease U.S. service to the Confederacy on the same date.

On June 1, postmasters found themselves without Confederate stamps. In response to his advertisement for bids, Reagan gave the contract to supply stamps to the Richmond firm Hoyer & Ludwig Printers, the only Southern firm to bid among the many Northern bidders. Later, printers Archer & Daly of Richmond also secured a contract from Reagan. For the moment, however, no stamps were available. In this period of nearly twenty weeks, postmasters produced provisional issues or used handstamps to fill the void.

The first Confederate stamp, a green five-center with the likeness of Jefferson Davis, was sold in Richmond on October 16, 1861. One month later it was being used throughout the South. This and later Confederate issues were inconsistent in quality and had varying shades of color owing to shortages of pigments and paper. In addition, the supply of stamps never kept pace with demand and postmasters often reverted to emergency provisionals. In an attempt to make up for the shortages, Reagan ordered stamps and plates from the London firm of Thomas de la Rue & Company. The first order was dumped overboard from the blockade runner *Bermuda* just before its capture by USS *Mercidita.* A reorder for 12 million five-centers and new plates reached Richmond safely and cost $1,007.88 in gold—Confederate currency and bonds being unacceptable to foreign firms. These lithographed English stamps were of a fine quality unattainable by Confederate printers, who lacked the materials, tools, and expertise to turn out high-resolution stamps.

The general issues of Confederate stamps bore images of Jefferson Davis, Thomas Jefferson, Andrew Jackson, and John C. Calhoun. There is no evidence of counterfeit stamps being made or used during the war. Few people entrusted letters of value or envelopes containing money to the post office, for it provided no insurance. Instead, these letters were sent via the Southern Express Company, which provided faster and safer transportation.

Although Southerners praised Reagan's efforts, they were never satisfied with the efficiency of the postal service. Frequent delays, lost letters, and high postal rates brought much criticism of the department. In the year after First Manassas, citizens' complaints steadily increased, although after mid-1862, these declined dramatically. Newspaper editors, on the other hand, never halted their criticism of high rates and late service. Blaming false economy and lack of clerks to handle the great increase in mail, some editors claimed that two of every three letters were lost. Disenchantment over late or lost mails even led several congressmen to support a motion to abolish the post office and turn the mail service over to the Southern Express Company. This motion was defeated on February 5, 1862, as most people realized the difficulties imposed by the transition, the economy, and the war.

Certainly the war itself led to delays and poor service, as few trains met schedules and troop transport took priority over letter delivery. Union raids and armies increasingly pushed south, destroying trainloads of mail, setting fire to postal facilities, and tearing up tracks and roads, so that mail had to be rerouted. In addition, the depletion in the ranks of qualified postal workers, who dropped the mail to pick up guns, left inexperienced replacements to learn the business. Most editorial attacks on the postal service were in response to Reagan's elimination of wasteful offices and superfluous routes, and his bare-bones budget. Wartime service never matched antebellum delivery in the North or the South.

In late 1862, with expenses outnumbering receipts, Reagan asked for higher rates. The hike was deemed unnecessary because it failed to allow for evaluation of the July rate hike, which had doubled existing rates. And as the Confederacy ran short of coins, Southerners bought postage stamps for use as petty cash and thereby helped Reagan balance his budget. Congress augmented the income of the Post Office Department by establishing an express mail service for government correspondence at a rate of one dollar for a half-ounce letter traveling over five hundred miles. After December 8, 1863, the department met congressional demands; Reagan reported expenses for the fiscal year ending in June 1863 to be $2,662,804.67 and receipts, $3,337,853.01, for a profit of $675,048.34. The surplus continued to grow, and the department operated at an overall profit for the entire period of its existence.

Low postal worker salaries, low hauling charges, and high postage rates in a time of enormous inflation helped produce the profit that probably could not have been achieved in other than wartime. Certainly, Reagan mismanaged the department in that he did not use the profits to improve service. The express mail service payment for government letters was taken from the Treasury to pay the post office—thereby hiding the true costs on Reagan's balance sheet. Economy was valued over service at a time when war casualties and grief begged that service come first. But Congress had pushed for economy and Reagan followed its demands as well as he could.

Some politicians, however, felt that service should come first and proposed allowing soldiers to send and receive letters and newspapers free of postage. In various votes, these measures were defeated in the House or Senate, or vetoed by Davis as too costly. In a compromise, soldiers were permitted to send letters postage due to the recipient. Not until January 28, 1865, did Congress override a presidential veto and allow newspapers to be sent to the front postage-free.

Mail transport from outside the Confederacy was fraught with complications. With the Union navy blockading Southern ports, the Confederacy had difficulty receiving and shipping foreign mail. Blockade runners carried the shipments past the naval cordon to Cuba, Bermuda, Nassau, Canada, and Mexico where English and French vessels took on or off-loaded the cargo. Confederate stamps were not recognized by foreign countries—to accept its stamps would imply recognition of the Confederacy—so ship captains arranged to take the mail and have suitable postage affixed at the port of entry. Mail delivery with the United States was handled by private express companies, primarily through the Adams–Southern Express connections that ebbed and flowed in response to the changing fronts.

After Vicksburg fell to Ulysses S. Grant and the Confederacy was cut in two, Reagan had Congress establish a Trans-Mississippi office at Marshall, Texas, under the direction of James H. Starr, former secretary of the treasury for the state of Texas. Reagan and Starr sent mail east and west in rowboats that crossed the Mississippi at night to avoid Federal patrols.

On August 20, 1863, four months after local bread riots, Richmond postal employees went on strike for higher wages. They made as little as sixty dollars a month and inflation had advanced prices over 500 percent. The *Richmond Examiner* railed against the workers and said they should be forced back to work or conscripted into the army. Reagan settled the matter by admitting that the grievances were real. After he promised to support their demand for better salaries, the employees returned to work on August 23. When the department showed a profit in 1863, Congress raised salaries for postal employees.

Reagan's efforts to deliver the mail brought him into conflict with other cabinet officers. A three-month squabble with Secretary of the Treasury Christopher G. Memminger was the most acrimonious. Reagan needed gold coin to pay English suppliers, but Memminger insisted that he could release only Confederate scrip. Reagan argued that his department had put at least fifty thousand in specie into the Treasury and that it must have coin to maintain routes. Davis finally let the attorney general settle the dispute in Reagan's favor.

Reagan also had a four-year struggle with the secretary of war over the military seizure of trains, the takeover of post office property, and the drafting of postal employees. Congress did exempt postal workers from military service, but after passage of the 1862 Conscription Act, only those employees nominated by the president and confirmed by the Senate were exempt. Davis supported Reagan's demands for high-quality personnel, and Congress extended the postal exemptions, but with many exceptions. After Secretary of War James A. Seddon accused Reagan of accepting low bids from those who could not give good service but simply wanted exemptions, Reagan countered that he often refused contracts if he believed the bid was only an effort to avoid conscription. Reagan insisted that the War Department granted as many exemptions to able-bodied men as did his department, which had less than five hundred men so exempted. Furthermore, he pointed out, mail was important to morale and must have strong men to deliver it. In 1864, Robert E. Lee, looking for all available men, complained that exemption of postal employees helped to drain his army. As the Confederacy crumbled, Reagan dropped the controversy and did the best he could with an increasingly limited staff.

Overall, Davis trusted Reagan implicitly and did not interfere with his programs. In return he got a devoted friend who believed strongly in Davis's administration of civilian and military policies. Along with Secretary of the Navy Stephen R. Mallory, Reagan was one of only two cabinet members to serve for the full war. He was with the president when Davis was taken prisoner on May 10, 1865, near Irwinville, Georgia. Reagan had been stable and sensible in his counsel, and he made the post office one of the major successes of the Confederate nation.

[*See also* Newspapers; Reagan, John H.; Southern Express Company; Stamps.]

BIBLIOGRAPHY

Crown, Francis J., Jr., ed. *Confederate Postal History.* Lawrence, Mass., 1976.

Deitz, August. *The Postal Service of the Confederate States of America.* Richmond, Va., 1929.

Garrison, L. R. "Administrative Problems of the Confederate Post Office Department." *Southwestern Historical Quarterly* 19 (1915–1916): 111–142, 232–251.

Patrick, Rembert. *Jefferson Davis and His Cabinet.* Baton Rouge, La., 1944.

Post Office Department of the Confederate States of America. Record of Letters and Other Communications from March 7, 1861, to October 12, 1863, and Reports of the Postmaster General. Manuscripts Division, Library of Congress, Washington, D.C.

Procter, Ben H. *Not without Honor: The Life of John H. Reagan.* Austin, Tex., 1962.

Reagan, John H. "An Account of the Organization and Operations of the Post Office Department of the Confederate States of America, 1861–1865." *Publications of the Southern Historical Association* 6 (1902): 314–327.

Reagan, John H. *Memoirs: With Special Reference to Secession and the Civil War.* New York, 1906.

RUSSELL DUNCAN

POVERTY. Poverty became a serious problem in the Confederacy and ultimately deprived the struggling Southern nation of the active allegiance of many individuals. Though initially unexpected, poverty was so widespread by 1862 that thousands of private persons and officials of state and local government labored to alleviate it. Eventually even the Confederate government became involved in relief efforts. Yet the scope of the problem was so great that it overwhelmed relief activities. Poverty exacerbated class resentments, and hunger caused many Southerners to put the welfare of their families above loyalty to the cause.

A variety of factors contributed to the poverty that descended on the Confederacy. The South had always depended on the North or foreign suppliers for manufactured goods. As the war and blockade disrupted trade, shortages developed in diverse commodities such as iron rails and sewing needles, nails and scythe blades, glass and medicines, cloth and coffee. Salt, an essential preservative, became scarce and remained so, despite large-scale Confederate efforts to acquire it.

Shortages grew worse as a result of hoarding. Merchants and panicky citizens often bought large quantities of potentially scarce items. The *Richmond Enquirer* reported that one man purchased seven hundred barrels of flour, and another planter carted in wagon loads of supplies until his "lawn and paths looked like a wharf covered with a ship's loads." Early in the war speculators hoarded salt, bacon, and leather, and six men gained control of the Confederacy's two nail factories. Newspapers and citizens hotly denounced known instances of speculation and extortion, but deficiencies in the Southern transportation network also hampered distribution of those commodities that were available. As a result, Confederates had to develop an ersatz economy, employing their ingenuity to substitute for many items.

Most Southerners assumed that food would not be a problem for their agricultural nation. Why, then, were shortages of food the primary cause of poverty and suffering? Some food rotted in depots, never reaching soldiers or urban markets. Civilians also lost food to the government through policies such as the tax-in-kind and impressment. Secretary of War James A. Seddon called impressment "a harsh, unequal, and odious mode of supply," yet the War Department depended upon it to supply the armies. Impressment aroused intense anger among the people, as did unauthorized foraging by soldiers, especially troops of cavalry. The *Richmond Enquirer* reported in August 1862 that people were saying, "*The Yankees cannot do us any more harm than our own soldiers have done.*" Drought and crop failures also affected crops in some sections of the Confederacy. But the greatest cause of food shortages was also the most general: the presence in the army of hundreds of thousands of yeoman farmers.

Slave owners could keep their unfree labor force at work while they fought, but non-slave-owning soldiers had to rely on their wives and children or other relatives to cultivate the fields. For many families this burden proved too great, especially as the war dragged on. In a typical plea to the War Department, a Georgia woman wrote, "I can't manage a farm well enough to make a surporte," and an elderly man in Virginia said of his son, "if you dount send him home I am bound to louse my crop and cum to suffer." Zebulon Vance, governor of North Carolina, informed President Jefferson Davis in 1863 that conscription had carried away "a large class whose labor was, I fear, absolutely necessary to the existence of the women and children left behind." Similarly, Governor Milledge L. Bonham of South Carolina opposed a call-up of troops in 1864 on the grounds that it would cause "great suffering next year, and possible starvation." The absence of key artisans, such as blacksmiths who could repair farming tools, aggravated the labor shortage, and the files of the War Department contain hundreds of letters appealing for the detail or exemption of blacksmiths and other artisans.

By the fall of 1862 alarming cries of hunger were being heard in the South. "Want and starvation are staring thousands in the face," declared the *Atlanta Daily Intelligencer.* "What shall we do for something to eat?" asked a paper in the hill country of Georgia in 1863. Tens, even hundreds of thousands of yeoman families, who had always prided themselves on their independence, fell into poverty and suffering. The dimensions of the problem are indicated by the governor of Alabama's admission at the end of the war that more than one-quarter of the white citizens in his state were on relief. A study of surviving records from several counties in North Carolina found that from one-fifth to two-fifths of the white population depended on government relief efforts for cornmeal and pork.

The South's response to this unprecedented social problem was significant but ultimately inadequate. In the Confederacy's straitened circumstances, not enough food, clothing, and other necessary items were available to serve the armies and the civilian population. The resulting poverty had significant effects. An anonymous Virginian wrote to the War Department in 1863 and asked a critical question: "What man is there that would stay in the armey and no that his family is sufring at home?" Later that year W. S. Keen, a provost marshal in Allegheny County, Virginia, answered the question in a letter to the secretary of war. "When our brave and true men, shall hear that their wives and little ones are actually suffering for bread," he warned, "they will naturally become restless and dissatisfied, and mutiny in our army will result, as naturally and as certainly as gravitation."

Provost Marshall Keen's prediction proved to be correct, as poverty stimulated desertion and caused many frustrated and suffering people to withdraw their cooperation or their allegiance from the government. Thus the problem of poverty was a crucial internal problem for the Confederacy.

[*See also* Bread Riots; Class Conflict; Conscription; Desertion; Extortion; Free Markets; Impressment; Inflation; Labor; Morale; Poor Relief; Salt; Speculation; State Socialism; Substitutes; Tax-in-Kind; Transportation.]

BIBLIOGRAPHY

Escott, Paul D. *After Secession: The Failure of Confederate Nationalism.* Baton Rouge, La., 1978.

Escott, Paul D. " 'The Cry of the Sufferers': The Problem of Welfare in the Confederacy." *Civil War History* 23, no. 3 (September 1977): 228–240.

Escott, Paul D. "Poverty and Governmental Aid for the Poor in Confederate North Carolina." *North Carolina Historical Review* 61, no. 4 (October 1984): 462–480.

Massey, Mary Elizabeth. *Ersatz in the Confederacy.* Columbia, S.C., 1952.

Ringold, May Spencer. *The Role of the State Legislatures in the Confederacy.* Athens, Ga., 1966.

Thomas, Emory M. *The Confederate State of Richmond: A Biography of the Capital.* Austin, Tex., 1971.

PAUL D. ESCOTT

POWDER WORKS. To supply gunpowder to their growing armies and coastal defenses, both the Confederate and state governments contracted in the war's first months with small, private powder mills in Tennessee, Virginia, the Carolinas, and Louisiana.

But Chief of Ordnance Col. Josiah Gorgas saw that a

Powder Works

Location	Name or Proprietor	Dates of Operation	Capacity
New Orleans (barracks)	City of New Orleans	Sept. '61–Apr. '62	3,000 lbs./day (projected) 1,500 lbs./day (reported)
Gretna, La. (marine hospital)	Private (unknown)	Dec. '61 (destroyed by explosion)	1,500 lbs./day (reported)
New Orleans (moved from Handsboro, Miss.)	Private (unknown)	Jan. '62–Apr. '62	1,200–1,600 lbs./day (reported)
Manchester, Tenn.	Whitman	Oct. '61–Feb. '62	1,500 lbs./day (reported)
Nashville, Tenn.	Sycamore Mill	?–Feb. '62	500 lbs./day (reported)
Raleigh, N.C.	Waterhouse & Bowes	Feb. '62–?	Unknown
Pendleton, S.C.	Bowen & Co.	Unknown	150 lbs./day (projected)
Walhalla, S.C.	J. M. Ostendorff	Unknown	150 lbs./day (projected)
Lewisburg, Va.	Gen. Davis	Unknown	Unknown
Augusta, Ga.	Augusta Powder Works	Apr. '62–Apr. '65	2,750,000 lbs. in three yrs. (reported)
Columbia, S.C.	Navy Powder Works	'63–Mar. '65	20,000 lbs./month (projected)

large, permanent national gunpowder work would be required. He assigned Maj. George W. Rains to select a site and design, build, and manage the work. Rains proved an excellent choice. A West Point graduate, he had construction and manufacturing experience, expertise in chemistry, and exceptional management ability.

Rains chose Augusta, Georgia, as his factory location, impressed with its combination of temperate climate, good water and rail transportation, and security from attack. Along a two-mile stretch of the Augusta canal he designed and built a world-class gunpowder factory. His complex of brick, granite, glass, and wood structures was architecturally attractive and designed for efficiency, quality, and volume in production. The array of buildings (situated on both sides of the canal) included a laboratory, charcoal kiln, preparation facilities, incorporating mills, and drying and granulating houses and magazines, as well as offices, blacksmith and carpentry shops, repair facilities, forges, and a cannon range for testing grades of powder.

Production began with raw materials: potassium nitrate, sulphur, and charcoal, all purified to Rains's exacting quality standards. These were ground and sized, then steamed for safety and mixed in massive rolling mills. The incorporating mills, each with two five-ton rollers running in circular iron beds, were built by foundries in Atlanta, Chattanooga, and Richmond. They were housed in a dozen bays, each with three massive brick walls, light roofs, and a fourth wall of wood and glass, designed to direct accidental blasts out and up with as little peripheral damage as possible. A large steam engine turned a subterranean power shaft that ran the length of the factory grounds, providing most of the motive power to the complex.

The mill first ran on April 10, 1862, production starting in doorless, windowless—even roofless—shells of buildings still under construction. Production continued uninterrupted until April 18, 1865. In those three years the plant, usually running twenty-four hours a day, manufactured 2,750,000 pounds of top-quality gunpowder. While prepared ammunition might sometimes run short in the front lines, at no time after April 1862 did the Confederate arsenals suffer a shortage of gunpowder.

In 1863 the Confederate navy opened its own gunpowder mill in Columbia, South Carolina, under a civilian manager, P. Baudery Garésche. Similar in operation to Rains's work, but much smaller, the mill had the capacity to produce 20,000 pounds per month. It ran until the fall of Columbia in March 1865.

[*See also* Niter and Mining Bureau; Saltpeter.]

BIBLIOGRAPHY

Goff, Richard D. *Confederate Supply.* Durham, N.C., 1969.

Melton, Maurice. " 'A Grand Assemblage': George W. Rains and the Augusta Powder Works." *Civil War Times Illustrated* 11 (1973): 28–37.

Milgram, Joseph P., and Norman P. Gentieu. *George Washington Rains: Gunpowdermaker to the Confederacy.* Philadelphia, 1961.

Rains, George W. *History of the Confederate Powder Works.* Augusta, Ga., 1882.

Vandiver, Frank E. *Ploughshares into Swords: Josiah Gorgas and Confederate Ordnance.* Austin, Tex., 1952.

MAURICE K. MELTON

PRAIRIE GROVE, ARKANSAS. Confederate Maj. Gen. Thomas C. Hindman, hoping to block a Union invasion of northwestern Arkansas, attacked a Federal army under Brig. Gen. Francis J. Herron at Prairie Grove, Washington County, on December 7, 1862. Before the Southerners could gain the victory, however, Herron was reinforced by Brig. Gen. James G. Blunt. The fighting lasted all day, but when night came the Confederates withdrew from the field leaving the region under Union control.

Hindman, in command of the First Corps, Army of the Trans-Mississippi, wanted to stop the Union advance into the state. In mid-November Blunt, with the First Division, Army of the Frontier, comprising around 5,000 Union troops, had moved toward Fayetteville while Herron had taken the rest of the army to Springfield, Missouri. On November 28, a small Confederate cavalry force under Brig. Gen. John S. Marmaduke engaged in a battle with Blunt at Cane Hill about thirty-five miles northeast of Van Buren, but being outnumbered, Marmaduke was forced to retire. Nevertheless, Hindman, with around 9,000 infantry and 2,300 cavalry, hoped to destroy Blunt before he was reinforced.

On December 3, as the Confederates left Van Buren to attack Blunt, Herron received orders to march the rest of the Army of the Frontier to Arkansas. Hindman planned to attack Blunt on December 7, unaware that Herron was on his way from Missouri with around 4,000 infantry and 2,000 cavalry. When Hindman learned that Herron was approaching, he knew his original strategy must be changed; if the two Union armies united, their artillery strength would be superior to his. In a hastily reworked plan based on speed and surprise, Hindman decided to move between the two, locate and attack Herron first, and then turn and defeat Blunt.

When the fighting began on December 7 it did not take Blunt long to realize he had been deceived, and the feint in his front was a ruse. In the meantime the main Confederate force had found Herron; although the Federals had just completed a forced march of about a hundred miles, Hindman failed to use this to his advantage. Rather than attacking the tired troops as planned, Hindman's infantry took up a defensive position along the Illinois River near Prairie Grove and waited for Herron to attack. The battle began around 9:30 in the morning and lasted until 7:00 P.M. with the armies alternately advancing and retreating along

Prairie Grove valley. Although Blunt reinforced Herron early in the afternoon, neither side was able to gain control of the field before the fighting ended at dusk. But the Confederate wagons were far to the rear, and lacking sufficient food and ammunition to renew the fighting the next day, Hindman quietly withdrew during the night.

The combined Federal commands sustained 174 men killed, 813 wounded, and 263 captured or missing out of a total engaged of around 8,000; about 3,000 cavalry did not participate. Hindman, who claimed less than 10,000 effectives, reported 164 killed, 817 wounded, and 336 missing. Although the battle was a tactical draw, it was a strategic defeat for the Confederates. With demoralized Southerners deserting, Hindman's army began to evaporate. On December 28, with scarcely 4,000 men left, Hindman was forced out of Van Buren and on to Little Rock, abandoning northwestern Arkansas to the Union and setting the stage for Union domination of the state.

BIBLIOGRAPHY

Edwards, John N. *Shelby and His Men: Or the War in the West.* Cincinnati, Ohio, 1867.

Hartsell, Henry F. "Battle of Prairie Grove, Arkansas, December 7, 1862." In *Civil War Battles in the West.* Edited by LeRoy H. Fischer. Manhattan, Kans., 1981.

Monaghan, Jay. *Civil War on the Western Border, 1854–1865.* Boston, 1955.

Oates, Stephen B. *Confederate Cavalry West of the River.* Austin, Tex., 1961.

Oates, Stephen B. "The Prairie Grove Campaign, 1862." *Arkansas Historical Quarterly* 19 (1960): 119–141.

Anne J. Bailey

PRESBYTERIAN CHURCH. Fifty-three ministers and thirty-eight ruling elders met in Augusta, Georgia, on December 4, 1861, to organize the new Presbyterian Church in the Confederate States of America. But in some respects, Southern Presbyterians had already broken with their Northern brethren in 1837 in a theological schism exacerbated by the slavery issue. The breach of 1861 simply stiffened Southern Presbyterians in their conviction that the church was a "pure theocracy" in which "the mediator is King and all power under Him is simply ministerial."

Yet the commissioners who organized the new church were profoundly disturbed by slavery and determined to use their allegiance to the Confederacy as a lever to nudge the region toward radical reform of slavery along Christian utopian lines. "If this government is His Ordinance, and the people His instruments," the commissioners stated, "they must see to it that they serve him with no unwashed or undefiled hands," a blunt admonition that the conversion, religious instruction, and loving nurturing of slaves had to take precedence over laboring in the masters' fields. By infusing the slave-master relationship with love and piety, Presbyterian proslavery theorists had become convinced by the 1850s that Christianity could "eat the heart out of slavery even as slavery continues."

Southern Presbyterian clergymen were, to be sure, fierce opponents of abolitionism because Northern antislavery zealots disrespected the sovereignty of God. "Slavery," Woodrow Wilson's father, Thomas Ruggles Wilson, told his Augusta, Georgia, parishioners in 1861, "is embedded in the very heart of the moral law itself, a law which constitutes . . . the very *constitution* of that royal kingdom whose regulations begin and end in the infinite holiness of Jehovah." "A gracious Providence," the new denomination declared, "brought [slaves] to our shores, and redeemed [them] from the bondage of barbarism and sin."

The Civil War tested this theological and ideological consensus. An effort in the first General Assembly to unite the Presbyterian Church in the Confederate States (which constituted the bulk of the Old School branch from the 1837 schism) with New School United Synod in Virginia and Tennessee foundered when James Henley Thornwell, the preeminent Old School theologian, warned that the New School clergy were still tainted with heretical views about the capacity of sinners to participate in their own redemption. An overture to the Associate Reformed Presbyterians, a Scottish traditionalist sect, offering to include the entire Psalter in the new Presbyterian hymnbook, elicited no response. Strenuous effort to continue missionary work overseas and in Indian Territory collapsed during the war, and a campaign to intensify evangelizing of slaves—including condemnation of cruelty by masters and of denial of legal protection for slaves—similarly atrophied in the heat of anti-Northern and proslavery sentiment. Isolated instances of Unionist sentiment among clergymen brought swift removal from pulpits and presbyteries.

While Methodist and Baptist chaplains were in the forefront of revivalism in the Confederate army, Presbyterians viewed the souls of soldiers with melancholy pessimism. Thomas J. ("Stonewall") Jackson, a Presbyterian, who incorporated chaplains into the structure of his forces more systematically than any other Southern commander, thought of himself as an instrument of God's sovereign Providence.

BIBLIOGRAPHY

Farmer, James O. "Southern Presbyterians and Southern Nationalism: A Study in Ambivalence." *Georgia Historical Quarterly* 75 (1991): 275–294.

Thompson, Ernest Trice. *Presbyterians in the South, Volume Two: 1861–1890.* Richmond, Va., 1973.

Robert M. Calhoon

PRESIDENCY. The office of the chief executive officer of the Confederacy derived its powers from the Provisional and Permanent Constitutions. Both documents prescribed an office almost exactly like the presidency of the United States, though they gave the Confederate president the item veto in appropriation bills. The Permanent Constitution gave him direct removal power over department heads and diplomats.

Since the Confederacy was at war, the powers of the presidency were used mainly to sustain military activities. President Jefferson Davis noted impending martial problems in his inaugural address, and in shaping his administration turned his attention first toward creating armies and a navy. Civil functions were not neglected, but were harnessed finally to sustaining a besieged nation.

As "commander-in-chief of the army and navy . . . and of the militia or the several States, when called into the actual service of the Confederate States," Davis found his responsibilities growing with the conflict. His concerns extended from raising and supporting armies and navies to providing supplies, providing commanders for soldiers and sailors, commissioning all Confederate officers, and devising a national strategy for victory. Fortunately for the Confederacy, the president had considerable military experience and knew how to begin.

He picked a cabinet with care, and it was part of the presidency. For war secretary Davis selected Alabamian Leroy P. Walker, whose apparent incapacity led to a long line of succeeding secretaries—but Davis really served as his own war minister. For secretary of the navy Davis picked Floridian Stephen R. Mallory and left most sea operations in his highly capable hands. Christopher G. Memminger took the treasury portfolio.

Judah P. Benjamin, regarded as the brilliant man of the cabinet, had an uncanny ability to get along with an increasingly besieged president. Benjamin cruised through several departments—Justice, War, finally State—and his management of secondary diplomacy (blockade running, foreign purchasing, diplomatic negotiations for increased belligerency) was sound. The Treasury Department, late in the war, came under George A. Trenholm, a South Carolina banker possessed of toughness and acumen.

While organizing military departments, the president considered strategy in a state rights context: governors were jealous of state territory and authority, and any national strategy had to be shaped around that reality. Davis adopted the "offensive-defensive" as the Confederacy's war plan. Weaker Southern forces would stand on the defensive when necessary to husband resources; when the right chance came, they would concentrate against smaller or isolated enemy forces. A look at Confederate operations from First Manassas to the end of the war will show the president's adherence to his strategy. There were those who argued for a more defensive posture—Braxton Bragg, Joseph E. Johnston, and P. G. T. Beauregard, for instance. And clearly the idea of standing on the defensive and receiving attack had an important precedent in American revolutionary history. But it is doubtful that such a strategy would have been better, given the growing strength of Union forces. Davis's plan probably best fitted the Southern situation.

Davis recognized that power came to his office from the Constitution, and he used the supreme law of the land to centralize war government—to secure Confederate assumption of all military operations (taking them out of state hands), to create a strong national army (the best prop for federal authority over the states), and to frame a national tax structure to underwrite the war.

Taxation proved the most difficult problem for the presidency. Secretary Memminger had hard-money penchants in a soft-money environment. And a laissez-faire Congress could never quite face up to the harsh decisions war demanded. Land, cotton, and slaves were the Confederacy's wealth resources, and the president urged their taxation. Congress dodged that necessity for a time with bond issues, loans, and some fairly innovative measures such as the tax-in-kind, the produce loan, and other levies. Finally a tough value-added tax came, along with an income tax, an excise tax, and taxes on virtually everything. But it was too late; expenses ran away with the currency. By early 1864 the Treasury Department did not know how many notes were circulating.

As Confederate money lost value, so did the foreign credibility of the cause. The president sponsored the important loan through Emile Erlanger and Co. in 1863 for $15 million. Discounted almost from the outset, the loan actually produced somewhere between $6 million and $10 million. More would have been lent by the Erlangers, but a conscientious, if whimsical, Congress did not want to encumber future generations.

A recent scholar, Douglas Ball, in *Financial Failure and Confederate Defeat* (1991), echoes a lingering theme in showing that financial chaos might have been avoided and lays the blame for failing to come to a modern financial system on the executive branch. Davis and Memminger, he says, had every reason to know better. That is probably true, but blame needs softening with sympathy. These men were caught up in the daily rigors of war; they were pushing an agrarian system into modern times and trying to shove a reluctant Congress the same way. That anything was done to sustain the currency is a triumph for the presidency and its branches.

Davis embodied the presidency. He is flayed often for aloofness, for petty defense of incompetent friends—General Bragg, Commissary Gen. Lucius B. Northrop, Gen. John Pemberton—and, like most presidents, he did rely on cronies. But he deserves much credit for changing himself from a private to something of a public man. Though he thought politicking distasteful, and surely unnecessary in a warring nation, he took several "swings around the Confederacy" to speak about the war, to sustain public morale. He lacked Abraham Lincoln's language in persuasion, but he had a zealot's fiery eloquence at times when he talked of the cause he tried to win.

War powers expanded from the moment the war began. The role of the commander in chief enlarged by necessity as Davis pushed military organization, recruiting, strategy, and logistics. Davis did not, despite later accusations, overcommand his forces. Some field commanders received special direction if the chief executive thought they needed it, but trusted ones like Lee, Albert Sidney Johnston, Bragg, and E. Kirby Smith enjoyed wide discretionary powers. Presidential attention went to strategical and logistical support of major campaigns (Albert Sidney Johnston's operations in Tennessee in 1862, for instance), but tactics were left to battle commanders.

Confederate affairs increasingly involved the presidency in state affairs. State rights supporters frayed Confederate nationalism and President Davis conducted wide correspondence with various governors in an effort to prop up their commitment to the war. Governors Joseph E. Brown of Georgia and Zebulon Vance of North Carolina worked almost openly against the cause, and Davis fought them with letters, speeches, and proclamations. State rights governors hampered a national strategy by forcing the president to fragment concentration of forces in defense of particular states. As the executive branch grew in power, it confronted these governors with increasing zeal but uneven results. Important legislation aimed at increasing national power (conscription, impressment, partial commandeering of space on blockade runners, heavy taxation) received presidential support before a fractious and reluctant congress.

Acutely aware of the need for centralized national power, the president fought for a strong war program. He expanded war powers by giving authority to the military departments and supported patriotic governors with such aid as a beleaguered executive could give. Congress followed the executive lead in much war legislation. But it balked at suspending habeas corpus by fiat and grudgingly moved toward a federalism that seemed too much like Abraham Lincoln's Union.

The presidency intruded into almost every phase of Confederate life as regulations abounded to manage the draft, impressment, taxation, manufacturing, transportation, even state legislative matters affecting the war. A presidential hand increasingly touched logistics. Influenced by such able logisticians as Gen. Josiah Gorgas, the chief of ordnance, the president worked to improve roads and railroads and to break or elude the blockade.

That the war lasted for four years is largely the result of Davis's expansion of the powers of his office. Presidential zeal transformed a fragmented feudalism into a small, modern martial nation. Because that happened, the Confederate executive is worth examining as an important facet of the American presidency.

[*See also* Cabinet; Davis, Jefferson.]

BIBLIOGRAPHY

Commager, Henry Steele, ed. *Documents of American History.* 5th ed. New York, 1949.

Coulter, E. Merton. *The Confederate States of America, 1861–1865.* A History of the South, vol. 7. Baton Rouge, La., 1950.

Davis, William C. *Jefferson Davis: The Man and His Hour.* New York, 1991.

Journal of the Congress of the Confederate States of America, 1861–1865. 7 vols. Washington, D.C., 1904–1905.

Matthews, James M., ed. *Statutes at Large of the Provisional Government of the Confederate States of America.* Richmond, Va., 1864.

Patrick, Rembert W. *Jefferson Davis and His Cabinet.* Baton Rouge, La., 1944.

Yearns, Wilfred B. *The Confederate Congress.* Athens, Ga., 1960.

Frank E. Vandiver

PRESTON, JOHN SMITH (1809–1881), superintendent of the Bureau of Conscription and brigadier general. As a lawyer in Abingdon, Virginia, the owner of a sugar plantation in Louisiana, and later a member of the South Carolina State Senate, Preston was an early advocate of state rights. In 1860 he served as the chairman of the South Carolina delegation to the Democratic convention in Charleston, and after South Carolina seceded, he acted as a commissioner to Virginia to encourage that state to secede also.

Preston volunteered for Confederate service in 1861. He became an aide to P. G. T. Beauregard during the Fort Sumter crisis and the fighting at First Manassas, where he earned recognition for his efficiency. He continued to receive promotions and in 1862 transferred to Columbia to take command of Confederate prison camps in the city.

In July 1863 Confederate Secretary of War James A. Seddon chose Preston to serve in the controversial position of superintendent of the Bureau of Conscription in Richmond, where he eventually earned a promotion to brigadier general. As superintendent of conscription, he faced criticism and hostility from commanders in the field. Preston envisioned the Conscription Bureau as a means of coordinating military and industrial efforts. But military personnel felt excluded from the bureau's decision-making process and fought with him over the assignment and placement of troops. Ultimately, the Confederacy closed the Conscription Bureau in March 1865.

In the years following the war, Preston remained vehemently unreconstructed. He became infamous for his speaking tours in which he continued to defend secession.

BIBLIOGRAPHY

Brooks, Robert Preston. *Conscription in the Confederate States of America, 1862–1865.* Cambridge, Mass., 1917.

Evans, Clement A., ed. *Confederate Military History.* 12 vols. Atlanta, 1899. Extended ed. in 19 vols. Wilmington, N.C., 1987–1989.

Wakelyn, Jon L. *Biographical Dictionary of the Confederacy.* Edited by Frank E. Vandiver. Westport, Conn., 1977.

JENNIFER LUND

PRESTON, WALTER (1819–1867), congressman from Virginia. A member of a large, well-to-do family of southwestern Virginia, Preston graduated from Princeton and Harvard Law School before returning to his hometown, Abingdon, Virginia, to practice. Running as a Whig candidate, he lost his attempt in 1857 to win election as attorney general.

After Virginia seceded, the state convention selected him to sit in the Provisional Congress. He was thereafter elected over Fayette McMullen to the First Congress. In turn, McMullen defeated him by a close margin in his bid for reelection in 1863. Preston was not a leader in the Congress, though he served on important committees, including Foreign Affairs and Quartermaster's and Commissary. As chairman of the latter committee, he was asked in late 1863 to investigate a charge that prisoners of war were not receiving adequate food. In February 1864 his committee concluded, not surprisingly, that the allegation was "entirely without foundation" and that, indeed, prisoners received rations at least as good as Confederate soldiers.

The Davis administration could count on his support generally for those measures designed to prosecute the war. On the other hand, Preston recoiled from endorsing stern actions, preferring instead to add qualifications. For example, though he supported conscription, he favored many categories of exemptions from service, and though he agreed on the need for suspension of habeas corpus, he wanted qualifications.

Preston returned home in 1863 and died there in 1867.

BIBLIOGRAPHY

Report of the Committee on Quartermaster and Commissary Departments (February 13, 1864). Richmond, Va., 1864.

Warner, Ezra J., and W. Buck Yearns. *Biographical Register of the Confederate Congress.* Baton Rouge, La., 1975.

NELSON D. LANKFORD

PRESTON, WILLIAM (1816–1887), brigadier general. Born October 16, 1816, in Louisville, Kentucky, Preston graduated from Harvard in 1838. He practiced law in Louisville and fought in the Mexican War. He served in the Kentucky legislature and in 1852 the U.S. Congress. In 1858 he was appointed minister to Spain but returned to Kentucky when the secession crisis began. He was prominent in the movement to persuade Kentuckians to join the Confederacy.

When the Civil War began, Preston joined his brother-in-law Albert Sidney Johnston and served as colonel on John C. Breckinridge's staff. Following the Battle of Shiloh he was promoted to brigadier general (to date from April 14, 1862), and fought at Corinth and Murfreesboro. Because of his diplomatic skill, he was named Confederate minister to the Mexican government of Maximilian. The war ended before his arrival there, however. Some sources indicate that he was promoted to major general in January 1865, but no official record of the promotion exists.

After the war, Preston traveled to Mexico, England, and Canada before returning home. He served as a Democrat in the Kentucky legislature in 1868 and 1869. Preston died on September 21, 1887, in Lexington, and is buried in Louisville.

BIBLIOGRAPHY

Connelly, Thomas L. *Army of the Heartland: The Army of Tennessee, 1861–1862.* Baton Rouge, La., 1967.

Davis, William C. *Breckinridge: Statesman, Soldier, Symbol.* Baton Rouge, La., 1974.

Johnston, William Preston. *The Life of Albert Sidney Johnston.* New York, 1878.

ANNE J. BAILEY

PRESTON, WILLIAM BALLARD (1805–1862), U.S. secretary of the navy and congressman from Virginia. Born in Smithfield, Montgomery County, Virginia, on November 25, 1805, Preston graduated from William and Mary in 1823 and then studied law at the University of Virginia before being admitted to the bar in 1826. During the 1830s and 1840s he served in both houses of the Virginia legislature as well as a brief period in the U.S. House (1847–1849). He was an antislavery Whig and became secretary of the navy for President Zachary Taylor in 1849. After Taylor's death in 1850, he returned to private life and resumed his law practice.

Like many Virginians, Preston opposed secession and did not support the Confederacy until he felt he had no other choice. He was a member of the state secession convention but opposed action until it became clear that war was unavoidable. Nevertheless, as a former Unionist, he seemed the perfect person to present the ordinance of secession to the convention.

After Virginia joined the Confederacy, Preston was sent to

the Provisional Congress from his district in the western part of the state. He later was a senator in the First Congress. He opposed giving the Confederate government too much power over the states and disliked excessive government regulation. He sat on several committees, including Military Affairs, Flag and Seal, and Foreign Affairs. Along with other members of the Preston family, he was a member of the Western bloc and a strong supporter of Gen. P. G. T. Beauregard.

Preston did not live long after he took his seat in the Confederate Senate. He died on November 16, 1862, at his home in Montgomery County.

BIBLIOGRAPHY

Alexander, Thomas B., and Richard E. Beringer. *The Anatomy of the Confederate Congress: A Study of the Influences of Member Characteristics on Legislative Voting Behavior, 1861–1865.* Nashville, Tenn., 1972.

Connelly, Thomas L., and Archer Jones. *The Politics of Command: Factions and Ideas in Confederate Strategy.* Baton Rouge, La., 1973.

ANNE J. BAILEY

PRICE, STERLING (1809–1867), U.S. congressman, antebellum governor of Missouri, and major general. Born in Virginia to a wealthy, slave-owning family, Price moved with them to Missouri in 1830. Elected to Congress in 1844, he left his seat to lead a regiment in the Mexican War, during which he received promotion to brigadier general and became military governor of Chihuahua. After he had served one term as governor of Missouri, his popularity and moderate Unionist stance earned him election as president of the 1861 state convention charged with deciding the issue of secession; the convention voted against it. But Price became angered by radical Unionists in St. Louis, in particular Congressman Frank P. Blair and Federal army captain Nathaniel Lyon, who were working to forestall secessionist efforts in the state. As a result, Price offered his services to secessionist Governor Claiborne F. Jackson as commander of state militia forces.

STERLING PRICE. LIBRARY OF CONGRESS

In an effort to prevent war in Missouri, Price signed an agreement with Federal Western Department commander William S. Harney that both sides would maintain neutrality. Blair and Lyon promptly abrogated the agreement by persuading President Abraham Lincoln to remove Harney from command. After a famous conference with Union leaders on June 11 at St. Louis's Planters' House Hotel, Price mobilized his state troops to oppose the Federal force Lyon was leading toward the state capital. Defeated at Boonville (Price was not present), the state troops retreated with Price to the southwestern corner of the state, where he collected and trained nearly 10,000 state guard recruits. While there, Price traveled to Arkansas and persuaded Confederate commander Ben McCulloch to enter neutral Missouri and join forces to attack Lyon, encamped at Springfield. On August 10, at Oak Hills, the Southern forces defeated Lyon's Federal troops in a battle that resulted in Lyon's death and a Union withdrawal. Buoyed by his ensuing popularity, Price in September marched northward, besieging and capturing 3,000 Federal troops and supplies at Lexington. Pressed by troops under John C. Frémont, he then retreated into Arkansas.

In March 1862, Price (called "Old Pap" by his men) again joined forces with McCulloch in the newly formed Army of the West, under overall command of Earl Van Dorn, to drive Federal forces from northern Arkansas. After being defeated at Elkhorn Tavern, he and his troops officially joined the Confederate army, and Price was commissioned a major general. Against the Missourian's wishes, Van Dorn transferred the army to northern Mississippi to assist Confederate defensive operations in the area against Federal forces under Ulysses S. Grant. Angered by this apparent abandonment of the Trans-Mississippi theater, Price twice traveled to Richmond and confronted President Jefferson Davis, engendering poor relations between the two. Davis called Price the vainest man he had ever met.

Price led forces in successive defeats at Iuka and Corinth before receiving transfer again to Arkansas in the spring of 1863. After leading a mismanaged attack on Helena, Price wintered his troops at Camden. The following spring he and

E. Kirby Smith took part at Jenkins' Ferry in successful defensive operations against Union forces under Frederick Steele in the Red River campaign. In an effort to liberate his home state and raise recruits, Price invaded Missouri in the fall of 1864 with a force of 12,000, mostly cavalry. While advancing on St. Louis in September, Price fought a bloody engagement at Pilot Knob and then headed west along the Missouri River pursued by a large Union force. After being defeated in a battle at Westport, he retreated in late October with his troops as far as Texas before turning back to Arkansas.

After the war, rather than surrender, Price escaped to Mexico, where he founded Carlota, a colony of ex-Confederates. When Maximilian's Mexican empire collapsed, Price returned to Missouri in early 1867, where he died suddenly less than a year later.

BIBLIOGRAPHY

Castel, Albert. *General Sterling Price and the Civil War in the West.* Baton Rouge, La., 1968.

Monaghan, Jay. *Civil War on the Western Border, 1854–1865.* Lincoln, Nebr., 1955.

Phillips, Christopher. *Damned Yankee: The Life of General Nathaniel Lyon.* Columbia, Mo., 1990.

Rea, Ralph. *Sterling Price: The Lee of the West.* Little Rock, Ark., 1959.

Shalhope, Robert E. *Sterling Price: Portrait of a Southerner.* Columbia, Mo., 1971.

CHRISTOPHER PHILLIPS

PRICE'S MISSOURI RAID. This grand though ultimately unsuccessful cavalry raid in September and October 1864 was conducted by Sterling Price, major general and commander of the District of Arkansas and Missouri, and E. Kirby Smith, commander of the Trans-Mississippi Department. They planned to capture St. Louis and recover Missouri, controlled by Union troops since the fall of 1861, for the Confederacy. In July 1864, when transfer of two Union corps to Mississippi weakened Federal strength in Louisiana, exiled Missouri Governor Thomas C. Reynolds wrote Price proposing a cavalry raid into Missouri. Eager to lead an expedition into his home state, Price met with Smith at Shreveport, Louisiana, in early August. Price had become convinced by members of the Order of American Knights, a secret organization loyal to the Confederacy, that such an invasion would cause thousands of recruits to swarm into the Southern ranks. Moreover, Price believed that a successful raid would exacerbate Northern dissatisfaction with the war and contribute to Abraham Lincoln's defeat in the upcoming presidential election. Then Lincoln's Peace Democrat successor, George B. McClellan, would recognize the Confederacy and sue for peace.

On August 4, 1864, Price received orders to make arrangements to invade Missouri, providing him with command of all cavalry west of the Mississippi. Three weeks later, he turned over command of his district to Maj. Gen. John B. Magruder and ordered Brig. Gen. Joseph O. Shelby to attack DeVall's Bluff, Arkansas, located on the White River, to divert the attention of Federal forces at nearby Helena. On August 28, Price left Camden, Arkansas, assuming command of cavalry divisions under Maj. Gens. John Sappington Marmaduke and James F. Fagan the next day. Proceeding to the Arkansas River, the column crossed on September 6 at Dardanelle. On September 12, the force made its way over the White River and the next day rendezvoused with Shelby's force at Pocahontas. While there, Price organized the Army of Missouri into three divisions under Marmaduke, Fagan, and Shelby, totaling 12,000 men and fourteen guns. Over 4,000 of his troops were unarmed, since Shelby had only recently conscripted them from northeastern Arkansas. Price hoped to obtain supplies and arms in Missouri.

Traveling in three parallel columns in order to gather forage and provisions, the force entered Missouri on September 19 and arrived at Fredericktown five days later. There Price received word that 1,500 Federals under Brig. Gen. Thomas Ewing lay poised at Ironton, twenty miles west. Moreover, he learned that a Union infantry corps under Maj. Gen. A. J. Smith had been diverted from Mississippi and was now encamped south of St. Louis. Price dispatched Shelby's division to Mineral Point to wreck railroad bridges between Ironton and St. Louis in order to prevent Smith from reinforcing Ewing. Price himself advanced toward Ironton on September 26. His force encountered slight resistance at Arcadia and quickly pushed Federal troops into Fort Davidson, a hexagonal earthen structure at nearby Pilot Knob.

The fort was armed with sixteen cannon and protected by nearly 900 yards of open meadow. But rather than position artillery on the mountains surrounding it and shelling it into submission, Price unwisely ordered a frontal assault at 2:00 P.M. Within twenty minutes, the Southern troops suffered more than 1,000 casualties, many from Price's most experienced brigades who had advanced several times to the very walls of the fort. Dismayed, he canceled further assaults, opting to use artillery from the heights. During the night, Ewing blew up the powder magazine and escaped with his command to Potosi, 25 miles distant, leaving the fort, cannons, and supplies to the Confederates. In all, the Federals had suffered less than 100 casualties. Discovering the following morning that Ewing had escaped, Price sent Shelby and Marmaduke in pursuit. When they learned that 4,500 Federal cavalry under Brig. Gen. Alfred Pleasonton were advancing from St. Louis to reinforce Ewing, both units withdrew.

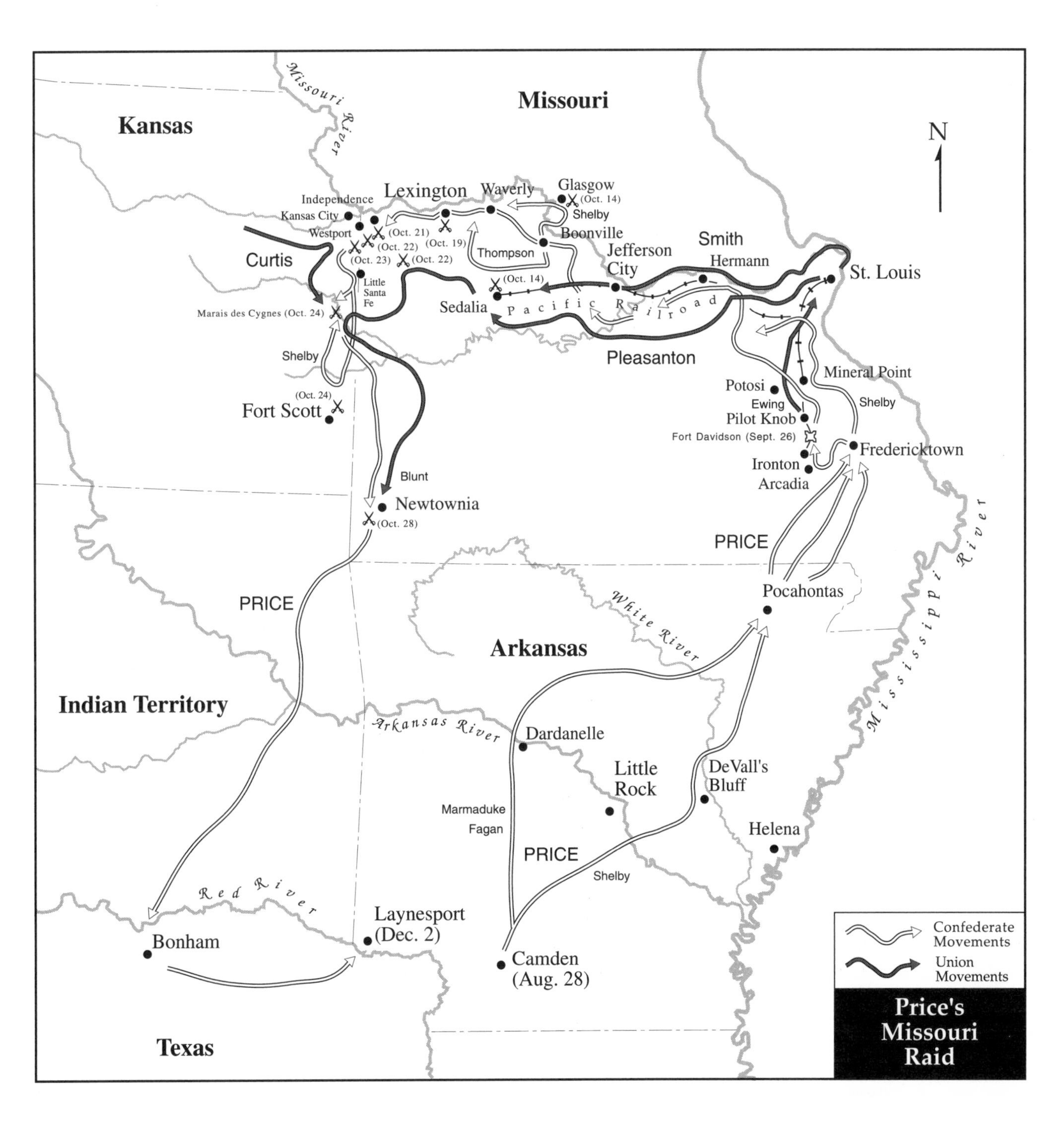

The decimation of his best troops at Pilot Knob and the arrival of Smith's 8,000-strong veteran corps at St. Louis convinced Price that any hope of capturing the city had passed. Yet, despite the obvious setback, Price believed that the continued presence of a large, supplied army would not only entice volunteers but might yet stir public opinion and affect the outcome of the November election. On September 30, after sending Shelby's cavalry as a feint toward St. Louis, Price began a slow march westward along the south bank of the Missouri River, hoping to gain recruits and foraging for supplies. As they moved toward the state capital, Jefferson City, the columns destroyed bridges and miles of the Pacific Railroad's track, avoiding all conflict other than minor skirmishes. Despite the supreme commander of the Order of American Knights' calling on members to enlist in Price's Army of Missouri, recruits proved sparse and many of those taken were unwilling to be disciplined. Moreover, Price's languid pace allowed nearly

7,000 Federal militia and regular troops to fortify the capital, rendering its capture difficult. On October 5, Price occupied Hermann, but shaken by the debacle at Pilot Knob and harassed by Pleasonton's cavalry, he bypassed Jefferson City and proceeded toward Boonville, which he occupied four days later.

At Boonville, Price added some 2,000 recruits, bringing his total force to 15,000, though many were unarmed and untrained. Moreover, looters and pillagers, including seasoned guerrillas and bushwhackers, abounded among new recruits. Their exploits had become so notorious that Governor Reynolds wrote Price in disgust, claiming that his troops' ravaging of the river counties would make it difficult to supplant the state's provisional Unionist government. Desperate for arms, Price on October 14 sent Shelby with a brigade to Glasgow, where locals reported that Federals had stored a large cache of weapons. Though Shelby captured more than 500 troops, the Union soldiers were able to destroy the arms before surrendering. Meanwhile, the rest of the army took up the march westward, with a detachment under Confederate partisan leader M. Jeff Thompson raiding Sedalia and capturing the militia there. Throughout, Union elements skirmished with Price's rear guard, which was protecting his cumbersome five-hundred-wagon supply train loaded with booty.

As Price plodded through the center of the state, Maj. Gen. William Rosecrans, commander of the Department of Missouri, mobilized forces to trap and destroy the invading army. In addition to instructing Pleasonton to dog Price in an effort to slow him, Rosecrans sent A. J. Smith's infantry to Sedalia in pursuit of the Confederate column and ordered 4,500 veterans under Maj. Gen. Joseph A. Mower to move from Arkansas to assist. Finally, he tried to communicate with Maj. Gen. Samuel Curtis, commander of the Department of Kansas, and have him send troops to trap Price between the converging Federal forces. Though ignorant of Rosecrans's plan, Curtis was well aware of Price's whereabouts and massed more than 15,000 militiamen and regulars near the border. On October 15, he ordered forward three brigades under Maj. Gen. James G. Blunt to Lexington, Missouri. Because most of Blunt's force were militia and would go no farther than the Big Blue River, six miles east of Kansas City, only 2,000 regulars reached Lexington.

Price's army reached Waverly, Missouri, on October 18 and the next day moved toward Lexington. Shelby encountered Blunt's lead units and pushed them back easily. Now aware that separate Union forces numbering more than twice his own were encircling him, Price moved quickly both to prevent Smith and Blunt from effecting a juncture and to leave himself an avenue of escape. He turned southward, planning to position his men between the two Union forces and defeat each in turn, and then to confront Curtis. On October 21, at the Little Blue River, Price encountered 400 dismounted horsemen with two howitzers, a token contingent of Blunt's troops. Blunt's main force had fallen back on the Big Blue, where Curtis's militia was entrenched on the steep west bank of the river. After a sharp skirmish, Price's men forced the small group of Federals to retreat to the hills behind the river. But as the Confederates continued their assault, Blunt returned with the rest of his infantry and artillery, most of whom were armed with repeating rifles and breechloaders. The Federals' superior firepower pushed back the advancing Confederates briefly, but Price's superior numbers soon threatened to turn both of Blunt's flanks, forcing the Union troops to retreat. That night, Blunt rejoined Curtis at the Big Blue.

On October 22, Price sent Marmaduke's division to the east to keep Pleasonton at bay and sent one brigade of Shelby's division to feint against Curtis at the main crossing ford of the Big Blue. Price's major thrust, made by brigades under Thompson and Sidney D. Jackman, came at Byram's Ford, the next upstream crossing, but in three hours of hard fighting, they were unable to prevail. Late in the afternoon, Alonzo Slayback's regiment found an uncontested crossing farther upriver. Taking that route, they fell upon the exposed right of Curtis's line. As the Union line withdrew, Shelby pushed his entire division across and drove the Federals toward Westport. With nightfall, the Confederates were forced to break off the attack before they could complete the victory, allowing Curtis to re-form his line just south of Westport.

While Price successfully forced a crossing of the Big Blue, Marmaduke in the rear experienced defeat. Pleasonton crossed the Little Blue and mauled William L. Cabell's brigade, taking nearly 400 prisoners and two cannons. Fighting through Independence, Pleasonton's cavalry pushed Marmaduke's division almost to the Big Blue. Marmaduke fell back to the west side of the river at nightfall and sent word to Price that the army was in danger of being trapped and destroyed. Fearing the loss of his men and his valuable wagon train, Price made preparations for a fighting withdrawal to the south.

At daybreak on October 23, Price sent Shelby's division, supported by two of Fagan's brigades, to attack the Federals at Westport. During two brutal hours of fighting, the opposing lines of horsemen charged and countercharged in the rolling woodlands along Brush Creek. Meanwhile, Pleasonton hurled a savage assault against Marmaduke at Byram's Ford, both sides taking heavy losses. By noon, Marmaduke's troops had spent all their ammunition, and they broke into a rout across the prairie, with Federal horsemen thundering after and capturing hundreds of them. Simultaneously, Blunt launched an attack on Shelby's line, nearly breaking the Confederate right. Learning of the collapse of Marmaduke's division, Price ordered all troops to retreat southward while Shelby fought for time. As Marmaduke and Fagan streamed toward Little Santa Fe, only Shelby's dogged withdrawal saved Price's army from complete destruction. The Battle of Westport proved to be Price's high-water mark, the last major action to take place in the Trans-Mississippi region. The exact number of casualties is unavailable, but Shelby estimated he had left at least eight hundred dead and wounded on the field. Price fled southward with a disorganized mass of horsemen, cattle, refugees, wagons, and unarmed men.

Curtis failed to order a pursuit for twelve hours, enabling Price to escape the Union pincers and secure his wagon train. Ultimately Price would regret this decision, for the ponderously slow wagons retarded his mounted forces' retreat, allowing the Federals to overtake them just one day later at the Marais des Cygnes River, sixty miles south. While Marmaduke and Fagan held off the advancing Federals, Shelby returned with his command from a foray to Fort Scott, Kansas, surprising Pleasonton and allowing Price to cross the river. In the fray, Marmaduke was captured. That night, Price burned nearly a third of his wagons. Skirmishing continued the entire next day and night, and on the afternoon of October 28, Blunt (now leading the pursuit) caught up with Price's retreating column near Newtonia, Missouri. Again, Shelby managed to drive off the advancing Federals before assistance could arrive. On October 29, Rosecrans recalled all troops belonging to the Department of Missouri, leaving Curtis with just 3,500 cavalry to continue the chase.

Before the situation could be rectified, Price had crossed the Arkansas River and dispersed his forces, marching into Indian Territory. On November 23, they arrived at Bonham, Texas. When the column returned to Laynesport, Arkansas, on December 2, 1864, Price's army had marched an incredible 1,488 miles. Though it had destroyed miles of railroad in Missouri and had diverted a corps of Federal infantry destined for William Tecumseh Sherman in Georgia, Price's raid had failed largely to achieve any of its objectives, and his army had lost an estimated 4,000 casualties, mostly to desertion.

BIBLIOGRAPHY

Britton, Wiley. *The Civil War on the Border.* New York, 1890.

Buresh, Lumir F. *October 25th and the Battle of Mine Creek.* Edited by Dan L. Smith. Kansas City, Mo., 1977.

Castel, Albert. *General Sterling Price and the Civil War in the West.* Baton Rouge, La., 1968.

Hinton, Richard J. *Rebel Invasion of Missouri and Kansas, and the Campaign of the Army of the Border, against General Sterling Price, in October and November, 1864.* Chicago, 1865.

Jenkins, Paul. *The Battle of Westport.* Kansas City, Mo., 1906.

Monaghan, Jay. *Civil War on the Western Border, 1854–1865.* Lincoln, Nebr., 1955.

Peterson, Cyrus A., and Joseph M. Hanson. *Pilot Knob: The Thermopylae of the West.* New York, 1914. Reprint, Cape Girardeau, Mo., 1964.

Shalhope, Robert E. *Sterling Price: Portrait of a Southerner.* Columbia, Mo., 1971.

CHRISTOPHER PHILLIPS

PRINTMAKING. The publication of engravings and lithographs dwindled and eventually ceased altogether in the Confederacy as the war drained the printmaking industry of essential resources as well as manpower. Paper and ink fell into short supply, and artists, engravers, and lithographers enlisted in the army along with other able-bodied men. But printmaking did not die for want of an audience for celebratory graphics or for an overall lack of nationalistic fervor among Southern audiences, as some historians have suggested. Rather, a unique confluence of adverse commercial, human, and geographic circumstances doomed Confederate printmaking, although for a time a few publishers did manage to produce a handful of spirited renderings.

At the outset of the war, vigorous printmaking enterprises could be found in such Southern cities as Baltimore, New Orleans, and Richmond. Baltimore's great potential as a Confederate printmaking center, however, ended when Maryland failed to secede. Thereafter Union censorship limited such production there. Local pro-Confederate artist Adalbert Volck produced brilliant etchings, some viciously assailing the Union and its leaders, others vivifying crucial Confederate myths with sentiment and sympathy. But Volck was compelled to publish his prints covertly for only a select group of fellow Southern sympathizers. He would surely have emerged as the leading printmaker of the Confederate cause had Baltimore become a Confederate city.

New Orleans, too, might have provided fertile ground for Confederate printmaking, but the city fell early to the Union in April 1862. Thereafter Federal censors prevented the dissemination of "disloyal" art. One local artist there was arrested merely for painting a portrait of Thomas J. ("Stonewall") Jackson.

Thus Richmond, by default, became the sole center of Confederate printmaking, a status that wartime shortages, together with government publishing priorities, quickly deflated. Local picture publishers like Hoyer & Ludwig were pressed into service printing stamps and currency, leaving little time for the production of icons for the family parlor, despite their propaganda potential for an image-starved public. The locally produced *Southern Illustrated News* did thrive for a time, offering weekly woodcut engravings of military heroes. But its artists were eventually lost to the army, and the paper, reduced to advertising for replacements who never appeared, shut down.

In this atmosphere of distraction and deprivation, Confederate publishers were able to produce only a handful of wartime graphics, nearly all in the first flush of enthusiasm for secession and nationhood. Several firms issued facsimiles of their states' secession ordinances, and others portrayed local regiments in camp. Hoyer & Ludwig, along with Tucker & Perkins of Augusta and Blelock & Co. of New Orleans, put out portraits optimistically entitled "Our First President," all depicting Jefferson Davis, the country's first and last chief executive, in 1861. In Savannah, R. H. Howell issued a scene of the first flag of independence raised in that city in 1860. "But few copies were struck off," according to one who owned a print, "—say a thousand . . . circulated throughout the country."

Aside from the *News*'s crude efforts, few portraits were available. An exception, Ernest Crehen's small image of J. E. B. Stuart, published in 1863, was probably intended as a book frontispiece and only a single copy survived. And a Vicksburg publisher who issued a scene of the Union bombardment there advertised it as "executed in the best style of art" despite its primitive appearance. It sold for five dollars, no doubt too expensive for the impoverished South. This lithograph may well have been the last print produced in the Confederacy. No evidence testifies more convincingly to the failure of Confederate printmaking than the industry's inability to manufacture a single separate sheet print of its greatest general, Robert E. Lee.

[*See also* Burial of Latane; Lost Cause, *article on* Iconography; Magazines, *article on* Southern Illustrated News; Volck, Adalbert.]

BIBLIOGRAPHY

Neely, Mark E., Jr., Harold Holzer, and Gabor S. Boritt. *The Confederate Image: Prints of the Lost Cause.* Chapel Hill, N.C., 1987.

Southern Illustrated News (Richmond, Va.), 1862–1865.

HAROLD HOLZER

PRISONERS OF WAR. Since neither the Confederacy nor the Union expected a long war, both sides failed to plan for the enemy soldiers they would capture. There were in existence U.S. Army regulations known to both combatants, which placed upon the quartermaster general the duty of taking charge of prisoners and provided for a commissary general of prisoners to carry out responsibilities for them. Such an officer had served during the War of 1812, providing a precedent familiar to North and South. But people on both sides also knew that the War of 1812 and the Revolutionary War had been characterized by charges of atrocious treatment of American captives. Confederates and Federals therefore were suspicious from the start of how their foe would treat prisoners.

Before the outbreak of fighting, the two sides released most potential enemies whom they took into custody. The Confederates, though they held enlisted men as prisoners, paroled U.S. Army officers captured in Texas upon their promise not to serve against the South. The Union similarly paroled captured Missouri militia.

Once fighting began both the Confederacy and the Union improvised arrangements for prisoners. The United States was the first to create a formal system, naming in 1861 Lt. Col. William H. Hoffman as commissary general of prisoners. Hoffman, who was one of the paroled prisoners from Texas, was a veteran army officer with experience only in managing the limited number of men in the peacetime army as economically as possible. Like his Confederate counterpart, John H. Winder, who during most of the war was the officer principally responsible for prisoners, Hoffman was preoccupied with preventing prisoners from escaping. To hold his captives, Hoffman began by leasing Johnson's Island on Lake Erie near Sandusky, Ohio. Though Hoffman originally intended it to be the main depot for Confederate prisoners, the rapid expansion of the war outstripped the capacity of the barracks, and it came to be used mainly to hold officers.

Hoffman then pressed into service Union training camps at Camp Randall (Madison, Wisconsin), Camp Douglas (Chicago), Camp Butler (Springfield, Illinois), Camp Morton (Indianapolis), and Camp Chase (Columbus, Ohio). Existing barracks were fenced in and new ones hastily constructed. The Union also used vacant buildings in St. Louis and seacoast forts such as Delaware on that river and Warren in Boston Harbor. Meanwhile the Confederates commandeered empty warehouses and similar structures for prisons. Both sides selected sites in considerable part because of proximity to transportation facilities, including rivers, bays, and especially railroads.

Prisoner Exchanges

As prisoners accumulated, they and their relatives pressed for their release on parole and exchange. An impediment was the insistence of the United States that it would take no action that recognized the legitimacy of secession or the legality of the Confederate States government. The Federals tolerated the generals in the field making exchanges with their opponents, and they permitted an informal system under which captured officers went on parole to the opposing capital and sought to arrange special exchanges for particular (often influential) captives.

But the Union declined to recognize the authority of the Confederates to license privateering by their people, and it proceeded in 1861 to bring captured privateers to trial as pirates. The Confederates, however, had captured at First Manassas over a thousand Union prisoners, putting the South in a position to retaliate if the privateers were executed. In November 1861, General Winder selected by lot high-ranking prisoners to undergo the same fate as the privateers. Although the Federal authorities concluded that exchanging privateers for hostages would not be equivalent to recognizing the Confederate government, and the Confederates for their part wanted even the limited recognition implicit in a plan for general exchange, the respective army commanders were unwilling to make this special exchange.

Since both sides had an incentive to end the controversy and be relieved of the growing burden of providing for prisoners, they agreed on July 22, 1862, to a cartel modeled on that between the United States and the British in the War of 1812. Gen. D. H. Hill on behalf of the South and Gen. John A. Dix on behalf of the North made an arrangement whereby all prisoners were to be paroled within ten days and sent to their own lines; a formal exchange would take place as soon as equivalent numbers had reached the lines. Agents for both sides were to administer the cartel, keeping records for an elaborate system under which men who could not be exchanged for enemies of equal rank would be matched according to a sliding scale of equivalents. (For example, a general commanding in chief or admiral equaled sixty privates or common seamen.) The cartel stated that it would continue during the war regardless of which side held the most prisoners and that no "misunderstanding" would interrupt the release of prisoners on parole. After the exchange began, both sides closed all but a few transient prisons.

But the belligerents discovered that they would have to create parole camps to house their men awaiting formal exchange, and sometimes they adapted facilities previously used for enemy prisoners. Both sides had difficulty in maintaining discipline among these idle men, who were prohibited from doing military duty, and they feared the likelihood that some of their soldiers in the field would readily surrender in order to obtain a vacation from combat. Moreover, a system resting on mutual trust was difficult to carry out between combatants who had gone to war partly because of their mistrust. Almost from the start, Robert Ould, the Confederate agent of exchange, was embroiled in

CONFEDERATE PRISONERS. Union guards watching over Southern troops captured in the Shenandoah Valley, 1862.

NATIONAL ARCHIVES

a controversy with his Union counterparts characterized by interminable bickering letters.

One issue that arose in these disputes involved a Confederate protest against Gen. Benjamin F. Butler's execution of William B. Mumford for hauling down the U.S. flag at New Orleans. Believing that the threat of retaliation had forced the United States to back down in such episodes as that of the imprisoned privateers, Ould's superior, President Jefferson Davis, made a major tactical blunder. On December 24, 1862, he issued a proclamation declaring Butler to be an outlaw and ordering that no captured U.S. commissioned officer should be released on parole until Butler had been caught and hanged. At the same time he ordered that black troops when captured should be turned over to the authorities of the state in which they were taken. He and the Confederate Congress subsequently resolved that captured white officers of black units were to be tried and put to death. The Confederates thus had taken actions that effectively ended the release of officers under the cartel, after May 25, 1863. Moreover, Confederate threats to retaliate against captured Union officers for the execution of two Confederates captured while recruiting, allegedly behind the Union lines, proved ineffective. Although the Confederates held another lottery among their prisoners, they found that the Federals by capturing Brig. Gen. William Henry Fitzhugh Lee, son of Robert E. Lee, had obtained a hostage that could not be topped in the game of threatened retaliation.

Meanwhile the exchange of noncommissioned officers and privates had continued. But the belligerents' exchange agents became involved in controversy over the legality of paroles of prisoners associated with the great battles of the summer of 1863, and in July the United States decided to cease further deliveries of prisoners. Butler, despite his status as an outlaw imposed by President Davis, claimed that he could break the deadlock over exchange, and in early 1864 the Union authorities permitted him to try. He succeeded only in exchanging two experimental boatloads of prisoners. In March 1864, he and Ould came to a final parting of the ways over the status of black soldiers. Ould agreed that those blacks who had been free before the war would be treated as prisoners of war but refused to grant such status to those who had been slaves. Inconsistent with this declaration, however, the two navy departments exchanged several naval prisoners without raising questions of race or slave status.

Indeed, though the new Federal general in chief, Ulysses S. Grant, urged Butler to insist on equal treatment for black troops, he privately raised several objections to exchanges. He indicated that ceasing exchanges would have the effect of discouraging easy surrenders and desertions to the enemy. He also pointed out that the Confederate conscription system permitted them to put into the field anyone released by the United States. "If we commence a system of exchange, which liberates all prisoners taken," he argued, "we will have to fight on until the whole South is exterminated." Instead of openly acknowledging this brutally realistic argument, Butler and Grant repeatedly demanded that the Confederates agree that their proposals for a man-for-man exchange include ex-slaves as well as other prisoners. Regular exchanges were not resumed during the 1864 campaign season.

Prison Conditions

As the unexchanged prisoners accumulated, both sides crowded more men into existing prisons and built new ones. The Union opened camps at Rock Island, Illinois, and Point Lookout, Maryland (the latter being the only Federal facility to use tents exclusively), and in July 1864, began to move prisoners into a fenced camp at Elmira, New York, which quickly became one of the more overcrowded and deadly Union prisons. Meanwhile, the Confederates had built a stockade at Andersonville, Georgia, which grew into the largest and most notorious Civil War prison. The overflow was sent to several smaller prisons. By the end of 1864, the incidence of deaths at one of these, the camp at Salisbury, North Carolina, began to rival that at Andersonville.

Officers. The inmates of both sides' prisons, new and old, henceforth experienced for a prolonged period conditions that previously had been mostly temporary. A prisoner's treatment was strongly affected by whether or not he was a commissioned officer. Both sides tried to house officers separately from enlisted men and usually in different prisons. One reason was the military tradition that officers had every interest in upholding—they were to be treated as gentlemen. Moreover, segregation of imprisoned officers from enlisted men had the practical effect of disrupting enemy military organization and discipline, facilitating control of the prisoners. (Indeed, the relatively few instances in which officers and men were temporarily held close to one another resulted in their increased plotting to escape, which convinced authorities of the importance of separation according to rank.)

Since officers were less numerous than enlisted men, their prisons were always smaller, which made for better sanitation. Moreover, because officers usually came from above average economic backgrounds and were better paid, they could buy additional food and comforts, and during most of the war both sides permitted them to do so. Thus, though mortality was high among officers on Civil War battlefields, it was relatively low in the prisons. Nonetheless, highly literate officers, resentful of their captivity, often wrote complaints about their treatment, which added to the notoriety of the Confederates' Libby Prison and the Union's Johnson's Island.

One of the few areas in which officers might suffer more than enlisted men was in that of retaliation. As mentioned above, their status made them obvious targets when either side wished to put pressure on the other. The most notorious instance of their literally becoming targets occurred in the summer of 1864. The Confederate commander at Charleston proposed to discourage the Union bombardment of the city from Morris Island by confining in it fifty high-ranking Union prisoners. With the approval of President Davis, the men were taken into the city. When the local Union commander learned of this and requested that fifty Confederate hostages be sent to him for the same purpose, the Confederates disingenuously denied that they had intended to place captives under fire and agreed to a special exchange of the two groups. Grant, upon learning of this violation of his suspension of exchanges, forbade its repetition.

Thus the Confederates did not succeed in an attempt to reopen exchanges by sending six hundred more captured officers to Charleston. Instead, Union officers, believing that the Confederates intended to place these prisoners under fire, ordered six hundred Confederate officers to be confined after September 7 in a hastily built stockade near the batteries on Morris Island. Housed in crowded tents on short rations, they were guarded by those men of the black Fifty-fourth Massachusetts who had survived the previous year's assault on Battery Wagner. Though most of the Confederates here and elsewhere resented and reacted hostilely to black guards, a few got along better with their keepers than their fellows liked. In October, the Federal authorities had the hostages transferred to Fort Pulaski, Georgia. For many years, this group of ex-Confederate officers recalled their sufferings as the objects of retaliation and proclaimed themselves "The Immortal Six Hundred."

Security Problems. Like the Confederate officers on Morris Island, prisoners of both sides and of all ranks often complained about their guards and the arrangements for security. As might be anticipated in a war involving strong popular emotion, the prisoners were often the focus of animus. As they were marched through enemy cities, civilians mocked and insulted them. In the prisons, officers and guards often treated them as despised enemies. Yet, though clearly some prison personnel acted the part of brutes and sadists, there is abundant evidence that many on both sides behaved with perhaps surprising kindness toward the men under their control. In several instances, clergymen, nuns, and members of the Masonic Order ministered to prisoners.

The problems of prison security that proved so controversial on both sides stemmed less from sadism than from the prison authorities' lack of confidence in their ability to maintain control. Neither side was willing to use first-class officers or men to run prisons. By 1864 when the prisons were especially crowded, they were guarded in the Confederacy mostly by reserves composed of boys and old men, and in the United States by men on short-term enlistments or unfit for field service. Commanders on both sides complained of their guards' lack of training and discipline. These outnumbered, mediocre guards were expected to keep throngs of prisoners within often flimsy fences and stockades. Should any number of prisoners break out, it was unlikely that guards armed with single-shot muskets could intimidate them. To discourage outbreaks, several prisons directed artillery pieces at their inmates, and Johnson's Island issued revolvers to its guards. But the most common security precaution was to lay out "deadlines" along the fences, which prisoners were forbidden to cross. Considering the quality of many of the guards, it was probably inevitable that some shot on almost any pretext at prisoners near the deadline. Neither side made any serious effort to enforce discipline in such cases.

Like prisoners in all times, those of the Civil War thought much about and often attempted escapes. The largest and best known was the exodus of 109 Union officers from Libby through a tunnel on February 9, 1864. Inmates of other prisons, Southern and Northern, also dug tunnels, sometimes successfully. Given the inadequacies of the guards, some prisoners found it possible to pass out in various disguises. At the unfenced camp at Columbia, South Carolina, some 373 prisoners simply ran the guard lines. Once out, prisoners on both sides often received help from sympathetic civilians, with Union escapees receiving assistance from mountain whites and slaves. Organized uprisings were less common, but a large one occurred on November 25, 1864, at Salisbury. Most prisoners simply endured prison life.

Prisoners' Lives. Their physical setting contributed to the captives' misery. The Union usually housed its prisoners in flimsily built, scantily heated barracks. The Confederates used some warehouses and similar buildings but far more camps, with tents for only a minority of the prisoners. Large numbers were forced to burrow into the earth with little or no shelter from the weather. When critics of the Confederacy asked why the prisoners could not have been permitted to cut timber to build their own huts, a partial explanation was the inability to guard working parties. A further problem at all of the larger prisons was the lack of facilities for disposing of human waste if the prison was not located along a large stream (as at Salisbury) or authorities were unwilling to spend money to build sewers (as at Chicago and Elmira). Inadequate shelter and sanitation contributed to the diseases that filled the insufficient hospitals.

Lack of clothing made conditions worse. Confederates often reached Northern prisons in garments badly worn and unsuited to winter weather. Federal commanders issued

PRISONERS AT FORT WARREN. Officers of the Confederate ship *Tacony*, held at Fort Warren in Boston harbor, 1863 or 1864.
NAVAL HISTORICAL CENTER, WASHINGTON, D.C.

limited amounts of substandard clothing and sometimes permitted prisoners to receive clothing from relatives and friends. Confederate prison keepers, on the other hand, supplied no clothing to their captives whose distress mounted as their uniforms wore out. Neither side provided prisoners with more than a limited number of blankets, and the plight of Northern prisoners was worsened by the Confederates' policy of systematically stripping newly captured men of bedding and other equipment. The typical prisoner was ragged and cold.

The most controversial aspect of the treatment of prisoners was the matter of food. Both the Confederacy and the Union claimed that they provided their prisoners with the same rations issued to their own troops; yet their captives claimed to be hungry and in many cases demonstrably lost weight. These contentions were less contradictory than they might seem. Although controversialists would later argue in precise terms about the ounces issued of various foods, the wartime records make it clear that the actual amounts were approximations. Moreover, both sides deducted a portion of the ration to create a so-called camp or hospital fund, theoretically for the prisoners' benefit. The keepers diverted additional rations to those captives willing to work around the prison. Thus no individual prisoner could count on receiving the officially announced quantity. And when the food available for the army as a whole was insufficient, as in the Confederacy, the needs of the guards were met first.

Ultimately, however, quantity was only part of the food problem. The basic ration of both sides consisted mainly of bread and meat. Unless supplemented with vegetables, the diet resulted in nutritional deficiencies and such diseases as scurvy. Guards could supplement from several sources; prisoners had only severely limited opportunities to buy vegetables. The Confederates issued none; the Union mainly did so only when scurvy actually appeared. As the cornbread issued by the Confederates was very rough and caused diarrhea, it is not surprising that their captives sickened and that many died.

Despite their hardships, most prisoners had an overabundance of leisure. Neither side attempted to compel them to work. The men read, participated in classes and religious meetings, and wrote diaries and letters. Many made jewelry or other small items as souvenirs for relatives or for sale to their captors. A significant minority seeking better treatment gave their paroles not to escape and agreed to do physical or clerical work for the prison keepers. Both sides thereby reduced the cost of running their prisons.

The prison life of blacks was very different. As the Confederacy declined to recognize them as legitimate soldiers, they often did not survive to reach the prisons; in several well-documented cases Confederate soldiers refused to give them quarter. But hundreds of black soldiers and civilian employees of the United States did reach the Confederate prisons where they were required to perform the more menial tasks. Others were sent to labor in niter works or to construct fortifications. Some were advertised in the newspapers in an effort to return them to slavery.

Prisoners as Manpower

White as well as black prisoners seemed to offer a source of manpower to both belligerents in the desperate year of 1864. The numerically inferior Confederates could gain particular advantage because their more rigorous conscription made it likely that they could return to the field a higher proportion of any exchanged prisoners. Hence the Confederates permitted prisoners in their hands to publicize their sufferings in Southern prisons and petition their government for an exchange. Grant and the Union leadership, however, believed that this would play into the hands of the South. Privately the Union commander admitted, "It is hard on our men held in Southern prisons not to exchange them, but it is humanity to those left in the ranks to fight our battles. Every man we hold, when released . . . becomes an active soldier against us. . . . If we hold those caught they amount to no more than dead men." He persistently asked the Confederates whether their proposed man-for-man exchange included equal treatment for black prisoners. As the Confederates were unwilling to agree to this, they were unable to obtain reinforcements through exchange.

The Confederates then concocted schemes to recapture their soldiers in Northern prisons. Rebel agents in Canada with the aid of Northern sympathizers devoted considerable time and money to plots to release prisoners in Camps Douglas and Morton. All their plans proved abortive, including an attempt to capture a Federal warship and then release the Confederate officers imprisoned on Johnson's Island. Also futile were hopes of conducting a naval expedition against Point Lookout and an attempt as part of Jubal Early's 1864 raid on Washington to continue to that prison.

Unable to retrieve their own men, the Confederates in desperation attempted to recruit soldiers from the Union prisoners in their camps. The War Department authorized recruiting foreign-born soldiers whose loyalty to the United States was presumed to be relatively low. In the summer and fall of 1864, Confederate recruiters visited the Eastern prison camps for enlisted men, told the inmates their government had abandoned them, and offered extra rations and pay if they joined the Confederate army. They were able to persuade about 4,500 men, not all foreign-born, to join several battalion-sized units led by Confederate officers. The Southerners hoped to use these men behind the lines and for peripheral military operations. Unsurprisingly, their record was mixed and sometimes disastrous, though some did labor effectively as engineers for the Confederacy.

It was as workers rather than soldiers that the prisoners supplied the Confederates with additional manpower. As mentioned above, the South, like the Union, used parolees to help run their prisons. Without such aid the Confederate system could not have functioned. General Winder estimated that the services of some eight hundred captive workers at Andersonville alone saved the Confederacy a million dollars yearly. And the Confederates recruited skilled men for a variety of enterprises besides prison-related work. They attempted to run shoemaking shops at several prisons. At Richmond over one hundred prisoners worked in the quartermaster shops, making shoes, clothing, and other equipment for the Confederates. Others worked for public and private manufacturers of a wide variety of war-related goods.

Although the Union with its abundance of skilled labor made little attempt to use its prisoners thus, it recruited even more Confederate prisoners for combat duty. Confronted with an outbreak of Indian warfare on the Great Plains, the Federals met part of their need for troops by enlisting prisoners to fight there rather than against their fellow Confederates. Organized into six regiments under Northern officers, the United States recruited about six thousand men, including several hundred recaptured Union prisoners who had previously joined the Confederates. Both sides tended to refer to their prisoner recruits as "Galvanized Yankees," verbal evidence of the suspicion that their new loyalty represented a thin coating. But those who fought for the United States for over a year after the war's end often rendered effective service.

The Effects of Politics

As unexchanged prisoners accumulated on both sides, the belligerents exploited their treatment for political purposes. In 1864 both the U.S. Congress's Committee on the Conduct of the War and a committee of the U.S. Sanitary Commission interviewed returned Union prisoners about conditions in Southern prisons. In addition to their verbal descriptions of horrors, both committees' reports included ghastly pictures of individual returnees.

The Lincoln administration used charges of mistreatment of prisoners to arouse bitter feeling against the South. Arguing that Confederate prisoners should be subject to the same treatment, the War Department reduced rations and forbade the sending of parcels from friends. Meanwhile Democrats and other opponents of the administration blamed Abraham Lincoln and Secretary of War Edwin M. Stanton for the lack of exchange and sought to use the prisoners' suffering as an issue in the 1864 presidential election.

The Confederates attempted to rebut Union propaganda and counterattacked with their own. To remind the world

BASEBALL GAME BETWEEN UNION PRISONERS. Salisbury, North Carolina, 1863. Lithograph of a drawing by Maj. Otto Boetticher.
NATIONAL ARCHIVES

that Confederates also were spending long months in prison, President and Mrs. Davis proudly displayed in their White House objects made by time-killing prisoners. In October 1864, English sympathizers held a Southern Bazaar at Liverpool to publicize the sufferings of Confederate prisoners and raise money for their relief. In March 1865, a joint congressional committee denounced the Union reports of prisoner mistreatment as mere sensationalism. It claimed that the reports' illustrations showing almost skeletal men were not typical of the prisoners, and though not furnishing pictures of returned Confederates, the committee asserted that many of them were in as bad or worse condition as the Federals.

The Confederates denied any deliberate mistreatment of their prisoners and attributed any shortages of supplies to the uncivilized nature of the warfare being waged by the United States against the Confederate economy, citing such operations as Gen. Philip Sheridan's devastation of the Shenandoah Valley. Moreover, they sought to attribute the sufferings on both sides to the Union's refusal to exchange prisoners. The Confederates' belated reply to Northern charges, however, received only limited circulation before or after the war's end.

Meanwhile, the warring powers had agreed upon measures to mitigate the prisoners' condition. To reduce political pressure for a general exchange, the Union authorities agreed to release the sick. In September 1864, General Butler proposed the exchange of men believed to be unfit for field service within sixty days. Reports of the bad condition of the several thousand men released under this arrangement built pressure to relieve the remaining prisoners. Confederate exchange agent Ould suggested and Grant agreed to an arrangement whereby each side would be allowed to forward food and clothing to be distributed by paroled officers to its own prisoners. To make this possible for the Confederates, they were permitted to send through the blockade a shipload of cotton for sale in the North. One load was sent and both sides distributed large amounts of goods early in 1865.

At almost the same time, general exchange resumed. Beginning the process in January 1865, Grant accepted a previous Confederate proposal to exchange all prisoners being held in close confinement under various attempts at retaliation. The Confederates—so unable to care for their prisoners that General Winder had unsuccessfully suggested paroling them and simply sending them across the lines—now again attempted to reopen exchange. On February 11, Ould proposed to Grant the delivery of "all the Federal prisoners now in our custody" if the Union would deliver an equal number of Confederates. Grant quickly agreed and both sides notified their overjoyed captives that they would be released.

Why was the Union now willing to exchange? With the administration under increasing attack in and out of Congress for the failure to exchange, Grant had been given personal public responsibility for the controversial matter. He knew that the resumption of active campaigning was still weeks away and that the approach of William Tecum-

ISSUING RATIONS AT ANDERSONVILLE PRISON, GEORGIA. Photograph taken on August 17, 1864, by A. J. Riddle. NATIONAL ARCHIVES

seh Sherman who was about to capture Columbia, South Carolina, made reinforcements for the collapsing Confederate armies a less critical concern. But what of the black prisoners whose plight the Federals had used to explain the earlier refusal to exchange anyone? Did the Confederate offer to free all prisoners include ex-slaves? Previously the Federal authorities had pressed the Confederates to be specific regarding the fate of former slaves. In 1865, the Union did not raise the question, and though the Confederates exchanged several hundred blacks, they never acknowledged returning one who had been a slave before the war. Lincoln's reelection and the anticipated end of the war had reduced the immediate political significance of the status of imprisoned former slaves.

Even as the war entered its final days, both sides continued to manipulate the prisoners for maximum advantage. Grant, correctly believing that his opponents were putting released prisoners into their ranks as quickly as possible, ordered that when possible physically unfit men should be sent first and that prisoners whose homes were in the West should be sent to the East. The Confederates, while too disorganized and harried to discriminate effectively, sought to send Union men who were sick or whose enlistments had expired. Like the Union, the dying Confederacy anticipated taking new prisoners and improvised facilities to hold them. As the surrender of Robert E. Lee marked the beginning of the end, however, the bulk of the remaining Confederate armies were paroled in the field without being held as prisoners of war.

Postwar Issues

It fell to the United States to provide for the repatriation of the prisoners on both sides. Federal prisoners released in the South were fed, reclothed, and returned either to their units or to their home states to be mustered out. As for the imprisoned Confederates, the Union authorities on May 8 ordered the release of all below the rank of colonel who were willing to take the amnesty oath of future allegiance to the United States, a privilege subsequently extended to all prisoners. Out of practical necessity, the Federals paid for their transportation home. The abandoned facilities that had held prisoners on both sides mostly disappeared except for the graves for which the United States ultimately assumed responsibility.

The Federal authorities also took charge of investigating alleged mistreatment of Union soldiers while in Confederate hands and of attempting to punish those responsible. The principal official in charge was Brig. Gen. Joseph Holt, judge advocate general. This Kentucky Unionist, moved by a passionate animus against the Confederates, ordered the arrest of a number of prison keepers and through his Bureau of Military Justice collected evidence and supervised trials by military commission. The flight from the country of several of the accused and the difficulty of finding witnesses after the demobilization of the Union army limited Holt's success. The best-known outcome of his efforts was the trial of Andersonville commandant Capt. Henry Wirz. After a military trial at Washington whose outcome was all but predetermined, Wirz was convicted of conspiring with "others unknown"—presumably the Confederate leadership—to mistreat Union prisoners and was hanged. More fortunate was the commander of Salisbury Prison, Major John H. Gee. After trial in the field, he was acquitted.

The trials came quickly to an end, but the government continued to make its case in the forum of public opinion. In the published records of the Wirz trial and other proceedings such as the trial of the Lincoln assassins, high Confederate officials from Jefferson Davis on down were linked with prison atrocities. In 1869 under Republican auspices, a committee of the House of Representatives investigated conditions in the former Confederate prisons, seeking evidence of Southern "barbarism" stemming from slavery. After hearing some three thousand witnesses, the committee produced a voluminous and highly negative report.

Ex-prisoners often drew upon these government documents to supplement their own recollections and diaries as they wrote memoirs of their prison days. Though a minority believed that their keepers had done their best, most were convinced that they had been the victims of a deliberate plot to destroy the prisoners. Some of them reflected the political partisanship of Reconstruction; others tried to make a case for pensioning the ex-prisoners.

Apologists for the Confederacy struggled against the tide. In memoirs, Jefferson Davis and others sought to show that they had tried to care for the prisoners. Minimizing their own roles in the attempts at retaliation, they blamed the Federal officials for the breakdown of exchange and the resultant suffering of prisoners of both sides. Former Confederates imprisoned in the North also wrote complaints about how they had been treated. No Northern prison, however, could equal the unique horror of Andersonville; moreover, fewer of the nation's publishers and readers of books were in the South. Thus the Confederacy's defenders were never able effectively to answer the Northern prisoners' charges.

The Confederacy's case fared somewhat better in the hands of professional historians. The Ohioan James Ford Rhodes, while doing research for his history of the Civil War, sought from the U.S. adjutant general statistics on the mortality rates in the prisons. He was told by Gen. Fred C. Ainsworth in 1903 that according to the best information obtainable, 211,411 Union soldiers were captured in the Civil War, of whom 16,668 were paroled in the field and 30,218 died in captivity; on the other hand, 462,634 Confederates were captured, of whom 247,769 were paroled and 25,976 died in prison. Rhodes concluded that the prison mortality rate was a bit over 12 percent in the North and 15.5 percent in the South, a difference less than he had expected. Though these percentages rested on admittedly incomplete records, they have been repeated by scholars ever since. Thus historians, including William B. Hesseltine, author of an old but still useful history of Civil War prisons, have not judged harshly the Confederacy's treatment of its captives.

Such has not been true of the popular literature. Even after the deaths of the prisoners, their memoirs and diaries have continued to appear in print to heap shame on their captors. After World War II, MacKinlay Kantor's widely circulated novel *Andersonville* (1955), based on the familiar charges against the Confederacy, suggested a contrived comparison with the horrors of the Nazi death camps and the culpability of their keepers. Interest in the treatment of American prisoners in later wars has helped keep alive the memory of those of the Civil War, ensuring that this topic will remain one of the more controversial aspects of the Confederacy.

[*See also* African American Troops in the Union Army; Andersonville Prison; Belle Isle Prison; Castle Thunder Prison; Enchantress Affair; Fort Delaware Prison; Galvanized Yankees; Johnson's Island Prison; Libby Prison; Northwestern Conspiracy; Point Lookout Prison; Prisons; Privateers; Provost Marshal; Salisbury Prison; Tories; Winder, John H.; Wirz, Henry.]

BIBLIOGRAPHY

Blakey, Arch Frederic. *General John H. Winder, C.S.A.* Gainesville, Fla., 1990.

Brown, Louis A. *The Salisbury Prison: A Case Study of Confederate Military Prisons, 1861–1865.* Wendell, N.C., 1980.

Bryant, William O. *Cahaba Prison and the Sultana Disaster.* Tuscaloosa, Ala., and London, 1990.

Byrne, Frank L. "Prison Pens of Suffering." In *Fighting for Time.* Vol. 4 of *The Image of War, 1861–1865.* Edited by William C. Davis. Garden City, N.Y., 1983.

Futch, Ovid L. *History of Andersonville Prison.* Gainesville, Fla., 1968.

Hesseltine, William B. *Civil War Prisons: A Study in War Psychology.* Columbus, Ohio, 1930. Reprint, New York, 1964.

Hesseltine, William B. "The Propaganda Literature of Confederate Prisons." *Journal of Southern History* 1 (1935): 56–66.

Hesseltine, William B., ed. *Civil War Prisons.* Kent, Ohio, 1962.

Shriver, Philip R., and Donald J. Breen. *Ohio's Civil War Prisons in the Civil War.* Columbus, Ohio, 1964.

Frank L. Byrne

PRISONS. The Confederate prisons began and ended more as a series of improvisations than as a systematic organization. Even before the outbreak of fighting, the Confederates held in temporary camps enlisted men of the U.S. Army taken prisoner in Texas. After the war began, the Confederates captured over a thousand Unionists at their victory at First Manassas and shipped them to Richmond. These they housed in Ligon's Warehouse and Tobacco Factory and in several similar structures. The officer responsible for these captives as well as for the Confederate soldiers and civilians held in other Richmond prisons was the city's provost marshal, Brig. Gen. John H. Winder. Winder had attended West Point and served in the U.S. Army. Because of his age (he was sixty-one when the war started) and probably because he had been lieutenant governor of Vera Cruz during the Mexican War, Winder received his behind-the-lines assignment and quickly became commander of the District of Henrico which surrounded the capital. Stern and unsympathetic, his attempts to regulate civilian life soon made him an object of hatred. Although at first some prisoners found him acceptable, his concern for security combined with the hardships of prolonged captivity in time caused the Union captives to blame him for their woes.

CASTLE PINCKNEY, SOUTH CAROLINA, AUGUST 1861. Confederate soldiers guarding prisoners taken at First Manassas.

LIBRARY OF CONGRESS

To reduce crowding, the Confederates almost immediately began to disperse their prisoners. They had acquired a cotton factory building in Salisbury, North Carolina, which they put into use. They housed others at Castle Pinckney in Charleston Harbor and at jails there and in Columbia, South Carolina. Seeking yet more space, the Confederates also used an abandoned paper mill at Tuscaloosa, Alabama, and the parish prison at New Orleans. Winder remained generally responsible for all these men, although on a rather vague basis. Unlike the Union, the Confederacy did not then have an office of commissary general of prisoners.

In 1862, Winder expanded his Richmond prisons. He took possession of the brick storehouse of Libby and Son, which became notorious as Libby Prison. Besides housing prisoners, it provided office space for Winder's subordinates who managed the local prisons. By midsummer, Winder had found additional space on Belle Isle in the James River on which he opened a rapidly growing camp. Besides the facilities for Union captives, Winder controlled Castle Thunder, a group of tobacco factories used to confine Confederate deserters, civilians, and political prisoners.

Feeding and providing for all these prisoners presented problems the Confederates very much wanted to eliminate. Hence on July 16, 1862, they agreed with the Union army authorities on a cartel providing for prompt paroling and exchange. They rapidly released the inmates of their prisons and closed or abandoned many of them. For some months, Winder was able to make do with a few temporary holding places (notably Libby) while retaining Castle Thunder and Salisbury as prisons for limited numbers of Confederate offenders. But by 1863, quarrels over the execution of the cartel had led to a breakdown of the exchange, and captives were again accumulating. The Confederates still did not appoint a central authority, and Winder continued to improvise prisons.

Because so many prisoners were in or near Richmond when exchange ceased, the Confederate capital became increasingly crowded. Winder converted Libby into a prison mainly for Union officers. To hold enlisted men, he impressed additional warehouses and enlarged the camp on Belle Isle. The presence of thousands of prisoners added to the war-swollen population of Richmond and made it difficult to provide food for all. By the winter of 1863–1864, soldiers and prisoners alike complained of hunger, and the prison authorities worried whether they could control their

LIBBY PRISON, RICHMOND, VIRGINIA. May 1865. NATIONAL ARCHIVES

embittered charges. Moreover, they realized that so many enemies within the capital created a security problem, the gravity of which was underscored by a cavalry raid on February 28 to March 4, 1864, which reached the city's outskirts. To reduce the prison population, the Confederates removed hundreds to six tobacco warehouses in Danville, Virginia.

Seeking a more substantial solution, Winder sent several officers to Georgia to locate sites for additional prisons. He hoped to reduce the difficulty in obtaining food and simultaneously to move the prisoners as far as possible from Union forces who could free them. Andersonville was chosen for a stockade (officially named Camp Sumter for its county) that became the most heavily populated and notorious Confederate prison for enlisted men. In February 1864, the authorities at Richmond began shipping trainloads of prisoners to the still unfinished stockade. In May, they moved the imprisoned officers from Richmond to a camp at Macon, Georgia. Enclosed by a high board fence, the camp had only one small building, which was used as a hospital and as housing for generals; the rest improvised as best they could. Some fifteen hundred officers were at Macon in the summer of 1864.

To control the new prisons, the Confederacy sent General Winder who had been relieved of his Richmond command. Setting his headquarters at Andersonville, he showed some concern over the wretched conditions of the pen and its inmates but devoted most of his attention to worry over its security, fearing breakouts, treachery by local residents, and Union rescue attempts. In July 1864, he was placed in command of all prisons in Georgia and Alabama, including an unfinished cotton warehouse surrounded by a fence on the Alabama River at Cahaba. Set up in 1863 as a temporary holding facility, the Cahaba Prison, which prisoners often informally called "Castle Morgan," held at one time over two thousand enlisted men. Though its prisoners were transferred several times, the Alabama facility remained in use until the war's end. It was less well known than others in the postwar period because of its smaller size and because a large number of its released inmates were killed in the destruction of the Mississippi steamboat *Sultana*.

At the same time Winder took charge of the Deep South prisons, Gen. W. M. Gardner was put in command of prisons in the other states east of the Mississippi. A Georgian who earlier had been wounded, Gardner, from headquarters at Richmond, supervised prisons in Virginia and North Carolina, which continued to be used largely for transients. When the Confederate War Department ordered the suspension of shipments to overcrowded Andersonville, the prisons farther north again began to overflow. Considering the deteriorating conditions, it is not inappropriate to compare the prisons to ill-constructed, partially blocked sewers.

Meanwhile conditions were slightly better in the Trans-Mississippi region of the Confederacy where prisons, like every other aspect of life, were run independently of the Richmond authorities after 1863. The Confederates selected as sites for prisons training camps in Texas, which offered a supply of guards. One was Camp Groce at Hempstead; another and more important one was Camp Ford at Tyler. Its stockade enclosed five acres and was later enlarged to ten. As at Andersonville, the prisoners had to improvise their own shelter and received no clothing from their captors. They were issued rations of cornmeal and beef. Unlike most prisons, Camp Ford confined both army officers and enlisted men, as well as navy men and enemy civilians. At maximum it held over 4,500 prisoners at one time, but because of its abundant water, only 286 died out of a total of 6,000.

Meanwhile, General Winder struggled to create new prisons and to shift captives to more remote locations. In August 1864, at a site near the railroad at Millen, Georgia, he ordered work to begin on a stockade enclosing forty-two acres, which he called Camp Lawton after the Confederate quartermaster general, Alexander R. Lawton, a Georgian. With a strange pride, Winder remarked, "I presume it is the largest prison in the world." Although the interior was laid out in a more orderly fashion than was Andersonville (from which most of its inmates were transferred), the prisoners again were left to improvise shelter. By November 8, 1864, some 10,299 prisoners had been incarcerated there under the command of Capt. D. W. Vowles. But a week later the approach of Gen. William Tecumseh Sherman's raiding troops forced the hasty abandonment of Millen. Winder had some of the prisoners shifted to temporary camps at Blackshear and Thomasville in southern Georgia and then returned some to Andersonville, where the Confederates belatedly erected a few sheds to shelter a minority of the inmates.

When the Confederates had sent some Andersonville prisoners to Millen, they had dispersed others to Savannah where they were held in a fenced camp. Still others were transported to a similar encampment at the fairgrounds in Charleston, with some crowding into the yard of the city jail. Earlier in the summer, the Confederates had moved the imprisoned officers at Macon to the same two cities. At Charleston the officers gave their paroles not to escape and were lodged comfortably in the Roper Hospital. Southern commanders at the besieged seaports objected to the accumulation of prisoners and moved quickly to rid themselves of them.

These movements of prisoners were decided upon by local commanders rather than by the man who on November 21, 1864, was placed in charge of all prisoners. The Confederate adjutant general issued an order putting General Winder in command of all guard personnel and inmates in prisons east of the Mississippi. Officers were warned not to interfere with his charges. At last the Confederacy had a commissary general of prisoners, but it was too late to do much good. The South's diminishing resources and Sherman's armies made it all but impossible to provide adequately for the prisoners or indeed to move them to places safe from recapture. Nonetheless the elderly general established headquarters at Augusta, Georgia, and set about his job.

The commander at Charleston, Gen. Samuel Jones, had begun in September 1864 to send off prisoners to the interior rail junction at Florence. There thousands were held in an open field while the local military built a stockade surrounded by an earthwork from which guards could keep watch. As at Andersonville and Millen, a stream ran through it, around which developed a swamp occupying six out of twenty-six acres. The men received rations so limited that by late January 1865, the commandant pronounced them near starvation. Of a total of 12,000 men at Florence, 2,802 died. While enlisted men suffered at Florence, their officers were only a little better off at Columbia, South Carolina. There in an open field they were directed to build huts before winter. When syrup was substituted for the meat ration, the prisoners called it "Camp Sorghum." Because so many escaped, the South Carolina state authorities consented to the transfer of the officers to a more secure location on the grounds of a local institution for the insane, which became known as Camp Asylum.

Meanwhile the government at Richmond decided on desperate action to free their capital of imprisoned officers and enlisted men. To eliminate the drain on the food supply of the besieged city before the winter of 1864–1865, they sent the officers to the tobacco warehouses at Danville where 2,400 prisoners of all ranks were crowded. Early in October they emptied the camp of enlisted men on Belle Isle, sending about 7,500 to Salisbury. Given the 800 military and political prisoners already there, the prison was instantly overcrowded. It was rather like someone trying to pour a gallon of water into a quart bottle. General Winder reported in December that conditions at Salisbury were worse than at Florence (indeed, both resembled Andersonville on a smaller scale).

Winder's solution was to build another prison. He sought property on the railroad fourteen miles above Columbia, and there at Killian's Mills began to construct a new stockade, which he hoped would, with Andersonville and Millen, house all his captives. Hence he moved his headquarters to Columbia. But unable either to supply his prisoners or to move them to safety from recapture by Sherman's troops advancing through the Carolinas, he suggested paroling the prisoners and sending them home without exchange. On February 6, 1865, just before the resumption of exchange, Winder died suddenly of a massive heart attack while inspecting the prison at Florence.

The prisoners rejoiced at the death of Winder, whom they viewed as the chief villain responsible for their sufferings. They circulated a rumor that his last words were "Cut off the molasses, boys." On February 14, the Confederates replaced him with Brig. Gen. Gideon Pillow, who had been largely inactive since being discredited by his involvement in the surrender of Fort Donelson. On March 20, he in turn was replaced by the invalided W. M. Gardner, superseded four days later by the more vigorous Gen. Daniel Ruggles. Under the supervision of these men, the prisoners in the Carolinas were moved up to a temporary holding site at Charlotte. Union forces subsequently seized the prisons at Columbia and Salisbury.

Meanwhile exchanges were occurring at Wilmington, North Carolina; City Point, Virginia; Vicksburg; and the mouth of the Red River. The Richmond prisons, including Libby and Castle Thunder, continued to hold mostly transient inmates until the city's fall. Even then, General Ruggles continued construction of the new prison at Killian's Mills and expected to house at Danville prisoners captured by Robert E. Lee.

With Lee's surrender and the collapse of the Confederacy, the prison system was abandoned. The last to close was Camp Ford, evacuated on May 17. Later the Federal authorities arrested a number of the prison officials. Though they were blamed then and later for the terrible conditions, far more responsibility lay with their superiors. They had delayed until too late the systematizing of the prisons and, like their Union counterparts, never gave enough attention to the welfare of the helpless pawns with which they were playing.

[*For further discussion of Confederate prisons, see* Andersonville Prison; Belle Isle Prison; Castle Thunder Prison; Libby Prison; Salisbury Prison. *For discussion of Federal prisons, see* Fort Delaware Prison; Johnson's Island Prison; Point Lookout Prison. *See also* Enchantress Affair; Prisoners of War; Provost Marshal; Winder, John H.]

BIBLIOGRAPHY

Blakey, Arch Frederic. *General John H. Winder, C.S.A.* Gainesville, Fla., 1990.

Brown, Louis A. *The Salisbury Prison: A Case Study of Confederate Military Prisons, 1861–1865.* Wendell, N.C., 1980.

Bryant, William O. *Cahaba Prison and the Sultana Disaster.* Tuscaloosa, Ala., and London, 1990.

Byrne, Frank L. "Prison Pens of Suffering." In *Fighting for Time.* Vol. 4 of *The Image of War, 1861–1865.* Edited by William C. Davis. Garden City, N.Y., 1983.

Futch, Ovid L. *History of Andersonville Prison.* Gainesville, Fla., 1968.

Hesseltine, William B. *Civil War Prisons: A Study in War Psychology.* Columbus, Ohio, 1930. Reprint, New York, 1964.

Lawrence, F. Lee, and Robert W. Glover. *Camp Ford, C.S.A.: The Story of Union Prisoners in Texas.* Austin, Tex., 1964.

Parker, Sandra V. *Richmond's Civil War Prisons.* Lynchburg, Va., 1990.

FRANK L. BYRNE

PRIVATEERS. Privately owned armed vessels authorized to prey upon enemy shipping were used in every American war prior to 1861. Convinced that privateering could help the Confederacy, President Jefferson Davis on April 17, 1861, published a proclamation offering letters of marque and reprisal to all interested parties. Initial response was enthusiastic, especially from New Orleans and Charleston. Privateers ranged from the little *Sea Hawk,* with its crew of 9, cruising Chesapeake Bay, to the ten-gun steamer *Isabella* of New Orleans, carrying 175 sailors and 50 marines.

The first of the New Orleans privateers was the 509-ton sidewheel steamer *Calhoun,* armed with five cannon and manned by a crew of 85. The six prizes it captured during May 1861 brought a considerable profit in New Orleans to its owners. Although other privateers—the 273-ton steamer *Music,* the 454-ton steamer *V. H. Ivy,* a former towboat, and the 95-ton schooner *J. O. Nixon*—also hunted off the mouth of the Mississippi, the operation of the New Orleans privateers ended in July 1861 as the Federal blockade tightened.

At Charleston, during the summer of 1861, the former pilot boat *Savannah* and the brig *Jefferson Davis* were commissioned as privateers. Commanded by one of its owners, Capt. Louis M. Coxetter, *Jefferson Davis* (the former slave ship *Echo*) took eight prizes before being wrecked off St. Augustine that August. Prize crew members aboard two of the prizes—*Enchantress* and *S. J. Waring*—became prisoners when the vessels were retaken while being brought to port. The men were tried and found guilty of piracy in compliance with President Abraham Lincoln's policy toward privateering (despite U.S. refusal in 1856 to join other maritime nations in condemning privateering and commerce raiding). Although Lincoln was apparently willing to allow the execution of convicted "pirates," he backed off when Davis prepared to execute Northern military prisoners in reprisal. Henceforth, prisoners taken from Southern privateers were treated as ordinary prisoners of war.

Another Charleston privateer, the 110-ton schooner *Dixie,* successfully brought one of its prizes to Moorhead City, North Carolina, and a second to Charleston; a third was retaken by USS *Wabash.* Although privateers *Gordon* and *Sallie* of Charleston took several prizes, another—*Beauregard*—was captured, and *Rattlesnake* sank after striking a mine.

Hatteras, North Carolina, became a cruising ground for privateers—*York, Mariner,* and *Gordon*—and North Carolina navy gunboats until the capture of Hatteras Inlet by Federal forces in August 1861. By then, *York* had been run ashore and set afire by its crew.

As Federal naval forces tightened the blockade and the threat of invasion increased, privateering vessels were subject to forced sale or charter to the Confederacy. This was the fate of *Ivy, Music,* and *Manassas I,* a 387-ton former tugboat converted to an ironclad ram at Algiers, Louisiana, and intended for use as a privateer. This formidible ram, taken over by Confederate authorities in December 1861, engaged a Federal squadron the following April.

A submarine, *Pioneer,* commissioned in March 1862, was also meant for use as a privateer. The two-man submersible, however, was deliberately sunk the following month to prevent its capture.

Eventually, the privateers *Dixie, Sallie, Gordon,* and *Mariner* became blockade runners. And, following their capture by blockaders, *Calhoun, Savannah,* and *Beauregard* became U.S. warships.

Among privateer captains, Coxetter and John C. Brain are particularly renowned for their exploits. In December 1863 the English-born Brain and sixteen companions commandeered the cargo-passenger vessel *Chesapeake* after boarding as passengers at New York. He had earlier obtained official authorization for his action by a letter of marque. Brain later used the same method to capture the U.S. mail steamer *Roanoke.* After transferring to the captured schooner *St. Mary's,* he continued to Jamaica, where he abandoned his prize.

Several vessels earmarked for use as privateers were, in fact, never used, and plans to use Confederate privateers in the Pacific never materialized.

Despite the success of a few privateers operating out of Southern ports early in the war, their activities ended as the blockade became more effective. As a result, Southern investors turned from privateering to blockade running as a less risky business venture. And commerce raiders, commissioned as Confederate warships, became more effective than privateering in preying upon the North's ocean commerce.

[*See also* Enchantress Affair *and entry on the ship* Jefferson Davis.]

BIBLIOGRAPHY

Hay, David, and Joan Hay. *The Last of the Confederate Privateers.* Edinburgh, 1977.

Robinson, William M. *The Confederate Privateers.* New Haven, 1928.

Silvertone, Paul H. *Warships of the Civil War Navies.* Annapolis, 1989.

NORMAN C. DELANEY

PRODUCE LOAN. A series of produce loans contributed to financing the Confederate war effort. The concept had its origin when many people became aware that the Confederacy had to acquire supplies for the military; that it had to secure funds sooner than it could establish a tax system; and that it had to pay for those supplies when possible with bonds instead of Treasury notes in order to limit the currency and thus forestall inflation. Commodities, still in the hands of their producers, might be exchanged for twenty-year, 8 percent bonds. The produce loan was designed to persuade farmers and planters to lend to the Confederacy a portion of the proceeds from the sale of such staples as cotton, tobacco, and sugar; it might secure military provisions, too. The Confederate Treasury could employ the anticipated receipts as the basis for establishing credit in Europe and across the South.

The Confederate Congress inaugurated the plan in a measure approved May 16, 1861, and expanded its terms to $100 million from $50 million on August 19. Additional acts of April 21, 1862, February 20, 1863, and April 30, 1863, expanded it further. Many planters proved enthusiastic about the plan, though smaller farmers typically had greater need for cash for their crops. In any case, the produce loan had as its premise a sale of commodities, and the Federal blockade rendered the export of cotton problematic. In addition, volunteer personnel failed to canvass some parts of the Deep South, and with much of the upper South the scene of military action, tobacco remained only marginal to the plan's operation. Finally, conditions for many producers had changed mightily between the time in the summer of 1861 when they pledged a loan and the time that fall when the crops came in.

Like so much of Confederate finance, the produce loan was flawed in both conception and implementation. That the 1861 acts generated only $34 million, one-third the stipulated amount (and 1.1 percent of the $3 billion in aggregate Confederate revenue), points to the limited success of the program. To a degree, however, the plan achieved its objectives. The produce loan operated to restrain the issue of Treasury notes and thus postponed destabilization of the currency, and the cotton thus obtained helped secure the Erlanger loan.

[*See also* Erlanger Loan.]

BIBLIOGRAPHY

Ball, Douglas, B. *Financial Failure and Confederate Defeat.* Urbana, Ill., 1991.

Schwab, John Christopher. *The Confederate States of America, 1861–1865: A Financial and Industrial History of the South during the Civil War.* New York, 1901. Reprint, New York, 1968.

Todd, Richard Cecil. *Confederate Finance.* Athens, Ga., 1954.

PETER WALLENSTEIN

PROPAGANDA. The South chose correctly to focus its propaganda effort on Great Britain because, as the world's greatest power, that nation's action or inaction could not only decide the outcome of the American war but also influence the position of France and other European states. Yet, despite its obvious importance, the Southern campaign to obtain British intervention was delayed until 1862 owing to the understandable but mistaken belief that Britain's dependence upon Southern raw cotton would force its hand. Confederate complacency was also strengthened by the knowledge that most of the English press, a majority of the Parliament, and the ministerial leaders were either anti-Northern or pro-Southern. Although Confederate leaders knew that many of the English hated slavery, President Abraham Lincoln had weakened that barrier to favorable relations by declaring that his objective was to save the Union, not destroy slavery.

Organized propaganda began inauspiciously when twenty-seven-year-old Henry Hotze, a naturalized Swiss journalist from Mobile, returned to Richmond from Europe late in 1861 and persuaded a skeptical Robert M. T. Hunter, secretary of state, to send him to England to educate British writers about the South. Arriving in January 1862 Hotze quickly succeeded in obtaining the help of several English journalists. He either wrote articles for them or assisted them in their preparation while permitting them to collect the customary fee. Soon there was a marked increase in pro-Southern materials in leading London newspapers. Hotze also boldly helped Southern sympathizers in Parliament prepare their speeches and supplied them with timely and accurate information.

Much encouraged, the opportunistic young Swiss decided to publish a weekly newspaper called the *Index.* While providing employment, money, and education for the English writers, it also served as a much needed repository for collecting and controlling Southern news. Given this monopoly, Hotze designed the *Index* to reach not the mass public but a select readership of the most influential groups in Great Britain such as the cabinet, Parliament, business leaders, and the print media. To instill confidence in the *Index,* he made the paper thoroughly English in style and appearance and moderate in its content.

Hotze faced some serious problems, however. Inadequate government funding forced him to depend on uncertain private contributions. Some impatient Southerners and English friends withheld support because they disliked the paper's temperate tone or doubted its effectiveness. It was also difficult to obtain timely and accurate information. But Hotze persevered. He published the *Index* until August 1865 and succeeded in making it the centerpiece of the Confederate propaganda program.

Meanwhile, a South Carolinian, Edwin de Leon, while in Europe had also observed a need for propaganda. Returning to Richmond, he persuaded President Jefferson Davis, an old friend, to appoint him chief Confederate propagandist overseas. His large contingency fund and instructions left no doubt that much was expected of him. At the time, President Davis, Judah P. Benjamin (recently appointed secretary of state), and de Leon were unaware of Hotze's success.

Arriving in London in late June 1862, de Leon observed Hotze's thriving operation and quickly moved on to France. There he incurred the wrath of John Slidell, Confederate commissioner to France, by delivering to him dispatches from Richmond with broken seals. But undaunted and confident of President Davis's friendship and support, de Leon pushed ahead. He hired French writers, thereby substantially increasing the flow of pro-Southern articles in French papers. He prepared a brochure called *La vérité sur les Etats Confédérés d'Amérique,* which served as source material for French journalists. Taking a cue from Hotze, de Leon subsidized Felix Aucaigne, editor of the *Paris Patrie,* making that journal a Confederate paper.

He ventured across the English Channel, inserted articles in English newspapers and magazines, countered Federal attacks on the Southern cotton loan, and supported Hotze in the distribution of an important piece entitled *An Address of the Southern Clergy to Christians.*

De Leon's mission ended abruptly late in 1863 when the Federals intercepted a dispatch of his to Richmond in which he criticized Slidell and denounced the French press as mercenary. After publication in the *New York Daily Tribune,* it created such a stir that Davis was forced to remove de Leon, much to the delight of Slidell and the relief of Hotze.

Benjamin, by now a strong supporter of Hotze, promptly asked him to extend operations to the Continent. In France he reversed de Leon's practice of hiring French writers and canceled the subsidy to Aucaigne's *Patrie.* He persuaded Auguste Havas, director of the Havas Agency, which enjoyed a monopoly in supplying foreign news to French editors, to accept pro-Southern articles previously published in England. He thus succeeded in expanding the dissemination of the Southern version of the conflict at little cost. Late in 1864 in the German states Hotze attempted to thwart the sale of Union bonds but with little success.

The efforts of Hotze and de Leon were bolstered by a contingent of English propagandists. Among the more prominent and effective of them were Alexander James Beresford Hope, who published two influential pieces: *A Popular View of the American War* and *The American Disruption;* F. W. Tremblett, an Anglican minister, who organized the Society for Cessation of Hostilities in America; and James Spence, by far the most important, who published in 1861 *The American Union* in which he vindicated the South but upset Southerners by suggesting that an independent Confederacy would abandon slavery. The book quickly went through four editions and became the most influential propaganda tract produced during the war. Spence also wrote many letters to the London *Times,* organized numerous Southern Clubs, staged pro-Southern rallies, and vigorously supported Tremblett's peace movement.

Still another aspect of Confederate propaganda involved efforts in 1863 and 1864 to counter Federal recruiting of Irishmen and Germans to relieve labor shortages and replenish the ranks of Northern armies. The alert Hotze hired private detectives to shadow Federal recruiters in Ireland to obtain evidence of violations of the British Foreign Enlistment Act (which forbade recruitment for foreign armies). But he found that Northern agents recruited Irishmen as laborers and did not offer them enlistment in the army until after they had left Ireland. In response to urgent pleas from James Mason, Confederate commissioner to Great Britain, and A. Dudley Mann, Confederate envoy to Belgium, Benjamin sent several agents to Ireland to operate under Hotze's supervision. Among them were Father John Bannon, a Confederate army chaplain, and Bishop P. N. Lynch from Charleston who worked directly with Irish priests to discourage parishioners from leaving. No agents were sent to the German states, but Mann himself undertook several small projects there, and at Benjamin's request he successfully petitioned Pope Pius IX to appeal directly to Irishmen and Germans not to emigrate. These measures may have slowed emigration, but harsh living conditions in the Old World coupled with the lure of Northern job opportunities and enlistment bounties were simply too great to overcome.

In the meantime, on both sides of the Atlantic, Confederate supporters by 1864 were noting with growing interest and anticipation the unrest and clamor for peace in the North, especially in the Old Northwest. The reports of disaffection gained increased credibility when Republicans, fearing Lincoln's defeat in the upcoming presidential election, charged vociferously that peacemongers and opponents of the war were traitors to the Union cause.

The swelling uproar convinced Southern leaders that with encouragement war-weary northwesterners, joined in a tenuous alliance with the East, might revolt and perhaps establish a separate government. Failing that, they could provide sufficient votes, in combination with those of dissident easterners, to defeat Lincoln and install in the White House a peace Democrat who would negotiate a settlement on Southern terms.

Consequently efforts toward this end were launched both in Great Britain and in the South. Hotze called the attention of *Index* readers to Northern disenchantment and the emerging peace movement, and Spence and Tremblett gathered several hundred thousand signatures for a peace petition. In Richmond, Davis commissioned Jacob Thompson of Mississippi and Clement C. Clay of Alabama to set up a base in Canada. There they were in touch with many Northerners including the notorious copperhead Clement L. Vallandigham; Benjamin Wood, owner and editor of the

CLEMENT C. CLAY. Confederate Secret Service operative in Canada. *HARPER'S PICTORIAL HISTORY OF THE GREAT REBELLION*

New York Daily News, vigorously pro-Southern and a contributor of news and articles to Hotze's *Index;* and Horace Greeley, the eccentric editor of the *New York Tribune.* Greeley succeeded with the help of the Southern commissioners in inducing Lincoln to discuss peace negotiations. The president was politically afraid to refuse peace overtures outright and was lured by the possibility that peace talks could weaken Peace Democrat opposition while strengthening his support among moderate Republicans. But when he insisted that reunion and abolition must be preconditions for negotiations, Lincoln's obstinacy produced instead a backlash that exacerbated the peace movement.

Thompson and Clay also helped plan and finance plots to promote an insurrection in the Old Northwest to liberate Confederate prisoners in Northern prison camps, to create a financial panic by buying gold and shipping it to Europe, to burn New York City, and to raid towns along the Canadian border. But their plots came to nothing. Although operational plans were well conceived, there were frequent communication breakdowns, and close surveillance by Union and Canadian authorities constantly plagued the conspirators. Above all else Confederate operations backfired because, as Thompson and Clay discovered time and again, agitated Northerners, Republican allegations to the contrary, were not prepared to take the bold leap from political rhetoric to insurrection and disunion.

After Gen. George B. McClellan, the Democratic nominee for president, openly repudiated the peace plank in the party's platform and Federal military fortunes improved dramatically in the fall of 1864, any hope for a Northern insurrection or peace negotiations evaporated, Lincoln's reelection was assured, and the fate of the Confederacy sealed.

In retrospect, the Southern propaganda program, though belated, was accurately focused and, despite the ineptness of de Leon and the failure of the Thompson and Clay mission, surprisingly well coordinated, owing chiefly to the spirited, imaginative, and tireless efforts of Henry Hotze and James Spence.

[*See also* Clay, Clement C.; Hotze, Henry; Index; Leon, Edward de; Northwestern Conspiracy; Thompson, Jacob.]

BIBLIOGRAPHY

Cullop, Charles P. *Confederate Propaganda in Europe, 1861–1865.* Coral Gables, Fla., 1969.

Jenkins, Brian. *Britain and the War for the Union.* 2 vols. Montreal, 1980.

Kinchen, Oscar A. *Confederate Operations in Canada and the North.* North Quincy, Mass., 1970.

Nelson, Lawrence. *Bullets, Ballots, and Rhetoric.* University, Ala., 1980.

Owsley, Frank L. *King Cotton Diplomacy: Foreign Relations of the Confederate States of America.* 2d ed. Revised by Harriet C. Owsley. Chicago, 1959.

CHARLES P. CULLOP

PROSLAVERY. The term *proslavery,* as used by antebellum abolitionists and proponents of slavery, and by historians, encompasses two historical phenomena: first, the attitude of favoring slavery (particularly black slavery) and its continuance and of opposing any interference with it, and second, the emergence in the United States from the 1830s through the Civil War of a literature vigorously arguing that the institution of slavery was beneficial for both slaves and society. The term has also been used incorrectly and inconsistently to describe certain writings that denigrate the role of African Americans, Hispanics, Asiatics, and other ethnic groups in the United States.

Once believed to be peculiar to the Old South and the Confederacy, proslavery literature, recent studies have shown, appeared wherever slavery existed; in the United States proslavery books, tracts, and pamphlets were produced prior to the Civil War by a great variety of individuals in both the North and the South. Particularly important in the early articulation of America's proslavery outlook, for example, were individuals who were born or educated in New England and Northern states, well educated (especially at such institutions as Yale and Princeton), professional (clergy, lawyers, journalists), and among the nation's most eminent nonpolitical leaders. As time passed, however, America's proslavery writers more frequently tended to be individuals native to and educated in the South. Many were members of the intellectual and cultural elite of the period.

A number of the more important pieces of proslavery literature appeared in the 1830s and 1840s. Although some historians have cited an 1832 essay by Thomas R. Dew, *Review of the Debate in the Virginia Legislature of 1831 and 1832,* as the launching pad for the aggressive Southern defense of slavery, it was actually an argument against African colonization as a permanent solution to what were seen as the dual problems of slavery and a large African population in the United States. William Harper's *Anniversary Oration* (1836) is often noted as one of the next major articulations of a proslavery perspective. James H. Hammond's *Two Letters on Slavery in the United States, Addressed to Thomas Clarkson, esq.* (1845) expressed the widely held position in the South that not only was slavery not evil; it was a positive benefit to society.

Other studies of the arguments that slavery was a positive good have noted that they also appeared in contexts other than the Old South, including the British West Indies and Great Britain itself. As early as the 1790s, in the course of parliamentary debates on the African slave trade and the future of slavery in the West Indies, numerous British writers held that slavery was not only a benefit to the West Indian plantation economy. They also held that it was a benefit to Africans who were thereby saved from the "savagery" of their native lands to live in peace within the Christian religion under the guidance of enlightened Englishmen. Even at this early period of the Industrial Revolution, these writers argued that the lot of the slave was superior to that of factory workers and their families.

Some of the most widely distributed and frequently cited proslavery publications during and just before the Civil War were the following:

From the North: Nehemiah Adams (Congregational clergyman, Boston), *A South-side View of Slavery* (1854); Charles Hodge (professor, Princeton Theological Seminary), *The Bible Argument on Slavery* (1857); John Henry Hopkins (Episcopal bishop of Vermont), *Bible View of Slavery* (1861) and *Scriptural, Ecclesiastical, and Historical View of Slavery* (1864); Charles Jared Ingersoll (lawyer and congressman, Philadelphia), *African Slavery in America* (1856); Nathan Lord (president of Dartmouth College), *A Letter of Inquiry to Ministers of the Gospel of all Denominations on Slavery* (1860) and *A True Picture of Abolition* (1863); Samuel F. B. Morse (inventor, artist, and manufacturer, New York), *Present Attempt to Dissolve the American Union* (1862); Nathan L. Rice (editor and college professor, Chicago), *Lectures on Slavery* (1860); Stuart Robinson (editor and clergyman, Louisville, Kentucky), *Slavery as Recognized in the Mosaic Civil Law* (1856) (1865); Samuel Seabury (Episcopal clergyman and college professor, New York City), *American Slavery Distinguished from the Slavery of English Theorists and Justified by the Law of Nature* (1861); and Hubbard Winslow (editor and author, Brooklyn), *Elements of Moral Philosophy* (1856).

From the South: E. N. Elliott (lawyer and college president, Mississippi), *Cotton Is King, and Pro-Slavery Arguments* (1860); George Dodd Armstrong (Presbyterian clergyman, Norfolk, Virginia), *The Christian Doctrine of Slavery* (1857); Albert Taylor Bledsoe (college professor at the University of Virginia), *Essay on Liberty and Slavery* (1856); George Fitzhugh (lawyer and author, Virginia), *Sociology for the South* (1854) and *Cannibals All!* (1859); James Henry Hammond (planter, governor, and U.S. senator), *Speech at Barnwell Courthouse, Oct. 29, 1858* (1858) and *Speech on the Admission of Kansas* (1858); Josiah Nott (physician, Mobile, Alabama), *Types of Mankind* (1854); Frederick A. Ross (manufacturer, clergyman, Alabama), *Slavery Ordained of God* (1857); Edmund Ruffin (planter, agronomist, Virginia), *The Political Economy of Slavery* (1857); William A. Smith (clergyman, president of Randolph-Macon College), *Lectures on the Philosophy & Practice of Slavery* (1856); Thornton Stringfellow (clergyman, planter), *Scriptural and Statistical Views in Favor of Slavery* (1856); and James H. Thornwell (clergyman, president of South Carolina College), *The Rights and Duties of Masters* (1850).

Wherever proslavery literature appeared, virtually identical arguments were used to justify the perpetuation of the institution. Because most American slaves were African Americans, many arguments related to their African past. Proslavery authors generally maintained that Africans historically had lived in uncivilized, barbaric, and degraded conditions, that many had always been held in slavery, and that therefore they did not find slavery an unusual or irksome condition. Many also held that Africans were racially inferior and were incapable of being civilized or of functioning well in situations where they would have to compete with European Americans. In their view, Africans would always require supervision and control. Indeed, some argued, Africans were happier in an enslaved than in a free condition.

Other proslavery authors maintained that slavery was the most perfect labor and welfare system ever devised: because slaves were property—a capital investment—slaveholders had a direct interest in treating them kindly. To preserve their investment, slaveholders would provide housing, food, and clothing and guard their chattels' health and welfare. No other form of labor—especially "wage slavery"—provided such protection.

The institution, it was argued, also benefited society at large. Because slaves were controlled by laws and occupied a dependent condition, societies with slavery were ensured against radical and revolutionary movements. Whereas capitalism tended to abandon the indigent and the ill, ran the reasoning, slavery provided a place and a caretaker for every individual.

Its advocates also held that American slavery was qualitatively different from other slave systems in history. Given the enlightened, religious, and freedom-loving character of Americans, they argued that slavery in the United States was the mildest and most benevolent form of slavery that had ever existed. The American system tended to civilize and Christianize barbaric Africans. The writers asserted that slaveholders, guided by the examples of slavery in the Bible, by Christian teachings, and by principles of the American Revolution, looked upon slavery as a "divine trust" practiced as God would have it for all ages.

Slavery, they further argued, was clearly a moral institution. This they supported by reference to the Bible. God had sanctioned slavery by placing his curse on Ham, by issuing laws for the governance of slavery among the patriarchs and the people of Israel, and by countenancing the practice in both the Old and the New Testaments. Not only did Christ and his apostles not condemn the practice of slavery; they admonished slaves to obey their masters and decreed that fugitive slaves should be returned to their owners.

Whereas many in America held with Thomas Jefferson and other framers of the Declaration of Independence that all men have the right to life, liberty, and the pursuit of happiness, proslavery writers insisted that such a right did not extend to the enslaved. Since, in these men's minds, slavery was a humane institution that provided for the comfort and care of those enslaved, it followed that it was a reasonable and fair practice, not inconsistent with the laws of nature. Essay after essay contended that the Founding Fathers never intended to argue that the enslavement of a servile race was inconsistent with the laws of nature.

Nor, they argued, was it theologically incorrect. God would not decree sin into existence. Indeed, it seemed to them that God specifically brought slavery into existence as a tool to save the "heathen." The master-slave relationship seemed just as divinely ordained as that of husband and wife or father and child; it would end only with the millennium or the end of time.

Most proslavery writers went beyond the mere justification of slavery as a moral and viable institution. They also held that in the master-slave relationship certain duties and responsibilities fell to the master. Whatever legal authority he had, the master was also morally responsible to provide the comforts of life to slaves, to give them just and fair treatment, to protect their families, and to provide religious instruction. When all was said and done, proslavery writers contended, masters were answerable to God for carrying out their divinely ordained roles.

Within the broad field of proslavery history there developed an American school of ethnology that—through pseudoscientific methods and theories—found the Negro to be a separate species from Caucasian whites. Dr. Samuel George Morton published *Crania Americana* in 1839 documenting his measurements and analyses of human skulls from all parts of the world. George R. Glidden, America's premier Egyptologist; Louis Agassiz, Swiss-born Harvard biologist; and many others added endless data intended to confirm the theory of separate species among humankind.

Although these ethnological treatises suggested separate origins for various races and thereby flew in the face of the biblical account of a single creation, the burgeoning field of scientific studies attracted clergymen who attempted to resolve the disparities among theology, science, and racial theory. Moses Ashley Curtis in North Carolina and John Bachman and Thomas Smyth in Charleston—all Northern-born and educated clergy—wrote profusely on the subject in religious as well as scientific publications.

Others made use of this pseudoscience either to defend slavery or to argue for the expulsion of blacks from America. Dr. Josiah C. Nott, a physician in Mobile, Alabama, and Dr. John H. Van Evrie, a physician in New York City, were among the most prolific popularizers of the theory. But the numbers of disciples were legion and included Sidney George Fisher of Philadelphia, Thomas Ewbank of Washington (U.S. commissioner of patents), and even Boston's Charles Eliot Norton, a conservative intellectual at Harvard.

Despite the abundance of arguments in the proslavery arsenal and the emergence of popular theory about racial disparities, typical proslavery literature wasted little space in recounting arguments that were largely part and parcel of the Western heritage. Most proslavery writers were concerned with other issues relating to the world of slaveholding. Many felt that those who opposed slavery were in actuality "jacobins," "infidels," and revolutionaries who wanted to upend not only slavery but also American society and government. Some were fearful that if slavery were abolished, America would forever harbor an alien population that might rise against whites or descend into "bestiality" and sap the energy and financial resources of the nation. Others looked with disfavor at the effects of laissez-faire capitalism on the nation's work force, wishing to avert what they saw as a system of wage slavery in the United States. Still others argued that slavery and the future of blacks in America were such divisive issues that they would lead to the Union's disruption.

Moreover, most proslavery literature in America not specifically intended to argue issues of race, ethnology, scripture, theology, or the economy contained a specific worldview that was conservative socially and philosophically, that was reformist and positive in purpose, and that promoted order and responsibility in society. It was not allied with any political party or movement; rather, it was an outgrowth of reactions to disruptive and revolutionary forces in the Western world. Fearful of the chaos they associated particularly with the French and Haitian revolutions, most proslavery writers excoriated abolitionists as irresponsible revolutionaries bent on destroying the American republic. To avoid such disruption, they espoused the reform of slavery, urging masters to exercise their proper duties and responsibilities to slaves and to bring their slaves into religious institutions.

Eventually the problems of slavery and Union became so intertwined that they could no longer be avoided. The election of Abraham Lincoln as president in 1860 brought the issues to a head. Immediately following his election, hundreds of orators and clergymen throughout the nation addressed the future of slavery and the Union in furious speeches and sermons. In the South, such men as Benjamin Morgan Palmer of New Orleans called for the Southern states to leave the Union and protect the "divine trust" of slavery. In the North, other voices concurred, including such prominent clergy as Henry J. Van Dyke of the First Presbyterian Church of Brooklyn and Rabbi Morris Jacob Raphall at B'nai Jeshurum in New York City.

As the nation's political institutions faltered, Southerners thought the time at hand when the South could pursue the practice of slavery without interference from outside forces. Proslavery ideas and arguments fused with religious images, as speakers envisioned the Confederacy building the Kingdom of God on earth complete with a perfected form of slavery. The new nation would become a harmonious organic unity with places for masters and slaves, capital and labor, merchants and craftsmen. Some men, such as Leonidas Spratt of Charleston, a proponent for the reopening of the African slave trade, thought that the time was at hand to augment the South's work force with fresh hands from Africa. Others, such as Henry Hughes of Mississippi, called the South's perfected form of slavery "warranteeism"; slaveholders, he said, owned not the person but his productive labor.

Alexander H. Stephens, Confederate vice president, took a contrary point of view in 1861 in what came to be known as the "cornerstone speech." Believing the popular literature classifying whites and blacks as separate species, Stephens asserted that the Confederacy provided an opportunity to enforce the laws of nature: "Our system commits no . . . violation of nature's laws. With us, all the white race, however high or low, rich or poor, are equal in the eyes of the law. Not so with the Negro. Subordination is his place. He, by nature, or by the curse against Canaan, is fitted for that condition which he occupies in our system."

Euphoria surrounding the creation of the Confederacy complete with slavery continued despite the onset of the war. In dozens of fast days and thanksgiving days proclaimed by President Jefferson Davis to celebrate military victories or contemplate the meaning of defeats, the barrage of proslavery pronouncements continued apace. Among the thousands of Confederate imprints still in existence—pamphlets, books, sermons, broadsides, and the like—half or more are reiterations of the centrality of slavery in Southern life and the appropriateness of the institution in the Confederacy.

Nor did the opening of a war for Southern independence halt the publication of proslavery literature throughout the North. After the election of Lincoln, Samuel F. B. Morse gathered like-minded individuals in first the American Society for Promoting National Unity (1861) and later the Society for the Diffusion of Political Knowledge (1863) to issue tracts in support of slavery and the right of the South to secede from the Union. He and his colleagues continued to defend slavery as a moral institution throughout the Civil War period.

And even with the end of the war and the abolition of slavery, some continued to argue the issue. In the South, disgruntled souls such as Robert L. Dubney, clergyman and former aide to Thomas J. ("Stonewall") Jackson, carried on the debate. His *Defense of Virginia (and through Her of the South) in Recent and Pending Contests* (1867) was an angry digest of virtually every proslavery argument. Dr. John H. Van Evrie of New York presented the racist perspective on slavery as he had for many years in a new book entitled *White Supremacy and Negro Subordination* (1868). Evidence of the tenacity of the issue in America is further indicated by the fact that as late as 1868 Norwegian Lutherans meeting in convention in Chicago attempted—unsuccessfully—to rescind a church tenet originally adopted in 1861 declaring the practice of slavery both moral and consistent with scripture.

[*See also* Cornerstone Speech.]

BIBLIOGRAPHY

Elliott, E. N., ed. *Cotton Is King, and Pro-Slavery Arguments.* Augusta, Ga., 1860.

Farmer, James Oscar, Jr. *The Metaphysical Confederacy.* Macon, Ga., 1986.

Faust, Drew Gilpin. *Confederate Nationalism: Ideology and Identity in the Civil War South.* Baton Rouge, La., 1988.

Faust, Drew Gilpin, ed. *The Ideology of Slavery: Proslavery Thought in the Antebellum South, 1830–1860.* Baton Rouge, La., 1981.

Fredrickson, George M. *The Black Image in the White Mind: The Debate on Afro-American Character and Destiny, 1817–1914.* New York, 1971.

Jenkins, William Sumner. *Pro-slavery Thought in the Old South.* Chapel Hill, N.C., 1935.

Takaki, Ronald T. *A Pro-slavery Crusade: The Agitation to Reopen the African Slave Trade.* New York, 1971.

Tise, Larry E. *Proslavery: A History of the Defense of Slavery in America, 1701–1840.* Athens, Ga., 1987.

LARRY E. TISE

PROSTITUTION. The Civil War created a climate that contributed to the widespread growth of brothels and prostitution, especially in the Confederate states. The large number of unattached men gathered into regiments at camps were targeted by the professional class of women who sold sexual favors, while the length of the war and its devastating effects upon the South led to the displacement of thousands of women, many of whom were forced into prostitution for economic survival.

By June 1863 Maj. W. J. Mims, stationed in eastern Tennessee, complained to his wife that "female virtue if it ever existed in this Country seems now almost a perfect wreck. Prostitutes are thickly crowded through mountain & valley, in hamlet & city." Mims was able to concede that "the influence of the armies has largely contributed to this state of things, as soldiers do not seem to feel the same restraints away from home, which at home regulated their intercourse with the gentler sex." A less charitable Northern hospital steward commented, "The lower class (both black & white in the south) seem to be totally ignorant of the meaning of the word 'Virtue' & both officers & men appear to have cast off all the restraints of home & indulge their passions to the fullest extent."

These relationships fueled vice and disease. Washington, D.C., boasted 450 bordellos by 1862, and over 7,000 prostitutes worked in the district. Richmond, the Confederate capital, was equally a mecca for sin, although it could not match the numbers attributed to D.C. By 1864 the Virginia city's mayor was forced to confess, "Never was a place more changed than Richmond. Go on the Capital Square any afternoon, and you may see these women promenading up and down the shady walks jostling respectable ladies into the gutters."

Many citizens were horrified and the *Richmond Enquirer* was full of complaints—one protester advocated horsewhipping to reduce this activity—but the paper argued that prostitutes, like buzzards and vultures, were simply a part of the army's entourage. Nevertheless, the YMCA hospital superintendent was able to mobilize against a madam who opened her bawdy house directly across from his hospital and encouraged her prostitutes to expose themselves in the windows to lure potential customers out of their hospital beds.

Evidence as to the extent and particulars of prostitution is difficult to determine. Historian Bell Wiley complained of the "veil of reticence" that shrouded the subject, quoting a veteran who confided, "Confederate soldiers were too much gentlemen to stoop to such things." Most material on the topic can be culled only from court records and newspaper accounts rather than private correspondence, which many family members and descendants were likely to censor.

Rare glimpses do emerge despite censorship. A journalist traveling with Confederate Gen. Albert Sidney Johnston reported, "It is really curious to observe how well and how strictly the three classes of women in camp keep aloof from each other." He goes on to distinguish wives and daughters of officers from the cooks and washers, and then concludes:

> The third and last class is happily the smallest; here and there a female of elegant appearance and unexceptionable manners; truly wife-like in their tented seclusion, but lacking that great and only voucher of respectability for females in camp—the marriage tie.

Increasingly, precautions were taken to rid the army of these camp followers. Army regulations restricted the number of laundresses per company and required them to furnish documentation of their good character. Further, in September 1862 near Vicksburg, an order was issued that provided that "company laundresses who do not actually wash for the men must be discharged." This kind of camp cleaning appears irregularly in the military records. In the spring of 1864 General Johnston demanded that the surrounding countryside in Tennessee be searched and all women who were unable to provide "proof of respectability" be shipped outside the reach of his soldiers.

Many prostitutes served the troops as seamstresses, washerwomen, and nurses, and some were female sutlers, like a woman described by Mary Chesnut: "She was dressed in the uniform of her regiment, but wore Turkish pantaloons. She frisked about in her hat and feathers. . . . She was followed at every step by a mob of admiring soldiers and boys." Although they may have been celebrated by the ranks, many met less favorable fates confronted by the brass. Mary and Mollie Bell posed as Confederate soldiers, assuming the aliases of Tom Parker and Bob Morgan, and worked the ranks for two years before they were charged with "aiding in the demoralization of General Early's veterans." The two women were put on trial, found guilty, and sentenced to terms in military prison.

Without comprehensive statistics, the scope of the problem of venereal disease arising from prostitution can only be guessed from irregular reports filed by regimental surgeons. In July 1861 nearly 11,500 men in 12 regiments reported 204 new cases of gonorrhea and 44 new cases of syphilis. By December of 1861, 43 regiments with nearly 35,000 men reported only 36 new cases of gonorrhea and 40 of syphilis. In September 1862 only 8 regiments with 6,200 men reported 36 new cases of gonorrhea and 10 of syphilis. After reviewing these and other compilations, Bell Wiley concluded that the high rate in the summer of 1861 was due to the concentration of troops in Richmond. In December 1862 the *Richmond Examiner* editorialized:

> If the Mayor of Richmond lacks any incentive to stimulate . . . breaking up the resorts of ill-fame in the city, let him visit the military hospitals where sick and disabled soldiers are received for treatment, and look upon the human forms lying there, wrecked upon the treacherous shoals of vice and passion which encounters the soldier at the corner of every street, lane and alley of the city.

For example, after a single month, the Tenth Alabama, while stationed in Richmond, reported 68 new cases of venereal disease.

Wiley believed that increased outbreaks in sexually transmitted diseases could be traced directly to proximity to towns with brothels, as when the North Carolina Fifty-fifth moved to Petersburg in October 1862. The town of Petersburg was legendary, and in the fall of 1863 a North Carolinian reported: "about two weeks ago there was a woman come from petersburg and stoped about 200 yards from our camp several of the boys went up and had lots of fun with her. it was about drill time and one of the boys missed drill and they put him on double duty."

Nashville was another town with a deservedly lewd reputation. In July 1863 Union Gen. William Rosecrans, desperate to stem the tide of disease, commandeered a boat, rounded up 111 prostitutes (there were over 450 licensed prostitutes in the city), forced them onto the cruiser, and shipped them to Louisville (where they were refused permission to disembark). By October 1864, Nashville supported both a hospital for prostitutes and another for syphilitic soldiers.

As for the lives of the prostitutes themselves, we have no testimony and few insights—only observations from unsympathetic commentators, such as the Alabama private Orville Bumpass who wrote to his wife about local "whoredom" who were "the ugliest, sallowfaced, shaggy headed, bare footed dirty wretches you ever saw." When W. C. McClellan wrote to his sister about a male burlesque show among the troops at Fredericksburg, he insisted that the prostitutes in the audience "ware dresses [but there is about them] not much of the Lady."

Although prostitution was remarkably common, we know very little about the economics of the sex trade within the Confederacy. Further, although gonorrhea and syphilis contributed to the debilitation of troops on both sides through frequent contact with these women who sold sexual favors, the immediate impact and subsequent consequences of this behavior remain unexplored in historical literature. For a society so obsessed with the purity of its women, the sullying effects of wartime might have rewrought the complex web of virtue and reputation that kept white Southern women on the pedestal. The history of prostitutes could contribute significantly to our appreciation of the war's impact on postwar society as a whole, but especially on the lives of Southern women.

BIBLIOGRAPHY

Massey, Mary. *Bonnet Brigades: American Women and the Civil War.* New York, 1966.

Wiley, Bell. *The Life of Johnny Reb: The Common Soldier of the Confederacy.* Indianapolis, 1943.

CATHERINE CLINTON

PROVOST MARSHAL. Provost marshals commanded military police in camps or on active service within the Confederacy and in occupied territories. They and their provost guards, collectively called "provost," served as the Confederate version of the Union Provost Marshal General's Department.

Military courts and provost marshals, as authorized by the Articles of War in March 1861, accompanied some armies even before First Manassas. Eventually, to help improve discipline, commanders established provost at every level from brigade to army and at each level within the military departments. Unlike the Union, however, the Confederacy did not immediately appoint a provost marshal general. Brig. Gen. Daniel Ruggles was so appointed in February 1865, and held the appointment until the end of the war in April.

Before that, Brig. Gen. John H. Winder functioned as de facto provost marshal general, in addition to being provost marshal of Richmond in 1861 and 1862 and afterward commissary-general for prisons. Winder, widely regarded as a martinet, was said to have been the most hated man in the Confederacy, a description based, no doubt, on his personal traits—belligerence, irascibility, abrasiveness, and arrogance—and his overzealous, high-handed execution of his duties, which, by their very nature, were difficult, contentious, and thankless. While he was roundly criticized and generally scorned by the public, many of his military contemporaries praised him as energetic, upright, and efficient. His operation of the passport system was commendable, resulting in thorough control of civilian and military movement. It is debatable, however, how effective the system was in achieving another of its chief aims, the apprehension of the spies, subversives, and traitors that were assumed to have infested Richmond. While Winder had some success in coping with crime in Richmond, and his police did reduce, for a time, the level of violence, he was unable to impose consistent or permanent law and order. Overall, Winder deserves credit for his devotion to duty and for his energetic performance as provost marshal. It is difficult to see, in view of the paucity of resources, how another officer could have done better. The task assigned him was probably beyond the capacity and talents of any officer.

A separate provost corps did not exist; rather, officers and men and units were detailed to provost duty, most units only temporarily, although a few served more or less permanently. The Twenty-fifth Georgia Battalion (Atlanta Provost Battalion) was one such unit, as were the First North Carolina, the Fifth Alabama, and the First Virginia Battalions—respectively, the provost guards of the Second Corps, the Third Corps, and the headquarters of the Army of Northern Virginia.

The absence of comprehensive provost strength records and the often ad hoc and transitory nature of such employment prevents definitive compilation of provost strength. The evidence does show that provost duty was manpower-intensive: in 1864 there were 1,200 men on provost duty in Richmond and some 2,200 in the Department of Alabama, Mississippi, and East Louisiana. Two years earlier, provost strength in the Army of Northern Virginia had been about 2,000. Assuming similar manpower allocations in other armies and departments, several thousand or more men experienced provost service.

The primary provost duty—to assist commanders in maintaining good order and discipline—eventually incorporated responsibility for arrest of offenders against military law (and often their custody); apprehension and return to their units of stragglers and deserters (perhaps the most important duty once the armies were in the field); operation on the railroads and throughout the nation of the passport system that was instituted to help the provost identify and capture stragglers, deserters, spies, and subversives; administration of martial law; initial custody of prisoners of war; and enforcement of conscription.

Performance of such intrusive duties, often with excessive zeal, made the provost odious to soldiers and civilians alike. Passports, for example, were seen as an intolerable oppression. Enforcement of martial law, which entailed such unpopular measures as prohibitions on liquor, caused more public outrage. Enforcement of conscription similarly tarnished the provost image. One particularly explosive issue was military arrest of civilians, which, although less common than in the United States, stood condemned as interference with state rights.

Other provost tasks included mobilizing and controlling black laborers; taking custody of captured black soldiers and Union deserters to the Confederacy; guarding hospitals and other vital installations and captured equipment and matériel pending salvage for Confederate use; stopping unauthorized departure from Confederate ports; and preventing valuable commodities like cotton or tobacco reaching the enemy through illicit trade or by seizure.

The provost frequently participated in operations, too, acting as advance and rear guards, reconnoitering the enemy, controlling the activities of scouts and spies, and, when necessary, joining in hard fighting, as they did in the Wilderness in May 1864.

After the Conscription Act of 1862, and more frequently after the 1864 act, many regular soldiers employed as provost returned to the various fronts, leaving disabled men, reserves, and over- and underage men to fill their place. This posed an insoluble dilemma: using the less able as provost would degrade Confederate ability to keep order and maintain front-line strength; on the other hand, using able-bodied regulars would maintain provost effectiveness at the cost of reducing front-line fighting strength.

Notwithstanding insufficient manpower and the use of incompetent men; sometimes bad or indifferent leadership; abuses of power, which created controversy and dissension; and the inconsistencies of the military judicial system, the provost made a significant contribution to the war effort. Despite their mixed record, they were an important element in the maintenance of Confederate strength.

The enormous vituperation directed at the provost was, in effect, a backhand tribute to them. Although the public often regarded provost as useless, their vigorous execution of their duties also won them a reputation as efficient and ubiquitous. In any case, they became a pervasive feature of life in a beleaguered Confederate States of America.

[*See also* File Closers; Habeas Corpus; Military Justice; Ruggles, Daniel; Winder, John H.]

BIBLIOGRAPHY

Blakey, Arch Fredric. *General John H. Winder, C.S.A.* Gainesville, Fla., 1990.

Radley, Kenneth. *Rebel Watchdog: The Confederate States Army Provost Guard.* Baton Rouge, La., 1989.

KENNETH RADLEY

PRYOR, ROGER A. (1828–1919), U.S. congressman and brigadier general. Born near Petersburg, Virginia, Pryor graduated from Hampden-Sydney College and received a law degree from the University of Virginia. Before the war he was widely known as an editor, politician, and orator.

An ultra-secessionist, Pryor urged the attack on Fort Sumter but declined the invitation to fire the first gun. He resigned from the U.S. House of Representatives on March 3, 1861, and in April was commissioned a colonel in the Provisional Army of the Confederate States. On May 3 he was appointed to command the Third Regiment of Virginia Infantry. He was admitted to the Provisional Congress in July and was elected to the First Congress, where he was a member of the Committee on Military Affairs. Pryor resigned his seat in April 1862 and was appointed a brigadier general. He led his brigade at Williamsburg, the

ROGER A. PRYOR. LIBRARY OF CONGRESS

Seven Days' Battles, Second Manassas, and Sharpsburg. In November 1862, the brigade was broken up, and he was given a small command south of the James River. Dissatisfied with so few troops, he resigned on August 26, 1863, and enlisted as a private in the Third Virginia Cavalry.

On November 27, 1864, Pryor was captured while exchanging newspapers with the enemy and was confined at Fort Lafayette. Through the influence of Horace Greeley, Abraham Lincoln in February 1865 ordered Pryor's parole and release. He returned to Petersburg and in the fall went to New York City, where he spent the remainder of his life. Pryor distinguished himself as a jurist and, in 1896, became a New York Supreme Court justice. He was buried at Princeton, New Jersey.

BIBLIOGRAPHY

Holzman, Robert S. *Adapt or Perish: The Life of General Roger A. Pryor, C.S.A.* Hamden, Conn., 1976.

Pryor, Mrs. Roger A. *My Day: Reminiscences of a Long Life.* New York, 1909.

Pryor, Mrs. Roger A. *Reminiscences of Peace and War.* New York, 1908.

Wallace, Lee A., Jr. *Third Virginia Infantry.* Lynchburg, Va., 1986.

LEE A. WALLACE, JR.

PUBLIC FINANCE. The Confederate era involved many innovations in public finance, for the Civil War was not just the end of the slavery era. It was also a transitional period characterized by a partial retrogression to past practices and simultaneously by innovative new procedures that looked forward to the Reconstruction epoch.

Money in Circulation

When the U.S. Constitution was debated and written in 1787, James Madison's proposal to allow the Federal government to issue its own currency (then styled "bills of credit") was voted down by a large majority. So too was a section prohibiting such issues. Simultaneously, the states were prohibited from issuing their notes as a currency, and this prohibition was thought to extend to any local government erected under their authority. (Because of these prohibitions, paper currency at this time consisted largely of notes emitted by state-chartered private banks.)

Despite these legal impediments, the United States during the War of 1812 did put out a few circulating notes. From 1837 to 1861, interest-bearing notes, originally intended to be closely held as an investment, were retained after their interest ceased to accumulate in order that they might be used as internal bills of exchange to make remittances to New York.

State governments, from 1789 to 1860, particularly in the South, issued small amounts of currency. North Carolina was the most serious offender, but Alabama, Kentucky, Mississippi, Florida, and Texas also circulated their own notes. Florida, as a territory, did so apparently with Congress's approval. Texas put out quite a few notes, presumably in its capacity as an independent republic. Practically all the other Southern states, except Virginia and Texas, chartered wholly owned state banks. The bills of these institutions were made tax receivable and their payment was guaranteed by the states. Chief Justice John Marshall declared, in *Craig v. Missouri,* that state notes were bills of credit within the meaning of the Constitution. He died, however, before a decision could be reached on state bank notes, and his successors upheld the validity of such issues.

Various counties and municipalities issued due bills in fractional parts of a dollar during the 1814–1821 and 1837–1842 depressions. This action was in part necessitated by the need to provide the public with a currency under the denomination of five dollars. The banks, for the most part, were prohibited from issuing such notes, and the hoarding of gold and silver coins meant that without local government note issues, there would not have been any currency between the copper cent pieces and the bank five-dollar notes. In light of this, they were urgently required for the needs of commerce.

These experiences played an important role in influencing the Southern people's currency policies from 1861 to 1865. Moreover, when it is remembered that John C. Calhoun, the intellectual father of the secession, had advocated a central government currency in 1837 as a cure for a crash and depression, it is not surprising that the Confederate, state, and local governments all issued their own currency.

Confederate Currency. The Confederate government, in a reprise of events during the American Revolution, proceeded to issue a large quantity of paper currency, which depreciated heavily. To begin with, however, the South copied the antebellum practices of the United States by issuing interest-bearing Treasury notes. But on May 16, 1861, the Confederate Congress, contrary to the recommendations of Secretary of the Treasury Christopher G. Memminger, inaugurated a policy of issuing non-interest-bearing notes in denominations as low as five dollars. Such bills were clearly intended to serve as currency.

Subsequently, in 1862, Congress again took the initiative by ordering the issue of one-dollar and two-dollar notes. Only in 1863 was a fifty-cent note authorized. No lower-denomination note was ever issued because by that time the purchasing power of the Confederate currency had fallen to the point where anything under fifty cents would have been practically worthless.

Congress was encouraged in this policy by three considerations. First, it was recognized that taxes were unpopular and that in any case there would be delays before even a well-digested and comprehensive fiscal program could be put into effect. Thus, at a minimum, the issue of Treasury notes was necessary to provide mobilization funds.

Second, there was also pressure to issue such notes because, unlike those emitted by the state banks, the states, or the local governments, Confederate Treasury notes were receivable throughout the country at their face value without being made subject to bank and note broker collection charges.

Finally, the popularity of such notes with the financial community and the public differed markedly from the bitter opposition to them in the United States. The Northern banks did not want a more popular rival currency in opposition to their own notes. And in any event, prior to the end of 1861, the Northern banks were still exchanging coin for their notes. The Federal demand notes, by drawing coin from their vaults, threatened them with an ultimate suspension of gold payments on their notes and deposits.

On the other hand, the Southern banks had suspended the payment of gold and silver coin on their obligations (with the notable exception of New Orleans) by the end of 1860. Everyone by mid-1861 was used to an exclusively paper money currency and wanted to have the best available. A currency put out by the central government clearly fell into that category, and so the Confederacy, unlike the United States, never had to pass a legal tender law compelling creditors to receive its notes.

Once started down the slippery path of currency issues, the Congress passed act after act, steadily enlarging the amount authorized. It was hoped that the right of the note holders to purchase bonds paying 8 percent interest in coin would prevent the currency from becoming redundant. But as neither Congress nor Secretary Memminger took any positive steps to assure long-term coin payments, this protective device ceased to function after July 1, 1862, when specie payments on the debt ceased.

Under these circumstances, the prewar circulation, which had had a face value in coin of approximately $150 million, soon underwent a rapid expansion. The Confederate-issued currency amounted to $96 million by February 1862. Act followed act until October 13, 1862, when Congress ceased to put any limits on the amount of currency to be issued. By the act of March 23, 1863, the secretary was allowed to emit $50 million a month. Under these circumstances, it was not surprising that the total amount of such notes in circulation had reached nearly $800 million on April 1, 1864.

Since there was no effective tax legislation passed until April 1863, and few collections were made before the beginning of 1864, efforts to prevent a redundant currency were limited solely to making such notes voluntarily exchangeable for bonds. Despite efforts in 1863 to compel the purchase of bonds with notes by a reduction in interest rates, the currency continued to grow. Then by the act of February 17, 1864, Congress required the note holders to exchange all of their currency for 4 percent registered bonds. Despite the large sums taken in, the issue of a further $460 million of notes dated February 17, 1864, kept the Confederate Treasury notes outstanding in excess of $800 million up to the collapse of the government in April 1865.

It must also be noted that, despite the large sums emitted, the Confederate government as the years passed fell ever further behind in its efforts to meet its obligations. Such arrears were $26 million in early 1862, rising by the war's end to $350 million.

Most of this deficit arose from the Treasury's inability to procure the necessary notes from the Confederate security printers and from the department's inefficiency in distributing its funds to the paymasters. The failure to pay soldiers and contractors in a timely manner promoted supply shortages and massive desertion.

State Government Currency Issues. The state governments were at first limited in their note emissions

Confederate Government Actions. In the years between 1789 and 1829, in keeping with Alexander Hamilton's view that the government should create an identity of interest between itself and its wealthier citizens, the Federal government chartered two Federal banks, sponsored the construction of canals, built post roads, and took other steps to encourage the economic development of the United States.

After President Andrew Jackson entered the White House in 1829, these activities more or less ceased. The Democrats adopted the doctrine of laissez-faire, which opposed government intervention. This, combined with the South's growing fear of Northern economic power exercised through the Washington regime, and with the popular doctrine of state rights, led many Southerners to adopt the view that economic development or regulation was beyond the proper scope of the central government's powers.

These attitudes found their reflection in both Confederate Constitutions. The general welfare clause present in the Federal Constitution was deleted and provisions inserted against what were then styled "internal improvements." These put a crimp on what the Confederate government might legitimately do either for itself or for its citizens.

Nonetheless, the Davis administration did take a number of actions that had far-reaching effects on the national economy and war efforts. Belatedly, in 1863 and 1864, the government asserted its control over interstate and foreign commerce by prohibiting the import of foreign luxury goods and by commandeering for government use both the incoming and the outgoing cargo space of blockade-running ships. This program, known as the "New Plan," effected a great improvement in governmental supply operations and finances, but it was adopted so late that most ports had been effectively closed before it could be put into operation.

At home, the administration undertook a variety of actions in keeping with the suggestions made by John C. Calhoun in 1816. Without waiting for private enterprise to deal with its various problems, the War Department created powder mills, nitrate beds, and a variety of manufacturing plants to provide the armed forces with weapons, munitions, clothing, shoes, and other equipment. The quantities furnished were never adequate, outside of munitions, but the army could hardly have endured its unequal contest with the Union forces without them.

In another departure from previous practice, the War Department also assumed increasing control over the South's ill-assorted railroad system. Companies were required, where possible, to share equipment, spare parts, and rolling stock. Railroad schedules were regulated. The government also built three important connecting lines. One provided a third route south from Richmond to North Carolina, and another from Georgia tied up with Florida's railroads and cattle supply. The third involved an attempt to complete the line between Montgomery, Alabama, and Jackson, Mississippi.

Despite widespread public clamor for a government advance on the cotton crop, all efforts to enact such a program were opposed by Secretary Memminger. As a result, the so-called 1861 Produce Loan (a scheme whereby the planters lent the government money secured by a pledge of the proceeds of the sale of their crops) produced a paltry $20 million. Only on April 14, 1862, did Congress enact and Jefferson Davis approve a law allowing the government to buy $35 million of produce with bonds. This action was too limited and too late to be of much benefit to either the Confederacy or the planters.

For the most part, the central government confined its activities to the military sphere and did little for the civilian sector of the economy. The government might have done more and done it earlier, but public suspicion of and state government opposition to any display of activism by the central regime go far to explain its apparent passivity. By 1863, the Richmond regime was seen as a necessitous body, always making demands on the people and giving nothing in exchange.

State and Local Government Activities. Although the Confederate government had to work carefully to placate or get around local sentiment and opposition to the exercise of governmental powers even in wartime, the state and local governments faced fewer obstacles in their efforts to intervene in the economy. Prior to the war, the states had lent money or their credit to banks, bridge and turnpike companies, railroads, and even manufacturing facilities. State leadership in economic development was taken for granted, and local governments supported the building of transportation facilities. Thus, when hostilities broke out, Southerners looked instinctively to their governors and state legislatures for relief.

In addition to their contribution to mobilizing the South's manpower for war, state governments undertook a variety of other activities. State and local governments were active in many cases in furnishing cash and food supplies to the impoverished families of soldiers. Without such programs, spotty and inadequate as many of them were, desertion among the Confederate troops would have been far worse than it was.

Southern state governments also manufactured, secured, and distributed scarce salt with which people preserved their meat supplies. Wool cards were made available in order that families might weave their own woolen cloth. State governments also attempted to regulate the distribution of scarce goods and to make contracts with manufacturers in order to prevent speculators from cornering supplies. A well-intended but crude effort was also made in some states to impose for the duration of the war a form of prohibition, but without much success. Mississippi was the only state that attempted to assist the blockaded planters by advancing them $5 million in Treasury notes secured by the pledge of cotton.

Nor did the more active states, particularly North Carolina and Georgia, neglect actions intended to maintain the morale of their citizens serving with the Confederate army. They purchased or leased vessels to ship state-owned cotton abroad. They sent supplies to the states' troops, an action necessitated by the fact that, because of the inefficiency of Confederate quartermaster and commissary authorities, troops were frequently left without uniforms, shoes, blankets, or food.

State agents also purchased and ran through the blockade supplies needed by the civilian population. These were in many cases distributed practically at cost. Significantly, these actions were undertaken within a year or so after hostilities broke out and a year and a half before President Davis promulgated the New Plan, which was the Confederate government's equivalent of the states's actions.

The management of the South's public finances exhibited wide-ranging errors of omission and commission. Many important opportunities were allowed to slip away, particularly in regulating trade and in enacting and enforcing effective tax legislation. The central government, more concerned with legalistic considerations than practical realities, did very little to help the South's planters or to smuggle goods in through the blockade.

The state governments, albeit with fewer resources and larger initial debts, did more, and they encountered fewer objections from the public regarding their interventionist policies. Whether they could have accomplished more had the Confederate government reimbursed them for their military expenditures is a moot point. The fact was that the two levels of government went pretty much their own way and failed to coordinate their efforts. The result was a declining economy riddled with inflation, suffering from a shortage of foreign goods, and unable to move goods internally. It was a classical prescription for the collapse of civilian morale, desertion from the army, and military defeat.

[*See also* Bonds; Currency, *overview article;* Debt; Erlanger Loan; Inflation; New Plan; Produce Loan; State Socialism; Taxation.]

BIBLIOGRAPHY

Ball, Douglas B. *Financial Failure and Confederate Defeat.* Urbana, Ill., 1991.

Ballagh, James Curtis. *The South in the Building of the Nation.* Vol. 5 of *Southern Economic History.* Richmond, Va., 1909.

Black, Robert C., III. *The Railroads of the Confederacy.* Chapel Hill, N.C., 1952.

Coulter, E. Merton. *The Confederate States of America, 1861–1865.* A History of the South, vol. 7. Baton Rouge, La., 1950.

Easton, Clement. *A History of the Southern Confederacy.* New York, 1954.

Hawk, Emory Q. *Economic History of the South.* New York, 1934.

Hill, Louise B. *State Socialism in the Confederate States of America.* Charlottesville, Va., 1936.

Schwab, John Christopher. *The Confederate States of America, 1861–1865: A Financial and Industrial History of the South during the Civil War.* New York, 1901.

Thorton, Mills. "Fiscal Policy and the Failure of Radical Reconstruction." In *Region, Race, and Reconstruction: Essay in Honor of C. Vann Woodward.* Edited by J. Morgan Kousser and James M. McPherson. New York, 1982.

Todd, Richard Cecil. *Confederate Finance.* Athens, Ga., 1954.

Wallenstein, Peter. "Rich Man's War, Rich Man's Fight." *Journal of Southern History* 50, no. 1 (February 1964): 15–42.

Woolfolk, George Ruble. "Taxes and Slavery in the Antebellum South." *Journal of Southern History* 26, no. 2 (May 1960): 180–200.

DOUGLAS A. BALL

PUBLISHING. *See* Book Publishing; Magazines; Newspapers.

PUGH, JAMES LAWRENCE (1820?–1907), congressman from Alabama. Pugh was born near Waynesboro in Burke County, Georgia, on December 12, 1820. Some sources give his birthdate as May 3, 1819. His mother died in 1824 and his father moved the family to an area called the Hobdy Plantation, west of the Pea River in Pike County, Alabama. Pugh was orphaned in 1830 and went to live with relatives in Louisville, Barbour County, Alabama. He spent the next ten years studying and working. In 1836 hostilities broke out between the Indians and frontier settlers, and the Alabama militia was called out to end the disturbance. In answer to the call, Pugh enlisted in the Eufaula Rifles under the command of Seth Lowe. At the end of the fighting, he was honorably discharged.

After reading law and being admitted to the bar, Pugh opened a private practice at Eufaula, which he maintained for thirty-nine years. Involving himself in Alabama politics, Pugh supported the Whig candidate William Henry Harrison in the 1840 presidential campaign and Henry Clay in 1844. In the 1848 election he was a presidential elector-at-large from Alabama and voted for Zachary Taylor and Millard Fillmore. In 1856 he again served as an elector-at-large for the Democratic candidate James Buchanan. In 1849 Pugh ran for the U.S. House of Representatives as a Whig but was narrowly defeated. William Lowndes Yancey campaigned on his behalf. After this election, Pugh joined the Democratic party and in 1859 was elected to Congress without opposition.

When Alabama seceded from the Union, Pugh resigned,

returned home, and enlisted as a private in the Eufaula Rifles, Company A, First Alabama Infantry. Pugh's unit, the first regiment authorized by the Alabama General Assembly, escorted Jefferson Davis to his inauguration as president of the Confederate States of America. The First Alabama was organized at Pensacola, Florida, in February and March 1861 and on April 1 was mustered into the Confederate army. Pugh remained with the unit at Pensacola until he was elected without opposition to the Confederate House of Representatives in December 1861.

When he took his seat on February 22, 1862, he was assigned to the Military, Public Buildings, and Currency committees. He was reelected in 1863 over three other candidates in a close vote. Pugh was a staunch supporter of President Davis while in Congress and continually supported efforts to strengthen the central government.

Pugh was also interested in the South's economy and often clashed with Secretary of the Treasury Christopher G. Memminger over his financial policies. Memminger was coping with an almost impossible situation, for the Confederacy had little money, and only loans from New Orleans bankers and the state of Alabama allowed the South to start the war fiscally sound. Memminger had little time to develop plans for a balanced budget; instead, he was forced to utilize a makeshift policy that depended largely on credit and taxation.

Memminger's policy of financing the war through expanding taxation directly opposed Pugh's approach of improving the South's economy by increasing its industrial and agricultural output. To Pugh, Memminger's ever-increasing demands for an expansion of the tax base stifled the Confederacy's economic development. He thought the main concern of the Confederate Congress should be the encouragement of increased production to offset the North's huge industrial advantage. To accomplish this goal, Pugh wanted to finance the war by increasing existing taxes instead of creating new ones. Because of the opposition of Pugh and his supporters, taxation was never a major source of Confederate finances, and the direct tax legislation enacted in 1861 provided the South with only about $17.5 million in revenue.

Memminger was successful in securing the passage of a comprehensive tax act in April 1863, however. It placed a levy on naval stores, salt, liquors, and agricultural products as well as requiring licenses for a wide variety of occupations. In addition, it established a graduated income tax and a tax-in-kind. This was precisely the type of repressive taxation that Pugh believed was preventing the South from reaching its full industrial and agricultural production, which he saw as necessary to wage a successful war. In January 1864, Pugh pushed for a reduction of the tax on industry and agriculture in the hope of improving output. Additional legislation was passed by Congress in February 1864, which allowed tax rebates and the paying of taxes in depreciated Confederate notes. Pugh also supported free trade in the hope of stimulating the Confederacy's economy and opposed expanding the ages for military conscription, which would remove older men from the South's labor force.

At the end of the Civil War, Pugh returned to his legal practice in Eufaula. By 1874 he was involved heavily in Alabama Reconstruction politics and was a major factor in ending Radical Reconstruction in the state. He was chosen as the head of the 1874 state convention of the Democratic and Conservative party. Under his leadership, the party nominated George S. Houston for the 1874 gubernatorial race to run against the incumbent Republican David Peter Lewis. The convention prepared a platform stating that the major issue of the campaign was "white vs. black" and called for white Alabamians to unite behind Houston. The election was filled with fraud on both sides and was marked by riots.

Pugh's candidate, Houston, won the election. Once he was in office, he proposed rewriting the Alabama Constitution of 1868, which most white Alabamians viewed as a document which they had had no voice in preparing. The question was put to a vote of the people, who ordered a new constitutional convention. When the election for delegates was held, Pugh was chosen, along with seventy-nine other Democrats, twelve Republicans, and seven independents. With the completion of the constitutional convention of 1875, Radical Reconstruction came to an end in Alabama.

Afterward Pugh remained active in the state's Democratic politics. He ran for the U.S. Senate in 1878 against Houston and lost by only two votes in the Alabama Senate. Upon Houston's death in 1880 the Alabama Senate chose Pugh to complete Houston's unexpired term. Pugh was reelected to the Senate in 1884, this time without opposition. In 1888 President Grover Cleveland offered him a seat on the U.S. Supreme Court, but he declined because of his age. He was reelected to the Senate in 1890.

Pugh left Congress on March 3, 1897, but continued to live in Washington, where he practiced law. He died there on March 9, 1907, and was buried in Fairview Cemetery in Eufaula.

BIBLIOGRAPHY

Brewer, W. *Alabama: Her History, Resources, War Record, and Public Men from 1540 to 1872.* Montgomery, Ala., 1872.

Connelly, Thomas L., and Archer Jones. *The Politics of Command.* Baton Rouge, La., 1973.

Fleming, Walter L. *Civil War and Reconstruction in Alabama.* New York, 1949.

Moore, Albert Burton. *History of Alabama and Her People.* 3 vols. New York, 1927.

Owen, Thomas M. *History of Alabama and Dictionary of Alabama Biography.* 4 vols. Chicago, 1921.

PAUL F. LAMBERT

PUNISHMENT. *See* Crime and Punishment.

PURCHASING. *See* Anglo-Confederate Purchasing; Erlanger Loan; New Plan.

PURYEAR, RICHARD C. (1801–1867), U.S. congressman from North Carolina. Born in Mecklenburg County, Virginia, February 9, 1801, Richard Clauselle Puryear moved as a child to Surry (present-day Yadkin) County, North Carolina. After receiving a rudimentary education, he entered the mercantile business in Huntsville and eventually became a substantial landowner and slaveholder. He served as a Whig in the North Carolina House of Commons (1838–1839, 1844–1847, and 1852) and in the state senate (1840–1841). Elected to the U.S. Congress in 1853 and 1855, he was defeated in 1857, in part because of his opposition to the Kansas-Nebraska Act.

A Unionist until Lincoln's call for troops, Puryear never became totally reconciled to the idea of Southern independence. In May 1861 he was elected by the secession convention to the Provisional Congress, where he served as a member of the Naval Affairs Committee. He opposed the economic policies of the Davis administration, voting to reduce the war tax and to add to the number of exemptions, but he supported the administration on most other measures. Puryear took little interest in the proceedings of Congress, however, and did not seek reelection. Reflecting the traditional Whig antipathy toward executive power, he privately opposed the Conscription Act and the suspension of the writ of habeas corpus, but he did not play an active role in public affairs after his service in Congress.

In 1866 Puryear served as a delegate to the National Union Convention in Philadelphia. He died at his plantation, Shallow Ford, on July 30, 1867.

BIBLIOGRAPHY

Alexander, Thomas B., and Richard E. Beringer. *The Anatomy of the Confederate Congress: A Study of the Influences of Member Characteristics on Legislative Voting Behavior, 1861–1865.* Nashville, Tenn., 1972.

Wakelyn, Jon L. *Biographical Dictionary of the Confederacy.* Edited by Frank E. Vandiver. Westport, Conn., 1977.

Warner, Ezra J., and W. Buck Yearns. *Biographical Register of the Confederate Congress.* Baton Rouge, La., 1975.

THOMAS E. JEFFREY

QUAKERS. *See* Society of Friends.

QUANTRILL, WILLIAM CLARKE (1837–1865), pro-Confederate Missouri guerrilla. At age sixteen, following the death of his father, an Ohio school principal, Quantrill drifted west, teaching school in Illinois, Indiana, and finally, in 1857, in Tuscarora Lake, Kansas, a settlement of Ohio migrants. Expelled from Tuscarora Lake as a thief, Quantrill joined an army expedition to Utah as a teamster, from where, late in 1858, he joined a gold party headed for Pikes Peak. Twelve of the nineteen men in the party died of exposure in the Rocky Mountains, and Quantrill's survival led him to believe that he was a man of destiny. Back in Kansas in 1859, Quantrill became something of a double agent, consorting with political bandits of both antislavery Kansans and proslavery Missourians, before finally throwing in his lot with the proslavery camp.

When the war began, the area around Independence, Missouri, went up in flames. Kansas Jayhawkers (antislavery Unionists, some enrolled in the militia, some freebooters) crossed the Missouri River to burn and plunder. In retaliation, many young Missourians took to the bush and spontaneously organized guerrilla bands. Quantrill, a bit older than most of these boys, a fine horseman and dead shot, and with a little military experience and a lot of self-confidence, led one of the most active gangs in attacking Union troops and raiding Kansas border towns. Such bands had the support of many local citizens, a difficult terrain in which to hide, and a cunning ability to attack the enemy at his weak spots, and then to scatter and melt back into the countryside.

In the summer of 1863, Union authorities began expelling or imprisoning suspected guerrilla sympathizers. On August 13, a rickety Kansas City prison collapsed, killing five young female kin of the Quantrill band. In retaliation, Quantrill gathered about 450 guerrillas and, on the morning of August 21, burst into Lawrence, Kansas, burning, looting, and killing about 150 unarmed men and boys, a raid that gained him national notoriety.

When his men sojourned in Texas that winter, Confederate authorities could neither enroll them nor control them. Quantrill's cohort disintegrated into smaller groups, led by younger and even more reckless men, notably George Todd and "Bloody" Bill Anderson, who carried on in 1864 in Missouri as before, while Quantrill sat out the summer in hiding. In October, Todd and Anderson were both killed, and Quantrill reassembled about thirty of his old band for an expedition into Kentucky. On May 10, 1865, Quantrill, surprised while sleeping in a barn, was shot, paralyzed, and captured. He was taken to a military prison hospital in nearby Louisville where, following his conversion to Roman Catholicism, he died on June 6.

Among Quantrill's fighters had been the James and Younger brothers; as their reputations rose during their postwar careers, so did his. Noble guerrillas had become noble outlaws, fighting those dreaded outsiders—bankers and railroad men—particularly in the historical fiction of the alcoholic newspaperman, John N. Edwards. By 1888, mythically rehabilitated Quantrill veterans were organizing annual reunions, at which they would have their pictures taken, always holding up a portrait of their fallen captain, Quantrill. In the twentieth century, Hollywood would utilize this romance in films about the Old West. Finally, some of his bones were buried with full Confederate military honors on October 24, 1992, in Higginsville, Missouri, by a rather macabre group of historical romanticists.

WILLIAM CLARKE QUANTRILL. LIBRARY OF CONGRESS

BIBLIOGRAPHY

Brownlee, Richard S. *Gray Ghosts of the Confederacy: Guerrilla Warfare in the West, 1861–1865.* Baton Rouge, La., 1958.

Castel, Albert. *William Clarke Quantrill: His Life and Times.* New York, 1962.

Connelley, William Elsey. *Quantrill and the Border Wars.* Cedar Rapids, Iowa, 1909. Reprint, New York, 1956.

Edwards, John N. *Noted Guerrillas, or the Warfare on the Border.* St. Louis, 1877.

Fellman, Michael. *Inside War: The Guerrilla Conflict in Missouri during the American Civil War.* New York, 1989.

MICHAEL FELLMAN

QUAPAWS. Residing initially along the Mississippi River in eastern Arkansas, 350 Quapaw Indians in 1861 occupied a 150-section reservation in what is now northeastern Oklahoma. Another 100 lived 180 miles southwest on the Canadian River. Influenced by their former Federal agent, A. J. Dorn, Chiefs War-te-she and Ki-he-cah-te-da of the reservation band signed a treaty of alliance with the Confederate States of America on October 4, 1861. Negotiated by Confederacy commissioner Albert Pike, the treaty bound the Southern states, among other things, to provide $2,000 in goods annually and to continue a $1,000 educational annuity paid by the United States, in return for which the Quapaws acknowledged the authority of the Southern government, recognized black slavery (the tribespeople had never owned slaves), and agreed to become parties to the existing war.

The Quapaws never honored the treaty. The off-reservation band joined 7,000 other Indians who refused to recognize any of Pike's treaties and in late 1861, under attack by Confederate troops, retreated northward to Kansas. There they were joined in February 1862 by the larger body of their kinsmen, who fled from the reservation to seek protection from marauding bands out of Arkansas and Missouri.

The united Quapaws remained as refugees in Kansas until the end of the war. Some 60 of their warriors did join the First Regiment of the Indian Home Guards, USA, which advanced into Indian Territory in June 1862; 80 Quapaw members of the Second Indian Regiment were absent "buffalo hunting" when it marched southward the following year.

On September 14, 1865, the Quapaws signed the Fort Smith peace treaty that terminated hostilities in Indian Territory. Later that fall they returned to their old reservation in northeastern Oklahoma and in February 1867 negotiated a new treaty with the United States.

BIBLIOGRAPHY

Baird, W. David. *The Quapaw Indians: A History of the Downstream People.* Norman, Okla., 1980.

Nieberding, Velma. *The History of Ottawa County.* Miami, Okla., 1983.

W. DAVID BAIRD

QUARLES, WILLIAM ANDREW (1825–1893), brigadier general. Quarles was born near Jamestown, Virginia, on July 4, 1825, but his parents moved to Christian County, Kentucky, when he was five years old. After studying law at the University of Virginia, he was admitted to the bar in 1848 and opened a legal practice in Clarksville, Tennessee. Quarles also was president of the Memphis, Clarksville, and Louisville Railroad. Active in Democratic politics, Quarles was an elector for Franklin Pierce in 1852, a delegate to the Democratic National Convention in 1856 and 1860, and an unsuccessful congressional candidate in 1858. He also served as a circuit court judge and the Tennessee supervisor of banks.

In 1861, Quarles was commissioned colonel of the Forty-second Tennessee Infantry and served under Albert Sidney Johnston until February 1862 when the regiment was ordered to Fort Donelson. Quarles's command arrived after the Federal assault on the position was under way, and he participated in the vicious fighting from February 13 through 15. Captured during the battle, Quarles later was exchanged and given command of the Ninth Tennessee Battalion, which included four regiments and was stationed at Port Hudson.

At the beginning of the siege of Vicksburg, Quarles's unit was transferred to Joseph E. Johnston's command at Jackson, Mississippi. Quarles was promoted to brigadier general on August 25, 1863, and sent as a part of Confederate reinforcements to Missionary Ridge; he arrived too late to participate in the fighting, however. Ordered to Georgia to protect Atlanta, he saw action in the protracted fighting between Dalton and Atlanta and at Pickett's Mill.

Quarles was in the vanguard of the Confederate assault at the Battle of Franklin. The fighting was so bitter that all of his staff officers who participated in the assault were killed. The highest ranking officer surviving the battle in Quarles's brigade was a captain. Quarles himself suffered a severe wound to the head while leading the assault, and the wound prevented further military service.

When the fighting ended, Quarles returned to Clarksville, Tennessee, where he practiced law and served in the state legislature. Quarles died in Clarksville on December 28, 1893, and was buried in Christian County.

BIBLIOGRAPHY

Evans, Clement A., ed. *Confederate Military History*. 12 vols. Atlanta, 1899. Extended ed. in 19 vols. Wilmington, N.C., 1987–1989.

Johnson, Robert U., and C. C. Buel, eds. *Battles and Leaders of the Civil War*. 4 vols. New York, 1887–1888. Reprint, Secaucus, N.J., 1982.

Warner, Ezra J. *Generals in Gray: Lives of the Confederate Commanders*. Baton Rouge, La., 1959.

PAUL F. LAMBERT

QUARTERMASTER BUREAU. Established February 26, 1861, the Quartermaster Bureau was responsible for providing the Confederate armies with nonfood and nonordnance items, as well as transportation functions. Thus, the production of uniforms, shoes, shirts, hats, tents, saddles, and wagons and their transportation were quartermaster functions, as was the transportation of the armies themselves. The bureau was headed first by Col. Abraham C. Myers of South Carolina (March 25, 1861–August 10, 1863) and then by Brig. Gen. Alexander R. Lawton of Georgia (August 10, 1863, to the end of the war).

The act establishing the department stipulated that it be manned by a colonel as quartermaster general, six majors as quartermasters, and as many lieutenants (subalterns) as assistant quartermasters as were necessary. All the quartermasters were authorized to act as paymasters.

The department was organized in the same manner as its prewar Federal counterpart. It was to run a simple senior office. The subordinate officers were to oversee functional areas such as shoes or uniforms for the major Confederate armies. Each of the major armies usually had a staff officer assigned to handle quartermaster functions, thus relieving the commanding general of what most officers considered an onerous task. Custom dictated that each division, brigade, and regimental commander assign quartermaster duties to an officer. Those assigned were rarely professional or experienced in supply matters, and those who were often faced the conflict of dual allegiance to their commander in the field and their superior, the quartermaster general, in Richmond. Consequently, supply problems related to the internal functioning of the quartermasters grew as the war progressed. At the company level, quartermaster functions, such as the actual distribution of uniforms to individual soldiers, were handled by a designated sergeant, who was often overseen by an officer.

What appeared to be the simple task of supplying soldiers in the field rapidly became extremely complicated as the number of soldiers and the distance over which they served increased. The quartermasters' problems were exacerbated by a number of factors: declining means of transportation, lack of coordination, spiraling wartime inflation, corruption, divisive politics, shortage of manpower, and the lack of glamour associated with nonbattle staff duties.

Following in the tradition of the Federal army, the Quartermaster Bureau was the senior department and the quartermaster general the ranking staff officer after the adjutant general. Because of seniority, he and his subordinates could and did usurp the assets of other staff departments, particularly in the functional area of transportation. This practice led to friction, rivalry, and an intense competition for limited assets that continued to the war's end. The combat efficiency of the Confederate armies was often affected by departments that rerouted scheduled trains, only to have the rerouted trains rescheduled by a local quartermaster. The lack of clear direction and coordination by the president and secretary of war accentuated this deadly problem.

Wartime inflation was another factor in the failure of the bureau to carry out its mission. The well-known tales of Confederate civilians having to pay incredible prices for goods and services also reflected the situation of the quartermasters, but they had a partial remedy—impressment. Using constitutional powers delegated by the secretary of war, they could commandeer private property, be it cloth for tents and uniforms or leather for shoes and saddles. Necessary goods could be impressed as long as the quartermaster provided just compensation. But given the rapidly spiraling inflation of the Confederacy, quartermasters often paid only half of an item's true market value. Civilians complained vehemently to the Congress, which eventually enacted legislation to curtail and regulate the process. The practice of impressment did nothing to enhance the quartermasters' reputation and stimulated charges of corruption.

Starting in the summer of 1862 and continuing until the end of the war, the Quartermaster Bureau was under almost continual investigation by Congress. Anger about quartermaster practices and in particular corruption led to the introduction of numerous resolutions and acts regarding their activities. One of the most telling was an Act to Protect the Confederate States against Frauds, Etc. The Senate debated the act on December 31, 1864, and the comments of Senator George N. Lester of Georgia reveal the deep-seated anger the Confederacy felt for the quartermasters. Lester admitted that there were some honest men in the bureau but asserted that the rest had been "engaged in plundering the government from the beginning of the war till now."

This sentiment led to legislation that was designed to destroy the department. An act submitted to President Jefferson Davis in March 1865 would have sent all able-bodied quartermasters under the age of forty-five to field positions. Davis vetoed the bill because it would have been a disaster for the already faltering war effort and would have added only two hundred men to the army.

Divisive politics was another factor in the quartermasters' failure. Almost as soon as the war began, state governors withheld vital supplies for their own states' use. Quartermaster General Lawton recognized the problem as soon as he took the job. He wrote two letters in 1864 to the secretary of war complaining that the governors controlled assets, like cotton and woolen factories, that the bureau needed:

> We draw not a single yard of any kind of material.... It would be better for the State authorities to allow this department to control factory production so far as they may be needed for military purposes.... The necessities of the people and the objects of charity must be postponed to the wants of the Army.

In the state rights–oriented Confederacy many governors would continue to control necessary supplies even to the detriment of the war effort.

Another problem for the bureau was manpower. In February 1865, it reported that it needed 2,299 white males, 3,451 blacks full time, and 5,000 women for part-time or piecework. Many important people thought that the department controlled too many skilled white males who in the manpower-short Confederacy were needed on the battlefront. President Davis, however, usually disagreed.

The last factor affecting the performance of the quartermasters was the lack of respect for their specialty. Often not the highest caliber officers, they had a poor reputation. In fact, Lawton, a former brigadier and division commander under Thomas J. ("Stonewall") Jackson, complained at length when he was assigned to his new billet. The comments of Gen. Richard S. Ewell at the Battle of Cedar Mountain reflected the feeling of most Confederate officers regarding quartermasters. When Ewell saw a well-dressed officer on the battlefield, he asked, "I do say, young man with the fine clothes on! Who are you and where do you belong?" Being informed that he was a quartermaster with a Virginia regiment, Ewell exploded: "Great Heavens! A Quartermaster on the battle-field; who ever heard of such a thing before?"

Nevertheless, given the difficulties they faced, it is amazing that the quartermasters accomplished as much as they did. Both Myers and Lawton struggled against impossible odds. Myers did a creditable job and Lawton's work bordered on superb.

[*See also* Impressment; Lawton, Alexander R.; Myers, Abraham C.]

BIBLIOGRAPHY

Coulter, Merton E. *The Confederate States of America, 1861–1865.* A History of the South, vol. 7. Baton Rouge, La., 1950.

Davis, Jefferson. *Jefferson Davis, Constitutionalist: His Letters, Papers and Speeches.* Jackson, Miss., 1923.

Eaton, Clement. *A History of the Southern Confederacy.* New York, 1954.

Goff, Richard D. *Confederate Supply.* Durham, N.C., 1969.

U.S. War Department. *War of the Rebellion: A Compilation of the Official Records of the Union and Confederate Armies.* Washington, 1880–1901. Ser. 4, vol. 3, pp. 556–557.

Vandiver, Frank E. *Rebel Brass: The Confederate Command System.* Baton Rouge, La., 1956.

Weinert, Richard P. *The Confederate Regular Army.* Shippensburg, Pa., 1991.

P. Neal Meier

RAIDERS. *See* Commerce Raiders.

RAILROADS. The decade of the 1850s was one of the most important periods in the history of American railroads. What had been at the beginning of the decade a scattering of short lines from Maine to Georgia had become by 1860 an iron network serving all the states east of the Mississippi. New construction in the ten years resulted in a growth from 9,021 to 30,626 miles. The mileage in 1850 was concentrated in a network stretching from Portland, Maine, and Buffalo, New York, south to Richmond, Virginia, and Wilmington, North Carolina. A separate 900-mile system served the major cities in South Carolina and Georgia. West of the mountains the only states with 100 miles or more of line were Michigan, Ohio, Indiana, Illinois, and Alabama.

Antebellum Sectional Differences. In the early 1830s railroad mileage in the Southern states (those south of the Potomac and Ohio rivers) had nearly matched that of the North, but by 1850 the North had 5,612 miles of line and the South only 2,133 miles. Clearly the industrial states in the North felt a greater need for the new mode of transport than did the more agrarian South. But in the 1850s the South did much to catch up. Arkansas and Texas laid their first track and the South (the future Confederate states plus Kentucky) built 7,402 miles of railroad, climbing to a total of 9,535 miles, or an increase of 347 percent.

Probably more significant was the new construction in the West. During the 1850s mileage in the eight Western states (the Old Northwest plus Iowa, Missouri, and California) increased from 1,276 to 11,078 miles. And by the end of the Civil War the network from western Pennsylvania to the Mississippi River seemed complete. Most of the new mileage ran east and west and connected with one or more major trunk lines.

For a generation prior to mid-century steamboats had had a monopoly on commerce and transportation in the Mississippi-Ohio basin, but the major railroad construction in the Old Northwest soon resulted in a new east-west trade axis that replaced the earlier north-south traffic of the Ohio and Mississippi River steamboats. The economic shift is noted by William and Bruce Catton in their *Two Roads to Sumter:* "Southerners who dreamed that the Northwest might be neutral or even an ally in the event of a civil conflict should have looked more closely at the endless parade of freight trains clattering across the mountains between the ocean and the lakes."

Certainly there was no lack of enthusiasm for railroads in the South. On the eve of the Civil War over a hundred companies shared the 9,000 miles of line in the Confederacy. The average length was 85 miles, with a third over 100 miles in length, and nine over 200 miles. Most of the Confederate lines represented a single state, with all their mileage within the state. In 1860 the average investment per mile of road was about $27,000 in the South, $36,000 in the West, and $48,000 in the Northeast. Southern railroads cost less for several reasons: cheaper slave labor, lighter and often inferior rails, easier terrain along the coastal plains of the South, and smaller amounts of rolling stock per mile of road. Financial support for the construction in the decade had come from some cities and counties and a few states, especially Virginia, North Carolina, and Tennessee, but most lines were chiefly financed by the private sector. A Federal land grant pushed through Congress by William R. King, senator from Alabama, and his colleague, Stephen A. Douglas of Illinois, had provided aid for the Mobile and Ohio and the Illinois Central in Illinois.

Construction of the 7,000 miles of new line in the eleven Southern states in the fifties was rather even during the ten years, but more than half of the new track was put down in the four years 1857 through 1860. This was in contrast to the pattern north of the Ohio River where nearly three-quarters was laid between 1852 and 1856. Southern lines, like those in the rest of the nation, were built in a variety of track gauges. The 5-foot gauge was dominant, but three states, with modest mileage, favored the 5-foot 6-inch gauge, and two states favored the 4-foot 8½-inch gauge, which was fairly standard in the North.

The Civil War was the first major conflict in which railroads played an important role. In 1861 the Union and Confederate rail systems were in some ways a study in contrast. The eleven Southern states with their 9,000 miles of line had nearly a third of the nation's rail mileage, but employed less than a fifth of the country's railroad work force. Many workers from the North were employed on Southern lines in 1861, probably because of the Southerners' traditional dislike for mechanical pursuits. When war came, many Northerners returned home, and those who remained were often viewed with suspicion, sometimes rightly so.

The South was also at a disadvantage in motive power, rolling stock, and track materials. The entire Confederacy had hardly as many locomotives as those found on the combined motive power rosters of the New York Central, the Pennsylvania, and the Erie. The states north of the Potomac had a dozen locomotive factories for every one located in the South. The few locomotive factories in the South, such as the Tredegar Iron Works at Richmond, were pressed by the Davis government into the production of ordnance. The states of Virginia, South Carolina, and Tennessee had produced a fair number of railroad cars, but Pennsylvania produced twice as many as the entire Confederacy. Obtaining replacement rail and spikes was also soon a problem. Before the war Southern railroad presidents preferred English to Northern rails, claiming the English to be superior and cheaper. The South produced some rail, but its production of 26,000 tons in 1860 was about a ninth of the Northern output. The Union blockade of Southern ports, plus the Confederate priority given to ordnance production, soon had Southern track maintenance officials hoarding their iron.

While the Confederate railways lagged well behind Northern roads in the quantity and maintenance of equipment, the types of engines and cars used by the rivals varied only slightly. Both North and South relied heavily on the American-type locomotive (a swiveled four-wheel truck in front plus four drivers) with its functional cowcatcher, balloon stack, and large headlight. This kind of engine (4-4-0) had a name rather than a number, weighed from fifteen to twenty-five tons, cost $8,000 to $10,000 new, used wood or coal for fuel, and was the pride and joy of the engine crew to whom it was assigned. Northern lines shifted to coal for fuel far faster than the Southern roads; nearly all Confederate railroads depended on cord wood. A few Northern railroads owned some engines with six rather than four drivers, but such locomotives were rare in the South.

The typical freight car, either Northern or Southern, had two four-wheel trucks, was from twenty-four to thirty-four feet in length, and had a load capacity of eight to twelve tons. First-class boxcars rarely cost more than $400 to $500 per car and often were built in company shops for much less. Passenger cars on the eve of the war normally came equipped with corner toilet, water tank, a wood-burning stove, and inadequate lighting. In 1860 first-class cars were about fifty feet in length, could hold fifty passengers, and were stopped with hand brakes. New cars cost from $1,500 to $3,000 each. Dining cars had not yet been introduced, and sleeping cars were almost unknown on Southern lines.

The principal railroad centers in the Confederacy were Richmond, Chattanooga, and Atlanta. Richmond was served by five roads, whereas the Union capital, a hundred miles to the north, depended upon a single branch line of the Baltimore and Ohio. Chattanooga and Atlanta both were served by three roads, but each was a vital line serving much of the region. At the start of the war, Richmond had two major routes to the south. An eastern coastal line, formed of six railroads, reached Wilmington, Charleston, and Savannah, the major Confederate eastern seaports. A second transmountain route via Petersburg, Lynchburg, Bristol, and Knoxville reached Chattanooga in the southeastern corner of Tennessee. Late in the war Richmond was served by a third line via Danville and Greensboro, which became a vital supply route for Robert E. Lee. West of Chattanooga the 296-mile Memphis and Charleston ran to Corinth and Memphis with connections serving Tennessee, Alabama, Mississippi, Louisiana, and New Orleans. South of Chattanooga the Georgia state-owned 138-mile Western and Atlantic reached Atlanta and several lines serving the Carolinas, Georgia, and Florida. The Western and Atlantic later would be a bone of contention between Joseph E. Brown, state rights governor of Georgia, and Jefferson Davis. These three junction cities were in states that had the greatest rail mileage in the Confederacy.

War's Effect on Southern Lines. In the spring of 1861 the *American Railroad Journal* predicted that the majority of the railroads would be unaffected by the Civil War, a mistaken prophecy, indeed. Southern lines leading toward the Virginia and Tennessee fronts soon were overwhelmed with a flood of excited soldiers and ancient ordnance moving north. South of Richmond the Petersburg Railroad doubled its gross revenue by 1862 and in that year had a record low operating ratio under 28 percent. Between 1861 and 1863 the Georgia Railroad lowered its operating ratio from 57 to 42 percent. The Wilmington and Weldon paid a 31 percent dividend in 1863, and between 1860–1861 and 1862–1863

Railroad Construction in the South during the 1850s

State	Mileage in 1850	Mileage in 1860	Increase in Decade	Investment per Mile	Dominant Gauge
Virginia	481	1,731	1,250	$36,679	4′8½″
North Carolina	283	937	654	18,796	4′8½″
South Carolina	289	973	684	22,675	5′0″*
Georgia	643	1,420	777	20,696	5′0″*
Florida	21	402	381	21,356	5′0″*
Tennessee	–	1,253	1,253	24,677	5′0″*
Alabama	183	743	560	25,022	5′0″
Mississippi	75	862	787	27,982	5′0″
Louisiana	80	335	255	35,988	5′6″
Arkansas	–	38	38	30,394	5′6″*
Texas	–	307	307	36,706	5′6″
Total	2,055	9,001	6,946		

*Only gauge in the state

total receipts on the North Carolina Railroad increased nearly fourfold. The operating ratio dropped to 38 percent, and dividends doubled. Of course, the lower operating ratios and higher dividends resulted in part from the scarcity of labor and replacement parts.

In these years military personnel made up well over a third of the passenger traffic. But freight traffic was declining on many Confederate lines in the early war months, especially in the cotton-producing states where the rail movement of cotton was reduced by the effective Union blockade of the Southern coastline. Also the early indications of rail prosperity must be discounted because the growing receipts and dividends were expressed in Confederate dollars, which were rapidly declining in real value.

Certainly much of the seeming prosperity was false, given the persistent inflation. The costs of railway operation generally rose faster than did the freight rates and passenger fares. In the first two or three years of war, mechanics' wages climbed from $2.50 to $20.00 a day, nails from 4 cents to $4.00 a pound, shovels from $10.50 to $300.00 per dozen, coal from 12 cents to $2.00 per bushel, and lubricating oil from $1.00 to $50.00 a gallon. Railroad officials found it hard to raise rates fast enough to match these rising costs. John P. King, the president of the 232-mile Georgia Railroad, long a prosperous line, complained in 1864 that because of inflation his road had been losing money for two years. He wrote of his railroad: "The more business it does, the more money it loses, and the greatest favor that could be conferred upon it—if public wants permitted—would be the privilege of quitting business until the end of the war!"

Early in the war major problems faced two railroads in border states—the Louisville and Nashville in Kentucky and Tennessee, and the Baltimore and Ohio in Maryland and Virginia. Both lines had major mileage in the Confederacy—the L & N in Tennessee on its way to Nashville, and the B & O in northern and western Virginia. As the war came to Kentucky in the spring of 1861, the L & N was enjoying prosperity, with merchants and public officials in Tennessee and points farther south ordering vast amounts of Northern goods. James Guthrie, its president, found his road so clogged with south-bound freight that he imposed a ten-day embargo late in April to clear his tracks. Through the summer of 1861 the cagey Guthrie tried to serve two masters at once. But by the end of the summer, he was forced to choose, and he broke with the Confederacy. Parts of his lines were in Confederate hands, but before too long northern Tennessee was again under Union control. Guthrie fully supported the Union, and he may have received higher than normal rates for his Federal business.

In a way the first violence of the Civil War had come to the B & O eighteen months before the capture of Fort Sumter, when John Brown made his raid on Harpers Ferry in 1859. In Baltimore John W. Garrett, president of the line, wired the Secretary of War, who sent Col. Robert E. Lee with a detachment of U.S. Marines to subdue Brown. All of Garrett's 379-mile railroad was located in slave states, and the majority of the line was in Virginia, a state soon to secede. Garrett had long considered the B & O to be a Southern railroad, but he knew that the future of his road lay with the North and the Union rather than the South. Western flour and Cumberland coal, both headed north, not the tobacco and cotton from Southern plantations, had made Baltimore and the B & O prosperous. In the troubled days of late April and early May 1861, Garrett and the B & O were regarded suspiciously and pressured by both the Union and the Confederacy.

Col. Thomas J. ("Stonewall") Jackson and his Confederate forces started to occupy the Harpers Ferry area in May

1861. Soon he was in effective control of forty-four miles of B & O track west of Harpers Ferry. On May 23, 1861, he captured fifty-six B & O engines and three hundred freight cars. Many of the locomotives were put to the torch, but a few were dragged on wagons behind dozens of horses to other Virginia lines to serve the Confederate war effort. Jackson also destroyed dozens of bridges and other B & O equipment west of Harpers Ferry. The B & O was not able to restore service in the region fully until March 1862. It is not surprising that during the spring months of 1861 Garrett's language describing the Confederacy shifted from "our southern friends" to "misguided friends" and finally to "damned rebels."

Confederate Administration. During the entire conflict the Confederate government's control of the railroads was far from effective. The widespread belief that the war would be short, the early failure to recognize the importance of the railroads in the war effort, and the reluctance of the Davis administration to override state authority contributed to the lack of effective regulation. Late in April 1861, thirty-three railroad presidents met in Montgomery and agreed to a uniform fare of two cents a mile for troops, and half the normal freight rate for the shipping of war munitions and provisions. They also agreed to accept Confederate bonds at par in payment for military transportation. A second convention of presidents at Chattanooga in October 1861 modified the Montgomery agreement, and the new rate structure was approved by Quartermaster General Abraham C. Myers. As the currency depreciated, steadily higher fares and rates were approved. The government never tried to control railroad charges for the general public.

On the eve of First Manassas, President Jefferson Davis believed rail congestion so severe that he commissioned as a major and assistant quartermaster William S. Ashe, former president of the Wilmington and Weldon. Ashe was

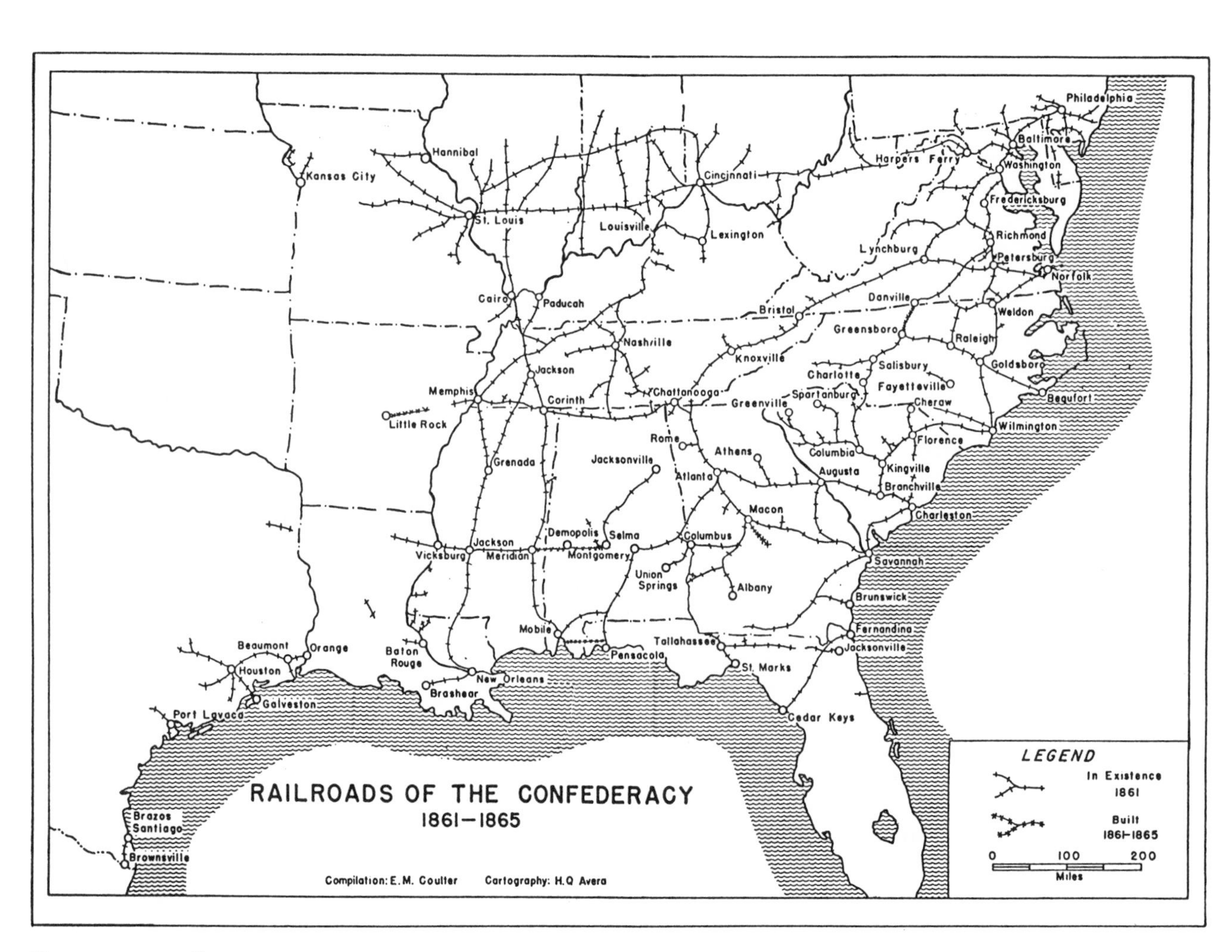

RAILROADS OF THE CONFEDERACY.

placed in charge of military rail transportation in Virginia, especially the lines serving Richmond. Major Ashe quickly set up his Richmond office, but Myers retained real control of railroad traffic, employing Ashe only as a subordinate. Confederate rail traffic problems were little improved, and in December 1862, Secretary of War George Wythe Randolph assigned Col. William M. Wadley to the supervision of "all the railroads in the Confederate States." But Wadley's appointment was never approved, and a third man, Capt. Frederick W. Sims, replaced him in May 1863. Sims had no greater success than his predecessors, however.

Some problems, such as changes of gauge at transfer points, were incapable of solution. At such cities as Richmond, Petersburg, and Lynchburg in Virginia; Wilmington and Charlotte in North Carolina; Columbus in Georgia; and Montgomery in Alabama, the connecting lines were of different gauges: 5 feet or 4 feet $8\frac{1}{2}$ inches. At these points the shifting of freight from one car to another could not be avoided. Even when connecting lines were in the same gauge, few railroad officials would permit their cars to be used on a foreign road. In many cities, such as Petersburg, Bristol, Knoxville, Chattanooga, Savannah, and Augusta, the terminating lines did not actually connect, and freight had to be hauled by wagon from one station to another. In June 1861, General Lee had urged that connecting track be laid in Petersburg. Many lines had earlier sought such tracks but had been stopped by strong transfer and hotel interests. During the war rail connections were achieved in some cities, but delays in the movement of troops and supplies persisted.

Early in the war both Davis and Lee were aware of several major gaps in the rail system. The 300-mile system in Texas was not tied to the Confederate rail network, and only a weak connecting line on the Georgia border eventually gave service to the 400 miles of railroad in Florida. Far more serious were smaller gaps—one along the Virginia–North Carolina border and a second in Alabama. In November 1861, Davis strongly urged the construction of a 48-mile connecting line between Danville, the southern terminal of the 143-mile Richmond and Danville, and Greensboro, located on the North Carolina Railroad. The building of such a link would give Richmond a third rail route with the states to the south, located between the exposed Weldon-Wilmington coastal line and the mountain route through eastern Tennessee. The Confederate Congress, in February 1862, appropriated $1 million to aid a private company, the Piedmont Railroad, to build such a line. But prominent leaders like Robert Barnwell Rhett, Sr., and Robert Toombs strongly protested the action. North Carolina planters along the route would not permit their slaves to work on the line, and North Carolina Governor Zebulon Vance, a firm advocate of state rights, also opposed it. As a result the project lagged and was finished only in the spring of 1864. The completion was timely since the Weldon-Wilmington coastal route was broken by Union troops later in the year. In the last year of the war a major portion of Lee's supplies moved north over the Piedmont Railroad.

The other major gap closed was between Selma, Alabama, and Meridian, Mississippi, a distance of under a hundred miles. Upon the recommendation of Davis the Confederate Congress on February 15, 1862, provided $150,000 to finish the partially built road between the two cities. The completion of this link late in 1862 provided both a shorter rail route from Vicksburg to Richmond and rail transportation well removed from the vulnerable Gulf coast. But during the war the Confederacy built no more than 200 miles of new line while over 3,000 miles were constructed in the United States.

The most pressing problem facing Confederate railroad officials was simply keeping their lines operating. Proper maintenance grew more difficult with every passing month. Rail, ties, fuel, replacement parts, and labor became more scarce as the war progressed. With all sources for new iron rail exhausted early in the war, managers were desperate to find iron. Though the Southern lines should have had about 4,000 tons of replacement rail each month, not a single new rail was produced in the Confederacy between 1862 and 1865.

The Western and Atlantic stumbled upon 1,100 tons of rail in Savannah and quickly bought it for $50 a ton, giving the line enough for about 15 miles of track. Late in 1861 Stonewall Jackson removed much of the rail from 19 miles of B&O double track between Harpers Ferry and Martinsburg and sent it south for the hard-pressed Confederate roads. In 1862 it was said there were 1,200 broken rails on the line from Nashville to Chattanooga, and many roads were so hard up for replacements they took up rail from side tracks, and later even branch lines, to repair their main stems.

Even the Confederate navy sought railroad iron. In June 1862, the Navy Department, headed by Stephen R. Mallory, impressed 1,100 tons of rail belonging to the 109-mile Atlantic and Gulf Railroad in Georgia to be used for the manufacture of ship's armor. In January 1863, the Iron Commission was created to determine what railroad iron could "best be dispensed with." Soon whole railroads were being taken over so their rail could be used on more important routes. Short lines were seized in North Carolina, Georgia, Florida, and Texas, but this only created new problems: as short or branch lines were dismantled, supplies for the army correspondingly declined.

By the middle years of the war, wood for cross ties and fuel grew scarce because of a shortage of labor to cut the wood. Often train crews made frequent stops on their routes to gather wood. In 1863 the North Carolina Railroad found cordwood so scarce it purchased wooded acres to ensure a steady supply and for a while demanded that half of any wood it hauled had to be sold to it.

The care and repair of locomotives and cars was another problem. Longer trains, the shortage of replacement parts, and the lack of skilled labor combined to make engines deteriorate more rapidly. By 1863 and 1864 a quarter of the locomotives of many lines needed repairs, and at least fifty engines were laid up because of the lack of tires for their drivers. The quality of passenger service also declined. By midwar many passenger cars were operating with broken windows, no water for the passengers, and no firewood for the coach's stove. Army use of passenger cars was often cited as the cause of missing seats, stoves, lamps, and water barrels when the coaches were finally returned to the owning road. The vast numbers of soldiers being moved by rail made it frequently necessary to use boxcars fitted with plank seats. In winter weather the troops often built fires on the floors of freight cars and left them burning when they debarked. When Gen. James Longstreet's men rode the rails to Chickamauga in September 1863, the soldiers pried boards from the side walls of the boxcars to improve the ventilation and the view. Passenger trains that had traveled 15 to 20 miles an hour in 1860 had dropped to 6 miles an hour by the end of the war.

The shortage of labor that started in 1861 when Northerners returned home grew worse when wages in munition plants outstripped the pay scales of most railroads. Eventually railroads raised wages but still lagged well behind the growing inflation rate. Several Confederate generals aggravated the shortage of skilled mechanics by keeping such men in uniform when they would have been more useful in railroad work. The Conscription Act of 1862 treated rail workers generously, exempting some six thousand. But the 1864 act was stiffer; it raised the draft age to fifty, and permitted no railroad to have more employees than miles of road.

Though there are no firm figures for the number of railroad employees, it seems probable that the number of employees early in the war was much larger than the number of miles of line (5,500–6,000) in operation in 1864. Of course, slaves made up an important portion of all railroad workers. Usually performing the less skilled jobs, they were either owned by the railroad or rented from slaveholders. Certainly all railroad workers at the end of the war were paid far less in real dollars than they were receiving in 1861. Thomas Webb, president of the North Carolina Railroad, made $6,000 a year in 1864, a figure worth no more at that point than $300 in gold. Before the war locomotive firemen were paid $300 a year, and the president received $2,500 a year.

But even with all their problems, rail lines on several occasions moved large bodies of Confederate troops long distances. When George B. McClellan's Union army threatened Richmond in early June 1862, Lee felt secure enough to send two brigades (nearly 10,000 men) by rail west to Charlottesville to strengthen Stonewall Jackson in the Shenandoah Valley. Later Jackson's enlarged forces returned by rail to face McClellan's left flank and pushed the Union army away from Richmond in the Seven Days' Battles. The entire operation lasted just over three weeks, with the troops moving more than 250 miles over seven or eight railroads.

Two massive troop movements were carried out later near Chattanooga. By the summer of 1862 Corinth and a large portion of the Memphis and Charleston line were in Union hands. In the last days of June, Braxton Bragg decided to move his army of about 25,000 men from northeastern Mississippi to Chattanooga, which was threatened by Union forces under Don Carlos Buell. The distance from Tupelo to Chattanooga is a little over 200 miles as the crow flies. Bragg's route by railroad covered 775 miles via the Mobile and Ohio to Mobile and then northeast over five short Alabama and Georgia lines to Atlanta and Chattanooga. The entire operation took a little more than a week. A year later, in mid-September, Bragg was reinforced during the Battle of Chickamauga when James Longstreet's First Corps of the Army of Virginia arrived from Richmond. The 12,000 Confederate troops had moved south about 900 miles in ten days using a dozen railroads in Virginia, the Carolinas, and Georgia. Confederate railroads were still in reasonable shape in the fall of 1863.

Union Capture and Destruction. During the four years of the war Union forces slowly but steadily encroached upon the northern and western frontiers of the Confederacy. During 1861 the Union armies reclaimed the northwestern counties of Virginia. In 1862 the South lost more of what would become West Virginia, half of Arkansas, the western half of Tennessee, a portion of Mississippi, and the area around New Orleans. The loss of the Mississippi River cut the Confederacy in two, and most of Arkansas and Tennessee plus large portions of Mississippi and Louisiana came under Union control. These Union gains were accompanied by the destruction of hundreds of miles of Confederate railways. The more important of the lines were rebuilt by the U.S. Military Railroad, an agency of the War Department created in 1862, under the supervision of Gen. Daniel C. McCallum.

One of the first railroad raids—colorful but totally ineffective—was the Andrews Raid of April 1862, in which a band of disguised Union soldiers stole the locomotive General and tried to wreck the Western and Atlantic Railroad. Two years later, in spring 1864, William Tecumseh Sherman with a strong Union army left Chattanooga and headed for Atlanta, following the track of the Western and Atlantic. For several months the normal daily flow of supplies to the 100,000 men and 35,000 animals in

Sherman's army consisted of sixteen trains, each composed of ten cars (10-ton capacity). This daily total of 1,600 tons was in marked contrast to the pitiful rations reaching Lee's army defending Richmond in 1864 and 1865. In the last months of the war Lee's supply trains were often delayed and his army was frequently reduced to two or three days of rations.

After taking Atlanta late in the summer of 1864 Sherman destroyed the rail line back to Chattanooga and set out for Savannah. On his march to the sea he left the railroads in central Georgia in tatters. He destroyed hundreds of miles of line, especially hitting the 191-mile Central of Georgia and the 102-mile Macon and Western. After leaving Savannah early in 1865, Sherman wreaked equal havoc on the rail system of South Carolina, including the railroads serving Columbia, the state capital.

By 1865 the U.S. Military Railroad controlled 2,100 miles of line, most of it former Confederate railroads. Hundreds of miles of railroads were out of operation by March and April. When Union forces cut the South Side Railroad near Richmond early in April, the end of the long conflict was near. As Lee's exhausted army moved toward Appomattox, the railroads were as crippled and defeated as the Southern armies they had vainly sought to support.

The long war had broken or destroyed the great majority of the Southern railroads, leaving twisted rails, burnt ties, gutted shops and depots, ruined bridges, and dilapidated or lost rolling stock. In May 1865, Chief Justice Salmon P. Chase visited North Carolina. The judge was provided with a train described by the correspondent Whitelaw Reid as "a wheezy little locomotive and an old mail agent's car, with all the windows smashed out and half the seats gone." Some lines were out of operation for many months. But a rehabilitation program aided by the Federal government resulted in both the fast return of the Southern roads General McCallum had rebuilt and the sale of government-owned cars and equipment to private parties. Most Southern roads were offering some kind of service by Christmas, 1865.

The inability of the Southern railways to support the Confederacy adequately resulted from several factors. In 1861 Confederate railroads were generally weak and inferior to Northern lines. Shortages of materials and labor made proper maintenance more difficult with each passing year. But a fundamental factor was the Southern belief in state rights. Since most railroads represented a single state, the individual lines subscribed to this doctrine with the same vigor as the governors and cabinet members who quarreled with Jefferson Davis. As a result the Richmond government was never able to provide a strong centralized supervision of the railroads and failed to support them when they were in peril.

[*See also entries on numerous battles and campaigns mentioned herein, particularly* Andrews Raid.]

BIBLIOGRAPHY

Black, Robert C., III. *The Railroads of the Confederacy.* Chapel Hill, N.C., 1952.
Coulter, E. Merton. *The Confederate States of America, 1861–1865.* A History of the South, vol. 7. Baton Rouge, La., 1950.
Johnston, Angus James, II. *Virginia Railroads in the Civil War.* Chapel Hill, N.C., 1961.
Ramsdell, C. W. "The Confederate Government and the Railroads." *American Historical Review* 22 (1916–17): 494–810.
Stover, John F. *Iron Road to the West: American Railroads in the 1850s.* New York, 1978.
Stover, John F. *The Railroads of the South, 1865–1900: A Study in Finance and Control.* Chapel Hill, N.C., 1955.
Trelease, Allen W. *The North Carolina Railroad, 1849–1871, and the Modernization of North Carolina.* Chapel Hill, N.C., 1991.
Turner, George Edgar. *Victory Rode the Rails.* Indianapolis, 1953.
Lash, Jeffrey N. *Destroyer of the Iron Horse: General Joseph E. Johnston and Confederate Rail Transport.* Kent, Ohio, 1991.

JOHN F. STOVER

RAINS, GABRIEL J. (1803–1881), brigadier general. A native of Craven County, North Carolina, Rains graduated from West Point in 1827. He distinguished himself in the Seminole War (1839–1842, 1849–1850) and

GABRIEL J. RAINS. LIBRARY OF CONGRESS

the Mexican War. Resigning from the U.S. Army with a rank of lieutenant colonel on July 1, 1861, Rains began his Confederate service as a colonel of infantry in the army. On September 23, 1861, he received a brigadier general's commission and a brigade on the Virginia Peninsula. He saw action at Yorktown (April 4–May 3), Williamsburg (May 4–5), and Seven Pines (May 31–June 1). During the retreat from Williamsburg and Yorktown, Rains planted shells with percussion caps in the road, which caused considerable destruction as the Federals advanced. Controversy surrounded his booby traps in the North and the South, and Gen. James Longstreet prohibited him from further engaging in such questionable means of warfare.

Shortly after Seven Pines, George Wythe Randolph, the secretary of war, placed Rains under the War Department so that he could experiment with explosives. Commanding Richmond's Bureau of Conscription during the winter of 1862–1863, Rains convinced Jefferson Davis that mines had military value and were not immoral. Rains reasoned that each new weapon was declared "barbarous" when first introduced, but eventually "each took its place according to its efficacy in human slaughter." On May 25, he began supervising the defense of a number of harbors—namely, Mobile, Charleston, and Savannah. For his efforts, Rains was assigned the superintendency of the Torpedo Bureau on June 17, 1864. His innovative development of an explosive sub terra shell demonstrated the future potential of mines.

After the war, Rains worked as a chemist in Augusta, Georgia. He died on August 6, 1881, and was buried in Aiken, South Carolina.

BIBLIOGRAPHY

Hill, D. H., Jr. *North Carolina.* Vol. 4 of *Confederate Military History.* Edited by Clement A. Evans. Atlanta, 1899. Vol. 5 of extended ed. Wilmington, N.C., 1987.

Perry, Milton F. *Infernal Machines.* Baton Rouge, La., 1965.

Rain, G. J. "Torpedoes." *Southern Historical Society Papers* 3 (1887): 255–260. Reprint, Wilmington, N.C., 1990.

Vandiver, Frank E. *Ploughshares into Swords: Josiah Gorgas and Confederate Ordnance.* Austin, Tex., 1952.

PETER S. CARMICHAEL

RAINS, JAMES EDWARDS (1833–1862), politician, editor, and brigadier general. Born April 10, 1833, in Nashville, Tennessee, Rains graduated from Yale Law School in 1854. He opened his practice in Nashville and soon became active in the middle Tennessee Whig party. He was elected city attorney in 1858 and in 1860 won election as district attorney for Davidson and two of its neighboring counties. He also served his party during this period as associate editor of the *Nashville Daily Republican Banner,* a strong voice of the Whig party in middle Tennessee.

In the spring of 1861 Rains enlisted as a private in the Hermitage Guards, Company D, Eleventh Tennessee, and quickly became its captain. On May 10, 1861, the men of the Eleventh elected him colonel of this Davidson County and western Tennessee regiment. They remained at Cumberland Gap for a year until maneuvered away from it in June 1862. Operating under Gen. Carter Stevenson, Rains, now commanding a brigade, distinguished himself in the recapture of Cumberland Gap and the march to join Braxton Bragg's army at Harrodsburg, Kentucky, in October 1862. Although the Eleventh did not participate in the fighting at Perryville, Rains's abilities and services were recognized by his promotion to brigadier general in November. In his first real battle at Murfreesboro, Rains commanded a mixed brigade of Tennesseans, Georgians, and North Carolinians under Gen. John P. McCown in William J. Hardee's sweeping envelopment on December 31. Leading the extreme left of the Confederate flanking move, the twenty-nine-year-old Rains eagerly advanced to the front of his brigade and was killed instantly by enemy rifle fire.

BIBLIOGRAPHY

Connelly, Thomas L. *Army of the Heartland: The Army of Tennessee, 1861–1862.* Baton Rouge, La., 1967.

Connelly, Thomas L. *Autumn of Glory: The Army of Tennessee, 1862–1865.* Baton Rouge, La., 1971.

Porter, James. *Tennessee.* Vol. 8 of *Confederate Military History.* Edited by Clement A. Evans. Atlanta, 1899. Vol. 10 of extended ed. Wilmington, N.C., 1987.

NATHANIEL CHEAIRS HUGHES, JR.

RALEIGH, NORTH CAROLINA. The capital of North Carolina was authorized by the General Assembly in 1792 and laid out on a wooded tract near the center of the state. An early example of a planned town, it had wide streets in a regular grid. A new state capitol completed in 1840 replaced the first one that burned in 1831; a handsome granite structure in the Doric style, it is located on a six-acre plot at the center of the city. Union soldiers arriving in the spring of 1865 commented on the white houses, picket fences, and gardens that appeared "real Northern-like."

Even after ten years the new town had a population of only 669 and little more than government offices and modest trade to attract newcomers. By 1860 its population had grown to 4,780 of whom 1,624 were slaves. Merchants, grocers, clerks, printers, and carpenters were major occupations. The town was a center of rail transportation, and a number of engineers, conductors, clerks, and other employees lived there. It was also the headquarters of the State Bank of North Carolina and supported branches of the Bank of New Bern and the Bank of Cape Fear. The capital was visited by those who had business with state officials, and hotels (one of which had a rare shower bath) provided accommodations for them. Members of the General Assembly took rooms in the hotels or stayed in private homes and ate at some of the numerous boardinghouses. At least two express companies did business in the town, and telegraph service had been available since 1848.

Perhaps the quality of life for some of the residents who could afford their services or goods is indicated by the presence of occupation lists of gardeners, governesses, mantua-makers, tailors, milliners, jewelers, and confectioners, as well as an artist, an architect, a music teacher, a bookseller, a man who made daguerreotypes, and two men who installed gas fixtures—a luxury only recently available. A large number of clergymen and almost as many lawyers, together with five druggists, four doctors, and three dentists, practiced their professions.

In addition to two public schools for boys and one for girls, there were several private academies and seminaries as well as others operated by the Baptist, Methodist, Presbyterian, and Episcopal churches. A college for young women operated by Episcopalians opened in 1842, and when the war began one supported by Presbyterians was under construction; although this college did not open until 1872, its building was used as a Confederate hospital.

Between 1861 and 1865 eleven newspapers appeared. Editors received news by telegraph, and with rival editors holding different points of view, readers were well informed. Nine periodicals pertaining to agriculture, religion, education, and other subjects were also published. A mill on the outskirts of town provided paper for the town's presses.

Despite its small size and lack of a varied economic base, the town undoubtedly had a metropolitan air. Among its residents were natives of eight foreign countries. There were no citizens from other Southern states except South Carolina, but people born in Vermont, Massachusetts, Connecticut, New York, Delaware, Pennsylvania, Maryland, and Tennessee lived in Raleigh.

North Carolina was largely Unionist in sentiment until Abraham Lincoln's call for volunteer troops. Afterward Southern sympathies prevailed. A convention in Raleigh took the state out of the Union on May 20, 1861, and adopted the state's first flag. At least half a dozen training camps were established along the railroad in and around the city; troops were also accommodated in the parks in town or in buildings cleared for their use. A powder mill and a bayonet factory opened, and the paper mill turned to production for the government. Raleigh became a hub of activity as officials prepared the state for war. They set up warehouses for supplies, and equipment soon was being shipped to troops in training and in the field. When the need arose, a large hospital was established on the state fairgrounds, and in time other buildings were put to the same use.

Zebulon Vance was governor from 1862 until the end of the war. In his relations with the Confederate government he upheld the principle of state rights and resisted directives from President Jefferson Davis and the Congress that he considered improper. This feud, it was widely asserted, denied promotion to military leaders from the state. A Raleigh newspaper editor, William W. Holden, opposed secession, called for the election of Vance, and even during the war advocated personal liberty. By 1863, however, he supported the peace movement and was quickly denounced as a traitor. Georgia troops passing through Raleigh in September 1863 burned his office. The next day about two hundred of Holden's followers retaliated by destroying the office of the rival conservative newspaper.

The hardships of war affected Raleigh as they did the rest of the South. Shortages of food and clothing, inflation, and news from the battlefront of illness, wounds, and death took their toll on civilian morale. Although some Union prisoners were confined in the city, the enemy posed no serious military threat until the spring of 1865. With Richmond under siege, Mrs. Jefferson Davis and her children moved to Raleigh, as did other refugees from Richmond and eastern North Carolina. It was even rumored that the Confederate capital might be moved to Raleigh.

Following the Battle of Bentonville from March 19 through 21, Union troops began to move toward Raleigh. State officials hastily shipped state records and other valuables by train to the west. Governor Vance permitted three emissaries to go by locomotive to intercept and confer with Gen. William Tecumseh Sherman; they secured a "suspension of hostilities" and his pledge not to damage Raleigh if his troops met no resistance. Sherman arrived in Raleigh on April 13, 1865, and set up headquarters in the governor's mansion. Nearly 100,000 Federal troops occupied the city and surrounding countryside. There was a single act of defiance when a Lieutenant Walsh from Texas fired on approaching Union troops. He was seized and hanged within ten minutes. Surplus horses, mules, and wagons from the Union army were released for the use of farmers in the area in readying their land for planting.

Raleigh, unlike the capitals of the four surrounding states, suffered virtually no damage during the war. Life quickly returned to normal as rail lines were repaired, shops were freshly stocked, newspapers resumed publication, schools and churches continued to operate, and doctors and other professional people returned home from the war. State records, which had been sent out of town as federal troops approached, were returned and the government began operating again.

BIBLIOGRAPHY

Carroll, Grady Lee Ernest. *The City of Raleigh, North Carolina, and the Civil War Experience.* [Raleigh, N.C.], 1979.

Harris, William C. *William Woods Holden: Firebrand of North Carolina Politics.* Baton Rouge, La., 1987.
Murray, Elizabeth Reid. *Wake, Capital County of North Carolina.* Raleigh, N.C., 1983.
Writers' Program, Work Projects Administration. *Raleigh, Capital of North Carolina.* Raleigh, N.C., 1942.

WILLIAM S. POWELL

RALLS, JOHN PERKINS (1822–1904), congressman from Alabama. Born on January 1, 1822, in Greene County, Georgia, Ralls received his early education in Greensboro and Cassville, Georgia, and graduated from the Medical College at Augusta, Georgia, in 1845. He opened his medical practice at Cassville before receiving additional medical training in Paris, France, during 1846 and 1847. After his return from Europe, he became county and city physician in Gadsden, Alabama, where he developed a successful medical practice. An immediate secessionist, he was a delegate to the Alabama convention and was a representative in the Second Confederate Congress in 1862, where he was a member of the Indian Affairs, Medical Department, and Special committees. He authored a resolution declaring that the Confederacy would never rejoin the United States. A supporter of President Jefferson Davis, Ralls favored enlarging the powers of the Confederate central government. Ralls was defeated in a bid for reelection in 1863. He served as a delegate to the 1875 Alabama Constitutional Convention and as a representative in the Alabama legislature in 1878. He died in Gadsden on November 23, 1904.

BIBLIOGRAPHY

Fleming, Walter L. *Civil War and Reconstruction in Alabama.* New York, 1905. Reprint, Spartanburg, S.C., 1978.
Owen, Thomas McAdory. *History of Alabama and Dictionary of Alabama Biography.* 4 vols. Chicago, 1921.
Wakelyn, Jon L. *Biographical Directory of the Confederacy.* Edited by Frank E. Vandiver. Westport, Conn., 1977.
Warner, Ezra J., and W. Buck Yearns. *Biographical Register of the Confederate Congress.* Baton Rouge, La., 1975.

SARAH WOOLFOLK WIGGINS

RAMS. The ship-killing ram of the ancient Mediterranean was given new life during the Civil War: steam power replaced the human muscles of the rowed galleys of antiquity, and iron armor protected rams from enemy gunfire. Southern leaders recognized that they would be unable to equal the North in numbers of warships, so they sought to build a fleet that was qualitatively superior. Armored rams provided an equalizing weapon. Existing vessels and power plants (propulsion machineries) were reinforced for ramming and rebuilt with iron armor. In addition, new vessels were built with rams and armored casemates; most had simplified hull forms designed to be built by carpenters unfamiliar with ship construction. Steam propulsion was universal, but rams built for service on the coast used screw propellers; those on the western rivers usually used paddle wheels in armored housings.

The first armored ram to see service was the propeller tugboat *Enoch Train,* which was rebuilt by private parties in New Orleans to become the privateer *Manassas.* It was seized by the Confederate navy and led the Confederate fleet in the Battle of the Mississippi, below New Orleans. *Manassas* rammed two Union warships but ran aground and was destroyed by its crew to prevent capture.

The most famous and influential ram was CSS *Virginia,* rebuilt from the burned steam frigate *Merrimack. Virginia* enjoyed a single day of success in Hampton Roads, Virginia, sinking two powerful Union vessels before meeting the Union ironclad *Monitor,* which had been built particularly to counter the threat posed by *Virginia. Monitor* and the turreted ironclads that followed it were designed with a projecting knuckle or "raft" to protect against Confederate rams. The two ironclads, the ram and the antiram, stalemated each other for over two months before Norfolk was captured, forcing the destruction of *Virginia.*

Rams were built on the shores of all the major navigable rivers of the Confederacy. They were intended to protect the rivers as interior lines of communication and to prevent the North from dividing the country by taking the rivers. Ironclads were built on the James River; on the North Carolina sounds; at Wilmington, Charleston, Savannah, and Mobile; and on the Mississippi and Red rivers. They were feared by Federal sailors, inducing in many the fearful condition derisively known as "ram fever."

Many vessels on the Western Rivers—the Mississippi, Missouri, Ohio, Red, Yellow, Yazoo, and their tributaries—were heavily reinforced and rebuilt with projecting ram bows. These river rams were usually paddle-wheel river steamers, with fragile hulls and superstructures. Lightly armed because their light hulls could not support the shock of firing heavy guns, they were protected with whatever materials were available: many Southern riverboats were covered with compressed bales of cotton, becoming cottonclads. Both sides also added heavy wood walls (woodclads) or sheets of half- to one-inch iron plates (tinclads). All depended on the ram as their main weapon.

Most Confederate rams were built with a strong armored beak ram on the bow, an armored knuckle protecting the waterline, and a sloping armored casemate to protect a small number of heavy guns. The ram was intended to be the main offensive weapon. The fatal flaw of most Southern rams was their low speed and poor maneuverability. Few foundries were capable of producing marine engines, and those that could were already producing at capacity.

CSS *Atlanta*. NATIONAL ARCHIVES

Confederate naval engineers adapted engines from other vessels, but few rams could steam over five knots.

Five powerful oceangoing steam rams were built abroad for the Confederate navy. James Dunwoody Bulloch ordered two rams from the shipyards of England and two from France. The first two, to be named *North Carolina* and *Mississippi,* were built by the shipyard of John Laird and Sons, Birkenhead, England. Their destination became known before delivery, however, leading to a lengthy court case and seizure by the British government to prevent the violation of neutrality. Bulloch, at the urging of John Slidell, also ordered a pair of ironclad rams from the shipyard of Lucien Arman of France. The rams were given the cover names *Sphinx* and *Cheops,* but they were prevented from sailing when their destination became known. Through a complicated arrangement, one ram was sold to Denmark, resold to the Confederacy, and delivered at sea. This ram was armed, commissioned CSS *Stonewall,* and taken to Havana, where it was delivered to the Spanish authorities at the end of the war. The fifth and largest ram was ordered by James H. North from the shipyard of James and George Thomson, of Govan, Glasgow, Scotland. It was built using the cover name *No. 61,* but proved too expensive and grand for Confederate needs. The ship was sold and became *Danmark* in the Danish navy. The Thomsons also proposed building a double-turret armored ram that was not ordered.

Only one Confederate ironclad ram was sunk in action by the enemy: *Albemarle,* defending Plymouth, North Carolina, and much of the interior of the state, was sunk by a small boat expedition using a spar torpedo. Two were captured in action: the rams *Atlanta,* near Savannah, and *Tennessee,* in Mobile Bay, were taken after they were rammed repeatedly and heavily shelled by Union vessels.

Many Confederate rams were destroyed to prevent capture. *Virginia* was blown up when Norfolk was abandoned. The large rams *Louisiana* and *Mississippi* were destroyed near New Orleans after the forts and city surrendered. *Arkansas* was set afire when it lost power and capture appeared imminent. Retreating forces destroyed four ironclad rams of the James River Fleet, two on Mobile Bay, two in Charleston Harbor, and one each on the Chattahoochee, Savannah, and Neuse rivers. Other, incomplete ironclad rams were destroyed across the South before advancing Union ground forces could take possession.

Confederate rams were the capital ships of the navy: fleets were built around the armored juggernauts that could convey naval force anywhere on the rivers. Rams offered the only possible counter to Union seapower and were successful in defending many areas of the South. Despite the small amount of action they saw, the Confederate ironclad rams *Chicora* and *Palmetto State* at Charleston; *Virginia II, Richmond, Fredricksburg,* and *Texas* in the James River Fleet; and *Huntsville, Tuscaloosa, Tennessee, Nashville,* and *Phoenix* in Mobile Bay all protected large seaboard cities for most of the war. Ironclad rams were an integral part of Confederate coastal defense plans. Those defenses allowed the South to retain control of important seaport cities, prevented the enemy from using the easy routes inland along the rivers, and kept seaports open for trade with other areas.

[*See also* Laird Rams *and entries on the ships* Albemarle,

Atlanta, Arkansas, Ironclads, Jackson, Nashville, Neuse, Stonewall, Tennessee, Tuscaloosa, Virginia, *and* Webb.]

BIBLIOGRAPHY

Baxter, James P., III. *The Introduction of the Ironclad Warship.* Cambridge, Mass., 1933. Reprint, New York, 1968.

Crandall, W. D., and I. D. Newell. *History of the Ram Fleet and the Mississippi Marine Brigade.* St. Louis, 1907.

Gosnell, A. Allen. *Guns on the Western Waters: The Story of River Gunboats in the Civil War.* Baton Rouge, La., 1949.

Mahan, Alfred T. *The Navy in the Civil War: The Gulf and Inland Waters.* New York, 1883.

Still, William N., Jr. *Iron Afloat: The Story of the Confederate Armorclads.* Columbia, S.C., 1985.

KEVIN J. FOSTER

RAMSAY, JAMES GRAHAM (1823–1903), congressman from North Carolina. Ramsay was born in Iredell County, North Carolina. After an early education in local schools, Ramsay entered Davidson College and graduated in 1841. Initially selecting medicine as a profession, he traveled to Philadelphia and enrolled in Jefferson Medical College. Upon graduation in 1848, Ramsay returned to his native state to practice in Rowan County. His local reputation as an able doctor and successful farmer grew, and in 1856, he won election to the state senate as a Whig. Espousing strong Unionist sentiment, Ramsay opposed secession. He chose, nevertheless, to remain in state politics after North Carolina voted to leave the Union.

In 1863, with the backing of his district's peace party and the support of the *North Carolina Standard* and its conservative editor, William Woods Holden, Ramsay was elected to the Second Confederate Congress. He assumed his new duties in the House of Representatives on May 2, 1864, and was appointed five days later to both the Medical Department and the Naval Affairs committees. While in Congress, Ramsay generally voted to weaken the power of the central government over the states. He opposed suspension of the writ of habeas corpus, impressment, and the arming of free blacks and slaves. Ramsay even offered a resolution in January 1865 to broaden the exemption list to the point of discharging from military duty all "blacksmiths, tanners, millwrights, public millers, hatters, and shoemakers" who could prove that they were "regularly engaged in the performance of their duties" on February 17, 1864.

Yet, in spite of his frequent opposition to any expansion of the power of the central government, there is no reason to question Ramsay's loyalty to the Confederacy. In November 1864 the North Carolina congressman voted in favor of the repetition of a declaration made by Congress in March 1862 stating that the people of the Confederacy will "suffer all the calamities of the most protracted war, but that they will never, on any terms, politically affiliate with a people who are guilty of an invasion of their soil and the butchery of their citizens." Even in late February 1865, when hopes for victory were all but gone, Ramsay voted in favor of a bill to levy additional taxes for the year to support the government.

After the war, Ramsay returned to the medical profession, this time in Charlotte. He became an active Republican and was chosen as an elector for the Grant ticket in 1872. Ramsay ran successfully for the state senate in 1883 and served one term. He died in Salisbury.

BIBLIOGRAPHY

Brawley, James S. *The Rowan Story, 1753–1953: A Narrative History of Rowan County, North Carolina.* Salisbury, N.C., 1953.

Journal of the Congress of the Confederate States of America, 1861–1865. 7 vols. Washington, D.C., 1904–1905.

Wakelyn, Jon L. *Biographical Dictionary of the Confederacy.* Edited by Frank E. Vandiver. Westport, Conn., 1977.

Warner, Ezra J., and W. Buck Yearns. *Biographical Register of the Confederate Congress.* Baton Rouge, La., 1975.

ALAN C. DOWNS

RAMSEUR, DODSON (1837–1864), major general. Born May 31, 1837, in Lincolnton, North Carolina, Stephen Dodson Ramseur graduated fourteenth in West Point's class of 1860. He resigned from the army in April 1861,

DODSON RAMSEUR. LIBRARY OF CONGRESS

enlisting as an artillery officer with his own state. He quickly moved up the ranks: to major of the Tenth North Carolina on May 16, 1861, and to colonel of the Forty-ninth North Carolina on April 12, 1862. At Malvern Hill in Virginia on July 1, 1862, Ramseur sustained a severe wound to the right arm that kept him from the army until January 1863. The promise he had shown won him the commission of brigadier general on November 1, 1862.

The North Carolinian became prominent in the Second Corps, leading a brigade under Maj. Gen. Robert Rodes and then a division under Lt. Gen. Jubal Early. Ramseur drilled troops hard and they responded well to severe tests at Chancellorsville, Gettysburg, and the Mule Shoe at Spotsylvania—the last of which elicited Robert E. Lee's personal gratitude and earned Ramseur promotion to major general on June 1, 1864. Superiors noted how the young man infused soldiers with his personal enthusiasm in generating an effective offensive punch. His initiative sometimes prompted assaults without adequate preparation, but overall Ramseur displayed tremendous ability as a divisional commander. In the Shenandoah Valley in 1864, the North Carolinians fought tenaciously at Winchester, Fisher's Hill, and Cedar Creek where Ramseur fell mortally wounded. He died October 20, 1864, and was buried in Lincolnton.

BIBLIOGRAPHY

Cox, William R. "Major General Stephen D. Ramseur: His Life and Character." *Southern Historical Society Papers* 18 (1890): 217–260. Reprint, Wilmington, N.C., 1990.

Gallagher, Gary W. *Stephen Dodson Ramseur: Lee's Gallant General.* Chapel Hill, N.C., 1985.

William Alan Blair

RANDAL, HORACE (1831–1864), brigadier general. Randal, a native of McNairy County, Tennessee, was born January 1, 1831. In 1839, his family moved to the vicinity of San Augustine, Texas. He received an appointment to the U.S. Military Academy and graduated in 1854. His first assignment took him to the frontier, where he served in western Texas and New Mexico.

Upon the secession of Texas, Randal resigned his commission on February 27, 1861. Refusing a Confederate commission as a lieutenant, he fought in the ranks in Virginia that year. Upon his return to Texas in 1862, Randal was appointed colonel of the Twenty-eighth Texas Cavalry Regiment and then commanded a brigade of Texas cavalry in Ben McCulloch's division in the Trans-Mississippi Department. His dash and efficiency as a commander during the Battle of Milliken's Bend (part of the Vicksburg campaign) prompted E. Kirby Smith to recommend him for promotion to brigadier general in November 1863. This high opinion of his skills in leading the brigade was echoed in Gen. Richard Taylor's reports of the Battles of Mansfield and Pleasant Hill, Louisiana, during the successful Confederate repulse of Nathaniel Banks's Red River campaign. Randal's commission as brigadier general was dated April 8, 1864, but he never received word of his promotion. He was killed leading his brigade during the Battle of Jenkins's Ferry on April 30, 1864. He was buried in Marshall, Texas.

Randal was a highly competent commander idolized by his soldiers. His death devastated his brigade, which never returned to the efficiency it had shown under his command.

BIBLIOGRAPHY

Fitzhugh, Lester N., comp. *Texas Batteries, Battalions, Regiments, Commanders, and Field Officers, Confederate States, Army, 1861–1865.* Midlothian, Tex., 1959.

Oates, Stephen B. *Confederate Cavalry West of the River.* Austin, Tex., 1961.

Roberts, O. M. *Texas.* Vol. 11 of *Confederate Military History.* Edited by Clement A. Evans. Atlanta, 1899. Vol. 15 of extended ed. Wilmington, N.C., 1989.

Taylor, Richard. *Destruction and Reconstruction: Personal Experiences of the Late War.* New York, 1879.

Roy R. Stephenson

RANDOLPH, GEORGE WYTHE (1818–1867), brigadier general and secretary of war. Randolph was the most successful of Thomas Jefferson's grandsons. Educated at home, in Boston, and in Washington, he entered the U.S. Navy as a midshipman at the age of thirteen. He became a charismatic leader, toured the ports of the Mediterranean and Caribbean, and attended David Farragut's school at Norfolk. On the USS *Constitution* he contracted tuberculosis, followed by a long period of remission. After qualifying as a passed midshipman, he attended the University of Virginia, where in 1841 he took one of its first law degrees and studied engineering and science. For a decade he practiced law at Charlottesville before moving to Richmond. Randolph was an officer of the Virginia Historical Society, a founder of the Richmond Mechanics Institute, and a leading criminal and admiralty lawyer.

Alarmed by John Brown's raid at Harpers Ferry, Randolph in 1859 organized the Richmond Howitzers, which he took to Charles Town in present-day West Virginia to act as guards until Brown was hanged. In 1860 Randolph served as a Virginia commissioner to contract for armaments in the North. Predicting Abraham Lincoln's election and arguing that neutrality was impossible, he urged that Virginia join in a Southern republic. He was a member of the Virginia convention of 1861, which sent him, William Ballard Preston, and A. H. H. Stuart to confer with President

GEORGE WYTHE RANDOLPH. LIBRARY OF CONGRESS

Lincoln. On April 12, Lincoln told them that he would meet force with force. After his call for troops, Virginia seceded.

Colonel Randolph then oversaw the enlargement of the Richmond Howitzers, which he led in winning the Battle of Big Bethel on June 10, 1861. As Gen. John B. Magruder's chief of ordnance, he helped design and arm fortifications at Yorktown. He was promoted to brigadier general and given a command in southeastern Virginia.

Randolph made three major contributions to the Confederacy. The first was his drafting of Virginia's conscription law, based on European models. It, in turn, became the model for Confederate conscription. His second was his work as secretary of war, a post he assumed in March 1862. At the outset of the Peninsular campaign, he and Robert E. Lee advised against Joseph E. Johnston's proposal for a hasty abandonment of Yorktown and retreat toward Richmond. Randolph delayed execution of Johnston's order to evacuate Norfolk until war matériel could be removed.

In organizing the War Office, Randolph named his nephew-in-law Garlick Kean chief of the Bureau of War and Josiah Gorgas chief of the Bureau of Ordnance. To solve problems of procuring war matériel and foodstuffs, he recruited specialists in foreign trade, agriculture, and railroads, as well as a number of lawyers who were alumni of the University of Virginia and Yale. These technocrats administered centralized planning and control from Richmond. Randolph increased the importation of war goods, including tinned bully-beef and Enfield rifles, by offering foreign suppliers and blockade runners greater profits for essential goods. To encourage manufacturers to convert to war goods, he assigned low priorities on the railroads for shipping civilian goods.

Randolph believed that Confederate armies were under strength not because governors hoarded troops but because lenient officers condoned absenteeism. His proposed remedy was to send missions authorized to investigate and punish offenders. When he became convinced that he could not provide enough food for the Confederate armies, he tried to persuade President Davis to permit the exchange of Confederate cotton for Union bacon. Although Randolph was secretary only nine months, his organization of the War Office endured for the life of the Confederacy.

Randolph's third contribution was his advising Davis to devote more attention to the West. Relying on information from his New Orleans recruits, he devised a scheme to liberate that city in the summer of 1862 through a combination of conventional means and a fifth-column uprising. Military events in Tennessee and Virginia occupied the Southern troops, however. From the outset of his secretaryship, he had declared that, unless there were radical changes in policy, he would be unable to provision adequately the Army of Northern Virginia, much less the other military units or the civilian population. Denying this, Davis procrastinated in authorizing Randolph's plans to recover New Orleans, the South's greatest port, and to import foodstuffs from Europe and the U.S. The secretary and the president did not make a good team. Davis's indecisiveness wore Randolph down, and he finally seized on a procedural pretext to resign in November 1862, leaving no possibility of reconsideration.

No longer in the Confederate army, Randolph assumed command of volunteers to defend Richmond from a threatened Union raid in May 1863. As a member of the city council at the time of the bread riots, he encouraged workers to demand increased wages to meet inflation. In November 1864 his health had so deteriorated that he and his wife ran the blockade and sailed for Europe. He consulted doctors in London, conferred with manufacturers, and wintered in southern France. Randolph delayed his return to the United States until September 1866 when he received a pardon. He died in April 1867 in Albemarle County, Virginia.

BIBLIOGRAPHY

Kean, Robert Garlick Hill. *Inside the Confederate Government.* Edited by Edward Younger. New York, 1957.

Patrick, Rembert W. *Jefferson Davis and His Cabinet.* Baton Rouge, La., 1944.

Shackelford, George Green. *George Wythe Randolph and the Confederate Elite.* Athens, Ga., 1988.

GEORGE GREEN SHACKELFORD

his native state, Reade never accepted the idea of an independent Southern nation. In February 1862 he introduced a plan calling for the immediate suspension of hostilities and a meeting of the belligerents in Norfolk. In 1863 he was appointed by Governor Zebulon Vance to fill the remaining month of George Davis's term in the Confederate Senate. There he distinguished himself as an energetic advocate of peace and a vigorous opponent of the Davis administration. In December 1864 he ran as a peace candidate for a full term in the Senate but was easily defeated by Thomas S. Ashe.

After the war Reade served as president of the Reconstruction convention and was subsequently elected associate justice of the state supreme court. By 1868 he had aligned himself with the Republican party. Following his retirement from the bench in 1879, he became a successful banker. He died in Raleigh on October 18, 1894.

BIBLIOGRAPHY

Alexander, Thomas B., and Richard E. Beringer. *The Anatomy of the Confederate Congress: A Study of the Influences of Member Characteristics on Legislative Voting Behavior, 1861–1865.* Nashville, 1972.

Hamilton, Joseph G. de Roulhac, and Max R. Williams, ed. *The Papers of William Alexander Graham.* 7 vols. to date. Raleigh, N.C., 1957–.

Wakelyn, Jon L. *Biographical Dictionary of the Confederacy.* Edited by Frank E. Vandiver. Westport, Conn., 1977.

Warner, Ezra J., and W. Buck Yearns. *Biographical Register of the Confederate Congress.* Baton Rouge, La., 1975.

THOMAS E. JEFFREY

REAGAN, JOHN H. (1818–1905), congressman from Texas and postmaster general. John Henninger Reagan, a native of Tennessee, was born October 8, 1818, and moved to Texas in 1839. He had a farm in Kaufman County and was an attorney, judge, and Democratic politician in the prewar years. He served two terms in the U.S. House of Representatives, 1857 to 1861. Although an advocate of Southern rights, he was not a radical Southerner in Congress and opposed such controversial issues as reopening the African slave trade and the acquisition of territory in Cuba, Mexico, and Central America. His experiences in the Thirty-fifth and Thirty-sixth Congresses convinced him, however, that the Republican majority would not look after the interests of his state or the South.

Reagan returned to the national capital following the election of Abraham Lincoln as president with some hope that the Union could be preserved, but that optimism quickly dissolved as he observed the efforts in Washington to reach a compromise. On December 14, 1860, he and twenty-nine other Southern congressmen composed a joint letter to their constituents. The group concluded that

JOHN H. REAGAN. LIBRARY OF CONGRESS

compromise with the Republican majority was impossible and that separation from the Union was necessary. Convinced that he could do nothing more to help achieve a solution to the sectional conflict, Reagan returned to Texas in January 1861.

On the way home Reagan learned that he had been elected to the Texas secession convention. He went directly to Austin but did not arrive there until January 30, two days after the convention began. Reagan nevertheless played a critical role in the proceedings. Believing that Governor Sam Houston, who remained loyal to the Union, might cause trouble for the secessionists, Reagan met with the governor on the day he arrived and tried to persuade him not to obstruct the proceedings of the convention. Houston informed Reagan that he would not oppose the will of the people and that he would meet with a delegation from the convention. Reagan headed the committee sent the next day to confer with the governor. Houston provided a formal announcement that he recognized the results of the election of delegates and the legitimacy of the convention. This paved the way for the passage of an ordinance of secession on February 1.

The convention elected Reagan as a member of the Provisional Congress at Montgomery. Personal business required him to remain in Texas until that March, however; thus he missed the establishment of the Confederacy and the election of Jefferson Davis as provisional president. He arrived in Montgomery on March 1 and took his seat in Congress the next day. There he earned the admiration of

President Davis and a reputation for bluntness. Reagan told the newly elected president that he would not have voted for him had he been present. Reagan explained that his decision was not based on any question concerning Davis's fitness for the office; rather, he would have preferred that Davis head the army.

Reagan's encounter with the president may have helped the executive make his decision to appoint the congressman as postmaster general. The cabinet post was a critical one for the new government. Good mail service was essential for the dissemination of information, particularly the distribution of newspapers. The mails were also a potentially important factor in the event of war; letters between soldiers in the field and their families at home could help morale.

The task faced by the postmaster general, however, would be extremely difficult for two reasons: the constitutional provision that the Post Office Department must pay its own expenses out of revenue after March 1, 1863, and the strain a war would place on the system. When the president's first two choices turned the job down, Davis turned to Reagan, who had been a member of the Postal Committee in the U.S. House of Representatives and had been recommended by the Texas delegation. On March 6, Davis asked Reagan to accept the post. Reagan initially turned it down but finally accepted, despite his reluctance to take on such a difficult job. His nomination was immediately confirmed by the Congress.

The new postmaster general began building his system by raiding the Washington offices of the U.S. Post Office for men with knowledge of that system's operations. His department heads brought with them the annual reports of the postmaster general, blank forms, and postal maps and modeled their post office on that of the United States. As much as possible those connected with the Federal post offices in the South were integrated into the Confederate department, although some individuals and contractors refused to remain with it.

From the beginning the constitutional provision requiring the post office to be self-supporting was a major concern for Reagan. Figures showing the cost of mail service in the South during the last full year of peace indicated the extent of his problem. In 1860 the Post Office Department had spent nearly $3 million while producing revenues of less than $1 million. Reagan would not be able to continue that system, but would have to both cut costs and increase revenues. He kept his own office staff at a minimum, closed some post offices, reduced the number of mail routes, discontinued duplicate service, and cut service on some routes from daily to triweekly delivery. He also negotiated a 50 percent reduction in the rates railroads charged to deliver the mail and cut mail service on the roads. In addition, he raised postage rates with the approval of Congress.

The U.S. postal system continued to operate in the South until Reagan ordered the inauguration of Confederate mail service on June 1, 1861, and provided for a final accounting and the return of all Federal property to the U.S. Post Office Department. From the beginning of its operations Reagan's system elicited complaints. It could not duplicate the service that Southerners had been used to receiving. Inadequate staffing, elimination of routes, reduction of the number of post offices, plus problems associated with creating a new system—contractors could not be found to deliver the mail in Texas and Arkansas, for example—produced a decline in service. Delays in delivery, loss of mail, thefts, lack of stamps and mail supplies, and high postal rates plagued the Confederate post office.

By the autumn of 1861 the press was filled with complaints. Even members of the cabinet expressed concern about the service. Burdened by the illness of his wife and upset by the criticism, Reagan submitted his resignation in 1862. President Davis persuaded him to remain in the cabinet, however, arguing that if he left, the public might see it as an expression of dissatisfaction with the administration. Reagan continued in office, but though he earned a reputation for hard work and personal integrity, the postmaster general was never able to satisfy the system's numerous critics.

Producing satisfactory service and adhering to the constitutional provision of self-sufficiency became even more difficult as the war progressed. The destruction of railroads and the cutting of communication lines by the movement of the armies inevitably disrupted service. Many materials necessary for postal operations, ranging from stamps to mail bags, were difficult to obtain. Confederate conscription policy, however, proved to be one of the post office's most onerous burdens. This problem developed as the result of a supplemental Confederate conscription law passed in October 1862. The initial law, passed in April 1862, had provided extensive exemptions from conscription, including postal employees, but the October legislation exempted only those postmasters and contractors nominated for their positions by the president and confirmed by the Senate. Reagan reported that the number of individuals available to deliver the mails was thus reduced by some seven-eighths. He lobbied Congress for legislation that ultimately restored many of the exemptions for post office personnel, but as the Confederate army faced growing manpower shortages, conscript officers continued to impress employees. The postmaster general finally became involved in a virtual war with the military, encouraging his men to resist conscription by securing writs of habeas corpus and then suing the conscript officers for false arrest. The fight between Reagan and Secretary of War James A. Seddon over the conscription of post office personnel continued into the autumn of 1864 and ended only when Reagan decided that conditions in the

Confederacy were so bad there was no point in pursuing the issue further.

The struggle between the post office and the military did have one favorable result. Reagan was able to obtain staff who would work for low wages and who bid low for mail delivery contracts so long as postal workers were exempt from military service. Mail service may have been inefficient, but the cost was low. This, combined with Reagan's early reduction in the overall size of the system, meant that the postmaster general was able to make the post office self-sustaining in the time allotted to him. By the end of 1863, his report indicated, the department was operating at a surplus.

Despite the criticism leveled at the postal service, many observers from the beginning considered Reagan to be one of the most capable of Davis's cabinet appointees. Even while accusing him of inefficiency, no critic ever considered Reagan to be anything other than of the most upstanding character. Considering the overwhelming problems of creating the new system, Reagan accomplished much, and the Confederacy never experienced within his department the same problems that developed in other government offices.

Reagan's duties as a cabinet officer went beyond his official role as postmaster general. He was one of the men Davis turned to for advice on the general problems facing the Confederacy. Despite his personal loyalty to the president, Reagan was forthright in his opposition to administration policies with which he disagreed. In 1863, the postmaster general found himself consistently in the minority on military matters. In particular, he opposed Robert E. Lee's invasion of Pennsylvania in the summer of that year and argued instead for moving more forces west in order to destroy Ulysses S. Grant's army, which was maneuvering to capture Vicksburg and cut the Confederacy in two. The differences between Reagan and other cabinet officials reached a point where Reagan offered to resign for a second time. But President Davis held his services to be too valuable and dissuaded him from this course.

On April 2, 1865, Postmaster General Reagan abandoned Richmond with President Davis in the hope of establishing the seat of government farther in the Confederate interior—a plan that went awry when Lee surrendered his army in northern Virginia. Another course was taken when Gen. Joseph E. Johnston began negotiating the surrender of his army. Reagan and Secretary of War John C. Breckinridge were sent to assist in the talks, where they offered a total Confederate surrender if the United States preserved the existing state governments, respected the political and property rights of Confederate citizens, and promised to impose no penalties on participants or to persecute them. After presenting this proposal, Reagan rejoined the president at Charlotte, North Carolina. When William Tecumseh Sherman ultimately offered only the terms Grant gave to Lee at Appomattox, the remaining cabinet members and the president resumed their flight, recommending that Johnston simply disband so that the army could reorganize elsewhere. Johnston chose to accept Sherman's terms.

At this point they hoped to reach Texas, where E. Kirby Smith's army remained intact. Other cabinet members resigned and returned home as the South's ultimate fate became obvious, but Reagan remained with the president. He was captured with the president's party on the evening of May 10, 1865, near Irwinville, Georgia.

Reagan was imprisoned until December 1865 at Fort Warren, where he wrote two important letters. The first, on May 28, urged President Andrew Johnson to adopt a lenient policy toward the defeated South, warning that a more radical approach would end in evil. A more controversial letter, on August 11, advised Texans to accept the results of the war, including the end of slavery and the guarantee of civil rights and suffrage—restricted with educational and property qualifications—for blacks. The second letter was condemned by his constituents, but Reagan believed that such a course was necessary to avoid military rule and unqualified black suffrage.

After his release, Reagan returned to Texas and practiced law. He was also active in Democratic politics. He served in the Texas constitutional convention in 1875 and was a U.S. congressman (1875–1877) and senator (1887–1891). He died at Palestine, Texas, March 6, 1905.

BIBLIOGRAPHY

McCaleb, Walter Flavius. "John H. Reagan." *Texas Historical Association Quarterly* 5 (July 1905): 41–50.

Patrick, Rembert W. *Jefferson Davis and His Cabinet.* Baton Rouge, La., 1944.

Proctor, Ben H. *Not without Honor: The Life of John H. Reagan.* Austin, Tex., 1962.

Reagan, John H. *Memoirs with Special Reference to Secession and the Civil War.* New York, 1906.

CARL H. MONEYHON

RECTOR, HENRY M. (1816–1899), governor of Arkansas. Rector was a native of Kentucky, born on May 1, 1816. Moving to Arkansas in 1835, he became a resident of Hot Springs where he was a prominent attorney and jurist. In the 1860 state election he ran for governor and led a revolt within the Democratic party against the dominant party faction known as the Family. In the campaign, Rector expressed few sentiments on national issues. As governor, however, he became a strong proponent of secession. In December 1860, he encouraged the General Assembly to call a state convention. When the legislature did not move fast enough, Rector himself practically declared war on the United States when he encouraged local militia companies to assemble at Little Rock and seize the U.S. arsenal in February 1861.

Arkansas finally seceded on May 6, and the secession convention created a military board with broad authority to raise and equip troops. As head of the board, Rector quickly found himself at odds with the policies of Confederate officials. He wanted to use the troops raised in Arkansas within the state, but Confederate authorities called for them to be sent east as rapidly as they were raised. Rector protested the removal of these troops but was unable to stop it.

In 1862 he was in another fight with the Confederacy, this time with Gen. Thomas C. Hindman, who had imposed martial law in the state during the Federal invasion in the spring and then maintained the suspension of civil authority in order to enforce conscription the following autumn. Rector threatened to secede from the Confederacy unless something was done. With support of part of the congressional delegation he finally obtained Hindman's replacement by Gen. Theophilus H. Holmes, but Holmes also proved reluctant to end martial law until instructed to do so by the president in the spring of 1863.

Rector had to fight political foes at home, too. In the state constitution written in 1861 his enemies included a provision that shortened his term, forcing him to run for reelection in October 1862. Because of his problems with the central government and the opposition of the Family, Rector was defeated overwhelmingly by Harris Flanagin. Rector tried to join the Confederate army after his defeat but was denied a commission. He served in the state reserve corps for the rest of the war.

After the war Rector returned to planting and was active in Democratic politics, serving in the constitutional conventions of 1868 and 1874. He died at Hot Springs on August 12, 1899.

BIBLIOGRAPHY

Hallum, John. *Biographical and Pictorial History of Arkansas.* Albany, N.Y., 1887.

Moore, Waddy W. "Henry Massie Rector." In *The Governors of Arkansas.* Edited by Timothy P. Donovan and Willard B. Gatewood, Jr. Fayetteville, Ark., 1980.

Obituary. *Arkansas Gazette* (Little Rock), August 13, 1899.

Yearns, W. Buck, ed. *The Confederate Governors.* Athens, Ga., 1985.

CARL H. MONEYHON

RED RIVER CAMPAIGNS. Two ill-fated Union campaigns along central Louisiana's Red River, a natural invasion route into Texas, were fought for political, economic, ideological, and diplomatic reasons rather than for purely military objectives. The liberation of Texas by the Union would placate Northern antislavery forces who considered Texas's 1845 admission as a slave state the culmination of a conspiracy led by Southern slave owners. Once freed, Texas, it was believed, would provide free-labor-grown cotton, which would simultaneously demonstrate the inferiority of slave labor and keep Northern mills running. This in turn would cement political support for the Republican party. Moreover, the occupation of Texas would eliminate Mexico's role in breaking the blockade and lessen the likelihood of French interference in Mexico. Last, the Red River valley itself contained large supplies of cotton, the capture of which offered huge financial and political incentives to the invading forces.

In the course of the campaigns, the Union lost 5,200 men and the Confederates, 4,200. Most important, these campaigns forced Gen. Ulysses S. Grant to delay his planned attack on Mobile, Alabama, for ten months and denied Gen. William Tecumseh Sherman 10,000 veterans when he marched against Gen. Joseph E. Johnston in Georgia. The campaigns ended in great controversy in both the North and the South.

The 1863 campaign was a sideline to the Union effort to capture Port Hudson, Louisiana, on the Mississippi River. In December 1862 Maj. Gen. Nathaniel P. Banks took command of the Department of the Gulf. He had been sent ostensibly to occupy any part of Texas in order to show the U.S. flag to the French in Mexico. But the more pressing matter of controlling the Mississippi claimed his attention. From April through July 1863 Banks cooperated with army and navy forces under Grant and Rear Adm. David G. Farragut operating against Port Hudson. Determined to clear all Confederate opposition to his west before moving on Port Hudson, Banks advanced up the Atchafalaya River and Bayou Teche as he headed for Alexandria, Louisiana. He defeated a small force under Maj. Gen. Richard Taylor at the Battles of Irish Bend and Fort Bisland on April 12 through 14. Banks then moved unopposed into Alexandria. At this point, Union General in Chief Henry W. Halleck reminded Banks of his orders. As a result Banks's planned move up the Red River to collect cotton and livestock ceased. In late May he left the Red River and moved against Port Hudson, which fell July 9.

With the Mississippi cleared, Banks was free to move against Texas; instead he and Grant wanted to attack Mobile. Halleck, however, now insisted on the campaign against Texas via the Red River, and with President Abraham Lincoln's strong backing, he ordered the campaign. The plan called for Banks with his 17,000 troops to be joined by 10,000 of Sherman's men commanded by Brig. Gen. Andrew Jackson Smith, Brig. Gen. Frederick Steele's force of 15,000 from the Department of Arkansas, and a

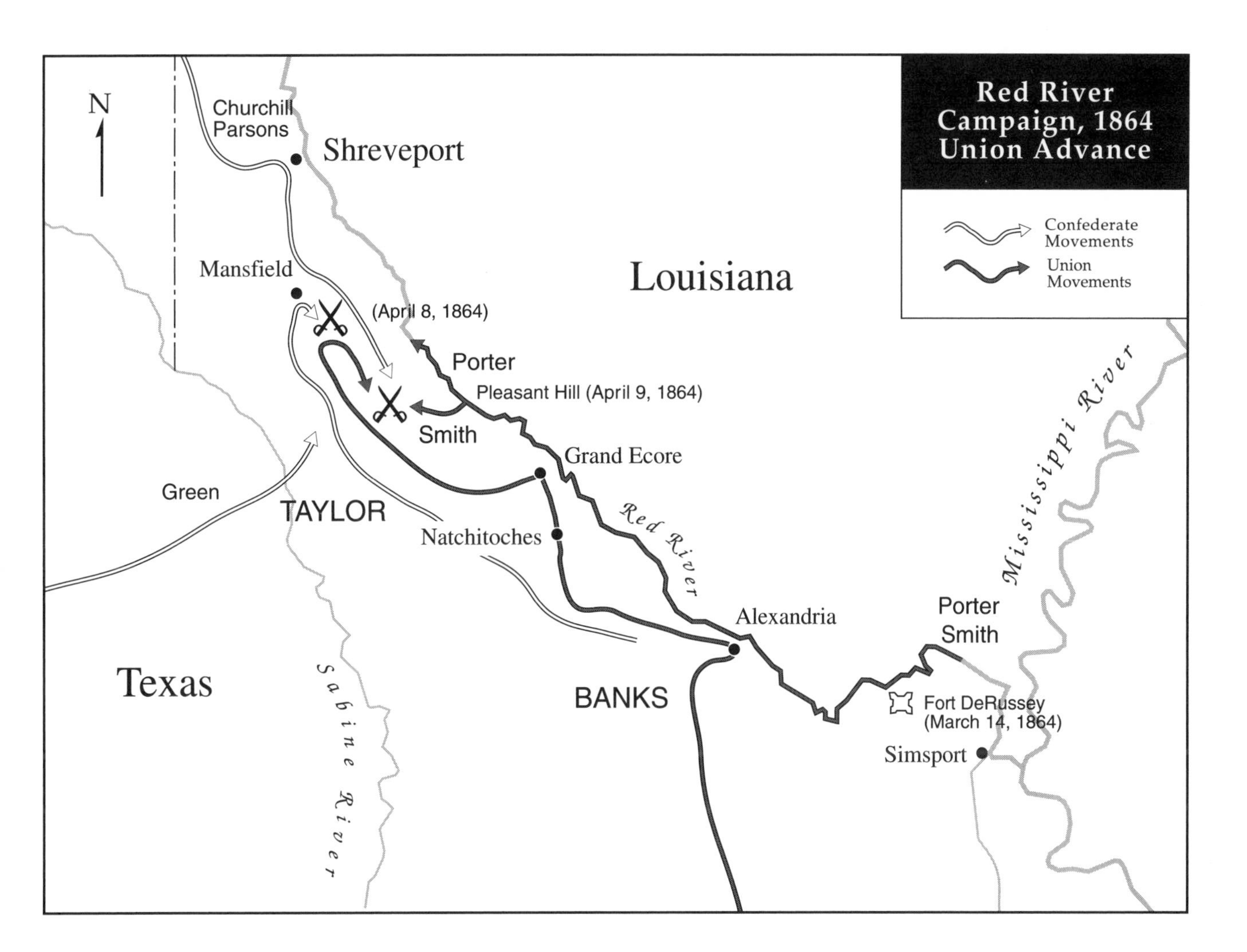

naval flotilla that included thirteen ironclads under Rear Adm. David D. Porter. Banks was to move north up Bayou Teche, Smith and Porter to steam up the Red River, and Steele to move south from Little Rock. The first two groups were to meet at Alexandria and advance on Shreveport, the ultimate goal of the campaign, where they would join Steele. In opposition, Gen. E. Kirby Smith could concentrate between 25,000 and 30,000 men taken from his commands in Texas, Louisiana, and Arkansas. Smith instructed Taylor, commanding in Louisiana, to decline any offer for a general engagement until all the reinforcements arrived.

The Union plan fell apart from the outset. Banks and A. J. Smith were to meet at Alexandria by March 17, 1864. Timing was crucial for two reasons: first, Porter's vessels required the high water brought by the spring rains to navigate the river; second, Grant released Sherman's men only with the promise that they would be returned no later than April 10. Porter entered the Red River on March 12 and moved upstream. Smith's corps, landed at Simsport by Porter, marched on and captured Fort DeRussy on March 14 after a brief engagement. Porter then steamed unopposed to Alexandria, arriving on the fifteenth, Smith's men joining them the next day. In the meantime, Banks was detained in New Orleans supervising elections to install a new free state government, and he did not arrive until the twenty-fourth; his men were not present until the twenty-sixth.

While the Union forces were assembling in Alexandria, Kirby Smith had ordered all but 2,300 men of Maj. Gen. John B. Magruder's Texas force to join Taylor and also instructed Maj. Gen. Sterling Price's entire Arkansas command of 14,000 to move to Shreveport. Taylor offered only token resistance as he waited for the promised help.

Banks advanced despite the late date. After reaching Grand Encore, he made the key mistake of the campaign. Rather than advancing along the Red River in concert with Porter's powerful fleet, he ordered the bulk of his army to move inland, which gave Porter the opportunity to scour the surrounding countryside for contraband. The two armies skirmished continually through the end of March

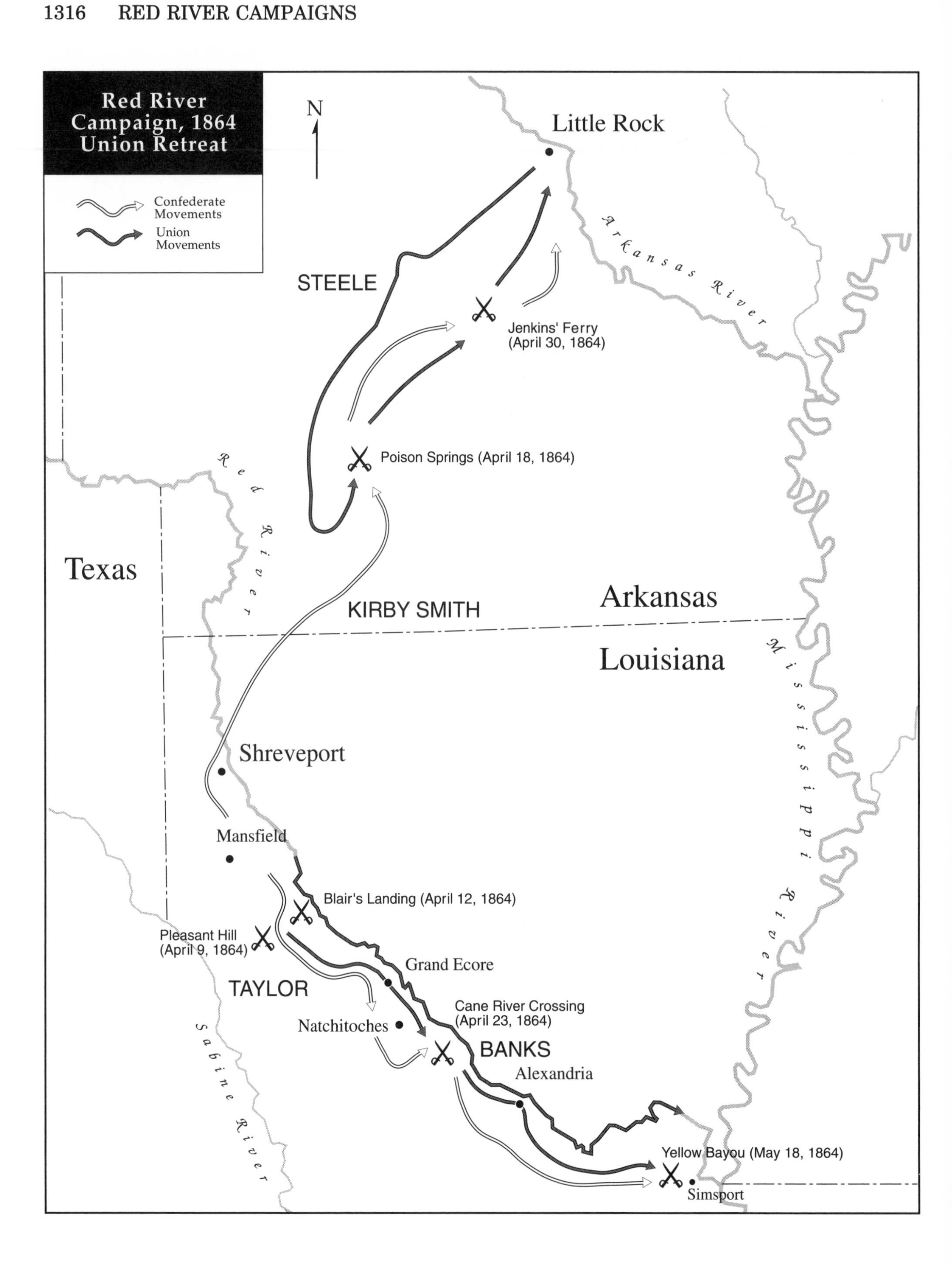
Red River Campaign, 1864 Union Retreat
Confederate Movements
Union Movements
N
Little Rock
Arkansas River
STEELE
Jenkins' Ferry (April 30, 1864)
Poison Springs (April 18, 1864)
Red River
Texas
KIRBY SMITH
Arkansas
Louisiana
Mississippi River
Shreveport
Mansfield
Blair's Landing (April 12, 1864)
Pleasant Hill (April 9, 1864)
Grand Ecore
TAYLOR
Cane River Crossing (April 23, 1864)
Natchitoches
BANKS
Alexandria
Sabine River
Yellow Bayou (May 18, 1864)
Simsport

and into early April as Taylor ordered his forces back, first to Natchitoches, then to Pleasant Hill, and finally to Mansfield.

At Mansfield, Taylor established a strong defensive position with his own men and the recently arrived reinforcements. On the morning of April 8 Banks's advance force encountered Taylor's cavalry under Gen. Tom Green, just in from Texas. Green offered stiff resistance as he fell back to the main defensive line. Banks, thinking his opponent would retreat as he had for the past two weeks, pressed on. Taylor, despite Kirby Smith's orders to avoid a pitched battle, attacked. Gen. Alfred Mouton's division led the Confederate charge that routed Banks's army. Union losses at Mansfield numbered almost 2,900, while Confederate casualties totaled 1,000. During the night Banks fell back to Pleasant Hill. On the afternoon of the ninth, Taylor again attacked, but the Union lines held. Union losses at Pleasant Hill numbered almost 1,400, Confederate losses, nearly 1,500.

Each side considered Pleasant Hill a defeat, and both Banks and Kirby Smith—recently arrived on the battlefield—ordered a withdrawal. When Smith learned that Banks was retreating, he ordered all of Taylor's force except Brig. Gen. Camille J. Polignac's infantry division (formerly under Mouton, who was killed at Mansfield) and Brig. Gen. John Austin Wharton's cavalry to join Price so that he could "dispose of Steele." Taylor pleaded to keep the force together and to pursue Banks, but to no avail.

The Battles of Mansfield and Pleasant Hill marked Banks's farthest advance. The two defeats, the rapidly falling river, the overdue date for A. J. Smith's departure, and the inability to link up with Steele convinced Banks that he had to withdraw. Taylor continued to attack—at Blair's Landing (April 12), and Cane River Crossing (April 23)—but his remaining force was too small to stop Banks. Porter's fleet, meanwhile, faced the dual problems of low water and Confederate attacks. Only the engineering feats of Col. Joseph Bailey, who constructed a series of dams near Alexandria, saved the fleet. Taylor's and Banks's forces skirmished until May 13, the day the fleet finally floated by the rapids in Alexandria. The final engagement of the campaign was at Yellow Bayou on May 18. The next day an improvised bridge of ships allowed Banks's men and wagons to cross the Atchafalaya River. The campaign was over; it was time for the controversy.

In the South, Richard Taylor asked to be and was relieved of his command because of his dispute with Kirby Smith over the latter's deployment of Confederate forces. In the North, Banks, for his failures, was replaced, and the congressional Joint Committee on the Conduct of the War investigated the campaign, infamous for its cotton speculation as well as its military shortcomings.

[*See also* Arkansas Campaign of 1864; Mansfield, Louisiana.]

BIBLIOGRAPHY

Harrington, Fred H. *Fighting Politician: Major General N. P. Banks.* Philadelphia, 1948.

Johnson, Ludwell H. *Red River Campaign: Politics and Cotton in the Civil War.* Baltimore, 1958.

Johnson, Robert U., and C. C. Buel, eds. *Battles and Leaders of the Civil War.* 4 vols. New York, 1887–1888. Reprint, Secaucus, N.J., 1982.

Taylor, Richard. *Destruction and Reconstruction: Personal Experiences of the Late War in the United States.* New York, 1879. Reprint, Philadelphia, 1955.

Winters, John S. *The Civil War in Louisiana.* Baton Rouge, La., 1963.

THOMAS J. LEGG

RED STRINGS. *See* Heroes of America.

REENACTMENTS. In the heat and humidity of midsummer Virginia, hundreds of Union soldiers mill down a dusty road past the bodies of men lying along the sides. Behind the exhausted troops the crash of musketry and the roar of cannons can be heard. Suddenly a horse-drawn battery gallops toward the men with artillerists shouting to them to clear the road; the Northerners scatter in every direction. On the battlefront Union and Confederate officers desperately try to maintain the integrity of their lines amid clouds of gunsmoke and the dust of a dry July. Just out of range of artillery sit civilian picnickers out for a summer's day of excitement. As the defeated Federals stream wordlessly by the civilians look on incredulously: how could their army be beaten so handily? Then the gunfire dies away, the battle smoke clears, and the rival armies march back to camp and head for their automobiles.

The time was 1986; the soldiers, reenactors; the occasion, the 125th anniversary of First Manassas. Tens of thousands of people from all over the world volunteered to wear an army uniform or civilian costume from the Civil War. Australian Confederates fought Federals from Germany; Californians shared hardtack with soldiers from Maine. Each year hundreds of such reenactments and living history demonstrations take place throughout the United States.

Reenactments started almost immediately after Robert E. Lee surrendered at Appomattox. Veterans of the Grand Army of the Republic and the United Confederate Veterans often donned their uniforms for reunions and were photographed reliving the battles they had fought. As these men died, they were succeeded by the next generation of organizations, the Sons of Union Veterans and the Sons of Confederate Veterans, who continued to honor their fathers with ceremonies and reenactments. In the 1990s hundreds of organizations with memberships of as few as five to as many as three thousand carried on the tradition.

The reenactors themselves are responsible for the creation of what is called an "impression"—the look the reenactor chooses to portray to the public. Meticulously researched, the impression can range from that of a civilian child to a particular general. All the clothing and equipment, privately purchased and custom-made, are careful reproductions of the originals. An average infantry soldier's impression includes a rifled musket, cartridge box and sling, cap box and waist belt, canteen, haversack, knapsack or blanket roll, brogans, cotton shirt, and woolen trousers, coat, and cap. Most reenactors also collect smaller items such as a pocket Bible, a comb, a "housewife" (sewing kit), and hardtack to provide the details for a well-rounded impression needed to re-create an individual from the past. The desire to honor and understand the Civil War from the perspective of the participants is the primary motivation for reenactors. They also wish to bring history to life, to make vivid the courage and sacrifice of the participants in an ugly war.

Re-creating a Civil War battle is a difficult, time-consuming, labor-intensive operation. In late June 1988, for example, over 12,000 reenactors participated in the largest re-creation of a battle ever staged on the 125th anniversary of the Battle of Gettysburg. The week-long event featured five scripted battles, authentic soldier and civilian camps, field hospital programs, seminars on nineteenth-century life, filming for a motion picture and a documentary, courses for college credit, and the assembling of two armies of soldiers not seen since 1865.

The phenomenon of reenacting has continued to grow, finding new avenues of expression. In the 1990s, over 30,000 people were engaged in bringing to life America's past to ensure that it would not die.

BIBLIOGRAPHY

Camp Chase Gazette. Lancaster, Ohio, 1964–.
The Civil War News. Arlington, Mass., 1979–.

DALE FETZER, JR.

REFUGEEING. Beginning with northern Virginia families in the spring of 1861, perhaps as many as 200,000 Southerners became refugees during the Civil War. As the Confederacy shrank, people left Kentucky, Tennessee, New Orleans, the Virginia peninsula, the Shenandoah Valley, and other areas to avoid the Northern invaders. Later on, many more fled from William Tecumseh Sherman's advancing army in Georgia and the Carolinas. Raids, skirmishes, and larger military campaigns all sent Southerners into short-term or long-term exile.

Simple fear of the enemy was the most powerful impetus: newspapers carried frightening tales of depredations and assaults on civilians. But food shortages and widespread suffering also forced families to move, even though some debated, planned, and hesitated for months before finally departing.

Refugees constituted a rough cross section of Southern society, and as the war dragged on, the planter class increasingly joined the exodus. Officers' families, state political leaders, and many professional men added a certain sophistication to this bedraggled group. Cities naturally attracted the most refugees, though yeoman and poor white families generally moved only short distances.

Packing (for those lucky enough to have sufficient warning of approaching Federals) became a major chore and a psychological ordeal as families tried to pile all their worldly possessions onto wagons or boxcars. Sifting through possessions accumulated during a lifetime could add to the distress, but if the refugees tried to take too much with them, they often had to leave surplus baggage along the roads. Given the scarcity and expense of transportation, Southerners traveled by any available means including train, wagon, horse, or on foot. Hazardous river crossings and washed-out roads made for tortuous journeys. Along the way, filthy rooms and poor food were standard, and the more aristocratic resented hobnobbing with their social inferiors.

Cities, towns, and rural areas lacked the housing and even the food necessary to accommodate the flood of newcomers. "Shew me a safe point and I'll go tomorrow," South Carolinian Jane Pringle wrote, "but no such happy valley exists in the Confederacy." Richmond's population doubled during the war's first year, and displaced persons continued to arrive for the next three years. Other families chose surrounding towns and rural areas, making Virginia the state with the largest refugee population. Those fleeing the Carolina coast flocked to Raleigh, North Carolina, and Columbia, South Carolina. Georgia—especially Atlanta—attracted refugees from Kentucky, Tennessee, and the Deep South. Texas offered a spacious and relatively secure haven for families in the Trans-Mississippi Confederacy.

Refugees who managed to find a new home complained of spartan conditions and extortionate rents. By any standards their housing was uncomfortable, but a simple frame house must have looked magnificent to the poor souls who slept on church pews or in stables, carriage houses, tents, caves and even abandoned boxcars. Landlords seldom provided board and often raised rents, driving families to seek more affordable accommodations. With families often forced to cook in their rooms, speculators soon raised prices for all kinds of provisions. Grits, bacon, and cornbread became staples of the refugee diet, but the more destitute sometimes lived on berries, tomatoes, or fish. Bedding, clothing, and firewood were in equally short supply. The

REFUGEE FAMILY. NATIONAL ARCHIVES

desperately poor finally had to rely on handouts from tight-fisted natives.

Often the social adjustment was even more difficult. Loneliness and despair dogged the lives of normally optimistic people. Families regularly welcomed kinfolk from distant places, but these new living arrangements caused considerable tension. Blood ties were often not strong enough to withstand the strain. Especially for women used to running their own households, living with relatives, much less strangers, could be frustrating. Natives begrudged sharing scarce housing and food with newcomers, particularly those from other states. Newspaper editors sympathized with the refugees' plight but often criticized their behavior. Even churches sometimes shunned them. A social cold war erupted, especially when displaced plantation families tried to lord it over their poorer neighbors. Provincialism and suspicion on both sides reinforced this hostility. So too boredom and homesickness made some refugees into chronic malcontents. "Everyone speaks of the high spirits and cheerfulness of the refugees," wrote Louisianian Sidney Harding, "They little know of how many sad hours we have."

Refugees who idled away their time sparked resentment, but doctors, lawyers, bankers, and artisans tried to establish their old professions in their new homes. Ministers set up new churches; refugee newspaper editors kept changing their mastheads; in desperation, displaced housewives turned to teaching, though most found their new profession neither profitable nor satisfying. Governors had to move state capitals to more secure locations. Although the Confederate government hired some refugees in the various departments, many had to settle for work as farm or day laborers. Women had few opportunities other than sewing or domestic service but still donated their mite to relief funds and labored long for charitable associations.

Regardless of these problems, refugees did manage to have a social life, notably in the towns and cities. Shared suffering could build a sense of community and even provide opportunity for pleasant diversions. Reading, writing letters, keeping a diary, and going to church filled in the times between special events. Among the fashionable set, parties, dances, and amateur theatricals, including the popular tableaux vivants (staged, motionless representations of famous scenes), helped the lonely and disheartened wile away the hours. Food was scarce and decorations limited, but weddings and holidays offered some relief from the drab lives led by most refugees. Christmas became the occasion for recalling happier times and perhaps momentarily forgetting the war, but makeshift gifts and disappointed children also served as painful reminders of the Confederacy's desperate straits.

Although refugees sometimes became revelers, such pleasures were transitory. Families who thought they had found safety and security were threatened again by the invaders or banished by Federal commanders. Under the best circumstances, crossing enemy lines entailed passes, oaths of allegiance, bureaucratic hassles, and some danger. For both Union and Confederate armies, dealing with refugees created logistical and security headaches.

With their property at the Federals' mercy and their lives disrupted, refugees sought public relief. Although indigent soldiers' families received some help, state and local governments discriminated against refugee families. Many disheartened Confederates returned to their homes before the end of the war even if they had to live under military occupation. Others had to wait weeks or even months after Appomattox to begin rebuilding lives that had been shattered by the war.

[*See also* Poor Relief; Poverty.]

BIBLIOGRAPHY

Andrews, Matthew Page. *The Women of the South in War Times.* Baltimore, 1920.

Massey, Mary Elizabeth. *Refugee Life in the Confederacy.* Baton Rouge, La., 1964.

Rable, George C. *Civil Wars: Women and the Crisis of Southern Nationalism.* Urbana, Ill., 1989.

George C. Rable

RELIGION. Antebellum Southern Protestants—by 1860 approximately two million strong—generally agreed on an evangelical theology of individual personal salvation, divine justification for all actions, opposition to secular activities, a literal reading of the Scriptures, and a just and benevolent Providence overseeing a chosen people. A number of clergy, however, advocated missionary reform, which included opposition to alcohol, religious instruction for slaves, and admonitions to masters to treat their slaves decently.

Slavery also divided the Northern and Southern branches of the Protestant churches, and by 1845 the two largest denominations, the Methodist Episcopal Church South and the Southern Baptist Convention, had been organized after separation from their Northern brethren. When the Civil War began, the other major denominations, Presbyterians, Lutherans, and Episcopalians, also formed separate Southern churches. While the Roman Catholic church avoided a split during the Civil War, Catholic clergy in the South firmly supported the Confederate cause. Despite the belief that churches should keep out of secular politics, the evangelical clergy supported Southern rights during the sectional crisis, while a number led in the movement to secede.

During the Civil War most Southern Protestant and Roman Catholic clergy called for civilian and military sacrifices for unity of purpose, and many held out to the very end for Confederate victory. Many clergy preached and wrote on the idea of a new nation, while some of them advocated a Christian Confederate nation. Churches supported the civil leaders' proclamations of fast days of abstinence and contrition, and clergy conducted services during the fasts. Churches assigned ministers to preach to and care for the souls of their soldiers. Chaplains in the front lines led prayer groups, held rousing evangelical revivals, and carried out mass baptisms, which at times turned the Confederate armies into religious crusaders. A religious revival swept through the Confederate armies in 1863. Church-owned presses published religious tracts, hymn books, and Bibles to distribute among the troops. Printed sermons often stirred the soldiers to regard the Northerners as infidels. Individual preachers used their multiple talents in military service. Presbyterian theologian Robert L. Dabney served on Gen. Thomas J. ("Stonewall") Jackson's staff, from which he helped to bring young college men into the army. Dr. Charles T. Quintard, later Episcopal bishop of Tennessee, gained fame as a chaplain and surgeon in the First Tennessee Regiment. Roman Catholic chaplain Abraham Ryan ministered to the religious needs of the Catholic soldiers and preached continued resistance against the invading Yankees.

Behind the lines women and clergy held rallies in churches, where they urged enlistees to sacrifice all to protect faith, honor, and home. Women worked in local churches, making clothing, blankets, and bandages for the soldiers. They organized Home Missionary Societies to care for slaves, to feed the poor, and to provide education for children of deceased veterans. Women also helped found church-related hospitals and served as nurses and aides near the front lines. A few women even preached to the troops.

The Civil War also produced divisions among the Southern churches and religious leaders over support for the Confederate cause. Tennessee Methodist William G. Brownlow and Kentucky Presbyterian Robert J. Breckinridge remained loyal to the Union and preached against Confederate victory. In middle Tennessee, David Lipscomb of the Disciples of Christ believed in Christian pacifism and opposed all war. Southerners as well as Northerners accused the Jewish people of war profiteering, and despite the fact that some ten thousand Southern Jews fought in Confederate ranks, clergy quoted New Testament admonitions against them, which unleashed waves of anti-Semitic activities. German Catholic Unionists in central Texas faced hostile nativists and had to fight or flee for their lives. Some clergy seized the moment to advocate decent treatment of the slaves, with a few even calling for eventual abolition of slavery. Black churches confronted wartime restrictions and hardships by advocating mutual support among slaves. Black clergy preached self-discipline and resisted white control by demanding the right to travel freely to serve their people.

As the fighting wore on, disruptions in the Southern churches abounded: property was lost, membership declined, and the war's devastation made clergy and laity alike question the central evangelical belief in a providential God. Border and upper South churchgoers often had to flee before approaching armies. Northern troops used churches as stables, staff headquarters, and hospitals. Both by mistake and deliberately, advancing Union armies pillaged and burned churches, church schools, and church orphanages. Lasting wounds were created as Northern Methodist clergy came south to take over abandoned churches, preach to the slaves, and proselytize among the worried citizenry. In West Virginia, Northern Methodist ministers at the state constitutional convention of 1863 led the movement to abolish slavery. Church schools and colleges lost students and were forced to close down; a number shut their doors permanently. Clergy and the faithful alike believed that defeat in battle meant that the Lord had deserted his chosen people. Many came to doubt the justice of their cause. Chaplains, too, noticed that their influence had declined among the soldiers. The resultant loss of religious faith no doubt undermined Confederate civilian and military morale.

At war's end, church leaders had to confront the demise of slavery. Some clergy deserted the South to settle with parishioners in such places as Brazil where slavery was still legal. Others sought to control the religious life of the ex-slaves. But the churches made little effort to assist the black people and soon segregated them in the rear of churches. The freed people founded their own churches. Northern black clergy came south to organize the African Methodist Episcopal church. In 1867 Georgia black clergy formed a separate Presbyterian church, and black Baptists founded Atlanta Baptist College (later Morehouse College) to train black preachers. Before the end of Reconstruction, the Southern Methodist and Baptist churches had lost most of their black members to separate denominations.

Church leaders attempted to ease the postwar guilt over defeat and to stem the loss of faith in a benevolent deity. For them, defeat in the war meant only that the Southern people had been tested to see whether they would remain true to their faith and heritage. Mainstream preachers joined ex-military leaders to advance the theme of a glorious Lost Cause, a past worthy of sacrifice. The concept of the Lost Cause soon prevailed among Protestants, as churches became centers for the rituals of Confederate heroics and the perpetuation of Old South religious values. Those who sought reform and the growth of a New South seemed lost in that atmosphere, which turned defeat into a victory for nostalgia. This marriage of reaction and piety resulted in the deepening of fundamentalism, proliferation of sectarianism, rapid growth in evangelical church membership, and continued separation of major northern and southern Protestant churches.

[*See also* Baptist Church; Bible Societies; Chaplains; Episcopal Church; Fast Days; Jews; Lost Cause, *overview article;* Lutheran Church; Mennonites; Methodist Church; Moravian Church; Presbyterian Church; Roman Catholic Church; Sermons; Society of Friends.]

BIBLIOGRAPHY

Beringer, Richard E., et al. *Why the South Lost the Civil War.* Athens, Ga., 1986.

Clebsch, William A. *Christian Interpretations of the Civil War.* Philadelphia, 1969.

Connelly, Thomas L., and Barbara L. Bellows. *God and General Longstreet: The Lost Cause in the Southern Mind.* Baton Rouge, La., 1982.

Faust, Drew Gilpin. *The Creation of Confederate Nationalism.* Baton Rouge, La., 1988.

Hill, Samuel S., Jr., ed. *Religion in the Southern States: A Historical Study.* Macon, Ga., 1983.

Mohr, Clarence L. *On the Threshold of Freedom: Masters and Slaves in Civil War Georgia.* Athens, Ga., 1986.

Jon L. Wakelyn

REPUBLICAN PARTY. At its birth, the Republican party was an avowedly sectional party. Arising out of the Northern protest over the Kansas-Nebraska Act (1854), the party opposed the expansion of slavery and called on Congress to exclude the institution from all the territories. Although Republicans denied any intention to interfere with slavery in the Southern states, the party had little strength in the South before 1865.

In the 1856 presidential election, the Republican party polled about one thousand votes in the border states and Virginia, but it had no viable organization below the Mason-Dixon Line. During the next four years, some Republican leaders sought to deflect the issue of sectionalism by building up the party in the South, and the party attracted a few notable Southern adherents, including Francis P. Blair, Jr., in Missouri, his brother Montgomery in Maryland, Cassius Clay in Kentucky, and Archibald Campbell in Virginia. Southern Republicans generally emphasized slavery's adverse effects on Southern whites and disavowed any concern for the welfare of blacks. Yet the

CAMPAIGN BANNER OF 1864. Printed to promote the Republican presidential ticket of 1864, the banner could also serve as a shade for a political lantern or torch. Lithograph printed in red, blue, and black on wove paper. Published by Oakley and Thompson, Boston, October 11, 1864. LIBRARY OF CONGRESS

party made little headway in the region. In 1860 Abraham Lincoln polled a mere twenty-six thousand votes in the slave states; his Southern support was confined to the border states and the western counties of Virginia.

During the war, the Unionist coalitions that took power in the border states eventually fragmented. Calling for immediate emancipation, the use of black troops, and stringent penalties against Confederates, radical organizations emerged led by such men as Henry Winter Davis in Maryland and Benjamin Gratz Brown in Missouri. Aided by military officials and federal patronage, the radicals won control of Maryland and Missouri and abolished slavery. They provided the nucleus of the full-fledged Republican parties that formed in the border states after the war. In the 1864 presidential election, Lincoln carried Maryland, West Virginia, and Missouri.

In the Confederacy the Republican movement was closely tied to the advance of the Union army. Shadow Republican parties, made up of a handful of die-hard Unionists and propped up by military support, had developed by 1864 in the occupied areas of Virginia, Arkansas, and Tennessee. The most serious attempt to establish the foundation for a postwar Republican party in a Confederate state occurred in Louisiana under the direction of Nathaniel P. Banks, the Union military commander. Wishing to create a white-only party, Banks backed the moderate faction led by Michael Hahn, who was elected governor of the reconstructed government. The moderates wrote a new state constitution that abolished slavery but rejected black suffrage. Prominent state leaders held aloof from the Union party, however, and it attracted support primarily from urban groups in the Union-controlled region around New Orleans.

The Republican party confronted major difficulties in establishing a Southern wing before 1865. Intimidation and violence, Southern whites' hostility to the party's program, the race issue, and factional squabbles all limited the Republican party's strength in the South. When the war ended, the party lacked any organization in most of the former Confederate states, and where it did exist in some guise, it represented only a very small minority of the white population.

[*See also* Kansas-Nebraska Act.]

BIBLIOGRAPHY

Abbott, Richard H. *The Republican Party and the South, 1855–1877.* Chapel Hill, N.C., 1986.

McCrary, Peyton. *Abraham Lincoln and Reconstruction: The Louisiana Experiment.* Princeton, N.J., 1978.

WILLIAM E. GIENAPP

REYNOLDS, ALEXANDER WELCH (1816–1876)

REYNOLDS, ALEXANDER WELCH (1816–1876), brigadier general. Reynolds was born in April 1816 in Frederick County, Virginia. He graduated from the U.S. Military Academy in 1838 and participated in the Seminole War. In 1847, Reynolds transferred to the Quartermaster Corps. Although dismissed from the service in 1856 for his inability to explain discrepancies in his accounts, he was restored to duty two years later.

In March of 1861 Reynolds was appointed captain in the Confederate service and the following July was commissioned colonel of the Fiftieth Virginia Infantry. On October 4, 1861, he was dismissed from the Federal service for having "absented himself from duty." Reynolds served with John B. Floyd in western Virginia in 1861 and 1862 and with E. Kirby Smith in Knoxville. Captured and paroled with John C. Pemberton's command at Vicksburg, he was later exchanged. After his promotion to brigadier general on September 14, 1863, he participated in the Battle of Chattanooga. While serving with Carter Stevenson's division during the Atlanta campaign, Reynolds was wounded at New Hope Church, but during the last months of the war he served in northern Alabama and middle Tennessee.

After the war Reynolds entered the service of the khedive of Egypt. He died in Alexandria, Egypt, on May 26, 1876. In his military record, Reynolds appears as a capable, steady soldier. He managed his brigade efficiently, but not exceptionally enough for his superiors to consider him for divisional command.

BIBLIOGRAPHY

Connelly, Thomas L. *Autumn of Glory: The Army of Tennessee, 1862–1865.* Baton Rouge, La., 1971.

Horn, Stanley F. *The Army of Tennessee: A Military History.* 2d ed. Norman, Okla., 1953.

Warner, Ezra J. *Generals in Gray: Lives of the Confederate Commanders.* Baton Rouge, La., 1959.

ROY R. STEPHENSON

REYNOLDS, DANIEL HARRIS (1832–1902), brigadier general. In the spring of 1861, Reynolds left his law practice in Lake Village, Arkansas, to become captain of the Chicot Rangers, a cavalry unit from Chicot County. In June, the group was mustered into Confederate service at Fort Smith and became part of Company A of the First Arkansas Cavalry Regiment.

During the first years of the war, Reynolds and his Rangers encountered a number of disappointing defeats. In March 1862 they took part in the Confederate disaster at Elkhorn Tavern, Arkansas. As members of the Army of Mississippi, they played a role in the invasion of Kentucky under Braxton Bragg. Reynolds and his men stayed with Sterling Price to defend Mississippi while Bragg and E. Kirby Smith moved into Kentucky. Under Price, Reynolds took part in the Battles of Iuka and Corinth in the fall of 1862.

Reynolds did experience the flush of success when he participated in the Confederate victory at Chickamauga in September 1863. In March 1864 he received a promotion to brigadier general.

Reynolds commanded his brigade during the last years of the war. He led his troops through the Atlanta campaign in 1864 and into Tennessee under John Bell Hood. After the disaster at the Battle of Nashville, Reynolds and his men joined Gen. Joseph E. Johnston in his impossible attempt to halt William Tecumseh Sherman's march through the Carolinas. At the decisive Battle of Bentonville, Reynolds lost his left leg.

After the war, Reynolds returned to Lake Village. He served one term in the Arkansas senate prior to Radical Reconstruction, before finally returning to his law practice.

BIBLIOGRAPHY

Harrell, John. *Arkansas*. Vol. 10 of *Confederate Military History*. Edited by Clement A. Evans. Atlanta, 1899. Vol. 14 of extended ed. Wilmington, N.C., 1988.

Johnson, Rossiter, ed. *Twentieth Century Biographical Dictionary of Notable Americans*. Boston, 1904.

Warner, Ezra J. *Generals in Gray: Lives of the Confederate Commanders*. Baton Rouge, La., 1959.

JENNIFER LUND

REYNOLDS, THOMAS C. (1821–1887), governor of Missouri. Born in Charleston, Thomas Caute Reynolds graduated from the University of Virginia in 1842. He settled in St. Louis in 1850 and was elected Missouri's lieutenant governor on the Democratic ticket in 1860.

An ardent secessionist, Reynolds conferred in Washington with various Southern congressmen as to the best course for Missouri to follow. Thereafter he worked strenuously in the legislature for a convention to decide the issue of secession. That convention, when it met, opted for a neutral stance, much to the disappointment of Reynolds and Governor Claiborne F. Jackson. Following the loss of Camp Jackson to Federals and subsequent rioting in May 1861, Reynolds went south to urge Jefferson Davis to supply Confederate troops with which to hold the state.

In July the state government, including Reynolds, was deposed by the state convention after Jackson had abandoned Jefferson City to the Union military under Nathaniel Lyon. Reynolds now retired to his native South Carolina where he remained until Jackson's death in December 1862. He quickly assumed the governorship and hastened to Richmond to confer with the Missouri congressional delegation. Then he headed west to pick up the scattered pieces of Missouri's government-in-exile. For the remainder of the war he held that government together, cooperating with Gen. E. Kirby Smith and the other Trans-Mississippi governors in matters affecting the region. Reynolds accompanied Sterling Price on his Missouri raid in 1864, hoping to be inaugurated at Jefferson City; but this proved impossible as the Confederates were driven back into Arkansas.

At war's end, Reynolds went to Mexico. He returned to St. Louis in 1868 and thereafter held several political posts before taking his own life in 1887.

BIBLIOGRAPHY

Castel, Albert. *General Sterling Price and the Civil War in the West*. Baton Rouge, La., 1968.

Kirkpatrick, Arthur R. "Missouri's Secessionist Government, 1861–1865." *Missouri Historical Review* 45 (January 1951): 124–137.

Parrish, William E. *A History of Missouri*. Vol. 3. Columbia, Mo., 1973.

Parrish, William E. "Missouri." In *The Confederate Governors*. Edited by W. Buck Yearns. Athens, Ga., 1985.

Snead, Thomas L. *The Fight for Missouri from the Election of Lincoln to the Death of Lyon*. New York, 1888.

WILLIAM E. PARRISH

RHETT, ROBERT BARNWELL, SR. (1800–1876), congressman from South Carolina and editor. Born in Beaufort, South Carolina, on December 21, 1800, Robert Barnwell Rhett was a classic Southern fire-eater whose uncompromising devotion to Southern independence earned him the title of "the father of secession." Although Rhett could claim a distinguished Carolina lineage, his father failed as a planter, and the young Rhett had to make his own fortune and carve out his own career. He chose the traditional path of law and politics. He was admitted to the South Carolina bar in 1821 and soon established a thriving legal business, but his real love was politics. As a member of the South Carolina legislature from 1826 to 1832, he quickly stamped himself as a bold and self-assured leader when he championed the cause of nullification. From the very start of his public career, he was identified as a firebrand eager to challenge established authority.

In 1837, the same year that he went along with the wishes of his brothers and changed the family name from Smith to Rhett in recognition of a distinguished ancestor, Rhett entered Congress as a state rights Democrat. Until 1844 he served as John C. Calhoun's lieutenant in Congress and tried to work through the national Democratic organization in an effort to control it in the interests of the South. When Calhoun's bid for the presidency faltered in 1844, and the old issues of the tariff and abolitionism flared up once again, Rhett reverted to the intransigence that had first characterized his political reputation. He led the ultraradicals of the Carolina low country in the Bluffton movement, a political protest that threatened nullification and even secession if the demands of South Carolina for a lower tariff and an end to abolitionist agitation were not met. The Bluffton movement soon faded, but Rhett's call for separate state action to protect Southern interests became the rallying cry of South Carolina secessionists in the prolonged crisis from 1849 to 1852 that was touched off by Southern demands for equal access to the territories recently won in the Mexican War.

In the midst of this crisis Rhett realized his long-cherished goal of reaching the U.S. Senate. In 1851 the South Carolina legislature elected him to fill the seat vacated by Calhoun's death. By this time Rhett was a confirmed secessionist committed to a permanent Southern confederacy. This goal eluded him, however, when his stand on separate state secession in opposition to the Compromise of 1850 was rejected in South Carolina. True to his state rights principles, Rhett then resigned from the Senate in 1852 after his state had repudiated his policies. With his leadership and his party defeated, he retired from politics. When he reemerged in 1857 with all his old radicalism, he worked closely with William Lowndes Yancey of Alabama and Edmund Ruffin of Virginia to fire the Southern imagination in favor of secession. He now owned the *Charleston Mercury* and, with a son as the editor, he used the paper as a pulpit for his secessionist views.

Rhett's unrelenting radicalism finally came to fruition in the fall of 1860. Abraham Lincoln's election triggered a successful secession movement in South Carolina and throughout the lower South, and, as Rhett had long preached that they must, the radicals pursued a strategy of separate state secession. Southern unity in favor of independence, Rhett had concluded as early as the Bluffton movement, could be achieved only if one state took the lead in secession and pulled the others along in its wake.

Rhett played a major role at the South Carolina secession convention. He wrote the *Address to the Slave-Holding States,* a formal statement of South Carolina's justification for secession. Rhett stressed the inalienable right of Southern whites to self-government, a right they must now seize to free themselves from the centralizing despotism of a Federal government dominated by a hostile Northern majority. Slavery, he reasoned, could not long survive a Union controlled by Lincoln's Republican party. On December 26 Rhett also proposed the calling of a Southern convention of the slaveholding states at the earliest possible date. Now that South Carolina had seceded and other states apparently were soon to follow, Rhett's great fear was that an independent South would be stillborn, the victim of scheming politicians who would use secession as leverage to exact concessions from the North with the aim of reconstructing the Union on a basis more favorable to the South. Thus, for Rhett, it was imperative that a new and permanent Southern confederacy be formed as soon as possible. Moreover, such a government had to be irrevocably wedded to the interests of that slave civilization to which Rhett had given his undying devotion.

Rhett headed the South Carolina delegation to the convention that met at Montgomery, Alabama, in early February 1861 to form a provisional government for the Confederate States of America. He went to Montgomery determined to shape the new Confederacy in the image of his beloved Carolina low country. Complete security for the slave society of his Beaufort district required not only separation from the threatening North but the political reshaping of the South into a homogeneous slave society approximating what Rhett knew at home. In pursuit of this goal he pushed a four-pronged program designed to safeguard the revolution of 1860 that he had been so instrumental in fomenting. He wanted a constitutional provision prohibiting the admission of any nonslave state, an opening of the African slave trade when desired by the planters, and full political representation of all slaves as a substitute for the old three-fifths clause in the U.S. Constitution. Since the profits from slave-produced staples were to be the engine of economic growth for the Confederacy, he insisted on a policy of free trade with the outside world so as to maximize the market for Southern exports. Free trade, Rhett believed, would quickly lead to an alliance with Britain, ever eager to guarantee its chief supply of raw cotton. Such an alliance would eliminate any talk of reconstructing the old Union and provide British military protection for Southern independence.

Perhaps more than any other delegate at the Montgomery convention, Rhett had a vision of what he wanted the new Southern republic to be. As he feared, however, his vision was rejected. At the urging of the Mississippi and Georgia delegations, Jefferson Davis of Mississippi, a late convert to secession and a reconstructionist in Rhett's view, was chosen as president. When he organized his administration, Davis pointedly did not offer Rhett either of the two posts he most wanted, that of secretary of state or commissioner to England. Rhett distrusted Davis, and the feeling was mutual. Despite serving on the committees for Foreign Affairs, Financial Independence, and a Permanent Constitution, Rhett was unable to implement the fundamental changes he felt were essential for the success of the Confederacy. The U.S. Constitution was adopted virtually without change by the Confederacy. The three-fifths clause for slave representation, the prohibition on the African slave trade, and the Federal tariff of 1857 were all retained. Most galling of all for Rhett was his defeat on the issue of admitting only slave states to the Confederacy. About all that Rhett could claim as victories were constitutional prohibitions against protective tariffs and Confederate expenditures for internal improvements.

Honored in Charleston as a prophet in the heady days of secession, Rhett was spurned in Montgomery as a spokesman for the Confederacy. Unlike Rhett, Davis expected a war with the North, and he rejected Rhett's program at Montgomery in part because he did not want a radically proslavery Confederacy to scare off the states of the upper South that had not yet left the Union. The economic and military resources of the upper South would be essential for any successful defense of the Confederacy against Northern armies. The war came in April 1861 with the firing on Fort Sumter, and five states in the upper South joined the original seven states of the Confederacy. Although heartened by the apparent Southern unity that accompanied the outbreak of war, Rhett remained deeply suspicious of Davis, and he set out as a congressman in the Provisional Congress to shape the policy of the Davis administration.

Rhett first tried to seize the initiative on foreign policy. He introduced resolutions calling for a diplomacy offering favorable and long-term trading ties to Europe in return for Confederate recognition. Unwilling to tie Davis's hands in foreign relations, Congress rejected the resolutions. In June, after Congress had adjourned, Rhett began a campaign through the *Charleston Mercury* to formulate war policy for the Confederacy. The *Mercury* attacked Davis for indecision and delay in waging the war. Frustrated by Union successes in Maryland, Missouri, and Kentucky, and concerned by the ominous signs of extensive war preparations in the North, Rhett called for a rapid and massive Confederate offensive. The war must be carried to the Yankees, proclaimed the *Mercury*. Any delay would favor the North by giving it time to mobilize its superior manpower and industrial resources. Once launched, a Confederate offensive would capitalize on the enthusiasm and innate fighting skills of Southern troops and smash Northern armies before they were disciplined into effective fighting units.

The Confederate victory at First Manassas on July 12, 1861, confirmed Rhett's belief in an offensive policy. Despite the success of Southern armies in the first major test of the war, Rhett stepped up his criticisms of the administration. The *Mercury* charged that a great opportunity for an advance on Washington after First Manassas had been lost because of Davis's timid generalship and inability to adequately supply Gen. P. G. T. Beauregard's troops. Rhett also returned to his claim that Davis was a reconstructionist at heart. The Northern rout at Manassas led to rumors that Northern commercial interests, especially those in the lower Midwest, were eager for an economic alliance with the Confederacy. Fearful that any commercial reunion would be but the first step toward eventual political reunion, Rhett lashed out at Davis for allegedly restraining Confederate armies in the hopes of a reconciliation with the North. As confirmation of his view, Rhett cited the blockage by the administration in Congress of his July resolutions imposing additional duties on Northern goods and banning trade in any European goods imported through the North.

Foreign policy continued to be a divisive issue between Rhett and Davis. Rhett was both angered and surprised by Britain's refusal to recognize Confederate independence. With his initial policy of diplomatic conciliation rejected by the Davis administration, Rhett switched to a policy of coercion in the summer of 1861. His resolutions in Congress called for an embargo of trade with all nations that did not recognize the Confederacy. Britain, he argued, must be forced to choose sides, and he was confident that the power of King Cotton would force the British to align with the Confederacy. Once again, Rhett met defeat. Most congressmen, as well as the Davis administration, wavered between conciliation and coercion. The result was a voluntary embargo, a withholding of cotton from the seaports by the planters. A compromise that reflected divided sentiment within the South, this policy was favored by the administration because it put economic pressure on Britain without being specifically identified with a hard-line policy by the Confederate government.

By the fall of 1861, the time of the elections for the First Congress, Rhett's unrelenting criticism of Davis was beginning to backfire. In the absence of a formal opposition party to serve as an institutional outlet for attacks on the administration's handling of the war, Rhett's opposition came to be seen as a personal vendetta and a drain on Confederate morale. Public opinion in his own state of South Carolina turned against him. Rhett had no interest in running for the Confederate House. His eyes were on the Senate, but he failed to secure either of the two Senate seats chosen by the legislature. On top of this political defeat, his plantation and hometown of Beaufort fell to the Federals in November 1861, when an amphibious invasion occupied much of the Carolina low country.

Chastened but hardly bowed, Rhett returned to Richmond in December for the last session of the Provisional Congress. Consistent with his earlier record, he assailed the administration but was unable to gain passage of the changes he favored. His navigation bill concerning direct trade with Europe, which would have restricted foreign trade to ships built in the Confederacy or by the countries that were supplying imports, was rejected by Congress. He failed to carry a new naturalization bill that would have made it more difficult for Northerners to become Confederate citizens, a measure prompted by Rhett's constant dread of reconstruction. Over Rhett's constitutional objections, the administration won passage of an act permitting the Confederate government to construct connecting lines for railroads in the name of national defense. The constitutional issue of centralization versus state rights involved in the railroad bill also dominated debate over legislation to raise fresh troops for the army now that the enlistments of the original twelve-month volunteers were about to expire. Rhett supported a bill introduced by Robert Toombs of Georgia, which, though requiring the states to raise fresh troops, left the appointment of the new officers for these troops up to the states. The administration blocked the Toombs bill and subsequently pushed through national conscription in April 1862.

The end of the Provisional Congress in the winter of 1861–1862 severed Rhett's only official link with the Confederacy. For all his sharp criticism of Davis, Rhett had never wavered in his commitment to Southern independence. Indeed, on crucial financial and military matters, he was a surprisingly strong supporter of the administration. Despite the obvious challenge to state rights in the Conscription Act of 1862, Rhett backed the measure as essential for military victory. By now he had teamed with his son, Barnwell, Jr., in running the *Charleston Mercury*. For the remainder of the war, the two Rhetts mounted a propaganda offensive in a desperate attempt to effect fundamental changes in the Confederate government and its prosecution of the war.

Their editorials were especially vitriolic in early 1862 after the Confederacy had been staggered by a series of military reverses that opened up Tennessee and the lower Mississippi valley to Union forces. After leading the call for a congressional investigation of the military losses, the Rhetts were bitterly disappointed when Davis vetoed a bill creating the office of commander in chief. The successful defense of Richmond in the Peninsular campaign in the spring of 1862 did little to change their opinion that Davis was utterly unfit to be setting military policy.

As the war reached its midpoint in 1863, Rhett was still confident of Southern victory. Indeed, he worried more about a reconciliation with the North and the subsequent loss of the opportunity to establish a thoroughly slave-based society than he did about the possibility of a vanquished South. When his confidence in victory was badly shaken by the twin Confederate disasters at Gettysburg and Vicksburg in July 1863, he turned on Davis with a renewed vehemence and accused him of criminal incompetence. Rhett now argued that only the South's best men, leaders such as Toombs and himself who had heretofore played but minor roles in the Confederate government, could save the South. Consequently, he ran for Congress in the fall elections of 1863. The result was the most stunning defeat of his political career. Contrary to his expectations, the incumbent in Rhett's Third Congressional District, Lewis M. Ayer, refused to step aside. Ayer won reelection by depicting Rhett as a divisive, if not disloyal, opponent of Davis and the war effort.

Gloom and demoralization permeated South Carolina in the last year and a half of the war. Although he welcomed any actions directed against the administration, Rhett viewed with alarm the peace movements that swelled in neighboring North Carolina and Georgia and gave signs of stirring even in South Carolina. Once Lincoln's reelection in November 1864 apparently ended once and for all the threat of reconciliation, Rhett called on his fellow South Carolinians to rely on their own resources in a last-ditch bid to achieve their independence. Davis and his government, Rhett believed, were now nearly as much to be feared as Lincoln's invading armies. Rhett was aghast when he heard of the plans coming out of Richmond to arm the slaves as Confederate soldiers. In what was to be the last public act of his career, he published a letter in November 1864 damning Davis for destroying the constitutional liberties and institution of slavery that Southerners had gone to war to protect. He hoped against hope that Congress and the states could still bring Davis to his senses and force him to wage the war within the confines of the Confederate Constitution.

At the end of the war all of Rhett's hopes had turned to ashes, but to the end of his life he remained as proud, obstinate, and self-righteous as he had been while fighting for the cause of Southern independence first as an American and then as a Confederate citizen. Many of his last years were spent in writing an unpublished history of the Confederacy, his final testament to the correctness of his views and the failures of Davis. Too proud to seek a pardon from the U.S. government after the war, he retired from public life. He moved to Louisiana in the early 1870s and lived at the plantation of a son-in-law in St. James Parish. He died on September 14, 1876, in the centennial year of the republic whose liberties he had always professed to celebrate.

BIBLIOGRAPHY

Cauthen, Charles Edward. *South Carolina Goes to War, 1861–1865.* Chapel Hill, N.C., 1950.

Escott, Paul D. *After Secession: Jefferson Davis and the Failure of Confederate Nationalism.* Baton Rouge, La., 1978.

Schultz, Harold S. *Nationalism and Sectionalism in South Carolina, 1852–1860.* Durham, N.C., 1950.

White, Laura A. *Robert Barnwell Rhett: Father of Secession.* New York, 1931.

Yearns, Wilfred B. *The Confederate Congress.* Athens, Ga., 1960.

WILLIAM L. BARNEY

RICE. Although never king of Southern agricultural staples, rice has been of central importance to the region's economy since the early eighteenth century. Moreover, it has retained its place in the royal retinue long after cotton's departure from the throne. Prior to the Civil War, furthermore, the major rice-producing area in the South—the low country of South Carolina and Georgia—was perhaps the wealthiest and most heavily commercialized plantation district in North America.

Domestication of the cereal *Oryza sativa* began in Southeast Asia seven millennia ago, whence it spread to other parts of Asia, the Middle East, Africa, and, much later, Mediterranean Europe. The cereal was transferred to the Western Hemisphere during the early modern period as part of the so-called Columbian exchange of biogens.

Some rice may have been grown in Spanish Florida in the sixteenth century, and the English experimented with the crop in Virginia in the early seventeenth century. It was not until the last decade of the latter century, however, that rice became firmly established in the American South, and it did so neither in Florida nor in Virginia, but in the youthful English settlement of Carolina.

From the time of initial settlement in 1670, the white colonists in the precociously commercialized Carolina colony searched hard for a viable export commodity. After more than two decades of experiments, failures, and false starts with a variety of minerals, raw materials, and plant and animal products, they began to have some success with rice. The precise origins of rice cultivation in the southern part of the colony (Carolina did not split into two separate entities, North Carolina and South Carolina, until 1729) are controversial, but relatively unimportant. Whether one believes that rice cultivation initially owed more to Europeans or to Africans ultimately matters little. The cereal was well known throughout the Old World by the late seventeenth century, and small quantities had already been grown successfully in the New. Whichever foundation myth one prefers, it was not until the mid-1690s that the colony possessed sufficient stocks of labor, capital, and local knowledge to begin cultivating, processing, and marketing successfully a staple agricultural commodity such as rice.

For a short period of time, apparently, rice was grown in Carolina without irrigation on dry and relatively high ground in the low country, that is, the easternmost third of what is now South Carolina. By the 1720s, production had shifted almost entirely to freshwater swamps in the area, where rudimentary irrigation works could be employed. Cultivation remained centered in these inland swamps in the low country of South Carolina and, after roughly 1750, Georgia until the last quarter of the eighteenth century, when the locus of activity shifted again, this time to swampland on or adjacent to the area's principal tidal rivers. Indeed, rice production in South Carolina and Georgia, and, to a lesser extent, in the Cape Fear region of North Carolina and parts of northeastern Florida, became increasingly concentrated geographically in the narrow zone on each of this area's major tidal rivers, close enough to the coast to be affected significantly by tidal action, but far enough inland to run with fresh water. It was along such rivers—six major ones in South Carolina and five in Georgia—that American rice production would be concentrated until the late nineteenth century when production shifted increasingly to the Old Southwest.

Rice cultivation in South Carolina and Georgia was arduous in nature—the crop demanded a great deal of hoeing and weeding—and was characterized by tight labor controls and considerable coercion throughout its history. No area in the entire South, in fact, was so thoroughly dominated by the institution of slavery as the low country under the rice regime and in no area were the role of African Americans and the influence of African American culture so profound.

To say this is not to suggest, as some have, that African Americans were alone responsible for the technical evolution of the low-country rice industry. If some slaves were from rice countries in West Africa and some technology—fanner baskets, for example—was clearly of African origin, much of the technology employed was generic in nature, and, thus, familiar to cereal producers throughout the world. The origins of even the task system, the distinguishing feature of labor organization in the low country, are open to question. Under this system, which evolved gradually after the mid-eighteenth century, a slave was responsible for completing a specified amount of work daily, a certain number of specified tasks as it were, upon the completion of which he or she was free to do what he or she so chose. This system most likely grew out of an ongoing process of informal negotiations between laborers bargaining for greater autonomy, and managers hoping to raise productivity and to lessen labor unrest by injecting the incentive of free time into the labor equation. However uncertain the origins of the system, its results are clear: over time, slaves used the relative freedom gained through the task system to work for themselves or to sell their free time to others. In so doing, they were often able to accumulate considerable amounts of personal property, which was, of course, only one of many ironies under slavery.

In any case, with the shift in the early eighteenth century to irrigation, rice production technology became increasingly elaborate and costly. In combination with the geographical limits imposed by nature, such technological considerations helped create an agricultural complex dominated by a relatively small number of capital-intensive plantations, which utilized sizable numbers of dependent laborers to produce rice and, at times, other staples for distant, largely foreign, markets.

The main markets for rice produced in the Southeast were never local. Until the late antebellum period, they usually were not even domestic, for most of the crop produced each year was destined for shipment abroad, particularly to the grain markets of northern Europe. In these markets, rice was viewed as a cheap commodity with numerous uses. It was sold as a dietary supplement or complement, for example, and as an animal feed. It was used in distilling and, by the mid-nineteenth century, in brewing and found employment in the starch, paper, and paste industries. Its most common use, however, was as a source of cheap, bulk calories for the poor and for soldiers, sailors, inmates, and schoolchildren in the absence of, or instead of, more desirable but often more expensive foodstuffs.

Prior to the entrance of American rice in European markets, most of the Continent's supply came from the Italian states of Lombardy and Piedmont, or from the Levant. By the mid-eighteenth century, though, rice from South Carolina and, later, Georgia had supplanted other suppliers in the principal European markets, and American rice maintained this position until the 1830s, when exports from the United States were surpassed by those from India and Southeast Asia.

Given the character of European demand, it is not surprising that Southeast Asia, the lowest-cost supplier in the market, could outcompete other supply sources. As a result of this penetration of its major markets, U.S. producers shifted their attention in the late antebellum period to the domestic market and others in the Western Hemisphere. Despite some success with this strategy, the rice industry of the South Atlantic states was clearly mature well before the Civil War: the rate of growth in output was slowing down, soil fertility was declining, costs (particularly for labor) were rising, and profit possibilities in the industry were diminishing—all of this before the disruption of four years of civil war.

Until recently, historians believed that the problems of the South Atlantic rice industry began in 1861 and that the industry's demise was a direct outgrowth of the Civil War and emancipation. It is now clear, however, that its problems were both structural and long-term in nature, having as much to do with the expansion and elaboration of capitalism and with shifts in international comparative advantage as with Federal occupation, wartime destruction of production facilities, and postwar shortages of capital and changes in labor relations.

To be sure, the latter short-term factors impeded the South Atlantic rice industry. Production in the four South Atlantic states of North Carolina, South Carolina, Georgia, and Florida fell from an all-time high of 179.4 million pounds of clean rice in 1859 (95.9 percent of the U.S. total) to 57 million pounds in 1869. But production in the area rose by nearly 48 percent between 1869 and 1879, and even as late as 1899 almost 69 million pounds of clean rice were produced in the South Atlantic region. By that time, however, Southeast Asian competition had not only knocked U.S. rice out of Europe but had penetrated the domestic market as well. The United States, in fact, was a major importer of rice for a half century after the Civil War.

One important long-term result of such competition was the gradual migration of the U.S. rice industry to Louisiana, Texas, and Arkansas. Here, highly mechanized production technology was employed, particularly after the so-called rice revolution of the mid-1880s, which raised productivity and minimized the problems posed by scarce or restive labor. Although rice *could* still be grown in the South Atlantic region at the turn of the century, highly mechanized production technology was not introduced on the reconstituted plantations, tenant plots, and yeoman freeholdings in the area. Consequently, production no longer meant profits, and the low country of South Carolina and Georgia lapsed into generations of stagnation and decline. In the last analysis, however, the evolution of the U.S. rice industry owed as much to European imperialism and to developments in Calcutta, Batavia, and Rangoon, as to more familiar events closer to home.

BIBLIOGRAPHY

Coclanis, Peter A. *The Shadow of a Dream: Economic Life and Death in the South Carolina Low Country, 1670–1920.* New York, 1989.

Dethloff, Henry C. *A History of the American Rice Industry, 1685–1985.* College Station, Tex., 1988.

Joyner, Charles W. *Down by the Riverside: A South Carolina Slave Community.* Urbana, Ill., 1984.

Smith, Julia Floyd. *Slavery and Rice Culture in Low Country Georgia, 1750–1860.* Knoxville, Tenn., 1985.

PETER A. COCLANIS

RICHARDSON, ROBERT VINKLER (1820–1870), colonel and acting brigadier general. Richardson was born in Granville County, North Carolina, on November 4, 1820. He moved as a child to Hardeman County, Tennessee, where he was reared and educated. After passing the bar,

Richardson in 1847 moved to Memphis, where he practiced law and engaged in business until the outbreak of the Civil War.

Richardson served early in the war under Brig. Gen. Gideon Pillow. Subsequently, he recruited the First Tennessee Partisan Rangers and, as colonel, led the regiment at Shiloh and Corinth. In November 1863, Richardson and his men became part of Maj. Gen. Nathan Bedford Forrest's newly created cavalry command in Mississippi. On December 3, he received an appointment as brigadier general and served with Forrest in a December raid into western Tennessee and at the Battle of Okolona in March 1864. But just prior to the Confederate operations in western Tennessee in March and April, Forrest relieved Richardson of his command "on account of charges preferred against him by Colonel [J. U.] Green," who was commanding one of Richardson's regiments.

Richardson also fared poorly with his promotion to brigadier general. Although the Confederate Congress confirmed the promotion, President Jefferson Davis refused to sign his commission in February 1864. Despite the rejection, Richardson remained in the service until the end of the war.

Following the war, Richardson went abroad and then returned to Memphis to engage in business and railroad building. While traveling in connection with his railroad interests, he stopped at a tavern in the village of Clarkton, Missouri, on the night of January 5, 1870, where an unknown assailant shot and mortally wounded him. He lingered briefly, dying early the next morning.

BIBLIOGRAPHY

Henry, Robert Selph. *"First with the Most" Forrest.* Indianapolis, 1944.

Warner, Ezra J. *Generals in Gray: Lives of the Confederate Commanders.* Baton Rouge, La., 1959.

Wills, Brian Steel. *A Battle from the Start: The Life of Nathan Bedford Forrest.* New York, 1992.

Wyeth, John Allan. *Life of General Nathan Bedford Forrest.* New York, 1899. Reprint, Baton Rouge, La., 1989.

BRIAN S. WILLS

RICHMOND, VIRGINIA.

RICHMOND, VIRGINIA. In 1860, Richmond was the twenty-fifth largest American city, with a population of 37,910. Its manufactures ranked thirteenth in value, far above those of Charleston, which it soon surpassed in size, and even those of New Orleans, a much larger city. Its industry, and its status since the Revolution as the seat of Virginia's government, impelled the leaders of the infant Confederacy to suggest that Richmond become the permanent capital if the Old Dominion seceded.

The Confederacy's move from Montgomery, the first capital city, in May 1861 was appropriate for a conservative revolution, for Richmond had long been a bastion of Whigs "who knew each other by the instincts of gentlemen." They so dominated antebellum politics that the city's few Democrats were called "the Spartan band." Know-Nothings triumphed in the 1855–1856 elections because of national Whiggery's disintegration and conservative fears of the city's growing ethnic and religious mix, noted by contemporary observer Frederick Law Olmsted. In the 1860 presidential election, the Constitutional Union ticket won 20 percent more of the 6,555 votes cast than the two Democratic slates combined.

Richmond's population was 62 percent white, over a fifth

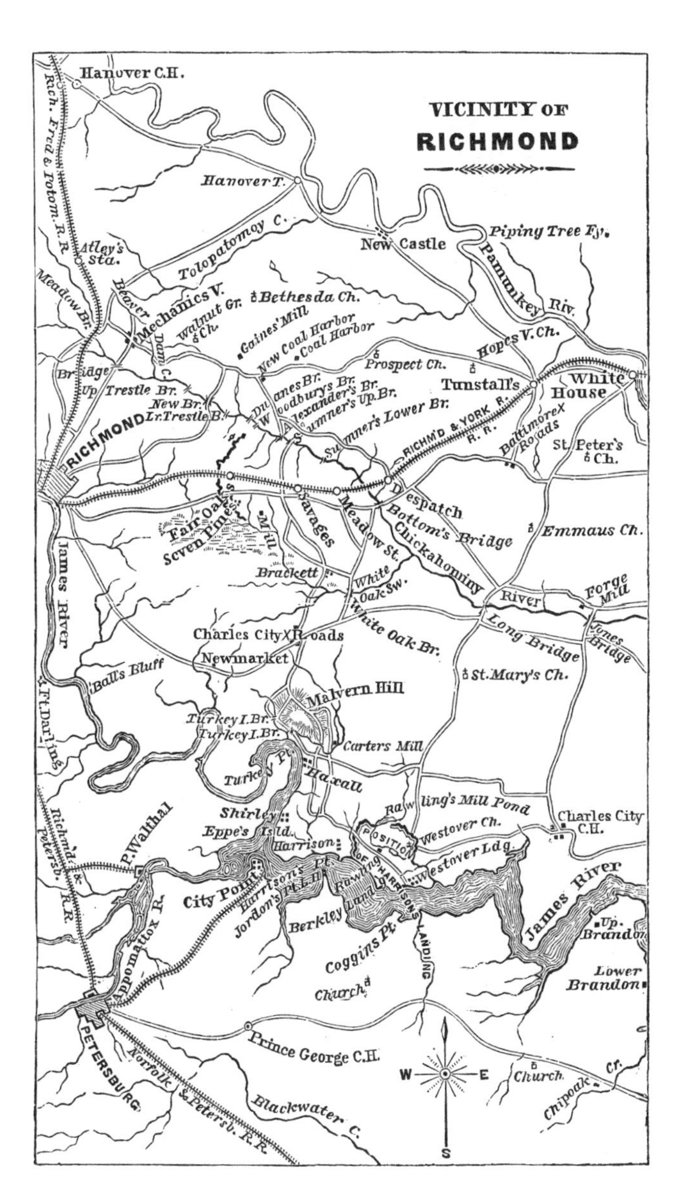

VICINITY OF RICHMOND, VIRGINIA.

HARPER'S PICTORIAL HISTORY OF THE GREAT REBELLION

of which was foreign-born, chiefly Irish Catholics, and Germans, many of whom were Lutherans. Catholics had three churches, including a cathedral. Wealthy Methodists, Presbyterians, and Baptists dominated, with Episcopalians at the pinnacle of prestige. There was also a significant Jewish minority with three synagogues.

African Americans, 18 percent of whom were free, had declined from 45 percent of the 1850 population. Corporations owned more slaves and in larger concentrations than did white families, two-thirds of whom owned none. Slaves and free blacks were essential to the city's major industries, where many held skilled jobs. Others worked in the trades and service occupations. There were active charitable and fraternal associations, large churches, and distinct gradations in black society as in white.

Richmond rivaled Baltimore as a milling center, with annual sales of $3 million from its twelve flour and meal mills, including the Gallego, largest in the world. Highly regarded for its quality, city flour was shipped to Australia and South America. Return cargoes of Brazilian coffee made Richmond the leading importer in 1860. In its tobacco market, the world's largest, sixty factories and related firms processed tobacco worth $5 million, making it the city's most profitable sector. Joseph R. Anderson's Tredegar Iron Works, the second largest foundry in the United States, was half of a substantial industry that employed one-fifth of the labor force and included dozens of firms with total sales of over $2 million. Profits from the city's slave trade, described by Charles Dickens and other visitors, probably exceeded those derived from milling or metal working. Only New Orleans was a larger slave mart. To this business and industrial complex, which was already diversifying, the war added powder mills, armories, laboratories, government offices, and huge troop encampments.

Richmond, Virginia's largest port, was a transportation hub. There were overnight steamship connections to Washington and Baltimore down the James River. Ocean and coasting vessels crowded Rocketts, the city's harbor. Five railroads terminated here, bringing passengers and freight from all directions. The Richmond and York River Railroad ran east to West Point, another deep-water port. The Richmond, Fredericksburg, and Potomac went north to Aquia Creek, with steamship connections to Washington and Baltimore via the Potomac. The Virginia Central also ran north to Gordonsville below Manassas Junction, continuing south and west to Charlottesville and Staunton. The Richmond and Petersburg connected to Wilmington via Weldon. The Richmond and Danville was the city's main direct link with the Deep South, although this line also crossed the Virginia and Tennessee, which ran through Bristol. The James River and Kanawha Canal extended west beyond Lynchburg more than two hundred miles from the Richmond docks. As late as 1859 the canal brought more freight tonnage into Richmond than all the railroads combined.

Edgar Allan Poe had lived here and edited the *Southern Literary Messenger,* which continued until 1864. George W. Bagby, George Fitzhugh, Edmund Ruffin, John R. Thompson, and Nathaniel Beverly Tucker all published in Richmond. The city boasted four major dailies, with total circulation of almost 84,000, including the *Whig, Enquirer, Examiner,* and *Dispatch,* and a German daily, *Taglicher Anzeiger.* It added a sixth, the *Sentinel,* during the war, as well as Confederate journals like the *Southern Illustrated News, Magnolia Weekly,* and *Southern Punch.* The city had several theaters and public halls but no library.

Richmond was the social center for Virginia east of the mountains and for much of the Mid-Atlantic seaboard. Genteel antebellum society became rougher in wartime. Entertainment included elegant receptions at the presidential mansion; "starvation parties" for young soldiers and beautiful belles, at which only water was served; and saloons, brothels, and gambling dens or "tigers," all of which ranged from the posh to the squalid. Writers as diverse as Mary Boykin Chesnut, Thomas C. DeLeon, J. B. Jones, and Sallie Brock Putnam described the Confederate citadel.

Schools included the Medical College of Virginia; Richmond College, a Baptist institution; the Richmond Female Institute; and the Virginia Mechanics Institute. All were taken over for military use. There were dozens of private academies, but no true public school system.

The state arsenal, armory, and penitentiary were here, and Richmond became the prison and hospital center of the South. The city held thirteen thousand prisoners in November 1863. Libby Prison, for Union officers, was located in a Maine ship chandler and slave trader's warehouse. Belle Isle, for enlisted men, was on a low island in the middle of the James. There were smaller prisons like Castle Thunder and Castle Lightning for spies, deserters, rowdies, political prisoners, and women.

Camp Winder, west of the city, was the largest hospital, and Phoebe Yates Pember's Chimborazo, on an eastern hill, was the most famous. There were at least sixty smaller military hospitals, run by the Confederate government, states, private individuals, and churches and other institutions.

The influx of politicians, clerks, office seekers, soldiers, and camp followers from all over the Confederacy, along with Southern refugees from the North, tripled or quadrupled the 1860 population, straining municipal services, including the markets, water and gas works, and police and fire protection. City employees were subject to conscription.

Tension between Richmonders and Confederate officials can be seen in the early furor over Provost Marshal John Winder's enforcement of martial law and resentment of his feared detectives or "plug-uglies," in John M. Daniel's bitter criticism of the Davis administration in his *Examiner,* and in the minutes of the city council.

Rampant inflation caused severe suffering for those on fixed incomes, and even regular increases in government salaries failed to keep pace, resulting in such ironies as a free black cobbler earning more than Confederate congressmen. The April 1863 bread riot was the most serious of the Southern food protests over shortages and high prices.

Organized resistance to the Confederacy by a Union underground included the spy Elizabeth Van Lew and Richmond, Fredericksburg, and Potomac Railroad Superintendent Samuel Ruth, who delayed beef shipments to Robert E. Lee's army. Unionists helped slaves and Federal prisoners to escape, committed arson and other sabotage, and chalked pro-Northern slogans on walls.

More than 7,300 men from the area served in the Confederate army, furnishing over forty companies of infantry, artillery, and cavalry, including two regiments, the First and Fifteenth Virginia infantries. Confederate dead filled the city's cemeteries, Shockoe, Oakwood, and Hollywood; the latter, the most famous after the war, is the burial site of J. E. B. Stuart, George E. Pickett and his men, and eventually Jefferson Davis and his family.

Although it may have been a strategic error for Confederate leaders to move their capital so close to the North, a decision still argued by Civil War historians, Richmond's location made it inevitable that Virginia would become the main battleground. Richmond was the goal of the Army of the Potomac for four years. After Irvin McDowell's drive ended at First Manassas in July 1861, George B. McClellan's Peninsular campaign threatened Richmond in 1862. Lee's Army of Northern Virginia pushed the front lines back in 1862 and 1863 in the Seven Days' Battles and at Second Manassas, Fredericksburg, and Chancellorsville. A series of star forts and three concentric lines of trenches encircled Richmond. There were never enough troops to man these earthworks fully, but they were used against major campaigns and raids, notably Stoneman's in May 1863 and Kilpatrick-Dahlgren's in March 1864.

The city was again threatened by Ulysses S. Grant's massive offensive that same spring. He was unable to take Richmond after the Wilderness, Spotsylvania, and Cold Harbor, but his siege of Petersburg eventually cut the city's direct rail link with Wilmington. Forced to evacuate after his lines were finally broken at Five Forks on April 1, 1865, Lee notified Jefferson Davis that Richmond must be abandoned. His army did not survive the loss of its capital for even a week.

The Confederate government evacuated the night of April 2, 1865. The Southerners blew up ironclads in the James and munitions in the city, including its powder magazine. The explosions caused more than a dozen fatalities. Custis Lee's rear guard burned Mayo's Bridge, the only vehicular and pedestrian link, as well as the two railroad viaducts. Fires set to destroy supplies of tobacco and cotton, despite the objections of city officials, were spread by high winds. Hindered by penitentiary inmates who cut their hoses, Richmond's few firemen were unable to control the flames. A mob of thousands of hungry civilians, as well as Confederate stragglers and deserters and Union prisoners, swarmed through the streets ahead of the blaze, looting stores and warehouses.

The evacuation fire consumed much of Richmond's industrial and business district, including all of the banks and most of the food suppliers. Property loss estimates ranged as high as $30 million. Residential neighborhoods were largely spared, but more than eight hundred buildings

RICHMOND, VIRGINIA. View from Gamble's Hill, April 1865. Visible from left to right are St. Paul's, the Second Baptist church, the Presbyterian church, City Hall, the First Baptist church, and the Capitol. *HARPER'S PICTORIAL HISTORY OF THE GREAT REBELLION*

THE BURNT DISTRICT OF RICHMOND, APRIL 1865. LIBRARY OF CONGRESS

burned in four dozen blocks, and the downtown area was a smoking wasteland when Union forces entered the city early on April 3, restoring order and putting out fires that were still burning.

Reconstruction in Richmond was moderate, despite legends to the contrary, but the impact of war and defeat was enormous. Rebuilding of the burned district began almost immediately after the Union occupation (largely financed by Northern backers who remain mostly unidentified), although ruins from the evacuation fire could still be seen in the 1870s. Economic recovery was slower and only partially successful. Panics in 1873 and 1893, lack of capital and access to raw materials, failure to adopt new technology, continued reliance on erratic water power from the James, the shift of the wheat belt farther west, and corporate consolidations all had their effect. The Tredegar Iron Works never recovered its antebellum stature. The city's mills declined after 1883, although the last lingered until 1932. Richmond's once-dominant industry was taken over in 1890 by James B. Duke's trust, the American Tobacco Company. Efforts to deepen the river channel failed, and Norfolk had surpassed the port of Richmond by 1881. Canal owners struggled to repair war damage but were stymied by floods, the 1873 depression, and rail competition. The towpath became a railroad right-of-way. The railroads fell under the control of outside interests or built extensions so that the city ceased to be a terminus.

No longer a major industrial center or transport hub, Richmond remained Virginia's capital and became the mausoleum of the Lost Cause, with thousands of Confederate graves, monuments to Southern heroes, and shrines like the White House of the Confederacy, the Lee House, the soldiers' homes, the Southern Historical Society at Battle Abbey (now the Virginia Historical Society), the Home for

Confederate Women, and the headquarters of the United Daughters of the Confederacy. Battlefields and other historic sites, most administered by the National Park Service, still ring the capital, and trenches greet the visitor leaving the airport. Richmond's population in the last half of the twentieth century has been roughly one-half black, and African Americans have often controlled the government and elected mayors in Virginia's "Holy City," the capital of a vanished nation.

[*See also* Belle Isle Prison; Bread Riots; Castle Thunder Prison; Libby Prison.]

BIBLIOGRAPHY

Bill, Alfred H. *The Beleaguered City: Richmond, 1861–1865.* New York, 1946.

Chesson, Michael B. *Richmond after the War, 1865–1890.* Richmond, Va., 1981.

Jones, Katherine M., ed. *Ladies of Richmond, Confederate Capital.* Indianapolis, 1962.

Jones, Virgil Carrington. *Eight Hours before Richmond.* New York, 1957.

Manarin, Louis H., ed. *Richmond at War: The Minutes of the City Council, 1861–1865.* Chapel Hill, N.C., 1966.

Manarin, Louis H., and Lee A. Wallace, Jr., eds. *Richmond Volunteers: The Volunteer Companies of the City of Richmond and Henrico County, Virginia, 1861–1865.* Richmond, Va., 1969.

Patrick, Rembert. *The Fall of Richmond.* Baton Rouge, La., 1960.

Thomas, Emory M. *The Confederate State of Richmond: A Biography of the Capital.* Austin, Tex., 1971.

MICHAEL B. CHESSON

RILLIEUX, NORBERT (1806–1894), inventor. Rillieux was born free in New Orleans, son of a French engineer-inventor, Vincent Rillieux, and a free mulatto woman, Constance Vivant. He was sent to school in Paris, where he was so outstanding in engineering that he became an instructor and published scientific papers on steam and engines.

Heretofore, sugar came out brown and lumpy. Rillieux invented the multiple-effect vacuum-chamber evaporation process by which sugar came out white and grainy. His system was first installed successfully at Myrtle Grove Plantation near New Orleans. During the 1840s and 1850s, he installed his process at many plantations, such as Bellechasse, home of Judah P. Benjamin, who later held several positions in Jefferson Davis's cabinet. While at a plantation installing and explaining the machinery, Rillieux usually stayed in a special house where he was waited upon by slave servants.

Meanwhile, Rillieux devised a brilliant plan to drain the lowlands of New Orleans, but, before it could be implemented, the increasing restrictions on free blacks in the South caused him to return to France in 1861. After the South Carolina slave conspiracy of 1822 led by a free black, Denmark Vesey, and the publication in 1829 of the abolitionist tract *Walker's Appeal* by David Walker, a free black from North Carolina living in Boston, Southern states had passed increasingly restrictive laws. Such laws barred free blacks from entering the state, made it more difficult to set slaves free, and ordered free blacks to leave the state or be made into slaves. The harshest laws, expelling free blacks, were passed in the 1850s.

In France, Rillieux followed a new career, Egyptology, for several decades, but returned to engineering in the early 1880s. He then perfected his vacuum-chamber evaporation process, which became the basic manufacturing technique up to the present time in the processing not only of sugar but also of condensed milk, soap, gelatin, glue, and other products.

BIBLIOGRAPHY

Haber, Louis. *Black Pioneers of Science and Invention.* New York, 1970.

Klein, Aaron E. *The Hidden Contributors: Black Scientists and Inventors in America.* Garden City, N.Y., 1971.

Meade, George P. "A Negro Scientist of Slavery Days." *Scientific Monthly* 62 (April 1946): 317–326.

EDGAR A. TOPPIN

RIPLEY, ROSWELL SABINE (1823–1887), brigadier general. Born in Ohio and a graduate of West Point in 1843, Ripley served with distinction in the Mexican War. While stationed at Sullivan's Island he married into a prominent Charleston family, resigned his commission, and settled there. In December 1860 after Maj. Robert Anderson moved his forces from Fort Moultrie to Fort Sumter, Major Ripley led state troops to seize Fort Moultrie. When the commanding officer at Charleston, P. G. T. Beauregard, ordered the bombardment of Fort Sumter, Ripley, now a lieutenant colonel, fired hot shot at the fort, which set ablaze its barracks. He was commended for his actions.

Promoted to the rank of brigadier general, Ripley commanded the Department of South Carolina during the first year of the war. He strengthened the defenses around Charleston for which he never had enough arms or men. In March 1862 Gen. John C. Pemberton replaced Ripley and ordered the batteries guarding the mouth of the Stono River dismantled. The hot-tempered Ripley opposed it. But the guns were removed, the Stono opened to Union gunboats, and Ripley was transferred to Virginia. On September 17 at Sharpsburg, Ripley sustained a serious wound in the throat; after having it bandaged, he returned to the field.

When Beauregard returned to Charleston in late 1862, Ripley was reassigned to him and supervised the placing of torpedoes in the harbor. His troops at Fort Wagner on

ROSWELL SABINE RIPLEY. LIBRARY OF CONGRESS

Morris Island withstood fifty-eight days of fierce bombardments and infantry assaults. These defenses made Federal officers reassess their invasion plans. But now Ripley accused Beauregard of allowing the seizure of Morris Island itself. A mutual dislike developed. Ripley was accused of insubordination and intoxication during an attack on James Island in July 1864. In February 1865 Ripley's request for a transfer from Charleston was approved by Beauregard who considered himself "fortunate to be rid of such an element of discord." Ripley joined General Joseph E. Johnston's army in North Carolina where at war's end he received his parole.

Subsequently, Ripley participated in an unsuccessful manufacturing project in England, engaged in several business ventures in Charleston and then moved to New York City where he conducted business for several years. He died there in 1887, but was buried in Charleston.

BIBLIOGRAPHY

Burton, E. Milby. *The Siege of Charleston, 1861–1865.* Columbia, S.C., 1976.

Fraser, Walter J., Jr. *Charleston! Charleston!: The History of a Southern City.* Columbia, S.C., 1989.

WALTER J. FRASER, JR.

RIVER DEFENSE FLEET. To defend the Mississippi south of New Orleans and to the north as far as Memphis, Confederates assembled fourteen river steamers, pilot boats, and tugs under the appellation the River Defense Fleet.

The large, well-armed Union force that threatened the entire Mississippi in 1861 set state legislators in Missouri and Mississippi clamoring for protection. Kentucky boatmen James Edward Montgomery and James H. Townsend originated the idea for the fleet, and Secretary of War Judah P. Benjamin engineered a million-dollar appropriation by late 1861.

In the loosely structured Confederate command system, naval officers assigned to the Mississippi had little or no part in plans or operations for the fleet. In January 1862, orders to purchase the boats went to Maj. Gen. Mansfield Lovell. Gen. M. Jeff Thompson of the Missouri State Guard later added his daring temperament to the enterprise.

The ships were first rechristened for Confederate army leaders. Armed with one 24- or 32-pounder mounted astern, they were not designed to engage the enemy as gunboats. Instead, reinforcing the prow of each boat with iron created a ram that could damage and sink a Union ship in a collision. "Cottonclad" came into the vocabulary of the Civil War when cotton was stuffed inside the hulls; this was done so that a cannonball that pierced the hull would bury itself in the matted fibers.

Six of the boats stood below New Orleans to meet the Union's April 24, 1862, assault on Forts Jackson and St. Philip. Five were run aground and abandoned by their untrained crews: *Defiance, General Breckenridge, General Lovell, Resolute,* and *Warrior. Stonewall Jackson* rammed and sank the Union *Varuna* before being burned by its fleeing crew.

The eight boats upriver saw more action. On May 10, *General Bragg, General Price, General Sumter, General Van Dorn,* and *Little Rebel* engaged the Union fleet at Plum Point, Tennessee, ramming and damaging U.S. ships *Cincinnati* and *Mound City.*

On June 5 and 6, other boats of the fleet joined in the Battle of Memphis. Of the veterans of the May 10 encounter, all were captured except *Van Dorn,* which was later destroyed at its mooring up the Yazoo River. Of the remaining four, *Colonel Lovell* was sunk with great loss of life; *General Thompson* exploded; *General Beauregard* was badly damaged when it and *Price* missed USS *Monarch* and rammed each other.

Thus ended the story of the River Defense Fleet—like so many Confederate naval efforts, better conceived than constructed and operated with a certain raffish optimism in the face of a much superior Union force.

BIBLIOGRAPHY

Civil War Naval Chronology, 1861–1865. 6 vols. Washington, D.C., 1961–1965.

Gillespie, Michael L. "The Novel Experiment: Cottonclads and

Steamboatmen." *Civil War Times Illustrated* 22 (December 1983): 34–39.
Pratt, Fletcher. *Guns on the Western Waters.* New York, 1956.

MAXINE TURNER

RIVERS, PRINCE (1822–?), sergeant, Thirty-third U.S. Colored Infantry. Rivers, born a slave in Edgefield County, South Carolina, fled to Union forces in Beaufort early in the Civil War. In May 1862, Rivers joined Gen. David Hunter's First Regiment of South Carolina Volunteers and was made a sergeant. He accompanied Hunter to New York City to win public support for the employment of black troops. But white troops, infuriated at the sight of a black man wearing sergeant's stripes, attacked Rivers. Rivers successfully resisted their assault until police arrived. Hunter, however, was forced to disband the black regiment in August 1862 when he failed to receive political or military support from Abraham Lincoln and Secretary of War Edwin M. Stanton.

Within two weeks, Stanton ordered Brig. Gen. Rufus Saxton to form a black regiment in South Carolina. Saxton directed Col. Thomas Wentworth Higginson to organize the First South Carolina Infantry, which would become the Thirty-third U.S. Colored Infantry. Higginson designated Rivers as color sergeant as well as provost sergeant. Higginson characterized Rivers as handsome, six feet tall, "jet black . . . perfectly proportioned, and of apparently inexhaustible strength and activity." Favorably impressed with the sergeant's modest education and administrative skills, Higginson tried unsuccessfully to obtain an officer's commission for Rivers.

Rivers's men were not as impressed with their sergeant. They gave him grudging respect but regarded him as a martinet who was overly diligent in pursuing deserters. On Emancipation Day, January 1, 1863, the Thirty-third participated in a moving ceremony and parade in Beaufort. Rivers delivered one of the speeches during the day's activities. The Thirty-third later distinguished itself in combat in expeditions up the St. Marys River in Georgia and Florida and the St. Johns River in Florida.

After the war, Rivers returned to Edgefield and played an influential role in Republican politics. He was elected to the 1868 constitutional convention and to three terms in the state house of representatives.

BIBLIOGRAPHY

Cornish, Dudley Taylor. *The Sable Arm: Negro Troops in the Union Army, 1861–1865.* New York, 1956.
Higginson, Thomas Wentworth. *Army Life in a Black Regiment.* New York, 1869. Reprint, Boston, 1962.

WILLIAM C. HINE

WILLIAM C. RIVES. LIBRARY OF CONGRESS

RIVES, WILLIAM C. (1793–1868), U.S. diplomat, representative to the Washington peace conference, and congressman from Virginia. William Cabell Rives was born May 4, 1793, at Union Hill in Amherst County, Virginia. He was educated at Hampden-Sydney College and the College of William and Mary. After his graduation from the latter in 1809, he studied law under Thomas Jefferson and became an intimate of James Madison. During the War of 1812 he served as aide-de-camp to John H. Cocke on the Chickahominy River. In 1817 Rives was elected to the first of several terms in Virginia's House of Delegates, where he served on the Courts and Justice, Executive Expenditures, and Finance committees.

Rives married Judith Page Walker on March 24, 1819. As heiress to the Castle Hill estate in Albemarle County, she brought Rives a four-thousand-acre plantation and almost a hundred slaves. After moving to Castle Hill, Rives served an additional year in the House of Delegates as a representative of Albemarle County before being elected to Congress in 1823. During the next six years, he ardently supported the cause of Andrew Jackson. The president rewarded Rives's loyalty by naming him minister to France in 1829.

During his time in Paris, Rives witnessed the deposing of Charles X in favor of Louis Philippe at the head of a new constitutional monarchy, scenes he would replay many times in his mind during the secession winter of 1860–1861. Under the Berlin and Milan decrees, the American minister negotiated a settlement of spoliation claims under which the French agreed to pay a $5 million indemnity and the Americans, in turn, agreed to reduce the duty on French wine imported into the United States.

On his return to America in 1832, Rives was elected to the U.S. Senate. His support for the Force Bill angered a number of members of the state legislature. On January 17, 1834, he rose to support Jackson's removal of Federal deposits from the Second Bank of the United States. Virginia's General Assembly instructed its congressional delegation to vote for censuring the president for his actions. Refusing to bow to pressure, Rives chose to resign his seat.

In 1835 Rives campaigned behind the scenes to win the vice presidential nomination on the Democratic ticket. Jackson, however, backed Richard M. Johnson of Kentucky for the office. Thwarted in his ambitions, Rives sought to return to the Senate. He lobbied the General Assembly to instruct the state's congressional delegation to vote for Thomas Hart Benton's resolution asking that the censure of Jackson for removing deposits be expunged. Senator John Tyler refused to do as instructed and resigned his seat, to which Rives was then elected.

Soon after his return to Washington in 1836, Rives found himself at loggerheads with President Martin Van Buren over what to do about the country's fiscal situation. Rives favored placing the Federal surplus in state banks and vehemently opposed both Jackson's specie circular and Van Buren's subtreasury system. A group calling itself the Conservative Democrats began to coalesce around Rives's leadership and in the 1838 elections won control of the Virginia General Assembly.

In 1839 Rives came up for reelection and was nominated by the Conservative Democrats. He faced former senator John Tyler, nominated by the Whigs, and John Young Mason, the regular Democratic nominee. Henry Clay, the national leader of the Whigs, wanted the support of the Conservative Democrats in 1840, so he offered Tyler a deal: if Tyler would withdraw from the race in favor of Rives, then Clay would see that Tyler received the Whig vice presidential nomination the next year. Tyler refused. None of the three candidates could win a majority, so the election was postponed until the next session. As a result, Virginia had but one senator until 1841, when Rives finally won reelection after Tyler became vice president.

Once in Washington, Rives consistently supported former rival Tyler against Clay until the question of the annexation of Texas came up. Rives maintained that Texas was a foreign nation and that as such, it was unconstitutional to admit it to the Union. By the end of Tyler's term, Rives had aligned himself with the Whig party, and he gave his support to Clay's candidacy in the presidential election of 1844.

When his senatorial term expired in 1845, Rives retired to Castle Hill and private life. Several works from his pen were published in Richmond, including *Discourse on the Character and Services of John Hampden* (1845) and *Discourse on the Uses and Importance of History* (1847). During this time he served a second stint as a member of the board of visitors of the University of Virginia. His first appointment to the board in 1828 had ended with his departure for France in 1829. His second term, begun in 1834, lasted until 1849, when he again stepped down upon receiving another appointment as minister to France, this one from President Zachary Taylor.

For the second time Rives went to turbulent Paris. Louis Philippe, whose relationship with Rives had been so cordial that his queen had consented to act as godmother to Rives's elder daughter, had been forced to abdicate in February 1848 after a series of revolts. In June a bloody uprising of Parisian workers marred the unstable peace of the newly proclaimed Second Republic. All around him Rives witnessed the aftermath of the bloody nationalist uprisings that erupted in Europe in 1848. He watched as the French moved into Italy to quell Garibaldi's risorgimento. He carried the memories with him when the United States stood on the brink of its own crisis a dozen years later.

Rives returned to Castle Hill in 1853 and again resumed the life of a private citizen. John Brown's raid on Harpers Ferry in October 1859 and Brown's subsequent canonization by radical elements in the North alarmed Rives about the safety of the Union. Fearing what would happen if the Republicans won the White House in 1860, Rives was instrumental in organizing the Constitutional Union party and was mentioned as a possible nominee for president. The party eventually selected as its candidate John Bell, whom Rives supported but did not actively campaign for because of feeble health. After Abraham Lincoln's victory, Rives issued a public *Letter from the Hon. William C. Rives to a Friend, on the Important Questions of the Day* (Richmond, 1860). He condemned the Northern reaction to what he termed "the bloody and revolting tragedy at Harper's Ferry" but believed it was the temporary triumph of a vociferous and radical minority. Calling for "dignity and coolness," he enumerated the legal means of self-protection and defense accorded the states under the Constitution. He called for Virginia to reorganize its militia, form volunteer units, procure arms for its state guard, and encourage domestic manufacture to reduce dependence on the North. He advocated an end to sectionally based parties, both North and South, and the removal of the slavery issue from agitation on the national political level. Finally, he pointed to the lack of feasibility of creating a nation out of the states in which slavery was legal. The differences between the economies of the lower South and the upper South and the ties of the border states to the Old Northwest would, in his opinion, be impossible to overcome.

On December 8 Rives called for a national peace conference to halt the secession crisis in its tracks. In mid-January he traveled to the nation's capital at the urging of several Virginia Unionists, including Winfield Scott, to lobby for such a national convention. During five days of social calls and dinners, Rives capitalized on his position as an elder statesman of the defunct Whig party and as a former intimate of Jefferson and Madison to meet informally with leaders of the Republican party, including Secretary of State-designate William H. Seward. On January 17, Rives advised Unionist Alexander H. H. Stuart to push the resolution calling for a national peace convention through the Virginia General Assembly. Two days later, the state legislature passed the resolution in the wording suggested by Rives and chose the former diplomat and senator as one of the Old Dominion's five delegates. At the same time, however, the General Assembly voted to summon a state convention to consider secession. Rives agreed to stand for election to this convention from Albemarle County and campaigned as well for Unionist Valentine W. Southall. Although Rives was not selected to attend the Richmond convention, he rejoiced at the enormous majority Unionist delegates held.

Rives returned to Washington on February 4 for the opening of the peace conference. He was unhappy with the composition of Virginia's delegation. He and George W. Summers were Unionists; John Tyler and John White Brockenbrough were moderate conditional Unionists but fast moving toward the secessionist position; and James A. Seddon was a fire-eater. To Rives's distress, Tyler was elected president of the convention on February 5, and Tyler, Brockenbrough, and Seddon finagled the selection of Seddon as Virginia's single representative to the Guthrie committee, which was assigned the task of drawing up compromise resolutions to keep the peace and reconcile the sections. To counteract any damage that Seddon might do, Rives began a series of private meetings with members of the Guthrie committee. Although most of the Republicans believed that a second constitutional convention was the only viable solution to the disagreements between the Union and the seceded states, Rives argued that immediate concessions were necessary to halt the spread of secession and to defuse the crisis.

Most of Rives's lobbying was carried on behind the scenes. He made only two major speeches in the course of the peace conference. The first, on February 13, was a eulogy of delegate John C. Wright of Ohio, with whom Rives had served in Congress in the 1820s. The second, on February 19, was a plea for concessions. Secession, he believed, was illegal, but it was a fait accompli. To keep Virginia, the upper South, and the border states in the Union would require only a guarantee of the rights of the slaveholding states. He painted for the conference delegates vivid pictures of what civil war looked like. "I have seen," he reminded them, "the pavements of Paris covered, and her gutters running with fraternal blood: God forbid that I should see this horrid picture repeated in my own country."

With other delegates from the conference, Rives called on Lincoln at the Willard Hotel on February 23. The former senator left the meeting convinced that the president-elect's views had been misrepresented in the Southern press but also that Lincoln did not understand the gravity of the situation facing his administration.

Three days after the delegates' interview with Lincoln, the conference voted on the Guthrie report. Although Rives and Summers supported the resolution calling for a constitutional amendment to extend the Missouri Compromise line to the Pacific Ocean, they were outvoted by the other three members of the Virginia delegation. After the resolution went down in defeat, eight states to eleven, a reconsideration was moved and carried. The conference then adjourned for the day. When the delegates reconvened on February 27, Virginia still voted in the negative, but the resolution passed, nine states to eight. The other proposals of the Guthrie committee also carried, though in most instances the votes of Tyler, Brockenbrough, and Seddon put Virginia in opposition. The convention then rose.

That afternoon Rives received an invitation to call on Lincoln with Alexander Doniphan of Missouri and Charles Morehead and James Guthrie of Kentucky. The president-elect promised he had no intentions to attack slavery in the states in which it already existed and that he would enforce the Fugitive Slave Laws. He would not, however, heed Morehead's pleas for concessions to the border states. Rives warned that if Lincoln did not abandon Fort Sumter, war was inevitable and that if violence broke out, Virginia would secede. Rives stated that if Virginia left the Union, "in that event I go, with all my heart and soul." Lincoln responded that he would withdraw Federal troops from Fort Sumter if Virginia would vote to remain in the Union. Rives said that he could not speak for his state and could make no promises, though he would work to prevent the secession of the Old Dominion.

Worn out by his exertions, Rives slept for twenty hours and then headed not for home but for Richmond, where the secession convention was then sitting. In a two-hour oration at Metropolitan Hall on March 8, he pleaded the cause of Union. He urged the approval of the resolutions of the peace conference as a just and equitable settlement to the sectional crisis. Rives met privately with convention president Robert Young Conrad and other delegates and returned, exhausted, to Albemarle County.

After the attack on Fort Sumter and Virginia's secession, Rives was selected as one of the commonwealth's delegates to the Provisional Confederate Congress, in which he sat until February 1862. In May 1864 he took a seat in the Second Congress. Because of his experience as minister to

France, he served on the Committee on Foreign Relations and succeeded Henry S. Foote of Tennessee as chairman. Rives also sat on the Flag and Seal Committee. His activity was limited by poor health, but he generally supported the policies of the Davis administration.

His only major speech during his second term was a two-hour argument on May 20 opposing Foote's resolution to repeal the suspension of habeas corpus. Rives maintained that the Magna Carta, the Constitution, and the Bill of Rights all allowed the suspension of the writ in wartime. Those who protested the suspension as "a dangerous inroad" on personal liberty and free speech, he declaimed, were ignoring the larger crisis of "an exterminating war of the most tremendous magnitude, waged by a ruthless foe, governed by no rules of humanity, obeying no laws of war." The congressman in fact attributed Richmond's deliverance from the most recent Union assaults at the Wilderness, Spotsylvania, and Yellow Tavern to the suspension of habeas corpus.

On November 21 Rives voted yea on a unanimous resolution reaffirming that the Confederacy would accept no peace terms that did not recognize its independence. The next month, he unsuccessfully opposed a bill to increase the salaries of members of the House by 50 percent. As the year closed, he endorsed a measure for the reduction and redemption of the currency and another for sequestering the property of men fleeing the Confederacy to escape military service. His support was critical in the adoption of a bill authorizing generals commanding departments to consolidate companies, battalions, and regiments; the bill passed by only one vote on January 9, 1865. The next day, he voted to kill the motion to reconsider the measure and return it to the Military Committee. In one of his final official acts, he reported on sundry resolutions on peace negotiations from the Committee on Foreign Relations. Rives was granted a leave of absence on January 28 and resigned his seat on March 2, 1865, citing failing health.

Three days after his resignation, Rives met in Richmond with Robert E. Lee to review a survey of the military situation drawn up by Assistant Secretary of War John A. Campbell. According to Rives, Lee maintained that the only hope for the Confederacy was to come to terms with the United States. The Confederate States could then marshal their resources and await more favorable circumstances to resume the fight for independence. With Lee's assessment in mind, Rives drew up a resolution for the Senate stating that prosecution of the war had become "impracticable" and advising Jefferson Davis to propose, through Lee, "an armistice preliminary to the re-establishment of peace & union." Rives, no longer part of Congress, intended that Senators William A. Graham of North Carolina, James L. Orr of South Carolina, and Robert M. T. Hunter of Virginia should shepherd the resolution through their chamber. The senators considered the resolution but decided in the end that pushing it through Congress would change nothing. Rives returned, for the last time, to Castle Hill and private life.

In the course of his duties as the third president of the Virginia Historical Society (an office he held from 1847 until his death), Rives had been persuaded to undertake a multivolume biography of his old friend James Madison, the Father of the Constitution. The first volume of the *History of the Life and Times of James Madison* had appeared in 1859. The Civil War delayed the composition and publication of volume two until 1866; volume three, which brought Madison up to 1797, made its appearance in 1868. Rives did not live to complete the fourth volume of the work Henry Cabot Lodge called "one of the most solemn, learned and respectable biographies ever penned by the hand of man." He died April 25, 1868, at Castle Hill and was buried in the family cemetery there. His four-volume edition of *Letters and Other Writings of James Madison* was completed by Philip R. Fendall and appeared in 1884.

BIBLIOGRAPHY

Brown, Alexander. *The Cabells and Their Kin: A Memorial Volume of History, Biography, and Genealogy.* Boston and New York, 1895.

Gunderson, Robert G. "William C. Rives and the 'Old Gentlemen's Convention.' " *Journal of Southern History* 22 (1956): 459–476.

Moore, John Hammond. "The Rives Peace Resolution—March, 1865." *West Virginia History* 26 (1964–1965): 153–160.

Rives, William Cabell. *Letter from the Hon. William C. Rives to a Friend, on the Important Questions of the Day.* Richmond, Va., 1860.

Rives, William Cabell. *Speech of Hon. William C. Rives on the Proceedings of the Peace Conference and the State of the Union, Delivered in Richmond, Virginia, March 8, 1861.* Richmond, Va., 1861.

Sowle, Patrick. "The Trials of a Virginia Unionist: William Cabell Rives and the Secession Crisis, 1860–1861." *Virginia Magazine of History and Biography* 80 (1972): 3–20.

Wingfield, Russell Stewart. "William Cabell Rives: A Biography." *Richmond College Historical Papers* 1 (1915): 57–72.

Sara B. Bearss

ROADS. Only a few interstate roads traversed the area of the Confederacy. One, dating from colonial times, was the Boston Post Road that ran all the way to Savannah. This road, which south of Washington came to be called Coastal Traffic, later was extended to St. Augustine, Florida.

By 1812, the Great Valley Road connected with the Valley Turnpike, running from Hagerstown, as well as with a connecting road from Richmond at Lynchburg, Virginia, and ran through Abingdon to Knoxville, Tennessee, where the Nashville road made a connection to Nashville. Then

ANTIETAM BRIDGE, MARYLAND. Photograph by Alexander Gardner, September 1862. NATIONAL ARCHIVES

General Jackson's Military Road ran from Nashville to Madisonville, Louisiana, opposite New Orleans. Another road, known as the Unicoy Road, connected Nashville with Augusta.

One of the most important roads in the West was the Old Natchez Road that ran from Natchez to Nashville. For years this route had been known as the Natchez Trace, and many of the flatboatmen, after selling their boats and cargoes on the lower Mississippi, had returned by this route to prepare again for a trip down the rivers. In 1801 the United States concluded treaties with the Chickasaw and Choctaw Nations to give their consent for the president of the United States to "lay out, open and make a convenient wagon road through their lands." For a time this road was as important for this area as was the Cumberland Road for Ohio, Pennsylvania, and Maryland. But soon the steamboats on the rivers reduced reliance on the Natchez Road for north-south transportation.

In the period from 1850 the only other long-distance highways in the South were minimally improved roads from Nashville to Memphis and on to Little Rock and Fort Smith, Arkansas; the segment of the Butterfield Overland Mail that crossed Texas between Washita and El Paso; and a Florida road from Pensacola to St. Augustine. A projected Federal highway from Washington to New Orleans never got beyond the felling of trees along the way.

Other roads were local, built by the states or communities. Several states chartered companies to build turnpikes with the understanding that they could charge tolls for their use. Often enterprising travelers would find or make byroads, sometimes nicknamed "shun pikes" to go around the toll stations and thus avoid payments.

Some stretches of the main roads, notably the Valley Turnpike in Virginia, were fully macadamized. That is, they had a firm bed of stone six to eight inches thick, and then a surface of small broken stones or pebbles two to three inches thick. Under traffic these would settle into a firm mosaic. Sometimes the joints were masked with a thin coating of hardened mud worn from the stone. For most roads gravel was used when available in the region. Some roads were nothing but clearings joined by wooden bridges over intervening streams. In some places plank roads or corduroy served as a shield against mud. Pavement of cobblestones or of roughly squared blocks of stone was found in city streets, though often towns and cities the size of Vicksburg had little or no paving at all, and in times of rain their dirt streets became so thick with mud as to be impassable for wheeled vehicles.

Traffic and weather quickly rippled the gravel roads with washboardlike ruts and chuck holes. Maintenance depended mostly on local inhabitants who were required by law to give two to three days of labor on the roads each year or pay a proportional head tax. But too often this amounted to little more than a desultory filling of chuckholes. Then when the war came no one was left to do the road work at a time when the roads needed more attention than ever.

Major obstacles on the roads were the streams that traversed them. On local roads, and when banks were not too steep, fords, often built up with gravel, were enough. Sometimes there were bridges improvised of logs and planks. But the main roads had more substantial bridges, some of stone, some of wood with stone piers and anchorages. From the earlier days there had been a substantial bridge across the 2,100-foot-wide James River in Virginia. There, in an early form, one section from the south shore to an island in midstream was laid on fifteen large boats held in place by anchors and chains, while the other section from the island to the north shore rested on piers. In some localities, especially in the West, covered bridges—that is, bridges with, in effect, houses built over them—were popular. Later generations were never sure whether bridges were covered to prevent horses from shying at the moving waters or to provide temporary shelter in case of storm. Most likely their purpose was to protect the wooden bridges from the weather. During the war bridges all over the country deteriorated, and wooden bridges in the combat zones were subject to burning.

In many places one had to rely on ferries to get across the rivers. Some of these were flat boats, manned by two men with paddles and poles. Some depended on the current of the stream for crossing: a cable from the boat was hooked to a ring on a cable that was secured to trees on the opposite sides of the stream, and the pressure of the current moved the boat across.

[*See also* Horses and Mules.]

BIBLIOGRAPHY

The American Heritage Pictorial Atlas of United States History. New York, 1966.

Dunbar, Seymour. *A History of Travel in America.* Indianapolis, 1915.

Meyer, B. H. *A History of Transportation in the United States before 1860.* Washington, D.C., 1917.

Nevins, Allan. *The War for Union.* 4 vols. New York, 1959–1960.

Phillips, U. B. *History of Transportation in the Eastern Cotton Belt to 1860.* New York, 1908.

Phillips, U. B. *Life and Labor in the Old South.* Boston, 1929.

Taylor, G. R. *The Transportation Revolution.* Boston, 1951.

James A. Huston

ROANE, JOHN SELDEN (1817–1867), brigadier general. Born January 8, 1817, in Wilson County, Tennessee, Roane attended Cumberland College in Kentucky and then moved to Arkansas. He was elected to the Arkansas legislature in 1844 and eventually became its Speaker. He fought in the Mexican War as a lieutenant colonel in Col. Archibald Yell's Arkansas volunteers, and when Yell died at Buena Vista, Roane took command. Because of a controversy over that battle, he fought a duel with the future Confederate Brigadier General Albert Pike in which neither was injured. Roane served as governor of Arkansas from 1849 to 1852.

Although Roane opposed secession, when the Civil War came he sided with the South. He was appointed a brigadier general on March 20, 1862, and was in command of Confederate troops when Maj. Gen. Samuel R. Curtis marched the Federal Army of the Southwest through Arkansas after the Battle of Elkhorn Tavern, Arkansas. When Roane received orders to stop Curtis, he declared martial law, intercepted the Texas cavalry en route to join Earl Van Dorn in Mississippi, and diverted them to Little Rock. This, along with other factors, prevented Little Rock's fall in the summer of 1862. Roane's brief command in Arkansas was cut short when Maj. Gen. Thomas C. Hindman replaced him, but he fought under Hindman at Prairie Grove in December 1862. He remained in the Trans-Mississippi until the end of the war and was paroled at Shreveport, Louisiana, on June 11, 1865.

Roane returned to his home in Pine Bluff, where he died on April 8, 1867. He is buried in Little Rock.

BIBLIOGRAPHY

Donovan, Timothy P., and Willard B. Gatewood, Jr., eds. *The Governors of Arkansas: Essays in Political Biography.* Fayetteville, Ark., 1981.

Harrell, John M. *Arkansas.* Vol. 10 of *Confederate Military History.* Edited by Clement A. Evans. Atlanta, 1899. Vol. 14 of extended ed. Wilmington, N.C., 1988.

Kerby, Robert L. *Kirby Smith's Confederacy: The Trans-Mississippi South, 1863–1865.* New York, 1972.

Anne J. Bailey

ROBERT E. LEE. Launched May 16, 1860, by James and George Thomson of Glasgow, Scotland, the sidewheel steamer *Giraffe* was intended for passenger service between

Glasgow and Belfast. The steamer measured 268 feet in length, 26 feet in beam, 12 feet in depth of hold, and 677 gross tons, and its sidewheels were driven by a two-cylinder oscillating engine of 290 nominal horse power. Unable to attain speeds suitable for a passenger steamer on that route, *Giraffe* was sold to Alexander Collie and Company. Collie in turn sold the steamer to the Confederate government, which converted it for blockade running.

Upon arrival in the Bahamas, the steamer was renamed *Robert E. Lee*. Under Capt. John Wilkinson, CSN, the steamer made twenty-two successful trips through the blockade. On its first trip through the blockade under another captain, November 9, 1863, *Lee* was captured by the blockaders *Iron Age* and *James Adger*. *Robert E. Lee* was condemned by the prize court and sold to the Federal navy. After conversion into a gunboat, the vessel was renamed USS *Fort Donelson* and served in the North Atlantic Blockading Squadron.

In 1865 the navy sold *Fort Donelson* to private parties who renamed it *Isabella* and operated it until 1869. It was then sold to the Chilean navy, who rearmed and renamed the steamer *Concepción*. The ship was apparently disposed of early in the 1870s following the war against Spain.

BIBLIOGRAPHY

Wilkinson, John. *The Narrative of a Blockade Runner*. New York, 1877. Reprint, Lexington, Mass., 1983.

Wise, Stephen R. *Lifeline of the Confederacy: Blockade Running during the Civil War*. Columbia, S.C., 1988.

KEVIN J. FOSTER

ROBERTS, WILLIAM PAUL

ROBERTS, WILLIAM PAUL (1841–1910), brigadier general and U.S. diplomat. Roberts was the youngest general officer in the Confederacy, being commissioned a brigadier at twenty-three. Born in Gates County, North Carolina, July 11, 1841, he was a schoolteacher before the war.

He enlisted as a private in the Nineteenth North Carolina Volunteers, later the Second North Carolina Cavalry, when the war started. He was promoted third lieutenant, August 30, 1861; first lieutenant, September 13, 1862; and captain, November 19, 1863. On May 7, 1864, he claimed the rank of major and was promoted to colonel a month later.

Shortly thereafter when dissatisfaction arose in a North Carolina brigade commanded by James Dearing, a Virginian, Robert E. Lee recommended that Roberts be placed in charge of the brigade. Lee wrote to the secretary of war that it would "remove the dissatisfaction that has arisen on account of the brigade, which is composed chiefly of North Carolina troops . . . being commanded by an officer from another state." The choice for the post was left to Rufus Barringer, a North Carolinian in the officer corps. Barringer selected Roberts because he "had many times proven himself a tenacious and effective fighter [and] was more regular in the enforcement of camp discipline." Roberts's commission as brigadier was dated February 23, 1865, nearly five months before his twenty-fourth birthday. In recognition of the promotion, Lee was said to have presented him with his own gauntlets.

Roberts's early service was in North Carolina. He transferred to the Army of Northern Virginia in the fall of 1862 and took part in the Battles of Fredericksburg and Brandy Station as well as the Suffolk campaign. His most notable achievement occurred at Reams' Station, August 25, 1864, when, according to D. H. Hill, he led his dismounted regiment in "a gallant charge upon the enemy's rifle-pits, carrying them handsomely and capturing a number of prisoners."

Roberts returned to North Carolina after receiving his parole at Appomattox. He was a member of the state constitutional convention, served in the state legislature, was elected auditor by the largest majority accorded a candidate at that time, and was appointed consul general to Victoria, British Columbia, by President Grover Cleveland. He died at a Norfolk, Virginia, hospital, March 28, 1910, following a fall at his home and was buried in Gatesville, North Carolina.

BIBLIOGRAPHY

Compiled Military Service Records. William Paul Roberts. Microcopy M331, Roll 213. Record Group 109. National Archives, Washington, D.C.

Hill, D. H., Jr. *North Carolina*. Vol. 4 of *Confederate Military History*. Edited by Clement A. Evans. Atlanta, 1899. Vol. 5 of extended ed. Wilmington, N.C., 1987.

Keys, Thomas Bland. *Tarheel Cossack: W. P. Roberts, Youngest Confederate General*. N.p., 1983.

Warner, Ezra J. *Generals in Gray: Lives of the Confederate Commanders*. Baton Rouge, La., 1959.

LOWELL REIDENBAUGH

ROBERTSON, BEVERLY HOLCOMBE

ROBERTSON, BEVERLY HOLCOMBE (1826–1910), brigadier general. Robertson was born in Amelia County, Virginia, on June 5, 1826. He graduated twenty-fifth in the class of 1849 at West Point and then served on the frontier with the Second Dragoons.

After the capture of Fort Sumter, Robertson returned to Virginia. In the fall he was named colonel of the Fourth Virginia Cavalry and commanded the regiment until the spring of 1862. During a reorganization, he lost the election for commander and was replaced because the troopers disliked his stern discipline and propensity for drill and military bearing. On June 9 Robertson was promoted to brigadier general and given command of the Laurel Brigade

BEVERLY HOLCOMBE ROBERTSON. LIBRARY OF CONGRESS

in order to bring some discipline to the troopers. With this command, Robertson participated at Cedar Mountain, Second Manassas, and the Maryland campaign. He was relieved of his command on September 5 and ordered to North Carolina to organize and instruct the cavalry in that department. It seems that Robertson was considered a good organizer and disciplinarian at drill, but unpredictable and lax in battle. During Brandy Station, as Stuart's entire cavalry engaged the Federals, Robertson's force did not engage the enemy at all. He missed the biggest cavalry battle of the war. A historian later noted that Robertson then "lost all self possession and [became] perfectly unreliable."

By February 1863 Robertson had fallen into disfavor with Maj. Gen. D. H. Hill, who wanted Robertson transferred back to Virginia. Hill described his cavalry as "the wonderfully inefficient brigade of Robertson." Lt. Gen. James Longstreet held a similar view of the man: he said that Robertson was "not . . . a very efficient officer in the field" and added that the cavalry could be better used "in proper hands." In May, Robertson was transferred to Virginia, as his cavalry had been parceled out by Hill to the different commands in Carolina. Once again in Virginia, Robertson led a brigade, but in early August he was relieved of this command, too. On October 15 Robertson was given command of the Second Military District of South Carolina, Georgia, and Florida, which he commanded until the end of the war. He had led his troops north and joined up with Joseph E. Johnston's army in North Carolina before surrendering there.

After the war Robertson moved to Washington and worked in insurance until his death on November 12, 1910.

BIBLIOGRAPHY

Eliot, Ellsworth, Jr. *West Point in the Confederacy.* New York, 1941.

Faust, Patricia L., ed. *Historical Times Illustrated Encyclopedia of the Civil War.* New York, 1986.

Thomas, Emory M. *Bold Dragon: The Life of J. E. B. Stuart.* New York, 1986.

Warner, Ezra J. *Generals in Gray: Lives of the Confederate Commanders.* Baton Rouge, La., 1959.

KENNETH L. STILES

ROBERTSON, FELIX HUSTON (1839–1928), lieutenant colonel and acting brigadier general. Born at Washington-on-the-Brazos, Texas, March 9, 1839, Robertson attended Baylor University before enrolling in the U.S. Military Academy in 1857. He withdrew on January 29, 1861, to join the Confederate army.

Robertson led artillery units during a number of engagements during the war. Commissioned a second lieutenant in March 1861, he participated in the bombardment of Fort Sumter before transferring to Pensacola, where he served as acting adjutant general for Gen. Adley Hogan Gladden. Robertson became a captain in October 1861, commanding the Alabama Battery at Shiloh and the Florida Battery at Murfreesboro. He rose to major on July 1, 1863, and led a battalion in James Longstreet's corps at Chickamauga.

In January 1864, Robertson gained the rank of lieutenant colonel, and he was placed in charge of artillery in Joseph Wheeler's cavalry corps during the Atlanta campaign. Promoted to brigadier general on July 26, he commanded a cavalry brigade in Tennessee and in Georgia following the fall of Atlanta. In November, Robertson suffered a wound at Buckhead Creek, Georgia, and saw no field action for the remainder of the war. The Confederate Senate rejected his nomination to brigadier general on February 22, 1865, but he claimed that rank when he surrendered at Macon on April 20.

Robertson returned to Texas and became a successful attorney and farmer. He worked actively in the Texas Division of Confederate Veterans, serving as commander in 1911. The last surviving Confederate general, he died in Waco on April 20, 1928, and was buried in Salado.

BIBLIOGRAPHY

Connelly, Thomas L. *Army of the Heartland: The Army of Tennessee, 1861–1862.* Baton Rouge, La., 1967.

Connelly, Thomas L. *Autumn of Glory: The Army of Tennessee, 1862–1865.* Baton Rouge, La., 1971.

Spencer, James, comp. *Civil War Generals: Categorical Listings and a Biographical Directory.* New York, 1986.

Warner, Ezra J. *Generals in Gray: Lives of the Confederate Commanders.* Baton Rouge, La., 1959.

Webb, Walter Prescott, and H. Bailey Carroll, eds. *The Handbook of Texas.* 2 vols. Austin, Tex., 1952.

MARVIN SCHULTZ

ROBERTSON, JEROME BONAPARTE (1815–1891), brigadier general. Robertson was born March 14, 1815, in Woodford County, Kentucky. Because of the early death of his father, he became a hatter's apprentice but studied medicine and graduated from Transylvania University in 1835. The next year he fought with Kentucky volunteers in the Texas Revolution and decided to relocate there as a doctor. He served in the legislature and became a delegate to the secession convention.

When the Civil War began, Robertson was elected captain of the First Company, Fifth Texas Infantry, which became part of the famed Texas Brigade in the Army of Northern Virginia. Robertson rose rapidly, led the regiment in the Seven Days' Battles, was wounded at Second Manassas, and was promoted to brigadier general on November 1, 1862. By the time of the Gettysburg engagement, he had succeeded John Bell Hood in command; he was slightly wounded in the battle. When the Texans accompanied James Longstreet to Georgia, Robertson fought at Chickamauga. Because Robertson was a Hood protégé, complex command rivalries caused Longstreet to become dissatisfied with him, and in January 1864 Robertson was arrested for "conduct highly prejudicial to good order and military discipline." Robertson, however, was transferred to Texas where he took command of the Reserve Corps.

Following the war, Robertson practiced medicine, served as state superintendent of the Bureau of Immigration, and engaged in railroad building. He died at the home of his son, Felix Huston Robertson, in Waco on January 7, 1891, and is buried there in Oakwood Cemetery.

BIBLIOGRAPHY

McMurry, Richard M. *John Bell Hood and the War for Southern Independence.* Lexington, Ky., 1982.

Piston, William Garrett. *Lee's Tarnished Lieutenant: James Longstreet and His Place in Southern History.* Athens, Ga., 1987.

Simpson, Harold B. *Hood's Texas Brigade: Lee's Grenadier Guard.* Waco, Tex., 1970.

Wright, Marcus J., comp., and Harold B. Simpson, ed. *Texas in the War, 1861–1865.* Hillsboro, Tex., 1965.

ANNE J. BAILEY

ROBINSON, CORNELIUS (1805–1867), congressman from Alabama. Born on September 25, 1805, in Wadesboro, North Carolina, Robinson received his LL.B. in 1824 from the University of North Carolina but never practiced law. He served in the Indian War of 1836 as a captain and in the Mexican War as a brigadier general. Throughout the antebellum period he operated a planting and commission business in Mobile, Alabama. A supporter of secession, he served in the Alabama secession convention and in the Provisional Confederate Congress after the resignation of John G. Shorter, who became Alabama governor. Robinson was a member of the Post Office Committee. He resigned in January 1862 because of poor health. He did not seek election to the permanent Confederate Congress and held minor military posts through the remainder of the war. After the war he was a planter in Lowndes County, Alabama. He died on July 29, 1867, at Church Hill, Alabama.

BIBLIOGRAPHY

Owen, Thomas McAdory. *History of Alabama and Dictionary of Alabama Biography.* 4 vols. Chicago, 1921.

Wakelyn, Jon L. *Biographical Dictionary of the Confederacy.* Edited by Frank E. Vandiver. Westport, Conn., 1977.

Warner, Ezra J., and W. Buck Yearns. *Biographical Register of the Confederate Congress.* Baton Rouge, La., 1975.

SARAH WOOLFOLK WIGGINS

RODDEY, PHILIP DALE (1826–1897), brigadier general. Roddey was born at Moulton, Alabama, on April 2, 1826. He had little or no formal education and tried a variety of jobs: tailor, sheriff, and steamboat deckhand.

In 1861, Roddey organized a cavalry company and was elected its captain. During the first years of the war, his men served largely as scouts, although they acted as Gen. Braxton Bragg's personal escort during the Battle of Shiloh. Roddey fought in Mississippi during the latter part of 1862, earning a commission as colonel of the Fourth Alabama Cavalry in December.

In April and May 1863, Roddey performed with distinction in Maj. Gen. Nathan Bedford Forrest's pursuit of Col. Abel D. Streight's Federal raiders. He received a promotion to brigadier general on August 3, 1863, and saw action at Chickamauga and Chattanooga as part of Brig. Gen. Joseph Wheeler's cavalry command. In 1864, he fought with Forrest at Brice's Cross Roads and in Gen. John Bell Hood's Tennessee campaign. Finally, in the spring of 1865, Roddey assisted Forrest in the defense of Selma, Alabama.

Following Roddey's surrender in May 1865, he engaged in business in New York. He died while in London, England, on business on July 20, 1897.

Philip Dale Roddey. Library of Congress

BIBLIOGRAPHY

Bearss, Edwin C. *Forrest at Brice's Cross Roads.* Dayton, Ohio, 1979.

Henry, Robert Selph. *"First with the Most" Forrest.* Indianapolis, 1944.

Johnson, Allen, and Dumas Malone, eds. *Dictionary of American Biography.* New York, 1937–1964.

Wills, Brian Steel. *A Battle from the Start: The Life of Nathan Bedford Forrest.* New York, 1992.

Wyeth, John Allan. *Life of General Nathan Bedford Forrest.* New York, 1899. Reprint, Baton Rouge, La., 1989.

Brian S. Wills

RODES, ROBERT (1829–1864), major general. Robert Emmett Rodes was born March 29, 1829, in Lynchburg, Virginia, and was educated at Virginia Military Institute. He was working as a civil engineer in Alabama just before the war and early in 1861 raised a company of volunteer infantry that became part of the Fifth Alabama Infantry. Rodes was commissioned colonel of that regiment on May 11 and led it to Virginia the following month. Colonel Rodes had no opportunity for distinction at First Manassas, being on the quiet far right with Richard S. Ewell, but he so impressed his superiors during the early stages of the war that he won promotion to brigadier general to date from October 21, 1861.

Rodes fought with distinction at Seven Pines despite a painful and serious wound. He returned to command briefly during the Seven Days' Battles but reopened the wound and was forced to convalesce for more than two months. Rodes rejoined the army in Maryland just in time to coordinate brilliantly the defense of the northern flank of Turner's Gap at South Mountain. At Sharpsburg three days later, Rodes's Brigade desperately defended half of the famous Bloody Lane. He played a minor role at Fredericksburg, but at Chancellorsville he occupied center stage in Thomas J. ("Stonewall") Jackson's mighty flank attack, commanding the leading division as its senior brigadier. Immediately after the battle Rodes received promotion to major general.

As a division commander, Robert Rodes became one of the most popular and respected officers in Robert E. Lee's army. A member of Stonewall Jackson's staff wrote home of Rodes: "I like him so much. He is very much admired by all and very popular." A subordinate who described Rodes's stern discipline (including holding a loaded pistol to the head of a cowardly officer) also called the general "one of the bravest and best officers" in the service. Part of his appeal derived from his strongly martial appearance. A member of J. E. B. Stuart's staff called Rodes one of the two "most splendid looking soldiers of the war" and an artillery major described him as "a man of very striking appearance . . . and martial bearing."

Rodes's first battle at his new rank opened spectacularly

Robert Rodes. Library of Congress

at Gettysburg, where his division arrived at a propitious time and place to attack the exposed Federal position on Oak Ridge on July 1. The general's performance on July 2, during which he accomplished little, has been the subject of the sole recurring criticism of his activities during the entire war. He commanded ably in the small-scale operations of late 1863 and early 1864 and then stood as one of Lee's strongest bulwarks in the campaign through the Wilderness and Spotsylvania toward Richmond.

Rodes and his division accompanied Jubal Early to the Shenandoah Valley in June 1864, and in that theater they added notably to their reputation. On September 19 a bullet in the head instantly killed Rodes during fighting east of Winchester. The army's chief of artillery later asserted that the loss of the battle that day was directly traceable to the general's death. In fitting encomium to the fallen leader, a member of Early's staff wrote in a letter to his wife, "Rodes was the best Division commander in the Army of N. Va. & was worthy of & capable for any position in it." That judgment still rings true after the passage of more than a century.

BIBLIOGRAPHY

Freeman, Douglas S. *Lee's Lieutenants: A Study in Command.* 3 vols. New York, 1942–1944. Reprint, New York, 1986.

Grimes, Bryan. *Extracts of Letters of Major-General Grimes to His Wife.* Raleigh, N.C., 1883.

Peyton, Green. "Robert E. Rodes." In *Memorial, V.M.I.* Edited by Charles D. Walker. Philadelphia, 1875.

ROBERT K. KRICK

ROGERS, SAMUEL ST. GEORGE (1832–1880), lieutenant colonel and congressman from Florida.

ROGERS, SAMUEL ST. GEORGE (1832–1880), lieutenant colonel and congressman from Florida. Born in Pulaski, Tennessee, Rogers moved to Columbus, Georgia, where he became a wealthy planter and lawyer. He moved again to Ocala, Florida, in 1851, and served as colonel of the Marion County militia during the conflicts with the Indians in the late 1850s.

A Democrat and ardent secessionist, Rogers served as lieutenant colonel of the Second Florida Infantry from July 1861 until the regiment was reorganized on May 10, 1862. He saw limited action at Yorktown, but was not active in the Peninsular campaign. In 1863, he was a member of the military court of the Department of South Carolina, Georgia, and Florida.

After he resigned from the Second Florida Infantry, he was elected to the Confederate House of Representatives in 1862 and was an active and effective member of many committees including Indian Affairs, Naval Affairs, and Impressments. He supported the Davis administration for the duration and returned to his plantation when the war ended. He campaigned actively for Democratic candidates after the war but held no political office. He died in Terre Haute, Indiana, on September 11, 1880.

BIBLIOGRAPHY

Alexander, Thomas B., and Richard E. Beringer. *The Anatomy of the Confederate Congress: A Study of the Influences of Member Characteristics on Legislative Voting Behavior, 1861–1865.* Nashville, Tenn., 1972.

Ott, Eloise R., and Louis Hickman Chazal. *Ocali Country, Kingdom of the Sun: A History of Marion County, Florida, 1559–1965.* Ocala, Fla., 1966.

Wakelyn, Jon L. *Biographical Dictionary of the Confederacy.* Edited by Frank E. Vandiver. Westport,Conn., 1977.

Warner, Ezra J., and W. Buck Yearns. *Biographical Register of the Confederate Congress.* Baton Rouge, La., 1975.

ARCH FREDRIC BLAKEY

ROMAN, ANDRÉ BIENVENU (1795–1866), governor of Louisiana and member of the 1861 peace commission. Born on March 5, 1795, in St. Landry Parish, Roman was the son of creole planter Jacques Etienne Roman and Marie Louise Patin. He grew up in St. James Parish and, in 1815, graduated from St. Mary's College in Maryland. The next year he married Aimee Françoise Parent and settled on a sugar plantation in St. James Parish.

In 1818, Roman won election to the Louisiana House of Representatives, serving as Speaker for several years. In 1831 he wrestled his way to the leadership of the creole political faction in Louisiana and was elected governor in a campaign directed by Henry Clay. Roman served until 1835 and won reelection in 1839. As governor, he presided over numerous improvements in the state. Also a noted agriculturalist, Roman built Oak Alley Plantation and established experimental farms.

A Whig, Roman was moderate on the abolition issue and opposed disunion. As a delegate to the Louisiana secession convention, he voted against leaving the Union. Nevertheless, the former governor could not abandon his home state and cast his lot with the Confederacy. In 1861, Roman accepted an appointment from the Confederate Congress to serve as a peace commissioner. Composed of Roman, John Forsyth, and Martin J. Crawford, the commission tried to reach a peaceful compromise with the United States. Secretary of State William H. Seward delayed meeting with them, and the firing on Fort Sumter ended the commission's mission.

Too old to further serve the Confederacy, Roman retired to his plantation. His home area fell to Union forces in 1862, but he refused to take an oath of allegiance. By the end of the war his fortune was wrecked, and he accepted an appointment as recorder of deeds and mortgages in New

Orleans. He died in that city while walking down Dumaine Street on January 28, 1866.

[*See also* Washington Peace Conference.]

BIBLIOGRAPHY

"A. B. Roman of Louisiana." *De Bow's Review* 11 (October 1851): 436–443.

Arthur, S. C., and G. C. H. Kernion. *Old Families of Louisiana.* New Orleans, 1931.

Gayarre, Charles E. A. *History of Louisiana.* Vol. 4. New York, 1866.

Tregle, Joseph G., Jr. "André Bienvenu Roman." In *The Louisiana Governors.* Edited by Joseph G. Dawson III. Baton Rouge, La., 1990.

KEVIN S. FONTENOT

ROMAN CATHOLIC CHURCH. Clustered in southern Maryland, in the Kentucky bluegrass region, along the Gulf coast, and along the lower south Atlantic coast, Roman Catholics had been among the earliest settlers and slave owners in the Old South. The mixture of Spanish, French, and, by the early nineteenth century, Irish inhabitants of New Orleans and southern Louisiana created divisions among those ethnic Catholics. But those Louisianans, who made up a majority of the Catholics in slaveholding states, would contribute important political, military, planter, and business leaders to the antebellum South.

During the antebellum period poor Irish Catholic immigrants held laboring jobs in the inland river towns, and German Catholics moved to the rich farmlands of central Texas. There seemed never enough priests and churches to tend the growing flock. On the eve of the Civil War, despite class and ethnic divisions, and hostility from Protestants, over fifty thousand parishioners and eleven bishops lived in the nine Southern dioceses. In the secession crisis the priests and bishops remained neutral, although they defended state rights and the scriptural arguments for slavery.

The Northern and Southern branches went their separate ways during the war, as a number of Northern bishops opposed the Southern church leaders' position on slavery. But the Catholic doctrine of loyalty to regional interests and deference to local hierarchy discouraged the formation of a separate Southern church. Most Southern bishops and twenty-eight priest-chaplains actively supported the Confederate cause. On behalf of the Confederate government Bishop Patrick Lynch of Charleston traveled to Rome to request that the pope oppose recruitment of Irish to fight for the Union. Perhaps because they were fearful of undue Protestant influence, the bishops distributed a number of religious pamphlets to appeal to Catholic troops. Chaplain Abram Ryan of Georgia wrote angry war poems defending Southern values and urging Catholic soldiers to resist the Union aggressors to the bitter end. Other clergy and nuns served as nurses and hospital administrators near the front lines. Nuns often traveled with the armies as nurses.

The Civil War proved costly to both the church and lay Catholics. Northern troops occupied and often destroyed church orphanages, convents, and schools. The German Catholics of Texas who opposed the war felt the brunt of Southern nativist sentiment. Bishop William H. Elder of Natchez was arrested and imprisoned for refusing in his sermons to recognize the Union president.

When the war ended, Bishop Augustin Verot of Savannah continued his earlier support for reforms of black life, calling for the education of former slaves and their inclusion in the life of the church. At the Second Plenary Council at Baltimore in 1866, the Northern and Southern church leaders talked of mutual cooperation to rebuild the Southern church, but no one offered a plan of missionary outreach to the ex-slaves. Southern priests even refused communion to black soldiers. Hierarchical teachings and lack of a preaching tradition also diminished the church's appeal for blacks. Church interest in the ex-slaves also waned because of the need to minister to the growing numbers of immigrants from the Northern states and western Europe. The clergy again grew concerned with the religious and ethnic tensions that existed in the heavily Protestant South. The Roman Catholic church thus remained marginal to both blacks and whites in a postwar South of religious piety and fundamentalism.

BIBLIOGRAPHY

Blied, Benjamin J. *Catholics in the Civil War.* Milwaukee, 1945.

Maxwell, John. *Slavery and the Catholic Church.* London, 1975.

Stepsis, Ursula, and Dolores Liptak, eds. *Pioneer Healers: The History of Women Religious in American Health Care.* New York, 1989.

Wakelyn, Jon L. "Catholic Elites in the Slaveholding South." In *Catholics in the Old South.* Edited by Randall M. Miller and Jon L. Wakelyn. Macon, Ga., 1983.

JON L. WAKELYN

ROSS, LAWRENCE SULLIVAN (1838–1898), major general and postwar governor of Texas. Born September 27, 1838, in Bretonsport, Iowa, "Sul" Ross moved with his family to the Republic of Texas the following year. He studied at Baylor University in Texas and completed his education at Wesleyan University in Florence, Alabama. As a young man, Ross earned a reputation as a dashing Indian fighter and Texas Ranger captain.

Upon secession Ross volunteered for duty but took time to marry Elizabeth Tinsely of Waco. In the fall of 1861, he became major of the Sixth Texas Cavalry and the next spring participated in the Elkhorn Tavern campaign. On May 24, he became colonel of the regiment. In the fall 1862 campaign for Corinth, Mississippi, Ross distinguished himself on several occasions. The following spring, he was again at the forefront of battle, leading his men at the Battle of Thompson's Station on March 5, 1863, and earning command of a brigade including the Sixth Texas and First Mississippi cavalries. For the next several months, Ross's brigade raided Union supply lines in central Tennessee. He was promoted to brigadier general on December 21, his command composed of four Texas cavalries.

In early 1864, Ross and his men again served in Mississippi, resisting William Tecumseh Sherman's advance on Meridian and engaging in several heated fights. In late spring, Ross and his men returned to Georgia, again to oppose Sherman. The engagement at Rome on May 17 began three months of constant skirmishing for the Texans. Ross narrowly escaped capture at Newnan on July 30. He served in Tennessee and Mississippi for the rest of the war, surrendering his command at Jackson on May 13, 1865.

Ross returned to Texas where he served alternately as a sheriff and state senator, and as governor from 1887 to 1891. Afterward he became president of Texas A&M University. Ross died on January 3, 1898.

BIBLIOGRAPHY

Benner, Judith Ann. *Sul Ross: Soldier, Statesman, Educator.* College Station, Tex., 1983.

Davis, William C., ed. *The Confederate General.* Gettysburg, Pa., 1991.

Evans, Clement A., ed. *Confederate Military History.* 12 vols. Atlanta, 1899. Extended ed. in 19 vols. Wilmington, N.C., 1987–1989.

DONALD S. FRAZIER

ROSSER, THOMAS LAFAYETTE (1836–1910), major general. Rosser, who was born October 15, 1836, near Lynchburg, Virginia, stood within a few weeks of graduating from the U.S. Military Academy when his adopted state of Texas seceded. He served the Confederacy as a lieutenant and then as a captain in the Washington Artillery of New Orleans for more than a year before being elected colonel of the Fifth Virginia Cavalry on June 24, 1862. The young officer caught J. E. B. Stuart's eye and prospered under the cavalry chief's steady support and recommendations—though grumbling the entire time that Stuart was not pressing his case firmly enough. Stuart's constant applause for Rosser resulted finally in a commission as brigadier general to date from September 28, 1863.

Rosser's subordinates invariably attested to the general's bravery, but with almost as much unanimity they complained of his incompetence, particularly when he assumed division command in 1864. Rosser "knows no more about putting a command into a fight than a school boy," wrote one field-grade officer who also openly admired the general's valor. During Jubal Early's 1864 campaign in the Shenandoah Valley, Rosser undertook the unenviable task of controlling the undisciplined Confederate cavalry in that theater. At Tom's Brook on October 9, 1864, Rosser suffered the most thorough thrashing any large Confederate cavalry force endured in Virginia during the war. Despite that reverse and others, late in October Robert E. Lee, calling Rosser "gallant & zealous," promoted him to major general to date from November 1, 1864. Rosser remained in the valley until March 1865 and then escaped from Appomattox just before Lee's surrender.

After the war Rosser spent some time in the West, where he was closely associated with George Armstrong Custer. He died March 29, 1910, in Charlottesville, Virginia.

BIBLIOGRAPHY

Beane, Thomas O. "Thomas Lafayette Rosser." *Magazine of Albemarle County History* 16 (1957–1958): 25–46.

McDonald, William N. *A History of the Laurel Brigade.* Baltimore, 1907. Reprint, Gaithersburg, Md., 1988.

Rosser, Thomas L. Papers. University of Virginia, Charlottesville.

ROBERT K. KRICK

ROST, PIERRE A. (1797–1868), diplomat. Born in France and a veteran of Napoleon's army, Rost immigrated to Natchez, Mississippi, in 1816 and studied law with Joseph E. Davis, elder brother of the future Confederate president. Moving to Louisiana, he married into a wealthy creole family and secured a state supreme court judgeship (1839 and 1846–1853). These personal connections were Rost's principal credentials, for he is commonly regarded as one of the Confederacy's weakest appointments.

Jefferson Davis named Rost to the Confederacy's first diplomatic mission to Europe with William Lowndes Yancey and A. Dudley Mann on February 27, 1861. The delegation failed to elicit recognition or assistance. Rost participated in England but spent most of his time in France. There he became something of a figure of ridicule because of his naive manner and unwarranted enthusiasm. *"Tout va bien"* ("All goes well") was his standard catchphrase—a posture that became particularly foolish after Union troops captured his own plantation in Louisiana.

Transferred to Spain as envoy extraordinary on August 24, 1861, Rost had no success arguing for aid on the supposed grounds of a "community of Spanish and Southern systems" and "the proximity of the Confederacy to Cuba." Furthermore, Rost found the Iberian climate uncongenial and was debilitated by diabetes. He kept finding spurious excuses to linger in Paris until ordered back to Madrid in March 1862.

By then, Rost's exuberance had turned to despair. He resigned on May 29, 1862, and spent the rest of the war in retirement in France, occasionally corresponding with Davis on diplomatic issues. Afterward, he returned to New Orleans, where he died on September 6, 1868.

BIBLIOGRAPHY

Owsley, Frank L. *King Cotton Diplomacy.* Chicago, 1959.

White, William W., and Joseph O. Baylen. "Pierre A. Rost's Mission to Europe, 1861–1863." *Louisiana History* 2 (Summer 1961): 322–331.

James J. Horgan

ROUDANEZ BROTHERS. Jean-Baptiste Roudanez (1815–1895) and Dr. Louis Charles Roudanez (1823–1890) were newspaper publishers in Louisiana. After the Union occupation of New Orleans in April 1862, Dr. Louis Charles Roudanez joined with several other influential free men of color to launch *L'Union,* a biweekly French-language newspaper. In the inaugural issue, Roudanez and his colleagues condemned slavery, blasted the Confederacy, and expressed solidarity with French and Haitian radicals. They urged free men of color to enlist in the Union army. Roudanez's radicalism stemmed in part from his experiences abroad.

The son of Louis Roudanez, a white, well-to-do French merchant, and Aimée Potens, a free woman of color, Roudanez was born in St. James Parish and educated in New Orleans. Sent to France to study medicine, he attended the Faculté de Médecine de Paris, where his two most important mentors were renowned proponents of French republicanism. In the 1848 French revolution, Roudanez and his classmates took to the barricades. During the 1850s, he returned to New Orleans to pursue a career despite the deteriorating status of the city's free black population. By the time of the Civil War, he had established a highly successful medical practice.

With the Confederate army's retreat from the city, Roudanez and his associates proposed to revolutionize race relations. In the pages of *L'Union,* they demanded voting rights and urged the nation to follow the example of France under the Second Republic when the French government abolished slavery and extended suffrage to free men of color and former slaves.

In the winter of 1863, when Gen. Nathaniel P. Banks, commander of the Department of the Gulf and the architect of wartime reconstruction in Louisiana, stymied free black demands for voting rights, Roudanez and his colleagues prepared to take their claims to Washington. In December they collected the signatures of a thousand free black property holders and twenty-two white Unionists. In their resolution, the petitioners urged the president and the Congress to extend suffrage to free blacks.

In mid-February 1864 Roudanez's older brother, Jean-Baptiste, a mechanical engineer who had worked on sugar plantations before the war, and E. Arnold Bertonneau, a former Union officer who had resigned in protest over the army's treatment of black soldiers, carried the petition to the nation's capital. On March 12 Louis Roudanez and Bertonneau met with Abraham Lincoln. Though they failed to obtain a commitment, the two men impressed the president. After the meeting, Lincoln privately encouraged Louisiana Governor Michael Hahn to introduce limited black suffrage. The president's influence notwithstanding, the Louisiana constitutional convention of 1864 rejected black voting rights.

The Roudanezes redoubled their efforts. Simultaneous with the adjournment of the convention in July, the brothers inaugurated a new newspaper, the *New Orleans Tribune.* The French and English-language triweekly, owned by Dr. Roudanez and published by Jean-Baptiste Roudanez, replaced the financially troubled *L'Union.* During the war, the Roudanezes and their supporters advanced a program of social, economic, and political change that included equal access to public schools and transportation, land ownership and farmer cooperatives for the freedmen, and universal male suffrage.

Though the Roudanezes played a key role in organizing Louisiana's Republican party in the aftermath of the war, they opposed the state's Reconstruction governor, Henry Clay Warmoth, a Republican moderate who stymied civil rights legislation and courted white Democrats at the expense of black Republicans. With the state on the verge of anarchy after Warmoth's impeachment in 1872, Dr. Roudanez appeared at the head of a bipartisan, biracial reform effort, the 1873 Louisiana unification movement, in an ill-fated attempt to secure social and political equality for black Louisianians.

BIBLIOGRAPHY

Blassingame, John W. *Black New Orleans, 1860–1880.* Chicago, 1973.

Desdunes, Rodolphe Lucien. *Our People and Our History.* Edited by Dorothea Olga McCants. Baton Rouge, La., 1973.

Hirsch, Arnold R., and Joseph Logsdon. *Creole New Orleans: Race and Americanization.* Baton Rouge, La., 1992.

Houzeau, Jean-Charles. *My Passage at the New Orleans "Tribune."* Edited by David C. Rankin. Baton Rouge, La., 1984.

Roussève, Charles B. *The Negro in Louisiana.* New Orleans, La., 1937.

Caryn Cossé Bell

ROUSSEAU, LAWRENCE (1790–?), navy captain. Rousseau was an early candidate for secretary of the navy because of his long experience as a Union officer. He had been appointed midshipman on January 16, 1809, and promoted to captain in 1837; but he had served at sea only two years after his promotion and not at all since the Mexican War.

As a Louisiana native, he was assigned the task of planning the defense of New Orleans. To assemble a squadron, he inspected a number of vessels for their suitability for conversion to naval service. Organization of the New Orleans station was in disarray, however, and areas of command were ill defined. As naval commander, he was subordinate to the army commander. Rousseau did not act incisively to secure the navy's position, and he is therefore assessed a share of responsibility for the fall of New Orleans.

On August 1, 1861, Rousseau took command of the Bureau of Orders and Detail, where his long experience in the U.S. Navy would serve him well in managing the personnel decisions handled by this office. The seniority of the position and its authority over assignments, promotions, and discipline made him the highest ranking adviser to the secretary of the navy. But scarcely three weeks after his assignment, on August 23, Rousseau was relieved of active command because of ill health. He was posted to Jackson and Savannah in 1862, to Selma from 1862 to 1863, and to Mobile from 1864 to 1865. Except for his service on the board of inquiry appointed to investigate the destruction of *Virginia,* he receives little or no further mention in the official records of naval activity in the Confederacy.

BIBLIOGRAPHY

Register of Officers of the Confederate States Navy, 1861–1865. Washington, D.C., 1931.

Wells, Tom H. *The Confederate Navy: A Study in Organization.* University, Ala., 1971.

MAXINE TURNER

ROYSTON, GRANDISON D. (1809–1889), congressman from Arkansas. Grandison Delaney Royston was born December 9, 1809, in Tennessee and moved to Arkansas in 1832. He ultimately settled at Washington, Hempstead County, where he was a prominent attorney, planter, and educator. He was a member of the state constitutional convention of 1836 and served periodically in the state legislature through the antebellum period. In 1860 he opposed secession, although after the election of Abraham Lincoln he supported a petition in the legislature asking Congress for constitutional amendments guaranteeing the protection of slavery. Royston ran for the secession convention but was defeated by A. H. Carrigan and Rufus K. Garland. Like most other prominent Arkansas Unionists, Royston went with his state in 1861.

In November 1861, he was elected to the House of Representatives of the First Congress, where he joined other state congressmen in protesting martial law in the state in 1862 and generally looked after measures of interest to the state. He was a supporter of legislation introduced by the Davis administration, including the controversial Conscription Act of April 1862. He backed increased taxation to support the military. With the rest of the Arkansas delegation, however, he opposed the suspension of the writ of habeas corpus, particularly after Gen. Thomas C. Hindman's actions within the state. In 1863 he ran for reelection but refused to campaign because he believed that to do so would be divisive. He was defeated again by Garland, who campaigned on an anti-Davis platform. Royston returned to Washington where he practiced law.

After the war Royston participated in Democratic politics and the return of that party to power in 1874. He died at Washington, August 14, 1889.

BIBLIOGRAPHY

Hallum, John. *Biographical and Pictorial History of Arkansas.* Albany, N.Y., 1887.

Newberry, Farrar. "The 'Grand Old Roman.'" *Arkansas Historical Quarterly* 18 (Spring 1951): 26–43.

CARL H. MONEYHON

RUFFIN, EDMUND (1794–1865), agricultural reformer, proslavery ideologue, and Southern nationalist. Born into a prominent Tidewater Virginia planter family, Ruffin earned wide acclaim during the first half of the nineteenth century as the preeminent agricultural reformer in the Old South.

When his inherited lands on the James River proved unresponsive to traditional ameliorative practices, Ruffin, in 1818, inaugurated a series of experiments with marl, a shell-like deposit containing calcium carbonate which neutralized soil acidity and enabled sterile soils to become once again productive. When the results proved efficacious, he published his findings, first in *An Essay on Calcareous Manures* (1832) and then in his celebrated agricultural journal, the *Farmers' Register* (1833–1842). After conducting an agricultural survey of South Carolina at the request of Governor James H. Hammond, Ruffin acquired a new tract of land on the Pamunkey River, naming it appropriately Marlbourne, and proceeded to transform it into a model estate. Subsequently, he was instrumental in reviving the Virginia State Agricultural Society and was four times elected president of that body.

Upon retiring from the management of his agricultural enterprises in the mid-1850s, Ruffin turned his attention to politics. Strongly opinionated, little disposed to compromise, and sharply critical of democracy, Ruffin had eschewed active participation in politics, serving only an abbreviated term as state senator in the 1820s. By mid-

EDMUND RUFFIN. *HARPER'S PICTORIAL HISTORY OF THE GREAT REBELLION*

century, however, he, like many others in his class, had become alarmed by the increasingly intemperate attacks upon Southern institutions by the abolitionists and their political allies in the North. Sufficiently moderate in 1831 to have interceded on behalf of a black wrongfully accused of complicity in the Nat Turner revolt, Ruffin later assumed an inflexible proslavery posture. Convinced that slavery was the very cornerstone of Southern society and that its future could not be guaranteed within the existing Union, Ruffin became an outspoken secessionist.

Although he had adopted a secessionist stance at least as early as 1850, it was during the last four years of the antebellum period that Ruffin's crusade for disunion became most intense. Lacking the oratorical skills of fellow fire-eater William Lowndes Yancey or the political influence of Robert Barnwell Rhett, Sr., Ruffin resorted instead to personal conversation and the power of his written prose to influence the course of events. Just as he had earlier propagated the gospel of marl so now he proselytized for his dream of Southern independence. In hotel lobbies from Washington to Charleston, at Virginia summer resorts, at the Southern Commercial Convention in Montgomery, on trains and steamboats—everywhere he traveled—Ruffin was indefatigable in his effort to persuade Southerners that their only salvation lay in separate nationhood. Even more significant were his voluminous writings. In addition to numerous articles and editorials prepared for newspapers in Richmond and Charleston, these included three lengthy pamphlets and two major articles, one of them serialized in *De Bow's Review,* as well as a 426-page political novel, *Anticipations of the Future,* which had been inspired by John Brown's raid on Harpers Ferry.

Despite such herculean efforts, Ruffin appears to have had only minimal influence in effecting secession. Certainly he had little in his home state of Virginia, as he later bitterly lamented. His writings, prolific as they were, seem to have attracted little notice from the public, and his attempt in 1858, in concert with Yancey, to mobilize public opinion behind the secessionist cause through a League of United Southerners proved ineffectual. Still, he remained active and highly visible. Excited by the events at Harpers Ferry, he enlisted in the Corps of Cadets of the Virginia Military Institute for one day in order to witness the execution of Brown. Subsequently, he dispatched pikes seized from the conspirators to the governors of all slaveholding states with the injunction that they be displayed as a "sample of the favors designed for us by our Northern Brethren."

It was only after the sectional crisis reached a climax in 1860 and 1861 that Ruffin finally received the public adulation so long denied him. Although he began to receive compliments and honors wherever he traveled outside of Virginia, it was in South Carolina that he was most appreciated. When that state became the first to secede he was there to participate in the celebration, and, on the eve of Abraham Lincoln's inauguration, he again departed for Charleston, vowing never to return to his native state until it joined the Confederacy. With his destiny now bound inextricably to that of his adopted state, it was altogether fitting that the venerable Ruffin was accorded the honor of firing the first artillery shot against Fort Sumter—a distinction that, though still controversial, was recognized generally by his contemporaries on both sides.

The notoriety engendered by Ruffin's role in the Sumter engagement elevated him to the status of a popular hero in the South. Rejoining his South Carolina unit, the Palmetto Guard, in time for the Manassas campaign, the aging fire-eater once again performed symbolic military service for his beloved Confederacy, firing several artillery rounds at the fleeing Federals as they retreated over the suspension bridge at Cub Run. Plagued, however, by physical infirmities and wartime tribulations, he was soon reduced to the role of a passive observer of the momentous conflict he had helped to instigate. Family properties were pillaged during the successive Federal campaigns against Richmond, and Ruffin was compelled to seek refuge as an exile, settling eventually at Redmoor, a small farm situated about thirty-five miles west of the capital. Despite the deteriorating military situation, the increasingly embittered Ruffin remained steadfast in his commitment to the cause of

Southern independence until that dream was shattered at nearby Appomattox.

With the demise of the Confederacy, Ruffin no longer had any reason to live. Despondent over the deaths of family members and his own declining health, reduced to virtual destitution by enemy depredations during the war, and fearful lest he become both a political and a pecuniary burden to his eldest son, Ruffin had long contemplated suicide. After the fall of Richmond his resolve became fixed, and for more than two months he planned methodically for the act of self-destruction, which he carried out shortly after noon on June 17, 1865. Thus did Ruffin, despite numerous reverses and disappointments, once again assume command of his own destiny. Contrary to popular belief, Ruffin did not wrap himself in a Confederate flag before firing the shot that ended his life.

BIBLIOGRAPHY

Allmendinger, David F., Jr. *Ruffin: Family and Reform in the Old South.* New York, 1990.

Allmendinger, David F., Jr., and William K. Scarborough. "The Day Ruffin Died." *Virginia Magazine of History and Biography* 97 (1989): 75–96.

Craven, Avery O. *Edmund Ruffin, Southerner: A Study in Secession.* New York, 1932. Reprint, Baton Rouge, La., 1966.

Mitchell, Betty L. *Edmund Ruffin: A Biography.* Bloomington, Ind., 1981.

Scarborough, William K., ed. *The Diary of Edmund Ruffin.* 3 vols. Baton Rouge, La., 1972–1989.

Walther, Eric H. *The Fire-Eaters.* Baton Rouge, La., 1992.

WILLIAM K. SCARBOROUGH

RUFFIN, THOMAS (1820–1863), congressman from North Carolina and colonel. Born near Louisburg, North Carolina, September 9, 1820, Ruffin was a distant cousin of Thomas Ruffin, chief justice of the North Carolina Supreme Court. He graduated from the University of North Carolina in 1841 and began practicing law in Goldsboro, but moved to Missouri soon afterward. Returning to North Carolina in 1850, he ran unsuccessfully as a Democrat for the U.S. House of Representatives in 1851. Elected to Congress in 1853, he served until March 1861.

A staunch advocate of Southern rights, Ruffin had publicly declared in 1859 that North Carolina should secede if a Republican won the presidency. In May 1861 he was elected by the secession convention to the Provisional Congress. Despite his long experience in the national legislature, Ruffin did not play a leading role in the Confederate Congress. Unimpressive as a debater, he seldom spoke and offered no bill or amendment. There is no record of his service on any congressional committee. He was an early opponent of the centralizing tendencies of the Davis administration and voted against a majority of its measures.

Declining to run for reelection, Ruffin entered the army as a captain in the First North Carolina Cavalry Regiment and rose to the rank of colonel. He served with the Army of Northern Virginia and was wounded at Gettysburg. After briefly returning to Goldsboro, he rejoined the army and was wounded at Auburn (Catlett's Station), Virginia, in a cavalry skirmish preceding the Battle of Bristoe Station. Taken prisoner, Ruffin died in Alexandria, Virginia, on October 13, 1863.

BIBLIOGRAPHY

Alexander, Thomas B., and Richard E. Beringer. *The Anatomy of the Confederate Congress: A Study of the Influences of Member Characteristics on Legislative Voting Behavior, 1861–1865.* Nashville, Tenn., 1972.

Hill, D. H., Jr. *North Carolina.* Vol. 4 of *Confederate Military History.* Edited by Clement A. Evans. Atlanta, 1899. Vol. 5 of extended ed. Wilmington, N.C., 1987.

Wakelyn, Jon L. *Biographical Dictionary of the Confederacy.* Edited by Frank E. Vandiver. Westport, Conn., 1977.

Warner, Ezra J., and W. Buck Yearns. *Biographical Register of the Confederate Congress.* Baton Rouge, La., 1975.

THOMAS E. JEFFREY

RUGGLES, DANIEL (1810–1897), brigadier general. A native of Barre, Massachusetts, where he was born January 31, 1810, Ruggles graduated in the 1833 class at West Point. He served in the Fifth Infantry in the Seminole and Mexican wars and emerged from the latter as brevet lieutenant colonel because of gallantry at Churubusco and Chapultepec. He married Richardetta Hooe of King George County, Virginia, and bought a home in Fredericksburg. While on sick leave there in 1859 and 1860, Ruggles encouraged the organization of local militia companies for the defense of his adopted state. After Virginia's secession, Ruggles took charge of the state's defenses along the Rappahannock River line.

On August 9, 1861, Ruggles was promoted to brigadier general and sent to the western theater. He fought at Shiloh, where Braxton Bragg reprimanded him for letting his troops get out of hand, and at Baton Rouge, where John C. Breckinridge praised his efforts. Heavy-bearded and stern-looking in appearance, gruff by nature, Ruggles was not a popular leader. His military secretary called him "an *old brute*" and added: "Being an old army officer and a New Englander, he had no conscience nor mercy on anyone."

Largely because of his personality, Ruggles spent the next two years performing administrative duties in western districts and departments. On March 30, 1865, after a long and embarrassing period of waiting for a new assignment, Ruggles became commissary general of prisoners.

DANIEL RUGGLES. LIBRARY OF CONGRESS

With the exception of a four-year residence in Texas, he lived quietly in Fredericksburg after the war. In the 1880s Ruggles served a term on West Point's board of visitors. He died June 1, 1897, at the age of eighty-eight and was buried in Fredericksburg.

BIBLIOGRAPHY

Hotchkiss, Jed. *Virginia.* Vol. 3 of *Confederate Military History.* Edited by Clement A. Evans. Atlanta, 1899. Vol. 4 of extended ed. Wilmington, N.C., 1987.

Stuart, Meriwether, ed. "The Military Orders of Daniel Ruggles." *Virginia Magazine of History and Biography* 69 (1961): 149–180.

JAMES I. ROBERTSON, JR.

RULES OF WAR. Even after a full year of fighting, few officers on either side of the Civil War had more than a functional understanding of the customary principles of war and the rights of combatants and noncombatants. In April 1863, Abraham Lincoln approved General Orders No. 100 (the Lieber Code) establishing guidelines for field commanders and soldiers of the Union army, but Confederate Secretary of War James A. Seddon rejected them out of hand in June, saying they encouraged unrestricted warfare. Thereafter, although both sides continued to stake out severely conflicting theoretical interpretations of the rules of war, they in fact worked toward the middle and treated each other with a remarkable degree of civility until the summer of 1864.

The war began taking an ugly turn for the South then, but only several months after Ulysses S. Grant had changed his predecessors' strategy from attacking at various weak points to a cordon offensive that attacked along the entire southern perimeter. The Confederates, who had been so good at drawing Union forces into set piece battles at places of their choosing, were now forced onto the defensive because manpower shortages left them unable to respond effectively to broad Northern thrusts. In addition, the extensive use of rifled bores, repeating rifles, machine guns, and even flamethrowers had been exacting especially heavy tolls on Confederate formations, which were still practicing massed assaults. When this change in the North's strategic doctrine and its deployment of increasingly destructive weapons were coupled with the South's own use of land mines and guerrillas, the reasonably humane war conducted up to that point could legitimately be described as having become a total war.

Nowhere was this more evident than during Philip H. Sheridan's Shenandoah campaign in 1864, when John S. Mosby's raids so ravaged Union supply columns that Sheridan destroyed everything in his path on his way out of the valley. A few months later in November, this scorched-earth policy was repeated on the roads to Atlanta, Savannah, and Columbia (which was truly savaged) after William Tecumseh Sherman concluded—correctly, as it turned out—that subjecting Southern civilians to the psychological stresses of military action would break their will. The South had been holding on until then in the vain hope that Lincoln would be upset in November, but with his reelection, based largely on the results of Sheridan's and Sherman's campaigns, vanished what little hope remained in Richmond for reaching some accommodation with peace advocates in the North.

In effect, while total war for the North in late 1864 meant utilizing every offensive means possible, it forced the South into an almost exclusively defensive strategy that came to rely on units like Mosby's—one of the few innovative tools still left at Robert E. Lee's disposal. At this point, Confederate regiments were so depleted that strategic retaliation on a small scale was the only form of offense showing any positive returns. That many professional soldiers on either side looked with great disfavor upon the activities of Confederate and pro-Confederate guerrillas did little to inhibit these scattered, but well-led and highly imaginative groups from holding down tens of thousands of Union troops in guard duty—several thousand in Missouri alone after 1862. Since this form of combat could be so brutal, however, the South felt a certain moral obligation not to employ it in an unrestricted manner, and its generally restrained use of this alternative may well have been one reason it lost the war.

It was also during the summer campaigns of 1864 that the North hardened its view on total war after learning of the treatment of its prisoners. Few had been taken by either side in the first year of conflict, so opposing field commanders often were able to work out paroles and exchanges immediately after skirmishes that included the wounded, their chaplains, and medical personnel; but after 1862, large battles accounted for such enormous numbers of captives that more permanent structures had to be hastily built. Although conditions at Libby (Richmond, Virginia) were slightly better than average, life in Confederate prisons like Andersonville (Georgia) and Belle Isle (North Carolina) was extremely harsh at best; overcrowding and inadequate supplies of food, water, clothing, medicine, trained guards, and competent administrators led to a 15.5 percent mortality rate. Confederate prisoners, though generally better off than their Union counterparts, still lost about 12 percent of their men in camps like Elvira (New York) and Point Lookout (Maryland).

Unknown to Northern troops, however, the South could barely treat its own wounded by late 1864 because of inadequate hospital facilities. This once led Union Gen. George B. McClellan to offer medical supplies for his wounded being held by Lee. Black Union captives fared the worst, though. Confederate policy in late 1862 denying them and their white officers prisoner-of-war status led initially to their occasional summary execution in the field and to a subsequent suspension of exchanges by the Union in May 1863; but well-publicized retaliations against Confederate prisoners compelled the South, by January 1865, to offer the unrestricted exchange of all prisoners. In fact, the use of cartels for formal exchanges thrived from 1862 until Grant became general in chief in the spring of 1864 and decided that he needed his prisoners back much less than Lee needed his. Ending the cartel was a tough decision to make, but in this attempt to shorten the war, Grant may inadvertently have helped create the very conditions that led to prisons like Andersonville and Fort Delaware.

Maritime law was infinitely more formalized than the corpus of agreements dictating military conduct on land. Lincoln announced a blockade of Southern ports a week after the war began, thus ignoring the advice of U.S. Secretary of the Navy Gideon Welles, who insisted that in doing so, the president had inadvertently conferred the status of belligerency upon the Confederacy. A municipal closure of the ports to commerce would have been preferable, Welles felt, because a blockade was legal only in a time of war, and technically, this was nothing more than a domestic insurrection.

Lincoln, though, realized that a policy of port closure—or "paper blockade" in the words of British Foreign Secretary John Russell—was unenforceable and would serve only to antagonize Great Britain by completely destroying its trade with the South, while coincidentally not legally obligating the British, as neutrals, to honor the act.

Neutral crew members serving aboard neutral blockade runners that had been captured by Union ships were seldom even detained, and the penalty was confined solely to the ship and its cargo. Both were sold after a prize court determined the legitimacy of their capture, and the proceeds were divided among Union crew members. Consequently, even Confederate blockade runners were seldom harmed—and then only if they resisted—making this form of war far less risky than what was happening on the fields of Franklin, Cold Harbor, and the Wilderness.

Following the Crimean War, the Declaration of Paris (April 1856) had established four rules that defined a blockade, abolished privateering, protected enemy goods on neutral carriers, and protected neutral goods on enemy carriers. But because it had failed to exempt from capture by privateer the private property of citizens of belligerent nations, Washington withheld its formal acceptance. After all, the United States could (and, of course, would) attain belligerent status sometime in the future and did not want the property of its subjects confiscated at sea. When Confederate privateers began terrorizing Union shipping in 1861, the Federal government debated hanging their crews as pirates, but reconsidered when faced with the certainty of reprisals by the South. Thereafter, the prosecution of privateers as civilian criminals was abandoned and they were afforded prisoner-of-war status with the same rights of parole and exchange as their landlubber colleagues.

[*See also* Blockade, *overview article;* Guerrilla Warfare; Hand Grenades and Land Mines; Prisoners of War; Torpedoes and Mines.]

BIBLIOGRAPHY

Beringer, Richard E., et al. *Why the South Lost the Civil War.* Athens, Ga., 1986.

Hoffman, Michael H. "The Customary Law of Non-international Armed Conflict: Evidence from the United States Civil War." *International Review of the Red Cross* 277 (July-August 1990): 322–344.

Johnson, Ludwell H. "The Confederacy: What Was It? A View from the Courts." *Civil War History* 32 (1986): 5–13.

Jones, Archer. *Civil War Command and Strategy.* New York, 1992.

McPherson, James C. *Battle Cry of Freedom.* New York, 1988.

Royster, Charles. *The Destructive War: William Tecumseh Sherman, Stonewall Jackson, and the Americans.* New York, 1991.

U.S. War Department. *War of the Rebellion: A Compilation of the Official Records of the Union and Confederate Armies.* Washington, D.C., 1880–1901. Ser. 2, vols. 3, 4, and 6.

JOHN R. CRONIN

RUSSELL, CHARLES WELLS (1818–1867), congressman from Virginia. Russell was born of Irish immigrant parents in Sisterville, Tyler County, Virginia (present-day West Virginia). After attending school in

Wheeling and at Jefferson College in Pennsylvania, Russell taught school in Richmond and then began law practice in Wheeling. He served in the Virginia House of Delegates between 1850 and 1853.

A secessionist Democrat, he represented Wheeling in the Provisional, First, and Second Congresses. For nearly his whole service, he was in the forlorn position of being a refugee congressman for a district under Federal control. Partly as a result, he staunchly supported the Davis administration throughout, and he served ably on the Naval Affairs, Judiciary, and Conference committees. Russell overcame his initial skepticism about conscription and strongly defended it. Similarly, he warmed to the need, as he saw it, for high taxes to underwrite the war effort. In 1864 he advocated a confiscatory in-kind levy on all agricultural production. A constant, and natural, interest for him was the futile effort to win western Virginia for the Confederacy. In the South's extremity, he supported arming the slaves and argued against peace negotiations. In January 1865 Russell succeeded in passing a measure to remove the draft exemption of overseers.

After the war Russell did not return to his native region but prudently spent some time in Canada and then settled in Baltimore, where he practiced law and wrote two novels. He died on November 22, 1867.

BIBLIOGRAPHY

Wakelyn, Jon L. *Biographical Dictionary of the Confederacy.* Edited by Frank E. Vandiver. Westport, Conn., 1977.

Warner, Ezra J., and W. Buck Yearns. *Biographical Register of the Confederate Congress.* Baton Rouge, La., 1975.

NELSON D. LANKFORD

RUSSELL, WILLIAM H. (1820–1907), journalist. Although internationally famous for his coverage of the Crimean War, Russell quickly alienated North and South with his accounts of the early months of the Civil War. He arrived in the United States in March 1861 representing the London *Times.* Concerned about the effect Russell would have on British opinion, Abraham Lincoln personally welcomed him. Present in Charleston during the Fort Sumter crisis, Russell talked with Governor Francis Pickens and other prominent South Carolinians. They impressed him with their belief in victory and their strong conviction (not shared by Russell) that cotton diplomacy would lead to British intervention and recognition of the Confederacy. In May, Russell visited Montgomery where he interviewed Jefferson Davis and other leaders who steadfastly maintained that the South would never return to the Union. Russell's criticism of slavery offended many Southerners, and Mary Boykin Chesnut called him "a licensed slanderer." He became even less popular in the North, however.

Russell's graphic portrayal of the panicked Yankee retreat from First Manassas wounded Northern pride. An enraged *New York Times* labeled him "Bull Run Russell," and he not only received threatening letters but was actually shot at. An irate Secretary of War Edwin Stanton denied Russell a pass to accompany the army. This inability to get to the front probably was responsible for his recall to London in April 1862.

Russell then edited the *Army and Navy Gazette.* It occasionally predicted final victory for the North but consistently argued that a permanent split in the Union was inevitable. As late as mid-November 1864 Russell maintained that despite the South's declining fortunes, Confederate independence was still likely.

BIBLIOGRAPHY

Atkins, John Black. *Life of Sir William Howard Russell.* 2 vols. London, 1911.

Chapman, Caroline. *Russell of the Times: War Dispatches and Diaries.* London, 1984.

Knightley, Phillip. *The First Casualty from Crimea to Vietnam: The War Correspondent as Hero, Propagandist and Myth Maker.* New York, 1975.

Russell, William Howard. *My Diary North and South.* New York, 1863.

Starr, Louis M. *Bohemian Brigade: Civil War Newsmen in Action.* New York, 1954.

CHARLES MCARVER

RUSSIA. Although a major European power, Russia appeared too remote and commercially unimportant to elicit the concern of Confederate leaders. With the outbreak of war in April 1861, moreover, Russian foreign minister Prince Alexander M. Gorchakov announced that Russia would support the Union cause. Russia's pro-Union attitude received reaffirmation when, in November 1862, Russia rejected Louis Napoleon's tripartite proposal for joint French, British, and Russian mediation in the American Civil War. Even so, that month the Confederate government appointed L. Q. C. Lamar as commissioner to Russia on the supposition that the Confederacy could now ask for recognition as a right, not as a favor. "We have," wrote Secretary of State Judah P. Benjamin in his instructions, "conquered our position by the sword." Benjamin encouraged Lamar to confer with commissioners James M. Mason and John Slidell in Europe to determine both the status of European affairs and the wisdom of complying with his instructions.

Lamar reached London in March 1863 only to discover that the governments of Europe were little concerned with America's future. "Lord Palmerston," he wrote, "is far more deeply engrossed with the conferences, jealousies, and rivalries between the leading powers of Europe than with the fate of constitutional government in America." Indeed, the Polish crisis of 1863 seemed to rivet Europe's attention. Although the Russian legation in London was encouraging, Lamar refused to challenge the North's entrenched position in St. Petersburg. In June the Confederate Senate, sharing Lamar's own resentment toward Europe's demeaning behavior, refused to confirm his appointment. This terminated the Confederacy's belated effort to seek recognition in Russia.

BIBLIOGRAPHY

Crook, David Paul. *The North, the South, and the Powers, 1861–1865.* New York, 1974.

Owsley, Frank Lawrence. *King Cotton Diplomacy: Foreign Relations of the Confederate States of America.* Revised by Harriet Chappell Owsley. Chicago, 1959.

NORMAN A. GRAEBNER

RUST, ALBERT (1818–1870), congressman from Arkansas and brigadier general. Born in Virginia, Rust moved to Arkansas in 1837 and became a prominent planter, attorney, and politician in El Dorado, Union County. He was a Democrat and represented his district in the U.S. Congress for two terms (1855–1857 and 1859–1861). In 1860 he supported Stephen A. Douglas for president and urged compromise in the secession crisis. In March 1861, he resigned from Congress and returned home. After the firing on Fort Sumter, Rust shifted his position to favor secession and joined the Confederacy.

ALBERT RUST. LIBRARY OF CONGRESS

The Arkansas secession convention adopted an ordinance of secession in its second session but selected a delegation to the Provisional Congress composed almost totally of men who had originally opposed secession. Rust, one of those chosen, went to Montgomery immediately. As a congressman, Rust was instrumental in having two companies of volunteers that had been raised in Ashley County accepted for Confederate service. He did little more in Congress before he returned to Arkansas to raise eight more companies to join the first two in July 1861, forming the Third Arkansas Infantry. Rust was elected colonel of the regiment. He participated in the Cheat Mountain campaign in the autumn and commanded the left wing of Gen. Henry Rootes Jackson's force in the Battle of Greenbrier River on October 3.

Rust left his regiment in November 1861 to attend a session of Congress at Richmond. When he returned in January 1862, Rust found his men outraged by orders to shift their winter quarters from an established camp to a new one at Romney, Virginia. Rust returned to Richmond to protest the matter to Jefferson Davis, showing a tendency to ignore the chain of command that recurred throughout his military career. Told to use proper channels, Rust resigned, but Davis appealed to him to withdraw his resignation. The president had already decided that he wanted Rust back in Arkansas to lead a brigade composed of several new regiments being raised there. Rust acceded to the president's wishes, and rather than being out of the army he found himself promoted to the rank of brigadier general.

Rust was appointed to the Army of the West and went to DeValls Bluff, Arkansas, where he assumed command of his new brigade, consisting of the Eighteenth, Nineteenth, and Twenty-second Infantry Regiments plus three battalions. He took his brigade to Corinth but then returned to Arkansas to help defend the state against an invading Federal army. Gen. Thomas C. Hindman assigned Rust to command his cavalry and sent them into the northeastern part of the state with orders to devastate the countryside and keep Gen. Samuel Curtis's column from being reinforced. In the Battle of the Cache, July 7, 1862, the Federals, moving toward the Mississippi River to secure their line of supplies, easily pushed Rust's force aside in a battle in which the Confederate units broke and ran. Hindman held Rust responsible for the poor performance of his men and also for Curtis's escape. Hindman complained in his report that General Rust had failed to carry out his assignment of destroying the countryside so that Curtis could not live off of it.

In September 1862, Rust was sent back to his old brigade, now a part of the division of Maj. Gen. John C. Breckinridge.

He was with the brigade in the Battle of Corinth in October 1862 but demonstrated no particular skills as a commander. He was popular among his men, however. When a vacancy at the head of the division opened up in January 1863, the officers of his brigade petitioned President Davis for his appointment as a major general and commander of their division. But his failure at the Cache, his unexceptional leadership of his brigade, and his reputation for not getting along with his senior officers ensured that he did not receive the promotion. These problems apparently limited his military career.

In March 1863, Rust seemed to have a new opportunity for promotion and a senior command when Gen. Sterling Price requested that he be reassigned to Little Rock to lead the Arkansas troops in Price's command. Price asked for Rust because he considered it important to name officers who enjoyed the confidence of the army and who would inspire hope among the people of the state. He believed Rust was such a man. In April 1863, Rust was sent to Arkansas and ordered to report to Price. Gen. E. Kirby Smith, however, wanted nothing to do with Rust. His reasons are not clear, but Smith told Theophilus H. Holmes that unless otherwise ordered by Richmond, Holmes should send Rust back to his command in Mississippi. Rust nevertheless remained in Arkansas, but he never received a command in the Trans-Mississippi Department.

In January 1864, he was sent to Texas, and Gen. John B. Magruder was asked to give him an assignment if Magruder wanted him. Once in Texas, Rust again found there was no command for him to assume. At the end of the war Rust still was listed as a part of E. Kirby Smith's force, but he was unassigned. In June 1865, Rust surrendered and was paroled at Galveston, Texas.

After the war Rust returned to Arkansas and settled at Little Rock. For a time he was active in state Republican politics. He died in Little Rock on April 3, 1870.

BIBLIOGRAPHY

Kerby, Robert L. *Kirby Smith's Confederacy: The Trans-Mississippi South, 1863–1865.* New York, 1972.

Morrow, John P., Jr. "Confederate Generals from Arkansas." *Arkansas Historical Quarterly* 21 (Autumn 1962): 240–241.

Obituary. *Arkansas Gazette* (Little Rock), April 7, 1870.

Carl H. Moneyhon

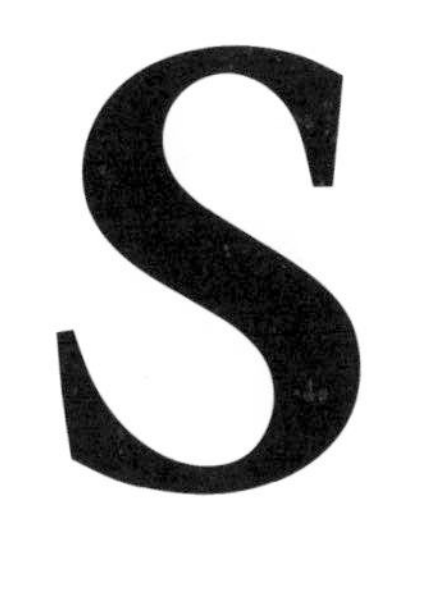

SABINE CROSS ROADS, LOUISIANA. *See* Mansfield, Louisiana.

SABINE PASS, TEXAS. The pass, an outlet for both the Sabine and the Neches rivers between Jefferson County, Texas, and Cameron Parish, Louisiana, provided a suitable route for a Federal expedition planning to cut the railroad between Houston and Beaumont. On September 8, 1863, a small group of Confederates overpowered a superior Union force in its attempt to invade the Texas coast, prompting President Jefferson Davis to call the battle "one of the most brilliant and most heroic achievements in the history of warfare."

This was not the first Union assault at Sabine Pass; in September 1862 Federal troops had forced the Confederates to abandon the position, but early in 1863 Texans drove Union gunboats away, reoccupied the pass, and constructed crude earthworks. After Vicksburg and Port Hudson fell, Federal authorities decided once more to "raise the flag in Texas." The attempt was to be a combined land and sea operation under Maj. Gen. Nathaniel P. Banks and Rear Adm. David G. Farragut. At New Orleans the Federals readied four gunboats, *Sachem, Clifton, Arizona,* and *Granite City,* and ordered some five thousand men of the Nineteenth Army Corps to board navy transports. In immediate command of the expedition was Maj. Gen. William B. Franklin.

To defend the pass the Confederates had forty-two men of the First Texas Heavy Artillery at Fort Griffin, an unfinished earthwork located about two miles above the entrance to the pass. The defenders, known as the Davis Guard, were mostly Irishmen from Houston, under the command of twenty-five-year-old Lt. Richard W. ("Dick") Dowling, a successful Houston saloon keeper born in Ireland.

On the night of September 7, the Union expedition arrived off the pass; the gunboats planned to silence the fort the next day in preparation for the landing of troops. During the afternoon on September 8, *Clifton* and *Sachem* moved up the channel, but a hit from one of the six Confederate cannons disabled *Sachem;* another shell struck the boiler, causing it to explode. *Clifton* was similarly disabled, and both vessels quickly surrendered. When an officer aboard *Granite City* mistakenly reported that Southern reinforcements were arriving, Franklin ordered a general withdrawal. The fighting lasted less than an hour, but the Federal losses included two gunboats, 19 men killed, 9 wounded, 37 missing, and 315 taken prisoner. The Confederates, who fired their artillery pieces over a hundred times, sustained no injuries.

This was the most significant battle in Texas during the war, and Dowling became a hero. The stunning Southern victory caused a temporary drop in the stock prices in New York City, and the *New York Herald* credited Dowling's victory, combined with the Federal defeat at Chickamauga, with drastically lowering the nation's credit. Franklin, who headed the expedition, was ridiculed as "the first American general . . . who managed to lose a fleet in contest with land batteries alone." As a result, Banks diverted his attack to southern Texas along the Rio Grande, and Sabine Pass was not used again as a route to invade Texas.

BIBLIOGRAPHY

Barr, Alwyn. "Sabine Pass, September 1863." *Texas Military History* 2 (1962): 17–22.

Barr, Alwyn. "Texas Coastal Defense, 1861–1865." *Southwestern Historical Quarterly* 65 (July 1962): 1–31.

Drummond, John A. "The Battle of Sabine Pass." *Confederate*

SABINE PASS, TEXAS. Capture of the Federal gunboat *Sachem* at Sabine Pass, Texas, September 8, 1863.
FRANK LESLIE'S ILLUSTRATED FAMOUS LEADERS AND BATTLE SCENES OF THE CIVIL WAR

Veteran 25 (August 1917): 364–365. Reprint, Wilmington, N.C., 1985.
McCormack, John. "Sabine Pass." *Civil War Times Illustrated* 12 (1973): 4–9, 34–37.
Muir, Andrew Forest. "Dick Dowling and Sabine Pass." *Civil War History* 4 (December 1958): 399–428.
Tolbert, Frank X. *Dick Dowling at Sabine Pass*. New York, 1962.
Young, Jo. "The Battle of Sabine Pass." *Southwestern Historical Quarterly* 52 (1948): 398–410.

ANNE J. BAILEY

SAILORS. The introduction of steam in 1802 had caused sweeping changes in the sea services, and with the introduction of ironclad warships, navies changed forever. Sailors no longer needed to be seamen. Engineers and coal heavers were beginning to replace sailing masters. Sailmakers and boatswains, the men responsible for ships' sails and rigging, found little to do in a vessel without sails. Confederate sailors, while facing these many changes, faced others equally deadly. In vessels primarily restricted to the rivers and bays of the South, they contended with malaria, typhus, yellow fever, and extremes of weather. Yet they still performed their duty.

From 1861 to 1865 the Confederate States Navy enlisted approximately six thousand seamen. Of these, only a small percentage were actually trained sailors. Seamen and marines were recruited at naval rendezvous and military and conscription camps throughout the South. Competition with the army deprived the navy of much-needed manpower. A fifty-dollar bounty, better pay, and better conditions prompted many to try to join the navy rather than the army, but army officers frequently refused to allow transfers to proceed.

Sailors inducted into the navy were first sent to a receiving ship, usually at the station they would serve. After being examined by a surgeon to determine their health and receiving a set of clothing, they were trained in the basic skills needed to run a ship of war. This was followed by a short, usually inadequate introduction to naval life, and then the men were transferred to the vessel that would be their home.

Once aboard ship the sailors were separated into two watch divisions: port and starboard. These divisions were again divided into two or three watch sections, each capable of keeping guard while in port. No more than one-sixth of the crew was allowed on liberty at any given time. Sailors were assigned berthing spaces and grouped into messes of eight to fourteen men. All unessential gear was stowed below, and the new sailors began their daily duties.

The sailor's day was separated into seven watches and regulated by the ship's bell. Following the morning watch (4:00 A.M. to 8:00 A.M.) was the forenoon watch (8:00 A.M. to 12:00 P.M.), the afternoon watch (12:00 P.M. to 4:00 P.M.), the first dogwatch (4:00 P.M. to 6:00 P.M.), the second dogwatch (6:00 P.M. to 8:00 P.M.), the evening watch (8:00 P.M. to 12:00 A.M.), and the night watch (12:00 A.M. to 4:00 A.M.). Sailors were expected to be on duty every other four hours.

To ensure that the men would not stand the same watch each day, the dogwatches, each two hours in length, were used. The time for each watch was kept by the ship's bell with the first bell of the watch being struck at the end of the first half-hour and a bell added for each half-hour after that until eight bells in all were struck and the four-hour watch ended.

Reveille aboard ship was 7:00 A.M. (six bells of the morning watch). All hands were called to scrub and clean the ship, pump out the bilges, wash clothes, clean and dry the decks, polish the ship's brass, wipe down the guns, and clear the ship for inspection. Breakfast, usually two ship's biscuits (hardtack) and water, was served at 8:00 A.M. Inspection was at 9:30 every day. Division officers examined the men for sickness, clothing deficiencies, and cleanliness and reported their findings to the executive officer. Any inadequacy was noted, and the men were required to make up their deficiency from the ship's paymaster in the case of clothing, or by seeing the ship's surgeon at sick call at 11:00 A.M.

At sick call the surgeon would examine the sailor, give him a "sick ticket," and place him on a sick list, which excused him from duty until he recovered. Chronically ill sailors were usually discharged quickly and sent home. Those wounded in the service could expect to receive the best medical attention available. All the naval surgeons and most of the assistant surgeons had to fulfill vigorous requirements and testing designed to screen out the incompetent. Most of the surgeons were from the old navy. Disabled seamen and those who recovered from a chronic illness were enlisted in the Naval Invalid Corps and given shore duty and half pay.

Deficiencies in clothing resulted in the sailor being issued new garments, with his pay account debited to reflect the purchase. Clothing prices could range from fifteen dollars to as little as fifty cents. A landsman's pay was sixteen dollars a month. Because the initial uniform purchase could cost as much as ninety-seven dollars, it took a new sailor a little over six months to pay for his uniform. After deducting their clothing issue from their pay, many sailors were left with no money, sometimes for the entire war. Pay for sailors was infrequent and usually inadequate. They could have an allotment sent home, but they were expected to keep six dollars for themselves to pay any debts incurred. A seaman could commute his unused spirit ration of four cents per day to supplement his pay, but it was seldom enough. Families of seamen often had insufficient funds and were faced with much hardship. In order to supplement their income, some sailors sold parts of their uniforms to civilians, a practice so rampant by 1864 that the Navy Department instructed officers to forbid it.

Shoes were of great importance in a navy powered by steam. Men on sailing vessels, who climbed rigging and worked sails, could go barefoot, but standing watch on ironclads and steamships required shoes. Fire and engine rooms and the decks adjacent to them became very hot, and conversely, in winter the iron armor was often covered by a thin layer of ice. The navy never solved the problem of shoes and clothing. By November 1864 the men of the James River Squadron were standing watch on freezing decks without shoes, coats, or blankets. And in December when Savannah fell, the seamen of the Savannah Squadron had to leave their belongings on the ships, which were scuttled. The Navy Department could not replace their lost clothing, and the men suffered much hardship on their march to Drewry's Bluff and the Appomattox campaign.

Formal duties aboard ship began at 11:00 A.M. with the crew, excluding those on watch, drilling on the use of heavy artillery, small arms, light artillery, or cutlasses and pistols. The division on watch worked the vessel and did a visual inspection of every line, sheet, sail, and seam to ensure that the ship was in operating condition. Lookouts were posted to watch for enemy warships, signals from the squadron's commander, and approaching vessels. All guns and gun carriages were inspected for any defects and repaired if necessary. In port or on a river defense vessel, sailors spent a great deal of time coaling the ship, loading firewood and provisions, transporting officers to the commander of the fleet in the ship's launch, and, especially during the summer months and to the sailors' consternation, taking visitors on trips in the ship's small boats.

Most jobs aboard ship were performed by gangs. Each warrant officer had a gang of men working for him. The carpenter's gang repaired the wooden parts of the vessel, including masts and spars. The gunner's gang inspected the ship's cannons, powder, cartridges, small arms ammunition, and signaling flares to ensure their serviceability. The boatswain's gang saw to the maintenance of the ropes, lines, sheets, and rigging. The sailmaker's gang repaired and maintained the ship's sails and awnings. The armorer's gang inspected the ship's small arms, rifles, pistols, revolvers, cutlasses, pikes, and swords and kept them in good condition.

Each petty officer was assigned a specific area or task to perform. To aid them, a "quarter-bill," or watch bill, was posted telling each sailor where to report to work. Some petty officers also had gangs. The master-at-arms, the ship's policeman, and his gang supervised the sailors being punished, kept discipline, and enforced the Articles of War. The captain-of-the-hold, a seaman, and his gang saw to the proper storage of supplies and the rotation of empty casks and containers. Improper storage could reduce the ship's speed, increase the ship's draft, or cause the vessel to handle poorly. The captain-of-the-tops, another seaman, and his gang inspected the topmasts of the vessel and made any repairs that were needed. Some duties could require the whole crew. If a gun carriage was found defective or the ship had to be coaled, the entire crew could be called to work under the direction of an officer until the job was completed.

At noon the crew was called to dinner, the largest meal of the day and the only one served hot. It usually consisted of meat, rice, beans, and bread. Sailors on the river squadrons could expect fresh meat and vegetables three times a week; those at sea got fresh meat and vegetables only while in port or from captured prizes. Although the acquisition of provisions at sea was precarious, men on the cruisers seemed to eat better than their counterparts at home. The portions of the meals as established by the Navy Department were much larger than those of soldiers. Each sailor was to receive ½ pound of meat, ½ cup of rice, ½ cup of beans, and ¼ pound of bread a day. These rations were supplemented by fresh vegetables, fowl, oysters, fish, molasses, spirits, and condiments. By pooling the men's rations, messes could provide a rather large meal. Monies specified for the mess but not used could purchase pepper, salt, mustard, and other spices and small stores from the paymaster. Menus were decided by the commanding officer, and the ship's cook drew rations from the steward. In 1864 the Navy Department cut the daily rations because, it was thought, the sailors were growing too fat. For the sake of morale it was decided that the navy's rations should be more in line with those of the army. The navy was then placed under the army's Commissary Department for provisions.

Afternoons were spent drilling, maintaining the ship, and finishing work begun in the morning. The only free time allowed the men was after the 6:00 P.M. roll call and supper. This was traditionally the time when sailors could freely talk, smoke, sing, or otherwise entertain themselves. Ships in port or on rivers usually allowed those not on duty to go ashore on a four-hour liberty. Sailors at Savannah, Charleston, and Richmond visited playhouses, taverns, and other centers of entertainment. Those who had not returned to their vessels by 11:00 P.M. could be punished for being late. All lights were ordered out by 8:00 P.M. (9:00 P.M. in the summer), signaling the end of the workday.

Sailors kept the evening and night watches on picket boats and in remote areas along rivers and streams, leaving the ship at nightfall and returning at daybreak. Naval pickets listened for Federal gunboats, launches, or infantry movements, working in conjunction with the army and supplementing the land forces performing the same duty. Because of the close proximity to Federal troops, many desertions occurred among those on picket duty.

Aboard a ship of war, regulations pertaining to the behavior of sailors and marines were strict. Unauthorized talking was not permitted, nor were sailors allowed to stand on the quarterdeck or bridge unless on watch or performing a specific duty. Officers' country, usually the stern of the vessel, was prohibited to enlisted men. Sailors of high rank, petty officers and warrant officers, were accorded some privileges. They ate separately from the rest of the crew, and their quarters were forward of the main mast or the forecastle. Sailors of lower rank were quartered aft of the main mast and were allowed only hammocks. Rules and regulations were posted and read weekly to the crew. Infractions were punished by anything from simple fines to courts-martial. Serious offenses, such as striking an officer or desertion, were punishable by death, although most sentences of this type were commuted by President Jefferson Davis.

Crews serving aboard ironclad warships and the Torpedo Battery Service had to brave the elements as well as work in temperatures that could reach 140 degrees. Ironclads were dark, damp, leaky, and poorly ventilated vessels that caused more deaths in the naval services than did combat. Because of the crowded conditions, men were prone to pulmonary diseases as well as other maladies. Disease in these ships was difficult to control, and sailors often were quartered ashore in warehouses where they could breathe fresh air. Those in the Torpedo Service spent most of their time in small boats or on shore. The task of building and placing torpedoes required constant attention, and sailors performing this service were usually detached from other duty.

Battle aboard the Confederate warship was much like that in the Federal navy. Sailors were detailed to specific duties at the guns and also assigned to "trimming" parties for operating the sails, boarding parties, fire parties, and powder divisions. The call to battle was sounded by the beat of a drum followed by two rolls. Rapid ringing of the ship's bell signaled a fire. Orders were passed verbally by the petty officers and boatswain. Marines were stationed at strategic places on the heavy guns and on the bridge to direct rifle fire at enemy officers. Aboard ironclads, the only personnel exposed to the enemy were the pilot and the captain; all others were protected by the heavy armor. With the advent of ironclads and rifled cannon, the importance of boarding parties decreased. Any need to board an enemy ship was far outweighed by the danger, for the common practice to repel boarders was for every ship in the fleet to fire on the boarded vessel. Boarders were used a few times, however, with positive results. The Confederate cutting-out expedition to board and capture USS *Waterwitch* in Ossabaw Sound, Georgia, in 1864 ended in the capture of a Federal warship; it was one of two successful attempts at boarding an enemy vessel during the war.

Confederate sailors and marines served with distinction for four years. Their lives were no less hard than those of their comrades in the army. Although they were few in number, their role was vital to the war effort. By keeping the ports open for much-needed supplies, the sailors of the

Confederate navy enabled the army to fight as long as it did.

[*See also* Marine Corps; Navy, *particularly articles on* Confederate Navy *and* Manpower; Uniforms, *articles on* Navy *and* Marine Uniforms.]

BIBLIOGRAPHY

Chapelle, Howard I. *The History of the American Sailing Navy: The Ships and their Development.* New York, 1949.

Confederate States Navy Department. *Regulations for the Navy of the Confederate States of America.* Richmond, Va., 1862.

Donnelly, Ralph W. *The Confederate States Marine Corps: The Rebel Leathernecks.* Shippingham, Pa., 1989.

Durkin, Joseph T. S. J. *Confederate Navy Chief Stephen R. Mallory.* Columbia, S.C., 1954.

Scales, Dabney, Midshipman, C.S.N. Unpublished Diary, 1863. Savannah River Squadron Papers. Emory University Manuscript Collection, Atlanta, Ga.

Upton, Commander U. P. *Manual of Internal Rules and Regulations for Men of War.* New York, 1862.

Watson, Thomas, Seaman. Unpublished diary, 1864–1865. Collections of the Coastal Heritage Society. Savannah, Ga.

Wells, Thomas H. *The Confederate Navy: A Study in Organization.* Tuscaloosa, Ala., 1971.

JOHN W. KENNINGTON, JR.

ST. JOHN, ISAAC M.

ST. JOHN, ISAAC M. (1827–1880), chief of the Niter and Mining Bureau, brigadier general, and commissary general. A native of Georgia raised in New York, St. John graduated from Yale in 1845 and experimented with law and journalism before settling on a career in civil engineering. He worked for railroad companies in several states and was in South Carolina when the Civil War began. Although he promptly joined a company as a private, he was soon assigned to duty as chief of engineers, supervising the development of Gen. John B. Magruder's defenses near Yorktown, Virginia. When Congress in April 1862 established a niter corps as an adjunct to the Ordnance Department, Gen. Josiah Gorgas appointed St. John to head the corps, which became the independent Niter and Mining Bureau in April 1863.

St. John was responsible for overseeing the procurement and manufacturing of niter (saltpeter), the major ingredient in gunpowder, as well as the mining of iron, copper, lead, coal, and zinc for military purposes. He thus supervised many widely separated installations, which often suffered from enemy depredations. Despite these and other war-related difficulties, St. John managed his bureau with such organization and efficiency that on February 16, 1865, he was promoted to brigadier general and replaced Lucius B. Northrop as commissary general. In attempting to bring order out of chaos in this department, St. John instituted several new policies and increased morale by his energetic approach to the problems. His leadership was not fully tested, however, since Richmond fell only five weeks after he assumed the position.

After the war, St. John returned to civil engineering, serving as city engineer of Louisville, Kentucky, and working for a variety of railroad companies. He died at White Sulphur Springs, West Virginia, on April 7, 1880, and was buried in Richmond, Virginia.

BIBLIOGRAPHY

Compiled Military Service Records. Niter and Mining Bureau. Isaac M. St. John. Microcopy M258, Roll 113. Record Group 109. National Archives, Washington, D.C.

"Death of Gen. St. John." *Louisville Courier-Journal,* April 10, 1880.

Vandiver, Frank E. *Ploughshares into Swords: Josiah Gorgas and Confederate Ordnance.* Austin, Tex., 1952.

GLENNA R. SCHROEDER-LEIN

SALISBURY PRISON.

SALISBURY PRISON. In November 1861, the Confederacy bought an abandoned cotton factory with sixteen acres of land in Salisbury, North Carolina. Located on a railroad, the site was convenient for transferring the prisoners of war who had accumulated in Richmond. Around the three-and-a-half-story brick factory and several smaller buildings, the military authorities built a fence with a walkway outside for sentinels. Cannons aimed inside were placed at two corners. A well provided water and large trees offered shade. To some early prisoners, the facility suggested a college campus.

The Confederates quickly began to move about 1,500 prisoners of war into the new stockade, which they believed adequate for 2,500 men. Locally recruited troops guarded them. With the beginning of prisoner exchange in 1862, the Federal inmates left, and the prison began to be used for deserters from both sides, Confederates sentenced by courts-martial, and political prisoners. For the latter it became second only to Richmond's Castle Thunder as a place of imprisonment. Physical conditions within were relatively healthy and comfortable.

After William Tecumseh Sherman's Georgia campaign, the Confederates could no longer send many prisoners to that state, so a backlog again built up at Richmond. Beginning in October 1864, the authorities at the Confederate capital suddenly decided again to send prisoners of war to Salisbury. Of the more than 8,000 men shipped there, relatively few were officers, but most were enlisted men, including a few hundred blacks. On November 6, 1864, the prison reached its maximum population of 8,740 men. Guarding them were junior and senior reserves headed by a Floridian, Maj. John Henry Gee. In December 1864, Brig. Gen. Bradley Tyler Johnson became the post's overall commander.

Conditions within the overcrowded prison rapidly deteriorated. Since the few buildings were then largely used as hospitals and the Confederates provided only a few tents, many prisoners had only such shelter as they could obtain by burrowing in the ground. The chief of Confederate prisons, Gen. John H. Winder, considered the site so deficient that he proposed moving the prisoners elsewhere and thus was unwilling to make improvements. Among the problems was the lack of a running stream, which created a shortage of water and a nauseating sanitary condition.

The cold, suffering inmates received limited quantities of often uncooked cornmeal and refuse meat. The more desperate plotted escapes and on November 25 attempted an unsuccessful mass uprising. Far more yielded to the blandishments of Confederate recruiters, with some becoming artisans and over 1,700 mostly foreign-born joining the army of their captors. Even more died, mainly of diarrhea and pneumonia. About 3,955 were buried in unmarked graves in trenches. Though the 15,000 prisoners confined in Salisbury at one time or another was less than the total in Andersonville, the percentage of deaths was comparable.

In mid-February 1865, the resumption of exchange emptied the Salisbury Prison, though the inmates suffered additional hardships as they traveled to Wilmington and Richmond. Thereafter only a few hundred transients were held in the stockade until April 12 when Gen. George Stoneman's Union raiders captured Salisbury and burned the prison along with other Confederate property.

After the war, the Federals arrested Major Gee on a charge of mistreating prisoners. Unlike Andersonville's Henry Wirz, he was not taken to Washington. Instead he was tried by a U.S. military commission in North Carolina, received an able legal defense based on his inability to do more than he did for the prisoners, and was acquitted and released after some six months' imprisonment. All that remains of the prison is a small national cemetery.

BIBLIOGRAPHY

Blakey, Arch Fredric. *General John H. Winder, C.S.A.* Gainesville, Fla., 1990.

Brown, Louis A. *The Salisbury Prison: A Case Study of Confederate Military Prisons.* Wendell, N.C., 1980.

Hesseltine, William B. *Civil War Prisons: A Study in War Psychology.* Columbus, Ohio, 1930. Reprint, New York, 1978.

FRANK L. BYRNE

SALT.

SALT. This mineral was vital to the civilian population as well as the military forces of the Confederacy. In an era with no reliable method of refrigeration, salt was the primary means of preserving meat. In addition, salt was used to pack cheese and eggs and preserve hides during leather making, as well as being employed in numerous chemical processes, various medications, and livestock dietary supplements.

Prior to the war, the Southern states had bought much of their salt from the North or imported it from Europe. Once the war started, the Confederacy had to develop internal sources for its requirements. The primary areas for salt production were Great Kanawha River near Charleston, West Virginia; Goose Creek near Manchester, Kentucky; southwest Alabama; Avery Island, Louisiana; and southwest Virginia. Salt was also produced along the Confederate seacoast. The largest industry to develop in Florida, during the war, was salt making.

Several of these locations (in West Virginia, Kentucky, and Louisiana) were captured early in the war. By 1863, most of the Confederacy's salt, especially for those states east of the Mississippi, was being produced at the Stuart, Buchanan & Co. saltworks in Saltville, Virginia. In 1864, thirty-eight furnaces containing over 2,600 kettles were producing about 4 million bushels of salt per year at just this one saltworks.

There were three methods of producing salt in the 1860s: extracting it from brine wells, extracting it from seawater or inland salt ponds, and mining deposits of rock salt. The process for extracting salt from seawater and brine wells was the same—evaporation. At Saltville, the brine was pumped from a well by steam engine and transported to furnaces through wooden pipes. After the water had evaporated, the crystallized salt was placed in split baskets to dry and then stored in bulk.

Federal forces did not allow salt manufacturing to continue unchallenged. The navy raided coastal salt makers, especially along the Florida coast, and the army made a point of destroying all saltworks in its path.

In the fall of 1864, Federal cavalry made two raids against the Saltville saltworks. In October, the Federals were unsuccessful, and following the battle over one hundred captured black troops were killed by Confederate soldiers. This was one of the war's worst massacres. In December, the Federals were able to capture and temporarily put the saltworks out of operation.

Each Confederate state had its own salt commissioner or agent, who acquired salt from the available sources and then passed it along to local agents for public distribution. Although resources were sufficient to provide all the salt needed, there were shortages throughout the war, especially for civilians. Causes for these shortages included the blockade, speculation and corruption, and inadequate transportation. These shortages, however, were never severe enough to cause serious problems for the army. Lucius B. Northrop, commissary-general, stated on January 25, 1865, that "the supply of salt has always been sufficient and the Virginia works were able to meet the demand for the army."

BIBLIOGRAPHY

Johns, John E. *Florida during the Civil War.* Gainesville, Fla., 1963.

Lonn, Ella. *Salt as a Factor in the Confederacy.* University, Ala., 1965.
Rachal, William M. E. "Salt the South Could Not Savor." *Virginia Cavalcade,* Autumn 1953.

MICHAEL E. HOLMES

SALTPETER. Known to the Confederates as niter, this mineral, potassium nitrate (KNO_3), was crucial to the Confederate war effort because it comprised about 75 percent of the gunpowder used. (The other ingredients were about 12.5 percent sulphur and 12.5 percent charcoal.) Although some saltpeter had been mined in the United States for local use since before the War of 1812, most was imported. The Union blockade forced the Confederacy to consider other sources of the mineral, although substantial importation, both by sea and from Mexico, continued throughout the war.

Three possible domestic saltpeter sources were available to the Confederates: limestone caves, residue under old buildings, and artificial niter beds. Caves with appropriate mineral and climatic conditions for the natural production of saltpeter could be found primarily in the foothills of Tennessee, Georgia, Arkansas, Virginia, and Alabama, areas that tended to be occupied by Union troops fairly early in the war. The Sauta Cave in Jackson County, Alabama, and a cave near Kingston in Bartow County, Georgia, were among the most famous and productive of the sites.

The dirt under old buildings, tobacco barns, stables, outhouses, and manure piles could also bear saltpeter, but mining these sources required the cooperation of private citizens. A potentially more reliable source of the mineral was the artificial manufacture of saltpeter in niter beds. These beds were composed of heaps of earth, manure, rotted vegetable matter, and other waste products, which were carefully tended, moistened with urine, and turned over for a considerable period of time to produce a coating of the mineral. Although the Confederates were able to procure some saltpeter by this method, most of the niter beds, established in "nitriaries" near the major cities, were not mature enough by the time the war ended to produce to their full capacity. In all cases of mining and manufacturing, the raw product was still primarily dirt and had to go through a leaching and refining process before the saltpeter could be used in gunpowder.

The Confederate Niter and Mining Bureau, headed by Isaac M. St. John, supervised the collection and production of saltpeter, sponsoring a number of mining ventures and the thirteen or more nitriaries. But the government also encouraged private citizens to manufacture saltpeter and published pamphlets by George W. Rains and Joseph LeConte to instruct the novice in the proper procedures.

Although complete records for the bureau do not exist, those available indicate that private and government manufacturing had produced 1,735,531.75 pounds of saltpeter and that 1,720,072 pounds had been imported by September 30, 1864.

[*See also* Niter and Mining Bureau.]

BIBLIOGRAPHY

Donnelly, Ralph W. "The Bartow County Confederate Saltpetre Works." *Georgia Historical Quarterly* 54 (1970): 305–319.
LeConte, Joseph. *Instructions for the Manufacture of Saltpetre.* Columbia, S.C., 1862.
Rains, George W. *Notes on Making Saltpetre from the Earth of Caves.* Augusta, Ga., 1861.
Schroeder, Glenna R. " 'We Will Support the Govt. to the Bitter End': The Augusta Office of the Confederate Nitre and Mining Bureau." *Georgia Historical Quarterly* 70 (1986): 288–305.
Smith, Marion O. "The Sauta Cave Confederate Niter Works." *Civil War History* 29 (1983): 293–315.

GLENNA R. SCHROEDER-LEIN

SALTVILLE MASSACRE. On October 2, 1864, a Federal cavalry raid of 3,600 troopers led by Gen. Stephen Burbridge was stopped and repulsed by a force of no more than 2,800 Confederates under the immediate command of Gen. John S. Williams. Among the defeated Federals were 600 men of the Fifth U.S. Colored Cavalry, many of whom remained wounded on the southwestern Virginia battlefield while their forces hastily retreated back toward their base in Kentucky.

The next morning men from two Tennessee brigades were seen randomly roaming the field shooting wounded black Federals. "It was bang, bang, bang, all over the field," wrote a Kentuckian, "negroes dropping everywhere." Some Confederates, notably the guerrilla Tennesseean Champ Ferguson, also murdered white wounded men. Other black soldiers who had been captured the day before were also shot. In all, though estimates vary, about 100 members of the Fifth U.S. Colored Cavalry were probably murdered while wounded or prisoners. The number of white Federals killed was perhaps a dozen or more. Chiefly, Tennessee soldiers did the killing, with the knowledge and acquiescence of one of their commanders, Gen. Felix Huston Robertson. Indeed, one witness said that he ordered the murders, an act he is alleged to have repeated a few weeks later in the war. It is possible that he joined in the killing himself.

Gen. John C. Breckinridge attempted, with Robert E. Lee's assistance, to bring Robertson before a court for the crime, but the collapse of the Confederate came too swiftly. Ironically, though much more a genuine massacre than the famous Fort Pillow affair, Saltville never achieved much notoriety.

BIBLIOGRAPHY

Davis, William C. "The Massacre at Saltville." *Civil War Times Illustrated* 9 (1970–1971): 4–11, 43–48.

Lawson, Lewis A. *Wheeler's Last Raid.* Greenwood, Fla., 1986.

WILLIAM C. DAVIS

SANDERS, JOHN CALDWELL CALHOUN (1840–1864), colonel and acting brigadier general. Sanders was born in Tuscaloosa, Alabama, on April 4, 1840, and attended the University of Alabama in 1858. When war broke out he enlisted in the Eleventh Alabama Infantry and was elected captain of Company E, the "Confederate Guards." Though it saw no fighting in 1861, his unit's baptism of fire came at Seven Pines in May 1862. Sanders was severely wounded in the leg at Frayer's Farm on June 30. He returned to duty on August 11 and was given command of the regiment as he was the senior officer present. He was wounded again at Sharpsburg and afterward was promoted to colonel. Sanders's regiment fought at Fredericksburg in December 1862 and at Chancellorsville and Gettysburg in 1863, where he was wounded in the knee during the second day and became one of the regiment's seventy-five casualties. During his recuperation, he led the divisional court-martial.

When Sanders returned to active duty in August, he was placed in charge of the brigade. During the Battle of the Wilderness in May 1864, he temporarily commanded Abner Perrin's brigade, William Mahone's division, when Perrin was killed at the Mule Shoe. Temporarily promoted to brigadier general effective May 31, he participated in the siege of Petersburg, leading his unit in a counterattack during the Battle of the Crater on July 30. On August 21, Sanders was mortally wounded at Weldon Railroad. A bullet hit him in his thigh, severing the femoral artery. The general bled to death in minutes. He was buried in an unmarked grave in Hollywood Cemetery, Richmond, Virginia.

BIBLIOGRAPHY

Faust, Patricia L., ed. *Historical Times Illustrated Encyclopedia of the Civil War.* New York, 1986.

Warner, Ezra J. *Generals in Gray: Lives of the Confederate Commanders.* Baton Rouge, La., 1959.

KENNETH L. STILES

SANDERSON, JOHN PEASE (1816–1871), congressman from Florida. Born in Sunderland, Vermont, Sanderson graduated from Amherst in 1839 and moved to Jacksonville, Florida, where he became a wealthy planter, lawyer, and secessionist Democrat in the early 1850s. He was a promoter of railroads for the state and served in the Florida house in 1843 and the senate in 1848; he was solicitor of the Eastern Circuit from 1849 to 1854. Elected to the secession convention as representative of the Sixteenth Senatorial District, he voted for disunion.

During the war, Sanderson served for only fifteen days in the Provisional Confederate Congress, finishing the unexpired term of George T. Ward who resigned in February 1862. He was conscripted in 1864 but was found not fit for service in the field. He did work in the Quartermaster Corps as a clerk for six months and as an appraiser of confiscated property for the Conscript Bureau. In 1865, Federal troops seized his plantation, Ortega, on the St. Johns River, and confiscated all of his stock, equipment, and crops.

Sanderson, after the war, secured the return of his land and resumed the practice of law in Jacksonville until his death on June 28, 1871.

BIBLIOGRAPHY

Davis, William Watson. *The Civil War and Reconstruction in Florida.* New York, 1913.

Wakelyn, Jon L. *Biographical Dictionary of the Confederacy.* Edited by Frank E. Vandiver. Westport, Conn., 1977.

Warner, Ezra J., and W. Buck Yearns. *Biographical Register of the Confederate Congress.* Baton Rouge, La., 1975.

ARCH FREDRIC BLAKEY

SAVANNAH, GEORGIA. [*This entry includes two articles,* City of Savannah, *which profiles the city during the Confederacy, and* Savannah Campaign, *which discusses the capture of the city in 1864. See also* Fort Pulaski, Georgia; Savannah Squadron.]

City of Savannah

Many of the commercial interests of antebellum Georgia revolved around Savannah, the state's largest city, which enjoyed the benefits of a commercial and demographic boom in the years prior to 1860. Its population in 1860 totaled nearly 23,000, having doubled during these preceding two decades. The city attracted rural Georgians and South Carolinians, ambitious Northerners, and a growing number of foreign-born. The 1860 census counted 4,696 foreign-born individuals among a white population of 13,875; three in every four of these came from Ireland. The ethnic mix also included 705 free blacks and 7,712 slaves.

Commercial expansion drew most of these people to Savannah. Railroad connections between the port and the Georgia interior, completed in 1843, directed the state's growing output of cotton and lumber through the port at Savannah to customers throughout Europe and the northern United States. The value of Savannah's exports leapt from $6 million in 1840 to $18 million in 1860. In the last

SAVANNAH, GEORGIA. View from the cupola of the Exchange, looking east toward Fort Jackson.

FRANK LESLIE'S ILLUSTRATED FAMOUS LEADERS AND BATTLE SCENES OF THE CIVIL WAR

year of the Union, half a million bales of cotton and 40 million board feet of lumber left the state by way of Savannah. Slave labor produced these commodities, giving the city a powerful economic as well as social stake in the preservation of slavery. But worry over the safety of its trade connections figured along with the security of slavery in shaping Savannah's reactions to the crisis of 1860.

On November 8 of that year, over 3,000 citizens gathered at the Masonic Hall to the accompaniment of brass bands, fireworks, and bonfires. They heard speakers denounce the election of Abraham Lincoln and approved the formation of a vigilance committee to enforce public support for Southern resistance to the Republican regime in Washington. Julian Hartridge, their representative in the Georgia Assembly, offered resolutions condemning the election results and calling for steps "to alleviate any unusual embarrassment of the commercial interest of the state consequent upon the present political emergency."

When the news of South Carolina's secession reached the city in December, citizens broke out "secession cockades" made from palmetto leaves; they wore them to almost nightly public meetings throughout the Christmas season in the downtown public squares. The people raised a platform in front of the statue of Revolutionary hero Nathaniel Greene, in Johnson Square, and decorated it with placards depicting rattlesnakes with the legend, "Don't tread on me!" The trio of local notables who represented Savannah at the state secession convention in January 1861 had plenty of evidence of the public's opinion on the question.

A few merchants saw the municipal situation differently. Secession meant war, they believed, and war meant the disruption of trade. By diverting capital and labor resources, armed conflict would, at the least, diminish the supply of export commodities upon which the city's prosperity rested. Even before the firing on Fort Sumter, local merchants remarked on the decline of business activity as customers at home and abroad waited to see what would happen. The leaders of Savannah, as war approached, sought ways to balance their patriotic duty to the South with personal and municipal well-being—objectives that, in the course of the conflict, grew increasingly incompatible.

At first the priorities were clear enough. Even before secession, the city worried about its defense needs. The city council voted immediately after the presidential election to buy ammunition for the city's nine volunteer militia companies. The public, believing Savannah a primary target in any military showdown, badgered authorities for troops, weapons, and funds for its defense. The state government responded even before secession became official. On January 3, 1861, local militia authorized by Governor Joseph E. Brown seized nearby Fort Pulaski, which commanded the river passage from Savannah to the Atlantic. (In this action they overpowered and captured a garrison consisting of one elderly Federal sergeant.) By the end of the month local forces had also taken over the Oglethorpe Barracks and Fort Jackson. Fort Pulaski was garrisoned with 400 troops, Fort Jackson with 120. State and local militia used both facilities to acclimate new recruits to military discipline and camp life.

Georgia seceded from the Union on January 16, 1861, and in the following month joined the Confederacy. Savannah's citizens elected Francis S. Bartow to represent them in the First Congress, but he resigned on May 1 to join the Oglethorpe Light Infantry in Virginia. Governor Brown attacked Bartow for leaving the state without authorization, a charge Bartow dismissed with contempt, denying that he needed the state's permission to defend his country. Bartow was killed at Manassas on July 21, 1861, becoming Savannah's first war hero. His clash with Brown presaged the tug of war over troops and materials between the state of Georgia and the Confederacy that would last throughout the war.

Savannah for the most part took the more cosmopolitan view of the Confederacy in this matter. The city's nine volunteer militia companies went to Virginia as the First Volunteer Regiment of Georgia, despite efforts to persuade them to stay home. In April 1861, the War Department appointed Alexander R. Lawton brigadier general and commander at Savannah, charged with the defense of the city and the coastal region. Lawson oversaw the garrisoning of the forts along the coast and the construction of works in the rivers that cut through the district. Meanwhile, Brown tried to prevent the departure of the Georgia Hussars for the Virginia front by declaring their equipment state property and forbidding them to take it out of Georgia. In order to leave for the front without interference from the governor, the Hussars spent $25,000 of their own money on horses and weapons.

In November 1861, the public's fears for the safety of Savannah suddenly took on a new urgency. Federal forces captured Port Royal at the beginning of the month and by November 25 moved onto Tybee Island as well. Union troops threatened the mouth of the Savannah River from these positions, and artillery they installed on Tybee jeopardized local defensive installations. Robert E. Lee, commander of the Department of South Carolina, Georgia, and Florida since November 1861, responded by designing a network of defenses around the city's exterior perimeter to be built by squads of soldiers and slaves. Lee left for Virginia in March 1862 before the new works were finished. Within a few weeks, Fort Pulaski fell to the rifled cannon of Tybee Island. Its commander, Col. Charles Olmstead, surrendered the fort on April 11, 1862, after a bombardment that rattled windows in downtown Savannah and rendered Pulaski indefensible. His decision, taken on humanitarian as well as practical grounds, was extremely unpopular in the city. After the fall of Fort Pulaski, Savannah was cut off from its conventional outlet to the Atlantic. Civilian authorities debated the wisdom of abandoning the city, and in May, Gen. John C. Pemberton seriously recommended that the city council evacuate women and children, declare martial law, and demolish the buildings along the forty-foot bluff that raises Savannah above the banks of the river so that heavy artillery could be installed to defend the position. The Georgia Assembly contributed to the deliberations a call for house-to-house resistance, if necessary.

In fact, by May 1862, the issue of whether and how to defend Savannah was moot. With the fall of Fort Pulaski the city was too vulnerable to serve as a base for blockade running, shipbuilding, or any other strategically significant enterprises. The Confederate government recognized this and moved its Savannah arsenal to Macon in May. An effective Federal naval blockade rendered any direct attack on the city superfluous. Union Gen. David Hunter thought 30,000 troops held Savannah (the accurate figure as of June was 13,000) and elected not to challenge them. Fort McAllister, at the mouth of the Ogeechee River south of town, came under sporadic shelling during that tense summer, but it, and the city, stayed in Southern hands until William Tecumseh Sherman arrived two years later.

The blockade and the immediacy of the Federal threat certainly damaged the local economy. At the beginning of the war Governor Brown prohibited cotton exports, on the theory that the resulting cotton famine would hasten European intervention on behalf of the Confederacy. By 1863, when that prospect had faded, Brown switched to a policy promoting exports to raise needed money and goods, but by then the blockade had minimized the profits in trade. During the first half of 1862 no export fees were collected at Savannah, and import duties totaled only $112.92. The export trade did not rebound until after the war ended.

Other business activity also fell off sharply during the war. Industrial enterprise in support of the war effort was never extensive. Henry F. Willink operated one of the Confederacy's largest shipyards during the first year of fighting, and the Central Railroad's shops were used to manufacture gun carriages and rifled cannon for state and Confederate forces. But after spring 1862, neither the state nor the Confederacy permitted any essential production to continue, since Federal troops were so near.

By 1862 the most pressing economic concerns in Savannah revolved around the problems of inflation and scarcity. Disruption of the import trade, the region's loss of personnel to the armed forces, and the military's demand combined to create commodity shortages that hit the population especially hard. Fresh vegetables, wheat, beef, and dairy products, together with imports like coffee and sugar, practically vanished from local groceries. By 1862 clothing, shoes, and salt had become all but impossible to buy. The scarcity drove prices to unthinkable levels. In October 1863, consumers paid $1.50 for a dozen eggs, $5.00 to $6.00 for a pound of butter, and up to $100 for eight bushels of sweet potatoes. Rumors about hoarding accompanied the rising prices. George Mercer, son of Confederate Gen. Hugh Weedon Mercer, was one of many who blamed it on "sordid speculators, composed chiefly of German Jews, of aliens, of Yankees." In 1863 the city council set up a municipal store to combat inflation, promising to keep prices reasonable. But the scarcities driving prices up were real, not the result of conspiracy.

These pressures highlighted two critical social problems. The business collapse and induction of thousands of wage earners into the military left families all over the city with diminished income or none at all. The city government recognized the problem almost immediately. On May 27, 1861, a public meeting organized a system to gather donations and distribute them to needy military dependents, but by the following February, this fund was exhausted. During 1862 the city spent almost $23,000 on food and fuel for the destitute, and the following March, six banks lent the city $55,000 without interest to help the poor. Sometimes aid took other forms. The city council threatened to publish the names of landlords who evicted soldiers' families for delinquent rent in 1863. Apparently the prospect of publicity had the desired effect. But the problems of food and fuel, complicated by inflation and dwindling municipal resources, persisted.

The other problem exacerbated by wartime conditions was ethnic antagonism among whites. Some conflicts predated the outbreak of war. Irish and German workers had spearheaded a campaign in the 1850s to exclude slaves and free blacks from the skilled crafts. In January 1861, while most citizens were talking secession and war, the city's master bootmakers resolved "that we will not contract to employ, hire, or learn any Negro the bootmaking business from this date." Similar disputes left relations between immigrant craftspeople and slaveholding interests strained. When the war began, trouble developed over the reluctance of many European-born men to be drafted into the military. When the first Conscription Act passed in 1862, hundreds of aliens in Savannah signed affadavits denying they had ever had any intention of becoming citizens; as aliens, of course, they were exempt from the draft. While Charleston was under Federal attack in July 1863, Mayor Thomas Holcombe refused to issue passes to 30 foreigners desiring to leave town. That December, another 120 aliens forswore any plans to become citizens. Other residents reacted bitterly to what seemed, to many, no more than a combination of cowardice and avarice. In fact, when the war started, hundreds of immigrants enlisted either individually or through such ethnically based militia units as the Irish Jasper Greens. But the public's perception held that immigrants, along with Northern business types, represented Savannah's worst "internal security problem." Another vigilance committee appeared late in the war to enforce loyalty and encourage enrollments in the military.

In the long run, the effect of the war on slavery represented a far more serious threat to the status quo. The military challenged the principle of owners' control over slave property by trying repeatedly to draft slaves for work on the defensive fortifications. Slave owners fought such efforts, claiming their slaves were irreplaceable and risked injury when they worked for the army. Hazards notwithstanding, the slaveholders' were really supporting the autonomy of private property when they refused to let slaves help defend slavery. Slave discipline broke down as the war continued. Between 1862 and 1864, the number of mayor's court cases involving slave defendants increased by 400 percent. The number of slaves jailed, despite owners' protests on their behalf, grew by 50 percent. To replace these hands became a more expensive proposition as inflation affected the purchase price and hire rates of slaves along with the costs of commodities. And slaves did not necessarily feel any need to stand by their troubled owners. In 1863, a boatload of slaves trying to escape to Fort Pulaski drowned when their boat capsized in the Savannah River. Others, as persistent complaints indicated, were more successful.

The war ended for Savannah when Sherman arrived on December 21, 1864, but its consequences continued to be felt. Military action had eroded the property that citizens had fought to protect. Now Union soldiers reported mobs of looters in the streets. Federal soldiers promptly dispersed these and set up a military government that earned the citizens' respect for its fairness and commitment to order. Civilians, relieved that the city had been spared bombardment, cooperated with Sherman's program to appropriate privately held provisions for the relief of the needy. Federal soldiers observed that black citizens regularly sought interviews with the Union commander to pledge their loyalty and offer their assistance to the occupying force.

George Mercer was not the only resident to view this and other "social changes that progress[ed] with the revolution" uneasily. Still, if the people went into the war with enthusiasm, they came out with a sense of relief. Sherman offered the city a chance to recover, and by the end of 1864, Savannah was glad to have it.

BIBLIOGRAPHY

Gamble, Thomas, Jr., comp. *A History of the City Government of Savannah, Ga., from 1790 to 1901.* Savannah, Ga., 1900.

Griffin, J. David. "Benevolence and Malevolence in Confederate Savannah." *Georgia Historical Quarterly* 49 (1965): 347–368.

Harden, William. *A History of Savannah and South Georgia.* 2 vols. Chicago, 1913.

Jones, Charles C., O. F. Vedder, and Frank Weldon. *History of Savannah, Ga.* Syracuse, N.Y., 1890.

Lawrence, Alexander A. *A Present for Mr. Lincoln: The Story of Savannah from Secession to Sherman.* Macon, Ga., 1961.

Mohr, Clarence L. *On the Threshold of Freedom, Masters and Slaves in Civil War Georgia.* Athens, Ga., 1986.

Myers, Robert Manson, ed. *The Children of Pride: A True Story of Georgia and the Civil War.* New Haven, 1972.

Nichols, George Ward. *The Story of the Great March, From the Diary of a Staff Officer.* New York, 1865.

EDWARD M. SHOEMAKER

Savannah Campaign

Gen. William Tecumseh Sherman with an army of some 60,000 veterans departed Atlanta for Savannah with twenty days of rations on November 15, 1864. The right wing was commanded by Gen. O. O. Howard and the left by Gen. Henry W. Slocum; two cavalry brigades were commanded by Gen. Hugh H. Kilpatrick. Violating standard military procedure by operating without a line of communications and supply, the army had to forage across the state, and supplies were running low when Sherman arrived at Savannah on December 10.

Upon Sherman's approach, Gen. William J. Hardee, commanding 10,000 troops at Savannah, skillfully took advantage of the terrain to concentrate his primary defenses two and a half miles west of the city on a peninsula about thirteen miles wide, which was flanked on the north by the Savannah River and on the south by the Little Ogeechee River. Hardee ordered his men to construct earthen redoubts and emplace heavy artillery along this line; then they flooded the rice fields to the front. The right of the line was commanded by Maj. Gen. Gustavus W. Smith, the center by Maj. Gen. Lafayette McLaws, and the left by Maj. Gen. Ambrose Ransom Wright. Hardee relied on Confederate gunboats on the Savannah River to protect northern Savannah and his army. Gen. P. G. T. Beauregard had ordered him to evacuate the city, if necessary.

The only major fortification not linked directly with Savannah's defenses was Fort McAllister at the mouth of the Ogeechee River, about sixteen miles south of the city. It was here that Sherman decided to attack to open a sea route for the resupply of his army.

General Sherman ordered Brig. Gen. William B. Hazen's division of the Fifteenth Corps to take Fort McAllister. Maj.

EVACUATION OF SAVANNAH. Confederate evacuation of the city, December 1864. *HARPER'S PICTORIAL HISTORY OF THE GREAT REBELLION*

George W. Anderson, Jr., commanding 250 Confederates in the sand and timber fortification, had planted abatis and mines around the fort. On December 13, they were surprised by an attack from the landside by 4,300 troops under Hazen's command. The defenders fought hand to hand until they were overwhelmed by superior numbers. Twenty-four Union officers and men were killed and 110 wounded. The Confederates had 1 officer and 15 men killed, and 54 wounded; 17 officers and 178 enlisted men were taken prisoner.

General Hardee now decided to evacuate the city. Confederate engineers began building a pontoon bridge across the Savannah River to Hutchinson Island, a distance of about one thousand feet; next the engineers laid temporary spans across the Middle and Back Rivers to the shore of South Carolina. Joseph Wheeler and his cavalry kept open the line of retreat, which was threatened by Federal forces.

On December 17 Sherman formally demanded the surrender of the city. When Hardee refused, Sherman ordered an attack to begin in three days. But after dark on December 20 Confederate forces around the city spiked their guns and began withdrawing over the pontoon bridges. By the following morning Hardee's army had safely crossed into South Carolina.

Although disappointed that the army had escaped, Sherman was pleased that his troops had captured over two hundred artillery pieces, large quantities of ammunition, and thirty thousand bales of cotton with minimal loss of personnel. He had also ended his March to the Sea and established a supply base. General Sherman presented Savannah to President Abraham Lincoln as a Christmas present.

BIBLIOGRAPHY

Durham, Roger S. "Savannah: Mr. Lincoln's Christmas Present." *Blue and Gray Magazine*, February 1991.

Hughes, Nathaniel C., Jr. *General William J. Hardee: Old Reliable.* Baton Rouge, La., 1965.

Lawrence, Alexander A. *A Present for Mr. Lincoln: The Story of Savannah from Secession to Sherman.* Macon, Ga., 1961.

WALTER J. FRASER, JR.

SAVANNAH. On May 18, 1861, John Harleston and a consortium of eleven other investors obtained a commission for the privateer *Savannah.* The schooner was the former *Charleston Pilot Boat No. 7,* measuring only 53 tons burden. *Savannah* was refitted and armed with a short 18-pounder on a pivot mount amidships and muskets, pistols, and cutlasses. On the evening of June 2, 1861, with a crew and officers numbering twenty, *Savannah* set sail on a commerce-raiding voyage.

The privateer captured the brig *Joseph* of Rockland, Maine, loaded with sugar on the following day. Shortly after, *Savannah* sighted a second brig and set off in pursuit. Approaching closer, the brig was discerned to be a warship, and *Savannah* attempted to escape the much larger vessel. The U.S. brig *Perry* caught up with the privateer as night fell, and a short battle ensued with both sides firing at gun flashes. Most of *Savannah*'s crew hid below decks during the battle and the schooner was captured. The men were transferred to *Perry* and the privateer became a prize.

Savannah was sent to New York, where it was condemned and sold. The twelve privateersmen were eventually carried to New York as well, where the press popularized the story of the capture of the *Savannah* "pirates" and called for their speedy execution. Imprisoned in the Tombs, a civil prison, the privateersmen were treated as criminals awaiting trial for piracy. Shortly after Jefferson Davis had called for privateers, Abraham Lincoln had proclaimed that privateersmen would be treated as pirates and not accorded prisoner of war status. Now, on July 6, Davis sent Lincoln a letter of protest stating that the Confederate government would treat captured Union combatants in a manner similar to that of the *Savannah* crew. A group of high-ranking Union officers held by the Confederacy was transferred to a civil prison as hostages to carry out the first part of the pledge.

On July 16, the privateersmen were indicted on ten counts, all generally related to their having "piratically, feloniously, and violently" assaulted the ship and crew of *Joseph* on the high seas. After some delays, beginning October 23, a twelve-man jury heard the evidence. Eight days later the jury reported to the judge that they were unable to reach a conclusion and were dismissed.

Owing largely to the Union officer prisoners' being held as hostages, the U.S. government backed down from the threats to execute the men and a second trial was never held. In February 1862, all privateersmen held in civil jails were transferred to military prisons and thereafter treated as prisoners of war. Most were exchanged that year.

The issue forced by the *Savannah* trial had consequences far beyond the fate of twelve men. The decision reached by the Federal government weakened the argument that the war was a simple insurrection. By according belligerent status to the privateersmen, the Lincoln government was forced to accept the conventional rules of war in what had been considered a civil war.

BIBLIOGRAPHY

Robinson, William Morrison, Jr. *The Confederate Privateers.* New Haven, 1928.

Trial of the Officers and Crew of the Privateer Savannah, on the Charge of Piracy, in the United States Circuit Court for the Southern District of New York. Hon. Judges Nelson and

Shipman, Presiding. Reported by A. F. Warburton, stenographer, and corrected by the counsel. New York, 1862.

KEVIN J. FOSTER

SAVANNAH SQUADRON. In March 1861 three small wooden gunboats, *Savannah, Sampson,* and *Resolute,* armed with one 32-pounder smoothbore each, were turned over to the Confederate government by the state of Georgia. The vessels had composed the Georgia State Navy created shortly after Georgia seceded. In the Confederate navy they were designated the Savannah Squadron with Capt. Josiah Tattnall as flag officer. The squadron was concentrated on the Savannah River until the fall of 1861 when a powerful Union amphibious force threatened Port Royal, South Carolina. Tattnall shifted his small force, reinforced by the gunboat *Lady Davis* from Charleston, through the sounds and waterways to Port Royal, but his efforts were futile. The small Confederate squadron was forced to retire hastily by the fleet of Flag Officer Samuel DuPont. Port Royal was captured by the Federal force.

The threat to Savannah persuaded the Confederate Navy Department to reinforce the Savannah Squadron. In November 1861 two 150-foot wooden gunboats were laid down on the Savannah River; four months later three additional vessels 112 feet in length were contracted for. Only one of the larger class, *Macon,* and one of the smaller class, *Isondiga,* were completed. The others were unfinished primarily because of the navy's decision to concentrate on building ironclads. In March 1862 the large armored vessel *Georgia* was laid down; the 250-foot warship armed with ten naval guns was completed in the fall of 1862. Because her motive power was incapable of moving the vessel, she was moored in the river to guard the channel approaches to the port.

Shortly after *Georgia* joined the squadron, a second ironclad was completed. *Atlanta* was converted from the iron-hulled blockade runner *Fingal.* In July 1863 *Atlanta* attempted to leave the river and attack Union blockaders in the sounds. Steaming down river, she ran aground, came under fire from two monitors, and surrendered.

In the summer of 1863 a third ironclad, the 150-foot *Savannah,* joined the squadron. Two additional ironclads were laid down in Savannah but never completed.

The Savannah Squadron cooperated with the land fortifications in defending the river approaches to Savannah. In December 1864, however, the city was captured by Gen. William Tecumseh Sherman's army from the west. The ships in the squadron were destroyed by their crews after covering the withdrawal of Confederate troops to South Carolina.

[*See also* Port Royal, South Carolina; Savannah, Georgia.]

BIBLIOGRAPHY

Scharf, J. Thomas. *History of the Confederate States Navy.* New York, 1887. Reprint, New York, 1977.

Still, William N., Jr. *Savannah Squadron.* Savannah, Ga., 1989.

WILLIAM N. STILL, JR.

SCALES, ALFRED MOORE (1827–1892), U.S. congressman, brigadier general, and governor of North Carolina. Born in North Carolina and a former congressman, Scales supported John C. Breckinridge in the presidential election of 1860. He attended his state's secession convention in February 1861 but did not advocate immediate secession.

When Abraham Lincoln called for troops in April 1861, Scales enlisted in the service and in October was appointed colonel of the Thirteenth North Carolina. After a short assignment in the Norfolk area, he participated in the engagements at Yorktown, Williamsburg, and Seven Pines. He commanded his regiment with skill and distinction during the Seven Days' Battles, receiving praise from his superior officers. Scales fought at Fredericksburg in December 1862, taking temporary command of the brigade when Brig. Gen. William Dorsey Pender fell wounded. At Chancellorsville he and his regiment again performed with distinction, defending their position against superior forces and then advancing against the enemy, capturing a Federal brigadier general in the process. Wounded during the fighting of May 3, Scales was convalescing at home when he received notification on June 13, 1863, of his promotion to brigadier general. Leading Pender's former brigade at Gettysburg, he was wounded on Seminary Ridge in the first day of fighting. In 1864 he participated in the Battles of the Wilderness and Spotsylvania, and the siege of Petersburg. He was at home on sick leave when the war ended.

After the war, Scales served as a congressman (1874–1884) and governor of North Carolina (1884–1888). When his term as governor expired, he retired from public service and became president of the Piedmont Bank at Greensboro. He died there in February 1892.

BIBLIOGRAPHY

Freeman, Douglas S. *Lee's Lieutenants: A Study in Command.* 3 vols. New York, 1942–1944. Reprint, New York, 1986.

Hill, D. H., Jr. *North Carolina.* Vol. 4 of *Confederate Military History.* Edited by Clement A. Evans. Atlanta, 1899. Vol. 5 of extended ed. Wilmington, N.C., 1987.

U.S. War Department. *War of the Rebellion: A Compilation of the Official Records of the Union and Confederate Armies.* Washington, D.C., 1880–1901. Ser. 1, vol. 21, p. 647; ser. 1, vol. 25, pt. 1, pp. 935–936; ser. 1, vol. 27, pt. 2, pp. 669–670.

MICHAEL G. MAHON

SCHARF, JOHN THOMAS (1843–1898), midshipman and historian. Scharf is famous for his postwar achievement as historian of the Confederate navy, not for his wartime exploits as a young midshipman. He entered the navy in 1863, serving first aboard the school ship *Patrick Henry* and then aboard the ironclad *Chicora* in Charleston during 1863 and 1864. He participated in John Taylor Wood's raid upon USS *Underwriter* in February 1864 and later that year transferred to the wooden gunboat *Chattahoochee* in Columbus, Georgia.

In May his commander, Lt. George W. Gift, another veteran of the *Underwriter* action, mounted an unsuccessful attack upon the blockade at Apalachicola, Florida. That group was then transferred to Savannah for service aboard *Water Witch* and *Sampson*. Upon the fall of Savannah on December 30, 1864, Scharf was assigned to Richmond for duty aboard *Patrick Henry*. On March 5 he was captured in Prince George's County, Maryland, and after three weeks was released on bond from Old Capitol Prison in Washington.

Scharf returned home to Baltimore, where he became an enterprising journalist and historian. His histories of Baltimore, Maryland, and Philadelphia were well known, but none rivaled his comprehensive *History of the Confederate States Navy from Its Organization to the Surrender of Its Last Vessel*. The book remains a major resource for historians, although it shares with other immediate postwar histories a Confederate bias, an absence of complete or official records, and conflicting accounts from the veterans who contributed their papers and recollections. Its twenty-six chapters treat chronologically the organization of the navy and actions of 1862 to 1863 in Virginia waters and on the Mississippi. It then recounts other actions state by state, and ends the book with chapters on the torpedo service, the Confederate naval school, the cruisers, and an appendix listing officers and ships. Many of the illustrations are reprints from U.S. Adm. D. D. Porter's naval history of the Civil War.

BIBLIOGRAPHY

Civil War Naval Chronology, 1861–1865. 6 vols. Washington, D.C., 1961–1965.

Register of Officers of the Confederate States Navy, 1861–1865. Washington, D.C., 1931.

Scharf, J. Thomas. *History of the Confederate States Navy from Its Organization to the Surrender of Its Last Vessel.* New York, 1887. Reprint, New York, 1977.

Turner, Maxine. *Navy Gray: A Story of the Confederate Navy on the Chattahoochee and Apalachicola Rivers.* University, Ala., 1988.

Maxine Turner

SCOTT, ROBERT EDEN (1808–1862), congressman from Virginia. Born in Warrenton, Virginia, Scott graduated from the University of Virginia in 1827 and was admitted to the bar in his hometown two years later. A Whig, he sat in the House of Delegates (1839–1842, 1845–1852) and the Virginia constitutional convention of 1850 to 1851. Before his election to the 1861 Virginia convention, Scott was approached by Federal officials with an offer to make him Abraham Lincoln's secretary of the navy. He declined to be considered for the appointment.

Though Scott opposed secession, he, like other conditional Unionists at the Virginia convention, voted first against disunion and finally for it. Elected to the Provisional Congress, Scott became a strong advocate of state rights despite his Whig background. He did, however, support emergency powers for the president. In the legislature he was remembered for his curious habit of beginning a speech with near-inarticulate stammering that gradually evolved into eloquence. In the election for the First Congress, he lost to former governor William Smith. He returned home and was active in his local guard defending against Federal raiding parties and bands of deserters from both sides that terrorized Fauquier County almost until the end of the war. Sent with a patrol on May 3, 1862, to capture a gang of Union deserters, Scott was shot dead by one of the soldiers.

BIBLIOGRAPHY

Gaines, William H., ed. *Biographical Register of Members, Virginia State Convention of 1861, First Session.* Richmond, Va., 1969.

Scott, Robert E. "Robert Eden Scott." *Fauquier Historical Society Bulletin,* 1st ser. (1921–1924): 78–92.

Wakelyn, Jon L. *Biographical Dictionary of the Confederacy.* Edited by Frank E. Vandiver. Westport, Conn., 1977.

Warner, Ezra J., and W. Buck Yearns. *Biographical Register of the Confederate Congress.* Baton Rouge, La., 1975.

Nelson D. Lankford

SCOTT, THOMAS (1829–1876), brigadier general. Thomas Moore Scott was born in Georgia, probably in Athens. When the Civil War began he was farming in Claiborne Parish, Louisiana.

On August 13, 1861, he joined Company B of the Twelfth Louisiana Infantry Regiment as captain. He was soon elected colonel of the regiment. In 1862 and 1863 he and his command were stationed in western Tennessee. From mid-1863 to the spring of 1864 they served in Mississippi and in May were sent to reinforce the Army of Tennessee, which was then defending North Georgia. Scott was especially distinguished in the Battle of Peachtree Creek (July 20).

Meanwhile, Scott's superiors had been trying to get him promoted to fill the vacancy left by the transfer of Brig. Gen. Abraham Buford to the cavalry. The promotion to brigadier general was made May 24, 1864, with Scott's date of rank as brigadier general set at May 10.

Scott commanded his brigade through the Atlanta campaign and in the first part of the Franklin and Nashville campaign. On November 30, 1864, at Franklin, Tennessee, he was severely wounded. In January the next year he appeared before a board of medical officers, which found him unfit for duty "because of Concussion and Contusion from Shell involving Spine and kidneys." As far as the records show, he saw no further military duty.

After the war Scott resumed his agricultural pursuits in Louisiana. He died April 21, 1876, and was buried in Greenwood Cemetery in New Orleans.

BIBLIOGRAPHY

Jones, Terry L. "Thomas Moore Scott." In *The Confederate General.* Edited by William C. Davis. Vol. 5. Harrisburg, Pa., 1991.

Warner, Ezra J. *Generals in Gray: Lives of the Confederate Commanders.* Baton Rouge, La., 1959.

RICHARD M. MCMURRY

SCURRY, WILLIAM R. (1821–1864), brigadier general. Born February 10, 1821, in Tennessee, Scurry came to Texas in the late 1830s and supported his adopted state as a soldier in the Mexican War and as a delegate to the secession convention of 1861. He entered Confederate service as lieutenant colonel of the Fourth Texas Mounted Volunteers, seeing action in the New Mexico campaign under Brig. Gen. Henry H. Sibley. On February 21, 1862, he proved himself under fire at Valverde, New Mexico, making himself heard "above the din of battle and smoke . . . encouraging the men to stand by their posts." At Glorieta Pass (March 28, 1862), he held firm as minié balls twice grazed his cheek.

He was promoted to brigadier general on September 12, 1862, transferred to Texas, and commanded part of the land forces during the recapture of Galveston on January 1, 1863, for which he earned the praise of Maj. Gen. John B. Magruder. Scurry served under Magruder as commander of the Eastern Sub-District of Texas and then closed out the war leading a brigade in John G. Walker's division. His men contested the advance of Union Maj. Gen. Nathaniel P. Banks along the Red River, winning praise from Lt. Gen. Richard Taylor for stern fighting at the Battles of Mansfield and Pleasant Hill (April 8–9, 1864). Scurry's brigade then went to Arkansas to oppose forces under Union Maj. Gen. Frederick Steele. On April 30, 1864, Scurry bled to death on the battlefield from wounds received at Jenkins Ferry. He was buried in Texas State Cemetery at Austin.

BIBLIOGRAPHY

Roberts, O. M. *Texas.* Vol. 11 of *Confederate Military History.* Edited by Clement A. Evans. Atlanta, 1899. Vol. 15 of extended ed. Wilmington, N.C., 1989.

Wright, Marcus J. *Texas in the War, 1861–1865.* Hillsboro, Tex., 1965.

WILLIAM ALAN BLAIR

SEARS, CLAUDIUS WISTAR (1817–1891), brigadier general. Sears, born in Peru, Massachusetts, on November 8, 1817, graduated from the U.S. Military Academy in 1841 but left the service the next year to become a teacher.

In 1861, Sears resigned the presidency of St. Thomas Academy, Holly Springs, Mississippi, and enlisted in the Seventeenth Mississippi Infantry Regiment when that state seceded. He was elected captain of Company G. When the Forty-sixth Regiment was formed, Sears was commissioned its colonel and led the unit at Chickasaw Bayou and at Port Gibson, where he was captured. Exchanged in 1864, he returned to his command and on March 1 was appointed brigadier general. Ordered to the Army of Tennessee, Sears

CLAUDIUS WISTAR SEARS. LIBRARY OF CONGRESS

participated in the Atlanta campaign and was commended by Gen. Samuel G. French for his actions in the desperate fight for Alatoona. He and his command, as part of John Bell Hood's army, attacked into Tennessee, and at the battle for Nashville, he lost a leg to an enemy shell. Captured again, this time near Pulaski, Tennessee, he was not paroled until June 23, 1865.

After the war, Sears was elected to the University of Mississippi chair of mathematics, which he occupied until 1889. He died February 15, 1891, and is buried at Oxford, Mississippi.

Brave and competent, Sears was respected both by his men and his superiors. Had the opportunity presented itself, he would doubtlessly have proven an effective division commander.

BIBLIOGRAPHY

Connelly, Thomas L. *Autumn of Glory: The Army of Tennessee, 1862–1865.* Baton Rouge, La., 1971.

Hooker, Charles E. *Mississippi.* Vol. 7 of *Confederate Military History.* Edited by Clement A. Evans. Atlanta, 1899. Vol. 9 of extended ed. Wilmington, N.C., 1987.

Horn, Stanley F. *The Army of Tennessee: A Military History.* 2d ed. Norman, Okla., 1953.

Warner, Ezra J. *Generals in Gray: Lives of the Confederate Commanders.* Baton Rouge, La., 1959.

Roy R. Stephenson

SECESSION. The formal withdrawal of individual states from the Federal Union created at the Constitutional Convention of 1787 occurred in two distinct phases of separate state actions. The first took the seven states of the lower South out of the Union by February 1, 1861. This phase, triggered by Abraham Lincoln's election in November 1860, started when South Carolina withdrew on December 20, 1860. When Lincoln responded to the Confederate firing on Fort Sumter in April 1861 by calling upon the states to furnish seventy-five thousand militia to put down the Southern "insurrection," four additional states from the upper South left in the second phase of secession. These states—Virginia, North Carolina, Tennessee, and Arkansas—rounded out the political dimensions of the new Southern Confederacy. The other four slave states of Missouri, Kentucky, Maryland, and Delaware in the border South remained within the Union (the Confederacy claimed Missouri and Kentucky as member states, and both were represented in the Confederate Congress).

Secession rested on the constitutional doctrine of state sovereignty. According to this state rights position, the Union of 1787 was a confederation of sovereign states. The Federal government was simply the agent of the states entrusted with certain specified and limited powers. The individual states retained ultimate sovereign power, and they could leave the Union the same way they had entered it by calling a special state convention. Contrary to this view, most Northerners believed by 1860 that the Union was sovereign and perpetual. The states had surrendered their individual sovereignty when they joined the Union, and the legal right of secession did not exist. Far from residing within the Constitution, secession was a revolutionary act of defiance directed against the Constitution and the Union it had created.

The debate over the legal nature of the Union was as old as the Union itself. Both sides could turn to the Constitution for confirmation of their respective views because of its studied ambiguity over the ultimate locus of sovereign power in the Union. Such ambiguity was necessary in order to provide for a middle constitutional position that could blur the sharp differences between nationalists and state righters at the Philadelphia Convention. The Founding Fathers were able to secure the ratification of the Constitution only by agreeing to set up a Federal system in which power was divided and shared between the central government and the state governments.

Early Sectional Crises

The looseness of the Federal system left plenty of room for Jeffersonian Republicans and Hamiltonian Federalists to jockey for power in the early Republic. Although the Hamiltonians were associated with a broad construction of the Constitution and the Jeffersonians with a strict one, the slaveholding Virginia presidents during the era of Democratic-Republican dominance from 1802 to 1824 by no means sought to crimp Federal power. Indeed, their control of the Federal government, combined with an aggressive policy of territorial expansion and the imposition of economic sanctions and a declaration of war against Britain in 1812, placed New England in the position of a beleaguered sectional minority chafing under Federal dominance. New Englanders, not Southerners, muttered the first cries of secession.

Missouri Crisis. The Missouri crisis of 1819–1820 marked the first major sectional confrontation in which the South turned to the doctrine of state rights in the defense of slavery. Down to 1819 Congress had routinely admitted new slave states into the Union. Southerners were thus surprised when Representative James Tallmadge of New York, in February 1819, attached a resolution to the Missouri statehood bill banning the future introduction of slaves and providing for the emancipation at the age of twenty-five of all slaves born in Missouri after its admission as a state. Passed in the Northern-dominated House by nearly unanimous Northern votes, the Tallmadge proviso was blocked in the Senate where the slave and free states were in even balance.

Congress finally reached a compromise in March 1820. Missouri, part of the original Louisiana Purchase territory, was admitted as a slave state with no restrictions placed upon slavery, and Maine was admitted as a free state, thereby maintaining sectional parity in the Senate. Slavery was prohibited from the remainder of the Louisiana Purchase territory north of latitude 36° 30′, the southern boundary of Missouri. Only the threat of Southern disunion forced the Northern concessions that made possible the Missouri Compromise. Cries of secession became for the first time a weapon in the Southern arsenal of proslavery defenses. Few Southern whites, however, seriously contemplated secession in 1820. They remained confident of their ability to protect slavery by clinging more tightly to the strict constructionist doctrines of the original Jeffersonians.

Nullification Crisis. Despite Southern control of the Jacksonian Democratic party that captured the presidency in 1828, South Carolina planters precipitated another sectional crisis in the early 1830s. These planters insisted that high protective tariffs were sacrificing the export economy of the slave South in the interests of Northern manufacturing capital. Their resistance to Federal authority produced the nullification crisis of 1832 and 1833.

Extending the arguments put forth by James Madison and Thomas Jefferson in the Virginia and Kentucky Resolutions of 1798, John C. Calhoun of South Carolina developed an elaborate constitutional theory by which a state could legally nullify Federal legislation that it determined violated its interests. The most delicate of those interests in the South involved slavery. For all the economic opposition to the tariff, the underlying issue ran much deeper. The tariff was only symptomatic of the far greater threat of centralizing Federal power encroaching upon the prerogatives of slave owners and the perceived personal safety of Southern whites.

After the tariff of 1832 failed to reduce duties as much as the nullifiers demanded, a special South Carolina convention met in the fall of 1832 and nullified the tariffs of 1828 and 1832. The result was a major constitutional crisis that produced, for the first time, a firm case in the North for a perpetual Union. Although a compromise tariff in 1833 satisfied the nullifiers, their defiance of Federal authority had sharpened the ideological lines in the sectional conflict. Secessionist doctrines now began to attract a popular following in the South.

The Crisis of Slavery in the Territories

In the midst of the nullification controversy, abolitionism burst upon the national scene. It was a product both of evangelical Christianity and the radical idea in a racist society that equality of opportunity and the right of self-betterment should be color-blind. The abolitionists had an impact far greater than their numbers alone. Never more than a very small minority of Northern whites (Northern blacks, of course, were far more likely to be abolitionists), the abolitionists used every conceivable means to spread their message that slavery was a moral abomination. Most particularly, they targeted slaveholders as moral pariahs who were a disgrace to Christianity and the Republic's ideals of human rights as expressed in the Declaration of Independence.

Slaveholders, many of whom were evangelicals themselves, were stung to the quick. They lashed back at their accusers by using their political power to deny the abolitionists a hearing. Mails were censored in the South to keep out abolitionist literature, and Congress passed a series of gag rules that automatically tabled antislavery petitions. By enacting such measures, Southern politicians unwittingly strengthened the cause of antislavery. The image of the "Slave Power," a conspiratorial force of tyrannical slaveholders running roughshod over the civil liberties and constitutional rights of Northern whites, began to take root in the popular consciousness of the North.

The demands of Southern Democrats in the early 1840s for the annexation of Texas, an independent slaveholding republic since 1836, fed Northern fears of a Southern plot to spread slavery. The push for Texas ultimately led to the Mexican War of 1846 through 1848. In that war American armies added California and most of the present-day Southwest to the Union and secured American claims to Texas as far south as the Rio Grande. The price of these territorial gains was the nation's worst sectional crisis since the flare-up over the admission of Missouri.

In the early stages of the Mexican War, David Wilmot, a congressman from Pennsylvania, introduced a proviso that prohibited slavery from any territory acquired as a result of the war. A Northern antislavery majority immediately formed in the House in support of the proviso. In response, Southern congressmen, almost to a man, rose up in defense of their right to expand slavery into Federal territories. Although Southern votes in the Senate were sufficient to defeat the Wilmot Proviso, the issues it raised continued to fester until the passage of a series of measures known collectively as the Compromise of 1850.

Compromise of 1850. Congress, against a backdrop of secessionist activity in the lower South and a call for a Southern convention to meet in Nashville, Tennessee, hammered out a compromise in the late summer of 1850. Concessions by the Northern antislavery majority in the House made possible the compromise. To be sure, California was admitted as a free state, the slave trade in Washington, D.C., was abolished, and the slave state of Texas yielded its claim on New Mexico (the eastern half bordered by the Rio Grande) in return for a Federal buyout of its debt. But the principle of the Wilmot Proviso was abandoned. The remaining lands in the Mexican Cession were organized into the territories of New Mexico and Utah with no mention of slavery. Even more damaging to the cause of antislavery was Northern acquiescence to a strengthened Fugitive Slave Act. This legislation put the full weight of the Federal government behind the efforts of slaveholders to recover their escaped slaves.

The Compromise of 1850 neutralized the Nashville Convention, and the secessionists were checkmated. Their strongholds were in South Carolina and Mississippi, but the refusal of Georgia, politically the bellwether in the lower South, to go along made Unionism respectable and politically profitable once again in the South. Nonetheless, the case for secession was significantly advanced. Even most Southern Unionists were forced to acknowledge that secession was a legal right. In the lower South the Unionism that triumphed was of a decidedly conditional variety. As the Georgia legislature made explicit, Southern states reserved the right to weigh the value of the Union against the safety of the institution of slavery.

Kansas-Nebraska Act. Hopes in both sections that the Compromise of 1850 would be the final word on the sectional controversy shattered in 1854 with the passage of the Kansas-Nebraska Act. In order to gain Southern votes necessary for the passage of his bill organizing the Louisiana Purchase territory north of 36° 30′, Senator Stephen A. Douglas of Illinois had to write into the Kansas-Nebraska Act a repeal of the Missouri Compromise restriction on slavery. Northerners widely interpreted this repeal as confirmation of a plot by the "Slave Power" to monopolize the territories for slavery at the expense of free labor.

STEPHEN A. DOUGLAS. Proponent of the Kansas-Nebraska Act and Democratic candidate in the 1860 presidential election.

NATIONAL ARCHIVES

The Northern storm of protest over the Kansas-Nebraska Act led to the formation of a sectionalized Republican party committed to preventing the spread of slavery into the territories. By 1856 the Republicans were the strongest party in the North. The Democrats were still a national party, but they were increasingly dominated by their Southern wing. In 1856, and with nearly solid support from the South, James Buchanan of Pennsylvania was elected as the last of the antebellum Democratic presidents.

The Buchanan presidency was a disaster for what remained of national unity. The Supreme Court ruled in the *Dred Scott* case of 1857 that Congress had no constitutional authority to prohibit slavery in the territories. The decision enraged Northerners and lent further credence to the notion of a "Slave Power" controlling the highest councils of government. A year later Democratic unity collapsed when Buchanan attempted to bring Kansas into the Union as a slave state. Convinced that the Free Soil majority in Kansas had been denied a fair opportunity to express its wishes on slavery, Douglas led a party revolt against Buchanan and his Southern supporters. Although few Southerners felt that slavery could thrive on the plains of Kansas, they were determined to establish the principle that a slave state could still be added to the Union. Largely because of the Douglas-led revolt, a slave Kansas was kept out of the Union. Southern Democrats never again trusted Douglas, and they would wreck the party before they would submit to his presidential nomination in 1860.

Election of 1860. John Brown's raid against the Harpers Ferry arsenal in October 1859 heightened sectional tensions as the election of 1860 approached. Brown, the epitome of the fiery abolitionist, failed in his attempt to incite a slave uprising and was executed in early December. Most Northerners, including the Republicans, denounced Brown as a wild-eyed fanatic. But, the fact that Brown had mounted a frontal attack upon slavery and then was elevated to martyrdom by a handful of New England reformers sent paroxysms of fear and anger throughout the South. Rumors of conspiracies and slave uprisings were rampant during the winter of 1859–1860, and Southerners were convinced that the Republican party was dominated by abolitionists and was plotting with them to unleash a bloodbath in the slave states.

The presidential election of 1860 was a four-way race. After the Southern Democrats bolted the party's national convention in Charleston, South Carolina, over the refusal of the Douglas Democrats to support a congressional slave code for the protection of slavery in the territories, the separate wings of the party nominated their own candidates for the presidency—Douglas for the North and John C. Breckinridge of Kentucky for the South. The Republicans ran Abraham Lincoln of Illinois, the favorite son of a state

ABRAHAM LINCOLN. Republican candidate and winner of the 1860 presidential election. Portrait by Mathew Brady, c. 1863.
NATIONAL ARCHIVES

in the lower North that was crucial to Republican hopes for victory in 1860. The fourth candidate was John Bell of Tennessee who was backed by members of the now defunct Whig party in the upper South.

As expected, Lincoln was elected on November 6, 1860. With the exception of New Jersey, whose electoral vote was split, he swept the free states and commanded a clear majority in the electoral college though securing only 40 percent of the total popular vote. Breckinridge carried eleven of the fifteen slave states, including the entire lower South. Bell took Virginia, Kentucky, and Tennessee. Douglas, whose popular vote was second to Lincoln's, won only Missouri.

Lincoln's election was the signal the secessionists had been waiting for. Southerners had anticipated with dread the election of 1860, and on November 6 their worst fears were confirmed. Southern political power had shrunk to the point where an antislavery minority party with no pretense of support in the South could capture the presidency. It would be hard to imagine a greater insult to Southern honor than this demonstration of the South's political impotency in the face of a growing Northern majority. Here then was the first great advantage of the secessionists. Regardless of party affiliation or political beliefs, Southerners felt tremendously wronged. For more than a generation they had cast themselves as the aggrieved innocents in an unequal sectional struggle that unleashed more and more Northern aggressions on Southern rights. They believed they had been denied their fair share of the Federal territories and unfairly taxed through high tariffs to subsidize Northern industrial might. They were infuriated by the personal liberty laws passed by many Northern states that made it more difficult to recover fugitive slaves. Above all, they had been branded as moral monsters for upholding the institution of slavery. Their self-respect demanded that a stand be taken against the latest Northern outrage, the election of a Republican president.

Secession Looms

Young, slaveholding lawyers and planters spearheaded secession. They came to political maturity in the 1850s at a time of intensifying sectional hostilities, and they turned to the Breckinridge movement for vindication of their rights and status against the onslaughts of the antislavery North. The Breckinridge demand for Federal protection of slavery in the territories was their answer to the Republican commitment to free soil. Their recently acquired wealth in land and slaves rested on a rickety structure of credit that required rising slave prices to keep from collapsing. Economic self-interest, as well as wounded pride, drove them to secession once Lincoln's election threatened to limit Southern growth by ending the expansion of slavery.

The Fire-eaters. The most prominent secessionists were known as the fire-eaters. In particular, William Lowndes Yancey of Alabama, Edmund Ruffin of Virginia, and Robert Barnwell Rhett, Sr., of South Carolina had earned this label for their long and uncompromising devotion to the cause of Southern independence. Outside the inner circle of Southern political power at the national level, and hence free of the need to fashion a middle position to hold together a bisectional party coalition, the fire-eaters consistently had taken a hard line on Southern rights. They pushed sectional issues to their logical extreme and applauded the breakup of the national Democratic party in

1860. Aided immeasurably by the fears provoked by John Brown's raid, they popularized the right of secession among the Southern masses.

As veterans of sectional agitation, the fire-eaters had learned an invaluable lesson: a united South was a myth. South Carolina had stood alone during the nullification crisis, and Calhoun had called in vain for a monolithic South to rise up and demand its rights from the Yankee aggressors. In the crisis of 1850 and 1851, the secessionists were left isolated in South Carolina and Mississippi. Unity was impossible because of statewide and regional divisions that broke along lines of geography and social development. Virtually every slave state was rife with tensions between the yeoman-dominated backcountry and the planter-dominated black belts and lowcountry. A very broad division ran along a line from South Carolina westward to the Mississippi that differentiated the lower South from the slave states above it. In the upper South slaveholdings and percentages of slave owners were relatively smaller, fears of losing racial control less intense, and integration into the free-labor economies of the North tighter. Following the leadership of Virginia, the states of the upper South counseled moderation in the sectional confrontations of the 1850s.

Now that a Republican victory had fired the Southern resolve to resist, the radicals of the lower South were determined not to repeat their mistakes of the past by waiting for the upper South to act. They rejected any plan of prior cooperation among the slave states and launched secession on their own. They pursued a strategy of separate state action and confidently predicted that wavering states would be forced to join those that had already gone out. Separate state action was indeed the key to secession. It enabled the secessionists to lead from strength and create an irreversible momentum.

"Resistance or submission" was the rallying cry of the secessionists. The former, Southerners were told, was an honorable act of self-defense demanded by a love of liberty and equality. The latter was the slavish servility of a dishonorable coward. Frightened white males, often spurred on by white women, responded by rushing to join vigilance committees, military companies, and associations of "Minute Men." All these paramilitary groups pledged to defend the South against widely feared incursions of abolitionists incited by Lincoln's success. Southern communities were thrown into an emotional frenzy as they mobilized on an emergency footing.

The Republican Threat. For all the popular hysteria they were instrumental in whipping up, the secessionists quite rationally assessed the nature of the Republican threat. The Republican stand against the expansion of slavery struck at the vital interests of the slave South. Economically, it threatened to choke off the profits of plantation agriculture by denying it access to fresh, arable lands. As a consequence, Southerners told themselves, whites would flee the slave states, and to save themselves, the dwindling numbers of whites would have to wage a preemptive war of extermination against the growing black majority. Politically, as free states were carved out of the territories, Southern power in Congress would be reduced to the point where slavery in the states could be dismantled by the ever larger political majority in the North. Most degrading of all from the Southern perspective was the humiliation implicit in submitting to the rule of an antislavery party. To do so would be an admission to Northerners and the outside world that the Southern way of life was morally suspect. Only slaves, the secessionists insisted, acted in such a servile fashion.

The secessionists did not expect the Republicans to make an immediate and direct move against slavery. They were well aware that the Republicans did not control Congress or the Supreme Court. As a new and still untested party, the Republicans would have to cooperate with Southern and Democratic politicians. But, reasoned the secessionists, such a demonstration that the slave South could, in the short run, survive under a Republican administration, would establish the fatal precedent of submitting to Republican rule and blunt the spirit of Southern resistance. In the meantime, the Republicans could use what power they had to begin the slow dismantling of slavery. The whole purpose of the Republican determination to prohibit the expansion of slavery was to put it on the road to extinction in the states where it existed.

In addition to all the perceived horrors of encirclement by a swelling majority of free states, the secessionists warned of changes in the sectional balance that the Republicans could potentially implement. They could move against slavery in Washington, D.C., and in Federal forts and installations. They could force the introduction of antislavery literature into the South by banning censorship of the Federal mails and simultaneously position the Supreme Court to overturn the *Dred Scott* ruling. They could weaken or repeal the Fugitive Slave Act and prohibit the interstate slave trade, a key link in the profitability of slavery to the South as a whole. Most alarming of all from the standpoint of the secessionists was the possibility that the Republicans would use Federal patronage and appointments to build a free labor party in the South. Senator Robert Toombs of Georgia echoed the concerns of many secessionists when he predicted in 1860 that Republican control of Federal jobs would create an "abolition party" within a year in Maryland, within two years in Kentucky, Missouri, and Virginia, and throughout the South by the end of four years.

Southern Divisions over Slavery. The Toombs prediction went to the heart of secessionists' fears over the commitment to slavery *within* the South. To be sure, very few Southern whites by 1860 favored an immediate end to slavery. Most such whites had left the South in the preceding generation, either voluntarily or in response to community pressures forcing them out. Nonetheless, deep divisions existed over the future of slavery and the direction of Southern society itself.

The Jeffersonian dream of a gradual withering away of slavery persisted in the upper South. Many whites could contemplate and even accept the eventual end of the institution as long as there was no outside interference in the process of disentanglement. In this region, as the proportion of slaves in the total population steadily declined in the late antebellum decades, slavery was increasingly becoming a matter of expediency, not of necessity. The secessionists had every reason to believe that a Republican administration would encourage the emancipationist sentiment that had already emerged among the white working classes in such slave cities as St. Louis, Baltimore, and Richmond.

In the lower South the secessionists doubted the loyalty to slavery of the yeomanry, a class of nonslaveholding farmers who composed the largest single bloc in the electorate. Although tied to the planters by a mutual commitment to white supremacy and often by bonds of kinship, these farmers occupied an ambivalent position in Southern society. They fervently valued their economic independence and political liberties, and hence they resented the spread of the plantation economy and the planters' pretensions to speak for them. But as long as the yeomen were able to practice their subsistence-oriented agriculture and the more ambitious ones saw a reasonable chance of someday buying a few slaves, this resentment fell far short of class conflict. In the 1850s, however, both these safety valves were being closed off. The proportion of families owning slaves fell from 31 to 25 percent. Sharply rising slave prices prevented more and more whites from purchasing slaves. At the same time, railroads spread the reach of a plantation agriculture geared to market production. Rates of farm tenancy rose in the older black belts, and the yeomen's traditional way of life was under increasing pressure.

Distrustful of the upper South as a region and the yeomanry as a class, the secessionists pushed for immediate as well as separate state secession. By moving quickly, they hoped to prevent divisions within the South from coalescing into a paralyzing debate over the best means of resisting Republican rule. Since most of the rabid secessionists were Breckinridge Democrats, the party that controlled nearly all the governorships and state legislatures in the lower South, the secessionists were able to set their own timetable for disunion.

The South Secedes

South Carolina was in the perfect position to launch secession. Its governor, William H. Gist, was on record as favoring a special state convention in the event of a Republican victory, and the legislature, the only one in the Union that still cast its state's electoral votes, was in session when news of Lincoln's election first reached the state. Aware of South Carolina's reputation for rash, precipitate action and leery of the state's being isolated, Gist would have preferred that another state take the lead in secession. But having been rebuffed a month earlier in his attempt to convince other Southern governors to seize the initiative, he was now prepared to take the first overt step. The South Carolina legislature almost immediately approved a bill setting January 8 as the election day for a state convention to meet on January 15.

Secession might well have been stillborn had the original convention dates set by the South Carolina legislature held. A two-month delay, especially in the likely event that no Southern state other than South Carolina would dare to go out alone, would have allowed time for passions to subside and lines of communication to be opened with the incoming Republican administration. But on November 10 a momentous shift occurred in the timing of South Carolina's convention. Reports of large secession meetings in Jackson, Mississippi, and Montgomery, Alabama, and reports that Georgia's governor, Joseph E. Brown, had recommended the calling of a convention in his state emboldened the South Carolina secessionists to accelerate their own timetable. They successfully pressured the South Carolina legislature to move up the dates of the state's convention to December 6 for choosing delegates and December 17 for the meeting.

Secession in the Lower South. The speedy call for an early South Carolina convention triggered similar steps toward secession by governors and legislatures throughout the lower South. On November 14 Governors Andrew B. Moore of Alabama and J. J. Pettus of Mississippi issued calls for state conventions, both of which were to be elected on December 24 and meet on January 7. Moore had prior legislative approval for calling a convention, and Pettus was given his mandate on November 26. Once the Georgia legislature voted its approval on November 18, Governor Brown set January 2 for the election of Georgia's convention and January 16 for its convening. The Florida legislature in late November and the Louisiana legislature in early December likewise authorized their governors to set in motion the electoral machinery for January meetings of their conventions. Texas was a temporary exception to the united front developing in the lower South for secession. Its governor, Sam Houston, was a staunch Unionist who refused to call his legislature into special session. As a result, Texas secessionists resorted to the irregular, if not

The Process of Secession

	SECESSION ORDINANCE	POPULAR RATIFICATION	JOINED THE CONFEDERACY*
South Carolina	Dec. 20, 1860	None	Apr. 3, 1861
Mississippi	Jan. 9, 1860	None	Mar. 29, 1861
Florida	Jan. 10, 1861	None	Feb. 26, 1861
Alabama	Jan. 11, 1861	None	Mar. 13, 1861
Georgia	Jan. 19, 1861	None	Mar. 16, 1861
Louisiana	Jan. 26, 1861	None	Mar. 21, 1861
Texas	Feb. 1, 1861	Feb. 23, 1861	Mar. 23, 1861
Virginia	Apr. 17, 1861	May 23, 1861	Apr. 27, 1861
Arkansas	May 6, 1861	None	May 10, 1861
Tennessee	May 6, 1861	June 8, 1861	May 7, 1861
North Carolina	May 20, 1861	None	May 20, 1861

*With the exceptions of Tennessee and Virginia, these are the dates that the secession conventions ratified the Confederate Constitution. On April 27, the Virginia convention invited the Confederate government to shift its capital to Richmond, and on May 7 Governor Isham Harris of Tennessee committed his state to a military alliance with the Confederacy.

illegal, expedient of issuing their own call for a January convention.

Within three weeks of Lincoln's election the secessionists had generated a strong momentum for the breakup of the Union by moving quickly and decisively. In contrast, Congress, acting slowly and hesitantly, did nothing to derail the snowballing movement.

Congress convened on December 3, and the House appointed a Committee of Thirty-three (one representative from each state) to consider compromise measures. The committee, however, waited a week before calling its first meeting, and the creation of a similar committee in the Senate was temporarily blocked by bitter debates between Republicans and Southerners. When the House committee did meet on December 14, its Republican members failed (by a vote of eight to eight) to endorse a resolution calling for additional guarantees of Southern rights. Choosing to interpret this Republican stand as proof that Congress could accomplish nothing, thirty congressmen from the lower South then issued an address to their constituents declaring their support for an independent Southern confederacy. A week later, on December 20, South Carolina became the first state to leave the Union when its convention unanimously approved an ordinance of secession.

South Carolina provided the impetus, but the ultimate fate of secession in the lower South rested on the outcome of the convention elections held in late December and early January in the six other cotton states. The opponents of immediate secession in these states were generally known as cooperationists. Arguing that in unity there was strength, the cooperationists wanted to delay secession until a given number of states had agreed to go out as a bloc. Many of the cooperationists were merely cautious secessionists in need of greater assurances before taking their states out. But an indeterminate number of others clung to the hope that the Union could still be saved if the South as a whole forced concessions from the Republicans and created a reconstructed Union embodying safeguards for slavery.

Any delay, however, was anathema to the immediate secessionists. They countered the cooperationists' fears of war by asserting that the North would accept secession rather than risk cutting off its supply of Southern cotton. The secessionists also neutralized the cooperationist call for unanimity of action by appointing secession commissioners to each of the states considering secession. The commissioners acted as the ambassadors of secession by establishing links of communication between the individual states and stressing the need for a speedy withdrawal. In a brilliant tactical move, the South Carolina convention authorized its commissioners on December 31 to issue a call for a Southern convention to launch a provisional government for the Confederate States of America. Even before another state had joined South Carolina in seceding, the call went out on January 3 for a convention to meet in Montgomery, Alabama, on February 4, 1861.

The secessionists won the convention elections in the lower South, but their margins of victory were far narrower than in South Carolina. The cooperationists polled about 40 percent of the overall vote, and in Alabama, Georgia, and Louisiana they ran in a virtual dead heat with the straight-out secessionists. Somewhat surprisingly, given the issues involved and the high pitch of popular excitement, voter turnout fell by more than one-third from the levels in the November presidential election. The short time allotted for campaigning and the uncontested nature of many of the local races held down the vote. In addition, many conservatives boycotted the elections out of fear of reprisals if they publicly opposed secession. The key to the victory of the secessionists was their strength in the plantation districts. They carried four out of five counties in which the slaves comprised a majority of the population and ran weakest in counties with the fewest slaves. The yeomen, especially in the Alabama and Georgia mountains, were against immediate secession. Characteristically, they opposed a policy they associated with the black belt planters.

Mississippi, Florida, Alabama, Georgia, and Louisiana successively seceded in their January conventions. They were joined by Texas on February 1, 1861. Like falling dominoes, the secession of one state made it easier for the next to follow. In each convention the secessionists fought back efforts for a cooperative approach or last-ditch calls for a Southern conference to make final demands on the Republicans. They also defeated attempts by cooperationists to submit the secession ordinances to a popular referendum. Only in Texas, where the secessionists were sensitive to the dubious legality by which they had forced the calling of a convention, was the decision on secession referred to the voters for their approval. In the end the secession ordinances passed by overwhelming majorities in all the conventions. This apparent unanimity, however, belied the fact that in no state had the immediate secessionists carried enough votes to have made up a majority in the earlier presidential election. Once the decision for secession was inevitable, the cooperationists voted for the ordinances in a conscious attempt to impress the Republicans with Southern resolve and unity.

Delegates from the seven seceded states met in Montgomery, Alabama, in February. Here, on the seventh, they adopted a Provisional Constitution (one closely modeled on the U.S. Constitution) for an independent Southern government and, on the ninth, elected Jefferson Davis of Mississippi as president. Thus, nearly a month before Lincoln's inauguration on March 4, the secessionists had achieved one of their major goals. They had a functioning government in place before the Republicans had even assumed formal control of the Federal government.

The Northern Response. Buchanan, the lame-duck president, did nothing to stem the tide of disunion. He officially held the reins of power in the four-month period between the presidential election in early November and Lincoln's inauguration in early March, but he had lost any popular mandate to govern. The secessionists had anticipated his indecision and cited it as confirmation of their argument that secession would be peaceable. Buchanan—reasoning that just as secession was unconstitutional so was any attempt by the Federal government to resist it by force—preferred to leave the problem for the Republicans to settle. He thought they were chiefly responsible for the crisis, and he said as much in his last annual message of December 3, 1860. His policy was a negative one of doing nothing to provoke an armed conflict with the seceding states.

The Republicans initially denied the existence of any real crisis. They were acutely aware of the pattern of Southern bluster and Northern concessions that had characterized former sectional confrontations, and they were not about to surrender their integrity as an antislavery party by yielding to Southern demands. At Lincoln's urging they drew the line at sanctioning the territorial expansion of slavery. Such a sanction was the crucial feature of the Crittenden Compromise, a package of six proposed constitutional amendments that came out of a Senate committee led by John J. Crittenden of Kentucky in mid-December. Under Crittenden's plan, slavery would be recognized south of 36° 30′ in all present territories, as well as those "hereafter acquired." To a man, congressional Republicans rejected what they interpreted as a blank check for the future expansion of slavery into Mexico and the Caribbean.

Secession in the Upper South. The collapse of the Crittenden Compromise in late December eliminated the already slim possibility that the drive toward secession might end with the withdrawal of South Carolina. Still, when Lincoln took office on March 4, the Republicans had reason to believe that the worst of the crisis was over. February elections in the Upper South had resulted in Unionist victories. In January the legislatures of five states—Arkansas, Virginia, Missouri, Tennessee, and North Carolina—had issued calls for conventions. The secessionists suffered a sharp setback in all the elections.

On February 4, Virginia voters chose to send moderates of various stripes to their convention by about a three-to-one margin. In yet another defeat for the secessionists, who opposed the measure, they also overwhelmingly approved a popular referendum on any decision reached by the convention. On February 9, Tennessee voted against holding a convention. Had one been approved, the Unionists elected would have composed an 80-percent majority. Arkansas and Missouri voted on February 18, and both elected Unionist majorities. On February 28, North Carolinians repeated the Tennessee pattern. They rejected the calling of a convention, which, in any event, would have been dominated by Unionists.

By the end of February secession apparently had burnt itself out in the upper South. It was defeated either by a popular vote or, as in the case of the slave states of Kentucky, Delaware, and Missouri, by the inability of the secessionists to pressure the legislatures or governors to issue a call for a convention. Despite fiery speeches and persistent lobbying by secession commissioners appointed by the Confederate government, the antisecessionists held their ground. In a region that lacked the passionate commitment of the lower South to defending slavery, they were able to mobilize large Unionist majorities of nonslaveholders. In particular, they succeeded in detaching large numbers of the Democratic yeomanry from the secessionist, slaveholding wing of their party. The yeomanry responded to the fears invoked by the Unionists of being caught in the crossfire of a civil war, and nonslaveholders in general questioned how well their interests would be served in a planter-dominated Confederacy.

A final factor accounting for the Unionist victories in the upper South was the meeting in Washington of the so-called Peace Convention called by the Virginia legislature. The delegates spent most of February debating various proposals for additional guarantees for slave property in an effort to find some basis for a voluntary reconstruction of the Union. Although boycotted by some of the Northern states and all of the states that had already seceded, the convention raised hopes of a national reconciliation and thereby strengthened the hand of the Unionists in the upper South. In the end, however, the convention was an exercise in futility. All it could come up with was a modified version of the Crittenden Compromise. Just before Lincoln's inauguration, Republican votes in the Senate killed the proposal.

Pressures for Action Mount. Throughout March and early April the Union remained in a state of quiescence that no one expected to last indefinitely. Both of the new governments, Lincoln's and Davis's, were under tremendous pressure to break the suspense by taking decisive action. Davis was criticized for not moving aggressively enough to bring the upper South into the Confederacy. Without that region and especially Virginia, it was argued, the Confederacy was but a cipher of a nation. It had negligible manufacturing capacity and only one-third of the South's free population. It desperately needed additional slave states to have a viable chance for survival. Just as desperately, Lincoln's government needed to make good on its claim that the Union was indivisible. Buchanan had been mocked for his indecisiveness, and Lincoln knew that he had to take a stand on enforcing Federal authority.

The upper South now became a pawn in a power struggle between Lincoln and Davis. However much moderates in the upper South wanted to avoid a confrontation that would ignite a war, they were publicly committed to coming to the assistance of any Southern state that the Republicans attempted to coerce back into the Union. In short, Unionism in the upper South was always highly conditional in nature. This in turn made the region hostage to events beyond its control and gave the Confederacy the leverage it needed to pull in additional states.

The only major Federal installations in the Confederacy still under Federal control when Lincoln became president were Fort Pickens in Pensacola Harbor and Fort Sumter in Charleston Harbor. The retention of these forts thereby became a test of the credibility of the Republicans as the defenders of the Union. By the same token, the acquisition of these forts was essential if the Confederacy were to lay claim to the full rights of a sovereign nation.

On March 5, Lincoln learned from Maj. Robert Anderson, the commander at Fort Sumter, that dwindling food supplies would force an evacuation of the fort within four to six weeks. Lincoln decided against any immediate attempt to save the fort. On March 12, however, he issued orders for the reinforcement of Fort Pickens. More accessible to the Federal navy because of its location outside Pensacola Harbor beyond the range of Confederate artillery, Fort Pickens had the additional advantage of being overshadowed in the public consciousness by Fort Sumter, a highly charged symbol of Federal resolve in the state that had started secession. Presumably, it could be reinforced with less risk of precipitating a war than could Fort Sumter.

Lincoln's initial decision not to act on Fort Sumter was also a concession to William H. Seward, his secretary of state. Seward was the chief spokesman for what was called the policy of "masterly inactivity." He believed that Unionists in the upper South were on the verge of leading a process of voluntary reunion. If the upper South were not stampeded into joining the Confederacy by a coercive act by the Republicans, Seward argued, an isolated Confederacy would soon have no choice but to bargain to rejoin the Union. Everything depended, of course, on a conciliatory Republican policy.

In pursuing this strategy, Lincoln temporarily considered a withdrawal from Fort Sumter in exchange for a binding commitment from the upper South not to leave the Union. Seward then made the mistake of assuming that evacuation was a foregone conclusion. He was conducting informal negotiations with three Confederate commissioners who were in Washington seeking a transfer of Fort Pickens and Fort Sumter. On March 15 he informed them through an intermediary to expect a speedy evacuation of Fort Sumter. When no such evacuation was forthcoming, Confederate leaders felt betrayed, and they vowed never again to trust the word of the Lincoln administration.

Mounting demands in the North to take a stand at Fort Sumter, combined with Lincoln's growing disillusionment over Southern Unionism, convinced the president that he would have to challenge the Confederacy over the issue of Fort Sumter. On March 29 he told his cabinet that he was preparing a relief expedition. He delayed informing Major Anderson of that decision until after a meeting on April 4 with John Baldwin, a Virginia Unionist. Although no firsthand account of this meeting exists, the discussion apparently confirmed Lincoln's belief that the upper South could not broker a voluntary reunion on terms acceptable to the Republican party. The final orders for the relief expedition were issued on April 6, the day that Lincoln learned that Fort Pickens had not yet been reinforced because of a mix-up in the chain of command.

News of Lincoln's decision to reinforce Fort Sumter "with provisions only" reached Montgomery, the Confederate capital, on April 8. The next day Davis ordered Gen. P. G. T. Beauregard, the Confederate commander at Charleston, to demand an immediate surrender of the fort.

SECESSION COMMISSIONERS. Pictured, from left to right, are A. B. Roman of Louisiana, John Forsyth of Alabama, and Martin J. Crawford of Georgia, the trio sent to Washington in March 1861 to negotiate for the peaceful transfer of Forts Pickens and Sumter to the Confederacy.
THE SOLDIER IN OUR CIVIL WAR

If Major Anderson refused, Beauregard was to attack the fort. Davis always felt that war was inevitable, and for months the most radical of the secessionists had been insisting that a military confrontation would be necessary to force the upper South into secession. Davis was convinced that he had no alternative but to counter Lincoln's move with a show of force.

Confederate batteries opened fire on Fort Sumter on April 12, and the fort surrendered two days later. On April 15 Lincoln issued a call for seventy-five thousand state militia to put down what he described as an insurrection against lawful authority. It was this call for troops, and not just the armed clash at Fort Sumter, that specifically triggered secession in the upper South. The Unionist majorities there suddenly dissolved once the choice shifted from supporting the Union or the Confederacy to fighting for or against fellow Southerners.

The Virginia convention, which had remained in session after rejecting immediate secession on April 4, passed a secession ordinance on April 17. Its decision was overwhelmingly ratified on May 23 in a popular referendum. Three other states quickly followed. A reconvened Arkansas convention voted to go out on May 6. The Tennessee legislature, in a move later ratified in a popular referendum, also approved secession on May 6. A hastily called North Carolina convention, elected on May 13, took the Tarheel State out on May 20.

By the late spring of 1861 the stage was set for the bloodiest war in American history. The popular reaction to the firing on Fort Sumter and Lincoln's call for troops unified the North behind a crusade to preserve the Union and solidified, at least temporarily, a divided South behind the cause of Southern independence.

[*See also* Compromise of 1850; Constitutional Union Party; Cooperationists; Crittenden Compromise; Declaration of Immediate Causes; Democratic Party; Dred Scott Decision; Election of 1860; Fire-eaters; Fort Sumter, South Carolina; Fugitive Slave Law; Harpers Ferry, West Virginia, *article on* John Brown's Raid; Kansas-Nebraska Act; Missouri Compro mise; Montgomery Convention; Nullification Controversy; Republican Party; State Rights; Unionism; Washington Peace Conference; Wilmot Proviso; and *entries on particular states and biographies of numerous figures mentioned herein.*]

BIBLIOGRAPHY

Barney, William L. *The Road to Secession.* New York, 1972.

Channing, Steven A. *Crisis of Fear: Secession in South Carolina.* New York, 1970.

Craven, Avery O. *The Growth of Southern Nationalism, 1848–1861.* Baton Rouge, La., 1953.

Crofts, Daniel W. *Reluctant Confederates: Upper South Unionists in the Secession Crisis.* Chapel Hill, N.C., 1989.

Fehrenbacher, Don E. *The South and Three Sectional Crises.* Baton Rouge, La., 1980.

Ford, Lacy K., Jr. *Origins of Southern Radicalism: The South Carolina Upcountry, 1800–1860.* New York, 1988.

Freehling, William W. *The Road to Disunion: Secessionists at Bay, 1776–1854.* New York, 1990.

Genovese, Eugene D. *The Political Economy of Slavery.* New York, 1965.

Johnson, Michael P. *Toward a Patriarchal Republic: The Secession of Georgia.* Baton Rouge, La., 1977.

McCardell, John. *The Idea of a Southern Nation: Southern Nationalists and Southern Nationalism, 1830–1860.* New York, 1979.

Oakes, James. *The Ruling Race: A History of American Slaveholders.* New York, 1982.

Potter, David M. *The Impending Crisis, 1848–1861.* New York, 1976.

Stampp, Kenneth M. *And the War Came: The North and the Secession Crisis.* Baton Rouge, La., 1950.

Thornton, J. Mills, III. *Politics and Power in a Slave Society: Alabama, 1800–1860.* Baton Rouge, La., 1978.

Wooster, Ralph A. *The Secession Conventions of the South.* Princeton, N.J., 1962.

William L. Barney

SECRETARIES OF EXECUTIVE DEPARTMENTS. *For discussion of the duties and functions of the secretaries of the Confederate executive departments, see* Cabinet *and articles on the particular departments:* Navy, *article on* Navy Department; Post Office Department; State Department; Treasury Department; War Department. *See also* Judiciary.

SECRET SERVICE. *See* Espionage, *articles on* Confederate Secret Service *and* Federal Secret Service.

SEDDON, JAMES A. (1815–1880), Congressman from Virginia and secretary of war. Seddon was descended from English immigrants who arrived in Virginia in the eighteenth century and settled near Fredericksburg. Here they built Snowden, later destroyed by Union soldiers during the Civil War. Seddon was born in the town on July 13, 1815. He graduated from the University of Virginia law school with honors in 1835. Soon afterward, he opened a law office in Richmond and became active in the Calhoun wing of the Democratic party. In 1845 he married Sarah Bruce, daughter of a renowned Virginia family, and settled into the Clay Street mansion that later became the White House of the Confederacy. The couple quickly joined the social elite of the city. Shortly before, he had been elected to the U.S. House of Representatives.

Seddon served in Congress from 1845 to 1847, and again from 1849 to 1851. An ardent disciple of Calhoun, he adopted the state rights stance on most national issues in his first term. He supported the admission of Texas, the acquisition of Oregon, free trade over protectionism, and the necessity and value of slavery to the Southern way of life. He declined reelection in 1847 because of poor health. By 1849, when he returned to Congress, he had become a Southern expansionist, sharing the dream of a large slave-based empire embracing the Caribbean. He had despaired of securing Southern rights in the Union and secretly favored secession and the formation of a Southern republic. In all measures of the Compromise of 1850, he affirmed ultra-Southern demands, siding with such extremist leaders as Robert Barnwell Rhett, Sr., and Jefferson Davis (with whom he had earlier become acquainted).

After leaving Congress in 1851, Seddon led the life

JAMES A. SEDDON. NATIONAL ARCHIVES

of a planter in outlying Goochland County, where he acquired land, slaves, and a new twenty-six room home, Sabot Hill. He was infrequently in the public eye in the 1850s. Yet behind the scenes he corresponded, politicked, and championed the ambitions of friends, notably Robert M. T. Hunter (his closest political associate); gave strong support to opponents in the state against the Know-Nothings; and continued to be a power in the politics of the South. In 1856 he was a delegate to the Democratic National Convention at Cincinnati and was nominated for vice president on the Buchanan ticket, which he refused. In 1858 he spoke at a dinner in Richmond honoring Nicaragua filibusterer William Walker, whom Seddon praised as an evangel of progress and civilization. His own views on slavery and Southern nationalism deepened as he read the latest Southern theorists and promoted the distribution of their proslavery literature throughout the South.

He saw the election of Abraham Lincoln in 1860 as the death knell of the territorial ambitions of the South. Immediately he counseled resistance to expected Northern aggression and advised friends to prepare for the disruption of the Union. In January 1861 he was chosen as a delegate to the Washington peace conference. As a member of its committee on resolutions, he defended the right of secession (and the legitimacy of the new Southern Confederacy) and submitted a minority report seeking a constitutional amendment protecting the permanence of slavery in the Union. In the end, together with the majority of the Virginia delegation, he voted against the compromise proposals of the body. Throughout the debates he was a vigorous defender of Southern interests. To some he recalled one of his own heroes, John Randolph of Roanoke, while to others he was a firebrand secessionist. Two days before adjournment, a reception was given for the newly arrived President-elect Lincoln. Seddon was among those with questions for the Republican leader, and a heated exchange of views followed, especially regarding abolitionists, their objectives, and the "incendiary" press of the Northern states. Lincoln's response and humorous wit defused the debate.

Seddon returned to Richmond with ex-President John Tyler, also a delegate and old acquaintance, to urge their state to secede and join the Southern Confederacy. Nothing, they felt, of compromise or guarantees would be granted by the Republican-controlled Union. The Seddon-Tyler report to Governor John Letcher concluded that the conference had been a failure and "independent state action" was the only alternative to certain Northern coercion. In several speeches, Seddon urged crowds of frenzied Richmonders to prepare for the worst. He also implored the Virginia state convention, then sitting in the city, to act. On April 16, 1861, following the firing on Fort Sumter and Lincoln's call for troops, Seddon spoke before the "Spontaneous Peoples' Convention," demanding immediate secession. The following day, Virginia responded and left the Union. As Seddon observed to Charles Bruce, his brother-in-law, "The whole State is [now] in movement and the difficulty is rather to restrain any men at home than to fire them to the War." He was elated—the South had at long last been delivered from "Yankee Thralldom," and his dreams for an independent nation had finally been realized.

From April to early summer of 1861, the peace of the Virginia countryside was shattered by the bustle of military preparations. Many of Seddon's relatives responded to the call, and Seddon himself would have donned a uniform but for his health and feeble constitution. Soon after President Davis's arrival in Richmond and transfer of the Confederate capital to Virginia, he met several times with his old friend, perhaps to discuss Hunter's or Seddon's availability for the post of secretary of state. The question was on the lips of many of his friends. In June, he was chosen by Virginia for the Provisional Confederate Congress.

Seddon's eight months in Congress proved helpful to the new Davis administration and to his own political fortunes. In this critical time the unicameral body was setting up the government, recruiting and provisioning armies, and financing the war. Seddon gave special attention to the latter—the revision of the Produce Loan of 1861 to double its bond and currency issue to $100 million; passage of a law to make Treasury notes legal tender for all debts; and issuance of bonds to underwrite the currency and overall deficit spending. He also helped shape the Sequestration Act, in reprisal for similar Federal legislation; a strict embargo on cotton export; subsidies to arms manufacturers; impressment laws for military needs; railroad legislation to consolidate the lines and close major gaps in their routes; prisoner of war exchange and establishment of prison camps; and numerous military bills. As congressman, he had introduced ten bills, most enacted into law. He met not infrequently with the president and lobbied with colleagues to support the administration and a vigorous prosecution of the war. He saw the conflict in large terms and tried to imbue others with his own perception. He thus emerged as a strong Confederate nationalist rather than a narrow state rights advocate on most major issues.

In the summer of 1862, Seddon was approached through a lengthy correspondence by oceanographer Capt. Matthew Fontaine Maury with various schemes for promoting innovations in naval warfare, use of metal ships and torpedo weaponry, and government use, if not control, of blockade runners for the strategic needs of the South. Some of these ideas would later be enacted once Seddon was in charge of the War Department.

In mid-November, when Secretary of War George Wythe Randolph resigned, Davis prevailed upon Seddon to fill the office. The choice was a personal one for Davis: he wanted a solid friend in this difficult post and also another Virginian in his cabinet. Others did as well, including critically outspoken foes of the president. They applauded Seddon's appointment on November 20. He would hold his post almost to the end of the war, longer than the combined tenure of the three previous occupants. The choice proved an excellent one. Seddon brought to his task not only dedication and intelligence but also independence of thought and tact. A good judge of men, he impressed diarist Mary Boykin Chesnut as a warm and caring man and a fascinating conversationalist. Usually diplomatic, he was best as a sympathetic listener and convincing advocate. Seddon's cadaverous appearance was deceptive, for he was a tireless worker. Save for Robert E. Lee, he became Davis's most influential military adviser and devised much of the South's offensive strategy of concentration and total war. Together with Stephen R. Mallory and Judah P. Benjamin, he was one of the ablest of Davis's cabinet heads.

Unlike his predecessor, Seddon lacked military experience and at first relied heavily on the president, Assistant Secretary of War John A. Campbell, and Inspector General Samuel Cooper. Later he took upon himself the burdens of responsibility. One month after his appointment, he observed to Charles Bruce:

> The life is one rather of close confinement and incessant worry than of severe labor, and so far I have not suffered tho' giving daily from 9 a m to 9 or 10 p m to my duties. Indeed few persons are so well prepared by previous habits for [such] a sedatory life. . . . I trust to do reasonably well, as soon as I get a little more trained to the routine and versed in the military knowledge of the place.

Davis gave most of his cabinet members wide latitude in running their offices. He sought their advice and tolerated opinions contrary to his own. But having been a secretary of war himself and as an experienced military man, Davis naturally took a strong personal interest in the War Department and to a degree regarded it as his own domain. He carefully scrutinized the activities of this office and kept a tighter rein on its head than on other cabinet officers. As armies, strategy, and war itself were the chief concern of the Confederacy's leaders, the secretary and president had to work closely together.

Seddon found Davis not an impossible taskmaster at first, though often a difficult one. In working with him, he had to act by suggestion rather than command, relying on tact in his relations with the egocentric president. In lesser matters Seddon was seldom overruled, but when he was, he bowed to the will of his chief. An unselfish man without political ambition, Seddon did not seek power; rather, he was simply devoted to the Southern cause. He was in no way obsequious; he was much too proud to serve as a mere figurehead. He valued his appointment as an expression of Davis's respect and remained in the cabinet only as long as he shared the esteem of the president and the confidence of the people.

By November 1862 the enemy was again on the move in Virginia. Ambrose Burnside was advancing on the capital by way of Fredericksburg. Lee maneuvered to counter him. At the same time Charleston and Wilmington to the south feared imminent assault; but in the West there were even graver fears that the Union would soon seize the Mississippi and sever the Confederacy in two. Seddon was not long in responding to this impending crisis. With confidence in Lee in Virginia and while giving assurances of support to P. G. T. Beauregard and the Atlantic defenses, he focused major attention on the western theater. He believed that the decisive contest in the war at this time was to be waged there. His deep concern for this theater and the planning he put forth serve as a good index of the kind of strategist he could have been, had Davis given him greater latitude. His fears of a major debacle in the Trans-Mississippi and his recognition of the need for a reorientation of Confederate strategy there had in large measure been shared by his predecessor. But where Randolph had failed, Seddon succeeded. He not only won Davis's support for a newly organized Department of the West and persuaded him to visit the region (the following month) but got him to name Joseph E. Johnston to its command. It was a good solution to a large dilemma but depended for success upon the audacity and imagination of the chosen commander. Johnston failed to rise to the occasion. Seddon repeatedly pleaded with him to assert his authority over the entire area and to assume command of the scattered forces of Braxton Bragg, John C. Pemberton, and lesser units, but to no avail. Disappointment followed disappointment until Pemberton's large army was pent up in Vicksburg by the summer of 1863.

December 1862 had seen Lee again victorious, at Fredericksburg. It was a costly but timely victory. Virginia was freed of the invader until spring, and the capital yet secure. Another lesser triumph came on January 1, 1863, when John B. Magruder retook the vital Gulf port of Galveston. Seddon, in the meantime, "borrowed" troops and taxed the resources of lesser points to brace Beauregard's command at Charleston. On April 7 an ironclad fleet appeared before the city and, after a brisk battle, was turned back.

The year 1863 started out as the high watermark in the life of the Confederacy, but with the loss of Vicksburg and the Mississippi River and the simultaneous repulse at Gettysburg, the Confederates were thereafter on the defensive. Seddon had favored sending a part of Lee's army to the West, but after lengthy debate in the cabinet and with Lee, he abandoned his plan and gave support to a second invasion of the North. Years later he would declare in a letter that the "disaster of Vicksburg . . . was the fatal turning point of the war."

Seddon once again sought to snatch victory in the West. In the fall of 1863 he persuaded Davis and Lee to send James Longstreet from Virginia to Tennessee, where his timely arrival and generalship helped win the Battle of Chickamauga. But no one could single-handedly win the war, least of all the secretary. Only by mustering its resources could the South hope to drive off the invaders, and only through teamwork, which he sought to promote, was victory possible. Incompetents and malcontents had to be removed, and those with ability, experience, and a will to win be empowered to lead the fight. Pemberton, for instance, found no admirer in the secretary; numerous complaints had poured into Richmond questioning his competency and retention in command. Most tragic to Seddon was the prolonged retention of Bragg in the West. He tried repeatedly for Bragg's recall, but Johnston and later Davis himself blocked him. Only after the disastrous defeat at Chattanooga in November 1863 was Bragg finally removed. William J. Hardee, his most promising subordinate, refused his place. Seddon and a majority of the cabinet favored a second chance for Johnston, and he was returned to the Army of Tennessee. Barely a year later, he would be removed, this time before the defenses of Atlanta. Seddon, in general, supported the "fighting" generals—Lee, Longstreet, later John Bell Hood, and, despite Davis's disdain, Beauregard. One prime fighter that all overlooked was Nathan Bedford Forrest, whose recognition came too late for the West.

By 1864 the South was fighting a holding action. Two-thirds of its territory was gone, and a third of its armies was absent without leave (as Seddon admitted to the president in his annual report). The day for offensives was over. Seddon was now preoccupied with keeping the two major armies alive despite eroding morale, mass desertions, and widespread disaffection and starvation on the home front. He fought with Governors Joseph E. Brown of Georgia and Zebulon Vance of North Carolina over conscription, impressment, and martial law. He struggled to save worn-out railroads, which he commandeered for the government. He sequestered space on blockade runners and sent forth the department's own vessels to bring in vital supplies. He broke the rules and allowed cotton to be traded with the enemy for meat and other food for the army. And he assisted secret service and espionage ventures behind Northern lines to promote disaffection, peace movements, and the defeat of Lincoln's reelection—all this, and much more, during the last months of the war.

The cause was crumbling, yet Seddon could not admit it. There was talk of resignation, but friends urged him to hold on. He did, as he continued to live with only a single body servant, bearing alone the anguish of a lost child and the death from combat wounds of his brother, Maj. John Seddon. Even the threat to his own life, implicit with the Dahlgren raid on Richmond and its plot to kill Davis and his cabinet, he discounted. In February 1865, he saw his old Democrat friend Francis P. Blair, who came to the Confederate capital to promote peace. This and the subsequent Hampton Roads conference were the latest expressions of the reality of ultimate defeat. Nor was he able at this late date to think his way beyond Hunter and Cobb on the issue of black soldiers. (Earlier, in 1863, he had agreed with Davis to suppress Patrick Cleburne's proposal to arm the slaves.) Only when Lee urged the measure because of his desperate need for more men did Seddon reconsider—but it was too late.

Finally, when the Virginia congressional delegation, in anger over conditions generally and in hopes of restoring public confidence, requested the president to reorganize his cabinet, Seddon was piqued and immediately resigned. He had mistaken the motives of this body, who did not seek his ouster. But perhaps it was time for him to step aside and return to his family. Despite Davis's reassurances (and the lengthy correspondence that ensued), his resignation became final. On February 5, 1865, he quit his office and returned to Sabot Hill.

With his retirement, some now realized the breadth of the services he had rendered. Although his name had become a household word throughout the South, his popularity, like that of other politicians in this military-conscious society, never approached that of the fighting generals. But many recognized him as a man of dedication, will, and strength. Perhaps he was not the ideal man for the position, in view of his lack of military background and inexperience as an administrator, but he was the best the South had to offer. "His critics were numerous," wrote Douglas S. Freeman, "but a student will search the list vainly to find the name of one who could have done better than Seddon."

Out of office, he could do little more than witness the last acts of the struggle. He had little hope that Richmond would not fall, he told his sister in March. A week later, in a letter to Davis, he thought better of the cause, which he now believed would prevail; "the Liberties and Independence of your Country" will be achieved, he asserted. When the end finally came, he "was completely crushed . . . and considered his life to have been a complete failure" (as he told his son).

On May 20, Seddon took the oath of amnesty, but three days later he was suddenly arrested and confined in Libby Prison with Hunter and Campbell. On June 5, the three arrived at Fort Pulaski, Georgia, where they were joined by eight other former leaders. After Seddon's release in December, he returned to Sabot Hill. He was able largely to restore his fortunes through his law practice and his plantations in Virginia and Louisiana. He never wrote his memoirs, having destroyed most of his papers out of fear of their seizure by the Radical Republicans. Seddon died on August 19, 1880, and was buried in Hollywood Cemetery, Richmond.

BIBLIOGRAPHY

Curry, Roy Watson. "James A. Seddon: A Southern Prototype." *Virginia Magazine of History and Biography* 63 (1955): 123–150.

Dowdey, Clifford. *Experiment in Rebellion.* New York, 1946.

Escott, Paul D. *After Secession: Jefferson Davis and the Failure of Confederate Nationalism.* Baton Rouge, La., 1978.

Jones, J. B. *A Rebel War Clerk's Diary at the Confederate States Capital.* 2 vols. Philadelphia, 1866. Reprint, New York, 1958.

O'Brien, G. F. J. "James A. Seddon: Statesman of the Old South." Ph.D. diss., University of Maryland, 1963.

Patrick, Rembert W. *Jefferson Davis and His Cabinet.* Baton Rouge, La., 1944.

Strode, Hudson. *Jefferson Davis.* 3 vols. New York, 1955–1964.

Younger, Edward, ed. *Inside the Confederate Government: The Diary of Robert Garlick Hill Kean.* New York, 1957.

JOHN O'BRIEN

SELMA, ALABAMA. [*This entry includes three articles,* City of Selma, *which profiles the city during the Confederacy,* Selma Naval Ordnance Works, *which discusses the establishment and operations of the ordnance works, and* Wilson's Raid on Selma, *which discusses the Federal raid of 1865.*]

City of Selma

Founded in 1820 on a high bluff overlooking the Alabama River, Selma, Alabama, served as the seat of government for Dallas County during the Civil War. Before the conflict, the city was the focal point of trade, industry, education, and social life for local black belt planters. The cotton producers' African American labor force dominated the population of the surrounding county. By 1860, Dallas County's population numbered 30,197 people, consisting of 7,785 whites and 22,412 blacks; the city was populated by 1,132 whites and 2,516 blacks. As Selma's war industries grew, its population increased. At the end of the conflict, the city's factories and foundries employed at least 10,000 men who, as war industry employees, were exempt from conscription.

Social and cultural life for Selma's whites revolved around the city's schools and churches. Before the war, the Dallas Male and Female academies attracted over a hundred students each. The Male Academy folded at the outbreak of the war, but the women's school remained open until forced to close for financial reasons in 1864. Religion centered on Selma's six Protestant churches and one Roman Catholic institution.

The war made Selma an industrial center. Two railroads—the Alabama and Tennessee River and the Alabama and Mississippi lines—connected the city to northern Alabama's coal and iron reserves and the plantation regions of neighboring Mississippi. The Alabama River linked Selma to Montgomery, Mobile, and the Gulf of Mexico to the south. With easy access to iron-making resources and an efficient transportation network, the city quickly became the site of numerous war industries.

The Confederate arsenal was moved from Mount Vernon, Alabama, to Selma in 1862 for security reasons. Lt. Col. James L. White commanded the twenty-four-building facility that, toward the end of the war, became a major supply depot for the Confederate army. When Union troops seized the facility in 1865, they found fifteen siege guns, ten heavy carriages, ten field pieces, sixty field carriages, ten caissons, sixty thousand rounds of artillery ammunition, and a million rounds of small arms ammunition.

The Confederate government also established the Selma Naval Foundry in the city. Managed by Capt. Catesby Jones and employing over three thousand men, the foundry produced heavy artillery, siege guns, and gunboats. Selma workers built four Confederate ships—*Tennessee, Selma,*

Morgan, and *Gaines.* The ships' armor plating came from the Selma Iron Works, which produced thirty tons of iron a day. Additional firms, such as the Nitre Works, the Powder Mill and Magazine, and at least ten other ironworks and foundries, boosted the importance of Selma as an industrial center. Historians have estimated that during the last two years of the war approximately one-half of the Confederate army's cannons and two-thirds of its ammunition came from Selma.

The city was also a center for light manufacturing, locomotive repair and production, and food distribution. Local industries generated guns, bayonets, swords, shovels, knapsacks, and clothing. When Selma fell to Union soldiers, the troops found five locomotives and ninety-two railroad cars in the city's two railroad production centers. Throughout the war, the Confederate Subsistence Department used Selma's excellent railroad connections and location on the Alabama River to direct the flow of foodstuffs from the surrounding countryside to the Southern armies.

Although Selma's remote position from the fighting protected it from attack during the first four years of the war, the city's isolation ended in April 1865. At that time, Union Maj. Gen. James H. Wilson led over thirteen thousand cavalrymen on what one historian has described as a "Yankee Blitzkrieg" through central Mississippi, Alabama, and Georgia. Wilson's objective, like that of Gen. William Tecumseh Sherman, was to destroy the Confederacy's remaining production centers and to crush the Deep South's will to resist. His cavalry smashed into Selma on April 2, 1865, meeting a Confederate force led by Gen. Nathan Bedford Forrest. By nightfall, Wilson had routed Forrest's forces, capturing 2,700 men and wounding or killing an unknown number of others. Forty-six Union men were dead and 300 had been wounded. Before the attack, Selma residents had destroyed as much property as possible to keep it from falling into enemy hands.

Selma lay burned and its industries destroyed following Wilson's raid. As the war ended, the black belt slaveholders lost their human chattel and, as a result, much of their wealth. The freedmen received the franchise during the next ten years of Reconstruction and participated in local politics. But when the white elites returned to political power in 1874, white supremacy reappeared. Selma emerged from the Confederacy a poor farm town dominated by segregation and reactionary politics until the civil rights revolution in the 1960s.

BIBLIOGRAPHY

Fleming, Walter L. *Civil War and Reconstruction in Alabama.* New York, 1905.

Hardy, John. *Selma: Her Institutions and Her Men.* Selma, Ala., 1879. Reprint, Spartanburg, S.C., 1978.

Jackson, Walter M. *The Story of Selma.* Birmingham, Ala., 1954.

Jones, James P. *Yankee Blitzkrieg: Wilson's Raid through Alabama and Georgia.* Athens, Ga., 1976.

McMillan, Malcolm C. *The Alabama Confederate Reader.* Tuscaloosa, Ala., 1963.

RIC A. KABAT

Selma Naval Ordnance Works

Selma, on the Alabama River in south central Alabama, became a manufacturing center for the Confederacy early in the war. Access by water, rail, and stage (far from the early active theaters of combat) and nearby iron furnaces made Selma an attractive site. The overall complex included a shipyard, a niter facility, a foundry, and a machine shop.

The foundry and machine shop eventually became the Selma Naval Ordnance Works. Originally the Selma Manufacturing Company, the facilities were not well built and had failed financially. Colin J. McRae, a member of the Provisional Congress, undertook early in the war with other investors to sell the firm to the Confederate government. McRae intended to continue as manager and to use the new capital to construct a rolling mill and otherwise expand the facility. The Confederate government twice declined. McRae and his colleagues then purchased the works and used McRae's position to obtain contracts. In the fall of 1862, McRae was forced to cut back construction of expanded facilities for lack of skilled workers. Iron molders struck for higher wages, and McRae was able to retain only seven of eighteen needed molders.

The Confederate government bought McRae and his colleagues out in February 1863. Col. George W. Raines assumed command of the facility "in behalf of the Army and Navy." Raines personally disapproved of the facility and urged that it be turned over to the navy. On June 1, 1863, the navy took over sole operation.

The new commander was Catesby Jones, former executive officer of the ironclad *Virginia.* Jones, with the assistance of an experienced foundryman, George Peacock, completed renovation of the works by the end of January 1864, with the exception of the rolling mill.

The rolling mill never became a reality, and its machinery was leased to the nearby Shelby Iron Company. Once in production, the Selma works became the South's second major producer (after the Tredegar Iron Works in Richmond) of large rifled Brooke naval guns and cannon. The Brooke guns were made in two sizes: 6.4 inches weighing 10,000 pounds and 7 inches weighing 14,000 pounds. Over 100 were produced.

Secretary of the Navy Stephen R. Mallory in early 1865 estimated the capacity of the facility to be seven heavy guns and five fieldpieces per week with projectiles. Shortages of iron and skilled labor, however, reduced production to one or two heavy guns and one fieldpiece per week.

This output required day-and-night operations every day of the week except Sunday. By 1865 the facility employed over four hundred men, of whom three hundred were blacks. The Selma works shared the general problem of retaining skilled labor. When skilled white workers entered the army, the army controlled them. Requests from the navy to the army to have these men detailed back to navy facilities were slow in being answered and required renewal every two months.

The Selma facilities were raided by Maj. Gen. James H. Wilson's cavalry corps on April 3, 1865, and effectively destroyed.

BIBLIOGRAPHY

Layton, Edwin. "Colin J. McRae and the Selma Arsenal." *Alabama Review* 18 (1966): 125–136.

Still, William N., Jr. "Selma and the Confederate States Navy." *Alabama Review* 14 (1962): 19–37.

ROBERT H. MCKENZIE

Wilson's Raid on Selma

The 1865 raid on Selma by Union Brig. Gen. James Harrison Wilson resulted in the defeat of Confederate Lt. Gen. Nathan Bedford Forrest's cavalry and the capture of the city.

On January 24, Lt. Gen. Richard Taylor named Forrest commander of the cavalry in the Department of Alabama, Mississippi, and East Louisiana, and in February he was promoted to lieutenant general. He then reorganized his command and attempted to instill confidence and discipline in his men.

In the meantime, Wilson gathered a vast array of cavalry in two camps along the north bank of the Tennessee River, at Waterloo and Gravelly Springs, Alabama, and set about preparing for his campaign. He sent an officer to meet with Forrest under the guise of discussing a prisoner exchange, but for the main purpose of gathering intelligence on his adversary. Finally, on March 22, following two months of preparations, Wilson started south. The Union command of just under 14,000 troopers constituted the largest mounted force assembled during the war and was particularly well-armed and equipped.

From the start, Wilson enjoyed good fortune. A threatened Union movement from Pensacola, Florida, briefly diverted Forrest's attention and delayed the convergence of his scattered forces. Even so, Forrest hoped to concentrate his men near the vital industrial center of Selma.

By March 30, Wilson was in Elyton (Birmingham). He dispatched 1,100 men under Brig. Gen. John Croxton to march to Tuscaloosa, where they were to burn anything of supposed military value, including the University of Alabama. This expedition took Croxton's men out of the remainder of the Selma campaign.

Forrest attempted to throw various forces in the path of the Union column to delay its advance, but Wilson's men, under Brig. Gen. Emory Upton, brushed the Confederates aside near Montevallo. Only a timely counterthrust by Forrest, his 75-man escort, and some 200 troopers enabled the Southerners to stop their opponents temporarily. In the fighting, Col. Edward Crossland's Confederate brigade lost 100 men killed, wounded, and captured, or about one-sixth of the brigade's strength.

At some point on March 31 or April 1, Wilson's men captured a Confederate courier shuttling messages between Forrest and his subordinates. The captured dispatches revealed Forrest's plans and dispositions and gave Wilson a distinct advantage at a pivotal point in the campaign. He acted immediately on what he had learned by dispatching a force to destroy a critical bridge at Centerville, over which Forrest hoped to bring a substantial part of his scattered command. Brig. Gen. Edward M. McCook's troopers seized and destroyed the bridge, preventing Brig. Gen. William H. Jackson and his 3,000 veterans from uniting with Forrest in time to halt Wilson short of Selma. The Union commander could now concentrate his efforts upon defeating the Confederates in front of him and pushing on to Selma.

Forrest made a final stand in a strong position at Bogler's Creek, near Ebenezer Church. Here, following a brief but sharp fight, Union cavalry under Upton and Brig. Gen. Eli Long forced Forrest to retreat to Selma, when the Alabama State Militia broke under the weight of the combined Union assault. The Battle of Ebenezer Church cost Wilson 12 killed and 40 wounded, but cost Forrest 300 or more, mostly captured, and three artillery pieces. The Confederate commander himself suffered painful wounds when a Union captain slashed at him with his saber before Forrest got his pistol free and killed his assailant.

By 2:00 P.M. on April 2, the first of Wilson's men had arrived before Selma. Here, the Union commander received a last piece of good fortune when his men captured one of the designers of the city's defenses, which the prisoner willingly drew for his captors. At 5:00 P.M., Wilson sent Long and Upton against the Confederate defenses. Although the Southern fire was heavier and more effective than expected, the Federals soon drove their opponents out of their first line of works and into a second. A renewed assault shattered this line when the Southern militia broke for the final time. For Forrest and the rest of his men, the battle degenerated into hundreds of individual combats as the Confederates struggled to escape or gave in and surrendered.

By the end of the day, Wilson securely held the industrial center as well as some 2,700 Confederate prisoners, at a cost of 46 killed, 300 wounded, and 13 missing. Forrest had one final fight in which he killed his thirtieth man in personal combat before successfully evading capture and escaping from Selma.

BIBLIOGRAPHY

Jones, James Pickett. *Yankee Blitzkrieg: Wilson's Raid through Alabama and Georgia.* Athens, Ga., 1976.

Longacre, Edward G. *From Union Stars to Top Hat: A Biography of the Extraordinary General James Harrison Wilson.* Harrisonburg, Pa., 1972.

Wills, Brian Steel. *A Battle from the Start: The Life of Nathan Bedford Forrest.* New York, 1992.

Wilson, James Harrison. *Under the Old Flag: Recollections of Military Operations in the War for the Union, the Spanish War, the Boxer Rebellion, etc.* New York, 1912.

BRIAN S. WILLS

SEMINOLES. With a population of 2,500 to 2,600 (2,257 Indians and 200 to 300 blacks), the Seminoles lived in central Indian Territory (present-day Oklahoma) between the North Canadian and Canadian rivers west of modern Seminole County. Although divided politically and geographically between the Union and Confederacy, the Seminole government joined the Confederacy August 1, 1861. It provided about three hundred troops to the Confederate cause and was one of the last Confederate governments to surrender.

The Seminoles had been forcibly removed from Florida between 1838 and 1843. They had gone through a prolonged struggle to adjust to the new country and only recently had settled into their current homes at the outbreak of the Civil War.

Confederate governments in Texas and Arkansas began making advances to the Indians of Indian Territory in January 1861, but the Seminoles and other Indians determined to remain neutral in the American conflict. The withdrawal of Union troops from Indian Territory in May 1861 and the immediate occupation of all forts in the territory by Confederates from Texas altered the situation. In addition, civil representatives of the Federal government were absent, and the Seminole annuities due in 1860 under previous treaties had not been paid. New Union appointees were unable or unwilling to assume their posts in 1861, so that all current or former officials of the Indian Department in Indian Territory were Confederate sympathizers.

Albert Pike of Arkansas, Confederate commissioner to the Indians west of Arkansas, negotiated treaties with the Creeks, Choctaws, and Chickasaws in early July 1861. A five-man delegation from the Seminole National Council headed by the principal chief, John Jumper (Hiniha Mikko), signed a treaty with Pike on August 1, 1861. Union officials and others later falsely asserted that this treaty was improperly executed. The delegation was similar to others that had negotiated previous treaties and most members had served on similar delegations. The treaty provisions were also the most generous ever offered the Seminoles.

Despite the advantages of the treaty and the clear dangers of opposition to the Confederacy, dissident portions of the tribe began agitation in the fall of 1861. In November, eight hundred to nine hundred dissidents, under the leadership of Billy Bowlegs (Sonaki Mikko) and Ahalak Tastanaki, joined dissident Upper Creeks under Opothleyahola on the Deep Fork River preparatory to joining Union forces in Kansas.

Slavery was not an issue in this split, since there were few slaves among the Seminoles. Most black Seminoles belonged to free Maroon communities, which had allied with the Indians in Florida. Further, Billy Bowlegs and John Jumper, the leaders of the two factions, were the largest nominal slave owners. Divisions between those of mixed ancestry and those of wholly Indian descent, or between progressives and traditionalists, had no role either, since virtually all Seminoles were conservative full-bloods. The split reflected other political divisions within the tribe, with the factions based on band membership. Billy Bowlegs was a rival claimant to the position of principal chief, which was hereditary. The other Union leaders represented bands that resented the ascendancy of Jumper's band and previously had opposed him.

In September, the Seminoles mustered a battalion of about three hundred men, under Maj. John Jumper, into Confederate service. Overall command of troops in Indian Territory belonged to Brig. Gen. Albert Pike and Col. Douglas Hancock Cooper, both white. The Seminole battalion fought at the Battle of Round Mountain against Opothleyahola's Union forces on November 19, 1861, which earned Jumper a commendation. They also operated around Fort Larned, Kansas, in May 1862, attempting to seize Union supplies and cut supply lines. In November 1862, John Jumper was promoted to lieutenant colonel. Although Confederate Seminole troops were largely stationed in their own country from that time on, they fought guerrilla actions along with other Indian troops under Brig. Gen. Stand Watie after the fall of 1863.

The Seminoles, like other Confederate Indians in Indian Territory, suffered numerous problems. Supplies for their troops seldom reached the territory, and the men went unpaid for many months at a time. Confederate military officials in Arkansas routinely seized such supplies for their own troops. Annuity payments promised under the treaty with Pike were delayed and irregular. Conflicts within the Confederate command also fostered discontent. General Pike resigned in July 1862 and was replaced by Colonel Cooper, now promoted to brigadier general. These conditions led an additional two hundred to three hundred Seminoles to flee to Kansas and join the Union in April

1862, leaving the tribe about evenly divided between the Union and the Confederacy.

The first Union invasion of Indian Territory in June 1862 had little direct impact on the Seminoles, and Union troops withdrew in early August. A second invasion from Kansas in September forced all Confederate troops south to the Choctaw Nation. Union troops under Col. William A. Phillips began successful military operations north of the Canadian River in April 1863. The Confederacy replaced Cooper with Brig. Gen. William Steele in June. Steele, however, was unacceptable to the Indians and resigned in December. He was replaced by Brig. Gen. Samuel Bell Maxey. Maxey placed Jumper's Seminole battalion under the command of Brig. Gen. Stand Watie.

Military actions by Union troops based at Fort Gibson in the Cherokee Nation, the operations of Kansas Jayhawkers, and raids by Plains Indians to the west caused the abandonment of the Seminole Nation in 1863. Seminole civilians withdrew south to a refugee camp at Oil Springs on the Washita River in the Chickasaw Nation for the duration of the war. Conditions in this camp were grim, with irregular supplies, inadequate shelter, and widespread disease. Corrupt contractors and supply problems defeated the best efforts of the Confederate agent, J. S. Murrow, to provide for them.

On June 23, 1865, General Watie surrendered his command to the Union. This ended the war for the Seminoles, who formally capitulated to the United States on September 19, 1865. The Seminole Nation, however, was deserted and its property totally destroyed. Unable to return, the refugees remained in their camp until 1866. The formal treaty between the United States and the Seminoles in March 1866 was one of the most punitive of any following the Civil War.

BIBLIOGRAPHY

Abel, Annie Heloise. *The American Indian as Participant in the Civil War.* Cleveland, Ohio, 1919.

Abel, Annie Heloise. *The American Indian as Slaveholder and Secessionist: An Omitted Chapter in the Diplomatic History of the Southern Confederacy.* Cleveland, Ohio, 1915.

Fischer, LeRoy H., ed. *The Civil War Era in Indian Territory.* Los Angeles, 1974.

McReynolds, Edwin C. *The Seminoles.* Norman, Okla., 1957.

Rampp, Larry C., and Donald L. Rampp. *The Civil War in the Indian Territory.* Austin, Tex., 1975.

RICHARD A. SATTLER

SEMMES, PAUL J. (1815–1863), brigadier general. The Gettysburg campaign cost the Army of Northern Virginia many of its best officers and men. Casualties among Robert E. Lee's general officers were particularly high, with seventeen, or nearly one-third, killed, wounded, or captured. Six distinguished combat leaders—Lewis Armistead, William Barksdale, Richard Garnett, Dorsey Pender, Johnston Pettigrew, and Paul J. Semmes—were killed or mortally wounded.

PAUL J. SEMMES. CIVIL WAR LIBRARY AND MUSEUM, PHILADELPHIA

Semmes, a younger brother of Confederate Adm. Raphael Semmes, was born in Wilkes County, Georgia, on June 4, 1815. He attended the University of Virginia and spent the antebellum years as a planter and banker in Georgia. Semmes, with fifteen years' experience as a militia officer, was elected colonel of the Second Georgia Infantry when it organized in the summer of 1861.

He soon commanded a brigade as a colonel and then was promoted to brigadier general on March 18, 1862. Semmes's first combat was in the campaigns around Yorktown and Williamsburg and at Seven Pines that spring. He was often commended by his superiors for his performance in the army's major campaigns from the Seven Days' Battles to Chancellorsville. On July 2, 1863, while leading his brigade in the Wheat Field on the second day at Gettysburg, Semmes was mortally wounded. He was taken back toward Virginia in an ambulance, but he died at Martinsburg, in present-day West Virginia, on July 10, 1863.

BIBLIOGRAPHY

Compiled Military Service Records. Paul J. Semmes. Microcopy M331, Roll 222. Record Group 109. National Archives, Washington, D.C.

Derry, Joseph T. *Georgia*. Vol. 6 of *Confederate Military History*. Edited by Clement A. Evans. Atlanta, 1899. Vol. 7 of extended ed. Wilmington, N.C., 1987.

J. TRACY POWER

SEMMES, RAPHAEL (1809–1877), rear admiral. Semmes was captain of CSS *Sumter* and CSS *Alabama* and admiral of the James River Squadron. His duty on the two ships was to prey upon enemy merchant vessels, and he did that job better than any other naval captain in naval history, burning sixty-four U.S. registered merchant vessels and bonding thirteen others. On *Sumter* he was the first to show the Confederate flag on the high seas and in neutral ports; on *Alabama* he sank USS *Hatteras,* a new U.S. Navy ironclad side-wheeler.

The experiences of his youth foreshadowed the introspective and self-reliant captain of *Sumter* and *Alabama.* Born in Maryland and orphaned at age nine, Raphael and his younger brother moved to Georgetown, D.C., to live with two of their uncles. Raphael, influenced by a merchant shipping uncle, was drawn first to sea life and second to law. A third uncle, a Maryland politician and future congressman, secured an appointment for him as a midshipman in the U.S. Navy, dated April 1, 1826. Raphael was sixteen.

RAPHAEL SEMMES. Civil War–period engraving.

NAVAL HISTORICAL CENTER, WASHINGTON, D.C.

A second career was necessary in the old navy because officers frequently received long enforced leaves without pay. Thus, after Semmes spent five years as a trainee officer, he was promoted to passed midshipman and placed on extended leave. He seized the opportunity to read law, passed the bar exam in 1833, and established a law office in Cincinnati, Ohio.

When recalled to duty, now Lieutenant Semmes was assigned to the Pensacola, Florida, Navy Yard. He moved his family to nearby Alabama and from that moment considered himself a citizen of that state. To help his wife with their growing family, he purchased three household slaves. His conversion to the Southern way of life was complete.

Semmes's experiences in the U.S. Navy prepared him for his role in the Civil War. On various ships he sailed the Gulf coasts on survey duty, was lighthouse inspector on the Gulf and Atlantic coasts, and performed blockade duty off Vera Cruz during the Mexican War. He commanded four U.S. Navy vessels.

From the end of the Mexican War until 1855 he remained on leave, practicing law in Mobile and writing *Service Afloat and Ashore during the War with Mexico,* a best-seller in the early 1850s. He was promoted to the rank of commander (1855), assigned as inspector of the Eighth Lighthouse District, and then transferred to Washington as secretary of the Lighthouse Board (1858) and later as member of the board (February 1861). By then his survey and lighthouse assignments had provided him with a thorough knowledge of Gulf, Caribbean, and North Atlantic shorelines, tides, and winds.

When Alabama seceded from the Union, Semmes resigned from the U.S. Navy to offer his services to the Confederacy. In 1861 his appearance commanded respect. Slightly below medium height with an erect bearing, he wore his hair long over his ears, had a large waxed mustache and small goatee, and had piercing black eyes. Highly intelligent and a voracious reader, he based the decision to follow his adopted state out of the Union on the constitutional ground that the Federal government had no right to impose its will on the several Southern states.

While traveling by train to Montgomery, Alabama, where Jefferson Davis had established the Provisional Government, he rode through a pine-forest fire. The flames prompted him to muse that "civil war is a terrible crucible through which to pass character."

He arrived in Montgomery in February 1861, met with President Davis, and left a day later to shop for arms and munitions in Northern states. In Montgomery, on April 4, Secretary of the Navy Stephen R. Mallory appointed Semmes commander in the Confederate navy and chief of the Lighthouse Bureau.

The firing on Fort Sumter led Semmes to realize that "it

was time to leave the things of peace to the future." He asked Mallory for a ship suitable for commerce raiding, and Mallory showed him a file on a ship in New Orleans, already examined and condemned. "Give me that ship," Semmes said. On the newly converted *Sumter,* Semmes cleverly eluded USS *Brooklyn* and sailed into the Gulf of Mexico on June 30, 1861.

President Abraham Lincoln's proclamation of a blockade of Southern ports and Davis's statement of intent to issue letters of marque forced Great Britain and France to proclaim their neutrality, which effectively recognized the Confederacy as de facto belligerent with the same international rights and limitations as held by the United States.

Semmes's objective was to draw U.S. warships from blockade duty by sinking U.S. merchant ships. His success against merchantmen led merchants worldwide to refuse to ship under the U.S. flag. (In Singapore, Semmes found seventeen U.S. merchantmen lying without cargoes for over three months.) Still, the United States would not weaken the blockade, and its merchant fleet has never recovered its prewar second position in world commercial shipping.

The *Sumter* cruise was a learning experience for Semmes. The blockade of Southern ports and limitations imposed by neutral countries prevented him from taking a prize into any port for adjudication. He regretfully burned his first victim, *Golden Rocket,* and then vainly attempted to force the weak Caribbean neutrals to accept his captures for adjudication. Afterward, constituting himself a maritime court and carefully following international law, he condemned, bonded, or released his prizes (except for two) according to their flag or registration and ownership of their cargo (neutral ownership protected the ship). On *Alabama* he converted one prize into CSS *Tuscaloosa* (June 1863) and sold another in August 1863.

Sumter was small, slowed when under sail by the drag of her propeller, and could ship only an eight-day supply of coal. Yet in six months Semmes captured eighteen ships, seven of which he destroyed. He hunted along the currents and winds that merchant ships traveled. Only the vessel's limitations hampered his success. He was blockaded at St. Pierre, Martinique, by USS *Iroquois,* but drawing upon his experiences as a blockader he eluded the more powerful ship. Semmes then headed for Cadiz, Spain, to effect needed repairs. Frustrated by Spanish delays, he sailed to Gibraltar, making his last capture within sight of the rock. Unable to repair *Sumter*'s boilers and blockaded by three Union vessels, he abandoned the ship and with 1st Lt. John McIntosh Kell went to London.

In England he met Commdr. James Dunwoody Bulloch who had designed a ship (#290) being built in the Laird Shipyards on the Mersey River, Liverpool. Semmes admired the ship as being perfect for a commerce cruiser. Assuming Bulloch would command her, Semmes sailed for home. In Nassau on June 8, 1862, he learned of his promotion to captain and assignment to command #290. He returned to England.

Bulloch meanwhile had sent #290, unarmed, to the Azores Islands. Semmes and Bulloch with supplies, arms, officers, and sailors rendezvoused just off the islands in international waters. Semmes's first glimpse of #290 afloat with her "perfect symmetry" and "lifting device to prevent drag when under sail" excited him. From then on, Semmes referred to the ship as if she were his living partner in a great endeavor. The partnership would last for twenty-three months. Together they would set a record of merchant ship captures that still stands. On August 24, 1862, in neutral waters, Semmes commissioned *Alabama* as a regular warship of the Confederate navy.

Alabama's crew, an international mix, required a firm discipline tempered with mercy. Semmes rarely appeared on deck except to take readings of the ship's position and give orders of the day to 1st Lieutenant Kell, who controlled the crew. Most of the officers had served on *Sumter.*

Semmes began the cruise on nearby waters where Northern whalers were at work. His first victim, heavy with whale oil, was the first of 54 ships he would capture and of 447 he would speak or board. When hailing a ship he would fly the U.S. flag and, if answered by the same, raise the Confederate standard and command the ship to halt. Should she attempt to flee, he would fire a shot and send aboard an armed party whose officer would escort the victim's captain and papers to Semmes's cabin. Should the papers show the cargo to be neutral-owned, Semmes would bond the ship and allow it to continue its voyage; if enemy-owned, the boarding party would take off the victim's crew and passengers, if any, plus whatever *Alabama* could use—food, clothing, rigging, coal—and then set the ship afire. Semmes would cruise one area until he felt Northern warships might learn of his location and then seek other hunting grounds.

Semmes moved southward to the Caribbean Sea and the Gulf of Mexico. He resented the reputation Northern newspapers bestowed upon him: "He never fights, just plunders." Learning of a Union fleet off the Texas coast, he decided to disrupt it. Approaching it, he lured USS *Hatteras* from the fleet and sank her in a close exchange.

Later, Semmes, heading for the East Indies, crossed the South Atlantic for South Africa and in Simon's Town refurbished the ship and refreshed the men. En route he noted in his ship's journal that his time afloat "had produced a constant tension of the nervous system and a wear and tear of body. . . . I am supremely disgusted with the sea and all its belongings." After a stormy voyage to the East Indies, he sank three merchant ships, futilely sought combat with USS *Wyoming,* and sailed to Singapore for rest.

Despite disheartening news from America, on the return voyage his spirits were momentarily raised by his last capture. In the eastern Atlantic Ocean, *Alabama* chased a victim all night. "When the day dawned we were within a couple of miles of him. It was the old spectacle of the panting breathless fawn, and the inexorable staghound." But as Semmes read the latest newspapers taken from the victim and learned of the Northern victories—it was late May 1864—he saw himself, in the third person, as one on whose shoulders the stress and strain of three years had laid "a load of a dozen years." Now *Alabama* was only a "wearied foxhound." And above his visions of man and ship, he saw "shadows of a sorrowful future."

On June 11, 1864, Semmes and *Alabama* limped into the harbor of Cherbourg, France, seeking refuge in the imperial docks. Immediately, Semmes wrote to Comm. Samuel Barron in Paris: "My health has suffered so much from a constant and harassing service of three years almost continuously at sea, that I shall have to ask for relief [from command of *Alabama*]." But fate in the form of Capt. John A. Winslow and USS *Kearsarge* intervened. *Alabama* now faced a possible blockade. Semmes decided that the ship should fight rather than rot in a French port. So he sent a message to Winslow, a former shipmate: "If you will give me time to recoal, I will come out and give you battle."

On June 19, 1864, *Alabama,* her sailors and officers in full dress uniform, sailed out of the harbor before cheering crowds. About seven miles into the English Channel, the two ships began firing; after sixty-five minutes *Alabama* was foundering. As she sank stern first, Semmes threw his sword into the sea, and then he and Kell jumped from the ship and swam to a boat from the English yacht *Deerhound.* "We fought her until she could no longer swim," Semmes later wrote, "and then gave her to the waves."

In Southampton, Semmes wrote his report to Mallory. Devastated by defeat and slightly wounded, he tried to explain the loss of his ship. Noting that *Alabama*'s shells did little damage to the side of the *Kearsarge,* he later blamed the loss on *Kearsarge*'s chain-covered sides. He was entertained by pro-Confederate groups, presented with a new sword, and traveled on the Continent. Refreshed, he began a strenuous seven-and-one-half-week trip to his home in Mobile, arriving on December 19, 1864.

He left Mobile on January 2, 1865, for Richmond, where President Davis and Congress honored him, promoted him to rear admiral, and assigned him to command the James River Squadron. When Ulysses S. Grant turned Robert E. Lee's right flank, Semmes was ordered to destroy his fleet and join Davis in Danville, Virginia. There the president appointed him a brigadier general of artillery. Ordered to join Joseph E. Johnston's forces in North Carolina, Semmes received the generous pardon granted by William Tecumseh Sherman to Johnston at Guilford Courthouse.

Semmes returned to his home in Mobile, but on December 15, 1865, he was arrested and imprisoned in Washington, D.C., charged by Secretary of the Navy Gideon Welles with having fled from the *Kearsarge-Alabama* battle after having surrendered by showing a white flag and, later, "without having been exchanged as a prisoner engaged in hostilities against the United States." After four months of imprisonment, he was released for lack of proper evidence.

Semmes returned to Mobile and, forbidden to hold public office, attempted to make a living by teaching in the Louisiana Military Institute, editing a newspaper in Memphis, Tennessee, and lecturing for small fees. Finally, he practiced law in Mobile, specializing in maritime law. In 1869 he published the 833-page *Memoirs of Service Afloat during the War between the States.* He died in 1877 at his summer cottage on Point Clear, across the bay from Mobile, from food poisoning.

BIBLIOGRAPHY

Case, Lynn M., and Warren F. Spencer. *The United States and France: Civil War Diplomacy.* Philadelphia, 1970.

Humphreys, Anderson, and Curt Guenther. *Semmes America.* Memphis, Tenn., 1989.

Kell, John McIntosh. *Recollections of a Navy Life Including the Cruises of the Confederate States Steamers "Sumter" and "Alabama."* Washington, D.C., 1900.

Newman, Harry Wright. *The Maryland Semmes and Kindred Families.* Baltimore, 1936.

Roberts, W. Adolfe. *Semmes of the Alabama.* New York, 1938.

Summersell, Charles Grayson. *The Cruise of the C.S.S. Sumter.* Tuscaloosa, Ala., 1965.

Summersell, Charles Grayson. *CSS Alabama: Builder, Captain, and Plans.* University, Ala., 1985.

WARREN F. SPENCER

SEMMES, THOMAS (1824–1899), congressman from Louisiana. For the last fifty years of the nineteenth century, Thomas Jenkins Semmes was a prominent New Orleans lawyer, Democratic politician, and senior statesmen. Although seldom associated with any single piece of significant legislation, Semmes as a Confederate senator helped shape policy in the areas of martial law, conscription, retaliation, and finances.

Semmes, first cousin and foster brother of Confederate Adm. Raphael Semmes, was born and raised in Washington, D.C. His father, a prominent merchant, came from a wealthy, Catholic landholding family from Maryland's Western Shore. His mother had been on personal terms with every U.S. president from James Monroe to Abraham Lincoln. While in the White House, Martin Van Buren used to visit the family, playing games with young Thomas and his playmates. Semmes enrolled in Georgetown College at age eleven, finishing at the top of his class six years later. In

1845 he graduated from Harvard Law School, where his classmates included President John Tyler's nephew, Henry Semple, and future Republican president Rutherford B. Hayes. Semmes was well positioned to launch his own career in law and politics.

One of two defining moments in Semmes's early political career occurred while he was studying at Harvard. He chanced to read proslavery theorist and Virginia jurist Abel P. Upshur's *Brief Enquiry into the True Nature and Character of our Federal Government* (1840), arguably one of the strongest historical cases for state sovereignty ever written. Upshur's treatise was an extended attack upon the constitutional nationalism embedded in Harvard Professor and U.S. Supreme Court Justice Joseph Story's widely influential *Commentaries on the Constitution of the United States.* Impressed with Upshur's logic, Semmes abandoned his family's staunch allegiance to the Whig party and became a Democrat—presumably of the extreme state rights persuasion. Like many young Southern intellectuals coming of age just prior to the Civil War, Semmes was swept along by the growing popularity of Southern nationalism.

The other defining moment in Semmes's early political career occurred five years after he relocated to New Orleans. From 1850 to 1855 Semmes had built up a moderately successful commercial practice as an attorney to cotton factors and brokers, and he had moved his family into a fashionable uptown section of the city, upriver from the Catholic French Quarter and the mixed immigrant wards. New Orleans had just emerged from four decades of rancorous American-Creole rivalry when a heavy influx of potato-famine Irish immigrants triggered an explosion of nativist political violence that divided New Orleans into armed camps. As Whigs, most of Semmes's clients and neighbors had joined the anti-immigrant American, or Know-Nothing, party, but in 1855 Semmes delivered an impassioned antinativist speech that ended his law partnership with a former Harvard classmate. The address caught the attention of the city's and state's Democratic leadership, who doubtless recognized that Semmes combined political and social characteristics that were unusual for antebellum New Orleans. He was an Anglo-American transplant, yet a Catholic; an uptown lawyer, yet a Democrat. And he had excellent national connections. The Democratic sachems immediately tapped him for the State Central Committee. A short time later Semmes was elected to the Louisiana legislature that met in 1856 and 1857.

Thereafter Semmes's political star rose quickly. In 1858 Democratic President James Buchanan appointed him U.S. attorney for the Eastern District of New Orleans—a position that gave him the duty of prosecuting ex–New Orleanian William Walker for filibustering in Nicaragua (Semmes persuaded Buchanan to drop the charges). The following year Semmes was elected by a comfortable margin to be state attorney general. He was only thirty-five years old.

From secession through Appomattox, Semmes figured prominently in the politics of the short-lived Confederate nation. A member of the New Orleans Southern Rights Association, which helped tip a divided city toward disunion during the 1860–1861 secession winter, Semmes was elected as an "immediate secessionist"—that is, a believer in separate state action—to the Louisiana secession convention of 1861. As a member of the convention's important Committee of Fifteen, he helped draft the ordinance that severed the Pelican State's ties to the old Union. His action was almost predictable in light of his youthful Southern nationalism. Semmes's first Confederate service was as a district judge, advising President Jefferson Davis about the legality of suspending bank specie payments in New Orleans. To conserve scarce bullion and facilitate the circulation of Confederate currency, the central government ordered banks to cease paying drafts in gold and silver.

After several close ballots, the Louisiana legislature in November 1861 elected Semmes to the Confederate Senate. He took his seat in February 1862. As Semmes was the fifth youngest senator in a group whose average age was nearly ten years older than his own, his role in that body was as an auxiliary, not a principal. He served on the important Finance and Judiciary committees but did not chair a major committee until picked to head Judiciary late in the war. His most well-known (and apparently lengthiest) speech was one he delivered as chairman of the Committee on the Flag and the Seal, when he argued for a Latin word change on the Confederate seal, partly on the ground that the word choice for *God* was too "pagan."

Notwithstanding his junior status, Semmes played an active part in shaping important legislation. His contribution was as a conservative, which stemmed naturally from his upper-class background, Catholic fundamentalism, and experience as a lawyer serving the interests of the rich and powerful. He thus worked closely with Virginia's Robert M. T. Hunter, chairman of the Senate Finance Committee, in drafting the regressive tax-in-kind bill—the unpopular tithing law that generated the bulk of the Richmond government's tax revenues after 1863. He also assisted the effort by Louisiana's senior senator, Edward Sparrow, a fabulously wealthy slave-owning planter from the state's cotton delta, in getting overseers exempted from the wartime draft. Semmes's amendment to the 1862 Conscription Law was the chief impetus for the hated Twenty-Slave Law that subsequently fueled the "rich man's war, poor man's fight" backlash.

Semmes also played a pivotal role in shaping Confederate policy on retaliation. The running congressional debates as to how to respond to "Yankee atrocities" boiled over after Lincoln's Emancipation Proclamation took effect and the

Union began systematically enlisting black soldiers. Believing the Lincoln administration was trying to foment slave insurrections, Jefferson Davis made known his intention to hand over to state prosecutors captured white officers of black troops. The Senate Judiciary Committee, however, issued an adverse report on Davis's plan. Declaring retaliation was a belligerent right that could be exercised only by the central government, Semmes introduced and secured passage of a joint resolution assigning such cases to military tribunals rather than state courts. The Lincoln administration's threat to retaliate against retaliation, however, discouraged the Confederate government from carrying out its threat to execute white officers.

Although one study of the Confederate Congress places Semmes with the proadministration faction, the fact is the junior senator from Louisiana was consistently opposed to Davis on most issues where there was room for disagreement. The only important issue on which they apparently concurred was the establishment of a supreme court, which Davis favored and Semmes unsuccessfully tried to create by means of legislation. Otherwise, the two men were at policy loggerheads—on martial law, the military role of P. G. T. Beauregard, and cabinet term limitations. Given the Confederate president's tendency to personalize conflict, his relationship with Semmes doubtless became strained as early as August 1862, when the New Orleanian asked the Judiciary Committee to report a bill prohibiting military officers from usurping civilian authority. Semmes was acting at the behest of Vice President Alexander H. Stephens, who, along with such other anti-administration stalwarts as Sparrow and Arkansas Senator Augustus Hill Garland, boarded at Semmes's rented mansion across the street from Davis's official Richmond residence. The martial law controversy had first blown up when the president asked Congress to suspend indefinitely the writ of habeas corpus, in effect making martial law part of "the permanent war effort." Like most western senators, especially from states where Union armies had established a beachhead, Semmes felt strong constituent pressure to keep Confederate generals from seizing authority to fix prices and muzzle the press. Trying to finesse the argument, the Senate Judiciary Committee let its House counterpart conduct a thorough study of the points at issue. In the end Semmes's martial law limitation bill was narrowly defeated because of congressional reluctance to enact laws that would likely be disregarded under emergency conditions.

If the martial law debates did not completely strain Semmes's and Davis's relationship, the controversy over Davis's treatment of New Orleans Gen. P. G. T. Beauregard produced an open break between senator and president. The disagreement flared up after Davis, still trading recriminations with Beauregard over the aftermath of First Manassas, let the Creole general languish as commander of the inconsequential Department of South Carolina and Georgia rather than reassign him to the Army of the West, which he had commanded for a short spell after Albert Sidney Johnston's death at Shiloh. By agreement with their congressional colleagues, in September 1862 while the martial law controversy was simmering, Semmes and Sparrow personally presented Davis with a petition signed by sixty senators and representatives appealing for Beauregard's restoration to the western command. Davis gave the senators a cool reception. Reading the petition aloud, including all sixty names, and interweaving his interpretive disagreements into the running commentary, Davis ended the interview by declaring he would not turn over the western army to Beauregard even if *"the whole world united in the petition."* Semmes and Sparrow came away from the meeting obviously miffed.

By January 1864, Semmes had become closely identified with the loosely organized anti-administration faction's effort to circumscribe Davis's power and authority. The previous December the Senate Judiciary Committee had taken up a bill introduced by Senator Waldo Johnson of Missouri that would limit cabinet terms to two years; in effect, the president would have to secure Senate reconfirmation of his bureau heads at the beginning of each new Congress. Partly a reflection of fears that a British cabinet form of government was evolving from the practice of some cabinet officers serving concurrently in Congress, the bill sought to assert the rights of the states over those of the central government. Semmes wrote the Judiciary Committee's favorable report sending the legislation onto the floor, arguing that the bill was constitutionally necessary to brake the executive's propensity for retaining in high office "individuals obnoxious to the States, as represented in the Senate." The Confederate War Department clerk John B. Jones said the measure was a declaration of war between Davis and the Congress. Confederate diarist Mary Boykin Chesnut recorded that Davis would have resigned had the bill become law—which it failed to do.

It also fell to Senator Semmes to fire Congress's parting shot at the disgruntled president. In March 1865, Davis aroused congressional ire by scolding lawmakers for their grudging approval of his plan to enlist black soldiers and grant them freedom. His brief message rehearsing old arguments about congressional obstructionism provoked the Senate to set up a secret Committee of Five to answer Davis's charges. Semmes drafted a report that canvassed every area of disagreement between Congress and the executive—impressment, exemptions, martial law, taxes—and concluded by rebuking Davis for transmitting a message "calculated to excite discord and dissension." A short while later, the Confederate Congress adjourned—sine die as military events would soon dictate.

For all his important behind-the-scenes committee and

legislative floor work, Semmes's sociability made the most lasting impression on many of his contemporaries. At the time of his Richmond sojourn, Semmes was not a wealthy man by the standards of the Confederate Senate; he lost the wealth he had accumulated in New Orleans when Union authorities confiscated and sold his house and all his belongings shortly after occupying the city. But Semmes had married well. His wife, Myra Knox, was the daughter of a wealthy banker-planter from Montgomery, Alabama. Her father sent the hampers of food (and possibly the costly rent payments) that made Semmes's mansion in Richmond such an affordably popular boardinghouse for Confederate influentials. Myra furnished the hospitality and grace that made social occasions at the mansion the stuff of wartime legend—as well as the target of wrathful barbs from the Richmond press. Mary Chesnut's famous diary alludes frequently to the couple's charade-filled parties and soirees attended by the brass and class of Confederate Richmond. Of medium height and middle-class girth, the balding and mustachioed Semmes used to perform upper-class renditions of slave heel-and-toe hoedowns as parlor audiences in his home cried out "The Honorable Senator from Louisiana has the floor."

Indeed, Semmes's wartime memories were more vivid regarding Confederate social life than congressional legislation. Those days were, as he recalled in the 1890s, "the last chapter in the history of that olden life." More than thirty years later, Semmes and his wife could still remember the price they paid for the 1864 New Year's turkey banquet—"one of the last big dinners that we had at our house," Myra Semmes told a New Orleans reporter.

In October 1865, Semmes joined the stream of pardon-seekers appealing for amnesty from President Andrew Johnson. It required only a five-minute interview for Semmes to secure his pardon and Johnson's good wishes. With a hundred-dollar loan, Semmes returned to his private law practice and financial well-being by landing such lucrative clients as the notorious Louisiana Lottery Company whose case he argued before the U.S. Supreme Court in 1891. Semmes rose quickly to the head of the state bar. From 1873 to 1879 he served as professor of civil law at the University of Louisiana (now Tulane). Called "the incarnation of logic" by local lawyers who admired his grasp of Greek and Latin, Semmes was counsel on almost every leading case that came before the civil courts in the postbellum era. In 1887 Semmes was elected president of the American Bar Association, and in 1890 he was invited to address the centennial celebration of the founding of the U.S. Supreme Court. Semmes was also in contention for the Supreme Court seat eventually filled by Mississippian L. Q. C. Lamar.

The couple's social life after the Civil War also resumed its busy pace. Well into the twentieth century, New Orleans's society still remembered Myra Semmes's masked balls and strict social conventions; getting on her exclusive party call list was a clear sign one had arrived. Thomas Semmes also perched atop the carnival and social hierarchy of uptown New Orleans. His national connections (he entertained President Grover Cleveland when he visited the Crescent City) added to a social cachet already impeccable by virtue of his Confederate pedigree. Among his other social honors, Semmes served as president of New Orleans's exclusive Boston Club. While consolidating his authority in New Orleans's society, Semmes was also deepening his involvement with organized Catholicism, becoming active in the Jesuit Alumni Association, lending his legal expertise to the church, and befriending several of the city's archbishops. Semmes's Anglo-Catholicism helped bridge the ethnocultural divisions that had split the New Orleans upper class during the first five decades of the nineteenth century.

As for postwar politics, Semmes played the role of senior statesman. He served prominently in both state constitutional conventions of 1879 and 1898. In the earlier convention he was instrumental in defeating agrarian efforts to repudiate the Reconstruction bonded debt and thus damage state credit. As chairman of the 1898 convention's Judiciary Committee, Semmes helped enact Louisiana's sweeping disfranchisement provision—which by the early 1900s had resulted in purging nearly all blacks and a substantial number of illiterate poor whites from the voting lists. His conservatism was also felt on New Orleans's school board, to which Semmes had been appointed in 1877 by Governor Francis T. Nicholls. As board president, Semmes was in the forefront of the effort to end New Orleans's successful experiment with integrated public schools and to slash expenditures to the bone. As an upper-class, extremely conservative Catholic, Semmes believed, as he put it at the 1874 law school graduation, that "compulsory education ignores moral and religious culture, [and] sacrifices heart and soul on the altar of material science."

By the time of Jefferson Davis's death in 1889, the scars of wartime politics had not completely healed. Deliberately excluded from the carriages escorting the ex–Confederate president's funeral cortege, Semmes paid tribute to Davis by marching with the procession of Confederate veterans from New Orleans to Metairie Cemetery. When Semmes died ten years later, he, too, as the last surviving Confederate senator, was given full military rites. According to a contemporary, his funeral was "one of the largest and most imposing" ever witnessed in New Orleans.

BIBLIOGRAPHY

Alexander, Thomas B., and Richard E. Beringer. *The Anatomy of the Confederate Congress: A Study of the Influences of Member*

Characteristics on Legislative Voting Behavior, 1861–1865. Nashville, Tenn., 1972.
Biographical and Historical Memoirs of Louisiana. Vol. 2. Chicago, 1892.
Chesnut, Mary Boykin. *Mary Chesnut's Civil War.* Edited by C. Vann Woodward. New Haven, Conn., 1981.
"Hon. Thomas J. Semmes: An Evening with the Venerable Statesman and Jurist." *Southern Historical Society Papers* 25 (1897): 317–333. Reprint, Wilmington, N.C., 1991.
Humphreys, Anderson, and Curt Guenther. *Semmes America.* Memphis, Tenn., 1989.
"University of Louisiana, Law Department. Address of Hon. Thos. J. Semmes." *New Orleans Picayune,* April 28, 1874.
"When Mrs. Thomas J. Semmes Was Hostess." *New Orleans Item-Tribune,* March 24, 1929.
Yearns, Wilfred B. *The Confederate Congress.* Athens, Ga., 1960.

LAWRENCE N. POWELL

SENECAS. Known as Mingos during the colonial era, the Senecas of northeastern Indian Territory were unrelated to the New York tribe of that name. They were actually the Senecas of Sandusky, an industrious people who in 1831 exchanged their Ohio lands for a 67,000-acre tract in Indian Territory. Within a year, 275 of them had moved to their new homes. Influenced by their former Federal agent, A. J. Dorn, Seneca chiefs Little Town Spicer and Small Town Spicer, in conjunction with the Eastern Shawnee headmen, signed a treaty of alliance with the Confederate States on October 4, 1861. In the treaty, negotiated by commissioner Albert Pike, the Senecas agreed to recognize slavery and to become military allies of the Southern states, while the Confederacy assumed all the monetary commitments contained in earlier tribal treaties with the United States plus some new ones.

Although the Confederacy did make one annuity payment, the Senecas were never able to take the treaty seriously. Bordering Missouri, their reserve was soon overrun by thieves and toughs who plundered the tribespeople of their horses, cattle, and other possessions. Looking for protection, they fled to Kansas where they remained as refugees until the end of the war. Some of their young men joined the Indian Home Guard Regiments and accompanied Union expeditions into Indian Territory.

In September 1865, the Senecas signed the Fort Smith peace treaty that terminated hostilities in Indian Territory. In February 1867, tribal leaders negotiated a new treaty with the United States by which they received partial compensation for some of their wartime losses. But they were forced to sell part of their lands for the settlement of smaller tribes and to join with the Senecas of the Seneca-Shawnee band as a single tribe.

BIBLIOGRAPHY

Nieberding, Velma. *The History of Ottawa County.* Miami, Okla., 1983.
Wright, Muriel H. *A Guide to the Indian Tribes of Oklahoma.* Norman, Okla., 1951. Reprint, Norman, Okla., 1983.

W. DAVID BAIRD

SEQUESTRATION. *For discussion of confiscation and sequestration, see* Confiscation.

SERMONS. Prior to the summer and fall of 1860 the sermons of Southern clergymen, generally, were apolitical in content; they were evangelical and emphasized the theological importance of religious experience for the salvation of the individual. In this respect the sermons of Southern clergymen were similar to those of clergymen throughout the country. As sectional tensions increased and secession drew closer, however, the sermons of some Southern clergymen increasingly began to reflect the tensions polarizing the nation and to espouse the views, values, and opinions of their environment.

Political issues became the subject of many sermons during this period. Some espoused secession from the Union, whereas others urged a more moderate or cautious approach to the political situation. The sermons of two prominent Presbyterian clergymen illustrate this reflection of Southern sentiment. Robert Lewis Dabney, moderator of the Synod of Virginia, preached a fast-day sermon on the first Sunday in November 1860. He denounced the passionate men whom he said were agitating the country and advised his listeners to pray for peace, vote for virtuous men, and be calm in language and manner. About the same time, James H. Thornwell, the most influential person in Southern Presbyterianism and a professor of theology at the denomination's seminary in Columbia, South Carolina, preached a thanksgiving sermon in which he declared that the Federal Union had become intolerable and was synonymous with tyranny, oppression, and falsehood. He denounced the Federal government as corrupt and declared that it was no longer possible to live with self-respect in a Union with a Republican chief executive. He recommended that the state of South Carolina secede from the Union at once.

Prior to the firing on Fort Sumter in April 1861, sentiments similar to those of Dabney and Thornwell were expressed by Baptist, Episcopal, Lutheran, Methodist, and other clergy in the South. But once war erupted and Abraham Lincoln called for volunteers to subdue rebellion, most clergymen, including moderates like Dabney, espoused the cause of the South.

Sermons justifying secession were based on three arguments. One was the state sovereignty doctrine enunciated forcefully by John C. Calhoun and other politicians since the 1830s. A second was the alleviation of unjust economic exploitation. Basil Manly and James C. Furman, Baptist clergymen in Alabama and South Carolina, respectively, argued that the South, for years, had been unjustly treated by Federal tariff laws. A final argument offered to justify secession was based upon Holy Scripture. The creation of the Confederacy was described as the working of the hand of God in history in a manner not unlike his creation of the Kingdom of Israel under David. It was asserted that the prosperity, atheism, and materialism of the North had prompted the Almighty to move against the United States, to divide it and to set apart a righteous remnant in the South to preserve his truth, justice, and honor.

The clergy's arguments defending secession and the Confederacy and placing the blame for the breakup of the Union on the North reflected the opinions many Southern politicians had been expressing for decades. The sermons of the vast majority of churchmen were in harmony with their intellectual environment, indicating that the clergymen were more followers than leaders of events and opinion at this time in Southern history.

It should be noted, however, that even after the war began not all Southern clergymen were apologists for the Confederacy and its values and institutions. Scattered throughout the region were some clergy, found in all denominations, who opposed the course of the South, viewed it as a road to destruction, and remained pro-Union in their sympathies. This sentiment was greatest in the areas of southwestern Virginia, eastern Tennessee, and western North Carolina, but it could be heard in every Southern state. Perhaps the most prominent clergymen of this persuasion were the Methodist William G. Brownlow of Tennessee, the Presbyterian James A. Lyon of Columbus, Mississippi, and Protestant Episcopal Bishop Alexander Gregg of Texas.

Among the overwhelming majority of clergymen supporting the Confederacy, religion became practically synonymous with patriotism during the war. The struggle was portrayed from numerous pulpits as a just or holy cause against a tyrannical aggressor. Southern men were urged to defend their homes and were told that they could enter into the war without compunction and with the faith that, though the battles might be bloody and rugged, the God of Hosts would be with them. Some clergymen, in their sermons, urged men to volunteer for the army. A prominent Presbyterian clergyman, Benjamin Morgan Palmer, composed a sermon based on *Psalms* 144:1, "Blessed be the Lord, my strength, which teacheth my hands to war and my fingers to fight," which he preached on numerous occasions to arouse the people and stimulate men to join the army. Mary B. Chesnut once attended a fast-day service and confessed that the sermon "stirred my blood, my flesh crept and tingled. A red hot glow of patriotism passed over me. There was . . . exhortation to fight and die." Other clergymen such as David Sullins and Bishop George F. Pierce, both Methodists, would occasionally accompany recruiters and address gatherings, urging the people to keep the faith and young men to volunteer for the army.

It was customary for sermons to explain the role of Almighty God in every victory and defeat of Confederate forces. Defeats were usually portrayed as necessary preparations for peace and prosperity; they were God's means of testing and building character. Southerners were reminded that God always chastises those whom he loves the most. The people were implored to remain firm in the faith and were assured that God would grant them the ultimate victory and independence. On the other hand, Confederate victory in battle was considered a gift of God and the evidence of his good pleasure toward the South. When George B. McClellan was forced to withdraw from the vicinity of Richmond in the summer of 1862, clergymen from Virginia to Texas proclaimed to their congregations that God had delivered the South from the oppressor and that it was evident that he was on the side of the South.

Clergymen of all denominations participated in numerous days of fasting and thanksgiving. These days were usually designated by secular authorities, and at such times businesses were closed and worship services were held. These fast-day sermons might thank the Almighty for some victory; urge citizens to greater efforts for independence; implore the people to keep the faith; and assure their listeners of God's continual care, even in the face of a military defeat.

Although the churches in the South had been engaged in missions to convert the slaves prior to 1861, denominational leaders were not pleased with the success of their efforts. During the war church spokesmen urged their constituency not to neglect the religious instruction of their servants. Some churchmen in the South speculated that the war was partially God's wrath for their failure to devote sufficient time and resources to converting the blacks. During the war the conscience of Protestantism was stirred by certain aspects of slavery which it was believed were not in keeping with Biblical teachings. For example, in a fast-day sermon in 1863 Methodist Bishop George F. Pierce declared that slave owners should recognize the legality and sacredness of slave marriages. Various Baptist and Presbyterian spokesmen in the South echoed Pierce's sentiments. Other reforms requested by churchmen included removing the ban on teaching slaves to read and write, and repealing the laws prohibiting blacks from preaching the gospel. Before the end of the war a few churchmen expressed sympathy for emancipation, especially for those slaves who might serve in the Confederate military forces.

Sermons by prominent clergymen were published in denominational weekly newspapers and journals, and by tract organizations such as the Evangelical Tract Society of Petersburg, Virginia, and the General Tract Agency of Raleigh, North Carolina. Some sermons were also printed and distributed by denominational agencies such as the Sunday School and Bible Board of the Baptist General Association of Virginia or the Presbyterian Committee of Publications in Richmond, Virginia. An indeterminate number of sermons were published in the South during the war. Some sources list approximately one hundred; probably as many more were printed in religious newspapers and journals during the same period.

During the course of the war, ecumenical organizations printed and distributed to soldiers more than one hundred tracts totaling over 60,000,000 pages. These tracts, consisting of four to sixteen pages, contained sermons, devotionals, instructions for Christian conduct, and exegesis on various items of Christian doctrine. Some denominations also published religious newspapers intended specifically for the men in the armed forces. Two of these papers, *The Soldiers' Paper* and the *Army and Navy Herald,* claimed a monthly circulation of 40,000 copies in 1862.

When the Confederacy collapsed in the spring of 1865 the sermons did not reflect bitterness and despair. Clergymen explained that the outcome of the war was still the will of God. The people of the South were counseled to accept the surrender of their armies as a part of the inscrutable plan of Providence and to endeavor to be loyal and obedient to the powers that be. Perhaps James B. Taylor, a respected Baptist clergyman in Virginia, exemplified most clergymen at the end of the war. He had argued that secession and the war were just and that the Almighty would bless the South with victory and independence. Yet in the spring and summer of 1865 he accepted the verdict of arms as being the decision of God, and he counseled his fellow Southerners and Baptists to accept the collapse of the Confederacy.

[*See also* Bible Societies; Fast Days.]

BIBLIOGRAPHY

Chesebrough, David B., ed. *God Ordained This War: Sermons on the Sectional Crisis, 1830–1865.* Columbia, S.C., 1991.

Daniel, W. Harrison. *Southern Protestantism in the Confederacy.* Bedford, Va., 1989.

Faust, Drew G. *The Creation of Confederate Nationalism: Ideology and Identity in the Civil War South.* Baton Rouge, La., 1988.

Romero, Sidney J. *Religion in the Rebel Ranks.* Lanham, Md., 1983.

Shattuck, Gardiner Humphrey, Jr. *A Shield and Hiding Place: The Religious Life of the Civil War Armies.* Macon, Ga., 1987.

Silver, James W. *Confederate Morale and Church Propaganda.* Tuscaloosa, Ala., 1957.

W. Harrison Daniel

SEVEN DAYS' BATTLES. The battles that took place from June 25 to July 1, 1862, on the Virginia Peninsula were the culmination of Union Maj. Gen. George B. McClellan's Peninsular campaign, which had carried his Army of the Potomac to within seven miles of Richmond.

While McClellan positioned his 100,000-man army just outside the Confederate capital, Gen. Robert E. Lee, who had replaced wounded Gen. Joseph E. Johnston as commander of the newly designated Army of Northern Virginia, shored up the city's defenses and sought an opportunity to seize the initiative. That opportunity came when Brig. Gen. J. E. B. Stuart, following a cavalry reconnaissance that took him completely around McClellan's forces, reported that the Union right flank was unsecured and vulnerable to attack. The Chickahominy River separated Maj. Gen. Fitz John Porter's 30,000 men from the remainder of the Union army.

Lee decided to launch his attack before McClellan realized the flaw in his troop dispositions. Lee divided his smaller army in the face of the enemy, leaving a fraction of his forces to confront McClellan while sending the bulk of his troops to attack Porter. In addition to his own men, Lee would have the services of Maj. Gen. Thomas J. ("Stonewall") Jackson's veterans from the Shenandoah Valley.

The opposing forces clashed briefly at Oak Grove on June 25, the day before Lee planned to open his offensive. Despite this action, he still hoped to surprise Porter with attacks from three divisions under Maj. Gens. A. P. Hill, James Longstreet, and D. H. Hill, in cooperation with Jackson's troops. Uncharacteristically, Jackson failed to arrive, and an impatient A. P. Hill started the attack prematurely. Porter's men, well entrenched in prepared positions along Beaver Dam Creek, near Mechanicsville, easily repulsed the repeated Confederate assaults. The bold but bloody attacks cost the Southerners 1,484 casualties to the Federals' 361.

On the following day, June 27, Lee's Confederates attacked the Federals in their new positions near Gaines' Mill. Again the Southerners suffered heavy losses in brutal assaults on the Union lines. Lee continued to press McClellan, hoping to annihilate his army in one battle. McClellan, now anxious about his army's survival, ordered a change of base from the York River to the James and steadily retreated.

The opposing forces clashed again at Savage's Station on June 29, Frayser's Farm on June 30, and finally at Malvern Hill on July 1. Although Lee had failed to execute his complicated plans to destroy McClellan's army, he had forced the Federals farther from the gates of Richmond. By the time the Seven Days' Battles ended, the Army of the Potomac was thirty miles from the city. Lee had driven his enemy from position to position, but at a tremendous cost to the Southerners: 3,286 killed, 15,909 wounded, and 946

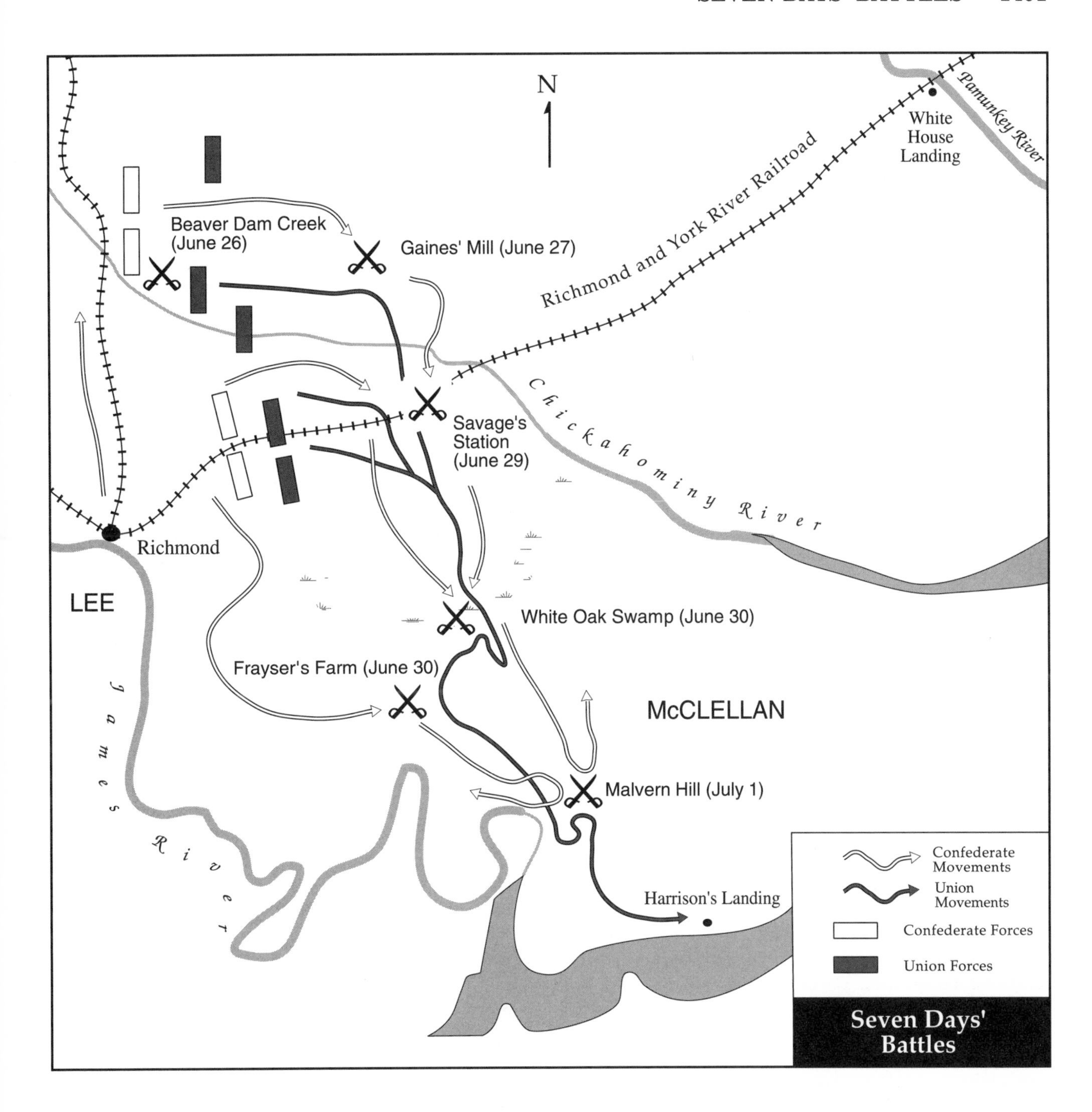

missing; the Federals lost 1,734 killed, 8,062 wounded, and 6,053 missing.

Robert E. Lee had saved Richmond from capture in 1862. In the process, he established a reputation for boldness and innovation and shook off the derogatory references to "Granny Lee" and the "King of Spades" (the latter for his use of defensive earthworks). McClellan remained at his base on the James River, assessing the campaign and placing blame on anyone other than himself.

[*See also* Frayser's Farm, Virginia; Gaines' Mill, Virginia; Malvern Hill, Virginia; Mechanicsville, Virginia; Savage's Station, Virginia.]

BIBLIOGRAPHY

Cullen, Joseph P. *The Peninsula Campaign, 1862: McClellan and Lee Struggle for Richmond.* Harrisburg, Pa., 1973.

Freeman, Douglas S. *Lee's Lieutenants: A Study in Command.* 3 vols. New York, 1942–1944. Reprint, New York, 1986.

Johnson, Robert U., and C. C. Buel, eds. *Battles and Leaders of the Civil War.* 4 vols. New York, 1887–1888. Reprint, Secaucus, N.J., 1982.

McPherson, James M. *Battle Cry of Freedom: The Civil War Era.* New York, 1988.

Sears, Stephen W. *George B. McClellan: The Young Napoleon.* New York, 1988.

Sears, Stephen W. *To the Gates of Richmond: The Peninsula Campaign.* New York, 1992.

BRIAN S. WILLS

SEVEN PINES, VIRGINIA. On May 31 and June 1, 1862, Confederate forces attempted to halt the advance of Gen. George B. McClellan's Army of the Potomac against the Southern capital. The battle, called either Seven Pines or Fair Oaks (from small villages some ten miles east of Richmond), illustrates the command-related difficulties inherent in Civil War combat, where armies occupied miles of space but information usually moved no faster than the speed of a horse. On the Confederate side, poor staff work, misunderstandings, and faulty execution robbed Gen. Joseph E. Johnston's well-designed plans of success.

Although McClellan had been delayed at Yorktown and bloodied at Williamsburg, by mid-May his slow, methodical Peninsula campaign seemed near success. Having advanced inland from Fortress Monroe, his flanks guarded by the York and James rivers, McClellan's 105,000-man army stood poised on the outskirts of Richmond, awaiting reinforcements under Gen. Irvin McDowell, who was scheduled to march overland from Washington. Although Johnston had barely 60,000 men, McClellan believed himself outnumbered.

As McClellan neared Richmond, the terrain necessitated that his large force straddle the rain-swollen Chickahominy River. Johnston realized that this split the Union army into two virtually isolated wings, and he seized the opportunity to strike McClellan's men north of the Chickahominy before McDowell joined them. The attack was slated for May 29. But when he learned that Thomas J. ("Stonewall") Jackson's campaign in the Shenandoah Valley had diverted McDowell, Johnston canceled his plans. He formulated instead an attack on the smaller, weaker portion of McClellan's army south of the river. This consisted of two corps, under Gens. Erasmus D. Keyes and Samuel P. Heintzelman, with Keyes's men occupying positions nearest the Confederates.

After a lengthy meeting on May 30, Johnston gave verbal instructions for the commander of his right wing, Gen. James Longstreet, to assault the center and flanks of Keyes's corps. The left wing under Gen. Gustavus W. Smith was to lend assistance if needed and prevent any Federal units from crossing the Chickahominy to support Keyes and Heintzelman.

Longstreet, however, advanced part of his troops over the wrong road. The confusion this caused combined with rain and a dispute over seniority with Gen. Benjamin Huger (who had not been notified that he was under Longstreet's command) to delay the attack until afternoon. Once the battle began, Longstreet's troop dispositions were so poor that only six of his thirteen brigades were effectively engaged.

Johnston realized quite early in the morning that coordination had broken down but could do little to restore it. The dispositions he had made, though typical of nineteenth-century attempts to control combat, actually added to his problems. Johnston had ordered some units to advance when Huger's division, marching from the rear, reached them. Others were to attack when they heard artillery fire. The delay caused by Longstreet's argument with Huger therefore pinned some brigades in place, while freakish acoustics prevented others from hearing the opening guns. Moreover, with only the small staff typical of Civil War commanders, Johnston could neither effectively ascertain nor correct Longstreet's errors. He shifted some of Smith's men to support Longstreet's attack, but Confederate divisions fought piecemeal. Although the Federals were mauled, the opportunity for a crushing blow was lost. Johnston was severely wounded late in the day, and command passed by seniority to Smith.

On the Federal side, McClellan, who was quite ill, exercised minimal control over the course of the battle. He knew that his advancing army was temporarily vulnerable as it straddled the Chickahominy, but in the unlikely event of a Confederate attack he expected his right wing, not his left, to be the target. When the sound of firing from the south reached his headquarters at New Bridge, on the north bank of the river, he did no more than alert Gen. Edward Sumner to ready his nearby command for action.

The Confederate attack, which began around 1:00 P.M., initially struck Keyes's men, who occupied the ground between Fair Oaks and Seven Pines. For much of the day they fought alone, as Keyes's messages to Heintzelman, who commanded the left wing, went astray. It was 2:30 P.M. or later before Heintzelman realized a major battle was underway. He then ordered his own corps to Keyes's support and around 3:00 P.M. telegraphed McClellan for help. Ironically, it was easier for Heintzelman to communicate with his commander across the river than with his subordinates at the front. McClellan promptly ordered Sumner's men to the south bank. Unimpeded by Smith, they crossed the swirling river on two rickety bridges and joined the battle in time to halt the Confederate advance.

The battle continued the next day, June 1, but events proved anticlimactic and did little but lengthen the casualty

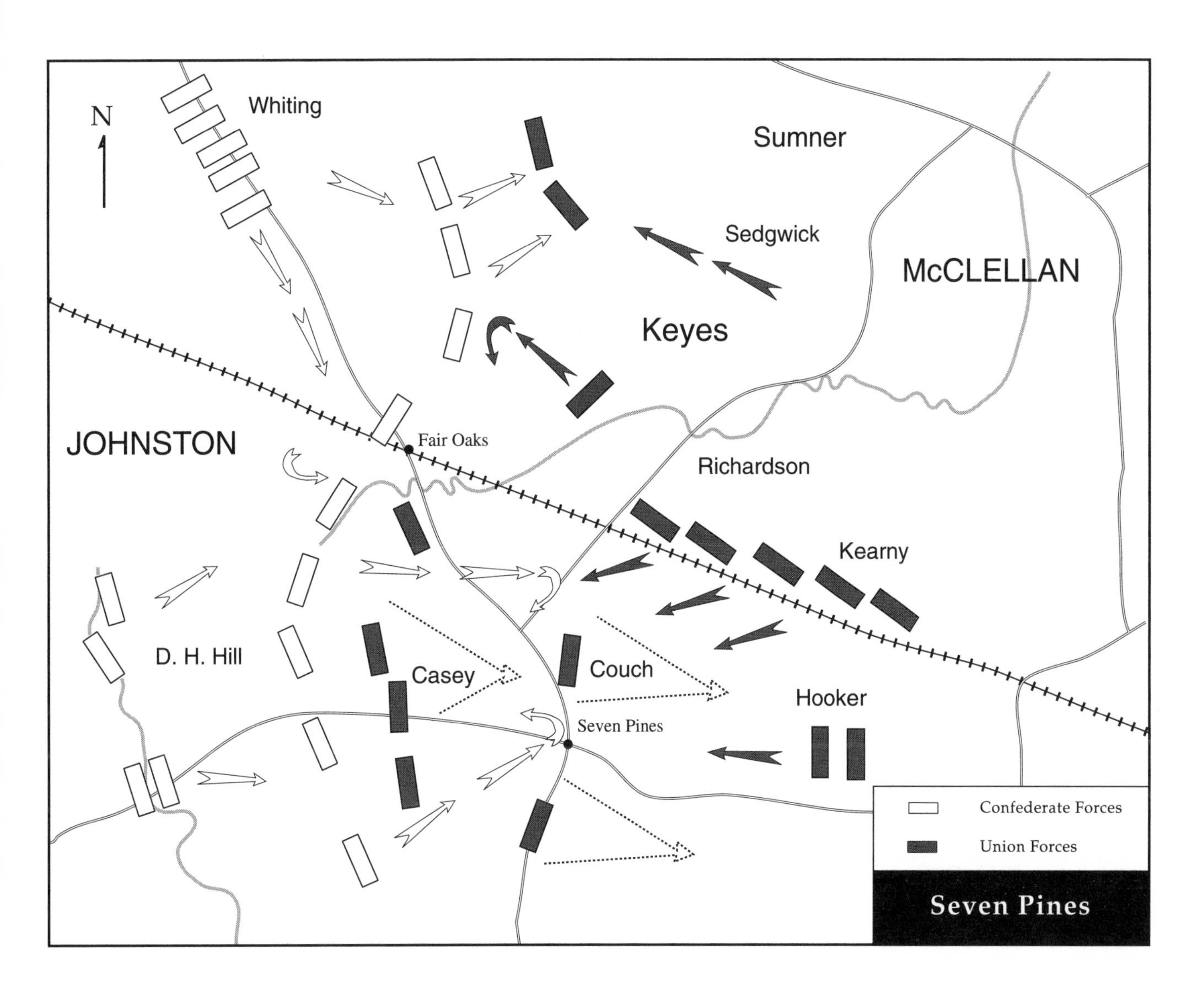

lists. Smith lacked both the physical and mental stamina needed to command an army. Although historians credit him too little for assuming command of a disorganized force and leading it into battle only a few hours later, he wasted Confederate strength in a series of uncoordinated assaults. McClellan had consulted carefully with Heintzelman during the night, and the Federals fought well. By the time McClellan reached the field in late morning, the Confederates had withdrawn and the battle was over. Federal losses for the two-day conflict were around 5,000, a full 1,100 fewer than those the Confederates suffered.

Most of the Federal army was never engaged, but the swollen Chickahominy prevented any immediate counterblow. Regardless, McClellan considered Seven Pines a Union victory. In its wake, he asked for and received reinforcements. His subsequent delay allowed the Confederates to recoup and reinforce as well. When the campaign for Richmond continued, McClellan faced a new opponent. Broken by the strain of command, Smith had asked to be relieved. As his successor Jefferson Davis chose Robert E. Lee.

BIBLIOGRAPHY

Freeman, Douglas S. *Lee's Lieutenants: A Study in Command.* 3 vols. New York, 1942–1944. Reprint, New York, 1986.

Govan, Gilbert G., and James W. Livingood. *A Different Valor: The Story of General Joseph E. Johnston.* Westport, Conn., 1973.

Johnston, Joseph E. *Narrative of Military Operations Directed during the late War between the States.* New York, 1872. Reprint, New York, 1969.

McClellan, George B. *McClellan's Own Story.* Edited by William C. Prime. New York, 1887.

Sears, Stephen W. *George B. McClellan: The Young Napoleon.* New York, 1988.

William Garrett Piston

SEXTON, FRANCIS B. (1828–1900), congressman from Texas. Sexton was born on April 29, 1828, in Indiana. His family settled in San Augustine, Texas, in 1831. Sexton, an attorney, slaveholding farmer, and politician, served as president of the 1860 state Democratic convention. He supported secession and after the war began entered the army. He was elected to the Texas Senate but returned to the state too late for the legislative session.

In 1861, he was elected from the Fourth Congressional District to the House of the First Congress. Although he generally supported the legislative program of the Davis administration, he opposed the impressment of slaves by the military and the removal of local reserves from the states. Sexton also had serious reservations about legislation allowing the president to suspend the writ of habeas corpus. During the first term he worked with the rest of his state's delegation to secure the creation of the Trans-Mississippi Department. He was reelected to the Second Congress in 1863 and during its sessions remained a supporter of Davis. Serving on the Post Office and Post Roads Committee, he was particularly interested in improving the Confederate mail service.

After the war Sexton returned to San Augustine and then moved to Harrison County within the state. He died at El Paso, Texas, on May 15, 1900.

BIBLIOGRAPHY

Estill, Mary S., ed. "Diary of a Confederate Congressman, 1862–1863." *Southwestern Historical Quarterly* 38 (April 1935): 270–301; 39 (July 1935): 33–65.

Yearns, Wilfred B. *The Confederate Congress.* Athens, Ga., 1960.

CARL H. MONEYHON

SHARP, JACOB HUNTER (1833–1907), brigadier general. Sharp was born in Pickensville, Alabama, February 6, 1833. While still a youth, he moved with his parents to Lowndes County, Mississippi. He attended the University of Alabama for one term (1850–1851) and then returned to Alabama. He was admitted to the bar and was practicing law in Columbus, Mississippi, when his adopted state seceded from the Union.

Sharp enlisted as a private in the First Battalion Mississippi Infantry (later part of the Forty-fourth Mississippi), which was formed late in 1861, and he was elected captain. The Forty-fourth, led by Sharp, fought in the Battles of Shiloh, Perryville, and Murfreesboro. Shortly before Chickamauga in September 1863, he was promoted to colonel of the Forty-fourth Mississippi Regiment, which he led through the first day's battle. During the second day's fighting, Sharp's regiment was involved in repulsing the right wing of the Union army, and when Maj. Gen. Thomas C. Hindman, division commander, was wounded, Sharp took over the brigade of Brig. Gen. James Patton Anderson, who replaced Hindman. His regiment was involved in the siege of Chattanooga, but Sharp was incapacitated for part of the time.

When the Atlanta campaign began, Sharp replaced the disabled Brig. Gen. William Feimster Tucker and led six Mississippi infantry units. "His tactical skill and ability to inspire troops" led to his promotion to brigadier general July 26, 1864. Within two days Sharp had distinguished himself at Ezra Church. He and his brigade participated in Hood's Tennessee campaign, followed by service in the Carolinas, where he fought his last battle at Bentonville with a spirited performance. He apparently surrendered with Joseph E. Johnston on April 26, 1865, although no record of his parole has been located.

After the war, Sharp resumed his legal career in Mississippi. He purchased the *Columbus Independent,* was active in the white supremacy movement during Reconstruction, and served as a member of the legislature from 1886 to 1890. He died at Columbus September 15, 1907, and was buried there.

BIBLIOGRAPHY

Crute, Joseph H., Jr. *Units of the Confederate Army.* Midlothian, Va., 1987.

Faust, Patricia L. ed. *Historical Times Encyclopedia of the Civil War.* New York, 1986.

Wheeler, Joseph. *Alabama.* Vol. 7 of *Confederate Military History.* Edited by Clement A. Evans. Atlanta, 1899. Vol. 8 of extended ed. Wilmington, N.C., 1987.

JOHN R. WOODARD

SHARPSBURG CAMPAIGN. Robert E. Lee's withdrawal from the passes of South Mountain on the night of September 14–15, 1862, signaled the end of a frustrating week of campaigning in Maryland. Following his day-long engagement with George B. McClellan at Fox's and Turner's gaps, Lee informed his subordinates, "The day has gone against us, and this army will go by way of Sharpsburg and cross the [Potomac] river." Lee thus canceled further continuation of his first invasion of the North.

Nothing had gone well for the Confederate army since it had entered the Old Line State during the first week of September. Western Marylanders greeted Lee with a cool reception rather than shouts of liberation. The Federals had not abandoned Harpers Ferry as expected, thus blocking critical supply and communication lines into the Shenandoah Valley. Thomas J. ("Stonewall") Jackson's subsequent operations against the Ferry had fallen behind schedule, and Lee's army remained dangerously divided into five parts as McClellan moved toward Frederick. McClellan's fortunate discovery of Special Order 191 on

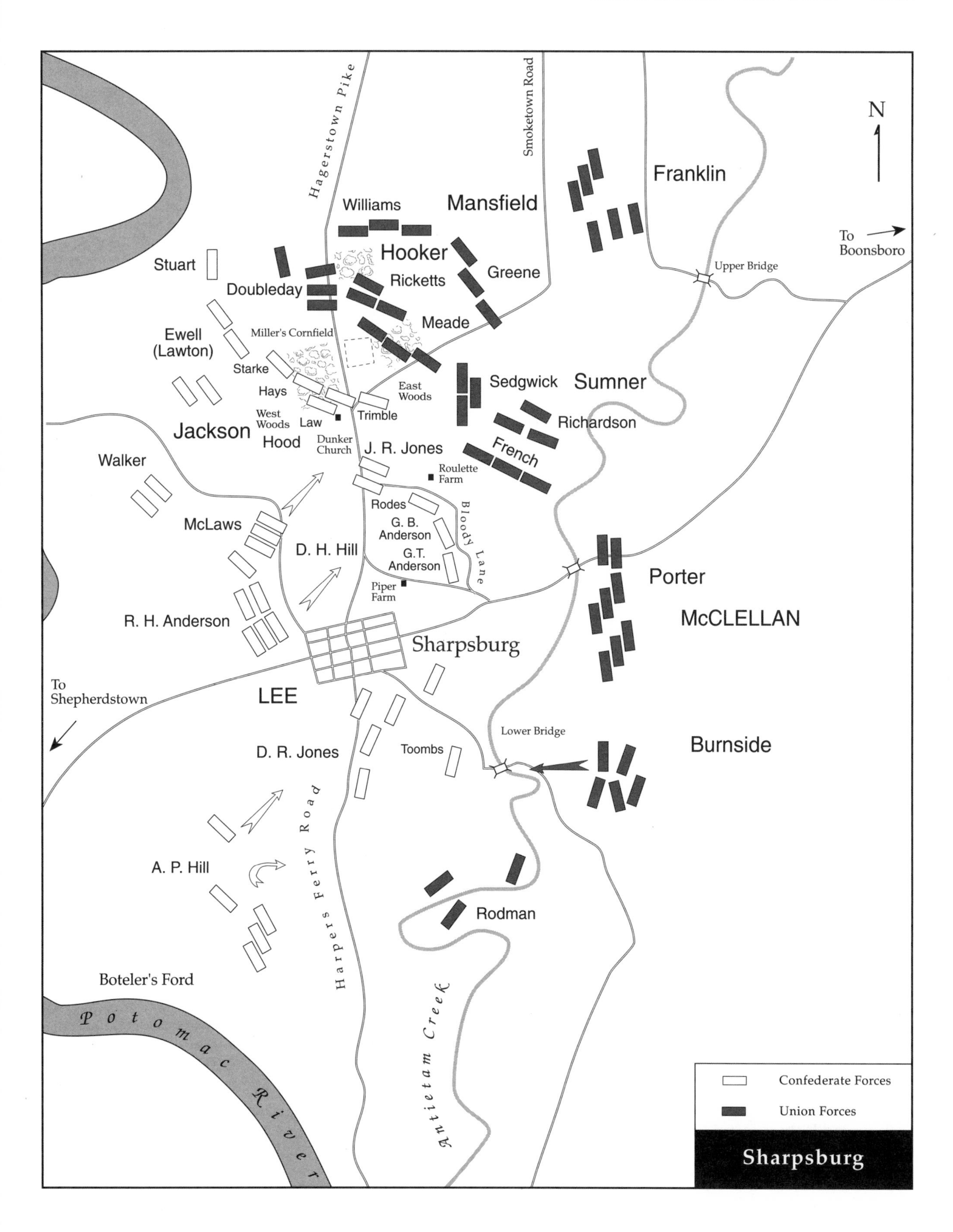
Hagerstown Pike
Smoketown Road
N
Franklin
Williams
Mansfield
To Boonsboro
Hooker
Stuart
Greene
Upper Bridge
Ricketts
Doubleday
Meade
Ewell (Lawton)
Miller's Cornfield
Starke
Sedgwick
Sumner
Hays
East Woods
West Woods
Law
Trimble
Richardson
Jackson
Hood
Dunker Church
J. R. Jones
French
Walker
Roulette Farm
Rodes
Bloody Lane
McLaws
G. B. Anderson
D. H. Hill
G.T. Anderson
Porter
Piper Farm
McCLELLAN
R. H. Anderson
Sharpsburg
To Shepherdstown
LEE
Lower Bridge
D. R. Jones
Toombs
Burnside
Harpers Ferry Road
A. P. Hill
Rodman
Boteler's Ford
Potomac River
Antietam Creek
Confederate Forces
Union Forces
Sharpsburg

September 13 provided him with "all the plans of the Rebels," and his drive toward South Mountain on the fourteenth was intended to "cut the enemy in two and beat him in detail." Stubborn Confederate resistance at the mountain passes foiled McClellan's plans, but Lee realized that further resistance on the fifteenth would prove futile. No choice remained but retreat from Maryland.

Yet during the withdrawal from South Mountain toward Sharpsburg, Lee received a message from Jackson. "I believe Harpers Ferry and its garrison will be surrendered on the morrow," Jackson reported. The commanding general, boosted by this possible good fortune, halted the retreat at Sharpsburg; and when word arrived of Stonewall's success late on the morning of the fifteenth, Lee gazed over the Antietam Creek and announced, "We will make our stand on these hills."

Lee's decision to stand at Sharpsburg was influenced by several factors. To begin with, the Southerners needed time to remove the large booty captured at Harpers Ferry. In addition, Boteler's (also known as Blackford's) Ford provided good access across the Potomac for Jackson's force of 23,000 marching seventeen miles north from Harpers Ferry. Lee also realized a stand in Maryland would gain time for the gathering of the fall harvest in the Shenandoah Valley. Foremost, however, was the opportunity to engage McClellan on Northern soil. A Confederate victory would embarrass the Republicans in an election year and perhaps provide the peace Democrats with an upper hand in Congress. The possibility of European diplomatic recognition for the South also loomed on the horizon.

Lee's determination to stand at Sharpsburg also carried great risks. If McClellan attacked before Lee's Harpers Ferry contingent arrived, the Federals would outnumber the Confederate commander five to one. In addition, with the Potomac River to his back and only one practicable crossing available at Boteler's Ford, Lee could be trapped along the Antietam if McClellan turned either flank. Lee's experience with and intuitive understanding of McClellan compelled him to gamble. Lee felt the Union general would not attack until the Confederates had reunited, and McClellan's cautious tendencies would forestall aggressive challenges to the Southern flanks.

Lee's belief that McClellan would not immediately attack proved correct. Although the Union commander pursued the Confederates to the east bank of the Antietam on the fifteenth, McClellan spent the sixteenth reconnoitering the terrain and deploying his 87,000 men. In the meantime, Jackson arrived on the afternoon of the sixteenth with his own division, and the divisions of Richard S. Ewell, and John G. Walker soon followed. The 8,000 men of Lafayette McLaws and Richard Heron Anderson were expected early on the morning of the seventeenth, and A. P. Hill's division, left behind at Harpers Ferry to arrange for the disposition of prisoners and booty, was half a day's march from Sharpsburg.

By the morning of September 17, with the exception of Hill's division, Lee's army of 35,000 sprawled over a four-mile line, anchored two miles north of Sharpsburg on the Potomac and stretching two miles south of the town to the lower bridge crossing of the Antietam. J. E. B. Stuart's horse artillery guarded the extreme left, while the infantry of Jackson's, Ewell's, and Hood's divisions covered the Confederate left in the cornfield and pastures of D. R. Miller and in the West Woods around a small Dunker church. D. H. Hill's division protected the middle, manning a sunken farm lane between the Roulette and Piper farms. D. R. Jones's and Walker's divisions initially defended the Confederate right on the high bluffs overlooking the Antietam. The Hagerstown Pike provided Lee with interior communications north of Sharpsburg, and the road leading west to Boteler's Ford, four miles from Lee's position, gave the Confederates their only avenue of escape.

McClellan, recognizing Lee's vulnerability with his back to the Potomac and with only one option for escape, devised an initial battle plan that primarily focused on the destruction of Lee's left flank. On the sixteenth, McClellan instructed Joseph Hooker's First Corps and the Twelfth Corps of Joseph Mansfield to cross the Antietam at the upper bridge and to swing north of Lee's line, and then return south at dawn on the seventeenth to smash Jackson and the left flank. Although the column of 20,000 made the flank march without detection, Hooker telegraphed the punch on the evening of the sixteenth when he pushed his advance too far south. Warned by this unexpected appearance of Federals on his left, Lee shifted Walker from his right to his left, and he poised the divisions of McLaws and Anderson, arriving on the seventeenth from Harpers Ferry at 3:00 A.M., toward the left.

At 5:30 A.M., Hooker's advance began. Although the Confederate left was outnumbered three to one, Hooker directed his three divisions badly, sending them forward piecemeal, thus negating his numerical superiority. The brigades of Hays, Laws, and Trimble smashed Hooker's first attack by James Ricketts's division in D. R. Miller's cornfield. Jackson's division crushed the assault by Abner Doubleday's division along the Hagerstown Pike. Hood's Texans drove the Pennsylvanians of George Meade's division backward through the cornfield and into the East Woods. With Hooker's corps demolished, Mansfield's Twelfth Corps began its advance. Piecemeal attacks by its two divisions again enabled the Confederates to stand their ground. To stop the attack of Alpheus Williams's division, Lee transferred three brigades from D. H. Hill's division north from the Confederate center. Then the Federal assault of George Greene's division stalled before the Dunker church.

Five Union divisions had failed to break Lee's left, but the Confederate carnage had been terrible. Almost half of Ewell's division had been slaughtered, and all but two of its regimental commanders had fallen. Brig. Gen. William E. Starke had been killed. Jackson's division suffered such extreme losses that a colonel now commanded a division. Hood's First Texas incurred 82 percent casualties during its assault. All totaled, 5,500 dead and wounded Union and Confederate soldiers lay in the cornfield and its environs after three hours of ferocious fighting.

Yet McClellan had not finished with the Confederate left. About 9:20 A.M., marching from the east toward the West Woods, came the three divisions of the Union Second Corps. At first, Southern resistance proved sporadic and light; but as John Sedgwick's division entered the West Woods in line formation, suddenly from its left and center was unleashed the fury of Lafayette McLaws's 4,000 Confederates. Lee had ordered McLaws up from the rear just in time to rout Sedgwick's advance, and the Confederate fire proved deadly—Sedgwick suffered 2,200 casualties in twenty minutes in the West Woods.

The morning phase of the Battle of Sharpsburg had ended. Lee's left remained intact, although tenuous, and attention now shifted south from the cornfield and the West Woods toward the sunken road defining the Confederate center. The 2,000 men in the brigades of George B. Anderson and Robert Rodes, reinforced by Richard Anderson's 4,000, defended the road against 8,000 men in two

CASUALTIES AT SHARPSBURG, MARYLAND. Photographed September 17, 1862, the single bloodiest day of the Civil War, behind the rail fence along the Hagerstown Pike, where Thomas J. ("Stonewall") Jackson's men met Gen. Joseph Hooker's charge. NATIONAL ARCHIVES

divisions of the Second Corps. William French's Union division struck first at 10:00 A.M. but, after repeated assaults, failed to dent the Confederate line. Israel Richardson's division followed and also failed to dislodge the stubborn Southerners. Finally at 1:00 P.M., after the death of G. B. Anderson and the wounding of Rodes, confusion developed in the Southern command, and the Confederates abandoned the lane owing to a misinterpreted order. The Federals quickly occupied the center of General Lee's line, and as one Southerner noted, "the end of the Confederacy was in sight." But McClellan refused to follow up on this breakthrough, and the battle for the Bloody Lane ended.

Attention now focused on the Confederate right. Defending the high bluffs overlooking the lower bridge across the Antietam were 500 Georgians of Robert Toombs's brigade. Facing Toombs were 12,000 men in the Ninth Corps, commanded by Ambrose Burnside. Fortunately for the Georgians, the bridge they defended was located in a narrow defile, making it impossible for Burnside to launch a large-scale frontal assault. For three hours, Toombs's men held off brigade-level attacks ordered by Burnside. At 1:00 P.M., however, a concerted charge by the Fifty-first New York and Fifty-first Pennsylvania finally established a bridgehead on the west bank of the Antietam. When Toombs discovered his right flank had been turned as well by I. P. Rodman's division, he abandoned his position, and the lower bridge belonged to Burnside.

For the next two hours, Burnside shuttled men, supplies, and food across the Antietam in preparation for a final assault against the Confederate right, now positioned along the Harpers Ferry Road just south of Sharpsburg. About 3:00 P.M., Burnside's corps began its advance, soon engaging D. R. Jones's thin division. The situation was desperate for General Lee. He could not maneuver Confederates from other parts of his line, and he had no reserves north of the Potomac. Suddenly, from the south, as Burnside methodically pressed forward, A. P. Hill and his Light Division arrived from Harpers Ferry, following a seventeen-mile forced march in seven hours. Lee ordered Hill to attack, and when his brigades smashed into Burnside's left flank, the stunned Federals retired toward the Antietam, ending the battle about dusk. Confederate Brig. Gen. Lawrence O'Bryan Branch was mortally wounded during Hill's assault.

It was the twelve bloodiest hours in American military history. In one day, almost 23,000 Union and Confederate casualties had fallen along the Antietam Creek. More than twice as many Americans lost their lives in one day at Sharpsburg as fell in the War of 1812, the Mexican War, and the Spanish-American War *combined.* Total casualties for the Federals included 12,410 (2,108 killed, 9,549 wounded, 753 missing). Confederate losses equaled 10,318 (1,546 killed, 7,754 wounded, 1,018 missing).

Despite the dangerous weakening of his army, Lee remained on the battlefield on the eighteenth, challenging McClellan to attack. The Union commander refused to reinitiate battle, however, and that night, the Army of Northern Virginia retired across Boteler's Ford and returned to Virginia.

Sharpsburg often is considered a turning point of the war. The Confederate military wave was at its peak in the fall of 1862, but with Braxton Bragg's failure in Kentucky and Lee's disappointing campaign in Maryland, hopes for diplomatic recognition and gains by the peace Democrats soon faded. In addition, Abraham Lincoln used McClellan's victory at Sharpsburg to announce his preliminary Emancipation Proclamation.

[*See also* Harpers Ferry, West Virginia, *article on* Battle of 1862; South Mountain, Maryland.]

BIBLIOGRAPHY

Cox, Jacob D. "The Battle of Antietam." In *Battles and Leaders of the Civil War.* Vol. 2. Edited by Robert U. Johnson and C. C. Buel. New York, 1888. Reprint, Secaucus, N.J., 1982.

Longstreet, James. "The Invasion of Maryland." In *Battles and Leaders of the Civil War.* Vol. 2. Edited by Robert U. Johnson and C. C. Buel. New York, 1888. Reprint, Secaucus, N.J., 1982.

Murfin, James V. *The Gleam of Bayonets.* New York, 1965.

Palfry, Francis. *The Antietam and Fredericksburg.* New York, 1881. Reprint, Wilmington, N.C., 1984.

Sears, Stephen. *Landscape Turned Red.* New York, 1983.

DENNIS E. FRYE

SHAWNEES. In 1861 there were two groups of Shawnees living in Indian Territory: those of the Seneca-Shawnee band and the Absentee Shawnees. Emigrants from Lewistown, Ohio, in 1832, and known subsequently as the Eastern Shawnees, the former group resided on a 60,000-acre tract near the Missouri border. The Absentee Shawnees, who had separated from the main body of the tribe after the American Revolution, lived in villages concentrated in southwestern Indian Territory near the Wichita Agency.

Influenced by their former Federal agent, A. J. Dorn, Eastern Shawnee chiefs Lewis Davis and Joseph Mohawk, in conjunction with the headmen of the Senecas of Sandusky, signed a treaty with the Confederate States on October 4, 1861. Negotiated by Albert Pike, the document, among other things, bound the Southern states to honor the provisions of former tribal treaties with the United States, legitimated slavery, and made the Indians partners in the existing war. Earlier, on August 12 at the Wichita Agency, Pike had negotiated a treaty with several tribes, including the Absentee Shawnees. Concerned only with "peace and brotherhood," these treaties promised no annuities and said nothing about becoming parties to a war.

Neither of the treaties involving the Shawnees was honored. The ruthless plundering of its reservation caused the Eastern Shawnee band to seek refuge in Kansas, where some of its young men joined the Indian Home Guard Regiments, USA. A similar exodus occurred in the West, with the Absentee Shawnee and other tribal groups moving to southwestern Kansas, only to return in October 1862 under Union encouragement to destroy the Confederate agency and nearly annihilate the defending Tonkawas.

On September 14, 1865, the Eastern Shawnees signed the Fort Smith peace treaty that terminated hostilities in Indian Territory. In February 1867, they negotiated a new treaty with the United States that gave them independence from the Senecas and partial compensation for war losses but required them to dispose of some of their land. An unratified treaty gave the Absentee Shawnees lands in what is now central Oklahoma.

BIBLIOGRAPHY

Nieberding, Velma. *The History of Ottawa County.* Miami, Okla., 1983.

Wright, Muriel H. *A Guide to the Indian Tribes of Oklahoma.* Norman, Okla., 1951. Reprint, Norman, Okla., 1983.

W. David Baird

Joseph O. Shelby. Library of Congress

SHELBY, JOSEPH O. (1830–1897), brigadier general. An educated, wealthy Missouri rope manufacturer, by the 1850s "Jo" Shelby was fast becoming one of the state's largest landholders and slave owners. During the Kansas-Missouri border troubles, he led two armed forays of proslavery activists into Kansas, one of which participated in the sack of Lawrence.

At the outbreak of the Civil War, he organized a company of cavalry and offered his services to the governor, Claiborne F. Jackson, commanding the pro-Southern State Guard forces. After serving as captain of cavalry in the Missouri State Guard, he received a commission as colonel in the Confederate service in June of 1862. During the next two years, Shelby led horsemen in every major battle west of the Mississippi, including Carthage, Oak Hills, and Lexington in Missouri, and Elkhorn Tavern in Arkansas, as well as in scores of minor actions. By war's end, his exploits as a cavalry commander west of the Mississippi had earned him a reputation comparable to that commanded by Nathan Bedford Forrest east of the river.

Once in Confederate service, Shelby organized a brigade of cavalry, which he named the "Iron Brigade." It proved one of the finest cavalry units in the Trans-Mississippi theater and participated in actions in Arkansas at St. Charles and DeVall's Bluff, as well as serving with John S. Marmaduke's cavalry division at Prairie Grove. Shelby was wounded in action at Helena in July 1863, but upon his recovery he raided Missouri, capturing stores in Boonville, Warsaw, Tipton, Stockton, and Neosho before retiring to Arkansas.

At Princeton, Arkansas, in March 1864, Shelby's force of one thousand horsemen delayed at least twelve thousand Federal infantry under Frederick Steele for an entire day, contributing to Steele's failure to take Little Rock during his Arkansas campaign. After successful raids along the White River that summer, Shelby participated in Sterling Price's raid into Missouri, engaging in the Battles of Pilot Knob, Big Blue River, and Westport, among others, after which he retreated to Clarksville, Texas.

Unwilling to surrender, Shelby and his loyal command crossed the Rio Grande into Mexico, but they did not participate in the conflict resulting in the overthrow of Mexican Emperor Maximilian. After assisting Price to form Carlota, a colony of ex-Confederates in Mexico, Shelby returned to Missouri where he lived out the remainder of his life.

BIBLIOGRAPHY

Britton, Wiley. *The Civil War on the Border.* New York, 1899.

Edwards, John N. *Shelby and His Men; or, The War in the West.* Kansas City, Mo., 1897.

Johnson, Robert U., and C. C. Buel, eds. *Battles and Leaders of the Civil War.* 4 vols. New York, 1887–1888. Reprint, Secaucus, N.J., 1982.

Monaghan, Jay. *Civil War on the Western Border, 1854–1865.* Lincoln, Neb., 1955.

O'Flaherty, Daniel. *General Jo Shelby: Undefeated Rebel.* Chapel Hill, N.C., 1954.

CHRISTOPHER PHILLIPS

SHELBY IRON COMPANY. Among the oldest and most prominent of the pioneer iron enterprises in Alabama, the Shelby Iron Company was located near the geographical center of the state some thirty miles southeast of present-day Birmingham. Founded in 1846 by Horace Ware, who soon took on a partner, it was incorporated by the state of Alabama in 1858. With the onset of the Civil War, Ware sold six-sevenths of his interest to local investors to raise capital for expansion.

The improved furnaces had a capacity of approximately 250 tons per week. The firm provided iron to both army and navy facilities in Selma, Mobile, Griswoldville (Georgia), Yazoo City (Mississippi), and Atlanta. Until January 1865, when a spur railroad was completed, all manufactured iron had to be shipped by wagon to the Alabama and Tennessee Rivers Railroad at Columbiana for reshipment.

Shelby experienced difficulty in getting a rolling mill in operation to produce two-inch armor plate for the navy and did not begin production for that purpose until March 1863. Shelby's iron, however, was in demand for producing guns, and most was used for that purpose.

Shelby employed 450 to 550 workers. Skilled white labor was recruited from throughout the South, and details from the army produced 40 to 75 men. Approximately three-fourths of the work force were hired slaves. One hundred or so skilled slave laborers were rented from industrial sites in Virginia, North Carolina, Tennessee, Georgia, and Mississippi, and unskilled slaves came from nearby sources.

The works were raided by forces of Maj. Gen. James H. Wilson's cavalry brigade on March 31, 1865.

BIBLIOGRAPHY

Armes, Ethel. *The Story of Coal and Iron in Alabama.* Birmingham, Ala., 1910. Reprint, Birmingham, Ala., 1972.

Vandiver, Frank E. "The Shelby Iron Company in the Civil War: A Study of a Confederate Industry." *Alabama Review* 1 (1948): 12–26, 111–127, 203–217.

ROBERT H. MCKENZIE

SHELLEY, CHARLES MILLER (1833–1907), brigadier general and U.S. congressman. Born December 28, 1833, in Sullivan County, Tennessee, Shelley moved with his family to Talladega, Alabama, in 1836. He became a contractor and builder.

A lieutenant in the Talladega Artillery, he spent several

CHARLES MILLER SHELLEY. LIBRARY OF CONGRESS

weeks at Fort Morgan, Alabama, early in 1861 until the company was reorganized as infantry and assigned to the Fifth Alabama. In May 1861 he was elected captain of the company (the regimental commander later called him "the best Captain in the regiment"). In 1862 he organized the Thirtieth Alabama Infantry Regiment and was chosen its colonel.

After participating with the Army of Tennessee in the Kentucky campaign of 1862, Shelley's unit was sent to reinforce Confederate troops in Mississippi. Captured at Vicksburg (July 1863), he was soon exchanged and returned to the Army of Tennessee. He served through the battles of late 1863 and the Atlanta campaign of 1864.

In September 1864 he was promoted to brigadier general. He commanded a brigade in the Franklin and Nashville campaign of late 1864 and in the Carolinas campaign of early 1865. After the surrender, he was paroled May 1, 1865, at Greensboro, North Carolina.

Shelley then returned to Alabama. A Democrat, he was elected sheriff of Dallas County in 1874 and in 1876 won the first of four consecutive terms in the U.S. House of Representatives. During the Cleveland administration he was appointed fourth auditor in the Treasury Department. He died in Birmingham January 20, 1907, and was buried in Oak Hill Cemetery, Talladega.

BIBLIOGRAPHY

Hewitt, Lawrence L. "Charles Miller Shelley." In *The Confederate General*. Edited by William C. Davis. Vol. 5. Harrisburg, Pa., 1991.

Warner, Ezra J. *Generals in Gray: Lives of the Confederate Commanders*. Baton Rouge, La., 1959.

RICHARD M. MCMURRY

SHENANDOAH. The steam-auxiliary cruiser *Shenandoah* was built as the china clipper *Sea King* in 1863. It was designed by noted London naval architect William Rennie and built by Alexander Stephen and Sons, Linthouse, Glasgow, Scotland, for Robertson & Company, London. It measured 2,190 tons, 220 feet long, 32.5 feet in breadth, and 20.5 feet in depth. *Sea King* made one trip to New Zealand before Confederate naval agent James Dunwoody Bulloch bought it for the Confederacy. The steamer *Laurel,* at Funchal, Madeira, provided crew, supplies, and armament (four 8-inch cannon, two Whitworth 32-pounder rifles, and two 12-pounders).

James Waddell commissioned CSS *Shenandoah* on October 20, 1864. The ship captured eleven prizes on the way to Melbourne, Australia. Refitted, it sailed for northern Pacific whaling grounds on February 19, 1865. The ship bonded four vessels and burned twenty-two, mostly whalers, on a continued voyage through the Caroline Islands, the seas of Japan and Okhotsk, and into the Bering Sea. There, on August 2, 1865, Waddell learned that the war had ended. He struck the armament down into the hold,

CSS SHENANDOAH. Flying the Confederate flag at the Williamstown dockyard in Melbourne, Australia, February 1865.

NAVAL HISTORICAL CENTER, WASHINGTON, D.C.

dismantled *Shenandoah* as a warship, and sailed for England.

The cruiser arrived in Liverpool on November 6, 1865, flying the Confederate flag, the last Southern military unit in service. Waddell paid the crew and turned the ship over to the British government. The U.S. consul in Liverpool brought suit, won ownership of the vessel, and sold it at auction to the sultan of Zanzibar. The ship led an adventurous life before its bottom was torn out on a reef near the island of Socotra in the northern Indian Ocean in 1879.

BIBLIOGRAPHY

Dalzell, George W. *The Flight from the Flag: The Continuing Effect of the Civil War upon the American Carrying Trade.* Chapel Hill, N.C., 1940.

Horan, James D., ed. *C.S.S. Shenandoah: The Memoirs of Lieutenant Commander James I. Waddell.* New York, 1960.

Hunt, Cornelius E. *The Shenandoah; or, The Last Confederate Cruiser.* New York, 1866.

Maffitt, Emma Martin. *The Life and Services of John Newland Maffitt.* New York, 1906.

KEVIN J. FOSTER

SHENANDOAH VALLEY. [*This entry includes three articles:* An Overview; Shenandoah Valley Campaign of Jackson, *which discusses the campaign of 1862; and* Shenandoah Valley Campaign of Sheridan, *which discusses the campaign of 1864. For further discussion of military action in the Shenandoah Valley, see* Cedar Creek, Virginia; Cross Keys and Port Republic, Virginia; Early's Washington Raid; Fisher's Hill, Virginia; Front Royal, Virginia; Lynchburg, Virginia; New Market, Virginia; Winchester, Virginia.]

An Overview

During the Civil War the Shenandoah Valley of Virginia was vital to the Confederacy for both military and economic reasons. Militarily, the region had a considerable influence on the campaigns in Virginia. The Shenandoah Valley was like a shield, protecting the Confederate capital. A Federal army could not advance against Richmond by the way of the valley because as it marched south it would be moving farther and farther away from its objective. Conversely, the valley was an asset for any Confederate army marching through it, for the army became an immediate threat to Washington, D.C., Baltimore, and other Northern cities. Nor did the Confederates have to maintain possession of the area to retain its advantages. In order to deny the Confederates the use of the valley, the Federals had to gain control of the entire region, which was beyond their capabilities.

Economically, the Shenandoah Valley was a major source of subsistence for the Confederacy. In the early stages of the war the farmers of the valley were called upon for large quantities of supplies, which they gave heartily. But as the war dragged on, their support faltered for several reasons, including adverse weather conditions and the valley's strategic location. It was the scene of continuous military operations; from the start of the war until October 1864, major portions were repeatedly fought over, marched through, or occupied.

Once the war started, the Confederate Subsistence Department began to accumulate the vast quantities of foodstuffs that would be required to sustain the armies in the field. In Virginia, the valley was one of the first regions they turned to for supplies. Its railroad lines were in constant use, so much so that the Virginia Central Railroad was limited at times exclusively to the transportation of supplies.

In the spring of 1862 the Shenandoah Valley was the scene of one of the major campaigns of the war—Confederate Maj. Gen. Thomas J. ("Stonewall") Jackson's famous Valley campaign. In a series of brilliant maneuvers from March 23 to June 9, Jackson's forces defeated three Federal armies in five battles. Jackson's exploits electrified the Southern populace and, more important, completely dismantled the Federal plan of operation in Virginia. Owing to the perceived threat to Washington, D.C., troops scheduled to be sent to Maj. Gen. George B. McClellan on the peninsula were diverted to the valley in an attempt to defeat Jackson. In the end, Jackson eluded his potential captors, united with Gen. Robert E. Lee outside of Richmond, and helped drive the Union forces back from the Confederate capital, while the troops slated to reinforce McClellan floundered in northern Virginia.

Although the valley was one of the major theaters of the war in Virginia in 1862, no major fighting occurred in the region the next year. For the most part, military operations were limited to Federal cavalry raids and scouting expeditions. The only time large bodies of troops were in the valley was during the Gettysburg campaign, when Lee used it as an avenue to invade Pennsylvania. Although the military operations in the valley had no major effect on the direction of the war in Virginia, they did have an adverse impact on agricultural production. Federal raiders destroyed crops, confiscated livestock and farm animals, and demoralized the civilian population.

Several other factors intervened now to reduce the valley's importance as a primary source of subsistence for the Confederacy. One was the weather. In 1862 a severe drought had diminished the year's harvest, and in 1863 there was excessive rain. Severe flooding destroyed most of the wheat crop in Virginia and negated any chance of accumulating a reserve for the army. Virginia experienced a 50- to 75-percent decline in crop production between 1862 and 1864. A second factor was the war's drain on manpower, as men of military age either joined the army or were later drafted. In many instances women and young children were the only ones left to work the farms. Yet another factor was the military situation. By 1863 a major portion of the valley was under the control of the Federal army. Military exigencies had compelled the Confederacy to abandon the entire lower valley to the enemy. And this loss was not temporary—throughout the rest of the war the lower valley remained in the hands of the Federals. As a result the resources of Berkeley, Clarke, Frederick, and Jefferson counties were lost to the Confederates.

With the commencement of active military operations in May 1864, the Shenandoah Valley once again became one of the major battlegrounds of the war. From May through October the valley was the scene of continuous military action. The Federal strategic plan called for simultaneous attacks against Confederate forces in Virginia from three directions. In one part of the operation, an army under the command of Maj. Gen. Franz Sigel was to march up the valley and destroy the Virginia Central Railroad. Sigel's march went smoothly until he reached the town of New Market on May 15, 1864. There outnumbered Confederate troops routed his army, forcing it to retreat back down the valley.

Lt. Gen. Ulysses S. Grant then replaced Sigel with Maj. Gen. David Hunter and directed him to carry out the previous orders. At first Hunter was successful in his advance. He had reached the outskirts of Lynchburg by June 15, destroying homes and crops as he went. His campaign, however, ended up even more of a disaster than Sigel's. To prevent Lynchburg from being captured and to reclaim the valley, Lee, on June 12, 1864, pulled the Second Corps of his army out of the trenches at Petersburg and sent it west under the command of Maj. Gen. Jubal Early. The reinforcements arrived at Lynchburg five days later. After making several attacks against the Confederate defenses on June 18, Hunter realized he was outnumbered and made a hasty retreat. But instead of retiring back down the valley, he retreated into West Virginia. This action took his command out of the war for several weeks and left the valley to the Confederates.

Early wasted no time in capitalizing on Hunter's error. After giving his army a day's rest he proceeded to advance down the valley. By the end of the first week in July, Early had traversed the entire valley, crossed over the Potomac River into Maryland, and begun to march on Washington, D.C. The Confederate army reached the outskirts of the city on July 11, but the Confederate commander knew he did not have the strength to capture it. So he began an orderly withdrawal back to Virginia and the valley the next day. By threatening Washington once more, Lee was hoping the Federals would be forced to lessen their hold on the Confederate capital. This time, however, the Confederate tactics were not successful, for Grant never relinquished his grip on Richmond.

Still, Early's continued presence in the valley had become a considerable annoyance to Grant in his efforts to defeat the Army of Northern Virginia. The Confederate advance on Washington had forced him to transfer two full army corps from the Petersburg front to quell the fears of the Lincoln administration. Determined to remove Early as a threat to the Northern capital and to close off the valley as an avenue of invasion and a source of supply, Grant placed Maj. Gen. Philip H. Sheridan in command of all military forces in northern Virginia.

Sheridan assumed command of the Army of the Shenandoah on the night of August 6, 1864, and began to make preparations to engage the enemy. In a series of battles between September 19 and October 19, 1864, the Federal army totally defeated the Confederate forces, routing them so completely that they were never again an effective fighting force. But the most dramatic aspect of Sheridan's campaign was the destruction of the valley's resources. Federal troops burned everything of value between Staunton and Winchester, leaving the valley a barren wasteland. This devastation, however, was not the loss it once would have been. For the last two years of the war the Confederacy had supported its military forces in Virginia with subsistence transported from the Deep South, not the valley.

By 1865 the Shenandoah Valley had become a reflection of the Confederacy itself. Before the war the valley had been one of the most fertile regions in Virginia, but in the course of the conflict its productivity vanished under the onslaught of modern armies. Four years of warfare had converted a fruitful countryside into one of charred homes and desolate farms.

BIBLIOGRAPHY

Catton, Bruce. *Terrible Swift Sword.* Garden City, N.Y., 1963.

Freeman, Douglas S. *Lee's Lieutenants: A Study in Command.* New York, 1942–1944. Reprint, New York, 1986.

McPherson, James M. *Ordeal by Fire: The Civil War and Reconstruction.* New York, 1982.

Vandiver, Frank E., ed. *The Civil War Diary of Josiah Gorgas.* Tuscaloosa, Ala., 1947.

Wert, Jeffry D. *From Winchester to Cedar Creek: The Shenandoah Campaign of 1864.* Carlisle, Pa., 1987.

MICHAEL G. MAHON

Shenandoah Valley Campaign of Jackson

Few areas in the Civil War had more strategic value for both sides than did the Shenandoah Valley of Virginia. The valley lies between the two most eastern ranges of the Allegheny Mountains. The eastern boundary of the valley is

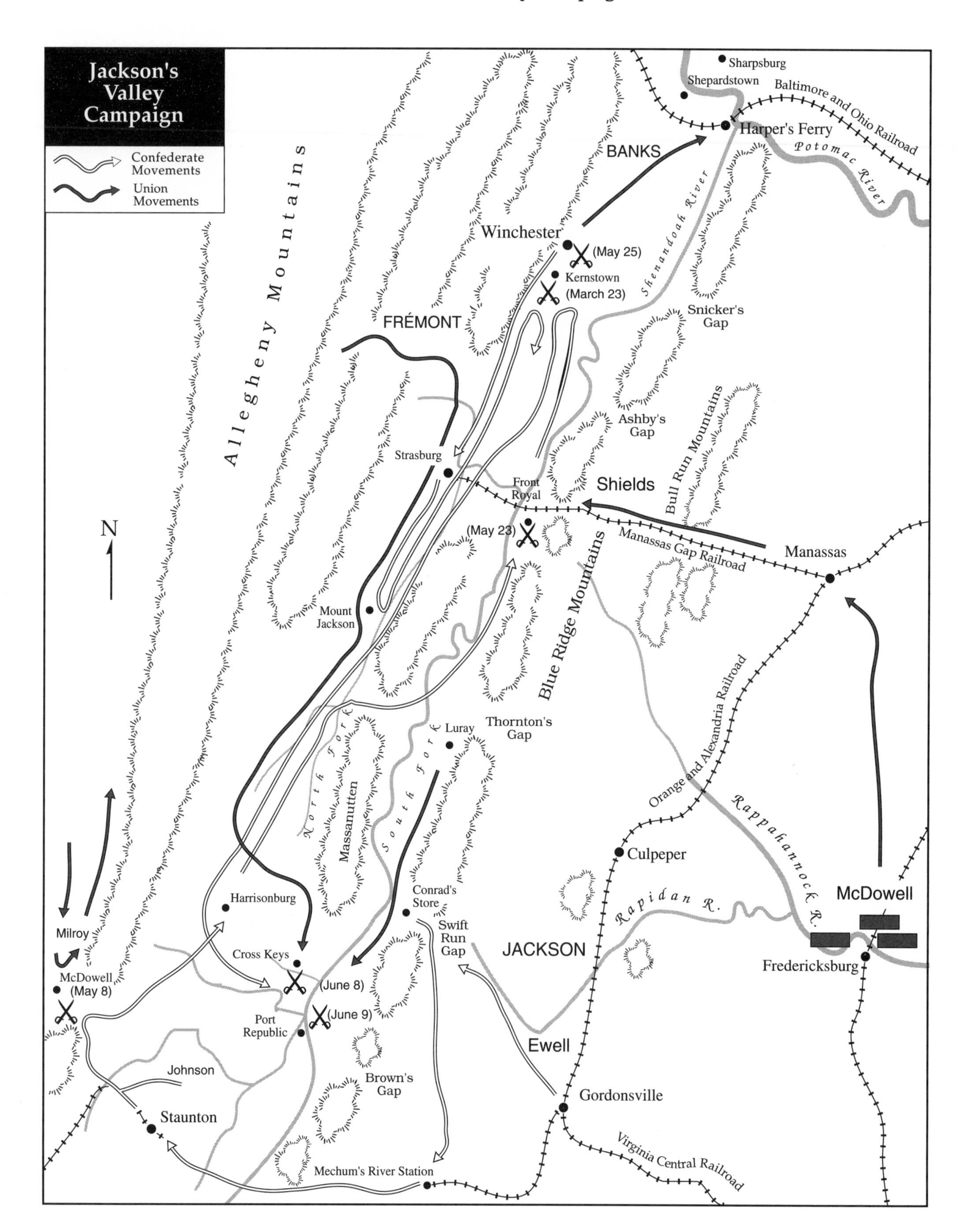
Jackson's Valley Campaign
Confederate Movements
Union Movements
Allegheny Mountains
Sharpsburg
Shepardstown
Baltimore and Ohio Railroad
Harper's Ferry
Potomac River
BANKS
Shenandoah River
Winchester
(May 25)
Kernstown
(March 23)
Snicker's Gap
FRÉMONT
Ashby's Gap
Bull Run Mountains
Strasburg
Front Royal
Shields
(May 23)
Manassas Gap Railroad
Manassas
Blue Ridge Mountains
N
Mount Jackson
Orange and Alexandria Railroad
Thornton's Gap
Luray
North Fork
South Fork
Massanutten
Rappahannock R.
Culpeper
McDowell
Conrad's Store
Harrisonburg
Rapidan R.
Swift Run Gap
Milroy
Cross Keys
JACKSON
Fredericksburg
McDowell
(May 8)
(June 8)
(June 9)
Port Republic
Ewell
Johnson
Brown's Gap
Gordonsville
Staunton
Virginia Central Railroad
Mechum's River Station

marked by the famed Blue Ridge Mountains, with the Alleghenies proper to the west. The valley stretches 165 miles from Lexington to Harpers Ferry and averages 30 miles in width. At the southern terminus the mountains on both sides press close upon Lexington. The ranges diverge at the other end around Harpers Ferry. There the Shenandoah River merges with the Potomac; there too the Baltimore and Ohio Railroad—then the main line of transportation between Washington and the West—crossed the Potomac. The Shenandoah loses altitude running south to north. Hence, and contrary to usual terminology, one travels northward down and southward up the valley.

Two factors gave the region important military value. The Shenandoah was a veritable breadbasket for the Confederacy. Grain, orchards, and livestock were in great abundance. The Army of Northern Virginia came to be all but totally dependent upon the produce of the area. Geographically the valley was a natural avenue into the heart of the North and the center of the Deep South. Any army that advanced into either Virginia or Maryland had to have control of the valley to protect its western flank against attack. With only eleven passes through the Blue Ridge, the Shenandoah was a long, natural fortress. It became the key to military movements, and military supremacy, in the eastern theater.

In the spring of 1862 the valley was the scene of one of the most brilliant campaigns in history. It was a campaign that made Confederate Gen. Thomas J. ("Stonewall") Jackson the hero of the South and a legend in his own time.

Jackson had returned to the Shenandoah in November 1861 to take charge of its defenses. His headquarters were at Winchester, twenty-six miles southwest of Harpers Ferry. Winchester guarded all the mountain passes in the lower Shenandoah and was a commercial center as well. Jackson's force at that time consisted of 3,600 infantry, 600 cavalry, and twenty-seven guns. Most of his soldiers were Virginians and familiar with the valley.

Late in February 1862, a Federal army slowly moved into the Shenandoah. It numbered 38,000 men, mostly hardy farmboys from the Midwest. Commanding the army was Maj. Gen. Nathaniel P. Banks, a Massachusetts political general with limited military capacities.

The small Confederate force in the valley seemed no threat to Banks's invaders. Yet Jackson was always a man who took responsibility very seriously. His instructions from the beginning had been to protect the left flank of the main Confederate force at Manassas, to guard the valley against all Federal intrusions, and to expect no reinforcements in the process. Determination outweighed concern by Jackson that he was outnumbered by ten-to-one odds. "If this valley is lost," he stated to a friend, "Virginia is lost."

With the Federal army slowly forming an arc around his small force, Jackson on March 11 abandoned Winchester. He retired slowly up the valley to Mount Jackson and encamped. Four Federal regiments of Gen. James Shields's division pursued cautiously at a distance. On a sleety March 21, those Federal units started back to Winchester. Jackson deduced that Shields was consolidating his troops with Banks's main command preparatory to uniting with Gen. George B. McClellan's massive army for a grand offensive against Richmond. He promptly put his brigades into motion heading north.

The Confederates covered forty-one miles in two days. A third of Jackson's men fell out along the way from exhaustion and sickness. On the afternoon of March 23, Jackson and barely two thousand soldiers reached the hamlet of Kernstown, two miles from Winchester. A crushing blow on Shields would stop Banks's withdrawal from the valley and possibly blunt McClellan's offensive as well.

Jackson quickly deployed his fatigued troops and attacked what he thought was only a segment of Shields's command. All too soon, owing to faulty intelligence reports, Jackson found himself locked in combat with a full Union division. Three hours of fighting brought his advance to a halt. After nightfall the Confederates retired up the valley. Yet Jackson's tactical failure proved a strategic success. Even though Shields's men moved on to Fredericksburg, Banks received orders to remain in the valley. This heretofore buffer zone now became a major theater of operations.

Grim resolution marked every step of Jackson's march as he led his forces to Conrad's Store, seventeen miles east of Harrisonburg. That point, at the base of Swift Run Gap, offered the Southern general a number of options. He could attack Banks's army if it sought to pass up the Valley Turnpike to the railroad town of Staunton; he could wage a strong defense if assailed at Conrad's Store; the mountain pass afforded a safe escape if needed. Banks halted at Harrisonburg and then backtracked forty-five miles to Strasburg so as to shorten his line of communication. The Federal general was convinced that Jackson was now a mere nuisance.

For most of April, as Confederate ranks filled and hardened into a tight military force, Jackson developed a master plan. He knew that a second Federal force of 15,000 soldiers under Gen. John C. Frémont was two ranges over in the Alleghenies. Another 40,000 bluecoats of Gen. Irvin McDowell's command were at Fredericksburg and poised to move easily toward Richmond or the valley. What Jackson first hoped to accomplish was to keep Banks and Frémont west of the Blue Ridge and isolated one from the other. At the same time, Jackson did not want McDowell leaving Fredericksburg. If Confederates in the valley could pin down Frémont, Banks, and McDowell, attack and defeat each, one by one, all other Southern defenders in Virginia could concentrate at Richmond and confront McClellan's 120,000 Federals.

The chances of this plan succeeding were slim. Yet "Old Jack" felt that deception, rapid marches, and unexpected attacks would accomplish his goals. As for the overwhelming numerical superiority of the enemy, Jackson would trust God to handle that problem.

Gen. Robert E. Lee, President Jefferson Davis's chief military adviser, was himself a gambler. He not only endorsed Jackson's proposal but sent badly needed reinforcements: 8,000 troops under eccentric, crusty, but highly dependable Gen. Richard S. Ewell. Another 2,000 Southerners, with gruff and profane Gen. Edward Johnson at their head, were in the mountains guarding the western approaches to Staunton. They were added to Jackson's command. By the end of April, Jackson was ready to go into action.

He ordered Ewell's division into the Conrad's Store encampment to keep an eye on Banks's movements. "Old Jack" then disappeared to the south with his own 6,000-man force. The men trudged three days through pouring rain and heavy mud. They finally reached Mechum's River Station on the Virginia Central Railroad and boarded trains with the belief that they were heading east to Richmond. Instead, the trains lumbered west. Confederates disembarked at Staunton to the surprise of townspeople answering the bells for Sunday church services. Jackson sealed the town to mask his presence. Meanwhile, Banks was reassuring officials in Washington that Jackson's "greatly demoralized and broken" army was fleeing toward the safety of Richmond.

On May 6, Jackson led his still-jaded troops in a hard thirty-five-mile march over rugged mountains to McDowell. His objective was Gen. Robert H. Milroy's 4,000 Federals comprising the vanguard of Frémont's army. At 4:00 P. M. on the eighth, from a commanding hilltop, the Confederates fired point-blank volleys of musketry into the advancing columns. The battle lasted until sundown. Though Federals inflicted twice their own losses, they could not pierce Jackson's lines. Milroy retreated. Jackson pursued for a distance. Confederate engineers closed the mountain passes, thus protecting Jackson's left flank in the upper valley. Now the stern and taciturn Southern commander was ready to clear the valley of Federal intruders.

Thanks in great part to his mapmaker, Maj. Jedediah Hotchkiss, Jackson could discuss valley terrain as easily as he could quote Scripture. He knew that it was eighty miles on the macadamized Valley Turnpike from Staunton to Winchester. East of that main thoroughfare, inside the valley from Harrisonburg to Strasburg, lay a dark ridge called Massanutten Mountain. To the east of it was a parallel and almost hidden road. It snaked through the narrow Luray Valley to Front Royal and beyond. More important, in that forty-mile stretch was only one point where the Massanutten could be crossed: the pass connecting the towns of New Market and Luray.

The next stage of Jackson's strategy was to unite his forces, sneak through and secure that pass, use the Massanutten as a screen, and head north. By hard marching he intended to strike unsuspecting advance positions at Front Royal and Strasburg; then he hoped to shatter Banks's army as he drove to the main Federal supply base at Winchester. Jackson swiftly merged the units of Ewell's and Johnson's forces into an army of 17,000 soldiers. That gave him an almost two-to-one superiority over Banks. Jackson drove his troops down the valley and disappeared across the Massanutten. The first Federal inkling that anything was amiss came on May 23, when a Confederate tidal wave appeared from nowhere and crushed the Union garrison at Front Royal.

Jackson spent the following day urging his near-exhausted soldiers to get between rapidly retreating Federals and Winchester. Confederates struck several times at the long and disjointed Union column but could not break it. Abandoned wagons loaded with goods littered the road for miles. Large numbers of the half-starved Southerners could not resist the temptation to pause for food.

On the morning of May 25, Jackson launched a full-scale assault at Winchester and by noon had Banks's entire army fleeing for the safety of the Potomac River. The three days of fighting had cost Jackson but 400 men. His army had seized 3,030 prisoners, 9,300 small arms, 2 rifled cannon, and such a wealth of quartermaster stores that Confederates scornfully referred thereafter to their Union opponent as "Commissary Banks."

Smashing victories by Jackson had now disrupted the entire Federal offensive in Virginia. With Banks cowering on the north bank of the Potomac and Jackson's army poised like a dagger at the north end of the Shenandoah, Union officials in Washington reacted sharply. McDowell's huge force at Fredericksburg, about to join McClellan, was to remain there as protection for the Northern capital. Shields's 20,000-man division, which had just reached Fredericksburg, was ordered to return to the valley. Frémont received instructions to advance with all haste into the Shenandoah. With Shields moving west and Frémont advancing east, both toward Strasburg, Jackson seemingly would be caught in the jaws of a massive vise.

The counterstrategy failed because of a combination of Federal vacillation and incredible marching by Jackson's "foot cavalry." In less than a day, Confederate units covered thirty-five to fifty miles and escaped the trap. Jackson retired to Harrisonburg and then to a point southeast of town where the North and South rivers came together to form the South Fork of the Shenandoah. Frémont was giving chase on the Valley Turnpike; Shields was advancing up the Luray Valley road.

On June 8, Ewell's division easily beat back feeble stabs by Frémont at Cross Keys. Jackson waited patiently three miles away at Port Republic. The next day he assailed Shields's force. Severe fighting occurred before the Federals broke off the engagement and headed northward. The great campaign was over; the Shenandoah Valley was still in Confederate hands.

Jackson and 17,000 men had totally thwarted the plans of 64,000 Federals in three different forces sent to destroy him. In forty-eight days his soldiers had marched 676 miles and fought four battles, six skirmishes, and a dozen delaying actions. Confederates had inflicted seven thousand casualties at a loss of half that number. Immense quantities of Union weapons and stores were in Confederate hands. The Federal military machine in Virginia was sputtering badly. Southerners everywhere took new faith in the success of the Confederate cause. Jackson would accept no accolades for his strategic masterpiece. He summarized the Valley campaign in a short note to his wife: "God has been our shield, and to His name be all the glory."

BIBLIOGRAPHY

Allan, William. *History of the Campaign of Gen. T. J. (Stonewall) Jackson in the Shenandoah Valley of Virginia.* Dayton, Ohio, 1987.

Henderson, G. F. R. *Stonewall Jackson and the American Civil War.* 2 vols. London, 1898. Reprint, Gloucester, Mass., 1968.

Hotchkiss, Jedediah. *Make Me a Map of the Valley.* Dallas, Tex., 1973.

Robertson, James I., Jr. *The Stonewall Brigade.* Baton Rouge, La., 1963.

Tanner, Robert G. *Stonewall in the Valley.* New York, 1976.

JAMES I. ROBERTSON, JR.

Shenandoah Valley Campaign of Sheridan

This Federal campaign, which took place from August to October 1864, effectively ended the Confederate presence in the Shenandoah Valley.

Following the near capture of Washington, D.C., by Lt. Gen. Jubal Early in mid-July 1864, and Early's subsequent burning of Chambersburg, Pennsylvania, on July 30, Gen. Ulysses S. Grant assigned Maj. Gen. Philip H. Sheridan to the Shenandoah Valley with instructions to "put himself south of the enemy and follow him to the death."

The thirty-three-year-old Irish-born Sheridan had been commanding Grant's cavalry, and although President Abraham Lincoln, Secretary of War Edwin M. Stanton, and Chief of Staff Henry W. Halleck all considered Sheridan too young and inexperienced for the Shenandoah position, Grant's opinion prevailed. Sheridan subsequently arrived at Harpers Ferry on August 6 to take command of the Army of the

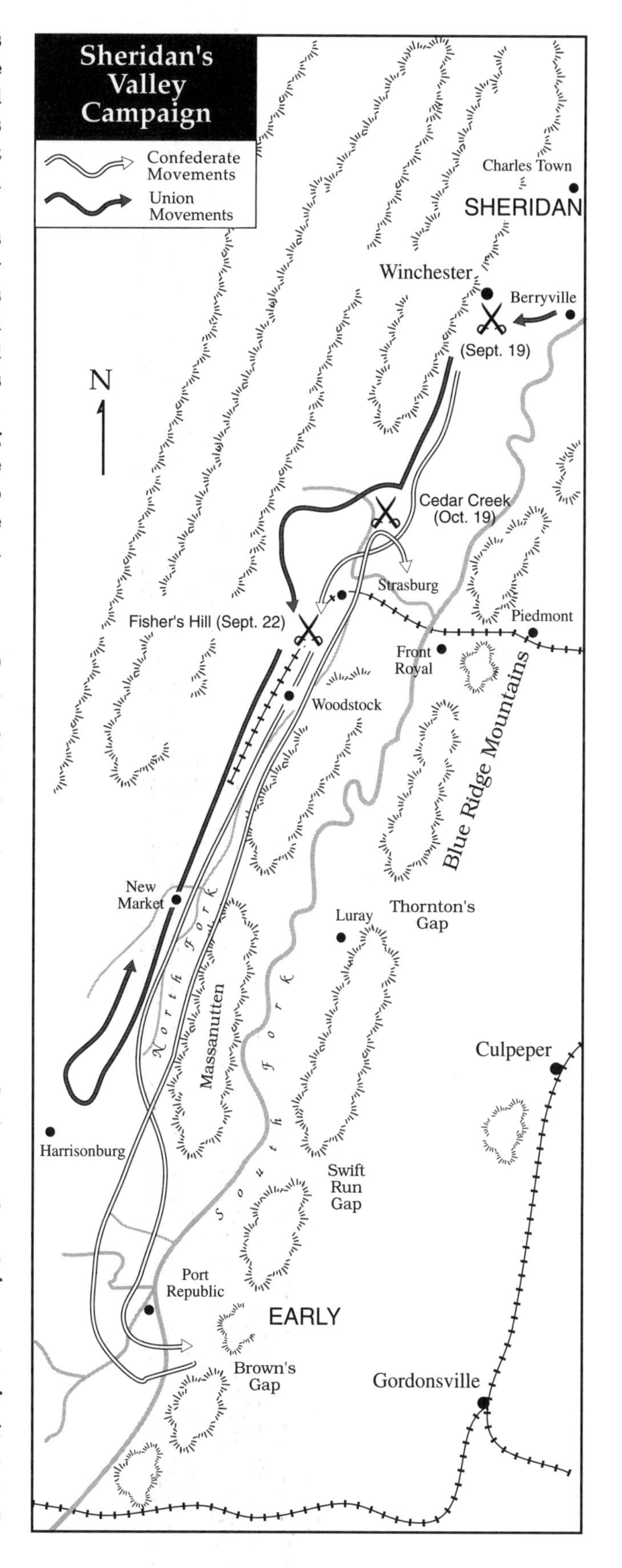

Shenandoah, composed of 35,000 infantry and artillery and 8,000 cavalry. The army's infantry consisted of three corps under Maj. Gen. Horatio G. Wright (Sixth Corps), Maj. Gen. George Crook (Eighth Corps), and Maj. Gen. William H. Emory (Nineteenth Corps). Brig. Gen. Alfred T. A. Torbert commanded the three divisions of cavalry.

Sheridan outnumbered Early three to one. Old Jube's Army of the Valley included 10,000 veterans from the Second Corps and 4,000 poorly equipped and ill-disciplined cavalrymen. Recognizing this disparity, Robert E. Lee on August 6 dispatched from the Richmond-Petersburg line the 3,500-man division of Maj. Gen. Joseph B. Kershaw, the artillery battalion of Maj. Wilfred E. Cutshaw, and the cavalry division of Maj. Gen. Fitzhugh Lee. When this additional force arrived at Front Royal on August 14, Sheridan, who had advanced fifty miles from Harpers Ferry to Cedar Creek, ordered a withdrawal north to Halltown, where he entrenched on a commanding ridge four miles west of Harpers Ferry.

From August 22 to September 18, Sheridan and Early marched and countermarched across the lower valley, conducting a "mimic war" that avoided major confrontation. Politics tempered Sheridan's usual aggressiveness; Secretary of War Stanton had informed him that the administration could not withstand one battlefield defeat. "I deemed it necessary to be very cautious," Sheridan wrote in his memoirs. "The fact that the Presidential election was impending made me doubly so . . . [since] the defeat of my army might be followed by the overthrow of the party in power." Sheridan's political sensitivity led Jubal Early to underestimate badly his dangerous opponent. Concluding that Sheridan "possessed an excessive caution which amounted to timidity," Early agreed to return to Petersburg the reinforcements he had received from Lee in mid-August.

When Sheridan on September 15 learned of this departure, he planned his strike. With Early's army scattered toward the Potomac on a raid to destroy the Baltimore and Ohio Railroad, Sheridan intended to smash Early's rear guard at Winchester and cut off the Confederate line of retreat south via the Valley Pike. Sheridan outlined this plan to Grant at Charles Town on September 17, and the commanding general responded, "Go in."

At 1:00 A.M. on September 19, Sheridan's army roused from its bivouac near Berryville and began marching west toward Winchester. Union cavalry seized the Opequon Creek crossing with little opposition, and Federal infantry soon splashed across the Opequon into the two-mile Berryville Canyon—a narrow defile through which passed the turnpike connecting Winchester and Berryville. Fortunately for Early, Sheridan's army became entangled in the canyon by the slow-moving wagons of the Sixth Corps. This delay robbed Sheridan of his tactical surprise and enabled Early to reconcentrate his army at Winchester.

Sheridan's infantry assault finally commenced at 11:40 A.M. with a blow against Maj. Gen. Dodson Ramseur's division on the Confederate right. A spirited Southern counterattack by Maj. Gen. Robert Rodes's division drove a wedge between the Sixth and Nineteenth Corps and nearly cost Sheridan the battle, but a stand by Maj. Gen. David Russell's division stalled the Confederate offensive. During this bloody action, Rodes lost his life, and General Russell died conducting the Union defense. Meeting failure on the Confederate right and center, Sheridan deployed Crook's Eighth Corps and two divisions of cavalry against the Confederate left flank. When the 10,000-man charge commenced at 4:00 P.M., Early's outnumbered and outflanked army cracked and went "whirling through Winchester" in headlong flight south on the Valley Pike. Early's defeat at the Third Battle of Winchester (known as the Battle of Opequon in the North) cost him 199 killed, 1,508 wounded, and 1,818 missing. Sheridan suffered 697 killed, 3,983 wounded, and 338 missing. For the first time in its history, the Second Corps, formerly commanded by Stonewall Jackson, had been driven from a field it defended.

During the night of September 19, Early retreated twenty miles south from Winchester to Fisher's Hill, a line of dominating ridges running perpendicular to the valley and anchored on the east by the North Fork of the Shenandoah River and to the west by North Mountain. Some considered it a Confederate "Gibraltar," but Early did not have enough men to hold the four-mile line. On September 21 and 22, while Sheridan feinted attack against the Confederate front, the 5,500 men of the Union's Eighth Corps under Crook secretly marched to North Mountain to attain a position behind Early's left flank. At 4:00 P.M. on the twenty-second, Crook's men smashed into the Confederate left held by Lunsford Lindsay Lomax's cavalry division. The panicked horsemen scattered in disarray, and with its left now exposed, Early's army fled from Fisher's Hill in a rout. Although Early's casualties were relatively light (30 killed, 210 wounded, 995 missing), he lost 14 guns to the Federals. He also lost his chief of staff, Lt. Col. William N. Pendleton, who was killed while attempting to rally his routed comrades. Sheridan accomplished his second victory in three days at a cost of 36 killed, 414 wounded, and 6 missing.

Following his September 22 defeat at Fisher's Hill, Early retreated 60 miles south and east to Brown's Gap in the Blue Ridge, where he awaited reinforcement from Kershaw's division and Cutshaw's battalion of artillery. Sheridan followed to Harrisonburg, arriving there on September 25. Concluding that Early's army was finished, Sheridan commenced burning the upper valley in accordance with Grant's orders to make the Shenandoah Valley a "barren waste." By October 7, as Sheridan's army moved north to

Woodstock, his cavalry had systematically destroyed 2,000 barns filled with wheat, hay, and farming implements and over 70 mills filled with flour and wheat. In addition, 3,000 sheep had been slaughtered and 4,000 cattle driven north. Sheridan notified Grant that the destruction was so thorough that the 92 miles from Winchester to Staunton "will have but little in it for man or beast."

As Sheridan retired north, Confederate Brig. Gen. Thomas Lafayette Rosser and his Laurel Brigade arrived in the valley and began menacing Sheridan's rear guard. At Tom's Brook, Sheridan tired of the harassment and ordered his cavalry to "whip the Rebel cavalry or get whipped." Subsequently, on October 9, Maj. Gen. George Armstrong Custer, in his first fight as a division commander, flanked Rosser's left while Maj. Gen. Wesley Merritt smashed Rosser's right, sending the Confederates reeling in a 26-mile chase known as the "Woodstock Races." Sheridan's horsemen captured 330 prisoners, 11 guns, and the headquarters wagons of four Confederate cavalry generals. The Federals lost 9 killed and 48 wounded.

Following the victory at Tom's Brook, Sheridan encamped north of Cedar Creek on October 10. Since he considered Early "disposed of," Sheridan began making plans to transfer his army back to Grant. To confer on future operations, Sheridan started for Washington on October 15, leaving the army in temporary command of General Wright. Meanwhile, Early had advanced north following his reinforcement at Brown's Gap. On October 17, Maj. Gen. John B. Gordon surveyed the Union army from Three Top Mountain and convinced Early that a surprise attack against the Union left flank at Cedar Creek was possible. Following an all-night march by the Second Corps along the base of Massanutten Mountain, Gordon's and Kershaw's 8,000 Confederates routed Crook's unsuspecting Eighth Corps at dawn on the nineteenth and then drove the Nineteenth Corps and Sixth Corps three miles north of their Cedar Creek camps. Early had seized twenty enemy cannon and 1,500 prisoners in the morning victory, but fatigue and rampant plundering stalled the Confederate offensive at about 11:00 A.M.

Meanwhile, Sheridan, who had returned by late morning, rallied his army and redeployed the cavalry on his flanks. At 4:00 P.M., the rejuvenated Federal army advanced. When Custer's cavalry division overran the Confederate left, Early's panicked line broke and a rout began. In one of the most remarkable one-day turnarounds in military history, Sheridan had snatched victory from defeat. As Early lamented, "The Yankees got whipped and we got scared."

Confederate losses in the Cedar Creek disaster included 320 killed, 1,540 wounded, and 1,050 missing; General Ramseur was mortally wounded. In addition, Early lost 43 cannon and at least 300 wagons and ambulances. Union casualties were 644 killed, 3,430 wounded, and 1,591 missing.

Early had faced Sheridan's overwhelming numbers and suffered four defeats in thirty days. With the Confederates routed and the valley breadbasket burned, Sheridan transferred much of his army to Grant, while Lee ordered all of Early's remaining infantry, with the exception of one division, to return to Petersburg.

BIBLIOGRAPHY

DuPont, Henry A. *The Campaign of 1864 in the Valley of Virginia and the Expedition to Lynchburg*. New York, 1925.

Early, Jubal A. *Autobiographical Sketch and Narrative of the War between the States*. Philadelphia, 1912. Reprint, Wilmington, N.C., 1989.

Gallagher, Gary W. *Struggle for the Shenandoah: Essays on the Valley Campaign of 1864*. Kent, Ohio, 1991.

Sheridan, Philip H. *Personal Memoirs of P. H. Sheridan*. New York, 1888.

Taylor, James E. *The James E. Taylor Sketchbook: With Sheridan in the Shenandoah in 1864*. Dayton, Ohio, 1989.

Wert, Jeffrey D. *From Winchester to Cedar Creek: The Shenandoah Campaign of 1864*. Carlisle, Pa., 1987.

DENNIS E. FRYE

SHEPLEY, GEORGE F. (1819–1878), Union general and military governor of Louisiana. When Republicans filled Federal offices in 1861, George Foster Shepley, a prominent lawyer and aspiring Democratic politician, lost his long-time appointment as U.S. attorney for Maine. By autumn, he had a new position, colonel of the Twelfth Maine Infantry. He accompanied his political friend, Gen. Benjamin F. Butler, to the Department of the Gulf and on May 20, 1862, became acting mayor of occupied New Orleans.

Serving under the imperious Butler was almost as difficult as administering martial law in the recalcitrant Crescent City, but Shepley successfully overcame the problems of terrible filth and worthless currencies that plagued this strategic metropolis. In July 1862, President Abraham Lincoln promoted him to brigadier general and appointed him military governor of the Union-controlled parts of Louisiana.

Expediting this fractious state's return to the Union was a formidable assignment for the cautious New Englander. Although tainted by the scandals associated with "Beast" Butler, Shepley remained military governor when Gen. Nathaniel P. Banks took command of the department. Shepley supervised the December 1862 elections for two congressional seats. His limited political powers, however, began eroding in 1863 when he supported the radical faction of Louisiana Unionists while Banks and Lincoln backed the moderates.

In March 1864, after an elected moderate Unionist governor assumed the office, Shepley took command of the District of Eastern Virginia in General Butler's Department of Virginia and North Carolina. In 1865, Shepley was chief-of-staff in Gen. Godfrey Weitzel's mostly black Twenty-fifth Army Corps; when they captured Richmond in April, he became that city's military governor. Resigning his commission on July 1, 1865, Shepley returned to Maine to practice law and to become a federal circuit judge in 1869.

BIBLIOGRAPHY

Dawson, Joseph G., III. *Army Generals and Reconstruction: Louisiana, 1862–1877.* Baton Rouge, La., 1982.

Ripley, C. Peter. *Slaves and Freedmen in Civil War Louisiana.* Baton Rouge, La., 1976.

Taylor, Joe Gray. *Louisiana Reconstructed, 1863–1877.* Baton Rouge, La., 1974.

Warner, Ezra J. *Generals in Blue: Lives of the Union Commanders.* Baton Rouge, La., 1964.

BLAKE TOUCHSTONE

SHERMAN'S MARCH TO THE SEA. *See* March to the Sea, Sherman's.

SHEWMAKE, JOHN TROUPE (1828–1898), congressman from Georgia. Shewmake was born on January 23, 1828, in Burke County, Georgia. A member of an affluent planter family, he was educated at home until he enrolled at Princeton College in 1846. He spent only a year there, after which he returned to Georgia and studied law in Augusta. He practiced for a short time near home in Waynesboro, but soon his ambitions led him back to Augusta. He established a successful practice and spent the rest of his life there, though he also operated a small plantation south of the city.

There is no record of Shewmake's antebellum political activity or views. His first elective position was a term in the Georgia Senate from 1861 to 1862. In October 1863, he was elected to represent the state's Fifth District in the Second Congress. Perhaps because so much of his district was plagued by Union forces during 1864, Shewmake was an avid supporter of any legislation strengthening the Confederate army and its defense measures. He opposed further government or military demands on the rural home front and proposed a variety of concessions for farmers, including payment at full market value for any goods impressed from Southern farms. In January 1865, he took a leave of absence from Congress and never returned to Richmond.

Once the war was over, Shewmake resumed his law practice in Augusta for several months but gave it up and moved to his plantation early in 1866. He served as the head of Augusta's board of education from 1874 to 1879, when he was again elected to the state Senate. He retired after two terms and died in Augusta in 1898.

BIBLIOGRAPHY

Memoirs of Georgia. Vol. 2. Atlanta, 1895.

Warner, Ezra J., and W. Buck Yearns. *Biographical Register of the Confederate Congress.* Baton Rouge, La., 1975.

Wakelyn, Jon L. *Biographical Dictionary of the Confederacy.* Edited by Frank E. Vandiver. Westport, Conn., 1977.

JOHN C. INSCOE

SHILOH CAMPAIGN. A small Methodist church gave its name to the first major land battle in the West on April 6 and 7, 1862. In February 1862, Gen. Ulysses S. Grant moved south against Confederate Forts Henry and Donelson guarding the Tennessee and Cumberland rivers. He had captured them by the sixteenth. Their loss forced the evacuation of parts of middle and western Tennessee by the Confederate army commanded by Gen. Albert Sidney Johnston. When Johnston abandoned Nashville, Gen. Don Carlos Buell's Army of the Ohio occupied the city. West of the Tennessee River, Gen. P. G. T. Beauregard, Johnston's deputy commander, withdrew the Southern forces from Columbus, Kentucky. He established a new line stretching from Island Number 10 on the Mississippi River to Corinth, Mississippi, and concentrated the bulk of his forces there.

After the surrender of the forts, the gunboats of the Union navy effectively controlled the Tennessee from its mouth to Muscle Shoals, Alabama. The Federals massed at Pittsburg Landing, the closest all-weather landing to Corinth, which, as a major rail junction, was the next Union target. Gen. Henry W. Halleck, now in command of Union forces west of the Appalachian Mountains, ordered Buell to march the Army of the Ohio west from Nashville and join the forces at Pittsburg Landing.

Johnston and Beauregard, to regain the initiative, decided to concentrate a large force at Corinth and attack Grant. Johnston ordered over 44,000 men to the town. These troops, however, were insufficiently trained on the division level. Johnston divided his army into four corps under the command of Gens. Leonidas Polk, Braxton Bragg, William J. Hardee, and John C. Breckinridge. The Reserve Corps, Breckinridge's unit, was no more than a large division.

While the Confederates concentrated at Corinth, four Union divisions were training at Pittsburg Landing. Another division, the Third, commanded by Gen. Lew Wallace, was stationed at Crump Landing seven miles to the north, and the Sixth Division under Gen. Joseph Prentiss was being assembled as new units arrived. Grant, confident that the battle at Corinth would be the last in the West and that

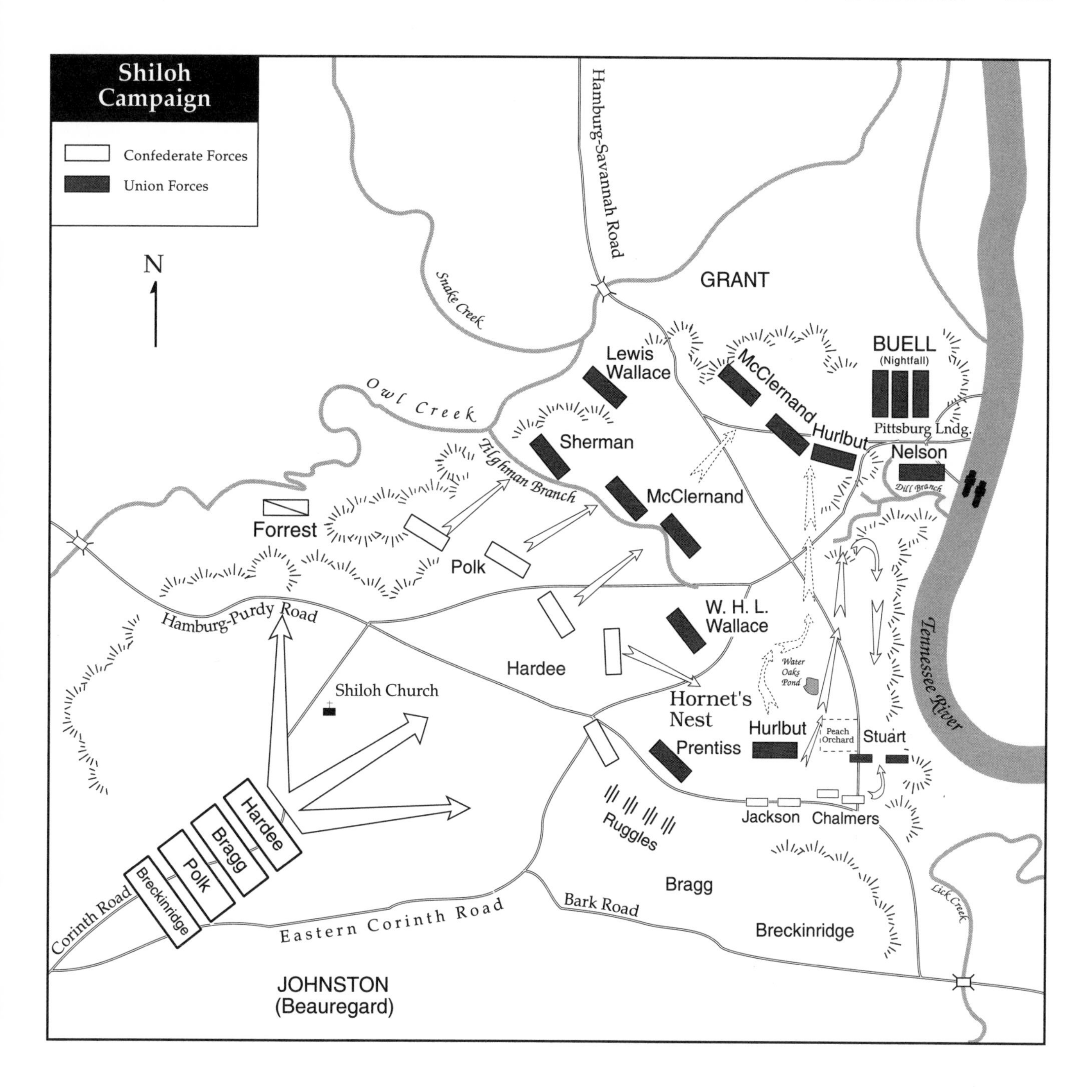

he would win it, did not take the necessary steps to keep informed of what was going on in his front.

On the evening of April 2, Beauregard received word from Bethel Springs that a portion of the Union army was moving out of its camps around Shiloh Church. He sent his chief of staff, Col. Thomas Jordan, to Johnston to recommend immediate attack. Johnston conferred with Bragg, who also advised attack, and sent Jordan back to Beauregard's headquarters, where he drafted Special Orders No. 8, the Confederate order of battle. On the morning of the third, Jordan presented this order to all corps commanders except Breckinridge. It called for marching that day and attacking on the fourth. Hardee's corps was to form one long line of battle and then press forward. A thousand yards behind it would be Bragg's corps also in the line of battle. Polk's and Breckinridge's corps would serve as reserves.

Owing to muddy roads and poor discipline during their march, the Confederates were not ready to attack on the fourth or on the fifth. That evening, Beauregard recommended calling the attack off, but Johnston refused. The attack would go on.

In the Union camps, Col. Everett Peabody, commander of

the First Brigade, Sixth Division, was not happy with the developments in his front. He sent out a patrol before dawn on the sixth to learn the true strength of the Southerners. These men, at 5:45 A.M., collided with the Third Mississippi Battalion serving as pickets under the command of Maj. Aaron Hardcastle. The patrol sent back word that it had met a major Confederate force and asked for reinforcements. Peabody sent out the Twenty-first Missouri, but before they arrived, the Southerners advanced, pushing the patrol back. Col. David Moore, commander of the Twenty-first, ordered the patrol to stand and fight. Further reinforced by elements of the Sixteenth Wisconsin, the patrol delayed the Confederates for about thirty minutes.

Meanwhile, Prentiss called his Sixth Division into the line of battle and prepared to meet the Confederates. The two forces met just south of the division camps. This was the first battle for most of these men, Northern or Southern. Prentiss's men held for a short while, but then Confederate brigades under John K. Jackson and James R. Chalmers got around their left flank. S. A. M. Woods's brigade found a hole to the left of their Fifth Division, forcing Prentiss to fall back. The Sixth held for a short time in their camps and then fell back again. Prentiss and about 3,000 men dug in at what came to be called the Hornet's Nest.

While the North's Sixth Division was under attack, its Fifth Division, to the right, was also meeting the enemy. First, Patrick Cleburne's brigade slammed into the brigades of Jessie Hildebrand and Ralph Buckland. Cleburne's right pushed back the Fifty-third Ohio, but was stopped cold by Buckland on the Southern left. S. A. M. Woods supported Cleburne on the right. Units from Bragg's and Polk's corps coming up to continue the drive forced Buckland and Hildebrand back.

By late morning, Confederate attacks had pushed the Union right back almost a mile to the Hamburg-Purdy Road. Here the North's First Division joined the line to protect the left of the Fifth. One brigade of the Fourth Division joined the left of the First. This concentration, however, had drawn the bulk of the Confederate troops. By 11:00 A.M., all but two brigades of the Southerners were massed against this line. It broke and was forced back about a half mile. John McDowell's brigade of the Fifth Division was cut off and had to fight its way back to the main force. Due to the shock of the Southern attack, the regiments of Hildebrand's and Buckland's brigades were scattered and ceased to exist as organized units.

On the Union left, Col. David Stuart's brigade of the Fifth Division guarded the eastern approaches to the battlefield. Stuart saw Confederate flags moving in Prentiss's camps and deployed his brigade to meet the expected attacks. Gen. Stephen D. Hurlbut brought his Fourth Division up to support Stuart. Gen. John McArthur's Brigade of the Second Division filled the gap between Stuart and Hurlbut. Behind Hurlbut, Prentiss was rallying the remains of his division, and at 11:00 A.M. they took up a position on Hurlbut's right. Gen. W. H. L. Wallace brought up the Second Division to extend the Union right toward the First Division's left. The First was commanded by Gen. John McClernand.

The first Confederate attacks against the Union left were made by Chalmers's and Jackson's brigades. Stuart's line stopped them at about 10:00 A.M. By using a heavy skirmish line and detaching troops to cover his left, Stuart led the Confederates to believe they were attacking a division. Johnston moved to the Southern right with Jackson's and Chalmers's brigades. There he took personal command of the eastern sector. All along the Confederate line, the various corps became hopelessly intermingled. As a result, the corps commanders split the line into sectors. Polk took the left, Hardee the center left, and Bragg the center right. Breckinridge assisted Johnston on the right.

Johnston began a series of probing attacks looking for the Union left flank. His intention was to turn this flank and force the Northerners to the west and away from Pittsburg Landing. But he was not able to bring enough strength to bear until about 2:00 P.M. Then he advanced five brigades. Aided by Stuart's running out of ammunition, Johnston forced the Union troops out of the Peach Orchard area, and they withdrew toward Pittsburg Landing. Unfortunately, Johnston was hit in the leg by a stray round and bled to death before his aides were able to find the wound.

On the Union right, McClernand and Gen. William Tecumseh Sherman (commanding the Union's Fifth Division) had fallen back to Jones Field. Here they organized a counterattack that forced the Southerners back, but they were unable to sustain the drive and had to withdraw. With Stuart withdrawing, McArthur was forced to fall back. This exposed Hurlbut's left to the attacks of Jackson's and Chalmers's brigades, as well as three other Confederate brigades. Hurlbut sent word to Prentiss that he would have to fall straight back for Pittsburg Landing. Prentiss realized this would leave his left in the air, but his orders from Grant were to hold the Hornet's Nest area at all costs.

Grant arrived on the battlefield in the middle of the morning. Earlier he had sent orders to Buell to march his lead division up the east bank of the river. He planned to ferry the men across to Pittsburg Landing. Grant also stopped at Crump Landing long enough to tell Lew Wallace to prepare his division for a quick move and then await orders. Once he arrived, Grant made a tour of the field and then sent orders to Wallace to move to Shiloh.

Polk and Hardee kept up the pressure against Sherman and McClernand, forcing them to fall back. Their left connected with Wallace's division in the Hornet's Nest. Their right guarded the River Road by which they expected Lew Wallace to arrive. As the pressure mounted, Sherman

ACTION AT SHILOH, TENNESSEE. By Shiloh Chapel, April 6, 1862.
FRANK LESLIE'S ILLUSTRATED FAMOUS LEADERS AND BATTLE SCENES OF THE CIVIL WAR

and McClernand fell back, breaking contact with Wallace on their left, which opened up a hole in the Union line. The Confederates poured through it and met their right flank brigades. The movement surrounded the Hornet's Nest.

In the Confederate center, Bragg threw attack after attack against Prentiss's and Wallace's divisions. They were all forced back until Gen. Daniel Ruggles took over the sector. A gun line established under his command pinned the Union troops down. This prevented many of them from withdrawing while the Confederates closed the purse on the Hornet's Nest.

With Prentiss's surrender, the Southerners regrouped for a final attack on Pittsburg Landing. Grant, however, had managed to establish a gun line of fifty-four cannons. This line, supported by those soldiers who were able to fall back, stopped the final Confederate attacks of the day. At dusk, Beauregard, who did not realize that Buell was arriving, called off the fighting. With Buell's arrival, along with that of Wallace, the Union losses of the day were more than made good.

On April 7 Grant went over to the offensive. Buell's fresh troops were on the left; the elements of the army that fought on the sixth were in the center; and Lew Wallace's Third Division was on the right. Beauregard tried to stop their advance, but with no fresh troops at hand, he didn't have a chance. Local counterattacks were successful (the most notable one was at Water Oaks Pond), but they did not stop the Union drive. At 2:30 Beauregard realized that the Confederates could not regain the offensive, and he ordered a withdrawal back to Corinth. Breckinridge took command of the rear guard. The Battle of Shiloh ended.

On the morning of the eighth, Grant sent out Sherman with some of his troops to discover how far the Confederates had withdrawn. At Fallen Timbers, just west of the battlefield, he ran into the rear guard under Col. Nathan Bedford Forrest. Forrest forced Sherman back. There was no further pursuit because Grant had lost the bulk of his ammunition and equipment. Buell's reserves were still downriver in Savannah awaiting shipment to Pittsburg Landing.

As a result of the battle, the Confederates' losses were 1,727 men killed, 8,012 wounded, and 959 missing for a total of 10,698 casualties. The Union losses were 1,254 killed, 8,408 wounded, and 2,885 missing for a total of 12,547 casualties. The Union did not relax its pressure on Corinth and on June 1, took the city. As a result, the Confederates lost Memphis and the rest of western Tennessee.

BIBLIOGRAPHY

Frank, Joseph A., and George A. Reaves. *Seeing the Elephant.* New York, 1989.

Johnson, Robert U., and C. C. Buel, eds. *Battles and Leaders of the Civil War.* 4 vols. New York, 1887–1888. Reprint, Secaucus, N.J., 1982.

McDonough, James L. *Shiloh: In Hell before Night.* Knoxville, Tenn., 1977.

Sword, Wiley. *Shiloh: Bloody April.* New York, 1974.

GEORGE A. REAVES III